IMAGINING
WORLDS

MARJORIE FORD graduated from the University of California at Berkeley and is currently a lecturer in English at Stanford University. This is her fourth year as the editor of the composition program's newsletter, *Notes in the Margins*. Marjorie Ford has taught freshman composition at San Jose State University and at a number of the community colleges in the Bay Area. Along with Jon Ford, she has written *Dreams and Inward Journeys* (1990/1994), *Writing as Revelation* (1991), and *Coming From Home* (1993). In collaboration with Ann Watters, she has written *Writing for Change: A Community Reader* (1994) and *A Guide for Change: Resources for Implementing Community Service Writing* (1994).

JON FORD graduated with a B.A. in English from the University of Texas and completed a Master's Degree in comparative literature at the University of Wisconsin, where he was a Woodrow Wilson Fellow. He also studied creative writing at San Francisco State University and started the successful poetry newsletter *Poetryflash*. Currently Jon Ford is chairman of English programs at the College of Alameda. Along with Marjorie Ford, he has written *Dreams and Inward Journeys* (1990/1994), *Writing as Revelation* (1991), and *Coming From Home* (1993).

for our children,
Michael and Maya

Contents

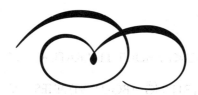

Imagining Worlds is designed for use in a second-semester, first-year composition course or in an introduction to literature course. As we chose the literature, helped our students to prepare the essays and short stories that serve as examples, and selected materials and wrote the apparatus for this text, our general goal was to produce a text that would engage the minds, hearts, and imagination of students and their teachers.

More specifically we believe that our presentation will encourage students to read more perceptively, think more critically, write more expressively and more intelligently, and see themselves as creative, imaginative human beings. We hope that students will learn to value and validate their feelings and ideas through understanding the works of other writers and through finding in writing itself an inner path toward self-understanding.

Imagining Worlds opens with two chapters on writing that explore reading, journal keeping, and writing as processes of discovery leading to the clarification and expression of ideas. In the student work included we show drafts to reinforce our belief that ideas are discovered as they are put into words and that drafts need to be revised repeatedly until clarity of expression is achieved.

After the two chapters on the writing process, we present chapters on the four genres of literature in the context of student casebooks, each of which illustrates one genre. The casebooks follow a similar pattern, with an introduction of the genre's form and then the presentation of student responses to a piece of literature from that genre. Some student responses are analytical or interpretive and text based, while other responses are creative. Each of the casebooks traces the student's process of finding a form of expression while working within traditional and creative guidelines. Although you will certainly decide to adapt the text to support your own objectives for a literature and composition class, we place emphasis on creative responses to validate the crucial role of the students' imagination in writing about literature.

Six thematic chapters then follow. These thematic chapters were shaped to help students focus and intensify their interests in universal human issues and concerns. We begin with "Creativity," because students are continually working to solve the complex issues implied in the creative process, and because in the beginning of a writing and literature course it is important for students to start to think of themselves as creators and writers, in the context of other creators and writers.

The second chapter, "Initiations and Passages," includes a range of classic works of literature that speak of the growth that an individual undergoes in a time of change and adjustment. From the changes that a student undergoes in school, to the celebrations and transformations that love, marriage, and family life bring, to the inevitability of loss and death, this chapter encourages students to look within themselves in order to understand better the ways that they are maturing. In the third chapter, "Relationships," the selections explore basic human relationship issues—bonds among peers, commitments between lovers, conflicts among family members, changing expectations in modern marriages, adjustment to separations and loss. Studying, discussing, writing, and sharing essays about these selections will help students to understand the complex fabric of relationships that characterizes our fast-paced and rapidly changing world.

The selections in the fourth chapter, "Struggles," present a range of conflicts faced by men and women from different cultural and religious backgrounds; conflicts relating to gender, race, work, economics, war, and personal inner struggles. The writing assignments in this chapter encourage students not only to analyze and understand social and cultural conflicts but also to reflect on the impact that these issues have had on their own lives. Because each individual's physical and spiritual sense of well-being is entwined with the natural world, the selections in "Natural Worlds," the fifth chapter, will help students to reflect on the ways that the natural world shapes their spiritual and philosophical perspectives and to realize that our country faces many serious environmental problems: increasing urbanization, abuse of natural resources, unpredictable and devastating natural disasters, and the like.

The theme for the sixth chapter is "Hauntings and Reflections." From the Ghost in Shakespeare's *Hamlet* to the angels in Annie Dillard's "Field of Silence," this chapter explores the realms of the unknown, of life after death, of guilt, and of revenge. This final chapter also shares the wisdom of many writers whose reflections may help students to understand better their own lives and to accept the limitations of the human condition.

Each of the thematic chapters includes works representing the four genres: stories, poems, essays, and plays. This range will help students to reflect on the ideas presented in each chapter from a number of formal perspectives. Each thematic chapter also includes a folk tale and several journal entries, as these types of writing help to engage students' imagination and feelings while giving them a sense of the mythical and personal origins of more sophisticated literary forms. The inclusion of journals kept by professional writers also demonstrates the integral role that journal keeping and prewriting play in a writer's creative process. The text's apparatus supports this concept as each selection begins with a prereading journal writing topic. Discussion questions and writing assignments, including prereading journals, expressive, analytical, interpretive, argumentative essays, and creative writing projects, as well as research assignments, follow each selection. At the end of each chapter comparative writing topics guide students toward a synthesis of the different perspectives and issues presented in the chapter selections. We believe that this range and mixture of types of assignments will encourage students to experiment with different forms of writing and help them to develop a sense of identity and voice as writers.

A wide range of ethnic backgrounds, cultures, and literary traditions is represented in *Imagining Worlds*—from contemporary to ancient, from American and Western European to African, Hispanic, and Asian. We hope students will learn from this diversity that, though the imagination may take many forms, there are also universal human concerns and patterns of development that connect us to one another.

ACKNOWLEDGMENTS

We would like to thank our editor, Steven Pensinger, for his supportive and imaginative spirit; Senior Editing Supervisor, James Belser, for his advice and guidance; Dane Johnson, for his help with biographical information on authors; Wesley Hall, for his assistance with permissions; and David Landow, who wrote the accompanying instructor's manual. Finally, we thank the students at the College of Alameda, De Anza College, and Stanford University who contributed their ideas and writings to the text.

McGraw-Hill and the authors would like to thank the following reviewers for their many helpful comments and suggestions: L. Bensel-Meyers, University of Tennessee; Kathleen Shine Cain, Merrimack College; Glenda Hudson, California State University–Bakersfield; Mary LaMattery, City College of San Francisco; Frank LaRosa, San Diego City College; Barry Maid, University of Arkansas at Little Rock; and Carolyn Pate, Southwest Texas State University.

Marjorie Ford
Jon Ford

Imagination is more important than knowledge. For knowledge is limited whereas imagination embraces the entire world.
Albert Einstein

I still have a dream. It is a dream deeply rooted in the American dream. I have a dream that one day this nation will rise up and live out the true meaning of its creed. . . . I have a dream that my four little children will one day live in a nation where they will not be judged by the color of their skin, but by the content of their character.
Martin Luther King, Jr., "I Have a Dream"

We do not know our own souls, let alone the souls of others. Human beings do not go hand in hand the whole stretch of the way. There is a virgin forest in each; a snowfield where even the print of bird's feet is unknown. Here we go alone.
Virginia Woolf

Poets, philosophers, politicians, artists, and scientists value the power of the imagination. Imagination has helped to create great works of art, to produce dreams and visions that have led to revolutionary insights and have changed the course of history. Our imagination can guide us on our journey along the path of life, as we travel to new cultures and encounter people with values different from our own, form friendships, raise families, build careers, and work to improve the quality of life in our communities. Our imagination can give us the courage and resourcefulness to face the trials and challenges of sickness, natural disasters, and loss of loved ones. Our imagination can help us to discover truths about the heart and the human spirit. As we face the unknown, imagination allows us to bring definition to solitude, what Virginia Woolf describes as "a snowfield where even the print of bird's feet in unknown."

Imagining Worlds presents the worlds created by writers who bring form to the journeys of their lives through words on paper, words that they shape into stories, essays, poems, or plays. As you read this text you will come to understand that imaginative literature asks you as a reader to collaborate, to complete and create meaning as you read. Your mind and imagination bring literature to life while encouraging reflection on your own identity and values. You may feel yourself changing and growing as you read, understanding and empathizing with the characters and the conflicts portrayed in literature. Like a telescope that allows astronomers to imagine life on stars in the galaxies, words as they are shaped into literature enlarge the mind and the spirit. Stories, poems, plays, and essays brought to life through a merging of your own imagination and the creativity of the writer can sustain you and help you to grow emotionally, intellectually, and spiritually.

As you think about the works in this text, search within yourself to decide what you value, both in yourself and in what you read. Try to find words of your own to express your particular responses to literary works. As you come to understand and appreciate the imagined worlds of others, your inner life will be enriched. To realize that words in the form of imaginative literature help each individual to clarify and to shape experience; to realize that words can help you to bear the pain of fear, anger, and loss; to realize that words as they articulate your joy also help you to extend and impassion the triumphs of being alive— this is the gift that *Imagining Worlds* offers to its readers.

One of our students expressed the fulfillment she found through writing and reading in the following journal entry:

    Through imagining the worlds of others I find it easier to
draw upon my own world in my writing. I have found that my world
is not much different from that of others. In coming to this
realization, my writing has come to have more meaning to me. I
feel more of a purpose to write, not just because it is a
requirement. So much is locked inside me; fears and hope, love
and hate. I have found that my writing has more personal meaning
because I have opened my mind and reached into my soul. Many of
the writers in this book have inspired me to do so. For the
first time in my life writing has become fulfilling for me.

Literature is a bridge that allows people to connect and communicate with one another. By reading others' works and sharing your writing with others, you will have the opportunity to become better acquainted with new people, many of whom will have grown up in different cultures. Just as your discussion of ideas about the meaning of a story, a poem, an image, a scene will be unpredictable, it will also be challenging—intellectually, culturally, and emotionally. In addition, working with a diversity of forms such as the short story, the journal, and the poem will help you find more complex and creative ways of presenting ideas both in your own personal and creative writing and in the essays you write for your coursework. Many students have found that looking within themselves to find a form and a style expressive of their own voice and intentions has empowered them to develop confidence as writers. We hope that *Imagining Worlds* will help you to develop this same confidence in your mind, in your imagination, and in your ability to express what you believe in and value.

Marjorie Ford
Jon Ford

IMAGINING WORLDS

IMAGINING WORLDS

The Reading and Writing Process

1

IMAGINING
WORLDS

The Reading and Writing Process

Chapter 1

KEEPING A JOURNAL

Many writers use their journals to explore and record new insights, special observations, private thoughts, and feelings. The process of putting thoughts into words and onto paper will help you clarify your ideas. Later, you can turn to your journal as a source of ideas for longer, more sustained writing projects. The following entry, from a student's journal, explores what keeping a journal has meant to her:

> I write in my journal about memories, values, morals, or thoughts and ideas which have taken me by surprise and have stayed with me. Some thoughts stay at the back of my mind and continue to grow until I write them down and fully explore them. I feel my thoughts and ideas becoming organized as I am writing in my journal. In writing journals in a free-flowing style, I often discover in the finished entry new ideas and viewpoints.

Writers keep many types of journals, depending on their interests and goals. Some writers use their journal simply as a way of reflecting on their private feelings and ideas, whereas others see it as a place to record ideas for and early drafts of essays, stories, and poems, as well as observations that may later find their way into finished works, whether fiction or nonfiction. Because one of the goals of this text is to help you to understand better the relationships between your inner world and imaginative literature, we recommend two different ways to develop your journal: as a dream journal and as a reader's journal. Both approaches will help you to increase your understanding of what you read, of your own writing process, and of yourself.

THE DREAM JOURNAL

Keeping a journal is in some ways like dreaming. The journal, like a dream, is a product of a private inner world, all your own. You can feel free about expressing and developing your thoughts and feelings in your dreams and in your journal. There are also similarities between vivid, sustained dreams and imaginative stories and poems. Centuries ago Plato pointed out that "art is a dream for awakened minds." Critic and teacher Northrop Frye has argued: "Art is a work of imagination withdrawn from ordinary life, dominated by the same forces that dominate the dream, and yet giving us a perspective and dimension on reality that we don't get from any other approach to reality." The similarities between dreams and literature make the practice of keeping a dream journal especially significant when working through a text, such as this one, that explores the role of the imagination in the creative process.

In "Professions for Women" which is included in the student casebook on essay writing, Virginia Woolf acknowledges the essential role that her unconscious, dream mind played in her writing: "I want you to imagine me writing a novel in a state of trance. . . . The image that comes to mind . . . is . . . [that] of a fisherman lying sunk in dreams on the verge of a deep lake with a rod held out over the water." Like the creative experience described by Woolf, many of the writers in *Imagining Worlds* have used their dreams and fantasies as sources for images and creative inspiration. Keeping a dream journal can help you to develop a sense of kinship with the imaginative worlds of professional writers.

Like literature, dreams express themselves through **characters, story lines, settings,** and **symbols.** Like literature, a dream will often reflect a dominant **mood:** slapstick farce, tragedy, adventure, horror. Dreams may include **allusions,** or references, to events, people, and places in the "waking world" and may even seem to explore philosophical ideas or themes. Understanding the symbolic language of your dreams will help you understand the connection between dreams and literary creations, as well as develop insight into the ways that literary concepts and strategies can act as keys to unlock your imagination. Keeping a dream journal will help you to refine your ability to understand and appreciate prose and literature. Learning to decode and working to understand dreams is similar to the process of unraveling and analyzing the meaning of a complex imaginative text. Like a literary work, a dream can be interpreted in a number of different ways. Just as it is important to spend time reflecting on a piece of literature, you can try to develop a fuller understanding of the dream rather than being satisfied with the first meaning you find.

Novelist John Steinbeck noted that "it is a common experience that a problem difficult at night is resolved in the morning after the committee of sleep has worked it out." Recording your dreams and thoughts upon waking can help you get in touch with your unconscious mind's solutions to problems that may puzzle or haunt you. By keeping a dream journal you can train your conscious mind to remember the insights brought to you from your unconscious mind, to increase your dream recall, as well as your ability to work through the concerns and insights that come to you in your sleep. Once you begin keeping a dream journal, you will realize that it is wasteful to allow the insights from your dreams and unconscious mind to slip away, unnoticed, as you prepare for the day to come.

We suggest that you write out your dreams immediately upon waking, perhaps in a small notebook kept beside your bed. First just try to capture the images and rhythms of a dream, rather than consciously shaping a story or coherent sequence of scenes. As you record your impressions, you will discover ideas, images, and metaphors for your writing; and you may find yourself revealing a new writer's voice, one that you may feel reflects your feelings and beliefs. You may be surprised and delighted by the originality and poetry of your own ideas. Later, you can review the journal and write interpretations of some of your dreams that seemed complex or of particular importance to you. After keeping your dream journal for several weeks, try to "read," or interpret, a particular dream as if it were a letter from your unconscious or a poem, short story, play, or film.

The following dream entry and interpretation were written by a student who was attending an urban college yet having a number of dreams about her childhood growing up close to nature in rural Sweden. She recorded this dream on the last day of school.

Dream

I'm standing by a lake in a forest. My hair is very long, down to my hips, and I'm wearing a greenish-brownish old dress. I'm looking at my reflection in the calm water; only a small movement in the water distorts my features. I feel the stillness around me and also inside of me. Curious, I observe the different yet similar images of myself reflected in the shimmering water. It seems like hours I'm standing there, taking in the beauty of the surroundings and my own reflections. I can see all kinds of faces, everything from a beautiful young princess to an ugly, old woman. Some of the faces look kind and happy, others seem uptight, angry and possessed. The vision drifts away, but stays in my mind. . . .

Interpretation

When I woke up I felt a sense of total acceptance and harmony. I think that it was really me there by the lakeside in an appearance of a little "forest elf," something I had wanted to be as a child. I stood there and looked at my own personality reflected in the water's magic mirror. It was interesting that I only looked; I did not criticize any part of myself. I just observed with a child's eyes, accepting all the different "faces" of my personality, old, young, kind, evil. The dream gave me a sense of oneness with my inner self, and a vision of the possibility of accepting who I am and the different parts of my personality.

After several weeks, reflect on the effect that keeping the journal is having on your writing in a journal entry. The dream journal project has helped students to visualize and describe scenes, as one student reported in his journal:

Reading and listening to other student essays, I have noticed that one of the keys to good descriptive writing that captivates the reader is the ability to imagine a clear, almost tangible picture, and then transcribe that image in the written word. Recalling the mental pictures dreams produce as I keep my dream journal has enhanced my ability to visualize both my dream world and my real world.

Students have come to understand themselves and their own writing processes better through keeping a dream journal. In his final paper, Frank Voci, a student in a literature class, shared the realizations that the process of writing down and reflecting on his dreams helped him to discover:

Keeping a dream journal has helped me . . . by providing a map . . . to my unconscious self, to a side of me less restricted by perceptions of those around me, to a side hidden from my waking reality. This has enabled me to become a fuller, more self-aware person.

Although keeping a dream journal brings many benefits, one valuable result is that it permits you as a writer to express yourself in an authentic writer's voice. This is difficult for even the most accomplished writers. One student explained:

Recording my dreams has helped me to speak more authentically in my writing. I am often startled by the voice that sometimes emerges in my dream journal and now in my essays, but I am pleased because this new voice expresses my point of view more accurately.

THE READING JOURNAL

Prereading Journal Writings

Because writing in your journal will help you to clarify your thoughts and feelings on the issues that you are studying, we have designed this text to encourage you to write before and after you read each selection. Writing before reading, sometimes just free-associating about the title of the work or writing a short, personal response to what you see as the theme or setting of the reading, is important because such brief, informal written responses initiate a dialogue between you and the text, encouraging you to read actively, thoughtfully, and imaginatively. As critics David Bartholomae and Anthony Petrosky put it, writing before reading places the student "in the position to author, or take responsibility for a reading. The enabling moment for the reader is the moment of silence, when a student sits down before a text . . . and must begin to write and begin to see what can be made of that writing." The journal writing suggestions we have included before reading selections can help you to create a connection with the text before you begin reading and to be receptive to what you read.

The reading journal will also suggest possible writing ideas that can later be developed into longer projects. As student writer Robert Hummel puts it, "The most important thing my reading journal did for me was to write—period. I have never had an easy time motivating myself to write, and it's always been a fairly painful struggle." Hummel's journal entry on the story "Lush Life" by John McCluskey (Chapter 7) explores, as does the original story, a night journey with a friend that led to a closer bond and to new insights about creativity and the meaning of life. The entry grew into the short story that follows.

Tapping

I remember tapping on my window. That was how my friend Jimmy used to get my attention if what he had to say was far too important for the grownups to hear, or if he just didn't feel like dealing with the adult population at all. That was the cause on that breezy summer's evening when we ran away for the night.

"I'm leaving, wanna come?" was all he said and I could tell he'd been crying.

"Yeah, okay." I said. Now was as good a time as any to declare my adulthood.

Running away was something he and I had talked about for quite a while. My mother was strung out on so many prescription drugs she passed out more often than she fell asleep. The only disease she really suffered from was chronic hypochondria and maybe a touch of loneliness, but all my twelve year old eyes could see was that I was being neglected and was simply better off on my own. Jimmy never said much about his home life, but the bruises he sometimes came to school with said more than he needed to. The two of us had a running fantasy about leaving home and becoming gangsters or high class con men. It seemed we were about ready to begin our lives of crime.

I put on some night clothes, tossed a few things into a backpack and slipped into the night with my friend.

"Where to?" I asked, fully knowing the answer.

"The dark streets of the city." He responded in that pulp private eye voice he did so well, but his heart wasn't in it and he sounded more drunk than tough.

"What's the matter, bud?" We were just reaching the corner
of our street, and I was already beginning to feel chilly.

He was silent for a long time, the question remaining
unanswered as we reached the foot of Brock's Hill where we'd
been known to recklessly ride our rickety Huffy bicycles at
something approaching Warp Five.

"Things couldn't be better." He finally said, this time
wearing a lousy Bogart impression. But his voice cracked,
betraying him.

We walked in silence for several blocks looking at the
sleeping houses as we passed them by. The moon was full and the
sky was clear so we had plenty of light. When we heard a car
coming we ducked into the bushes as though we'd been running
away all our lives.

We cut through Jackson Park and paused for a breather on
the playground where we'd won and lost countless imaginary
battles. I tried sitting on the monkey bars but they felt cold
and lifeless in the middle of the night so I just lay on the
grass counting stars.

"The Big Dipper, Little Dipper, Orion's Belt, Cassiopeia
. . ." I rattled off the names of all the Constellations I could
think of. Astronomy was my obsession at the time. "Leo the Lion,
Perseus, Pisces . . . "

"My father is a bastard." Jimmy's own voice this time,
barely a whisper.

The anger in his voice stopped me in the middle of my list.
"What?"

"My father is a first class shit." He said this with a
grin, but I could see tears shining in the blue moonlight.
"Tonight I decided I wasn't ever going to be like him."

"What'd he do?"

"Nothing, I mean, nothing worse than usual. Came home, got
drunk, bitched about work, bitched about the house, bitched
about me, bitched about . . . bitched about Mom." His mother had
left home a year earlier, just up and left. Jimmy hardly ever
talked about her any more.

"So after he passed out I figured I'd just see how far away
from that bastard I could get, just like I guess she did. Maybe
he'll get the hint. Probably be glad I'm gone, one less mouth to
feed, more money for beer. Probably won't even know I'm gone for
about a week." He chuckled at this, "In a week, I could be as
far as . . ."

"Detroit." I finished his sentence for him, just like I
sometimes would when we'd fantasize about running away.

"Or Houston, or New York, or Canada." At this point in our
lives, we both thought Canada was a state located somewhere on
the East Coast, and we were both saving up Canadian coins just
so we could go there and spend them. "Doesn't matter, just as
long as I get as far away from here as I can."

He looked at me and I could see by the pain in his face he
knew that we'd gotten about as far as we were going to get this
time.
     We ended up spending the night in the park, just talking.
He'd never been real open about his family and, for the first
time, he was letting it all out. He just seemed grateful to have
someone to spill it all to, I guess, and I could see his mood
get lighter as the evening progressed to dawn. When we walked
home, we did so feeling closer to any human beings than we ever
had, and perhaps, ever would.

Reading Process Journal Writings

Marking and Questioning the Text

After completing your prereading journal response, scan the selection to determine the purpose of the reading: to inform, to tell a story, to persuade or argue,
to reflect philosophically on an experience. Making this determination and asking yourself the following questions about the reading will help you to develop
clear expectations and prepare you to respond to what you are about to experience:

1. What do I expect the writer to accomplish in this selection?
2. What is my perspective on the issues raised?
3. What do I already know about this subject?
4. What questions do I have that I hope the reading will answer?

Make marginal notes as you read, bracketing crucial passages, using question marks or exclamation marks, writing brief comments such as "no," "yes," or
"why?" and putting in marginal comments such as "main idea" or "symbol." Develop a notation system that feels comfortable and suits your needs. As you
read, try to remember the major conventions of the genre of the selection, looking for relevant patterns of support, key scenes, examples, and images, as well as
any repeated words and phrases that reveal special emphasis. If you are reading
poetry, try reading the poem aloud. Listen to the way the sounds and rhythms
of the words contribute to the overall feeling or mood of the work. Comment in
your journal on difficult concepts; jot down words and place-names that need
looking up in a dictionary or encyclopedia; write down questions for your classmates and your instructor.

Postreading Responses

Writing in your journal just after reading a selection will help you deepen your
understanding of the text and your own reading process. You can answer questions about the readings that follow each selection or answer your own questions about passages in the readings that you find difficult. Some students prefer

to write a brief response statement after each reading of the same text, keeping track of the way that their responses vary and become more focused with each repeated reading. A second approach is to write a "summary response" after reading the selection and thinking about the questions included after the selection.

You can also use the journal productively by seeing it as a place to capture your reflections on and evaluation of your learning process as you read and study a text. Did you like or dislike the selection as a whole? Were there any ambiguities or contradictions in the text? Do you have any information that makes you doubt the writer's conclusions? What did you learn about literature, about the imagination, about other cultures, about how to read and interpret texts, about your own writing process?

Journal writings can be points of departure for further reading and study, as well as a way of developing insights and preliminary drafts for future essays. As the term progresses, and you look back through the pages of your journal, you are likely to realize that you have come to understand your writing, your reading, and yourself better. The student casebooks in this text include a number of examples of reader response writings. The following journal entry was written by a student after reading Carlos Fuentes' "The Doll Queen." The student describes her reading process and her struggle to find value in a story that disturbed her. She could develop this journal entry in a variety of ways—a full evaluation of the story, an examination of the author's style, an analysis of the characters and their motivations, or a research paper on the cultural issues the story explores.

```
"The Doll Queen" was certainly a surprise for me. I was long in
getting completely through it. I found it very thick with
details to wade through. But Fuentes is obviously a master of
creating a dream-like vapor of memory and imagination for the
reader, and the imagery he uses to describe his time with
Amilamia is very beautiful and realistic, a memory perfectly
evoked and recalled. I was not at all fond of Carlos' character,
but this was a snap judgment, a feeling not born out of
consideration. I am sure that my initial response to him has to
do with his possessiveness of Amilamia, his obsessive, really
self-centered love for her. Overall, I felt little sympathy for
any of the characters in the story except for Amilamia. There
was a sickness to Carlos' wild, obsessive hunt for Amilamia into
the private world of her family, a sickness about her cruel and
demented parents (although perhaps they are not so bizarre as
they might seem; I know many families that are similarly private
and controlling in their relationships with their children).
Though it was touching and well-executed, I was not personally
drawn by this story. I would recommend it, however, as a good
example of dream-like memory writing and for the feelings and
ideas it projects through its characters and images about Latin
American sensibility, history, and culture.
```

Chapter 2

FROM READER'S JOURNAL TO FINISHED TEXT

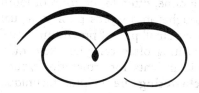

Imagining Worlds offers you the opportunity to write creatively, trying your hand at informal journal entries and freewritings, folk tales, poems, short stories, and dialogues. However, the majority of the suggested writing assignments involve some form of essay writing. The first casebook on essay writing that follows discusses the genre of the essay in greater detail. To start with, you need to know that an essay is an exploration of ideas, a fully developed statement written for a particular audience of readers, as opposed to a journal entry written exclusively for the writer. Classroom essays frequently have clear divisions: an engaging or provocative introduction; a clear thesis statement that indicates your purpose; a body section that develops your ideas thoroughly, often with personal examples and references to relevant texts; and an emphatic conclusion. Moving from reading and responding informally to texts to producing public, finished writing involves transforming your responses and reflections about your reading into ideas that your audience can understand and accept as valid. To get a sense of the variety of ways that these general concepts about writing an essay can be applied, read several of the student essays included in *Imagining Worlds*. You will notice that each student has a unique way of developing and organizing his or her experiences and ideas for maximum reader comprehension and engagement.

The essays you will write in this course will probably take many forms and may be directed at different audiences. Some of your writings will analyze and interpret fictional and nonfictional readings in the book; others may be narratives, expository essays, arguments, or research papers in response to fictional or nonfictional readings. You will probably need to write several drafts of the paper. Each subsequent draft may focus on a somewhat different aspect of the writing process, although in actual practice you will find that simply going back over your paper repeatedly, recopying it, and making changes that feel right at that particular moment can be an effective approach in itself. For the sake of discussion, the stages of the writing process can be divided into **prewriting, drafting, outlining,** and **revising** your drafts and then **rewriting** and **proofreading** the final version of your paper.

PREWRITING

Prewriting is the writing done, often in the form of journal entries, as you read and try to put your thoughts into words prior to actually beginning a formal draft of your paper. Only a small part of prewriting actually finds its way into a finished essay, but prewriting often can yield key images and phrases, thesis statements, and valuable insights for structuring your writing. **Freewriting, brainstorming,** and **clustering** are helpful techniques for generating and recording ideas in preparation for developing an essay. Such techniques can help you to silence the internal critic who may block your writing by expecting a perfect product immediately.

Freewriting

Freewriting involves writing rapidly without stopping for brief periods of time, between five and fifteen minutes. Some of the responses you have done already in your reading journal probably resemble freewriting. Freewriting, like any form of informal journal or response writing, will help you get in touch with what you really want to say about a subject, with your underlying feelings about a topic. After freewriting or reader response writing, reread what you have written and circle fresh, insightful ideas and expressions. Then try a second freewriting using the circled ideas and phrases as points of departure. You can try freewriting at any stage of the writing process. In the example that follows, the student had already done a journal response to the story "The Doll Queen" (see page 301); she now focuses in greater detail on the disturbing and repulsive characters in the story. As you read the student's freewriting, circle passages that you think could be further developed.

Freewriting: Why Were the Characters So Disturbing?

CARLOS--He was so scheming--the way he found out the owner of the building, etc. He appears no more of a redeemable character in his recollections of his times with Amilamia-- basically, he was a young man who liked to play childish games and yet was beginning to feel adult needs, and he becomes frustrated with Amilamia . . . he more or less forsakes her, and

innocently, she leaves believing he'll see her again. Now he
again constructs her for his own needs . . . he's "tired of
sleeping with secretaries" and hopes to find a beautiful,
mature, unspoiled Amilamia or perhaps a wholesome mother, and he
has a profound belief of the importance of these memories, that
these things solidify his self-view and he unthinkingly acts--
though he claims he doesn't believe--as though they will be
equally important to Amilamia. I can't help feeling that
Amilamia will be unimpressed by Carlos. Is her disinterest from
memory of the hurt of inexplicably losing her closest friend, or
is it because she is simply indifferent to Carlos? I can't
decide. In the end, he deserves his awful shock because he is
going there for another selfish reason--he believes that the
parents want yet another reminder of her--and wasn't he himself
disgusted with their preternatural obsession with the girl? Why
is he contributing to it again?

　　THE PARENTS--What needs to be said? This transcends
cultural barriers. Doesn't it? These people seem sick to me.
Thinking of the morals behind such behavior. Devil's Spawn?
Amilamia is physically deformed. Poor Parents. One should feel
sorry for them? For them? What about Amilamia? Their attitude is
unforgivable. It is vile the way they enshrine her, in a funeral
manner. I have little to say about the ultimate and definitive
wrongness in the way they treat their daughter. These are
Christian morals? I bet they sit around wondering why God did
this to them. The blind selfishness is too much.

Brainstorming

Begin by jotting down a list, on paper or computer screen, of whatever comes to
mind about a topic or a reading: an issue, a character, a particular point of view,
a vivid image. After completing your list, group related ideas and then do further
brainstorming on interesting groups of ideas; also delete information that seems
irrelevant or repetitious. A revised, reordered brainstorming list can lead to some
further insights for freewriting or to a scratch outline for an essay. The following
brainstorming list and accompanying comment were done by the student writing on the character Carlos in the story "The Doll Queen."

```
Brainstorming: On the Character of Carlos
  scheming                      observant
  self-centered                 thoughtless
  high-minded                   selfish
  romantic                      dreamy
  idealistic                    imaginative
  molds relationships to fit    concerned with his
     his needs                     own vision
```

Carlos is extremely well-educated, but his observations never
seem to leave the realm of importance of his own experience
. . . he is caught up in his own life, in his needs, and
somehow, although we would usually say that at fourteen he was
just confused and young, his actions seem somehow too brusque
. . . children often are . . . at 29, has he changed so much?
. . . What is he looking for in Amilamia? What does he expect
her to be . . . why does he seek her out? . . . why does he
invent such a story tell to Amilamia's parents? His schemes seem
so complete to me, it seems to me he is really working hard to
add drama to his life without thought to others, if not at their
expense . . . the end of the story doesn't say much to me . . .
it is clearly a comment on the dramatic difference between their
memories and the present . . . but what does Carlos do with
this? Does he become sad, angry, and is it anger at Amilamia's
parents or anger at himself?

Clustering

Clustering is another effective strategy to help you discover connections between ideas and to develop a sense of direction or outline for your essay. Place a
key word or short phrase in the center of a page. Draw a balloon around it and
create offshoots from the word or phrase like spokes from a wheel or blossoms
from the central stem of a plant. Each of these major associations can in turn become the point of origin for a further cluster of associations.

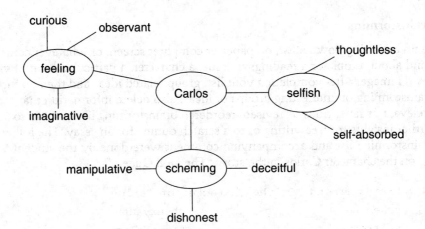

Outlining

Outlining helps writers in different ways. Some writers rely on just a few words
and notes as a guideline for a draft; others work from a scratch outline, similar
to a brainstorming list or a clustering with a few key points and phrases includ-

ed; and a few work best when they use their rough notes and prewritings to develop a full, formal outline before attempting to draft an essay. Whatever techniques of prewriting or outlining you decide to use, remember that it is important to gradually develop the threads, the images, the ideas that come to mind as you reflect on your readings and on your own feelings, experiences, and thoughts. Following is the statement of overall goal and a scratch outline for a paper on "The Doll Queen."

Outline

1. Concepts:

a) Goal: I want to write an essay that will examine one of the legitimate themes of the story in terms of my first response to it. I feel the flavor of my reading experience--the distaste for the main characters--must somehow tie into something Fuentes wanted to communicate about his main idea.

b) Main idea: Memory vs. reality

c) What about it? Memories are not always what they seem . . . when we see the truth of our memories, we see some truth in ourselves--how we always think, see, perceive . . . we selectively paint them to fit our needs.

d) How does my feeling that the Carlos is so disturbing fit into this theme? Memories are not always accurate representations of the past. We shape them and change them, selecting the most important elements to support our ideals. The same is true with our self-perceptions and our perceptions of others. We choose to see only what fits our perception. Like many of us, Carlos returns to his childhood playground to find that literally, his memory is larger than life. But he also uncovers deeper, more disturbing inconsistencies. Carlos looks to find the wonder of his childhood, and ends by revealing the truth of his abandonment of Amilamia, his deceitfulness as he goes to claim her in the present, his possessiveness. These are all unpleasant things, parts of himself he never expected to find, parts of him that are just as real as his intelligence, tenderness, and imagination. Carlos finds the same irony in his perceptions of Amilamia's parents. At first he sees them as tragic, loving, doting figures who love their dear, departed daughter into death. Despite their obsession, he can only grieve for them and try to repossess his happier memories of Amilamia. But when he keeps delving deeper into the past, into the memories of Amilamia, he finds these monsters that are not at all what they once seemed. Now he has completely destroyed his joyful memory of Amilamia, and has come to a real perception of the truth.

2. Scratch Outline:

a) Thesis paragraph: Fuentes' main purpose seems to be the exploration of the relationships between memories and reality. Through the course of the story, we come to see the disturbing realities of Carlos as he brings the gap between truth and memories closer and closer.

     Body paragraphs:

b) First level of Carlos' encounter with the present reality of his memories, using the park as example.

c) Background of story--why it is disturbing that Carlos searches in his past: it is a self-absorbed motivation; he cares little for the real Amilamia.

d & e) The next level down through the memory and the unpleasant things this brings out in Carlos: the entrance into the private family and Carlos' resulting deceit and manipulation, his consequent self-loathing.

f) Show that even further into the delusion of the memory, Carlos' idealism is still strong and he thoughtlessly returns to the home from which it has been requested he stay away. Here Carlos is face to face with his self-centered "love" for Amilamia, and with the ugly truth about Amilamia's family.

g) Conclusion: Reiterate introduction, use text from outline to tie up paper. Also comment on the symbolism of Amilamia's condition as Carlos finds her.

STRATEGIES FOR ORGANIZATION AND DEVELOPMENT

Collect your journal entries, notes, and prewritings for your essay; look over the material to select the particular idea that you want to develop further. Check your early prewriting for other ideas or examples that relate to the limited topic you have chosen for your focus.

    As you begin to draft, keep the purpose for your writing in mind and try to select a major strategy, or **mode,** of writing for your paper. Before you decide on a dominant writing strategy, consider the following questions:

1. Do you want to approach the subject from a **personal perspective,** reflecting on your topic or issue in the context of your personal experience?

2. Do you want to **explain** a concept, **tell** a story, **analyze** a character, or **persuade** your reader of your point of view?

3. Can you **illustrate** a concept with a **narrative,** such as a case history? Will you need to describe a scene, a person, an object? Will you need to develop dialogue to make your characters seem more real?

4. Can you **compare** two readings, characters, or techniques in order to understand both of them better?

5. Should you **analyze** or break down a reading, topic, issue, or problem into parts through a **process** analysis, a **cause and effect** analysis, or an extended **definition**?

6. Should you present a **cause** and then discuss its **effects?** Or should you begin with the effect and then trace back to the causes?

7. Should you analyze a **problem** and propose a **solution,** either in an expository problem-solution essay or a researched proposal that argues for a particular position or course of action?

Although thinking about these questions will help you find an appropriate central strategy it is likely that, in a longer essay, you will need to use more than one organization or developmental technique to clarify your purpose and facilitate your reader's understanding. In the case of the student who planned a paper on "The Doll Queen," she chose to develop her essay using analysis of character and relevant themes. She needed to support and develop her ideas through quotation and paraphrase of a series of key scenes in the story, taking care not simply to engage in a lengthy and pointless plot summary.

AUDIENCE

In drafting your essay, you will also need to consider the audience for your writing, your intended readers. Although most of the topics in *Imagining Worlds* assume that your audience is the students in your composition and literature class, sometimes a writing project may suggest or specify a more particular audience, such as an essay written in the form of a response directed to either the original author of a reading or the author's original readers. Develop an authentic sense of voice and use examples that provide evidence, as well as clear and effective logic, to capture the interest of your peers.

Considering your audience will guide your method of developing the essay and help you to make crucial decisions about word choice, facts, and arguments to include or leave out. Selecting topics and issues according to your own interest and knowledge, prewriting extensively on the selected issue, and letting purpose and audience help to guide the assertions you make and the mode of development you use will lead you to develop a rough draft that you can then review, reflect on, and refine through the revision process.

A STUDENT DRAFT OF A PAPER ON "THE DOLL QUEEN"

The draft that follows presents an analysis of Carlos' character in "The Doll Queen." After reflecting on her reader response journal and prewriting, the student decided to look more closely at Carlos' personal qualities, to think about them within the context of the major themes she now saw in the story and wanted to write about: memory and truth. She had come to perceive the negative qualities in Carlos' character as reflective in part of his naive relationship to the past and his unwillingness to understand and accept reality.

Rough Draft

The Doll Queen   *Find a title*

Carlos Fuentes, like many Latin American authors, ~~writes in a slightly surrealistic way, and he~~ likes to *should flow more*

explore the way that we alter and shape reality. This

reality can be in the past, as in memories, or in the

present, in our perceptions of others and ourselves. In

his story <u>The Doll Queen</u>, Fuentes allows us to follow

the journey of Carlos, a character who is trying to

find peace and happiness in reliving a childhood

memory. Unfortunately, in plumbing the depths of his

past, Carlos finds unpleasant realities about himself

and others. *flesh out; re-cap theme of memory & reality*

At first, Carlos' disappointment and realization are

on a very ~~surface~~ level. The story begins as Carlos   *superficial*

goes to a favorite park of his youth to reminisce about

his childhood. We learn that he is here because he

wants to discover the tranquility of the feeling he

shared with the little girl, Amilamia, with whom he

used to share his days in the park. He remembers her as a serious, beautiful, innocent and open child, who knew him at the time that he was passing between his "own irresolute childhood and the open world, the promised land" of young adulthood that Carlos found in his books. In going to the park, Carlos expects to find a wild garden, with open meadow and rolling hills thick with green grass. But when he arrives he finds his memories of the place were larger than life. The great hill he remembers is nothing more than "a barely elevated patch of dark stubble with not more heights and depth" than those of sheer imagination. His images of childhood are diminished by time and age, and every aspect of his park that seemed large and grand seem sad and pathetic.

either elaborate on past or leave out

~~Also in his first episode~~, Fuentes introduces us to the character of Carlos: the way he thinks, his sensibilities, and his lifestyle past and present. ~~We learn that~~ Carlos is a well-read, well-educated man of 29, who is "a bachelor still, with no family to maintain, slightly bored with sleeping with secretaries . . . feeling the lack of a central attraction such as those" he once had in youth, with Amilamia. It is natural for Carlos to be curious about his childhood friend, but we sense it is the loneliness and predictability of life that truly bring him in search

of Amilamia. Although in his childhood he abandoned *run-on . . .*
Amilamia because the discrepancy between their   *also, more*
descriptive
development was too great, Carlos has the feeling that *he was*
now, at 22, Amilamia will be just the excitement he *frustrated,*
needs to feel young and vital again. He does not give *we never saw*
her again
much thought to how Amilamia will feel about such a
reunion, only imagining her in terms of how much like
herself in childhood she will still be. Carlos is *awkward*
caught up in his elaborate memories of childhood, never
imagining what he may uncover as he continues his
search to mesh past with present. His self-absorption
becomes more evident as he goes to Amilamia's home to
inquire after her.

in the story
At each step, a slightly more distasteful element of
Carlos' character manifests itself. His once mild
obsession with a memory begins to bring out a *— For example,*
deceitful, manipulative side of himself. When Carlos
goes to Amilamia's house, he has no luck in speaking to
the tenants. But instead of returning at a later time
to try again, Carlos goes to the city hall and obtains
records which enable him to pose as a building
inspector in order to be admitted into Amilamia's *desperate (emphasize his obsession)*
home. *(.) ?* He also wrestles with his own sense of sanity as
memories of ~~the young~~ girl fill his thoughts. Carlos
fights with his imagination, pushing away the crazy *new*
notion that "in that house lived a seven-year-old girl *paragraph*
that [he] had known fourteen or fifteen years before." *¶*
It is clear in these kinds of illusions that Carlos is
much less interested in Amilamia as a person that in
her private meaning for him.

In his efforts
~~While looking~~ to recapture the wonder of his childhood, Carlos enters a deeply private play of characters in Amilamia's home and family. Here another layer of the distance between fact and fiction is lifted, and Carlos faces more truth about himself and the reality of Amilamia's fate. He meets Amilamia's parents, who though at first seem distan*t and strange* then seem tragic as they reveal their own reality of Amilamia. Carlos is forced to face the impropriety of his intrusion into their world, slapped with the reality of how despicable his behavior and deceit have been. His childhood friend is dead, it seems, and her family is in deepest mourning. They have created an unnatural effigy of her, and left her dark room filled with flowers, toys and candles to complete a macabre altar to their lost Amilamia. Carlos is discouraged, believing himself to have found only tragedy, sorrow, and self-loathing where he sought peace and harmony.

re-order

Nearly one year later, Carlos' romantic ideal of Amilamia again infiltrates his memory and he goes back to the girl's family to present them with a token of her youth. *ambiguous* Immediately we are struck by the discrepancy *awkward: the reality v. the memory* between his memory of his last visit and what we have just seen. He seems to have forgotten the morbid, ghastly atmosphere of the family home and the mother's plea to Carlos to leave them alone, and not to come back again. His selfish, dreamy nature propels him back to the house, and this time Carlos must face even more disturbing truths. Finding Amilamia alive, we sense in

Amilamia he knew, but because the cruelty of his

treatment of her ~~once~~ *in childhood* must come back to him ten-fold.

In his zealous quest for the pretty little Amilamia,

down through the years ~~to~~ *by way of* seemingly harmless memories,

Carlos finds not only his own weaknesses, but a badly

crippled woman and her monstrous, cruel parents. A *a separate paragraph*

picture of the true reality of Amilamia's world is

given to Carlos and to us in one instant, as the man

concerned with his own vision is forced to face a more

appalling redefinition of memory than he could have

ever imagined in all his afternoon daydreams.

Add more conclusion.
What does Amilamia's crippled state represent?
Wrap up theme: impact of delving all the way into
memory.
What impact will his experience have on Carlos?
What will his future be?

REVISING: STAGES AND ISSUES

After completing a draft, set it aside for a time before working on a revision. Also, share your draft with friends, peers, or your instructor; it is difficult for a writer to evaluate his or her work objectively and to trace the accuracy of the logic and examples without feedback from others. Some of the notations on the student draft reflect comments by the student's peers and her own further insights into the text. After sharing her paper with her friends, classmates, and instructor, the student realized that her initial attitude toward the character had changed. Whereas her first impression of him was critical, she came to see that Carlos seemed to grow in the course of the story from being naive, selfish, and deceptive to becoming more engaged with others, more aware of the nature of complex realities such as memory, truth, and change. She also came to understand that the future of the character could only be decided by the individual reader, that Carlos is, in a sense, "a work in progress."

Many of our students typically revise their papers several times. Keep copies of all your drafts to trace your progress and because you may decide to go back to an earlier version of your paper to reinsert a strong, original image or phrase that you had deleted.

The process of revision can be divided into several steps or stages that often overlap. Begin by asking yourself questions about the overall shape or form of the essay:

1. Is the **main idea,** or thesis, clear?
2. Have you developed your **thesis** throughout the paper? If you have included interesting but not strictly relevant ideas or details, this is the time to delete them.
3. Are there any contradictions or inconsistencies in your logic and point of view?
4. Have you developed **support** for your major points through references to the text, in the form of summaries, paraphrases, or brief quotations or through reference to personal experience or popular culture?
5. Does your draft have a **voice?** Change language, phrases, and sentences that sound mechanical or pretentious. Eliminate jargon and very informal language. Underline passages where you see your real voice as a writer shining through—places where you have come up with interesting turns of phrase, expressive sentences, original images. Try to build on the strengths of your voice as you work through your revision process.
6. Would **outlining** or reoutlining your original draft help? Even if you tried outlining before drafting your paper, your ideas may have changed so much as you wrote your draft that it may be worthwhile to outline once again.

Revising Paragraphs

Writers follow up their initial revision of a draft with a closer scrutiny of the **paragraphs** that make up their composition. Paragraphs are like the floors of a building: each must be solidly constructed, well secured to the floor immediately before and the one just beyond it, reflective of the goals and design of the whole structure. Once you have completed a draft, you will want to check that your topic sentences are in the most emphatic position in the paragraph. Also make sure that your transitional sentences help readers to follow your logic and organization.

The **introductory paragraph** is like the entry way of a home where you invite your reader to enter and feel comfortable; the **body paragraphs** are like the rooms that a good floor plan naturally leads us through; and the **conclusion** is like the peak of a roof, a natural culmination of the structure that often points beyond the limits of what you've just said, to suggest the future, to reflect on the implications of your thesis. Like a house, your paragraphs should also have beams—solid supporting ideas, examples, and direct and indirect references to text you are discussing, as well as repetitions and transitions that lead the reader back to your thesis.

Editing and Proofreading

During the final stage of revision you will need to pay careful attention to language and sentence structure. You might want to refer to a thesaurus and a dictionary; check and replace any words or expressions that are vague or unclear. Remember that you want to express your ideas concisely, precisely, and vividly. Fine-tune your sentences for variety, length, and rhythm; read them aloud to get a feel for the rhythm of your sentence structure.

Proofreading involves checking your grammar, punctuation, and spelling. Often the best writers are the most critical of their work, so if you find yourself going through several revisions, you can interpret this positively as a sign of your concern for your essay. Nevertheless, at some point you will need to stop revising. Although the end result of your efforts at revision should be an essay you can take pride in, it is difficult to know when your essay is at last finished. As one student put it:

Even after having written what seemed like the final draft of the essay, I found new things to change and new ways to improve the writing. . . . There is no such thing as a final draft. We use this term only because of time limits and deadlines that must end the rewriting process.

FINAL, EDITED PAPER ON "THE DOLL QUEEN"

Here is the student's revised, edited version of her essay on "The Doll Queen." Because she had done so much work in prewriting, her draft was very smooth and didn't need major restructuring, just some changes in wording, a clear title, a more developed thesis, and a stronger, more thoughtful conclusion. What other changes do you notice between the draft and the final version of the essay? Can you think of other suggestions for improving the essay even further?

Carlos, Memory, and Truth in Fuentes' "The Doll Queen"

Carlos Fuentes, like many Latin American authors, explores the way that our minds alter and shape reality. This reality can be in the past, as in memories, or in the present, in our perceptions of others and ourselves. In his story "The Doll Queen," Fuentes allows us to follow the journey of Carlos, a character who is trying to find peace and happiness in reliving a childhood memory. Unfortunately, in plumbing the depths of his past, Carlos encounters unpleasant realities about himself and others. As he peels away layers of memory and imagery, Fuentes shows us the darker, selfish, deceitful side of a young man who appears at first only nostalgic and somewhat bored, while revealing to the reader the terrible discoveries that Carlos makes about just how different memory and truth can be.

At first, Carlos' disappointment and realization are on a very superficial level. The story begins as he goes to a favorite park of his youth to reminisce about his childhood. We learn that he is here because he wants to recover the childhood feelings of tranquility and innocence that he once shared with a little girl, Amilamia, with whom he spent many afternoons in the park. He remembers her as a serious, beautiful, innocent and open child, who knew him at the time that he was passing between his "own irresolute childhood and the open world, the promised land" of young adulthood that Carlos found in his books and advanced schooling. In going to the park, Carlos expects to find a wild garden, with open meadow and rolling hills thick with green grass. But when he arrives, he finds his memories of the place were larger than life. The great hill he remembers is nothing more than "a barely elevated patch of dark stubble with not more heights and depths" than those of sheer imagination. His images of childhood are diminished by time and age, and every aspect of his park that seemed large and grand turns out to be sad and pathetic.

Also in this first episode, Fuentes introduces us to the character of Carlos: the way he thinks, his sensibilities, and his lifestyle. We learn that Carlos is a well-read, well-educated man of 29. He is "a bachelor still, with no family to maintain, slightly bored with sleeping with secretaries . . . feeling the lack of a central attraction such as those" that he once had in youth, with Amilamia. It is natural for Carlos to be curious about his childhood friend, but we sense it is the loneliness and predictability of adult life that truly bring him in search of Amilamia. In his childhood, Carlos abandoned Amilamia. We learn that, frustrated and confused by the situation created by the seven-years difference in their ages, he left her in the park one day, never to return. Carlos has the feeling that now Amilamia will be just the excitement he needs to feel young and vital again. He does not give much thought to how Amilamia will feel about such a reunion, only imagining her in terms of how much like herself in childhood she will still be. Carlos never imagines what he may uncover as he continues his search to mesh past with present. His self-absorption becomes more evident as he goes to Amilamia's home to inquire after her.

At each step in the story, a slightly more distasteful element of Carlos' character manifests itself. His once mild obsession with a memory begins to bring out a deceitful, manipulative side of his personality. For example, when Carlos

goes to Amilamia's house, he has no luck in speaking to the
tenants. However, instead of returning at a later time to try
again, he goes to the city hall and obtains records that enable
him to pose as a building inspector in order to be admitted into
Amilamia's home.

Carlos also wrestles with his own sense of sanity as
memories of the young girl fill his thoughts. He fights with his
imagination, pushing away the crazy notion that "in that house
lived a seven-year-old girl that [he] had known fourteen or
fifteen years before." It is clear in these kinds of illusions
that Carlos is much less interested in Amilamia as a person than
in her private meaning for him.

In his efforts to recapture the wonder of his childhood,
Carlos enters a deeply private play of characters in Amilamia's
home and family. Here another layer of the distance between fact
and fiction is lifted, and Carlos faces more truth about himself
and the reality of Amilamia's fate. He meets Amilamia's parents,
who at first appear distant and strange, and then seem tragic,
as they reveal their reality of Amilamia. Carlos is forced to
face the impropriety of his intrusion into their world, slapped
with the reality of how despicable his behavior and deceit have
been. His childhood friend is dead, it seems, and her family is
in deepest mourning. They have created an unnatural effigy of
her, and left her dark room filled with flowers, toys and
candles to complete a macabre shrine to their lost Amilamia.
Carlos is discouraged, believing himself to have found only
tragedy, sorrow, and self-loathing where he sought only peace
and harmony.

Nearly one year later, Carlos' romantic ideal of Amilamia
again infiltrates his memory, and he goes back to the girl's
family to give them a card she had given him in childhood, a
token of her youth to add to their "shrine." Immediately we are
struck by the discrepancy between his memory of his last visit
and what we have just seen. He seems to have forgotten the
morbid, ghastly atmosphere of the home and the mother's plea to
Carlos to leave the family alone, not to come back again. His
selfish, dreamy nature propels him back to the house, and this
time Carlos must face even more disturbing truths. Finding
Amilamia alive, we sense in Carlos the impact of seeing the real
girl, not only because her deformities make her so different
from the Amilamia he knew, but because the cruelty of his
treatment of her once must now come back to him ten-fold. In his
zealous quest for the pretty little Amilamia and to recapture
seemingly harmless memories, Carlos finds not only his own
weaknesses, but a badly crippled woman and her monstrous, cruel
parents.

A picture of the true reality of Amilamia's world is given
to Carlos and to the reader in one instant, as the man concerned
with his own vision is forced to face a more appalling
redefinition of memory than he could have ever imagined in his

daydreams. As we finish reading the story, Fuentes leaves us with many unanswered questions about Carlos and his future. Will he be shattered by his final vision of his little friend? Will he intervene to help the crippled Amilamia, or will he at last manage to put his childhood behind him, to use the dark realizations he has had in the course of the story to propel him into a full adult life, a life in which he may find it possible to confront the realities of love, commitment, and parenthood? The story provides no easy answers to these questions, and leaves it up to the reader to decide Carlos' fate.

PEER SHARING

Each student in your class has had very special life experiences and has developed an individual outlook on learning and on life. You can become a better reader and writer of literature through learning about the diversity of opinion in your own classroom. A literature class offers the opportunity for sharing; the classroom can become a safe place where each student's voice can contribute to a collaborative interpretation of texts by professional writers as well as to a sharing of knowledge and evaluative skills. Sharing and listening to your peers will help you to improve your own writing. To become a better listener, whether you are in a small group or participating in a discussion with the entire class, try to keep your attention focused on the issues at hand; take notes on what is being said rather than tuning out others' comments and focusing exclusively on what you would like to say. If you feel impatient and have something you want to share, write it down so that when it is your turn to speak, your ideas will be clearly expressed and to the point. In small group activities, such as discussing study questions or sharing a student's essay for comment, it's helpful to practice repeating or rephrasing aloud what each member has just finished saying, just so that you are clear that you heard him or her correctly.

To facilitate the flow of discussion in a small group, one person can be selected to take notes. In a computer classroom the notes can be written directly on the computer and printed at the end of the class. If your classroom does not have a computer, the notes can be photocopied for group members. Spelling, grammar, and punctuation are certainly not crucial; the challenge is for the transcriber to get the ideas brought up in the discussion down on paper. This frees the other group members to participate fully in the discussion. It can also assure that a sense of the continuity of discussion would develop over a number of class periods. The role of transcriber should be rotated, so that each group member gets a chance to practice the activity and has other opportunities to participate in the discussion. The group notes will come to represent a collaborative interpretation of the reading. Conflicting points of view that can't be resolved through discussion should be noted, honored as alternative visions of the work. Students can take the notes home and refer to them when they are writing their own essays.

Following is an example of the group notes kept by a transcriber for a brief group discussion of the story "My Son the Murderer," by Bernard Malamud. As you can see, the group discussion was intense and productive, leading to good insights about the relevance and emotional complexity of the story as well as to possible ideas for further writing.

```
This selection especially caught everybody's attention because
of its unexpected title, coupled with the fact that Malamud
actually meant "murder" in a non-physical, emotional sense. The
conflict between a snoopy, ineffectual yet concerned father and
Harry, the disturbed son in the story who is depressed about
being drafted and possibly sent to Vietnam, struck a familiar
chord among several members of the group. Reactions ranged from
anger towards the father for violating Harry's privacy by
reading his mail, to frustration with Harry's sullen attitude,
to a strong identification with both characters. We also
discussed the effectiveness of Malamud's use of imagery to
express the tension in the relationship and Harry's difficult
transition into the adult world. Group members were particularly
impressed by the power of the image in the story's climactic
scene: "The man on the shore was Harry, standing in water to the
top of his shoes": an image of a young man on the verge of life
or death choices. Our group was able to perceive, through our
discussion and sharing of responses, that the emotions involved
in "My Son the Murderer"--defiance, loneliness, love and hate--
are universal ones, and that the story is still quite relevant
even though it was written during the Vietnam-war years.
```

Peer Revisions in Small Groups

Student writers often benefit from sharing even their early drafts with their peers. If peer review happens frequently in your writing classroom, usually in small groups of four or five students, you may come to experience your writing group as a community with common interests and concerns. However, there are obstacles to be overcome for peer review to function successfully. Peer group participants need to listen to one another's work, to make both supportive and constructive comments about one another's writing. Begin with some basic issues for evaluating peer papers. After your group has worked together for a time, discussion of drafts will follow naturally along the lines suggested by the following questions:

1. Did the paper capture your attention and hold your interest? Why?
2. Does the paper have a clear thesis? Are the ideas interesting and well developed?
3. Does the essay have a voice that holds it together and gives it "personality"?

4. Does the student's interpretation of works you have read and discussed seem accurate and well supported by references to the texts?
5. Does the essay conclude on a strong note?
6. What is the paper's greatest writing strength? How could the writer improve his or her paper?

Always come prepared to your peer reviews. Your preparation will encourage others in your group to be prepared as well. Some groups like to select a leader to keep the group on track; other students prefer a decentralized structure with each member having equal responsibility and making individual reports back to the group or to the class as a whole. Although you will want to revise your paper after your peer review, it is helpful to make enough copies of your paper for all group members so that they can follow along as you read your paper aloud and make comments for you to consider later. Learning how to share your feelings and thoughts about one another's papers in an honest, supportive, and constructive way is both possible and worthwhile. Working on revisions in peer groups will reinforce a sense of camaraderie and community as you help and learn from one another and thus build your skills and confidence in writing. One student wrote in his journal about the changes in his writing process that came through listening to the advice of other group members and practicing multiple revisions:

```
    Peer advice helps in rewriting. My writing group's comments
on drafts proved valuable for improved versions. They also gave
me a more critical eye for my drafts and motivated me to rewrite
the paper to share it again with the group. In discussing my
argument paper, for instance, although I had originally thought
my draft was too subjective, Sonya and Heidi told me that I
needed more examples, especially from my own experience,
explaining my feelings about the issue further, yet presenting
some facts to back up my position so it didn't just seem as if I
was playing on the reader's emotions. I was at first nervous
about having to peer share my paper, but the advice and
constructive criticism helped me to reorganize and develop my
argument in my later drafts.
```

Through keeping your imagination active as you learn to read texts closely, through keeping a reader's journal to record your impressions and ideas for further writing, through sharing your responses to the texts with others, through taking the time and effort required to write and revise your impressions into essays that communicate your views with power and clarity, you will develop your own inner voice. What is writing if not the spirit of the imagination, the journey of the self created from within?

READING
AND WRITING
ABOUT LITERATURE

2

READING
AND WRITING
ABOUT LITERATURE

Chapter 3

READING
AND WRITING
ABOUT STORIES

QUESTIONS RAISED BY STORIES

Most people enjoy reading fiction, but when they think and talk about their reading experiences, as you are doing now in this class, certain questions may arise: What is a story, and how are stories related to the world of facts, of "reality"? Why do people enjoy telling and hearing stories? What is a "good story," and why do we like some stories better than others? What can we learn from reading stories, and how do they "teach"? Understanding the issues raised by these questions is fundamental to appreciating and evaluating fiction. Write down tentative answers to these questions; then read the story that follows, "Helping to Lie," a German tale similar to the folk tales that begin each of the chapters in Part Three of *Imagining Worlds*. After you finish reading the story, write a personal response to the tale in your reading journal.

Helping to Lie

There once was a nobleman who liked to tell terrible lies, but sometimes he got stuck. Once he wanted to hire a new servant. When one came to offer his services, the nobleman asked him if he could lie. "Well," he said, "if it's got to be!"

"Yes," said the nobleman, "I sometimes got stuck telling lies. Then you will have to help me."

One day they were in an inn, and the nobleman was as usual telling lies: "Once I went hunting and I shot down three hares in the air."

"This is not possible," said the others.

"Then you better fetch my coachman," he said, "to bear witness." They fetched him. "Johann, listen, I have just been telling these gentlemen about the three hares I shot in the air. Now you tell them how that was."

"Yes, sir. We were in the meadow, and a hare came jumping through the hedge, and while it was jumping out, you shot and it was dead. Afterward, when it was cut open, there were two young hares inside." Of course the others could say nothing to this.

On their way home the nobleman said that it was well done.

"Well, sir," said Johann, "the next time you tell lies, try to keep out of the air. On firm ground it will be easier for me to help you."

LITERARY QUALITIES OF THE STORY

Even though it is short and written in simple language, "Helping to Lie" has all of the qualities of a short story: a central theme, a consistent point of view, characters, dialogue, symbolism, and figurative language, as well as a plot sequence with beginning, development, high point, and resolution. Let's analyze some of the literary qualities that this folk narrative shares with more "artistic" fiction.

Theme

Themes are the ideas in literature. Sophisticated stories may have several themes. What a reader perceives to be the theme often reflects as much about the values and concerns of the reader as it does about the intentions of the author. "Helping to Lie," a folk tale designed to teach a practical lesson, has a strong central theme concerning truth, reality, and falsehood. The tale does not make subtle ethical distinctions, but it does point out that even a lie must have some qualities of truth or realism if it is to be believed. No thesis statement or "moral" is stated; there is just a series of events and the servant's final words, which read rather like a riddle: "On firm ground it will be easier for me to help you." We could paraphrase the servant's advice to his master as follows: "Try to make statements, even if they are lies, that make some degree of sense or that are based on accurate observations."

Plot

The **plot** of a story is the sequence of events through which the action moves. A plot almost always involves one or more central conflicts that grow in intensity. Traditional stories, often conclude with a clear resolution of the conflict. In "Helping to Lie" the main plot is simple, yet it carries the meaning of the story: A master hires a servant to help him lie more effectively; conflict arises when the master is trapped by an impossible lie. His servant helps him out, offering some useful advice that resolves the action. The story-within-a-story, or secondary plot of the lie itself, begun by the master and completed by the servant, is just as important as the frame plot. It dramatically reveals the servant's imagination and resourcefulness as well as the master's impulsiveness.

Characters

Characters in a story may be flat and unchanging, or "round," revealing different qualities of character that grow and change as the story moves through its complications. Although they are basically static and one-dimensional, the characters in "Helping to Lie" have different values, and the impulsive master, through listening to the servant's commonsense advice, may perhaps learn a valuable lesson about the art of lying and of getting along in social situations.

Point of View

Point of view refers to the teller of the story, either a character or an offstage narrator. Point of view in fiction can be first person, using an "I" narrator; third person (he, she, or they); third-person limited (limited to the awareness of one person); third-person omniscient (an all-knowing narrator); or third-person "objective," in which a third-person narrator sees events from the outside. "Helping to Lie," like most traditional folk tales, uses a third-person narrator who allows us to see the events in the story from an objective perspective, almost as if we were witnessing a play.

Dialogue

Because the story is written in the "objective" point of view, it uses **dialogue** rather than focusing on thoughts and feelings. The dialogue consists of a number of exchanges between servant and master, exchanges that reveal the values and personalities of each while helping to advance the story line.

Setting

Setting refers to where and when a story takes place. This story has several settings, but the most important one is the inn where the master tells his tall tales. The setting of the inn is not described in detail, as in more complex and fully developed stories, but we can imagine it to be a rowdy place where boasting and telling lies are common activities, a form of entertainment.

Symbolism and Figurative Language

Figurative language includes nonliteral, imaginative comparisons, whereas in **symbolism** an object is developed to represent an idea or feeling. Stories depend on such stylistic devices to present subtle meanings and emotions while engaging the senses, emotions, and imagination of the reader. "Helping to Lie" uses symbolism in its references to the hares shot in the air, which could be said to represent the folly of crude boastfulness, whereas the servant's last response to the master is an example of figurative language: "[T]ry to keep out of the air. On firm ground it will be easier for me to help you." Here the servant is speaking figuratively, using "the air" to represent impulsive talk, lying without forethought and "firm ground" to take care to keep one's remarks realistic and believable.

EVALUATING THE STORY

Is "Helping to Lie" a "good story?" That depends on what you mean by "good." Because the tale does seem to condone lying, we would probably say that the story isn't morally uplifting, yet it is realistic and honest in its portrayal of human nature. Because of its amusing, subtle, and imaginative handling of literary techniques and ideas, we would be likely to consider this tale worth reading and sharing with others. The story presents a valuable lesson for all people who feel the need to embellish the truth from time to time, including salespersons, politicians, and even writers. While "Helping to Lie" is about the art of effective lying, it can also be seen as a story about story telling which implies that while an effective story is not totally true to external reality, it can emphasize certain details to dramatize reality, to hold the interest of an audience, and to illuminate the complexity of life and thought. An effective story teller uses a number of strategies or conventions of fiction, such as those we have just seen in "Helping to Lie": theme, plot, character, dialogue, symbolism, point of view, and setting. The author of fiction applies such strategies artfully, with an understanding of the underlying laws of physical and human nature.

WRITING IN RESPONSE TO FICTION: A STUDENT CASEBOOK

There are many ways to write about fiction. You can apply the strategies discussed in our analysis of "Helping to Lie" in order to analyze, interpret, or evaluate a story, or you can share a personal experience called to mind by the original tale, one that seems to parallel it in significant ways. You can even choose to write a story of your own that develops an idea or plot line of the original tale. You will find that the discipline of writing about fiction sharpens your reading process, making you more aware of subtleties of language and literary strategy, as well as of your own values, heart, and imagination. Laurie Fiedler, the student who wrote the casebook that follows on Tim O'Brien's "Field Trip," a story about a veteran's return to Vietnam, wrote two papers in response to the original narrative: a creative response and an analytical essay. Before considering Fiedler's responses to the story, read the story and write down your first responses to it. Consider the meaning of the title, key symbols, figurative expressions, and any strong feelings, positive or negative, that the story's characters, plot, and subject matter encourage you to think about.

Field Trip

Tim O'Brien

Twenty years after leaving Vietnam, I returned with my daughter Kathleen. There we visited the site of Kiowa's death, that place where he had disappeared under mud and water, folded in with the war when the field exploded, and where I now looked for signs of forgiveness or personal grace or whatever else the land might offer. The field was still there, though not as I remembered it. Much smaller, I thought, and not nearly so menacing. And in the bright sunlight it was hard to picture what had happened on this ground some 20 years ago. Except for a few marshy spots along the river, everything was bone-dry. No ghosts—just a flat, grassy field. The place was at peace. There were yellow butterflies. There was a breeze and a wide blue sky. Along the river two old farmers stood in ankle-deep water repairing the same narrow dike where we had laid out Kiowa's body after pulling him from the muck. Things were quiet. At one point, I remember, one of the farmers looked up and shaded his eyes, staring across the field at us; then after a time he wiped his forehead and went back to work.

I stood with my arms folded, feeling the grip of sentiment and time. Amazing, I thought. Twenty years.

Behind me, in the jeep, Kathleen sat waiting with a government interpreter, and now and then I could hear the two of them talking in soft voices. They were already fast friends. Neither of them, I think, understood what all this was about, why I'd insisted that we search out this spot. It had been a hard two-hour ride from Quang Ngai City, bumpy dirt roads and a hot August sun, ending up at an empty field on the edge of nowhere.

I took out my camera, snapped a couple of pictures, then stood gazing out at the field. After a time Kathleen got out of the jeep and came to stand beside me.

"You know what I think?" she said. "I think this place stinks. It smells like . . . God, I don't even *know* what. It smells rotten."

"It sure does. I know that."

"So when can we go?"

"Pretty soon," I said.

She started to say something, but then hesitated. Frowning, she squinted out at the field for a second or so, then shrugged and walked back to the jeep.

Kathleen had just turned ten, and this trip was a kind of birthday present, showing her the world, offering a small piece of her father's history. For the most part she'd held up well—far better than I—and over the first two weeks she'd trooped along without complaint as we hit the obligatory tourist stops. Ho Chi Minh's mausoleum in Hanoi. A model farm outside Saigon. The tunnels at Cu Chi. The monuments and government offices and orphanages. Through most of this Kathleen had seemed to enjoy the foreignness of it all, the exotic food and animals, and even during those periods of boredom and discomfort she'd kept up a good-humored tolerance. At the same time, however, she'd seemed a bit puzzled. The war was as remote to her as cavemen and dinosaurs.

One morning in Saigon she'd asked what it was all about. "This whole war," she said, "why was everybody so mad at everybody else?"

I shook my head. "They weren't mad, exactly. Some people wanted one thing, other people wanted another thing."

"What did *you* want?"

"Nothing," I said. "To stay alive."

"That's all?"

"Yes."

Kathleen sighed. "Well, I don't get it. I mean, how come you were even here in the first place?"

"I don't know," I said. "Because I had to be."

"But *why*?"

I tried to find something to tell her, but finally I shrugged and said, "It's a mystery, I guess. I don't know."

For the rest of the day she was very quiet. That night, though, just before bedtime, Kathleen put her hand on my shoulder and said, "You know something? Sometimes you're pretty weird, aren't you?"

"Well, no," I said.

"You are *too*." She pulled her hand away and frowned at me. "Like coming over here. Some dumb thing happens a long time ago and you can't ever forget it."

"And that's bad?"

"No," she said quietly. "That's weird."

In the second week of August, near the end of our stay, I'd arranged for the side trip up to Quang Ngai. The tourist stuff was fine, but from the start I'd wanted to take my daughter to the places I'd seen as a soldier. I wanted to show her the Vietnam that kept me awake at night—a shady trail outside the village of My Khe, a filthy old pigsty on the Batangan Peninsula. Our time was short, however, and choices had to be made. In the end I decided to take her to this piece of ground where my friend Kiowa had died. It seemed appropriate. And, besides, I had business here.

Now, looking out at the field, I wondered if it was all a mistake. Everything was too ordinary. A quiet sunny day, and the field was not the field I remembered. I pictured Kiowa's face, the way he used to smile, but all I felt was the awkwardness of remembering.

Behind me, Kathleen let out a little giggle. The interpreter was showing her magic tricks.

Things change.

There were birds and butterflies, the soft rustlings of rural anywhere. Below, in the earth, the relics of our presence were no doubt still there, the canteens and bandoliers and mess kits. This little field, I thought, had swallowed so much. My best friend. My pride. My belief in myself as a man of some small dignity and courage. Still, it was hard to find any real emotion. It simply wasn't there. After that long night in the rain, I'd seemed to grow cold inside, all the illusions gone, all the old ambitions and hopes for myself sucked away into the mud. Over the years that coldness had never entirely disappeared. There were times in my life when I couldn't feel much, not sadness or pity or passion, and somehow I blamed this place for what I had become, and I blamed it for taking away the person I had once been. For 20 years this field had embodied all the waste that was Vietnam, all the vulgarity and horror.

Now it was just what it was. Flat and dreary and unremarkable. I walked up toward the river, trying to pick out specific landmarks, but all I recognized was a small rise where Jimmy Cross had set up his command post that night. Nothing else. For a while I watched the two old farmers working under the hot sun. I took a few more photographs, waved at the farmers, then turned and moved back to the jeep.

Kathleen gave me a little nod.

"Well," she said, "I hope you're having fun."

"Sure."

"Can we go now?"

"In a minute," I said. "Just relax."

At the back of the jeep I found the small cloth bundle I'd carried over from the States.

Kathleen's eyes narrowed. "What's that?"

"Stuff," I told her.

She glanced at the bundle again, then hopped out of the jeep and followed me back to the field. We walked past Jimmy Cross's command post, past the spot where Kiowa had gone under, down to where the field dipped into the marshland along the river. I took off my shoes and socks.

"Okay," Kathleen said, "what's going on?"

"A quick swim."

"Where?"

"Right here," I said. "Stay put."

She watched me unwrap the cloth bundle. Inside was Kiowa's old hunting hatchet.

I stripped down to my underwear, took off my wristwatch, and waded in. The water was warm against my feet. Instantly, I recognized the soft, fat feel of the bottom. The water here was eight inches deep.

Kathleen seemed nervous. She squinted at me, her hands fluttering. "Listen, this is stupid," she said, "you can't even hardly get *wet*. How can you *swim* out there?"

"I'll manage."

"But it's not . . . I mean, God it's not even *water,* it's like mush or something."

She pinched her nose and watched me wade out to where the water reached my knees. Roughly here, I decided, was where Mitchell Sanders had found Kiowa's rucksack when we went back to dig him out. I eased myself down, squatting at first, then sitting. There was again that sense of recognition. The water rose to midchest, a deep greenish brown, almost hot. Small water bugs skipped along the surface. Right here, I thought. Leaning forward, I reached in with the hatchet and wedged it handle-first into the soft bottom, letting it slide away, the blade's own weight taking it under. Tiny bubbles broke along the surface.

I tried to think of something decent to say, something meaningful and right, but nothing came to me.

I looked down into the field.

"Well," I finally managed. "There it is."

My voice surprised me. It had a rough, chalky sound, full of things I did not know were there. I wanted to tell Kiowa that he'd been a great friend, the very best, but all I could do was slap hands with the water.

The sun made me squint. Twenty years. A lot like yesterday, a lot like never. In a way, maybe, I'd gone under with Kiowa, and now after two decades I'd finally worked my way out. A hot afternoon, a bright August sun, and the war was over. For a few moments I could not bring myself to move. Like waking from a summer nap, feeling lazy and sluggish, the world collecting itself around me. fifty meters up the field one of the old farmers stood watching from along the dike. The man's face was dark and solemn. As we stared at each other, neither of us moving, I felt something go shut in my heart while something else swung open. Briefly, I wondered if the old man might walk over to exchange a few war stories, but instead he picked up a shovel, raised it over his head and held it there for a time, grimly, like a flag. Then he brought the shovel down and said something to his friend and began digging into the hard, dry ground.

I stood up and waded out of the water.

"What a mess," Kathleen said. "All that gunk on your skin, you look like. . . . Wait'll I tell Mommy, she'll probably make you sleep in the garage."

"You're right," I said. "Don't tell her."

I pulled on my shoes, took my daughter's hand and led her across the field toward the jeep. Soft heat waves shimmied up out of the earth.

When we reached the jeep, Kathleen turned and glanced out at the field.

"That old man," she said, "is he mad at you or something?"

"I hope not."

"He *looks* mad."

"No," I said. "All that's finished."

REACTIONS ON READING "FIELD TRIP"

Just before and after reading "Field Trip," student writer Laurie Fiedler wrote the following responses in her journal. Notice how Fiedler emphasizes ideas and experiences from her past before the first reading, which is a simple response to the title of the story.

Before Reading

The title reminds me of field trips I took with my class in the fourth grade to places like Steinhart Aquarium, where we peered into the rectangular tanks that illuminated the darkened hallways of the aquarium like rows of television sets in department stores . . . I see that the story is about Vietnam. A great many images come into my mind about Vietnam. Having just completed a course in Vietnamese history, I imagine that this is written by an American soldier who fought on the front lines of Vietnam. American soldiers had little understanding of the Vietnamese people and their history. The title suggests to me a young American soldier, naive, witnessing great destruction and massacre in the "field" of battle--a fox hole in combat in Vietnam . . .

After a First Reading

My first impression is that the story is "fluffier" than I had imagined; this made me feel let down. The story was sweet and lacked real punch. I felt the author was over romanticizing, and I felt like his daughter must have felt when she said, "Some dumb thing happens a long time ago and you can't ever forget it." I can't understand the character's self-indulgence in bringing a ten-year-old child for a two hour ride to a swamp where the axe he discards will probably injure some unsuspecting victim. Although I can empathize with the loss of a friend, what did he expect? He went to WAR. It seems a bit much to carry around an axe for twenty years only to dump it halfway around

the world. And if he chose to take his daughter along to teach
her about the harsh realities of life, why couldn't he explain
to her why he was there? What finally galls me is his attempt to
speak for the Vietnamese farmer, "No, that's all finished." He
has decided to resolve his own feelings, but what gives him the
right to speak for the farmer? The farmer has every right to
despise every "round eye" he comes in contact with. The narrator
is so self-involved that he still has no concept of the history
or culture, no respect or understanding of the rape of the
Vietnamese people. I find this sentimentalism arrogant and
ignorant, precisely the chauvanistic white male attitude that
helped instigate the war in Vietnam to begin with.

Fiedler's initial response to the story is negative. She had just finished a
course in Vietnamese history and had anticipated another type of story, one that
made a more overtly political statement. Fiedler felt that the story, which first
appeared in *McCall's*, did not take seriously enough the war in Vietnam and its
long-term influences on American veterans and on the Vietnamese people. She
especially disliked the central character, the veteran, whom she saw as having
little sensitivity to the Vietnamese.

After her initial rejection of the story, Fiedler discussed it with her instructor
and classmates. She then read "Field Trip" again, more slowly and reflectively.
Because she had had trouble connecting emotionally with the veteran, feeling
that his life experiences were quite different from her own, in subsequent readings she tried harder to identify with him. She began to imagine the path he had
traveled in his life, from his school days through being called up by the draft and
sent to Vietnam, to his experience of loss in the war, to the events after the war
as he began to struggle to make his adjustment to peacetime life. Laurie Fiedler
had never read any of Tim O'Brien's earlier Vietnam war fiction, but it would
have been interesting for her to have read other stories by O'Brien about the
war, such as the widely anthologized "The Things They Carry," based on his
own experiences in Vietnam.

As Fiedler developed her fantasies about the character, she was literally
bringing him to life in her mind, serving as a co-creator of the original story.
This process brought her closer to the protagonist in "Field Trip" and eventually
led her to write a short story about the character's life before the experiences
narrated in "Field Trip." In writing her story, Laurie made use of an old atlas she
owned that had been printed in the mid-1960s during the Vietnam war era. She
set her story, which she titled "Then," in a small midwestern town, and learned
as much as possible about life in that community in the mid-1960s, reviewing
her notes and texts from her Vietnam history class for information about the
war. In her story she used key details and symbols from the original story, such
as the hatchet, the marsh, and the field. She also developed the narrator's relationship with the character Kiowa in order to understand better the significance
of the hatchet. To gain more objectivity on the character and his world, she
changed the point of view from first person to third person.

As you read Fiedler's version of the Vietnam war era, which set in motion the events described in O'Brien's story, ask yourself if she has captured the feeling of this period in American history, as you know it through reading, conversation, and films. Does she use vivid, authentic-seeming details to bring her scenes and characters to life? Finally, consider whether her version of the main character's past seems logically connected to or implied by the plot and characters in the story "Field Trip."

Then

Summer of 1966 was coming to an end in Scott's Bluff, Nebraska, and Dennis Mercer was growing restless. He had spent most of his first summer as a high school graduate hooking cutthroats down at the Platte, hanging out at the Dairy Queen, and avoiding his father's store as much as possible; he now watched his friends leaving and felt a growing agitation. He thought about driving Susan McAllister to the bus depot earlier this morning where they had said their tearful goodbyes. Even though she had promised to return at winter break, he felt she was gone; it was over. Once people left Scott's Bluff, they seldom came back for very long.

Back at the deserted Dairy Queen, Dennis licked the last of the vanilla ice cream from his straw and started his car, burning rubber as he lunged out of the parking lot. As he drove home, he thought about his friends Eddie and Frank, who had already been drafted. At least they knew where they were going. Dennis knew it was his turn now.

His family had finished dinner by the time he returned home. As he walked in the house, his sister Molly was standing very tall as she was being fitted for a new dress by his mother. As Dennis stood for a moment watching Molly getting ready so seriously for second grade, he realized how much he would miss her when he left, and the familiar abyss of longing filled his chest again. Images of President Johnson flickered on a small black and white Magnavox while Dennis quietly informed his parents that he'd enlisted in the Army and would be leaving for Fort Sill in three days. His father remained quiet; his mother's eyes teared up. Molly pressed a small Arbor Day coin into his hand for good luck.

The six weeks of boot camp went by quickly. Dennis found Oklahoma much like Nebraska. The hardest part was the deafening sound of the artillery; every night Dennis went to bed with his ears ringing. He got along well with the other men in his unit and was surprised to find himself developing a friendship with an Indian, the first Dennis had ever met. Richard Kiowa's mother and father ran a general store in eastern Wyoming. The unlikely duo of Mercer and Kiowa was formed one night at

Sally's Place, a bar near Fort Sill. Forced outside of the bar
and knocked to the ground by two drunken cowboys, Dennis felt
the stranglehold of one of the drunks loosen around his neck as
he blacked out. He came to as his shoulders were shaken by two
strong hands, Kiowa's. Dennis, too drunk and embarrassed to
care, showed his savior his Arbor Day coin. Kiowa solemnly
pulled a small hatchet out of his knapsack. It had been his
grandfather's and was a symbol of bravery and strength. His
grandfather had used it to kill a bobcat in his manhood ritual.
Fascinated, Dennis dreamed that night of tracking, of hunting,
of becoming a man.

Dennis and Kiowa began their tour in Vietnam in November of
1966. The two arrived with 2,000 other men into Da Nang, about
100 miles from the 17th parallel. They remained there for two
weeks and then were transferred to Binh Son, a small farming
village about 95 miles south. The batallion watched over the
village and patrolled the nearby jungles. Days in the village
were hot and calm. Dennis and Kiowa befriended a small girl,
Trang, who was about Molly's age. Trang was very clever at
finding fresh food for them; she was playful and had an easy
smile. Dennis spent his time in the village playing hide and
seek with Trang and thinking about his future. He and Kiowa
planned to head west to California when their tour was up. They
planned every detail of the trip--the old pick-up they would buy
to haul their possessions in, the short visits back to their
folks to gather up the things they had left behind, the long
drive West, taking turns behind the wheel, rock music on the
radio, singing, visiting the Grand Canyon on a clear night,
riding into San Francisco on a sunny day. They planned this
dream to keep themselves sane and alive.

The Viet Cong never fought the way they were expected to.
There were no front lines. One never knew when the quiet of the
jungle would be ruptured by the clanging of machine guns or hand
grenades. Dennis saw men's legs severed in primitive looking,
but highly sophisticated booby traps. As bad as the days were in
the jungle, the nights were worse. By the time Dennis' artillery
was called in, the Viet Cong had often left their marks on the
flesh of the scouts who preceded the artillery. They would then
simply disappear back into the jungle, leaving Dennis and his
men to tend to the dying and to fire into dark vegetation at
whatever seemed to sway there in the shadows.

The men began to lose their sense of time and place, their
sense of purpose, of decency. Civilians who seemed like they
might be harboring the Cong were executed. Some young men
collected strange souvenirs from a killed Viet Cong (or
suspected Viet Cong--it was hard to be certain . . . .).

By January of 1968 the soldiers began to relax a bit. The
upcoming Tet Holiday had the villagers making elaborate

preparations, often heading north to Chu Lai for exotic goods,
some of which they would share with the soldiers. The ARVN were
preparing to return to their families for the truce. Brigadier
General William Desobry had announced that the Viet Cong were
"poorly motivated, poorly trained," and added that the ARVN had
"the upper hand completely." Jungle excursions had been halted,
and Dennis began to take great joy in learning from Trang how to
make paper lanterns shaped like animals and birds. Dennis and
Kiowa were now counting the weeks until their duty would be
over. After a brief stop at home, they were planning to start
their surfing lessons in California.

On January 31, the harmony came to an abrupt halt.
Mitchell Sanders burst into the mess tent yelling that Da Nang
had been bombed. There were now orders to send artillery
immediately to the North for back-up. Then the second report
came in: Hue had been taken over by at least 5,000 Viet Cong
with more VC on the way. Binh Son was soon under siege as well.
As Dennis fired his artillery, he saw Kiowa running west with
Trang in one hand and her infant brother in the other. Dennis
glanced over at what was left of Trang's hut. Maybe they would
be safe. He knew that Trang's uncle lived in a near-by village
close to Quang Ngai.

Within a few hours it was over. The devastation of South
Vietnam had turned into a military defeat for the North. While
the others preceded with the duty of disposing of the debris
that had once been a village, of shoveling what had once been
men into body bags, Dennis headed east to find Kiowa and Trang.
In an hour they came to the small village outside Quang Ngai. It
too had been hit. The familiar smoldering smell burnt Dennis'
nostrils as he viewed the landscape that had once supported
small huts. Dennis knew this village. He had come here often to
help stock Jimmy Cross's understaffed unit with supplies. As he
came to a marsh, Dennis spotted Kiowa's rucksack. There was no
mistaking it--it was not military issue, but a small pack that
Dennis knew carried only the legacy of Kiowa's grandfather.
Wading waist deep in the muck, Dennis at last found Kiowa, half
sunken, half floating. Trang and her brother would never be
found.

Somehow Dennis made it through the next few months and
arrived home in time for spring. Sprawled awkwardly on the
living-room couch, he heard once again the voice of President
Johnson, saw his worn-out, flabby image flickering from the old
Magnavox, his voice slowed to a crawl, "and will not accept the
nomination of my party. . . ." Dennis's family tried their best
to help him put the war out of his mind. Any reference to his
experiences in Vietnam were quickly quieted so as not to upset
the youngsters--or those older people who had lost sons in the
war. After a few weeks of feeling bored, irritable, and

displaced, Dennis began to follow the dream that he and Kiowa
had so painstakingly planned. He spent the next few years living
in the mountains of Santa Cruz in isolation.

        One night in his hunting dreams Kiowa's grandfather came to
Dennis, again leading him on the trail as Dennis tracked a deer.
On awakening, he knew that it was time to get on with his life
and become a man. He used his G.I. Bill to attend San Jose State
and then took a job teaching English at a high school in San
Francisco. He married Elyce, a young woman he had met while at
college who came to do a workshop at his school during the first
year he taught there. They had a daughter, Kathleen, whose
brightness and understanding continually amazed him.

        Kiowa's family wrote to Dennis telling him that they
considered him a brave man, a blood brother of their son. They
asked Dennis to keep the hatchet as a reminder of what the two
had shared, but he knew it would never truly belong to him. He
knew that he had to go back, to give his memories of Kiowa and
Trang back to the earth. With his wife's blessing, Dennis left
with Kathleen on a field trip to the past. Back to his strong,
brave friend.

        After the historic research and writing involved in writing "Then," Laurie
Fiedler felt ready to return with new understanding to the characters and events
portrayed in "Field Trip." She decided to write an interpretive analysis of the
story and the narrator's devastating experiences in order to answer some of the
questions and objections she had raised in her previous readings of the text. Her
second essay is called "Now," to reflect the present-day setting of the story. As
you read Fiedler's essay, notice how she interprets the symbolism in the story:
the field, the butterflies, the blue sky, Kiowa's hatchet, and the old man whose
ambiguous gesture with a shovel concludes the story. Ask yourself if you agree
with her analysis and evaluation of the narrator. Has he finally succeeded in his
quest to put his past in order? Does the student writer provide enough evidence
to convince you of her viewpoint?

Now

        In the story "Field Trip" Tim O'Brien creates a narrator
who describes his return to Vietnam with his 10 year old
daughter 20 years after a tour of duty in Vietnam. The narrator
has brought his daughter with him to help her to understand an
important part of her father's history. He has taken her on a
tour of some of the main tourist attractions of Vietnam, but has
difficulty answering her questions about the war and what he was
doing there: he can only say that he was trying "to stay alive."
The short story begins with O'Brien's narrator and his daughter
arriving at a half-dried-up pond in a field where his friend
Kiowa was killed in battle. As the scene at the pond develops,

the character discovers the value of his present-day life and
realizes that he has no more need to dwell on the past.

When the narrator enters the former field of battle, he
realizes that it is not at all as he remembers it to be: the
pond is much smaller, the field, quite ordinary. Although he
allows himself to be momentarily overtaken by remembered
emotions, he returns to the jeep, retrieves a small sack, and
proceeds, to his daughter's disbelief, to wade out into the
murky swamp. He drops a hatchet, a treasured memento of his
friend Kiowa, deep into the muck where he last saw Kiowa, then
glances up at an old Vietnamese farmer working in the field. The
farmer raises a shovel "grimly . . . like a flag" and then
begins to dig in the "hard, dry ground." Although the old man's
gesture could be interpreted as hostile, the narrator chooses
not to see it that way, to look beyond it and to leave the field
with his daughter in calm and dignity. "All that's finished" are
the narrator's last words, spoken in response to his daughter's
question about the old man's apparent anger. The war seems to
have ended at last for the narrator.

Why would a man with such pain and so many haunting
memories bring his daughter half-way around the world to a
place that represents to him only death and destruction? The
narrator thinks that the experience will be a "field trip," a
learning experience for his daughter. Yet the trip has no
lesson to teach his daughter about Vietnam. His daughter does
not need the trip; rather, he needs to have his daughter along,
as she is his link to the present and the future. He is aware
of his daughter's magical quality of joy and of forgiveness.
The daughter realizes that his pain has overshadowed his life,
but she doesn't judge him for it: "Some dumb thing happens a
long time ago and you can't ever forget it." When the narrator
asks her if "that's bad" she responds simply, "No. . . . That's
weird." The narrator has been afraid of what he might find back
in the pond. He has brought his daughter along to keep him
afloat.

The field itself is seen by the narrator as an extension of
his own inner life, his conscience. When he first sees the
field, he looks for "signs of forgiveness or personal grace." He
finds none--fields do not offer such things; they simply grow
and change in response to the natural elements. He expects the
field to be menacing, as it was during the war. It is not that
way now; instead, he finds a "place at peace. There were yellow
butterflies. There was a breeze and a wide blue sky." He has
come to find something, but it is not forgiveness. While he
doesn't realize it yet, he has already forgiven himself.
Although he has been obsessed with the war and Kiowa's death for
twenty years, he has already gotten on with his life; in fact,
he has created a new life. The yellow butterflies may represent
the joy and hope his daughter brings him, while the great blue

sky represents the hopes and dreams yet to be realized in the
narrator's life and in the life of his family.

The pond represents the narrator's worst nightmare, the
depth of his pain. He blames the pond for taking his pride,
dignity, and self-respect along with his friend. But the pond,
and its quicksand-like muck that once sucked down his dreams,
now is smaller than he had remembered it. As far in as he can
wade, he can't submerge himself. He must sit down to bring the
water to chest level. The pond no longer has the power to drag
him down. Only an odor left in the air, the stagnant stench of
the drying pond, suggests the faint memory of a terrible
experience long past, almost forgotten.

The Vietnamese farmer is a silent sentinel to the
narrator's struggle in the field. The abruptness of his gesture
in raising the shovel "like a flag" suggests anger and
resentment, but for the narrator the farmer seems to represent
the fears of the past, fears of the "other," the exotic-looking,
alien people whose presence loomed in the jungles and whose
anger killed the narrator's friend. Now the exotic, once
frightening "enemy" is only a farmer, his instrument of
aggression is simply a shovel that breaks new ground, both for
the Vietnamese as well as for the narrator, who chooses to see
the farmer's gesture as peaceful, as the sign of a new
beginning.

Although the main character in "Field Trip" returned to
Vietnam to bury the hatchet, he realizes at the end that he
buried it long ago. The field is full of life now; the pond of
death is almost dried up. The narrator is ready to get on with
his life. He has grown past his Vietnam years, so that his great
emotional journey is finally only an episode in his life, only a
field trip. But still it is a necessary ritual for him, a lesson
to be learned.

Chapter 4

READING AND WRITING ABOUT ESSAYS

FORMS AND PURPOSES OF THE ESSAY

Essays take different forms and have many purposes, from telling a story and exploring one's own experiences, to explaining causes and procedures, to arguing a position and critiquing the writings and ideas of others. Although it is considerably more polished and public, the essay is similar to the journal; in fact, as you read through the journal entries included in this text, many of them may remind you of the tone, language, and development of essays. This may be because the essay is the one type of writing taught so universally in schools that almost every literate adult has had some experience with the form; thus, when we sit down to write, our most intimate thoughts "naturally" find their way into language in the form of personal essays.

Most of the essays you have written for your previous composition and literature classes and for other academic courses were designed to help you clarify ideas and experiences, for yourself as well as for your peers and instructors, to create a strong intellectual or emotional focus, and to make a series of points about a subject through clear topic sentences and development of support and examples. Traditional classroom essays often begin with a short introduction that provides background information and a thesis or statement of the essay's main point. In the main part of the essay key supports are presented in well-developed paragraphs that maintain the attention of a reader through effective examples, persuasive evidence, vivid descriptive images, and original figures of speech. Finally, an effective conclusion is presented, often ending with a strong clincher sentence.

The classroom essay has its limitations, and it can be a stilted, inauthentic mode of writing, especially if it is written only to fulfill an instructor's assignment. Such "schoolwork" may lack a sense of genuine commitment to ideas, making predictable statements and arguments possibly designed to avoid offending a teacher rather than to speaking out boldly on a subject of vital concern to the writer.

WRITER'S VOICE IN THE ESSAY

If a student is only writing to fulfill an instructor's assignment and needs to learn more about how to use language expressively, his or her essay may lack a sense of voice, what Donna J. Hickey refers to in *Developing a Written Voice* as "the sound pattern of a distinct, engaging, human personality." The "sound pattern" that emerges as the dominant voice of an essay is easy to recognize; often only a few lines are enough to announce the presence of a writer who has a clear sense of voice, a personality expressed in words, sentences, and rhythms of speech. The writer's voice lingers with a reader long after particular points and arguments are forgotten; the voice is what makes reading the essay a pleasure rather than a task, an illumination rather than simply a means for acquiring knowledge, such as might be gained from reading a dictionary, an almanac, or an encyclopedia. A strong sense of voice will be be found in most of the essays in *Imagining Worlds;* as you read and write about these essays, consider what constitutes the unique quality of each writer's style of expression.

To identify what makes a writer's voice unique, ask the following questions about the selection that you are reading or writing:

1. What is the writer's fundamental outlook on life and relationship to the subject at hand? Is the writer's tone serious, sarcastic, cynical, highly emotional, rational?

2. How does the writer share experiences that are personal or that seem lived and authentic to help sustain a sense of connection, of dialogue with the reader?

3. What "conversational" uses of language does the writer develop? Is there any colloquial, informal language? Does the writer sometimes employ unusual words or slang expressions for special effects?

4. Does the writer develop any figurative (nonliteral) comparisons that reveal original thinking, an ability to perceive reality sharply and to make original, insightful connections?

5. How does the writer create rhythm or repetition within the structures of the sentences or throughout an entire paragraph or essay? Is there a pattern of sentences of increasing length and complexity, followed by one or more shorter sentences for emphasis, or do most of the sentences reflect a simple structure?

THE ESSAY AS EXPLORATION

In addition to a strong sense of voice, you will find that professional essays are often less structured and goal-directed than the classroom essay. Michel de Montaigne, who originated the essay form, described the form using a French word, *essai,* which means "attempt." Montaigne's definition suggests that writers think through developing language and may develop ambiguous, tentative, or speculative ideas in their essays; that an essay can be an exploration of a thought, a teasing out of an intellectual impulse, as well as a focused, directed series of points in defense of a thesis.

RELATIONSHIP BETWEEN THE ESSAY AND FICTION

Although we often think of the essay as "real," as nonfictional, even at times confessional in tone, essays and fiction share certain characteristics. For example, a short story writer may create an imaginary speaker who attempts to persuade another character, as Donald Barthelme does in "The Sandman," a story that consists of a boyfriend's rambling letter to his girlfriend's psychiatrist. The speaker in such a story may seem to be writing an essay that argues a position, but because the reader understands that the speaker is an imaginary person, a "character," the speaker's argument can be interpreted literally but understood as a means for revealing motives, values, and personality. On the other hand, some essays, such as Jonathan Swift's ironic satire, "A Modest Proposal," employ techniques of fiction. In "A Modest Proposal," Swift develops the persona or mask of an insensitive speaker, a "character" who argues that Irish children should be roasted and eaten to alleviate the food shortage in that country. Most readers soon realize that Swift is critical of his narrative, and that the essay as a whole is a satire of British attitudes toward the Irish. Modern essayists and columnists such as Art Hoppe and Art Buchwald also write essays using a persona whose views do not directly reflect their own. Readers know that the "speaker" in these essays and columns is really not the author but only a mask the writer has created to convey ideas effectively.

Many of the essays in this book can be referred to as "literary," in that they use the techniques and devices usually associated with literature in order to engage the attention of readers, to make points, and to create imaginary worlds.

The literary essay with a strong sense of individual voice and richness of imagery is vividly represented in Virginia Woolf's "Professions for Women." As you read the essay, consider the five questions about voice (on page 50).

Professions for Women

Virginia Woolf

When your secretary invited me to come here, she told me that your Society is concerned with the employment of women and she suggested that I might tell you something about my own professional experiences. It is true I am a woman; it is true I am employed; but what professional experiences have I had? It is difficult to say. My profession is literature; and in that profession there are fewer experiences for women than in any other, with the exception of the stage—fewer, I mean, that are peculiar to women. For the road was cut many years ago—by Fanny Burney, by Aphra Behn, by Harriet Martineau, by Jane Austen, by George Eliot—many famous women, and many more unknown and forgotten, have been before me, making the path smooth, and regulating my steps. Thus, when I came to write, there were very few material obstacles in my way. Writing was a reputable and harmless occupation. The family peace was not broken by the scratching of a pen. No demand was made upon the family purse. For ten and sixpence one can buy paper enough to write all the plays of Shakespeare—if one has a mind that way. Pianos and models, Paris, Vienna and Berlin, masters and mistresses, are not needed by a writer. The cheapness of writing is, of course, the reason why women have succeeded as writers before they have succeeded in the other professions.

But to tell you my story—it is a simple one. You have only got to figure to yourselves a girl in a bedroom with a pen in her hand. She had only to move that pen from left to right—from ten o'clock to one. Then it occurred to her to do what is simple and cheap enough for all—to slip a few of those pages into an envelope, fix a penny stamp in the corner, and drop the envelope into the red box at the corner. It was thus that I became a journalist; and my effort was rewarded on the first day of the following month—a very glorious day it was for me—by a letter from an editor containing a cheque for one pound ten shillings and sixpence. But to show you how little I deserve to be called a professional woman, how little I know of the struggles and difficulties of such lives, I have to admit that instead of spending that sum upon bread and butter, rent, shoes and stockings, or butcher's bills, I went out and bought a cat—a beautiful cat, a Persian cat, which very soon involved me in bitter disputes with my neighbours.

What could be easier than to write articles and to buy Persian cats with the profits? But wait a moment. Articles have to be about something. Mine, I seem to remember, was about a novel by a famous man. And while I was writing this review, I discovered that if I were going to review books I should need to do battle with a certain phantom. And the phantom was a woman, and when I came to know her better I called her after the heroine of a famous poem, "The Angel in the House." It was she who used to come between me and my paper when I was writing reviews. It was she who bothered me and wasted my time and so tormented me that at last I killed her. You who come of a younger and happier generation may not have heard of her—you may not know what I mean by the Angel in the House. I will describe her as shortly as I can. She was intensely sympathetic. She was immensely charming. She was utterly unselfish. She excelled in the difficult arts of family life. She sacrificed herself daily. If there was a chicken, she took the leg; it there was a draught she sat in it—in short she was so constituted that she never had a mind or a wish of her own, but preferred to sympathize always with the minds and wishes of others. Above all—I need not say it—she was pure. Her purity was supposed to be her chief beauty—her blushes, her great grace. In those days—the last of Queen Victoria—every house had its Angel. And when I came to write I encountered her with the very first words. The shadow of her wings fell on my page; I heard the rustling of her skirts in the room. Directly, that is to say, I took my pen in hand to review that novel by a famous man, she slipped behind me and whispered: "My dear, you are a young woman. You are writing about a book that has been written by a man. Be sympathetic; be tender; flatter; deceive; use all the arts and wiles of our sex. Never let anybody guess that you have a mind of your own. Above all, be pure." And she made as if to guide my pen. I now record the one act for which I take some credit to myself, though the credit rightly belongs to some excellent ancestors of mine who left me a certain sum of money—shall we say five hundred pounds a year?—so that it was not necessary for me to depend solely on charm for my living. I turned upon her and caught her by the throat. I did my best to kill her. My excuse, if I were to be had up in a court of law, would be that I acted in self-defence. Had I not killed her she would have killed me. She would have plucked the heart out of my writing. For, as I found, directly I put pen to paper, you cannot review even a novel without having a mind of your own, without expressing what you think to be the truth about human relations, morality, sex. And all these questions, according to the Angel in the House, cannot be dealt with freely and openly by women; they must charm, they must conciliate, they must—to put it bluntly— tell lies if they are to succeed. Thus, whenever I felt the shadow of her wing or the radiance of her halo upon my page, I took up the inkpot and flung it at her. She died hard. Her fictitious nature was of great assistance to her. It is far harder to kill a phantom than a reality. She was always creeping back when I thought I had despatched her. Though I flatter myself that I killed her in the end, the struggle was severe; it took much time that had better have been spent upon learning Greek grammar; or in roaming the world in search of adventures. But it was a real experience; it was an experience that was bound to befall all women writers at that time. Killing the Angel in the House was part of the occupation of a woman writer.

But to continue my story. The Angel was dead; what then remained? You may say that what remained was a simple and common object—a young woman in a bedroom with an inkpot. In other words, now that she had rid herself of falsehood, that young woman had only to be herself. Ah, but what is "herself"? I mean, what is a woman? I assure you, I do not know. I do not believe that you know. I do not believe that anybody can know until she has expressed herself in all the arts and professions open to human skill. That indeed is one of the reasons why I have come here—out of respect for you, who are in process of showing us by your experiments what a woman is, who are in process of providing us, by your failures and successes, with that extremely important piece of information.

But to continue the story of my professional experiences. I made one pound ten and six by my first review; and I bought a Persian cat with the proceeds. Then I grew ambitious. A Persian cat is all very well, I said; but a Persian cat is not enough. I must have a motor car. And it was thus that I became a novelist—for it is a very strange thing that people will give you a motor car if you will tell them a story. It is a still stranger thing that there is nothing so delightful in the world as telling stories. It is far pleasanter than writing reviews of famous novels. And yet, if I am to obey your secretary and tell you my professional experiences as a novelist, I must tell you about a very strange experience that befell me as a novelist. And to understand it you must try first to imagine a novelist's state of mind. I hope I am not giving away professional secrets if I say that a novelist's chief desire is to be as unconscious as possible. He has to induce in himself a state of perpetual lethargy. He wants life to proceed with the utmost quiet and regularity. He wants to see the same faces, to read the same books, to do the same things day after day, month after month, while he is writing, so that nothing may break the illusion in which he is living—so that nothing may disturb or disquiet the mysterious nosings about, feelings round, darts, dashes and sudden discoveries of that very shy and illusive spirit, the imagination. I suspect that this state is the same both for men and women. Be that as it may, I want you to imagine me writing a novel in a state of trance. I want you to figure to yourselves a girl sitting with a pen in her hand, which for minutes, and indeed for hours, she never dips into the inkpot. The image that comes to my mind when I think of this girl is the image of a fisherman lying sunk in dreams on the verge of a deep lake with a rod held out over the water. She was letting her imagination sweep unchecked round every rock and cranny of the world that lies submerged in the depths of our unconscious being. Now came the experience, the experience that I believe to be far commoner with women writers than with men. The line raced through the girl's fingers. Her imagination had rushed away. It had sought the pools, the depths, the dark places where the largest fish slumber. And then there was a smash. There was an explosion. There was foam and confusion. The imagination had dashed itself against something hard. The girl was roused from her dream. She was indeed in a state of the most acute and difficult distress. To speak without figure she had thought of something, something about the body, about the passions which it was unfitting for her as a woman to say. Men, her reason told her, would be shocked. The consciousness of what men will say of a woman who speaks the truth about her passions had roused her from her artist's state of unconsciousness. She could write no more. The trance was over. Her imagination could work no longer. This I believe to be a very common experience with women writers—they are impeded by the extreme conventionality of the other sex. For though men sensibly allow themselves great freedom in these respects, I doubt that they realize or can control the extreme severity with which they condemn such freedom in women.

These then were two very genuine experiences of my own. Those were two of the adventures of my professional life. The first—killing the Angel in the House—I think I solved. She died. But the second, telling the truth about my own experiences as a body, I do not think I solved. I doubt that any woman has solved it yet. The obstacles against her are still immensely powerful—and yet they are very difficult to define. Outwardly, what is simpler than to write books? Outwardly, what obstacles are there for a woman rather than for a man? Inwardly, I think, the case is very different; she has still many ghosts to fight, many prejudices to overcome. Indeed it will be a long time still, I think, before a woman can sit down to write a book without finding a phantom to be slain, a rock to be dashed against. And if this is so in literature, the freest of all professions for women, how is it in the new professions which you are now for the first time entering?

Those are the questions that I should like, had I time, to ask you. And indeed, if I have laid stress upon these professional experiences of mine, it is because I believe that they are, though in different forms, yours also. Even when the path is nominally open—when there is nothing to prevent a woman from being a doctor, a lawyer, a civil servant—there are many phantoms and obstacles, as I believe, looming in her way. To discuss and define them is I think of great value and importance; for thus only can the labour be shared, the difficulties be solved. But besides this, it is necessary also to discuss the ends and the aims for which we are fighting, for which we are doing battle with these formidible obstacles. Those aims cannot be taken for granted; they must be perpetually questioned and examined. The whole position, as I see it—here in this hall surrounded by women practising for the first time in history I know not how many different professions—is one of extraordinary interest and importance. You have won rooms of your own in the house hitherto exclusively owned by men. You are able, though not without great labour and effort, to pay the rent. You are earning your five hundred pounds a year. But this freedom is only a beginning; the room is your own, but it is still bare. It has to be furnished; it has to be decorated; it has to be shared. How are you going to furnish it, how are you going to decorate it? With whom are you going to share it, and upon what terms? These, I think are questions of the utmost importance and interest. For the first time in history you are able to ask them; for the first time you are able to decide for yourselves what the answers should be. Willingly would I stay and discuss those questions and answers—but not tonight. My time is up; and I must cease.

Theme and Tone of the Essay

Like the folktale "Helping to Lie," Woolf's essay explores the relationship between lying and truth telling. Woolf's thesis, that there are repressive forces within people which make it difficult for them to tell the truth when the truth might be shocking, is quite different from that of "Helping to Lie," which seemed to condone lying, at least in the form of tall tales for the entertainment of casual acquaintances. Woolf is reflecting on the intimate relationship between a woman and her writing, and she sees it as essential (yet almost impossibly challenging) that writers be honest, creating intense moments of intimacy and revelation in their work. A clear, serious, yet vulnerable voice comes across in Woolf's essay, as intense and engaged as the voice in a first-person narrative story or a lyric poem; in fact, Woolf was a widely published and highly acclaimed story writer and novelist.

Sharing Experience with the Reader

Much of the power of a strong literary essay develops from the author's ability to use example and illustration derived from authentic, lived experience. Notice how effectively Woolf begins her exploration of the subject of the need for privacy, honesty, and revelation in women's writing through a series of examples from her own life—incidents about mailing her writings off to be published, buying a cat, getting in disputes with neighbors. The examples contain storylike, precise detail, and above all, they seem believable—we assume they really happened.

Conversational Voice

One reason why we are receptive to Woolf's thesis is because of her open, direct sense of voice. Her essay retains its original direct address to members of a women's society, and she invites her audience to participate with her in her reflection on the difficulties involved in being a professional writer. She uses ordinary spoken language, with many dashes and asides ("But wait a moment") and even includes fragments ("The Angel in the House") for dramatic and intimate effect. Most of her language is down to earth, with a number of short sentences and common, concrete language.

Use of Figurative Language

Woolf uses metaphoric language to clarify the mental and emotional response of a woman trying to write honestly and deeply: "The image that comes to mind when I think of this girl [writing] is the image of a fisherman lying sunk in dreams on the verge of a deep lake. . . ." When she wants to describe the barriers to honesty in women's writing, she extends this metaphor: "The line . . .

sought the pools, the depths. And then there was a smash . . . foam and confusion." As the writer is confronted with her own inhibitions about "speak[ing] the truth about her passions. . . . She could write no more." Woolf uses the powerful central symbol of a "room of one's own" to represent the writer's sense of professionalism and privacy, while the disturbing character of "The Angel of the House" is used to objectify the voice of social decorum that undercuts the woman's writer's efforts to be a professional, to serve her own vision of truth and reality rather than to serve her family and to fill an accepted social role.

Use of Patterned Language

Woolf's sense of voice is intensified by her use of repeated phrases and clauses. She uses the sentence "It has to be furnished" (a reference to the "room of one's own" of the professional woman writer) to introduce a series of similar sentences which build the symbol of the room emphatically through their repeated form: "It has to be furnished; it has to be decorated; it has to be shared." She continues and builds to her conclusion by challenging her readers with a series of related, unanswered questions: "How are you going to furnish it, how are you going to decorate it? With whom are you going to share it, and on what terms?"

WRITING IN RESPONSE TO ESSAYS: A STUDENT CASEBOOK

Although it is possible to write analytically about essays, as we have just done about Woolf's essay, reading an essay more often evokes a strong response, a desire to "talk back" to the text in agreement or disagreement with the author's views, as in a letter to the editor. Students frequently find that writing in their journals informal, "opinionated" responses to what they read helps them to clarify and strengthen their own views on the subject of an essay and prepares them for more complex, analytical writing. Following is a series of responses by a student writer, Kim Carlson, to Virginia Woolf's "Professions for Women." Before reading the student's responses, you should write a journal entry of your own expressing your feelings and ideas about "Professions for Women." After you have finished writing, think about the student's response: On what aspects of the essay did Kim Carlson choose to focus? To what extent does she seem to accept the text's meaning, to create a dialogue with it, or to disagree with its ideas? How does she try to apply the issues raised in the text to the concerns of today's women? How is Kim Carlson's response to the essay similar to and yet different from your response?

REACTIONS ON READING "PROFESSIONS FOR WOMEN"

First Response

I've read this before; I know I have. I remember sitting in my sister's room on the edge of her bed and reading this a long time ago, not really fully understanding it. I must have been snooping through her schoolbooks. Anyway . . . this essay seems as if I could have heard it spoken yesterday at some meeting for women students at my college, on their way to becoming doctors, lawyers, politicians, whatever--the talk of overcoming the prejudices against women that exist within the working world of the male.

Why is it that a woman, on an average, still makes 60 cents to every dollar a man makes? When I think of stereotypical women's professions, I immediately come up with teacher, nurse, maid, housekeeper, baby-sitter: professions where the main objective is caring for people, oftentimes caring for children. It seems as if women in these professions are trading in time with their own families to take care of someone else's.

Women are the caretakers of the world, I firmly believe that, and they always will be. Every woman is instilled with the natural desire to nurture, to care for others, especially children. Despite all my higher level education, despite my liberal upbringing and the thousands of times that it was shown to me that I could be anything I wanted, do anything I wanted, when I see a little toddler smiling I want to drop everything and have my own children.

Professions for women are creeping forward, not shooting off the way they should be. There are still only a few women in Congress, far more male doctors than female, more professional men than women. Why? It is not that we lack the drive. Many of the women I know are the most ambitious, driven individuals I have ever met. Then why isn't it 50/50 yet? Because someone must raise our children, someone has to care for everyone else. And there is a core in every woman, a circle of wisdom that knows that raising two, or three, or four wonderful children and giving them the best of everything is more important than securing a partnership in the firm or getting tenure at the University. We all know that when it is all over, when the lights have dimmed and the air has calmed, we will be happy with our memories of the lives we have touched, and not with the money in the bank.

Second Response

In Kim Carlson's second reading and response to the text, she decided to explore another issue raised in Woolf's essay: its commentary on the world of literature and of women's writing in particular. Carlson raises a question here that is only hinted at in the original text; she shows a willingness to go beyond Woolf's focus on the difficulties of recognition for the woman writer to a reflection on the differences between male and female writing. She thinks about the problem of stereotyping in critical attempts to assess and categorize the style and concerns of women's writing and the female voice in writing.

My Second Reaction on Reading "Professions for Women"

My professor once lectured for an entire week on the "non-linearity" of women's writing, specifically Virginia Woolf's To the Lighthouse. Why must women's writing be categorized this way? Of course women's writing is going to be different from a man's, there are empirical differences which will divide their experiences and emotions from a man's, shaping their writing differently. But the same can be said for two different women writers, or for that matter, two different male writers. You cannot lump all of women's literature together--it simply defies that sort of categorizing. Can you imagine the absurdity of holding a class on the male writers of the 19th century, or attempting to characterize all of literature written by men as sharing certain characteristics? Impossible!

Virginia Woolf believes that writing is considered by society to be a good profession for a woman because it is relatively cheap and does not disrupt the household. There is a stereotype that a woman's writing will always be flowing, emotional, "touchy-feely," while a man's writing will be rational and coherent. Frankly, that is absurd. Women are capable of writing in any way they choose--and I hope that those women who are today aspiring to be writers ignore the walls pressing in on them and let their style breathe and expand in any way that it wishes. There may be a tendency to write "emotionally" because that is what is expected, or there may be a tendency to write dryly for the sole purpose of swinging the pendulum the other direction: fight it!! Writing is a personal expression, it should come from you and no one else, should be shaped by your expectations and ideals and no one else's. The Angel needs to be killed again and again, banished to the past where it belongs, as a relic of the restraints of women's writing which no longer apply.

After completing two responses to the essay, Kim Carlson began to take some notes for a paper on the figure of the Angel in the House, the imaginary woman who haunted Woolf, making it difficult for her to write freely about her thoughts and feelings. The Angel is a symbol, an internalized version of the "proper," obedient, repressed woman idealized by the Victorians. Although Carlson saw how the Angel limited women's power of accomplishment in the world, she could identify with some of the Angel's traditional values, such as the desire to have children. Carlson began to think about how the text might be read and responded to from the Angel's perspective, and decided finally to write a creative narrative in which she would allow the Angel to tell her own side of the story. She found a few key lines that captured the personality and values of the Angel: "Above all—she was pure . . . her blushes, her great grace . . ."; "[she] preferred to sympathize always with the mind and wishes of others"; "they must charm, they must conciliate . . . tell lies if they are to succeed. . . ."

As you read Carlson's essay, notice how she uses humor, images, dialogue, and physical interaction between the Angel and a youthful, rebellious "Ginny Woolf" to dramatize her retelling of Woolf's essay. Does this "creative" response lead you to interpret or to re-see the essay differently? Could Carlson have used other ideas and images from the original essay to enhance and deepen the retelling by the Angel? Did you feel that the point at which the Angel breaks off and concludes her narrative/argument is appropriate, or could other points have been made in defense of her life style?

No Respect

Well, of all the nerve I have ever seen in my entire life! Obviously little Ginny was not aware that I was trying to help her, trying to guide her gently to the path of a proper woman. That is my duty, you understand, to make sure the little darlings of the world don't run astray and trample the delicate blossoms of budding young gentlemen. I tried to tell her, "Now Virginia, our role as young women is to be gardeners--water the little seedlings, tend to their soil and nurture them lovingly, and one day they will spring up into the able-bodied men who will take care of you and provide for your every whim and fancy. And you must be careful not to tread on them, not to do anything that may damage their pride or hinder their growth." And what did that uncouth little creature do? She trampled all over the whole garden, writing article after article criticizing and deriding the literary works of men, mind you, leaving their flower carcasses crushed in her tracks.

It was a terrible sight, I tell you, just atrocious. Of course, I did not give up there; my mission to educate her and other women is far too pressing an issue to be abandoned so quickly. I followed her everywhere, constantly trying to impress upon her the attitudes and mannerisms she needed to adopt in order to be a genteel young lady. At parties, I would glide up behind her and whisper in her ear, reminding her to laugh at Mr. Hoffenpot's inconsequential joke, telling her to make sure that everyone was well cared for and entertained. And sometimes I did succeed, my efforts paying off in Virginia's conciliation to the gentlemen in the room, just as things should be. But more often than not she acted as if she hadn't heard a word I said. To tell you the truth, I began to think that maybe, just maybe, Ginny didn't agree with my beliefs, maybe she thought that these time-honored standards for a woman's behavior simply didn't apply to her.

But what a ridiculous thought! To think that any lady would want to conduct herself in a manner that was not sweet and kind, tender and feminine, and above all, self-sacrificing. It is the duty of a lady to make sure that everyone else is happy and provided for before she tends to her own needs. This is what keeps relationships, families, my goodness, <u>society</u> running smoothly and without confusion. Can you imagine the utter chaos that would arise if women began to lead their lives for themselves, putting their own comfort and needs and happiness before that of their families and the gentlemen in their lives? Simply unthinkable. In such a world how would we be able to tell the difference between the young ladies and the gentlemen? You might as well let the young ladies run around in men's britches and make complete fools of themselves--since they desire to behave as men, why not have them dress like men also?

You know, to tell you the God's honest truth, I think maybe she was just a little tiny bit jealous of me. Honestly now, can I help it if I look lovely in my long white skirts and my dainty, feathered wings? My radiance and beauty stem from my purity, naturally, and if only Ginny would have followed my example and behaved as coyly and sweetly as I do, then she could have become almost as beautiful as I (well, we can't all be the <u>most</u> beautiful, now, can we?). Of course I never flaunted my loveliness, for a proper young lady would never do such a thing, but I suspect that after seeing me day after day and being subjected to my charms, she was a little envious. I can't blame her for that, I suppose; no doubt any other young woman would feel the same. But maybe, just maybe the reason that she chose to behave so insolently towards me was because she knew she would never be as virtuous and angelic as I am. If only Ginny would have accepted my guidance, if only she had listened . . .

And then, it happened. She was sitting at that little desk of hers in the corner of the room, slaving away at some silly literary critique or another. No doubt she was criticizing, most improperly, a work by a male author when she <u>knows</u> that she ought to be praising him and heralding the wisdom of whatever little novel that he has written. Well, of course I couldn't let her get away with that--after all, she had been ignoring my invaluable advice for such a long time now. So I crept up behind her and suggested sweetly, "Ginny, dear, why don't you forget about that silly article and go downstairs to do some needlepoint with your sisters?" At that point she slowly laid her pen down next to her paper, turned away from the desk and looked me straight in the eye. That little wench--she gazed at me with the sweetest, most grateful look upon her face, and then she grabbed the inkpot off her desk and flung it right at me! The ink soaked into my beautiful white dress and even spotted my wings, my precious wings. It was all I could do to leave that room before she lost her senses entirely and would try to throw me from the window.

I tried for weeks to get those ink spots out of my gown.
They have faded somewhat, but I don't suppose that I will ever
be able to remove completely the stains that little Ginny Woolf
left upon me. And to my utter horror and amazement, she was not
the only young lady who attempted to rid me from their lives.
Others have tried to stab me with their pens and pencils, tie me
up with their typewriter ribbons, or gag me with their little
pink erasers. And I must admit that the damage has been done; I
will never be the same as the pristine young darling that
started this mission so many years ago. Unfortunately, it seems
that the longer time goes on, I am appreciated and worshipped
less and less. Perhaps women are beginning to question whether
they even need my strong moral guidance in their lives. It is
almost as if they don't even <u>want</u> to become representatives of
all that is sweet, pure, gracious, and docile. Is it possible
that my mission is no longer a fruitful one? I can't bear to
even consider the possibility. But don't you think for a minute
that I'm giving up the fight--oh, no, that certainly would not
do. I still have many, many years of work left in me, and
besides, a <u>real</u> lady never breaks her word.

After writing an imaginative monologue from the Angel's point of view,
Kim Carlson tried a more expository and argumentative approach. In the essay
that follows, "Angels, Devils, Angels, Devils . . . ," she reflects on the meanings
that Woolf's essay might have for a woman today, whose inner conflict is one
between the feminist self, which tends to be the dominant side of the personality, and the angel self, which may be subordinate but is still present in the
modern female. This essay went through a number of revisions. Carlson began
writing for an audience of women, as Woolf did in "Professions for Women"; in
later drafts she decided to use more examples and to broaden the focus of her
essay in order to explain the inner world of modern women to both male and
female readers. As you read Carlson's essay, ask yourself if she has succeeded in
clearly defining the two sides of the modern woman. Consider if the generalizations she draws in her essay are based on accurate observations and developed
with appropriate, effective examples.

"Angels, Devils, Angels, Devils . . ."

"Angels, devils, angels, devils . . ." So goes the old
nursery rhyme from the days of skipping rope on the playground.
In these modern days of women who divide themselves between
family and career, most women experience an inner conflict
between the "angelic," traditional aspect of themselves and the
antithesis to this persona, the devil. While the angel embodies
the more traditional goals of homemaking and caring for
children, the devil is often seen as the hard-nosed, ambitious
woman who abandons her family to climb the corporate ladder. Of
course, the aspect of a woman's character which drives her to

achieve career success is by no means evil or "devilish," but for many years it was seen as such. A woman's desire to move out of the home and find a place in the work force was viewed as leading to the downfall of the traditional nuclear family, and indeed, to the destruction of "family values." We now realize, however, that there is nothing devilish or destructive about this ambition. However, despite this realization that a woman's career ambition is a natural, beneficial trait, there is still an inevitable conflict between the extreme ends of the spectrum of choices: the complete angel who wants to do nothing but please everyone, and the devil who must think only of herself in order to "get ahead" in the work force.

Virginia Woolf originally wrote "Professions for Women" as a speech given to a group of young professional women. In the essay, Woolf introduces the image of the Angel in the House as representing all that is sweet, demure, and conceding in women. This Angel plagues Woolf as she attempts to escape from under the influence of powerful stereotypes about the manner in which women should always defer to the superiority of men. The image of the perfect, pious, virtuous, caring, selfless woman is amazingly powerful and compelling. The Angel always takes care of everything, never failing to yield her own wants and needs to those of others. No woman can say that she hasn't ever experienced the guilt of knowing that she didn't live up to the image of the Angel of the house--somehow she was just not caring enough, selfless enough, good, enough to pass the test. Of course, it would be impossible for any flesh-and-blood female to personify the one hundred percent purity and perfection of the Angel in the House, but this truth does not seem to stop us from trying, nor does it stop society from subtly making us believe that we should be capable of such perfection. "I'm perfect, I'm docile and submissive," whispers the Angel, "so why can't you be too?"

Nowadays, however, the Angel has competition from her alter ego. Call her a devil if you like; call her whatever you want, she probably wouldn't care much, because this woman has no time to waste playing the docile role. She's got goals: an education, a career. She wants to change the world, to make a difference. Along the way she has no plans to play caretaker to the egos, whims, wants, and needs of any man. She's fully liberated and unwilling to compromise her feminist ideals in any way. Most of the time it's nice to have the devil around. She certainly keeps women in line during those passing moments when trying to have it all--career, family, social life--seems much too overwhelming a proposition, when the "angel" starts to whisper too loud, "Why not just give up and stay at home? Women in the past were satisfied with such a lot, so why do you think that you deserve to have more?" Well, the devil certainly doesn't stand for such backsliding. Oh, no, she doesn't let a woman get away with that way of thinking for very long. Sneaking up behind a woman, the

devil whispers in her ears reminders of all those feelings and
aspirations that motivated her to try so hard in the first
place. She reminds women of what they're capable of and makes
sure they suppress any impulses to fully give in to the Angel.
Before long the woman is back to thinking about her career goals
and social responsibilities.

But is this really wise? The problem with the devil is
that, just like the angel, she tends to go too far in her
efforts. She wants women to drop all ties to the way women "used
to be." No more women who are homemakers and nothing else, no
more marriages where the man brings home the bacon and the woman
makes sure it's cooked to perfection. To move ahead into the
future, she believes, a woman must cut the ties with the past.
The devil sometimes tries to make women suppress fundamental
parts of their female-ness. She might tell a woman to stop being
so kind to people she doesn't know, to stop caring so much about
the feelings and concerns of co-workers, because such behavior
isn't "masculine" and certainly won't help in the struggle to
get ahead in the corporate/executive world.

Obviously, both the Angel and the Devil have a few
character flaws, to say the least. As representations of the
dichotomy of choices that are available to women, they each
embody the extreme positions of homemaker and career woman.
Somewhere between these two is the proper mixture which will
produce a well-balanced, modern woman. Some women may lean
toward the career side and choose not to marry or raise
children, and still others may opt to devote most of their time
to their family. Each woman must strive to discover her own
balance between these two forces, molding and shaping her own
life as she makes choices and selects certain options over
others. Today we are fortunate enough to have women role models
who dedicate themselves both to their careers and their
families, among them Anne Richardson and Hilary Rodham-Clinton.
However, the unfortunate reality is that some women are forced
into certain choices because of necessity or extenuating
circumstances, as in the case of women who must work
unwillingly outside the home to ensure the financial survival
of her family. But in an ideal world, all women would be able
to make their own decisions about how, when, and how much to
give of themselves to family and career. After all, every woman
has the right to listen to her own mind, and to follow her own
path in life, no matter what the angel, devil, or anyone else
might say. Woolf sums up this freedom of choice perfectly, as
she discusses the liberty to define one's own space: "this
freedom is only a beginning; the room is your own, but it is
still bare. . . . With whom are you going to share it, and on
what terms?"

Chapter 5

READING AND WRITING ABOUT POETRY

POETRY AND OTHER FORMS OF LITERATURE

Because of its brevity and compression, as well as its special conventions, such as rhyme and meter, poetry is distinct from the types of literature we have explored thus far. At the same time, poetry is also similar to other forms of fiction and nonfiction writing. A poem can develop a storylike narrative, with a "speaker" or narrative voice like that of a character in a book; it can also be confessional and personal, almost like journal entries set in lines. Poetry, like drama, can be a performance art form; poets often read their lyrics before large audiences. Finally, poetry can be essaylike in its use of persuasive rhetoric, sometimes using point-by-point support for a central argument or call to action, as in Dylan Thomas' moving poem to his father, "Do Not Go Gentle into that Good Night." A persuasive poem such as Thomas' may use repeated phrases and lines for emphasis, vivid examples, and a strong concluding "stanza" to reinforce its main point, like the conclusion of a speech or essay. Poems can explore a theme philosophically, using rhetorical strategies such as examples, definition, and comparison to communicate the poet's view of the world.

READING A POEM: UNDERSTANDING STRATEGIES AND CONVENTIONS

Just as there are different types of poetry, there are different ways of reading a poem. Some people like to read aloud or listen to others read poetry, for the sound of the language and to enter into the emotional mood that the poem creates. When reading poetry for ideas, it is important to study the text closely and carefully. For an example, let's take a look at a short poem by the nineteenth-century American poet Emily Dickinson, "Tell All the Truth but tell it slant—," which analyzes the relationship between truth and falsehood or distortion. First read Dickinson's poem aloud and write a brief response to it in your journal. Then try to restate the poem in your own words, taking into consideration some of the following questions: What is the speaker saying in the poem about truth and distortion? Do you agree or disagree with the poem's perspective on these issues? What did you like or dislike about the poem, and why? Does the poem seem difficult or perplexing? What makes this a poem, as opposed to an essay, on the subject of truth?

> Tell All the Truth but tell it slant—
> Success in Circuit lies
> Too bright for our infirm Delight
> The Truth's superb surprise
> As Lightning to the Children eased
> With explanation kind
> The Truth must dazzle gradually
> Or every man be blind—

Themes

The poem offers advice on "telling the truth." Although we may feel that a genuine relationship can be built only on truth, the speaker in the poem suggests that the truth is often too complicated to be stated in a simple, direct way: "Tell All the Truth but tell it slant." Sometimes the truth can shock, even hurt, others and may be so difficult to comprehend or accept that it must be revealed gradually: "The Truth must dazzle gradually/Or every man be blind—." The poem suggests that there is an art to telling the truth, just as the story "Helping to Lie" (Chapter 4) informs us that there is an art to lying. To convey the truth effectively, we must take special care in the choice of words we use, arranging and pacing our presentation of details and ideas so that the revelation emerges at just the right moment for our audience to "get it." Emily Dickinson's poem offers especially good advice for a writer who must plan a presentation and consider the feelings and background knowledge of the reader.

Compression and Intensity

Although the poem presents both an argument and its supports, there are several qualities that make it different from an essay on the subject of truth and lying. First, like most poetry, it is very brief—only ten lines, with each line alternating between eight and six syllables in length. The brevity of poetry puts special demands on both poet and reader. Every line must add to the meaning, and much of the meaning is implied rather than stated directly; thus the reader needs to mentally unpack or decode each image in the poem while reflecting on the poem's meaning. In studying poetry, it is important to read each poem several times, both aloud and silently, always assuming that every word and mark of punctuation in the poem are significant.

Rhythmic Patterns

Poetry is typically written in **lines.** The **rhythm** of a poem is achieved by patterning the beat or pulse of the lines as well as by creating a series of lines of about the same length. Even in modern poetry, which often uses speech patterns close to those of ordinary conversation, some heavily accented, rhythmical lines are used for effect. Dickinson's poem uses alternate four-beat and three-beat lines of eight and six syllables. The poem is written in **meter,** a regular pattern of accented and unaccented syllables typical in traditional poetry. Dickinson has chosen an **iambic** pattern consisting of an unaccented followed by an accented syllable:

> The Truth' must da'zzle gra'dually'
> Or ev'ery man' be blind'—

The regular pattern of meter helps to give an emphasis to the argument of the poem, while at the same time illustrating, through the controlled artfulness of meter, the main point of the poem: that truth can't just be "blurted out"; it needs to "dazzle gradually."

Sound

Notice that in addition to a regular meter, elements of repeated vowel and consonant sounds are used to pattern this poem more intricately, with every second line in the poem ending in either a full **rhyme** (lies, surprise, kind, blind) or a partial rhyme (*ea*sed, partial*ly*). The poet also has introduced a number of sound repetitions (known as **assonance** and **alliteration**) within each line, as seen in the repeated "u" and "s" sounds in the line "the Truth's superb surprise." All of the patterns of sound repetition in the poem help to create what is known as the music of poetry. In fact, poetry was originally a form of literature designed to be recited or sung to musical accompaniment, often with drumming or plucked strings. In addition to the rich sensory appeal of its sound patterns, Dickinson's sound effects also complement the meaning of the poem, as in the line "the Truth's superb surprise" above, where the "i" sound in "surprise" provides a literal surprise, breaking the rather somber pattern of the "u" sounds in the rest of the line.

Word Choice and Level of Diction

Notice that the order of words and phrases, as well as the diction, or word choice, of Dickinson's poem is different from that of normal speech and prose writing. To appreciate the subtlety of word choice in a poem requires frequent rereadings, and reference to a dictionary. You will notice in Dickinson's poem some words that are especially rich in connotation or shadings of meaning. For example, the word "slant" at the end of line 1 means literally to be at an angle, not straight. When applied to people and art, it implies a certain deviousness of character or telling. The word is commonly used as an adjective; "slanted" refers to a "version" of reality, a telling that is not totally objective, a biased vision of events. Dickinson is not recommending outright lying, just a sort of "angling in" of the truth, as opposed to a straight, direct line drawn from point a to point b.

In line 2 another word catches our attention: "Circuit." A circuit literally means a "circle," or a series of points one goes through before finally returning to the beginning. One doesn't usually think of success as going around in circles ("Success in Circuit lies"), so this line presents a **paradox,** a contradiction of ordinary reality or accepted wisdom. But what about the word "lies"? This word seems to be used in a deliberately ambiguous way, as in a pun: "lies" ordinarily would be taken to mean "contained within" or "can be found in," as success can be found in a circuit; however, there is a pun on another meaning, that of telling a lie. The poem thus implies that success is attained by telling circuitous lies. The need for artful caution in revealing the truth is clarified by the use of the words "infirm delight," another paradox, which implies that, though people can be delighted by knowing the truth, they can also be injured by truth if they are emotionally "infirm," or vulnerable, as is a person recuperating from an illness or a deep sadness.

Figurative Language

In addition to complex plays of language and intellectual challenges like paradoxes, poets often use figures of speech such as the **metaphor** and the **simile** to create meaning. A metaphor makes a direct equation between two items or realities that are literally different but have underlying similarities. Dickinson creates an implied metaphor when she recommends that the truth be "slant," like a slanted line, and she calls the truth "too bright for our infirm Delight"— suggesting that the truth is like the sun, capable of blinding us if taken in directly, and that our delight is weak, like that of a recuperating patient. The poet also uses a simile when she compares telling the truth to telling children about lightning: "*As Lightning* to the Children eased."

WRITING IN RESPONSE TO POETRY: A STUDENT CASEBOOK

The following casebook, by student writer Julian Castro, presents a response to Alberto Alvaro Rios' "Nani," a poem narrated by a man who has returned to his grandmother's home for a meal. While being served, he reflects on his grandmother's role in his life. Before you read Castro's responses, read the poem for yourself, first silently, just to get an overall sense of the subject matter; note any words, phrases, or comparisons that might seem unusual or that are used in a new or unfamiliar way. Then read the poem aloud, taking care to pause briefly at phrase and clause endings, punctuation points, and line breaks in order to become more dramatically engaged with the "voice" of the poem. After reading "Nani," write a brief response in your reading journal: What is the speaker saying about his relationship with Nani, about her values, about what she represents to him personally as well as culturally?

Nani
Alberto Alvaro Rios

Sitting at her table, she serves
the sopa de arroz[1] to me
instinctively, and I watch her,
the absolute mamá, and eat words
I might have had to say more   5
out of embarrassment. To speak,
now-foreign words I used to speak,
too, dribble down her mouth as she serves
me albóndigas.[2] No more
than a third are easy to me.   10
By the stove she does something with words
and looks at me only with her
back. I am full. I tell her
I taste the mint, and watch her speak
smiles at the stove. All my words   15
make her smile. Nani never serves
herself, she only watches me
with her skin, her hair. I ask for more.

[1] Rice soup
[2] Meatballs

I watch the mamá warming more
tortillas for me. I watch her   20
fingers in the flame for me.
Near her mouth, I see a wrinkle speak
of a man whose body serves
the ants like she serves me, then more words
from more wrinkles about children, words   25
about this and that, flowing more
easily from these other mouths. Each serves
as a tremendous string around her,
holding her together. They speak
nani was this and that to me   30
and I wonder just how much of me
will die with her, what were the words
I could have been, was. Her insides speak
through a hundred wrinkles, now, more
than she can bear, steel around her,   35
shouting, then, What is this thing she serves?

She asks me if I want more.
I own no words to stop her.
Even before I speak, she serves.

REACTIONS ON READING "NANI"

First Response

Julian Castro, who comes from a family that is in some ways similar to that of
the speaker in the poem, identified with the concerns expressed in the poem, as
can be seen in his first response to "Nani." In this entry, Castro informally explores issues of family obligation, cultural assimilation, and guilt that the poem
raised for him.

    The speaker considers Nani the ultimate giver of life and
his link to his past. Nani knows the family history, the
cultural traditions and achievements that make him who he is.
The speaker fears her death because a part of him will die with
her. Already he fails to understand the Spanish language (he
says he only understands a third of her words). He wonders what
else he will lose when she dies.
    Unfortunately, this is a common situation for many second
and third generation Mexican-Americans. My grandmother, who came
to the United States from Mexico, is seventy-seven years old.
She knows a great deal about my family history that neither my
mother nor I has ever found out. Since she is the last of my

grandparents alive, when she dies I may never know about my
great-grandparents and their parents and so on. If I fail to
understand my ties to Mexico, how can I identify with that part
of myself? The speaker seems to be uncovering this same conflict
in himself. Like him, I cannot speak Spanish well; still, I try
to communicate with my grandmother. But I wonder what reason I
will have to use the language when she is gone.

It's terrifying to think that we lose part of ourselves
with the death of a loved one. What makes it worse is that the
speaker, like myself, has had plenty of time to learn more from
his mother (in my case my grandmother), but he was too busy
advancing himself in the ways of another culture. Now he cannot
relate to Nani like he should be able to. Eventually, we may
become individuals who have lost part of ourselves and can only
identify with the American culture in which we live. If that
happens, then all that our mothers and grandmothers have done
for us will be lost, and we should be embarrassed and ashamed of
that.

Next Julian Castro reread the poem several times. In order to get a clear
sense of its overall form and the subtleties of the speaker's voice and feelings, he
decided to do a prose paraphrase of the text. Through this activity he was able
to go beyond simply responding personally to the poem. He understood more
deeply the dilemma of the culturally assimilated, nostalgic, and ill-at-ease speaker
in the poem.

Second Response: Paraphrase and Interpretation

After reading the poem several times, I get a sense that
the speaker is juxtaposing his life to Nani's. Lines like ". . .
what were the words I could have been, was" demonstrate the
speaker's curiosity about what he might have become if perhaps
he had not assimilated into the dominant culture. He elaborates
on how caring and giving Nani is, and the words he uses indicate
a great respect for her way of life. Perhaps she doesn't speak
English or have much formal schooling, but she did the best she
could. She continues to give him love and stability even in her
old age. The speaker, then, leaves the reader with a grand
question: Have I chosen the wrong life? He doesn't know if he
has done the right thing by removing himself from his Mexican
background. He wonders what it would be like for him to live his
life like Nani lived hers. Then he has to ask himself whether he
is unselfish enough to live a life like hers. I think he
realizes that he cannot be as giving as she has been. That's why
he is embarrassed that Nani continues to serve him. After all,
she is an old woman; he is an able-bodied young man. Lines 37-
39, "She asks me if I want more. I own no words to stop her.
Before I speak, she serves" demonstrate his dilemma. Here is a

man, probably in the prime of his life, who continues to take
and take, perhaps without giving back anything. He must be
thinking "How can I repay her for what she's given me? Money
means little to her, but what else do I have to give? Or is it
enough that I keep her company? Can I possibly refuse to
entertain her with my company?"

The speaker is confused about what to do in return for what
Nani gives. And although he may never be completely comfortable
with his inability to give much back, I think he rationalizes
when he says that Nani wants nothing in return. He wants to
accept how generous she is and just enjoy regaining what he has
lost--part of himself.

After exploring his personal response to the poem, Julian Castro decided to
develop an analytical essay about the poem, drawing on his journal entries to
give his readers an understanding of the poem's meaning and depth of feeling.
He did not explicate the text line by line and image by image but, rather, set out
to explore the major themes of the poem, particularly the speaker's alienation,
doubt, and confusion about his bicultural heritage, as well as the guilt he experiences about Nani's powerful emotional commitment to his welfare. In exploring
themes, however, the student writer's attention was drawn to a number of
strategies and techniques of the poet: his use of the formal line arrangement typical of the sestina, key elements of diction, including the poet's use of Spanish
words, and the central action of serving food as a metaphor for the service to
family that has given Nani's life its meaning. As you read Castro's analysis of
the poem, notice how he uses close references and paraphrase to back up his interpretation of the text.

"Nani": An Analysis

Alberto Rios has achieved success and acclaim as a writer
and scholar. However, his good fortune sharply contrasts with
the experiences of most first generation Mexican-American
immigrants. In his poem "Nani," the speaker, an assimilated
Mexian-American, acknowledges the distance between his life and
the life of his grandmother, Nani. As the speaker reflects on
his separation from her, his questions turn inward, and his
words uncover confusion about his bicultural heritage.

The poem begins at a dinner table, where the speaker is
being served by "the absolute mama," Nani. Right away the
language of the poem indicates the presence of a second culture.
She serves him sopa de arroz, the Spanish term for rice soup.
His use of the term "sopa de arroz" instead of the English term
gives a clue that he understands at least some words of Spanish
and that Nani is probably a Spanish speaker as well. However,
the next line is a perplexing one. "I watch her/the absolute
mama and eat words/I might have had to say more out of
embarrassment." Immediately, the reader wonders why the speaker

would be embarrassed by being served by Nani. Just as quickly,
the speaker explains why he feels uncomfortable.

In lines six through ten the speaker reveals his inability
to fully understand Nani's language, for when he speaks of her
words he says, "No more than a third are easy to me." But he
also mentions that he did understand her once. When he says, "To
speak/now foreign words I used to speak," we know that he once
felt a part of the ritual Nani is performing at the dinner
table. The speaker intensifies the separation by using
contrasting references. First, he describes how the words
"dribble down her mouth." That image makes her speech seem like
babbling, for it might as well be to him. But then he uses a
second Spanish term. ". . . as she serves me albondigas," he
states. His use of the Spanish term reveals how language used to
unite them through the eating ritual. Little bits of dialogue
remain in his vocabulary, but the language is now "foreign" to
him.

In lines eleven through eighteen the speaker changes his
focus and his perception on Nani. He uses imagery that puts her
in a mythical light: "By the stove she does something with her
words and looks at me only with her back," and "Nani never
serves/herself, she only watches me/with her skin, her hair.
. . ." These images illustrate how powerful, almost magical Nani
appears to the speaker. She serves him unselfishly and takes
nothing for herself. As his images liken her to a supernatural
being, a question arises about the past relationship between
Nani and the speaker. The speaker gives hints. He says that "All
my words/make her smile." Nani's every gesture expresses
feelings of great warmth and affection. Even though the speaker
is grown up, Nani continues to spoil him with her kindness.

In line thirteen, when the speaker says "I am full," the
meaning is ambiguous, suggesting the speaker's confusion--is his
stomach full, is he full of guilt, or is he full of love for
Nani? The next section of the poem, lines nineteen through
thirty-six, offer a tentative answer to the question of
fullness, although not a complete one. Here the speaker
elaborates on his relationship with Nani. She fills him with
love, having apparently given him everything that she ever
could, surviving others whom she has previously loved and served
as well: "I see a wrinkle speak/of a man whose body serves/the
ants like she serves me. . . ." Could that man be the speaker's
grandfather, or his own father? The speaker equates Nani's life
experiences and her fond memories of the past with her numerous
wrinkles, each of which "serves/as a crucial string around
her,/holding her together." He suggests here that those
experiences are what keep her going, and what she wants is to
pass her wisdom on to him, to "fill him up" in a far more
meaningful way than merely serving him a meal.

Herein lies the central theme of the poem. It becomes

obvious that the speaker is separated from Nani and from part of
himself. He has assimilated into the mainstream American
culture, and like so many second and third generation Mexican-
Americans, he has lost the ability to speak Spanish well. This
is the base of his separation from Nani. He no longer possesses
that knowledge of his culture, while Nani has lived her life by
its traditions. Thus, he ponders the consequences of Nani's
death: "I wonder just how much of me/will die with her . . ."
She knows everything about his past, and his future will be a
sad one if he cannot regain what he has lost, his culture.
Already he only speaks Spanish when he is with her; when will he
use it after she is gone?

The Spanish language here implies more than just a set of
sounds, words, and symbols for communication; it represents the
Mexican customs and traditions that contribute to the character
of an individual. He stands to lose part of his identity.
Therefore, when Nani speaks to him "through a hundred wrinkles,
now, more/than she can bear, steel around her,/shouting then,"
he realizes, as she does, that she may not have long to live,
that their conversation is perhaps a final opportunity for her
to teach him about that other side of him that he has lost, the
Mexican side. This may explain why it seems to him like Nani is
frantically "shouting" through her wrinkles. Because she is
doing so, the speaker has to ask himself, "What is this thing
she serves?" In that phrase alone it is evident that the speaker
knows Nani has given him more than just a home and good food.
She has given him his identity. From her he has learned about
his past and his present. She probably has helped him learn to
read and write, and now she teaches him about who he really is.

When the speaker realizes how removed his life is from
Nani's, he becomes confused and feels guilty. Throughout the
poem he contrasts his life with hers. When he states ". . . what
were the words/I could have been, was," he reveals his curiosity
about what might have become of him if he had not assimilated.
Nani has given him all that she possibly could, and his words
reflect a great respect for the way she has lived her life.
Perhaps she doesn't speak English or have much formal education,
but she did the best she could, and even in her old age, she
continues to provide him with love and stability. Because of
this, he feels guilty. He does not know if he has done the right
thing by separating himself from his native culture. He must ask
himself what his life would have been like if he had lived as
Nani has. Could he have been unselfish enough to live such a
life? Because he realizes that he cannot be as giving, he is
embarrassed in line six when she serves him. After all, Nani is
an old woman, but he is an able-bodied young man.

In lines thirty-seven through thirty nine ("She asks me if
I want more./I own no words to stop her/Before I speak, she
serves"), the speaker reveals his dilemma. Here is a man,

probably in the prime of his life, who continues to take and take without giving back much. He must be confused about how he can repay her for everything she has given him. Money means little to her, but what else does he have to give? Is his company enough for her? Although he may never be completely comfortable because of what he cannot give back, I think he believes that Nani wants only his company and attention. Therefore, he can accept how generous she is and just enjoy regaining part of his identity.

The structure of the poem, a sestina form that involves the repetition of six key words at the end of the lines, emphasizes the character of Nani and the conflict of the speaker. At every fifth line throughout much of the poem, one of the words is repeated at the end of consecutive lines. This form adds to the speaker's mythical portrayal of Nani, and it reveals something about her personality. The poem is split into two sections, lines one through eighteen and nineteen through thirty-nine. Words like "serves," "me," "more," "words," "her," and "speak" indicate that Nani is benevolent. Special attention should be paid to the word "serves" which occurs at the end of the first and last lines of the poem. The speaker clearly wants to emphasize how much Nani has given him, and the impact on him of her constant, selfless service. Other key words, like "speak," indicate what Nani does for him in terms of language. Her love keeps him close to her and to his culture of origin.

Alberto Rios puts his subject in familiar surroundings to have him realize how far he has drifted from them. That can be taken as a message to the children and grandchildren of immigrants, many of whom, like the speaker, have assimilated and lost much of their native heritage. Identity is made up of more than one part. Thus, the speaker's self-questioning is an invitation to these people to consider what they are giving up and at what price. To those of us who have experienced Mexican customs, Nani is a common figure. The way the poem presents her with dignity and pride illustrates a special respect for the women, who, although often unacknowledged, are our nurturers. What can we give back to them?

After analyzing and interpreting Rios' poem, Julian Castro returned to some of the thoughts in his first journal response and decided to write a creative essay that would take the form of a narrative based on his memories of a recent visit to his grandmother, a woman very much like Nani. Castro wanted his essay to stand on its own as a work of reflection and commentary on the gulf that divides the new generation of Mexican-Americans from their parents and grandparents. Castro wrote in a commentary on his essay that he wished in particular "to make the new generation . . . aware of how much of their identity has been lost. Perhaps then they can try to regain it." As you read his narrative, "Vas a Vivir a Dos Cien" (May you live to be two hundred), notice the attention he has paid to the voicing of inner thoughts, as well as his use of descriptive detail, symbolism, and dialogue, both in Spanish and English. Ask yourself if Castro has succeeded in achieving his purpose: to increase the awareness of young Mexican-Americans of their identity and the importance of their cultural traditions.

Vas a Vivir a Dos Cien

She watches me pour milk into my coffee. "Mamo," I call to her, "Do you want any?" Since she likes her coffee strong, I know the answer before I ask. "Only a little," she will say. We sit and talk on the old couch in front of her seven year old TV. She lives in the world of television these days and can recite the daily soap opera schedule. Some days I watch her absorbed in these programs. She chastises certain characters and praises others, acting as if they could hear her. I ask her why she believes in soap operas. "They aren't real," I say, but still she throws an occasional "Hmmm!" at the blaring TV. I wonder why she enjoys watching escapist fantasies, for her life has been nothing like a soap opera.

Mamo worked as a maid most of her life. Her thick-skinned hands and swollen feet tell me she has had a hard life; I can see the grief in her face that has accumulated over seventy years. She tells me that she often dreams about the ladies she used to work for. I smile back at her, and ask which one she dreamt of last night. "Mrs. Kirby," she answers; then she tells me that all but one of the women are dead. She has outlived them, but I remind myself that she has diabetes and other health problems. She tells me that she doesn't want to live too long. The thought of her death saddens me now. How long will she live?

"Vas a vivir a dos cien," I tell her in crude Spanish: You'll live to be two hundred. "No, no," she answers, her head shaking from side to side. "I only want to live long enough to see you and your brother grow up." Still, I insist jokingly that she is going to live longer than anyone ever has. But then I wonder why she doesn't want more. Mamo has had nothing all her life. She used to tell me stories of how her family ate only beans and tortillas for months at a time. I know she never made much money, for her prized possession is an old black storage chest with worn pictures and dresses in it. She still has a meager lifestyle. Her social security check helps pay the rent, but most months she has little left. Why doesn't she wish for something for herself--better clothes, nicer furniture, or an easier life?

Now I realize how much she loves us, and I want to tell her how much I care about her, but I can't. My mouth cannot express in English what her heart feels in Spanish. "I love you, Mamo," I think to myself, but my tongue cannot explain to her how I feel. So many years of schooling, and I cannot express myself.

She dropped out of school in the fourth grade, but now her
feelings touch me so perfectly. I can feel the age in her
coffee-brown skin. She starts speaking again; her tongue rolls
off word after word, and a few of them I cannot understand.
Those are the ones from her heart. They are not the English
words that I study in school, and that my mother speaks around
the house. While only small phrases of Mamo's Spanish words mean
something to me, I feel what she means.

Our lives are too different. I will not live like she does
in twenty years--these dirty floors, these little rooms--I will
live in a big house with many rooms. I will be successful--but
is that good? No amount of money can ever tell her what I feel.
TVs or dresses or big houses--none of them can say, "Te amo,
Abuelita," and make her feel it. I drink my coffee, lukewarm
now, and wonder how to return my love on her terms. What can I
give her back? Now, she speaks in her gentle voice about her own
mother, and of cities in Mexico where she grew up, so many miles
from here. "Only a weaker cup of coffee," I think somberly, and
look down at her swollen, round feet. Confused now, I listen
more attentively.

Chapter 6

READING AND WRITING ABOUT DRAMA

DRAMA AND OTHER LITERARY FORMS

Curtain going up! Although some people have never attended a live play, almost everyone is familiar with the dramatic form from television situation comedies that are often "staged" in a single room—a family room or apartment, an airport, an office, a bar, a police station. Such a single-room setting is similar to the basic set of a staged play. The experience of drama is similar in many ways to other types of literature. Like the short story, a play has characters, a setting, and a plot, as well as symbols and a range of emotional and intellectual themes. However, drama differs from other types of literature in a number of significant ways.

First, theater is a performance art. A live performance of a play can be compared to a book that, instead of being opened and read is revealed to the audience by the raising of a curtain or the dimming of house lights and the brightening of stage lights. When this ritual "opening" of the stage setting occurs, the audience *as a community* (rather than the individual as reader) is transported into the dream space of the play for the duration of the performance. This experience is very different from the way a person reads a book, as books allow us to reread a difficult passage, to insert a bookmark and take a break of several hours, or even days, before returning.

At the same time certain qualities of a dramatic performance parallel the "show" put on by the characters in a book. As we watch the play, we are attentive to the tone of voice of the actors. Whereas a writer of a story might let us know by saying, "The sheriff had a gruff voice," in a play, the effect is more immediate—the sheriff-actor simply raises his voice and out pours the gruff sound, as interpreted by the actor and director. As members of an audience we also notice the style of movement in the play, which is often carefully choreographed through the theatrical art of **blocking.** This corresponds to the stage movements and directions: upstage, downstage, right stage, stage center. In a play, blocking can be almost as subtle and pictorial as the choreography in a dance performance, and contributes enormously to the emotional and thematic impact of the live experience of the play. Theater is a visual art in many other ways. A major part of the impact of the drama is the appearance and costumes of the actors, as well as the sets and other stage objects, such as furniture and a variety of objects known as "properties" that often add symbolic significance to the themes of the play. In these ways the experience and meaning of drama are similar to those of other visual arts such as painting and film.

DRAMA AND THE SCRIPT

As a reader it is important to realize that a play begins with a **script;** the bright, loud, fast moving show you see in the theater is really just a director's and actors' collaborative "reading" of the original script, which, although it will be annotated, modified, or cut somewhat in rehearsal, is quite similar to the scripts of the plays you see in your textbook. Actors and directors interpret the same play quite differently, just as readers select different aspects of a work of fiction or an essay to concentrate on, using their own personal values as a sort of filter through which they read and interpret the text. For example, the play *Hamlet,* included in this text, has been performed countless times, over hundreds of years. Many directors cut parts of the script that they consider less important, placing emphasis on certain key scenes, moments of conflict, and revelation that reflect their own vision of Shakespeare's text. As you read the plays in *Imagining Worlds,* think of yourself as both actor and director. How would you produce this play? What elements would you focus on? Which characters would you present sympathetically? Who are the villians? How do you respond to the ideas and values of the script? What would you like to add to the author's script?

ELEMENTS OF DRAMA

Before writing about a dramatic script, it is important to read it carefully and thoughtfully. Try to get inside the dramatic world of the play; you might try "performing" a few scenes, perhaps doing a dramatic reading with one or more friends. As you read a play with care, you will notice that certain dramatic elements help to get the meaning and intense feeling behind the script across to the reader.

Speeches and Dialogue

Underline particularly interesting lines of dialogue and high points of conflict, as well as longer speeches, or "soliloquies," in which a character voices inner thoughts and feelings in a sustained way. Notice thematic ideas that recur throughout the play. In drama, dialogue is the primary way that the ideas and characters are created for the actors and the audience. As you read the play *Open Admissions,* in the student casebook, notice how the dialogue between Alice and Calvin helps to characterize their unique motivations, social classes, and educational levels and reveals the play's theme: misunderstanding and miscommunication between a teacher and student from diverse backgrounds.

Characters in Conflict

If a play involves a sustained conflict between two or three strong characters, you might try writing a brief list of qualities and points of difference between them, as the student in the casebook does with the two characters in Shirley Lauro's *Open Admissions.* Next, relate the conflicts to the themes and issues that the play explores.

Plot

Because a play is longer and more complex in its structure than the form of a story, you might try writing out a brief plot outline: What happens in each scene, and how does each scene advance the action and revelation of ideas in the play? Into how many acts is the play divided, and what movement of thought and feeling occurs in each act? What is the crisis, or turning point of the action, in the play? How does the conclusion resolve key issues and conflicts, if at all? Is the resolution positive and unifying, as in what is commonly called "comedy," or, as in tragedy, is the ending a series of defeats for the hero resulting in a revelation of error, loss, and a destructive pattern of human events beyond the ability of the characters to control? In *Open Admissions,* the plot is simple, yet it carries much of the meaning of the play: The speech teacher, Alice, and Calvin, her African-American student, are involved in a conflict over Calvin's progress in the course. Calvin demands more from Alice as a speech teacher than she is willing or able to give. The conflict accelerates, until the revelation that Calvin believes that he has been given grades by Alice that are inflated, that she's just "passing him on." Calvin's anger builds to a climax, but in the resolution Alice resumes control of the situation, forcing Calvin to submit to her view of education, which seems to be a matter of teaching students to repress their real nature by learning tricks to help them fit into mainstream society.

Setting and Dramatic Symbolism

Plays can be set indoors, in intimate places such as bedrooms and living rooms; outdoors, in a public forum, as in Greek tragedy such as *Antigone;* or in a desolate landscape, as in Beckett's *Waiting for Godot. Open Admissions* is set in a teacher's drab institutional office, a place where neither character really feels comfortable or at home. When you read a play, pay attention to the scenic directions, especially to the furnishings (or even to the absence of furnishings) in rooms where the different scenes and acts of the play take place. What do these furnishings suggest about the life style, social class, and values of the characters? Note that key objects often acquire symbolic properties, such as the piano that dominates the stage in August Wilson's *The Piano Lesson* or the blackboard in the teacher's office in *Open Admissions,* which intimidates the student Calvin while reassuring Alice Miller of her control.

WRITING IN RESPONSE TO DRAMA: A STUDENT CASEBOOK

The student whose work is included here, Julie Layard, chose to write about the play *Open Admissions.* Begin by reading the play for yourself and taking some notes on your responses to it. Be especially aware of the confining setting and the cultural gap between the characters, Calvin and Alice.

Open Admissions
Shirley Lauro,

THE CHARACTERS

PROFESSOR ALICE MILLER—	Professor of Speech Communications. Started out to be a Shakespearean scholar. Has been teaching Speech at a city college in New York for 12 years. She is overloaded with work and exhausted. Late thirties. Wears skirt, blouse, sweater, coat, gloves. Carries briefcases.
CALVIN JEFFERSON—	18, a Freshman in Open Admissions Program at the College. Black, powerfully built, handsome, big. At first glance a streetperson, but belied by his intensity. Wears jacket, jeans, cap, sneakers. Has been at the College 3 months, hoping it will work out.

THE PLACE

A cubicle Speech Office at a city college in New York.

THE TIME

The Present. Late fall. 6 o'clock in the evening.

The play begins on a very high level of tension and intensity and builds from there. The level of intensity is set by CALVIN who enters the play with a desperate urgency, as though he had arrived at the Emergency Room of a Hospital, needing immediate help for a serious problem. He also enters in a state of rage and frustration but is containing these feelings at first. The high level of tension is set by both ALICE and CALVIN and occurs from the moment CALVIN enters. ALICE wants to leave. She does not want the scene to take place. The audience's experience from the start should be as if they had suddenly turned in on the critical round of a boxing match.

CALVIN'S speech is "Street Speech" jargon. Run-on sentences and misspellings in the text are for the purpose of helping the actor with the pronunciations and rhythms of the language.

The Speech office of Professor Alice Miller in a city college in New York. A small cubicle with partitions going ¾ of the way up. Windowless, airless, with a cold antiseptic quality and a strong sense of impersonalness and transience. The cubicle has the contradictory feelings of claustrophobia and alienation at the same time. It is a space used by many teachers during every day of the week.

On the glass-windowed door it says:

SPEECH COMMUNICATIONS DEPT.

Prof. Alice Miller, B.A., M.A., Ph.D.

There are other names beneath that.

In the cubicle there is a desk with nothing on it except a phone, a chair with a rain coat on it, a swivel chair and a portable black board on which has been tacked a diagram of the "Speech Mechanism." Room is bare except for these things.

At Rise: Cubicle is in darkness. Muted light filters through glass window on door from hallway. Eerie feeling. A shadow appears outside door. Someone enters, snapping on light.

It is ALICE. She carries a loose stack of essays, a book sack loaded with books and a grade book, one Shakespeare book, two speech books, and a portable cassette recorder. She closes the door, crosses to the desk, puts the keys in her purse, puts purse and booksack down and dials "O."

ALICE: Outside please. (*Waits for this, then dials a number.*) Debbie? Mommy, honey . . . A "93"? Terrific! Listen, I just got through. I had to keep the class late to finish . . . So, I can't stop home for dinner. I'm going right to the meeting . . . no, I'll be safe . . . don't worry. But you go put the double lock on, ok? And eat the cold meatloaf. (*She puts essays in book sack.*) See you later. Love you too. (*She kisses the receiver.*) Bye.

(*She hangs up, puts on coat, picks up purse and book sack, crosses to door and snaps off light. Then opens door to go.* CALVIN *looms in doorway.*)

ALICE: OOHH! You scared me!

CALVIN: Yes ma'am, I can see I scared you okay. I'm sorry.

ALICE: Calvin Washington? 10:30 section?

CALVIN: Calvin Jefferson. 9:30 section.

ALICE: Oh, right. Of course. Well, I was just leaving. Something you wanted?

CALVIN: Yes, Professor Miller. I came to talk to you about my grades. My grade on that Shakespeare project especially.

ALICE: Oh. Yes. Well. What did you get, Calvin? A "B" wasn't it? Something like that?

CALVIN: Umhmm. Thass right. Somethin like that . . .

ALICE: Yes. Well, look, I don't have office hours today at all. It's very dark already. I just stopped to make a call. But if you'd like to make an appointment for a conference, I'm not booked yet next month. Up 'till then, I'm just jammed.

CALVIN: Thass two weeks! I need to talk to you right now!

ALICE: Well what exactly is it about? I mean the grade is self-explanatory— "Good"—"B" work. And I gave you criticism in class the day of the project, didn't I? So what's the problem?

CALVIN: I wanna sit down and talk about *why* I got that grade! And all my grades in point of fact.

ALICE: But I don't have office hours today. It's very late and I have another commitment. Maybe tomorrow—*(She tries to leave.)*

CALVIN *(voice rising):* I have to talk to you *now!*

ALICE: Look, tomorrow there's a Faculty Meeting. I can meet you here afterwards . . . around 12:30. Providing Professor Roth's not scheduled to use the desk.

CALVIN: I got a job tomorrow! Can't you talk to me right now?

ALICE: But what's it about? I don't see the emergen—

CALVIN *(voice rising loudly):* I jiss *tole* you what it's about! My project and my *grades* is what it's about!

ALICE *(glancing down the hall, not wanting a commotion overheard):* All right! Just stop shouting out here, will you? *(She snaps on light and crosses to desk.)* Come on in. I'll give you a few minutes now.

(He comes in.)

ALICE: *(She puts purse and book sack down and sits at desk.)* Okay. Now then. What?

CALVIN: *(Closes door and crosses UC. Silent for a moment, looking at her. Then:)* How come all I ever git from you is "B"?

ALICE *(stunned):* What?

CALVIN: This is the third project I did for you. An all I ever git is "B."

ALICE: Are you juking? This is what you wanted to talk about? "B" is an excellent grade!

CALVIN: No it's not! "A" is "excellent." "B" is "good."

ALICE: You don't think you deserved an "A" on those projects, do you?

CALVIN: No. But I got to know how to improve myself somehow, so maybe sometime I can try for a "A." I wouldn't even mind on one of those projects if I got a "C." Thass average—if you know what I mean? Or a "D." But all I ever git from you is "B." It don't matter what I do in that Speech Communications Class, seems like. I come in the beginnin a it three months ago? On the Open Admissions? Shoot, I didn't know which end was up. I stood up there and give this speech you assigned on "My Hobby." You remember that?

ALICE *(reads note on desk):* About basketball?

CALVIN: Huh-uh. That was Franklin Perkins give that speech. Sits in the back row?

ALICE *(tosses note in wastebasket):* Oh. Yes. Right. Franklin.

CALVIN: Umhmm. I give some dumb speech about "The Hobby a Makin Wooden Trays."

ALICE: Oh, yes. Right. I remember that.

CALVIN: Except I didn't have no hobby makin wooden trays, man. I made one in high school one time, thass all.

ALICE *(leafs through pages of speech books):* Oh, well, that didn't matter. It was the speech that counted.

CALVIN: Umhmm? Well, that was the sorriest speech anybody ever heard in their lives! I was scared to death and couldn't put one word in front a the other any way I tried. Supposed to be 5 minutes. Lasted 2! And you give me a "B"!

ALICE *(rises, crosses to DR table and puts speech books down):* Well, it was your first time up in class, and you showed a lot of enthusiasm and effort. I remember that speech.

CALVIN: Everybody's firss time up in class, ain't it?

ALICE: Yes. Of course.

CALVIN *(crosses DR to ALICE):* That girl sits nex to me, that Judy Horowitz—firss time she was up in class too. She give that speech about "How to Play the Guitar?" And man, she brought in charts and taught us to read chords and played a piece herself an had memorized the whole speech by heart. An you give *her* a "B."

ALICE *(crosses to desk, picks up book sack and puts it on desk):* Well, Judy's organization on her outline was a little shaky as I recall.

CALVIN *(crosses end of desk):* I didn't even turn no outline in.

ALICE *(picks up purse and puts it on desk):* You didn't?

CALVIN *(leans in):* Huh-uh. Didn't you notice?

ALICE: Of course! It's—just—well, it's been sometime—*(She quickly takes the grade book from the book sack and looks up his name.)* Let me see, oh, yes. Right. Here, I see. You didn't hand it in . . .

CALVIN: Thass right, I didn'.

ALICE: You better do that before the end of the term.

CALVIN: I can't. Because I don't know which way to do no outline!

ALICE *(looks up name in grade book and marks it with red pencil):* Oh. Well . . . that's all right. Don't worry about it, okay? *(She puts grade book away.)* Just work on improving yourself in other ways.

CALVIN: What other ways? Only thing you ever say about anything I ever done in there is how I have got to get rid of my "Substandard Urban Speech!"

ALICE *(picks up 2 files from desk and crosses to UCR file cabinet):* Well, yes, you do! You see, that's your real problem, Calvin! "Substandard Speech." It undercuts your "Positive Communicator's Image!" Remember how I gave a lecture about that? About how all of you here have Substandard Urban Speech because this is a Sub—an *Urban* College. *(She puts on gloves.)* Remember? But that's perfectly okay! It's okay! Just like I used to have Substandard Midwestern Speech when I was a student. Remember my explaining about that? How I used to say "crik" for "creek," and "kin" for "can" and "tin" for "ten?" *(She crosses in back of desk and chuckles at herself.)* Oh, and my breathiness! *(She picks up purse.)* That was just my biggest problem of all: Breathiness. I just about worked myself to death up at Northwestern U. getting it right straight out of my speech. Now, that's what you have to do too, Calvin. *(She picks up book sack and keys.)* Nothing to be ashamed of— but get it right straight out! *(She is ready to leave. She pats* CALVIN *on the shoulder and crosses UC.)*

CALVIN: *(Pause. Looks at her.)* Thass how come I keep on gittin "B"?

ALICE: "That's."

CALVIN *(steps in to* ALICE*):* Huh?

ALICE: "That's." Not "Thass." Can't you hear the difference? "That's" one of the words in the Substandard Black Urban Pattern. No final "T's." Undermining your Positive Image . . . labeling you. It's "Street Speech." Harlemese. Don't you remember? I called everyone's attention to your particular syndrome in class the minute you started talking?

(He looks at her, not speaking.)

ALICE: It's "last," not "lass;" "first," not "firss." That's your friend, that good old "Final T!" Hear *it* when I talk?

CALVIN: Sometimes. When you say *it,* hi*tt*in i*t* like tha*t!*

ALICE: Well, you should be going over the exercises on it in the speech book all the time, and recording yourself on your tape recorder. *(She pats book sack.)*

CALVIN: I don't got no tape recorder.

ALICE: Well, borrow one! *(She turns away.)*

CALVIN *(crosses in back of* ALICE *to her right):* On that Shakespeare scene I jiss did? Thass why I got a "B"? Because of the "Final T's?"

ALICE *(backs DS a step):* Well, you haven't improved your syndrome, have you?

CALVIN: How come you keep on answerin me by axin me somethin else?

ALICE: And that's the other one.

CALVIN: What "other one"?

ALICE: Other most prevalent deviation. You said: "ax-ing" me somethin else.

CALVIN: Thass right. How come you keep axin me somethin else?

ALICE: "Asking me," Calvin, "asking me!"

CALVIN: I jiss did!

ALICE: No, no. Look. That's classic Substandard Black! Text book case. *(She puts purse and book sack down and crosses to diagram on blackboard.)* See, the jaw and teeth are in two different positions for the two sounds, and they make two completely different words! *(She writes "ass-king," and "ax-ing" on the blackboard, pronouncing them in an exaggerated way for him to see.)* "ass-king" and "ax-ing." I am "ass-king" you the question. But, the woodcutter is "ax-ing" down the tree. Can't you hear the difference? *(She picks up his speech book from desk.)* Here.

(CALVIN *follows her to desk.*)

ALICE: Go over to page 105. It's called a "Sharp S" problem with a medial position "sk" substitution. See? "skin, screw, scream"—those are "sk" sounds in the Primary Position. "Asking, risking, frisking,—that's medial position. And "flask, task, mask"—that's final position. Now you should be working on those, Calvin. Reading those exercises over and over again. I mean the way you did the Othello scene was just ludicrous: "Good gentlemen, I *ax* thee—" (*She crosses to the board and points to "ax-ing". She chuckles.*) That meant Othello was chopping the gentlemen down!

CALVIN: How come I had to do the Othello scene anyhow? Didn git any choice. An Franklin Perkins an Sam Brown an Lester Washington they had to too.

ALICE: What do you mean?

CALVIN: An Claudette Jackson an Doreen Simpson an Melba Jones got themselves assigned to Cleopatra on the Nile?

ALICE: Everyone was assigned!

CALVIN: Uh-huh. But everybody else had a choice, you know what I mean? That Judy Horowitz, she said you told her she could pick outa five, six different characters. And that boy did his yesterday? That Nick Rizoli? Did the Gravedigger? He said he got three, four to choose off of too.

ALICE (*crosses to Calvin*): Well some of the students were "right" for several characters. And you know, Calvin, how we talked in class about Stanislavsky and the importance of "identifying" and "feeling" the part?

CALVIN: Well how Doreen Simpson "identify" herself some Queen sittin on a barge? How I supposed to "identify" some Othello? I don't!

ALICE (*crosses to blackboard, picks up fallen chalk*): Oh, Calvin, don't be silly.

CALVIN (*crosses center*): Well, I don'! I'm not no kind a jealous husband. I haven' got no wife. I don' even got no girlfriend, hardly! And thass what it's all about ain't it? So what's it I'm supposed to "identify" with anyhow?

ALICE (*turns to* CALVIN): Oh, Calvin, what are you arguing about? You did a good job!

CALVIN: "B" job, right?

ALICE: Yes.

CALVIN (*crosses to* ALICE): Well, what's that "B" standin for? Cause I'll tell you somethin you wanna know the truth: I stood up there didn' hardly know the sense a anythin I read, couldn't hardly even read it at all. Only you didn't notice. Wasn't even listenin, sittin there back a the room jiss thumbin through your book.

(ALICE *crosses to desk.*)

CALVIN: So you know what I done? Skip one whole paragraph, tess you out— you jiss kep thumbin through your book! An then you give me a "B"! (*He has followed Alice to desk.*)

ALICE (*puts papers in box and throws out old coffee cup*): Well that just shows how well you did the part!

CALVIN: You wanna give me somethin I could "identify" with, how come you ain' let me do that other dude in the play . . .

ALICE: Iago?

CALVIN: Yeah. What is it they calls him? Othello's . . .

ALICE: Subordinate.

CALVIN: Go right along there with my speech syndrome, wouldn' it now? See, Iago has to work for the Man. I identifies with him! He gits jealous man. Know what I mean? Or that Gravedigger? Shovelin dirt for his day's work! How come you wouldn't let me do him? Thass the question I wanna ax you!

ALICE *(turns to* CALVIN*):* "A**ᴣk me**," Calvin, "Ask me!"

CALVIN *(steps SR):* "Ax you?" Okay, man. *(turns to* ALICE*)* Miss Shakespeare, Speech Communications 1! *(crosses US of* ALICE*)* Know what I'll "ax" you right here in this room, this day, at this here desk right now? I'll "ax" you how come I have been in this here college 3 months on this here Open Admissions an I don't know nothin more than when I came in here? You know what I mean? This supposed to be some big break for me. This here is where all them smart Jewish boys has gone from the Bronx Science and went an become some Big Time Doctors at Bellvue. An some Big Time Judges in the Family Court an like that there. And now it's supposed to be my turn.

*(*ALICE *looks away and* CALVIN *crosses R of* ALICE*)*

CALVIN: You know what I mean? *(He crosses UR.)* An my sister Jonelle took me out of foster care where I been in 6 homes and 5 schools to give me my chance. *(He crosses DR.)* Livin with her an she workin 3 shifts in some "Ladies Restroom" give me my opportunity. An she say she gonna buss her ass git me this education I don't end up on the streets! *(crosses on a diagonal to* ALICE*)* Cause I have got *brains!*

*(*ALICE *sits in student chair.* CALVIN *crosses in back, to her left.)*

CALVIN: You understand what I am Communicatin to you? My high school has tole me I got brains an can make somethin outta my life if I gits me the chance! And now this here's supposed to be my chance! High school says you folks gonna bring me up to date on my education and git me even. Only nothin is happenin to me in my head except I am getting more and more confused about what I knows and what I don't know! *(He sits in swivel chair.)* So what I wanna "ax" you is: How come you don't sit down with me and teach me which way to git my ideas down instead of givin me a "B."

*(*ALICE *rises and crosses UR.)*

CALVIN: I don't even turn no outline in? Jiss give me a "B." *(He rises and crosses R of* ALICE*.)* An Lester a "B"! An Melba a "B"! An Sam a "B"! What's that "B" standin for anyhow? Cause it surely ain't standin for no piece of work!

ALICE: Calvin don't blame me!

*(*CALVIN *crosses DR.)*

ALICE: I'm trying! God knows I'm trying! The times are rough for everyone. I'm a Shakespearean scholar, and they have me teaching beginning Speech. I was supposed to have 12 graduate students a class, 9 classes a week, and they gave me 35 Freshmen a class, 20 classes a week. I hear 157 speeches a week! You know what that's like? And I go home late on the subway scared to death! In Graduate School they told me I'd have a first rate career. Then I started here and they said: "Hang on! Things will improve!" But they only got worse . . . and worse! Now I've been here for 12 years and I haven't written one word in my field! I haven't read 5 research books! I'm exhausted . . . and I'm finished! We all have to bend. I'm just hanging on now . . . supporting my little girl . . . earning a living . . . and that's all . . . *(She crosses to desk.)*

CALVIN *(faces* ALICE*):* What I'm supposed to do, feel sorry for you? Least you can *earn* a livin! Clean office, private phone, name on the door with all them B.A.'s, M.A.'s, Ph.D.'s.

ALICE: You can have those too. *(She crosses DR to* CALVIN.*)* Look, last year we got 10 black students into Ivy League Graduate Programs. And they were no better than you. They were just *perceived (points to blackboard)* as better. Now that's the whole key for you . . . to be perceived as better! So you can get good recommendations and do well on interviews. You're good looking and ambitious and you have a fine native intelligence. You can make it, Calvin. All we have to do is work on improving your Positive Communicator's Image . . . by getting rid of that Street Speech. Don't you see?

CALVIN: See what? What you axin *me* to see?

ALICE: *"Asking"* me to see, Calvin. *"Asking"* me to see!

CALVIN: *(Starts out of control at this, enraged, crosses UC and bangs on file cabinet.)* Ooooeee! Ooooeee! You wanna *see?* You wanna *see?* Ooooeee!

ALICE: Calvin stop it! STOP IT!

CALVIN: "Calvin stop it"? "Stop it"? *(picks up school books from desk)* There any black professors here?

ALICE *(crosses UR.):* No! They got cut . . . the budget's low . . . they got . . .

CALVIN *(interrupting):* Cut? *They* got CUT? *(crosses to* ALICE *and backs her to the DS edge of desk)* Gonna *cut you,* lady! Gonna cut you, throw you out the fuckin window, throw the fuckin books out the fuckin window, burn it all mother fuckin down. FUCKIN DOWN!!!

ALICE: Calvin! Stop it! STOP IT! YOU HEAR ME?

CALVIN *(turns away, center stage):* I CAN'T!! *YOU* HEAR *ME?* I CAN'T! *YOU* HEAR *ME!* I CAN'T! YOU GOTTA GIVE ME MY EDUCATION! GOTTA TEACH ME! GIVE ME SOMETHING NOW! GIVE ME NOW! NOW! NOW! NOW! NOW! NOW!

*(*CALVIN *tears up text book. He starts to pick up torn pages and drops them. He bursts into a wailing, bellowing cry in his anguish and despair, doubled over in pain and grief. It is a while before his sobs subside. Finally,* ALICE *speaks.)*

ALICE: Calvin . . . from the bottom of my heart . . . I want to help you . . .

CALVIN *(barely able to speak):* By changin my words? Thass nothin . . . nothin! I got to know them big ideas . . . and which way to git em down . . .

ALICE: But how can I teach you that? You can't write a paragraph, Calvin . . . or a sentence . . . you can't spell past 4th grade . . . the essay you wrote showed that . . .

CALVIN *(rises):* **What essay?**

ALICE *(crosses to UL files, gets essay and hands it to* CALVIN*):* **The autobiographical one . . . you did it the first day . . .**

CALVIN: **You said that was for *your* reference . . . didn't count . . .**

ALICE: **Here . . .**

CALVIN: *(Opens it up. Stunned.)* **"F"? Why didn't you tell me I failed?**

ALICE *(crosses to desk, puts essay down):* **For what?**

CALVIN *(still stunned):* **So you could teach me how to write.**

ALICE *(crosses DL):* **In 16 weeks?**

CALVIN *(still can't believe this):* **You my teacher!**

ALICE: **That would take years! And speech is my job. You need a tutor.**

CALVIN: **I'm your job. They outa tutors!**

ALICE *(turns to him):* **I can't do it, Calvin. And that's the real truth. I'm one person, in one job. And I can't. Do you understand? And even if I could, it wouldn't matter. All that matters is the budget . . . and the curriculum . . . and the grades . . . and how you look . . . and how you talk!**

CALVIN: *(Pause. Absorbing this.)* **Then I'm finished, man.**

(There is a long pause. Finally:)

ALICE *(gets essay from desk, refiles it and returns to desk):* **No, you're not. If you'll bend and take what I can give you, things will work out for you . . . Trust me . . . Let me help you Calvin . . . Please . . . I can teach you speech . . .**

CALVIN *(crosses to UC file cabinet. Long pause):* **Okay . . . all right, man . . .** *(Crosses to student chair and sits.)*

ALICE *(crosses to desk, takes off rain coat and sits in swivel chair):* **Now, then, we'll go through the exercise once then you do it at home . . . please, repeat after me, slowly . . . "asking" . . . "asking" . . . "asking" . . .**

CALVIN *(long pause):* **Ax-ing . . .**

ALICE: **Ass-king . . .**

CALVIN: *(During the following, he now turns from* ALICE*, faces front, and gazes out beyond the audience; on his fourth word, lights begin to fade to black.)* **Ax-ing . . . Aks-ing . . . ass-king . . . asking . . . asking . . . asking . . .**

BLACKOUT

END OF PLAY

REACTIONS ON READING
OPEN ADMISSIONS

Prereading and Writing

Julie Layard began by brainstorming and freewriting on her feelings about the general subject of Shirley Lauro's play, the open admissions concept of education.

Before Reading: Response to the Title

"Open Admissions"--A forgotten dream, chance to survive, a
support-system, an encouraging arm, a push to achieve,
acceptance of "different" students, a chance to mend mistakes,
to learn all life-long, amends made for poor primary and
secondary schools, redress, compensations, reparation,
restitution, a band-aid, overcrowded, overloaded, biased,
partial, corrupt, quota education, controversy, rehabilitation,
opportunity, future, multi-cultural, invisible students, racial
cliques, indirect apology, open admission of guilt of depriving
students of basic skills, generalized information, bad
reputation, cultural sensitivity, delicate balance, budget cuts,
transfer programs, inner-city planning, assembly-line education.
    But where would I be today if it were not for the open
admissions system established in the United States? I don't have
to worry about tuition at my school. I have the chance to follow
my dreams, I have the chance to do as well as I dare to do, to
pursue anything I could imagine, because of the programs at my
community college. Yet I can't help thinking about the word play
of an "open admission of guilt" vs. the "open admission" policy
seen in community colleges today. This double entendre is an
exact reflection of my feelings concerning the open admissions
system of education. Essentially, open admissions is an ideal;
underprivileged, undereducated, or otherwise previously unable
students are supposed to have a fair chance, but the quick-patch
system of education most instructors practice in schools
operating on the principle of open admission cannot provide
equal compensation for initial failure.

Responding to the Text

After recording her reactions to the title and the cultural implications of the subject matter of the work, Layard read through the play fairly rapidly. Then she
wrote a response to the two major characters and the major themes as she understood them.

Reading Response to Open Admissions

    Calvin Jefferson--Like so many of the students I see at
school--curious, ambitious, hopeful, tired of his world,
trusting, passionate, full of frustration, frightened that he
lost his chance when he sacrificed school in the past. He hopes
for the best, but something in him also doubts it will ever be.
He needs encouragement and assurance to keep trying.
    Prof. Alice Miller: I picture her youth: dreams of the
British Museum libraries, late nights of study, sleeping in
study lounges, early-morning lectures. Love of literature,

disassociation from the common world of commercialism: empty, dirty reality. Romantic, sharp-witted, strong. I imagine her single, living in an uptown one bedroom apartment with her walls lined with books. Loves to be in culturally rich surroundings; she saves enough to go back to London, drives out to Oxford. I see her with images of England in her eyes as she watches the students give their speeches, imagining the wide open spaces of north Britain instead of the heavy, claustrophobic classroom in New York City. She is tired, and she is disappointed.

This play reminds me of a teacher I had my first semester at college who graded on a curve to such an extent that he was delivering grades of "excellent" to students to whom he had never introduced the material. This instructor was cheating the "A" students as well as the "C" students--building for us a false sense that we had knowledge. Incidents like these are at the root of the injustice that truly disabled students like Calvin Jefferson are facing all over the United States today. How will these kids survive? From the start, our public school instructors seem intent on simply delivering us to the next level of education with passable skills, with the ability to sufficiently blend into our academic environment.

At the same time I can't help identifying with Professor Miller. She is right, of course; with over twenty classes a week, obligations to the school board, and a child of her own, she does not have time or energy to teach Calvin basic skills that take years to develop and that he needs so desperately. Yet I blame her apathy, her acceptance of the fate of such students that she knows is inevitable. Why are all the teachers keeping quiet? Where did their social conscience go? Doesn't it upset her? Doesn't she feel it is unfair? Can she sleep at night, knowing these students can barely read a television schedule? How difficult will it be for them to hold a job, much less enjoy the feeling that reading Shakespeare gives her?

I need to look more closely at the dialogue to analyze the full meaning of the play. What is literally being said? What does Calvin want from Alice? How does she justify her inaction? Why do the characters say what they do? Is Calvin really angry with Alice, or is he angry at the system? Does Alice really resent Calvin, or is she reacting out of frustration? Why do the characters say what they do when they do? Why does Alice wait until after Calvin has confronted her to give him an honest evaluation of his language skills? How does her timing change the information into a personal insult rather than an objective evaluation? Finally, how is Lauro using the dialogue to make secondary references to the theme of the play? What is the significance of Alice as a speech teacher and her obsession with a positive communicator's image? After answering these questions for myself I will be able to see more clearly the patterns that the theme of communication takes in Lauro's play--the positions

of the characters, the structure of their discussion. For Calvin
and many others like him, a war of miscommunication will forever
obscure the path to learning.

Developing an Essay

After completing the prewritings and doing some thinking and research on open
admissions policy, Julie Layard read over her work to find a focus for a short
essay on the play. She decided on the subject of communication, realizing that
the central conflict in the play involves a breakdown in communication between
the highly educated Miller and the demanding student, Calvin. Layard wrote a
scratch outline and an initial draft of her paper; she then revised her draft
significantly, after sharing it with her classmates and instructor. Following is the
final revision of her essay. Do you agree with her interpretation and evaluation
of the play? Does she support her ideas adequately? Can you think of ways she
could have improved her essay?

Communication in "Open Admissions"

Shirley Lauro, a playwright and teacher for many years, was
part of the faculty at the City University of New York in the
late 1970s when an open admissions policy was initiated. She saw
its beginning, and soon after, she saw its end. The one-act play
"Open Admissions" can be read as a statement about Lauro's
experiences in the program. In addition to taking a strong
position concerning cultural insensitivity in education today,
the play also explores the root cause of the failure of the open
admissions system. The identity of Lauro's characters, the
issues they confront in their discussion, and the conflicts that
arise in the action, are all closely tied to the theme of what
makes for good communication.

The play opens in a sterile, communal faculty office, where
we find Calvin Jefferson, a young, underprepared student in the
open admissions program, and Alice Miller, his speech teacher.
Alice has not discussed Calvin's individual learning problems
with him, and Calvin has waited until the end of the semester to
voice his own concerns. Both characters are caught up in the act
of discussing their personal anxieties about their own teacher-
student relationship. A confrontation ensues, and much of the
blame for the breakdown of their communication is placed on the
open admissions system itself.

Essentially, most students and teachers feel distant from
one another's emotional needs. Take Alice, for instance.
Clearly, she has spent very little time thinking about Calvin's
problems. Although Alice is very well educated, she is trained
as a Shakespearean scholar, not as a teacher. The stage
direction and her dialogue make it clear to us that Alice Miller
never intended to teach, so we have to assume that she has
little experience with education and little patience for

students with special needs. Alice is responsible for teaching, but the evidence from the text implies that she is not very interested in communicating to her students what she knows.

Calvin Jefferson, on the other hand, has trouble finding the words to express his needs. From the few clues we are given about his history, it would be fair to assume that he has not had very much experience with having his needs met, at all. Calvin may be bright, but for him, communicating with others is a purely emotional experience. In his dreams of educational success, which he describes to Alice, he can be specific about little but that he has great hope. "My high school has tole me I got brains an I can make somethin outta my life if I gits me the chance! . . . High school says you folks gonna bring me up to date on my education and git me even . . ." In his frustration, he becomes enraged; in his pain, he cries. Calvin tries to explain to Alice what he wants, but his methods alienate her.

Both characters are locked into their own dilemmas, unable to reach out to one another. Alice refuses to acknowledge that she has made a mistake, that she could have provided him with an honest evaluation of his skills at the beginning of the semester and referred him to tutors. Even in her insulting alternative suggestions to Calvin, she uses lofty jargon about "positive communicator's image" and sophisticated concepts about perceived value. Calvin does not know specifically what he needs, making ambiguous references to "them big ideas." Instead of communicating, the two of them spend their time punishing one another for their lack of mutual understanding.

Cultural patterns of confrontation also lead to conflict in the play. In the climax of the action, Calvin loses his composure under the strain of the argument. He shouts, cries, and acts out violently in his confusion and fear. This is the way that he has learned to be heard. Calvin threatens Alice and cries out in anguish, finally breaking down in tears. In the process of getting attention in this way, any valid needs are obscured, and Alice doesn't want to listen to Calvin anymore.

Although she appears polite and calm, it would be a mistake to see Alice as unemotional in her response to Calvin's tantrum. She puts just as much--or more--negative emotion into her lines as Calvin does in even his most bitter outburst. What he may act out in grief and frustration, she counters with controlled, vindictive hostility. While Calvin begs Alice for help, she quietly pulls from a file cabinet his initial writing sample, intended for her reference in student placement. When he looks at it, he is stunned to see it marked with an "F". Calvin does not understand why Alice did not advise him of his chances from the start. She turns to him. "For what? . . . You can't write a paragraph, Calvin . . . or a sentence . . . you can't spell past the fourth grade." He is crushed. He has asked for her guidance, but she offers none. Calvin makes no more argument, but answers her judgment in numb acceptance: "Then I'm finished, man."

In one moment, Alice has broken all of Calvin's dreams. Information that could have directed him to specialists and tutors at the beginning of the semester at this point can only fill him with a sense of overpowering shame and a feeling of defeat. Calvin's outburst was an essentially undirected emotional response to the system, but Alice's cold reaction is an act of emotional abuse.

As the focus of their confrontation moves from resolution to revenge, Alice and Calvin step into the rigidly defined roles they will play with one another. Alice gains control over Calvin once more, and finally offers her own terms, asking him to "bend and take what I can give you . . . I can teach you speech." Calvin realizes that lessons in elocution are all that Alice intends to offer him, but he has no choice but to accept her weak compromise. As the play closes, Calvin is heard attempting to perfect his pronunciation of the word "asking." One hopes Alice will be able to recognize the deeper meaning of the word, beyond the simple "correct" sounds. Calvin is truly "asking" for help in the play; he should not be made to feel like an "ass-king" or kiss-ass in order to gain the knowledge he so desperately seeks.

Alice and Calvin are embroiled in a war of emotions, rather than reason. They have lost the thread that ties them to the subject of education; they have embarked on a contest of personal attack. It becomes clear that Calvin's eventual failure in achieving his goal to learn will not be the result of Alice's busy schedule, or of his own staggering lack of previous education. It will most likely be because of ineffectual, damaging exchanges between student and teacher.

During conflicts, messages often become confused in their explanation. At crucial moments, we are unable to voice exactly how we feel, be it "Help me," or "I don't know how." In communicating, we build complex webs around our basic needs. Lauro is making a statement about why students slip through the cracks, year after year, without gaining a satisfactory education. Certainly, Alice Miller's complaints are valid. There is no real way for her to compensate in one semester of school for what Calvin does not know--basic skills that take many years to build. But her resignation turns to passive-aggression when she refuses to communicate with him, to offer what she can. It is what thousands of teachers in these kinds of situations have denied their students: interest enough to establish a forum of communication that might have led Calvin to people who could help, communication that might have made it possible for him to express his doubts immediately. Open admissions programs can work. Like Calvin, many of the students taking part in these first attempts were underprepared. That was to be expected; it was the reason the programs were initiated in the first place. What no one counted on was how underprepared the system would be for change.

Notice that Julie Layard includes an introduction in which she indicates what the play is about and clarifies the focus of the essay; it will examine how the characters and their conflict in the play reflect on the central theme of communication. She follows her introduction with a series of related paragraphs, developed with references to key lines and details, strong words, images, figurative language, and bits of dialogue from the play that add to and support the interpretation of the work and the central argument of the essay. Finally, she provides an effective conclusion that evaluates the situation explored in the play and indicates what she learned and what other readers could learn from *Open Admissions*.

3

THEMES
AND GENRES

Chapter 7

CREATIVITY

The poet's voice need not merely be the record of man, it can be one of the props, the pillars to help him endure and prevail.
William Faulkner, "Nobel Prize Acceptance Speech"

The Maker of a sentence launches out into the infinite and builds a road into Chaos and old Night, and is followed by those who hear . . . with something of wild, creative delight.
Ralph Waldo Emerson, *Journals*

[A] divine discontent, [a] disequilibrium, [a] state of inner tension is the source of artistic energy.
May Sarton, "The Journal of a Solitude"

I want to be with that tree and follow it to a place it knows, to the source of life, where one can be what he dreams, through the faith of the poem.
Jimmy Santiago Baca, "Pushing Through"

Creativity can take many forms: the production of a work of art or literature, the live performance of a play, the nurturing of new life, the maintenance of strong, caring relationships with other people. Creativity speaks to and touches the human spirit. Through creativity, individuals can connect with experiences outside of the present moment and the limits of their characters. As William Faulkner suggests, creativity gives us the courage to keep struggling, helping us to prevail even when life seems most depressing or cruel. Creativity, which inspires in its audience what Emerson refers to as "wild, creative delight," can be seen as the root of the human spirit.

Each of the essays, stories, and poems, as well as the play, selected for this

Pablo Picasso. *Three Musicians*. Fontainebleau, summer, 1921. Oil on canvas, 6'7" × 7'3¾". The Museum of Modern Art, New York. Mrs. Simon Guggenheim Fund. Photograph © 1993 The Museum of Modern Art, New York.

chapter provides a unique impression of the power of the creative spirit. These works explore the mysterious nature of creativity and the essentially collaborative relationship between the writer and his or her audience. The selections present a number of the concepts that are fundamental to an understanding of the creative process. How does an artist's heritage and culture influence his or her creative process? From what sources in the artist's past has the work been shaped? What is the relationship between the creative artist and his or her audience? How does each particular form of literature such as poetry, the short story, or drama affect the writer's creative process? In what ways is artistic creativity connected to other creative expressions of life such as the need to give birth and nurture human life, social and family relationships, and the human need to grow intellectually, emotionally, and spiritually? Each in its own way, the readings in this chapter will help you to understand better the nature of creativity.

Every work of art encourages the reader to consider the relationship of the artwork to the culture and values out of which it was born, the process through which it was shaped. In some of the selections a particular work of art comes to embody this very process. For example, in her essay "Ordinary Spirit," Joy Harjo discusses how her writing has helped her to understand, to value, and to transform creatively her family's culture. Similarly, in his elegiac poem "Yonosa House," R. T. Smith pays tribute to his Native American grandmother who "wove the myths of the race/in fevered patterns" on his young mind. August Wilson in his Pulitzer Prize–winning play, *The Piano Lesson,* develops the central metaphor of the play around an ornately carved antique piano that embodies the family's history of struggle: their values, their spirit, their creativity, their power.

Artists reach out to their audiences to complete the creative process; thus understanding the relationship between the author and his or her audience is always fundamental to an understanding of a piece of writing. Readers enter into a collaborative dialogue with the piece of literature they are reading, completing the work by interpreting it through their experiences, imagination, and values. An example of the collaborative relationship between writer and reader is seen in Grace Paley's story "A Conversation with My Father." Paley shows through the father's reading of and his daughter's response to his reading of her story how art reflects the perceptions of the artist as well as the interpretation of the audience, so that, ultimately, art, like a conversation, is a reciprocal process. In a similar way, in her poem "The Secret," Denise Levertov expresses the relationship between writer and audience as one of sharing and of knowing, both alone and together, as one of offering ideas or "secrets" that are reinterpreted and passed on, bringing happiness, connection, and change.

Artists try to understand the complexity of the creative process, which involves an unpredictable synthesis of conscious and unconscious thoughts. In his essay "Pushing Through" poet Jimmy Santiago Baca claims that "each true poem is a pearl-handled pistol you point at your heart." In his poem "The Thought-Fox," Ted Hughes expresses the elusive process of inspiration through the metaphor of a fox's arrival at midnight. Hughes' magical insight echoes another of Baca's: "A true poem is starlight that has reached the earth."

Directly related to the mysterious nature of the creative process is the question of how creativity is nourished and enhanced through relationships with other creators and works of art. In "Ode on a Grecian Urn," John Keats reflects on how a creator can deepen his or her powers and find inspiration in the presence of great works of art. In "Sailing to Byzantium" William Butler Yeats maintains that artistic power does not come from knowing the "rules" but from studying "monuments of its [the artistic soul's] own magnificence." In John McCluskey's short story "Lush Life," a night journey also becomes a journey into the unconscious minds of the two main characters, both jazz musicians, who weave the important lessons that they have learned about life and music into a new jazz song.

In periods of social upheaval, artists must redefine the relationship between creativity and the socioeconomic conditions that they struggle with in order to survive. In her essay "coming to voice," bell hooks argues that becoming a writer involves expressing one's feelings and thoughts, speaking out to an audience, especially if those thoughts and feelings represent a rebellion against the prevailing economic, social, and cultural values of one's community. In his short story, "B. Wordsworth," V. S. Naipaul creates a portrait of a penniless poet scorned by society; yet B. Wordsworth's actions and values affirm the spirit of love, caring, and forgiveness.

Many women writers today are exploring the interrelationships among artistic creation, childbirth, nurturing, and creative problem solving. For example, Nancy Willard, in her poem "Why I Never Answered Your Letter," illustrates some of the ways that a life of nurturing as a wife and mother can devour, and at the same time feed, a woman's creative energy for writing. Despite the changed perspectives of modern women on issues of traditional gender roles, many families and cultures continue to place a primary emphasis on women's roles as childbearers and nurturers. In her poem "The Quilt," Chitra Divakaruni provides vivid, ironic images of the way that East Indian culture values motherhood as the highest expression of a woman's creativity.

Perhaps most importantly, literature helps us to experience the ways in which creative works allow the individual to transcend the limits of temporal experience, to pass on a vital tradition to future generations. Along with many of the writers in this chapter, John Keats and J. R. R. Tolkien both address spiritual questions about the relationships between art and life. In his poem "Ode on a Grecian Urn" Keats perceives artistic beauty as unchanged by time, synonymous with the discovery of immortal truths, whereas Tolkien's short story "Leaf by Niggle" presents a parable of an unappreciated artist whose painting, after the artist's physical death, becomes a leaf on the tree of life.

The issues raised in this introduction will help you to begin your reading for this chapter; however, we encourage you to discover other issues and to share your special insights and knowledge with your classmates and instructor. Your experiences, ideas, and voice need to be heard by others in order to be understood and appreciated.

In the folk tale "How Spider Obtained the Sky God's Stories," which begins the chapter, Anansi the spider's daring, ingenuity, understanding of the past, and practical problem-solving skills help him gain possession of the stories of the sky god. As you begin this chapter, imagine that you are like Anansi: ingenious and persistent, intensely involved in your quest for knowledge but, at the same time, logical and pragmatic. Work to find a way to reinterpret, to make your own the stories, poems, essays, and plays that you read in the text, relating them to your own past, to the myths that have shaped your family, your community, and your culture. Gradually you will begin to feel that you possess an identity as a creative reader and writer engaged in a conversation with the poem, story, essay, or play that you are reading. Your writer's identity will come alive in this process of uncovering and expressing your feelings and thoughts, generating a dialogue with the blank piece of paper that you fill with words, with ideas, with feelings. As you connect yourself to the "imagined worlds" selected for this and the other chapters in this book, you will discover creative and spiritual strength as well as a more concrete understanding of how you can develop and refine your own processes of reading and writing.

Folk Tales

How Spider Obtained
The Sky God's Stories
Africa (Ashanti)

Journal

Write a story about a time when you wanted something very much and obtained it through enterprising and resourceful action.

Anansi the spider is the central figure in many African folk tales. Clever, vital, and cunning, he is a classic example of the "trickster" character in folk-mythology.

Kwaku Anansi, the spider, once went to Nyankonpon, the sky god, in order to buy the sky god's stories. The sky god said, "What makes you think *you* can buy them?" The spider answered and said, "I know I shall be able." Thereupon the sky god said, "Great and powerful towns like Kokofu, Bekwai, Asumengya, have come, but they were unable to purchase them, and yet you who are but a mere masterless man, you say you will be able?"

The spider said, "What is the price of the stories?" The sky god said, "They cannot be bought for anything except Onini, the python; Osebo, the leopard; Mmoatia, the fairy; and Mmoboro, the hornets." The spider said, "I will bring some of all these things, and, what is more, I'll add my old mother, Nsia, the sixth child, to the lot."

The sky god said, "Go and bring them then." The spider came back, and told his mother all about it, saying, "I wish to buy the stories of the sky god, and the sky god says I must bring Onini, the python; Osebo, the leopard; Mmoatia, the fairy; and Mmoboro, the hornets; and I said I would add you to the lot and give you to the sky god." Now the spider consulted his wife, Aso, saying, "What is to be done that we may get Onini, the python?" Aso said to him, "You go off and cut a branch of a palm tree, and cut some stringcreeper as well, and bring them." And the spider came back with them. And Aso said, "Take them to the stream." So Anansi took them; and, as he was going along he said, "It's longer than he is, it's not so long as he; you lie, it's longer than he."

The spider said, "There he is, lying yonder." The python, who had over-heard this imaginary conversation, then asked, "What's this all about?" To which the spider replied, "Is it not my wife, Aso, who is arguing with me that this palm branch is longer than you, and I say she is a liar." And Onini, the python, said, "Bring it, and come and measure me." Anansi took the palm branch and laid it along the python's body. Then he said, "Stretch yourself out." And the python stretched himself out, and Anansi took the rope-creeper and wound it and the sound of the tying was *nwenene! nwenene! nwenene!* until he came to the head. Anansi, the spider said, "Fool, I shall take you to the sky god and receive the sky god's tales in exchange." So Anansi took him off to Nyame, the sky god. The sky god then said, "My hand has touched it; there remains what still remains."

The spider returned and came and told his wife what had happened, say-ing, "There remain the hornets." His wife said, "Look for a gourd, and fill it with water and go off with it." The spider went along through the bush, when he saw a swarm of hornets hanging there, and he poured out some of the water and sprinkled it on them. He then poured the remainder upon himself and cut a leaf of plantain and covered his head with it. And now he addressed the hor-nets, saying, "As the rain has come, had you not better come and enter this, my gourd, so that the rain will not beat you; don't you see that I have taken a plantain leaf to cover myself?" Then the hornets said, "We thank you, Aku, we thank you, Aku." All the hornets flew disappearing into the gourd, *fom!*

Father Spider covered the mouth, and exclaimed, "Fools, I have got you, and I am taking you to receive the tales of the sky god in exchange." And he took the hornets to the sky god. The sky god said, "My hand has touched it; what remains still remains."

The spider came back once more, and told his wife, and said, "There remains Osebo, the leopard." Aso said, "Go and dig a hole." Anansi said, "That's enough, I understand." Then the spider went off to look for the leopard's tracks, and, having found them, he dug a very deep pit, covered it over, and came back home. Very early next day, when objects began to be visible, the spider said he would go off, and when he went, lo, a leopard was lying in the pit. Anansi said, "Little father's child, little mother's child, I have told you not to get drunk, and now, just as one would expect of you, you have become intoxicated, and that's why you have fallen into the pit. If I were to say I would get you out, next day, if you saw me, or likewise any of my children, you would go and catch me and them." The leopard said, "O! I could not do such a thing."

Anansi then went and cut two sticks, put one here, and one there, and said, "Put one of your paws here, and one also of your paws here." And the leopard placed them where he was told. As he was about to climb up, Anansi lifted up his knife, and in a flash it descended on his head, *gao!* was the sound it made. The pit received the leopard and *fom!* was the sound of the falling. Anansi got a ladder to descend into the pit to go and get the leopard out. He got the leopard out and came back with it, exclaiming, "Fool, I am taking you to exchange for the stories of the sky god." He lifted up the leopard to go and give to Nyame, the sky god. The sky god said, "My hands have touched it; what remains still remains."

Then the spider came back, carved an Akua's child, a black flat-faced wooden doll, tapped some sticky fluid from a tree and plastered the doll's body with it. Then he made *eto,* pounded yams, and put some in the doll's hand. Again he pounded some more and placed it in a brass basin; he tied string round the doll's waist, and went with it and placed it at the foot of the odum tree, the place where the fairies come to play. And a fairy came along. She said, "Akua, may I eat a little of this mash?" Anansi tugged at the string, and the doll nodded her head. The fairy turned to one of the sisters, saying, "She says I may eat some." She said, "Eat some, then." And she finished eating, and thanked her. But when she thanked her, the doll did not answer. And the fairy said to her sister, "When I thank her, she does not reply." The sister of the first fairy said, "Slap her crying-place." And she slapped it, *pa!* And her hand stuck there. She said to her sister, "My hand has stuck there." She said, "Take the one that remains and slap her crying-place again." And she took it and slapped her, *pa!* and this one, too, stuck fast. And the fairy told her sister, saying, "My two hands have stuck fast." She said, "Push it with your stomach." She pushed it and her stomach stuck to it. And Anansi came and tied her up, and he said, "Fool, I have got you, I shall take you to the sky god in exchange for his stories." And he went off home with her.

Now Anansi spoke to his mother, Ya Nsia, the sixth child, saying, "Rise up, let us go, for I am taking you along with the fairy to go and give you to the sky god in exchange for his stories." He lifted them up, and went off there to where the sky god was. Arrived there he said, "Sky god, here is a fairy and my old woman whom I spoke about, here she is, too." Now the sky god called his elders, the Kontire and Akwam chiefs, the Adonten, the Gyase, the Oyoko, Ankobea, and Kyidom. And he put the matter before them, saying, "Very great kings have come and were not able to buy the sky god's stories, but Kwaku Anansi, the spider, has been able to pay the price: I have received from him Osebo, the leopard; I have received from him Onini, the python; and of his own accord, Anansi has added his mother to the lot; all these things lie here." He said, "Sing his praise." *"Eee!"* they shouted. The sky god said, "Kwaku Anansi, from today and going on forever, I take my sky god's stories and I present them to you, *kose! kose! kose!* my blessing, blessing, blessing! No more shall we call them the stories of the sky god, but we shall call them spider stories."

This, my story, which I have related, if it be sweet, or if it be not sweet, take some elsewhere, and let some come back to me.

QUESTIONS AND CONSIDERATIONS

1. Why are the sky god's stories so important to Anansi? How does he set out to obtain them?

2. How do you interpret the significance of the process that Anansi must go through in order to obtain the stories? For example, what might each stage in the quest represent?

3. Why is Anansi successful?

4. Discuss how the meaning of the tale is completed by the last two lines. If the tale has a "moral" about art, creativity, and its sources or process, what might that moral be?

Journals

How I Came
To Write Fiction

George Eliot

From the Journal, 6 December, 1857

September 1857 made a new era in my life, for it was then I began to write Fiction. It had always been a vague dream of mine that some time or other I might write a novel, and my shadowy conception of what the novel was to be, varied, of course, from one epoch of my life to another. But I never went farther towards the actual writing of the novel than an introductory chapter describing a Staffordshire village and the life of the neighboring farm houses, and as the years passed on I lost any hope that I should ever be able to write a novel, just as I desponded about everything else in my future life. I always thought I was deficient in dramatic power, both of construction and dialogue, but I felt I should be at my ease in the descriptive parts of a novel. My "introductory chapter" was pure description though there were good materials in it for dramatic presentation. It happened to be among the papers I had with me in Germany and one evening in Berlin, something led me to read it to George. He was struck with it as a bit of concrete description, and it suggested to him the possibility of my being able to write a novel, though he distrusted—indeed disbelieved in, my possession of any dramatic power. Still, he began to think that I might as well try, some time, what I could do in fiction, and by and bye, when we came back to England and I had greater success than he had ever expected in other kinds of writing, his impression that it was worth while to see how far my mental power would go towards the production of a novel, was strengthened. He began to say very positively, "You must try and write a story," and when we were at Tenby he urged me to begin at once. I deferred it, however, after my usual fashion, with work that does not present itself as an absolute duty. But one morning as I was lying in bed, thinking what should be the subject of my first story, my thoughts merged themselves into a dreamy doze, and I imagined myself writing a story of which the title was—"The Sad Fortunes of the Reverend Amos Barton." I was soon wide awake again, and told G. He said, "O what a capital title!" and from that time I had settled in my mind that this should be my first story. George used to say, "It may be a failure—it may be that you are unable to write fiction. Or perhaps, it may be just good enough to warrant your trying again." Again, "You may write a chef-d'oeuvre at once—there's no telling." But his prevalent impression was that though I could hardly write a *poor* novel, my effort would want the highest quality of fiction—dramatic presentation. He used to say, "You have wit, description and philosophy—those go a good way towards the production of a novel. It is worth while for you to try the experiment."

We determined that if my story turned out good enough, we would send it to Blackwood, but G. thought the more probable result was, that I should have to lay it aside and try again.

But when we returned to Richmond I had to write my article on Silly Novels ("Silly Novels by Lady Novelists," Westminster Review) and my review of Contemporary Literature, so that I did not begin my story till September 22. After I had begun it, as we were walking in the Park, I mentioned to G. that I had thought of the plan of writing a series of stories containing sketches drawn from my own observation of the Clergy, and calling them "Scenes from Clerical Life" opening with "Amos Barton." He at once accepted the notion as a good one—fresh and striking; and about a week afterwards when I read him the early part of "Amos," he had no longer any doubt about my ability to carry out the plan. The scene at Cross Farm, he said, satisfied him that I had the very element he had been doubtful about—it was clear I could write good dialogue. There still remained the question whether I could command any pathos, and that was to be decided by the mode in which I treated Milly's death. One night G. went to town on purpose to leave me a quiet evening for writing it. I wrote the chapter from the news brought by the shepherd to Mrs. Hackit, to the moment when Amos is dragged from the bedside and I read it to G. when he came home. We both cried over it, and then he came up to me and kissed me saying, "I think your pathos is better than your fun."

So when the story was finished G. sent it to Blackwood, who wrote in reply, that he thought the "Clerical reminiscences would do," congratulated the author of being "worthy the honours of print and pay," but would like to see more of the series before he undertook to print. However, when G. wrote that the author was discouraged by this editorial caution, Blackwood disclaimed any distrust and agreed to print the story at once. The first appeared in the January number 1857. . . . When the story was concluded he wrote me word how Albert Smith had sent him a letter saying he had never read anything that affected him more than Milly's death, and, added Blackwood, "the men at the club seem to have mingled their tears and their tumblers together. It will be curious if you should be a member and be hearing your own praises!" There was clearly no suspicion that I was a woman. It is interesting, as an indication of the value there is in such conjectural criticism generally, to remember that when G. read the first part of "Amos" to a party . . . they were all sure I was a clergyman—a Cambridge man.

Dec. 31 (the last night of 1857.)

The dear old year is gone with all its *Weben* and *Streben*. Yet not gone either: for what I have suffered and enjoyed in it remains to me an everlasting possession while my soul's life remains. This time last year I was alone, as I am now, and dear George was at Vernon Hill. I was writing the introduction to "Mr. Gilfil's Love-Story." What a world of thoughts and feelings since then! My life has deepened unspeakably during the last year; I feel a greater capacity for moral and intellectual enjoyment; a more acute sense of my deficiencies in the past; a more solemn desire to be faithful to coming duties than I remember at any former period of my life. And my happiness has deepened too: the blessedness of a perfect love and union grows daily. I have had some severe suffering this year from anxiety about my sister, and what will probably be a final separation from her—there has been no other real trouble. Few women, I fear, have had such reason as I have to think the long sad years of youth were worth living for the sake of middle age. Our prospects are very bright too. I am writing my new novel. G. is full of his "Physiology of Common Life." . . . So good-by, dear 1857! May I be able to look back on 1858 with an equal consciousness of advancement in work and in heart.

From *A Writer's Diary*
Virginia Woolf

Tuesday, May 11th [1920]

It is worth mentioning, for future reference, that the creative power which bubbles so pleasantly in beginning a new book quiets down after a time, and one goes on more steadily. Doubts creep in. Then one becomes resigned. Determination not to give in, and the sense of an impending shape keep one at it more than anything. I'm a little anxious. How am I to bring off this conception? Directly one gets to work one is like a person walking, who has seen the country stretching out before. I want to write nothing in this book [*Jacob's Room*] that I don't enjoy writing. Yet writing is always difficult.

Sunday, May 12th [1929]

Here, having just finished what I call the final revision of *Women and Fiction* [*A Room of One's Own*], so that L. can read it after tea, I stop; surfeited. And the pump, which I was so sanguine as to think ceased, begins again. About *Women and Fiction*, I am not sure—a brilliant essay?—I daresay: it has much work in it, many opinions boiled down into a kind of jelly, which I have stained red as far as I can. But I am eager to be off—to write without any boundary coming slick in one's eyes: here my public has been too close; facts; getting them malleable, easily yielding to each other.

Tuesday, May 28th

Now about this book, *The Moths*. How am I to begin it? And what is it to be? I feel no great impulse; no fever; only a great pressure of difficulty. Why write it then? Why write at all? Every morning I write a little sketch, to amuse myself. I am not saying, I might say, that these sketches have any relevance. I am not trying to tell a story. Yet perhaps it might be done in that way. A mind thinking. They might be islands of light—islands in the stream that I am trying to convey; life itself going on. The current of the moths flying strongly this way. A lamp and a flower pot in the center. The flower can always be changing. But there must be more unity between each scene than I can find at present. Autobiography it might be called. . . . .

Saturday, February 7th [1931]

Here in the few minutes that remain, I must record, heaven be praised, the end of *The Waves*. I wrote the words O Death fifteen minutes ago, having reeled across the last ten pages with some moments of such intensity and intoxication that I seemed only to stumble after my own voice, or almost, after some sort of speaker (as when I was mad) I was almost afraid, remembering the voices that used to fly ahead. Anyhow, it is done; and I have been sitting these 15 minutes in a state of glory, and calm, and some tears. . . . How physical the sense of triumph and relief is! Whether good or bad, it's done; and as I certainly felt at the end, not merely finished, but rounded off, completed, the thing stated—how hastily, how fragmentarily I know. . . .

What interests me in the last stage was the freedom and boldness with which my imagination picked up, used and tossed aside all the images, symbols which I had prepared. I am sure that this is the right way of using them—not in set pieces, as I had tried at first, coherently, but simply as images, never making them work out; only suggest. Thus I hope to have kept the sound of the sea and the birds, dawn and garden subconsciously present, doing their work underground.

Friday, July 27th [1934]

. . . Odd how the creative power at once brings the whole universe to order. I can see the day whole, proportioned—even after a long flutter of the brain such as I've had this morning it must be a physical, moral, mental necessity, like setting the engine off. A wild windy hot day—a tearing wind in the garden; all the July apples on the grass. I'm going to indulge in a series of quick sharp contrasts: breaking my moulds as much as ever I like. Trying every kind of experiment. Now of course I can't write diary or letters or read because I am making up all the time. Perhaps Bob T. was right in his poem when he called me fortunate above all—I mean in having a mind that can express—no, I mean in having mobilised my being—learned to give it complete outcome—I mean, that I have to some extent forced myself to break every mold and find a fresh form of being, that is of expression, for everything I feel or think. So that when it is working I get the sense of being fully energised—nothing stunted. But this needs constant effort, anxiety and rush.

From the Dalva
Notebooks: 1985–1987

Jim Harrison

The thirteen-year-old girl walks out into the damp moonlight. It's after midnight and I'm trying to imagine the freshness of her emotions.

Only when I'm fatigued do I worry about being vindicated.

I explained to Ms.—that life was a vastly mysterious process to which our culture inures us so we won't become useless citizens.

I'm inventing a country song, "Gettin' too Old to Run Away." In the middle of these sloppy ironies I remembered the tremendous silence of the midday eclipse last summer. Nature was confused & the birds roosted early. I was full of uncontrollable anger because I had to leave for L.A. in a few days for a screenplay conference. No one liked my idea of the life of Edward Curtis except me.

In a dream a ranch foreman named Samuel Creekmouth appeared to me and told me how to behave. I became irritable but in the morning had a lush & jubilant vision of what the novel was to be.

On the walk there were two small beaver, a huge black snake, a great blue heron feathering into a S.W. wind, sand dunes caving into a furious sea, on a rare hot day in late April.

Hard to keep the usual inferior balance when the dream life is kicking the shit out of you during, as usual, the waxing moon. In the same place I saw an actual wolf last year I found a female wolf in a dream, her back broken. I went to her, knelt down and gathered her up, and she disappeared into me. This experience was frightening.

That peculiar but very beautiful girl I saw in a dress shop in Key West ten years ago reappeared. She told me you can't give up Eros. Then, as with most of my dream women, she turned into a bird (this time a mourning dove), and flew away.

Awoke in the middle of the night and wrote down that it is important not to accept life as a brutal approximation. This was followed by a day of feeling quite hopelessly incapable of writing my "vision" of the novel which I haven't begun to compose.

In New York City staying with my agent Bob Dattila over by the river on East 72nd. We are trying to make business deals on the phone, and play gin rummy though we can't quite remember the rules of the game. Bob asked me what was even deeper than the bedrock in the huge excavation next door. I told him watery grottos full of blind, albino dolphins. Then in the night, in a dream, I climbed out of the excavation in the form of a monster: my eyes were lakes, my hair trees, my cheek was a meadow across which a river ran like a rippling scar. In the morning it was a comfort to walk the dog up to Ray's for a breakfast slice of pizza. Since I have three at home it is a considerable solace to have a dog friend in NYC, and when I come to town Bob's dog knows she can count on me for a slice of pizza. In short, we make each other happy.

What I don't want for myself is called a "long ending" with the vital signs not altogether there. This thought occurred to me after reading a biography by John Dos Passos.

Upset that this novel is going to make me too "irrational" to earn a living. In my background it is inconceivable for a man not to offer the full support for his family. A half dozen years ago I made a great deal of money but didn't have the character appropriate to holding on to any of it. This must take training. Now the accretion of beloved objects & images in my life and dreams has become more totemistic & shamanistic: grizzly bear turd & tooth, coyote skull, crow and heron wings, a pine cone from the forest where García Lorca was executed. Probably nothing to worry about as it began when I was half-blinded as a child, and for comfort wandered around the forest and lake and you don't find any trinkets there.

Always surprised on these days when the mind makes her shotgun, metaphoric leaps for reasons I've never been able to trace. Remembered that Wang Wei said a thousand years ago, "Who knows what causes the opening and closing of the door?"

Alliance: Nebraska reminds me of what America was supposed to look like before it became something else. Along Rte. 20 the almost unpardonable beauty of desolation. I could live along a creek in the Sandhills. I've established no strengths outside the field of the imagination, which is a fancy way of saying I'm hungover from an American Legion barn dance a waitress invited me to. She disappeared with a cowpoke who could wrestle a truck. Woke at first light laughing. Stepped on a steak bone.

Re: the banality of behavioral and emotional weather reports. My life is still killing me but I am offering less cooperation. I want to know what you do, rather than what you quit doing.

Up at my cabin more attacks of irrationality. Been here too long in solitude. Blurred peripheries so I "am" the bitch coyote that killed the rabbit in the yard. My longest & strongest literary relationship is with McGuane—twenty years of letters and we don't even see each other once a year.

Rode an enormous crow, flying down to the Manistee River to drink from a sandbar. Used a martingale. Easier to stay on than a horse and a better view! James Hillman says that dream animals are soul doctors. Bet I'm the only one around here who reads Cioran & Kierkegaard after working his bird dogs.

Disturbed that I am creating this heroine because I'm lonely and wish to have someone I can utterly love. Relieved of sanity fears by reading Angus Fletcher on the subject of the borders of consciousness.

There are many hidden, unnumbered floors in the apartment buildings in NYC, or so I have thought.

My coffin was made of glass and she ran out of the woods and shattered it! She is E. Hopper's girl at the window.

This must be a novel written from the cushion—silence, out of water, the first light, twilight, the night sky, the furthest point in the forest, from the bottom of a lake, the bottom of the river, northern lights, from the clouds and loam, also the city past midnight, Los Angeles at dawn when the ocean seems less tired having slept in private, from the undisturbed prairie, from attics and root cellars, the girl hiding in the thicket for no reason, the boy looking in the wrong direction for the rising moon.

At the cabin the fog is so dense you can hear it. A rabbit near woodpile, fly sound, crackle of fire in the hush. Can't drink much or my heroine escapes, evades me. The voice just beyond hearing.

Hot tip from Taisen Deshimaru on the writing of this book. "You must concentrate upon and consecrate yourself wholly to each day, as though a fire were raging in your hair." Reminded me again of the injurious aspects of protestantism for an artist—one's life as inevitable, or predestined, causing a looseness in the joints, the vast difference between Calvin (and John Bunyan). You must transfer these banal energies toward self-improvement to your work.

The postmodern novel suffocates from ethical mandarinism. It is almost totally white middle class, a product of writer's schools, the National Endowment, foundations, academia. The fact that this doesn't matter one little bit is interesting. Who could possibly give a fuck during this diaspora. The literary world is one of those unintentionally comic movies they used to make about voodoo and zombies.

Who said, "You can't do something you don't know if you keep doing what you do know." Drinking prevents vertigo and that's why I can't get her voice if I drink. A trip to NYC restored my vertigo. If you enter a bookstore or a publisher's office your life again becomes incomprehensible. Fear refreshes. Luckily you can head immediately for a good restaurant.

Back home the troubling dream image of myself emerging like the "Thing" from a block of ice full of sticks and leaves.

In another dream she ran backward nakedly into history which was an improbable maze. Another night an unpleasant visit with Herman Melville who didn't look well.

Went up to my winter retreat at a hotel in Escanaba to edit *Paris Review* interview. Can't get beyond first page by the second day because I'm not currently interested in anything I've ever said, what with a hot eyeball from being two-thirds done. Zero degrees and a five-hour walk in the woods because I got lost, followed by rigatoni & Italian sausage, and two bottles of red wine. Next day I walk miles out onto the frozen harbor ice—a marvelous polar landscape of glittering sun & ice as far as you can see. Fishermen have driven their pick-up trucks out on the ice and are pulling nets where the ice was divided by a fuel oil tanker. They are Chippewas and offer me a partially frozen beer that thunks in the bottle.

A strange March walk: broke, can't write, sick from new blood-pressure medicine, out in an area of juniper, dunes, pine culverts out of the wind. Thoughts about the degree to which I'm a slave or lowly employee of the system I've created: cigarettes smoke me, food eats me, alcohol drinks me, house swallows me, car drives me, etc.

"She" comes and goes. I had to talk to Hollywood today (to say why I was fired from the last project) and she fled top speed. An utterly enervating & fatal game of pursuit.

It seems that severe emotional problems, neuroses, are born, thrive, multiply in areas where language never enters. The writer thinks that if he can solve these problems his quality of language will vastly improve. This is the fallacy of writing as therapy. Dostoyevski maintained that to be acutely conscious is to be diseased. One could imagine a novel that murders the writer. You don't want to discover a secret your persona can't bear up under. But then you can't rid yourself of the hubris of wanting to create a hero or heroine of consciousness.

Completely flipped from nervous exhaustion on page 430. Take my wife and daughter to Key West, a place I had feared returning to after so much "disorder and early sorrow" from a dozen previous trips. Turned out pleasantly. Good chats with Brinnin, mostly on how to determine pathology when everything is pathological. Studied the giant ocean river, the gulfstream, where Duane committed suicide on his buckskin horse. We forget we have blood in us until it starts coming out.

All your aggression is directed toward discovering new perceptions, and consequently against yourself when you fail to come up with anything new. But then I "made her up" knowing very well we will abandon each other.

Bernard Fontana warned me about getting the "Indian disease." It takes a great deal of discipline not to shatter into fragments. The wonders of negative capability & allowing her to decide what she's going to do next. What Fontana meant is the intense anxiety I felt at the Umbanda session seventy miles outside of Rio de Janeiro when the ladies went into their whirling trance to heal the black drummer who was a drunk. If you've seen and lived the supposed best the white world has to offer it's "harmless" to check out the rest of the world. We are all in the *Blue Angel* in that respect. The actual world is Dietrich's thighs.

Startled to read in Jung that violently colorful dreams & psychic events occur to people in psychic flux who need more consciousness.

At the cabin just saw a chipmunk leap off the picnic table & tear the throat out of a mouse, lapping vigorously at the blood. I am chock-full of conclusions. Must write Quammen to find out what's going on here. Lopez told me the only way to feed ravens is to gather road kills, a rather smelly business. Peacock has studied bears so long he has become one, not entirely a happy situation. Dalva is probably my twin sister who was taken away at birth.

Nearly finished. It's like going outside to estimate the storm damage. Want to avoid stepping into a thousand-storey elevator shaft. As a ninth grader I was very upset to discover that Ross Lockridge committed suicide when he finished *Raintree County*.

My friend _____ thought that all of his concessions, like the Eucharist, were rites of passage. He forgot how easy it is to earn the contempt of your fellow writers.

Was amused to realize that the mess I am always trying to extricate myself from is actually my life. The other night I played ranchero music & thought how different the music is in areas of fruit, hot peppers, garlic, hot sun, giant moths, & butterflies. An old woman in Brazil had a worn photo of a group of men ice fishing in Minnesota which she thought was amusing. We drank rum and I tried to explain away the lugubrious masochism of life in the upper midwest.

For almost ten minutes I looked forward to the second volume when North-ridge's voice will become mangled & intolerable, a prairie Lear.

Finishing any large piece of work makes one dense and irascible. I cooked the fucking brook trout too long! I demand more of myself and life than it is suited to offer. I look for the wrong form the reward is to come in—thus it is a full year before I realize how good a certain meal was: during bird season we stopped by a river, started our portable grill and watched four English Setters and a Lab swim lazily in an eddy in the October sunlight. We grilled woodcock and grouse over split maple, had a clumsy salad, bread, and a magnum of wine, napped on the grass surrounded by wet dogs.

Nearly done at the cabin, a specific giddiness. Last night wild pale-green northern lights above scudding thunderheads. On the way home from the tavern I saw a very large bear on the two-track to the cabin, thus hesitated to take a midnight stroll, possibly disturbing both of us. He was not my friend, but a great bear, a Beowulf, trundling across the path & swiveling for a look at me, his head higher than mine was in the car.

Hard to develop the silence and humility necessary for creating good art if you are always yelling "look at me" like a three-year-old who has just shit in the sandbox.

Postscript. Finished the novel in July and have since driven 27,000 miles to get over it. Perhaps it is easier to write a novel than survive it. Driving is a modest solution as the ego dissipates in the immensity of the landscape, slips out into the road behind you. Watched an Indian, Jonathan Windyboy, dance seven hours in a row in New Mexico. That might work but as a poet I work within the skeleton of a myth for which there is no public celebration. Publication parties aren't quite the same thing. I can imagine the kiva late at night under a summery full moon; the announcer asks the drum group from the Standing Rock Sioux to play a round from the Grass Dance for Jim's beloved Dalva! But perhaps our rituals as singers are as old as theirs. Caged my epigraph from Loren Eiseley's tombstone—"We loved the earth but could not stay."

From *Strong Songs*

Keith H. Basso

July 14th

I walked to the trading post and saw Leon Beatty sitting on the porch. The eminent medicine man did not cut an impressive figure. A small man, stooped and heavyset, he has a fleshy face and peers at the world through very thick glasses. He was wearing a battered old hat and a pair of delapidated sneakers. An eagle feather was attached to his shirt with a safety pin. He was eating an orange Popsicle. As he sat in the morning sun, a thin black puppy approached him and lay down inches from his feet. He spoke to the dog and it moved away. Then he called it back and gave it half the Popsicle.

Don Cooley told me that Leon Beatty is fifty-six years old. His first wife died three years ago. His new wife, whom he married several months ago, is just eighteen.

July 16

Leon Beatty sings tonight. I will attend the ceremony with Dudley Patterson and Ernest Murphy. Although I am eager to see what happens, I know I will feel conspicuous and self-conscious. When I asked Dudley how I should conduct myself, a quizzical expression crossed his face. "Show respect," he said. Then he grinned. "And don't talk to nobody about grasshoppers."

We arrived at the camp of Warren Gregg's mother just as the sun was setting. Three wickiups, two shades, a tar-papered shack. There was considerable activity. A knot of women, seated on blankets beneath an apple tree, prepared stacks of white tortillas, while four men, sweating hard, chopped firewood nearby. Small children raced about happily—playing tag, chasing after dogs, laughing, kicking up clouds of dust. Other people waited quietly beside their horses. A flock of crows clattered by overhead.

As the sky began to darken, two men carrying drums emerged from a wickiup and walked toward one of the shades. This was where the ceremony would take place. The interior of the shade had been cleared of all personal belongings, and a fire was burning in a shallow pit near the main entrance. A few feet from the fire, Warren Gregg's clothes hung on a coat hanger suspended from a beam, and directly beneath them, resting on top of a broken wooden cupboard, was a pair of his shoes. Next to the cupboard, neatly arranged on the seat of a chair, I saw the tail of a Mule deer, a ceramic butter dish filled with holy yellow powder, and four sprigs of some leafy plant. Beside the chair, attached to the tip of a five-foot stake, an eagle's wingfeather extended parallel to the ground. The feather was pointed south, toward Phoenix.

More and more people entered the shade. They stood in total silence and all I could hear was the crackling of the fire and a dog barking outside. Presently, Leon Beatty came in, accompanied by two assistants. He went straight to the chair in the front of the shade. Speaking softly in Apache, he picked up the deer's tail, dipped it into the dish of yellow powder, and brushed it over Warren Gregg's clothes and shoes. He repeated this blessing four times. Then he walked to a bench about six feet away and sat down between the two men with drums. Moments later, the drummers had established their beat and the medicine man began to sing. His voice sounded thin and reedy, as if strained from overuse, and it was difficult to hear over the thumping of the drums. He sang for a couple of minutes and stopped abruptly. He cleared his lungs and spat. Then, cupping his hand around his mouth, he began to sing again. This time his voice was strong. In flawless unison with the drums his song came pouring forth—an ancient song, compelling in the architecture of its unfamiliar sound, a modern song, squarely addressed to the needs of a fellow man in trouble. His voice rose and fell, rose and fell, and the song gathered force. He was singing louder now, well beyond the reach of the drums, and the power of his words—his work—his prayer—filled the shade completely. On the wingfeather of an eagle, his song was headed for Phoenix.

QUESTIONS AND CONSIDERATIONS

1. Compare the writing processes of George Eliot, Virginia Woolf, and Jim Harrison as discussed in their journals.

2. What obstacles and challenges have Harrison, Woolf, and Eliot had to face and overcome to be successful writers?

3. Woolf says "Odd how the creative power at once brings the whole universe to order." What positive impact does creativity seem to have on the inner worlds of Woolf, Eliot, Harrison, and Basso?

4. Write in your journal about the way that you organize your day in order to allow yourself time and concentration for your creative projects.

Fiction

A Conversation with My Father
Grace Paley

Journal

Do you enjoy creating stories about your experiences? Why or why not?

My father is eighty-six years old and in bed. His heart, that bloody motor, is equally old and will not do certain jobs any more. It still floods his head with brainy light. But it won't let his legs carry the weight of his body around the house. Despite my metaphors, this muscle failure is not due to his old heart, he says, but to a potassium shortage. Sitting on one pillow, leaning on three, he offers last-minute advice and makes a request.

"I would like you to write a simple story just once more," he says, "the kind de Maupassant wrote, or Chekhov, the kind you used to write. Just recognizable people and then write down what happened to them next."

I say, "Yes, why not? That's possible." I want to please him, though I don't remember writing that way. I *would* like to try to tell such a story, if he means the kind that begins: "There was a woman . . ." followed by plot, the absolute line between two points which I've always despised. Not for literary reasons, but because it takes all hope away. Everyone, real or invented, deserves the open destiny of life.

Finally I thought of a story that had been happening for a couple of years right across the street. I wrote it down, then read it aloud. "Pa," I said, "how about this? Do you mean something like this?"

Once in my time there was a woman and she had a son. They lived nicely, in a small apartment in Manhattan. This boy at about fifteen became a junkie, which is not unusual in our neighborhood. In order to maintain her close friendship with him, she became a junkie too. She said it was part of the youth culture, with which she felt very much at home. After a while, for a number of reasons, the boy gave it all up and left the city and his mother in disgust. Hopeless and alone, she grieved. We all visit her.

"O.K., Pa, that's it," I said, "an unadorned and miserable tale."

"But that's not what I mean," my father said. "You misunderstood me on purpose. You know there's a lot more to it. You know that. You left everything out. Turgenev wouldn't do that. Chekhov wouldn't do that. There are in fact Russian writers you never heard of, you don't have an inkling of, as good as anyone, who can write a plain ordinary story, who would not leave out what you have left out. I object not to facts but to people sitting in trees talking senselessly, voices from who knows where. . . ."

"Forget that one, Pa, what have I left out now? In this one?"

"Her looks, for instance."

"Oh. Quite handsome, I think. Yes."

"Her hair?"

"Dark, with heavy braids, as though she were a girl or a foreigner."

"What were her parents like, her stock? That she became such a person. It's interesting, you know."

"From out of town. Professional people. The first to be divorced in their county. How's that? Enough?" I asked.

"With you, it's all a joke," he said. "What about the boy's father? Why didn't you mention him? Who was he? Or was the boy born out of wedlock?"

"Yes," I said. "He was born out of wedlock."

"For Godsakes, doesn't anyone in your stories get married? Doesn't anyone have the time to run down to City Hall before they jump into bed?"

"No," I said. "In real life, yes. But in my stories, no."

"Why do you answer me like that?"

"Oh, Pa, this is a simple story about a smart woman who came to N.Y.C. full of interest love trust excitement very up to date, and about her son, what a hard time she had in this world. Married or not, it's of small consequence."

"It is of great consequence," he said.

"O.K.," I said.

"O.K. O.K. yourself," he said, "but listen. I believe you that she's good-looking, but I don't think she was so smart."

"That's true," I said. "Actually that's the trouble with stories. People start out fantastic. You think they're extraordinary, but it turns out as the work goes along, they're just average with a good education. Sometimes the other way around, the person's a kind of dumb innocent, but he outwits you and you can't even think of an ending good enough."

"What do you do then?" he asked. He had been a doctor for a couple of decades and then an artist for a couple of decades and he's still interested in details, craft, technique.

"Well, you just have to let the story lie around till some agreement can be reached between you and the stubborn hero."

"Aren't you talking silly now?" he asked. "Start again," he said. "It so happens I'm not going out this evening. Tell the story again. See what you can do this time."

"O.K.," I said. "But it's not a five-minute job." Second attempt:

Once, across the street from us, there was a fine handsome woman, our neighbor. She had a son whom she loved because she'd known him since birth (in helpless chubby infancy, and in the wrestling, hugging ages, seven to ten, as well as earlier and later) This boy, when he fell into the fist of adolescence, became a junkie. He was not a hopeless one. He was in fact hopeful, and wrote persuasive articles for his high-school newspaper. Seeking a wider audience, using important connections, he drummed into Lower Manhattan newsstand distribution a periodical called *Oh! Golden Horse!*

In order to keep him from feeling guilty (because guilt is the stony heart of nine tenths of all clinically diagnosed cancers in America today, she said), and because she had always believed in giving bad habits room at home where one could keep an eye on them, she too became a junkie. Her kitchen was famous for a while—a center for intellectual addicts who knew what they were doing. A few felt artistic like Coleridge and others were scientific and revolutionary like Leary. Although she was often high herself, certain good mothering reflexes remained, and she saw to it that there was lots of orange juice around and honey and milk and vitamin pills. However, she never cooked anything but chili, and that no more than once a week. She explained, when we talked to her, seriously, with neighborly concern, that it was her part in the youth culture and she would rather be with the young, it was an honor, than with her own generation.

One week, while nodding through an Antonioni film, this boy was severely jabbed by the elbow of a stern and proselytizing girl, sitting beside him. She offered immediate apricots and nuts for his sugar level, spoke to him sharply, and took him home.

She had heard of him and his work and she herself published, edited, and wrote a competitive journal called *Man Does Live by Bread Alone*. In the organic heat of her continuous presence he could not help but become interested once more in his muscles, his arteries, and nerve connections. In fact he began to love them, treasure them, praise them with funny little songs in *Man Does Live. . . .*

the fingers of my flesh transcend
my transcendental soul
the tightness in my shoulders end
my teeth have made me whole

To the mouth of his head (that glory of will and determination) he brought hard apples, nuts, wheat germ, and soybean oil. He said to his old friends, From now on, I guess I'll keep my wits about me. I'm going on the natch. He said he was about to begin a spiritual deep-breathing journey. How about you too, Mom? he asked kindly.

His conversion was so radiant, splendid, that neighborhood kids his age began to say that he had never been a real addict at all, only a journalist along for the smell of the story. The mother tried several times to give up what had become without her son and his friends a lonely habit. This effort only brought it to supportable levels. The boy and his girl took their electronic mimeograph and moved to the bushy edge of another borough. They were very strict. They said they would not see her again until she had been off drugs for sixty days.

At home alone in the evening, weeping, the mother read and reread the seven issues of *Oh! Golden Horse!* They seemed to her as truthful as ever. We often crossed the street to visit and console. But if we mentioned any of our children who were at college or in the hospital or dropouts at home, she would cry out, My baby! My baby! and burst into terrible, face-scarring, time-consuming tears. The End.

First my father was silent, then he said, "Number One: You have a nice sense of humor. Number Two: I see you can't tell a plain story. So don't waste time." Then he said sadly, "Number Three: I suppose that means she was alone, she was left like that, his mother. Alone. Probably sick?"

I said, "Yes."

"Poor woman. Poor girl, to be born in a time of fools, to live among fools. The end. The end. You were right to put that down. The end."

I didn't want to argue, but I had to say, "Well, it is not necessarily the end, Pa."

"Yes," he said, "what a tragedy. The end of a person."

"No, Pa," I begged him. It doesn't have to be. She's only about forty. She could be a hundred different things in this world as time goes on. A teacher or a social worker. An ex-junkie! Sometimes it's better than having a master's in education."

"Jokes," he said. "As a writer that's your main trouble. You don't want to recognize it. Tragedy! Plain tragedy! Historical tragedy! No hope. The end."

"Oh, Pa," I said. "She could change."

"In your own life, too, you have to look it in the face." He took a couple of nitroglycerin. "Turn to five," he said, pointing to the dial on the oxygen tank. He inserted the tubes into his nostrils and breathed deep. He closed his eyes and said, "No."

I had promised the family to always let him have the last word when arguing, but in this case I had a different responsibility. That woman lives across the street. She's my knowledge and my invention. I'm sorry for her. I'm not going to leave her there in that house crying. (Actually neither would Life, which unlike me has no pity.)

Therefore: She did change. Of course her son never came home again. But right now, she's the receptionist in a storefront community clinic in the East Village. Most of the customers are young people, some old friends.

"The doctor said that?" My father took the oxygen tubes out of his nostrils and said, "Jokes. Jokes again."

"No, Pa, it could really happen that way, it's a funny world nowadays."

"No," he said. "Truth first. She will slide back. A person must have character. She does not."

"No, Pa," I said. "That's it. She's got a job. Forget it. She's in that storefront working."

"How long will it be?" he asked. "Tragedy! You too. When will you look it in the face?"

QUESTIONS AND CONSIDERATIONS

1. Why does the narrator's father want his daughter to write a simple story like the ones by de Maupassant or Chekhov? Why does the daughter dislike writing this type of story? Do you agree or disagree with the narrator's point of view?

2. Why is the narrator's father dissatisfied with his daughter's first story? Why does the daughter rewrite her story? How does the narrator feel about her father?

3. Contrast the first and second versions of the story. Which ideas about how to write a story are demonstrated through the conversation between the father and the daughter? What does the development of the daughter's story reveal about the creative process?

4. Who is more "realistic" about interpreting life experiences, the father or the daughter? Who has a more "tragic" viewpoint?

5. Whose approach to interpreting life experiences, that of the father or the daughter, is closer to your own? Explain.

6. Imagine that you are a teacher or a student in a creative writing workshop. How would you respond to the central character's story that she presents to her father? What advice would you have for the narrator?

IDEAS FOR WRITING

1. Write an essay in which you analyze the relationships between art and life as they are revealed through the father-daughter conversation in this story. Refer to specific lines in the text as you develop your analysis.

2. Write both a tragic and a comic portrait of one of your neighbors. Which version do you prefer? Why?

B. Wordsworth

V. S. Naipaul

Journal

Write about a conversation or an experience that you have shared with an older person who helped you to develop wisdom about the importance of laughter, loving, and forgiveness.

Three beggars called punctually every day at the hospitable houses in Miguel Street. At about ten an Indian came in his dhoti and white jacket, and we poured a tin of rice into the sack he carried on his back. At twelve an old woman smoking a clay pipe came and she got a cent. At two a blind man led by a boy called for his penny.

Sometimes we had a rogue. One day a man called and said he was hungry. We gave him a meal. He asked for a cigarette and wouldn't go until we had lit it for him. That man never came again.

The strangest caller came one afternoon at about four o'clock. I had come back from school and was in my home-clothes. The man said to me, "Sonny, may I come inside your yard?"

He was a small man and he was tidily dressed. He wore a hat, a white shirt, and black trousers.

I asked, "What you want?"

He said, "I want to watch your bees."

We had four small gru-gru palm trees and they were full of uninvited bees.

I ran up the steps and shouted, "Ma, it have a man outside here. He say he want to watch the bees."

My mother came out, looked at the man, and asked in an unfriendly way, "What you want?"

The man said, "I want to watch your bees."

His English was so good, it didn't sound natural, and I could see my mother was worried.

She said to me, "Stay here and watch him while he watch the bees."

The man said, "Thank you, Madam. You have done a good deed today."

He spoke very slowly and very correctly as though every word was costing him money.

We watched the bees, this man and I, for about an hour, squatting near the palm trees.

The man said, "I like watching bees. Sonny, do you like watching bees?"

I said, "I ain't have the time."

He shook his head sadly. He said, "That's what I do, I just watch. I can watch ants for days. Have you ever watched ants? And scorpions, and centipedes, and *congorees*—have you watched those?"

I shook my head.

I said, "What you does do, mister?"

He got up and said, "I am a poet."

I said, "A good poet?"

He said, "The greatest in the world."

"What your name, mister?"

"B. Wordsworth."

"B for Bill?"

"Black. Black Wordsworth. White Wordsworth was my brother. We share one heart. I can watch a small flower like the morning glory and cry."

I said, "Why you does cry?"

"Why, boy? Why? You will know when you grow up. You're a poet, too, you know. And when you're a poet you can cry for everything."

I couldn't laugh.

He said, "You like your mother?"

"When she not beating me."

He pulled out a printed sheet from his hip-pocket and said, "On this paper is the greatest poem about mothers and I'm going to sell it to you at a bargain price. For four cents."

I went inside and I said, "Ma, you want to buy a poetry for four cents?"

My mother said, "Tell that blasted man to haul his tail away from my yard, you hear."

I said to B. Wordsworth, "My mother say she ain't have four cents."

B. Wordsworth said, "It is the poet's tragedy."

And he put the paper back in his pocket. He didn't seem to mind.

I said, "Is a funny way to go round selling poetry like that. Only calypsonians do that sort of thing. A lot of people does buy?"

He said, "No one has yet bought a single copy."

"But why you does keep on going round, then?"

He said, "In this way I watch many things, and I always hope to meet poets."

I said, "You really think I is a poet?"

"You're as good as me," he said.

And when B. Wordsworth left, I prayed I would see him again.

About a week later, coming back from school one afternoon, I met him at the corner of Miguel Street.

He said, "I have been waiting for you for a long time."

I said, "You sell any poetry yet?"

He shook his head.

He said, "In my yard I have the best mango tree in Port of Spain. And now the mangoes are ripe and red and very sweet and juicy. I have waited here for you to tell you this and to invite you to come and eat some of my mangoes."

He lived in Alberto Street in a one-roomed hut placed right in the centre of the lot. The yard seemed all green. There was the big mango tree. There was a coconut tree and there was a plum tree. The place looked wild, as though it wasn't in the city at all. You couldn't see all the big concrete houses in the street.

He was right. The mangoes were sweet and juicy. I ate about six, and the yellow mango juice ran down my arms to my elbows and down my mouth to my chin and my shirt was stained.

My mother said when I got home, "Where you was? You think you is a man now and could go all over the place? Go cut a whip for me."

She beat me rather badly, and I ran out of the house swearing that I would never come back. I went to B. Wordsworth's house. I was so angry, my nose was bleeding.

B. Wordsworth said, "Stop crying, and we will go for a walk."

I stopped crying, but I was breathing short. We went for a walk. We walked down St Clair Avenue to the Savannah and we walked to the racecourse.

B. Wordsworth said, "Now, let us lie on the grass and look up at the sky, and I want you to think how far those stars are from us."

I did as he told me, and I saw what he meant. I felt like nothing, and at the same time I had never felt so big and great in my life. I forgot all my anger and all my tears and all the blows.

When I said I was better, he began telling me the names of the stars, and I particularly remembered the constellation of Orion the Hunter, though I don't really know why. I can spot Orion even today, but I have forgotten the rest.

Then a light was flashed into our faces, and we saw a policeman. We got up from the grass.

The Policeman said, "What you doing here?"

B. Wordsworth said, "I have been asking myself the same question for forty years."

We became friends, B. Wordsworth and I. He told me, "You must never tell anybody about me and about the mango tree and the coconut tree and the plum tree. You must keep that a secret. If you tell anybody, I will know, because I am a poet."

I gave him my word and I kept it.

I liked his little room. It had no more furniture than George's front room, but it looked cleaner and healthier. But it also looked lonely.

One day I asked him, "Mister Wordsworth, why you does keep all this bush in your yard? Ain't it does make the place damp?"

He said, "Listen, and I will tell you a story. Once upon a time a boy and girl met each other and they fell in love. They loved each other so much they got married. They were both poets. He loved words. She loved grass and flowers and trees. They lived happily in a single room, and then one day, the girl poet said to the boy poet, 'We are going to have another poet in the family.' But this poet was never born, because the girl died, and the young poet died with her, inside her. And the girl's husband was very sad, and he said he would never touch a thing in the girl's garden. And so the garden remained, and grew high and wild."

I looked at B. Wordsworth, and as he told me this lovely story, he seemed to grow older. I understood his story.

We went for long walks together. We went to the Botanical Gardens and the Rock Gardens. We climbed Chancellor Hill in the late afternoon and watched the darkness fall on Port of Spain, and watched the lights go on in the city and on the ships in the harbour.

He did everything as though he were doing it for the first time in his life. He did everything as though he were doing some church rite.

He would say to me, "Now, how about having some ice-cream?"

And when I said, yes, he would grow very serious and say, "Now, which café shall we patronize?" As though it were a very important thing. He would think for some time about It, and finally say, "I think I will go and negotiate the purchase with that shop."

The world became a most exciting place.

One day, when I was in his yard, he said to me, "I have a great secret which I am now going to tell you."

I said, "It really secret?"

"At the moment, yes."

I looked at him, and he looked at me. He said, "This is just between you and me, remember. I am writing a poem."

"Oh." I was disappointed.

He said, "But this is a different sort of poem. This is the greatest poem in the world."

I whistled.

He said, "I have been working on it for more than five years now. I will finish it in about twenty-two years from now, that is, if I keep on writing at the present rate."

"You does write a lot, then?"

He said, "Not any more. I just write one line a month. But I make sure it is a good line."

I asked, "What was last month's good line?"

He looked up at the sky, and said, *"The past is deep."*

I said, "It is a beautiful line."

B. Wordsworth said, "I hope to distil the experiences of a whole month into that single line of poetry. So, in twenty-two years, I shall have written a poem that will sing to all humanity."

I was filled with wonder.

Our walks continued. We walked along the sea-wall at Docksite one day, and I said, "Mr. Wordsworth, if I drop this pin in the water, you think it will float?"

He said, "This is a strange world. Drop your pin, and let us see what will happen."

The pin sank.

I said, "How is the poem this month?"

But he never told me any other line. He merely said, "Oh, it comes, you know. It comes."

Or we would sit on the sea-wall and watch the liners come into the harbour.

But of the greatest poem in the world I heard no more.

I felt he was growing older.

"How you does live, Mr. Wordsworth?" I asked him one day.

He said, "You mean how I get money?"

When I nodded, he laughed in a crooked way.

He said, "I sing calypsoes in the calypso season."

"And that last you the rest of the year?"

"It is enough."

"But you will be the richest man in the world when you write the greatest poem?"

He didn't reply.

One day when I went to see him in his little house, I found him lying on his little bed. He looked so old and so weak, that I found myself wanting to cry.

He said, "The poem is not going well."

He wasn't looking at me. He was looking through the window at the coconut tree, and he was speaking as though I wasn't there. He said, "When I was twenty I felt the power within myself." Then, almost in front of my eyes, I could see his face growing older and more tired. He said, "But that—that was a long time ago."

And then—I felt it so keenly, it was as though I had been slapped by my mother. I could see it clearly on his face. It was there for everyone to see. Death on the shrinking face.He looked at me, and saw my tears and sat up.

He said, "Come." I went and sat on his knees.

He looked into my eyes, and he said, "Oh, you can see it, too. I always knew you had the poet's eye."

He didn't even look sad, and that made me burst out crying loudly.

He pulled me to his thin chest, and said, "Do you want me to tell you a funny story?" and he smiled encouragingly at me.

But I couldn't reply.

He said, "When I have finished this story, I want you to promise that you will go away and never come back to see me. Do you promise?"

I nodded.

He said, "Good. Well, listen. That story I told you about the boy poet and the girl poet, do you remember that? That wasn't true. It was something I just made up. All this talk about poetry and the greatest poem in the world, that wasn't true, either. Isn't that the funniest thing you have heard?"

But his voice broke.

I left the house, and ran home crying, like a poet, for everything I saw.

I walked along Alberto Street a year later, but I could find no sign of the poet's house. It hadn't vanished, just like that. It had been pulled down, and a big, two-storeyed building had taken its place. The mango tree and the plum tree and the coconut tree had all been cut down, and there was brick and concrete everywhere.

It was just as though B. Wordsworth had never existed.

QUESTIONS AND CONSIDERATIONS

1. How does Naipaul use dialect and Standard English to emphasize the difference between the characters' social status and class? B. Wordsworth's use of language suggests that he is well educated. What do you think B. Wordsworth did before becoming a poet? Where do you think he was educated?

2. Why does the main character call himself B. Wordsworth? What kind of poetry does he write? Why does B. Wordsworth try to sell his poetry?

3. Why does the young boy like B. Wordsworth? Why does B. Wordsworth think that the young boy is a poet? Do you agree with B. Wordsworth? Why or why not? Why is it important that their friendship remain a secret?

4. Why does B. Wordsworth tell the boy at their final visit that the story about the young lovers and the garden was a lie?

5. What has B. Wordsworth taught the boy? What has the boy learned about what it means to be a poet through his relationship with B. Wordsworth?

6. Explain the significance of B. Wordsworth's home, his mango and coconut trees, and his garden. What replaces B. Wordsworth's home? Why does the young boy conclude that "it was just as though B. Wordsworth had never existed"?

IDEAS FOR WRITING

1. Write an essay or a short story about a person who has taught you an important lesson about living or about the importance of being true to a creative vision, as B. Wordsworth taught the boy in the story.

2. In this story what relationships are developed between laughter and tears, anger and peace of mind? Refer to specific lines in the story to support your response.

Lush Life
John McCluskey

Journal

Write about a night trip you took with a friend that led you to new insights about creativity or about the meaning of life.

Dayton, Ohio

Behind the dance hall the first of the car doors were banging shut, motors starting up, and from somewhere—a backyard, an alley—dogs barked. The band's bus was parked at one darkened corner of the parking lot. Empty, it was a mute and hulking barn in this hour. Along its side in slanted, bold-red letters was painted a sign: EARL FERGUSON AND AMERICA'S GREATEST BAND.

Suddenly the back door to the dance hall swung open and loud laughter rushed out on a thick pillow of cigarette smoke. Ahead of others, two men in suits—the taller one in plaids and the other in stripes—walked quickly, talking, smoking. They stopped at a convertible, a dark-red Buick, dew already sprouting across its canvas top. Other men, all members of the band, in twos or threes, would come up, slap their backs, share a joke or two, then drift toward the bus. In the light over the back door, moths played.

The shorter man, Billy Cox, took off his glasses, fogged the lenses twice, then cleaned them with his polka-dot silk square. He reached a hand toward Tommy, the bassist, approaching.

"I'm gone say, 'See y'all further up the road in Cleveland,'" Tommy said. "But after a night like tonight, it's gone be one hell of a struggle to tear ourselves from this town. Am I right about that, Billy C.?"

Tommy laughed, gold tooth showing, and patted his impeccable "do." More than once it had been said that Tommy sweated ice water. With his face dry, hair in place, tie straightened after three hours of furious work, no one could doubt it now.

Tommy spoke again, this time stern, wide-legged, and gesturing grandly. "Just you two don't get high and dry off into some damn ditch." His usual farewell slid toward a cackle. Billy waved him off.

In the Scout Car, Billy and Earl Ferguson would drive through the night to the next date. Throughout the night they would stay at least an hour or so ahead of the bus. They would breakfast and be nearly asleep by the time the bus pulled into the same hotel parking lot, the men emerging, looking stunned from a fitful sleep on a noisy bus.

From a nearby car a woman's throaty laugh lit up the night. They turned to see Pretty Horace leaning into a car, the passenger's side, smoothing down the back edges of his hair and rolling his rump as he ran his game.

"Man, stop your lying!" came her voice. She, too, was toying with the ends of her hair, dyed bright red and glowing in that light. Her friend from the driver's seat, with nothing better to do perhaps, leaned to hear, to signify, her face round as the moon's.

Moving with a pickpocket's stealth and slow grin spreading, Poo moved up to the driver's side of the car and whispered something. The driver jerked back, then gave him her best attention, smiling. One hand to her throat, she moistened her lips, glistened a smile.

In unison, Billy and Earl shook their heads while watching it all. Billy slid one hand down a lapel, pulled a cigarette from the corner of his mouth. "Some of the boys gone make a long night of this one."

Earl nodded. "Some mean mistreaters fixing to hit that bus late and do a whole lot of shucking, man."

Yes, some would dare the bus's deadline by tipping into an after-hours party, by following some smiling woman home. The rules were simple, however: if you missed the bus and could not make practice the next day, you were fined fifty dollars. If you missed the date because you missed the bus or train, you were fired. Daring these, you could seek adventure that broke the monotony of long road trips. You could bring stories that released bubbles of laughter throughout an overheated and smoke-filled bus.

Cars were rolling out of the side parking lot and, passing members of the band, the drivers honked in appreciation. Earl bowed slowly and waved an arm wide and high toward his men, some still walking out of the back door of the dance hall. Then he embraced Billy, mugged, and pointed to Billy's chest as if branding there all the credit for a magnificent night. After all, they had done Basie and Ellington to perfection. Their own original tunes had been wonders to behold. From the very beginning the audience had been with them and danced and danced, heads bobbing and shoulders rocking, cheering every solo. The dancers had fun on the stair step of every melody; hugging tightly, they did the slow grind to the promise of every ballad. Now they thanked the band again with the toot of their horns, shouts, and the wave of their hands.

Within an hour the bus would start up, all the equipment packed and stored below. Then it would roll slowly out of the parking lot. Some of the men would already be snoring. By the outskirts of town, a car might catch up to it, tires squealing as the car rocked to a stop. One of the men—usually McTee or "Rabbit" Ousley, as myth might have it—would climb out and blow a kiss to some grinning woman behind the wheel and strut onto the bus like some wide-legged conqueror. The doors to the bus would close behind him, sealing his stories from any verification and sealing them against the long, long night.

But it was the Buick, Earl and Billy inside, pulling away first. They would leave before these tales of triumph, outright lies about quick and furious love in a drafty back room or tales of a young wife whispering, "Run! Run!" and the scramble for a window after the husband's key slid into the lock downstairs. Yes, before all that, Earl and Billy would pull from the parking lot and start away, slow at first, like they had all the time in the world.

Well before the edge of town, they would have checked for cigarettes, surely, and from some magical place on a side street, a jukebox blaring and the smell of fried chicken meeting them at the door with its judas hole, they would find their coffee in Mason jars, coffee heavily sugared and creamed, and steaming chicken sandwiches wrapped neatly in waxed paper.

Older women, who would do double duty at Sunday church dinners, would smile and wipe their hands on their aprons. And bless them, these good and prodigal sons with conked hair. Then, moving toward the door, Billy and Earl would be greeted by achingly beautiful women with late night joy lacing their hoarse voices. Billy and Earl would take turns joking and pulling each other away, then, outside and laughing, climb back into the car for the journey through the night.

For the first few minutes, the lights of Dayton thinning, used car lots and a roller rink as outposts, they were silent before nervous energy swept over them. It was that unsettling bath of exhaustion and exuberance, rising to a tingle at the base of the neck, so familiar at the end of a performance. With Earl at the wheel, they began to harmonize and scat their way through "Take the A Train," "One O'Clock Jump," and their own wonderful collaboration, "October Mellow." In this way they would ride for a while. They would sing in ragged breaths before they gave out in laughter. The radio might go on, and there would be mostly the crackle of static, or, faintly, a late night gospel concert with harmonies rising and falling, like a prayer song tossed to the wind. Stray cars would rush past in the next lane, headed back toward Dayton. They passed a trailer groaning under its load, one or two squat Fords, then settled back. The night's first chapter was closed behind them with the noise from the motor, with smears of light.

Like a sudden tree in the car's lights, a sign sprouted and announced the city limits of Springfield.

Billy started nodding as if answering some ancient question. "Springfield got more fine women than they got in two St. Louises or five New Orleanses, I'm here to tell you."

"Wake up, Billy. Find me a place with women finer than they got in St. Louis or New Orleans or Harlem—think I'm gone let Harlem slide?—find me such a place and you got a easy one-hundred-dollar bill in your hand and I'll be in heaven. I'm talking serious now."

Billy snorted, sitting up straight and shaking his head. "I ain't hardly sleeping. Just remembering is all. See, I ain't been through here since 1952, but I can call some preacher's daughter right now—brown skin and about yeah-tall—yeah, at this very hour. Lord, she would be so fine that you and me both would run up the side of a mountain and holler like a mountain jack."

Then Earl blew a smoke ring and watched its rise; maybe it would halo the rearview mirror. "Well, okay, I'll take your word for it now, but if we're ever back through here, I definitely want to stop and see if these women are as pretty as you say."

"They pretty, they mamas pretty, they grandmamas pretty. . . ."

Earl laughed his high-pitched laugh. "You get crazier every day, Billy Cox." He pushed the accelerator, slamming them deeper into their seats.

Earl leveled off at sixty and for minutes was content to enjoy the regular beat of the wheels hitting the seams across the pavement, *pa-poom, pa-poom, pa-poom.* It was on the next stretch of road, ten miles outside of Springfield, that they truly sensed the flatness of the place. In the darkness there were no distant hills promising contour, variety, or perspective. Fields to the left? Woods to the right? They were silent for a minute or so. Crackling music flared up once again from the radio, then died.

"What do you think of the new boy's work tonight?" Billy asked.

"Who, 'Big City'? Not bad, man. Not bad at all." Earl snapped his fingers. "He's swinging more now. Matter of fact, he's driving the entire trumpet section, Big Joe included. You get the prize on that one, you brought him in. I remember you kept saying he could play the sweetest ballads, could curl up inside something like Strayhorn's 'Daydream' as easy as a cat curl up on a bed."

Billy nodded and looked out the side window. "I knew he had it in him the first time I heard him. His problem was hanging around Kansas City too long with that little jive band and just playing careful music. Sometimes you can't tell what's on the inside—just fast or slow, just hard or soft, just mean or laughing sweet. Can't never tell with some. But I had that feeling, know what I'm saying? Had the feeling that if we cut him loose, let him roam a little taste, that he could be all them combinations, that he could be what a tune needed him to be."

Earl tossed a cigarette stub out the window. He remembered the night he had met young Harold. The band was on break, and Harold walked up slowly, head down. The trumpet player had been nervous in his too-tight suit. Earl had later confided to Billy that he looked like he had just come in from plowing a cornfield and that if he joined the band he would have to learn how to dress, to coordinate his colors of his ties and suits, shine his shoes. When you joined the Ferguson band, you joined class. Style was more than your sound. It was your walk, the way you sat during the solos by others, the way you met the night. Earl had promptly nicknamed him "Big City."

"He said meeting you was like meeting God," Billy had said the next morning over hash browns and lukewarm coffee.

Earl smiled now. He was not God, true. He did know that among bandleaders roaming with their groups across this country, he was one of the best. He knew, too, that soft-spoken Billy Cox, five years younger, was the best composer in the business, period. Together they worked an easy magic. Few could weave sounds the way they could, few could get twelve voices, twelve rambunctious personalities, to shout or moan as one. And with it all was the trademark sound: the perfect blend of brass and reeds. Basie might have had a stronger reed section, with the force of a melodic hurricane; Ellington, a brass section with bite and unmatchable brightness. But they had the blend. Within the first few notes you knew that it was Earl Ferguson's band and nobody else's. Now and then players would leave to join other caravans inching across the continent, but the sound, their mix, stayed the same.

The scattered lights of Springfield were far behind them now, merged to a dull electric glow in the rearview mirror. And out from the town there were only occasional lights along State Route 42, one or two on front porches, lights bathing narrow, weathered, and wooded fronts, wood swings perfectly still in that time. Tightly closed shutters, silences inside. Both tried to imagine the front of the houses at noon—children pushing the porch swing? A dog napping in the shade nearby? Clothes flapping on a line running from behind the house? Gone suddenly, a blur to pinpoint, then out.

From a pocket Billy had taken out a matchbook. A few chord progressions had been scribbled on the inside cover. Then, drawing out a small lined tablet from beneath the seat, he quickly drew a bass staff and started humming.

"You got something going?" Earl asked.

"I think, yeah. A little light something, you know, like bright light and springtime and whatnot."

Earl tapped the wheel lightly with the palm of his free hand. "Toss in a small woman's bouncy walk, and I might get excited with you."

"Well, help me then. This time you use the woman—tight yellow skirt, right?—and I'll use the light, the light of mid-May, and when they don't work together, I think we'll both know."

"Solid. What you got so far?"

Billy did not answer. He kept a finger to his ear, staring from the matchbook cover to the tablet. Earl let it run. You don't interrupt when the idea is so young.

More often than not, Billy and Earl brought opposites or, at least, unlikely combinations together. One of the band's more popular numbers, a blues, was the result of Billy's meditations on the richly perfumed arms of a large and fleshy woman, arms tightly holding a man who mistook her short laugh for joy. To this, Earl had brought the memory of a rainy night and a long soft moan carried on the wind, something heard from the end of an alley. They used only the colors and sounds from these images, and only later, when the songs were fully arranged, did the smell and the touch of them sweep in. There had been other songs that resolved the contrasts, the differences, between the drone of a distant train and an empty glass of gin, a lipstick print at its rim, fingerprints around it. A baby's whimpering, and a man grinning as he counted a night's big take from the poker table, painted bright red fingernails tapping lightly down a lover's arm, and the cold of a lonely apartment. How much did the dancing couples, those whispering and holding close as second skins or those bouncing and whirling tirelessly, feel these things, too? Or did they bring something entirely different to the rhythms, something of their own?

Earl and Billy had talked about this many times. They had concluded that it was enough to bring contexts to dreams, to strengthen those who listened and danced. And there were those moments, magical, alive, when the dance hall was torn from the night and whirled, spinning like a top, a half mile from heaven.

Billy started whistling and tapping his thigh. Then he hummed a fragment of a song loudly.

Earl was nodding. "Nice. Already I can hear Slick Harry taking off with Ousley just under him with the alto. In triplets? Let's see, go through it again right quick."

Again Billy hummed and Earl brought in high triplets, nervous wings snagged to the thread of the melody, lifting the piece toward brightness. They stopped, and Billy, smiling now, worked quickly, a draftsman on fire, adding another line or two, crossing out, scribbling notes. He would look up to follow the front edges of the car's lights, then away to the darkness and back to the page.

"Listen up." Billy gave the next lines, flats predominating, while offering harsh counterpoint to the first two lines and snatching the song away from a tender playfulness for a moment. He scratched his chin and nodded. Pointed to the darkness.

"This is what I got so far." And he sang the line in a strong tenor voice, his melody now seeming to double the notes from the last line, though the rhythm did not vary. It was the kind of thing Art Tatum might do with "Tea for Two" or something equally simple. The song moved swiftly from a lyrical indulgence to a catch-me-if-you-can show of speed.

"Watch it now," Earl said, "or they will figure us for one of those beboppers." He chuckled. The woman in his mind walked faster, traffic about her thickened, the streets sent up jarring sounds. Those would be trumpets, probably. Surroundings leaned in. Trombones and tenor saxophones playing in the lowest octaves announced their possibilities.

Earl offered a line of his own. His woman walked quickly up the steps of a brownstone. In. Common enough sequence, but no surprise there. Whatever prompted it, though, was fleeting. Gone. Then he said, "Okay, forget mine for now. Let's stay with what you got."

Billy shrugged and marked off another staff, then glanced again to the match cover. He let out a long, low whistle. "Now we come to the bridge.

"This is when we need a piano, Earl. I bet the closest one to here is probably some ol' beat-up thing in one of these country churches out here. Or something sitting in the front parlor of one of these farmer's houses, and the farmer's daughter playing 'Jingle Bells' after bringing in the eggs."

Hip and arrogant city was in their laughter, they of funky cafés where fights might break out and beer bottles fly as the piano man bobbed and weaved, keeping time on a scarred piano that leaned and offered sticky keys in the lowest and highest octaves.

Then the Earl of Ferguson told the story of a piano search years before Billy had joined the band. With two other men in the car and barely an hour east of St. Louis, when the puzzle of a chord progression struck with the force of a deep stomach cramp. Spotting one light shining in the wilderness, a small neon sign still shining over a door, he ordered the car stopped. Trotting up, Earl noticed the sign blink off. He banged on the door, the hinges straining from each blow. Nobody turned off a sign in his face. The door swung open and up stepped an evil-looking, red-haired farmer in overalls, a man big enough to fill the doorway.

"I said to this giant, 'Quick, I got to get on your piano.' Not 'I got to find your toilet,' or 'I got to use your phone,' but 'I got to use your piano.'" He shook his head as he laughed now.

"That giant rocked on his heels like I had punched him square in the chest. He left just enough room for me to squeeze in and sure enough there was a little raggedy piano in the corner of his place.

"P.M. had enough sense to offer to buy some of the man's good whiskey while I'm sitting there playing and trying to figure out the good chord. P.M. always did have good common sense. Most folks try to remember what just happened, but Past was already on what's happening next. I'm forgetting you never knew P.M. The guys called him Past Midnight because he was so dark-skinned. The shadow of a shadow. Next thing they calling him Past, then one day Rabbit showed up calling him P.M., and it stuck. His real name was Wiley Reed, and he was one of the best alto players in the world."

He paused now, glanced out his side window. "Anyway, he showed him class that night. The giant steady looking around suspiciouslike at first. I mean, he didn't know us from Adam, didn't know how many more of us was waiting outside to rush in and turn out the joint. But he loosened up and took his mess of keys out and go to his cabinet. I'm just playing away because this is the greatest song of my life, don't care if it is in some country roadhouse way out in Plumb Nelly. I'm cussing, too, Billy, because this song is giving me fits, do you hear me? It just wouldn't let me go. All I wanted was to make it through the bridge. I figured the rest would come soon as I'm back in the car.

"Well, P.M. and the man making small talk, and Leon trying to get slick on everybody and tipping over to get him a few packs of Old Golds. I'm checking all this, see, and closing in on something solid and oh-so-sweet, and hearing the big guy go on and on about getting home because his wife already thinking he's sniffing around the new waitress—I remember that part clear as I'm sitting here—when, *boom!* Leon open up the closet, a mop and a jug of moonshine fell out and this woman inside trying to button up her blouse. She give a scream like she done seen the boogeyman. All hell commence to break loose. Next thing you know Leon backing off and telling the woman he ain't meant no harm, just trying to get some cigarettes, he lie. Big Boy running over and telling me we got to take our whiskey and go, song or no song. I look up, and two white guys running down the steps from just over our heads, one of them holding some cards in his hands. The other one run to the telephone like he reporting a robbery. I mean from the outside it's just a little-bitty place on the side of the road, but inside all kinds of shit going on. Well, I found the chords I wanted, did a quick run-through and called out to the fellows to haul ass. If some man's wife or some woman's man don't come in there shooting up the place, then the sheriff might raid the place for all-night gambling. Either way we lose."

Earl was laughing now. A light rain had started to fall just as he ended his tale. The windshield wipers clicked rhythmically; the bump of the road seemed a grace note: *bachoo-choo, bachoo-choo.*

"Never know when you get the tune down right. Go too early and you pluck it raw. Go too late and you got rotten fruit." Earl coughed. "Don't go at all and you put a bad hurt on yourself."

From across the highway a rabbit darted toward them, then cut away. Earl had turned the car just slightly before straightening it without letting up on the accelerator.

"Almost had us one dead rabbit."

Billy did not answer. He was tapping his pencil on the tablet. Up ahead and to the east they would discover the electric glow of Columbus. Beyond that they would have three more hours before Cleveland and breakfast at the Majestic Hotel on Carnegie Avenue. There might be a new singer or two waiting to try out with the band. Who knows? Somebody—another Billy or Sassy Sarah—might get lucky and ride back with them to New York, her life changed forever. Some young woman, prettier than she would ever know, would otherwise be serving up beef stew or spareribs in some tiny smoky place on Cedar Avenue, notes running through her head or thoughts of a sickly mother and two children she and her husband were trying to feed. How many times Billy and Earl had seen it, how many times they had heard the hope there, the sweat mustaches sprouting, the need to escape the routine nights. It was common ground. They had all been there, falling to sleep in clothes that smelled of cigarette smoke, the world a place of slow mornings with traffic starting and a door slamming, a baby crying, and an "Oh, goddamn, one more funky morning, but I'm alive to see it through anyhow.

There was a bump beneath the car. "You clipped something for sure that time, sportey-otee."

"All kinds of stuff out here at night," Earl said. "They like the warm road. Coons, possums, snakes, cows."

"Cows?"

"Yeah, cows." Billy had lit a cigarette. Earl tapped the end of the fresh one he had just placed in his mouth, and Billy reached to light it. "Thanks. Don't tell me you done forgot that cow we nicked on the road up to Saratoga Springs."

Yes, yes, Billy remembered. "Cow must have thought we was the Midnight Special, much noise as I was making trying to scare him off the road. Probably just out to get him a little side action in the next field." The car had knocked it to one knee before it struggled back up and, in the rearview mirror, slipped into the darkness.

They were quiet for long moments. After music, after hours, different thoughts could struggle to life. If there was an easiness earlier, swift terror could strike them in the darkest hours before dawn. They could grow suddenly uneasy in the silences. They could sense it together like a bone-deep chill starting. For now Billy pushed the wing shut on his side, rolled his window up another inch.

In a small town just west of Columbus, they passed a café, the lone light in that stretch. A man behind a long counter—white apron, white T-shirt—was scrubbing the counter and talking with a customer. He stopped his work to make a point, head moving from side to side. The customer nodded. Another man stood over a table at the window, dunking a doughnut. With his free hand, he waved as the car passed. Surprised, Earl honked once, then turned to glance back.

"That back there reminds me of something."

"Huh?"

"That man right back there waving. You didn't see him? Standing back there, waving at us and probably every car coming through here this late."

"Don't tell me you want to get some food," Billy said. "Hell, Earl, I thought those chicken sandwiches and pound cake—"

"No, no. That ain't what I'm thinking. Had a guy in the band by the name of Boonie years ago, way before you joined the band. Boonie could play him some mean trombone, I'm here to tell you. Fact, he could play trumpet and cornet, too. Probably would have played the tuba if I would have asked him to. Like you, he was the master of horns. Anyway, something happened—could have been bad gin or something else nobody will ever know about. He just snapped, and they found him one morning standing on a corner cussing at folks and swearing up and down that he was the governor of Africa. They took him to the jailhouse first, then the crazy house. They didn't keep him there long, six, seven months maybe.

"I went up to see him, way out in the country, Billy, you know where they put those places. Well, just past the gate was this man, and he waved at me when I first came in, and, while I was walking around with Boonie, he waved a couple more times. At first I thought he was just part of the staff because he was all over the place. But then I noticed he's wearing the same kind of clothes as Boonie. And he keeps smiling, you know? By the time I left, he was back out by the gate and waving again. It didn't take me long to figure out that all he had to do was wave at whatever was new and moving by. Like that man back there waving at the night."

Billy only glanced at him, then looked back to his notebook. Earl shook his head and chuckled. "Governor of Africa, can you beat that? Boonie was lucky, though; I mean, the way he wound up. He never got his chops back after he got out. He worked around a little, then finally left the life. He got a foundry job and raised his family in Detroit. Others ain't been so lucky."

Earl glanced ahead to more lights showing up through the rain. He knew some who entered hospitals, never to emerge. And many, too many, died before the age of fifty. Just last March, young "Bird" Parker had died in New York, not yet thirty-five. He whose notes surprised like shooting stars. Playing this music could be as risky as working in a steel mill or coal mine. But what were the choices? What could he do about it, leader of some? Perhaps only show them a lesson or two through his example. Now he did limit himself to one large and long drink per night—one part scotch and three parts water—from an oversized coffee mug. Soon he would cut down on his cigarettes. Beyond that he let the rules pronounce the purpose: you needed a clear head and a sound body to play the music he lived for.

Their talk of work and women—the incomplete song still a bright ribbon over their heads—pulled them well beyond the glow of Columbus. Coffee and sandwiches finished, they were down to three cigarettes each and figured there was nothing open between Columbus and Cleveland. Billy took over at the wheel. Twenty miles or so north of Columbus, they neared a car in trouble at the side of the road. The hood was up and in the swath of the front head-lights was a man—very young, thin, white—kneeling at the back tire.

"Keep going, Billy. That cracker'll get help."

Billy slowed. "Well, Earl, it won't hurt. . . ."

Earl stared at him, hard. "You getting softhearted on me? That boy could be the Klan, see? You remember what happened to the Purnell band down in Tennessee just last month? Huh, remember that stuff? Got beat up by a bunch of rednecks, one of them getting his nose broke, and they still winding up in jail for disturbing the peace and impersonating a band? No, let him get help from his own kind."

Billy pulled the car off the road. "He's just a kid, Earl."

"You go without me, then." He watched Billy leave, then quickly felt under his seat.

Billy was approaching the car, and Earl could hear him ask, "Need a hand?"

"Sure do," the boy said loudly "If you got a jack on you, we can do this in no time."

Beneath his seat in the Buick, Earl had found the gun wrapped in a towel. He opened the glove compartment and placed it inside, unwrapping the towel and leaving the small door open. He began to hum the new song slowly, softly, watching his friend, smiling Billy, trusting Billy, help a stranger.

Billy brought the jack from their trunk and set it up. He could smell alcohol on the boy, and, straightening up, he saw a girl in the car sip from a flask. Neither could have been older than eighteen. She was trying to hum something, missing, then tried again.

"Dumb me out here without a jack, I swear," the boy said. Billy only nodded as they set the jack under the frame.

The boy called the girl out of the car, and she stood apart shyly, both hands holding up the collar of her light coat.

"Your friend back there under the weather?" the boy asked.

"He just don't need the exercise," Billy said. "How about her? She feeling all right?"

The boy looked up in surprise, then he smiled. "No, she all right. She don't need no exercise either." He leaned closer to Billy as they pulled off the wheel and started to set the spare. "Course, me and her just about exercised out." Then he laughed. "Whoo-ee!"

The tire was on now, and the boy was tightening the lugs. "Pretty nice car you got back there. You a undertaker or a preacher?"

"No, neither one. I'm a musician."

The boy whistled low. "Musicians make enough for a car like that? I need to learn me some music. You get to travel a lot and see them big-city women and all like that?"

"Sure do."

The boy glanced at the girl and said loudly, "Course, a man could go all over the world and never find a woman sweet as my Josie there."

Her hair needed a brush, her dress was wrinkled, and her shoes were old and run-over. She was plain and drunk. In the morning she might be in the choir of a tiny church and by evening making biscuits to the staccato of radio news broadcasts. Billy was folding up the jack and turning away.

"Ain't she about the prettiest doggone thing a man could ever see?"

"I know how you feel, sport. I got one just as sweet back in New York."

Billy walked away and waved good-bye with his back turned. He slammed the trunk closed, then settled behind the wheel. He pulled the car back onto the highway.

Earl was whistling. "Feel better?" he asked, not looking up.

"What's that for?" Billy pointed to the gun.

"I thought about cleaning it. Ain't been cleaned in a year." Then: "My daddy told me once that it takes more than a smile and a good heart to get through this world. Told me sometimes you can reach out a helping hand and get it chopped off."

Billy was shivering. "Hide it, Earl. Please."

"Okay, okay. Look, while you were playing the Good Samaritan with Jethro back there, I finished the song. Listen up, young-blood."

Earl hummed through the opening key, stretching the note, then moved through the bright afternoon of the melody, repeated the line in the thinning light of its early evening. The song soon lifted to the bridge, a vivid golden stair step on which to linger briefly. Then the return to the opening line that suggested new possibilities: the smell of a pine forest after a rain, a meadow, too, a deer or two frozen at one edge. There was a street, glistening, a small oil slick catching dull rainbows, and a stranger's laughter like a bright coin spinning at their feet. Yes, all of that.

The small and proud woman walking, her hips working against yellow wool, had been lost to Earl. She would return, surely, to move through another song, walking to a different rhythm. For now she had brought Earl excited to Billy's first thoughts. Provided a spirit. Together, they hummed the song through, speeding it up, slowing. Each time, they tried different harmonies—the bass stronger here, the trombones higher there. Most of the parts had been worked through by the time they noticed the hills near Medina taking shape.

"Got it," Billy said finally. He slapped the wheel with relief.

"It's nice," Earl said.

"Think the people will like it?" Billy asked.

Earl yawned and looked out the window. Maybe he could get twenty minutes or so of sleep before they touched the edges of the city. "You worry too much, Billy. Course they gone like it. They got no choice. We did the best we could. We'll run through it this afternoon, do it again in Pittsburgh, and maybe have it ready by the time we hit Philly. Can't you just hear Big City's solo already?" He settled back, eyes closed.

Cars, trees, cornfields just harvested were explosions of dull colors. Signs placed one hundred feet apart, a shaving cream ad suddenly claimed Billy's attention. *The big blue tube's/Just like Louise/You get a thrill/From every squeeze.* He laughed aloud, then started whistling. Then the car roared into a stretch of light fog. Billy leaned forward, his head almost touching the windshield. Then he stiffened.

"Earl, wake up. I got something to tell you."

"Let it slide. Tell me over grits and coffee." Earl kept his eyes closed.

"No, it can't wait. It happened back there in Dayton. I just now remembered. You know on that second break? Well, I stepped outside to get a little air, take a smoke, you understand. A couple folk stroll past and tell me how much they like our playing, so I'm talking with them a while and then I see this woman—short with a red wig and she standing off to the side. She look up every now and then like she want to come over and say something. But she wait until nobody's around and she walk over real quicklike. Something about her make me think about a bird hopping, then resting, hopping some more. She told me she really like the music, like some of the songs really get a hold of her. . . ."

Earl opened one eye. "Yeah, and she just want to take a cute little man like you home to make music to her all the time."

"No, no, no. Nothing like that, but you better believe I was hoping for some action."

Forehead still to the windshield, Billy fumbled for words, worked a hand like he was flagging down a car. "No, she's smiling but not smiling, if you know what I mean. We talk about a lot of things, then she gets down to the thing she really wanted to talk about, I figure. She told me about her baby. She told me about hearing her baby screaming one day and she rush from her ironing and found him in the next room bleeding. He fell on a stick or glass or something, cut his belly, and blood going every which way. Said her son's belly was thin, like a balloon, but not going down when it's poked. She put her hand there, she said, and could feel each beat of the heart. Every time the heart beat, more blood would spurt out between her fingers. She screamed for help, screamed for her neighbors next door, just screamed and screamed. Blood was all over her, too, she said, but she never saw that until later. All she could do is tell her child not to die and press on that thin belly. And pray and pray, even after he in the ambulance. She told me that baby was all she got in this world."

Billy shook his head slowly. "What could I say to all that? Here I go outside for some fresh air and a draw or two on my Lucky Strikes. She brings me this story when I want to know whether my shoes are shined, my front still holding up, or whether some big-legged woman want to pull me home with her. I touched her on the shoulder, was all I could do. She told me the baby lived, and she smiled this dopey smile. Then she left."

Earl's eyes were closed. He waved his hand as if shooing a fly from his forehead. "It's this music we play, Billy. It opens people up, makes them give up secrets. Better than whiskey or dope for that. It don't kill you, and you can't piss it away. You can whistle it the next day in new places. You can loan it to strangers, and they thank you for it."

Then he shrugged. "It's what keeps us going all night."

Sitting back, fog thinning, Billy nodded and started back whistling. Before long they would sight the giant mills pumping smoke into the gray morning. At Lakewood Billy might swing closer to the gray and glassy Erie. Then he would pick up speed and head toward the east side, through a world raging to light outside their windows. Finally they would gain Carnegie Avenue and weave their way among the early church traffic. They would find the Majestic Hotel, breakfast, and attempt sleep, two wizards before the band.

QUESTIONS AND CONSIDERATIONS

1. Characterize Billy and Earl. What unique attitudes about music and about life does each represent?

2. Explain the significance of the stop to help change the white couple's flat tire. How are Billy's and Earl's values exemplified by their attitudes toward the couple's predicament?

3. Why does Earl have to tell Billy about what he learned from the woman in Dayton? What has Earl learned, and how has he incorporated his new insights into his art?

4. How do Earl and Billy create their song? What do they come to understand about music, collaboration, and creativity through their adventure into the night?

5. Why is the story's title appropriate? How does exploring the different meanings of the words "lush" and "life" help you to understand better the story's meaning?

6. Did reading this story bring you new insights about the creative process?

IDEAS FOR WRITING

1. Analyze and interpret several of the major issues explored in this story—for example, the role of collaboration in creativity, the relationship between life and art, the particular challenges and rewards of the artistic life. Refer to specific scenes in the story to support your major points.

2. Write a story about a nighttime journey and adventure that you took with a friend. Reflect on what you learned about friendship, collaboration, and creativity from your trip.

Janus
Ann Beattie

Journal

Write about an object that holds complex meaning for you.

The bowl was perfect. Perhaps it was not what you'd select if you faced a shelf of bowls, and not the sort of thing that would inevitably attract a lot of attention at a crafts fair, yet it had real presence. It was as predictably admired as a mutt who has no reason to suspect he might be funny. Just such a dog, in fact, was often brought out (and in) along with the bowl.

Andrea was a real-estate agent, and when she thought that some prospective buyers might be dog-lovers, she would drop off her dog at the same time she placed the bowl in the house that was up for sale. She would put a dish of water in the kitchen for Mondo, take his squeaking plastic frog out of her purse and drop it on the floor. He would pounce delightedly, just as he did every day at home, batting around his favorite toy. The bowl usually sat on a coffee table, though recently she had displayed it on top of a pine blanket chest and on a lacquered table. It was once placed on a cherry table beneath a Bonnard still-life, where it held its own.

Everyone who has purchased a house or who has wanted to sell a house must be familiar with some of the tricks used to convince a buyer that the house is quite special: a fire in the fireplace in early evening; jonquils in a pitcher on the kitchen counter, where no one ordinarily has space to put flowers; perhaps the slight aroma of spring, made by a single drop of scent vaporizing from a lamp bulb.

The wonderful thing about the bowl, Andrea thought, was that it was both subtle and noticeable—a paradox of a bowl. Its glaze was the color of cream and seemed to glow no matter what light it was placed in. There were a few bits of color in it—tiny geometric flashes—and some of these were tinged with flecks of silver. They were as mysterious as cells seen under a microscope; it was difficult not to study them, because they shimmered, flashing for a split second, and then resumed their shape. Something about the colors and their random placement suggested motion. People who liked country furniture always commented on the bowl, but then it turned out that people who felt comfortable with Biedemeier loved it just as much. But the bowl was not at all ostentatious, or even so noticeable that anyone would suspect that it had been put in place deliberately. They might notice the height of the ceiling on first entering a room, and only when their eye moved down from that, or away from the refraction of sunlight on a pale wall, would they see the bowl. Then they would go immediately to it and comment. Yet they always faltered when they tried to say something. Perhaps it was because they were in the house for a serious reason, not to notice some object.

Once, Andrea got a call from a woman who had not put in an offer on a house she had shown her. That bowl, she said—would it be possible to find out where the owners had bought that beautiful bowl? Andrea pretended that she did not know what the woman was referring to. A bowl, somewhere in the house? Oh, on a table under the window. Yes, she would ask, of course. She let a couple of days pass, then called back to say that the bowl had been a present and the people did not know where it had been purchased.

When the bowl was not being taken from house to house, it sat on Andrea's coffee table at home. She didn't keep it carefully wrapped (although she transported it that way, in a box); she kept it on the table, because she liked to see it. It was large enough so that it didn't seem fragile, or particularly vulnerable if anyone sideswiped the table or Mondo blundered into it at play. She had asked her husband to please not drop his house key in it. It was meant to be empty.

When her husband first noticed the bowl, he had peered into it and smiled briefly. He always urged her to buy things she liked. In recent years, both of them had acquired many things to make up for all the lean years when they were graduate students, but now that they had been comfortable for quite a while, the pleasure of new possessions dwindled. Her husband had pronounced the bowl "pretty," and he had turned away without picking it up to examine it. He had no more interest in the bowl than she had in his new Leica.

She was sure that the bowl brought her luck. Bids were often put in on houses where she had displayed the bowl. Sometimes the owners, who were always asked to be away or to step outside when the house was being shown, didn't even know that the bowl had been in their house. Once—she could not imagine how—she left it behind, and then she was so afraid that something might have happened to it that she rushed back to the house and sighed with relief when the woman owner opened the door. The bowl, Andrea explained—she had purchased a bowl and set it on the chest for safekeeping while she toured the house with the prospective buyers, and she . . . She felt like rushing past the frowning woman and seizing her bowl. The owner stepped aside, and it was only when Andrea ran to the chest that the lady glanced at her a little strangely. In the few seconds before Andrea picked up the bowl, she realized that the owner must have just seen that it had been perfectly placed, that the sunlight struck the bluer part of it. Her pitcher had been moved to the far side of the chest, and the bowl predominated. All the way home, Andrea wondered how she could have left the bowl behind. It was like leaving a friend at an outing—just walking off. Sometimes there were stories in the paper about families forgetting a child somewhere and driving to the next city. Andrea had only gone a mile down the road before she remembered.

In time, she dreamed of the bowl. Twice, in a waking dream—early in the morning, between sleep and a last nap before rising—she had a clear vision of it. It came into sharp focus and startled her for a moment—the same bowl she looked at every day.

She had a very profitable year selling real estate. Word spread, and she had more clients than she felt comfortable with. She had the foolish thought that if only the bowl were an animate object she could thank it. There were times when she wanted to talk to her husband about the bowl. He was a stockbroker, and sometimes told people that he was fortunate to be married to a woman who had such a fine aesthetic sense and yet could also function in the real world. They were a lot alike, really—they had agreed on that. They were both quiet people—reflective, slow to make value judgments, but almost intractable once they had come to a conclusion. They both liked details, but while ironies attracted her, he was more impatient and dismissive when matters became many-sided or unclear. But they both knew this; it was the kind of thing they could talk about when they were alone in the car together, coming home from a party or after a weekend with friends. But she never talked to him about the bowl. When they were at dinner, exchanging their news of the day, or while they lay in bed at night listening to the stereo and murmuring sleepy disconnections, she was often tempted to come right out and say that she thought that the bowl in the living room, the cream-colored bowl, was responsible for her success. But she didn't say it. She couldn't begin to explain it. Sometimes in the morning, she would look at him and feel guilty that she had such a constant secret.

Could it be that she had some deeper connection with the bowl—a relationship of some kind? She corrected her thinking: how could she imagine such a thing, when she was a human being and it was a bowl? It was ridiculous. Just think of how people lived together and loved each other . . . But was that always so clear, always a relationship? She was confused by these thoughts, but they remained in her mind. There was something within her now, something real, that she never talked about.

The bowl was a mystery, even to her. It was frustrating, because her involvement with the bowl contained a steady sense of unrequited good fortune; it would have been easier to respond if some sort of demand were made in return. But that only happened in fairy tales. The bowl was just a bowl. She did not believe that for one second. What she believed was that it was something she loved.

In the past, she had sometimes talked to her husband about a new property she was about to buy or sell—confiding some clever strategy she had devised to persuade owners who seemed ready to sell. Now she stopped doing that, for all her strategies involved the bowl. She became more deliberate with the bowl, and more possessive. She put it in houses only when no one was there, and removed it when she left the house. Instead of just moving a pitcher or a dish, she would remove all the other objects from a table. She had to force herself to handle them carefully, because she didn't really care about them. She just wanted them out of sight.

She wondered how the situation would end. As with a lover, there was no exact scenario of how matters would come to a close. Anxiety became the operative force. It would be irrelevant if the lover rushed into someone else's arms, or wrote her a note and departed to another city. The horror was the possibility of the disappearance. That was what mattered.

She would get up at night and look at the bowl. It never occurred to her that she might break it. She washed and dried it without anxiety, and she moved it often, from coffee table to mahogany corner table or wherever, without fearing an accident. It was clear that she would not be the one who would do anything to the bowl. The bowl was only handled by her, set safely on one surface or another; it was not very likely that anyone would break it. A bowl was a poor conductor of electricity: it would not be hit by lightning. Yet the idea of damage persisted. She did not think beyond that—to what her life would be without the bowl. She only continued to fear that some accident would happen. Why not, in a world where people set plants where they did not belong, so that visitors touring a house would be fooled into thinking that dark corners got sunlight—a world full of tricks?

She had first seen the bowl several years earlier, at a crafts fair she had visited half in secret, with her lover. He had urged her to buy the bowl. She didn't *need* any more things, she told him. But she had been drawn to the bowl, and they had lingered near it. Then she went on to the next booth, and he came up behind her, tapping the rim against her shoulder as she ran her fingers over a wood carving. "You're still insisting that I buy that?" she said. "No," he said. "I bought it for you." He had bought her other things before this—things she liked more, at first—the child's ebony-and-turquoise ring that fitted her little finger; the wooden box, long and thin, beautifully dovetailed, that she used to hold paper clips; the soft gray sweater with a pouch pocket. It was his idea that when he could not be there to hold her hand she could hold her own—clasp her hands inside the lone pocket that stretched across the front. But in time she became more attached to the bowl than to any of his other presents. She tried to talk herself out of it. She owned other things that were more striking or valuable. It wasn't an object whose beauty jumped out at you; a lot of people must have passed it by before the two of them saw it that day.

Her lover had said that she was always too slow to know what she really loved. Why continue with her life the way it was? Why be two-faced, he asked her. He had made the first move toward her. When she would not decide in his favor, would not change her life and come to him, he asked her what made her think she could have it both ways. And then he made the last move and left. It was a decision meant to break her will, to shatter her intransigent ideas about honoring previous commitments.

Time passed. Alone in the living room at night, she often looked at the bowl sitting on the table, still and safe, unilluminated. In its way, it was perfect: the world cut in half, deep and smoothly empty. Near the rim, even in dim light, the eye moved toward one small flash of blue, a vanishing point on the horizon.

QUESTIONS AND CONSIDERATIONS

1. Why do you think the story is entitled "Janus"?

2. The story begins, "The bowl was perfect." What makes the bowl perfect? What is paradoxical and what is mysterious about the bowl?

3. Why does Andrea's lover buy her the bowl? Why do you think the author develops parallels between the bowl and Andrea's lover?

4. How does the bowl help Andrea to be a successful realtor? Why does Andrea feel that she must choose between the bowl and a lover?

5. Does Andrea's relationship to the bowl help you to recall relationships that you have had with important objects and people in your life?

6. Why does the author leave the ending ambiguous?

IDEAS FOR WRITING

1. Write an essay in which you interpret the bowl as a "muse," an inspirational force. Refer to the text as well as to personal experiences, observations, literature, and forms of popular culture to support your interpretation.

2. Write a sequel to this story that predicts the fate of the bowl, of the narrator's career, and of her relationship with her boyfriend.

Leaf by Niggle
J. R. R. Tolkien

Journal

Write about how appreciating or creating a work of art has helped you to understand better your own feelings about mortality or the afterlife.

There was once a little man called Niggle, who had a long journey to make. He did not want to go, indeed the whole idea was distasteful to him; but he could not get out of it. He knew he would have to start some time, but he did not hurry with his preparations.

Niggle was a painter. Not a very successful one, partly because he had many other things to do. Most of these things he thought were a nuisance; but he did them fairly well, when he could not get out of them: which (in his opinion) was far too often. The laws in his country were rather strict. There were other hindrances, too. For one thing, he was sometimes just idle, and did nothing at all. For another, he was kindhearted, in a way. You know the sort of kind heart: it made him uncomfortable more often than it made him do anything; and even when he did anything, it did not prevent him from grumbling, losing his temper, and swearing (mostly to himself). All the same, it did land him in a good many odd jobs for his neighbour, Mr. Parish, a man with a lame leg. Occasionally he even helped other people from further off, if they came and asked him to. Also, now and again, he remembered his journey, and began to pack a few things in an ineffectual way: at such times he did not paint very much.

He had a number of pictures on hand; most of them were too large and ambitious for his skill. He was the sort of painter who can paint leaves better than trees. He used to spend a long time on a single leaf, trying to catch its shape, and its sheen, and the glistening of dewdrops on its edges. Yet he wanted to paint a whole tree, with all of its leaves in the same style, and all of them different.

There was one picture in particular which bothered him. It had begun with a leaf caught in the wind, and it became a tree; and the tree grew, sending out innumerable branches, and thrusting out the most fantastic roots. Strange birds came and settled on the twigs and had to be attended to. Then all round the Tree, and behind it, through the gaps in the leaves and boughs, a country began to open out; and there were glimpses of a forest marching over the land, and of mountains tipped with snow. Niggle lost interest in his other pictures; or else he took them and tacked them on to the edges of his great picture. Soon the canvas became so large that he had to get a ladder; and he ran up and down it, putting in a touch here, and rubbing out a patch there. When people came to call, he seemed polite enough, though he fiddled a little with the pencils on his desk. He listened to what they said, but underneath he was thinking all the time about his big canvas, in the tall shed that had been built for it out in his garden (on a plot where once he had grown potatoes).

He could not get rid of his kind heart. 'I wish I was more strong-minded' he sometimes said to himself, meaning that he wished other people's troubles did not make him feel uncomfortable. But for a long time he was not seriously perturbed. 'At any rate, I shall get this one picture done, my real picture, before I have to go on that wretched journey,' he used to say. Yet he was beginning to see that he could not put off his start indefinitely. The picture would have to stop just growing and get finished.

One day, Niggle stood a little way off from his picture and considered it with unusual attention and detachment. He could not make up his mind what he thought about it, and wished he had some friend who would tell him what to think. Actually it seemed to him wholly unsatisfactory, and yet very lovely, the only really beautiful picture in the world. What he would have liked at that moment would have been to see himself walk in, and slap him on the back and say (with obvious sincerity): 'Absolutely magnificent! I see exactly what you are getting at. Do get on with it, and don't bother about anything else! We will arrange for a public pension, so that you need not.'

However, there was no public pension. And one thing he could see: it would need some concentration, some *work,* hard uninterrupted work, to finish the picture, even at its present size. He rolled up his sleeves, and began to concentrate. He tried for several days not to bother about other things. But there came a tremendous crop of interruptions. Things went wrong in his house; he had to go and serve on a jury in the town; a distant friend fell ill; Mr. Parish was laid up with lumbago; and visitors kept on coming. It was springtime, and they wanted a free tea in the country: Niggle lived in a pleasant little house, miles away from the town. He cursed them in his heart, but he could not deny that he had invited them himself, away back in the winter, when he had not thought it an 'interruption' to visit the shops and have tea with acquaintances in the town. He tried to harden his heart; but it was not a success. There were many things that he had not the face to say *no* to, whether he thought them duties or not; and there were some things he was compelled to do, whatever he thought. Some of his visitors hinted that his garden was rather neglected, and that he might get a visit from an Inspector. Very few of them knew about his picture, of course; but if they had known, it would not have made much difference. I doubt if they would have thought that it mattered much. I dare say it was not really a very good picture, though it may have had some good passages. The Tree, at any rate, was curious. Quite unique in its way. So was Niggle; though he was also a very ordinary and rather silly little man.

At length Niggle's time became really precious. His acquaintances in the distant town began to remember that the little man had got to make a troublesome journey, and some began to calculate how long at the latest he could put off starting. They wondered who would take his house, and if the garden would be better kept.

The autumn came, very wet and windy. The little painter was in his shed. He was up on the ladder, trying to catch the gleam of the westering sun on the peak of a snow-mountain, which he had glimpsed just to the left of the leafy tip of one of the Tree's branches. He knew that he would have to be leaving soon: perhaps early next year. He could only just get the picture finished, and only so so, at that: there were some corners where he would not have time now to do more than hint at what he wanted.

There was a knock on the door. 'Come in!' he said sharply, and climbed down the ladder. He stood on the floor twiddling his brush. It was his neighbour, Parish: his only real neighbour, all other folk lived along way off. Still, he did not like the man very much: partly because he was so often in trouble and in need of help; and also because he did not care about painting, but was very critical about gardening. When Parish looked at Niggle's garden (which was often) he saw mostly weeds; and when he looked at Niggle's pictures (which was seldom) he saw only green and grey patches and black lines, which seemed to him nonsensical. He did not mind mentioning the weeds (a neighbourly duty), but he refrained from giving any opinion of the pictures. He thought this was very kind, and he did not realise that, even if it was kind, it was not kind enough. Help with the weeds (and perhaps praise for the pictures) would have been better.

'Well, Parish, what is it?' said Niggle.

'I oughtn't to interrupt you, I know,' said Parish (without a glance at the picture). 'You are very busy, I'm sure.'

Niggle had meant to say something like that himself, but he had missed his chance. All he said was: 'Yes.'

'But I have no one else to turn to,' said Parish.

'Quite so,' said Niggle with a sigh: one of those sighs that are a private comment, but which are not made quite inaudible. 'What can I do for you?'

'My wife has been ill for some days, and I am getting worried,' said Parish. 'And the wind has blown half the tiles off my roof, and water is pouring into the bedroom. I think I ought to get the doctor. And the builders, too, only they take so long to come. I was wondering if you had any wood and canvas you could spare, just to patch me up and see me through for a day or two.' Now he did look at the picture.

'Dear, dear!' said Niggle. 'You *are* unlucky. I hope it is no more than a cold that your wife has got. I'll come round presently, and help you move the patient downstairs.'

'Thank you very much,' said Parish, rather coolly. 'But it is not a cold, it is a fever. I should not have bothered you for a cold. And my wife is in bed downstairs already. I can't get up and down with trays, not with my leg. But I see you are busy. Sorry to have troubled you. I had rather hoped you might have been able to spare the time to go for the doctor, seeing how I'm placed; and the builder too, if you really have no canvas you can spare.'

'Of course,' said Niggle; though other words were in his heart, which at the moment was merely soft without feeling at all kind. 'I could go. I'll go, if you are really worried.'

'I am worried, very worried. I wish I was not lame,' said Parish.

So Niggle went. You see, it was awkward. Parish was his neighbour, and everyone else a long way off. Niggle had a bicycle, and Parish had not, and could not ride one. Parish had a lame leg, a genuine lame leg which gave him a good deal of pain: that had to be remembered, as well as his sour expression and whining voice. Of course, Niggle had a picture and barely time to finish it. But it seemed that this was a thing that Parish had to reckon with and not Niggle. Parish, however, did not reckon with pictures; and Niggle could not alter that. 'Curse it!' he said to himself, as he got out his bicycle.

It was wet and windy, and daylight was waning. 'No more work for me today!' thought Niggle, and all the time that he was riding, he was either swearing to himself, or imagining the strokes of his brush on the mountain, and on the spray of leaves beside it, that he had first imagined in the spring. His fingers twitched on the handlebars. Now he was out of the shed, he saw exactly the way in which to treat that shining spray which framed the distant vision of the mountain. But he had a sinking feeling in his heart, a sort of fear that he would never now get a chance to try it out.

Niggle found the doctor, and he left a note at the builder's. The office was shut, and the builder had gone home to his fireside. Niggle got soaked to the skin, and caught a chill himself. The doctor did not set out as promptly as Niggle had done. He arrived next day, which was quite convenient for him, as by that time there were two patients to deal with, in neighbouring houses. Niggle was in bed, with a high temperature, and marvellous patterns of leaves and involved branches forming in his head and on the ceiling. It did not comfort him to learn that Mrs Parish had only had a cold, and was getting up. He turned his face to the wall and buried himself in leaves.

He remained in bed some time. The wind went on blowing. It took away a good many more of Parish's tiles, and some of Niggle's as well: his own roof began to leak. The builder did not come. Niggle did not care; not for a day or two. Then he crawled out to look for some food (Niggle had no wife). Parish did not come round: the rain had got into his leg and made it ache; and his wife was busy mopping up water, and wondering if 'that Mr. Niggle' had forgotten to call at the builder's. Had she seen any chance of borrowing anything useful, she would have sent Parish round, leg or no leg; but she did not, so Niggle was left to himself.

At the end of a week or so Niggle tottered out to his shed again. He tried to climb the ladder, but it made his head giddy. He sat and looked at the picture, but there were no patterns of leaves or visions of mountains in his mind that day. He could have painted a far-off view of a sandy desert, but he had not the energy.

Next day he felt a good deal better. He climbed the ladder, and began to paint. He had just begun to get into it again, when there came a knock on the door.

'Damn!' said Niggle. But he might just as well have said 'Come in!' politely, for the door opened all the same. This time a very tall man came in, a total stranger.

'This is a private studio,' said Niggle. 'I am busy. Go away!'

'I am an Inspector of Houses,' said the man, holding up his appointment-card, so that Niggle on his ladder could see it.

'Oh!' he said.

'Your neighbour's house is not satisfactory at all,' said the Inspector.

'I know,' said Niggle. 'I took a note to the builders a long time ago, but they have never come. Then I have been ill.'

'I see,' said the Inspector. 'But you are not ill now.'

'But I'm not a builder. Parish ought to make a complaint to the Town Council, and get help from the Emergency Service.'

'They are busy with worse damage than any up here,' said the Inspector. 'There has been a flood in the valley, and many families are homeless. You should have helped your neighbour to make temporary repairs and prevent the damage from getting more costly to mend than necessary. That is the law. There is plenty of material here: canvas, wood, waterproof paint.'

'Where?' asked Niggle indignantly.

'There!' said the Inspector, pointing to the picture.

'My picture!' exclaimed Niggle.

'I dare say it is,' said the Inspector. 'But houses come first. That is the law.'

'But I can't . . .' Niggle said no more, for at that moment another man came in. Very much like the Inspector he was, almost his double: tall, dressed all in black.

'Come along!' he said. 'I am the Driver.'

Niggle stumbled down from the ladder. His fever seemed to have come on again, and his head was swimming; he felt cold all over.

'Driver? Driver?' he chattered. 'Driver of what?'

'You, and your carriage,' said the man. 'The carriage was ordered long ago. It has come at last. It's waiting. You start today on your journey, you know.'

'There now!' said the Inspector. 'You'll have to go; but it's a bad way to start on your journey, leaving your jobs undone. Still, we can at least make some use of this canvas now.'

'Oh, dear!' said poor Niggle, beginning to weep. 'And it's not even finished!'

'Not finished!' said the Driver. 'Well, it's finished with, as far as you're concerned, at any rate. Come along!'

Niggle went, quite quietly. The Driver gave him no time to pack, saying that he ought to have done that before, and they would miss the train; so all Niggle could do was to grab a little bag in the hall. He found that it contained only a paint-box and a small book of his own sketches: neither food nor clothes. They caught the train all right. Niggle was feeling very tired and sleepy; he was hardly aware of what was going on when they bundled him into his compartment. He did not care much: he had forgotten where he was supposed to be going, or what he was going for. The train ran almost at once into a dark tunnel.

Niggle woke up in a very large, dim railway station. A Porter went along the platform shouting, but he was not shouting the name of the place; he was shouting *Niggle!*

Niggle got out in a hurry, and found that he had left his little bag behind. He turned back, but the train had gone away.

'Ah, there you are!' said the Porter. 'This way! What! No luggage? You will have to go to the Workhouse.'

Niggle felt very ill, and fainted on the platform. They put him in an ambulance and took him to the Workhouse Infirmary.

He did not like the treatment at all. The medicine they gave him was bitter.

The officials and attendants were unfriendly, silent, and strict; and he never saw anyone else, except a very severe doctor, who visited him occasionally. It was more like being in a prison than in a hospital. He had to work hard, at stated hours: at digging, carpentry, and painting bare boards all one plain colour. He was never allowed outside, and the windows all looked inwards. They kept him in the dark for hours at a stretch, 'to do some thinking,' they said. He lost count of time. He did not even begin to feel better, not if that could be judged by whether he felt any pleasure in doing anything. He did not, not even in getting into bed.

At first, during the first century or so (I am merely giving his impressions), he used to worry aimlessly about the past. One thing he kept on repeating to himself, as he lay in the dark: 'I wish I had called on Parish the first morning after the high winds began. I meant to. The first loose tiles would have been easy to fix. Then Mrs Parish might never have caught cold. Then I should not have caught cold either. Then I should have had a week longer.' But in time he forgot what it was that he had wanted a week longer for. If he worried at all after that, it was about his jobs in the hospital. He planned them out, thinking how quickly he could stop that board creaking, or rehang that door, or mend that table-leg. Probably he really became rather useful, though no one ever told him so. But that, of course, cannot have been the reason why they kept the poor little man so long. They may have been waiting for him to get better, and judging 'better' by some odd medical standard of their own.

At any rate, poor Niggle got no pleasure out of life, not what he had been used to call pleasure. He was certainly not amused. But it could not be denied that he began to have a feeling of—well satisfaction: bread rather than jam. He could take up a task the moment one bell rang, and lay it aside promptly the moment the next one went, all tidy and ready to be continued at the right time. He got through quite a lot in a day, now; he finished small things off neatly. He had no 'time of his own' (except alone in his bed-cell), and yet he was becoming master of his time; he began to know just what he could do with it. There was no sense of rush. He was quieter inside now, and at resting-time he could really rest.

Then suddenly they changed all his hours; they hardly let him go to bed at all; they took him off carpentry altogether and kept him at plain digging, day after day. He took it fairly well. It was a long while before he even began to grope in the back of his mind for the curses that he had practically forgotten. He went on digging, till his back seemed broken, his hands were raw, and he felt that he could not manage another spadeful. Nobody thanked him. But the doctor came and looked at him.

'Knock off!' he said. 'Complete rest—in the dark.'

Niggle was lying in the dark, resting completely; so that, as he had not been either feeling or thinking at all, he might have been lying there for hours or for years, as far as he could tell. But now he heard Voices: not voices that he had ever heard before. There seemed to be a Medical Board, or perhaps a Court of Inquiry, going on close at hand, in an adjoining room with the door open, possibly, though he could not see any light.

'Now the Niggle case,' said a Voice, a severe voice, more severe than the doctor's.

'What was the matter with him?' said a Second Voice, a voice that you might have called gentle, though it was not soft—it was a voice of authority, and sounded at once hopeful and sad. 'What was the matter with Niggle? His heart was in the right place.'

'Yes, but it did not function properly,' said the First Voice. 'And his head was not screwed on tight enough: he hardly ever thought at all. Look at the time he wasted, not even amusing himself! He never got ready for his journey. He was moderately well-off, and yet he arrived here almost destitute, and had to be put in the paupers' wing. A bad case, I am afraid. I think he should stay some time yet.'

'It would not do him any harm, perhaps,' said the Second Voice. 'But, of course, he is only a little man. He was never meant to be anything very much; and he was never very strong. Let us look at the Records. Yes. There are some favourable points, you know.'

'Perhaps,' said the First Voice; 'but very few that will really bear examination.'

'Well,' said the Second Voice, 'there are these. He was a painter by nature. In a minor way, of course; still, a Leaf by Niggle has a charm of its own. He took a great deal of pains with leaves, just for their own sake. But he never thought that that made him important. There is no note in the Records of his pretending, even to himself, that it excused his neglect of things ordered by the law.'

'Then he should not have neglected so many,' said the First Voice.

'All the same, he did answer a good many Calls.'

'A small percentage, mostly of the easier sort, and he called those Interruptions. The Records are full of the word, together with a lot of complaints and silly imprecations.'

'True; but they looked like interruptions to him, of course, poor little man. And there is this: he never expected any Return, as so many of his sort call it. There is the Parish case, the one that came in later. He was Niggle's neighbour, never did a stroke for him, and seldom showed any gratitude at all. But there is no note in the Records that Niggle expected Parish's gratitude; he does not seem to have thought about it.'

'Yes, that is a point,' said the First Voice; 'but rather small. I think you will find Niggle often merely forgot. Things he had to do for Parish he put out of his mind as a nuisance he had done with.'

'Still, there is this last report,' said the Second Voice, 'that wet bicycle-ride. I rather lay stress on that. It seems plain that this was a genuine sacrifice: Niggle guessed that he was throwing away his last chance with his picture, and he guessed, too, that Parish was worrying unnecessarily.'

'I think you put it too strongly,' said the First Voice. 'But you have the last word. It is your task, of course, to put the best interpretation on the facts. Sometimes they will bear it. What do you propose?'

'I think it is a case for a little gentle treatment now,' said the Second Voice.

Niggle thought that he had never heard anything so generous as that Voice. It made Gentle Treatment sound like a load of rich gifts, and the summons to a King's feast. Then suddenly Niggle felt ashamed. To hear that he was considered a case for Gentle Treatment overwhelmed him, and made him blush in the dark. It was like being publicly praised, when you and all the audience knew that the praise was not deserved. Niggle hid his blushes in the rough blanket.

There was a silence. Then the First Voice spoke to Niggle, quite close. 'You have been listening,' it said.

'Yes,' said Niggle.

'Well, what have you to say?'

'Could you tell me about Parish?' said Niggle. 'I should like to see him again. I hope he is not very ill? Can you cure his leg? It used to give him a wretched time. And please don't worry about him and me. He was a very good neighbour, and let me have excellent potatoes, very cheap which saved me a lot of time.'

'Did he?' said the First Voice. 'I am glad to hear it.'

There was another silence. Niggle heard the Voices receding. 'Well, I agree,' he heard the First Voice say in the distance. 'Let him go on to the next stage. Tomorrow, if you like.'

Niggle woke up to find that his blinds were drawn, and his little cell was full of sunshine. He got up, and found that some comfortable clothes had been put out for him, not hospital uniform. After breakfast the doctor treated his sore hands, putting some salve on them that healed them at once. He gave Niggle some good advice, and a bottle of tonic (in case he needed it). In the middle of the morning they gave Niggle a biscuit and a glass of wine; and then they gave him a ticket.

'You can go to the railway station now,' said the doctor. 'The Porter will look after you. Good-bye.'

Niggle slipped out of the main door, and blinked a little. The sun was very bright. Also he had expected to walk out into a large town, to match the size of the station; but he did not. He was on the top of a hill, green, bare, swept by a keen invigorating wind. Nobody else was about. Away down under the hill he could see the roof of the station shining.

He walked downhill to the station briskly, but without hurry. The Porter spotted him at once.

'This way!' he said, and led Niggle to a bay, in which there was a very pleasant little local train standing: one coach, and a small engine, both very bright, clean, and newly painted. It looked as if this was their first run. Even the track that lay in front of the engine looked new: the rails shone, the chairs were painted green, and the sleepers gave off a delicious smell of fresh tar in the warm sunshine. The coach was empty.

'Where does this train go, Porter?' asked Niggle.

'I don't think they have fixed its name yet,' said the Porter. 'But you'll find it all right.' He shut the door.

The train moved off at once. Niggle lay back in his seat. The little engine puffed along in a deep cutting with high green banks, roofed with blue sky. It did not seem very long before the engine gave a whistle, the brakes were put on, and the train stopped. There was no station, and no signboard, only a flight of steps up the green embankment. At the top of the steps there was a wicket-gate in a trim hedge. By the gate stood his bicycle; at least, it looked like his, and there was a yellow label tied to the bars with NIGGLE written on it in large black letters.

Niggle pushed open the gate, jumped on the bicycle, and went bowling downhill in the spring sunshine. Before long he found that the path on which he had started had disappeared, and the bicycle was rolling along over a mar-vellous turf. It was green and close; and yet he could see every blade distinct-ly. He seemed to remember having seen or dreamed of that sweep of grass somewhere or other. The curves of the land were familiar somehow. Yes: the ground was becoming level, as it should, and now, of course, it was beginning to rise again. A great green shadow came between him and the sun. Niggle looked up, and fell off his bicycle.

Before him stood the Tree, his Tree, finished. If you could say that of a Tree that was alive, its leaves opening, its branches growing and bending in the wind that Niggle had so often felt or guessed, and had so often failed to catch. He gazed at the Tree, and slowly he lifted his arms and opened them wide.

'It's a gift!' he said. He was referring to his art, and also to the result; but he was using the word quite literally.

He went on looking at the Tree. All the leaves he had ever laboured at were there, as he had imagined them rather than as he had made them; and there were others that had only budded in his mind, and many that might have budded, if only he had had time. Nothing was written on them, they were just exquisite leaves, yet they were dated as clear as a calendar. Some of the most beautiful—and the most characteristic, the most perfect examples of the Nig-gle style—were seen to have been produced in collaboration with Mr. Parish: there was no other way of putting it.

The birds were building in the Tree. Astonishing birds: how they sang! They were mating, hatching, growing wings, and flying away singing into the Forest, even while he looked at them. For now he saw that the Forest was there too, opening out on either side, and marching away into the distance. The Mountains were glimmering far away.

After a time Niggle turned towards the Forest. Not because he was tired of the Tree, but he seemed to have got it all clear in his mind now, and was aware of it, and of its growth, even when he was not looking at it. As he walked away, he discovered an odd thing: the Forest, of course, was a distant Forest, yet he could approach it, even enter it, without its losing that particular

charm. He had never before been able to walk into the distance without turning it into mere surroundings. It really added a considerable attraction to walking in the country, because, as you walked, new distances opened out; so that
you now had double, treble, and quadruple distances, doubly, trebly, and
quadruply enchanting. You could go on and on, and have a whole country in a
garden, or in a picture (if you preferred to call it that). You could go on and on,
but not perhaps for ever. There were the Mountains in the background. They
did get nearer, very slowly. They did not seem to belong to the picture, or only
as a link to something else, a glimpse through the trees of something different,
a further stage: another picture.

Niggle walked about, but he was not merely pottering. He was looking
round carefully. The Tree was finished, though not finished with—'Just the
other way about to what it used to be,' he thought—but in the Forest there
were a number of inconclusive regions, that still needed work and thought.
Nothing needed altering any longer, nothing was wrong, as far as it had gone,
but it needed continuing up to a definite point. Niggle saw the point precisely,
in each case.

He sat down under a very beautiful distant tree—a variation of the Great
Tree, but quite individual, or it would be with a little more attention—and he
considered where to begin work, and where to end it, and how much time was
required. He could not quite work out his scheme.

'Of course!' he said. 'What I need is Parish. There are lots of things about
earth, plants, and trees that he knows and I don't. This place cannot be left
just as my private park. I need help and advice: I ought to have got it sooner.'

He got up and walked to the place where he had decided to begin work. He
took off his coat. Then, down in a little sheltered hollow hidden from a further
view, he saw a man looking round rather bewildered. He was leaning on a
spade, but plainly did not know what to do. Niggle hailed him. 'Parish!' he called.

Parish shouldered his spade and came up to him. He still limped a little.
They did not speak, just nodded as they used to do, passing in the lane, but
now they walked about together, arm in arm. Without talking, Niggle and
Parish agreed exactly where to make the small house and garden, which
seemed to be required.

As they worked together, it became plain that Niggle was now the better of
the two at ordering his time and getting things done. Oddly enough, it was Niggle who became most absorbed in building and gardening, while Parish often
wondered about looking at trees, and especially at the Tree.

One day Niggle was busy planting a quickset hedge, and Parish was lying
on the grass near by, looking attentively at a beautiful and shapely little yellow
flower growing in the green turf. Niggle had put a lot of them among the roots
of his Tree long ago. Suddenly Parish looked up: his face was glistening in the
sun, and he was smiling.

'This is grand!' he said. 'I oughtn't to be here, really. Thank you for putting
in a word for me.'

'Nonsense,' said Niggle. 'I don't remember what I said, but anyway it was
not nearly enough.'

'Oh yes, it was,' said Parish. 'It got me out a lot sooner. That Second Voice, you know: he had me sent here; he said you had asked to see me. I owe it to you.'

'No. You owe it to the Second Voice,' said Niggle. 'We both do.'

They went on living and working together: I do not know how long. It is no use denying that at first they occasionally disagreed, especially when they got tired. For at first they did sometimes get tired. They found that they had both been provided with tonics. Each bottle had the same label: *A few drops to be taken in water from the Spring, before resting.*

They found the Spring in the heart of the Forest; only once long ago had Niggle imagined it, but he had never drawn it. Now he perceived that it was the source of the lake that glimmered, far away and the nourishment of all that grew in the country. The few drops made the water astringent, rather bitter, but invigorating; and it cleared the head. After drinking they rested alone; and then they got up again and things went on merrily. At such times Niggle would think of wonderful new flowers and plants, and Parish always knew exactly how to set them and where they would do best. Long before the tonics were finished they had ceased to need them. Parish lost his limp.

As their work drew to an end they allowed themselves more and more time for walking about, looking at the trees, and the flowers, and the lights and shapes, and the lie of the land. Sometimes they sang together; but Niggle found that he was now beginning to turn his eyes, more and more often, towards the Mountains.

The time came when the house in the hollow, the garden, the grass, the forest, the lake, and all the country was nearly complete, in its own proper fashion. The Great Tree was in full blossom.

'We shall finish this evening,' said Parish one day. 'After that we will go for a really long walk.'

They set out next day, and they walked until they came right through the distances to the Edge. It was not visible, of course: there was no line, or fence, or wall; but they knew that they had come to the margin of that country. They saw a man, he looked like a shepherd; he was walking towards them, down the grass-slopes that led up into the Mountains.

'Do you want a guide?' he asked. 'Do you want to go on?'

For a moment a shadow fell between Niggle and Parish, for Niggle knew that he did now want to go on, and (in a sense) ought to go on; but Parish did not want to go on, and was not yet ready to go.

'I must wait for my wife,' said Parish to Niggle. 'She'd be lonely. I rather gathered that they would send her after me, some time or other, when she was ready, and when I had got things ready for her. The house is finished now, as well as we could make it; but I should like to show it to her. She'll be able to make it better, I expect: more homely. I hope she'll like this country, too.' He turned to the shepherd. 'Are you a guide?' he asked. 'Could you tell me the name of this country?'

'Don't you know?' said the man. 'It is Niggle's Country. It is Niggle's Picture, or most of it: a little of it is now Parish's Garden.'

'Niggle's Picture!' said Parish in astonishment. 'Did *you* think of all this, Niggle? I never knew you were so clever. Why didn't you tell me?'

'He tried to tell you long ago,' said the man, 'but you would not look. He had only got canvas and paint in those days, and you wanted to mend your roof with them. This is what you and your wife used to call Niggle's Nonsense, or That Daubing.'

'But it did not look like this then, not *real*,' said Parish.

'No, it was only a glimpse then,' said the man; 'but you might have caught the glimpse, if you had ever thought it worth while to try.'

'I did not give you much chance,' said Niggle. 'I never tried to explain. I used to call you Old Earth-grubber. But what does it matter? We have lived and worked together now. Things might have been different, but they could not have been better. All the same, I am afraid I shall have to be going on. We shall meet again, I expect: there must be many more things we can do together. Goodbye!' He shook Parish's hand warmly: a good, firm, honest hand it seemed. He turned and looked back for a moment. The blossom on the Great Tree was shining like flame. All the birds were flying in the air and singing. Then he smiled and nodded to Parish and went off with the shepherd.

He was going to learn about sheep, and the high pasturages, and look at a wider sky, and walk ever further and further towards the Mountains, always uphill. Beyond that I cannot guess what became of him. Even little Niggle in his old home could glimpse the Mountains far away, and they got into the borders of his picture; but what they are really like, and what lies beyond them only those can say who have climbed them.

'I think he was a silly little man,' said Councillor Tompkins. 'Worthless, in fact; no use to Society at all.'

'Oh, I don't know,' said Atkins, who was nobody of importance, just a schoolmaster. 'I am not so sure: it depends on what you mean by use.'

'No practical or economic use,' said Tompkins. 'I dare say he could have been made into a serviceable cog of some sort, if you schoolmasters knew your business. But you don't, and so we get useless people of his sort. If I ran this country I should put him and his like to some job that they're fit for, washing dishes in a communal kitchen or something, and I should see that they did it properly. Or I would put them away. I should have put *him* away long ago.'

'Put him away? You mean you'd have made him start on the journey before his time?'

'Yes, if you must use that meaningless old expression. Push him through the tunnel into the great Rubbish Heap: that's what I mean.'

'Then you don't think painting is worth anything, not worth preserving, or improving, or even making use of?'

'Of course, painting has uses,' said Tompkins. 'But you couldn't make use of his painting. There is plenty of scope for bold young men not afraid of new ideas and new methods. None for this old-fashioned stuff. Private daydreaming. He could not have designed a telling poster to save his life. Always fiddling with leaves and flowers. I asked him why, once. He said he thought they were pretty! Can you believe it? He said *pretty*! 'What, digestive and genital organs of plants?' I said to him; and he had nothing to answer. Silly footler.'

'Footler,' sighed Atkins. 'Yes, poor little man, he never finished anything. Ah well, his canvases have been put to "better uses", since he went. But I am not so sure, Tompkins. You remember that large one, the one they used to patch the damaged house next door to his, after the gales and floods? I found a corner of it torn off, lying in a field. It was damaged, but legible: a mountain-peak and a spray of leaves. I can't get it out of my mind.'

'Out of your what?' said Tompkins.

'Who are you two talking about?' said Perkins, intervening in the cause of peace: Atkins had flushed rather red.

'The name's not worth repeating,' said Tompkins. 'I don't know why we are talking about him at all. He did not live in town.'

'No,' said Atkins; 'but you had your eye on his house, all the same. That is why you used to go and call, and sneer at him while drinking his tea. Well, you've got his house now, as well as the one in town, so you need not grudge him his name. We were talking about Niggle, if you want to know, Perkins.'

'Oh, poor little Niggle!' said Perkins. 'Never knew he painted.'

That was probably the last time Niggle's name ever came up in conversation. However, Atkins preserved the odd corner. Most of it crumbled; but one beautiful leaf remained intact. Atkins had it framed. Later he left it to the Town Museum, and for a long time while 'Leaf: by Niggle' hung there in a recess, and was noticed by a few eyes. But eventually the Museum was burnt down, and the leaf, and Niggle, were entirely forgotten in his old country.

'It is proving very useful indeed,' said the Second Voice. 'As a holiday, and a refreshment. It is splendid for convalescence; and not only for that, for many it is the best introduction to the Mountains. It works wonders in some cases. I am sending more and more there. They seldom have to come back.'

'No, that is so,' said the First Voice. 'I think we shall have to give the region a name. What do you propose?'

'The Porter settled that some time ago,' said the Second Voice. '*Train for Niggle's Parish in the bay*: he has shouted that for a long while now. Niggle's Parish. I sent a message to both of them to tell them.'

'What did they say?'

'They both laughed. Laughed—the Mountains rang with it!'

QUESTIONS AND CONSIDERATIONS

1. What are Niggle's strengths and weaknesses as a painter? What relationships do you see between Niggle's personal struggles and his creative process? Why does Niggle want to finish his painting before leaving on his inevitable journey?

2. Why and how does Niggle help his neighbor Parish? Why does the Inspector make further demands on Niggle, claiming that he is legally obligated to help Parish re-

build his house, even if it means relinquishing his painting? Do you agree with the Inspector? Contrast the values of Niggle, Parish, and the Inspector.

3. What is significant about the way that Niggle's journey begins? Why does Niggle
get confused at the train station, lose his baggage, and end up in the workhouse
infirmary? What does Niggle's time in the infirmary symbolize? What does he learn
there? Who do the first and second voices at his trial represent? Why is Niggle allowed to
leave the workhouse?

4. How does Niggle see the tree he tried to finish painting in a new light after his release from the workhouse and his journey home? Why does Niggle see the forest bordering his own home in a new way after returning from the workhouse? Why are Niggle
and Parish able to appreciate one another's talents in the forest?

5. Where are the scenes in the forest and the mountains taking place—in reality, in
Niggle's imagination, or in the afterlife? Is the story an allegory or a dream? If the workhouse, forest, and mountains represent the afterlife or heaven, interpret the distinct
meaning of each of the three places.

6. Why does Atkins preserve the odd corner of Niggle's painting? How do the people of the community regard Niggle after he is gone?

IDEAS FOR WRITING

1. Write an interpretive analysis of the symbolic meaning of Niggle's painting.

2. Write an essay or short story about a painting or sculpture. Develop the story in a
literal and symbolic way. Turn in a copy of the painting with your writing.

Essays

Memory and Imagination
Patricia Hampl

Journal

*Write about a memory that you often think about but have never written down
on paper. After recording your memory in words, re-read it and write about how
writing it down has changed your understanding of the memory.*

When I was seven, my father, who played the violin on Sundays with a nicely
tortured flair which we considered artistic, led me by the hand down a long,
unlit corridor in St. Luke's School basement, a sort of tunnel that ended in a
room full of pianos. There many little girls and a single sad boy were playing

truly tortured scales and arpeggios in a mash of troubled sound. My father gave me over to Sister Olive Marie, who did look remarkably like an olive.

Her oily face gleamed as if it had just been rolled out of a can and laid on the white plate of her broad, spotless wimple. She was a small, plump woman; her body and the small window of her face seemed to interpret the entire alphabet of olive: her face was a sallow green olive placed upon the jumbo ripe olive of her black habit. I trusted her instantly and smiled, glad to have my hand placed in the hand of a woman who made sense, who provided the satisfaction of being what she was: an Olive who looked like an Olive.

My father left me to discover the piano with Sister Olive Marie so that one day I would join him in mutually tortured piano-violin duets for the edification of my mother and brother who sat at the table meditatively spooning in the last of their pineapple sherbet until their part was called for: they put down their spoons and clapped while we bowed, while the sweet ice in their bowls melted, while the music melted, and we all melted a little into each other for a moment.

But first Sister Olive must do her work. I was shown middle C, which Sister seemed to think terribly important. I stared at middle C and then glanced away for a second. When my eye returned, middle C was gone, its slim finger lost in the complicated grasp of the keyboard. Sister Olive struck it again, finding it with laughable ease. She emphasized the importance of middle C, its central position, a sort of North Star of sound. I remember thinking, "Middle C is the belly button of the piano," an insight whose originality and accuracy stunned me with pride. For the first time in my life I was astonished by metaphor. I hesitated to tell the kindly Olive for some reason; apparently I understood a true metaphor is a risky business, revealing of the self. In fact, I have never, until this moment of writing it down, told my first metaphor to anyone.

Sunlight flooded the room; the pianos, all black, gleamed. Sister Olive, dressed in the colors of the keyboard, gleamed; middle C shimmered with meaning and I resolved never—never—to forget its location: it was the center of the world.

Then Sister Olive, who had had to show me middle C twice but who seemed to have drawn no bad conclusions about me anyway, got up and went to the windows on the opposite wall. She pulled the shades down, one after the other. The sun was too bright, she said. She sneezed as she stood at the windows with the sun shedding its glare over her. She sneezed and sneezed, crazy little convulsive sneezes, one after another, as helpless as if she had the hiccups.

"The sun makes me sneeze," she said when the fit was over and she was back at the piano. This was odd, too odd to grasp in the mind. I associated sneezing with colds, and colds with rain, fog, snow and bad weather. The sun, however, had caused Sister Olive to sneeze in this wild way, Sister Olive who gleamed benignly and who was so certain of the location of the center of the world. The universe wobbled a bit and became unreliable. Things were not, after all, necessarily what they seemed. Appearance deceived: here was the sun acting totally out of character, hurling this woman into sneezes, a woman so mild that she was named, so it seemed, for a bland object on a relish tray.

I was given a red book, the first Thompson book, and told to play the first piece over and over at one of the black pianos where the other children were crashing away. This, I was told, was called practicing. It sounded alluringly adult, practicing. The piece itself consisted mainly of middle C, and I excelled, thrilled by my savvy at being able to locate that central note amidst the cunning camouflage of all the other white keys before me. Thrilled too by the shiny red book that gleamed, as the pianos did, as Sister Olive did, as my eager eyes probably did. I sat at the formidable machine of the piano and got to know middle C intimately, preparing to be as tortured as I could manage one day soon with my father's violin at my side.

But at the moment Mary Katherine Reilly was at my side, playing something at least two or three lessons more sophisticated than my piece. I believe she even struck a chord. I glanced at her from the peasantry of single notes, shy, ready to pay homage. She turned toward me, stopped playing, and sized me up.

Sized me up and found a person ready to be dominated. Without introduction she said, "My grandfather invented the collapsible opera hat."

I nodded, I acquiesced, I was hers. With that little stroke it was decided between us—that she should be the leader, and I the side-kick. My job was admiration. Even when she added, "But he didn't make a penny from it. He didn't have a patent"—even then, I knew and she knew that this was not an admission of powerlessness, but the easy candor of a master, of one who can afford a weakness or two.

With the clairvoyance of all fated relationships based on dominance and submission, it was decided in advance: that when the time came for us to play duets, I should always play second piano, that I should spend my allowance to buy her the Twinkies she craved but was not allowed to have, that finally, I should let her copy from my test paper, and when confronted by our teacher, confess with convincing hysteria that it was I, I who had cheated, who had reached above myself to steal what clearly belonged to the rightful heir of the inventor of the collapsible opera hat. . . .

There must be a reason I remember that little story about my first piano lesson. In fact, it isn't a story, just a moment, the beginning of what could perhaps become a story. For the memoirist, more than for the fiction writer, the story seems already *there,* already accomplished and fully achieved in history ("in reality," as we naively say). For the memoirist, the writing of the story is a matter of transcription.

That, anyway, is the myth. But no memoirist writes for long without experiencing an unsettling disbelief about the reliability of memory, a hunch that memory is not, after all, *just* memory. I don't know why I remembered this fragment about my first piano lesson. I don't, for instance, have a single recollection of my first arithmetic lesson, the first time I studied Latin, the first time my grandmother tried to teach me to knit. Yet these things occurred too, and must have their stories.

It is the piano lesson that has trudged forward, clearing the haze of forget-fulness, showing itself bright with detail more than thirty years after the event. I did not choose to remember the piano lesson. It was simply there, like a book that has always been on the shelf, whether I ever read it or not, the binding and title showing as I skim across the contents of my life. On the day I wrote this fragment I happened to take that memory, not some other, from the shelf and paged through it. I found more detail, more event, perhaps a little more entertainment than I had expected, but the memory itself was there from the start. Waiting for me.

Or was it? When I reread what I had written just after I finished it, I real-ized that I had told a number of lies. I *think* it was my father who took me the first time for my piano lesson—but maybe he only took me to meet my teacher and there was no actual lesson that day. And did I even know then that he played the violin—didn't he take up his violin again much later, as a result of my piano playing, and not the reverse? And is it even remotely accurate to de-scribe as "tortured" the musicianship of a man who began every day by belting out "Oh What a Beautiful Morning" as he shaved?

More: Sister Olive Marie did sneeze in the sun, but was her name Olive? As for her skin tone—I would have sworn it was olive-like; I would have been willing to spend the better part of an afternoon trying to write the exact descrip-tion of imported Italian or Greek olive her face suggested: I wanted to get it right. But now, were I to write that passage over, it is her intense black eye-brows I would see, for suddenly they seem the central fact of that face, some indicative mark of her serious and patient nature. But the truth is, I don't re-member the woman at all. She's a sneeze in the sun and a finger touching middle C. That, at least, is steady and clear.

Worse: I didn't have the Thompson book as my piano text. I'm sure of that because I remember envying children who did have this wonderful book with its pictures of children and animals printed on the pages of music.

As for Mary Katherine Reilly. She didn't even go to grade school with me (and her name isn't Mary Katherine Reilly—but I made that change on pur-pose). I met her in Girl Scouts and only went to school with her later, in high school. Our relationship was not really one of leader and follower; I played first piano most of the time in duets. She certainly never copied anything from a test paper of mine: she was a better student, and cheating just wasn't a possi-bility with her. Though her grandfather (or someone in her family) did invent the collapsible opera hat and I remember that she was proud of that fact, she didn't tell me this news as a deft move in a childish power play.

So, what was I doing in this brief memoir? Is it simply an example of the curious relation a fiction writer has to the material of her own life? Maybe. That may have some value in itself. But to tell the truth (if anyone still believes me capable of telling the truth), I wasn't writing fiction. I was writing memoir—or was trying to. My desire was to be accurate. I wished to embody the myth of memoir: to write as an act of dutiful transcription.

Yet clearly the work of writing narrative caused me to do something very different from transcription. I am forced to admit that memoir is not a matter of transcription, that memory itself is not a warehouse of finished stories, not a static gallery of framed pictures. I must admit that I invented. Buy why?

Two whys: why did I invent, and then, if a memoirist must inevitably invent rather than transcribe, why do I—why should anybody—write memoir at all?

I must respond to these impertinent questions because they, like the bumper sticker I saw the other day commanding all who read it to QUESTION AUTHORITY, challenge my authority as a memoirist and as a witness.

It still comes as a shock to realize that I don't write about what I know: I write in order to find out what I know. Is it possible to convey to a reader the enormous degree of blankness, confusion, hunch and uncertainty lurking in the act of writing? When I am the reader, not the writer, I too fall into the lovely illusion that the words before me (in a story by Mavis Gallant, an essay by Carol Bly, a memoir by M. F. K. Fisher), which *read* so inevitably, must also have been *written* exactly as they appear, rhythm and cadence, language and syntax, the powerful waves of the sentences laying themselves on the smooth beach of the page one after another faultlessly.

But here I sit before a yellow legal pad, and the long page of the preceding two paragraphs is a jumble of crossed-out lines, false starts, confused order. A mess. The mess of my mind trying to find out what it wants to say. This is a writer's frantic, grabby mind, not the poised mind of a reader ready to be edified or entertained.

I sometimes think of the reader as a cat, endlessly fastidious, capable, by turns, of mordant indifference and riveted attention, luxurious, recumbent, and ever poised. Whereas the writer is absolutely a dog, panting and moping, too eager for an affectionate scratch behind the ears, lunging frantically after any old stick thrown in the distance.

The blankness, of a new page never fails to intrigue and terrify me. Sometimes, in fact, I think my habit of writing on long yellow sheets comes from an atavistic fear of the writer's stereotypic "blank white page." At least when I begin writing, my page isn't utterly blank; at least it has a wash of color on it, even if the absence of words must finally be faced on a yellow sheet as truly as on a blank white one. Well, we all have our ways of whistling in the dark.

If I approach writing from memory with the assumption that I know what I wish to say, I assume that intentionality is running the show. Things are not that simple. Or perhaps writing is even more profoundly simple, more telegraphic and immediate in its choices than the grating wheels and chugging engine of logic and rational intention. The heart, the guardian of intuition with its secret, often fearful intentions, is the boss. Its commands are what a writer obeys—often without knowing it. Or, I do.

That's why I'm a strong adherent of the first draft. And why it's worth pausing for a moment to consider what first draft really is. By my lights, the piano lesson memoir is a first draft. That doesn't mean it exists here exactly as I first wrote it. I like to think I've cleaned it up from the first time I put it down on paper. I've cut some adjectives here, toned down the hyperbole there, smoothed a transition, cut a repetition—that sort of housekeeperly tidying-up. But the piece remains a first draft because I haven't yet gotten to know it, haven't given it a chance to tell me anything. For me, writing a first draft is a little like meeting someone for the first time. I come away with a wary acquaintanceship, but the real friendship (if any) and genuine intimacy—that's all down the road. Intimacy with a piece of writing, as with a person, comes from paying attention to the revelations it is capable of giving, not by imposing my own preconceived notions, no matter how well-intentioned they might be.

I try to let pretty much anything happen in a first draft. A careful first draft is a failed first draft. That may be why there are so many inaccuracies in the piano lesson memoir: I didn't censor, I didn't judge. I kept moving. But I would not publish this piece as a memoir on its own in its present state. It isn't the "lies" in the piece that give me pause, though a reader has a right to expect a memoir to be as accurate as the writer's memory can make it. No, it isn't the lies themselves that makes the piano lesson memoir a first draft and therefore "unpublishable."

The real trouble: the piece hasn't yet found its subject; it isn't yet about what *it* wants to be about. Note: what *it* wants, not what I want. The difference has to do with the relation a memoirist—any writer, in fact—has to unconscious or half-known intentions and impulses in composition.

Now that I have the fragment down on paper, I can read this little piece as a mystery which drops clues to the riddle of my feelings, like a culprit who wishes to be apprehended. My narrative self (the culprit who has invented) wishes to be discovered by my reflective self, the self who wants to understand and make sense of a half-remembered story about a nun sneezing in the sun. . . .

We only store in memory images of value. The value may be lost over the passage of time (I was baffled about why I remembered that sneezing nun, for example), but that's the implacable judgment of feeling: *this*, we say somewhere deep within us, is something I'm hanging on to. And of course, often we cleave to things because they possess heavy negative charges. Pain likes to be vivid.

Over time, the value (the feeling) and the stored memory (the image) may become estranged. Memoir seeks a permanent home for feeling and image, a habitation where they can live together in harmony. Naturally, I've had a lot of experiences since I packed away that one from the basement of St. Luke's School; that piano lesson has been effaced by waves of feeling for other moments and episodes. I persist in believing the event has value—after all, I remember it—but in writing the memoir I did not simply relive the experience. Rather, I explored the mysterious relationship between all the images I could round up and the even more impacted feelings that caused me to store the images safely away in memory. Stalking the relationship, seeking the congruence between stored image and hidden emotion—that's the real job of memoir.

By writing about the first piano lesson, I've come to know things I could not know otherwise. But I only know these things as a result of reading this first draft. While I was writing, I was following the images, letting the details fill the room of the page and use the furniture as they wished. I was their dutiful servant—or thought I was. In fact, I was the faithful retainer of my hidden feelings which were giving the commands.

I really did feel, for instance, that Mary Katherine Reilly was far superior to me. She was smarter, funnier, more wonderful in every way—that's how I saw it. Our friendship (or she herself) did not require that I become her vassal, yet perhaps in my heart that was something I wanted; I wanted a way to express my feeling of admiration. I suppose I waited until this memoir to begin to find the way.

Just as, in the memoir, I finally possess that red Thompson book with the barking dogs and bleating lambs and winsome children. I couldn't (and still can't) remember what my own music book was, so I grabbed the name and image of the one book I could remember. It was only in reviewing the piece after writing it that I saw my inaccuracy. In pondering this "lie," I came to see what I was up to: I was getting what I wanted. At last.

The truth of many circumstances and episodes in the past emerges for the memoirist through details (the red music book, the fascination with a nun's name and gleaming face), but these details are not merely information, not flat facts. Such details are not allowed to lounge. They must work. Their work is the creation of symbol. But it's more accurate to call it the *recognition* of symbol. For meaning is not "attached" to the detail by the memoirist; meaning is revealed. That's why a first draft is important. Just as the first meeting (good or bad) with someone who later becomes the beloved is important and is often reviewed for signals, meanings, omens and indications.

Now I can look at that music book and see it not only as "a detail," but for what it is, how it *acts*. See it as the small red door leading straight into the dark room of my childhood longing and disappointment. That red book *becomes* the palpable evidence of that longing. In other words, it becomes symbol. There is no symbol, no life-of-the-spirit in the general or the abstract. Yet a writer wishes—indeed all of us wish—to speak about profound matters that are, like it or not, general and abstract. We wish to talk to each other about life and death, about love, despair, loss, and innocence. We sense that in order to live together we must learn to speak of peace, of history, of meaning and values. Those are a few.

We seek a means of exchange, a language which will renew these ancient concerns and make them wholly and pulsingly ours. Instinctively, we go to our store of private images and associations for our authority to speak of these weighty issues. We find, in our details and broken and obscured images, the language of symbol. Here memory impulsively reaches out its arms and embraces imagination. That is the resort to invention. It isn't a lie, but an act of necessity, as the innate urge to locate personal truth always is.

All right. Invention is inevitable. But why write memoir? Why not call it fiction and be done with all the hashing about, wondering where memory stops and imagination begins? And if memoir seeks to talk about "the big issues," about history and peace, death and love—why not leave these reflections to those with expert and scholarly knowledge? Why let the common or garden variety memoirist into the club? I'm thinking again of that bumper sticker: why Question Authority?

My answer, of course, is a memoirist's answer. Memoir must be written because each of us must have a created version of the past. Created: that is, real, tangible, made of the stuff of a life lived in place and in history. And the down side of any created thing as well: we must live with a version that attaches us to our limitations, to the inevitable subjectivity of our points of view. We must acquiesce to our experience and our gift to transform experience into meaning and value. You tell me your story, I'll tell you my story.

If we refuse to do the work of creating this personal version of the past, someone else will do it for us. That is a scary political fact. "The struggle of man against power," a character in Milan Kundera's novel *The Book of Laughter and Forgetting* says, "is the struggle of memory against forgetting." He refers to willful political forgetting, the habit of nations and those in power (Question Authority!) to deny the truth of memory in order to disarm moral and ethical power. It's an efficient way of controlling masses of people. It doesn't even require much bloodshed, as long as people are entirely willing to give over their personal memories. Whole histories can be rewritten. As Czeslaw Milosz said in his 1980 Nobel Prize lecture, the number of books published that seek to deny the existence of the Nazi death camps now exceeds one hundred.

What is remembered is what *becomes* reality. If we "forget" Auschwitz, if we "forget" My Lai, what then do we remember? And what is the purpose of our remembering? If we think of memory naively, as a simple story, logged like a documentary in the archive of the mind, we miss its beauty but also its function. The beauty of memory rests in its talent for rendering detail, for paying homage to the senses, its capacity to love the particles of life, the richness and idiosyncrasy of our existence. The function of memory, on the other hand, is intensely personal and surprisingly political.

Our capacity to move forward as developing beings rests on a healthy relation with the past. Psychotherapy, that widespread method of mental health, relies heavily on memory and on the ability to retrieve and organize images and events from the personal past. We carry our wounds and perhaps even worse, our capacity to wound, forward with us. If we learn not only to tell our stories but to listen to what our stories tell us—to write the first draft and then return for the second draft—we are doing the work of memoir.

Memoir is the intersection of narration and reflection, of story-telling and essay-writing. It can present its story *and* reflect and consider the meaning of the story. It is a peculiarly open form, inviting broken and incomplete images, half-recollected fragments, all the mass (and mess) of detail. It offers to shape this confusion—and in shaping, of course it necessarily creates a work of art, not a legal document. But then, even legal documents are only valiant attempts to consign the truth, the whole truth and nothing but the truth to paper. Even they remain versions.

Locating touchstones—the red music book, the olive Olive, my father's violin playing—is deeply satisfying. Who knows why? Perhaps we all sense that we can't grasp the whole truth and nothing but the truth of our experience. Just can't be done. What can be achieved, however, is a version of its swirling, changing wholeness. A memoirist must acquiesce to selectivity, like any artist. The version we dare to write is the only truth, the only relationship we can have with the past. Refuse to write your life and you have no life. At least, that is the stern view of the memoirist.

Personal history, logged in memory, is a sort of slide projector flashing images on the wall of the mind. And there's precious little order to the slides in the rotating carousel. Beyond that confusion, who knows who is running the projector? A memoirist steps into this darkened room of flashing, unorganized images and stands blinking for a while. Maybe for a long while. But eventually, as with any attempt to tell a story, it is necessary to put something first, then something else. And so on, to the end. That's a first draft. Not necessarily the truth, not even *a* truth sometimes, but the first attempt to create a shape.

The first thing I usually notice at this stage of composition is the appalling inaccuracy of the piece. Witness my first piano lesson draft. Invention is screamingly evident in what I intended to be transcription. But here's the further truth: I feel no shame. In fact, it's only now that my interest in the piece truly quickens. For I can see what isn't there, what is shyly hugging the walls, hoping not to be seen. I see the filmy shape of the next draft. I see a more acute version of the episode or—this is more likely—an entirely new piece rising from the ashes of the first attempt.

The next draft of the piece would have to be a true re-vision, a new seeing of the materials of the first draft. Nothing merely cosmetic will do—no rouge buffing up the opening sentence, no glossy adjective to lift a sagging line, nothing to attempt covering a patch of gray writing. None of that. I can't say for sure, but my hunch is the revision would lead me to more writing about my father (why was I so impressed by that ancestral inventor of the collapsible opera hat? Did I feel I had nothing as remarkable in my own background? Did this make me feel inadequate?). I begin to think perhaps Sister Olive is less central to this business than she is in this draft. She is meant to be a moment, not a character.

And so I might proceed, if I were to undertake a new draft of the memoir. I begin to feel a relationship developing between a former self and me.

And, even more compelling, a relationship between an old world and me.

Some people think of autobiographical writing as the precious occupation of a particularly self-absorbed person. Maybe, but I don't buy that. True memoir is written in an attempt to find not only a self but a world.

The self-absorption that seems to be the impetus and embarrassment of autobiography turns into (or perhaps always was) a hunger for the world. Actually, it begins as hunger for *a* world, one gone or lost, effaced by time or a more sudden brutality. But in the act of remembering, the personal environment expands, resonates beyond itself, beyond its "subect," into the endless and tragic recollection that is history.

We look at old family photographs in which we stand next to black, boxy Fords and are wearing period costumes, and we do not gaze fascinated because there we are young again, or there we are standing, as we never will again in life, next to our mother. We stare and drift because there we are . . . historical. It is the dress, the black car that dazzle us now and draw us beyond our mother's bright arms which once caught us. We reach into the attractive impersonality of something more significant than ourselves. We write memoir, in other words. We accept the humble position of writing a version rather than "the whole truth."

I suppose I write memoir because of the radiance of the past—it draws me back and back to it. Not that the past is beautiful. In our commercial memoir, in history, the death camps *are* back there. In intimate life too, the record is usually pretty mixed. "I could tell you stories . . ." people say and drift off, meaning terrible things have happened to them.

But the past is radiant. It has the light of lived life. A memoirist wishes to touch it. No one owns the past, though typically the first act of new political regimes, whether of the left or the right, is to attempt to re-write history, to grab the past and make it over so the end comes out right. So their power looks inevitable.

No one owns the past, but it is a grave error (another age would have said a grave sin) not to inhabit memory. Sometimes I think it is all we really have. But that may be a trifle melodramatic. At any rate, memory possesses authority for the fearful self in a world where it is necessary to have authority in order to Question Authority.

There may be no more pressing intellectual need in our culture than for people to become sophisticated about the function of memory. The political implications of the loss of memory are obvious. The authority of memory is a personal confirmation of selfhood. To write one's life is to live it twice, and the second living is both spiritual and historical, for a memoir reaches deep within the personality as it seeks its narrative form and also grasps the life-of-the-times as no political treatise can.

Our most ancient metaphor says life is a journey. Memoir is travel writing, then, notes taken along the way, telling how things looked and what thoughts occurred. But I cannot think of the memoirist as a tourist. This is the traveller who goes on foot, living the journey, taking on mountains, enduring deserts, marveling at the lush green places. Moving through it all faithfully, not so much a survivor with a harrowing tale to tell as a pilgrim, seeking, wondering.

QUESTIONS AND CONSIDERATIONS

1. Why does Hampl begin with the story about Sister Olive Marie and her piano lessons? What insights into Hampl's personality and values does the story reveal? Did you identify with Hampl while reading her story? Why or why not?

2. How do your feelings about Hampl and her story change as she begins to develop her theory about the writing process and the relationship between writing and the imagination? Which of Hampl's ideas about the writing process interest you the most? For example, do you agree with her that a first draft should not be a careful draft? Do you believe that the heart is the "boss" of your writing?

3. How does Hampl define the difference between memoir and fiction in this essay? Does Hampl believe that one's memory and imagination can record the truth of an event? When you write or tell about your experiences, how conscious are you of shaping the events to reflect a factual or an objective truth?

4. Why does Hampl believe it is important to write about the important events in one's life? According to Hampl, in what sense is writing about one's memories a process of self-discovery and self-understanding? Do you agree with Hampl?

5. Discuss several of Hampl's metaphors or images that you thought were effective. Explain how these images helped to emphasize her meaning.

6. How has reading this essay changed your understanding of the relationships among truth, fact, and the imagination of the writer?

IDEAS FOR WRITING

1. Develop Question 4 into an essay. Use examples from your own experiences and from selections in the text to support your point of view.

2. Develop Question 6 into an essay. Use examples from your own experiences and from selections in the text to support your point of view.

Ordinary Spirit

Joy Harjo

Journal

Discuss a time when your family or your heritage encouraged you to write. Why did you value what you produced?

I was born in Tulsa, Oklahoma, on May 9, 1951, after a long, hard labor that occurred sporadically for over a week. My mother didn't know it was labor because I wasn't due until mid-July. I also surprised her because I was a single birth; she had been told to possibly expect twins. The birth was hard on both of us. I was kept alive on a machine for the first few days of my life until I made a decision to live. When I looked around I saw my mother, only nineteen, of mixed Cherokee and French blood, who had already worked hard for her short life. And my father, a few years older, a tall, good-looking Creek man who was then working as a mechanic for American Airlines. I don't think I was ever what they expected, but I am grateful that they made my life possible and honor them for it.

I was the first of four children who were born evenly spaced over the next eight years or so. And much later had my own children, Phil and Rainy Dawn. We are descended from a long line of tribal speakers and leaders from my father's side. Menawa, who led the Red Stick War against Andrew Jackson, is our great-great (and possibly another great) grandfather. I don't know much about the family on my mother's side except there were many rebels and other characters. They are all part of who I am, the root from which I write, even though I may not always name them.

I began writing around the time I was twenty-two years old. I am now thirty-four and feel that after all this time I am just beginning to learn to write. I am only now beginning to comprehend what poetry is, and what it can mean. Each time I write I am in a different and wild place, and travel toward something I do not know the name of. Each poem is a jumping-off edge and I am not safe, but I take more risks and understand better now how to take them. They do not always work, but when they do it is worth it. I could not live without writing and/or thinking about it. In fact, I don't have to think about it; it's there, some word, concept always being born or, just as easily, dying.

I walk in and out of many worlds. I used to see being born of this mixed-blood/mixed-vision a curse, and hated myself for it. It was too confusing and destructive when I saw the world through that focus. The only message I got was not belonging anywhere, not to any side. I have since decided that being familiar with more than one world, more than one vision, is a blessing, and know that I make my own choices. I also know that it is only an illusion that any of the worlds are separate.

It is around midnight. I often write at this time in my workroom near the front of an old Victorian-style house near downtown Denver. Tonight a thick snow has muffled the sounds of traffic. The world is quiet except for the sound of this typewriter humming, the sometimes dash of metallic keys, and the deep breathing of my dog who is asleep nearby. And then, in the middle of working, the world gives way and I see the old, old Creek one who comes in here and watches over me. He tries to make sense of this world in which his granddaughter has come to live. And often teases me about my occupation of putting words on paper.

I tell him that it is writing these words down, and entering the world through the structure they make, that has allowed me to see him more clearly, and to speak. And he answers that maybe his prayers, songs, and his belief in them has allowed him to create me.

We both laugh, and continue our work through many seasons.

This summer, during one of those sultry summer evenings when the air hums with a chorus of insects and there's the sound of children playing in the street, I sat, writing. Not actually writing but staring into that space above the typewriter where vision telescopes. I began remembering the way the world was before speech in childhood. A time when I was totally conscious of sound and conscious of being in a world in which the webbed connections between us all were translucent yet apparent. I remember what it felt like to live within that space, where every live thing had a voice, and each voice/sound an aurora of color. It was sometime during that reminiscence that I began this poem:

Summer Night

The moon is nearly full,
      the humid air sweet like melon.
Flowers that have cupped the sun all day
          dream of iridescent wings
under the long dark sleep.
      Children's invisible voices call out
in the glimmering moonlight.
        Their parents play wornout records
of the *cumbia*. Behind the screendoor
        their soft laughter swells
into the rhythm of a smooth guitar.
        I watch the world shimmer
inside this globe of a summer night,
        listen to the wobble of her
spin and dive. It happens all the time, waiting for you
        to come home.
There is an ache that begins
      in the sound of an old blues song.
It becomes a house where all the lights have gone out
        but one.
And it burns and burns
      until there is only the blue smoke of dawn
and everyone is sleeping in someone's arms
        even the flowers
even the sound of a thousand silences.
        And the arms of night
in the arms of day.
      Everyone except me.
But then the smell of damp honeysuckle twisted on the vine.
And the turn of the shoulder
      of the ordinary spirit who keeps watch
over this ordinary street
      And there you are, the secret
of your own flower of light
      blooming in the miraculous dark.
(from *Furious Light,* Watershed Foundation cassette, 1986)

For years I have wanted to capture that ache of a summer night. This summer in Denver was especially humid, reminded me of Oklahoma. I wanted to feel, in the poem, of a thick, sweet air. And I wanted the voices I remembered, my parents' talking and scratchy, faint music of the radio. In the poem it is my neighbors I hear, and their old records of the *cumbia*. I also wanted to sustain a blues mood, pay homage to the blues because I love the blues. There was the sound of a sensuous tenor saxophone beneath the whole poem. I also added the part of everyone being in someone else's arms, "everyone except me," for the blues effect.

But I did not want to leave the poem there, in the center of the ache; I wanted to resolve it. I looked out the front door into the night and caught a glimpse of someone standing near the streetlight, a protecting spirit who was keeping watch over the street. I could have made that up, but I believe it is true. And I knew the spirit belonged in the poem and, because the spirit lives in the poem, too, helps turn the poem around to a place of tender realization. Hence, "And there you are, the secret / of your own flower of light / blooming in the miraculous dark."

When I first began writing, poetry was simply a way for me to speak. I was amazed that I could write anything down and have it come out a little more than coherently. Over the years the process has grown more complicated, more intricate, and the world within the poem more immense. In another recent poem the process is especially important:

Transformations

This poem is a letter to tell you that I
have smelled the hatred you have tried
to find me with; you would like to destroy me.
Bone splintered in the eye of one you choose
to name your enemy won't make it better for you
to see. It could take a thousand years if you name it
that way, but then, to see after all that time, never
could anything be so clear. Memory has many forms.
When I think of early winter I think of a blackbird
laughing in the frozen air; guards a piece of light. I
saw the whole world caught in that sound. The sun
stopped for a moment because of tough belief. I don't
know what that has to do with what I am trying to tell you
except that I know you can turn a poem into something
else. This poem could be a bear treading the far northern
tundra, smelling the air for sweet alive meat. Or a piece
of seaweed stumbling in the sea. Or a blackbird, laughing.
What I mean is that hatred can be turned into something
else, if you have the right words, the right meanings
buried in that tender place in your heart where
the most precious animals live. Down the street
an ambulance has come to rescue an old man who is slowly
losing his life. Not many can see that he is already
becoming the backyard tree he has tended for years,
before he moves on. He is not sad, but compassionate

for the fears moving around him.
That's what I mean to tell you. On the other side
of the place you live stands a dark woman.
She has been trying to talk to you for years.
You have called the same name in the middle of a nightmare,
from the center of miracles. She is beautiful.
This is your hatred back. She loves you.

When I began writing the poem, I knew I wanted an actual transformation to be enacted within it. I began with someone's hatred, which was a tangible thing, and wanted to turn it into love by the end of the poem. I was also interested in the process of becoming. I tried to include several states of becoming. The "process of the poem" becoming was one. I entered the poem very consciously with lines such as, "I don't know what that has to do with what I am trying to tell you," and "What I mean is . . ." I also consciously switched tenses partly for that reason, and others. I often change tense within a poem and do so knowing what I am doing. It isn't by accident that it happens. Time doesn't realistically work in a linear fashion.

Within the poem is also the process of the "hater" becoming one who is loved, and who ultimately loves. The "I" is also involved in the process.

Earlier in the day an ambulance came into the neighborhood to pick up an elderly neighbor who had suffered a stroke and was near death. It was a major event. All who witnessed it walked carefully through the rest of the day. I was still thinking of him when I wrote the poem and knew that somehow he, too, belonged in the poem, for he was also part of the transformation.

I was not sure how the poem would end when I began writing it, but looking back I realize the ending must have originated in one of two places. One was a story I heard from a woman who during times of deep emotional troubles would be visited by a woman who looked just like her. She herself would never see her, but anyone passing by her room while she was asleep would see this imaginary woman, standing next to her bed. I always considered the "imaginary" woman as her other self, the denied self who wanted back in.

And I was reminded, too, of the woman who had followed me around at an all-night party in Santa Fe a few years before. We had all drifted around the house, talking, dancing, filled with music and whatever else we had tasted. She finally caught up with me around dawn and told me that she was sorry she was white, and then told me that she believed white people had no souls. I was shocked and sad. And I saw her soul, starved but thinly beautiful, knocking hard on the wall of cocaine and self-hatred she was hiding behind.

So the poem becomes a way of speaking to her.

It is now very late and I will let someone else take over this story. Maybe the cricket who likes to come in here and sing and who probably knows a better way to write a poem than me.

It is not the last song, but to name anything that, only means that I would continue to be amazed at the creation of any new music.

QUESTIONS FOR DISCUSSION

1. Why does Harjo begin by sharing her family's heritage? How has her family's heritage influenced and helped her to develop an identity as a writer? In what ways has your own family's heritage influenced you? Did your family encourage you to value writing?

2. How does Harjo experience and define the process of writing poetry?

3. What solace does writing bring Harjo? Does writing sometimes bring you solace or peace of mind? When and how?

4. How does Harjo come to accept and value her cultural heritage?

5. How does the inclusion of the poems "Summer Night" and "Transformations" enrich the meaning of Harjo's essay?

6. Why is the title, "Ordinary Spirit," appropriate? How does Harjo define and show that she values her "ordinary" spirit in her essay?

IDEAS FOR WRITING

1. Compare and contrast your reasons for writing and your writing process with Harjo's. How might you apply her ideas and strategies to your own writing?

2. Write a poem or short story about an important transformation in your life that illustrates your particular cultural and emotional dilemmas.

Coming to Voice
Bell Hooks

Journal

Discuss an experience in which expressing your point of view felt like an act of liberation, a breaking free from limiting social or cultural expectations.

Angela Davis spoke these words. They moved me. I say them here and hope to say them in many places. This is how deeply they touched me—evoking memories of innocence, of initial passionate commitment to political struggle. They were spoken in a talk she gave at a conference focussing on "Poetry and Politics: Afro-American Poetry Today." I began writing poetry when I was young, ten years old. Poetry came into my life, the sense of poetry, with reading scripture with those awkward and funny little rhymes we would memorize and recite on Easter Sunday. Then it came into my life at Booker T. Washington grade school where I learned that poetry was no silent subject. That moment of learning was pure enchantment, for we learned by listening and reciting that words put together just so, said just so, could have the same impact on our psyches as song, could lift and exalt our spirits, enabling us to feel tremendous joy, or carrying us down into that most immediate and violent sense of loss and grief.

Like many African-Americans, I became a writer through making poems. Poetry was one literary expression that was absolutely respected in our working-class household. Nights when the lights would go out, when storms were raging, we would sit in the dim candlelight of our living room and have a talent show. I would recite poems: Wordsworth, James Weldon Johnson, Langston Hughes, Elizabeth Barrett Browning, Emily Dickinson, Gwendolyn Brooks, poetry by white writers was always there in schools and on family bookshelves in anthologies of "great" works sold to us by door-to-door salesmen, book peddlers, who came spreading their wares as though we were a dark desert people and they weary travelers bringing us light from a faraway place. Poetry by black writers had to be searched for, a poem copied from books no one would let you borrow for fear of loss, or taken from books found by puzzled white southern librarians eager to see that you "read right." I was in high school before I discovered James Weldon Johnson's collection of *American Negro Poetry*. It had never been checked out of the library even though it had been on the shelves for some time. I would keep this book as long as I could, working to memorize every poem so I would know them all by heart.

For me, poetry was the place for the secret voice, for all that could not be directly stated or named, for all that would not be denied expression. Poetry was privileged speech—simple at times, but never ordinary. The magic of poetry was transformation; it was words changing shape, meaning, and form. Poetry was not mere recording of the way we southern black folks talked to one another, even though our language was poetic. It was transcendent speech. It was meant to transform consciousness, to carry the mind and heart to a new dimension. These were my primitive thoughts on poetry as I experienced and knew it growing up.

When I became a student in college creative writing classes, I learned a notion of "voice" as embodying the distinctive expression of an individual writer. Our efforts to become poets were to be realized in this coming into awareness and expression of one's voice. In all my writing classes, I was the only black student. Whenever I read a poem written in the particular dialect of southern black speech, the teacher and fellow students would praise me for using my "true," authentic voice, and encouraged me to develop this "voice," to write more of these poems. From the onset this troubled me. Such comments seemed to mask racial biases about what my authentic voice would or should be.

In part, attending all-black segregated schools with black teachers meant that I had come to understand black poets as being capable of speaking in many voices, that the Dunbar of a poem written in dialect was no more or less authentic than the Dunbar writing a sonnet. Yet it was listening to black musicians like Duke Ellington, Louis Armstrong, and later John Coltrane that impressed upon our consciousness a sense of versatility—they played all kinds of music, had multiple voices. So it was with poetry. The black poet, as exemplified by Gwendolyn Brooks and later Amiri Baraka, had many voices—with no single voice being identified as more or less authentic. The insistence on finding one voice, one definitive style of writing and reading one's poetry, fit all too neatly with a static notion of self and identity that was pervasive in university settings. It seemed that many black students found our situations problematic precisely because our sense of self, and by definition our voice, was not unilateral, monologist, or static but rather multi-dimensional. We were as at home in dialect as we were in standard English. Individuals who speak languages other than English, who speak patois as well as standard English, find it a necessary aspect of self-affirmation not to feel compelled to choose one voice over another, not to claim one as more authentic, but rather to construct social realities that celebrate, acknowledge, and affirm differences, variety. In *Borderlands: La Frontera,* Gloria Anzaldúa writes of the need to claim all the tongues in which we speak, to make speech of the many languages that give expression to the unique cultural reality of a people:

> For a people who are neither Spanish nor live in a country in which Spanish is the first language; for a people who live in a country in which English is the reigning tongue but who are not Anglo, for a people who cannot entirely identify with either standard (formal, Castilian) Spanish nor standard English, what recourse is left to them but to create their own language? A language which they can connect their identity to, one capable of communicating the realities and values true to themselves . . .

In recent years, any writing about feminism has overshadowed writing as a poet. Yet there are spaces where thoughts and concerns converge. One such space has been the feminist focus on coming to voice—on moving from silence into speech as revolutionary gesture. Once again, the idea of finding one's voice or having a voice assumes a primacy in talk, discourse, writing, and action. As metaphor for self-transformation, it has been especially relevant for groups of women who have previously never had a public voice, women who are speaking and writing for the first time, including many women of color. Feminist focus on finding a voice may seem clichéd at times, especially when the insistence is that women share a common speech or that all women have something meaningful to say at all times. However, for women within oppressed groups who have contained so many feelings—despair, rage, anguish—who do not speak, as poet Audre Lorde writes, "for fear our words will not be heard nor welcomed," coming to voice is an act of resistance. Speaking becomes both a way to engage in active self-transformation and a rite of passage where one moves from being object to being subject. Only as subjects can we speak. As objects, we remain voiceless—our beings defined and interpreted by others. It is this liberating speech that Mariana Romo-Carmona writes about in her introduction to *Compañeras: Latina Lesbians:*

> Each time a woman begins to speak, a liberating process begins, one that is unavoidable and has powerful political implications. In these pages we see repeated the process of self-discovery, of affirmation in coming out of the closet, the search for a definition of our identity within the family and out community, the search for answers, for meaning in our personal struggles, and the com-

mitment to a political struggle to end all forms of oppression. The stages of increasing awareness become clear when we begin to recount the story of our lives to someone else, someone who has experienced the same changes. When we write or speak about these changes we establish our experiences as valid and real, we begin to analyze, and that analysis gives us the necessary perspective to place our lives in a context where we know what to do next.

Awareness of the need to speak, to give voice to the varied dimensions of our lives, is one way women of color begin the process of education for critical consciousness.

Need for such speech is often validated in writings by people engaged in liberation struggles in the Third World, in the literatures of people struggling globally from oppression and domination. El Salvadoran writer Manlio Argueta structures his powerful novel, *One Day Of Life,* around the insistence on the development of political awareness, the sharing of knowledge that makes the revolutionary thinker and activist. It is the character José who is most committed to sharing his awareness with family and community, and most importantly with Lupé, his friend and wife, to whom he says:

> that's why the problems can't be solved by a single person, but only by all of us working together, the humble, the clearheaded ones. And this is very important; you can be humble and live in darkness. Well, the thing is not a matter of being or not being humble. The problem lies in our awareness. The awareness we will have. Then life will become as clear as spring water.

I first read this novel in a course I taught on Third World literature and it was clear then that speaking freely, openly has different meaning for people from exploited and oppressed groups.

Non-literary works by writers opposing domination also speak to the primacy of coming to voice, of speaking for the oppressed. In keeping with this emphasis on speech, Alicia Partnoy proclaims, in her brave work, *The Little School: Tales of Disappearance and Survival in Argentina,* "They cut off my voice so I grew two voices, into different tongues my songs I pour." Here speech has a dual implication. There is the silence of the oppressed who have never learned to speak and there is the voice of those who have been forcefully silenced because they have dared to speak and by doing so resist. Egyptian writer Nawal el Sa'adawi protests against such silences in her *Memoirs From The Women's Prison.* She dedicated her book "To all who have hated oppression to the point of death, who have loved freedom to the point of imprisonment, and have rejected falsehood to the point of revolution." Or the resistance to being silenced Theresa Had Cha describes in *Dictee:*

> Mother, you are a child still. At eighteen. More of a child since you are always ill. They have sheltered you from the others. It is not your own. Even if it not you know you must. You are bi-lingual. You are tri-lingual. The tongue that is forbidden is your own mother tongue. You speak in the dark, in the secret. The

one that is yours. Your own . . . Mother tongue is your refuge. It is being home. Being who you are. Truly. To speak makes you sad. To utter each word is a privilege you risk by death.

In fiction as well as in confessional writing, those who understand the power of voice as gesture of rebellion and resistance urge the exploited, the oppressed to speak.

To speak as an act of resistance is quite different than ordinary talk, or the personal confession that has no relation to coming into political awareness, to developing critical consciousness. This is a difference we must talk about in the United States, for here the idea of finding a voice risks being trivialized or romanticized in the rhetoric of those who advocate a shallow feminist politic which privileges acts of speaking over the content of speech. Such rhetoric often turns the voices and beings of non-white women into commodity, spectacle. In a white-supremacist, capitalist, patriarchal state where the mechanisms of co-optation are so advanced, much that is potentially radical is undermined, turned into commodity, fashionable speech as in "black women writers are in right now." Often the question of who is listening and what is being heard are not answered. When reggae music became popular in the United States, I often pondered whether the privileged white people who listened were learning from this music to resist, to rebel against white supremacy and white imperialism. What did they hear when Bob Marley said, "we refuse to be what you wanted us to be"—did they think about colonization, about internalized racism? One night at a Jimmy Cliff concert attended predominantly by young white people, Cliff began a call and response refrain where we the listeners were to say "Africa for Africans." There was suddenly a hush in the room, as though the listeners finally heard the rebellion against white supremacy, against imperialism in the lyrics. They were silent, unable apparently to share in this gesture affirming black solidarity. Who is listening and what do they hear?

Appropriation of the marginal voice threatens the very core of self-determination and free self-expression for exploited and oppressed peoples. If the identified audience, those spoken to, is determined solely by ruling groups who control production and distribution, then it is easy for the marginal voice striving for a hearing to allow what is said to be overdetermined by the needs of that majority group who appears to be listening, to be tuned in. It becomes easy to speak about what that group wants to hear, to describe and define experience in a language compatible with existing images and ways of knowing, constructed within social frameworks that reinforce domination. Within any situation of colonization, of domination, the oppressed, the exploited develop various styles of relating, talking one way to one another, talking another way to those who have power to oppress and dominate, talking in a way that allows one to be understood by someone who does not know your way of speaking, your language. The struggle to end domination, the individual struggle to resist colonization, to move from object to subject, is expressed in the effort to establish the liberatory voice—that way of speaking that is no longer determined by one's status as object—as oppressed being. That way of speaking is characterized by opposition, by resistance. It demands that paradigms shift—that we learn to talk—to listen—to hear in a new way.

To make the liberated voice, one must confront the issue of audience—we must know to whom we speak. When I began writing my first book, *Ain't I A Woman: black women and feminism,* the initial completed manuscript was excessively long and very repetitious. Reading it critically, I saw that I was trying not only to address each different potential audience—black men, white women, white men, etc.—but that my words were written to explain, to placate, to appease. They contained the fear of speaking that often characterizes the way those in a lower position within a hierarchy address those in a higher position of authority. Those passages where I was speaking most directly to black women contained the voice I felt to be most truly mine—it was then that my voice was daring, courageous. When I thought about audience—the way in which the language we choose to use declares who it is we place at the center of our discourse—I confronted my fear of placing myself and other black women at the speaking center. Writing this book was for me a radical gesture. It not only brought me face-to-face with this question of power; it forced me to resolve this question, to act, to find my voice, to become that subject who could place herself and those like her at the center of feminist discourse. I was transformed in consciousness and being.

When the book was first published, white women readers would often say to me, "I don't feel this book is really talking to me." Often these readers would interpret the direct, blunt speech as signifying anger and I would have to speak against this interpretation and insist upon the difference between direct speech and hostility. At a discussion once where a question about audience was raised, I responded by saying that while I would like readers to be diverse, the audience I most wanted to address was black women, that I wanted to place us at the center. I was asked by a white woman, "How can you do that in a cultural context where black women are not primary book buyers and white women are the principle buyers of feminist books?" It seemed that she was suggesting that audience should be determined by who buys certain books. It had never occurred to me that white women would not buy a book if they did not see themselves at the center because, more than any group of people I could identify, white people have travelled the globe consuming cultural artifacts that did not place them at the center. My placement of black women at the center was not an action to exclude others but rather an invitation, a challenge to those who would hear us speak, to shift paradigms rather than appropriate, to have all readers listen to the voice of a black woman speaking a subject and not as underprivileged other. I wrote *Ain't I A Woman* not to inform white women about black women but rather as an expression of my longing to know more and think deeply about our experience.

In celebrating our coming to voice, Third World women, African-American women must work against speaking as "other," speaking to difference as it is constructed in the white-supremacist imagination. It is therefore crucial that we search our hearts and our words to see if our true aim is liberation, to make sure they do not suppress, trap, or confine. Significantly, knowing who is listening provides an indication of how our voices are heard. My words are heard differently by the oppressive powerful. They are heard in a different way by black women who, like me, are struggling to recover ourselves from the ravages of colonization. To know our audience, to know who listens, we must be in dialogue. We must be speaking with and not just speaking to. In hearing responses, we come to understand whether our words act to resist, to transform, to move. In a consumer culture where we are all led to believe that the value of our voice is not determined by the extent to which it challenges, or makes critical reflection possible, but rather by whether or not it (and sometimes even we) is liked, it is difficult to keep a liberatory message. It is difficult to maintain a sense of direction, a strategy for liberated speaking, if we do not constantly challenge these standards of valuation. When I first began to talk publicly about my work, I would be disappointed when audiences were provoked and challenged but seemed to disapprove. Not only was my desire for approval naive (I have since come to understand that it is silly to think that one can challenge and also have approval), it was dangerous precisely because such a longing can undermine radical commitment, compelling a change in voice so as to gain regard.

Speaking out is not a simple gesture of freedom in a culture of domination. We are often deceived (yes, even those of us who have experienced domination) by the illusion of free speech, falsely believing that we can say whatever we wish in an atmosphere of openness. There would be no need to even speak of the oppressed and exploited coming to voice, articulating and redefining reality, if there were not oppressive mechanisms of silencing, suppressing, and censoring. Thinking we speak in a climate where freedom is valued, we are often shocked to find ourselves assaulted, our words devalued. It should be understood that the liberatory voice will necessarily confront, disturb, demand that listeners even alter ways of hearing and being. I remember talking with Angela Davis a few years ago about the death threats that she often received before speaking. Our conversation had a profound effect on my consciousness, on me as a listener; it changed my understanding of what it means to speak from a radical position in this society. When one threatens—one is at risk.

Often I am amazed as a teacher in the classroom at the extent to which students are afraid to speak. A young black woman student wrote these words to me:

> My voice is not fit to be heard by 120 people. To produce such a voice, my temperature increases and my hands shake. My voice is calm and quiet and soothing; it is not a means of announcing the many secrets my friends have told me—it quiets the rush of the running stream that is their life, slowing to make a mirror to reflect their worries, so that they can be examined and prob-

lems rectified. I am not relieved by voicing my opinions. Placing my opinion up to be judged by the public is a form of opening myself to criticism and pain. Those who do not share my eyes cannot see where to tread lightly on me.

I am afraid. I am, and will always be afraid. My fear is that I will not be understood. I try to learn the vocabulary of my friends to ensure my communication on their terms. There is no singular vocabulary of 120 people. I will be misunderstood; I will not be respected as a speaker; they will name me Stupid in their minds; they will disregard me. I am afraid.

Encouraging students to speak, I tell them to imagine what it must mean to live in a culture where to speak one risks brutal punishment—imprisonment, torture, death. I ask them to think about what it means that they lack the courage to speak in a culture where there are few if any consequences. Can their fear be understood solely as shyness or is it an expression of deeply embedded, socially constructed restrictions against speech in a culture of domination, a fear of owning one's words, of taking a stand? Audre Lorde's poem, "Litany for Survival," addresses our fear of speech and urges us to overcome it:

and when we speak we are afraid
our words will not be heard
nor welcomed
but when we are silent
we are still afraid

So it is better to speak
remembering
we were never meant to survive.

To understand that finding a voice is an essential part of liberation struggle—for the oppressed, the exploited a necessary starting place—a move in the direction of freedom, is important for those who stand in solidarity with us. That talk which identifies us as uncommitted, as lacking in critical consciousness, which signifies a condition of oppression and exploitation, is utterly transformed as we engage in critical reflection and as we act to resist domination. We are prepared to struggle for freedom only when this groundwork has been laid.

When we dare to speak in a liberatory voice, we threaten even those who may initially claim to want our words. In the act of overcoming our fear of speech, of being seen as threatening, in the process of learning to speak as subjects, we participate in the global struggle to end domination. When we end our silence, when we speak in a liberated voice, our words connect us with anyone, anywhere who lives in silence. Feminist focus on women finding a voice, on the silence of black women, of women of color, has led to increased interest in our words. This is an important historical moment. We are both speaking of our own volition, out of our commitment to justice, to revolutionary struggle to end domination, and simultaneously called to speak, "invited" to share our words. It is important that we speak. What we speak about is more important. It is our responsibility collectively and individually to distinguish be-tween mere speaking that is about self-aggrandizement, exploitation of the ex-otic "other," and that coming to voice which is a gesture of resistance, an affir-mation of struggle.

QUESTIONS AND CONSIDERATIONS

1. Why does hooks believe that hearing poetry read aloud brings it to life? Do you agree with her?

2. Why is poetry "the place for the secret voice"? How does hooks explain the trans-formative power of poetry? Have you ever experienced the transformative power of po-etry as hooks describes it?

3. Why is hooks critical of the concept of voice as it is defined by her creative writ-ing teachers? According to hooks, how do feminists understand the power of voice? How did hooks find the power of her own voice?

4. Why does hooks think that her audience plays a crucial role in helping her to ar-ticulate her ideas and feelings? Do you ever consider the audience for your writing in a way that is similar to the way hooks is responsive to her audience?

5. According to hooks, when is coming to voice a "gesture of resistance, affirmation and struggle"? Do you agree with her on this point?

6. Discuss several examples and key images in hooks' essay that clarify her relation-ship to the dominant class and to her inner life.

IDEAS FOR WRITING

1. Write about an incident in which you spoke out honestly, when your voice be-came a gesture of resistance and an affirmation of struggle. Were you changed by this ex-perience? How?

2. Discuss the concept of voice in writing? Discuss several different but effective uses of voice by writers in this text.

Pushing Through

Jimmy Santiago Baca

Journal

Why do you think a person becomes a writer? How does a person develop his or her sense of identity and role as a writer?

I was never much for taking advice, although I think that in a great many in-stances it would have helped. I wanted to experience everything, even at the risk of making big mistakes. I wanted to explore the interior of people's minds, to understand why they did what they did, and I wanted to find this out for myself. When anyone tried to give me advice, their words coming towards me melted away like snowflakes touching fire. My character was formed through adversity and tender hope, like initials scratched into prison walls.

Young poet, you who may read these lines, let me tell you honestly how it was with me in my youth, in the hope that it may help in your own struggle. I wanted to embrace all of life, the beautiful and the ugly, to sit with cowards and warriors and listen to them all. I never aspired to be right, or govern my life by theory, imperiously pointing at others the finger of righteousness.

I love struggle, and my wounds are the proud insignia from encounters into which I have flung myself fully, with no holding back. And this life, lived in the moment without reservation, has been packed with glittering success and bleak misfortune. I've played both, shaved the thickness from both, as a blues pianist wears down the black and white keys, as a hobo wears down the soles of his shoes with the miles.

I've looked for a place in America where I could say, "Ah, this is it, yes, I'll settle here. I'll stay." I never came to that place, but along the way I have met with remarkable people who nourished my poems. When I am an old man looking back on my life, there'll be no regrets for roads not taken.

Don't depend on America to tell you who you are. Don't let yourself be tempted to become a mere linguist who dabbles in poetry for thrills or academic distinction. Reject the killing safety of literary workshops, of universities. Don't fear the jagged emotion, but tongue the sweet sap of your terror and joy; follow the tap-root that drives deep into your soul and touches the primal core of molten light that feeds all life in the universe.

Write to the maddened drum of your own passions, and don't let your imagination be tamed by the sterile pronouncements of critics. Let the hours cocoon in your heart and grow wings to fly across the continents of your imagination till they die at your feet.

Each true poem is a pearl-handled pistol you point at your heart. You twirl the cylinder of language and squeeze the trigger. The poem may reveal your weaknesses, but it will tell you how to live. It will bring you face to face with the truth. Real poems disarm us and lift us out of ourselves. They shoot sparks as from fire-blackened logs, and for an instant we leave the darkness and become scintillant beings.

There is a boulder suspended in the middle of me. The crude substance of which we are made, what is given to us genetically, is like a dense boulder. The exercise of creativity wears the stone down to a pebble, to dust and steam and air, volcano-breath.

A true poem is starlight that has reached earth.

I had a dream in a time when I was trying to kick the lingering effects of drug abuse. I would do okay for a month or so, but then I would start to use again. It was hard to deal the last blow to my habit.

In this dream there appeared a beautiful horse at my half-opened back door. I knew I had to go out and ride the horse, to mount it and ride it down, but it was wild. Probably I would get thrown and kicked and break a bone or two, but I had to risk it, it was my task to tame that horse by my own sheer power. But I was afraid.

As I was staring at the horse, it reared and stamped, challenging me. Then my wife appeared behind me and her eyes told me that there was another way. Stepping past me, she held the door open and lifted and extended her hand. She walked toward the horse slowly, until she had covered half the distance to where he stood. And the horse then went to meet her, uncertainly, hesitantly, until the two were face to face. My wife reached out and caressed his nose and went to his side and brushed his mane with her fingertips. He had become tame and trusting.

I knew that the dream was telling me that all my life I had taken on my problems by force, trying to change my life with force and through confrontation. But now it was time to try a different way, a deeper and more peaceful way, of love, and trust, and surrender.

As I walked out toward him, the horse lifted his head suddenly and his eyes were full of mistrustful fury. But when I reached out my hand he allowed me slowly to touch his head.

I was changed by that dream. Young poet, listen to your dreams.

In the orphanage one bright Sunday morning, the sun shone through all the dining hall windows. That extraordinary light made life seem a fairy tale for a small boy of six. Sundays were visiting days and hard for me, because I had no one to visit me. We had just come from Mass and I sat down at a table with five other boys. We fought over the bread on the platter in the middle of the table and we poured out fresh milk from a silver pitcher.

I looked out the window and saw a group of women in pretty dresses who had just arrived to visit. The thought came to me that one of them was my mother. I left the room to get a closer look, walking down the long corridors to where the guests would enter. Halfway down the hall, Sister Anna Louise stopped me and ordered me back to the dining hall. I started to obey, but as soon as I reached the loud dining hall I turned away to run back down the corridor. I was compelled to see the face of that woman, to be near her, to sniff her perfume and let my eyes devour her.

But Sister Anna Louise caught me again and, grasping my shirt to hold me still, began to beat me, flailing at my body and slapping my face until it went numb. I looked at her, and I knew she was out of control. Her face was contorted, swollen and crimson, and her eyes were blue beads of ice lit with small points of flame. She was unleashing upon me the fury of all that was unfulfilled in her. At last I went limp; and a part of myself fled to hide where no one could touch it.

I couldn't return to the dining hall. I lay crumpled on the hall tiles, dizzy and hot and bruised from the beating. But my one burning thought was that now I would not get to see the woman I hoped was my mother. That was the horrible, unacceptable reality. My whole universe fell in upon itself, black and toxic.

Now I would not see, maybe never see, that woman who meant all life and all love to me.

Finding no outlet for my rage, I spent years in a drug-haze, endless lost days of drug-taking, crazy partying. In our drug-blitzes, all things straight and good were branded by my friends and me as hypocrisy, to us the worst of sins. We created our own distorted code that reversed the order of the universe. We believed that our suffering gave us that license.

In the drug world, night and day were one. Loud music was always blaring, the phones were always ringing, there was always food cooking, and people talking at each other in wild soliloquies.

We could not live with our failures and our doubts. So we turned up the music, turned on the booze and drugs, deceiving ourselves that in so doing we were creating another and better world. But it was a world that lacked all meaning. You must have meaning to live, and meaning comes only from long and honest struggle of the soul.

I made a paper airplane of my youthful heart. Its innocence burned in the fires of violence. But my heart never forgot its first innocence and hunger for beauty.

Cry out when the heart yearns to do so, young poet, and love your loneliness. Trust in the wisdom not accessible to reason. Let nothing be more important to you than the process of the poem. Read the poets; and eschew political theories, religious systems. Let poetry be your open space that you traverse with courage. Be true to your calling. Then may your words touch the multitudes, as a mother's kiss falls on the face of a dreaming child.

But advice, all advice, is like stale meat turning bad. I like my meals freshly cooked, by my own flame. So here I am, simply standing next to you, side by side, sharing with you some things that have inspired me to dance and forget myself in song. For all that, I still stumble like a fool, trying to make sense of my life.

To the poet has been given the power to conjure up winter in midsummer, if his heart so desires. He can sing the most hidden secrets of the heart. And these are gifts from God, before whom I lay prone, my face to the earth, in thanksgiving.

I have been a convict, an addict to booze and drugs; and the lover of life and juggler of words I am still. Here, in the park, see the man selling ice cream, the balloon man. Over there people are sitting on the grass. Two little girls screech with happiness at the pigeons following them. The church bells greet the sauntering crowds in their Sunday best. Upstairs, in a room off the common square, a man rises and pukes his guts into the toilet, the bitterness of last night's whiskey stings his chapped lips. Next door a man covers a woman, their hastily shed clothing mixed together on the floor. They whisper and sigh, grunt, and gyrate into each other as the sun illumines the floating dust motes that drift through the window.

I have given myself a lot of bad advice, but things are getting better. I don't hurt myself as much as I used to. Now, when I dive into an image of life, into the glistening metaphor, into the water, I don't crack my head as often. I believe that the water is deeper than I can see. I can't see bottom and I never will, but sometimes I can touch it. Now when I write, it's like the first time I felt my fingertips touch the bottom of a swimming pool. There was triumph in that, bravery and accomplishment. I don't come up bleeding anymore.

My life is a musical score, and each dawn I wake to play my trumpet notes to the new day, a new page turned. I step out among the trees like a child who has wandered far from his parents, into a forest. I don't understand why certain leaves are turning gray. I want to be with that tree and follow it to a place it knows, to the source of life, where one can be what he dreams, through the faith of the poem.

QUESTIONS AND CONSIDERATIONS

1. According to Baca, what drives people to want to write and express themselves? How did Baca learn to write?

2. Interpret both of Baca's claims about what a poem is: "Each true poem is a pearl-handled pistol you point at your heart" and "A true poem is starlight that has reached earth." In what ways do the meanings of the two metaphors contrast with and embellish each other?

3. What is the effect of Baca's use of similes and metaphors? List and discuss several of the images that you found expressive and that helped you to understand better his ideas and experiences.

4. Baca gives an example of one of his dreams that changed his life and interprets it for his readers. Is his approach (the presentation and interpretation of the dream) effective? Why or why not? Write down one of your dreams that helped you to understand yourself better and to change. Try to interpret your dream and then share your dream and interpretation with your class.

5. What is the interrelationship among Baca's beating by Sister Anna Louise, his drug abuse, his recovery, and his commitment to life as a poet?

6. How does Baca feel about advice? What advice does he have for himself and for other writers?

IDEAS FOR WRITING

1. In his essay Baca suggests that writing is an act closely related to one's dreams and unconscious mind. After explaining how you think that Baca understands the relationships between his dreams and his writing, explore the relationships you have experienced between the writing process and dreaming and the unconscious mind.

2. Write an essay similar to Baca's in which you discuss some of the strong experiences that influenced your character and your sense of yourself as a writer.

Poetry

Ode on a Grecian Urn

John Keats

Journal

*Write about an experience of looking at an old painting or sculpture that
captured your imagination and "transported" you out of your own life and into
another time and culture.*

I

Thou still unravish'd bride of quietness,
    Thou foster-child of silence and slow time,
Sylvan historian, who canst thus express
    A flowery tale more sweetly than our rhyme:
What leaf-fring'd legend haunts about thy shape   5
    Of deities or mortals, or of both,
        In Tempe or the dales of Arcady?
    What men or gods are these? What maidens loth?
What mad pursuit? What struggle to escape?
        What pipes and timbrels? What wild ecstasy?   10

II

Heard melodies are sweet, but those unheard
    Are sweeter; therefore, ye soft pipes, play on;
Not to the sensual ear, but, more endear'd,
    Pipe to the spirit ditties of no tone:
Fair youth, beneath the trees, thou canst not leave   15
    Thy song, nor ever can those trees be bare;
        Bold Lover, never, never canst thou kiss,
Though winning near the goal—yet, do not grieve;
    She cannot fade, though thou hast not thy bliss,
        For ever wilt thou love, and she be fair!   20

III

Ah, happy, happy boughs! that cannot shed
    Your leaves, nor ever bid the Spring adieu;
And, happy melodist, unwearied,

For ever piping songs for ever new;
    More happy love! more happy, happy love!   25
        For ever warm and still to be enjoy'd,
            For ever panting, and for ever young;
    All breathing human passion far above,
        That leaves a heart high-sorrowful and cloy'd,
            A burning forehead, and a parching tongue.   30

IV

Who are these coming to the sacrifice?
    To what green altar, O mysterious priest,
Lead'st thou that heifer lowing at the skies,
    And all her silken flanks with garlands drest?
What little town by river or sea shore,   35
    Or mountain-built with peaceful citadel,
        Is emptied of this folk, this pious morn?
And, little town, thy streets for evermore
    Will silent be; and not a soul to tell
        Why thou art desolate, can e'er return.   40

V

O Attic shape! Fair attitude! with brede
    Of marble men and maidens overwrought,
With forest branches and the trodden weed;
    Thou, silent form, dost tease us out of thought
As doth eternity: Cold Pastoral!   45
    When old age shall this generation waste,
        Thou shalt remain, in midst of other woe
    Than ours, a friend to man, to whom thou say'st,
"Beauty is truth, truth beauty,"—that is all
    Ye know on earth, and all ye need to know.   50

QUESTIONS AND CONSIDERATIONS

1. In the first stanza Keats personifies the urn. To what different types of people does he compare the urn? Why does he make these comparisons?

2. What questions does the speaker ask about the urn in stanza I and stanza IV? Are the questions answered through the development of the poem?

3. What image on the surface of the urn does the second stanza capture? What comment does the stanza make on the "unheard" melodies? Do you agree with the speaker's point of view on "unheard" melodies?

4. What lines in the third stanza suggest that the love and beauty imagined by the mind and spirit are more powerful and enduring than human passions? Do you agree with the speaker on this point?

5. Are you convinced by the poem's conclusion: "Beauty is truth, truth beauty, that is all/Ye know on earth, and all ye need to know"?

6. What does the poem imply about the relationships between the individual human lover and the creator and the role of art?

IDEAS FOR WRITING

1. Write an essay in which you agree or disagree with the idea that the perception of truth and beauty by the spirit and the imagination are more rewarding and meaningful than the human experience of passion and love.

2. Write a poem or a personal essay in which you enter into the world of a work of art imaginatively, describing and re-creating it in words as Keats does.

The Secret
Denise Levertov

Journal

*Write about a time when you felt imaginatively and creatively involved
in a work you were reading. What did you learn from this
experience?*

Two girls discover
the secret of life
in a sudden line of
poetry.

I who don't know the   5
secret wrote
the line. They
told me

(through a third person)
they had found it   10
but not what it was,
not even

what line it was. No doubt
by now, more than a week
later, they have forgotten   15
the secret,

the line, the name of
the poem. I love them

for finding what
I can't find,   20

and for loving me
for the line I wrote:
and for forgetting it
so that

a thousand times, till death   25
finds them, they may
discover it again, in other
lines,

in other
happenings. And for   30
wanting to know it,
for

assuming there is
such a secret, yes,
for that   35
most of all.

QUESTIONS AND CONSIDERATIONS

1. What secret do the two girls discover in a line of poetry?

2. Who is the speaker in the poem? How does the speaker feel about the girls' "discovery"?

3. Why is it significant that the girls reveal neither the poem, the line of the poem that contained the secret, "or what the "secret" is?

4. Does the fact that the girls are likely to forget the secret in a week make its discovery less significant? Is this "forgetting" an important part of the act of reading?

5. Why is it particularly significant that the secret of life that the girls have found through reading is something the author herself can't find? What does this suggest about the role of imagination and creativity in the act of reading?

6. Why do you think this poem about "the secret of life" is written in such a simple, style, with short words, lines, and stanzas?

IDEAS FOR WRITING

1. Using examples from poems or stories you have read, write an essay in which you discuss how literature can reveal "secrets of life" to its readers.

2. Reading literature is a very personal and individual experience, and it can be argued that it isn't so important that people read precisely and remember much of what they read; rather, what counts is the imaginative growth and creative stimulus that

comes through reading. Write an essay in which you state whether you agree or disagree with this view of the act of reading, providing examples from your own reading experience.

The Harlem Dancer
Claude McKay

Journal

Write about a dance performance that you remember well. What was the relationship between the dancer and the audience? What was your emotional response to the dancer and his or her performance?

Applauding youths laughed with young prostitutes
And watched her perfect, half-clothed body sway;
Her voice was like the sound of blended flutes
Blown by black players upon a picnic day.
She sang and danced on gracefully and calm,   5
The light gauze hanging loose about her form;
To me she seemed a proudly-swaying palm
Grown lovelier for passing through a storm.
Upon her swarthy neck black shiny curls
Luxuriant fell; and tossing coins in praise,   10
The wine-flushed, bold-eyed boys, and even the girls,
Devoured her shape with eager, passionate gaze;
But looking at her falsely-smiling face,
I knew her self was not in that strange place.

QUESTIONS AND CONSIDERATIONS

1. Describe the setting where the performance takes place. What influence does the setting seem to have on the speaker's response to the performance and to the dance? What effect does the setting have on your response to the dancer's performance?

2. Describe the dancer. What images and verbs does the speaker use to capture her movements?

3. How does the speaker feel about the dancer? Does he respect or understand her?

4. Discuss the conflicts between art and life and between the dancer and her audience that are presented in the poem.

5. The speaker says, "I knew her self was not in that strange place." Where do you think the dancer's self might be? Explain your interpretation.

6. How do the final two lines add new complications to the poem's meaning? What do these lines reveal both about the attitude of the dancer and the values of the speaker in the poem?

IDEAS FOR WRITING

1. Develop an essay, story, or poem that describes a dance, musical, or theatrical performance that you enjoyed. What did you learn from the experience?

2. Rewrite the poem from the dancer's point of view.

The Quilt
Chitra Divakaruni

Journal

In what ways do you think that the creativity involved in the process of bearing and nurturing children is similar to the creative process of the artist?

> *The parrot flies to the custard-apple tree.*
> *The bees are among the pomegranates.*
> *I call and call you, little bride.*
> *Why do you not speak?*
> Bengali Folk Song

Blue and sudden as beginning,
a quilt at the bottom
of the small mahogany chest
which holds her things.

She died in childbirth,   5
this grandmother whose name
no one can tell me.

He married again,
a strong woman this time,
straight backed, wide-hipped   10
for boy-children.
In the portrait downstairs
she wears the family diamonds
and holds her fourth son.

There are no pictures   15
of the wife who failed.

Her quilt leaves on my fingers
satin dust
as from a butterfly wing.

I spread it against   20
the floor's darkness, see her fingers
working it into the world-design,
the *gul-mobur* tree
bright yellow against the blue,
the river winding through rice fields   25
into a horizon where men with swords
march to a war
or a wedding.

As the baby grew she stitched in
a drifting afternoon boat   30
with a peacock sail.
In the foreground, young grass.
A woman with a deer.
She is left unfinished,
no eyes, no mouth,   35
her face a smooth blankness
tilted up at birds
that fall like flames from the sky.

QUESTIONS AND CONSIDERATIONS

1. How does the epigram from the Bengali folk song support the themes of the poem?

2. How does the opening image, "Blue and sudden as beginning," establish and foreshadow the conflict explored throughout the poem between giving birth to a child and creating art?

3. What do we learn about the wife who died in childbirth from the quilt that the speaker discovers in the mahogany chest? Why is the "woman with a deer . . . left unfinished"? How are the quilt and its story contrasted with the "portrait downstairs" of the second wife? What does this poem suggest about the personal nature of creativity?

4. The family in the poem values the second wife who bore four male children more highly than the wife who died in childbirth: "There are no pictures/of the wife who failed." What does the speaker suggest that the first mother contributed to the family? Why does the poem's speaker value the first mother's contribution?

5. What does the picture in the unfinished quilt symbolize?

6. What relationships between artistic creativity and childbearing does the poem establish?

IDEAS FOR WRITING

1. Write an essay that discusses different ways that childbirth and raising children are similar to and yet different from the artist's creative process.

2. Write an essay in which you discuss the gender-related assumptions about the role and definition of creativity presented in this poem or other works in this chapter. Do

you think women and men are valued equally as artists in our society? Does your culture continue to value women as creators within the sphere of home and family?

3. Write an essay in which you contrast the purpose of crafts such as quilting and sewing with that of "fine" art such as portrait painting or sculpture. What different needs, public and private, are filled by crafts as opposed to "fine" art?

Sailing to Byzantium
William Butler Yeats

That is no country for old men. The young
In one another's arms, birds in the trees
—Those dying generations—at their song,
The salmon-falls, the mackerel-crowded seas,
Fish, flesh, or fowl, commend all summer long   5
Whatever is begotten, born, and dies.
Caught in that sensual music all neglect
Monuments of unaging intellect.

An aged man is but a paltry thing,
A tattered coat upon a stick, unless   10
Soul clap its hands and sing, and louder sing
For every tatter in its mortal dress,
Nor is there singing school but studying
Monuments of its own magnificence;
And therefore I have sailed the seas and come   15
To the holy city of Byzantium.

O sages standing in God's holy fire
As in the gold mosaic of a wall,
Come from the holy fire, perne in a gyre,
And be the singing-masters of my soul.   20
Consume my heart away; sick with desire
And fastened to a dying animal
It knows not what it is; and gather me
Into the artifice of eternity.

Once out of nature I shall never take   25
My bodily form from any natural thing,
But such a form as Grecian goldsmiths make
Of hammered gold and gold enameling

To keep a drowsy Emperor awake;
Or set upon a golden bough to sing   30
To lords and ladies of Byzantium
Of what is past, or passing, or to come.

QUESTIONS

1. What is the function of art in Byzantium, Yeats' version of paradise? Why is Byzantium "no country for old men"? Why has the speaker come to Byzantium? Why does the speaker want to take on a "bodily form" made from "hammered gold"? What will he sing of in Byzantium and to whom will he sing?

2. Do you agree with the speaker in the poem that it is possible for art to help people to accept their own mortality? Write a poem or an essay in which you develop your ideas on art and mortality.

[Maggie and Milly and Molly and May]

e. e. cummings

maggie and milly and molly and may
went down to the beach (to play one day)

and maggie discovered a shell that sang
so sweetly she couldn't remember her troubles, and

milly befriended a stranded star   5
whose rays five languid fingers were;

and molly was chased by a horrible thing
which raced sideways while blowing bubbles: and

may came home with a smooth round stone
as small as a world and as large as alone.   10

For whatever we lose (like a you or a me)
it's always ourselves we find in the sea

QUESTIONS

1. What object does each child in the poem discover at the beach? How does the object reflect her personality, fears, and values? What perspective on the nature and origins of creativity and artistic taste does the poem present?

2. Write an essay or poem about finding or creating an object or art. Why was this experience important to you?

Poetry

Marianne Moore

I, too, dislike it: there are things that are important beyond all
                                        this fiddle.
  Reading it, however, with a perfect contempt for it, one
                              discovers in
    it after all, a place for the genuine.
      Hands that can grasp, eyes
        that can dilate, hair that can rise   5
          if it must, these things are important not because a

high-sounding interpretation can be put upon them but because
                              they are
    useful. When they become so derivative as to become
                        unintelligible,
    the same thing may be said for all of us, that we
      do not admire what   10
      we cannot understand: the bat
        holding on upside down or in quest of something to

eat, elephants pushing, a wild horse taking a roll, a tireless wolf
                                under
    a tree, the immovable critic twitching his skin like a horse that
                     feels a flea, the base-
    ball fan, the statistician—   15
      nor is it valid
        to discriminate against "business documents and

school-books"; all these phenomena are important. One must
                        make a distinction
    however: when dragged into prominence by half poets, the
                     result is not poetry,
    nor till the poets among us can be   20
      "literalists of
      the imagination"—above
        insolence and triviality and can present

for inspection, "imaginary gardens with real toads in them,"
                        shall we have
    it. In the meantime, if you demand on the one hand,   25
    the raw material of poetry in
      all its rawness and
      that which is on the other hand
        genuine, you are interested in poetry.

QUESTIONS

1. What does the speaker dislike about poetry? What does the speaker find "genuine" and "useful"? What does the speaker mean by the phrase "imaginary gardens with real toads in them"?

2. Write an essay in which you discuss the type of poetry that you like. Do you dislike any kind of poetry? Why? Contrast your views of poetry with those of the speaker in Moore's poem.

Of Modern Poetry

Wallace Stevens

The poem of the mind in the act of finding
What will suffice. It has not always had
To find: the scene was set; it repeated what
Was in the script.
          Then the theatre was changed
To something else. Its past was a souvenir.   5

It has to be living, to learn the speech of the place.
It has to face the men of the time and to meet
The women of the time. It has to think about war
And it has to find what will suffice. It has
To construct a new stage. It has to be on that stage   10
And, like an insatiable actor, slowly and
With meditation, speak words that in the ear,
In the delicatest ear of the mind, repeat,
Exactly, that which it wants to hear, at the sound
Of which, an invisible audience listens,   15
Not to the play, but to itself, expressed
In an emotion as of two people, as of two
Emotions becoming one. The actor is
A metaphysician in the dark, twanging
An instrument, twanging a wiry string that gives   20
Sounds passing through sudden rightnesses, wholly
Containing the mind, below which it cannot descend,
Beyond which it has no will to rise.
                It must
Be the finding of a satisfaction, and may
Be of a man skating, a woman dancing, a woman   25
Combing. The poem of the act of the mind.

QUESTIONS

1. How does the speaker think that modern poetry has changed since it "repeated what/Was in the script"? Starting with the first "it has" in line 6, what qualities are listed? According to the speaker, in what sense do "two/Emotions becom[e] one" in modern poetry? How is the modern poet like an actor? Like a "metaphysician in the dark"? How is the modern poem musical? How is it "the finding of a satisfaction"?

2. Write an essay in which you either discuss Stevens' ideas on modern poetry, explaining why you agree or disagree with him, or evaluate Stevens' poem as an example of the type of "modern poetry" it celebrates. Is it an effective poem?

The Thought-Fox
Ted Hughes

I imagine this midnight moment's forest:
Something else is alive
Beside the clock's loneliness
And this blank page where my fingers move.

Through the window I see no star: 5
Something more near
Though deeper within darkness
Is entering the loneliness:

Cold, delicately as the dark snow
A fox's nose touches twig, leaf;   10
Two eyes serve a movement, that now
And again now, and now, and now

Sets neat prints into the snow
Between trees, and warily a lame
Shadow lags by stump and in hollow   15
Of a body that is bold to come

Across clearings, an eye,
A widening deepening greenness,
Brilliantly, concentratedly,
Coming about its own business   20

Till, with a sudden sharp hot stink of fox,
It enters the dark hole of the head.
The window is starless still; the clock ticks,
The page is printed.

QUESTIONS

1. Hughes' speaker is involved in the act of creating. What does he imagine as his "fingers move" on the "blank page"? How does the speaker reveal the process through which he perceives the fox and writes about it? What does the poem suggest about inspiration and the act of creation?

2. Write an essay about the inspiration and the creative process involved in a piece of writing you have done. How did you use your physical experiences, memories, imagination, and problem solving to produce the finished work?

In My Craft
or Sullen Art

Dylan Thomas

In my craft or sullen art
Exercised in the still night
When only the moon rages
And the lovers lie abed
With all their griefs in their arms,   5
I labor by singing light
Not for ambition or bread
Or the strut and trade of charms
On the ivory stages
But for the common wages   10
Of their most secret heart.

Not for the proud man apart
From the raging moon I write
On these spindrift pages
Nor for the towering dead   15
With their nightingales and psalms
But for the lovers, their arms
Round the griefs of the ages,
Who pay no praise or wages
Nor heed my craft or art.   20

QUESTIONS

1. Why does the speaker refer to his poetry as "my craft or sullen art"? What audiences for his art does the speaker reject? For whom is the speaker in Thomas' poem creating? Why is the speaker not concerned about his audience failing to "heed my craft or art"?

2. Write an essay about the audience you create for most often when you write or produce other art forms. Do you agree with Thomas that it doesn't matter if your chosen audience fails to "pay no praise or wages" for your art?

The Artist

William Carlos Williams

Mr. T.
             bareheaded
                          in a soiled undershirt
        his hair standing out
             on all sides
                          stood on his toes
        heels together
                     arms gracefully
                     for the moment
curled above his head.
             Then he whirled about
                     bounded
into the air
             and with an *entrechat*
                     perfectly achieved
completed the figure.
             My mother
                     taken by surprise
where she sat
             in her invalid's chair
                     was left speechless.
Bravo! she cried at last
             and clapped her hands.
                     The man's wife
came from the kitchen:
             What goes on here? she said.
             But the show was over.

QUESTIONS

1. Does the poem suggest that an artist needs an appreciative audience? Would Mr. T.'s *entrechat* have been as meaningful if the woman in the wheelchair had not applauded or if a larger audience had been present?

2. Write an essay or poem about an artistic performance in dance, music, song, or theater that you felt was underappreciated or perhaps only witnessed by yourself. What made this moment special and the performance unique?

Ego-tripping (there may be a reason why)

Nikki Giovanni

I was born in the congo
I walked to the fertile crescent and built
   the sphinx
I designed a pyramid so tough that a star
   that only glows every one hundred years falls   5
   into the center giving divine perfect light
I am bad
I sat on the throne
   drinking nectar with allah
I got hot and sent an ice age to europe   10
   to cool my thirst
My oldest daughter is nefertiti
   the tears from my birth pains
   created the nile
I am a beautiful woman   15

I gazed on the forest and burned
   out the sahara desert
   with a packet of goat's meat
   and a change of clothes
I crossed it in two hours   20
I am a gazelle so swift
   so swift you can't catch me

   For a birthday present when he was three
I gave my son hannibal an elephant
   He gave me rome for mother's day   25
My strength flows ever on

My son noah built new/ark and
I stood proudly at the helm
   as we sailed on a soft summer day

I turned myself into myself and was   30
   jesus
   men intone my loving name

All praises All praises
I am the one who would save

I sowed diamonds in my back yard   35
My bowels deliver uranium
    the filings from my fingernails are
    semi-precious jewels
    On a trip north
I caught a cold and blew   40
My nose giving oil to the arab world
I am so hip even my errors are correct
I sailed west to reach east and had to round off
    the earth as I went
    The hair from my head thinned and gold was   45
    laid across three continents

I am so perfect so divine so ethereal so surreal
I cannot be comprehended
    except by my permission
I mean . . . I can fly   50
    like a bird in the sky . . .

QUESTIONS

1. What does this "boast" poem suggest about the relationship between creativity and self-esteem? About creativity and free association or mental play? About creativity and cultural diversity? About creativity and "correctness" versus the acceptance of mistakes and errors? About creativity and the awareness of history?

2. Create your own free-association ego trip in the form of a poem or freewriting in which you brag about your accomplishments, real or imaginary.

Poem for the Creative
Writing Class, Spring 1982
Merle Woo

The silence in the classroom
of people I've grown to respect—
seems like so much potential here:
men and women
brown black yellow jewish white   5
gay and straight.

Classrooms are ugly,
cages with beautiful birds in them.
scraped, peeling walls

empty bookcases   10
an empty blackboard—
no ideas here.

And one window.
One writer comes in
from sitting on the sill,   15
three stories up.
We all want to fly
and feel the sun on the backs of our wings—

Inhale the breath
pulling in the energy of   20
seventeen people around me
and exhale
putting out my ideas, ideas, ideas.
We all want to fly out that window.
A breeze comes in once in a while,   25
we want to go out with it
to where the birds are.

To take flight
using the words
that give us wings.   30

What is language after all
but the touching and uplifting
one to the others:
scenes
poems   35
dreams
our own natural imagery:
coins
a train to El Salvador   40
sleeping, pregnant mothers
menacing garages/a fist pounding/voices yelling
a yogi
cops being the bowery boys
roller coasters
blood   45
a girl on a swing
roses
water, streams, rivers, oceans
rise. rise.

Who can keep us caged?   50

QUESTIONS

1. How does the speaker contrast the ugliness and sterility of the classroom with the creative spirit and aspiration of the writing students and their instructor? How is the metaphor of flight used in the poem to emphasize its ideas on creativity and learning?

2. Write a poem or essay about an exciting and creative classroom learning experience. What made this learning experience positive?

Why I Never Answered Your Letter
Nancy Willard

It's true I make books, but not often.
Mostly I am always feeding someone,
nine cats whose tails flag me down each morning
and who know a soft touch when they feel one,
and who write on my door in invisible milk: 5
Good for a handout. Good for a night's lodging.

Mostly I'm taking from Peter and not paying Paul.
My man comes home, dreaming of sirloin.
I ravage the house: three eggs and half a potato.
I embalm them in amorous spices with beautiful names.   10
It's true I make books, but mostly I make do.
The chapters of hunger are filled but nothing is finished.

At night a baby calls me for comfort and milk.
Someday I'll teach him to sing, to dance, and to draw,
to learn his letters, to speak like an honest man.   15
Right now I teach him to eat, and I tell him a story,
how an angel came to Saint John with a book in its hands,
saying, *Take and eat. It shall make thy belly bitter,*
but thou shalt know all people, all prophets, and all lands.

QUESTIONS

1. What prevents the speaker in the poem from finishing her books? How does she express her creativity? How does she plan to help her child become creative? Discuss the meaning of the final lines of the poem, quoted from the Gospel of St. John?

2. Write an essay in which you contrast the creativity involved in completing a specific product, such as a book or a painting, to the creativity involved in nurturing children?

Yonosa House

R. T. Smith

She stroked molten tones
from the heart-carved maple dulcimer
and sat like a stately sack of bones
withered within coarse skin,
rocking to corn chants, snake   5
songs, music of passing seasons.

Her old woman's Tuscarora hair
hung like waxed flax ready to spin
till she wove and knotted it
to lie like ropes on her shoulders.   10
Through my young mind she wove
the myths of the race
in fevered patterns, feather colors:
Sound of snow, kiss of rock,
the feel of bruised birch bark,   15
the call of the circling hawk.

Her knotted hands showing blue rivers
jerked nervously through cornbread frying,
pressed fern patterns on butter pats,
brewed sassafras tea in the hearth.   20

They buried Yonosa in a deerskin skirt,
beads and braids, but featherless.
I cut hearts in her coffin lid,
wind-slain maple like the dulcimer.
The mountain was holy enough for her.   25
We kept our promise and raised no stone.
She sank like a root to be Georgia clay.
No Baptist churchyard caught her bones.

I thank her hands when the maples turn,
hear her chants in the thrush's song.   30

QUESTIONS

1. In what ways was the speaker's grandmother creative? How does her creativity survive after her physical death? How did her creativity as a tribal person differ from the creativity of modern people who perceive themselves in more individualistic terms?

2. Write a poem or essay about a parent or older relative whom you believe was creative but would not be appreciated or understood in today's world.

Drama

The Piano Lesson
August Wilson

Journal

*Write about an object that has been in your family for many generations and
that embodies the struggles or traditions of your family.*

THE SETTING

The action of the play takes place in the kitchen and parlor of the house where
DOAKER CHARLES lives with his niece, BERNIECE, and her eleven-year-old daughter, MARETHA. The house is sparsely furnished, and although there is evidence
of a woman's touch, there is a lack of warmth and vigor. BERNIECE and MARETHA
occupy the upstairs rooms. DOAKER's room is prominent and opens onto the
kitchen. Dominating the parlor is an old upright piano. On the legs of the piano,
carved in the manner of African sculpture, are mask-like figures resembling
totems. The carvings are rendered with a grace and power of invention that
lifts them out of the realm of craftsmanship and into the realm of art. At left is a
staircase leading to the upstairs.

ACT ONE

Scene 1

*(The lights come up on the Charles household. It is five o'clock in the morning. The dawn
is beginning to announce itself, but there is something in the air that belongs to the night.
A stillness that is a portent, a gathering, a coming together of something akin to a storm.
There is a loud knock at the door.)*

BOY WILLIE *(off stage, calling):* Hey, Doaker . . . Doaker!

(He knocks again and calls.)

   Hey, Doaker! Hey, Berniece! Berniece!

*(DOAKER enters from his room. He is a tall, thin man of forty-seven, with severe features,
who has for all intents and purposes retired from the world though he works full-time as a
railroad cook.)*

DOAKER: Who is it?

BOY WILLIE: Open the door, nigger! It's me . . . Boy Willie!

DOAKER: Who?

BOY WILLIE: Boy Willie! Open the door!

(DOAKER *opens the door and* BOY WILLIE *and* LYMON *enter.* BOY WILLIE *is thirty years old. He has an infectious grin and a boyishness that is apt for his name. He is brash and impulsive, talkative and somewhat crude in speech and manner.* LYMON *is twenty-nine.* BOY WILLIE'*s partner, he talks little, and then with a straightforwardness that is often disarming.)*

DOAKER: What you doing up here?

BOY WILLIE: I told you, Lymon. Lymon talking about you might be sleep. This is Lymon. You remember Lymon Jackson from down home? This my Uncle Doaker.

DOAKER: What you doing up here? I couldn't figure out who that was. I thought you was still down in Mississippi.

BOY WILLIE: Me and Lymon selling watermelons. We got a truck out there. Got a whole truckload of watermelons. We brought them up here to sell. Where's Berniece?

(Calls.)

Hey, Berniece!

DOAKER: Berniece up there sleep.

BOY WILLIE: Well, let her get up.

(Calls.)

Hey, Berniece!

DOAKER: She got to go to work in the morning.

BOY WILLIE: Well she can get up and say hi. It's been three years since I seen her.

(Calls.)

Hey, Berniece! It's me . . . Boy Willie.

DOAKER: Berniece don't like all that hollering now. She got to work in the morning.

BOY WILLIE: She can go on back to bed. Me and Lymon been riding two days in that truck . . . the least she can do is get up and say hi.

DOAKER *(looking out the window):* Where you all get that truck from?

BOY WILLIE: It's Lymon's. I told him let's get a load of watermelons and bring them up here.

LYMON: Boy Willie say he going back, but I'm gonna stay. See what it's like up here.

BOY WILLIE: You gonna carry me down there first.

LYMON: I told you I ain't going back down there and take a chance on that truck breaking down again. You can take the train. Hey, tell him Doaker, he can take the train back. After we sell them watermelons he have enough money he can buy him a whole railroad car.

DOAKER: You got all them watermelons stacked up there no wonder the truck broke down. I'm surprised you made it this far with a load like that. Where you break down at?

BOY WILLIE: We broke down three times! It took us two and a half days to get here. It's a good thing we picked them watermelons fresh.

LYMON: We broke down twice in West Virginia. The first time was just as soon as we got out of Sunflower. About forty miles out she broke down. We got it going and got all the way to West Virginia before she broke down again.

BOY WILLIE: We had to walk about five miles for some water.

LYMON: It got a hole in the radiator but it runs pretty good. You have to pump the brakes sometime before they catch. Boy Willie have his door open and be ready to jump when that happens.

DOY WILLIC: Lymon think that's funny. I told the nigger I give him ten dollars to get the brakes fixed. But he thinks that funny.

LYMON: They don't need fixing. All you got to do is pump them till they catch.

(BERNIECE enters on the stairs. Thirty-five years old, with an eleven-year-old daughter, she is still in mourning for her husband after three years.)

BERNIECE: What you doing all that hollering for?

BOY WILLIE: Hey, Berniece. Doaker said you was sleep. I said at least you could get up and say hi.

BERNIECE: It's five o'clock in the morning and you come in here with all this noise. You can't come like normal folks. You got to bring all that noise with you.

BOY WILLIE: Hell, I ain't done nothing but come in and say hi. I ain't got in the house good.

BERNIECE: That's what I'm talking about. You start all that hollering and carry on as soon as you hit the door.

BOY WILLIE: Aw hell, woman, I was glad to see Doaker. You ain't had to come down if you didn't want to. I come eighteen hundred miles to see my sister I figure she might want to get up and say hi. Other than that you can go back upstairs. What you got, Doaker? Where your bottle? Me and Lymon want a drink.

(To BERNIECE.)

This is Lymon. You remember Lymon Jackson from down home.

LYMON: How you doing, Berniece. You look just like I thought you looked.

BERNIECE: Why you all got to come in hollering and carrying on? Waking the neighbors with all that noise.

BOY WILLIE: They can come over and join the party. We fixing to have a party. Doaker, where your bottle? Me and Lymon celebrating. The Ghosts of the Yellow Dog got Sutter.

BERNIECE: Say what?

BOY WILLIE: Ask Lymon, they found him the next morning. Say he drowned in his well.

DOAKER: When this happen, Boy Willie?

BOY WILLIE: About three weeks ago. Me and Lymon was over in Stoner County when we heard about it. We laughed. We thought it was funny. A great big old three-hundred-and-forty-pound man gonna fall down his well.

LYMON: It remind me of Humpty Dumpty.

BOY WILLIE: Everybody say the Ghosts of the Yellow Dog pushed him.

BERNIECE: I don't want to hear that nonsense. Somebody down there pushing them people in their wells.

DOAKER: What was you and Lymon doing over in Stoner County?

BOY WILLIE: We was down there working. Lymon got some people down there.

LYMON: My cousin got some land down there. We was helping him.

BOY WILLIE: Got near about a hundred acres. He got it set up real nice. Me and Lymon was down there chopping down trees. We was using Lymon's truck to haul the wood. Me and Lymon used to haul wood all around them parts.

(To BERNIECE.*)*

Me and Lymon got a truckload of watermelons out there.

*(*BERNIECE *crosses to the window to the parlor.)*

Doaker, where your bottle? I know you got a bottle stuck up in your room. Come on, me and Lymon want a drink.

*(*DOAKER *exits into his room.)*

BERNIECE: Where you all get that truck from?

BOY WILLIE: I told you it's Lymon's.

BERNIECE: Where you get the truck from, Lymon?

LYMON: I bought it.

BERNIECE: Where he get that truck from, Boy Willie?

BOY WILLIE: He told you he bought it. Bought it for a hundred and twenty dollars. I can't say where he got that hundred and twenty dollars from . . . but he bought that old piece of truck from Henry Porter. *(To* LYMON.*)* Where you get that hundred and twenty dollars from, nigger?

LYMON: I got it like you get yours. I know how to take care of money.

*(*DOAKER *brings a bottle and sets it on the table.)*

BOY WILLIE: Aw hell, Doaker got some of that good whiskey. Don't give Lymon none of that. He ain't used to good whiskey. He liable to get sick.

LYMON: I done had good whiskey before.

BOY WILLIE: Lymon bought that truck so he have him a place to sleep. He down there wasn't doing no work or nothing. Sheriff looking for him. He bought that truck to keep away from the sheriff. Got Stovall looking for him too. He down there sleeping in that truck ducking and dodging both of them. I told him come on let's go up and see my sister.

BERNIECE: What the sheriff looking for you for, Lymon?

BOY WILLIE: The man don't want you to know all his business. He's my company. He ain't asking you no questions.

LYMON: It wasn't nothing. It was just a misunderstanding.

BERNIECE: He in my house. You say the sheriff looking for him, I wanna know what he looking for him for. Otherwise you all can go back out there and be where nobody don't have to ask you nothing.

LYMON: It was just a misunderstanding. Sometimes me and the sheriff we don't think alike. So we just got crossed on each other.

BERNIECE: Might be looking for him about that truck. He might have stole that truck.

BOY WILLIE: We ain't stole no truck, woman. I told you Lymon bought it.

DOAKER: Boy Willie and Lymon got more sense than to ride all the way up here in a stolen truck with a load of watermelons. Now they might have stole them watermelons, but I don't believe they stole that truck.

BOY WILLIE: You don't even know the man good and you calling him a thief. And we ain't stole them watermelons either. Them old man Pitterford's watermelons. He give me and Lymon all we could load for ten dollars.

DOAKER: No wonder you got them stacked up out there. You must have five hundred watermelons stacked up out there.

BERNIECE: Boy Willie, when you and Lymon planning on going back?

BOY WILLIE: Lymon say he staying. As soon as we sell them watermelons I'm going on back.

BERNIECE (starts to exit up the stairs): That's what you need to do. And you need to do it quick. Come in here disrupting the house. I don't want all that loud carrying on around here. I'm surprised you ain't woke Maretha up.

BOY WILLIE: I was fixing to get her now.

(Calls.)

Hey, Maretha!

DOAKER: Berniece don't like all that hollering now.

BERNIECE: Don't you wake that child up!

BOY WILLIE: You going up there . . . wake her up and tell her her uncle's here. I ain't seen her in three years. Wake her up and send her down here. She can go back to bed.

BERNIECE: I ain't waking that child up . . . and don't you be making all that noise. You and Lymon need to sell them watermelons and go on back.

(BERNIECE exits up the stairs.)

BOY WILLIE: I see Berniece still try to be stuck up.

DOAKER: Berniece alright. She don't want you making all that noise. Maretha up there sleep. Let her sleep until she get up. She can see you then.

BOY WILLIE: I ain't thinking about Berniece. You hear from Wining Boy? You know Cleotha died?

DOAKER: Yeah, I heard that. He come by here about a year ago. Had a whole sack of money. He stayed here about two weeks. Ain't offered nothing. Berniece asked him for three dollars to buy some food and he got mad and left.

LYMON: Who's Wining Boy?

BOY WILLIE: That's my uncle. That's Doaker's brother. You heard me talk about Wining Boy. He play piano. He done made some records and everything. He still doing that, Doaker?

DOAKER: He made one or two records a long time ago. That's the only ones I ever known him to make. If you let him tell it he a big recording star.

BOY WILLIE: He stopped down home about two years ago. That's what I hear. I don't know. Me and Lymon was up on Parchman Farm doing them three years.

DOAKER: He don't never stay in one place. Now, he been here about eight months ago. Back in the winter. Now, you subject not to see him for another two years. It's liable to be that long before he stop by.

BOY WILLIE: If he had a whole sack of money you liable never to see him. You ain't gonna see him until he get broke. Just as soon as that sack of money is gone you look up and he be on your doorstep.

LYMON (noticing the piano): Is that the piano?

BOY WILLIE: Yeah . . . look here, Lymon. See how it got all cash money. He don't know I found out the most Stovall how it's carved up real nice and polished and everything? You never find you another piano like that.

LYMON: Yeah, that look real nice.

BOY WILLIE: I told you. See how it's polished? My mama used to polish it every day. See all them pictures carved on it? That's what I was talking about. You can get a nice price for that piano.

LYMON: That's all Boy Willie talked about the whole trip up here. I got tired of hearing him talk about the piano.

BOY WILLIE: All you want to talk about is women. You ought to hear this nigger, Doaker. Talking about all the women he gonna get when he get up here. He ain't had none down there but he gonna get a hundred when he get up here.

DOAKER: How your people doing down there, Lymon?

LYMON: They alright. They still there. I come up here to see what it's like up here. Boy Willie trying to get me to go back and farm with him.

BOY WILLIE: Sutter's brother selling the land. He say he gonna sell it to me. That's why I come up here. I got one part of it. Sell them watermelons and get me another part. Get Berniece to sell that piano and I'll have the third part.

DOAKER: Berniece ain't gonna sell that piano.

BOY WILLIE: I'm gonna talk to her. When she see I got a chance to get Sutter's land she'll come around.

DOAKER: You can put that thought out your mind. Berniece ain't gonna sell that piano.

BOY WILLIE: I'm gonna talk to her. She been playing on it?

DOAKER: You know she won't touch that piano. I ain't never known her to touch it since Mama Ola died. That's over seven years now. She say it got blood on it. She got Maretha playing on it though. Say Maretha can go on and do everything she can't do. Got her in an extra school down at the Irene Kaufman Settlement House. She want Maretha to grow up and be a schoolteacher. Say she good enough she can teach on the piano.

BOY WILLIE: Maretha don't need to be playing on no piano. She can play on the guitar.

DOAKER: How much land Sutter got left?

BOY WILLIE: Got a hundred acres. Good land. He done sold it piece by piece, he kept the good part for himself. Now he got to give that up. His brother come down from Chicago for the funeral . . . he up there in Chicago got some kind of business with soda fountain equipment. He anxious to sell the land, Doaker. He don't want to be bothered with it. He called me to him and said cause of how long our families done known each other and how we been good friends and all, say he wanted to sell the land to me. Say he'd rather see me with it than Jim Stovall. Told me he'd let me have it for two thousand dollars cash money. He don't know I found out the most Stovall would give him for it was fifteen hundred dollars. He trying to get that extra five hundred out of me telling me he doing me a favor. I thanked him just as nice. Told him what a good man Sutter was and how he had my sympathy and all. Told him to give me two weeks. He said he'd wait on me. That's why I come up here. Sell them watermelons. Get Berniece to sell that piano. Put them two parts with the part I done saved. Walk in there. Tip my hat. Lay my money down on the table. Get my deed and walk on out. This time I get to keep all the cotton. Hire me some men to work it for me. Gin my cotton. Get my seed. And I'll see you again next year. Might even plant some tobacco or some oats.

DOAKER: You gonna have a hard time trying to get Berniece to sell that piano. You know Avery Brown from down there don't you? He up here now. He followed Berniece up here trying to get her to marry him after Crawley got killed. He been up here about two years. He call himself a preacher now.

BOY WILLIE: I know Avery. I know him from when he used to work on the Willshaw place. Lymon know him too.

DOAKER: He after Berniece to marry him. She keep telling him no but he won't give up. He keep pressing her on it.

BOY WILLIE: Avery think all white men is bigshots. He don't know there some white men ain't got as much as he got.

DOAKER: He supposed to come past here this morning. Berniece going down to the bank with him to see if he can get a loan to start his church. That's why I know Berniece ain't gonna sell that piano. He tried to get her to sell it to help him start his church. Sent the man around and everything.

BOY WILLIE: What man?

DOAKER: Some white fellow was going around to all the colored people's houses looking to buy up musical instruments. He'd buy anything. Drums. Guitars. Harmonicas. Pianos. Avery sent him past here. He looked at the piano and got excited. Offered her a nice price. She turned him down and got on Avery for sending him past. The man kept on her about two weeks. He seen where she wasn't gonna sell it, he gave her his number and told her if she ever wanted to sell it to call him first. Say he'd go one better than what anybody else would give her for it.

BOY WILLIE: How much he offer her for it?

DOAKER: Now you know me. She didn't say and I didn't ask. I just know it was a nice price.

LYMON: All you got to do is find out who he is and tell him somebody else wanna buy it from you. Tell him you can't make up your mind who to sell it to, and if he like Doaker say, he'll give you anything you want for it.

BOY WILLIE: That's what I'm gonna do. I'm gonna find out who he is from Avery.

DOAKER: It ain't gonna do you no good. Berniece ain't gonna sell that piano.

BOY WILLIE: She ain't got to sell it. I'm gonna sell it. I own just as much of it as she does.

BERNIECE: *(offstage, hollers)*: Doaker! Go on get away. Doaker!

DOAKER: *(calling)*: Berniece?

(DOAKER and BOY WILLIE rush to the stairs, BOY WILLIE runs up the stairs, passing BERNIECE as she enters, running.)

DOAKER: Berniece, what's the matter? You alright? What's the matter?

(BERNIECE tries to catch her breath. She is unable to speak.)

DOAKER: That's alright. Take your time. You alright. What's the matter?

(He calls.)

Hey, Boy Willie?

BOY WILLIE *(offstage)*: Ain't nobody up here.

BERNIECE: Sutter . . . Sutter's standing at the top of the steps.

DOAKER *(calls)*: Boy Willie!

(LYMON crosses to the stairs and looks up. BOY WILLIE enters from the stairs.)

BOY WILLIE: Hey Doaker, what's wrong with her? Berniece, what's wrong? Who was you talking to?

DOAKER: She say she seen Sutter's ghost standing at the top of the stairs.

BOY WILLIE: Seen what? Sutter? She ain't seen no Sutter.

BERNIECE: He was standing right up there.

BOY WILLIE *(entering on the stairs)*: That's all in Berniece's head. Ain't nobody up there. Go on up there, Doaker.

DOAKER: I'll take your word for it. Berniece talking about what she seen. She say Sutter's ghost standing at the top of the steps. She ain't just make all that up.

BOY WILLIE: She up there dreaming. She ain't seen no ghost.

LYMON: You want a glass of water, Berniece? Get her a glass of water, Boy Willie.

BOY WILLIE: She don't need no water. She ain't seen nothing. Go on up there and look. Ain't nobody up there but Maretha.

DOAKER: Let Berniece tell it.

BOY WILLIE: I ain't stopping her from telling it.

DOAKER: What happened, Berniece?

BERNIECE: I come out my room to come back down here and Sutter was standing there in the hall.

BOY WILLIE: What he look like?

BERNIECE: He look like Sutter. He look like he always look.

BOY WILLIE: Sutter couldn't find his way from Big Sandy to Little Sandy. How he gonna find his way all the way up here to Pittsburgh? Sutter ain't never even heard of Pittsburgh.

DOAKER: Go on, Berniece.

BERNIECE: Just standing there with the blue suit on.

BOY WILLIE: The man ain't never left Marlin County when he was living . . . and he's gonna come all the way up here now that he's dead?

DOAKER: Let her finish. I want to hear what she got to say.

BOY WILLIE: I'll tell you this. If Berniece had seen him like she think she seen him she'd still be running.

DOAKER: Go on, Berniece. Don't pay Boy Willie no mind.

BERNIECE: He was standing there . . . had his hand on top of his head. Look like he might have thought if he took his hand down his head might have fallen off.

LYMON: Did he have on a hat?

BERNIECE: Just had on that blue suit . . . I told him to go away and he just stood there looking at me . . . calling Boy Willie's name.

BOY WILLIE: What he calling my name for?

BERNIECE: I believe you pushed him in the well.

BOY WILLIE: Now what kind of sense that make? You telling me I'm gonna go out there and hide in the weeds with all them dogs and things he got around there . . . I'm gonna hide and wait till I catch him looking down his well just right . . . then I'm gonna run over and push him in. A great big old three-hundred-and-forty-pound man.

BERNIECE: Well, what he calling your name for?

BOY WILLIE: He bending over looking down his well, woman . . . how he know who pushed him? It could have been anybody. Where was you when Sutter fell in his well? Where was Doaker? Me and Lymon was over in Stoner County. Tell her, Lymon. The Ghosts of the Yellow Dog got Sutter. That's what happened to him.

BERNIECE: You can talk all that Ghosts of the Yellow Dog stuff if you want. I know better.

LYMON: The Ghosts of the Yellow Dog pushed him. That's what the people say. They found him in his well and all the people say it must be the Ghosts of the Yellow Dog. Just like all them other men.

BOY WILLIE: Come talking about he looking for me. What he come all the way up here for? If he looking for me all he got to do is wait. He could have saved himself a trip if he looking for me. That ain't nothing but in Berniece's head. Ain't no telling what she liable to come up with next.

BERNIECE: Boy Willie, I want you and Lymon to go ahead and leave my house. Just go on somewhere. You don't do nothing but bring trouble with you everywhere you go. If it wasn't for you Crawley would still be alive.

BOY WILLIE: Crawley what? I ain't had nothing to do with Crawley getting killed. Crawley three time seven. He had his own mind.

BERNIECE: Just go on and leave. Let Sutter go somewhere else looking for you.

BOY WILLIE: I'm leaving. Soon as we sell them watermelons. Other than that I ain't going nowhere. Hell, I just got here. Talking about Sutter looking for me. Sutter was looking for that piano. That's what he was looking for. He had to die to find out where that piano was at . . . If I was you I'd get rid of it. That's the way to get rid of Sutter's ghost. Get rid of that piano.

BERNIECE: I want you and Lymon to go on and take all this confusion out of my house!

BOY WILLIE: Hey, tell her, Doaker. What kind of sense that make? I told you, Lymon, as soon as Berniece see me she was gonna start something. Didn't I tell you that? Now she done made up that story about Sutter just so she could tell me to leave her house. Well, hell, I ain't going nowhere till I sell them watermelons.

BERNIECE: Well why don't you go out there and sell them! Sell them and go on back!

BOY WILLIE: We waiting till the people get up.

LYMON: Boy Willie say if you get out there too early and wake the people up they get mad at you and won't buy nothing from you.

DOAKER: You won't be waiting long. You done let the sun catch up with you. This the time everybody be getting up around here.

BERNIECE: Come on, Doaker, walk up here with me. Let me get Maretha up and get her started. I got to get ready myself. Boy Willie, just go on out there and sell them watermelons and you and Lymon leave my house.

(BERNIECE *and* DOAKER *exit up the stairs.*)

BOY WILLIE: *(Calling after them.)* If you see Sutter up there . . . tell him I'm down here waiting on him.

LYMON: What if she see him again?

BOY WILLIE: That's all in her head. There ain't no ghost up there.

(Calls.)

Hey, Doaker . . . I told you ain't nothing up there.

LYMON: I'm glad he didn't say he was looking for me.

BOY WILLIE: I wish I would see Sutter's ghost. Give me a chance to put a whupping on him.

LYMON: You ought to stay up here with me. You be down there working his land . . . he might come looking for you all the time.

BOY WILLIE: I ain't thinking about Sutter. And I ain't thinking about staying up here. You stay up here. I'm going back and get Sutter's land. You think you ain't got to work up here. You think this the land of milk and honey. But I ain't scared of work. I'm going back and farm every acre of that land.

(DOAKER enters from the stairs.)

I told you there ain't nothing up there, Doaker. Berniece dreaming all that.

DOAKER: I believe Berniece seen something. Berniece level-headed. She ain't just made all that up. She say Sutter had on a suit. I don't believe she ever seen Sutter in a suit. I believe that's what he was buried in, and that's what Berniece saw.

BOY WILLIE: Well, let her keep on seeing him then. As long as he don't mess with me.

(DOAKER starts to cook his breakfast.)

I heard about you, Doaker. They say you got all the women looking out for you down home. They be looking to see you coming. Say you got a different one every two weeks. Say they be fighting one another for you to stay with them.

(To LYMON.*)*

Look at him, Lymon. He know it's true.

DOAKER: I ain't thinking about no women. They never get me tied up with them. After Coreen I ain't got no use for them. I stay up on Jack Slattery's place when I be down there. All them women want is somebody with a steady payday.

BOY WILLIE: That ain't what I hear. I hear every two weeks the women all put on their dresses and line up at the railroad station.

DOAKER: I don't get down there but once a month. I used to go down there every two weeks but they keep switching me around. They keep switching all the fellows around.

BOY WILLIE: Doaker can't turn that railroad loose. He was working the railroad when I was walking around crying for sugartit. My mama used to brag on him.

DOAKER: I'm cooking now, but I used to line track. I pieced together the Yellow Dog stitch by stitch. Rail by rail. Line track all up around there. I lined track all up around Sunflower and Clarksdale. Wining Boy worked with me. He helped put in some of that track. He'd work it for six months and quit. Go back to playing piano and gambling.

BOY WILLIE: How long you been with the railroad now?

DOAKER: Twenty-seven years. Now, I'll tell you something about the railroad. What I done learned after twenty-seven years. See, you got North. You got West. You look over here you got South. Over there you got East. Now, you can start from anywhere. Don't care where you at. You got to go one of them four ways. And whichever way you decide to go they got a railroad that will take you there. Now, that's something simple. You think anybody would be able to understand that. But you'd be surprised how many people trying to go North get on a train going West. They think the train's supposed to go where they going rather than where it's going.

Now, why people going? Their sister's sick. They leaving before they kill somebody . . . and they sitting across from somebody who's leaving to keep from getting killed. They leaving cause they can't get satisfied. They going to meet someone. I wish I had a dollar for every time that someone wasn't at the station to meet them. I done seen that a lot. In between the time they sent the telegram and the time the person get there . . . they done forgot all about them.

They got so many trains out there they have a hard time keeping them from running into each other. Got trains going every whichaway. Got people on all of them. Somebody going where somebody just left. If everybody stay in one place I believe this would be a better world. Now what I done learned after twenty-seven years of railroading is this . . . if the train stays on the track . . . it's going to get where it's going. It might not be where you going. If it ain't, then all you got to do is sit and wait cause the train's coming back to get you. The train don't never stop. It'll come back every time. Now I'll tell you another thing . . .

BOY WILLIE: What you cooking over there, Doaker? Me and Lymon's hungry.

DOAKER: Go on down there to Wylie and Kirkpatrick to Eddie's restaurant. Coffee cost a nickel and you can get two eggs, sausage, and grits for fifteen cents. He even give you a biscuit with it.

BOY WILLIE: That look good what you got. Give me a little piece of that grilled bread.

DOAKER: Here . . . go on take the whole piece.

BOY WILLIE: Here you go, Lymon . . . you want a piece?

(He gives LYMON *a piece of toast.* MARETHA *enters from the stairs.)*

BOY WILLIE: Hey, sugar. Come here and give me a hug. Come on give Uncle Boy Willie a hug. Don't be shy. Look at her, Doaker. She done got bigger. Ain't she got big?

DOAKER: Yeah, she getting up there.

BOY WILLIE: How you doing, sugar?

MARETHA: Fine.

BOY WILLIE: You was just a little old thing last time I seen you. You remember me, don't you? This your Uncle Boy Willie from down South. That there's Lymon. He my friend. We come up here to sell watermelons. You like watermelons?

*(*MARETHA *nods.)*

We got a whole truckload out front. You can have as many as you want. What you been doing?

MARETHA: Nothing.

BOY WILLIE: Don't be shy now. Look at you getting all big. How old is you?

MARETHA: Eleven. I'm gonna be twelve soon.

BOY WILLIE: You like it up here? You like the North?

MARETHA: It's alright.

BOY WILLIE: That there's Lymon. Did you say hi to Lymon?

MARETHA: Hi.

LYMON: How you doing? You look just like your mama. I remember you when you was wearing diapers.

BOY WILLIE: You gonna come down South and see me? Uncle Boy Willie gonna get him a farm. Gonna get a great big old farm. Come down there and I'll teach you how to ride a mule. Teach you how to kill a chicken, too.

MARETHA: I seen my mama do that.

BOY WILLIE: Ain't nothing to it. You just grab him by his neck and twist it. Get you a real good grip and then you just wring his neck and throw him in the pot. Cook him up. Then you got some good eating. What you like to eat? What kind of food you like?

MARETHA: I like everything . . . except I don't like no black-eyed peas.

BOY WILLIE: Uncle Doaker tell me your mama got you playing that piano. Come on play something for me.

(BOY WILLIE crosses over to the piano followed by MARETHA.)

Show me what you can do. Come on now. Here . . . Uncle Boy Willie give you a dime . . . show me what you can do. Don't be bashful now. That dime say you can't be bashful.

(MARETHA plays. It is something any beginner first learns.)

Here, let me show you something.

(BOY WILLIE sits and plays a simple boogie-woogie.)

See that? See what I'm doing? That's what you call the boogie-woogie. See now . . . you can get up and dance to that. That's how good it sound. It sound like you wanna dance. You can dance to that. It'll hold you up. Whatever kind of dance you wanna do you can dance to that right there. See that? See how it go? Ain't nothing to it. Go on you do it.

MARETHA: I got to read it on the paper.

BOY WILLIE: You don't need no paper. Go on. Do just like that there.

BERNIECE: Maretha! You get up here and get ready to go so you be on time. Ain't no need you trying to take advantage of company.

MARETHA: I got to go.

BOY WILLIE: Uncle Boy Willie gonna get you a guitar. Let Uncle Doaker teach you how to play that. You don't need to read no paper to play the guitar. Your mama told you about that piano? You know how them pictures got on there?

MARETHA: She say it just always been like that since she got it.

BOY WILLIE: You hear that, Doaker? And you sitting up here in the house with Berniece.

DOAKER: I ain't got nothing to do with that. I don't get in the way of Berniece's raising her.

BOY WILLIE: You tell your mama to tell you about that piano. You ask her how them pictures got on there. If she don't tell you I'll tell you.

BERNIECE: Maretha!

MARETHA: I got to get ready to go.

BOY WILLIE: She getting big, Doaker. You remember her, Lymon?

LYMON: She used to be real little.

(There is a knock on the door. DOAKER goes to answer it. AVERY enters. Thirty-eight years old, honest and ambitious, he has taken to the city like a fish to water, finding in it opportunities for growth and advancement that did not exist for him in the rural South. He is dressed in a suit and tie with a gold cross around his neck. He carries a small Bible.)

DOAKER: Hey, Avery, come on in. Berniece upstairs.

BOY WILLIE: Look at him . . . look at him . . . he don't know what to say. He wasn't expecting to see me.

AVERY: Hey, Boy Willie. What you doing up here?

BOY WILLIE: Look at him, Lymon.

AVERY: Is that Lymon? Lymon Jackson?

BOY WILLIE: Yeah, you know Lymon.

DOAKER: Berniece be ready in a minute, Avery.

BOY WILLIE: Doaker say you a preacher now. What . . . we supposed to call you Reverend? You used to be plain old Avery. When you get to be a preacher, nigger?

LYMON: Avery say he gonna be a preacher so he don't have to work.

BOY WILLIE: I remember when you was down there on the Willshaw place planting cotton. You wasn't thinking about no Reverend then.

AVERY: That must be your truck out there. I saw that truck with them watermelons, I was trying to figure out what it was doing in front of the house.

BOY WILLIE: Yeah, me and Lymon selling watermelons. That's Lymon's truck.

DOAKER: Berniece say you all going down to the bank.

AVERY: Yeah, they give me a half day off work. I got an appointment to talk to the bank about getting a loan to start my church.

BOY WILLIE: Lymon say preachers don't have to work. Where you working at, nigger?

DOAKER: Avery got him one of them good jobs. He working at one of them skyscrapers downtown.

AVERY: I'm working down there at the Gulf Building running an elevator. Got a pension and everything. They even give you a turkey on Thanksgiving.

LYMON: How you know the rope ain't gonna break? Ain't you scared the rope's gonna break?

AVERY: That's steel. They got steel cables hold it up. It take a whole lot of breaking to break that steel. Naw, I ain't worried about nothing like that. It ain't nothing but a little old elevator. Now, I wouldn't get in none of them airplanes. You couldn't pay me to do nothing like that.

LYMON: That be fun. I'd rather do that than ride in one of them elevators.

BOY WILLIE: How many of them watermelons you wanna buy?

AVERY: I thought you was gonna give me one seeing as how you got a whole truck full.

BOY WILLIE: You can get one, get two. I'll give you two for a dollar.

AVERY: I can't eat but one. How much are they?

BOY WILLIE: Aw, nigger, you know I'll give you a watermelon. Go on, take as many as you want. Just leave some for me and Lymon to sell.

AVERY: I don't want but one.

BOY WILLIE: How you get to be a preacher, Avery? I might want to be a preacher one day. Have everybody call me Reverend Boy Willie.

AVERY: It come to me in a dream. God called me and told me he wanted me to be a shepherd for his flock. That's what I'm gonna call my church . . . The Good Shepherd Church of God in Christ.

DOAKER: Tell him what you told me. Tell him about the three hobos.

AVERY: Boy Willie don't want to hear all that.

LYMON: I do. Lots a people say your dreams can come true.

AVERY: Naw. You don't want to hear all that.

DOAKER: Go on. I told him you was a preacher. He didn't want to believe me. Tell him about the three hobos.

AVERY: Well, it come to me in a dream. See . . . I was sitting out in this railroad yard watching the trains go by. The train stopped and these three hobos got off. They told me they had come from Nazareth and was on their way to Jerusalem. They had three candles. They gave me one and told me to light it . . . but to be careful that it didn't go out. Next thing I knew I was standing in front of this house. Something told me to go knock on the door. This old woman opened the door and said they had been waiting on me. Then she led me into this room. It was a big room and it was full of all kinds of different people. They looked like anybody else except they all had sheep heads and was making noise like sheep make. I heard some-body call my name. I looked around and there was these same three hobos. They told me to take off my clothes and they give me a blue robe with gold thread. They washed my feet and combed my hair. Then they showed me these three doors and told me to pick one.

I went through one of them doors and that flame leapt off that candle and it seemed like my whole head caught fire. I looked around and there was four or five other men standing there with these same blue robes on. Then we heard a voice tell us to look out across this valley. We looked out and saw the valley was full of wolves. The voice told us that these sheep people that I had seen in the other room had to go over to the other side of this valley and somebody had to take them. Then I heard another voice say, "Who shall I send?" Next thing I knew I said, "Here I am. Send me." That's when I met Jesus. He say, "If you go, I'll go with you." Something told me to say, "Come on. Let's go." That's when I woke up. My head still felt like it was on fire . . . but I had a peace about myself that was hard to explain. I knew right then that I had been filled with the Holy Ghost and called to be a servant of the Lord. It took me a while before I could accept that. But then a lot of little ways God showed me that it was true. So I be-came a preacher.

LYMON: I see why you gonna call it the Good Shepherd Church. You dreaming about them sheep people. I can see that easy.

BOY WILLIE: Doaker say you sent some white man past the house to look at that piano. Say he was going around to all the colored people's houses looking to buy up musical instruments.

AVERY: Yeah, but Berniece didn't want to sell that piano. After she told me about it . . . I could see why she didn't want to sell it.

BOY WILLIE: What's this man's name?

AVERY: Oh, that's a while back now. I done forgot his name. He give Berniece a card with his name and telephone number on it, but I believe she throwed it away.

(BERNIECE *and* MARETHA *enter from the stairs.*)

BERNIECE: Maretha, run back upstairs and get my pocketbook. And wipe that hair grease off your forehead. Go ahead, hurry up.

(MARETHA *exits up the stairs.*)

How you doing, Avery? You done got all dressed up. You look nice. Boy
Willie, I thought you and Lymon was going to sell them watermelons.

BOY WILLIE: Lymon done got sleepy. We liable to get some sleep first.

LYMON: I ain't sleepy.

DOAKER: As many watermelons as you got stacked up on that truck out there,
you ought to have been gone.

BOY WILLIE: We gonna go in a minute. We going.

BERNIECE: Doaker. I'm gonna stop down there on Logan Street. You want anything?

DOAKER: You can pick up some ham hocks if you going down there. See if you
can get the smoked ones. If they ain't got that get the fresh ones. Don't
get the ones that got all that fat under the skin. Look for the long ones.
They nice and lean.

(He gives her a dollar.)

Don't get the short ones lessen they smoked. If you got to get the fresh
ones make sure that they the long ones. If they ain't got them smoked
then go ahead and get the short ones.

(Pause.)

You may as well get some turnip greens while you down there. I got some
buttermilk . . . if you pick up some cornmeal I'll make me some cornbread
and cook up them turnip greens.

(MARETHA enters from the stairs.)

MARETHA: We gonna take the streetcar?

BERNIECE: Me and Avery gonna drop you off at the settlement house. You mind
them people down there. Don't be going down there showing your color.
Boy Willie, I done told you what to do. I'll see you later, Doaker.

AVERY: I'll be seeing you again, Boy Willie.

BOY WILLIE: Hey, Berniece . . . what's the name of that man Avery sent past
say he want to buy the piano?

BERNIECE: I knew it. I knew it when I first seen you. I knew you was up to something.

BOY WILLIE: Sutter's brother say he selling the land to me. He waiting on me
now. Told me he'd give me two weeks. I got one part. Sell them watermelons get me another part. Then we can sell that piano and I'll have the third
part.

BERNIECE: I ain't selling that piano, Boy Willie. If that's why you come up here
you can just forget about it.

(To DOAKER.)

Doaker, I'll see you later. Boy Willie ain't nothing but a whole lot of mouth. I
ain't paying him no mind. If he come up here thinking he gonna sell that
piano then he done come up here for nothing.

(BERNIECE, AVERY, and MARETHA exit the front door.)

BOY WILLIE: Hey, Lymon! You ready to go sell these watermelons.

*(*BOY WILLIE *and* LYMON *start to exit. At the door* BOY WILLIE *turns to* DOAKER*.)*

Hey, Doaker . . . if Berniece don't want to sell that piano . . . I'm gonna cut it in half and go on and sell my half.

*(*BOY WILLIE *and* LYMON *exit.)*

(The lights go down on the scene.)

Scene 2

(The lights come up on the kitchen. It is three days later. WINING BOY *sits at the kitchen table. There is a half-empty pint bottle on the table.* DOAKER *busies himself washing pots.* WINING BOY *is fifty-six years old.* DOAKER's *older brother, he tries to present the image of a successful musician and gambler, but his music, his clothes, and even his manner of presentation are old. He is a man who looking back over his life continues to live it with an odd mixture of zest and sorrow.)*

WINING BOY: So the Ghosts of the Yellow Dog got Sutter. That just go to show you I believe I always lived right. They say every dog gonna have his day and time it go around it sure come back to you. I done seen that a thousand times. I know the truth of that. But I'll tell you outright . . . if I see Sutter's ghost I'll be on the first thing I find that got wheels on it.

*(*DOAKER *enters from his room.)*

DOAKER: Wining Boy!

WINING BOY: And I'll tell you another thing . . . Berniece ain't gonna sell that piano.

DOAKER: That's what she told him. He say he gonna cut it in half and go on and sell his half. They been around here three days trying to sell them watermelons. They trying to get out to where the white folks live but the truck keep breaking down. They go a block or two and it break down again. They trying to get out to Squirrel Hill and can't get around the corner. He say soon as he can get that truck empty to where he can set the piano up in there he gonna take it out of here and go sell it.

WINING BOY: What about them boys Sutter got? How come they ain't farming that land?

DOAKER: One of them going to school. He left down there and come North to school. The other one ain't got as much sense as that frying pan over yonder. That is the dumbest white man I ever seen. He'd stand in the river and watch it rise till it drown him.

WINING BOY: Other than seeing Sutter's ghost how's Berniece doing?

DOAKER: She doing alright. She still got Crawley on her mind. He been dead three years but she still holding on to him. She need to go out here and let one of these fellows grab a whole handful of whatever she got. She act like it done got precious.

WINING BOY: They always told me any fish will bite if you got good bait.

DOAKER: She stuck up on it. She think it's better than she is. I believe she messing around with Avery. They got something going. He a preacher now. If you let him tell it the Holy Ghost sat on his head and heaven opened up with thunder and lightning and God was calling his name. Told him to go out and preach and tend to his flock. That's what he gonna call his church. The Good Shepherd Church.

WINING BOY: They had that joker down in Spear walking around talking about he Jesus Christ. He gonna live the life of Christ. Went through the Last Supper and everything. Rented him a mule on Palm Sunday and rode through the town. Did everything . . . talking about he Christ. He did everything until they got up to that crucifixion part. Got up to that part and told everybody to go home and quit pretending. He got up to the crucifixion part and changed his mind. Had a whole bunch of folks come down there to see him get nailed to the cross. I don't know who's the worse fool. Him or them. Had all them folks come down there . . . even carried the cross up this little hill. People standing around waiting to see him get nailed to the cross and he stop everything and preach a little sermon and told everybody to go home. Had enough nerve to tell them to come to church on Easter Sunday to celebrate his resurrection.

DOAKER: I'm surprised Avery ain't thought about that. He trying every little thing to get him a congregation together. They meeting over at his house till he get him a church.

WINING BOY: Ain't nothing wrong with being a preacher. You got the preacher on one hand and the gambler on the other. Sometimes there ain't too much difference in them.

DOAKER: How long you been in Kansas City?

WINING BOY: Since I left here. I got tied up with some old gal down there.

(Pause.)

You know Cleotha died.

DOAKER: Yeah, I heard that last time I was down there. I was sorry to hear that.

WINING BOY: One of her friends wrote and told me. I got the letter right here.

(He takes the letter out of his pocket.)

I was down in Kansas City and she wrote and told me Cleotha had died. Name of Willa Bryant. She say she know cousin Rupert.

(He opens the letter and reads.)

Dear Wining Boy: I am writing this letter to let you know Miss Cleotha Holman passed on Saturday the first of May she departed this world in the loving arms of her sister Miss Alberta Samuels. I know you would want to know this and am writing as a friend of Cleotha. There have been many hardships since last you seen her but she survived them all and to the end was a good woman whom I hope have God's grace and is in His Paradise. Your cousin Rupert Bates is my friend also and he give me your address and I pray this reaches you about Cleotha. Miss Willa Bryant. A friend.

(He folds the letter and returns it to his pocket.)

They was nailing her coffin shut by the time I heard about it. I never knew she was sick. I believe it was that yellow jaundice. That's what killed her mama.

DOAKER: Cleotha wasn't but forty-some.

WINING BOY: She was forty-six. I got ten years on her. I met her when she was sixteen. You remember I used to run around there. Couldn't nothing keep me still. Much as I loved Cleotha I loved to ramble. Couldn't nothing keep me still. We got married and we used to fight about it all the time. Then one day she asked me to leave. Told me she loved me before I left. Told me, Wining Boy, you got a home as long as I got mine. And I believe in my heart I always felt that and that kept me safe.

DOAKER: Cleotha always did have a nice way about her.

WINING BOY: Man that woman was something. I used to thank the Lord. Many a night I sat up and looked out over my life. Said, well, I had Cleotha. When it didn't look like there was nothing else for me, I said, thank God, at least I had that. If ever I go anywhere in this life I done known a good woman. And that used to hold me till the next morning.

(Pause.)

What you got? Give me a little nip. I know you got something stuck up in your room.

DOAKER: I ain't seen you walk in here and put nothing on the table. You done sat there and drank up your whiskey. Now you talking about what you got.

WINING BOY: I got plenty money. Give me a little nip.

(DOAKER carries a glass into his room and returns with it half-filled. He sets it on the table in front of WINING BOY.)

WINING BOY: You hear from Coreen?

DOAKER: She up in New York. I let her go from my mind.

WINING BOY: She was something back then. She wasn't too pretty but she had a way of looking at you made you know there was a whole lot of woman there. You got married and snatched her out from under us and we all got mad at you.

DOAKER: She up in New York City. That's what I hear.

(The door opens and BOY WILLIE and LYMON enter.)

BOY WILLIE: Aw hell . . . look here! We was just talking about you. Doaker say you left out of here with a whole sack of money. I told him we wasn't going see you till you got broke.

WINING BOY: What you mean broke? I got a whole pocketful of money.

DOAKER: Did you all get that truck fixed?

BOY WILLIE: We got it running and got halfway out there on Centre and it broke down again. Lymon went out there and messed it up some more. Fellow told us we got to wait till tomorrow to get it fixed. Say he have it running like new. Lymon going back down there and sleep in the truck so the people don't take the watermelons.

LYMON: Lymon nothing. You go down there and sleep in it.

BOY WILLIE: You was sleeping in it down home, nigger! I don't know nothing about sleeping in no truck.

LYMON: I ain't sleeping in no truck.

BOY WILLIE: They can take all the watermelons. I don't care. Wining Boy, where you coming from? Where you been?

WINING BOY: I been down in Kansas City.

BOY WILLIE: You remember Lymon? Lymon Jackson.

WINING BOY: Yeah, I used to know his daddy.

BOY WILLIE: Doaker say you don't never leave no address with nobody. Say he got to depend on your whim. See when it strike you to pay a visit.

WINING BOY: I got four or five addresses.

BOY WILLIE: Doaker say Berniece asked you for three dollars and you got mad and left.

WINING BOY: Berniece try and rule over you too much for me. That's why I left. It wasn't about no three dollars.

BOY WILLIE: Where you getting all these sacks of money from? I need to be with you. Doaker say you had a whole sack of money . . . turn some of it loose.

WINING BOY: I was just fixing to ask you for five dollars.

BOY WILLIE: I ain't got no money. I'm trying to get some. Doaker tell you about Sutter? The Ghosts of the Yellow Dog got him about three weeks ago. Berniece done seen his ghost and everything. He right upstairs.

(Calls.)

Hey Sutter! Wining Boy's here. Come on, get a drink!

WINING BOY: How many that make the Ghosts of the Yellow Dog done got?

BOY WILLIE: Must be about nine or ten, eleven or twelve. I don't know.

DOAKER: You got Ed Saunders. Howard Peterson. Charlie Webb.

WINING BOY: Robert Smith. That fellow that shot Becky's boy . . . say he was stealing peaches . . .

DOAKER: You talking about Bob Mallory.

BOY WILLIE: Berniece say she don't believe all that about the Ghosts of the Yellow Dog.

WINING BOY: She ain't got to believe. You go ask them white folks in Sunflower County if they believe. You go ask Sutter if he believe. I don't care if Berniece believe or not. I done been to where the Southern cross the Yellow Dog and called out their names. They talk back to you, too.

LYMON: What they sound like? The wind or something?

BOY WILLIE: You done been there for real, Wining Boy?

WINING BOY: Nineteen thirty. July of nineteen thirty I stood right there on that spot. It didn't look like nothing was going right in my life. I said everything can't go wrong all the time . . . let me go down there and call on the Ghosts of the Yellow Dog, see if they can help me. I went down there and right there where them two railroads cross each other . . . I stood right there on that spot and called out their names. They talk back to you, too.

LYMON: People say you can ask them questions. They talk to you like that?

WINING BOY: A lot of things you got to find out on your own. I can't say how they talked to nobody else. But to me it just filled me up in a strange sort of way to be standing there on that spot. I didn't want to leave. It felt like the longer I stood there the bigger I got. I seen the train coming and it seem like I was bigger than the train. I started not to move. But something told me to go ahead and get on out the way. The train passed and I started to go back up there and stand some more. But something told me not to do it. I walked away from there feeling like a king. Went on and had a stroke of luck that run on for three years. So I don't care if Berniece believe or not. Berniece ain't got to believe. I know cause I been there. Now Doaker'll tell you about the Ghosts of the Yellow Dog.

DOAKER: I don't try and talk that stuff with Berniece. Avery got her all tied up in that church. She just think it's a whole lot of nonsense.

BOY WILLIE: Berniece don't believe in nothing. She just think she believe. She believe in anything if it's convenient for her to believe. But when that convenience run out then she ain't got nothing to stand on.

WINING BOY: Let's not get on Berniece now. Doaker tell me you talking about selling that piano.

BOY WILLIE: Yeah . . . hey, Doaker, I got the name of that man Avery was talking about. The man what's fixing the truck gave me his name. Everybody know him. Say he buy up anything you can make music with. I got his name and his telephone number. Hey, Wining Boy, Sutter's brother say he selling the land to me. I got one part. Sell them watermelons get me the second part. Then . . . soon as I get them watermelons out that truck I'm gonna take and sell that piano and get the third part.

DOAKER: That land ain't worth nothing no more. The smart white man's up here in these cities. He cut the land loose and step back and watch you and the dumb white man argue over it.

WINING BOY: How you know Sutter's brother ain't sold it already? You talking about selling the piano and the man's liable to sold the land two or three times.

BOY WILLIE: He say he waiting on me. He say he give me two weeks. That's two weeks from Friday. Say if I ain't back by then he might gonna sell it to somebody else. He say he wanna see me with it.

WINING BOY: You know as well as I know the man gonna sell the land to the first one walk up and hand him the money.

BOY WILLIE: That's just who I'm gonna be. Look, you ain't gotta know he waiting on me. I know. Okay. I know what the man told me. Stoval already done tried to buy the land from him and he told him no. The man say he waiting on me . . . he waiting on me. Hey, Doaker . . . give me a drink. I see Wining Boy got his glass.

(DOAKER *exits into his room.*)

Wining Boy, what you doing in Kansas City? What they got down there?

LYMON: I hear they got some nice-looking women in Kansas City. I sure like to go down there and find out.

WINING BOY: Man, the women down there is something else.

(DOAKER *enters with a bottle of whiskey. He sets it on the table with some glasses.*)

DOAKER: You wanna sit up here and drink up my whiskey, leave a dollar on the table when you get up.

BOY WILLIE: You ain't doing nothing but showing your hospitality. I know we ain't got to pay for your hospitality.

WINING BOY: Doaker say they had you and Lymon down on the Parchman Farm. Had you on my old stomping grounds.

BOY WILLIE: Me and Lymon was down there hauling wood for Jim Miller and keeping us a little bit to sell. Some white fellows tried to run us off of it. That's when Crawley got killed. They put me and Lymon in the penitentiary.

LYMON: They ambushed us right there where that road dip down and around that bend in the creek. Crawley tried to fight them. Me and Boy Willie got away but the sheriff got us. Say we was stealing wood. They shot me in my stomach.

BOY WILLIE: They looking for Lymon down there now. They rounded him up and put him in jail for not working.

LYMON: Fined me a hundred dollars. Mr. Stovall come and paid my hundred dollars and the judge say I got to work for him to pay him back his hundred dollars. I told them I'd rather take my thirty days but they wouldn't let me do that.

BOY WILLIE: As soon as Stovall turned his back, Lymon was gone. He down there living in that truck dodging the sheriff and Stovall. He got both of them looking for him. So I brought him up here.

LYMON: I told Boy Willie I'm gonna stay up here. I ain't going back with him.

BOY WILLIE: Ain't nobody twisting your arm to make you go back. You can do what you want to do.

WINING BOY: I'll go back with you. I'm on my way down there. You gonna take the train? I'm gonna take the train.

LYMON: They treat you better up here.

BOY WILLIE: I ain't worried about nobody mistreating me. They treat you like you let them treat you. They mistreat me I mistreat them right back. Ain't no difference in me and the white man.

WINING BOY: Ain't no difference as far as how somebody supposed to treat you. I agree with that. But I'll tell you the difference between the colored man and the white man. Alright. Now you take and eat some berries. They taste real good to you. So you say I'm gonna go out and get me a whole pot of these berries and cook them up to make a pie or whatever. But you ain't looked to see them berries is sitting in the white fellow's yard. Ain't got no fence around them. You figure anybody want something they'd fence it in. Alright. Now the white man come along and say that's my land. Therefore everything that grow on it belong to me. He tell the sheriff, "I want you to put this nigger in jail as a warning to all the other niggers. Otherwise first thing you know these niggers have everything that belong to us."

BOY WILLIE: I'd come back at night and haul off his whole patch while he was sleep.

WINING BOY: Alright. Now Mr. So and So, he sell the land to you. And he come to you and say, "John, you own the land. It's all yours now. But them is my berries. And come time to pick them I'm gonna send my boys over. You got the land . . . but them berries, I'm gonna keep them. They mine." And he go and fix it with the law that them is his berries. Now that's the difference between the colored man and the white man. The colored man can't fix nothing with the law.

BOY WILLIE: I don't go by what the law say. The law's liable to say anything. I go by if it's right or not. It don't matter to me what the law say. I take and look at it for myself.

LYMON: That's why you gonna end up back down there on the Parchman Farm.

BOY WILLIE: I ain't thinking about no Parchman Farm. You liable to go back before me.

LYMON: They work you too hard down there. All that weeding and hoeing and chopping down trees. I didn't like all that.

WINING BOY: You ain't got to like your job on Parchman. Hey, tell him, Doaker, the only one got to like his job is the waterboy.

DOAKER: If he don't like his job he need to set that bucket down.

BOY WILLIE: That's what they told Lymon. They had Lymon on water and everybody got mad at him cause he was lazy.

LYMON: That water was heavy.

BOY WILLIE: They had Lymon down there singing:

(Sings.)

O Lord Berta Berta O Lord gal oh-ah
O Lord Berta Berta O Lord gal well

(LYMON and WINING BOY join in.)

Go 'head marry don't you wait on me oh-ah
Go 'head marry don't you wait on me well
Might not want you when I go free oh-ah
Might not want you when I go free well

BOY WILLIE: Come on, Doaker. Doaker know this one.

(As DOAKER joins in the men stamp and clap to keep time. They sing in harmony with great fervor and style.)

O Lord Berta Berta O Lord gal oh-ah
O Lord Berta Berta O Lord gal well

Raise them up higher, let them drop on down oh-ah
Raise them up higher, let them drop on down well
Don't know the difference when the sun go down oh-ah
Don't know the difference when the sun go down well

Berta in Meridan and she living at ease oh-ah
Berta in Meridan and she living at ease well

I'm on old Parchman, got to work or leave oh-ah
I'm on old Parchman, got to work or leave well

O Alberta, Berta, O Lord gal oh-ah
O Alberta, Berta, O Lord gal well

When you marry, don't marry no farming man oh-ah
When you marry, don't marry no farming man well
Everyday Monday, hoe handle in your hand oh-ah
Everyday Monday, hoe handle in your hand well

When you marry, marry a railroad man, oh-ah
When you marry, marry a railroad man, well
Everyday Sunday, dollar in your hand oh-ah
Everyday Sunday, dollar in your hand well

O Alberta, Berta, O Lord gal oh-ah
O Alberta, Berta, O Lord gal well

BOY WILLIE: Doaker like that part. He like that railroad part.

LYMON: Doaker sound like Tangleye. He can't sing a lick.

BOY WILLIE: Hey, Doaker, they still talk about you down on Parchman. They ask
me, "You Doaker Boy's nephew?" I say, "Yeah, me and him is family." They
treated me alright soon as I told them that. Say, "Yeah, he my uncle."

DOAKER: I don't never want to see none of them niggers no more.

BOY WILLIE: I don't want to see them either. Hey, Wining Boy, come on play
some piano. You a piano player, play some piano. Lymon wanna hear
you.

WINING BOY: I give that piano up. That was the best thing that ever happened
to me, getting rid of that piano. That piano got so big and I'm carrying it
around on my back. I don't wish that on nobody. See, you think it's all fun
being a recording star. Got to carrying that piano around and man did I
get slow. Got just like molasses. The world just slipping by me and I'm
walking around with that piano. Alright. Now, there ain't but so many
places you can go. Only so many road wide enough for you and that
piano. And that piano get heavier and heavier. Go to a place and they find
out you play piano, the first thing they want to do is give you a drink, find
you a piano, and sit you right down. And that's where you gonna be for
the next eight hours. They ain't gonna let you get up! Now, the first three
or four years of that is fun. You can't get enough whiskey and you can't
get enough women and you don't never get tired of playing that piano.
But that only last so long. You look up one day and you hate the whiskey,
and you hate the women, and you hate the piano. But that's all you got.
You can't do nothing else. All you know how to do is play that piano. Now,
who am I? Am I me? Or am I the piano player? Sometime it seem like the

only thing to do is shoot the piano player cause he the cause of all the trouble I'm having.

DOAKER: What you gonna do when your troubles get like mine?

LYMON: If I knew how to play it, I'd play it. That's a nice piano.

BOY WILLIE: Whoever playing better play quick. Sutter's brother say he waiting on me. I sell them watermelons. Get Berniece to sell that piano. Put them two parts with the part I done saved . . .

WINING BOY: Berniece ain't gonna sell that piano. I don't see why you don't know that.

BOY WILLIE: What she gonna do with it? She ain't doing nothing but letting it sit up there and rot. That piano ain't doing nobody no good.

LYMON: That's a nice piano. If I had it I'd sell it. Unless I knew how to play like Wining Boy. You can get a nice price for that piano.

DOAKER: Now I'm gonna tell you something, Lymon don't know this . . . but I'm gonna tell you why me and Wining Boy say Berniece ain't gonna sell that piano.

BOY WILLIE: She ain't got to sell it! I'm gonna sell it! Berniece ain't got no more rights to that piano than I do.

DOAKER: I'm talking to the man . . . let me talk to the man. See, now . . . to understand why we say that . . . to understand about that piano . . . you got to go back to slavery time. See, our family was owned by a fellow named Robert Sutter. That was Sutter's grandfather. Alright. The piano was owned by a fellow named Joel Nolander. He was one of the Nolander brothers from down in Georgia. It was coming up on Sutter's wedding anniversary and he was looking to buy his wife . . . Miss Ophelia was her name . . . he was looking to buy her an anniversary present. Only thing with him . . . he ain't had no money. But he had some niggers. So he asked Mr. Nolander to see if maybe he could trade off some of his niggers for that piano. Told him he would give him one and a half niggers for it. That's the way he told him. Say he could have one full grown and one half grown. Mr. Nolander agreed only he say he had to pick them. He didn't want Sutter to give him just any old nigger. He say he wanted to have the pick of the litter. So Sutter lined up his niggers and Mr. Nolander looked them over and out of the whole bunch he picked my grandmother . . . her name was Berniece . . . same like Berniece . . . and he picked my daddy when he wasn't nothing but a little boy nine years old. They made the trade off and Miss Ophelia was so happy with that piano that it got to be just about all she would do was play on that piano.

WINING BOY: Just get up in the morning, get all dressed up and sit down and play on that piano.

DOAKER: Alright. Time go along. Time go along. Miss Ophelia got to missing my grandmother . . . the way she would cook and clean the house and talk to her and what not. And she missed having my daddy around the house to fetch things for her. So she asked to see if maybe she could trade back that piano and get her niggers back. Mr. Nolander said no. Said a deal was a deal. Him and Sutter had a big falling out about it and Miss Ophelia took sick to the bed. Wouldn't get out of the bed in the morning. She just lay there. The doctor said she was wasting away.

WINING BOY: That's when Sutter called our granddaddy up to the house.

DOAKER: Now, our granddaddy's name was Boy Willie. That's who Boy Willie's named after . . . only they called him Willie Boy. Now, he was a worker of wood. He could make you anything you wanted out of wood. He'd make you a desk. A table. A lamp. Anything you wanted. Them white fellows around there used to come up to Mr. Sutter and get him to make all kinds of things for them. Then they'd pay Mr. Sutter a nice price. See, everything my granddaddy made Mr. Sutter owned cause he owned him. That's why when Mr. Nolander offered to buy him to keep the family together Mr. Sutter wouldn't sell him. Told Mr. Nolander he didn't have enough money to buy him. Now . . . am I telling it right, Wining Boy?

WINING BOY: You telling it.

DOAKER: Sutter called him up to the house and told him to carve my grandmother and my daddy's picture on the piano for Miss Ophelia. And he took and carved this . . .

(DOAKER *crosses over to the piano.*)

See that right there? That's my grandmother, Berniece. She looked just like that. And he put a picture of my daddy when he wasn't nothing but a little boy the way he remembered him. He made them up out of his memory. Only thing . . . he didn't stop there. He carved all this. He got a picture of his mama . . . Mama Esther . . . and his daddy, Boy Charles.

WINING BOY: That was the first Boy Charles.

DOAKER: Then he put on the side here all kinds of things. See that? That's when him and Mama Berniece got married. They called it jumping the broom. That's how you got married in them days. Then he got here when my daddy was born . . . and here he got Mama Esther's funeral . . . and down here he got Mr. Nolander taking Mama Berniece and my daddy away down to his place in Georgia. He got all kinds of things what happened with our family. When Mr. Sutter seen the piano with all them carvings on it he got mad. He didn't ask for all that. But see . . . there wasn't nothing he could do about it. When Miss Ophelia seen it . . . she got excited. Now she had her piano and her niggers too. She took back to playing it and played on it right up till the day she died. Alright . . . now see, our brother Boy Charles . . . that's Berniece and Boy Willie's daddy . . . he was the oldest of us three boys. He's dead now. But he would have been fifty-seven if he had lived. He died in 1911 when he was thirty-one years old. Boy Charles used to talk about that piano all the time. He never could get it off his mind. Two or three months go by and he be talking about it again. He be talking about taking it out of Sutter's house. Say it was the story of our whole family and as long as Sutter had it . . . he had us. Say we was still in slavery. Me and Wining Boy tried to talk him out of it but it wouldn't do any good. Soon as he quiet down about it he'd start up again. We seen where he wasn't gonna get it off his mind . . . so, on the Fourth of July, 1911 . . . when Sutter was at the picnic what the county give every year . . . me and Wining Boy went on down there with him and took that piano out of Sutter's house. We put it on a wagon and me and Wining Boy carried it over into the next county with Mama Ola's people. Boy Charles decided to stay around there and wait until Sutter got home to make it look like business as usual.

Now, I don't know what happened when Sutter came home and found that piano gone. But somebody went up to Boy Charles's house and set it on fire. But he wasn't in there. He must have seen them coming cause he went down and caught the 3:57 Yellow Dog. He didn't know they was gonna come down and stop the train. Stopped the train and found Boy Charles in the boxcar with four of them hobos. Must have got mad when they couldn't find the piano cause they set the boxcar afire and killed everybody. Now, nobody know who done that. Some people say it was Sutter cause it was his piano. Some people say it was Sheriff Carter. Some people say it was Robert Smith and Ed Saunders. But don't nobody know for sure. It was about two months after that that Ed Saunders fell down his well. Just upped and fell down his well for no reason. People say it was the ghost of them men who burned up in the boxcar that pushed him in his well. They started calling them the Ghosts of the Yellow Dog. Now, that's how all that got started and that why we say Berniece ain't gonna sell that piano. Cause her daddy died over it.

BOY WILLIE: All that's in the past. If my daddy had seen where he could have traded that piano in for some land of his own, it wouldn't be sitting up here now. He spent his whole life farming on somebody else's land. I ain't gonna do that. See, he couldn't do no better. When he come along he ain't had nothing he could build on. His daddy ain't had nothing to give him. The only thing my daddy had to give me was that piano. And he died over giving me that. I ain't gonna let it sit up there and rot without trying to do something with it. If Berniece can't see that, then I'm gonna go ahead and sell my half. And you and Wining Boy know I'm right.

DOAKER: Ain't nobody said nothing about who's right and who's wrong. I was just telling the man about the piano. I was telling him why we say Berniece ain't gonna sell it.

LYMON: Yeah, I can see why you say that now. I told Boy Willie he ought to stay up here with me.

BOY WILLIE: You stay! I'm going back! That's what I'm gonna do with my life! Why I got to come up here and learn to do something I don't know how to do when I already know how to farm? You stay up here and make your own way if that's what you want to do. I'm going back and live my life the way I want to live it.

(WINING BOY *gets up and crosses to the piano.*)

WINING BOY: Let's see what we got here. I ain't played on this thing for a while.

DOAKER: You can stop telling that. You was playing on it the last time you was through here. We couldn't get you off of it. Go on and play something.

(WINING BOY sits down at the piano and plays and sings. The song is one which has put many dimes and quarters in his pocket, long ago, in dimly remembered towns and way stations. He plays badly, without hesitation, and sings in a forceful voice.)

WINING BOY *(singing):*

> I am a rambling gambling man
> I gambled in many towns
> I rambled this wide world over
> I rambled this world around
> I had my ups and downs in life
> And bitter times I saw
> But I never knew what misery was
> Till I lit on old Arkansas.
>
> I started out one morning
> to meet that early train
> He said, "You better work for me
> I have some land to drain.
> I'll give you fifty cents a day,
> Your washing, board and all
> And you shall be a different man
> In the state of Arkansas."
>
> I worked six months for the rascal
> Joe Herrin was his name
> He fed me old corn dodgers
> They was hard as any rock
> My tooth is all got loosened
> And my knees begin to knock
> That was the kind of hash I got
> In the state of Arkansas.
>
> Traveling man
> I've traveled all around this world
> Traveling man
> I've traveled from land to land
> Traveling man
> I've traveled all around this world
> Well it ain't no use
> writing no news
> I'm a traveling man.

(The door opens and BERNIECE enters with MARETHA.)

BERNIECE: Is that . . . Lord, I know that ain't Wining Boy sitting there.

WINING BOY: Hey, Berniece.

BERNIECE: You all had this planned. You and Boy Willie had this planned.

WINING BOY: I didn't know he was gonna be here. I'm on my way down home. I stopped by to see you and Doaker first.

DOAKER: I told the nigger he left out of here with that sack of money, we thought we might never see him again. Boy Willie say he wasn't gonna see him till he got broke. I looked up and seen him sitting on the doorstep asking for two dollars. Look at him laughing. He know it's the truth.

BERNIECE: Boy Willie, I didn't see that truck out there. I thought you was out selling watermelons.

BOY WILLIE: We done sold them all. Sold the truck too.

BERNIECE: I don't want to go through none of your stuff. I done told you to go back where you belong.

BOY WILLIE: I was just teasing you, woman. You can't take no teasing?

BERNIECE: Wining Boy, when you get here?

WINING BOY: A little while ago. I took the train from Kansas City.

BERNIECE: Let me go upstairs and change and then I'll cook you something to eat.

BOY WILLIE: You ain't cooked me nothing when I come.

BERNIECE: Boy Willie, go on and leave me alone. Come on, Maretha, get up here and change your clothes before you get them dirty.

(BERNIECE *exits up the stairs, followed by* MARETHA.)

WINING BOY: Maretha sure getting big, ain't she, Doaker. And just as pretty as she want to be. I didn't know Crawley had it in him.

(BOY WILLIE *crosses to the piano.*)

BOY WILLIE: Hey, Lymon . . . get up on the other side of this piano and let me see something.

WINING BOY: Boy Willie, what is you doing?

BOY WILLIE: I'm seeing how heavy this piano is. Get up over there, Lymon.

WINING BOY: Go on and leave that piano alone. You ain't taking that piano out of here and selling it.

BOY WILLIE: Just as soon as I get them watermelons out that truck.

WINING BOY: Well, I got something to say about that.

BOY WILLIE: This my daddy's piano.

WINING BOY: He ain't took it by himself. Me and Doaker helped him.

BOY WILLIE: He died by himself. Where was you and Doaker at then? Don't come telling me nothing about this piano. This is me and Berniece's piano. Am I right, Doaker?

DOAKER: Yeah, you right.

BOY WILLIE: Let's see if we can lift it up, Lymon. Get a good grip on it and pick it up on your end. Ready? Lift!

(As they start to move the piano, the sound of SUTTER'S GHOST is heard. DOAKER is the only one to hear it. With difficulty they move the piano a little bit so it is out of place.)

BOY WILLIE: What you think?

LYMON: It's heavy . . . but you can move it. Only it ain't gonna be easy.

BOY WILLIE: It wasn't that heavy to me. Okay, let's put it back.

(The sound of SUTTER'S GHOST *is heard again. They all hear it as* BERNIECE *enters on the stairs.)*

BERNIECE: Boy Willie . . . you gonna play around with me one too many times. And then God's gonna bless you and West is gonna dress you. Now set that piano back over there. I done told you a hundred times I ain't selling that piano.

BOY WILLIE: I'm trying to get me some land, woman. I need that piano to get me some money so I can buy Sutter's land.

BERNIECE: Money can't buy what that piano cost. You can't sell your soul for money. It won't go with the buyer. It'll shrivel and shrink to know that you ain't taken on to it. But it won't go with the buyer.

BOY WILLIE: I ain't talking about all that, woman. I ain't talking about selling my soul. I'm talking about trading that piece of wood for some land. Get something under your feet. Land the only thing God ain't making no more of. You can always get you another piano. I'm talking about some land. What you get something out the ground from. That's what I'm talking about. You can't do nothing with that piano but sit up there and look at it.

BERNIECE: That's just what I'm gonna do. Wining Boy, you want me to fry you some pork chops?

BOY WILLIE: Now, I'm gonna tell you the way I see it. The only thing that make that piano worth something is them carvings Papa Willie Boy put on there. That's what make it worth something. That was my great-grandaddy. Papa Boy Charles brought that piano into the house. Now, I'm supposed to build on what they left me. You can't do nothing with that piano sitting up here in the house. That's just like if I let them watermelons sit out there and rot. I'd be a fool. Alright now, if you say to me, Boy Willie, I'm using that piano. I give out lessons on it and that help me make my rent or whatever. Then that be something else. I'd have to go on and say, well, Berniece using that piano. She building on it. Let her go on and use it. I got to find another way to get Sutter's land. But Doaker say you ain't touched that piano the whole time it's been up here. So why you wanna stand in my way? See, you just looking at the sentimental value. See, that's good. That's alright. I take my hat off whenever somebody say my daddy's name. But I ain't gonna be no fool about no sentimental value. You can sit up here and look at the piano for the next hundred years and it's just gonna be a piano. You can't make more than that. Now I want to get Sutter's land with that piano. I get Sutter's land and I can go down and cash in the crop and get my seed. As long as I got the land and the seed then I'm alright. I can always get me a little something else. Cause that land give back to you. I can make me another crop and cash that in. I still got the land and the seed. But that piano don't put out nothing else. You ain't got nothing working for you. Now, the kind of man my daddy was he would have understood that.

I'm sorry you can't see it that way. But that's why I'm gonna take that piano out of here and sell it.

BERNIECE: You ain't taking that piano out of my house.

(She crosses to the piano.)

Look at this piano. Look at it. Mama Ola polished this piano with her tears for seventeen years. For seventeen years she rubbed on it till her hands bled. Then she rubbed the blood in . . . mixed it up with the rest of the blood on it. Every day that God breathed life into her body she rubbed and cleaned and polished and prayed over it. "Play something for me, Berniece. Play something for me, Berniece." Every day. "I cleaned it up for you, play something for me, Berniece." You always talking about your daddy but you ain't never stopped to look at what his foolishness cost your mama. Seventeen years' worth of cold nights and an empty bed. For what? For a piano? For a piece of wood? To get even with somebody? I look at you and you're all the same. You, Papa Boy Charles, Wining Boy, Doaker, Crawley . . . you're all alike. All this thieving and killing and thieving and killing. And what it ever lead to? More killing and more thieving. I ain't never seen it come to nothing. People getting burned up. People getting shot. People falling down their wells. It don't never stop.

DOAKER: Come on now, Berniece, ain't no need in getting upset.

BOY WILLIE: I done a little bit of stealing here and there, but I ain't never killed nobody. I can't be speaking for nobody else. You all got to speak for yourself, but I ain't never killed nobody.

BERNIECE: You killed Crawley just as sure as if you pulled the trigger.

BOY WILLIE: See, that's ignorant. That's downright foolish for you to say something like that. You ain't doing nothing but showing your ignorance. If the nigger was here I'd whup his ass for getting me and Lymon shot at.

BERNIECE: Crawley ain't knew about the wood.

BOY WILLIE: We told the man about the wood. Ask Lymon. He knew all about the wood. He seen we was sneaking it. Why else we gonna be out there at night? Don't come telling me Crawley ain't knew about the wood. Them fellows come up on us and Crawley tried to bully them. Me and Lymon seen the sheriff with them and give in. Wasn't no sense in getting killed over fifty dollars' worth of wood.

BERNIECE: Crawley ain't knew you stole that wood.

BOY WILLIE: We ain't stole no wood. Me and Lymon was hauling wood for Jim Miller and keeping us a little bit on the side. We dumped our little bit down there by the creek till we had enough to make a load. Some fellows seen us and we figured we better get it before they did. We come up there and got Crawley to help us load it. Figured we'd cut him in. Crawley trying to keep the wolf from his door . . . we was trying to help him.

LYMON: Me and Boy Willie told him about the wood. We told him some fellows might be trying to beat us to it. He say let me go back and get my thirty-eight. That's what caused all the trouble.

BOY WILLIE: If Crawley ain't had the gun he'd be alive today.

LYMON: We had it about half loaded when they come up on us. We seen the sheriff with them and we tried to get away. We ducked around near the bend in the creek . . . but they was down there too. Boy Willie say let's give in. But Crawley pulled out his gun and started shooting. That's when they started shooting back.

BERNIECE: All I know is Crawley would be alive if you hadn't come up there and got him.

BOY WILLIE: I ain't had nothing to do with Crawley getting killed. That was his own fault.

BERNIECE: Crawley's dead and in the ground and you still walking around here eating. That's all I know. He went off to load some wood with you and ain't never come back.

BOY WILLIE: I told you, woman . . . I ain't had nothing to do with . . .

BERNIECE: He ain't here, is he? He ain't here!

(BERNIECE *hits* BOY WILLIE.)

I said he ain't here. Is he?

(BERNIECE *continues to hit* BOY WILLIE, *who doesn't move to defend himself, other than back up and turning his head so that most of the blows fall on his chest and arms.*)

DOAKER (*grabbing* BERNIECE): Come on, Berniece . . . let it go, it ain't his fault.

BERNIECE: He ain't here, is he? Is he?

BOY WILLIE: I told you I ain't responsible for Crawley.

BERNIECE: He ain't here.

BOY WILLIE: Come on now, Berniece . . . don't do this now. Doaker get her. I ain't had nothing to do with Crawley . . .

BERNIECE: You come up there and got him!

BOY WILLIE: I done told you now. Doaker, get her. I ain't playing.

DOAKER: Come on. Berniece.

(MARETHA *is heard screaming upstairs. It is a scream of stark terror.*)

MARETHA: Mama! . . . Mama!

(*The lights go down to black. End of Act One.*)

ACT TWO

Scene One

(*The lights come up on the kitchen. It is the following morning.* DOAKER *is ironing the pants to his uniform. He has a pot cooking on the stove at the same time. He is singing a song. The song provides him with the rhythm for his work and he moves about the kitchen with the ease born of many years as a railroad cook.*)

DOAKER:
Gonna leave Jackson Mississippi
and go to Memphis
and double back to Jackson
Come on down to Hattiesburg

Change cars on the Y.D.
coming through the territory to
Meridian
and Meridian to Greenville
and Greenville to Memphis
I'm on my way and I know where

Change cars on the Katy
Leaving Jackson
and going through Clarksdale
Hello Winona!
Courtland!
Bateville!
Como!
Senitobia!
Lewisberg!
Sunflower!
Glendora!
Sharkey!
And double back to Jackson
Hello Greenwood
I'm on my way Memphis
Clarksdale
Moorhead
Indianola
Can a highball pass through?
Highball on through sir
Grand Carson!
Thirty First Street Depot
Fourth Street Depot
Memphis!

(WINING BOY: *enters carrying a suit of clothes.*)

DOAKER: I thought you took that suit to the pawnshop?

WINING BOY: I went down there and the man tell me the suit is too old. Look at this suit. This is one hundred percent silk! How a silk suit gonna get too old? I know what it was he just didn't want to give me five dollars for it. Best he wanna give me is three dollars. I figure a silk suit is worth five dollars all over the world. I wasn't gonna part with it for no three dollars so I brought it back.

DOAKER: They got another pawnshop up on Wylie.

WINING BOY: I carried it up there. He say he don't take no clothes. Only thing he take is guns and radios. Maybe a guitar or two. Where's Berniece?

DOAKER: Berniece still at work. Boy Willie went down there to meet Lymon this morning. I guess they got that truck fixed, they been out there all day and ain't come back yet. Maretha scared to sleep up there now. Berniece don't know, but I seen Sutter before she did.

WINING BOY: Say what?

DOAKER: About three weeks ago. I had just come back from down there. Sutter couldn't have been dead more than three days. He was sitting over there at the piano. I come out to go to work . . . and he was sitting right there. Had his hand on top of his head just like Berniece said. I believe he broke his neck when he fell in the well. I kept quiet about it. I didn't see no reason to upset Berniece.

WINING BOY: Did he say anything? Did he say he was looking for Boy Willie?

DOAKER: He was just sitting there. He ain't said nothing. I went on out the door and left him sitting there. I figure as long as he was on the other side of the room everything be alright. I don't know what I would have done if he had started walking toward me.

WINING BOY: Berniece say he was calling Boy Willie's name.

DOAKER: I ain't heard him say nothing. He was just sitting there when I seen him. But I don't believe Boy Willie pushed him in the well. Sutter here cause of that piano. I heard him playing on it one time. I thought it was Berniece but then she don't play that kind of music. I come out here and ain't seen nobody, but them piano keys was moving a mile a minute. Berniece need to go on and get rid of it. It ain't done nothing but cause trouble.

WINING BOY: I agree with Berniece. Boy Charles ain't took it to give it back. He took it cause he figure he had more right to it than Sutter did. If Sutter can't understand that . . . then that's just the way that go. Sutter dead and in the ground . . . don't care where his ghost is. He can hover around and play on the piano all he want. I want to see him carry it out the house. That's what I want to see. What time Berniece get home? I don't see how I let her get away from me this morning.

DOAKER: You up there sleep. Berniece leave out of here early in the morning. She out there in Squirrel Hill cleaning house for some bigshot down there at the steel mill. They don't like you to come late. You come late they won't give you your carfare. What kind of business you got with Berniece?

WINING BOY: My business. I ain't asked you what kind of business you got.

DOAKER: Berniece ain't got no money. If that's why you was trying to catch her. She having a hard enough time trying to get by as it is. If she go ahead and marry Avery . . . he working every day . . . she go ahead and marry him they could do alright for themselves. But as it stands she ain't got no money.

WINING BOY: Well, let me have five dollars.

DOAKER: I just give you a dollar before you left out of here. You ain't gonna take my five dollars out there and gamble and drink it up.

WINING BOY: Aw, nigger, give me five dollars. I'll give it back to you.

DOAKER: You wasn't looking to give me five dollars when you had that sack of money. You wasn't looking to throw nothing my way. Now you wanna come in here and borrow five dollars. If you going back with Boy Willie you need to be trying to figure out how you gonna get train fare.

WINING BOY: That's why I need the five dollars. If I had five dollars I could get me some money.

(DOAKER goes into his pocket.)

Make it seven.

DOAKER: You take this five dollars . . . and you bring my money back here too.

(BOY WILLIE and LYMON enter. They are happy and excited. They have money in all of their pockets and are anxious to count it.)

DOAKER: How'd you do out there?

BOY WILLIE: They was lining up for them.

LYMON: Me and Boy Willie couldn't sell them fast enough. Time we got one sold we'd sell another.

BOY WILLIE: I seen what was happening and told Lymon to up the price on them.

LYMON: Boy Willie say charge them a quarter more. They didn't care. A couple of people give me a dollar and told me to keep the change.

BOY WILLIE: One fellow bought five. I say now what he gonna do with five water-melons? He can't eat them all. I sold him the five and asked him did he want to buy five more.

LYMON: I ain't never seen nobody snatch a dollar fast as Boy Willie.

BOY WILLIE: One lady asked me say, "Is they sweet?" I told her say, "Lady, where we grow these watermelons we put sugar in the ground." You know, she believed me. Talking about she had never heard of that before. Lymon was laughing his head off. I told her, "Oh, yeah, we put the sugar right in the ground with the seed." She say, "Well, give me another one." Them white folks is something else . . . ain't they, Lymon?

LYMON: Soon as you holler watermelons they come right out their door. Then they go and get their neighbors. Look like they having a contest to see who can buy the most.

WINING BOY: I got something for Lymon.

(WINING BOY goes to get his suit. BOY WILLIE and LYMON continue to count their money.)

BOY WILLIE: I know you got more than that. You ain't sold all them watermelons for that little bit of money.

LYMON: I'm still looking. That ain't all you got either. Where's all them quarters?

BOY WILLIE: You let me worry about the quarters. Just put the money on the table.

WINING BOY *(entering with his suit)*: Look here, Lymon . . . see this? Look at his eyes getting big. He ain't never seen a suit like this. This is one hundred percent silk. Go ahead . . . put it on. See if it fit you.

(LYMON tries the suit coat on.)

Look at that. Feel it. That's one hundred percent genuine silk. I got that in Chicago. You can't get clothes like that nowhere but New York and

Chicago. You can't get clothes like that in Pittsburgh. These folks in Pittsburgh ain't never seen clothes like that.

LYMON: This is nice, feel real nice and smooth.

WINING BOY: That's a fifty-five-dollar suit. That's the kind of suit the bigshots wear. You need a pistol and a pocketful of money to wear that suit. I'll let you have it for three dollars. The women will fall out their windows they see you in a suit like that. Give me three dollars and go on and wear it down the street and get you a woman.

BOY WILLIE: That looks nice, Lymon. Put the pants on. Let me see it with the pants.

(LYMON *begins to try on the pants.*)

WINING BOY: Look at that . . . see how it fits you? Give me three dollars and go on and take it. Look at that, Doaker . . . don't he look nice?

DOAKER: Yeah . . . that's a nice suit.

WINING BOY: Got a shirt to go with it. Cost you an extra dollar. Four dollars you got the whole deal.

LYMON: How this look, Boy Willie?

BOY WILLIE: That look nice . . . if you like that kind of thing. I don't like them dress-up kind of clothes. If you like it, look real nice.

WINING BOY: That's the kind of suit you need for up here in the North.

LYMON: Four dollars for everything? The suit and the shirt?

WINING BOY: That's cheap. I should be charging you twenty dollars. I give you a break cause you a homeboy. That's the only way I let you have it for four dollars.

LYMON (*Going into his pocket*): Okay . . . here go the four dollars.

WINING BOY: You got some shoes? What size you wear?

LYMON: Size nine.

WINING BOY: That's what size I got! Size nine. I let you have them for three dollars.

LYMON: Where they at? Let me see them.

WINING BOY: They real nice shoes, too. Got a nice tip to them. Got pointy toe just like you want.

(WINING BOY *goes to get his shoes.*)

LYMON: Come on, Boy Willie, let's go out tonight. I wanna see what it looks like up here. Maybe we go to a picture show. Hey, Doaker, they got picture shows up here?

DOAKER: The Rhumba Theater. Right down there on Fullerton Street. Can't miss it. Got the speakers outside on the sidewalk. You can hear it a block away. Boy Willie know where it's at.

(DOAKER *exits into his room.*)

LYMON: Let's go to the picture show, Boy Willie. Let's go find some women.

BOY WILLIE: Hey, Lymon, how many of them watermelons would you say we got left? We got just under a half a load . . . right?

LYMON: About that much. Maybe a little more.

BOY WILLIE: You think that piano will fit up in there?

LYMON: If we stack them watermelons you can sit it up in the front there.

BOY WILLIE: I'm gonna call that man tomorrow.

WINING BOY *(returns with his shoes):* Here you go . . . size nine. Put them on. Cost you three dollars. That's a Florsheim shoe. That's the kind Staggerlee wore.

LYMON *(trying on the shoes):* You sure these size nine?

WINING BOY: You can look at my feet and see we wear the same size. Man, you put on that suit and them shoes and you got something there. You ready for whatever's out there. But is they ready for you? With them shoes on you be the King of the Walk. Have everybody stop to look at your shoes. Wishing they had a pair. I'll give you a break. Go on and take them for two dollars.

*(*LYMON *pays* WINING BOY *two dollars.)*

LYMON: Come on, Boy Willie . . . let's go find some women. I'm gonna go upstairs and get ready. I'll be ready to go in a minute. Ain't you gonna get dressed?

BOY WILLIE: I'm gonna wear what I got on. I ain't dressing up for these city niggers.

*(*LYMON *exits up the stairs.)*

That's all Lymon think about is women.

WINING BOY: His daddy was the same way. I used to run around with him. I know his mama too. Two strokes back and I would have been his daddy! His daddy's dead now . . . but I got the nigger out of jail one time. They was fixing to name him Daniel and walk him through the Lion's Den. He got in a tussle with one of them white fellows and the sheriff lit on him like white on rice. That's how the whole thing come about between me and Lymon's mama. She knew me and his daddy used to run together and he got in jail and she went down there and took the sheriff a hundred dollars. Don't get me to lying about where she got it from. I don't know. The sheriff *looked at that hundred dollars and turned his nose up* Told her, say, "That ain't gonna do him no good. You got to put another hundred on top of that." She come up *there and got me where I was playing at this saloon* . . . said she had all but fifty dollars and asked me if I could help. Now the way I figured it . . . without that fifty dollars the sheriff was gonna turn him over to Parchman. The sheriff turn him over to Parchman it be three years before anybody see him again. Now I'm gonna say it right . . . I will give anybody fifty dollars to keep them out of jail for three years. I give her the fifty dollars and she told me to come over to the house. I ain't asked her. I figure if she was nice enough to invite me I ought to go. I ain't had to say a word. She invited me over just as nice. Say, "Why don't you come over to the house?" She ain't had to say nothing else. Them words rolled off her tongue just as nice. I went on down there and sat about three hours. Started to leave and changed my mind. She grabbed hold to me and say,

"Baby, it's all night long." That was one of the shortest nights I have ever spent on this earth! I could have used another eight hours. Lymon's daddy didn't even say nothing to me when he got out. He just looked at me funny. He had a good notion something had happened between me an' her. L. D. Jackson. That was one bad-luck nigger. Got killed at some dance. Fellow walked in and shot him thinking he was somebody else.

(DOAKER enters from his room.)

Hey, Doaker, you remember L. D. Jackson?

DOAKER: That's Lymon's daddy. That was one bad-luck nigger.

BOY WILLIE: Look like you ready to railroad some.

DOAKER: Yeah, I got to make that run.

(LYMON enters from the stairs. He is dressed in his new suit and shoes, to which he has added a cheap straw hat.)

LYMON: How I look?

WINING BOY: You look like a million dollars. Don't he look good, Doaker? Come on, let's play some cards. You wanna play some cards?

BOY WILLIE: We ain't gonna play no cards with you. Me and Lymon gonna find some women. Hey, Lymon, don't play no cards with Wining Boy. He'll take all your money.

WINING BOY *(to LYMON)*: You got a magic suit there. You can get you a woman easy with that suit . . . but you got to know the magic words. You know the magic words to get you a woman?

LYMON: I just talk to them to see if I like them and they like me.

WINING BOY: You just walk right up to them and say, "If you got the harbor I got the ship." If that don't work ask them if you can put them in your pocket. The first thing they gonna say is, "It's too small." That's when you look them dead in the eye and say, "Baby, ain't nothing small about me." If that don't work then you move on to another one. Am I telling him right, Doaker?

DOAKER: That man don't need you to tell him nothing about no women. These women these days ain't gonna fall for that kind of stuff. You got to buy them a present. That's what they looking for these days.

BOY WILLIE: Come on, I'm ready. You ready, Lymon? Come on, let's go find some women.

WINING BOY: Here, let me walk out with you. I wanna see the women fall out their window when they see Lymon.

(They all exit and the lights go down on the scene.)

Scene 2

(The lights come up on the kitchen. It is late evening of the same day. BERNIECE *has set a tub for her bath in the kitchen. She is heating up water on the stove. There is a knock at the door.)*

BERNIECE: Who is it?

AVERY: It's me, Avery.

(BERNIECE *opens the door and lets him in.*)

BERNIECE: Avery, come on in. I was just fixing to take my bath.

AVERY: Where Boy Willie? I see that truck out there almost empty. They done sold almost all them watermelons.

BERNIECE: They was gone when I come home. I don't know where they went off to. Boy Willie around here about to drive me crazy.

AVERY: They sell them watermelons . . . he'll be gone soon.

BERNIECE: What Mr. Cohen say about letting you have the place?

AVERY: He say he'll let me have it for thirty dollars a month. I talked him out of thirty-five and he say he'll let me have it for thirty.

BERNIECE: That's a nice spot next to Benny Diamond's store.

AVERY: Berniece . . . I be at home and I get to thinking you up here an' I'm down there. I get to thinking how that look to have a preacher that ain't married. It makes for a better congregation if the preacher was settled down and married.

BERNIECE: Avery . . . not now. I was fixing to take my bath.

AVERY: You know how I feel about you, Berniece. Now . . . I done got the place from Mr. Cohen. I get the money from the bank and I can fix it up real nice. They give me a ten cents a hour raise down there on the job . . . now Berniece, I ain't got much in the way of comforts. I got a hole in my pockets near about as far as money is concerned. I ain't never found no way through life to a woman I care about like I care about you. I need that. I need somebody on my bond side. I need a woman that fits in my hand.

BERNIECE: Avery, I ain't ready to get married now.

AVERY: You too young a woman to close up, Berniece.

BERNIECE: I ain't said nothing about closing up. I got a lot of woman left in me.

AVERY: Where's it at? When's the last time you looked at it?

BERNIECE (*stunned by his remark*): That's a nasty thing to say. And you call yourself a preacher.

AVERY: Anytime I get anywhere near you . . . you push me away.

BERNIECE: I got enough on my hands with Maretha. I got enough people to love and take care of.

AVERY: Who you got to love you? Can't nobody get close enough to you. Doaker can't half say nothing to you. You jump all over Boy Willie. Who you got to love you, Berniece?

BERNIECE: You trying to tell me a woman can't be nothing without a man. But you alright, huh? You can just walk out of here without me—without a woman—and still be a man. That's alright. Ain't nobody gonna ask you, "Avery, who you got to love you?" That's alright for you. But everybody gonna be worried about Berniece. "How Berniece gonna take care of herself? How she gonna raise that child without a man? Wonder what she do with herself. How she gonna live like that?" Everybody got all kinds of questions for Berniece. Everybody telling me I can't be a woman unless I got a man. Well, you tell me, Avery—you know—how much woman am I?

AVERY: It wasn't me, Berniece. You can't blame me for nobody else. I'll own up

to my own shortcomings. But you can't blame me for Crawley or nobody
else.

BERNIECE: I ain't blaming nobody for nothing. I'm just stating the facts.

AVERY: How long you gonna carry Crawley with you, Berniece? It's been over
three years. At some point you got to let go and go on. Life's got all kinds
of twists and turns. That don't mean you stop living. That don't mean you
cut yourself off from life. You can't go through life carrying Crawley's ghost
with you. Crawley's been dead three years. Three years, Berniece.

BERNIECE: I know how long Crawley's been dead. You ain't got to tell me that. I
just ain't ready to get married right now.

AVERY: What is you ready for, Berniece? You just gonna drift along from day to
day. Life is more than making it from one day to another. You gonna look
up one day and it's all gonna be past you. Life's gonna be gone out of your
hands—there won't be enough to make nothing with. I'm standing here
now, Berniece—but I don't know how much longer I'm gonna be standing
here waiting on you.

BERNIECE: Avery, I told you . . . when you get your church we'll sit down and
talk about this. I got too many other things to deal with right now. Boy
Willie and the piano . . . and Sutter's ghost. I thought I might have been
seeing things, but Maretha done seen Sutter's ghost, too.

AVERY: When this happen, Berniece?

BERNIECE: Right after I came home yesterday. Me and Boy Willie was arguing
about the piano and Sutter's ghost was standing at the top of the stairs.
Maretha scared to sleep up there now. Maybe if you bless the house he'll
go away.

AVERY: I don't know, Berniece. I don't know if I should fool around with something like that.

BERNIECE: I can't have Maretha scared to go to sleep up there. Seem like if you
bless the house he would go away.

AVERY: You might have to be a special kind of preacher to do something like
that.

BERNIECE: I keep telling myself when Boy Willie leave he'll go on and leave with
him. I believe Boy Willie pushed him in the well.

AVERY: That's been going on down there a long time. The Ghosts of the Yellow
Dog been pushing people in their wells long before Boy Willie got grown.

BERNIECE: Somebody down there pushing them people in their wells. They ain't
just upped and fell. Ain't no wind pushed nobody in their well.

AVERY: Oh, I don't know. God works in mysterious ways.

BERNIECE: He ain't pushed nobody in their wells.

AVERY: He caused it to happen. God is the Great Causer. He can do anything.
He parted the Red Sea. He say I will smite my enemies. Reverend
Thompson used to preach on the Ghosts of the Yellow Dog as the hand of
God.

BERNIECE: I don't care who preached what. Somebody down there pushing
them people in their wells. Somebody like Boy Willie. I can see him doing

something like that. You ain't gonna tell me that Sutter just upped and fell in his well. I believe Boy Willie pushed him so he could get his land.

AVERY: What Doaker say about Boy Willie selling the piano?

BERNIECE: Doaker don't want no part of that piano. He ain't never wanted no part of it. He blames himself for not staying behind with Papa Boy Charles. He washed his hands of that piano a long time ago. He didn't want me to bring it up here—but I wasn't gonna leave it down there.

AVERY: Well, it seems to me somebody ought to be able to talk to Boy Willie.

BERNIECE: You can't talk to Boy Willie. He been that way all his life. Mama Ola had her hands full trying to talk to him. He don't listen to nobody. He just like my daddy. He get his mind fixed on something and can't nobody turn him from it.

AVERY: You ought to start a choir at the church. Maybe if he seen you was doing something with it—if you told him you was gonna put it in my church—maybe he'd see it different. You ought to put it down in the church and start a choir. The Bible say "Make a joyful noise unto the Lord." Maybe if Boy Willie see you was doing something with it he'd see it different.

BERNIECE: I done told you I don't play on that piano. Ain't no need in you to keep talking this choir stuff. When my mama died I shut the top on that piano and I ain't never opened it since. I was only playing it for her. When my daddy died seem like all her life went into that piano. She used to have me playing on it . . . had Miss Eula come in and teach me . . . say when I played it she could hear my daddy talking to her. I used to think them pictures came alive and walked through the house. Sometime late at night I could hear my mama talking to them. I said that wasn't gonna happen to me. I don't play that piano cause I don't want to wake them spirits. They never be walking around in this house.

AVERY: You got to put all that behind you, Berniece.

BERNIECE: I got Maretha playing on it. She don't know nothing about it. Let her go on and be a schoolteacher or something. She don't have to carry all of that with her. She got a chance I didn't have. I ain't gonna burden her with that piano.

AVERY: You got to put all of that behind you, Berniece. That's the same thing like Crawley. Everybody got stones in their passway. You got to step over them or walk around them. You picking them up and carrying them with you. All you got to do is set them down by the side of the road. You ain't got to carry them with you. You can walk over there right now and play that piano. You can walk over there right now and God will walk over there with you. Right now you can set that sack of stones down by the side of the road and walk away from it. You don't have to carry it with you. You can do it right now.

(AVERY *crosses over to the piano and raises the lid.*)

Come on, Berniece . . . set it down and walk away from it. Come on, play "Old Ship of Zion." Walk over here and claim it as an instrument of the Lord. You can walk over here right now and make it into a celebration.

(BERNIECE *moves toward the piano.*)

BERNIECE: Avery . . . I done told you I don't want to play that piano. Now or no other time.

AVERY: The Bible say, "The Lord is my refuge . . . and my strength!" With the strength of God you can put the past behind you, Berniece. With the strength of God you can do anything! God got a bright tomorrow. God don't ask what you done . . . God ask what you gonna do. The strength of God can move mountains! God's got a bright tomorrow for you . . . all you got to do is walk over here and claim it.

BERNIECE: Avery, just go on and let me finish my bath. I'll see you tomorrow.

AVERY: Okay, Berniece. I'm gonna go home. I'm gonna go home and read up on my Bible. And tomorrow . . . if the good Lord give me strength tomor-row . . . I'm gonna come by and bless the house . . . and show you the power of the Lord.

(AVERY *crosses to the door.*)

It's gonna be alright, Berniece. God say he will soothe the troubled waters. I'll come by tomorrow and bless the house.

(*The lights go down to black.*)

Scene 3

(*Several hours later. The house is dark.* BERNIECE *has retired for the night.* BOY WILLIE *enters the darkened house with* GRACE.)

BOY WILLIE: Come on in. This my sister's house. My sister live here. Come on, I ain't gonna bite you.

GRACE: Put some light on. I can't see.

BOY WILLIE: You don't need to see nothing, baby. This here is all you need to see. All you need to do is see me. If you can't see me you can feel me in the dark. How's that, sugar?

(*He attempts to kiss her.*)

GRACE: Go on now . . . wait!

BOY WILLIE: Just give me one little old kiss.

GRACE (*pushing him away*): Come on, now. Where I'm gonna sleep at?

BOY WILLIE: We got to sleep out here on the couch. Come on, my sister don't mind. Lymon come back he just got to sleep on the floor. He run off with Dolly somewhere he better stay there. Come on, sugar.

GRACE: Wait now . . . you ain't told me nothing about no couch. I thought you had a bed. Both of us can't sleep on that little old couch.

BOY WILLIE: It don't make no difference. We can sleep on the floor. Let Lymon sleep on the couch.

GRACE: You ain't told me nothing about no couch.

BOY WILLIE: What difference it make? You just wanna be with me.

GRACE: I don't want to be with you on no couch. Ain't you got no bed?

BOY WILLIE: You don't need no bed, woman. My granddaddy used to take women on the backs of horses. What you need a bed for? You just want to be with me.

GRACE: You sure is country. I didn't know you was this country.

BOY WILLIE: There's a lot of things you don't know about me. Come on, let me show you what this country boy can do.

GRACE: Let's go to my place. I got a room with a bed if Leroy don't come back there.

BOY WILLIE: Who's Leroy? You ain't said nothing about no Leroy.

GRACE: He used to be my man. He ain't coming back. He gone off with some other gal.

BOY WILLIE: You let him have your key?

GRACE: He ain't coming back.

BOY WILLIE: Did you let him have your key?

GRACE: He got a key but he ain't coming back. He took off with some other gal.

BOY WILLIE: I don't wanna go nowhere he might come. Let's stay here. Come on, sugar.

(He pulls her over to the couch.)

Let me heist your hood and check your oil. See if your battery needs charged.

(He pulls her to him. They kiss and tug at each other's clothing. In their anxiety they knock over a lamp.)

BERNIECE: Who's that . . . Wining Boy?

BOY WILLIE: It's me . . . Boy Willie. Go on back to sleep. Everything's alright.

(To GRACE.*)*

That's my sister. Everything's alright, Berniece. Go on back to sleep.

BERNIECE: What you doing down there? What you done knocked over?

BOY WILLIE: It wasn't nothing. Everything's alright. Go on back to sleep.

(To GRACE.*)*

That's my sister. We alright. She gone back to sleep.

(They begin to kiss. BERNIECE *enters from the stairs dressed in a nightgown. She cuts on the light.)*

BERNIECE: Boy Willie, what you doing down here?

BOY WILLIE: It was just that there lamp. It ain't broke. It's okay. Everything's alright. Go on back to bed.

BERNIECE: Boy Willie, I don't allow that in my house. You gonna have to take your company someplace else.

BOY WILLIE: It's alright. We ain't doing nothing. We just sitting here talking. This here is Grace. That's my sister Berniece.

BERNIECE: You know I don't allow that kind of stuff in my house.

BOY WILLIE: Allow what? We just sitting here talking.

BERNIECE: Well, your company gonna have to leave. Come back and talk in the morning.

BOY WILLIE: Go on back upstairs now.

BERNIECE: I got an eleven-year-old girl upstairs. I can't allow that around here.

BOY WILLIE: Ain't nobody said nothing about that. I told you we just talking.

GRACE: Come on . . . let's go to my place. Ain't nobody got to tell me to leave but once.

BOY WILLIE: You ain't got to be like that, Berniece.

BERNIECE: I'm sorry, Miss. But he know I don't allow that in here.

GRACE: You ain't got to tell me but once. I don't stay nowhere I ain't wanted.

BOY WILLIE: I don't know why you want to embarrass me in front of my company.

GRACE: Come on, take me home.

BERNIECE: Go on, Boy Willie. Just go on with your company.

(BOY WILLIE and GRACE exit. BERNIECE puts the light on in the kitchen and puts on the teakettle. Presently there is a knock at the door. BERNIECE goes to answer it. BERNIECE opens the door. LYMON enters.)

LYMON: How you doing, Berniece? I thought you'd be asleep. Boy Willie been back here?

BERNIECE: He just left out of here a minute ago.

LYMON: I went out to see a picture show and never got there. We always end up doing something else. I was with this woman she just wanted to drink up all my money. So I left her there and came back looking for Boy Willie.

BERNIECE: You just missed him. He just left out of here.

LYMON: They got some nice-looking women in this city. I'm gonna like it up here real good. I like seeing them with their dresses on. Got them high heels. I like that. Make them look like they real precious. Boy Willie met a real nice one today. I wish I had met her before he did.

BERNIECE: He come by here with some woman a little while ago. I told him to go on and take all that out of my house.

LYMON: What she look like, the woman he was with? Was she a brown-skinned woman about this high? Nice and healthy? Got nice hips on her?

BERNIECE: She had on a red dress.

LYMON: That's her! That's Grace. She real nice. Laugh a lot. Lot of fun to be with. She don't be trying to put on. Some of these woman act like they the Queen of Sheba. I don't like them kind. Grace ain't like that. She real nice with herself.

BERNIECE: I don't know what she was like. He come in here all drunk knocking over the lamp, and making all kind of noise. I told them to take that somewhere else. I can't really say what she was like.

LYMON: She real nice. I seen her before he did. I was trying not to act like I seen her. I wanted to look at her a while before I said something. She seen me when I come into the saloon. I tried to act like I didn't see her. Time I looked around Boy Willie was talking to her. She was talking to him kept looking at me. That's when her friend Dolly came. I asked her if she wanted to go to the picture show. She told me to buy her a drink while she thought about it. Next thing I knew she done had three drinks talking about she too tired to go. I bought her another drink, then I left. Boy Willie was gone and I thought he might have come back here. Doaker gone, huh? He say he had to make a trip.

BERNIECE: Yeah, he gone on his trip. This is when I can usually get me some peace and quiet, Maretha asleep.

LYMON: She look just like you. Got them big eyes. I remember her when she was in diapers.

BERNIECE: Time just keep on. It go on with or without you. She going on twelve.

LYMON: She sure is pretty. I like kids.

BERNIECE: Boy Willie say you staying . . . what you gonna do up here in this big city? You thought about that?

LYMON: They never get me back down there. The sheriff looking for me. All because they gonna try and make me work for somebody when I don't want to. They gonna try and make me work for Stovall when he don't pay nothing. It ain't like that up here. Up here you more or less do what you want to. I figure I find me a job and try to get set up and then see what the year brings. I tried to do that two or three times down there . . . but it never would work out. I was always in the wrong place.

BERNIECE: This ain't a bad city once you get to know your way around.

LYMON: Up here is different. I'm gonna get me a job unloading boxcars or something. One fellow told me say he know a place. I'm gonna go over there with him next week. Me and Boy Willie finish selling them watermelons I'll have enough money to hold me for a while. But I'm gonna go over there and see what kind of jobs they have.

BERNIECE: You shouldn't have too much trouble finding a job. It's all in how you present yourself. See now, Boy Willie couldn't get no job up here. Somebody hire him they got a pack of trouble on their hands. Soon as they find that out they fire him. He don't want to do nothing unless he do it his way.

LYMON: I know. I told him let's go to the picture show first and see if there was any women down there. They might get tired of sitting at home and walk down to the picture show. He say he wanna look around first. We never did get down there. We tried a couple of places and then we went to this saloon where he met Grace. I tried to meet her before he did but he beat me to her. We left Wining Boy sitting down there running his mouth. He told me if I wear this suit I'd find me a woman. He was almost right.

BERNIECE: You don't need to be out there in them saloons. Ain't no telling what you liable to run into out there. This one liable to cut you as quick as that one shoot you. You don't need to be out there. You start out that fast life you can't keep it up. It makes you old quick. I don't know what them women out there be thinking about.

LYMON: Mostly they be lonely and looking for somebody to spend the night with them. Sometimes it matters who it is and sometimes it don't. I used to be the same way. Now it got to matter. That's why I'm here now. Dolly liable not to even recognize me if she sees me again. I don't like women like that. I like my women to be with me in a nice and easy way. That way we can both enjoy ourselves. The way I see it we the only two people like us

in the world. We got to see how we fit together. A woman that don't want
to take the time to do that I don't bother with. Used to. Used to bother with
all of them. Then I woke up one time with this woman and I didn't know
who she was. She was the prettiest woman I had ever seen in my life. I
spent the whole night with her and didn't even know it. I had never taken
the time to look at her. I guess she kinda knew I ain't never really looked at
her. She must have known that cause she ain't wanted to see me no
more. If she had wanted to see me I believe we might have got married.
How come you ain't married? It seem like to me you would be married. I
remember Avery from down home. I used to call him plain old Avery. Now
he Reverend Avery. That's kinda funny about him becoming a preacher. I
like when he told about how that come to him in a dream about them
sheep people and them hobos. Nothing ever come to me in a dream like
that. I just dream about women. Can't never seem to find the right one.

BERNIECE: She out there somewhere. You just got to get yourself ready to meet
her. That's what I'm trying to do. Avery's alright. I ain't really got nobody in
mind.

LYMON: I get me a job and a little place and get set up to where I can make a
woman comfortable I might get married. Avery's nice. You ought to go
ahead and get married. You be a preacher's wife you won't have to work. I
hate living by myself. I didn't want to be no strain on my mama so I left
home when I was about sixteen. Everything I tried seem like it just didn't
work out. Now I'm trying this.

BERNIECE: You keep trying it'll work out for you.

LYMON: You ever go down there to the picture show?

BERNIECE: I don't go in for all that.

LYMON: Ain't nothing wrong with it. It ain't like gambling and sinning. I went to
one down in Jackson once. It was fun.

BERNIECE: I just stay home most of the time. Take care of Maretha.

LYMON: It's getting kind of late. I don't know where Boy Willie went off to. He's
liable not to come back. I'm gonna take off these shoes. My feet hurt. Was
you in bed? I don't mean to be keeping you up.

BERNIECE: You ain't keeping me up. I couldn't sleep after that Boy Willie woke
me up.

LYMON: You got on that nightgown. I likes women when they wear them fancy
nightclothes and all. It makes their skin look real pretty.

BERNIECE: I got this at the five-and-ten-cents store. It ain't so fancy.

LYMON: I don't too often get to see a woman dressed like that.

(There is a long pause. LYMON *takes off his suit coat.)*

Well, I'm gonna sleep here on the couch. I'm supposed to sleep on the
floor but I don't reckon Boy Willie's coming back tonight. Wining Boy sold
me this suit. Told me it was a magic suit. I'm gonna put it on again tomorrow. Maybe it bring me a woman like he say.

(He goes into his coat pocket and takes out a small bottle of perfume.)

I almost forgot I had this. Some man sold me this for a dollar. Say it come from Paris. This is the same kind of perfume the Queen of France wear. That's what he told me. I don't know if it's true or not. I smelled it. It smelled good to me. Here . . . smell it see if you like it. I was gonna give it to Dolly. But I didn't like her too much.

BERNIECE *(takes the bottle):* It smells nice.

LYMON: I was gonna give it to Dolly if she had went to the picture with me. Go on, you take it.

BERNIECE: I can't take it. Here . . . go on you keep it. You'll find somebody to give it to.

LYMON: I wanna give it to you. Make you smell nice.

(He takes the bottle and puts perfume behind BERNIECE's *ear.)*

They tell me you supposed to put it right here behind your ear. Say if you put it there you smell nice all day.

*(*BERNIECE *stiffens at his touch.* LYMON *bends down to smell her.)*

There . . . you smell real good now.

(He kisses her neck.)

You smell real good for Lymon.

(He kisses her again. BERNIECE *returns the kiss, then breaks the embrace and crosses to the stairs. She turns and they look silently at each other.* LYMON *hands her the bottle of perfume.* BERNIECE *exits up the stairs.* LYMON *picks up his suit coat and strokes it lovingly with the full knowledge that it is indeed a magic suit. The lights go down on the scene.)*

Scene 4

(It is late the next morning. The lights come up on the parlor. LYMON *is asleep on the sofa.* BOY WILLIE *enters the front door.)*

BOY WILLIE: Hey, Lymon! Lymon, come on get up.

LYMON: Leave me alone.

BOY WILLIE: Come on, get up, nigger! Wake up, Lymon.

LYMON: What you want?

BOY WILLIE: Come on, let's go. I done called the man about the piano.

LYMON: What piano?

BOY WILLIE *(dumps* LYMON *on the floor):* Come on, get up!

LYMON: Why you leave, I looked around and you was gone.

BOY WILLIE: I come back here with Grace, then I went looking for you. I figured you'd be with Dolly.

LYMON: She just want to drink and spend up your money. I come on back here looking for you to see if you wanted to go to the picture show.

BOY WILLIE: I been up at Grace's house. Some nigger named Leroy come by but I had a chair up against the door. He got mad when he couldn't get in. He went off somewhere and I got out of there before he could come back. Berniece got mad when we came here.

LYMON: She say you was knocking over the lamp busting up the place.

BOY WILLIE: That was Grace doing all that.

LYMON: Wining Boy seen Sutter's ghost last night.

BOY WILLIE: Wining Boy's liable to see anything. I'm surprised he found the right house. Come on, I done called the man about the piano.

LYMON: What he say?

BOY WILLIE: He say to bring it on out. I told him I was calling for my sister, Miss Berniece Charles. I told him some man wanted to buy it for eleven hundred dollars and asked him if he would go any better. He said yeah, he would give me eleven hundred and fifty dollars for it if it was the same piano. I described it to him again and he told me to bring it out.

LYMON: Why didn't you tell him to come and pick it up?

BOY WILLIE: I didn't want to have no problem with Berniece. This way we just take it on out there and it be out the way. He want to charge twenty-five dollars to pick it up.

LYMON: You should have told him the man was gonna give you twelve hundred for it.

BOY WILLIE: I figure I was taking a chance with that eleven hundred. If I had told him twelve hundred he might have run off. Now I wish I had told him twelve-fifty. It's hard to figure out white folks sometimes.

LYMON: You might have been able to tell him anything. White folks got a lot of money.

BOY WILLIE: Come on, let's get it loaded before Berniece come back. Get that end over there. All you got to do is pick it up on that side. Don't worry about this side. You wanna stretch you' back for a minute?

LYMON: I'm ready.

BOY WILLIE: Get a real good grip on it now.

(The sound of SUTTER's GHOST is heard. They do not hear it.)

LYMON: I got this end. You get that end.

BOY WILLIE: Wait till I say ready now. Alright. You got it good? You got a grip on it?

LYMON: Yeah, I got it. You lift up on that end.

BOY WILLIE: Ready? Lift!

(The piano will not budge.)

LYMON: Man, this piano is heavy! It's gonna take more than me and you to move this piano.

BOY WILLIE: We can do it. Come on—we did it before.

LYMON: Nigger—you crazy! That piano weighs five hundred pounds!

BOY WILLIE: I got three hundred pounds of it! I know you can carry two hundred pounds! You be lifting them cotton sacks! Come on lift this piano!

(They try to move the piano again without success.)

LYMON: It's stuck. Something holding it.

BOY WILLIE: How the piano gonna be stuck? We just moved it. Slide you' end out.

LYMON: Naw—we gonna need two or three more people. How this big old piano get in the house?

BOY WILLIE: I don't know how it got in the house. I know how it's going out though! You get on this end. I'll carry three hundred and fifty pounds of it. All you got to do is slide your end out. Ready?

(They switch sides and try again without success. DOAKER *enters from his room as they try to push and shove it.)*

LYMON: Hey, Doaker . . . how this piano get in the house?

DOAKER: Boy Willie, what you doing?

BOY WILLIE: I'm carrying this piano out the house. What it look like I'm doing? Come on, Lymon, let's try again.

DOAKER: Go on let the piano sit there till Berniece come home.

BOY WILLIE: You ain't got nothing to do with this, Doaker. This my business.

DOAKER: This is my house, nigger! I ain't gonna let you or nobody else carry nothing out of it. You ain't gonna carry nothing out of here without my permission!

BOY WILLIE: This is my piano. I don't need your permission to carry my belongings out of your house. This is mine. This ain't got nothing to do with you.

DOAKER: I say leave it over there till Berniece come home. She got part of it too. Leave it set there till you see what she say.

BOY WILLIE: I don't care what Berniece say. Come on, Lymon. I got this side.

DOAKER: Go on and cut it half in two if you want to. Just leave Berniece's half sitting over there. I can't tell you what to do with your piano. But I can't let you take her half out of here.

BOY WILLIE: Go on, Doaker. You ain't got nothing to do with this. I don't want you starting nothing now. Just go on and leave me alone. Come on, Lymon. I got this end.

*(*DOAKER *goes into his room.* BOY WILLIE *and* LYMON *prepare to move the piano.)*

LYMON: How we gonna get it in the truck?

BOY WILLIE: Don't worry about how we gonna get it on the truck. You got to get it out the house first.

LYMON: It's gonna take more than me and you to move this piano.

BOY WILLIE: Just lift up on that end, nigger!

*(*DOAKER *comes to the doorway of his room and stands.)*

DOAKER *(quietly with authority)*: Leave that piano set over there till Berniece come back. I don't care what you do with it then. But you gonna leave it sit over there right now.

BOY WILLIE: Alright . . . . I'm gonna tell you this, Doaker. I'm going out of here . . . I'm gonna get me some rope . . . find me a plank and some wheels . . . and I'm coming back. Then I'm gonna carry that piano out of here . . . sell it and give Berniece half the money. See . . . now that's what I'm gonna do. And you . . . or nobody else is gonna stop me. Come on, Lymon . . . let's go get some rope and stuff. I'll be back, Doaker.

*(*BOY WILLIE *and* LYMON *exit. The lights go down on the scene.)*

Scene 5

(The lights come up. BOY WILLIE *sits on the sofa, screwing casters on a wooden plank.* MARETHA *is sitting on the piano stool.* DOAKER *sits at the table playing solitaire.)*

BOY WILLIE *(to* MARETHA*):* Then after that them white folks down around there started falling down their wells. You ever seen a well? A well got a wall around it. It's hard to fall down a well. You got to be leaning way over. Couldn't nobody figure out too much what was making these fellows fall down their well . . . so everybody says the Ghosts of the Yellow Dog must have pushed them. That's what everybody called them four men what got burned up in the boxcar.

MARETHA: Why they call them that?

BOY WILLIE: Cause the Yazoo Delta railroad got yellow boxcars. Sometime the way the whistle blow sound like an old dog howling so the people call it the Yellow Dog.

MARETHA: Anybody ever see the Ghosts?

BOY WILLIE: I told you they like the wind. Can you see the wind?

MARETHA: No.

BOY WILLIE: They like the wind you can't see them. But sometimes you be in trouble they might be around to help you. They say if you go where the Southern cross the Yellow Dog . . . you go to where them two railroads cross each other . . . and call out their names . . . they say they talk back to you. I don't know, I ain't never done that. But Uncle Wining Boy he say he been down there and talked to them. You have to ask him about that part.

*(*BERNIECE *has entered from the front door.)*

BERNIECE: Maretha, you go on and get ready for me to do your hair.

*(*MARETHA *crosses to the steps.)*

Boy Willie, I done told you to leave my house.

(To MARETHA*.)*

Go on, Maretha.

*(*MARETHA *is hesitant about going up the stairs.)*

BOY WILLIE: Don't be scared. Here, I'll go up there with you. If we see Sutter's ghost I'll put a whupping on him. Come on, Uncle Boy Willie going with you.

*(*BOY WILLIE *and* MARETHA *exit up the stairs.)*

BERNIECE: Doaker—what is going on here?

DOAKER: I come home and him and Lymon was moving the piano. I told them to leave it over there till you got home. He went out and got that board and them wheels. He say he gonna take that piano out of here and ain't no-body gonna stop him.

BERNIECE: I ain't playing with Boy Willie. I got Crawley's gun upstairs. He don't know but I'm through with it. Where Lymon go?

DOAKER: Boy Willie sent him for some rope just before you come in.

BERNIECE: I ain't studying Boy Willie or Lymon—or the rope. Boy Willie ain't taking that piano out this house. That's all there is to it.

(BOY WILLIE *and* MARETHA *enter on the stairs.* MARETHA *carries a hot comb and a can of hair grease.* BOY WILLIE *crosses over and continues to screw the wheels on the board.)*

MARETHA: Mama, all the hair grease is gone. There ain't but this little bit left.

BERNIECE *(gives her a dollar):* Here . . . run across the street and get another can. You come straight back, too. Don't you be playing around out there. And watch the cars. Be careful when you cross the street.

(MARETHA *exits out the front door.)*

Boy Willie, I done told you to leave my house.

BOY WILLIE: I ain't in you' house. I'm in Doaker's house. If he ask me to leave then I'll go on and leave. But consider me done left your part.

BERNIECE: Doaker, tell him to leave. Tell him to go on.

DOAKER: Boy Willie ain't done nothing for me to put him out of the house. I told you if you can't get along just go on and don't have nothing to do with each other.

BOY WILLIE: I ain't thinking about Berniece.

(He gets up and draws a line across the floor with his foot.)

There! Now I'm out of your part of the house. Consider me done left your part. Soon as Lymon come back with that rope. I'm gonna take that piano out of here and sell it.

BERNIECE: You ain't gonna touch that piano.

BOY WILLIE: Carry it out of here just as big and bold. Do like my daddy would have done come time to get Sutter's land.

BERNIECE: I got something to make you leave it over there.

BOY WILLIE: It's got to come better than this thirty-two-twenty.

DOAKER: Why don't you stop all that! Boy Willie, go on and leave her alone. You know how Berniece get. Why you wanna sit there and pick with her?

BOY WILLIE: I ain't picking with her. I told her the truth. She the one talking about what she got. I just told her what she better have.

BERNIECE: That's alright, Doaker. Leave him alone.

BOY WILLIE: She trying to scare me. Hell, I ain't scared of dying. I look around and see people dying every day. You got to die to make room for somebody else. I had a dog that died. Wasn't nothing but a puppy. I picked it up and put it in a bag and carried it up there to Reverend C. L. Thompson's church. I carried it up there and prayed and asked Jesus to make it live like he did the man in the Bible. I prayed real hard. Knelt down and everything. Say ask in Jesus' name. Well, I must have called Jesus' name two hundred times. I called his name till my mouth got sore. I got up and looked in the bag and the dog still dead. It ain't moved a muscle! I say, "Well, ain't nothing precious." And then I went out and killed me a cat. That's when I discovered the power of death. See, a nigger that ain't afraid to die is the worse kind of nigger for the white man. He can't hold that power over you. That's what I learned when I killed that cat. I got the

power of death too. I can command him. I can call him up. The white man
don't like to see that. He don't like for you to stand up and look him square
in the eye and say, "I got it too." Then he got to deal with you square up.

BERNIECE: That's why I don't talk to him, Doaker. You try and talk to him and
that's the only kind of stuff that comes out his mouth.

DOAKER: You say Avery went home to get his Bible?

BOY WILLIE: What Avery gonna do? Avery can't do nothing with me. I wish
Avery would say something to me about this piano.

DOAKER: Berniece ain't said about that. Avery went home to get his Bible. He
coming by to bless the house see if he can get rid of Sutter's ghost.

BOY WILLIE: Ain't nothing but a house full of ghosts down there at the church.
What Avery look like chasing away somebody's ghost?

(MARETHA *enters the front door.*)

BERNIECE: Light that stove and set that comb over there to get hot. Get something to put around your shoulders.

BOY WILLIE: The Bible say an eye for an eye, a tooth for a tooth, and a life for a
life. Tit for tat. But you and Avery don't want to believe that. You gonna
pass up that part and pretend it ain't in there. Everything else you gonna
agree with. But if you gonna agree with part of it you got to agree with all
of it. You can't do nothing halfway. You gonna go at the Bible halfway. You
gonna act like that part ain't in there. But you pull out the Bible and open it
and see what it say. Ask Avery. He a preacher. He'll tell you it's in there.
He the Good Shepherd. Unless he gonna shepherd you to heaven with
half the Bible.

BERNIECE: Maretha, bring me that comb. Make sure it's hot.

(MARETHA *brings the comb.* BERNIECE *begins to do her hair.*)

BOY WILLIE: I will say this for Avery. He done figured out a path to go through
life. I don't agree with it. But he done fixed it so he can go right through it
real smooth. Hell, he liable to end up with a million dollars that he done got
from selling bread and wine.

MARETHA: OWWWWWW!

BERNIECE: Be still, Maretha. If you was a boy I wouldn't be going through this.

BOY WILLIE: Don't you tell that girl that. Why you wanna tell her that?

BERNIECE: You ain't got nothing to do with this child.

BOY WILLIE: Telling her you wished she was a boy. How's that gonna make her
feel?

BERNIECE: Boy Willie, go on and leave me alone.

DOAKER: Why don't you leave her alone? What you got to pick with her for?
Why don't you go on out and see what's out there in the streets? Have
something to tell the fellows down home.

BOY WILLIE: I'm waiting on Lymon to get back with that truck. Why don't you go
on out and see what's out there in the streets? You ain't got to work tomorrow. Talking about me . . . why don't you go out there? It's Friday night.

DOAKER: I got to stay around here and keep you all from killing one another.

BOY WILLIE: You ain't got to worry about me. I'm gonna be here just as long as it takes Lymon to get back here with that truck. You ought to be talking to Berniece. Sitting up there telling Maretha she wished she was a boy. What kind of thing is that to tell a child? If you want to tell her something tell her about that piano. You ain't even told her about that piano. Like that's something to be ashamed of. Like she supposed to go off and hide somewhere about that piano. You ought to mark down on the calendar the day that Papa Boy Charles brought that piano into the house. You ought to mark that day down and draw a circle around it . . . and every year when it come up throw a party. Have a celebration. If you did that she wouldn't have no problem in life. She could walk around here with her head held high. I'm talking about a big party!

Invite everybody! Mark that day down with a special meaning. That way she know where she at in the world. You got her going out here thinking she wrong in the world. Like there ain't no part of it belong to her.

BERNIECE: Let me take care of my child. When you get one of your own then you can teach it what you want to teach it.

(DOAKER *exits into his room.*)

BOY WILLIE: What I want to bring a child into this world for? Why I wanna bring somebody else into all this for? I'll tell you this . . . If I was Rockefeller I'd have forty or fifty. I'd make one every day. Cause they gonna start out in life with all the advantages. I ain't got no advantages to offer nobody. Many is the time I looked at my daddy and seen him staring off at his hands. I got a little older I know what he was thinking. He sitting there saying, "I got these big old hands but what I'm gonna do with them? Best I can do is make a fifty-acre crop for Mr. Stovall. Got these big old hands capable of doing anything. I can take and build something with these hands. But where's the tools? All I got is these hands. Unless I go out here and kill me somebody and take what they got . . . it's a long row to hoe for me to get something of my own. So what I'm gonna do with these big old hands? What would you do?"

See now . . . if he had his own land he wouldn't have felt that way. If he had something under his feet that belonged to him he could stand up taller. That's what I'm talking about. Hell, the land is there for everybody. All you got to do is figure out how to get you a piece. Ain't no mystery to life. You just got to go out and meet it square on. If you got a piece of land you'll find everything else fall right into place. You can stand right up next to the white man and talk about the price of cotton . . . the weather, and anything else you want to talk about. If you teach that girl that she living at the bottom of life, she's gonna grow up and hate you.

BERNIECE: I'm gonna teach her the truth. That's just where she living. Only she ain't got to stay there.

(*To* MARETHA.)

Turn you' head over to the other side.

BOY WILLIE: This might be your bottom but it ain't mine. I'm living at the top of life. I ain't gonna just take my life and throw it away at the bottom. I'm in the world like everybody else. The way I see it everybody else got to come up a little taste to be where I am.

BERNIECE: You right at the bottom with the rest of us.

BOY WILLIE: I'll tell you this . . . and ain't a living soul can put a come back on it. If you believe that's where you at then you gonna act that way. If you act that way then that's where you gonna be. It's as simple as that. Ain't no mystery to life. I don't know how you come to believe that stuff. Crawley didn't think like that. He wasn't living at the bottom of life. Papa Boy Charles and Mama Ola wasn't living at the bottom of life. You ain't never heard them say nothing like that. They would have taken a strap to you if they heard you say something like that.

(DOAKER *enters from his room.*)

Hey, Doaker . . . Berniece say the colored folks is living at the bottom of life. I tried to tell her if she think that . . . that's where she gonna be. You think you living at the bottom of life? Is that how you see yourself?

DOAKER: I'm just living the best way I know how. I ain't thinking about no top or no bottom.

BOY WILLIE: That's what I tried to tell Berniece. I don't know where she got that from. That sound like something Avery would say. Avery think cause the white man give him a turkey for Thanksgiving that makes him better than everybody else. That's gonna raise him out of the bottom of life. I don't need nobody to give me a turkey. I can get my own turkey. All you have to do is get out my way. I'll get me two or three turkeys.

BERNIECE: You can't even get a chicken let alone two or three turkeys. Talking about get out your way. Ain't nobody in your way.

(To MARETHA.)

Straighten your head, Maretha! Don't be bending down like that. Hold your head up!

(To BOY WILLIE.)

All you got going for you is talk. You' whole life that's all you ever had going for you.

BOY WILLIE: See now . . . I'll tell you something about me. I done strung along and strung along. Going this way and that. Whatever way would lead me to a moment of peace. That's all I want. To be as easy with everything. But I wasn't born to that. I was born to a time of fire.

The world ain't wanted no part of me. I could see that since I was about seven. The world say it's better off without me. See, Berniece accept that. She trying to come up to where she can prove something to the world. Hell, the world a better place cause of me. I don't see it like Berniece. I got a heart that beats here and it beats just as loud as the next fellow's. Don't care if he black or white. Sometime it beats louder. When it beats louder, then everybody can hear it. Some people get scared of that. Like Berniece. Some people get scared to hear a nigger's heart beating. They think you ought to lay low with that heart. Make it beat quiet and go along with everything the way it is. But my mama ain't birthed me for nothing. So what I got to do? I got to mark my passing on the road. Just like you write on a tree, "Boy Willie was here."

That's all I'm trying to do with that piano. Trying to put my mark on the road. Like my daddy done. My heart say for me to sell that piano and get me some land so I can make a life for myself to live in my own way. Other than that I ain't thinking about nothing Berniece got to say.

(There is a knock at the door. BOY WILLIE *crosses to it and yanks it open thinking it is* LYMON. AVERY *enters. He carries a Bible.)*

BOY WILLIE: Where you been, nigger? Aw . . . I thought you was Lymon. Hey, Berniece, look who's here.

BERNIECE: Come on in, Avery. Don't you pay Boy Willie no mind.

BOY WILLIE: Hey . . . Hey, Avery . . . tell me this . . . can you get to heaven with half the Bible?

BERNIECE: Boy Willie . . . I done told you to leave me alone.

BOY WILLIE: I just ask the man a question. He can answer. He don't need you to speak for him. Avery . . . if you only believe on half the Bible and don't want to accept the other half . . . you think God let you in heaven? Or do you got to have the whole Bible? Tell Berniece . . . if you only believe in part of it . . . when you see God he gonna ask you why you ain't believed in the other part . . . then he gonna send you straight to Hell.

AVERY: You got to be born again. Jesus say unless a man be born again he cannot come unto the Father and who so ever heareth my words and believeth them not shall be cast into a fiery pit.

BOY WILLIE: That's what I was trying to tell Berniece. You got to believe in it all. You can't go at nothing halfway. She think she going to heaven with half the Bible.

(To BERNIECE.*)*

You hear that . . . Jesus say you got to believe in it all.

BERNIECE: You keep messing with me.

BOY WILLIE: I ain't thinking about you.

DOAKER: Come on in, Avery, and have a seat. Don't pay neither one of them no mind. They been arguing all day.

BERNIECE: Come on in, Avery.

AVERY: How's everybody in here?

BERNIECE: Here, set this comb back over there on that stove.

(To AVERY.*)*

Don't pay Boy Willie no mind. He been around here bothering me since I come home from work.

BOY WILLIE: Boy Willie ain't bothering you. Boy Willie ain't bothering nobody. I'm just waiting on Lymon to get back. I ain't thinking about you. You heard the man say I was right and you still don't want to believe it. You just wanna go and make up anythin'. Well there's Avery . . . there's the preacher . . . go on and ask him.

AVERY: Berniece believe in the Bible. She been baptized.

BOY WILLIE: What about that part that say an eye for an eye a tooth for a tooth and a life for a life? Ain't that in there?

DOAKER: What they say down there at the bank, Avery?

AVERY: Oh, they talked to me real nice. I told Berniece . . . they say maybe they let me borrow the money. They done talked to my boss down at work and everything.

DOAKER: That's what I told Berniece. You working every day you ought to be able to borrow some money.

AVERY: I'm getting more people in my congregation every day. Berniece says she gonna be the Deaconess. I get me my church I can get married and settled down. That's what I told Berniece.

DOAKER: That be nice. You all ought to go ahead and get married. Berniece don't need to be by herself. I tell her that all the time.

BERNIECE: I ain't said nothing about getting married. I said I was thinking about it.

DOAKER: Avery get him his church you all can make it nice.

(To AVERY.)

Berniece said you was coming by to bless the house.

AVERY: Yeah, I done read up on my Bible. She asked me to come by and see if I can get rid of Sutter's ghost.

BOY WILLIE: Ain't no ghost in this house. That's all in Berniece's head. Go on up there and see if you see him. I'll give you a hundred dollars if you see him. That's all in her imagination.

DOAKER: Well, let her find that out then. If Avery blessing the house is gonna make her feel better . . . what you got to do with it?

AVERY: Berniece say Maretha seen him too. I don't know, but I found a part in the Bible to bless the house. If he is here then that ought to make him go.

BOY WILLIE: You worse than Berniece believing all that stuff. Talking about . . . if he here. Go on up there and find out. I been up there I ain't seen him. If you reading from that Bible gonna make him leave out of Berniece imagi- nation, well, you might be right. But if you talking about . . .

DOAKER: Boy Willie, why don't you just be quiet? Getting all up in the man's business. This ain't got nothing to do with you. Let him go ahead and do what he gonna do.

BOY WILLIE: I ain't stopping him. Avery ain't got no power to do nothing.

AVERY: Oh, I ain't got no power. God got the power! God got power over everything in His creation. God can do anything. God say, "As I comman- deth so it shall be." God said, "Let there be light," and there was light. He made the world in six days and rested on the seventh. God's got a wonderful power. He got power over life and death. Jesus raised Lazareth from the dead. They was getting ready to bury him and Jesus told him say, "Rise up and walk." He got up and walked and the people made great rejoicing at the power of God. I ain't worried about him chasing away a little old ghost!

(There is a knock at the door. BOY WILLIE *goes to answer it.* LYMON *enters carrying a coil of rope.)*

BOY WILLIE: Where you been? I been waiting on you and you run off somo-where.

LYMON: I ran into Grace. I stopped and bought her drink. She say she gonna go to the picture show with me.

BOY WILLIE: I ain't thinking about no Grace nothing.

LYMON: Hi, Berniece.

BOY WILLIE: Give me that rope and get up on this side of the piano.

DOAKER: Boy Willie, don't start nothing now. Leave the piano alone.

BOY WILLIE: Get that board there, Lymon. Stay out of this, Doaker.

(BERNIECE exits up the stairs.)

DOAKER: You just can't take the piano. How you gonna take the piano? Berniece ain't said nothing about selling that piano.

BOY WILLIE: She ain't got to say nothing. Come on, Lymon. We got to lift one end at a time up on the board. You got to watch so that the board don't slide up under there.

LYMON: What we gonna do with the rope?

BOY WILLIE: Let me worry about the rope. You just get up on this side over here with me.

(BERNIECE enters from the stairs. She has her hand in her pocket where she has Crawley's gun.)

AVERY: Boy Willie . . . Berniece . . . why don't you all sit down and talk this out now?

BERNIECE: Ain't nothing to talk out.

BOY WILLIE: I'm through talking to Berniece. You can talk to Berniece till you get blue in the face, and It don't make no difference. Get up on that side, Lymon. Throw that rope around there and tie it to the leg.

LYMON: Wait a minute . . . wait a minute, Boy Willie. Berniece got to say. Hey, Berniece . . . did you tell Boy Willie he could take this piano?

BERNIECE: Boy Willie ain't taking nothing out of my house but himself. Now you let him go ahead and try.

BOY WILLIE: Come on, Lymon, get up on this side with me.

(LYMON stands undecided.)

Come on, nigger! What you standing there for?

LYMON: Maybe Berniece is right, Boy Willie. Maybe you shouldn't sell it.

AVERY: You all ought to sit down and talk it out. See if you can come to an agreement.

DOAKER: That's what I been trying to tell them. Seem like one of them ought to respect the other one's wishes.

BERNIECE: I wish Boy Willie would go on and leave my house. That's what I wish. Now, he can respect that. Cause he's leaving here one way or another.

BOY WILLIE: What you mean one way or another? What's that supposed to mean? I ain't scared of no gun.

DOAKER: Come on, Berniece, leave him alone with that.

BOY WILLIE: I don't care what Berniece say. I'm selling my half. I can't help it if her half got to go along with it. It ain't like I'm trying to cheat her out of her half. Come on, Lymon.

LYMON: Berniece . . . I got to do this . . . Boy Willie say he gonna give you half of the money . . . say he want to get Sutter's land.

BERNIECE: Go on, Lymon. Just go on . . . I done told Boy Willie what to do.

BOY WILLIE: Here, Lymon . . . put that rope up over there.

LYMON: Boy Willie, you sure you want to do this? The way I figure it . . . I might be wrong . . . but I figure she gonna shoot you first.

BOY WILLIE: She just gonna have to shoot me.

BERNIECE: Maretha, get on out the way. Get her out the way, Doaker.

DOAKER: Go on, do what your mama told you.

BERNIECE: Put her in your room.

(MARETHA *exits to* DOAKER's *room.* BOY WILLIE *and* LYMON *try to lift the piano. The door opens and* WINING BOY *enters. He has been drinking.*)

WINING BOY: Man, these niggers around here! I stopped down there at Seefus. . . . These folks standing around talking about Patchneck Red's coming. They jumping back and getting off the sidewalk talking about Patchneck Red this and Patchneck Red that. Come to find out . . . you know who they was talking about? Old John D. from up around Tyler! Used to run around with Otis Smith. He got everybody scared of him. Calling him Patchneck Red. They don't know I whupped the nigger's head in one time.

BOY WILLIE: Just make sure that board don't slide, Lymon.

LYMON: I got this side. You watch that side.

WINING BOY: Hey, Boy Willie, what you got? I know you got a pint stuck up in your coat.

BOY WILLIE: Wining Boy, get out the way!

WINING BOY: Hey, Doaker. What you got? Gimme a drink. I want a drink.

DOAKER: It look like you had enough of whatever it was. Come talking about "What you got?" You ought to be trying to find somewhere to lay down.

WINING BOY: I ain't worried about no place to lay down. I can always find me a place to lay down in Berniece's house. Ain't that right, Berniece?

BERNIECE: Wining Boy, sit down somewhere. You been out there drinking all day. Come in here smelling like an old polecat. Sit on down there, you don't need nothing to drink.

DOAKER: You know Berniece don't like all that drinking.

WINING BOY: I ain't disrespecting Berniece. Berniece, am I disrespecting you?

I'm just trying to be nice. I been with strangers all day and they treated me like family. I come in here to family and you treat me like a stranger. I don't need your whiskey. I can buy my own. I wanted your company, not your whiskey.

DOAKER: Nigger, why don't you go upstairs and lay down? You don't need nothing to drink.

WINING BOY: I ain't thinking about no laying down. Me and Boy Willie fixing to party. Ain't that right, Boy Willie? Tell him. I'm fixing to play me some piano. Watch this.

(WINING BOY *sits down at the piano.*)

BOY WILLIE: Come on, Wining Boy! Me and Lymon fixing to move the piano.

WINING BOY: Wait a minute . . . wait a minute. This a song I wrote for Cleotha. I wrote this song in memory of Cleotha.

(*He begins to play and sing.*)

Hey little woman what's the matter with you now
Had a storm last night and blowed the line all down

Tell me how long
Is I got to wait
Can I get it now
Or must I hesitate

It takes a hesitating stocking in her hesitating shoe
It takes a hesitating woman wanna sing the blues

Tell me how long
Is I got to wait
Can I kiss you now
Or must I hesitate.

BOY WILLIE: Come on, Wining Boy, get up! Get up, Wining Boy! Me and Lymon's fixing to move the piano.

WINING BOY: Naw . . . Naw . . . you ain't gonna move this piano!

BOY WILLIE: Get out the way, Wining Boy.

(WINING BOY, *his back to the piano, spreads his arms out over the piano.*)

WINING BOY: You ain't taking this piano out the house. You got to take me with it!

BOY WILLIE: Get on out the way, Wining Boy! Doaker get him!

(*There is a knock on the door.*)

BERNIECE: I got him, Doaker. Come on, Wining Boy. I done told Boy Willie he ain't taking the piano.

(BERNIECE *tries to take* WINING BOY *away from the piano.*)

WINING BOY: He got to take me with it!

(DOAKER goes to answer the door. GRACE enters.)

GRACE: Is Lymon here?

DOAKER: Lymon.

WINING BOY: He ain't taking that piano.

BERNIECE: I ain't gonna let him take it.

GRACE: I thought you was coming back. I ain't gonna sit in that truck all day.

LYMON: I told you I was coming back.

GRACE *(sees BOY WILLIE)*: Oh, hi, Boy Willie. Lymon told me you was gone back down South.

LYMON: I said he was going back. I didn't say he had left already.

GRACE: That's what you told me.

BERNIECE: Lymon, you got to take your company someplace else.

LYMON: Berniece, this is Grace. That there is Berniece. That's Boy Willie's sister.

GRACE: Nice to meet you.

(To LYMON.)

I ain't gonna sit out in that truck all day. You told me you was gonna take me to the movie.

LYMON: I told you I had something to do first. You supposed to wait on me.

BERNIECE: Lymon, just go on and leave. Take Grace or whoever with you. Just go on get out my house.

BOY WILLIE: You gonna help me move this piano first, nigger!

LYMON *(to GRACE)*: I got to help Boy Willie move the piano first.

(Everybody but GRACE suddenly senses SUTTER's presence.)

GRACE: I ain't waiting on you. Told me you was coming right back. Now you got to move a piano. You just like all the other men.

(GRACE now senses something.)

Something ain't right here. I knew I shouldn't have come back up in this house.

(GRACE exits.)

LYMON: Hey, Grace! I'll be right back, Boy Willie.

BOY WILLIE: Where you going, nigger?

LYMON: I'll be back. I got to take Grace home.

BOY WILLIE: Come on, let's move the piano first!

LYMON: I got to take Grace home. I told you I'll be back.

(LYMON exits. BOY WILLIE exits and calls after him.)

BOY WILLIE: Come on, Lymon! Hey . . . Lymon! Lymon . . . come on!

(Again, the presence of SUTTER is felt.)

WINING BOY: Hey, Doaker, did you feel that? Hey, Berniece . . . did you get cold? Hey, Doaker . . .

DOAKER: What you calling me for?

WINING BOY: I believe that's Sutter.

DOAKER: Well, let him stay up there. As long as he don't mess with me.

BERNIECE: Avery, go on and bless the house.

DOAKER: You need to bless that piano. That's what you need to bless. It ain't done nothing but cause trouble. If you gonna bless anything go on and bless that.

WINING BOY: Hey, Doaker, if he gonna bless something let him bless everything. The kitchen . . . the upstairs. Go on and bless it all.

BOY WILLIE: Ain't no ghost in this house. He need to bless Berniece's head. That's what he need to bless.

AVERY: Seem like that piano's causing all the trouble. I can bless that. Berniece, put me some water in that bottle.

(AVERY takes a small bottle from his pocket and hands it to BERNIECE, who goes into the kitchen to get water. AVERY takes a candle from his pocket and lights it. He gives it to BERNIECE as she gives him the water.)

Hold this candle. Whatever you do make sure it don't go out.

O Holy Father we gather here this evening in the Holy Name to cast out the spirit of one James Sutter. May this vial of water be empowered with thy spirit. May each drop of it be a weapon and a shield against the presence of all evil and may it be a cleansing and blessing of this humble abode.

Just as Our Father taught us how to pray so He say, "I will prepare a table for you in the midst of mine enemies," and in His hands we place ourselves to come unto his presence. Where there is Good so shall it cause Evil to scatter to the Four Winds.

(He throws water at the piano at each commandment.)

AVERY: Get thee behind me, Satan! Get thee behind the face of Righteousness as we Glorify His Holy Name! Get thee behind the Hammer of Truth that breaketh down the Wall of Falsehood! Father. Father. Praise. Praise. We ask in Jesus' name and call forth the power of the Holy Spirit as it is written. . . .

(He opens the Bible and reads from it.)

I will sprinkle clean water upon thee and ye shall be clean.

BOY WILLIE: All this old preaching stuff. Hell, just tell him to leave.

(AVERY continues reading throughout BOY WILLIE's outburst.)

AVERY: I will sprinkle clean water upon you and you shall be clean: from all your uncleanliness, and from all your idols, will I cleanse you. A new heart also will I give you, and a new spirit will I put within you: and I will take out of your flesh the heart of stone, and I will give you a heart of flesh. And I will put my spirit within you, and cause you to walk in my statutes, and ye shall keep my judgments, and do them.

(BOY WILLIE grabs a pot of water from the stove and begins to fling it around the room.)

BOY WILLIE: Hey Sutter! Sutter! Get your ass out this house! Sutter! Come on and get some of this water! You done drowned in the well, come on and get some more of this water!

(BOY WILLIE is working himself into a frenzy as he runs around the room throwing water and calling SUTTER's name. AVERY continues reading.)

BOY WILLIE : Come on, Sutter!

(He starts up the stairs.)

Come on, get some water! Come on, Sutter!

(The sound of SUTTER's GHOST *is heard. As* BOY WILLIE *approaches the steps he is suddenly thrown back by the unseen force, which is choking him. As he struggles he frees himself, then dashes up the stairs.)*

BOY WILLIE: Come on, Sutter!

AVERY *(continuing):* A new heart also will I give you and a new spirit will I put within you: and I will take out of your flesh the heart of stone, and I will give you a heart of flesh. And I will put my spirit within you, and cause you to walk in my statutes, and ye shall keep my judgments, and do them.

(There are loud sounds heard from upstairs as BOY WILLIE *begins to wrestle with* SUTTER's GHOST. *It is a life-and-death struggle fraught with perils and faultless terror.* BOY WILLIE *is thrown down the stairs.* AVERY *is stunned into silence.* BOY WILLIE *picks himself up and dashes back upstairs.)*

AVERY: Berniece, I can't do it.

(There are more sounds heard from upstairs. DOAKER *and* WINING BOY *stare at one another in stunned disbelief. It is in this moment, from somewhere old, that* BERNIECE *realizes what she must do. She crosses to the piano. She begins to play. The song is found piece by piece. It is an old urge to song that is both a commandment and a plea. With each repetition it gains in strength. It is intended as an exorcism and a dressing for battle. A rustle of wind blowing across two continents.)*

BERNIECE *(singing):*
    I want you to help me
    I want you to help me
    I want you to help me
    I want you to help me
    I want you to help me
    I want you to help me
    Mama Berniece
    I want you to help me
    Mama Esther
    I want you to help me
    Papa Boy Charles
    I want you to help me
    Mama Ola
    I want you to help me

    I want you to help me
    I want you to help me
    I want you to help me
    I want you to help me
    I want you to help me
    I want you to help me

I want you to help me
I want you to help me

(The sound of a train approaching is heard. The noise upstairs subsides.)

BOY WILLIE: Come on, Sutter! Come back, Sutter!

(BERNIECE begins to chant:)

BERNIECE:

Thank you.
Thank you.
Thank you.

(A calm comes over the house. MARETHA enters from DOAKER's room. BOY WILLIE enters on the stairs. He pauses a moment to watch BERNIECE at the piano.)

BERNIECE:

Thank you.
Thank you.

BOY WILLIE: Wining Boy, you ready to go back down home? Hey, Doaker, what time the train leave?

DOAKER: You still got time to make it.

(MARETHA crosses and embraces BOY WILLIE.)

BOY WILLIE: Hey Berniece . . . if you and Maretha don't keep playing on that piano . . . ain't no telling . . . me and Sutter both liable to be back.

(He exits.)

BERNIECE: Thank you.

(The lights go down to black.)

QUESTIONS AND CONSIDERATIONS

1. What do the carvings on the piano represent?

2. Why is the play entitled *The Piano Lesson?* What lessons does the piano embody for the family in the play? For the audience?

3. Why does Boy Willie want to sell the piano? Why won't Berniece agree to let him? What is significant about their dispute?

4. Why is the family haunted by Sutter's Ghost? Is the ghost finally exorcised?

5. Why do the African-Americans and the white people interpret the law differently? Refer to specific scenes in the play to support your points.

6. Contrast Boy Willie's and Avery's attitudes toward Jesus. What power do Jesus and the Christian religion have in the play?

7. Why does Boy Willie leave at the close of the play without the piano? What values triumph with his departure?

IDEAS FOR WRITING

1. Write a reflective essay about an object of value that has been in your family for a long time. Explore the reasons underlying any conflict or struggle over the heirloom or property. How was the struggle resolved? What values did you reflect on more deeply as

you analyzed the conflict? Did you discover new insights into human nature and the human spirit from your process of reflection?

2. Write an essay in which you relate the author's point of view about the status and role of African-Americans in the world of the play to the status and role of blacks in your own community. Does this play give you new insights into the spiritual and creative legacy, character, and status of African-Americans?

3. Arrange a play reading of one of the acts of *The Piano Lesson.* If possible, use actual stage movements and a real piano as a central focus. Write an essay about the differences between experiencing the play read aloud in a dramatic setting and reading it analytically in your textbook. What different kinds of creativity are involved in reading a play, viewing it as a performance, and actually staging or acting in it?

Student Writing

"The Beginning"
Kay Luo

Kay Luo, a first-year student from Renton, Washington, wrote the following story for her composition class. Luo is interested in issues of creativity, work, and relationships. She initially read Beattie's tale as the story of a woman whose creativity has been misdirected into negotiating difficult relationships while trying to balance her unfulfilling personal life. Luo wrote "The Beginning" as a prequel to Ann Beattie's "Janus," which becomes the first story written by a frustrated real estate agent named Janis. In Luo's story, discontent with her current life is reflected in Janis's writing and her creation of an alter ego, a character called "Andrea." In effect, "The Beginning" is Luo's "creation myth" of how the story "Janus" came to be. Luo shifts the focus of attention in the story away from the sleek, lovely bowl, a finished work of art beyond the average person's powers to produce, and onto an object that, although ugly and rather primitive, might serve as a tool for focusing and directing creative efforts: an old-fashioned typewriter.

As you read Luo's story, ask yourself how much of Beattie's style she has succeeding in capturing and whether you prefer her vision to that of the original version. Consider particularly what this student work reveals about the nature of creativity and the creative process in writing.

    Janis propped open the door to the McCarthy house after
having inspected it one last time to make sure that everything

was in order for the afternoon's showing. Satisfied that the
rooms radiated with neatness yet retained a hint of lived-in
modesty, she found herself with nothing else to do for the
remaining twenty minutes before the open house was to start.
Before long though, while nervously running down her mental
checklist, Janis realized that she had forgotten to inspect the
garage area and rushed out to do so.

As Janis lifted up the rolling door the sunlight began to
reveal a garage as tidy as the house itself. However, as the
door pulled itself all the way open, it exposed a clutter of
shopping bags that leaned up against two overflowing garbage
cans. Annoyed by the disarray, she went in to clean up the small
mess.

Peering into one bag, Janis found a collection of faded,
rainbow-colored, alphabet refrigerator magnets, a green turtle-
shaped cookie jar, a pretty little hand-stitched sign with red
hearts and the words "Home is where the heart is," and a pink
plastic bread box--items which would surely clash with the newly
remodeled peach and white colored kitchen.

As Janis sorted through the jumble of household misfits she
came across a little typewriter. It was an old typewriter, with
round black buttons--the kind which one had to peck at in order
to send the character's long metal arm up to punch itself onto
the paper. It would make loud clicking sounds as one typed and
chimed at the end of a line, announcing to everyone that someone
was writing. Janis had not used such a machine since high
school, when computers and word processors had not yet
simplified the world.

Writing with such a typewriter was tedious and frustrating,
as it required one's full concentration. Unlike today's
technology it was unforgiving of mistakes and the completion of
a flawless page was indeed, artwork. Janis could remember a time
when, while struggling through grade school she had actually
toyed with the idea of becoming a writer. But then, as her
husband would half teasingly remark, "The real world doesn't
have room for such silly ideas!" CLICK, CLICK, CLICK, CLICK . . .

Once upon a time there was a

"Hello . . . is there a Realtor here?" interrupted a voice.
The first viewers had arrived and Janis fled back into the house
to attend to them. The day dragged by and it was with great
relief that she finally finished up and hastily locked up the
house.

CLICK, CLICK, CLICK . . . sounded the machine. Janis had
rescued the typewriter from the trash pile and was now at home
playing with the new treasure. "Hmm, that's interesting . . .
are we having leftovers for dinner?" remarked her husband, who
had returned home from work.

Hours later, while her husband had drifted off into a deep
slumber, Janis continued away on the machine. She was entranced

by the melodic clicking and it was almost as if the machine were recording her dream.

It was the half-real, half-imagined product of a wandering mind, she thought as she read her words the next day. Random items in her house found their way onto the sheets of paper: the picture on her refrigerator of Andrea, her niece; a dog food advertisement in the newspaper; a bowl in the pantry; her furniture. She didn't know what to make of what she had written and would day after day ponder her creation with a raised brow.

Finally, one evening as she and her husband were preparing to go to sleep she remarked, "There's an interesting story that I thought you might like to read." He climbed into bed and responded with a yawn, "That's nice, dear. What is it called?" Janis paused briefly before saying, "Well, I don't know that it has a title." She went to her drawer and pulled her work out, offering it to him. "Oh honey, maybe tomorrow, I'm really rather tired," he said. "It's short," she urged, "why don't I read it to you?" He gave a tired sigh and agreed so she began to read her story.

Janis read the story with a casual and lighthearted tone-- as if it was just another magazine article she had come across. It was strange though, for it was the first time she had given a voice to her words. Starting to feel uncomfortable, Janis hesitated to look over at her husband and would not have known that he had fallen asleep had his quiet snores not interrupted her reading.

Why, she hadn't even reached the second page! Or the part about the . . . suddenly, pieces started to fall together. As she continued reading with a calm inner voice, it all made sense. For she now understood the feelings that her mind had intended.

As the last few words left her lips, an astounded Janis reached over to the night stand for a pen. She turned back to the first page and there, in the space she had saved for a title, she scrawled in *Janus*. Her story now completed, she returned it to the drawer and left the bedroom, shutting the door firmly behind her.

Connections: Ideas for Discussion and Writing

1. Develop an essay in which you discuss several of the ideas presented by authors in this chapter that have helped you to understand and enhance your own writing process. Refer to specific readings and to your own writing process to support your ideas. How will your new perception of the writing process encourage you to draw on your creative and unconscious mind?

2. Discuss your new insights into the role of the imagination and the creative process in the completion of a work of art or in some other area of life in which you feel that creativity plays a major role. Use references to readings in the text as well as your own creative experiences to support your ideas.

3. Compare two or more selections in this chapter that explore relationships between creativity and the life-death cycle. How have these readings helped you to understand more about the relationship among creativity, life, and death?

4. Discuss several selections in this chapter that have deepened your understanding of the relationships between artistic creativity and the process of birth and childrearing. How did your views on these subjects evolve through reading the selections?

5. Write an essay in which you describe or present a cultural or religious ritual, familiar to you from your family or childhood, that relies on an artistic form such as narrative, music, dance, drama, or poetry. After describing or presenting the ritual, discuss how it has helped you and your family to maintain your own sense of culture and spiritual well-being. What can you conclude about the importance of such artistic forms?

6. Narrate a story that was told to you by an older family member, a story that involves an issue of controversy for your generation and your culture. Contrast your own values or those of your generation with the values implied in the original story.

7. Discuss ways in which the chapter has linked differences in cultural/mythological or ethnic identity to differing views and definitions of creativity and the role of the creator. Make reference to particular readings to support your ideas.

8. Compare two selections in this chapter that present different definitions of the function of art and creativity in the life of the individual or of society. With which do you most agree, and why?

9. Compare two selections in this section from different genres: a play and a poem, a story and a poem or essay, etc. How do they demonstrate similar views of creativity and its function? What impact does the genre in which each of these works is written have on your understanding of and response to the ideas on creativity of the two works you have chosen to compare?

10. Using brief quotations to support your ideas, discuss, analyze, and compare the voices of several writers in the chapter whose characteristic style and creative stance reflect resistance, an affirmation of struggle, and a desire for liberation. How have their voices influenced and inspired you?

Chapter 8

INITIATION
AND PASSAGES

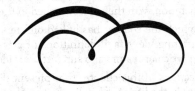

[U]ntil each individual maintains a responsible relationship to his or her own losses and changes, there will be no such thing as a hopeful future. . . . [O]ne's future depends . . . on those invisible elements from the past, those things we are missing, are grieving for, have forgotten and left behind, so that they may be recovered.
Tess Gallagher, "The Poem As a Reservoir for Grief"

Rage for the world as it is
But for what it may be
More love now than last year.
Muriel Rukeyser, "This Place in the Ways"

Through loyalty to the past, our mind refuses to realize that tomorrow's joy is possible only if today's makes way for it; that each wave owes the beauty of its line only to the withdrawal of the preceding one.
Andre Gide, *Journals,* 1928, tr. Justin O'Brien

Initiations and passages are implicit in the cycle of life. From tribal celebrations and sacrifices, to christenings, bar mitzvahs, wedding ceremonies, birthing rooms, and mourners' services, every culture marks the sequence of human development with rituals of passage, ceremonies of initiation into the next stage of life. Such rites acknowledge both continuity and change: from the moment a mother gives birth to a child, to the days when children start school; from the adolescent's struggle to establish him- or herself in a peer group, to the good-byes when a young adult leaves home for college; from the day parents witness their children marry and start families of their own, to the days when grown

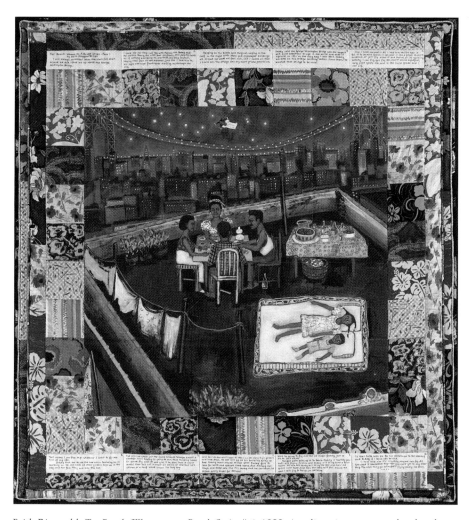

Faith Ringgold. *Tar Beach (Woman on a Beach Series #1)*. 1988. Acrylic paint on canvas bordered with printed and painted quilted and pieced cloth, 74⅝ × 68½". Solomon R. Guggenheim Museum, New York. Gift of Mr. and Mrs. Gus and Judith Lieber, 1988. Photograph by David Heald © The Solomon R. Guggenheim Foundation, New York. (88.3620)

children attend the funerals of their siblings, children, cherished friends, or parents. At the same time that these rites of passage acknowledge cultural tradition and the inevitability of change, they also celebrate the individual's contribution to the human and spiritual community. Through the power of language—metaphor, images, rhythms, the voice that captures a song—literature and nonfiction help people to understand and accept the complex and sometimes frightening transformations that occur in their lives, joyous triumphs as well as losses and sorrow. Particularly in our complex and culturally diverse society, the traditional rites of passage need to be modified and at the same time cherished as links with the past.

Each of the selections in this chapter speaks of a unique issue of initiation and passage. They can be thematically grouped according to the stages of a life: the initiation experiences of childhood, of adolescence, of early adulthood, of middle age, and finally, of aging and bereavement. The reading selections will help you reflect on the initiations and passages you have already traveled through as well as those you have yet to experience.

For children, school presents a challenging passage into a larger world beyond the confines of the home. In "Chike's School Days" African author Chinua Achebe maintains a complex adult view of the ironic impact of a routine education in an emerging, postcolonial third world country, while at the same time he sees that the insatiable curiosity of schoolchildren has the potential to make the initiation into education a revelation. In her story "Celia Behind Me," Isabel Huggan captures the cruelty of the power in peer groups that ostracize those children who are misfits or who have apparent physical weaknesses. Philip Levine's speaker in the poem "The Life Ahead" reminisces about the way that a child's imagination opens doors to the world beyond his home, neighborhood, and school.

As the body and mind of an adolescent begin to mature, the emotional turmoil related to these changes can be confusing and overwhelming. Many of the selections explore these intense, tumultuous experiences of adolescence. "Araby," a short story by James Joyce, voices the feelings and conflicts of a Catholic adolescent's first infatuation with a young woman in his neighborhood, while in "Am I Blue," playwright Beth Henley brings together two adolescents who feel confused and lost as they struggle against peer pressure to become involved in adult vices. As readers identify with the characters' fears and hopes, they also begin to imagine how they might feel and react in a similar situation. In the poem "Saturday at the Canal," Gary Soto expresses the longing for independence of the small-town teenager: "This loneliness. . . . We wanted to get out." In her poem "The Moment," Sharon Olds explores the realization of the passage into womanhood of a young adolescent girl who becomes aware of "the dark Egyptian stain" of menstruation.

The adjustment to mainstream American culture is a kind of initiation that many immigrants and minorities face. In "Silent Dancing," Judith Ortiz Cofer traces the difficult balancing act that newcomers must manage as they try to integrate two cultures, the one that shaped their past and the one that they will live with in the future. Cofer acknowledges that this struggle involves a grappling with the fears that haunt the immigrant's dreams in spite of what he or she may want to become. In her autobiographical essay "Graduation," Maya Angelou's initiation into the power of prejudice and of educational inequality leads her to a deeper courage to overcome the obstacles in her path.

Like adolescence, childbirth is a profound moment of transformation that changes a woman's life irrevocably. Several of the poems in this chapter chart the paths that women have taken through this passage. In "Metaphors," Sylvia Plath sees her physical transformation during pregnancy as symbolic of the inevitability of the realities of motherhood that lie ahead; and Denise Levertov's "Who He Was" presents the reflections of a pregnant woman who thinks about her unborn child, as yet uninitiated into life and laughter. The speaker in Adrianne Marcus' poem, "The Woman in the Next Room," proclaims her sisterhood with other mothers who have "cheated death" by surviving difficult childbirths.

Middle age is often a time when men and women stop to evaluate, reflect, and reconsider their paths through life; many times new roads appear on the horizon of middle age just as others seem to close off. In his short story "The Doll Queen," Carlos Fuentes' narrator tells of the innocence and hope of a childhood infatuation that he attempts to recapture in later life. The narrator in Tillie Olsen's "I Stand Here Ironing" reflects on the struggles and victories that she has shared with her daughter. In his classic essay "Once More to the Lake" E. B. White writes of a trip with his own son to the lake where White had vacationed with his father. As White shares this important part of his childhood with his son, he relives his childhood only to face the consequences of his own middle age.

As middle age brings a new awareness beyond the passionate hopes and demanding goals of youth, this deeper awareness of one's existence is directly challenged by the death of a loved one. A number of the poems reflect on the process of coming to terms with loss. For example the speaker in Li-Young Lee's poem "Eating Together" finally comes to acknowledge and accept his recently deceased father's absence at a family meal.

The human spirit prevails through the voices of writers who are receptive and patient as they record and interpret their passages through times of crisis and transition. Writing thus can be seen both as an act of celebration as well as an act of healing. Muriel Rukeyser captures the writer's process in her poem "This Place in the Ways": "I wait for song,/My poem-hand still, on the paper, .../ My heart beating strong/all night long!"

Folk Tale

Hansel and Grettel
The Brothers Grimm

Journal

Write about a time when you felt abandoned, nelgected or ignored by your family. What did you learn about yourself, your family, and your values from this experience? How did the experience help you to grow and mature?

"Hansel and Grettel" is one of the stories of the Brothers Grimm, early nineteenth-century German linguists who collected European folk tales. Although "Hansel and Grettel" reminds one of a nightmare because the uncaring stepmother forces her husband to abandon his children, who must struggle against an evil witch, the story ends, as do many folk tales, on a note of triumph and reconciliation.

Once upon a time there dwelt on the outskirts of a large forest a poor woodcutter with his wife and two children; the boy was called Hansel and the girl Grettel. He had always little enough to live on, and once, when there was a great famine in the land, he couldn't even provide them with daily bread. One night, as he was tossing about in bed, full of cares and worry, he sighed and said to his wife: "What's to become of us? How are we to support our poor children, now that we have nothing more for ourselves?"

"I'll tell you what, husband," answered the woman, who was the children's step-mother. "Early tomorrow morning we'll take the children out into the thickest part of the wood; there we shall light a fire for them and give them each a piece of bread; then we'll go on to our work and leave them alone. They won't be able to find their way home, and we shall thus be rid of them."

"No, wife," said her husband, "that I won't do; how could I find it in my heart to leave my children alone in the wood? The wild beasts would soon come and tear them to pieces."

"Oh! you fool," said she, "then we must all four die of hunger, and you may just as well go and plane the boards for our coffins"; and she left him no peace till he consented.

"But I can't help feeling sorry for the poor children," added the husband.

The children, too, had not been able to sleep for hunger, and had heard what their stepmother had said to their father. Grettel wept bitterly and spoke to Hansel: "Now it's all up with us."

"No, no, Grettel," said Hansel, "don't fret yourself; I'll be able to find a way of escape, no fear." And when the old people had fallen asleep he got up, slipped on his little coat, opened the back door and stole out.

The moon was shining clearly, and the white pebbles which lay in front of the house glittered like bits of silver. Hansel bent down and filled his pocket with as many of them as he could cram in. Then he went back and said to Grettel, "Be comforted, my dear little sister, and go to sleep. God will not desert us"; and he lay down in bed again.

At daybreak, even before the sun was up, the woman came and woke the two children: "Get up, you lie-abeds, we're all going to the forest to fetch wood." She gave them each a bit of bread and spoke: "There's something for your luncheon, but don't eat it up before, for it's all you'll get."

Grettel took the bread under her apron, as Hansel had the stones in his pocket. Then they all set out together on the way to the forest. After they had walked for a little, Hansel stood still and looked back at the house, and this manœuvre he repeated again and again.

His father observed him, and spoke: "Hansel, what are you gazing at there, and why do you always remain behind? Take care, and don't lose your footing."

"Oh! Father," said Hansel, "I am looking back at my white kitten, which is sitting on the roof, waving me a farewell."

The woman exclaimed: "What a donkey you are! That isn't your kitten, that's the morning sun shining on the chimney." But Hansel had not looked back at his kitten, but had always dropped one of the white pebbles out of his pocket onto the path.

When they had reached the middle of the forest the father said: "Now, children, go and fetch a lot of wood, and I'll light a fire that you mayn't feel cold."

Hansel and Grettel heaped up brushwood till they had made a pile nearly the size of a small hill. The brushwood was set fire to, and when the flames leaped high the woman said: "Now lie down at the fire, children, and rest yourselves; we are going into the forest to cut down wood; when we've finished we'll come back and fetch you."

Hansel and Grettel sat down beside the fire, and at midday ate their little bits of bread. They heard the strokes of the axe, so they thought their father was quite near. But it was no axe they heard, but a bough he had tied onto a dead tree, and that was blown about by the wind. And when they had sat for a long time their eyes closed with fatigue, and they fell fast asleep. When they awoke at last, it was pitch dark.

Grettel began to cry, and said: "How are we ever to get out of the wood?"

But Hansel comforted her. "Wait a bit," he said, "till the moon is up, and then we'll find our way sure enough." And when the full moon had risen he took his sister by the hand and followed the pebbles, which shone like new threepenny bits, and showed them the path. They walked all through the night, and at daybreak reached their father's house again.

They knocked at the door, and when the woman opened it she exclaimed: "You naughty children, what a time you've slept in the wood! We thought you were never going to come back." But the father rejoiced, for his conscience had reproached him for leaving his children behind by themselves.

Not long afterwards there was again great dearth in the land, and the children heard their step-mother address their father thus in bed one night: "Everything is eaten up once more; we have only half a loaf in the house, and when that's done it's all up with us. The children must be got rid of; we'll lead them deeper into the wood this time, so that they won't be able to find their way out again. There is no other way of saving ourselves."

The man's heart smote him heavily, and he thought: "Surely it would be better to share the last bite with one's children!" But his wife wouldn't listen to his arguments, and did nothing but scold and reproach him. If a man yields once, he's done for, and so, because he had given in the first time, he was forced to do so the second.

But the children were awake, and had heard the conversation. When the old people were asleep Hansel got up, and wanted to go out and pick up pebbles again, as he had done the first time; but the woman had barred the door, and Hansel couldn't get out. But he consoled his little sister, and said: "Don't cry, Grettel, and sleep peacefully, for God is sure to help us."

At early dawn the woman came and made the children get up. They received their bit of bread, but it was even smaller than the time before. On the way to the wood Hansel crumbled it in his pocket, and every few minutes he stood still and dropped a crumb on the ground.

"Hansel, what are you stopping and looking about you for?" said the father.

"I'm looking back at my little pigeon, which is sitting on the roof waving me a farewell," answered Hansel.

"Fool!" said the wife. "That isn't your pigeon, it's the morning sun glittering on the chimney." But Hansel gradually threw all his crumbs onto the path. The woman led the children still deeper into the forest, farther than they had ever been in their lives before.

Then a big fire was lit again, and the stepmother said: "Just sit down there, children, and if you're tired you can sleep a bit; we're going into the forest to cut down wood, and in the evening when we're finished we'll come back to fetch you."

At midday Grettel divided her bread with Hansel, for he had strewed his all along their path. Then they fell asleep, and evening passed away, but nobody came to the poor children.

They didn't awake till it was pitch dark, and Hansel comforted his sister, saying: "Only wait, Grettel, till the moon rises, then we shall see the bread crumbs I scattered along the path; they will show us the way back to the house." When the moon appeared they got up, but they found no crumbs, for the thousands of birds that fly about the woods and fields had picked them all up.

"Never mind," said Hansel to Grettel. "You'll see, we'll still find a way out." But all the same they did not.

They wandered about the whole night, and the next day, from morning till evening, but they could not find a path out of the wood. They were very hungry, too, for they had nothing to eat but a few berries they found growing on the ground. And at last they were so tired that their legs refused to carry them any longer, so they lay down under a tree and fell fast asleep.

On the third morning after they had left their father's house they set about their wandering again, but only got deeper and deeper into the wood, and now they felt that if help did not come to them soon they must perish. At midday they saw a beautiful little snow-white bird sitting on a branch, which sang so sweetly that they stopped still and listened to it. And when its song was finished it flapped its wings and flew on in front of them. They followed it and came to a little house, on the roof of which it perched; and when they came quite near they saw that the cottage was made of bread and roofed with cakes, while the window was made of transparent sugar.

"Now we'll set to," said Hansel, "and have a regular blow-out. I'll eat a bit of the roof, and you, Grettel, can eat some of the window, which you'll find a sweet morsel."

Hansel stretched up his hand and broke off a little bit of the roof to see what it was like, and Grettel went to the casement and began to nibble at it. Thereupon a shrill voice called out from the room inside:

"Nibble, nibble, little mouse,
Who's nibbling my house?"

The children answered:

"'Tis Heaven's own child,
The tempest wild,"

and went on eating, without putting themselves about. Hansel, who thoroughly appreciated the roof, tore down a big bit of it, while Grettel pushed out a whole round window-pane, and sat down the better to enjoy it. Suddenly the door opened, and an ancient dame leaning on a staff hobbled out. Hansel and Grettel were so terrified that they let what they had in their hands fall.

But the old woman shook her head and said: "Oh, ho! you dear children, who led you here? Just come in and stay with me, no ill shall befall you." She took them both by the hand and led them into the house, and laid a most sumptuous dinner before them—milk and sugared pancakes, with apples and nuts. After they had finished, two beautiful little white beds were prepared for them, and when Hansel and Grettel lay down in them they felt as if they had got into heaven.

The old woman had appeared to be most friendly, but she was really an old witch who had waylaid the children, and had only built the little bread house in order to lure them in. When anyone came into her power she killed, cooked, and ate him, and held a regular feast-day for the occasion. Now witch-es have red eyes, and cannot see far, but, like beasts, they have a keen sense of smell, and know when human beings pass by. When Hansel and Grettel fell into her hands she laughed maliciously, and said jeeringly: "I've got them now; they shan't escape me."

Early in the morning, before the children were awake, the old woman rose up, and when she saw them both sleeping so peacefully, with their round rosy cheeks, she muttered to herself, "That'll be a dainty bite."

Then she seized Hansel with her bony hand and carried him into a little stable, and barred the door on him. He might scream as much as he liked, it did him no good.

Then she went to Grettel, shook her till she awoke, and cried: "Get up, you lazy-bones, fetch water and cook something for your brother. When he's fat I'll eat him up." Grettel began to cry bitterly, but it was of no use: she had to do what the wicked witch bade her.

So the best food was cooked for poor Hansel, but Grettel got nothing but crab-shells. Every morning the old woman hobbled out to the stable and cried: "Hansel, put out your finger, that I may feel if you are getting fat." But Hansel always stretched out a bone, and the old dame, whose eyes were dim, couldn't see it, and thinking always it was Hansel's finger, wondered why he fattened so slowly. When four weeks passed and Hansel still remained thin, she lost patience and determined to wait no longer.

"Hi! Grettel," she called to the girl, "be quick and get some water. Hansel may be fat or thin, I'm going to kill him tomorrow and cook him." Oh! how the poor little sister sobbed as she carried the water, and how the tears rolled down her cheeks!

"Kind heaven help us now!" she cried. "If only the wild beasts in the wood had eaten us, then at least we should have died together."

"Just hold your peace," said the old hag. "Crying won't help you."

Early in the morning Grettel had to go out and hang up the kettle full of water, and light the fire. "First we'll bake," said the old dame. "I've heated the oven already and kneaded the dough." She pushed Grettel out to the oven, from which fiery flames were already issuing. "Creep in," said the witch, "and see if it's properly heated, so that we can shove in the bread." For when she had got Grettel in she meant to close the oven and let the girl bake, that she might eat her up too.

But Grettel perceived her intention, and spoke: "I don't know how I'm to do it; how do I get in?"

"You silly goose!" said the hag. "The opening is big enough. See, I could get in myself." And she crawled toward it, and poked her head into the oven. Then Grettel gave her a shove that sent her right in, shut the iron door, and drew the bolt. Gracious! how she yelled! it was quite horrible; but Grettel fled, and the wretched old woman was left to perish miserably.

Grettel flew straight to Hansel, opened the little stable-door, and cried: "Hansel, we are free; the old witch is dead."

Then Hansel sprang like a bird out of a cage when the door is opened. How they rejoiced, and fell on each other's necks, and jumped for joy, and kissed one another! And as they had no longer any cause for fear, they went into the old hag's house, and there they found, in every corner of the room, boxes with pearls and precious stones.

"These are even better than pebbles," said Hansel, and crammed his pockets full of them.

Grottol said: "I too will bring something home"; and she filled her apron full.

"But now," said Hansel, "let's go and get well away from the witches' wood."

When they had wandered about for some hours they came to a big lake. "We can't get over," said Hansel; "I see no bridge of any sort or kind."

"Yes, and there's no ferry-boat either," answered Grettel; "but look, there swims a white duck; if I ask her she'll help us over"; and she called out:

> "Here are two children, mournful very,
> Seeing neither bridge nor ferry;
> Take us upon your white back,
> And row us over, quack, quack!"

The duck swam toward them, and Hansel got on her back and bade his little sister sit beside him.

"No," answered Grettel, "we should be too heavy a load for the duck; she shall carry us across separately."

The good bird did this, and when they were landed safely on the other side and had gone on for a while, the wood became more and more familiar to them, and at length they saw their father's house in the distance. Then they set off to run and, bounding into the room, fell on their father's neck. The man had not passed a happy hour since he left them in the wood, but the woman had died. Grettel shook out her apron so that the pearls and precious stones rolled about the room, and Hansel threw down one handful after the other out of his pocket. Thus all their troubles were ended, and they all lived happily ever afterwards.

QUESTIONS AND CONSIDERATIONS

1. Why do you think the father agrees to his wife's plan? Why is it significant that his wife is the children's stepmother? What relationship do you see between the witch and the stepmother?

2. In what sense is this a story of initiation and passage? Which of the events and/or issues raised in the tale seem most relevant to your own life experiences?

3. How do the elements of magic and fantasy affect the meaning that the story holds for you?

4. Why are Hansel and Grettel successful in defeating the witch and finding their way back home? What have Hansel and Grettel learned? What have you learned from reading the tale?

Journals

"My Yearning to Talk to Someone"
From *Diary of a Young Girl*

Anne Frank

Thursday, 6 January, 1944

Dear Kitty,

My longing to talk to someone became so intense that somehow or other I took it into my head to choose Peter.

Sometimes if I've been upstairs into Peter's room during the day, it always struck me as very snug, but because Peter is so retiring and would never turn anyone out who became a nuisance, I never dared stay long, because I was afraid he might think me a bore. I tried to think of an excuse to stay in his room and get him talking, without it being too noticeable, and my chance came yesterday. Peter has a mania for crossword puzzles at the moment and hardly does anything else. I helped him with them and we soon sat opposite each other at his little table, he on the chair and me on the divan.

It gave me a queer feeling each time I looked into his deep blue eyes, and he sat there with that mysterious laugh playing round his lips. I was able to read his inward thoughts. I could see on his face that look of helplessness and uncertainty as to how to behave, and, at the same time, a trace of his sense of manhood. I noticed his shy manner and it made me feel very gentle; I couldn't refrain from meeting those dark eyes again and again, and with my whole heart I almost beseeched him: oh, tell me, what is going on inside you, oh, can't you look beyond this ridiculous chatter?

But the evening passed and nothing happened, except that I told him about blushing—naturally not what I have written, but just so that he would become more sure of himself as he grew older.

When I lay in bed and thought over the whole situation, I found it far from encouraging, and the idea that I should beg for Peter's patronage was simply repellent. One can do a lot to satisfy one's longings, which certainly sticks out in my case, for I have made up my mind to go and sit with Peter more often and to get him talking somehow or other.

Whatever you do, don't think I'm in love with Peter—not a bit of it! If the Van Daans had had a daughter instead of a son, I should have tried to make friends with her too. . . .

"How Shall I Say It?"
From *The Journals of Ruth Benedict*

Ruth Benedict

November, 1912.

I have been reading Walt Whitman, and Jeffries' *Story of My Heart.* They are alike in their superb enthusiasm for life—for actual personal living. To Jeffries nothing, literally nothing, is of worth except as it feeds his "soul-life, his psyche," and as a fantastic appendage, his fevered, exotic dream of the soul-life of future generations. Whitman is far sturdier and more healthful; but it is their common ground that impresses me: their unwavering, ringing belief that the *Me* within them is of untold worth and importance. I read in wonder and admiration—in painful humility. Does this sense of personal worth, this enthusiasm for one's own personality, belong only to the great expressive souls? or to a mature period of life I have not yet attained? or may I perhaps be shut from it by eternal law because I am a woman and lonely? It seems to me the one priceless gift of this life:—of all blessings on earth I would choose to have a man-child who possessed it. . . .

August 20.

How shall I say it? That I have attained to the zest for life? That I have looked in the face of God and had five days of magnificent comprehension? . . . It happened when Stanley came down last week. He had been here one week in July—a glorious week of tramping and rowing and reading, of lying on the hilltops and dreaming over the valleys. But I let him go again.

And last week he came down for two days on his way to Europe. And Oh I was so glad to see him! I think I knew it that night. But he did not see it. We went down to the Collins' Woods in the boat, and still he did not see. It was afternoon when I told him—I had hoped he would see for himself. But it had happened, and I'd rather be with him than anywhere else in God's universe.

He had been lying on the ground. He sat up and moved toward me, and said with a tenderness and awe I had never heard before, "Oh, Ruth, is it true?" And then he put his arms around me, and rested his head against me. In the long minute we sat there, he asked in the same hushed voice, "Ruth, will you marry me?" And I answered him, "Yes Stanley." After that we did not speak. Later it was I who told him first that I loved him.—And so the whole world changed. Is it not awesome—wonderful beyond expression? Every day I have grown surer, happier. Nothing in all my life would be worth setting over against our Sunday afternoon drive through Lyon Brook or our last afternoon together on the towpath.

We turn in our sleep and groan because we are parasites—we women—because we produce nothing, say nothing, find our whole world in the love of a man. —For shame! We are become the veriest Philistines—in this matter of woman's sphere. I suppose it is too soon to expect us to achieve perspective on the problem of woman's rights—but surely there is no other problem of human existence where we would be childish enough to believe in the finality of our little mathematical calculations of "done" or "not done." But here in the one supremely complicated relation of man and woman which involves the perpetual interchange of all that is most difficult to be reckoned—here we thrust in "the world's coarse thumb and finger," here we say "to the eyes of the public shalt thou justify thy existence." —Oh no! do we care whether Beatrice formed clubs, or wrote a sonnet? In the quiet self-fulfilling love of Wordsworth's home, do we ask that Mary Wordsworth should have achieved individual self-expression? In general,—a woman has one supreme power—to love. If we are to arrive at any blythness in facing life, we must have faith to believe that it is in exercising this gift, in living it out to its fullest that she achieves herself, that she "justifies her existence."

From *Fragments from a Journal*

Czeslaw Milosz

Berkeley / August 6, 1987

Adventures of my life. "A revolving bard," as I have called myself. For thirty years in Poland an Orwellian non-person, then a reception in my honor at the Summer Royal Palace in Warsaw given by the Minister of Culture, and soon after, at the time of martial law, again to an attic. Yet my adventure with Oscar Milosz is even more surprising. A couple of months ago, on May 24, 1987, I take a train from the Gare de Lyon to Fontainebleau. After a few minutes I recognize to the right of the track familiar escarpments and trees; my station, Montgeron, flashes by, and later, when the train passes Brunoy and runs through the fields, I search the horizon for the cathedral tower of Brie-Comte Robert.

The first time I sat in a train to Fontainebleau was in 1931. I was twenty. A young elegant woman, a Parisienne, on the opposing seat intrigued me, a provincial. It is not so that now, in this train, I do not give her thought. On the contrary, I am counting: she might have been around thirty then; to add fifty-six years makes eighty-six, so probably she has already died. . . .

Thus, May 1987. La Societé des Amis de Milosz celebrates with an annual luncheon precisely in the Hôtel de l'Aigle Noir, and I go there as a newly elected *président d'honneur* after the death of Jean Cassou. Probably the only sunny day in this May. We depose flowers on the tomb which bears an inscription in Lithuanian and in French: "The first representative of independent Lithuania in Paris." A little crowd is composed of Frenchmen and Lithuanians. Andrzej, who arrived from Warsaw a few days ago, startles the latter by addressing them in pure Lithuanian. After that, a visit to Place Milosz and to the house where Oscar died, at rue Royale, with a garden surrounded by a wall, where we are allowed to enter by the present owner, a retired shoe merchant. A long luncheon, speeches, next a promenade in the Parc du Château, where I wonder whether I am identical to the young man guided here by my cousin fifty-six years ago.

Berkeley / August 9, 1987

In Walnut Creek at the wedding of Ewa, then a party arranged in Danville at a park. When I came to Berkeley in 1960 with Janka and the children and Alfred Tarski was driving us around to show us the region, east of the Berkeley Hills there was only the country—in valleys, the orchards of walnuts; higher, slopes of straw color throughout most of the year, dotted by black oaks. Now the city is everywhere: streets and houses amidst the green, lawns, tennis courts, pools, parks. Also, a metro line, here not underground, leading from San Francisco. I am not sure whether I am strongly for conservation and against development. These landscapes were once rather sterile: dry grass and prickly oaks. The climate is different than in Berkeley, the fog from the sea does not reach here, the sky is always blue, everything is parched, and only people bring water and verdure here.

My childhood differed from childhood today. Mainly because of clouds of insects which buzzed, jumped, stung, bit, entered your eyes. Naked legs covered with scars and blisters from constant scratching. Crickets sputtered in the grass, beetles were running, plenty of red ants (those had the strongest sting), black ants of various sizes; on leaves caterpillars of many colors and shapes were spotted; in the kitchen or in some rooms, for instance those by the dairy, walls hardly visible under a moving fur of flies; glass fly traps filled with whey made dense by layers of drowned bodies. Chemicals have gotten rid of that swarming multiplicity which distinguished my childhood by one more thing: a great number of birds. Today insectivore birds have a hard life, though their scarcity probably does not strike people lacking comparisons.

Berkeley / August 10, 1987

There is a peculiar quality of light in the north and I discovered it after we (Janka and me) lifted our tent in the Canadian Rockies, at Jasper National Park, from where (in August) we had been chased by the first snow. The year was 1969. The road to Edmonton goes first north and only later turns east. There, by the Athabasca, I met this quality of light, so normal for many inhabitants of our planet that they do not even notice it. The first time I had that perception was shortly before World War II when I came from Warsaw on a visit to a small town, Glebokie, where my father was working. Glebokie is not farther north than my native district, but much farther to the east; thence, possibly, a difference. I have never described that town. It was surrounded by the most essential Byelorussian countryside; it had two baroque Jesuit churches and a *shtetl,* known from Yiddish literature and Chagall's paintings. But I have never seen, before or afterward, such an agglomeration of wooden shops. They looked like one barge or ark divided into small cubicles.

Accustomed to the light of California, probably I would now adapt myself to the light of the north with a certain difficulty. Already I found the last gray May in Europe depressing. Yesterday a blue sky (from around 1:00 P.M.) assuaged various despairs to which I bar access. Though I guess I would also like the climate of the Caribbean, those violent rains lasting a few minutes and again the splendor of wet, glimmering verdure in the sun.

QUESTIONS AND CONSIDERATIONS

1. Compare the way that Ruth Benedict and Anne Frank comment in their diaries on the difficulties of feeling emotional closeness with a person while maintaining one's own sense of self.

2. Does the confusion experienced by Benedict and Frank remind you of similar feelings you have experienced about emotional closeness and the power of love? If so, write about such an experience in your journal.

3. How does Milosz comment on the way he perceives change in his life through noting the changes in nature? How does he feel about the way the environment has changed in recent years?

4. Write in your journal about changes in the physical or ecological environment in your neighborhood, or elsewhere, that you have noted over the years. How do you respond to these changes?

5. Do Milosz' comments on the quality of light in California and Europe remind you of any similar contrast of awareness in light or seeing as you have moved or grown older? If so, write about such an awareness in your journal.

Fiction

Chike's School Days
Chinua Acheke

Journal

Write about what you remember enjoying and fearing in your first days at elementary school.

Sarah's last child was a boy, and his birth brought great joy to the house of his father, Amos. The child received three names at his baptism—John, Chike,

Obiajulu. The last name means "the mind at last is at rest." Anyone hearing this name knew at once that its owner was either an only child or an only son. Chike was an only son. His parents had had five daughters before him.

Like his sisters Chike was brought up "in the ways of the white man," which meant the opposite of traditional. Amos had many years before bought a tiny bell with which he summoned his family to prayers and hymn-singing first thing in the morning and last thing at night. This was one of the ways of the white man. Sarah taught her children not to eat in their neighbours' houses because "they offered their food to idols." And thus she set herself against the age-old custom which regarded children as the common responsibility of all so that, no matter what the relationship between parents, their children played together and shared their food.

One day a neighbour offered a piece of yam to Chike, who was only four years old. The boy shook his head haughtily and said, "We don't eat heathen food." The neighbour was full of rage, but she controlled herself and only muttered under her breath that even an *Osu* was full of pride nowadays, thanks to the white man.

And she was right. In the past an *Osu* could not raise his shaggy head in the presence of the free-born. He was a slave to one of the many gods of the clan. He was a thing set apart, not to be venerated but to be despised and almost spat on. He could not marry a free-born, and he could not take any of the titles of his clan. When he died, he was buried by his kind in the Bad Bush.

Now all that had changed, or had begun to change. So that an *Osu* child could even look down his nose at a free-born, and talk about heathen food! The white man had indeed accomplished many things.

Chike's father was not originally an *Osu,* but had gone and married an *Osu* woman in the name of Christianity. It was unheard of for a man to make himself *Osu* in that way, with his eyes wide open. But then Amos was nothing if not mad. The new religion had gone to his head. It was like palm-wine. Some people drank it and remained sensible. Others lost every sense in their stomach.

The only person who supported Amos in his mad marriage venture was Mr. Brown, the white missionary, who lived in a thatch-roofed, red-earth-walled parsonage and was highly respected by the people, not because of his sermons, but because of a dispensary he ran in one of his rooms. Amos had emerged from Mr. Brown's parsonage greatly fortified. A few days later he told his widowed mother, who had recently been converted to Christianity and had taken the name of Elizabeth. The shock nearly killed her. When she recovered, she went down on her knees and begged Amos not to do this thing. But he would not hear; his ears had been nailed up. At last, in desperation, Elizabeth went to consult the diviner.

This diviner was a man of great power and wisdom. As he sat on the floor of his hut beating a tortoise shell, a coating of white chalk round his eyes, he saw not only the present, but also what had been and what was to be. He was called "the man of the four eyes." As soon as old Elizabeth appeared, he cast his stringed cowries and told her what she had come to see him about. "Your son has joined the white man's religion. And you too in your old age when you should know better. And do you wonder that he is stricken with insanity? Those who gather ant-infested faggots must be prepared for the visit of lizards." He cast his cowries a number of times and wrote with a finger on a bowl of sand, and all the while his *nwifulu,* a talking calabash, chatted to itself. "Shut up!" he roared, and it immediately held its peace. The diviner then muttered a few incantations and rattled off a breathless reel of proverbs that followed one another like the cowries in his magic string.

At last he pronounced the cure. The ancestors were angry and must be appeased with a goat. Old Elizabeth performed the rites, but her son remained insane and married an *Osu* girl whose name was Sarah. Old Elizabeth renounced her new religion and returned to the faith of her people.

We have wandered from our main story. But it is important to know how Chike's father became an *Osu,* because even today when everything is upside down, such a story is very rare. But now to return to Chike who refused heathen food at the tender age of four years, or maybe five.

Two years later he went to the village school. His right hand could now reach across his head to his left ear, which proved that he was old enough to tackle the mysteries of the white man's learning. He was very happy about his new slate and pencil, and especially about his school uniform of white shirt and brown khaki shorts. But as the first day of the new term approached, his young mind dwelt on the many stories about teachers and their canes. And he remembered the song his elder sisters sang, a song that had a somewhat disquieting refrain:

Onye nkuzi ewelu itali piagbusie umuaka.

One of the ways an emphasis is laid in Ibo is by exaggeration, so that the teacher in the refrain might not actually have flogged the children to death. But there was no doubt he did flog them. And Chike thought very much about it.

Being so young, Chike was sent to what was called the "religious class" where they sang, and sometimes danced, the catechism. He loved the sound of words and he loved rhythm. During the catechism lesson the class formed a ring to dance the teacher's question. "Who was Caesar?" he might ask, and the song would burst forth with much stamping of feet.

Siza bu eze Rome
Onye nachi enu uwa dum.

It did not matter to their dancing that in the twentieth century Caesar was no longer ruler of the whole world.

And sometimes they even sang in English. Chike was very fond of "Ten Green Bottles." They had been taught the words but they only remembered the first and the last lines. The middle was hummed and hie-ed and mumbled:

Ten grin botr angin on dar war,
Ten grin botr angin on dar war,
Hm, hm hm hm hm
Hm, hm hm hm hm hm,
An ten grin botr angin on dar war.

In this way the first year passed. Chike was promoted to the "Infant School," where work of a more serious nature was undertaken.

We need not follow him through the Infant School. It would make a full story in itself. But it was no different from the story of other children. In the Primary School, however, his individual character began to show. He developed a strong hatred for arithmetic. But he loved stories and songs. And he liked particularly the sound of English words, even when they conveyed no meaning at all. Some of them simply filled him with elation. "Periwinkle" was such a word. He had now forgotten how he learned it or exactly what it was. He had a vague private meaning for it and it was something to do with fairyland. "Constellation" was another.

Chike's teacher was fond of long words. He was said to be a very learned man. His favourite pastime was copying out jaw-breaking words from his *Chambers' Etymological Dictionary.* Only the other day he had raised applause from his class by demolishing a boy's excuse for lateness with unanswerable erudition. He had said: "procrastination is a lazy man's apology." The teacher's erudition showed itself in every subject he taught. His nature study lessons were memorable. Chike would always remember the lesson on the methods of seed dispersal. According to teacher, there were five methods: by man, by animals, by water, by wind, and by explosive mechanism. Even those pupils who forgot all the other methods remembered "explosive mechanism."

Chike was naturally impressed by teacher's explosive vocabulary. But the fairyland quality which words had for him was of a different kind. The first sentences in his *New Method Reader* were simple enough and yet they filled him with a vague exultation: "Once there was a wizard. He lived in Africa. He went to China to get a lamp." Chike read it over and over again at home and then made a song of it. It was a meaningless song. "Periwinkles" got into it, and also "Damascus." But it was like a window through which he saw in the distance a strange, magical new world. And he was happy.

QUESTIONS AND CONSIDERATIONS

1. What is the significance of Chike's name?

2. Why is it important for the reader to understand how Chike's father was converted to Christianity?

3. Does the diviner seem like a man of great power and wisdom? Refer to specific passages in the text to support your answer.

4. How does Chike behave at school? What does he fear? Why does he like school? What is he learning? Although this is a story of initiation into the social world of school, how is Chike also initiated into the spiritual world?

5. Define the story's tone, referring to passages in the text to support your response. How does the tone reinforce Achebe's perspective on the impact of Christianity on the native African culture?

6. What is the narrator's evaluation of Chike's Christian education? What is your evaluation of his education?

IDEAS FOR WRITING

1. Write an essay that analyzes and interprets "Chike's School Days." Discuss its comments about education and its impact on the child.

2. Write an ironic essay or story about an educational experience that you had as a child.

Celia Behind Me
Isabel Huggan

Journal

Write about an incident during your childhood or adolescence when you were part of or witnessed a peer group that victimized another child who had been labeled an outsider and a misfit.

There was a little girl with large smooth cheeks and very thick glasses who lived up the street when I was in public school. Her name was Celia. It was far too rare and grownup a name, so we always laughed at it. And we laughed at her because she was a chubby, diabetic child, made peevish by our teasing.

My mother always said, "You must be nice to Celia, she won't live forever," and even as early as seven I could see the unfairness of that position. Everybody died sooner or later, I'd die too, but that didn't mean everybody was nice to me or to each other. I already knew about mortality and was prepared to go to heaven with my two aunts who had died together in a car crash with their heads smashed like overripe melons. I overheard the bit about the melons when my mother was on the telephone, repeating that phrase and sobbing. I used to think about it often, repeating the words to myself as I did other things so that I got a nice rhythm: "Their heads smashed like melons, like melons, like melons." I imagined the pulpy insides of muskmelons and watermelons all over the road.

I often thought about the melons when I saw Celia because her head was so round and she seemed so bland and stupid and fruitlike. All rosy and vulnerable at the same time as being the most *awful* pain. She'd follow us home from school, whining if we walked faster than she did. Everybody always walked faster than Celia because her short little legs wouldn't keep up. And she was bundled in long stockings and heavy underwear, summer and winter, so that even her clothes held her back from our sturdy, leaping pace over and under hedges and across backyards and, when it was dry, or when it was frozen, down the stream bed and through the drainage pipe beneath the bridge on Church Street.

Celia, by the year I turned nine in December, had failed once and was behind us in school, which was a relief because at least in class there wasn't someone telling you to be nice to Celia. But she'd always be in the playground at recess, her pleading eyes magnified behind those ugly lenses so that you couldn't look at her when you told her she couldn't play skipping unless she was an ender. "Because you can't skip worth a fart," we'd whisper in her ear. "Fart, fart, fart," and watch her round pink face crumple as she stood there, turning, turning, turning the rope over and over.

As the fall turned to winter, the five of us who lived on Brubacher Street and went back and forth to school together got meaner and meaner to Celia. And, after the brief diversions of Christmas, we returned with a vengeance to our running and hiding and scaring games that kept Celia in a state of terror all the way home.

My mother said, one day when I'd come into the kitchen and she'd just turned away from the window so I could see she'd been watching us coming down the street, "You'll be sorry, Elizabeth. I see how you're treating that poor child, and it makes me sick. You wait, young lady. Some day you'll see how it feels yourself. Now you be nice to her, d'you hear?"

"But it's not just me," I protested. "I'm nicer to her than anybody else, and I don't see why I have to be. She's nobody special, she's just a pain. She's really dumb and she can't do anything. Why can't I just play with the other kids like everybody else?"

"You just remember I'm watching," she said, ignoring every word I'd said. "And if I see one more snowball thrown in her direction, by you or by anybody else, I'm coming right out there and spanking you in front of them all. Now you remember that!"

I knew my mother, and knew this was no idle threat. The awesome responsibility of now making sure the other kids stopped snowballing Celia made me weep with rage and despair, and I was locked in my room after supper to "think things over."

I thought things over. I hated Celia with a dreadful and absolute passion. Her round guileless face floated in the air above me as I finally fell asleep, taunting me: "You have to be nice to me because I'm going to die."

I did as my mother bid me, out of fear and the thought of the shame that a public spanking would bring. I imagined my mother could see much farther up the street than she really could, and it prevented me from throwing snowballs or teasing Celia for the last four blocks of our homeward journey. And then came the stomach-wrenching task of making the others quit.

"You'd better stop," I'd say. "If my mother sees you she's going to thrash us all."

Terror of terrors that they wouldn't be sufficiently scared of her strapwielding hand; gut-knotting fear that they'd find out or guess what she'd really said and throw millions of snowballs just for the joy of seeing me whipped, pants down in the snowbank, screaming. I visualized that scene all winter, and felt a shock of relief when March brought such a cold spell that the snow was too crisp for packing. It meant a temporary safety for Celia, and respite for me. For I knew, deep in my wretched heart, that were it not for Celia I was next in line for humiliation. I was kind of chunky and wore glasses too, and had sucked my thumb so openly in kindergarten that "Sucky" had stuck with me all the way to Grade 3 where I now balanced at a hazardous point, nearly accepted by the amorphous Other Kids and always at the brink of being laughed at, ignored or teased. I cried very easily, and prayed during those years—not to become pretty or smart or popular, all aims too far out of my or God's reach, but simply to be strong enough not to cry when I got called Sucky.

During that cold snap, we were all bundled up by our mothers as much as poor Celia ever was. Our comings and goings were hampered by layers of flannel bloomers and undershirts and ribbed stockings and itchy wool against us no matter which way we turned; mitts, sweaters, scarves and hats, heavy and wet-smelling when the snot from our dripping noses mixed with the melting snow on our collars and we wiped, in frigid resignation, our sore red faces with rough sleeves knobbed over with icy pellets.

Trudging, turgid little beasts we were, making our way along slippery streets, breaking the crusts on those few front yards we'd not yet stepped all over in glee to hear the glorious snapping sound of boot through hard snow. Celia, her glasses steamed up even worse than mine, would scuffle and trip a few yards behind us, and I walked along wishing that some time I'd look back and she wouldn't be there. But she always was, and I was always conscious of the abiding hatred that had built up during the winter, in conflict with other emotions that gave me no peace at all. I felt pity, and a rising urge within me to cry as hard as I could so that Celia would cry too, and somehow realize how bad she made me feel, and ask my forgiveness.

It was the last day before the thaw when the tension broke, like northern lights exploding in the frozen air. We were all a little wingy after days of switching between the extremes of bitter cold outdoors and the heat of our homes and school. Thermostats had been turned up in a desperate attempt to combat the arctic air, so that we children suffered scratchy, tingly torment in our faces, hands and feet as the blood in our bodies roared in confusion, first freezing, then boiling. At school we had to go outside at recess—only an act of God would have ever prevented recess, the teachers had to have their cigarettes and tea—and in bad weather we huddled in a shed where the bicycles and the janitor's outdoor equipment were stored.

During the afternoon recess of the day I'm remembering, at the end of the shed where the girls stood, a sudden commotion broke out when Sandra, a rich big girl from Grade 4, brought forth a huge milk-chocolate bar from her pocket. It was brittle in the icy air, and snapped into little bits in its foil wrapper, to be divided among the chosen. I made my way cautiously to the fringe of her group, where many of my classmates were receiving their smidgens of sweet chocolate, letting it melt on their tongues like dark communion wafers. Behind me hung Celia, who had mistaken my earlier cries of "Stop throwing snowballs at Celia!" for kindness. She'd been mooning behind me for days, it seemed to me, as I stepped a little farther forward to see that there were only a few pieces left. Happily, though, most mouths were full and the air hummed with the murmuring sound of chocolate being pressed between tongue and palate.

Made bold by cold and desire, I spoke up. "Could I have a bit, Sandra?" She turned to where Celia and I stood, holding the precious foil in her mittened hand. Wrapping it in a ball, she pushed it over at Celia. Act of kindness, act of spite, vicious bitch or richness seeking expiation? She gave the chocolate to Celia and smiled at her. "This last bit is for Celia," she said to me.

"But I can't eat it," whispered Celia, her round red face aflame with the sensation of being singled out for a gift. "I've got di-a-beet-is." The word. Said so carefully. As if it were a talisman, a charm to protect her against our rough healthiness.

I knew it was a trick. I knew she was watching me out of the corner of her eye, that Sandra, but I was driven. "Then could I have it, eh?" The duress under which I acted prompted my chin to quiver and a tear to start down my cheek before I could wipe it away.

"No, no, no!" jeered Sandra then. "Suckybabies can't have sweets either. Di-a-beet-ics and Suck-y-ba-bies can't eat chocolate. Give it back, you little fart, Celia! That's the last time I ever give you anything!"

Wild, appreciative laughter from the chocolate-tongued mob, and they turned their backs on us, Celia and me, and waited while Sandra crushed the remaining bits into minuscule slivers. They had to take off their mitts and lick their fingers to pick up the last fragments from the foil. I stood there and prayed: "Dear God and Jesus, I would please like very much not to cry. Please help me. Amen." And with that the clanging recess bell clanked through the playground noise, and we all lined up, girls and boys in straight, straight rows, to go inside.

After school there was the usual bunch of us walking home and, of course, Celia trailing behind us. The cold of the past few days had been making us hurry, taking the shortest routes on our way to steaming cups of Ovaltine and cocoa. But this day we were all full of that peculiar energy that swells up before a turn in the weather and, as one body, we turned down the street that meant the long way home. Past the feed store where the Mennonites tied their horses, out the back of the town hall parking-lot and then down a ridge to the ice-covered stream and through the Church Street culvert to come out in the unused field behind the Front Street stores; the forbidden adventure we indulged in as a gesture of defiance against the parental "come right home."

We slid down the snowy slope at the mouth of the pipe that seemed immense then but was really only five feet in diameter. Part of its attraction was the tremendous racket you could make by scraping a stick along the corrugated sides as you went through. It was also long enough to echo very nicely if you made good booming noises, and we occasionally titillated each other by saying bad words at one end that grew as they bounced along the pipe and became wonderfully shocking in their magnitude . . . poopy, Poopy, POOpy, POOOOPy, POOOOPPYYY!

I was last because I had dropped my schoolbag in the snow and stopped to brush it off. And when I looked up, down at the far end, where the white plate of daylight lay stark in the darkness, the figures of my four friends were silhouetted as they emerged into the brightness. As I started making great sliding steps to catch up, I heard Celia behind me, and her plaintive, high voice: "Elizabeth! Wait for me, okay? I'm scared to go through alone. Elizabeth?"

And of course I slid faster and faster, unable to stand the thought of being the only one in the culvert with Celia. Then we would come out together and we'd really be paired up. What if they always ran on ahead and left us to walk together? What would I ever do? And behind me I heard the rising call of Celia, who had ventured as far as a few yards into the pipe, calling my name to come back and walk with her. I got right to the end, when I heard another noise and looked up. There they all were, on the bridge looking down, and as soon as they saw my face began to chant, "Better wait for Celia, Sucky. Better get Celia, Sucky."

The sky was very pale and lifeless, and I looked up in the air at my breath curling in spirals and felt, I remember this very well, an exhilarating, clear-headed instant of understanding. And with that, raced back into the tunnel where Celia stood whimpering half-way along.

"You little fart!" I screamed at her, my voice breaking and tearing at the words. "You little diabetic fart! I hate you! I hate you! Stop it, stop crying, I hate you! I could bash your head in I hate you so much, you fart, you fart! I'll smash your head like a melon! And it'll go in pieces all over and you'll die. You'll die, you diabetic. You're going to die!" Shaking her, shaking her and banging her against the cold, ribbed metal, crying and sobbing for grief and gasping with the exertion of pure hatred. And then there were the others, pulling at me, yanking me away, and in the moral tones of those who don't actually take part, warning me that they were going to tell, that Celia probably was going to die now, that I was really evil, they would tell what I said.

And there, slumped in a little heap, was Celia, her round head in its furry bonnet all dirty at the back where it had hit against the pipe, and she was hiccupping with fear. And for a wild, terrible moment I thought I had killed her, that the movements and noises her body made were part of dying.

I ran.

I ran as fast as I could back out the way we had come, and all the way back to the schoolyard. I didn't think about where I was going, it simply seemed the only bulwark to turn to when I knew I couldn't go home. There were a few kids still in the yard but they were older and ignored me as I tried the handle of the side door and found it open. I'd never been in the school after hours, and was stricken with another kind of terror that it might be a strappable offence. But no-one saw me, even the janitor was blessedly in another part of the building, so I was able to creep down to the girls' washroom and quickly hide in one of the cubicles. Furtive, criminal, condemned.

I was so filled with horror I couldn't even cry. I just sat on the toilet seat, reading all the things that were written in pencil on the green, wooden walls. *G.R. loves M.H.* and *Y.F. hates W.S. for double double sure. Mr. Becker wears ladies pants.* Thinking that I might die myself, die right here, and then it wouldn't matter if they told on me that I had killed Celia.

But the inevitable footsteps of retribution came down the stone steps before I had been there very long. I heard the janitor's voice explaining he hadn't seen any children come in and then my father's voice saying that the others were sure this is where Elizabeth would be. And they called my name, and then came in, and I guess saw my boots beneath the door because I suddenly thought it was too late to scrunch them up on the seat and my father was looking down at me and grabbed my arm, hurting it, pulling me, saying "Get in the car, Elizabeth."

Both my mother and my father spanked me that night. At first I tried not to cry, and tried to defend myself against their diatribe, tried to tell them when they asked, "But whatever possessed you to do such a terrible thing?" But whatever I said seemed to make them more angry and they became so soured by their own shame that they slapped my stinging buttocks for personal revenge as much as for any rehabilitative purposes.

"I'll never be able to lift my head on this street again!" my mother cried, and it struck me then, as it still does now, as a marvellous turn of phrase. I thought about her head on the street as she hit me, and wondered what Celia's head looked like, and if I had dented it at all.

Celia hadn't died, of course. She'd been half-carried, half-dragged home by the heroic others, and given pills and attention and love, and the doctor had come to look at her head but she didn't have so much as a bruise. She had a dirty hat, and a bad case of hiccups all night, but she survived.

Celia forgave me, all too soon. Within weeks her mother allowed her to walk back and forth to school with me again. But, in all the years before she finally died at seventeen, I was never able to forgive her. She made me discover a darkness far more frightening than the echoing culvert, far more enduring than her smooth, pink face.

QUESTIONS AND CONSIDERATIONS

1. Why does the narrator use the image of the smashed, overripe melons to express her feelings for Celia and her anxieties about death?

2. How does Elizabeth come to protect and identify with Celia? Why does she have such mixed feelings about Celia? How and why has Elizabeth been stigmatized by her association with Celia?

3. Why is the narrator's detailed description of the division of the chocolate bar at the end of winter after "the tension broke, like northern lights exploding in the frozen air" especially effective? Does it remind you of incidents in your childhood or in your present life?

4. Why does Elizabeth attack Celia? Explore several possible explanations.

5. What image does Elizabeth develop to reveal the irony she sees in the retribution her parents' sought against her as they punished her for hurting Celia? Why does Celia forgive Elizabeth quickly, while Elizabeth never forgives Celia or herself?

6. Have you ever been through a situation in which, as Elizabeth did, you "discovered a darkness" within you that frightened you?

IDEAS FOR WRITING

1. Write an essay in which you discuss how during your childhood or adolescence you came to realize an inner darkness or potential for cruel behavior. In your conclusion discuss the impact that writing about the incident had on your self-understanding and your self-esteem.

2. Write an essay in which you discuss several trials or initiations that you were subjected to by your peers when you were in elementary or junior high school. Compare your own experiences to those explored in the story, and draw some conclusions about the impact of peer pressure on adolescents.

Araby
James Joyce

Journal
---

*Write about your first romantic crush or infatuation: the circumstances, your
feelings, and the long-term impact that the relationship had on your
development.*

North Richmond Street, being blind, was a quiet street except at the hour when the Christian Brothers' School set the boys free. An uninhabited house of two storeys stood at the blind end, detached from its neighbours in a square ground. The other houses of the street, conscious of decent lives within them, gazed at one another with brown imperturbable faces.

The former tenant of our house, a priest, had died in the back drawing-room. Air, musty from having been long enclosed, hung in all the rooms, and the waste room behind the kitchen was littered with old useless papers. Among these I found a few paper-covered books, the pages of which were curled and damp: *The Abbot,* by Walter Scott, *The Devout Communicant* and *The Memoirs of Vidocq.* I liked the last best because its leaves were yellow. The wild garden behind the house contained a central apple-tree and a few straggling bushes under one of which I found the late tenant's rusty bicycle-pump. He had been a very charitable priest; in his will he had left all his money to institutions and the furniture of his house to his sister.

When the short days of winter came dusk fell before we had well eaten our dinners. When we met in the street the houses had grown sombre. The space of sky above us was the colour of ever-changing violet and towards it the lamps of the street lifted their feeble lanterns. The cold air stung us and we played till our bodies glowed. Our shouts echoed in the silent street. The career of our play brought us through the dark muddy lanes behind the houses where we ran the gauntlet of the rough tribes from the cottages, to the back doors of the dark dripping gardens where odours arose from the ashpits, to the dark odorous stables where a coachman smoothed and combed the horse or shook music from the buckled harness. When we returned to the street light from the kitchen windows had filled the areas. If my uncle was seen turning the corner we hid in the shadow until we had seen him safely housed. Or if Mangan's sister came out on the doorstep to call her brother in to his tea we watched her from our shadow peer up and down the street. We waited to see whether she would remain or go in and, if she remained, we left our shadow and walked up to Mangan's steps resignedly. She was waiting for us, her figure defined by the light from the half-opened door. Her brother always teased her before he obeyed and I stood by the railings looking at her. Her dress swung as she moved her body and the soft rope of her hair tossed from side to side.

Every morning I lay on the floor in the front parlour watching her door. The blind was pulled down to within an inch of the sash so that I could not be seen. When she came out on the doorstep my heart leaped. I ran to the hall, seized my books and followed her. I kept her brown figure always in my eye and, when we came near the point at which our ways diverged, I quickened my pace and passed her. This happened morning after morning. I had never spoken to her, except for a few casual words, and yet her name was like a summons to all my foolish blood.

Her image accompanied me even in places the most hostile to romance. On Saturday evenings when my aunt went marketing I had to go to carry some of the parcels. We walked through the flaring streets, jostled by drunken men and bargaining women, amid the curses of labourers, the shrill litanies of shop-boys who stood on guard by the barrels of pigs' cheeks, the nasal chanting of street-singers, who sang a *come-all-you* about O'Donovan Rossa, or a ballad about the troubles in our native land. These noises converged in a single sensation of life for me: I imagined that I bore my chalice safely through a throng of foes. Her name sprang to my lips at moments in strange prayers and praises which I myself did not understand. My eyes were often full of tears (I could not tell why) and at times a flood from my heart seemed to pour itself out into my bosom. I thought little of the future. I did not know whether I would ever speak to her or not or, if I spoke to her, how I could tell her of my confused adoration. But my body was like a harp and her words and gestures were like fingers running upon the wires.

One evening I went into the back drawing-room in which the priest had died. It was a dark rainy evening and there was no sound in the house. Through one of the broken panes I heard the rain impinge upon the earth, the fine incessant needles of water playing in the sodden beds. Some distant lamp or lighted window gleamed below me. I was thankful that I could see so little.

All my senses seemed to desire to veil themselves and, feeling that I was about to slip from them, I pressed the palms of my hands together until they trembled, murmuring: *"O love! O love!"* many times.

At last she spoke to me. When she addressed the first words to me I was so confused that I did not know what to answer. She asked me was I going to *Araby.* I forgot whether I answered yes or no. It would be a splendid bazaar, she said she would love to go.

"And why can't you?" I asked.

While she spoke she turned a silver bracelet round and round her wrist. She could not go, she said, because there would be a retreat that week in her convent. Her brother and two other boys were fighting for their caps and I was alone at the railings. She held one of the spikes, bowing her head towards me. The light from the lamp opposite our door caught the white curve of her neck, lit up her hair that rested there and, falling, lit up the hand upon the railing. It fell over one side of her dress and caught the white border of a petticoat, just visible as she stood at ease.

"It's well for you," she said.

"If I go," I said, "I will bring you something."

What innumerable follies laid waste my waking and sleeping thoughts after that evening! I wished to annihilate the tedious intervening days. I chafed against the work of school. At night in my bedroom and by day in the class-room her image came between me and the page I strove to read. The syllables of the word *Araby* were called to me through the silence in which my soul luxuriated and cast an Eastern enchantment over me. I asked for leave to go to the bazaar on Saturday night. My aunt was surprised and hoped it was not some Freemason affair. I answered few questions in class. I watched my master's face pass from amiability to sternness; he hoped I was not beginning to idle. I could not call my wandering thoughts together. I had hardly any patience with the serious work of life which, now that it stood between me and my desire, seemed to me child's play, ugly monotonous child's play.

On Saturday morning I reminded my uncle that I wished to go to the bazaar in the evening. He was fussing at the hallstand, looking for the hat-brush, and answered me curtly:

"Yes, boy, I know."

As he was in the hall I could not go into the front parlour and lie at the window. I left the house in bad humour and walked slowly towards the school. The air was pitilessly raw and already my heart misgave me.

When I came home to dinner my uncle had not yet been home. Still it was early. I sat staring at the clock for some time and, when its ticking began to irritate me, I left the room. I mounted the staircase and gained the upper part of the house. The high cold empty gloomy rooms liberated me and I went from room to room singing. From the front window I saw my companions playing below in the street. Their cries reached me weakened and indistinct and, leaning my forehead against the cool glass, I looked over at the dark house where she lived. I may have stood there for an hour, seeing nothing but the brown-clad figure cast by my imagination, touched discreetly by the lamplight at the curved neck, at the hand upon the railings and at the border below the dress.

When I came downstairs again I found Mrs. Mercer sitting at the fire. She was an old garrulous woman, a pawnbroker's widow, who collected used stamps for some pious purpose. I had to endure the gossip of the tea-table. The meal was prolonged beyond an hour and still my uncle did not come. Mrs. Mercer stood up to go: she was sorry she couldn't wait any longer, but it was after eight o'clock and she did not like to be out late, as the night air was bad for her. When she had gone I began to walk up and down the room, clenching my fists. My aunt said:

"I'm afraid you may put off your bazaar for this night of Our Lord."

At nine o'clock I heard my uncle's latchkey in the halldoor. I heard him talking to himself and heard the hallstand rocking when it had received the weight of his overcoat. I could interpret these signs. When he was midway through his dinner I asked him to give me the money to go to the bazaar. He had forgotten.

"The people are in bed and after their first sleep now," he said.

I did not smile. My aunt said to him energetically:

"Can't you give him the money and let him go? You've kept him late enough as it is."

My uncle said he was very sorry he had forgotten. He said he believed in the old saying: "All work and no play makes Jack a dull boy." He asked me where I was going and, when I had told him a second time he asked me did I know *The Arab's Farewell to his Steed.* When I left the kitchen he was about to recite the opening lines of the piece to my aunt.

I held a florin tightly in my hand as I strode down Buckingham Street towards the station. The sight of the streets thronged with buyers and glaring with gas recalled to me the purpose of my journey. I took my seat in a third-class carriage of a deserted train. After an intolerable delay the train moved out of the station slowly. It crept onward among ruinous houses and over the twinkling river. At Westland Row Station a crowd of people pressed to the carriage doors; but the porters moved them back, saying that it was a special train for the bazaar. I remained alone in the bare carriage. In a few minutes the train drew up beside an improvised wooden platform. I passed out on to the road and saw by the lighted dial of a clock that it was ten minutes to ten. In front of me was a large building which displayed the magical name.

I could not find any sixpenny entrance and, fearing that the bazaar would be closed, I passed in quickly through a turnstile, handing a shilling to a weary-looking man. I found myself in a big hall girdled at half its height by a gallery. Nearly all the stalls were closed and the greater part of the hall was in darkness. I recognised a silence like that which pervades a church after a service. I walked into the centre of the bazaar timidly. A few people were gathered about the stalls which were still open. Before a curtain, over which the words *Café Chantant* were written in coloured lamps, two men were counting money on a salver. I listened to the fall of the coins.

Remembering with difficulty why I had come I went over to one of the stalls and examined porcelain vases and flowered tea-sets. At the door of the stall a young lady was talking and laughing with two young gentlemen. I remarked their English accents and listened vaguely to their conversation.

"O, I never said such a thing!"

"O, but you did!"

"O, but I didn't!"

"Didn't she say that?"

"Yes. I heard her."

"O, there's a . . . fib!"

Observing me the young lady came over and asked me did I wish to buy anything. The tone of her voice was not encouraging; she seemed to have spoken to me out of a sense of duty. I looked humbly at the great jars that stood like eastern guards at either side of the dark entrance to the stall and murmured:

"No, thank you."

The young lady changed the position of one of the vases and went back to the two young men. They began to talk of the same subject. Once or twice the young lady glanced at me over her shoulder.

I lingered before her stall, though I knew my stay was useless, to make my interest in her wares seem the more real. Then I turned away slowly and walked down the middle of the bazaar. I allowed the two pennies to fall against the sixpence in my pocket. I heard a voice call from one end of the gallery that the light was out. The upper part of the hall was now completely dark.

Gazing up into the darkness I saw myself as a creature driven and derided by vanity; and my eyes burned with anguish and anger.

QUESTIONS AND CONSIDERATIONS

1. Joyce's narrator carefully creates the setting and mood of the story in the first two paragraphs. Discuss several of the details in these two paragraphs that gave you clues about the world of the narrator, the values of his family and community.

2. What details foreshadow the narrator's attraction to Mangan's sister? Why does the narrator promise to bring Mangan's sister something from the Araby bazaar? Why is it significant that Mangan's sister is not allowed to go?

3. Discuss the significance of the reactions of the schoolmaster, the uncle, and the aunt to the narrator's decision to attend the bazaar. How do their reactions give a more complete perspective on the narrator's motivations and expectations?

4. Interpret the significance of the narrator's observations of the bazaar. Why do you think the bazaar makes him think of the silence after a church service?

5. After all of his anticipation and desire to please Mangan's sister, why doesn't the narrator buy her a gift? What does the narrator learn about himself through his trip to the bazaar? Why does he see himself "as a creature driven and derided by vanity?"

6. How did the religious setting and mood of the story affect the way that you related to the narrator's crisis of conscience and his initiation? What aspects of the narrator's quest and struggles did you find most compelling and accurate?

IDEAS FOR WRITING

1. Write an essay or a short story about your first infatuation, emphasizing your feelings, your conflicts, and your realizations.

2. Write an essay in which you discuss several of the images developed in the story to show how they help to create the story's mood and its major themes. Refer specifically to the text as you develop your points.

The Doll Queen

Carlos Fuentes
Translated from the Spanish by Margaret S. Peden

Journal

Write about a meeting or unexpected encounter with a childhood friend whom you had not seen in a number of years.

I

I went because that card—such a strange card—reminded me of her existence. I found it in a forgotten book whose pages had revived the ghost associated with the childish calligraphy. For the first time in a long time I was rearranging my books. I met surprise after surprise since some, placed on the highest shelves, had not been read for a long time. So long a time that the edges of the leaves were grainy, and a mixture of gold dust and greyish scale fell onto my open palm, reminiscent of the lacquer covering certain bodies glimpsed first in dreams and later in the deceptive reality of the first ballet performance to which we're taken. It was a book from my childhood—perhaps from that of many children—that related a series of more or less truculent exemplary tales which had the virtue of precipitating us upon our elders' knees to ask them, over and over again: Why? Children who are ungrateful to their parents; maidens kidnapped by flashy horsemen and returned home in shame— as well as those who willingly abandon hearth and home; old men who in exchange for an overdue mortgage demand the hand of the sweetest and most long-suffering daughter of the threatened family. . . . Why? I do not recall their answers, I only know that from among the stained pages fell, fluttering, a white card in Amilamia's atrocious hand: *Amilamia wil not forget her good frend—com see me her lik I draw it.*

And on the other side was that map of a path starting from an X that indicated, doubtlessly, the park bench where I, an adolescent rebelling against prescribed and tedious education, forgot my classroom schedule in order to spend several hours reading books which if not actually written by me, seemed to be: who could doubt that only from *my* imagination could spring all those corsairs, those couriers of the tsar, all those boys slightly younger than I who rowed all day up and down the great American rivers on a raft. Clutching the arm of the park bench as if it were the frame of a magical saddle, at first I didn't hear the sound of the light steps and of the little girl who would stop behind me after running down the graveled garden path. It was Amilamia, and I don't know how long the child would have kept me silent company if her mischievous spirit, one afternoon, had not chosen to tickle my ear with down from a dandelion she blew towards me, her lips puffed out and her brow furrowed in a frown.

She asked my name and after considering it very seriously, she told me hers with a smile which if not candid, was not too rehearsed. Quickly I realized that Amilamia had discovered, if discovered is the word, a form of expression midway between the ingenuousness of her years and the forms of adult mimicry that well-brought-up children have to know, particularly those for the solemn moments of introduction and of leave-taking. Amilamia's seriousness, apparently, was a gift of nature, whereas her moments of spontaneity, by contrast, seemed artificial. I like to remember her, afternoon after afternoon, in a succession of snapshots that in their totality sum up the complete Amilamia. And it never ceases to surprise me that I cannot think of her as she really was, or remember how she actually moved, light, questioning, constantly looking around her. I must remember her fixed forever in time, as in a photograph album. Amilamia in the distance, a point on the spot where the hill began to descend from a lake of clover towards the flat meadow where I, sitting on the bench, used to read: a point of fluctuating shadow and sunshine and a hand that waved to me from high on the hill. Amilamia frozen in her flight down the hill, her white skirt billowing, the flowered panties gathered around her thighs with elastic, her mouth open and eyes half-closed against the streaming air, the child crying with pleasure. Amilamia sitting beneath the eucalyptus trees, pretending to cry so that I would go over to her. Amilamia lying on her stomach with a flower in her hand: the petals of a flower which I discovered later didn't grow in this garden, but somewhere else, perhaps in the garden of Amilamia's house, since the single pocket of her blue-checked apron was often filled with those white blossoms. Amilamia watching me read, holding with both hands to the bars of the green bench, asking questions with her grey eyes: I recall that she never asked me what I was reading, as if she could divine in my eyes the images born of the pages. Amilamia laughing with pleasure when I lifted her by the waist and whirled her around my head; she seemed to discover a new perspective on the world in that slow flight. Amilamia turning her back to me and waving goodbye, her arm held high, the fingers waving excitedly. And Amilamia in the thousand postures she affected around my bench, hanging upside down, her bloomers billowing; sitting on the gravel with her legs crossed and her chin resting on her fist; lying on the grass, baring her belly-button to the sun; weaving tree branches, drawing animals in the mud with a twig, licking the bars of the bench, hiding beneath the seat, silently breaking off the loose bark from the ancient treetrunks, staring at the horizon beyond the hill, humming with her eyes closed, imitating the voices of birds, dogs, cats, hens, and horses. All for me, and nevertheless, nothing. It was her way

of being with me, all these things I remember, but at the same time her manner of being alone in the park. Yes, perhaps my memory of her is fragmentary
because reading alternated with the contemplation of the chubby-cheeked
child with smooth hair changing in the reflection of the light: now wheat-
colored, now burnt chestnut. And it is only today that I think how Amilamia in
that moment established the other point of support for my life, the one that created the tension between my own irresolute childhood and the open world, the
promised land that was beginning to be mine through my reading.

Not then. Then I dreamed about the women in my books, about the quin-
tessential female—the word disturbed me—who assumed the disguise of the
Queen in order to buy the necklace secretly, about the imagined beings of
mythology—half recognizable, half white-breasted, damp-bellied salaman-
ders—who awaited monarchs in their beds. And thus, imperceptibly, I moved
from indifference towards my childish companion to an acceptance of the
child's gracefulness and seriousness and from there to an unexpected rejection of a presence that became useless to me. She irritated me, finally. I who
was fourteen was irritated by that child of seven who was not yet memory or
nostalgia, but rather the past and its reality. I had let myself be dragged along
by weakness. We had run together, holding hands, across the meadow. Together we had shaken the pines and picked up the cones that Amilamia guarded jealously in her apron pocket. Together we had constructed paper boats
and followed them, happy and gay, to the edge of the drain. And that afternoon
amidst shouts of glee, when we tumbled together down the hill and rolled to a
stop at its foot, Amilamia was on my chest, her hair between my lips; but when
I felt her panting breath in my ear and her little arms sticky from sweets around
my neck, I angrily pushed away her arms and let her fall. Amilamia cried, rubbing her wounded elbow and knee, and I returned to my bench. Then Amilamia went away and the following day she returned, handed me the paper
without a word, and disappeared, humming, into the woods. I hesitated
whether to tear up the card or keep it in the pages of the book: *Afternoons on
the Farm.* Even my reading had become childish because of Amilamia. She
did not return to the park. After a few days I left for my vacation and when I returned it was to the duties of my first year of prep school. I never saw her
again.

II

And now, almost rejecting the image that is unaccustomed without being fantastic, but is all the more painful for being so real, I return to that forgotten park
and stopping before the grove of pines and eucalyptus I recognize the small-
ness of the bosky enclosure that my memory has insisted on drawing with an
amplitude that allowed sufficient space for the vast swell of my imagination.
After all, Strogoff and Huckleberry, Milady de Winter and Geneviève de Bra-
bante were born, lived and died here: in a little garden surrounded by mossy
iron railings, sparsely planted with old, neglected trees, barely adorned by a
concrete bench painted to look like wood that forces me to believe that my

beautiful wrought-iron green-painted bench never existed, or else was a part of my orderly, retrospective delirium. And the hill . . . How could I believe the promontory that Amilamia climbed and descended during her daily coming and going, that steep slope we rolled down together, was *this.* A barely elevated patch of dark stubble with no more heights and depths than those my memory had created.

Com see me here lik I draw it. So I would have to cross the garden, leave the woods behind, descend the hill in three loping steps, cut through that narrow grove of chestnuts—it was here, surely, where the child gathered the white petals—open the squeaking park gate and suddenly recall . . . , know . . . , find oneself in the street, realize that every afternoon of one's adolescence, as if by a miracle, he had succeeded in suspending the beat of the surrounding city, annulling that flood-tide of whistles, bells, voices, sobs, engines, radios, imprecations. Which was the true magnet, the silent garden or the feverish city?

I wait for the light to change and cross to the other sidewalk, my eyes never leaving the red iris detaining the traffic. I consult Amilamia's paper. After all, that rudimentary map is the true magnet of the moment I am living, and just thinking about it startles me. I was obliged, after the lost afternoons of my fourteenth year, to follow the channels of discipline; now I find myself, at twenty-nine, duly certified with a diploma, owner of an office, assured of a moderate income, a bachelor still, with no family to maintain, slightly bored with sleeping with secretaries, scarcely excited by an occasional outing to the country or to the beach, feeling the lack of a central attraction such as those once afforded me by my books, my park, and Amilamia. I walk down the street of this grey, low-buildinged suburb. The one-story houses with their doorways scaling paint succeed each other monotonously. Faint neighborhood sounds barely interrupt the general uniformity: the squeal of a knife-sharpener here, the hammering of a shoe-repairman there. The children of the neighborhood are playing in the dead-end streets. The music of an organ-grinder reaches my ears, mingled with the voices of children's rounds. I stop a moment to watch them with the sensation, also fleeting, that Amilamia must be among these groups of children, immodestly exhibiting her flowered panties, hanging by her knees from some balcony, still fond of acrobatic excesses, her apron pocket filled with white petals. I smile, and for the first time I am able to imagine the young lady of twenty-two who, even if she still lives at this address, will laugh at my memories, or who perhaps will have forgotten the afternoons spent in the garden.

The house is identical to all the rest. The heavy entry door, two grilled windows with closed shutters. A one-story house, topped by a false neoclassic balustrade that probably conceals the practicalities of the flat-roofed *azotea:* clothes hanging on lines, tubs of water, servants' quarters, a chicken coop. Before I ring the bell, I want to free myself of any illusion. Amilamia no longer lives here. Why would she stay fifteen years in the same house? Besides, in spite of her precocious independence and aloneness, she seemed like a well-brought-up, well-behaved child, and this neighborhood is no longer elegant;

Amilamia's parents, without doubt, have moved. But perhaps the new renters will know where.

I press the bell and wait. I ring again. Here is another contingency: no one is home. And will I feel the need again to look for my childhood friend? No. Because it will not be possible a second time to open a book from my adolescence and accidentally find Amilamia's card. I would return to my routine, I would forget the moment whose importance lay in its fleeting surprise.

I ring once more. I press my ear to the door and am surprised: I can hear a harsh and irregular breathing on the other side; the sound of labored breathing, accompanied by the disagreeable odor of stale tobacco, filters through the cracks in the hall.

"Good afternoon. Could you tell me . . . ?"

As soon as he hears my voice, the person moves away with heavy and unsure steps. I press the bell again, shouting this time:

"Hey! Open up! What's the matter? Don't you hear me?"

No response. I continue ringing the bell, without result. I move back from the door, still staring at the small cracks, as if distance might give me perspective, or even penetration. With all my attention fixed on that damned door, I cross the street, walking backwards; a piercing scream, followed by a prolonged and ferocious blast of a whistle, saves me in time; dazed, I seek the person whose voice has just saved me. I see only the automobile moving down the street and I hang on to a lamp post, a hold that more than security offers me a point of support during the sudden rush of icy blood to my burning, sweaty skin. I look towards the house that has been, that was, that must be, Amilamia's. There, behind the balustrade, as I had known there would be, fluttering clothes are drying. I don't know what else is hanging there—skirts, pajamas, blouses—I don't know. All I can see is that starched little blue-checked apron, clamped by clothespins to the long cord that swings between an iron bar and a nail in the white wall of the *azolea*.

III

In the Bureau of Records they have told me that the property is in the name of a Señor R. Valdivia, who rents the house. To whom? That they don't know. Who is Valdivia? He has declared himself a businessman. Where does he live? Who are *you?* the young lady asked me with haughty curiosity. I haven't been able to present a calm and sure appearance. Sleep has not relieved my nervous fatigue. Valdivia. As I leave the Bureau the sun offends me. I associate the repugnance provoked by the hazy sun sifting through the clouds—therefore all the more intense—with the desire to return to the damp, shadowy park. No. It is only the desire to know whether Amilamia lives in that house and why they refuse to let me enter. But the first thing I must do is reject the absurd idea that kept me awake all night. Having seen the apron drying on the flat roof, the one where she kept the flowers, and so believing that in that house lived a seven-year-old girl that I had known fourteen or fifteen years before. . . . She must have a little girl! Yes. Amilamia, at twenty-two, is the mother of a girl who dressed the same, looked the same, repeated the same games, and—who knows—perhaps even went to the same park. And deep in thought I again arrived at the door of the house. I ring the bell and await the whistling breathing on the other side of the door. I am mistaken. The door is opened by a woman who can't be more than fifty. But wrapped in a shawl, dressed in black and in black low-heeled shoes, with no make-up and her salt and pepper hair pulled into a knot, she seems to have abandoned all illusion or pretext of youth; she is observing me with eyes so indifferent they seem almost cruel.

"You want something?"

"Señor Valdivia sent me." I cough and run my hand over my hair. I should have picked up my briefcase at the office. I realize that without it I cannot play my role very well.

"Valdivia?" the woman asks without alarm, without interest.

"Yes. The owner of this house."

One thing is clear. The woman will reveal nothing in her face. She looks at me, calmly.

"Oh, yes. The owner of the house."

"May I come in?"

I think that in bad comedies the traveling salesman sticks a foot in the door so they can't close the door in his face. I do the same, but the woman steps back and with a gesture of her hand invites me to come into what must have been a garage. On one side there is a glass-paned door, its paint faded. I walk towards the door over the yellow tiles of the entryway and ask again, turning towards the woman who follows me with tiny steps:

"This way?"

I notice for the first time that in her white hands she is carrying a chaplet which she toys with ceaselessly. I haven't seen one of those old-fashioned rosaries since my childhood and I want to comment on it, but the brusque and decisive manner with which the woman opens the door precludes any gratuitous conversation. We enter a long narrow room. The woman hastens to open the shutters. But because of four large perennial plants growing in porcelain and crusted glass pots the room remains in shadow. The only other objects in the room are an old high-backed cane-trimmed sofa and a rocking chair. But it is neither the plants nor the sparseness of the furniture that draws my attention.

The woman invites me to sit on the sofa before she sits in the rocking chair. Beside me, on the cane arm of the sofa, there is an open magazine.

"Señor Valdivia sends his apologies for not having come in person."

The woman rocks, unblinkingly. I peer at the comic book out of the corner of my eye.

"He sends his greetings and. . . ."

I stop, awaiting a reaction from the woman. She continues to rock. The magazine is covered with red-penciled scribbling.

". . . and asks me to inform you that he must disturb you for a few days. . . ."

My eyes search rapidly.

". . . A new evaluation of the house must be made for the tax lists. It seems it hasn't been done for. . . . You have been living here since . . . ?"

Yes. That is a stubby lipstick lying under the chair. If the woman smiles, it is only with the slow-moving hands caressing the chaplet; I sense, for an instant, a swift flash of ridicule that does not quite disturb her features. She still does not answer.

". . . for at least fifteen years, isn't that true?"

She does not agree. She does not disagree. And on the pale thin lips there is not the least sign of lipstick. . . .

". . . you, your husband, and . . . ?"

She stares at me, never changing expression, almost daring me to continue. We sit a moment in silence, she playing with the rosary, I leaning forwards, my hands on my knees. I rise.

"Well, then, I'll be back this afternoon with the papers. . . ."

The woman nods while, in silence, she picks up the lipstick and the comic book and hides them in the folds of her shawl.

IV

The scene has not changed. This afternoon, while I am writing down false figures in my notebook and feigning interest in establishing the quality of the dulled floor-boards and the length of the living room, the woman rocks, as the three decades of the chaplet whisper through her fingers. I sigh as I finish the supposed inventory of the living room and I ask her for permission to go to the other rooms in the house. The woman rises, bracing her long black-clad arms on the seat of the rocking chair and adjusting the shawl on her narrow bony shoulders.

She opens the opaque glass door and we enter a dining room with very little more furniture. But the table with the aluminum legs and the four nickel and plastic chairs lack even the slight hint of distinction of the living room furniture. Another window with wrought-iron grille and closed shutters must at times illuminate this bare-walled dining room, bare of either shelves or bureau. The only object on the table is a plastic fruit dish with a cluster of black grapes, two peaches, and a buzzing corona of flies. The woman, her arms crossed, her face expressionless, stops behind me. I take the risk of breaking the order of things: it is evident that these rooms will not tell me anything that I really want to know.

"Couldn't we go up to the roof?" I ask. "I believe that is the best way of measuring the total area."

The woman's eyes light up as she looks at me, or perhaps it is only the contrast with the penumbra of the dining room.

"What for?" she says finally. "Señor . . . Valdivia . . . knows the dimensions very well."

And those pauses, one before and one after the owner's name, are the first indications that something is at last perturbing the woman and forcing her, in defense, to resort to a certain irony.

"I don't know." I make an effort to smile. "Perhaps I prefer to go from top to bottom and not . . . " my false smile drains away, ". . . from bottom to top."

"You will go the way I show you," the woman says, her arms crossed across her chest, the silver cross hanging against her dark belly.

Before smiling weakly, I force myself to think how, in this shadow, my gestures are useless, not even symbolic. I open the notebook with a crunch of the cardboard cover and continue making my notes with the greatest possible speed, never glancing up, the numbers and estimates of this task whose fiction—the light flush in my cheeks and the perceptible dryness of my tongue tell me—is deceiving no one. And after filing the graph paper with absurd signs, with square roots and algebraic formulas, I ask myself what is preventing me from getting to the point, from asking about Amilamia and getting out of here with a satisfactory answer. Nothing. And nevertheless, I am sure that even if I obtained a response, the truth does not lie along this road. My slim and silent companion is a person I wouldn't look twice at in the street, but in this almost uninhabited house with the coarse furniture, she ceases to be an anonymous face in the crowd and is converted into a stock character of mystery. Such is the paradox, and if memories of Amilamia have once again awakened my appetite for the imaginary, I shall follow the rules of the game, I shall exhaust all the appearances, and I shall not rest until I find the answer—perhaps simple and clear, immediate and evident—that lies beyond the unexpected veils the señora of the rosary places in my path. Do I bestow a more-than-justified strangeness upon my reluctant Amphitryon? If that is so, I shall only take more pleasure in the labyrinths of my own invention. And the flies are still buzzing around the fruit dish, occasionally pausing on the damaged end of the peach, a nibbled bite—I lean closer using the pretext of my notes—where little teeth have left their mark in the velvety skin and ochre flesh of the fruit. I do not look towards the señora. I pretend I am taking notes. The fruit seems to be bitten but not touched. I crouch down to see it better, rest my hands upon the table, moving my lips closer as if I wished to repeat the act of biting without touching. I look down and I see another sign close to my feet: the track of two tires that seem to be bicycle tires, the print of two rubber tires that come as far as the edge of the table and then lead away, growing fainter, the length of the room, towards the señora. . . .

I close my notebook.

"Let us continue, señora."

As I turn towards her, I find her standing with her hands resting on the back of a chair. Seated before her, coughing the smoke of his black cigarette, is a man with heavy shoulders and hidden eyes: these eyes, hardly visible behind swollen wrinkled lids as thick and droopy as the neck of an ancient turtle, seem nevertheless to follow my every movement. The half-shaven cheeks, criss-crossed by a thousand grey furrows, hang from protruding cheekbones, and his greenish hands are folded beneath his arms. He is wearing a coarse blue shirt, and his rumpled hair is so curly it looks like the bottom of a barnacle-covered ship. He does not move, and the true sign of his existence is that difficult whistling breathing (as if every breath must breach a flood-gate of phlegm, irritation, and abuse) that I had already heard through the chinks of the entry hall.

Ridiculously, he murmurs: "Good afternoon . . . ," and I am disposed to forget everything: the mystery, Amilamia, the assessment, the bicycle tracks. The apparition of this asthmatic old bear justifies a prompt retreat. I repeat "Good afternoon," this time with an inflection of farewell. The turtle's mask dissolves into an atrocious smile: every pore of that flesh seems fabricated of brittle rubber, of painted, peeling oilcloth. The arm reaches out and detains me.

"Valdivia died four years ago," says the man in a distant, choking voice that issues from his belly instead of his larynx: a weak, high-pitched voice.

Held by that strong, almost painful, claw, I tell myself it is useless to pretend. But the wax and rubber faces observing me say nothing and for that reason I am able, in spite of everything, to pretend one last time, to pretend that I am speaking to myself when I say:

"Amilamia. . . ."

Yes; no one will have to pretend any longer. The fist that clutches my arm affirms its strength for only an instant, immediately its grip loosens, then it falls, weak and trembling, before rising to take the waxen hand touching the shoulder: the señora, perplexed for the first time, looks at me with the eyes of a violated bird and sobs with a dry moan that does not disturb the rigid astonishment of her features. Suddenly the ogres of my imagination are two solitary, abandoned, wounded old people, scarcely able to console themselves in the shuddering clasp of hands that fills me with shame. My fantasy has brought me to this stark dining room to violate the intimacy and the secret of two human beings exiled from life by something I no longer have the right to share. I have never despised myself more. Never have words failed me in such a clumsy way. Any gesture of mine would be in vain: shall I approach them, shall I touch them, shall I caress the woman's head, shall I ask them to excuse my intrusion? I return the notebook to my jacket pocket. I toss into oblivion all the clues in my detective story: the comic book, the lipstick, the nibbled fruit, the bicycle tracks, the blue-checked apron. . . . I decide to leave this house in silence. The old man, from behind those thick eyelids, must have noticed me. The high breathy voice says:

"Did you know her?"

That past, so natural they must use it every day, finally destroys my illusions. There is the answer. Did you know her? How many years? How many years must the world have lived without Amilamia, assassinated first by my forgetfulness, and revived, scarcely yesterday, by a sad impotent memory? When did those serious grey eyes cease to be astonished by the delight of an always solitary garden? When did those lips cease to pout or press together thinly in that ceremonious seriousness with which, I now realize, Amilamia must have discovered and consecrated the objects and events of life that, she knew perhaps intuitively, was fleeting?

"Yes, we played together in the park. A long time ago."

"How old was she?" says the old man, his voice even more muffled.

"She must have been about seven. No, older than seven."

The woman's voice rises, along with the arms that seem to implore:
"What was she like, señor? Tell us what she was like, please."

I close my eyes. "Amilamia is my memory, too. I can only compare her to
the things that she touched, that she brought, that she discovered in the park.
Yes. Now I see her, coming down the hill. No. It isn't true that it was a barely
elevated patch of stubble. It was a hill, with grass, and Amilamia's coming and
going had traced a path, and she waved to me from the top before she started
down, accompanied by the music, yes, the music I saw, the painting I smelled,
the tastes I heard, the odors I touched . . . my hallucination. . . ." Do they
hear me? "She came, waving, dressed in white, in a blue-checked apron . . .
the one you have hanging on the *azotea* . . . ."

They take my arms and still I do not open my eyes.

"What was she like, señor?"

"Her eyes were gray and the color of her hair changed in the reflection of
the sun and the shadow of the trees. . . ."

They lead me gently, the two of them; I hear the man's labored breathing,
the cross on the rosary hitting against the woman's body.

"Tell us, please. . . ."

"The air brought tears to her eyes when she ran; when she reached my
bench her cheeks were silvered with happy tears. . . ."

I do not open my eyes. Now we are going upstairs. Two, five, eight, nine,
twelve steps. Four hands guide my body.

"What was she like, what was she like?"

"She sat beneath the eucalyptus and wove garlands from the branches
and pretended to cry so I would quit my reading and go over to her. . . ."

Hinges creak. The odor overpowers everything else: it routs the other
senses, it takes its seat like a yellow Mogul upon the throne of my hallucination; heavy as a coffin, insinuating as the slither of draped silk, ornamented as
a Turkish sceptre, opaque as a deep, lost vein of ore, brilliant as a dead star.
The hands no longer hold me. More than the sobbing, it is the trembling of the
old people that envelops me. Slowly, I open my eyes: first through the dizzying
liquid of my cornea then through the web of my eyelashes, the room suffocated in that enormous battle of perfumes is disclosed, effluvia and frosty, almost
flesh-like petals; the presence of the flowers is so strong here they seem to
take on the quality of living flesh—the sweetness of the jasmine, the nausea of
the lilies, the tomb of the tuberose, the temple of the gardenia. Illuminated
through the incandescent wax lips of heavy sputtering candles, the small windowless bedroom with its aura of wax and humid flowers assaults the very
center of my plexus, and from there, only there at the solar center of life, am I
able to revive and to perceive beyond the candles, among the scattered flowers, the accumulation of used toys: the colored hoops and wrinkled balloons,
cherries dried to transparency, wooden horses with scraggly manes, the scoot-
er, blind and hairless dolls, bears spilling their sawdust, punctured oilcloth

ducks, moth-eaten dogs, wornout jumping ropes, glass jars of dried candy, wornout shoes, the tricycle (three wheels? no, two, and not like a bicycle—two *parallel* wheels below), little woolen and leather shoes; and, facing me, within reach of my hand, the small coffin raised on paper flower-decorated blue boxes, flowers of life this time, carnations and sunflowers, poppies and tulips, but like the others, the ones of death, all part of a potion brewed by the atmosphere of this funeral hot-house in which reposes, inside the silvered coffin, between the black silk sheets, upon the pillow of white satin, that motionless and serene face framed in lace, highlighted with rose-colored tints, eyebrows traced by the lightest trace of pencil, closed lids, real eyelashes, thick, that cast a tenuous shadow on cheeks as healthy as those of the days in the park. Serious red lips, set almost in the angry pout that Amilamia feigned so I would come to play. Hands joined over the breast. A chaplet identical to the mother's, strangling that cardboard neck. Small white shroud on the clean, prepubescent, docile body.

The old people, sobbing, have knelt.

I reach out my hand and run my fingers over the porcelain face of my friend. I feel the coldness of those painted features, of the doll-queen who presides over the pomp of this royal chamber of death. Porcelain, cardboard, and cotton. *Amilamia wil not forget her good frend—com see me here lik I draw it.*

I withdraw my fingers from the false cadaver. Traces of my fingerprints remain where I touched the skin of the doll.

And nausea crawls in my stomach where the candle smoke and the sweet stench of the lilies in the enclosed room have settled. I turn my back on Amilamia's sepulchre. The woman's hand touches my arm. Her wildly staring eyes do not correspond with the quiet, steady voice.

"Don't come back, señor. If you truly loved her, don't come back again."

I touch the hand of Amilamia's mother. I see through nauseous eyes the old man's head buried between his knees, and I go out of the room to the stairway, to the living room, to the patio, to the street.

V

If not a year, nine or ten months have passed. The memory of that idolatry no longer frightens me. I have forgotten the odor of the flowers and the image of the petrified doll. The real Amilamia has returned to my memory and I have felt, if not content, sane again: the park, the living child, my hours of adolescent reading, have triumphed over the spectres of a sick cult. The image of life is the more powerful. I tell myself that I shall live forever with my real Amilamia, the conqueror of the caricature of death. And one day I dare look again at that notebook with graph paper where I wrote the information of the false assessment. And from its pages, once again, falls Amilamia's card with its terrible childish scrawl and its map for getting from the park to her house. I smile as I pick it up. I bite one of the edges, thinking that in spite of everything, the poor old people would accept this gift.

Whistling, I put on my jacket and knot my tie. Why not visit them and offer them this paper with the child's own writing?

I am running as I approach the one-story house. Rain is beginning to fail in large isolated drops that bring from the earth with magical immediacy an odor of damp benediction that seems to stir the humus and precipitate the fermentation of everything living with its roots in the dust.

I ring the bell. The shower increases and I become insistent. A shrill voice shouts: "I'm going!" and I wait for the figure of the mother with her eternal rosary to open the door for me. I turn up the collar of my jacket. My clothes, my body, too, smell different in the rain. The door opens:

"What do you want? How wonderful you've come!"

The misshapen girl sitting in the wheelchair lays one hand on the doorknob and smiles at me with an indecipherably wry grin. The hump on her chest converts the dress into a curtain over her body, a piece of white cloth that nonetheless lends an air of coquetry to the blue-checked apron. The little woman extracts a pack of cigarettes from her apron pocket and rapidly lights a cigarette, staining the end with orange-painted lips. The smoke causes the beautiful grey eyes to squint. She arranges the coppery, wheat-colored, permanently waved hair: She stares at me all the time with a desolate, inquisitive, and hopeful—but at the same time fearful—expression.

"No Carlos. Go away. Don't come back."

And from the house, at the same moment, I hear the high breathy breathing of the old man, coming closer and closer.

"Where are you? Don't you know you're not supposed to answer the door? Go back! Devil's spawn! Do I have to beat you again?"

And the water from the rain trickles down my forehead, over my cheeks, and into my mouth, and the little frightened hands drop the comic book onto the damp stones.

QUESTIONS AND CONSIDERATIONS

1. Why does the 29-year-old narrator seek out Amilamia again after so many years? What does he hope to gain?

2. Why does the narrator lie to Amilamia's parents? Why do you think that Amilamia's parents act as if they believe the narrator's claim that he is there to assess their apartment's value when they know that he is lying about the purpose of his visit?

3. Discuss several passages that characterize Amilamia's parents. What writing techniques does Fuentes use to create a strong physical and emotional impression of them? How do you feel about Amilamia's parents?

4. Why have Amilamia's parents constructed a false shrine to their "doll queen"? How does the shrine function as a symbol? Discuss several meanings that you see in the title after reading and thinking about the story.

5. Why do you think that Amilamia has become disabled? How and why do the narrator's feelings about Amilamia, her parents, and himself change at the end of the story? Why is this a story of initiation and passage for the narrator?

6. Although this story resembles a dream or fantasy in its distortions of time and the grotesque details about Amilamia's home life, what aspects of the story make it seem believable, true to actual parent-child relationships?

IDEAS FOR WRITING

1. Write an essay in which you compare the narrator's relationship with Amilamia to your own memories of a childhood friend who helped you to make a transition in life. Would you like to see this friend again, as the narrator attempts to do in the story? What would you say to this friend if you could see him or her?

2. Develop an essay that explores several realistic insights about what adults learn when they try to relive or revisit their childhood. To support your main ideas, use references to the story and/or experiences that you have had.

I Stand Here Ironing
Tillie Olsen

Journal

Write about obstacles that you have had to overcome because of the economic circumstances of your family. What strengths have you gained as an individual because of your struggles?

I stand here ironing, and what you asked me moves tormented back and forth with the iron.

"I wish you would manage the time to come in and talk with me about your daughter. I'm sure you can help me understand her. She's a youngster who needs help and whom I'm deeply interested in helping."

"Who needs help." Even if I came, what good would it do? You think because I am her mother I have a key, or that in some way you could use me as a key? She has lived for nineteen years. There is all that life that has happened outside of me, beyond me.

And when is there time to remember, to sift, to weigh, to estimate, to total? I will start and there will be an interruption and I will have to gather it all together again. Or I will become engulfed with all I did or did not do, with what should have been and what cannot be helped.

She was a beautiful baby. The first and only one of our five that was beautiful at birth. You do not guess how new and uneasy her tenancy in her now-loveliness. You did not know her all those years she was thought homely, or see her poring over her baby pictures, making me tell her over and over how beautiful she had been—and would be, I would tell her—and was now, to the seeing eye. But the seeing eyes were few or non-existent. Including mine.

I nursed her. They feel that's important nowadays. I nursed all the children, but with her, with all the fierce rigidity of first motherhood, I did like the books then said. Though her cries battered me to trembling and my breasts ached with swollenness, I waited till the clock decreed.

Why do I put that first? I do not even know if it matters, or if it explains anything.

She was a beautiful baby. She blew shining bubbles of sound. She loved motion, loved light, loved color and music and textures. She would lie on the floor in her blue overalls patting the surface so hard in ecstasy her hands and feet would blur. She was a miracle to me, but when she was eight months old I had to leave her daytimes with the woman downstairs to whom she was no miracle at all, for I worked or looked for work and for Emily's father, who "could no longer endure" (he wrote in his good-bye note) "sharing want with us."

I was nineteen. It was the pre-relief, pre-WPA world of the depression. I would start running as soon as I got off the streetcar, running up the stairs, the place smelling sour, and awake or asleep to startle awake, when she saw me she would break into a clogged weeping that could not be comforted, a weeping I can hear yet.

After a while I found a job hashing at night so I could be with her days, and it was better. But it came to where I had to bring her to his family and leave her.

It took a long time to raise the money for her fare back. Then she got chicken pox and I had to wait longer. When she finally came, I hardly knew her, walking quick and nervous like her father, looking like her father, thin, and dressed in a shoddy red that yellowed her skin and glared at the pockmarks. All the baby loveliness gone.

She was two. Old enough for nursery school they said, and I did not know then what I know now—the fatigue of the long day, and the lacerations of group life in the nurseries that are only parking places for children.

Except that it would have made no difference if I had known. It was the only place there was. It was the only way we could be together, the only way I could hold a job.

And even without knowing, I knew. I knew the teacher that was evil because all these years it has curdled into my memory, the little boy hunched in the corner, her rasp, "why aren't you outside, because Alvin hits you? that's no reason, go out, scaredy." I knew Emily hated it even if she did not clutch and implore "don't go Mommy" like the other children, mornings.

She always had a reason why she should stay home. Momma, you look sick, Momma. I feel sick. Momma, the teachers aren't there today, they're sick. Momma, we can't go, there was a fire there last night. Momma, it's a holiday today, no school, they told me.

But never a direct protest, never rebellion. I think of our others in their three-, four-year-oldness—the explosions, the tempers, the denunciations, the demands—and I feel suddenly ill. I put the iron down. What in me demanded that goodness in her? And what was the cost, the cost to her of such goodness?

The old man living in the back once said in his gentle way: "You should smile at Emily more when you look at her." What *was* in my face when I looked at her? I loved her. There were all the acts of love.

It was only with the others I remembered what he said, and it was the face of joy, and not of care or tightness or worry I turned to them—too late for Emily. She does not smile easily, let alone almost always as her brothers and sisters do. Her face is closed and sombre, but when she wants, how fluid. You must have seen it in her pantomimes, you spoke of her rare gift for comedy on the stage that rouses a laughter out of the audience so dear they applaud and applaud and do not want to let her go.

Where does it come from, that comedy? There was none of it in her when she came back to me that second time, after I had had to send her away again. She had a new daddy now to learn to love, and I think perhaps it was a better time.

Except when we left her alone nights, telling ourselves she was old enough.

"Can't you go some other time, Mommy, like tomorrow?" she would ask. "Will it be just a little while you'll be gone? Do you promise?"

The time we came back, the front door open, the clock on the floor in the hall. She rigid awake. "It wasn't just a little while. I didn't cry. Three times I called you, just three times, and then I ran downstairs to open the door so you could come faster. The clock talked loud. I threw it away, it scared me what it talked."

She said the clock talked loud again that night I went to the hospital to have Susan. She was delirious with the fever that comes before red measles, but she was fully conscious all the week I was gone and the week after we were home when she could not come near the new baby or me.

She did not get well. She stayed skeleton thin, not wanting to eat, and night after night she had nightmares. She would call for me, and I would rouse from exhaustion to sleepily call back: "You're all right, darling, go to sleep, it's just a dream," and if she still called, in a sterner voice, "now go to sleep, Emily, there's nothing to hurt you." Twice, only twice, when I had to get up for Susan anyhow, I went in to sit with her.

Now when it is too late (as if she would let me hold and comfort her like I do the others) I get up and go to her at once at her moan or restless stirring. "Are you awake, Emily? Can I get you something?" And the answer is always the same: "No, I'm all right, go back to sleep, Mother."

They persuaded me at the clinic to send her away to a convalescent home in the country where "she can have the kind of food and care you can't manage for her, and you'll be free to concentrate on the new baby." They still send children to that place. I see pictures on the society page of sleek young women planning affairs to raise money for it, or dancing at the affairs, or decorating Easter eggs or filling Christmas stockings for the children.

They never have a picture of the children so I do not know if the girls still wear those gigantic red bows and the ravaged looks on the every other Sunday when parents can come to visit "unless otherwise notified"—as we were notified the first six weeks.

Oh it is a handsome place, green lawns and tall trees and fluted flower beds. High up on the balconies of each cottage the children stand, the girls in their red bows and white dresses, the boys in white suits and giant red ties. The parents stand below shrieking up to be heard and the children shriek down to be heard, and between them the invisible wall "Not To Be Contaminated by Parental Germs or Physical Affection."

There was a tiny girl who always stood hand in hand with Emily. Her parents never came. One visit she was gone. "They moved her to Rose College," Emily shouted in explanation. "They don't like you to love anybody here."

She wrote once a week, the labored writing of a seven-year-old. "I am fine. How is the baby. If I write my leter nicly I will have a star. Love." There never was a star. We wrote every other day, letters she could never hold or keep but only hear read—once. "We simply do not have room for children to keep any personal possessions," they patiently explained when we pieced one Sunday's shrieking together to plead how much it would mean to Emily, who loved so to keep things, to be allowed to keep her letters and cards.

Each visit she looked frailer. "She isn't eating," they told us.

(They had runny eggs for breakfast or mush with lumps, Emily said later, I'd hold it in my mouth and not swallow. Nothing ever tasted good, just when they had chicken.)

It took us eight months to get her released home, and only the fact that she gained back so little of her seven lost pounds convinced the social worker.

I used to try to hold and love her after she came back, but her body would stay stiff, and after a while she'd push away. She ate little. Food sickened her, and I think much of life too. Oh she had physical lightness and brightness, twinkling by on skates, bouncing like a ball up and down up and down over the jump rope, skimming over the hill; but these were momentary.

She fretted about her appearance, thin and dark and foreign-looking at a time when every little girl was supposed to look or thought she should look a chubby blonde replica of Shirley Temple. The doorbell sometimes rang for her, but no one seemed to come and play in the house or be a best friend. Maybe because we moved so much.

There was a boy she loved painfully through two school semesters. Months later she told me how she had taken pennies from my purse to buy him candy. "Licorice was his favorite and I brought him some every day, but he still like Jennifer better'n me. Why, Mommy?" The kind of question for which there is no answer.

School was a worry to her. She was not glib or quick in a world where glibness and quickness were easily confused with ability to learn. To her overworked and exasperated teachers she was an overconscientious "slow learner" who kept trying to catch up and was absent entirely too often.

I let her be absent, though sometimes the illness was imaginary. How different from my now-strictness about attendance with the others. I wasn't working. We had a new baby, I was home anyhow. Sometimes, after Susan grew old enough, I would keep her home from school, too, to have them all together.

Mostly Emily had asthma, and her breathing, harsh and labored, would fill the house with a curiously tranquil sound. I would bring the two old dresser mirrors and her boxes of collections to her bed. She would select beads and single earrings, bottle tops and shells, dried flowers and pebbles, old postcards and scraps, all sorts of oddments; then she and Susan would play Kingdom, setting up landscapes and furniture, peopling them with action.

Those were the only times of peaceful companionship between her and Susan. I have edged away from it, that poisonous feeling between them, that terrible balancing of hurts and needs I had to do between the two, and did so badly, those earlier years.

Oh there are conflicts between the others too, each one human, needing, demanding, hurting, taking—but only between Emily and Susan, no, Emily toward Susan that corroding resentment. It seems so obvious on the surface, yet it is not obvious. Susan, the second child, Susan, golden- and curly-haired and chubby, quick and articulate and assured, everything in appearance and manner Emily was not; Susan, not able to resist Emily's precious things, losing or sometimes clumsily breaking them; Susan telling jokes and riddles to company for applause while Emily sat silent (to say to me later: that was *my* riddle, Mother, I told it to Susan); Susan, who for all the five years' difference in age was just a year behind Emily in developing physically.

I am glad for that slow physical development that widened the difference between her and her contemporaries, though she suffered over it. She was too vulnerable for that terrible world of youthful competition, of preening and parading, of constant measuring of yourself against every other, of envy, "If I had that copper hair," "If I had that skin. . . ." She tormented herself enough about not looking like the others, there was enough of the unsureness, the having to be conscious of words before you speak, the constant caring—what are they thinking of me? without having it all magnified by the merciless physical drives.

Ronnie is calling. He is wet and I change him. It is rare there is such a cry now. That time of motherhood is almost behind me when the ear is not one's own but must always be racked and listening for the child cry, the child call. We sit for a while and I hold him, looking out over the city spread in charcoal with its soft aisles of light *"Shoogily,"* he breathes and curls closer. I carry him back to bed, asleep. *Shoogily.* A funny word, a family word, inherited from Emily, invented by her to say: *comfort.*

In this and other ways she leaves her seal, I say aloud. And startle at my saying it. What do I mean? What did I start to gather together, to try and make coherent? I was at the terrible, growing years. War years. I do not remember them well. I was working, there were four smaller ones now, there was not time for her. She had to help be a mother, and housekeeper, and shopper. She had to set her seal. Mornings of crisis and near hysteria trying to get lunches packed, hair combed, coats and shoes found, everyone to school or Child Care on time, the baby ready for transportation. And always the paper scribbled on by a smaller one, the book looked at by Susan then mislaid, the homework not done. Running out to that huge school where she was one, she was lost, she was a drop; suffering over the unpreparedness, stammering and unsure in her classes.

There was so little time left at night after the kids were bedded down. She would struggle over books, always eating (it was in those years she developed her enormous appetite that is legendary in our family) and I would be ironing, or preparing food for the next day, or writing V-mail to Bill, or tending the baby. Sometimes, to make me laugh, or out of her despair, she would imitate happenings or types at school.

I think I said once: "Why don't you do something like this in the school amateur show?" One morning she phoned me at work, hardly understandable through the weeping: "Mother, I did it. I won, I won; they gave me first prize; they clapped and clapped and wouldn't let me go."

Now suddenly she was Somebody, and as imprisoned in her difference as she had been in anonymity.

She began to be asked to perform at other high schools, even in colleges, then at city and statewide affairs. The first one we went to, I only recognized her that first moment when thin, shy, she almost drowned herself into the curtains. Then: Was this Emily? The control, the command, the convulsing and deadly clowning, the spell, then the roaring, stamping audience, unwilling to let this rare and precious laughter out of their lives.

Afterwards: You ought to do something about her with a gift like that—but without money or knowing how, what does one do? We have left it all to her, and the gift has as often eddied inside, clogged and clotted, as been used and growing.

She is coming. She runs up the stairs two at a time with her light graceful step, and I know she is happy tonight. Whatever it was that occasioned your call did not happen today.

"Aren't you ever going to finish the ironing, Mother? Whistler painted his mother in a rocker. I'd have to paint mine standing over an ironing board." This is one of her communicative nights and she tells me everything and nothing as she fixes herself a plate of food out of the icebox.

She is so lovely. Why did you want me to come in at all? Why were you concerned? She will find her way.

She starts up the stairs to bed. "Don't get me up with the rest in the morning." "But I thought you were having midterms." "Oh, those," she comes back in, kisses me, and says quite lightly, "in a couple of years when we'll all be atom-dead they won't matter a bit."

She has said it before. She *believes* it. But because I have been dredging the past, and all that compounds a human being is so heavy and meaningful in me, I cannot endure it tonight.

I will never total it all. I will never come in to say: She was a child seldom smiled at. Her father left me before she was a year old. I had to work her first six years when there was work, or I sent her home and to his relatives. There were years she had care she hated. She was dark and thin and foreign-looking in a world where the prestige went to blondeness and curly hair and dimples, she was slow where glibness was prized. She was a child of anxious, not proud, love. We were poor and could not afford for her the soil of easy growth. I was a young mother, I was a distracted mother. There were the other children pushing up, demanding. Her younger sister seemed all that she was not. There were years she did not want me to touch her. She kept too much in herself, her life was such she had to keep too much in herself. My wisdom came too late. She has much to her and probably nothing will come of it. She is a child of her age, of depression, of war, of fear.

Let her be. So all that is in her will not bloom—but in how many does it? There is still enough left to live by. Only help her to know—help make it so there is cause for her to know—that she is more than this dress on the ironing board, helpless before the iron.

QUESTIONS AND CONSIDERATIONS

1. Who is the audience for this story? Is the mother speaking to herself, to her daughter's counselor, or to a larger audience?

2. Although Emily, the narrator's 19-year-old daughter, "was a beautiful baby," her life didn't turn out ideally. What circumstances in the narrator's family and economic pressures influenced Emily's childhood?

3. The mother asks, "Where does it come from, that comedy?" What situations in Emily's life helped to make her a talented comedian?

4. Do you think that the narrator in the story has been a responsible, realistic parent? Do you think she tries to rationalize her failures? Do you think that mothers whose children are in late adolescence often experience doubts similar to those that the narrator expresses?

5. How do the title and the narrator's final comments about not wanting her child to be "helpless before the iron" reinforce the meaning of the story?

6. What initiations and passages are explored in this story, both for the mother and the daughter?

IDEAS FOR WRITING

1. Retell the narrator-mother's story from the point of view of her daughter, Emily. Why would Emily's perspective differ from her mother's?

2. Write a narrative about a specific situation when you were forced to realize that your character and resources were limited to some extent. Discuss this realization as an initiation into adulthood, a passage from innocence to experience.

My Man Bovanne
Toni Cade Bambara

Journal

What contribution do older people make to your family?
Why do you value them?

Blind people got a hummin jones if you notice. Which is understandable completely once you been around one and notice what no eyes will force you into
to see people, and you get past the first time, which seems to come out of
nowhere, and it's like you in church again with fat-chest ladies and old gents
gruntin a hum low in the throat to whatever the preacher be saying. Shakey
Bee bottom lip all swole up with Sweet Peach and me explainin how come the
sweetpotato bread was a dollar-quarter this time stead of dollar regular and he
say uh hunh he understand, then he break into this *thizzin* kind of hum which
is quiet, but fiercesome just the same if you ain't ready for it. Which I wasn't.
But I got used to it and the onliest time I had to say somethin bout it was when
he was playin checkers on the stoop one time and he commenst to hummin
quite churchy seem to me. So I says, "Look here Shakey Bee, I can't beat you
and Jesus too." He stop.

  So that's how come I asked My Man Bovanne to dance. He ain't my man
mind you, just a nice ole gent from the block that we all know cause he fixes
things and the kids like him. Or used to fore Black Power got hold their minds
and mess em around till they can't be civil to ole folks. So we at this benefit for
my niece's cousin who's runnin for somethin with this Black party somethin or
other behind her. And I press up close to dance with Bovanne who blind and
I'm hummin and he hummin, chest to chest like talkin. Not jammin my breasts
into the man. Wasn't bout tits. Was bout vibrations. And he dug it and asked
me what color dress I had on and how my hair was fixed and how I was doing
without a man, not nosy but nice-like, and who was at this affair and was the
canapes dainty-stingy or healthy enough to get hold of proper. Comfy and
cheery is what I'm trying to get across. Touch talkin like the heel of the hand
on the tambourine or on a drum.

  But right away Joe Lee come up on us and frown for dancin so close to
the man. My own son who knows what kind of warm I am about; and don't
grown men call me long distance and in the middle of the night for a little
Mama comfort? But he frown. Which ain't right since Bovanne can't see and
defend himself. Just a nice old man who fixes toasters and busted irons and
bicycles and things and changes the lock on my door when my men friends
get messy. Nice man. Which is not why they invited him. Grassroots you see.
Me and Sister Taylor and the woman who does heads at Mamies and the
man from the barber shop, we all there on account of we grassroots. And I
ain't never been souther than Brooklyn Battery and no more country than the
window box on my fire escape. And just yesterday my kids tellin me to take

them countrified rags off my head and be cool. And now can't get Black enough to suit em. So everybody passin sayin My Man Bovanne. Big deal, keep stepping and don't even stop a minute to get the man a drink or one of them cute sandwiches or tell him what's goin on. And him standin there with a smile ready case someone do speak he want to be ready. So that's how come I pull him on the dance floor and we dance squeezin past the tables and chairs and all them coats and people standin round up in each other face talkin bout this and that but got no use for this blind man who mostly fixed skates and skooters for all these folks when they was just kids. So I'm pressed up close and we touch talkin with the hum. And here come my daughter cuttin her eye at me like she do when she tell me about my "apoliti-cal" self like I got hoof and mouf disease and there ain't no hope at all. And I don't pay her no mind and just look up in Bovanne shadow face and tell him his stomach like a drum and he laugh. Laugh real loud. And here come my youngest, Task, with a tap on my elbow like he the third-grade monitor and I'm cuttin up on the line to assembly.

"I was just talkin on the drums," I explained when they hauled me into the kitchen. I figured drums was my best defense. They can get ready for drums what with all this heritage business. And Bovanne stomach just like that drum Task give me when he come back from Africa. You just touch it and it hum thizzim, thizzim. So I stuck to the drum story. "Just drummin that's all."

"Mama, what are you talkin about?"

"She had too much to drink," say Elo to Task cause she don't hardly say nuthin to me direct no more since that ugly argument about my wigs.

"Look here, Mama," say Task, the gentle one. "We just tryin to pull your coat. You were makin a spectacle of yourself out there dancing like that."

"Dancin like what?"

Task run a hand over his left ear like his father for the world and his father before that.

"Like a bitch in heat," say Elo.

"Well uhh, I was goin to say like one of them sex-starved ladies gettin on in years and not too discriminating. Know what I mean?"

I don't answer cause I'll cry. Terrible thing when your own children talk to you like that. Pullin me out the party and hustlin me into some stranger's kitchen in the back of a bar just like the damn police. And ain't like I'm old old. I can still wear me some sleeveless dresses without the meat hangin off my arm. And I keep up with some thangs through my kids. Who ain't kids no more. To hear them tell it. So I don't say nuthin.

"Dancin with that tom," say Elo to Joe Lee, who leanin on the folks' freez-er. "His feet can smell a cracker a mile away and go into their shuffle number post haste. And them eyes. He could be a little considerate and put on some shades. Who wants to look into them blown-out fuses that—"

"Is this what they call the generation gap?" I say.

"Generation gap," spits Elo, like I suggested castor oil and fricassee pos-sum in the milk shakes or somethin. "That's a white concept for a white phe-nomenon. There's no generation gap among Black people. We are a col—"

"Yeh, well never mind," says Joe Lee. "The point is Mama . . . well, it's pride. You embarrass yourself and us too dancin like that."

"I wasn't shame." Then nobody say nuthin. Them standin there in they pretty clothes with drinks in they hands and gangin up on me, and me in the third-degree chair and nary a olive to my name. Felt just like the police got hold to me.

"First of all," Task say, holding up his hand and tickin off the offenses, "the dress. Now that dress is too short, Mama, and too low cut for a woman your age. And Tamu's going to make a speech tonight to kick off the campaign and will be introducin you and expecting you to organize the council of elders—"

"Me? Didn nobody ask me nuthin. You mean Nisi? She change her name?"

"Well, Norton was supposed to tell you about it. Nisi wants to introduce you and then encourage the older folks to form a Council of the Elders to act as an advisory—"

"And you going to be standing there with your boobs out and that wig on your head and that hem up to your ass. And people'll say, 'Ain't that the horny bitch that was grindin with the blind dude?'"

"Elo, be cool a minute," say Task, gettin to the next finger. "And then there's the drinkin. Mama, you know you can't drink cause next thing you know you be laughin loud and carryin on," and he grab another finger for the loudness. "And then there's the dancin. You been tattooed on the man for four records straight and slow draggin even on the fast numbers. How you think that look for a woman your age?"

"What's my age?"

"What?"

"I'm axin you all a simple question. You keep talkin bout what's proper for a woman my age. How old am I anyhow?" And Joe Lee slams his eyes shut and squinches up his face to figure. And Task run a hand over his ear and stare into his glass like the ice cubes goin calculate for him. And Elo just starin at the top of my head like she goin rip the wig off any minute now.

"Is your hair braided up under that thing? If so, why don't you take it off? You always did do a neat cornroll."

"Uh huh," cause I'm think how she couldn't undo her hair fast enough talking bout cornroll so countrified. None of which was the subject. "How old, I say?"

"Sixtee-one or—"

"You a damn lie Joe Lee Peoples."

"And that's another thing," say Task on the fingers.

"You know what you all can kiss," I say, gettin up and brushin the wrinkles out my lap.

"Oh, Mama," Elo say, puttin a hand on my shoulder like she hasn't done since she left home and the hand landin light and not sure it supposed to be there. Which hurt me to my heart. Cause this was the child in our happiness fore Mr. Peoples die. And I carried that child strapped to my chest till she was nearly two. We was close is what I'm tryin to tell you. Cause it was more me in the child than the others. And even after Task it was the girl-child I covered in the night and wept over for no reason at all less it was she was a chub-chub like me and not very pretty, but a warm child. And how did things get to this, that she can't put a sure hand on me and say Mama we love you and care about you and you entitled to enjoy yourself cause you a good woman?

"And then there's Reverend Trent," say Task, glancin from left to right like they hatchin a plot and just now lettin me in on it. "You were suppose to be talking with him tonight, Mama, about giving us his basement for campaign headquarters and—"

"Didn nobody tell me nuthin. If grassroots mean you kept in the dark I can't use it. I really can't. And Reven Trent a fool anyway the way he tore into the widow man up there on Edgecombe cause he wouldn't take in three of them foster children and the woman not even comfy in the ground yet and the man's mind messed up and—"

"Look here," say Task. "What we need is a family conference so we can get all this stuff cleared up and laid out on the table. In the meantime I think we better get back into the other room and tend to business. And in the meantime, Mama, see if you can't get to Reverend Trent and—"

"You want me to belly rub with the Reven, that it?"

"Oh damn," Elo say and go through the swingin door.

"We'll talk about all this at dinner. How's tomorrow night, Joe Lee?" While Joe Lee being self-important I'm wonderin who's doin the cookin and how come nobody ax me if I'm free and do I get a corsage and things like that. Then Joe nod that it's O.K. and he go through the swingin door and just a little hubbub come through from the other room. Then Task smile his smile, lookin just like his daddy, and he leave. And it just me in this stranger's kitchen, which was a mess I wouldn't never let my kitchen look like. Poison you just to look at the pots. Then the door swing the other way and it's My Man Bovanne standin there saying Miss Hazel but lookin at the deep fry and then at the steam table, and most surprised when I come up on him from the other direction and take him on out of there. Pass the folks pushing up toward the stage where Nisi and some other people settin and ready to talk, and folks gettin to the last of the sandwiches and the booze fore they settle down in one spot and listen serious. And I'm thinkin bout tellin Bovanne what a lovely long dress Nisi got on and the earrings and her hair piled up in a cone and the people bout to hear how we all gettin screwed and gotta form our own party and everybody there listenin and lookin. But instead I just haul the man on out of there, and Joe Lee and his wife look at me like I'm terrible, but they ain't said boo to the man yet. Cause he blind and old and don't nobody there need him since they grown up and don't need they skates fixed no more.

"Where we goin, Miss Hazel?" Him knowin all the time.

"First we gonna buy you some dark sunglasses. Then you comin with me to the supermarket so I can pick up tomorrow's dinner, which is goin to be a grand thing proper and you invited. Then we goin to my house."

"That be fine. I surely would like to rest my feet." Bein cute, but you got to let men play out they little show, blind or not. So he chat on bout how tired he is and how he appreciate me taking him in hand this way. And I'm thinkin I'll have him change the lock on my door first thing. Then I'll give the man a nice warm bath with jasmine leaves in the water and a little Epsom salt on the sponge to do his back. And then a good rubdown with rosewater and olive oil. Then a cup of lemon tea with a taste in it. And a little talcum, some of that fancy stuff Nisi mother sent over last Christmas. And then a massage, a good face massage round the forehead which is the worryin part. Cause you gots to take care of the older folks. And let them know they still needed to run the mimeo machine and keep the spark plugs clean and fix the mailboxes for folks who might help us get the breakfast program goin, and the school for the little kids and the campaign and all. Cause old folks is the nation. That what Nisi was sayin and I mean to do my part.

"I imagine you are a very pretty woman, Miss Hazel."

"I surely am," I say just like the hussy my daughter always say I was.

QUESTIONS AND CONSIDERATIONS

1. Characterize the narrator in the story. What is her attitude toward her children, toward Bovanne, and toward the other people in her community? What is your response to the narrator? Do you agree with her perspective on Bovanne and her children?

2. Discuss Bovanne's role in the community, both when he was young and now that he is older. How have he and his community changed?

3. Discuss the children's attitude toward their mother, particularly her behavior with Bovanne. Are they acting with her best interests in mind, as they suggest, or in their own interest? Why don't the children want her "dancing so close" to Bovanne? In what ways do the children's and the narrator's responses suggest that both they and their mother are going through transitions in their lives?

4. How does the author establish the narrator's voice? Refer to examples and details in the text that illustrate her use of African-American dialect. Was the dialect a barrier to understanding the story for you, or did it make the story more realistic and believable?

5. The author uses imagery and figurative language in the story, such as "a tap on my elbow like the third grade monitor and I'm cutting up on the line to assembly." Why is this image effective? Discuss several other images that help make the story's meaning richer.

6. Do you agree with Elo that there is "no generation gap" among black people? Does the story support Elo's position?

IDEAS FOR WRITING

1. Discuss the meaning of the narrator's assertion that "old folks is the nation." Do you agree with her? Support your point of view with examples from your own experiences and from the experiences of friends, literature, and popular culture.

2. Write an essay in which you discuss the different issues that you have seen people facing as they make the passage from middle age into old age. Refer to your own experiences to support your ideas.

Essays

Silent Dancing
Judith Ortiz Cofer

Journal

Write about a family photograph, home movie, or video that brings back memories of conflicts you felt as a child.

We have a home movie of this party. Several times my mother and I have watched it together, and I have asked question about the silent revellers coming in and out of focus. It is grainy and of short duration but a great visual aid to my first memory of life in Paterson at that time. And it is in color—the only complete scene in color I can recall from those years.

We lived in Puerto Rico until my brother was born in 1954. Soon after, because of economic pressures on our growing family, my father joined the United States Navy. He was assigned to duty on a ship in Brooklyn Yard, New York City—a place of cement and steel that was to be his home base in the States until his retirement more than twenty years later. He left the Island first, tracking down his uncle who lived with his family across the Hudson River, in Paterson, New Jersey. There he found a tiny apartment in a huge apartment building that had once housed Jewish families and was just being transformed into a tenement by Puerto Ricans overflowing from New York City. In 1955 he sent for us. My mother was only twenty years old, I was not quite three, and my brother was a toddler when we arrived at *El Building,* as the place had been christened by its new residents.

My memories of life in Paterson during those first few years are in shades of gray. Maybe I was too young to absorb vivid colors and details, or to discriminate between the slate blue of the winter sky and the darker hues of the snow-bearing clouds, but the single color washes over the whole period. The building we lived in was gray, the streets were gray with slush the first few months of my life there, the coat my father had bought for me was dark in color and too big. It sat heavily on my thin frame.

I do remember the way the heater pipes banged and rattled, startling all of us out of sleep until we got so used to the sound that we automatically either shut it out or raised our voices above the racket. The hiss from the valve punctuated my sleep, which has always been fitful, like an nonhuman presence in the room—the dragon sleeping at the entrance of my childhood. But the pipes were a connection to all the other lives being lived around us. Having come from a house made for single family back in Puerto Rico—my mother's extended-family home—it was curious to know that strangers lived under our floor and above our heads, and that the heater pipe went through everyone's apartments. (My first spanking in Paterson came as a result of playing tunes on the pipes in my room to see if there would be an answer). My mother was as new to this concept of beehive life as I was, but had been given strict orders by my father to keep the doors locked, the noise down, ourselves to ourselves.

It seems that Father had learned some painful lessons about prejudice while searching for an apartment in Paterson. Not until years later did I hear how much resistance he had encountered with landlords who were panicking at the influx of Latinos into a neighborhood that had been Jewish for a couple of generations. But it was the American phenomenon of ethnic turnover that was changing the urban core of Paterson, and the human flood could not be held back with an accusing finger.

"You Cuban?" the man had asked my father, pointing a finger at his name tag on the Navy uniform—even though my father had the fair skin and light brown hair of his northern Spanish family background and our name is as common in Puerto Rico as Johnson is in the U.S.

"No," my father had answered looking past the finger into his adversary's angry eyes "I'm Puerto Rican."

"Same shit." And the door closed. My father could have passed as European, but we couldn't. My brother and I both have our mother's black hair and olive skin, and so we lived in El Building and visited our great-uncle and his fair children on the next block. It was their private joke that they were the German branch of the family. Not many years later that area too would be mainly Puerto Rican. It was as if the heart of the city map were being gradually colored in brown—*café-con-leche* brown. Our color.

The movie opens with a sweep of the living room. It is "typical" immigrant Puerto Rican decor for the time: the sofa and chairs are square and hard-looking, upholstered in bright colors (blue and yellow in this instance, and covered in the transparent plastic) that furniture salesmen then were adept at making women buy. The linoleum on the floor is light blue, and if it was subjected to the spike heels as it was in most places, there were dime-sized indentation all over it that cannot be seen in this movie. The room is full of people dressed in mainly two colors: dark suits for the men, red dresses for the women. I have asked my mother why most of the women are in red that night, and she shrugs, "I don't remember. Just a coincidence." She doesn't have my obsession for assigning symbolism to everything.

The three women in red sitting on the couch are my mother, my eighteen-year-old cousin, and her brother's girlfriend. The "novia" is just up from the Island, which is apparent in her body language. She sits up formally, and her dress is carefully pulled over her knees. She is a pretty girl but her posture makes her look insecure, lost in her full skirted red dress which she has carefully tucked around her to make room for my gorgeous cousin, her future sister-in-law. My cousin has grown up in Paterson and is in her last year of high school. She doesn't have a trace of what Puerto Ricans call "la mancha" (literally, the stain: the mark of the new immigrant—something about the posture, the voice, or the humble demeanor making it obvious to everyone that that person has just arrived on the mainland; has not yet acquired the polished look of the city dweller). My cousin is wearing a tight red-sequined cocktail dress. Her brown hair has been lightened with peroxide around the bangs, and she is holding a cigarette very expertly between her fingers, bringing it up to her mouth in a sensuous arc of her arm to her as she talks animatedly with my mother, who has come up to sit between the two women, both only a few years younger than herself. My mother is somewhere halfway between the poles they represent in our culture.

It became my father's obsession to get out of the barrio, and thus we were never permitted to form bonds with the place or with the people who lived there. Yet the building was a comfort to my mother, who never got over yearning for *la isla*. She felt surrounded by her language: the walls were thin, and voices speaking and arguing in Spanish could be heard all day. *Salsas* blasted out of radios turned on early in the morning and left on for company. Women seemed to cook rice and beans perpetually—the strong aroma of red kidney beans boiling permeated the hallways.

Though Father preferred that we do our grocery shopping at the supermarket when he came home on weekend leaves, my mother insisted that she could cook only with products whose labels she could read, and so, during the week, I accompanied her and my little brother to *La Bodega*—a hole-in-the-wall grocery store across the street from *El Building*. There we squeezed down three narrow aisles jammed with various products. Goya and Libby's—those were the trademarks trusted by her Mamá, and so my mother bought cans of Goya beans, soups and condiments. She bought little cans of Libby's fruit juices for us. And she bought Colgate toothpaste and Palmolive soap. (The final *e* is pronounced in both those products in Spanish, and for many years I believed that they were manufactured on the Island. I remember my surprise at first hearing a commercial on television for the toothpaste in which Colgate rhymed with "ate.") We would linger at La Bodega, for it was there that mother breathed best, taking in the familiar aromas of the foods she knew from Mamá's kitchen, and it was also there that she got to speak to the other women of El Building without violating outright Father's dictates against fraternizing with our neighbors.

But he did his best to make our "assimilation" painless. I can still see him carrying a Christmas tree up several flights of stairs to our apartment, leaving a trail of aromatic pine. He carried it formally, as if it were a flag in a parade. We were the only ones in El Building that I knew of who got presents on both Christmas Day and on *Día de Reyes,* the day when the Three Kings brought gifts to Christ and to Hispanic children.

Our greatest luxury in El Building was having our own television set. It must have been a result of Father's guilty feelings over the isolation he had imposed on us, but we were one of the first families in the barrio to have one. My brother quickly became an avid watcher of Captain Kangaroo and Jungle Jim. I loved all the family series, and by the time I started first grade in school, I could have drawn a map of Middle America as exemplified by the lives of characters in "Father Knows Best," "The Donna Reed Show," "Leave It to Beaver," "My Three Sons," and (my favorite) "Bachelor Father," where John Forsythe treated his adopted teenage daughter like a princess because he was rich and had a Chinese houseboy to do everything for him. Compared to our neighbors in El Building, we were rich. My father's Navy check provided us with financial security and a standard of life that the factory workers envied. The only thing his money could not buy us was a place to live away from the barrio—his greatest wish and Mother's greatest fear.

In the home movie the men are shown next, sitting around a card table set up in one corner of the living room, playing dominoes. The clack of the ivory pieces is a sound familiar. I heard it in many houses on the Island and in many apartments in Paterson. In "Leave It To Beaver," the Cleavers played bridge in every other episode; in my childhood, the men started every social occasion with a hotly debated round of dominoes: the women would sit around and watch, but they never participated in the games.

Here and there you can see a small child. Children were always brought to parties and, whenever they got sleepy, put to bed in the host's bedrooms. Babysitting was a concept unrecognized by the Puerto Rican women I knew: a responsible mother did not leave her children with any stranger. And in a culture where children are not considered intrusive, there is no need to leave the children at home. We went where our mother went.

Of my pre-school years I have only impressions: the sharp bite of the wind in December as we walked with our parents towards the brightly lit stores downtown, how I felt like a stuffed doll in my heavy coat, boots and mittens; how good it was to walk into the five-and-dime and sit at the counter drinking hot chocolate.

On Saturdays our whole family would walk downtown to shop at the big department stores on Broadway. Mother bought all our clothes at Penny's and Sears, and she liked to buy her dresses at the women's specialty shops like Lerner's and Diana's. At some point we would go into Woolworth's and sit at the soda fountain to eat.

We never ran into other Latinos at these stores or eating out, and it became clear to me only years later that the women from El Building shopped mainly at other places—stores owned either by other Puerto Ricans, or by Jewish merchants who had philosophically accepted our presence in the city and decided to make us their good customers, if not neighbors and friends. These establishments were located not downtown, but in the blocks around our street, and they were referred to generically as *La Tienda, El Bazar, La Bodega, La Botánica.* Everyone knew what was meant. These were the stores where your face did not turn a clerk to stone, where your money was as green as anyone else's.

On New Year's Eve we were dressed up like child models in the Sears catalogue—my brother in a miniature man's suit and bow tie, and I in a black patent leather shoes and a frilly dress with several layers of crinolines underneath. My mother wore a bright red dress that night, I remember, and spike heels; her long black hair hung to her waist. Father, who usually wore his Navy uniform during his short visits home, had put on a dark civilian suit for the occasion: we had been invited to his uncle's house for a big celebration. Everyone was excited because my mother's brother, Hernán—a bachelor who could indulge himself in such luxuries—had bought a movie camera which he would be trying out that night.

Even the home movie cannot fill in the sensory details such a gathering left imprinted in a child's brain. The thick sweetness of women's perfume mixing with the ever-present smells of food cooking in the kitchen: meat and plantain *pasteles,* the ubiquitous rice dish made special with pigeon peas—*gandules*—and seasoned with the precious *sofrito* sent up from the island by somebody's mother or smuggled in by a recent traveler. *Sofrito* was one of the items that women hoarded, since it was hardly ever in stock at La Bodega. It was the flavor of Puerto Rico.

The men drank Palo Viejo rum and some of the younger ones got weepy. The first time I saw a grown man cry was at a New Year's Eve party. He had been reminded of his mother by the smells in the kitchen. But what I remember most were the boiled *pasteles*—boiled until the plantain or yucca rectangles stuffed with corned beef or other meats, olives, and many other savory ingredients, all wrapped in banana leaves. Everyone had to fish one out with a fork. There was always a "trick" pastel—one without stuffing—and whoever got that one was the "New Year's Fool."

There was also the music. Long-playing albums were treated like precious china in these homes. Mexican recordings were popular, but the songs that brought tears to my mother's eyes were sung by the melancholic Daniel Santos, whose life as a drug addict was the stuff of legend. Felipe Rodríguez was a particular favorite of couples. He sang about faithless women and broken-hearted men. There is a snatch of a lyric that has stuck in my mind like a needle on a worn groove: "De piedra ha de ser mi cama, de piedra la cabecera . . . la mujer que a mi me quiera . . . ha de quererme dc voras. Ay, Ay, corazón, ¿por qué no amas . . . ?" I must have heard it a thousand times since the idea of a bed made of stone, and its connection to love, first troubled me with its disturbing images.

The five-minute home movie ends with people dancing in a circle. The creative filmmaker must have asked them to do that so that they could file past him. It is both comical and sad to watch silent dancing. Since there is no justification for the absurd movements that music provides for some of us, people appear frantic, their faces embarrassingly intense. It's as if you were watching sex. Yet for years, I've had dreams in the form of this home movie. In a recurring scene, familiar faces push themselves forward into my mind's eye, plastering their features into distorted close-ups. And I'm asking them: "Who is she? Who is the woman I don't recognize? Is she an aunt? Somebody's wife? Tell me who she is. Tell me who these people are."

"No, see the beauty mark on her cheek as big as a hill on the lunar land- scape of her face—well, that runs in the family. The women on your father's side of the family wrinkle early; it's the price they pay for that fair skin. The young girl with the green stain on her wedding dress is *La Novia*—just up from the island. See, she lowers her eyes as she approaches the camera like she's supposed to. Decent girls never look you directly in the face. *Humilde,* humble, a girl should express humility in all her actions. She will make a good wife for your cousin. He should consider himself lucky to have met her only weeks after she arrived here. If he married her quickly, she will make him a good Puerto Rican-style wife; but if he waits too long, she will be corrupted by the city, just like your cousin there."

"She means me. I do what I want. This is not some primitive island I live on. Do they expect me to wear a black *mantilla* on my head and go to mass every day? Not me. I'm an American woman and I will do as I please. I can type faster than anyone in my senior class at Central High, and I'm going to be a secretary to a lawyer when I graduate. I can pass for an American girl any- where—I've tried it—at least for Italian, anyway. I never speak Spanish in pub- lic. I hate these parties, but I wanted the dress. I look better than any of these *humildes* here. My life is going to be different. I have an American boyfriend. He is older and has a car. My parents don't know it, but I sneak out of the house late at night sometimes to be with him. If I marry him, even my name will be American. I hate rice and beans. It's what makes these women fat."

"Your *prima* is pregnant by that man she's been sneaking around with. Would I lie to you? I'm your great-uncle's common-law wife—the one he aban- doned on the island to marry your cousin's mother. I was not invited to this party, but I came anyway. I came to tell you that story about your cousin that you've always wanted to hear. Remember that comment your mother made to a neighbor that has always haunted you? The only thing you heard was your cousin's name and then you saw your mother pick up your doll from the couch and say: 'It was as big as this doll when they flushed it down the toilet.' This image has bothered you for years, hasn't it? You had nightmares about babies being flushed down the toilet, and you wondered why anyone would do such a horrible thing. You didn't dare ask your mother about it. She would only tell you that you had not heard her right and yell at you for listening to adult conversa- tions. But later, when you were old enough to know about abortions, you sus- pected. I am here to tell you that you were right. Your cousin was growing an *Americanito* in her belly when this movie was made. Soon after she put some- thing long and pointy into her pretty self, thinking maybe she could get rid of the problem before breakfast and still make it to her first class at the high school. Well, *Niña,* her screams could be heard downtown. Your aunt, her Mamá, who had been a midwife on the Island, managed to pull the little thing out. Yes, they probably flushed it down the toilet, what else could they do with it—give it a Christian burial in a little white casket with blue bows and ribbons?

Nobody wanted that baby—least of all the father, a teacher at her school with a house in West Paterson that he was filling with real children, and a wife who was a natural blond.

Girl, the scandal sent your uncle back to the bottle. And guess where you cousin ended up? Irony of ironies. She was sent to a village in Puerto Rico to live with a relative on her mother's side: a place so far away from civilization that you have to ride a mule to reach it. A real change in scenery. She found a man there. Women like that cannot live without male company. But believe me, the men in Puerto Rico know how to put a saddle on a woman like her. *La Gringa,* they call her. ha, ha. ha. *La Gringa* is what she always wanted to be . . .

The old woman's mouth becomes a cavernous black hole I fall into. And as I fall, I can feel the reverberations of her laughter. I hear the echoes of her last mocking words: *La Gringa, La Gringa!* And the conga line keeps moving silently past me. There is no music in my dream for the dancers.

When Odysseus visits Hades asking to see the spirit of his mother, he makes an offering of sacrificial blood, but since all of the souls crave an audience with the living, he has to listen to many of them before he can ask questions. I, too, have to hear the dead and the forgotten speak in my dream. Those who are still part of my life remain silent, going around and around in their dance. The others keep pressing their faces forward to say things about the past.

My father's uncle is last in line. He is dying of alcoholism, shrunken and shriveled like a monkey, his face is a mass of wrinkles and broken arteries. As he comes closer I realize that in his features I can see my whole family. If you were to stretch that rubbery flesh, you could find my father's face, and deep within *that* face—mine. I don't want to look into those eyes ringed in purple. In a few years he will retreat into silence, and take a long, long time to die. *Move back, Tío,* I tell him. *I don't want to hear what you have to say. Give the dancers room to move, soon it will be midnight. Who is the New Year's Fool this time?*

QUESTIONS AND CONSIDERATIONS

1. After being raised as a young child in Puerto Rico, of what contrasts in life style is Cofer most conscious when she arrives in Paterson, New Jersey? What prejudice does her family experience in the new neighborhood? Did your family, or families that you know, have to face similar types of prejudice? In what ways is the realization of prejudice a passage of initiation?

2. How does Cofer's use of language help her to recapture her childhood? Give several examples of Cofer's images and details that are especially effective in dramatizing her responses to the American way of life.

3. What do Cofer and her brother learn about the myth of mainstream American family life from watching television? How does this knowledge affect both her assimilation into the American neighborhoods in which she lives and her evaluation of traditional Puerto Rican values?

4. Why does Cofer's father forbid his family to shop or socialize in their immediate neighborhood? Why does Cofer's mother feel more comfortable at the neighborhood markets? Why does she violate her husband's dictates? With whose point of view are you more sympathetic? Which parent's point of view does Cofer adopt as she matures into womanhood?

5. Why is Cofer haunted by the dream story her great aunt tells about La Gringa? What cultural and gender assumptions does La Gringa's fate demonstrate?

6. Why is the selection entitled "Silent Dancing"? What meaning does Cofer read into the silent dancing that she watches at the end of the home movie? What meaning do you read into the image? In what sense is the silent dancing an image of initiation?

IDEAS FOR WRITING

1. Write an essay that explores several ways in which adjusting to a new culture is a process of initiation. You can write about your own experiences or experiences that you have learned about through the readings in this textbook, other literature, or popular culture.

2. Write an essay in which you discuss a conflict that you or a close friend experienced because you or the friend was not a member of the dominant cultural group in your community. What did you learn from this conflict? How did it help you to shape your understanding of community life and your expectations or goals for your future? In what ways was this conflict a passage of initiation?

Graduation
Maya Angelou

Journal

Describe your graduation from elementary or secondary school. How did it mark a turning point in your life?

The children in Stamps trembled visibly with anticipation. Some adults were excited too, but to be certain the whole young population had come down with graduation epidemic. Large classes were graduating from both the grammar school and the high school. Even those who were years removed from their own day of glorious release were anxious to help with preparations as a kind of dry run. The junior students who were moving into the vacating classes' chairs were tradition-bound to show their talents for leadership and management. They strutted through the school and around the campus exerting pressure on the lower grades. Their authority was so new that occasionally if they pressed a little too hard it had to be overlooked. After all, next term was coming, and it never hurt a sixth grader to have a play sister in the eighth grade, or a tenth-year student to be able to call a twelfth grader Bubba. So all was endured in a spirit of shared understanding. But the graduating classes themselves were the nobility. Like travelers with exotic destinations on their minds, the graduates were remarkably forgetful. They came to school without their books, or tablets, or even pencils. Volunteers fell over themselves to secure replacements for the missing equipment. When accepted, the willing workers might or might not be thanked, and it was of no importance to the pregraduation rites. Even teachers were respectful of the now quiet and aging seniors, and tended to speak to them, if not as equals, as beings only slightly lower than themselves. After tests were returned and grades given, the student body, which acted like an extended family, knew who did well, who excelled, and what piteous ones had failed.

Unlike the white school, Lafayette County Training School distinguished itself by having neither lawn, nor hedges, nor tennis court, nor climbing ivy. Its two buildings (main classrooms, the grade school, and home economics) were set on a dirt hill with no fence to limit either its boundaries or those of bordering farms. There was a large expanse to the left of the school which was used alternately as a baseball diamond or a basketball court. Rusty hoops on the swaying poles represented the permanent recreational equipment, although bats and balls could be borrowed from the P.E. teacher if the borrower was qualified and if the diamond wasn't occupied.

Over this rocky area relieved by a few shady tall persimmon trees the graduating class walked. The girls often held hands and no longer bothered to speak to the lower students. There was a sadness about them, as if this old world was not their home and they were bound for higher ground. The boys, on the other hand, had become more friendly, more outgoing. A decided change from the closed attitude they projected while studying for finals. Now they seemed not ready to give up the old school, the familiar paths and classrooms. Only a small percentage would be continuing on to college—one of the South's A & M (agricultural and mechanical) schools, which trained Negro youths to be carpenters, farmers, handymen, masons, maids, cooks, and baby nurses. Their future rode heavily on their shoulders, and blinded them to the collective joy that had pervaded the lives of the boys and girls in the grammar school graduating class.

Parents who could afford it had ordered new shoes and ready-made clothes for themselves from Sears and Roebuck or Montgomery Ward. They also engaged the best seamstresses to make the floating graduating dresses and to cut down secondhand pants which would be pressed to a military slickness for the important event.

Oh, it was important, all right. Whitefolks would attend the ceremony, and two or three would speak of God and home, and the Southern way of life, and Mrs. Parsons, the principal's wife, would play the graduation march while the lower-grade graduates paraded down the aisles and took their seats below the platform. The high school seniors would wait in empty classrooms to make their dramatic entrance.

In the Store I was the person of the moment. The birthday girl. The center. Bailey* had graduated the year before, although to do so he had had to forfeit all pleasures to make up for his time lost in Baton Rouge.

My class was wearing butter-yellow piqué dresses, and Momma launched out on mine. She smocked the yoke into tiny crisscrossing puckers, then shirred the rest of the bodice. Her dark fingers ducked in and out of the lemony cloth as she embroidered raised daisies around the hem. Before she considered herself finished she had added a crocheted cuff on the puff sleeves, and a pointy crocheted collar.

I was going to be lovely. A walking model of all the various styles of fine hand sewing and it didn't worry me that I was only twelve years old and merely graduating from the eighth grade. Besides, many teachers in Arkansas Negro schools had only that diploma and were licensed to impart wisdom.

The days had become longer and more noticeable. The faded beige of former times had been replaced with strong and sure colors. I began to see my classmates' clothes, their skin tones, and the dust that waved off pussy willows. Clouds that lazed across the sky were objects of great concern to me. Their shiftier shapes might have held a message that in my new happiness and with a little bit of time I'd soon decipher. During that period I looked at the arch of heaven so religiously my neck kept a steady ache. I had taken to smiling more often, and my jaws hurt from the unaccustomed activity. Between the two physical sore spots, I suppose I could have been uncomfortable, but that was not the case. As a member of the winning team (the graduating class of 1940) I had outdistanced unpleasant sensations by miles. I was headed for the freedom of open fields.

Youth and social approval allied themselves with me and we trammeled memories of slights and insults. The wind of our swift passage remodeled my features. Lost tears were pounded to mud and then to dust. Years of withdrawal were brushed aside and left behind, as hanging ropes of parasitic moss.

My work alone had awarded me a top place and I was going to be one of the first called in the graduating ceremonies. On the classroom blackboard, as well as on the bulletin board in the auditorium, there were blue stars and white stars and red stars. No absences, no tardinesses, and my academic work was among the best of the year. I could say the preamble to the Constitution even faster than Bailey. We timed ourselves often: "WethepeopleoftheUnited-Statesinordertoformamoreperfectunion . . . " I had memorized the Presidents of the United States from Washington to Roosevelt in chronological as well as alphabetical order.

My hair pleased me too. Gradually the black mass had lengthened and thickened, so that it kept at last to its braided pattern, and I didn't have to yank my scalp off when I tried to comb it.

---

* The author's brother.

Louise and I had rehearsed the exercises until we tired out ourselves. Henry Reed was class valedictorian. He was a small, very black boy with hooded eyes, a long, broad nose, and an oddly shaped head. I had admired him for years because each term he and I vied for the best grades in our class. Most often he bested me, but instead of being disappointed I was pleased that we shared top places between us. Like many Southern Black children, he lived with his grandmother, who was as strict as Momma and as kind as she knew how to be. He was courteous, respectful, and soft-spoken to elders, but on the playground he chose to play the roughest games. I admired him. Anyone, I reckoned, sufficiently afraid or sufficiently dull could be polite. But to be able to operate at a top level with both adults and children was admirable.

His valedictory speech was entitled "To Be or Not to Be." The rigid tenth-grade teacher had helped him to write it. He'd been working on the dramatic stresses for months.

The weeks until graduation were filled with heady activities. A group of small children were to be presented in a play about buttercups and daisies and bunny rabbits. They could be heard throughout the building practicing their hops and their little songs that sounded like silver bells. The older girls (non-graduates, of course) were assigned the task of making refreshments for the night's festivities. A tangy scent of ginger, cinnamon, nutmeg, and chocolate wafted around the home economics building as the budding cooks made samples for themselves and their teachers.

In every corner of the workshop, axes and saws split fresh timber as the woodshop boys made sets and stage scenery. Only the graduates were left out of the general bustle. We were free to sit in the library at the back of the building or look in quite detachedly, naturally, on the measures being taken for our event.

Even the minister preached on graduation the Sunday before. His subject was, "Let your light so shine that men will see your good works and praise your Father, Who is in Heaven." Although the sermon was purported to be addressed to us, he used the occasion to speak to backsliders, gamblers, and general ne'er-do-wells. But since he had called our names at the beginning of the service we were mollified.

Among Negroes the tradition was to give presents to children going only from one grade to another. How much more important this was when the person was graduating at the top of the class. Uncle Willie and Momma had sent away for a Mickey Mouse watch like Bailey's. Louise gave me four embroidered handkerchiefs. (I gave her three crocheted doilies.) Mrs. Sneed, the minister's wife, made me an underskirt to wear for graduation, and nearly every customer gave me a nickel or maybe even a dime with the instruction "Keep on moving to higher ground," or some such encouragement.

Amazingly the great day finally dawned and I was out of bed before I knew it. I threw open the back door to see it more clearly, but Momma said, "Sister, come away from that door and put your robe on."

I hoped the memory of that morning would never leave me. Sunlight was itself still young, and the day had none of the insistence maturity would bring it in a few hours. In my robe and barefoot in the backyard, under cover of going to see about my new beans, I gave myself up to the gentle warmth and thanked God that no matter what evil I had done in my life He had allowed me to live to see this day. Somewhere in my fatalism I had expected to die, accidentally, and never have the chance to walk up the stairs in the auditorium and gracefully receive my hard-earned diploma. Out of God's merciful bosom I had won reprieve.

Bailey came out in his robe and gave me a box wrapped in Christmas paper. He said he had saved his money for months to pay for it. It felt like a box of chocolates, but I knew Bailey wouldn't save money to buy candy when we had all we could want under our noses.

He was as proud of the gift as I. It was a soft-leather-bound copy of a collection of poems by Edgar Allan Poe, or, as Bailey and I called him, "Eap." I turned to "Annabel Lee" and we walked up and down the garden rows, the cool dirt between our toes, reciting the beautifully sad lines.

Momma made a Sunday breakfast although it was only Friday. After we finished the blessing, I opened my eyes to find the watch on my plate. It was a dream of a day. Everything went smoothly and to my credit. I didn't have to be reminded or scolded for anything. Near evening I was too jittery to attend to chores, so Bailey volunteered to do all before his bath.

Days before, we had made a sign for the Store and as we turned out the lights Momma hung the cardboard over the doorknob. It read clearly: CLOSED. GRADUATION.

My dress fitted perfectly and everyone said that I looked like a sunbeam in it. On the hill, going toward the school, Bailey walked behind with Uncle Willie, who muttered, "Go on, Ju." He wanted him to walk ahead with us because it embarrassed him to have to walk so slowly. Bailey said he'd let the ladies walk together, and the men would bring up the rear. We all laughed, nicely.

Little children dashed by out of the dark like fireflies. Their crepe-paper dresses and butterfly wings were not made for running and we heard more than one rip, dryly, and the regretful "uh uh" that followed.

The school blazed without gaiety. The windows seemed cold and unfriendly from the lower hill. A sense of ill-fated timing crept over me, and if Momma hadn't reached for my hand I would have drifted back to Bailey and Uncle Willie, and possibly beyond. She made a few slow jokes about my feet getting cold, and tugged me along to the now-strange building.

Around the front steps, assurance came back. There were my fellow "greats," the graduating class. Hair brushed back, legs oiled, new dresses and pressed pleats, fresh pocket handkerchiefs and little handbags, all homesewn. Oh, we were up to snuff, all right. I joined my comrades and didn't even see my family go in to find seats in the crowded auditorium.

The school band struck up a march and all classes filed in as had been rehearsed. We stood in front of our seats, as assigned, and on a signal from the choir director, we sat. No sooner had this been accomplished than the band started to play the national anthem. We rose again and sang the song, after which we recited the pledge of allegiance. We remained standing for a brief minute before the choir director and the principal signaled to us, rather desperately I thought, to take our seats. The command was so unusual that our carefully rehearsed and smooth-running machine was thrown off. For a full minute we fumbled for our chairs and bumped into each other awkwardly. Habits change or solidify under pressure, so in our state of nervous tension we had been ready to follow our usual assembly pattern: the American National Anthem, then the pledge of allegiance, then the song every Black person I knew called the Negro National Anthem. All done in the same key, with the same passion and most often standing on the same foot.

Finding my seat at last, I was overcome with a presentiment of worse things to come. Something unrehearsed, unplanned, was going to happen, and we were going to be made to look bad. I distinctly remember being explicit in the choice of pronoun. It was "we," the graduating class, the unit, that concerned me then.

The principal welcomed "parents and friends" and asked the Baptist minister to lead us in prayer. His invocation was brief and punchy, and for a second I thought we were getting back on the high road to right action. When the principal came back to the dais, however, his voice had changed. Sounds always affected me profoundly and the principal's voice was one of my favorites. During assembly it melted and lowed weakly into the audience. It had not been in my plan to listen to him, but my curiosity was piqued and I straightened up to give him my attention.

He was talking about Booker T. Washington, our "late great leader," who said we can be as close as the fingers on the hand, etc. . . . Then he said a few vague things about friendship and the friendship of kindly people to those less fortunate than themselves. With that his voice nearly faded, thin, away. Like a river diminishing to a stream and then to a trickle. But he cleared his throat and said, "Our speaker tonight, who is also our friend, came from Texarkana to deliver the commencement address, but due to the irregularity of the train schedule, he's going to, as they say, 'speak and run.'" He said that we understood and wanted the man to know that we were most grateful for the time he was able to give us and then something about how we were willing always to adjust to another's program, and without more ado—"I give you Mr. Edward Donleavy."

Not one but two white men came through the door offstage. The shorter one walked to the speaker's platform, and the tall one moved over to the center seat and sat down. But that was our principal's seat, and already occupied. The dislodged gentleman bounced around for a long breath or two before the Baptist minister gave him his chair, then with more dignity than the situation deserved, the minister walked off the stage.

Donleavy looked at the audience once (on reflection, I'm sure that he wanted only to reassure himself that we were really there), adjusted his glasses, and began to read from a sheaf of papers.

He was glad "to be here and to see the work going on just as it was in the other schools."

At the first "Amen" from the audience I willed the offender to immediate death by choking on the word. But Amens and Yes, sir's began to fall around the room like rain through a ragged umbrella.

He told us of the wonderful changes we children in Stamps had in store. The Central School (naturally, the white school was Central) had already been granted improvements that would be in use in the fall. A well-known artist was coming from Little Rock to teach art to them. They were going to have the newest microscopes and chemistry equipment for their laboratory. Mr. Donleavy didn't leave us long in the dark over who made these improvements available to Central High. Nor were we to be ignored in the general betterment scheme he had in mind.

He said that he had pointed out to people at a very high level that one of the first-line football tacklers at Arkansas Agricultural and Mechanical College had graduated from good old Lafayette County Training School. Here fewer Amen's were heard. Those few that did break through lay dully in the air with the heaviness of habit.

He went on to praise us. He went on to say how he had bragged that "one of the best basketball players at Fisk sank his first ball right here at Lafayette County Training School."

The white kids were going to have a chance to become Galileos and Madame Curies and Edisons and Gauguins, and our boys (the girls weren't even in on it) would try to be Jessie Owenses and Joe Louises.

Owens and the Brown Bomber were great heroes in our world, but what school official in the white-goddom of Little Rock had the right to decide that those two men must be our only heroes? Who decided that for Henry Reed to become a scientist he had to work like George Washington Carver, as a bootblack, to buy a lousy microscope? Bailey was obviously always going to be too small to be an athlete, so which concrete angel glued to what country seat had decided that if my brother wanted to become a lawyer he had to first pay penance for his skin by picking cotton and hoeing corn and studying correspondence books at night for twenty years?

The man's dead words fell like bricks around the auditorium and too many settled in my belly. Constrained by hard-learned manners I couldn't look behind me, but to my left and right the proud graduating class of 1940 had dropped their heads. Every girl in my row had found something new to do with her handkerchief. Some folded the tiny squares into love knots, some into triangles, but most were wadding them, then pressing them flat on their yellow laps.

On the dais, the ancient tragedy was being replayed. Professor Parsons sat, a sculptor's reject, rigid. His large, heavy body seemed devoid of will or willingness, and his eyes said he was no longer with us. The other teachers examined the flag (which was draped stage right) or their notes, or the windows which opened on our now-famous playing diamond.

Graduation, the hush-hush magic time of frills and gifts and congratulations and diplomas, was finished for me before my name was called. The accomplishment was nothing. The meticulous maps, drawn in three colors of ink, learning and spelling decasyllabic words, memorizing the whole of *The Rape of Lucrece*—it was nothing. Donleavy had exposed us.

We were maids and farmers, handymen and washerwomen, and anything higher that we aspired to was farcical and presumptuous. Then I wished that Gabriel Prosser and Nat Turner had killed all whitefolks in their beds and that Abraham Lincoln had been assassinated before the signing of the Emancipation Proclamation, and that Harriet Tubman had been killed by that blow on her head and Christopher Columbus had drowned in the *Santa Maria.*

It was awful to be Negro and have no control over my life. It was brutal to be young and already trained to sit quietly and listen to charges brought against my color with no chance of defense. We should all be dead. I thought I should like to see us all dead, one on top of the other. A pyramid of flesh with the whitefolks on the bottom, as the broad base, then the Indians with their silly tomahawks and teepees and wigwams and treaties, the Negroes with their mops and recipes and cotton sacks and spirituals sticking out of their mouths. The Dutch children should all stumble in their wooden shoes and break their necks. The French should choke to death on the Louisiana Purchase (1803) while silkworms ate all the Chinese with their stupid pigtails. As a species, we were an abomination. All of us.

Donleavy was running for election, and assured our parents that if he won we could count on having the only colored paved playing field in that part of Arkansas. Also—he never looked up to acknowledge the grunts of acceptance—also, we were bound to get some new equipment for the home economics building and the workshop.

He finished, and since there was no need to give any more than the most perfunctory thank-you's, he nodded to the men on the stage, and the tall white man who was never introduced joined him at the door. They left with the attitude that now they were off to something really important. (The graduation ceremonies at Lafayette County Training School had been a mere preliminary.)

The ugliness they left was palpable. An uninvited guest who wouldn't leave. The choir was summoned and sang a modern arrangement of "Onward, Christian Soldiers," with new words pertaining to graduates seeking their place in the world. But it didn't work. Elouise, the daughter of the Baptist minister, recited "Invictus," and I could have cried at the impertinence of "I am the master of my fate, I am the captain of my soul."

My name had lost its ring of familiarity and I had to be nudged to go and receive my diploma. All my preparations had fled. I neither marched up to the stage like a conquering Amazon, nor did I look in the audience for Bailey's nod of approval. Marguerite Johnson, I heard the name again, my honors were read, there were noises in the audience of appreciation, and I took my place on the stage as rehearsed.

I thought about colors I hated: ecru, puce, lavender, beige, and black.

There was shuffling and rustling around me, then Henry Reed was giving his valedictory address, "To Be or Not to Be." Hadn't he heard the whitefolks? We couldn't *be,* so the question was a waste of time. Henry's voice came out clear and strong. I feared to look at him. Hadn't he got the message? There was no "nobler in the mind" for Negroes because the world didn't think we had minds, and they let us know it. "Outrageous fortune"? Now, that was a joke. When the ceremony was over I had to tell Henry Reed some things. That is, if I still cared. Not "rub," Henry, "erase." "Ah, there's the erase." Us.

Henry had been a good student in elocution. His voice rose on tides of promise and fell on waves of warnings. The English teacher had helped him to create a sermon winging through Hamlet's soliloquy. To be a man, a doer, a builder, a leader, or to be a tool, an unfunny joke, a crusher of funky toadstools. I marveled that Henry could go through the speech as if we had a choice.

I had been listening and silently rebutting each sentence with my eyes closed; then there was a hush, which in an audience warns that something unplanned is happening. I looked up and saw Henry Reed, the conservative, the proper, the A student, turn his back to the audience and turn to us (the proud graduating class of 1940) and sing, nearly speaking,

Lift ev'ry voice and sing
Till earth and heaven ring
Ring with the harmonies of Liberty . . .

It was the poem written by James Weldon Johnson. It was the music composed by J. Rosamond Johnson. It was the Negro National Anthem. Out of habit we were singing it.

Our mothers and fathers stood in the dark hall and joined the hymn of encouragement. A kindergarten teacher led the small children onto the stage and the buttercups and daisies and bunny rabbits marked time and tried to follow:

Stony the road we trod
Bitter the chastening rod
Felt in the days when hope, unborn, had died.
Yet with a steady beat
Have not our weary feet
Come to the place for which our fathers sighed?

Every child I knew had learned that song with his ABCs and along with "Jesus Loves Me This I Know." But I personally had never heard it before.

Never heard the words, despite the thousands of times I had sung them. Never thought they had anything to do with me.

On the other hand, the words of Patrick Henry had made such an impression on me that I had been able to stretch myself tall and trembling and say, "I know not what course others may take, but as for me, give me liberty or give me death."

And now I heard, really for the first time:

We have come over a way that with tears has been watered,
We have come, treading our path through the blood
                    of the slaughtered.

While echoes of the song shivered in the air, Henry Reed bowed his head, said "Thank you," and returned to his place in the line. The tears that slipped down many faces were not wiped away in shame.

We were on top again. As always, again. We survived. The depths had been icy and dark, but now a bright sun spoke to our souls. I was no longer simply a member of the proud graduating class of 1940; I was a proud member of the wonderful, beautiful Negro race.

Oh, Black known and unknown poets, how often have your auctioned pains sustained us? Who will compute the lonely nights made less lonely by your songs, or by the empty pots made less tragic by your tales?

If we were a people much given to revealing secrets, we might raise monuments and sacrifice to the memories of our poets, but slavery cured us of that weakness. It may be enough, however, to have it said that we survive in exact relationship to the dedication of our poets (include preachers, musicians, and blues singers).

QUESTIONS AND CONSIDERATIONS

1. Why does Angelou contrast the white school and her black school, the attitudes of the graduating girls and the graduating boys? Do the gender and ethnic assumptions implied by the striking contrasts still exist in American culture and in your own community?

2. How does the black community in Stamps feel about the graduation and the graduates? What does an education represent to the black citizens of Stamps?

3. Why does Angelou feel proud of herself and of Henry Reed, the class valedictorian?

4. Why do Donleavy's expectations of the graduation class of Lafayette County Training School dampen the spirits of the students and their relatives? Which images does Angelou use to convey a sense of disillusionment and defeat after the speech?

5. Why does Henry Reed decide to lead the class in the Negro National Anthem? Why does Angelou hear and understand for the first time the meaning behind the words of the poem? How have black poets inspired the black community to have faith?

6. In what ways is Angelou's graduation a passage from innocence to experience?

IDEAS FOR WRITING

1. Write an essay about your graduation as an experience of initiation and passage. Did your graduation give you faith in your power to succeed in spite of the obstacles that you realized you would have to overcome?

2. Write an essay in which you compare and contrast the social attitudes toward African-Americans portrayed in Angelou's story with attitudes commonly held today. You might draw on your own experiences during your elementary and secondary education, as well as what you have learned from reading or from popular culture.

Life Stories
Michael Dorris

Journal

Write about a job you held in high school or college that helped you to make a transition in your life and to become more self-reliant.

In most cultures, adulthood is equated with self-reliance and responsibility, yet often Americans do not achieve this status until we are in our late twenties or early thirties—virtually the entire average lifespan of a person in a traditional non-Western society. We tend to treat prolonged adolescence as a warm-up for real life, as a wobbly ladder between childhood and legal maturity. Whereas a nineteenth-century Cheyenne or Lakota teenager was expected to alter self-conception in a split-second vision, we often meander through an analogous rite of passage for more than a decade—through high school, college, graduate school.

Though he had never before traveled alone outside his village, the Plains Indian male was expected at puberty to venture solo into the wilderness. There he had to fend for and sustain himself while avoiding the menace of unknown dangers, and there he had absolutely to remain until something happened that would transform him. Every human being, these tribes believed, was entitled to at least one moment of personal, enabling insight.

Anthropology proposes feasible psychological explanations for why this flash was eventually triggered: fear, fatigue, reliance on strange foods, the anguish of loneliness, stress, and the expectation of ultimate success all contributed to a state of receptivity. Every sense was quickened, alerted to perceive deep meaning, until at last the interpretation of an unusual event—a dream, a chance encounter, or an unexpected vista—reverberated with significance. Through this unique prism, abstractly preserved in a vivid memory or song, a boy caught foresight of both his adult persona and his vocation, the two inextricably entwined.

The best approximations that many of us get to such a heady sense of eventuality come in the performance of the jobs we hold during summer vacation. Summers are intermissions, and once we hit our teens it is during these breaks in our structured regimen that we initially taste the satisfaction of remuneration that is earned, not merely doled. Tasks defined as work are not graded, they are compensated; they have a worth that is inarguable because it translates into hard currency. Wage labor—and in the beginning, this generally means a confining, repetitive chore for which we are quickly overqualified—paradoxically brings a sense of blooming freedom. At the outset, the complaint to a peer that business supersedes fun is oddly liberating—no matter what drudgery requires your attention, it is by its very required nature serious and adult.

At least that's how it seemed to me. I come from a line of people hard hit by the Great Depression. My mother and her sisters went to work early in their teens—my mother operated a kind of calculator known as a comptometer while her sisters spent their days, respectively, at a peanut factory and at Western Union. My grandmother did piecework sewing. Their efforts, and the Democratic Party, saw them through, and to this day they never look back without appreciation for their later solvency. They take nothing for granted. Accomplishments are celebrated, possessions are valuable, in direct proportion to the labor entailed to acquire them; anything easily won or bought on credit is suspect. When I was growing up we were far from wealthy, but what money we had was correlated to the hours one of us had logged. My eagerness to contribute to, or at least not diminish, the coffer was countered by the arguments of those whose salaries kept me in school: my higher education was a sound group investment. The whole family was adamant that I have the opportunities they had missed and, no matter how much I objected, they stinted themselves to provide for me.

Summer jobs were therefore a relief, an opportunity to pull a share of the load. As soon as the days turned warm I began to peruse the classifieds, and when the spring semester was done, I was ready to punch a clock. It even felt right. Work in June, July, and August had an almost biblical aspect: in the hot, canicular weather your brow sweats, just as God had ordained. Moreover, summer jobs had the luxury of being temporary. No matter how onerous, how off my supposed track, employment terminated with the falling leaves and I was back to real life. So, during each annual three-month leave from secondary school and later from the university, I compiled an eclectic resumé: lawn cutter, hair sweeper in a barber shop, lifeguard, delivery boy, mail carrier, file clerk, youth program coordinator on my Montana reservation, ballroom dance instructor, theater party promoter, night-shift hospital records keeper, human adding machine in a Paris bank, encyclopedia salesman, newspaper stringer, recreation bus manager, salmon fisherman.

The summer I was eighteen a possibility arose for a rotation at the post office, and I grabbed it. There was something casually sophisticated about work that required a uniform, about having a federal ranking, even if it was GS-1

(Temp/Sub), and it was flattering to be entrusted with a leather bag containing who knew what important correspondence. Every day I was assigned a new beat, usually in a rough neighborhood avoided whenever possible by regular carriers, and I proved quite capable of complicating what would normally be fairly routine missions. The low point came on the first of August when I diligently delivered four blocks' worth of welfare checks to the right numbers on the wrong streets. It is no fun to snatch unexpected wealth from the hands of those who have but moments previously opened their mailboxes and received a bonus.

After my first year of college, I lived with relatives on an Indian reservation in eastern Montana and filled the only post available: Coordinator of Youth Programs. I was seduced by the language of the announcement into assuming that there existed Youth Programs to be coordinated. In fact, the Youth consisted of a dozen bored, disgruntled kids—most of them my cousins—who had nothing better to do each day than to show up at what was euphemistically called "the gym" and hate whatever Program I had planned for them. The Youth ranged in age from fifteen to five and seemed to have as their sole common ambition the determination to smoke cigarettes. This put them at immediate and ongoing odds with the Coordinator, who on his first day naively encouraged them to sing the "Doe, a deer, a female deer" song from *The Sound of Music.* They looked at me, that bleak morning, and I looked at them, each boy and girl equipped with a Pall Mall behind an ear, and we all knew we faced a long, struggle-charged battle. It was to be a contest of wills, the hearty and wholesome versus prohibited vice. I stood for dodge ball, for collecting bugs in glass jars, for arts and crafts; they had pledged a preternatural allegiance to sloth. The odds were not in my favor and each waking dawn I experienced the lightheadedness of anticipated exhaustion, that thrill of giddy dissociation in which nothing seems real or of great significance. I went with the flow and learned to inhale.

The next summer, I decided to find work in an urban setting for a change, and was hired as a general office assistant in the Elsa Hoppenfeld Theatre Party Agency, located above Sardi's restaurant in New York City. The agency consisted of Elsa Hoppenfeld herself, Rita Frank, her regular deputy, and me. Elsa was a gregarious Viennese woman who established contacts through honesty, hard work, and personal charm, and she spent much of the time away from the building courting trade. Rita was therefore both my immediate supervisor and constant companion; she had the most incredible fingernails I had ever seen—long, carefully shaped pegs lacquered in cruel primary colors and hard as stone—and an attitude about her that could only be described as zeal.

The goal of a theater party agent is to sell blocks of tickets to imminent Broadway productions, and the likely buyers are charities, B'nai B'riths, Hadassahs, and assorted other fund-raising organizations. We received commissions on volume, and so it was necessary to convince a prospect that a play—preferably an expensive musical—for which we had reserved the rights to seats would be a boffo smash hit.

The object of our greatest expectation that season was an extravaganza called *Chu Chem,* a saga that aspired to ride the coattails of *Fiddler on the Roof* into entertainment history. It starred the estimable Molly Picon and told the story of a family who had centuries ago gone from Israel to China during the Diaspora, yet had, despite isolation in an alien environment, retained orthodox culture and habits. The crux of the plot revolved around a man with several marriageable daughters and nary a kosher suitor within five thousand miles. For three months Rita and I waxed eloquent in singing the show's praises. We sat in our little office, behind facing desks, and every noon while she redid her nails I ordered out from a deli that offered such exotic (to me) delicacies as fried egg sandwiches, lox and cream cheese, pastrami, tongue. I developed of necessity and habit a telephone voice laced with a distinctly Yiddish accent. It could have been a great career. However, come November, *Chu Chem* bombed. Its closing was such a financial catastrophe for all concerned that when the following January one Monsieur Dupont advertised on the placement board at my college, I decided to put an ocean between me and my former trusting clientele.

M. Dupont came to campus with the stated purpose of interviewing candidates for teller positions in a French bank. Successful applicants, required to be fluent *en français,* would be rewarded with three well-paid months and a rent-free apartment in Paris. On my way to the language lab, I registered for an appointment.

The only French in the interview was *Bonjour, ça va?,* after which M. Dupont switched into English and described the wonderful deal on charter air flights that would be available to those who got the nod. Round-trip to Amsterdam, via Reykjavík, leaving the day after exams and returning in mid-September, no changes or substitutions. I signed up on the spot. I was to be a *banquier,* with *pied-à-terre* in Montparnasse!

Unfortunately, when I arrived with only $50 in traveler's checks in my pocket—the flight had cleaned me out, but who needed money since my paycheck started right away—no one in Paris had ever heard of M. Dupont. *Alors.*

I stood in the Gare du Nord and considered my options. There weren't any. I scanned a listing of Paris hotels and headed for the cheapest one: the Hotel Villedo, $10 a night. The place had an ambiance that I persuaded myself was antique, despite the red light above the sign. The only accommodation available was "the bridal suite," a steal at $20. The glass door to my room didn't lock and in the adjacent room there was a rather continual floor show, but at some point I must have dozed off. When I awoke the church bells were ringing, the sky was pink, and I felt renewed. No little setback was going to spoil my adventure. I stretched, then walked to a mirror that hung above the sink next to the bed. I leaned forward to punctuate my resolve with a confident look in the eye.

The sink disengaged and fell to the floor. Water gushed. In panic I rummaged through my open suitcase, stuffed two pairs of underpants into the pipe to quell the flow, and before the dam broke, I was out the door. I barreled through the lobby of the first bank I passed, asked to see the director, and told the startled man my sad story. For some reason, whether from shock or pity, he hired me at $1.27 an hour to be a cross-checker of foreign currency transactions, and with two phone calls found me lodgings at a commercial school's dormitory.

From 8 to 5 each weekday my duty was to sit in a windowless room with six impeccably dressed people, all of whom were totaling identical additions and subtractions. We were highly dignified with each other, very professional, no *tutoyer*ing. Monsieur Saint presided, but the formidable Mademoiselle was the true power; she oversaw each of our columns and shook her head sadly at my American-shaped numbers.

My legacy from that summer, however, was more than an enduring penchant for crossed 7s. After I had worked for six weeks, M. Saint asked me during a coffee break why I didn't follow the example of other foreign students he had known and depart the office at noon in order to spend the afternoon touring the sights of Paris with the Alliance Française.

"Because," I replied in my halting French, "that costs money. I depend upon my full salary the same as any of you." M. Saint nodded gravely and said no more, but then on the next Friday he presented me with a white envelope along with my check.

"Do not open this until you have left the Société Général," he said ominously. I thought I was fired for the time I had mixed up kroner and guilders, and, once on the sidewalk, I steeled myself to read the worst. I felt the quiet panic of blankness.

"Dear Sir," I translated the perfectly formed script. "You are a person of value. It is not correct that you should be in our beautiful city and not see it. Therefore we have amassed a modest sum to pay the tuition for a two-week afternoon program for you at the Alliance Française. Your wages will not suffer, for it is your assignment to appear each morning in this bureau and reacquaint us with the places you have visited. We shall see them afresh through your eyes." The letter had thirty signatures, from the director to the janitor, and stuffed inside the envelope was a sheaf of franc notes in various denominations.

I rushed back to the tiny office. M. Saint and Mademoiselle had waited, and accepted my gratitude with their usual controlled smiles and precise handshakes. But they had blown their Gallic cover, and for the next ten days and then through all the weeks until I went home in September, our branch was awash with sightseeing paraphernalia. Everyone had advice, favorite haunts, criticisms of the alliance's choices or explanations. Paris passed through the bank's granite walls as sweetly as a June breeze through a window screen, and ever afterward the lilt of overheard French, a photograph of Sacré-Coeur or the Louvre, even a monthly bank statement, recalls to me that best of all summers.

I didn't wind up in an occupation with any obvious connection to the careers I sampled during my school breaks, but I never altogether abandoned those brief professions either. They were jobs not so much to be held as to be weighed, absorbed, and incorporated, and, collectively, they carried me forward into adult life like an escalator, unfolding a particular pattern at once amazing and inevitable.

QUESTIONS AND CONSIDERATIONS

1. How does Dorris explain the rite of passage into adolescence for a Plains Indian male? What was your reaction to the Native American male's rite of passage?

2. Why do you think Dorris begins his essay by establishing a contrast between the Native American and American teenager's passages through adolescence?

3. According to Dorris, how does working help an adolescent to identify with the adult world?

4. Reflect on each employment opportunity that Dorris presents to determine what you think he learned as he moved into adulthood from his early work experiences.

5. How does the language, as well as the essay's humorous tone, support the theme and ideas? Refer to specific passages to support your points.

6. Although he begins his essay with a reference to the initiation rites of the Plains Indian, Dorris, a Native American, concludes with a narrative about his initiation into living abroad and the mysteries of French culture. In what ways are Dorris' summer job experiences and the rite of passage of the Plains Indian similar?

IDEAS FOR WRITING

1. Write a definition of adolescence that includes what you think are the crucial issues an adolescent must face; use examples from your own experiences, from the experiences of your peers, or from popular culture to support your main ideas. Also consider how your definition of adolescence is rooted in the cultural assumptions of your peers and family.

2. Like Dorris, write an essay that reflects on the ways that your summer jobs as an adolescent have shaped your character and values. Focus on how these jobs helped you to make the passage through adolescence into the adult world. You might want to compare your experiences to the work experiences of Michael Dorris.

Once More to the Lake
E. B. White

Journal

Write about a family ritual that you remember looking forward to as a child, such as going on a family vacation regularly. Why have the memories and the ritual remained important to you? Will you share this ritual with your children?

August 1941

One summer, along about 1904, my father rented a camp on a lake in Maine and took us all there for the month of August. We all got ringworm from some kittens and had to rub Pond's Extract on our arms and legs night and morning, and my father rolled over in a canoe with all his clothes on; but outside of that the vacation was a success and from then on none of us ever thought there was any place in the world like that lake in Maine. We returned summer after summer—always on August 1 for one month. I have since become a salt-water man, but sometimes in summer there are days when the restlessness of the tides and the fearful cold of the sea water and the incessant wind that blows across the afternoon and into the evening make me wish for the placidi-ty of a lake in the woods. A few weeks ago this feeling got so strong I bought myself a couple of bass hooks and a spinner and returned to the lake where we used to go, for a week's fishing and to revisit old haunts.

I took along my son, who had never had any fresh water up his nose and who had seen lily pads only from train windows. On the journey over to the lake I began to wonder what it would be like. I wondered how time would have marred this unique, this holy spot—the coves and streams, the hills that the sun set behind, the camps and the paths behind the camps. I was sure that the tarred road would have found it out, and I wondered in what other ways it would be desolated. It is strange how much you can remember about places like that once you allow your mind to return into the grooves that lead back. You remember one thing, and that suddenly reminds you of another thing. I guess I remembered clearest of all the early mornings, when the lake was cool and motionless, remembered how the bedroom smelled of the lumber it was made of and of the wet woods whose scent entered through the screen. The partitions in the camp were thin and did not extend clear to the top of the rooms, and as I was always the first up I would dress softly so as not to wake the others, and sneak out into the sweet outdoors and start out in the canoe, keeping close along the shore in the long shadows of the pines. I remembered being very careful never to rub my paddle against the gunwale for fear of dis-turbing the stillness of the cathedral.

The lake had never been what you would call a wild lake. There were cot-tages sprinkled around the shores, and it was in farming country although the shores of the lake were quite heavily wooded. Some of the cottages were owned by nearby farmers, and you would live at the shore and eat your meals at the farmhouse. That's what our family did. But although it wasn't wild, it was a fairly large and undisturbed lake and there were places in it that, to a child at least, seemed infinitely remote and primeval.

I was right about the tar: it led to within half a mile of the shore. But when I got back there, with my boy, and we settled into a camp near a farmhouse and into the kind of summertime I had known, I could tell that it was going to be pretty much the same as it had been before—I knew it, lying in bed the first morning smelling the bedroom and hearing the boy sneak quietly out and go off along the shore in a boat. I began to sustain the illusion that he was I, and therefore, by simple transposition, that I was my father. This sensation persist-ed, kept cropping up all the time we were there. It was not an entirely new feel-ing, but in this setting it grew much stronger. I seemed to be living a dual existence. I would be in the middle of some simple act, I would be picking up a bait box or laying down a table fork, or I would be saying something and suddenly it would be not I but my father who was saying the words or making the gesture. It gave me a creepy sensation.

We went fishing the first morning. I felt the same damp moss covering the worms in the bait can, and saw the dragonfly alight on the tip of my rod as it hovered a few inches from the surface of the water. It was the arrival of this fly that convinced me beyond any doubt that everything was as it always had been, that the years were a mirage and that there had been no years. The small waves were the same, chucking the rowboat under the chin as we fished at anchor, and the boat was the same boat, the same color green and the ribs broken in the same places, and under the floorboards the same fresh water leavings and débris—the dead hellgrammite, the wisps of moss, the rusty discarded fishhook, the dried blood from yesterday's catch. We stared silently at the tips of our rods, at the dragonflies that came and went. I lowered the tip of mine into the water, tentatively, pensively dislodging the fly, which darted two feet away, poised, darted two feet back, and came to rest again a little farther up the rod. There had been no years between the ducking of this dragonfly and the other one—the one that was part of memory. I looked at the boy, who was silently watching his fly, and it was my hands that held his rod, my eyes watching. I felt dizzy and didn't know which rod I was at the end of.

We caught two bass, hauling them in briskly as though they were mackerel, pulling them over the side of the boat in a businesslike manner without any landing net, and stunning them with a blow on the back of the head. When we got back for a swim before lunch, the lake was exactly where we had left it, the same number of inches from the dock, and there was only the merest suggestion of a breeze. This seemed an utterly enchanted sea, this lake you could leave to its own devices for a few hours and come back to, and find that it had not stirred, this constant and trustworthy body of water. In the shallows, the dark, water-soaked sticks and twigs, smooth and old, were undulating in clusters on the bottom against the clean ribbed sand, and the track of the mussel was plain. A school of minnows swam by, each minnow with its small individual shadow, doubling the attendance, so clear and sharp in the sunlight. Some of the other campers were in swimming, along the shore, one of them with a cake of soap, and the water felt thin and clear and unsubstantial. Over the years there had been this person with the cake of soap, this cultist, and here he was. There had been no years.

Up to the farmhouse to dinner through the teeming dusty field, the road under our sneakers was only a two-track road. The middle track was missing, the one with the marks of the hooves and the splotches of dried, flaky manure. There had always been three tracks to choose from in choosing which track to walk in; now the choice was narrowed down to two. For a moment I missed terribly the middle alternative. But the way led past the tennis court, and something about the way it lay there in the sun reassured me; the tape had loosened along the backline, the alleys were green with plantains and other weeds, and the net (installed in June and removed in September) sagged in the dry noon, and the whole place steamed with midday heat and hunger and emptiness. There was a choice of pie for dessert, and one was blueberry and one was apple, and the waitresses were the same country girls, there having been no passage of time, only the illusion of it as in a dropped curtain—the waitresses were still fifteen; their hair had been washed, that was the only difference—they had been to the movies and seen the pretty girls with the clean hair.

Summertime, oh, summertime, pattern of life indelible with fadeproof lake, the wood unshatterable, the pasture with the sweetfern and the juniper forever and ever, summer without end; this was the background, and the life along the shore was the design, the cottages with their innocent and tranquil design, their tiny docks with the flagpole and the American flag floating against the white clouds in the blue sky, the little paths over the roots of the trees leading from camp to camp and the paths leading back to the outhouses and the can of lime for sprinkling, and at the souvenir counters at the store the miniature birchbark canoes and the postcards that showed things looking a little better than they looked. This was the American family at play, escaping the city heat, wondering whether the newcomers in the camp at the head of the cove were "common" or "nice," wondering whether it was true that the people who drove up for Sunday dinner at the farmhouse were turned away because there wasn't enough chicken.

It seemed to me, as I kept remembering all this, that those times and those summers had been infinitely precious and worth saving. There had been jollity and peace and goodness. The arriving (at the beginning of August) had been so big a business in itself, at the railway station the farm wagon drawn up, the first smell of the pineladen air, the first glimpse of the smiling farmer, and the great importance of the trunks and your father's enormous authority in such matters, and the feel of the wagon under you for the long ten-mile haul, and at the top of the last long hill catching the first view of the lake after eleven months of not seeing this cherished body of water. The shouts and cries of the other campers when they saw you, and the trunks to be unpacked, to give up their rich burden. (Arriving was less exciting nowadays, when you sneaked up in your car and parked it under a tree near the camp and took out the bags and in five minutes it was all over, no fuss, no loud wonderful fuss about trunks.)

Peace and goodness and jollity. The only thing that was wrong now, really, was the sound of the place, an unfamiliar nervous sound of the outboard motors. This was the note that jarred, the one thing that would sometimes break the illusion and set the years moving. In those other summertimes all motors were inboard; and when they were at a little distance, the noise they made was a sedative, an ingredient of summer sleep. They were one-cylinder and two-cylinder engines, and some were make-and-break and some were jump-spark, but they all made a sleepy sound across the lake. The one-lungers throbbed and fluttered, and the twin-cylinder ones purred and purred, and that was a quiet sound, too. But now the campers all had outboards. In the daytime, in the hot mornings, these motors made a petulant, irritable sound; at night in the still evening when the afterglow lit the water, they whined about one's ears like mosquitoes. My boy loved our rented outboard, and his great desire was to achieve single-handed mastery over it, and authority, and he soon learned the trick of choking it a little (but not too much), and the adjustment of the needle valve. Watching him I would remember the things you could do with the old one-cylinder engine with the heavy flywheel, how you could have it eating out of your hand if you got really close to it spiritually. Motorboats in those days didn't have clutches, and you would make a landing by shutting off the motor at the proper time and coasting in with a dead rudder. But there was a way of reversing them, if you learned the trick, by cutting the switch and putting it on again exactly on the final dying revolution of the flywheel, so that it would kick back against compression and begin reversing. Approaching a dock in a strong following breeze, it was difficult to slow up sufficiently by the ordinary coasting method, and if a boy felt he had complete mastery over his motor, he was tempted to keep it running beyond its time and then reverse it a few feet from the dock. It took a cool nerve, because if you threw the switch a twentieth of a second too soon you would catch the flywheel when it still had speed enough to go up past center, and the boat would leap ahead, charging bull-fashion at the dock.

We had a good week at the camp. The bass were biting well and the sun shone endlessly, day after day. We would be tired at night and lie down in the accumulated heat of the little bedrooms after the long hot day and the breeze would stir almost imperceptibly outside and the smell of the swamp drift in through the rusty screens. Sleep would come easily and in the morning the red squirrel would be on the roof, tapping out his gay routine. I kept remembering everything, lying in bed in the mornings—the small steamboat that had a long rounded stern like the lip of a Ubangi, and how quietly she ran on the moonlight sails, when the older boys played their mandolins and the girls sang and we ate doughnuts dipped in sugar, and how sweet the music was on the water in the shining night, and what it had felt like to think about girls then. After breakfast we would go up to the store and the things were in the same place—the minnows in a bottle, the plugs and spinners disarranged and pawed over by the youngsters from the boys' camp, the Fig Newtons and the Beeman's gum. Outside, the road was tarred and cars stood in front of the store. Inside, all was just as it had always been, except there was more Coca-Cola and not so much Moxie and root beer and birch beer and sarsaparilla. We would walk out with the bottle of pop apiece and sometimes the pop would backfire up our noses and hurt. We explored the streams, quietly, where the turtles slid off the sunny logs and dug their way into the soft bottom; and we lay on the town wharf and fed worms to the tame bass. Everywhere we went I had trouble making out which was I, the one walking at my side, the one walking in my pants.

One afternoon while we were at that lake a thunderstorm came up. It was like the revival of an old melodrama that I had seen long ago with childish awe. The second-act climax of the drama of the electrical disturbance over a lake in America had not changed in any important respect. This was the big scene, still the big scene. The whole thing was so familiar, the first feeling of oppression and heat and a general air around camp of not wanting to go very far away. In midafternoon (it was all the same) a curious darkening of the sky, and a lull in everything that had made life tick; and then the way the boats suddenly swung the other way at their moorings with the coming of a breeze out of the new quarter, and the premonitory rumble. Then the kettle drum, then the snare, then the bass drum and cymbals, then crackling light against the dark, and the gods grinning and licking their chops in the hills. Afterward the calm, the rain steadily rustling in the calm lake, the return of light and hope and spirits, and the campers running out in joy and relief to go swimming in the rain, their bright cries perpetuating the deathless joke about how they were getting simply drenched, and the children screaming with delight at the new sensation of bathing in the rain, and the joke about getting drenched linking the generations in a strong indestructible chain. And the comedian who waded in carrying an umbrella.

When the others went swimming my son said he was going in, too. He pulled his dripping trunks from the line where they had hung all through the shower and wrung them out. Languidly, and with no thought of going in, I watched him, his hard little body, skinny and bare, saw him wince slightly as he pulled up around his vitals the small, soggy, icy garment. As he buckled the swollen belt, suddenly my groin felt the chill of death.

QUESTIONS AND CONSIDERATIONS

1. White feels that when he is with his son at the lake he exists on two levels of time simultaneously: "I seemed to be living a dual existence." Explain what White means by this observation. Have you ever had a similar type of realization?

2. Why does White feel that there have been no years between the time when he was a boy at the lake with his father and when he is at the lake as a father to his son? Why is this insight so significant to White?

3. "The only thing that was wrong now, really, was the sound of the place, an unfamiliar nervous sound of the outboard motors." Why do the sounds of the outboards upset White? What other changes does he notice at the lake?

4. What are the most significant events and feelings from his youth that White recalls during his days with his son at the lake?

5. What does the electrical storm over the lake symbolize? How does it remind White of his own aging and mortality?

6. In what ways do you think the lake holds new meanings for White now that he has visited it with his son? For White, what type of initiation does the trip to the lake with his son become?

IDEAS FOR WRITING

1. Write an essay about returning to a place that you loved during your childhood. Describe how it felt to return, reflecting on how the visit symbolizes a passage for you and an initiation into a new stage of your life.

2. Write an essay in which you discuss whether such "father and son" or "mother and daughter" vacation experiences as White explores in his essay are beneficial to the growth of both parents and children.

Poetry

Metaphors

Sylvia Plath

Journal

Create a series of imaginative comparisons that help to describe the way you currently perceive yourself.

I'm a riddle in nine syllables,
An elephant, a ponderous house,
A melon strolling on two tendrils.
O red fruit, ivory, fine timbers!
This loaf's big with its yeasty rising.   5
Money's new-minted in this fat purse.
I'm a means, a stage, a cow in calf.
I've eaten a bag of green apples,
Boarded the train there's no getting off.

QUESTIONS AND CONSIDERATIONS

1. Why does the speaker's riddle have nine syllables? How does the poem emphasize the number nine in its language, stanza structure, and images?

2. Examine the animal images and comparisons in the poem. Why does the speaker compare herself to animals such as the elephant and the cow?

3. The speaker uses several different types of food imagery in her riddle, comparing herself to a melon, a loaf, and to a person who has "eaten a bag of green apples." What impression do these images give you of the speaker, her self-image, and her inner-body sensations?

4. What impression of the speaker's state of mind is suggested through the comparison of the speaker as a "fat purse" carrying money, as well as the final line, "Boarded the train there's no getting off"?

5. How do you think the narrator feels about her pregnancy? In what ways is her pregnancy an initiation?

6. What insights into a woman's feelings about being pregnant does the poem help you to understand?

IDEAS FOR WRITING

1. Most readers interpret "Metaphors" as an expression of a woman's feelings about her pregnancy. Write an essay that discusses the narrator's feelings about pregnancy, based on the language and imagery of the poem. What did you learn about being pregnant and about yourself from studying and thinking about the poem?

2. Write a poem, story, or personal essay in which you develop a series of related metaphors or comparisons to express your feelings about a physical change and its accompanying psychological impact on your life.

The Journey
for Jane at thirteen
Maxine Kumin

Journal

Write about a journey you took during early adolescence that helped you to establish your independence from your family.

Papers in order; your face
accurate and on guard in the cardboard house
and the difficult patols you will speak
half-mastered in your jaw;
the funny make-up in your funny pocketbook—   5
pale lipstick, half a dozen lotions
to save your cloudless skin
in that uncertain sea
where no one charts the laws—
of course you do not belong to me   10
nor I to you
and everything is only true in mirrors.

I help to lock your baggage:
history book, lace collar and pink pearls
from the five-and-ten,   15
an expurgated text
of how the gods behaved on Mount Olympus,

and pennies in your shoes.
You lean as bland as sunshine on the rails.
Whatever's next— 20
the old oncoming uses
of your new troughs and swells—
is coin for trading among girls
in gym suits and geometry classes.

How can you know I traveled here, 25
stunned, like you, by my reflection
in forest pools;
hunted among the laurel
and whispered to by swans
in accents of my own invention? 30

It is a dangerous time.
The water rocks away the timber
and here is your visa stamped in red.
You lean down your confident head.
We exchange kisses; I call your name 35
and wave you off as the bridge goes under.

QUESTIONS AND CONSIDERATIONS

1. Why and how is the daughter's trip presented as both a literal and a symbolic journey?

2. Describe Jane's character, based on the information the poet gave us about her daughter. Does she seem like a typical adolescent? Why or why not? Explain.

3. The mother says, "of course you do not belong to me/nor I to you/and everything is only true in mirrors." What kind of a "truth" is reflected in mirrors? Why would a 13-year-old be susceptible to seeing the truth in mirrors?

4. Why does the mother feel that she will not be able to protect or help her daughter during her journey? Does the poem imply that the daughter will return? Do you think the daughter will return? Explain your response.

5. Why does the mother interpret her daughter's baggage as "an expurgated text/of how the gods behaved on Mount Olympus"?

6. The poem is told from a mother's point of view. How do you think Jane would describe the experience that her mother has written about?

IDEAS FOR WRITING

1. Write an essay about a journey away from your home and familiar environment which you took in your adolescence that had a special significance for you and your family. Narrate the literal journey and then reflect on what you learned from it and how the journey symbolized a transition in your life.

2. Write about a turning point or a separation experience that you went through during adolescence from two points of view, yours and that of one of your parents.

Saturday At The Canal
Gary Soto

Journal
---

*Write about a period of waiting and transition in your life, a period between
grades or after graduation from high school when you had fantasies of leaving
home but didn't feel quite ready.*

I was hoping to be happy by seventeen.
School was a sharp check mark in the roll book,
An obnoxious tuba playing at noon because our team
Was going to win at night. The teachers were
Too close to dying to understand. The hallways   5
Stank of poor grades and unwashed hair. Thus,
A friend and I sat watching the water on Saturday,
Neither of us talking much, just warming ourselves
By hurling large rocks at the dusty ground
And feeling awful because San Francisco was a postcard   10
On a bedroom wall. We wanted to go there,
Hitchhike under the last migrating birds
And be with people who knew more than three chords
On a guitar. We didn't drink or smoke,
But our hair was shoulder length, wild when   15
The wind picked up and the shadows of
This loneliness gripped loose dirt. By bus or car,
By the sway of train over a long bridge,
We wanted to get out. The years froze
As we sat on the bank. Our eyes followed the water,   20
White-tipped but dark underneath, racing out of town.

QUESTIONS AND CONSIDERATIONS

1. Why isn't the speaker "happy by seventeen," as he had hoped to be?

2. As the speaker reflects back on his first years of high school, which images and memories does he recall? Are his memories and feelings similar to those that you have about high school when you were seventeen?

3. Do you think the speaker is fair to the teachers who seem to him "Too close to dying to understand"? What is it the teachers can't understand?

4. The speaker and his friend maintain a fantasy of life in San Francisco. How would you fill in their fantasy from the few details presented in the poem? What does the speaker think that he might share with or learn from the people in San Francisco?

5. Although the speaker and his friend imagine various ways of getting away from the dull community where they live, they seem to be paralyzed, unable to make the final decision to leave: "the years froze." Why do you think that they feel paralyzed?

6. Discuss the significance of the setting of the poem (a Saturday, in the winter or late fall, above an irrigation canal) in terms of the theme of adolescent restlessness. Consider particularly the poem's last lines: "Our eyes followed the water,/White-tipped but dark underneath, racing out of town."

IDEAS FOR WRITING

1. Write a sequel to this poem, either in the form of a poem or a story. How do you imagine the speaker and his friend will change?

2. Based on the evidence given in the poem and on your own knowledge of adolescents, do you think it would be wise for the two friends to follow their fantasy and move to San Francisco or some other large, exciting city, or would it be better for them, if possible, to continue their education in their own community? What advice would you have for them?

The Wild Swans
At Coole
William Butler Yeats

Journal

Write about a familiar place you have returned to at different times in your life. How have your feelings about the place changed as you have grown older?

The trees are in their autumn beauty,
The woodland paths are dry,
Under the October twilight the water
Mirrors a still sky;
Upon the brimming water among the stones   5
Are nine-and-fifty swans.

The nineteenth autumn has come upon me
Since I first made my count;
I saw, before I had well finished,
All suddenly mount   10
And scatter wheeling in great broken rings
Upon their clamorous wings.

I have looked upon those brilliant creatures,
And now my heart is sore.
All's changed since I, hearing at twilight,   15
The first time on this shore,
The bell-beat of their wings above my head,
Trod with a lighter tread.

Unwearied still, lover by lover,
They paddle in the cold   20
Companionable streams or climb the air;
Their hearts have not grown old;
Passion or conquest, wander where they will,
Attend upon them still.

But now they drift on the still water,   25
Mysterious, beautiful;
Among what rushes will they build,
By what lake's edge or pool
Delight men's eyes when I awake some day
To find they have flown away?   30

QUESTIONS AND CONSIDERATIONS

1. What is the significance of the season in which the poem is set?

2. What is suggested by the mounting of the swans before the narrator has finished his count?

3. The narrator says that "All's changed" since the time 19 years ago when he first counted the swans. How has he changed? What losses do you imagine he has suffered?

4. The speaker creates a contrast in the poem between himself and the swans. How are they different? What does this suggest that the narrator now realizes about his place in nature?

5. What insight is suggested by the poem's concluding question? What is the ambiguous meaning of the word "awake"?

6. The poem uses a regular six-line metered and rhymed stanza, ending in rhymed couplets. How does the regular occurrence of the patterned stanza help to reinforce the poem's meaning and central theme?

IDEAS FOR WRITING

1. Write an essay in which you describe a familiar location you have returned to at different times over the years. Develop your essay through comparing some of the insights or perceptions you have had in this place at various times in your life.

2. Write about the role that natural creatures play in helping us to define ourselves and to give us solace as we move through the passages of life. Provide examples from works in the text as well as your own experiences.

The Life Ahead

Philip Levine

I wakened, still a child,
and dressed myself slowly
for the life ahead. It
came at two, after lunch,

the class quieted   5
and the teacher's eyes
clouded and closed.
I could smell our coats
on their hooks, I could
smell my own uncut hair,   10
the hair of a dog, and
when I looked down below
to the dark streets awash
with oil, a small boy—
alone and lost—wandered   15
across the playground.
He climbed the fence
and made it across
the avenue, past the closed
candy store, and down   20
the street that led to hell.
There was a river in Detroit
and if you crossed it you
were in another country,
but something always   25
called me back, a woman
who had no use for me
or a brother who did, or
the pure white aura
of steel before the forge   30
came down with a groan
like the sea's and we stood
back waiting for one more
leaf of a truck spring, thick
arched leaf of earth. Something   35
called me back to this life,
and I came home to wander
the schoolyard again
as a lost boy and find
above or below the world   40
was here and now, drowning
in oil, second by second
borrowed from the clock.

QUESTIONS

1. What discovery does the speaker make when, as a child in school in Detroit, he looks "down below to the dark streets"? Where does he want to go, and what prevents him from going? Why does he return to the playground later, and what new insight does he have there about the world?

2. Write an essay about a moment of childhood discovery or insight that came to you in a particular setting. Contrast your childhood perception with a new insight you had recently in similar surroundings.

Birches
Robert Frost

When I see birches bend to left and right
Across the lines of straighter darker trees,
I like to think some boy's been swinging them.
But swinging doesn't bend them down to stay.
Ice-storms do that. Often you must have seen them   5
Loaded with ice a sunny winter morning
After a rain. They click upon themselves
As the breeze rises, and turn many-colored
As the stir cracks and crazes their enamel.
Soon the sun's warmth makes them shed crystal shells   10
Shattering and avalanching on the snow-crust—
Such heaps of broken glass to sweep away
You'd think the inner dome of heaven had fallen.
They are dragged to the withered bracken by the load,
And they seem not to break; though once they are bowed   15
So low for long, they never right themselves:
You may see their trunks arching in the woods
Years afterwards, trailing their leaves on the ground
Like girls on hands and knees that throw their hair
Before them over their heads to dry in the sun.   20
But I was going to say when Truth broke in
With all her matter-of-fact about the ice-storm
I should prefer to have some boy bend them
As he went out and in to fetch the cows—
Some boy too far from town to learn baseball,   25
Whose only play was what he found himself,
Summer or winter, and could play alone.
One by one he subdued his father's trees
By riding them down over and over again
Until he took the stiffness out of them,   30
And not one but hung limp, not one was left
For him to conquer. He learned all there was
To learn about not launching out too soon
And so not carrying the tree away
Clear to the ground. He always kept his poise   35

To the top branches, climbing carefully
With the same pains you use to fill a cup
Up to the brim, and even above the brim.
Then he flung outward, feet first, with a swish,
Kicking his way down through the air to the ground. 40
So was I once myself a swinger of birches.
And so I dream of going back to be.
It's when I'm weary of considerations,
And life is too much like a pathless wood
Where your face burns and tickles with the cobwebs 45
Broken across it, and one eye is weeping
From a twig's having lashed across it open.
I'd like to get away from earth awhile
And then come back to it and begin over.
May no fate willfully misunderstand me 50
And half grant what I wish and snatch me away
Not to return. Earth's the right place for love:
I don't know where it's likely to go better.
I'd like to go by climbing a birch tree,
And climb black branches up a snow-white trunk 55
Toward heaven, till the tree could bear no more,
But dipped its top and set me down again.
That would be good both going and coming back.
One could do worse than be a swinger of birches.

QUESTIONS

1. What point is the speaker making about climbing birch trees? Why is this activity pleasurable for a young person, and why does it please the speaker, now an adult, to think about climbing the trees? How does the image of climbing and bending birches reflect the speaker's view of life?

2. Write an essay in which you develop an extended metaphor of a natural process, as Frost does in "Birches." Use the metaphor you develop to describe or explain one of your own beliefs or values.

The Moment

Sharon Olds

When I saw the dark Egyptian stain,
I went down into the house to find you, Mother—
past the grandfather clock, with its huge
ochre moon, past the burnt

sienna woodwork, rubbed and glazed.   5
I went deeper and deeper down into the
body of the house, down below the
level of the earth. It must have been
the maid's day off, for I found you there
where I had never found you, by the wash tubs,   10
your hands thrust deep in soapy water,
and above your head, the blazing windows
at the surface of the ground.
You looked up from the iron sink,
a small haggard pretty woman   15
of 40, one week divorced.
"I've got my period, Mom," I said,
and saw your face abruptly break open and
glow with joy. "Baby," you said,
coming toward me, hands out and   20
covered with tiny delicate bubbles like seeds.

QUESTIONS

1. What "moment" in her life does the speaker describe? What is its significance in her life as an individual and in relationship to her life with her mother, "a small haggard pretty woman/ . . . one week divorced"? How does the setting of the poem, a basement washroom, add to the poignancy and intensity of the moment of revelation and communion between the mother and daughter?

2. Write an essay about a time when you told your parents or grandparents about a change or growing process you were experiencing. What did you learn about yourself and about your relative through this moment of sharing?

Hanging Fire

Audre Lorde

I am fourteen
and my skin has betrayed me
the boy I cannot live without
still sucks his thumb
in secret   5
how come my knees are
always so ashy
what if I die
before morning
and momma's in the bedroom   10
with the door closed.

I have to learn how to dance
in time for the next party
my room is too small for me
suppose I die before graduation   15
they will sing sad melodies
but finally
tell the truth about me
There is nothing I want to do
and too much   20
that has to be done
and momma's in the bedroom
with the door closed.

Nobody even stops to think
about my side of it   25
I should have been on Math Team
my marks were better than his
why do I have to be
the one
wearing braces   30
I have nothing to wear tomorrow
will I live long enough
to grow up
and momma's in the bedroom
with the door closed.   35

QUESTIONS

1. What is the 14-year-old speaker worried about? What type of relationship does she have with her mother? Do the speaker's complaints seem typical of early adolescents? If you were her mother, would you be worried about her?

2. Write an essay or letter from the mother of the young girl speaking in this poem. What advice or explanations would you have for her?

The Woman in the Next Room

Adrianne Marcus

With each pain
She screams at God. Though the door
is shut and nurses try to quiet her
With talk, I hear her howling

For salvation. Another pain   5
Begins: I grip the bed, feeling
the flesh grow tight, intensely
Mount until I cannot breathe
To cry aloud; an alien head
Locks firm in the bones   10
And I and the woman in the next
Room are sisters in madness.
The white sweep of the clock
Shortens our breathing; a face
Sealed in a green mask peers   15
Down at me, looms in my nightmare
Like a rational voice. Doctors,
Midwives of living practice their deep
And hidden art while the women
They fear suffer and hasten   20
Their death. Oh sister, madness
Becomes us: these Gods are mortal,
We must endure them. Pain
And forgetting: the clock
Brings closer to that hour   25
When we cheat death
With our bodies.

QUESTIONS

1. What is the speaker's reaction to her labor pains and to those of other women in the hospital? How does the speaker feel about the hospital and the doctors? Why does the speaker imagine that she and the other women in labor will "cheat death"? Why does she call them her "sisters"?

2. Write an essay about childbirth. What do you think that women learn through childbirth? Do you think it is possible for men to have an understanding of the feelings women experience in childbirth?

Who He Was

Denise Levertov

One is already here whose life
bearing like seed its distant death, shall grow
through human pain, human joy, shall know,
music and weeping, only because
the strange flower of your thighs   5
bloomed in my body. From our joy
begins a stranger's history. Who

is this rider in the dark? We lie
in candlelight; the child's quick unseen movements
jerk my belly under your hand. Who,   10
conceived in joy, in joy,
lies nine months alone in a walled silence?

Who is this rider in the dark,
nine months the body's tyrant,
nine months alone in a walled silence   15
our minds cannot fathom?
Who is it will come out of the dark,
whose cries demand our mercy, tyrant
no longer, but alone still, in a solitude
memory cannot reach?   20
Whose lips will suckle at these breasts,
thirsting, unafraid, for life?
Whose eyes will look out of that solitude?

The wise face of the unborn
ancient and innocent   25
must change to infant ignorance
before we see it, irrevocable third
looking into our lives; the child
must hunger, sleep, cry, gaze, long weeks
before it learns of laughter. Love can never   30
wish a life no darkness; but may love
be constant in the life our love has made.

QUESTIONS

1. What does the speaker in the poem feel about her unborn child? How does she use the words "dark" and "darkness" to describe the life of both her unborn child and her infant? What is the speaker's final wish for the unborn?

2. Write an essay in which you discuss the experience of being pregnant. Make references to "Who He Was."

My Papa's Waltz
Theodore Roethke

The whiskey on your breath
Could make a small boy dizzy;
But I hung on like death:
Such waltzing was not easy.

We romped until the pans   5
Slid from the kitchen shelf;
My mother's countenance
Could not unfrown itself.

The hand that held my wrist
Was battered on one knuckle;   10
At every step you missed
My right ear scraped a buckle.

You beat time on my head
With a palm caked hard by dirt,
Then waltzed me off to bed   15
Still clinging to your shirt.

QUESTIONS

1. How does the speaker in the poem feel about his childhood "waltzing" with his father? Was the waltzing a pleasant experience? How was it painful in some ways? What mood do the rhythm, rhyme, and word choice of the poem help to create? What insights into the speaker's attitudes about his father do they provide?

2. Write an essay about an experience you remember from your childhood in which one or more of the adults involved was intoxicated and rowdy. How did you react to their behavior? Do you feel differently about the experience now than you did when it occurred? If so, how and why?

Big Bessie Throws Her Son into the Street

Gwendolyn Brooks

A day of sunny face and temper.
The winter trees
Are musical.

Bright lameness from my beautiful disease,
You have your destiny to chip and eat.   5

Be precise.
With something better than candles in the eyes.
(Candles are not enough.)

At the root of the will, a wild inflammable stuff.

New pioneer of days and ways, be gone.   10
Hunt out your own or make your own alone.

Go down the street.

QUESTIONS

1. How does Big Bessie feel about her son? Why does she refer to him as a "bright lameness from my beautiful disease"? Why does she advise him to "be precise"? What future does she wish for him?

2. Write an essay to a relative, friend, or lover whom you think needs to develop a more independent and separate life. What advice would you give the person about the future and about survival?

Happy Birthday
Frank Bidart

Thirty-three, goodbye—
the awe I feel

is not that you won't come again, or why—

or even that after
a time, we think of those who are dead   5

with a sweetness that cannot be explained—

but that I've read the trading-cards:
RALPH TEMPLE CYCLIST CHAMPION TRICK RIDER

WILLIE HARRADON CYCLIST
THE YOUTHFUL PHENOMENON   10

F. F. IVES CYCLIST
100 MILES 6 H. 25 MIN. 30 SEC.

—as the fragile metal of their
wheels stopped turning, as they

took on wives, children, accomplishments, all those   15
predilections which also insisted on ending,

they could not tell themselves from what they had done.

Terrible to dress in the clothes
of a period that must end.

They didn't plan it that way—   20
they didn't plan it that way.

QUESTIONS

1. Who is the speaker addressing? How does he feel about his age? About mortality? Why does he quote from cyclist trading cards? What is the significance of the poem's
repeated last line: "They didn't plan it that way"?

2. The speaker states that it is "Terrible to dress in the clothes/of a period that must
end." Write an essay about a time in your life when what you wore and what you did
were really only a "stage," a period that you now consider over, a part of your past. How
do you feel about this time in your life: the clothes you wore, the things you did, your attitudes? How have you changed?

Nightmare Begins
Responsibility
Michael Harper

I place these numbed wrists to the pane
watching white uniforms whisk over
him in the tube-kept
prison
fear what they will do in experiment   5

watch my gloved stickshifting gasolined hands
breathe *boxcar-information-please* infirmary tubes
distrusting white/pink mending paperthin
silkened end hairs, distrusting tubes
shrunk in his *trunk-skincapped*   10
shaven head, in thighs
distrusting-white-hands-picking-baboon-light
on this son who will not make his second night
of this wardstrewn intensive airpocket
where his father's asthmatic   15
hymns of *night-train,* train done gone
his mother can only know that he has flown
up into essential calm unseen corridor
going boxscarred home, *mamaborn, sweetsonchild*
gonedowntown into *researchtestingwarehousebatteryacid*   20
mama-son-done-gone / me telling her 'nother

train tonight, no music, no breathstroked
heartbeat in my infinite distrust of them:

and of my distrusting self
white-doctor-who-breathed-for-him-all-night   25
say it for two sons gone,
say nightmare, say it loud
panebreaking heartmadness:
nightmare begins responsibility.

QUESTIONS

1. Why is the speaker so full of distrust for the hospital and its doctors? In what way does the speaker mature or become more responsible? How is the speaker's sense of confusion and desperation emphasized by the interspersed italicized lines and phrases? How does the speaker's references to music underscore his emotional distress?

2. Write an essay in which you respond to the poem's title. Do you agree that a "nightmare," or an extremely negative experience, can create a sense of responsibility or obligation to react to the nightmare in waking life?

Eating Together

Li-Young Lee

In the steamer is the trout
seasoned with slivers of ginger,
two sprigs of green onion, and sesame oil.
We shall eat it with rice for lunch,
brothers, sister, my mother who will   5
taste the sweetest meat of the head,
holding it between her fingers
deftly, the way my father did
weeks ago. Then he lay down
to sleep like a snow-covered road   10
winding through pines older than him,
without any travelers, and lonely for no one.

QUESTIONS

1. How does eating the trout evoke memories of the speaker's father? Why is the father's death described as "like a snow-covered road"? How is the image of the road developed and resolved in the final lines of the poem?

2. Write an essay in which you develop an extended comparison between a type of food, physical object, or particular situation that reminds you of a loved one whom you have lost.

Bukit China

Shirley Geok-lin-Lim

Bless me, spirits, I am returning.
Stone marking my father's bones,
I light the joss. A dead land.
On noon steepness smoke ascends
Briefly. Country is important,   5
Is important. This knowledge I know
If it will rise with smoke, with the dead.

He did not live for my returning.
News came after burial.
I did not put on straw, black,   10
Gunny-sack, have not fastened
Grief on shoulder, walked mourning
Behind, pouring grief before him,
Not submitted to his heart.

This then must be enough, salt light   15
For nights, remembering bamboo
And bats cleared in his laughter.
My father's daughter, I pour
No brandy before memory,
But labor, constantly labor,   20
Bearing sunwards grave bitter smoke.

QUESTIONS

1. What is the speaker's relationship to her past and to her Chinese cultural heritage? Was she close to her father? What do the last four lines of the poem imply about her way of honoring her father's memory and her feelings of kinship with him?

2. Write an essay about the importance of rituals in maintaining one's sense of culture and family tradition. Provide examples from rituals practiced in your own culture.

This Place in the Ways

Muriel Rukeyser

Having come to this place
I set out once again
On the dark and marvelous way
From where I began:
Belief in the love of the world,   5
Woman, spirit, and man.

Having failed in all things
I enter a new age
Seeing the old ways as toys,
The houses of a stage   10
Painted and long forgot;
And I find love and rage.

Rage for the world as it is
But for what it may be
More love now than last year.   15
And always less self-pity
Since I know in a clearer light
The strength of the mystery.

And at this place in the ways
I wait for song,   20
My poem-hand still, on the paper,
All night long.
Poems in throat and hand, asleep,
And my storm beating strong!

QUESTIONS

1. How would you describe the "place" to which the speaker has come? What belief does she reaffirm at this stage of her life? What is the "new age" that she feels she is entering? Why does she see the "old ways as toys"? What does she mean by "the strength of the mystery"?

2. Write an essay on life in which you create a series of metaphors or comparisons to describe or explain your sense of several of the major "passages" people go through as they grow older and more experienced.

Drama

Am I Blue

Beth Henley

Journal

*Write about a time during your late adolescence when you felt peer pressure
to participate in an "adultlike" experience. Describe your feelings
about the situation. If you gave in to the peer pressure, discuss how
you felt about what happened.*

CHARACTERS

JOHN POLK   *Seventeen.*
ASHBE   *Sixteen.*
HILDA   *Thirty-five, a waitress.*
STREET CHARACTERS: BARKER, WHORE, BUM, CLAREECE

SETTINGS

A bar, the street, the living room of a run-down apartment

TIME

Fall 1968

The scene opens on a street in the New Orleans French Quarter on a rainy
blue bourbon night. Various people: a whore, bum, street barker, CLAREECE appear and disappear along the street. The scene then focuses on a bar where a
piano is heard from the back room playing softly and indistinctly "Am I Blue?"
The lights go up on JOHN POLK, who sits alone at a table. He is seventeen, a bit
overweight and awkward. He wears nice clothes, perhaps a navy sweater with
large white monograms. His navy raincoat is slung over an empty chair. While
drinking, JOHN POLK concentrates on the red-and-black card that he holds in his
hand. As soon as the scene is established, ASHBE enters from the street. She
is sixteen, wears a flowered plastic rain cap, red galoshes, a butterfly barrette,
and jeweled cat eyeglasses. She is carrying a bag full of stolen goods. Her
hair is very curly. Ashbe makes her way cautiously to JOHN POLK's table. As he
sees her coming, he puts the card into his pocket. She sits in the empty chair
and pulls his raincoat over her head.

ASHBE: Excuse me . . . do you mind if I sit here, please?

JOHN POLK: *(Looks up at her—then down into his glass.)* What are you doing hiding under my raincoat? You're getting it all wet.

ASHBE: Well, I'm very sorry, but after all, it is a raincoat. *(He tries to pull off coat.)* It was rude of me, I know, but look, I just don't want them to recognize me.

JOHN POLK: *(looking about):* Who to recognize you?

ASHBE: Well, I stole these two ashtrays from the Screw Inn, ya know, right down the street. *(She pulls out two glass commercial ashtrays from her white plastic bag.)* Anyway, I'm scared the manager saw me. They'll be after me, I'm afraid.

JOHN POLK: Well, they should be. Look, do you mind giving me back my raincoat? I don't want to be found protecting any thief.

ASHBE: *(coming out from under coat):* Thief—would you call Robin Hood a thief?

JOHN POLK: Christ.

ASHBE: *(back under coat):* No, you wouldn't. He was valiant—all the time stealing from the rich and giving to the poor.

JOHN POLK: But your case isn't exactly the same, is it? You're stealing from some crummy little bar and keeping the ashtrays for yourself. Now give me back my coat.

ASHBE: *(throws coat at him):* Sure, take your old coat. I suppose I should have explained—about Miss Marcey. *(Silence.)* Miss Marcey, this cute old lady with a little hump in her back. I always see her in her sun hat and blue print dress. Miss Marcey lives in the apartment building next to ours. I leave all the stolen goods as gifts on her front steps.

JOHN POLK: Are you one of those kleptomaniacs? *(He starts checking his wallet.)*

ASHBE: You mean when people all the time steal and they can't help it?

JOHN POLK: Yeah.

ASHBE: Oh, no. I'm not a bit careless. Take my job tonight, my very first night job, if you want to know. Anyway, I've been planning it for two months, trying to decipher which bar most deserved to be stolen from. I finally decided on the Screw Inn. Mainly because of the way they're so mean to Mr. Groves. He works at the magazine rack at Diver's Drugstore and is really very sweet, but he has a drinking problem. I don't think that's fair to be mean to people simply because they have a drinking problem—and, well, anyway, you see I'm not just stealing for personal gain. I mean, I don't even smoke.

JOHN POLK: Yeah, well, most infants don't, but then again, most infants don't hang around bars.

ASHBE: I don't see why not, Toulouse Lautrec did.

JOHN POLK: They'd throw me out.

ASHBE: Oh, they throw me out, too, but I don't accept defeat. *(Slowly moves into him.)* Why it's the very same with my pick-pocketing.

(JOHN POLK sneers, turns away.)

It's a very hard art to master. Why, every time I've done it I've been caught.

JOHN POLK: That's all I need is to have some slum kid tell me how good it is to steal. Everyone knows it's not.

ASHBE *(about his drink):* That looks good. What is it?

JOHN POLK: Hey, would you mind leaving me alone—I just wanted to be alone.

ASHBE: Okay. I'm sorry. How about if I'm quiet?

(JOHN POLK shrugs. He sips drink, looks around, catches her eye; she smiles and sighs.)

I was just looking at your pin. What fraternity are you in?

JOHN POLK: SAE.

ASHBE: Is it a good fraternity?

JOHN POLK: Sure, it's the greatest.

ASHBE: I bet you have lots of friends.

JOHN POLK: Tons.

ASHBE: Are you being serious?

JOHN POLK: Yes.

ASHBE: Hmm. Do they have parties and all that?

JOHN POLK: Yeah, lots of parties, booze, honking horns; it's exactly what you would expect.

ASHBE: I wouldn't expect anything. Why did you join?

JOHN POLK: I don't know. Well, my brother—I guess it was my brother—he told me how great it was, how the fraternity was supposed to get you dates, make you study, solve all your problems.

ASHBE: Gee, does it?

JOHN POLK: Doesn't help you study.

ASHBE: How about dates? Do they get you a lot of dates?

JOHN POLK: Some.

ASHBE: What were the girls like?

JOHN POLK: I don't know—they were like girls.

ASHBE: Did you have a good time?

JOHN POLK: I had a pretty good time.

ASHBE: Did you make love to any of them?

JOHN POLK: *(to self):* Oh, Christ—

ASHBE: I'm sorry—I just figured that's why you had the appointment with the whore—'cause you didn't have anyone else—to make love to.

JOHN POLK: How did you know I had the, ah, the appointment?

ASHBE: I saw you put the red card in your pocket when I came up. Those red cards are pretty familiar around here. The house is only about a block or so away. It's one of the best, though, really very plush. Only two murders and a knifing in its whole history. Do you go there often?

JOHN POLK: Yeah, I like to give myself a treat.

ASHBE: Who do you have?

JOHN POLK: What do you mean?

ASHBE: I mean which girl.

(JOHN POLK gazes into his drink.)

Look, I just thought I might know her is all.

JOHN POLK: Know her, ah, how would you know her?

ASHBE: Well, some of the girls from my high school go there to work when they get out.

JOHN POLK: G.G., her name is G.G.

ASHBE: G.G.—Hmm, well, how does she look?

JOHN POLK: I don't know.

ASHBE: Oh, you've never been with her before?

JOHN POLK: No.

ASHBE: *(confidentially):* Are you one of those kinds that likes a lot of variety?

JOHN POLK: Variety? Sure, I guess I like variety.

ASHBE: Oh, yes, now I remember.

JOHN POLK: What?

ASHBE: G.G., that's just her working name. Her real name is Myrtle Reims; she's Kay Reims's older sister. Kay is in my grade at school.

JOHN POLK: Myrtle? Her name is Myrtle?

ASHBE: I never liked the name, either.

JOHN POLK: Myrtle, oh, Christ. Is she pretty?

ASHBE *(matter-of-fact):* Pretty, no she's not real pretty.

JOHN POLK: What does she look like?

ASHBE: Let's see . . . she's, ah, well, Myrtle had acne, and there are a few scars left. It's not bad. I think they sort of give her character. Her hair's red, only I don't think it's really red. It sort of fizzles out all over her head. She's got a pretty good figure—big top—but the rest of her is kind of skinny.

JOHN POLK: I wonder if she has a good personality.

ASHBE: Well, she was a senior when I was a freshman; so I never really knew her. I remember she used to paint her fingernails lots of different colors—pink, orange, purple. I don't know, but she kind of scares me. About the only time I ever saw her true personality was around a year ago. I was over at Kay's making a health poster for school. Anyway, Myrtle comes busting in screaming about how she can't find her spangled bra anywhere. Kay and I just sat on the floor cutting pictures of food out of magazines while she was storming about slamming drawers and swearing. Finally, she found it. It was pretty garish—red with black and gold-sequined G's on each cup. That's how I remember the name—G.G.

(As ASHBE *illustrates the placement of the G's she spots* HILDA, *the waitress, approaching.* ASHBE *pulls the raincoat over her head and hides on the floor.* HILDA *enters through the beaded curtains spilling her tray.* HILDA *is a woman of few words.)*

HILDA: Shit, damn curtain. 'Nuther drink?

JOHN POLK: Ma'am?

HILDA: *(points to drink):* Vodka Coke?

JOHN POLK: No, thank you. I'm not quite finished yet.

HILDA: Napkins clean.

*(*ASHBE *pulls her bag off the table.* HILDA *looks at* ASHBE, *then to* JOHN POLK. *She walks around the table, as* ASHBE *is crawling along the floor to escape.* ASHBE *runs into* HILDA'S *toes.)*

ASHBE: Are those real gold?

HILDA: You again. Out.

ASHBE: She wants me to leave. Why should a paying customer leave? *(Back to* HILDA.*)* Now I'll have a mint julep and easy on the mint.

HILDA: This preteen with you?

JOHN POLK: Well—I—No—I—

HILDA: IDs.

ASHBE: Certainly, I always try to cooperate with the management.

HILDA *(looking at* JOHN POLK's *ID):* ID, 11-12-50. Date 11-11-68.

JOHN POLK: Yes, but—well, 11-12 is less than two hours away.

HILDA: Back in two-hours.

ASHBE: I seem to have left my identification in my gold lamé bag.

HILDA: Well, boo hoo. *(Motions for* ASHBE *to leave with a minimum of effort. She goes back to table.)* No tip.

ASHBE: You didn't tip her?

JOHN POLK: I figured the drinks were so expensive—I just didn't—

HILDA: No tip!

JOHN POLK: Look, miss, I'm sorry. *(Going through his pockets.)* Here, would you like a—a nickel—wait, wait here's a quarter.

HILDA: Just move ass, sonny. You, too, Barbie.

ASHBE: Ugh, I hate public rudeness. I'm sure I'll refrain from ever coming here again.

HILDA: Think I'll go in the back room and cry. *(*ASHBE *and* JOHN POLK *exit.* HILDA *picks up tray and exits through the curtain, tripping again.)* Shit. Damn curtain.

*(*ASHBE *and* JOHN POLK *are now standing outside under the awning of the bar.)*

ASHBE: Gee, I didn't know it was your birthday tomorrow. Happy birthday! Don't be mad. I thought you were at least twenty or twenty-one, really.

JOHN POLK: It's okay. Forget it.

ASHBE: *(As they begin walking, various blues are heard coming from the nearby bars):* It's raining.

JOHN POLK: I know.

ASHBE: Are you going over to the house now?

JOHN POLK: No, not till twelve.

ASHBE: Yeah, the pink-and-black cards—they mean all night. Midnight till morning. *(At this point a street barker beckons the couple into his establishment. Perhaps he is accompanied by a whore.)*

BARKER: Hey, mister, bring your baby on in, buy her a few drinks, maybe tonight ya get lucky.

ASHBE: Keep walking.

JOHN POLK: What's wrong with the place?

ASHBE: The drinks are watery rotgut, and the show girls are boys.

BARKER: Up yours, punk!

JOHN POLK *(who has now sat down on a street bench):* Look, just tell me where a cheap bar is. I've got to stay drunk, but I don't have much money left.

ASHBE: Yikes, there aren't too many cheap bars around here, and a lot of them check IDs.

JOHN POLK: Well, do you know of any that don't?

ASHBE: No, not for sure.

JOHN POLK: Oh, God, I need to get drunk.

ASHBE: Aren't you?

JOHN POLK: Some, but I'm losing ground fast. *(By this time a bum who has been traveling drunkenly down the street falls near the couple and begins throwing up.)*

ASHBE: Oh, I know! You can come to my apartment. It's just down the block. We keep one bottle of rum around. I'll serve you a grand drink, three or four if you like.

JOHN POLK *(fretfully):* No, thanks.

ASHBE: But look, we're getting all wet.

JOHN POLK: Sober, too, wet and sober.

ASHBE: Oh, come on! Rain's blurring my glasses.

JOHN POLK: Well, how about your parents? What would they say?

ASHBE: Daddy's out of town and Mama lives in Atlanta; so I'm sure they won't mind. I think we have some cute little marshmallows. *(Pulling on him.)* Won't you really come?

JOHN POLK: You've probably got some gang of muggers waiting to kill me. Oh, all right—what the hell, let's go.

ASHBE: Hurrah! Come on. It's this way. *(She starts across the stage, stops, and picks up an old hat.)* Hey look at this hat. Isn't it something! Here, wear it to keep off the rain.

JOHN POLK *(throwing hat back onto street):* No, thanks, you don't know who's worn it before.

ASHBE *(picking hat back up):* That makes it all the more exciting. Maybe it was a butcher's who slaughtered his wife or a silver pirate with a black bird on his throat. Who do you guess?

JOHN POLK: I don't know. Anyway, what's the good of guessing? I mean, you'll never really know.

ASHBE *(trying the hat on):* Yeah, probably not. *(At this point,* ASHBE *and* JOHN POLK *reach the front door.)* Here we are. *(*ASHBE *begins fumbling for her key.* CLAREECE, *a teeny-bopper, walks up to* JOHN POLK.*)*

CLAREECE: Hey, man, got any spare change?

JOHN POLK *(looking through his pockets):* Let me see—I—

ASHBE *(coming up between them, giving* CLAREECE *a shove):* Beat it, Clareece. He's my company.

CLAREECE *(walks away and sneers):* Oh, shove it, Frizzels.

ASHBE: A lot of jerks live around here. Come on in. *(She opens the door. Lights go up on the living room of a run-down apartment in a run-down apartment house. Besides being merely run-down, the room is a malicious pigsty with colors, paper hats, paper dolls, masks, torn-up stuffed animals, dead flowers and leaves, dress-up clothes, etc., thrown all about.)* My bones are cold. Do you want a towel to dry off?

JOHN POLK: Yes, thank you.

ASHBE: *(She picks a towel up off of the floor and tosses it to him.)* **Here.** *(He begins drying off as she takes off her rain things; then she begins raking things off the sofa.)* Please do sit down. *(He sits.)* I'm sorry the place is disheveled, but my father's been out of town. I always try to pick up and all before he gets in. Of course he's pretty used to messes. My mother never was too good at keeping things clean.

JOHN POLK: When's he coming back?

ASHBE: Sunday, I believe. Oh, I've been meaning to say—

JOHN POLK: What?

ASHBE: My name's Ashbe Williams.

JOHN POLK: Ashbe?

ASHBE: Yeah, Ashbe.

JOHN POLK: My name's John Polk Richards.

ASHBE: John Polk? They call you John Polk?

JOHN POLK: It's family.

ASHBE *(putting on socks):* These are my favorite socks, the red furry ones. Well, here's some books and magazines to look at while I fix you something to drink. What do you want in your rum?

JOHN POLK: Coke's fine.

ASHBE: I'll see do we have any. I think I'll take some hot Kool-Aid myself. *(She exits to the kitchen.)*

JOHN POLK: Hot Kool-Aid?

ASHBE: It's just Kool-Aid that's been heated, like hot chocolate or hot tea.

JOHN POLK: Sounds great.

ASHBE: Well, I'm used to it. You get so much for your dime it makes it worth your while. I don't buy presweetened, of course, it's better to sugar your own.

JOHN POLK: I remember once I threw up a lot of grape Kool-Aid when I was a kid. I've hated it ever since. Hey, would you check on the time?

ASHBE: *(She enters carrying a tray with several bottles of food coloring, a bottle of rum, and a huge glass.)* I'm sorry we don't have Cokes. I wonder if rum and Kool-Aid is good? Oh, we don't have a clock, either. *(She pours a large amount of rum into the large glass.)*

JOHN POLK: I'll just have it with water, then.

ASHBE: *(She finds an almost empty glass of water somewhere in the room and dumps it in with the rum.)* Would you like food coloring in the water? It makes a drink all the more aesthetic. Of course, some people don't care for aesthetics.

JOHN POLK: No, thank you, just plain water.

ASHBE: Are you sure? The taste is entirely the same. I put it in all my water.

JOHN POLK: Well—

ASHBE: What color do you want?

JOHN POLK: I don't know.

ASHBE: What's your favorite color?

JOHN POLK: Blue, I guess. *(She puts a few blue drops into the glass—as she has nothing to stir with, she blows into the glass, turning the water blue.)* **Thanks.**

ASHBE: *(Exits. She screams from kitchen.)* Come on, say come on, cat, eat your fresh good milk.

JOHN POLK: You have a cat?

ASHBE *(off):* No.

JOHN POLK: Oh.

ASHBE: *(She enters carrying a tray with a cup of hot Kool-Aid and Cheerios and colored marshmallows.)* Here are some Cheerios and some cute little colored marshmallows to eat with your drink.

JOHN POLK: Thanks.

ASHBE: I one time smashed all the big white marshmallows in the plastic bag at the grocery store.

JOHN POLK: Why did you do that?

ASHBE: I was angry. Do you like ceramics?

JOHN POLK: Yes.

ASHBE: My mother makes them. It's sort of her hobby. She is very talented.

JOHN POLK: My mother never does anything. Well, I guess she can shuffle the bridge deck okay.

ASHBE: Actually, my mother is a dancer. She teaches at a school in Atlanta. She's really very talented.

JOHN POLK *(indicates ceramics):* She must be to do all these.

ASHBE: Well, Madeline, my older sister, did the blue one. Madeline gets to live with Mama.

JOHN POLK: And you live with your father.

ASHBE: Yeah, but I get to go visit them sometimes.

JOHN POLK: You do ceramics, too?

ASHBE: No, I never learned . . . but I have this great pot holder set. *(Gets up to show him.)* See I make lots of multicolored pot holders and sent them to Mama and Madeline. I also make paper hats. *(Gets material to show him.)* I guess they're more creative, but making pot holders is more relaxing. Here, would you like to make a hat?

JOHN POLK: I don't know, I'm a little drunk.

ASHBE: It's not hard a bit. *(Hands him material.)* Just draw a real pretty design on the paper. It really doesn't have to be pretty, just whatever you want.

JOHN POLK: It's kind of you to give my creative drives such freedom.

ASHBE: Ha, ha, ha, I'll work on my pot holder set a bit.

JOHN POLK: What time is it? I've really got to check on the time.

ASHBE: I know. I'll call the time operator. *(She goes to the phone.)*

JOHN POLK: How do you get along without a clock?

ASHBE Well, I've been late for school a lot. Daddy has a watch. It's 11:03.

JOHN POLK: I've got a while yet.

ASHBE *(twirls back to her chair, drops, and sighs)*

JOHN POLK: Are you a dancer, too?

ASHBE *(delighted):* I can't dance a bit, really. I practice a lot is all, at home in the afternoon. I imagine you go to a lot of dances.

JOHN POLK: Not really, I'm a terrible dancer. I usually get bored or drunk.

ASHBE: You probably drink too much.

JOHN POLK: No, it's just since I've come to college. All you do there is drink more beer and write more papers.

ASHBE: What are you studying for to be?

JOHN POLK: I don't know.

ASHBE: Why don't you become a rancher?

JOHN POLK: Dad wants me to help run his soybean farm.

ASHBE: Soybean farm. Yikes, that's really something. Where is it?

JOHN POLK: Well, I live in the Delta, Hollybluff, Mississippi. Anyway, Dad feels I should go to business school first; you know, so I'll become, well, management minded. Pass the blue.

ASHBE: Is that what you really want to do?

JOHN POLK: I don't know. It would probably be as good as anything else I could do. Dad makes good money. He can take vacations whenever he wants. Sure it'll be a ball.

ASHBE: I'd hate to have to be management minded. (JOHN POLK *shrugs.*) I don't mean to hurt your feelings, but I would really hate to be a management mind. (*She starts walking on her knees, twisting her fists in front of her eyes, and making clicking sounds as a management mind would make.*)

JOHN POLK: Cut it out. Just forget it. The farm could burn down and I wouldn't even have to think about it.

ASHBE (*after a pause*): Well, what do you want to talk about?

JOHN POLK: I don't know.

ASHBE: When was the last dance you went to?

JOHN POLK: Dances. That's a great subject. Let's see, oh, I don't really remember. It was probably some blind date. God, I hate dates.

ASHBE: Why?

JOHN POLK: Well, they always say that they don't want popcorn and they wind up eating all of yours.

ASHBE: You mean, you hate dates just because they eat your popcorn? Don't you think that's kind of stingy?

JOHN POLK: It's the principle of the thing. Why can't they just say, yes, I'd like some popcorn when you ask them. But, no, they're always so damn coy.

ASHBE: I'd tell my date if I wanted popcorn. I'm not that immature.

JOHN POLK: Anyway, it's not only the popcorn. It's a lot of little things. I've finished coloring. What do I do now?

ASHBE: Now you have to fold it. Here . . . . like this. (*She explains the process with relish.*) Say, that's really something.

JOHN POLK: It's kind of funny looking. (*Putting the hat on.*) Yeah, I like it, but you could never wear it anywhere.

ASHBE: Well, like what, anyway?

JOHN POLK: Huh?

ASHBE: The things dates do to you that you don't like, the little things.

JOHN POLK: Oh, well just the way they wear those false eyelashes and put their hand on your knee when you're trying to parallel park and keep on giggling and going off to the bathroom with their girlfriends. It's obvious they don't want to go out with me. They just want to go out so that they can wear their new clothes and won't have to sit on their ass in the dormitory. They never want to go out with me. I can never even talk to them.

ASHBE: Well, you can talk to me and I'm a girl.

JOHN POLK: Well, I'm really kind of drunk and you're a stranger . . . Well, I probably wouldn't be able to talk to you tomorrow. That makes a difference.

ASHBE: Maybe it does. *(A bit of a pause, and then, extremely pleased by the idea, she says.)* You know we're alike because I don't like dances, either.

JOHN POLK: I thought you said you practiced . . . in the afternoons.

ASHBE: Well, I like dancing. I just don't like dances. At least not like—well, not like the one our school was having tonight. . . . They're so corny.

JOHN POLK: Yeah, most dances are.

ASHBE: All they serve is potato chips and fruit punch, and then this stupid baby band plays and everybody dances around thinking they're so hot. I frankly wouldn't dance there. I would prefer to wait till I am invited to an exclusive ball. It doesn't really matter which ball, just one where they have huge golden chandeliers and silver fountains and serve delicacies of all sorts and bubble blue champagne. I'll arrive in a pink silk cape. *(Laughing.)* I want to dance in pink!

JOHN POLK: You're mixed up. You're probably one of those people that live in a fantasy world.

ASHBE: I do not. I accept reality as well as anyone. Anyway, you can talk to me, remember. I know what you mean by the kind of girls it's hard to talk to. There are girls a lot that way in the small clique at my school. Really tacky and mean. They expect everyone to be as stylish as they are, and they won't even speak to you in the hall. I don't mind if they don't speak to me, but I really love the orphans, and it hurts my feelings when they are so mean to them.

JOHN POLK: What do you mean—they're mean to the orpheens? *(Notices pun and giggles to self.)*

ASHBE: Oh, well, they sometimes snicker at the orphans' dresses. The orphans usually have hand-me-down, drab, ugly dresses. Once Shelly Maxwell wouldn't let Glinda borrow her pencil, even though she had two. It hurt her feelings.

JOHN POLK: Are you best friends with these orphans?

ASHBE: I hardly know them at all. They're really shy. I just like them a lot. They're the reason I put spells on the girls in the clique.

JOHN POLK: Spells, what do you mean, witch spells?

ASHBE: Witch spells? Not really, mostly just voodoo.

JOHN POLK: Are you kidding? Do you really do voodoo?

ASHBE: Sure, here I'll show you my doll. *(Goes to get doll, comes back with straw voodoo doll. Her air as she returns is one of frightening mystery.)* I know a lot about the subject. Cora she used to wash dishes in the Moonlight Café, told me all about voodoo. She's a real expert on the subject, went to all the meetings and everything. Once she caused a man's throat to rot away and turn almost totally black. She's moved to Chicago now.

JOHN POLK: It doesn't really work. Does it?

ASHBE: Well, not always. The thing about voodoo is that both parties have to believe in it for it to work.

JOHN POLK: Do the girls in school believe in it?

ASHBE: Not really; I don't think. That's where my main problem comes in. I have to make the clique believe in it, yet I have to be very subtle. Mainly, I give reports in English class or Speech.

JOHN POLK: Reports?

ASHBE: On voodoo.

JOHN POLK: That's really kind of sick, you know.

ASHBE: Not really. I don't cast spells that'll do any real harm. Mainly, just the kind of thing to make them think—to keep them on their toes. *(Blue drink intoxication begins to take over and* JOHN POLK *begins laughing.)* What's so funny?

JOHN POLK: Nothing. I was just thinking what a mean little person you are.

ASHBE: Mean! I'm not mean a bit.

JOHN POLK: Yes, you are mean— *(Picking up color.)* and green, too.

ASHBE: Green?

JOHN POLK: Yes, green with envy of those other girls; so you play all those mean little tricks.

ASHBE: Envious of those other girls, that stupid, close-minded little clique!

JOHN POLK: Green as this marshmallow. *(Eats marshmallow.)*

ASHBE: You think I want to be in some group . . . a sheep like you? A little sheep like you that does everything when he's supposed to do it!

JOHN POLK: Me a sheep—I do what I want!

ASHBE: Ha! I've known you for an hour and already I see you for the sheep you are!

JOHN POLK: Don't take your green meanness out on me.

ASHBE: Not only are you a sheep, you are a *normal* sheep. Give me back my colors! *(Begins snatching colors away.)*

JOHN POLK *(pushing colors at her):* Green and mean! Green and mean! Green and mean! Et cetera.

ASHBE *(throwing marshmallows at him):* That's the reason you're in a fraternity and the reason you're going to manage your mind, and dates—you go out on dates merely because it's expected of you even though you have a terrible time. That's the reason you go to the whorehouse to prove you're a normal man. Well, you're much too normal for me.

JOHN POLK: Infant bitch. You think you're really cute.

ASHBE: That really wasn't food coloring in your drink, it was poison! *(She laughs, he picks up his coat to go, and she stops throwing marshmallows at him.)* Are you going? I was only kidding. For Christ sake, it wasn't really poison. Come on, don't go. Can't you take a little friendly criticism?

JOHN POLK: Look, did you have to bother me tonight? I had enough problems without— *(Phone rings. Both look at phone; it rings for the third time. He stands undecided.)*

ASHBE: Look, wait, we'll make it up. *(She goes to answer phone.)* Hello—Daddy. How are you? . . . I'm fine . . . Dad, you sound funny . . . what? . . . Come on, Daddy, you know she's not here. *(Pause.)* Look, I told you I wouldn't call anymore. You've got her number in Atlanta. *(Pause, as she sinks to the floor.)* Why have you started again? . . . Don't say that. I can tell it. I can. Hey, I have to go to bed now, I don't want to talk anymore, okay? *(Hangs up phone, softly to self.)* Goddamnit.

JOHN POLK: *(He has heard the conversation and is taking off his coat.)* Hey, Ashbe— *(She looks at him blankly, her mind far away.)* You want to talk?

ASHBE: No. *(Slight pause.)* Why don't you look at my shell collection? I have this special shell collection. *(She shows him collection.)*

JOHN POLK: They're beautiful, I've never seen colors like this. *(ASHBE is silent, he continues to himself.)* I used to go to Biloxi a lot when I was a kid . . . one time my brother and I, we camped out on the beach. The sky was purple. I remember it was really purple. We ate pork and beans out of a can. I'd always kinda wanted to do that. Every night for about a week after I got home, I dreamt about these waves foaming over my head and face. It was funny. Did you find these shells or buy them?

ASHBE: Some I found, some I bought. I've been trying to decipher their meaning. Here, listen, do you hear that?

JOHN POLK: Yes.

ASHBE: That's the soul of the sea. *(She listens.)* I'm pretty sure it's the soul of the sea. Just imagine when I decipher the language. I'll know all the secrets of the world.

JOHN POLK: Yeah, probably you will. *(Looking into the shell.)* You know, you were right.

ASHBE: What do you mean?

JOHN POLK: About me, you were right. I am a sheep, a normal one. I've been trying to get out of it, but now I'm as big a sheep as ever.

ASHBE: Oh, it doesn't matter. You're company. It was rude of me to say.

JOHN POLK: No, because it was true. I really didn't want to go into a fraternity, I didn't even want to go to college, and I sure as hell don't want to go back to Hollybluff and work the soybean farm till I'm eighty.

ASHBE: I still say you could work on a ranch.

JOHN POLK: I don't know. I wanted to be a minister or something good, but I don't even know if I believe in God.

ASHBE: Yeah.

JOHN POLK: I never used to worry about being a failure. Now I think about it all the time. It's just I need to do something that's—fulfilling.

ASHBE: Fulfilling, yes, I see what you mean. Well, how about college? Isn't it fulfilling? I mean, you take all those wonderful classes, and you have all your very good friends.

JOHN POLK: Friends, yeah, I have some friends.

ASHBE: What do you mean?

JOHN POLK: Nothing—well, I do mean something. What the hell, let me try to explain. You see it was my "friends," the fraternity guys that set me up with G.G., excuse me, Myrtle, as a gift for my eighteenth birthday.

ASHBE: You mean, you didn't want the appointment?

JOHN POLK: No, I didn't want it. Hey, ah, where did my blue drink go?

ASHBE (as she hands him the drink): They probably thought you really wanted to go.

JOHN POLK: Yeah, I'm sure they gave a damn what I wanted. They never even asked me. Hell, I would have told them a handkerchief, a pair of argyle socks, but, no, they have to get me a whore just because it's a cool-ass thing to do. They make me sick. I couldn't even stay at the party they gave. All the sweaty T-shirts and moron sex stories—I just couldn't take it.

ASHBE: Is that why you were at the Blue Angel so early?

JOHN POLK: Yeah, I needed to get drunk, but not with them. They're such creeps.

ASHBE: Gosh, so you really don't want to go to Myrtle's?

JOHN POLK: No, I guess not.

ASHBE: Then are you going?

JOHN POLK (pause): Yes.

ASHBE: That's wrong. You shouldn't go just to please them.

JOHN POLK: Oh, that's not the point anymore; maybe at first it was, but it's not anymore. Now I have to go for myself—to prove to myself that I'm not afraid.

ASHBE: Afraid? (Slowly, as she begins to grasp his meaning.) You mean, you've never slept with a girl before?

JOHN POLK: Well, I've never been in love.

ASHBE (in amazement): You're a virgin?

JOHN POLK: Oh, God.

ASHBE: No, don't feel bad, I am, too.

JOHN POLK: I thought I should be in love—

ASHBE: Well, you're certainly not in love with Myrtle. I mean, you haven't even met her.

JOHN POLK: I know, but, God, I thought maybe I'd never fall in love. What then? You should experience everything—shouldn't you? Oh, what's it matter, everything's so screwed.

ASHBE: Screwed? Yeah, I guess it is. I mean, I always thought it would be fun to have a lot of friends who gave parties and go to dances all dressed up. Like the dance tonight—it might have been fun.

JOHN POLK: Well, why didn't you go?

ASHBE: I don't know. I'm not sure it would have been fun. Anyway, you can't go—alone.

JOHN POLK: Oh, you need a date?

ASHBE: Yeah, or something.

JOHN POLK: Say, Ashbe, ya wanna dance here?

ASHBE: No, I think we'd better discuss your dilemma.

JOHN POLK: What dilemma?

ASHBE: Myrtle. It doesn't seem right you should—

JOHN POLK: Let's forget Myrtle for now. I've got a while yet. Here, have some more of this blue-moon drink.

ASHBE: You're only trying to escape through artificial means.

JOHN POLK: Yeah, you got it. Now, come on. Would you like to dance? Hey, you said you liked to dance.

ASHBE: You're being ridiculous.

JOHN POLK *(winking at her)*: Dance?

ASHBE: John Polk, I just thought—

JOHN POLK: Hmm?

ASHBE: How to solve your problem—

JOHN POLK: Well—

ASHBE: Make love to me!

JOHN POLK: What?!

ASHBE: It all seems logical to me. It would prove you weren't scared, and you wouldn't be doing it just to impress others.

JOHN POLK: Look, I—I mean I hardly know you—

ASHBE: But we've talked. It's better this way, really. I won't be so apt to point out your mistakes.

JOHN POLK: I'd feel great stripping a twelve-year-old of her virginity.

ASHBE: I'm sixteen! Anyway, I'd be stripping you of yours just as well. I'll go put on some Tiger Claw perfume. *(She runs out.)*

JOHN POLK: Hey, come back! Tiger Claw perfume, Christ.

ASHBE *(entering)*: I think one should have different scents for different moods.

JOHN POLK: Hey, stop spraying that! You know I'm not going to—well, you'd get neurotic or pregnant or some damn thing. Stop spraying, will you!

ASHBE: Pregnant? You really think I could get pregnant?

JOHN POLK: Sure, it'd be a delightful possibility.

ASHBE: It really wouldn't be bad. Maybe I would get to go to Tokyo for an abortion. I've never been to the Orient.

JOHN POLK: Sure, getting cut on is always a real treat.

ASHBE: Anyway, I might just want to have my dear baby. I could move to Atlanta with Mama and Madeline. It'd be wonderful fun. Why, I could take him to the supermarket, put him in one of those little baby seats to stroll him about. I'd buy peach baby food and feed it to him with a tiny golden spoon. Why, I could take colored pictures of him and send them to you through the mail. Come on— *(Starts putting pillows onto the couch.)* Well, I guess you should kiss me for a start. It's only etiquette; everyone begins with it.

JOHN POLK: I don't think I could even kiss you with a clear conscience. I mean, you're so small, with those little cat-eye glasses and curly hair—I couldn't even kiss you.

ASHBE: You couldn't even kiss me? I can't help it if I have to wear glasses. I got the prettiest ones I could find.

JOHN POLK: Your glasses are fine. Let's forget it, okay?

ASHBE: I know, my lips are too purple, but if I eat carrots, the dye'll come off and they'll be orange.

JOHN POLK: I didn't say anything about your lips being too purple.

ASHBE: Well, what is it? You're just plain chicken, I suppose—

JOHN POLK: Sure, right, I'm chicken, totally chicken. Let's forget it. I don't know how, but somehow this is probably all my fault.

ASHBE: You're darn right it's all your fault! I want to have my dear baby or at least get to Japan. I'm so sick of school I could smash every marshmallow in sight! *(She starts smashing.)* Go on to your skinny pimple whore. I hope the skinny whore laughs in your face, which she probably will because you have an easy face to laugh in.

JOHN POLK: You're absolutely right; she'll probably hoot and howl her damn fizzle red head off. Maybe you can wait outside the door and hear her, give you lots of pleasure, you sadistic little thief.

ASHBE: Thief—was Robin Hood—Oh, what's wrong with this world? I just wasn't made for it is all. I've probably been put in the wrong world, I can see that now.

JOHN POLK: You're fine in this world.

ASHBE: Sure, everyone just views me as an undesirable lump.

JOHN POLK: Who?

ASHBE: You for one.

JOHN POLK *(pause):* You mean because I wouldn't make love to you?

ASHBE: It seems clear to me.

JOHN POLK: But you're wrong, you know.

ASHBE *(to self, softly):* Don't pity me.

JOHN POLK: The reason I wouldn't wasn't that—it's just that—well, I like you too much to.

ASHBE: You like me?

JOHN POLK: Undesirable lump, Jesus. Your cheeks, they're—they're—

ASHBE: My cheeks? They're what?

JOHN POLK: They're rosy.

ASHBE: My cheeks are rosy?

JOHN POLK: Yeah, your cheeks, they're really rosy.

ASHBE: Well, they're natural, you know. Say, would you like to dance?

JOHN POLK: Yes.

ASHBE: I'll turn on the radio. *(She turns on radio. Ethel Waters is heard singing "Honey in the Honeycomb." ASHBE begins snapping her fingers.)* Yikes, let's jazz it out. *(They dance.)*

JOHN POLK: Hey, I'm not good or anything—

ASHBE: John Polk.

JOHN POLK: Yeah?

ASHBE: Baby, I think you dance fine! *(They dance on, laughing, saying what they want till end of song. Then a radio announcer comes on and says the 12:00 news will be in five minutes. Billie Holiday or Terry Pierce begins singing, "Am I Blue?")*

JOHN POLK: Dance?

ASHBE: News in five minutes.

JOHN POLK: Yeah.

ASHBE: That means five minutes till midnight.

JOHN POLK: Yeah, I know.

ASHBE: Then you're not—

JOHN POLK: Ashbe, I've never danced all night. Wouldn't it be something to—to dance all night and watch the rats come out of the gutter?

ASHBE: Rats?

JOHN POLK: Don't they come out at night? I hear New Orleans has lots of rats.

ASHBE: Yeah, yeah, it's got lots of rats.

JOHN POLK: Then let's dance all night and wait for them to come out.

ASHBE: All right—but, but how about our feet?

JOHN POLK: Feet?

ASHBE: They'll hurt.

JOHN POLK: Yeah.

ASHBE *(smiling):* Okay, then let's dance. *(He takes her hand, and they dance as lights black out and the music soars and continues to play.)*

QUESTIONS AND CONSIDERATIONS

1. Describe the main characters in the play, John and Ashbe. What crisis is each experiencing? Why is the age of the characters especially relevant in interpreting and evaluating their dilemmas and conflicts?

2. Did you find it easy to identify with these characters? Why or why not?

3. What situations described in the play suggest that the main characters are going through an initiation into adulthood?

4. Henley uses color to create the meanings and mood of the play. Interpret the title, "Am I Blue," the blue of John's drinks and clothing, his red and black card, the green of Ashbe's marshmallow, and the multiple colors of Ashbe's shells, ceramics, and potholders. Can you think of other color details that emphasize meanings in the play? How do the contrasting colors in the play help to define characters and clarify the play's central theme and mood?

5. How is the 1968 New Orleans French Quarter and the associations most people have with this area and time period used to underscore the events of the play? If the play were set elsewhere or in a different time period, would it have a different impact on you?

6. Why are John and Ashbe drawn to one another? Try to imagine what their lives will be like when they are in their early twenties.

7. The play explores a number of controversial types of behavior: theft, prostitution, underage drinking, abortion. What is the play's perspective on the central characters' involvement in these types of behavior and on how these issues impact on the lives of today's adolescents? Do you find your own views on these issues reflected in the play?

IDEAS FOR WRITING

1. Write another scene for the play, in dramatic or story form, in which you continue or resolve the relationship that has developed between the two characters.

2. Imagine that you are writing a letter to John or Ashbe. What advice would you give to help John or Ashbe through the crisis he or she is experiencing? You might share related experiences of your own that you have managed to get through successfully.

Student Writing

Jennifer Angel, from Tucson, Arizona, and Amanda Beacom of Visalia, California, were students in an introductory composition class when they read Tillie Olsen's "I Stand Here Ironing." Both students responded strongly to the text, but in different ways. Jennifer Angel identified more with the daughter, Emily, while Amanda Beacom, whose parents are high school teachers, related more strongly with the school counselor who is concerned about Emily's promise and achievement. Thus, when both students had the opportunity to retell the story from another narrative viewpoint, Angel chose to write using Emily's voice, and Beacom's response took the form of a "Letter to a Mother" from a concerned school counselor who genuinely wanted to help Emily. As you read the two essays, ask yourself how each each student attempts to capture an accurate sense of the dilemma that exists within the original story, and how the responses in the voices of characters seem to fit into the world created by Olsen while providing some thoughtful alternatives to the sense of limits and entrapment perceived by the mother who narrates "I Stand Here Ironing."

"The Shadow in the Spotlight"
Jennifer Angel

Suddenly, I was on stage. That eighth grade talent show in which I satirized all the teachers made me Emily Olsen. I recall my nervousness as I hunched my shoulders and wrinkled my nose to become Mr. Spear, croaking out the answers to imaginary math problems. I remember it wasn't long before the crowd was laughing, and my initial fear dissolved in the triumph of confidence. I had never felt so much pride in myself. My astonishment at the reception of the audience was magnified by the fact that they were strangers. I did not know them and yet I could make them smile. It seemed ironic that all my life, and still, although maybe just a little bit now, I could never give that same happiness, that gem of laughter to my loved ones. I could never get this kind of response, this understanding of me, Emily, from my own Mother.

Mother was always melancholy. Emerging from the kitchen with a cheese sandwich in my hand one Friday afternoon after school, I found her at the bottom of the stairs with a dustrag in her hand, staring listlessly into the hallway. Her eyes were red and her face pale with fatigue. I could only take the rag from her and finish going over the banister in silence. I did not understand Mother's plaintive moods.

"I forgot to pick up Susan from school for the doctor's appointment," she whispered. "When will it get done, now that the car's in the shop until Tuesday? When will I ever get Ronnie off the waiting list for that afterschool playtime so I can work the afternoon shift?"

Mother's head turned towards the kitchen as the potatoes boiled over, calling her back to work. The boiling water dripped into the flames and made them sizzle orange. "Emily?," her voice suggested that I see the dinner, so I dropped the rag on the stair and bounced into the kitchen, trying to be as enthusiastic as possible. After seeing to the potatoes, I opened the stove to check the roast and got a blast of hot air in my face. I was reminded of the hot, aching fever that left me in bed all those weeks while I was growing up, battling red measles and the flu.

Even now, Mother thinks of me as this frail creature who can't be cured. I had an awful fever last spring and Mother thought I was going to die, or at least be swept up by a wind and blown out a window. She complained about chills, and made sure every door and window were shut so tight there was hardly any fresh air left to breathe in the house. Because Susan had left the kitchen door open a minute as she was taking out the trash, Mother's brow wrinkled and her body stiffened with suppressed frustration for hours when my fever increased that night. Mother wouldn't leave my side for a minute. She didn't work all that week. I tried to explain to her through my half-stupor how silly it was that she should stay. I even mustered the energy to get agitated enough to have her stonily exit the room. I told her I was fine--"no chicken soup just now, Mother, please, just leave me alone"--and she got all rubbed the wrong way. She couldn't look me in the eye for a day. She never smiled and her eyes were vacant with apology. She didn't know that one

smile from her would have brought me back in about half the time
it took all that wives' tale chicken soup.

It was as a child that I needed Mother's love and concern.
It was in the Institute when I was not allowed even a teddy
bear, and missed so much the occasional bedtime kiss that Mother
used to give when I was sick in bed at home. Now overridden with
guilt, Mother tries to make up for those years. It's too late
for that. And I am not bitter for it. All I need now is for
mother to stop ironing a minute and see how her little, sickly
firstborn has grown into a strong woman.

Mother lives so much in the past. But just because there
was no hope for me then tells nothing of the future. Why is it I
can turn frowns to smiles, but not Mother's? I want to shake her
from her fantastical dreams: "I forgive you Mother! All hope is
not lost for your lanky, dark firstborn who was never Student of
the Month or Prom Queen!"

Just yesterday, I spoke to her about my going to college
after I work for a couple of years. She nodded her head, "My
Emily," she murmured. I cherished the tinge of pride in that
moment, in which what I thought would be her usual astonishment
at my aspirations was brushed aside. "Mother," I wanted to
implore her, "I do need your help." But I am patient for now.
Mother has all the right intentions, I know. Someday, she will
be jarred from her guilty past and share in my expectations for
the future.

"Letter to a Mother"
Amanda Beacom

From your silence I gather you doubt my sincerity or my
ability to help. Having received no indication that you plan to
act upon our telephone conversation of two weeks ago, I write
this letter to reiterate my message and convince you of its
worth. <u>I wish you would manage the time to come in and talk with
me about your daughter.</u>*

Emily seems to be swimming with her head above water now.
She walks into my office with a lighter step and a less furrowed
brow than that which I remember at the beginning of the school
year, and she speaks with enthusiasm of her budding talent as a
comedian. You notice these changes too. Perhaps you believe that
now the worst is over, or that with her goodbye to girlhood
comes your cue as mother to let go, to bow out from your
starring role in her life.

---

* Underscored sentence taken directly from the short story.

Neither I, nor the social institution that employs me, can tell you how to be a mother. But as a high school counselor, I can show you statistics compiled from the caseloads of other social workers, statistics which measure the success rates of students with poor study skills and attendance records; the percentage of welfare children who become welfare parents; the numbers of teenage mothers whose own mother gave birth to her before the age of 20. Drawing from my own files, I can cite case after case of students who failed to graduate from high school, sons whose dreams of transforming their childhood talent into a career in professional sports never materialized, daughters whose fleeting passion burnt out far too quickly.

What if Emily becomes pregnant at age 19? What if she must find low-paying work to support her child? What if she must put aside her promise as a performance artist? For Emily, perhaps the worst is over. But what if it's not? I want to help her, to provide a base of support for her and show her all her options.

Please help me. Encourage Emily to go to school regularly; she cannot hope to achieve a sense of stability if her attendance in class depends upon her whims and insecurities on a particular day. Your daughter is blessed with intelligence and a quick wit, but teachers who notice her ability in the initial assignments she completes tend to forget their positive first impressions when she exhibits the traits of inconsistency common to a "problem" student. Rather than receiving the praise her creative ideas could bring, she hears reprimands of her poor study skills and falls into a self-defeating circle of sporadic attendance, negative response from authority figures, low self-esteem, and thus worsening attendance habits.

Secondly, let me enroll Emily in a peer-counseling program. Ease her chores at home so that she can make the time to meet with an individual her own age after school--someone who will provide advice, sympathy, and encouragement; someone who will ground her in the reality of present school commitments and potential career opportunities. Allow Emily the chance to know someone to whom she can relate and in whom she may find a friend.

Lastly, and perhaps most importantly, join me in planning for your daughter's future. I have suggested to Emily that she apply to one of the several art institutes in this state; scholarship money is available for budding young performers in need of financial aid. I want to build upon her present success, and while I cannot guarantee that this effort will bear fruit, the application process in itself will cause her to think seriously about her present course in life and its relationship to where she wants to be several years from now. With your encouragement of this effort, we can open a window to her future. I do not want your daughter to become another statistic.

When you make your decision about my proposals in this letter, please consider one final point. After reviewing my

notes from Emily's file, I can guess at the reasons behind your
lack of response to my overtures. Barely beyond breast-feeding
at age two, Social Service recommended her as ready for the
impersonal, intimidating world of nursery school. Then they sent
her skeleton-thin to a convalescent home, from which she
returned even thinner, even more withdrawn. And throughout
Public School, teachers passed over her quiet presence or
assumed her reticence indicated stupidity. Now, as Social
Service quickly approaches the point at which its moral
obligation to Emily ends--having achieved nothing except perhaps
a negative impact upon the quality of her life--it solicits one
last chance to provide assistance.

     I offer no excuses for the past wrongs Emily suffered from
the "helping" hand of government programs. If in the future she
fulfills the prophecy of my statistics, both mother and
institution will share the blame. But must we chain ourselves
helplessly to the past when the opportunity remains to make a
positive impact upon the future? You may believe that it's too
late to reach out to your daughter, but must you impose the same
mentality upon others who wish to help? Please facilitate this
effort to right a wrong. After all, just as perfect parenting is
not always possible for a mother overburdened by work and
children, perfect social service is not always possible for a
system overburdened by obligations and responsibilities. My
efforts may prove unsuccessful, but I want to try.

Connections: Ideas for Discussion and Writing

1. Several of the readings in the chapter comment on the adjustments and insights
of young people during or at the end of their schooling. Compare two or more of these
readings and indicate which view of the impact of school on the life of a young person is
closest to your own, as well as which reading most closely reflects your own beliefs
about education.

2. For many young people, nature is a positive force that mirrors their growing
inner world and allows time for solitary contemplation and physical testing of a
strengthening body. Provide examples drawn from several of the selections in this chapter of the role of nature in the life of the child and adolescent. You might wish to consider such works as White's "Once More to the Lake," Frost's "Birches," and Fuentes'
"The Doll Queen."

3. Poverty and social inequality are major roadblocks in life. Compare several readings that present people of various ages coming to terms with the reality of social and
economic disparities in our world. Which authors have the most optimistic view of the
possibilities of triumphing in spite of these obstacles?

4. A major passage in life is the journey into sexuality. Compare the insights about
sexuality as a rite of passage made by several of the authors in the chapter.

5. Separating from one's family and leaving home can be traumatic experiences, yet
leaving home is a necessary and liberating passage into adulthood. Which works most

clearly explore the complex emotions involved in separating from home and family? Write an essay in which you compare several such works.

6. Pregnancy and motherhood necessitate major redefinitions of a woman's self-concept and life style. Compare several of the works in the chapter that explore women's feelings about pregnancy and motherhood.

7. A major life passage is the recognition and acceptance of one's mortality, which can become a preoccupation because of the death of a loved one or simply because of the passage of another year in one's life. Compare several selections in the chapter that explore aging and mortality.

Chapter 9

RELATIONSHIPS

I think we are all skydivers falling through our
separate spaces. We float, lie prone in a circle.
Reaching out, we hold hands for a moment . . .
Jim Wayne Miller, "Skydiving"

mother, i have worn your name like a shield
it has torn but protected me all these years . . .
Lucille Clifton, "February 13, 1980"

Clearly, a little permission is a dangerous thing.
But when you hug someone you want it
to be a masterpiece of connection . . .
Tess Gallagher, "The Hug"

Which ideas and images come to mind when you hear the word "relationship"? Each new, vital relationship necessitates reaching out and taking risks. In some types of formal relationships, such as those between a teacher and a student, a doctor and a patient, or a manager and an employee, it is possible to establish clear guidelines for commitment and behavior; however, a deeper and more intimate relationship is harder to understand objectively and to evaluate. Once one loves another person, one is changed by and becomes a part of that person. Feeling that one is joined to another individual emotionally makes it difficult to separate from him or her and may lead to possessiveness or jealousy, as well as to feelings of happiness and anticipation that may be difficult to keep in perspective.

Relationships imply caring, giving, feeling nourished, and being a significant

Marc Chagall. *Birthday [l'Anniversaire]*. 1915. Oil on cardboard, 31¾ × 39¼″. The Museum of Modern Art, New York. Acquired through the Lillie P. Bliss Bequest.

part of another person's life. Relationships change; just as one cannot go back and erase the history of a relationship, one cannot permanently possess or control another individual, even the person or people whom one loves most dearly. Everyone must face separations in the course of a relationship: when children leave home, when a good friend travels or moves to a different neighborhood, when a parent, child, close relative, dear friend, or partner breaks off a relationship or dies.

Reading through this chapter will provide you with the opportunity to reflect on the many different meanings that the word "relationship" has come to hold for you. The literature in this chapter focuses on the changing relationships between women and men, parents and children, siblings, and friends. Many of the writers emphasize the healing power that understanding, accepting, and forgiveness within a relationship can bring. We hope that your mind will be enriched and intrigued by learning about relationships that you have yet to encounter and by reflecting on those with which you already have had some experience. As you read and reflect on the selections, you will discover other significant issues within relationships that merit examination and reflection.

Each of the selections in this chapter is unique in its approach to describing and defining relationships. The Native American folk tale that opens the chapter, "How Men and Women Got Together," captures a fundamental pattern in the lives of many people, a pattern of discovering, acknowledging, and accepting both the differences and the powerful qualities of the opposite sex. The tale explores the way that sexual attraction, marriage, and the desire to raise children unite men and women: "This is surely the most wonderful thing that ever happened to me."

A number of the selections in the chapter question the traditional myth that love and marriage necessarily go hand-in-hand, leading inevitably to children and equal fulfillment for both partners. Modern experiences and understandings about marriage, sexuality, psychology, parenting, divorce, and alternative family groups have revealed some of the fallacies in such assumptions. Today many men and women are thoughtfully redefining traditional relationships as they struggle to build workable and fulfilling lives in our society. At the same time, as Deborah Tannen discusses in her essay, "Gossip," men and women may have difficulty understanding one another because of their different life experiences and communication styles.

The diversity of cultures within our cities or communities and the new opportunities in careers and in parenting for men and women encourage people to question seriously what qualities they want in the relationships that make up the fabric of their lives. For those individuals who reject the idea of marriage, the quest for a deeply satisfying emotional union still remains a concern. In the story by David Leavitt, "A Place I've Never Been," Nathan, a gay man who is fearful of AIDS, reveals his inner sense of emptiness, "Do you realize . . . I've never been in love? Never once in my life have I actually been in love?"

Other works in the chapter examine conflicts in relationships that are a consequence of cultural conflict and the rejection of traditional values. Although the main characters in Bharati Mukherjee's "A Wife's Story" were married for a number of years in India, the wife has left her home and her husband to earn a Ph.D. degree in New York City, where she lives on her own. The traditions that she grew up believing would guide her adult life are no longer entirely applicable; her husband, too, must grapple with the changes that his wife's new life style creates. Mukherjee leaves the reader to speculate on the future of this couple whose relationship seems to be lost in a changing world. Traditional culture also fails to provide enough emotional support for the two Japanese immigrant families who are struggling against poverty and cultural alienation in Wakako Yamauchi's short play "And the Soul Shall Dance."

A number of selections in this chapter explore relationships between parents and their children. Guilt, anger, and resentment are major sources of tension in parent-child relationships. Even as adults, many people expend enormous amounts of energy worrying about why they have not lived up to their parents' expectations, or harboring resentment and pain about the ways that their parents disappointed or neglected them. The speaker in Philip Levine's poem "Starlight" examines memories of his relationship with his father, reflecting deeply on the way that children understand intuitively and respond emotionally to their parents' disappointments in life. Michel Marriott, in his essay "Father Hunger," attributes feelings of anger, pain, and rejection to his father's emotional distance and disapproval. In Amy Tan's story "Two Kinds," the narrator, Jing-Mei Woo, seeks her mother's approval while at the same time rejecting many of her mother's values and plans for her. Ed Bullins explores a disillusioned son's deep longing for his mother and a home in his play "A Son, Come Home."

Along with the frustration, pain, and sadness that relationships bring, loving can be creative, healing, and enabling; love can nurture forgiveness, rebirth, and growth. Two of the selections suggest that sibling relationships can be resolved in a meaningful and hopeful way. Maria Howe's speaker in the poem "Letter to My Sister" reminds us of the importance of forgiveness: "Forgive me the circumstances of my life . . . / Perhaps this is the love we earn." James Baldwin's classic story, "Sonny's Blues," also ends positively, as the two main characters, both brothers, finally come to understand one another's very unique life styles and values, finding solace in forgiveness through renewing their bond.

Many fulfilling emotional relationships are developed outside of our immediate families. Individuals often maintain strong relationships with people who live in their neighborhood, with their students and teachers, with professional acquaintances and fellow workers, people with whom they share a special interest, political point of view, or talent. These relationships can provide reassurance and acceptance. The selections by Lorna Dee Cervantes, Dudley Randall, and David Leavitt explore the wide range of friendship that people develop during their lifetime. However, friendship, like any type of caring, loving relationship, involves risks as well as rewards. Many of us have felt like the narrator in Tess Gallagher's poem who finds that hugging a stranger can be a profound experience that changes her irrevocably: "when you hug someone you want it/to be a masterpiece of connection." Shakespeare captures the vulnerability at the core of human love in his poem "When my love swears that she is made of truth,/I do believe her, though I know she lies." Jim Wayne Miller envisions friendship and love as risk-taking ventures when he frames friendship in the image of sky-diving: "We float, lie prone in a circle./Reaching out, we hold hands for a moment." The skydivers float alone toward their shadows on the earth, leaving each reader to draw his or her own conclusions. The dangers of loving touch us all; yet, for most people, the risks of potential loss or betrayal continue to be worth taking.

On your journey through these readings you are likely to find more new questions than answers. The wealth of emotional realities and paradoxical truths, the joy, the sadness, and the wisdom that you will discover as you engage yourselves in the lives of the characters and speakers on these pages will be illuminating and rewarding. For each of us the meaning of "relationship" is intensely personal and meaningful.

Folk Tales

How Men and Women Got Together
Native American (Blood-Piegan)

Journal

Write about something you think that women and men don't understand about the "opposite sex" which makes communication between the sexes difficult.

Old Man had made the world and everything on it. He had done everything well, except that he had put the men in one place and the women in another, quite a distance away. So they lived separately for a while.

Men and women did everything in exactly the same way. Both had buffalo jumps—steep cliffs over which they chased buffalo herds so that the animals fell to their death at the foot of the cliff. Then both the men and the women butchered the dead animals. This meat was their only food; they had not yet discovered other things that were good to eat.

After a while the men learned how to make bows and arrows. The women learned how to tan buffalo hides and make tipis and beautiful robes decorated with porcupine quills.

One day Old Man said to himself, "I think I did everything well, but I made one bad mistake, putting women and men in different places. There's no joy or pleasure in that. Men and women are different from each other, and these different things must be made to unite so that there will be more people. I must make men mate with women. I will put some pleasure, some good feeling into it; otherwise the men won't be keen to do what is necessary. I myself must set an example."

Old Man went over to where the women were living. He traveled for four days and four nights before he saw the women in their camp. He was hiding behind some trees, watching. He said to himself, "Ho, what a good life they're having! They have these fine tipis made of tanned buffalo hide, while we men have only brush shelters or raw, stinking, green hides to cover us. And look what fine clothes they wear, while we have to go around with a few pelts around our loins! Really, I made a mistake putting the women so far away from us. They must live with us and make fine tents and beautiful clothes for us also. I'll go back and ask the other men how they feel about this."

So Old Man went back to his camp and told the men what he had seen. When they heard about all the useful and beautiful things the women had, the men said, "Let's go over there and get together with these different human beings."

"It's not only those things that are worth having," said Old Man. "There's something else—a very pleasurable thing I plan on creating."

Now, while this was going on in the men's camp, the chief of the women's village had discovered the tracks Old Man had made while prowling around. She sent a young woman to follow them and report back. The young woman arrived near the men's camp, hid herself, and watched for a short while. Then she hurried back to the women as fast as she could and told everybody, "There's a camp over there with human beings living in it. They seem different from us, taller and stronger. Oh, sisters, these beings live very well, better than us. They have a thing shooting sharp sticks, and with these they kill many kinds of game—food that we don't have. They are never hungry."

When they heard this, all the women said, "How we wish that these strange human beings would come here and kill all kinds of food for us!" When the women were finishing their meeting, the men were already over the hill toward them. The women looked at the men and saw how shabbily dressed they were, with just a little bit of rawhide around their loins. They looked at the men's matted hair, smelled the strong smell coming from their unwashed bodies. They looked at their dirty skin. They said to each other, "These beings called men don't know how to live. They have no proper clothes. They're dirty; they smell. We don't want people like these." The woman chief hurled a rock at Old Man, shouting "Go away!" Then all the women threw rocks and shouted "Go away!"

Old Man said, "It was no mistake putting these creatures far away from us. Women are dangerous. I shouldn't have created them." Then Old Man and all the men went back to their own place.

After the men left, the woman chief had second thoughts. "These poor men," she said, "they don't know any better, but we could teach them. We could make clothes for them. Instead of shaming them, maybe we could get them to come back if we dress as poorly as they do, just with a piece of hide or fur around our waist.

And in the men's camp, Old Man said, "Maybe we should try to meet these women creatures once more. Yes, we should give it another chance. See what I did on the sly." He opened his traveling bundle in which he kept his jerk meat and other supplies, and out of it took a resplendent white buckskin outfit. "I managed to steal this when those women weren't looking. It's too small for me, but I'll add on a little buffalo hide here and a little bear fur there, and put a shield over here, where it doesn't come together over my belly. And I'll make myself a feather headdress and paint my face. Then maybe this woman chief will look at me with new eyes. Let me go alone to speak with the women creatures first. You stay back a little and hide until I have straightened things out."

So Old Man dressed up as best he could. He even purified himself in a sweat bath which he thought up for this purpose. He looked at his reflection in the lake waters and exclaimed, "Oh, how beautiful I am! I never knew I was that good-looking! Now that woman chief will surely like me."

Then Old Man led the way back to the women's camp. There was one woman on the lookout, and even though the men were staying back in hiding, she saw them coming. Then she spotted Old Man standing alone on a hilltop overlooking the camp. She hurried to tell the woman chief, who was butchering with most of the other women at the buffalo jump. For this job they wore their poorest outfits: just pieces of rawhide with a hole for the head, or maybe only a strap of rawhide around the waist. What little they had on was stiff with blood and reeked of freshly slaughtered carcasses. Even their faces and hands were streaked with blood.

"We'll meet these men just as we are," said the woman chief. "They will appreciate our being dressed like them."

So the woman chief went up to the hill on which Old Man was standing, and the other women followed her. When he saw the woman chief standing there in her butchering clothes, her flint skinning knife still in her hand, her hair matted and unkempt, he exclaimed, "Hah! Hrumph! This woman chief is ugly. She's dressed in rags covered with blood. She stinks. I want nothing to do with a creature like this. And those other women are just like her. No, I made no mistake putting these beings far away from us men!" And having said this, he turned around and went back the way he had come, with all his men following him.

"It seems we can't do anything right," said the woman chief. "Whatever it is, those male beings misunderstand it. But I still think we should unite with them. I think they have something we haven't got, and we have something they haven't got, and these things must come together. We'll try one last time to get them to understand us. Let's make ourselves beautiful."

The women went into the river and bathed. They washed and combed their hair, braided it, and attached hair strings of bone pipes and shell beads.

They put on their finest robes of well-tanned, dazzling white doeskin covered with wonderful designs of porcupine quills more colorful than the rainbow. They placed bone and shell chokers around their necks and shell bracelets around their wrists. On their feet they put full quilled moccasins. Finally the women painted their cheeks with sacred red face paint. Thus wonderfully decked out, they started on their journey to the men's camp.

In the village of male creatures, Old Man was cross and ill-humored. Nothing pleased him. Nothing he ate tasted good. He slept fitfully. He got angry over nothing. And so it was with all the men. "I don't know what's the matter," said Old Man. "I wish women were beautiful instead of ugly, sweet-smelling instead of malodorous, good-tempered instead of coming at us with stones or bloody knives in their hands."

"We wish it too," said all the other men.

Then a lookout came running, telling Old Man, "The women beings are marching over here to our camp. Probably they're coming to kill us. Quick everybody, get your bows and arrows!"

"No, wait!" said Old Man. "Quick! Go to the river. Clean yourselves. Anoint and rub your bodies with fat. Arrange your hair pleasingly. Smoke yourselves up with cedar. Put on your best fur garments. Paint your faces with sacred red paint. Put bright feathers on your heads." Old Man himself dressed in the quilled robe stolen from the women's camp which he had made into a war shirt. He wore his great chief's headdress. He put on his necklace of bear claws. Thus arrayed, the men assembled at the entrance of their camp, awaiting the women's coming.

The women came. They were singing. Their white quilled robes dazzled the men's eyes. Their bodies were fragrant with the good smell of sweet grass. Their cheeks shone with sacred red face paint.

Old Man exclaimed, "Why, these women beings are beautiful! They delight my eyes! Their singing is wonderfully pleasing to my ears. Their bodies are sweet-smelling and alluring!"

"They make our hearts leap," said the other men.

"I'll go talk to their woman chief," said Old Man. "I'll fix things up with her."

The woman chief in the meantime remarked to the other women, "Why, these men beings are really not as uncouth as we thought. Their rawness is a sort of strength. The sight of their arm muscles pleases my eyes, the sound of their deep voices thrills my ears. They are not altogether bad, these men."

Old Man went up to the woman chief and said, "Let's you and I go someplace and talk."

"Yes, let's do that," answered the woman chief. They went someplace. The woman chief looked at Old Man and liked what she saw. Old Man looked at the woman chief and his heart pounded with joy. "Let's try one thing that has never been tried before," he said to the woman chief.

"I always like to try out new, useful things," she answered.

"Maybe one should lie down, trying this," said Old Man.

"Maybe one should," agreed the woman chief. They lay down.

After a while Old Man said, "This is surely the most wonderful thing that ever happened to me. I couldn't ever imagine such a wonderful thing."

"And I," said the woman chief, "I never dreamed I could feel so good. This is much better, even, than eating buffalo tongues. It's too good to be properly described."

"Let's go and tell the others about it," said Old Man.

When Old Man and the woman chief got back to the camp, they found nobody there. All the male creatures and the women beings had already paired off and gone someplace, each pair to their own spot. They didn't need to be told about this new thing; they had already found out.

When the men and women came back from wherever they had gone, they were smiling. Their eyes were smiling. Their mouths were smiling, their whole bodies were smiling, so it seemed.

Then the women moved in with the men. They brought all their things, all their skills to the men's village. Then the women quilled and tanned for the men. Then the men hunted for the women. Then there was love. Then there was happiness. Then there was marriage. Then there were children.

QUESTIONS AND CONSIDERATIONS

1. Why does the Old Man, whom we first hear about from the narrator of this tale, decide to bring the men and women together after separating them initially?

2. What do the men like and dislike about the women? What do the women like and dislike about the men? How do the men try to win over the women? How do the women try to win over the men?

3. What finally brings the men and women together? What definition of love is implied through the telling of this tale?

4. How do you imagine the story would have been told differently if the narrator of the tale were a woman?

Journals

Diaries
Käthe Kollwitz

September 1, 1911

I imagine the following sculpture as utterly beautiful: a pregnant woman chiseled out of stone. Carved only down to the knees so that she looks the way Lise said she did the time she was pregnant with Maria: "As if I am rooted to the ground." The immobility, restraint, introspection. The arms and hands dangling heavily, the head lowered, all attention directed inward. And the whole thing in heavy, heavy stone. Title: *Pregnancy*.

New Year's Day, 1912

. . . No progress in my relationship with Karl. What he always speaks of, what seems to him still the sole worthwhile goal of our long living together—that we should grow together in the deepest intimacy—I still do not feel and probably never will learn to feel.

Are not the ties with the boys also growing slacker? I almost think so. For the last third of life there remains only work. It alone is always stimulating, rejuvenating, exciting and satisfying. . . .

August 27, 1914

A piece by Gabriele Reuter in the *Tag* on the tasks of women today. She spoke of the joy of sacrificing—a phrase that struck me hard. Where do all the women who have watched so carefully over the lives of their beloved ones get the heroism to send them to face the cannon? . . .

[Peter Kollwitz was killed on October 22, 1914.]

December 9, 1914

My boy! On your memorial I want to have your figure on top, *above* the parents. You will lie outstretched, holding out your hands in answer to the call for sacrifice: "Here I am." Your eyes—perhaps—open wide, so that you see the blue sky above you, and the clouds and birds. Your mouth smiling. And at your breast the pink I gave you.

February 15, 1915

. . . I do not want to die, even if Hans and Karl should die. I do not want to go until I have faithfully made the most of my talent and cultivated the seed that was placed in me until the last small twig has grown. This does not contradict the fact that I would have died—smilingly—for Peter, and for Hans too, were the choice offered me . . . Peter was seed for the planting which should not have been ground. He was the sowing. I am the bearer and cultivator of seedcorn. What Hans will become, the future will show. But since I am to be the cultivator, I want to serve faithfully. Since recognizing that, I am almost serene and much firmer in spirit. It is not only that I am permitted to finish my work—I am obliged to finish it. This seems to me to be the meaning of all the babble about culture. Culture arises only when the individual fulfils his cycle of obligations. . . .

August 28, 1915

. . . How Karl and I are now growing more and more intimately used to one another . . . Yes, new flowers have grown up which would not have grown without the tears shed this year. . . .

January 17, 1916

. . . Where are my children now? What is left to their mother? One boy to the right and one to the left, my right son and my left son, as they called themselves. One dead and one so far away, and I cannot help him . . . My whole life as a mother is really behind me now. I often have a terrible longing to have it back again—to have children, my boys, one to the right and one to the left; to dance with them as formerly when spring arrived and Peter came with flowers and we danced a springtide dance.

For our silver wedding anniversary

Dear Husband: When we married, we took a leap in the dark. We were not building upon a firm foundation, or at least one firmly believed in. There were grave contradictions in my own feelings. In the end I acted on this impulse: jump in—you'll manage to swim. . . .

I have never been without your love, and because of it we are now so firmly linked after twenty-five years. Karl, my dear, thank you. I have so rarely told you in words what you have been and are to me. Today I want to do so, this once . . .

From the bottom of my heart I am thankful to the fate which gave us our children and in them such inexpressible happiness.

If Hans is let live, we shall be able to see his further development, and perhaps we may expect children of his. If he too is taken, then all the sunlight that out of him lighted, warmed and made everything golden will be smothered; but we shall still hold tight to one another's hands to the end. . . .

Your Käthe

October 1, 1918

. . . Wildly contradictory feelings. Germany is losing the war . . . Will the patriotic emotion flare up once more so powerfully that a last-ditch defense will start? . . . *not another day* of war when it is clear that the war is lost.

December 26, 1919

There are days when Mother sleeps most of the time, murmuring softly in her dreams and daydreaming when she is awake. Always about children . . . It is really so sweet to see how the dreams and visions and fantasies of so old a mother always return to her children. So after all they were the strongest emotion in her life.

February 26, 1920

I want to do a drawing of a man *who sees the suffering of the world.* That can only be Jesus, I suppose. In the drawing where Death seizes the children there is also a woman in the background who sees the suffering of the world. The children being seized by death are not hers; she is too old for that. Nor is she looking; she does not stir, but she knows about the world's suffering. . . .

End of October, 1921

A lovely, happy period of work. The *Mothers* is making progress day by day. How wonderful life is at such times.

Karl had a pleasant experience recently. He lectured to a group of women and young girls. I did not wait up for him, but went to bed. Around eleven o'clock I heard young voices singing, moving past our house and then fading away. The girls had accompanied Karl home, singing.

Karl is blithe. How good it is for me when I sometimes complain about too little time, and so on—the way he unsentimentally and yet with the greatest kindness thrusts my nonsense aside.

December 1922

. . . Peter [Hans's son] on the high chair, also at the table, with his back to me. All around his head the fine white hair, shot through with light. It so reminded me of our own children. Afterwards, when I held him on my lap, he kept pointing at me and saying, "Here, Gandmother." A pause between "Gand" and "mother," and then the word "mother" slipping out quickly, carelessly.

June 1924

The first day of Whitsun, a joyous and happy day for me. I went out to spend it with the children. Magnificent weather. . . . The twins are precious. Sturdy, droll, innocent little white heads. Babbling their own language. When Ottilie sits between them to feed them and gives each in turn a spoonful of pap, the one who doesn't have her turn clenches her fists and her face turns red at having to wait, while the other opens her mouth for the spoon with the smuggest air of contentment. It is wonderful to see. Happy Ottilie, who is so thoroughly maternal. Whatever comes later on, these three years of work with the babies will always give her a kind of satiated feeling. She is a mother through and through, much as she sometimes rants against being one.

Little Peter has given me a pink.

October 22, 1924

When I entered Mother's room today to bring her down to supper, I saw a strange scene. Like something out of a fairy tale. Mother sat at the table, under the lamp, in Grandfather's easy chair. In front of her were snapshots she was looking through. Diagonally across her shoulders sat Frau Klingelhof's big cat.

Mother used to be unable to stand cats. But now she likes to have the cat on her lap. The cat warms her hands. Sometimes it seems to me that Mother thinks the cat is a baby. When it wants to get down, Mother clasps it anxiously, as if she were afraid the baby will fall. Then her face is full of concern. She actually struggles with the cat.

In the picture Helmy Hart took of Mother, which shows only the head, Mother has a strange expression. The wisdom of great age is there. But it is not the wisdom that thinks in thoughts; rather it operates through dim feelings. These are not the "thoughts hitherto inconceivable" that Goethe had, but the summation of eighty-seven years of living, which are now unclearly felt. Mother muses. yet even that is not quite it, for musing implies, after all, thinking. It is hard to say what the picture expresses. The features themselves do not definitely express one thing or another. Precisely because Mother no longer thinks, there is a unity about her. A very old woman who lives within herself in undifferentiated perception. Yes, that is right; but in addition: who lives within herself according to an order that is pure and harmonious. As Mother's nature always was.

It seems more and more evident to me that Mother does not recognize the cat for what it is, but thinks it is a baby. Often she wraps it up in a blanket and holds it just like a child. It is touching and sweet to see my old mother doing this.

From *Journal of a Solitude*
May Sarton

September 15th

Begin here. It is raining. I look out on the maple, where a few leaves have turned yellow, and listen to Punch, the parrot, talking to himself and to the rain ticking gently against the windows. I am here alone for the first time in weeks, to take up my "real" life again at last. That is what is strange—that friends, even passionate love, are not my real life unless there is time alone in which to explore and to discover what is happening or has happened. Without the interruptions, nourishing and maddening, this life would become arid. Yet I taste it fully only when I am alone here and "the house and I resume old conversations."

On my desk, small pink roses. Strange how often the autumn roses look sad, fade quickly, frost-browned at the edges! But these are lovely, bright, singing pink. On the mantel, in the Japanese jar, two sprays of white lilies, recurved, maroon pollen on the stamens, and a branch of peony leaves turned a strange pinkish-brown. It is an elegant bouquet; *shibui,* the Japanese would call it. When I am alone the flowers are really seen; I can pay attention to them. They are felt as presences. Without them I would die. Why do I say that? Partly because they change before my eyes. They live and die in a few days; they keep me closely in touch with process, with growth, and also with dying. I am floated on their moments.

The ambience here is order and beauty. That is what frightens me when I am first alone again. I feel inadequate. I have made an open place, a place for meditation. What if I cannot find myself inside it?

I think of these pages as a way of doing that. For a long time now, every meeting with another human being has been a collision. I feel too much, sense too much, am exhausted by the reverberations after even the simplest conversation. But the deep collision is and has been with my unregenerate, tormenting, and tormented self. I have written every poem, every novel, for the same purpose—to find out what I think, to know where I stand. I am unable to become what I see. I feel like an inadequate machine, a machine that breaks down at crucial moments, grinds to a dreadful halt, "won't go," or, even worse, explodes in some innocent person's face.

Plant Dreaming Deep has brought me many friends of the work (and also, harder to respond to, people who think they have found in me an intimate friend). But I have begun to realize that, without my own intention, that book gives a false view. The anguish of my life here—its rages—is hardly mentioned. Now I hope to break through into the rough rocky depths, to the matrix itself. There is violence there and anger never resolved. I live alone, perhaps for no good reason, for the reason that I am an impossible creature, set apart by a temperament I have never learned to use as it could be used, thrown off by a word, a glance, a rainy day, or one drink too many. My need to be alone is balanced against my fear of what will happen when suddenly I enter the huge empty silence if I cannot find support there. I go up to Heaven and down to Hell in an hour, and keep alive only by imposing upon myself inexorable routines. I write too many letters and too few poems. It may be outwardly silent here but in the back of my mind is a clamor of human voices, too many needs, hopes, fears. I hardly ever sit still without being haunted by the "undone" and the "unsent." I often feel exhausted, but it is not my work that tires (work is a rest); it is the effort of pushing away the lives and needs of others before I can come to the work with any freshness and zest.

September 17th

Cracking open the inner world again, writing even a couple of pages, threw me back into depression, not made easier by the weather, two gloomy days of darkness and rain. I was attacked by a storm of tears, those tears that appear to be related to frustration, to buried anger, and come upon me without warning. I woke yesterday so depressed that I did not get up till after eight.

I drove to Brattleboro to read poems at the new Unitarian church there in a state of dread and exhaustion. How to summon the vitality needed? I had made an arrangement of religious poems, going back to early books and forward into the new book not yet published. I suppose it went all right—at least it was not a disaster—but I felt (perhaps I am wrong) that the kind, intelligent people gathered in a big room looking out on pine trees did not really want to think about God. His absence (many of the poems speak of that) or His presence. Both are too frightening.

On the way back I stopped to see Perley Cole, my dear old friend, who is dying, separated from his wife, and has just been moved from a Dickensian nursing home into what seems like a far better one. He grows more transparent every day, a skeleton or nearly. Clasping his hand, I fear to break a bone.

Yet the only real communication between us now (he is very deaf) is a hand-clasp. I want to lift him in my arms and hold him like a baby. He is dying a terri-bly lonely death. Each time I see him he says, "It is rough" or "I did not think it would end like this."

Everywhere I look about this place I see his handiwork: the three small trees by a granite boulder that he pruned and trimmed so they pivot the whole meadow; the new shady border he dug out for me one of the last days he worked here; the pruned-out stone wall between my field and the church. The second field where he cut brush twice a year and cleared out to the stone wall is growing back to wilderness now. What is done here has to be done over and over and needs the dogged strength of a man like Perley. I could have never managed it alone. We cherished this piece of land together, and fought together to bring it to some semblance of order and beauty.

I like to think that this last effort of Perley's had a certain ease about it, a game compared to the hard work of his farming years, and a game where his expert knowledge and skill could be well used. How he enjoyed teasing me about my ignorance!

While he scythed and trimmed, I struggled in somewhat the same way at my desk here, and we were each aware of the companionship. We each looked forward to noon, when I could stop for the day and he sat on a high stool in the kitchen, drank a glass or two of sherry with me, said, "Court's in session!" and then told me some tall tale he had been cogitating all morning.

It was a strange relationship, for he knew next to nothing about my life, re-ally; yet below all the talk we recognized each other as the same kind. He en-joyed my anger as much as I enjoyed his. Perhaps that was part of it. Deep down there was understanding, not of the facts of our lives so much as of our essential natures. Even now in his hard, lonely end he has immense dignity. But I wish there were some way to make it easier. I leave him with bitter re-sentment against the circumstances of this death. "I know. But I do not ap-prove. And I am not resigned."

Last Autumn of the War:
September–October 1944

Stephen Spender

September 13, 1944

Julian wrote to me some weeks ago from Wales that he was very depressed. A love affair had gone wrong, he had been disappointed in his hopes that he would have a position at the Peace Conference after the war. Evidently he has reached a crisis in his life. He is fifty-five. He has been living for several years on easy successes, journalism, committees, broadcasting, journeys to places about which he has written books. Planning and so on. All these are generalized activities, in which he has been able to live off his general intelligence, good will, and progressive opinions.

He has not done the scientific work in which he might have specialized. He has not thrown everything else up in order to lead a political crusade. He is not a teacher. He has the gifts to have done any of these, and he might also have become a distinguished writer. What is more important, he has never revised his assumption that one can be good merely by supporting progressive causes, and that the basis of morality is the evolution of the society in which one lives. The natural goodness in himself—which is considerable—remains childlike, charming, and unself-knowing, because he thinks of goodness as a kind of contribution made to a public cause, not the development of a potentiality within himself.

Now he has had, at the age of fifty-five, a real crisis. He has an illness, contracted in Africa, combined with a nervous breakdown. He was sent to the London Hospital. There he was given injections which put him to sleep for several days on end. His first night there, a bomb fell on a wing of the hospital. Julian was badly shaken and woken from his sleep. He was then moved to Harrow Hospital.

Juliette, his wife, went to see him after the move. He complained that the nurses were very unintelligent and could not even read to him correctly, confusing words such as "peasant" and "pheasant." He asked Juliette whether she could not come to the hospital and read to him every day. She explained matters to the doctor, who flew into a temper and said that she had called his nurses illiterate. He added that she must certainly not come and read to Julian as it was most important to keep him from his family. Julian, he added, had been sent to the hospital to be cured, not to be made worse.

After this several specialists were consulted as to the nature of J.'s illness. It was decided to give up the sleeping cure, and try electric-shock treatment. Juliette was sent for, to get her consent. The doctor came in while she was with Julian and asked whether she agreed to the treatment. She hesitated a moment, and said: "Well, it's rather a difficult thing to decide." The doctor said to Julian: "You see, your wife is trying to obstruct the treatment. I am confident that I can cure you, but she is trying to prevent me." Juliette protested: "I only wanted to think things over." The doctor left the room, and returning a few minutes later, said to Julian, "I have decided not to treat you. I cannot be responsible for you, in view of your wife's attitude."

September 15

Dunstan Thompson, the young American poet and a GI in London, came to spend the night with us. We talked much of Catholicism. He said that he believed in the supreme authority of the Church but that he could no longer be a Catholic. He was homosexual. He could not think that to be homosexual was a sin; therefore he convicted himself of the still worse sin of pride. He found it impossible for him to go to confession every week and confess always the same sin, of which he could not sincerely repent.

He shares a room in the Catholic college where he lives with a friend. They are lovers. Every week they confess, and after confession try for a few days to keep apart. Dunstan said he could not resolve this dilemma for himself by finding a pansy priest as confessor. So he left the Church.

I thought much of religion later because Adam von Trott had been sentenced to death by the Nazis, and I prayed for him all day. Passionate conviction that by concentrating my mind on Adam I could comfort him in his cell where he was waiting to be hanged.

During the night, I dreamt of God, or of light. I seemed to realize in my dream that the essential requirement of religious belief is belief in a spiritual force beyond the human. The idea of humanity is only the projection on an immense screen of the individual self, oneself magnified. The human race dies with each self that dies. The sense of God beyond humanity is the sine qua non of religion.

September 20

Saw Julian at his home. He looked white and tired, but less physically ill than I had expected. When we were alone he explained to me that his disease of the liver caused him the most frightful depression. He said: "What I can't explain to you is that I am obsessed by the most terrible longing to kill myself. I suppose that you, as a person outside my situation, think that suicide is an inexcusable crime?" I said I did not think this was necessarily so; but I was convinced that if he could overcome this impulse, he would probably do his best work in the coming years, work enriched by what he is experiencing now. Just as I was saying this, Juliette came in and suggested that we all three go for a walk on Hampstead Heath. We went for a short walk past the place where the flying bomb ("doodle bug") had fallen only a few days ago, just when we were all, having breakfast at their house. (Sometimes during air raids, Natasha and I would sleep in the Huxley's air raid shelter as we had none in our apartment.) I reminded Julian of this, but he did not seem to remember about it. Juliette asked: "Shall we walk a bit further on?" Julian said he didn't mind. Juliette: "But do you want to?" He said: "I do exactly what I'm told."

At lunch he seemed to have a return to his old self, and discussed this morning's leading article in the *Times*. He said, "Even they admit that International Control is necessary."

Over coffee, when Juliette was out of the room, I said to Julian: "In six months' time the war will be over, and you will be better, and everything will be quite different, if only you have the patience to endure these six months." He said in an almost surprised tone of voice: "Oh, but do you think everything will be better? I am sure it will all be much worse."

Harry Royall. Royall is the boy aged nineteen whom I met at Sidcup Hospital for patients suffering from pleural diffusion. He is so thin as to seem almost two-dimensional, but in his face like cardboard are brilliantly shining eyes. I have been trying to get him a place at Oxford University. He seems divided between wanting to be a schoolmaster and wilder ambitions—being an actor, going into politics. The London County Council have provided him with scholarships amounting to £150 a year. Recently Oxford University sent him a kind of preliminary bill for £15 to be paid before he goes up.

Two days ago he asked me if I would lend him £25, I said that I could not do so unless he would pay it back within six months. I also discussed with him the problem of going to Oxford with only £150 a year. I recommended him not to go unless he could raise another £100.

We dined at the Hamish Hamiltons. Sam Behrmann was there. Very friendly. An American, Captain Kennedy, badly burnt, with a beard to hide his scars, came in after dinner. He described the German P.O.W. camp where he is stationed. He said: "The Germans are gullible. They can be fooled. The thing is, always to shout at them."

September 27

Lunched with Cyril Connolly. E. M. Forster was there. Forster always gives me the impression that, in his extremely diffident way, he is making moral judgments on everyone in any room where he happens to be. The very reticence of his personality shows up everyone else, like a color besides which almost any other color seems tawdry and vulgar.

The effect of his presence on me was that I talked a great deal about myself. All the time I was thinking, while he looked at me—his head slightly on one side—how abominably vulgar I am. How often the word 'I' comes into my conversation.

After Forster had gone, I told Cyril this. Cyril said: "I quite agree. When I served the steak I wondered whether Morgan would notice that I had taken the largest piece, and I prayed that if he did he would also realize that his piece, though smaller, was juicier and more tender and had less fat on it. Then I also hoped that at dessert, he would realize that although I took the largest apple, it was a green one, whereas the one I gave him was the ripest."

October 3

Two days home with a cold.

On Sunday I got up to go to the Savile Club, as I could not get hold of Rudi—, my guest, to put him off. He was heavy and Germanic and dull, and I'm afraid I did little to encourage him. We joined the Australian poet and music critic W. J. Turner for coffee, and Turner and I, ignoring Rudi, discussed Alex

Comfort's novel, or, rather, Alex Comfort, for neither of us had read his novel. Turner said he had no sympathy with Comfort's brand of pacifism. He did not see why Comfort was so squeamish and why, on humanitarian grounds, he objected to killing Germans.

Turner went on to argue that there was nothing essentially more terrible in killing or being killed than in many other of the evils of the world. He also said that modern life had no more violence in proportion to the number of people living than life had always in the past. He quoted a story by James Stephens to illustrate that if one had three wishes which would change the world, one would end by wishing it to remain the same. The special case of the modern world and the cause of our present distress lay in our having acquired such an immense quantity of unmanageable knowledge, that we had lost faith in the idea that we could attain any universal final source of truth, which had comforted our ancestors.

Dunstan Thompson rang and said he had persuaded Harry Royall to accept money to help him get to Oxford. Dunstan added: "I also gave him two of your books, though I mentioned that two books by Auden might be a better investment." Although I think this myself, the remark annoyed and depressed me. Why? Because I was feeling ill and frustrated perhaps and it reminded me of my frustration? Because, although I do not consider myself better than Auden, I do feel that in my work I am unique; and the comparison suggests that I am trying to do the same thing as Auden, which he does better? Because the remark, coming from Dunstan, is depressingly familiar in a way that slightly jars me? It does not matter.

Another autumn of war. The longer blackout, the darkness beginning at seven or eight, the cold canopy of night packed and bristling with malice, the city exhausted and weary beneath. The sense of all the will and energy that has now gone into destruction, unable to stop until everything is destroyed. Fear. Exhaustion. All the people I know who are ill.

The world may not be any more miserable than it always has been, but the modern disorder outrages our intelligence and moral sense to a degree that oppresses the spirit perhaps more than ever before.

Yet all we pray in our hearts for is happiness. Stop the bombs. Give us security and the power to organize our material and human resources. Give us strength to make a deal with Russia and America. If this can be done, after all we may be happy. But happiness is piecemeal: goodness is the view of the whole good applied to all the separate particulars of life. The aim of happiness cannot make each one of us sacrifice enough for all to be happy or good.

Dunstan Thompson rang last night at about eleven, to ask whether he could stay the night, bringing a friend. I was unwilling, as N. has a bad cold. However I changed my mind when I learned that the friend was Harry Royall. The latest about Royall is that Oxford refused him a grant on the grounds of his health. Dunstan is anxious to raise him the money to go there from rich friends. Dunstan now seems very involved with Royall. However I have seen neither of them today, having to leave for the office* this morning before they got up.

October 4

Dined with Juliette, Anthony and Francis Huxley (her sons). Julian being back in hospital. The architect Jane Drew was there. She has just been appointed head of planning in Nigeria. Very excited about West African negroes whom she describes as spontaneous, creative, happy, polygamous, incapable of making anything ugly, etc., etc. She said that the English have the defects opposite to all these good qualities. At dinner she pronounced that married people should always be perfectly honest with each other about their love affairs. I said that honesty usually meant the guilty party putting responsibility for his/her infidelity on the shoulders of the innocent party. After dinner she criticized our civilization for its lack of "natural flowering"! She said that machinery was a mistake, etc., etc. People were without faith in any religion. Nevertheless most people were, by nature, good, and so on. We argued a bit about how many people were good and how many cared about having values of any kind. Juliette, Francis, Anthony and I agreed with her criticism of western civilization. Our difficulty, we said, was to know what to do about it. We could not transform ourselves into West African negroes.

I walked home with Anthony afterward. He said that the war had made him skeptical of people like Jane Drew with her simplicist primitivist view of life. He was convinced that the Germans had some very good ideas: given ten to twenty years in which to perfect rockets and flying bombs, they would be able to destroy England completely with robot weapons.

October 12

At the theater *(Pier Gynt!)* we saw Royall and Dunstan, whom we scarcely spoke to.

I felt convinced that they are having an affair. I was annoyed that Royall should not have written or talked to me about several changes in his plans. Thinking about this kept me awake several nights. At this stage of the war small worries tend to exaggerate themselves in one's mind. Knowing this, I decided to do nothing about Royall. However later in the week I decided that I really ought to concern myself about him, and risk quarreling with Dunstan. Accordingly I wrote Dunstan a letter saying that I did not think Royall's problems could be solved by taking him to night clubs. I pointed out that though the stage might seem a suitable career for him at the present moment, it might not seem so as soon as the war was over and that unless Royall was a genius at acting, it might be desirable for him to acquire a general education. Teaching might still be the best profession for him.

Dunstan rang and said he was not at all offended by my letter. We had tea

---

* At this stage of the war I was transferred from the National Fire Service to the Foreign Office.

to discuss Royall's future. We agreed that the best thing was to find out what Royall really wanted, putting all the advantages and disadvantages of teaching, acting, and Oxford before him; and then to raise the money to help him.

This morning Dunstan rang and said it was quite clear that what R. really wanted was to go to Oxford. Natasha rang Nevill Coghill at Exeter College, who said that if we could find the money, Exeter would take him. Two hours later, however, he rang to say that the Rector of Exeter told him that Royall had been rejected on grounds of health.

I want to be happy more than I want to be good. Or, rather, I think I do. Every time a buzz bomb flies over, every time I read the newspaper, I pray that the catastrophe will not strike *me* down, that somehow *we* will reach through these dark days to the bright sky months or years beyond, to where we can enjoy happiness in peace. My will is obsessed with happiness.

At the same time, though, I feel that I shall never escape from the unhappiness of *the others*. The trouble about happiness is that it is a purely selfish sensation. The innocent, the simple, and the selfish can be happy even amid general unhappiness. But those who are fully conscious will always be aware of the misery of *the others*, and of the too great price paid for their own good fortune. Sometimes I even wish for a universal catastrophe to occur, so as to involve me in the total sum of the surrounding unhappiness. This is because I feel that to escape from the unhappiness of *the others* is weakness, since one's mind is flooded all the time with the reality of their suffering. One should imagine in one's own life the unhappiness which is today's world.

This brings me back to the idea of goodness. But for me goodness seems *ausgeschlossen*. To begin with, I have to earn too much money. My whole way of life is too compromised, too much dissipated by a hundred concessions. Beside this, goodness repels me. Goodness is anti-social, to be good would be to be disloyal to my friends, my fellow conspirators—*mes semblables, mes frères*.

QUESTIONS AND CONSIDERATIONS

1. May Sarton explains why she finds satisfaction in journal writing: "I am here alone for the first time in weeks, to take up my 'real' life again at last." Compare Sarton's feeling of a need for solitude in her life with the attitudes toward solitude versus social life and involvement in close relationships expressed by Spender and Kollwitz.

2. What conclusions does Kollwitz come to about the role of mothering in a woman's life?

3. How do the journal writers express their feelings about loss, death, and spirituality? Whose point of view is closest to your own?

4. Compare the way that Spender is involved with his friends with the way Kollwitz expresses her involvement with family members. Who seems more intimately involved in caring and nurturing relationships?

5. Write in your journal about a time when you found it difficult to reconcile your commitment to personal relationships with others and your need for commitment to your writing or to your career. Have you been able to reconcile your conflict? How?

Fiction

Two Kinds

Amy Tan

Journal

Write about an experience that you had with a parent or relative who tried to push you into being a child prodigy or into performing beyond what you felt were your limits.

My mother believed you could be anything you wanted to be in America. You could open a restaurant. You could work for the government and get good retirement. You could buy a house with almost no money down. You could become rich. You could become instantly famous.

"Of course you can be prodigy, too," my mother told me when I was nine. "You can be best anything. What does Auntie Lindo know? Her daughter, she is only best tricky."

America was where all my mother's hopes lay. She had come here in 1949 after losing everything in China: her mother and father, her family home, her first husband, and two daughters, twin baby girls. But she never looked back with regret. There were so many ways for things to get better.

We didn't immediately pick the right kind of prodigy. At first my mother thought I could be a Chinese Shirley Temple. We'd watch Shirley's old movies on TV as though they were training films. My mother would poke my arm and say, *"Ni kan"*—You watch. And I would see Shirley tapping her feet, or singing a sailor song, or pursing her lips into a very round O while saying, "Oh my goodness."

"Ni kan," said my mother as Shirley's eyes flooded with tears. "You already know how. Don't need talent for crying!"

Soon after my mother got this idea about Shirley Temple, she took me to a beauty training school in the Mission district and put me in the hands of a student who could barely hold the scissors without shaking. Instead of getting big fat curls, I emerged with an uneven mass of crinkly black fuzz. My mother dragged me off to the bathroom and tried to wet down my hair.

"You look like Negro Chinese," she lamented, as if I had done this on purpose.

The instructor of the beauty training school had to lop off these soggy clumps to make my hair even again. "Peter Pan is very popular these days," the instructor assured my mother. I now had hair the length of a boy's, with straight-across bangs that hung at a slant two inches above my eyebrows. I liked the haircut and it made me actually look forward to my future fame.

In fact, in the beginning, I was just as excited as my mother, maybe even more so. I pictured this prodigy part of me as many different images, trying each one on for size. I was a dainty ballerina girl standing by the curtains, waiting to hear the right music that would send me floating on my tiptoes. I was like the Christ child lifted out of the straw manger, crying with holy indignity. I was Cinderella stepping from her pumpkin carriage with sparkly cartoon music filling the air.

In all of my imaginings, I was filled with a sense that I would soon become *perfect.* My mother and father would adore me: I would be beyond reproach. I would never feel the need to sulk for anything.

But sometimes the prodigy in me became impatient. "If you don't hurry up and get me out of here, I'm disappearing for good," it warned. "And then you'll always be nothing."

Every night after dinner, my mother and I would sit at the Formica kitchen table. She would present new tests, taking her examples from stories of amazing children she had read in *Ripley's Believe It or Not,* or *Good Housekeeping, Reader's Digest,* and a dozen other magazines she kept in a pile in our bathroom. My mother got these magazines from people whose houses she cleaned. And since she cleaned many houses each week, we had a great assortment. She would look through them all, searching for stories about remarkable children.

The first night she brought out a story about a three-year-old boy who knew the capitals of all the states and even most of the European countries. A teacher was quoted as saying the little boy could also pronounce the names of the foreign cities correctly.

"What's the capital of Finland?" my mother asked me, looking at the magazine story.

All I knew was the capital of California, because Sacramento was the name of the street we lived on in Chinatown. "Nairobi!" I guessed, saying the most foreign word I could think of. She checked to see if that was possibly one way to pronounce "Helsinki" before showing me the answer.

The tests got harder—multiplying numbers in my head, finding the queen of hearts in a deck of cards, trying to stand on my head without using my hands, predicting the daily temperatures in Los Angeles, New York, and London.

One night I had to look at a page from the Bible for three minutes and then report everything I could remember. "No Jehoshaphat had riches and honor in abundance and . . . that's all I remember, Ma," I said.

And after seeing my mother's disappointed face once again, something inside of me began to die. I hated the tests, the raised hopes and failed expectations. Before going to bed that night, I looked in the mirror above the bathroom sink and when I saw only my face staring back—and that it would always be this ordinary face—I began to cry. Such a sad, ugly girl! I made high-pitched noises like a crazed animal, trying to scratch out the face in the mirror.

And then I saw what seemed to be the prodigy side of me—because I had never seen that face before. I looked at my reflection, blinking so I could see more clearly. The girl staring back at me was angry, powerful. This girl and I were the same. I had new thoughts, willful thoughts, or rather thoughts filled with lots of won'ts. I won't let her change me, I promised myself. I won't be what I'm not.

So now on nights when my mother presented her tests, I performed listlessly, my head propped on one arm. I pretended to be bored. And I was. I got so bored I started counting the bellows of the foghorns out on the bay while my mother drilled me in other areas. The sound was comforting and reminded me of the cow jumping over the moon. And the next day, I played a game with myself, seeing if my mother would give up on me before eight bellows. After a while I usually counted only one, maybe two bellows at most. At last she was beginning to give up hope.

· · ·

Two or three months had gone by without any mention of my being a prodigy again. And then one day my mother was watching *The Ed Sullivan Show* on TV. The TV was old and the sound kept shorting out. Every time my mother got halfway up from the sofa to adjust the set, the sound would go back on and Ed would be talking. As soon as she sat down, Ed would go silent again. She got up, the TV broke into loud piano music. She sat down. Silence. Up and down, back and forth, quiet and loud. It was like a stiff embraceless dance between her and the TV set. Finally she stood by the set with her hand on the sound dial.

She seemed entranced by the music, a little frenzied piano piece with this mesmerizing quality, sort of quick passages and then teasing lilting ones before it returned to the quick playful parts.

"Ni kan," my mother said, calling me over with hurried hand gestures. "Look here."

I could see why my mother was fascinated by the music. It was being pounded out by a little Chinese girl, about nine years old, with a Peter Pan haircut. The girl had the sauciness of a Shirley Temple. She was proudly modest like a proper Chinese child. And she also did this fancy sweep of a curtsy, so that the fluffy skirt of her white dress cascaded slowly to the floor like the petals of a large carnation.

In spite of these warning signs, I wasn't worried. Our family had no piano and we couldn't afford to buy one, let alone reams of sheet music and piano lessons. So I could be generous in my comments when my mother badmouthed the little girl on TV.

"Play note right, but doesn't sound good! No singing sound," complained my mother.

"What are you picking on her for?" I said carelessly. "She's pretty good. Maybe she's not the best, but she's trying hard." I knew almost immediately I would be sorry I said that.

"Just like you," she said. "Not the best. Because you not trying." She gave a little huff as she let go of the sound dial and sat down on the sofa.

The little Chinese girl sat down also to play an encore of "Anitra's Dance" by Grieg. I remember the song, because later on I had to learn how to play it.

Three days after watching *The Ed Sullivan Show,* my mother told me what my schedule would be for piano lessons and piano practice. She had talked to Mr. Chong, who lived on the first floor of our apartment building. Mr. Chong was a retired piano teacher and my mother had traded housecleaning services for weekly lessons and a piano for me to practice on every day, two hours a day, from four until six.

When my mother told me this, I felt as though I had been sent to hell. I whined and then kicked my foot a little when I couldn't stand it anymore.

"Why don't you like the way I am? I'm *not* a genius! I can't play the piano. And even if I could, I wouldn't go on TV if you paid me a million dollars!" I cried.

My mother slapped me. "Who ask you be genius?" she shouted. "Only ask you be your best. For you sake. You think I want you be genius? Hnnh! What for! Who ask you!"

"So ungrateful," I heard her mutter in Chinese. "If she had as much talent as she has temper, she would be famous now."

Mr. Chong, whom I secretly nicknamed Old Chong, was very strange, always tapping his fingers to the silent music of an invisible orchestra. He looked ancient in my eyes. He had lost most of the hair on top of his head and he wore thick glasses and had eyes that always looked tired and sleepy. But he must have been younger than I thought, since he lived with his mother and was not yet married.

I met Old Lady Chong once and that was enough. She had this peculiar smell like a baby that had done something in its pants. And her fingers felt like a dead person's, like an old peach I once found in the back of the refrigerator; the skin just slid off the meat when I picked it up.

I soon found out why Old Chong had retired from teaching piano. He was deaf. "Like Beethoven!" he shouted to me. "We're both listening only in our head!" And he would start to conduct his frantic silent sonatas.

Our lessons went like this. He would open the book and point to different things, explaining their purpose: "Key! Treble! Bass! No sharps or flats! So this is C major! Listen now and play after me!"

And then he would play the C scale a few times, a simple chord, and then, as if inspired by an old, unreachable itch, he gradually added more notes and running trills and a pounding bass until the music was really something quite grand.

I would play after him, the simple scale, the simple chord, and then I just played some nonsense that sounded like a cat running up and down on top of garbage cans. Old Chong smiled and applauded and then said, "Very good! But now you must learn to keep time!"

So that's how I discovered that Old Chong's eyes were too slow to keep up with the wrong notes I was playing. He went through the motions in half-time. To help me keep rhythm, he stood behind me, pushing down on my right shoulder for every beat. He balanced pennies on top of my wrists so I would keep them still as I slowly played scales and arpeggios. He had me curve my hand around an apple and keep that shape when playing chords. He marched stiffly to show me how to make each finger dance up and down, staccato like an obedient little soldier.

He taught me all these things, and that was how I also learned I could be lazy and get away with mistakes, lots of mistakes. If I hit the wrong notes because I hadn't practiced enough, I never corrected myself. I just kept playing in rhythm. And Old Chong kept conducting his own private reverie.

So maybe I never really gave myself a fair chance. I did pick up the basics pretty quickly, and I might have become a good pianist at that young age. But I was so determined not to try, not to be anybody different that I learned to play only the most ear-splitting preludes, the most discordant hymns.

Over the next year, I practiced like this, dutifully in my own way. And then one day I heard my mother and her friend Lindo Jong both talking in a loud bragging tone of voice so others could hear. It was after church, and I was leaning against the brick wall wearing a dress with stiff white petticoats. Auntie Lindo's daughter, Waverly, who was about my age, was standing farther down the wall about five feet away. We had grown up together and shared all the closeness of two sisters squabbling over crayons and dolls. In other words, for the most part, we hated each other. I thought she was snotty. Waverly Jong had gained a certain amount of fame as "Chinatown's Littlest Chinese Chess Champion."

"She bring home too many trophy," lamented Auntie Lindo that Sunday. "All day she play chess. All day I have no time do nothing but dust off her winnings." She threw a scolding look at Waverly, who pretended not to see her.

"You lucky you don't have this problem," said Auntie Lindo with a sigh to my mother.

And my mother squared her shoulders and bragged: "Our problem worser than yours. If we ask Jing-mei wash dish, she hear nothing but music. It's like you can't stop this natural talent."

And right then, I was determined to put a stop to her foolish pride.

A few weeks later, Old Chong and my mother conspired to have me play in a talent show which would be held in the church hall. By then, my parents had saved up enough to buy me a secondhand piano, a black Wurlitzer spinet with a scarred bench. It was the showpiece of our living room.

For the talent show, I was to play a piece called "Pleading Child" from Schumann's *Scenes from Childhood*. It was a simple, moody piece that sounded more difficult than it was. I was supposed to memorize the whole thing, playing the repeat parts twice to make the piece sound longer. But I dawdled over it, playing a few bars and then cheating, looking up to see what notes followed. I never really listened to what I was playing. I daydreamed about being somewhere else, about being someone else.

The part I liked to practice best was the fancy curtsy: right foot out, touch the rose on the carpet with a pointed foot, sweep to the side, left leg bends, look up and smile.

My parents invited all the couples from the Joy Luck Club to witness my debut. Auntie Lindo and Uncle Tin were there. Waverly and her two older brothers had also come. The first two rows were filled with children both younger and older than I was. The littlest ones got to go first. They recited simple nursery rhymes, squawked out tunes on miniature violins, twirled Hula Hoops, pranced in pink ballet tutus, and when they bowed or curtsied, the audience would sigh in unison, "Awww," and then clap enthusiastically.

When my turn came, I was very confident. I remember my childish excitement. It was as if I knew, without a doubt, that the prodigy side of me really did exist. I had no fear whatsoever, no nervousness. I remember thinking to myself, This is it! This is it! I looked out over the audience, at my mother's blank face, my father's yawn, Auntie Lindo's stiff-lipped smile, Waverly's sulky expression. I had on a white dress layered with sheets of lace, and a pink bow in my Peter Pan haircut. As I sat down I envisioned people jumping to their feet and Ed Sullivan rushing up to introduce me to everyone on TV.

And I started to play. It was so beautiful. I was so caught up in how lovely I looked that at first I didn't worry how I would sound. So it was a surprise to me when I hit the first wrong note and I realized something didn't sound quite right. And then I hit another and another followed that. A chill started at the top of my head and began to trickle down. Yet I couldn't stop playing, as though my hands were bewitched. I kept thinking my fingers would adjust themselves back, like a train switching to the right track. I played this strange jumble through two repeats, the sour notes staying with me all the way to the end.

When I stood up, I discovered my legs were shaking. Maybe I had just been nervous and the audience, like Old Chong, had seen me go through the right motions and had not heard anything wrong at all. I swept my right foot out, went down on my knee, looked up and smiled. The room was quiet, except for Old Chong, who was beaming and shouting, "Bravo! Bravo! Well done!" But then I saw my mother's face, her stricken face. The audience clapped weakly, and as I walked back to my chair, with my whole face quivering as I tried not to cry, I heard a little boy whisper loudly to his mother, "That was awful," and the mother whispered back, "Well, she certainly tried."

And now I realized how many people were in the audience, the whole world it seemed. I was aware of eyes burning into my back. I felt the shame of my mother and father as they sat stiffly throughout the rest of the show.

We could have escaped during intermission. Pride and some strange sense of honor must have anchored my parents to their chairs. And so we watched it all: the eighteen-year-old boy with a fake mustache who did a magic show and juggled flaming hoops while riding a unicycle. The breasted girl with white makeup who sang from *Madama Butterfly* and got honorable mention. And the eleven-year-old boy who won first prize playing a tricky violin song that sounded like a busy bee.

After the show, the Hsus, the Jongs, and the St. Clairs from the Joy Luck Club came up to my mother and father.

"Lots of talented kids," Auntie Lindo said vaguely, smiling broadly.

"That was somethin' else," said my father, and I wondered if he was referring to me in a humorous way, or whether he even remembered what I had done.

Waverly looked at me and shrugged her shoulders. "You aren't a genius like me," she said matter-of-factly. And if I hadn't felt so bad, I would have pulled her braids and punched her stomach.

But my mother's expression was what devastated me: a quiet, blank look that said she had lost everything. I felt the same way, and it seemed as if everybody were now coming up, like gawkers at the scene of an accident, to see what parts were actually missing. When we got on the bus to go home, my father was humming the busy-bee tune and my mother was silent. I kept thinking she wanted to wait until we got home before shouting at me. But when my father unlocked the door to our apartment, my mother walked in and then went to the back, into the bedroom. No accusations. No blame. And in a way, I felt disappointed. I had been waiting for her to start shouting, so I could shout back and cry and blame her for all my misery.

I assumed my talent-show fiasco meant I never had to play the piano again. But two days later, after school, my mother came out of the kitchen and saw me watching TV.

"Four clock," she reminded me as if it were any other day. I was stunned, as though she were asking me to go through the talent-show torture again. I wedged myself more tightly in front of the TV.

"Turn off TV," she called from the kitchen five minutes later.

I didn't budge. And then I decided. I didn't have to do what my mother said anymore. I wasn't her slave. This wasn't China. I had listened to her before and look what happened. She was the stupid one.

She came out from the kitchen and stood in the arched entryway of the living room. "Four clock," she said once again, louder.

"I'm not going to play anymore," I said nonchalantly. "Why should I? I'm not a genius."

She walked over and stood in front of the TV. I saw her chest was heaving up and down in an angry way.

"No!" I said, and now I felt stronger, as if my true self had finally emerged. So this was what had been inside me all along.

"No! I won't!" I screamed.

She yanked me by the arm, pulled me off the floor, snapped off the TV. She was frighteningly strong, half pulling, half carrying me toward the piano as I kicked the throw rugs under my feet. She lifted me up and onto the hard bench. I was sobbing by now, looking at her bitterly. Her chest was heaving even more and her mouth was open, smiling crazily as if she were pleased I was crying.

"You want me to be someone that I'm not!" I sobbed. "I'll never be the kind of daughter you want me to be!"

"Only two kinds of daughters," she shouted in Chinese. "Those who are obedient and those who follow their own mind! Only one kind of daughter can live in this house. Obedient daughter!"

"Then I wish I wasn't your daughter. I wish you weren't my mother," I shouted. As I said these things I got scared. I felt like worms and toads and slimy things were crawling out of my chest, but it also felt good, as if this awful side of me had surfaced, at last.

"Too late change this," said my mother shrilly.

And I could sense her anger rising to its breaking point. I wanted to see it spill over. And that's when I remembered the babies she had lost in China, the ones we never talked about. "Then I wish I'd never been born!" I shouted. "I wish I were dead! Like them."

It was as if I had said the magic words. Alakazam!—and her face went blank, her mouth closed, her arms went slack, and she backed out of the room, stunned, as if she were blowing away like a small brown leaf, thin, brittle, lifeless.

It was not the only disappointment my mother felt in me. In the years that followed, I failed her so many times, each time asserting my own will, my right to fall short of expectations. I didn't get straight As. I didn't become class president. I didn't get into Stanford. I dropped out of college.

For unlike my mother, I did not believe I could be anything I wanted to be. I could only be me.

And for all those years, we never talked about the disaster at the recital or my terrible accusations afterward at the piano bench. All that remained unchecked, like a betrayal that was now unspeakable. So I never found a way to ask her why she had hoped for something so large that failure was inevitable.

And even worse, I never asked her what frightened me the most: Why had she given up hope?

For after our struggle at the piano, she never mentioned my playing again. The lessons stopped. The lid to the piano was closed, shutting out the dust, my misery, and her dreams.

So she surprised me. A few years ago, she offered to give me the piano, for my thirtieth birthday. I had not played in all those years. I saw the offer as a sign of forgiveness, a tremendous burden removed.

"Are you sure?" I asked shyly. "I mean, won't you and Dad miss it?"

"No, this your piano," she said firmly. "Always your piano. You only one can play."

"Well, I probably can't play anymore," I said. "It's been years."

"You pick up fast," said my mother, as if she knew this was certain. "You have natural talent. You could been genius if you want to."

"No I couldn't."

"You just not trying," said my mother. And she was neither angry nor sad. She said it as if to announce a fact that could never be disproved. "Take it," she said.

But I didn't at first. It was enough that she had offered it to me. And after that, every time I saw it in my parents' living room, standing in front of the bay windows, it made me feel proud, as if it were a shiny trophy I had won back.

Last week I sent a tuner over to my parents' apartment and had the piano reconditioned, for purely sentimental reasons. My mother had died a few months before and I had been getting things in order for my father, a little bit at a time. I put the jewelry in special silk pouches. The sweaters she had knitted in yellow, pink, bright orange—all the colors I hated—I put those in moth-proof boxes. I found some old Chinese silk dresses, the kind with little slits up the sides. I rubbed the old silk against my skin, then wrapped them in tissue and decided to take them home with me.

After I had the piano tuned, I opened the lid and touched the keys. It sounded even richer than I remembered. Really, it was a very good piano. Inside the bench were the same exercise notes with handwritten scales, the same second-hand music books with their covers held together with yellow tape.

I opened up the Schumann book to the dark little piece I had played at the recital. It was on the left-hand side of the page, "Pleading Child." It looked more difficult than I remembered. I played a few bars, surprised at how easily the notes came back to me.

And for the first time, or so it seemed, I noticed the piece on the right-hand side. It was called "Perfectly Contented." I tried to play this one as well. It had a lighter melody but the same flowing rhythm and turned out to be quite easy. "Pleading Child" was shorter but slower; "Perfectly Contented" was longer but faster. And after I played them both a few times, I realized they were two halves of the same song.

QUESTIONS AND CONSIDERATIONS

1. Why does the narrator's mother try to make her into a child prodigy? Why does the daughter want to fulfill her mother's fantasy of her? What part of her rebels against her mother's fantasy, and why?

2. How does the story integrate the cultural dreams of the Chinese immigrants and the dreams of mainstream Americans?

3. Contrast the values and personalities of the narrator and her mother. Do you think that the narrator is a fully Americanized young woman?

4. What do the narrator and her mother learn about themselves and one another at the piano recital and during the accusations at the piano bench the next day? In what ways does this scene capture a typical preadolescent identity struggle?

5. What frightened the narrator most about her mother's changed attitude about her becoming a great pianist? What does the narrator come to understand about her mother's belief in her daughter's natural talent at piano? How can the narrator be two kinds of daughters for her mother?

6. How does Amy Tan use humor and imagery in presenting the narrator's ordeal of fulfilling her mother's fantasy of being a child prodigy?

IDEAS FOR WRITING

1. Write an essay in which you discuss several of the issues in mother-daughter relationships that this story explores. First consider the issues in the context of the story and then from the perspective of your own life experiences.

2. Write a short story about a child or preadolescent who is groomed to become a child prodigy. Consider your own experiences, those of friends or relatives, and those presented in the media. Focus on the resentment and bitterness that can accompany an attempt to achieve stardom as well as the stress that success places on a child in this situation.

Hills Like White Elephants
Ernest Hemingway

Journal

Write about a trip or outing you went on with someone with whom you had a romantic relationship, an outing when you had a conflict or argument. What did you learn about your relationship with this person on the trip?

The hills across the valley of the Ebro were long and white. On this side there was no shade and no trees and the station was between two lines of rails in the sun. Close against the side of the station there was the warm shadow of the building and a curtain, made of strings of bamboo beads, hung across the open door into the bar, to keep out flies. The American and the girl with him sat at a table in the shade, outside the building. It was very hot and the express from Barcelona would come in forty minutes. It stopped at this junction for two minutes and went on to Madrid.

"What should we drink?" the girl asked. She had taken off her hat and put it on the table.

"It's pretty hot," the man said.

"Let's drink beer."

"Dos cervezas," the man said into the curtain.

"Big ones?" a woman asked from the doorway.

"Yes. Two big ones."

The woman brought two glasses of beer and two felt pads. She put the felt pads and the beer glasses on the table and looked at the man and the girl. The girl was looking off at the line of hills. They were white in the sun and the country was brown and dry.

"They look like white elephants," she said.

"I've never seen one," the man drank his beer.

"No, you wouldn't have."

"I might have," the man said. "Just because you say I wouldn't have doesn't prove anything."

The girl looked at the bead curtain. "They've painted something on it," she said. "What does it say?"

"Anis del Toro. It's a drink,"

"Could we try it?"

The man called "Listen" through the curtain. The woman came out from the bar.

"Four reales."

"We want two Anis del Toro."

"With water?"

"Do you want it with water?"

"I don't know," the girl said. "Is it good with water?"

"It's all right."

"You want them with water?" asked the woman.

"Yes, with water."

"It tastes like licorice," the girl said and put the glass down.

"That's the way with everything."

"Yes," said the girl. "Everything tastes of licorice. Especially all the things you've waited so long for, like absinthe."

"Oh, cut it out."

"You started it," the girl said. "I was being amused. I was having a fine time."

"Well, let's try and have a fine time."

"All right. I was trying. I said the mountains looked like white elephants. Wasn't that bright?"

"That was bright."

"I wanted to try this new drink: That's all we do, isn't it—look at things and try new drinks?"

"I guess so."

The girl looked across at the hills.

"They're lovely hills," she said. "They don't really look like white elephants. I just meant the coloring of their skin through the trees."

"Should we have another drink?"

"All right."

The warm wind blew the bead curtain against the table.

"The beer's nice and cool," the man said.

"It's lovely," the girl said.

"It's really an awfully simple operation, Jig," the man said. "It's not really an operation at all."

The girl looked at the ground the table legs rested on.

"I know you wouldn't mind it, Jig. It's really not anything. It's just to let the air in."

The girl did not say anything.

"I'll go with you and I'll stay with you all the time. They just let the air in and then it's all perfectly natural."

"Then what will we do afterward?"

"We'll be fine afterward. Just like we were before."

"What makes you think so?"

"That's the only thing that bothers us. It's the only thing that's made us unhappy."

The girl looked at the bead curtain, put her hand out, and took hold of two of the strings of beads.

"And you think then we'll be all right and be happy."

"I know we will. You don't have to be afraid. I've known lots of people that have done it."

"So have I," said the girl. "And afterward they were all so happy."

"Well," the man said, "if you don't want to you don't have to. I wouldn't have you do it if you didn't want to. But I know it's perfectly simple."

"And you really want to?"

"I think it's the best thing to do. But I don't want you to do it if you don't really want to."

"And if I do it you'll be happy and things will be like they were and you'll love me?"

"I love you now. You know I love you."

"I know. But if I do it, then it will be nice again if I say things are like white elephants, and you'll like it?"

"I'll love it. I love it now but I just can't think about it. You know how I get when I worry."

"If I do it you won't ever worry?"

"I won't worry about that because it's perfectly simple."

"Then I'll do it. Because I don't care about me."

"What do you mean?"

"I don't care about me."

"Well, I care about you."

"Oh, yes. But I don't care about me. And I'll do it and then everything will be fine."

"I don't want you to do it if you feel that way."

The girl stood up and walked to the end of the station. Across, on the other side, were fields of grain and trees along the banks of the Ebro. Far away, beyond the river, were mountains. The shadow of a cloud moved across the field of grain and she saw the river through the trees.

"And we could have all this," she said. "And we could have everything and every day we make it more impossible."

"What did you say?"

"I said we could have everything."

"We can have everything."

"No, we can't."

"We can have the whole world."

"No, we can't."

"We can go everywhere."

"No, we can't. It isn't ours any more."

"It's ours."

"No, it isn't. And once they take it away, you never get it back."

"But they haven't taken it away."

"We'll wait and see."

"Come on back in the shade," he said. "You mustn't feel that way."

"I don't feel any way," the girl said. "I just know things."

"I don't want you to do anything that you don't want to do—"

"Nor that isn't good for me," she said. "I know. Could we have another beer?"

"All right. But you've got to realize—"

"I realize," the girl said. "Can't we maybe stop talking?"

They sat down at the table and the girl looked across at the hills on the dry side of the valley and the man looked at her and at the table.

"You've got to realize," he said, "that I don't want you to do it if you don't want to. I'm perfectly willing to go through with it if it means anything to you."

"Doesn't it mean anything to you? We could get along."

"Of course it does. But I don't want anybody but you. I don't want any one else. And I know it's perfectly simple."

"Yes, you know it's perfectly simple."

"It's all right for you to say that, but I do know it."

"Would you do something for me now?"

"I'd do anything for you."

"Would you please please please please please please please stop talking?"

He did not say anything but looked at the bags against the wall of the station. There were labels on them from all the hotels where they had spent nights.

"But I don't want you to," he said, "I don't care anything about it."

"I'll scream," the girl said.

The woman came out through the curtains with two glasses of beer and put them down on the damp felt pads. "The train comes in five minutes," she said.

"What did she say?" asked the girl.

"That the train is coming in five minutes."

The girl smiled brightly at the woman, to thank her.

"I'd better take the bags over to the other side of the station," the man said. She smiled at him.

"All right. Then come back and we'll finish the beer."

He picked up the two heavy bags and carried them around the station to the other tracks. He looked up the tracks but could not see the train. Coming back, he walked through the barroom, where people waiting for the train were drinking. He drank an Anis at the bar and looked at the people. They were all waiting reasonably for the train. He went out through the bead curtain. She was sitting at the table and smiled at him.

"Do you feel better?" he asked.

"I feel fine," she said. "There's nothing wrong with me. I feel fine."

QUESTIONS AND CONSIDERATIONS

1. How does the physical setting of the story—a bar in a hot, desolate Spanish train station—contribute to the atmosphere of the story and help to reveal the relationship between the couple?

2. The name of this story, "Hills Like White Elephants," refers literally to the "long and white" hills the couple can see on the other side of the Ebro River valley. What else does this image suggest about the couple and their differences? What are the implications of the expression "white elephant"?

3. What is the "awfully simple operation" that the American in the story wants Jig to have? Why does she resist him at first and then finally give in?

4. What does Jig mean when she says, "And we could have everything and every day we make it more impossible"? What different definitions do Jig and the American have of the term "everything"? Do you think the relationship will survive after the operation?

5. Why is Jig so irritated by the American's "talking"? What seems to disturb her about the way he uses language?

6. Many of Jig's statements are ironic. Point out examples of irony in Jig's responses. Do you think that the American realizes that Jig is speaking ironically? Do you think he understands the irony of her final statement, "I feel fine"?

IDEAS FOR WRITING

1. Much of the impact of this story comes from the dialogue and images that present the two main characters and their different points of view on what a good relationship involves; in some ways, it resembles a one-act play or a short film. Rewrite the story as a play or film and then write a short analysis of the changes you have made. How did turning the story into another form change its meaning? Why do you think an audience would have responded differently to the story if they saw it on the screen or viewed it in a theater?

2. Write an essay in which you describe and analyze the relationship between Jig and the American. Why do they fail to communicate? Is there hope for their relationship? Provide examples from the text to support your point of view.

A Place I've Never Been

David Leavitt

Journal

Write about a game that you played with your high school or college peers that involved risk and the challenge of self-revelation.

I had known Nathan for years—too many years, since we were in college—so when he went to Europe I wasn't sure how I'd survive it; he was my best friend, after all, my constant companion at Sunday afternoon double bills at the Thalia, my ever-present source of consolation and conversation. Still, such a turn can prove to be a blessing in disguise. It threw me off at first, his not being there—I had no one to watch *Jeopardy!* with, or talk to on the phone late at night—but then, gradually, I got over it, and I realized that maybe it was a good thing after all, that maybe now, with Nathan gone, I would be forced to go out into the world more, make new friends, maybe even find a boyfriend. And I had started: I lost weight, I went shopping. I was at Bloomingdale's one day on my lunch hour when a very skinny black woman with a French accent asked me if I'd like to have a makeover. I had always run away from such things, but this time, before I had a chance, this woman put her long hands on my cheeks and looked into my face—not my eyes, my face—and said, "You're really beautiful. You know that?" And I absolutely couldn't answer. After she was through with me I didn't even know what I looked like, but everyone at my office was amazed. "Celia," they said, "you look great. What happened?" I smiled, wondering if I'd be allowed to go back every day for a makeover, if I offered to pay.

There was even some interest from a man—a guy named Roy who works downstairs, in contracts—and I was feeling pretty good about myself again, when the phone rang, and it was Nathan. At first I thought he must have been calling me from some European capital, but he said no, he was back in New York. "Celia," he said, "I have to see you. Something awful has happened."

Hearing those words, I pitched over—I assumed the worst. (And why not? He had been assuming the worst for over a year.) But he said, "No, no, I'm fine. I'm perfectly healthy. It's my apartment. Oh, Celia, it's awful. Could you come over?"

"Were you broken into?" I asked.

"I might as well have been!"

"Okay," I said. "I'll come over after work."

"I just got back last night. This is too much."

"I'll be there by six, Nathan."

"Thank you," he said, a little breathlessly, and hung up.

I drummed my nails—newly painted by another skinny woman at Bloomingdale's—against the black Formica of my desk, mostly to try out the sound.

In truth I was a little happy he was back—I had missed him—and not at all surprised that he'd cut his trip short. Rich people are like that, I've observed; because they don't have to buy bargain-basement tickets on weird charter airlines, they feel free to change their minds. Probably he just got bored tooting
around Europe, missed his old life, missed *Jeopardy!,* his friends. Oh, Nathan!
How could I tell him the Thalia had closed?

I had to take several buses to get from my office to his neighborhood—
a route I had once traversed almost daily, but which, since Nathan's departure, I hadn't had much occasion to take. Sitting on the Madison Avenue
bus, I looked out the window at the rows of unaffordable shops, some still
exactly what they'd been before, others boarded up, or reopened under new
auspices—such a familiar panorama, unfolding, block by block, like a Chinese scroll I'd once been shown on a museum trip in junior high school. It
was raining a little, and in the warm bus the long, unvarying progress of my
love for Nathan seemed to unscroll as well—all the dinners and lunches
and arguments, and all the trips back alone to my apartment, feeling ugly
and fat, because Nathan had once again confirmed he could never love me
the way he assured me he would someday love a man. How many hundreds of times I received that confirmation! And yet, somehow, it never occurred to me to give up that love I had nurtured for him since our earliest
time together, that love which belonged to those days just past the brink of
childhood, before I understood about Nathan, or rather, before Nathan understood about himself. So I persisted, and Nathan, in spite of his embarrassment at my occasional outbursts, continued to depend on me. I think he
hoped that my feeling for him would one day transform itself into a more
maternal kind of affection, that I would one day become the sort of woman
who could tend to him without expecting anything in return. And that was,
perhaps, a reasonable hope on his part, given my behavior. But: "If only,"
he said to me once, "you didn't have to act so crazy, Celia—" And that was
how I realized I had to get out.

I got off the bus and walked the block and a half to his building—its
façade, I noted, like almost every façade in the neighborhood, blemished by a
bit of scaffolding—and, standing in that vestibule where I'd stood so often,
waited for him to buzz me up. I read for diversion the now familiar list of tenants' names. The only difference today was that there were ragged ends of
Scotch tape stuck around Nathan's name; probably his subletter had put his
own name over Nathan's, and Nathan, returning, had torn the piece of paper
off and left the ends of the tape. This didn't seem like him, and it made me
suspicious. He was a scrupulous person about such things.

In due time—though slowly, for him—he let me in, and I walked the three
flights of stairs to find him standing in the doorway, unshaven, looking as if
he'd just gotten out of bed. He wasn't wearing any shoes, and he'd gained
some weight. Almost immediately he fell into me—that is the only way to describe it, his big body limp in my arms. "Oh, God," he murmured into my hair,
"am I glad to see you."

"Nathan," I said. "Nathan." And held him there. Usually he wriggled out of physical affection; kisses from him were little nips; hugs were tight, jerky chokeholds. Now he lay absolutely still, his arms slung under mine, and I tried to keep from gasping from the weight of him. But finally—reluctantly—he let go, and putting his hand on his forehead, gestured toward the open door. "Prepare yourself," he said. "It's worse than you can imagine."

He led me into the apartment. I have to admit, I was shocked by what I saw. Nathan, unlike me, is a chronically neat person, everything in its place, all his perfect furniture glowing, polished, every state-of-the-art fountain pen and pencil tip-up in the blue glass jar on his desk. Today, however, the place was in havoc—newspapers and old Entenmann's cookie boxes spread over the floor, records piled on top of each other, inner sleeves crumpled behind the radiator, the blue glass jar overturned. The carpet was covered with dark mottlings, and a stench of old cigarette smoke and sweat and urine inhabited the place. "It gets worse," he said. "Look at the kitchen." A thick, yellowing layer of grease encrusted the stovetop. The bathroom was beyond the pale of my descriptive capacity for filth.

"Those bastards," Nathan was saying, shaking his head.

"Hold on to the security deposit," I suggested. "Make them pay for it."

He sat down on the sofa, the arms of which appeared to have been ground with cigarette butts, and shook his head. "There *is* no security deposit," he moaned. "I didn't take one because supposedly Denny was my friend, and this other guy—Hoop, or whatever his name was—he was Denny's friend. And look at this!" From the coffee table he handed me a thick stack of utility and phone bills, all unopened. "The phone's disconnected," he said. "Two of the rent checks have bounced. The landlord's about to evict me. I'm sure my credit rating has gone to hell. Jesus, why'd I do it?" He stood, marched into the corner, then turned again to face me. "You know what? I'm going to call my father. I'm going to have him sick every one of his bastard lawyers on those assholes until they pay."

"Nathan," I reminded, "they're unemployed actors. They're poor."

"Then let them rot in jail!" Nathan screamed. His voice was loud and sharp in my ears. It had been a long time since I'd had to witness another person's misery, a long time since anyone had asked of me what Nathan was now asking of me: to take care, to resolve, to smooth. Nonetheless I rallied my energies. I stood. "Look," I said. "I'm going to go out and buy sponges, Comet, Spic and Span, Fantastik, Windex. Everything. We're going to clean this place up. We're going to wash the sheets and shampoo the rug, we're going to scrub the toilet until it shines. I promise you, by the time you go to sleep tonight, it'll be what it was."

He stood silent in the corner.

"Okay?" I said.

"Okay."

"So you wait here," I said. "I'll be right back."

"Thank you."

I picked up my purse and closed the door, thus, once again, saving him from disaster.

But there were certain things I could not save Nathan from. A year ago, his ex-lover Martin had called him up and told him he had tested positive. This was the secret fact he had to live with every day of his life, the secret fact that had brought him to Xanax and Halcion, Darvon and Valium—all crude efforts to cut the fear firing through his blood, exploding like the tiny viral time bombs he believed were lying in wait, expertly planted. It was the day after he found out that he started talking about clearing out. He had no obligations—he had quit his job a few months before and was just doing free-lance work anyway—and so, he reasoned, what was keeping him in New York? "I need to get away from all this," he said, gesturing frantically at the air. I believe he really thought back then that by running away to somewhere where it was less well known, he might be able to escape the disease. This is something I've noticed: The men act as if they think the power of infection exists in direct proportion to its publicity, that in places far from New York City it can, in effect, be outrun. And who's to say they are wrong, with all this talk about stress and the immune system? In Italy, in the countryside, Nathan seemed to feel he'd feel safer. And probably he was right; he would feel safer. Over there, away from the American cityscape with its streets full of gaunt sufferers, you're able to forget the last ten years, you can remember how old the world is and how there was a time when sex wasn't something likely to kill you.

It should be pointed out that Nathan had no symptoms; he hadn't even had the test for the virus itself. He refused to have it, saying he could think of no reason to give up at least the hope of freedom. Not that this made any difference, of course. The fear itself is a brutal enough enemy.

But he gave up sex. No sex, he said, was safe enough for him. He bought a VCR and began to hoard pornographic videotapes. And I think he was having phone sex too, because once I picked up the phone in his apartment and before I could say hello, a husky-voiced man said, "You stud," and then, when I said "Excuse me?" got flustered-sounding and hung up. Some people would probably count that as sex, but I'm not sure I would.

All the time, meanwhile, he was frenzied. I could never guess what time he'd call—six in the morning, sometimes, he'd drag me from sleep. "I figured you'd still be up," he'd say, which gave me a clue to how he was living. It got so bad that by the time he actually left I felt as if a great burden had been lifted from my shoulders. Not that I didn't miss him, but from that day on my time was, miraculously, my own. Nathan is a terrible correspondent—I don't think he's sent me one postcard or letter in all the time we've known each other—and so for months my only news of him came through the phone. Strangers would call me, Germans, Italians, nervous-sounding young men who spoke bad English, who were staying at the YMCA, who were in New York for the first time and to whom he had given my number. I don't think any of them actually wanted to see me; I think they just wanted me to tell them which bars were good and which subway lines were safe—information I happily dispensed. Of course, there was a time when I would have taken them on the subways, shown them around the bars, but I have thankfully passed out of that phase.

And of course, as sex became more and more a possibility, then a likelihood once again in my life, I began to worry myself about the very things that were torturing Nathan. What should I say, say, to Roy in contracts, when he asked me to sleep with him, which I was fairly sure he was going to do within a lunch or two? Certainly I wanted to sleep with him. But did I dare ask him to use a condom? Did I dare even broach the subject? I was frightened that he might get furious, that he might overreact, and I considered saying nothing, taking my chances. Then again, for me in particular, it was a very big chance to take; I have a pattern of falling in love with men who at some point or other have fallen in love with other men. All trivial, selfish, this line of worry, I recognize now, but at that point Nathan was gone, and I had no one around to remind me of how high the stakes were for other people. I slipped back into a kind of women's-magazine attitude toward the whole thing: for the moment, at least, *I* was safe, and I cherished that safety without even knowing it, I gloried in it. All my speculations were merely matters of prevention; that place where Nathan had been exiled was a place I'd never been. I am ashamed to admit it, but there was even a moment when I took a kind of vengeful pleasure in the whole matter—the years I had hardly slept with anyone, for which I had been taught to feel ashamed and freakish, I now wanted to rub in someone's face: I was right and you were wrong! I wanted to say. I'm not proud of having had such thoughts, and I can only say, in my defense, that they passed quickly—but a strict accounting of all feelings, at this point, seems to me necessary. We have to be rigorous with ourselves these days.

In any case, Nathan was back, and I didn't dare think about myself. I went to the grocery store, I bought every cleaner I could find. And when I got back to the apartment he was still standing where he'd been standing, in the corner. "Nate," I said, "here's everything. Let's get to work."

"Okay," he said glumly, even though he is an ace cleaner, and we began.

As we cleaned, the truth came out. This Denny to whom he'd sublet the apartment, Nathan had had a crush on. "To the extent that a crush is a relevant thing in my life anymore," he said, "since God knows, there's nothing to be done about it. But there you are. The libido doesn't stop, the heart doesn't stop, no matter how hard you try to make them."

None of this—especially that last part—was news to me, though Nathan had managed to overlook that aspect of our relationship for years. I had understood from the beginning about the skipping-over of the security payment, the laxness of the setup, because these were the sorts of things I would have willingly done for Nathan at a different time. I think he was privately so excited at the prospect of this virile young man, Denny, sleeping, and perhaps having sex, between his sheets, that he would have taken any number of risks to assure it. Crush: what an oddly appropriate word, considering what it makes you do to yourself. His apartment was, in a sense, the most Nathan could offer, and probably the most Denny would accept. I understood: You want to get as close as you can, even if it's only at arm's length. And when you come back, maybe, you want to breathe in the smell of the person you love loving someone else.

Europe, he said, had been a failure. He had wandered, having dinner with old friends of his parents, visiting college acquaintances who were busy with exotic lives. He'd gone to bars, which was merely frustrating; there was nothing to be done. "What about safe sex?" I asked, and he said, "Celia, please. There is no such thing, as far as I'm concerned." Once again this started a panicked thumping in my chest as I thought about Roy, and Nathan said, "It's really true. Suppose something lands on you—you know what I'm saying—and there's a microscopic cut in your skin. Bingo."

"Nathan, come on," I said. "That sounds crazy to me."

"Yeah?" he said. "Just wait till some ex-lover of yours calls you up with a little piece of news. Then see how you feel."

He returned to his furious scrubbing of the bathroom sink. I returned to my furious scrubbing of the tub. Somehow, even now, I'm always stuck with the worst of it.

Finally we were done. The place looked okay—it didn't smell anymore—though it was hardly what it had been. Some long-preserved pristineness was gone from the apartment, and both of us knew without saying a word that it would never be restored. We breathed in exhausted—no, not exhausted triumph. It was more like relief. We had beaten something back, yet again.

My hands were red from detergents, my stomach and forehead sweaty. I went into the now-bearable bathroom and washed up, and then Nathan said he would take me out to dinner—my choice. And so we ended up, as we had a thousand other nights, sitting by the window at the Empire Szechuan down the block from his apartment, eating cold noodles with sesame sauce, which, when we had finished them, Nathan ordered more of. "God, how I've missed these," he said, as he scooped the brown slimy noodles into his mouth. "You don't know."

In between slurps he looked at me and said, "You look good, Celia. Have you lost weight?"

"Yes, as a matter of fact," I said.

"I thought so."

I looked back at him, trying to recreate the expression on the French woman's face, and didn't say anything, but as it turned out I didn't need to. "I know what you're thinking," he said, "and you're right. Twelve pounds since you last saw me. But I don't care. I mean, you lose weight when you're sick. At least this way, gaining weight, I know I don't have it."

He continued eating. I looked outside. Past the plate-glass window that separated us from the sidewalk, crowds of people walked, young and old, good-looking and bad-looking, healthy and sick, some of them staring in at our food and our eating. Suddenly—urgently—I wanted to be out among them, I wanted to be walking in that crowd, pushed along in it, and not sitting here, locked into this tiny two-person table with Nathan. And yet I knew that escape was probably impossible. I looked once again at Nathan, eating happily, resigned, perhaps, to the fate of his apartment, and the knowledge that everything would work out, that this had, in fact, been merely a run-of-the-mill crisis. For the moment he was appeased, his hungry anxiety sated; for the moment. But who could guess what would set him off next? I steadied my chin on my palm, drank some water, watched Nathan eat like a happy child.

The next few weeks were thorny with events. Nathan bought a new sofa, had his place recarpeted, threw several small dinners. Then it was time for Lizzie Fischman's birthday party—one of the few annual events in our lives. We had known Lizzie since college—she was a tragic, trying sort of person, the sort who carries with her a constant aura of fatedness, of doom. So many bad things happen to Lizzie you can't help but wonder, after a while, if she doesn't hold out a beacon for disaster. This year alone, she was in a taxi that got hit by a bus; then she was mugged in the subway by a man who called her an "ugly dyke bitch"; then she started feeling sick all the time, and no one could figure out what was wrong, until it was revealed that her building's heating system was leaking small quantities of carbon monoxide into her awful little apartment. The tenants sued, and in the course of the suit, Lizzie, exposed as an illegal subletter, was evicted. She now lived with her father in one half of a two-family house in Plainfield, New Jersey, because she couldn't find another apartment she could afford. (Her job, incidentally, in addition to being wretchedly low-paying, is one of the dreariest I know of: proofreading accounting textbooks in an office on Forty-second Street.)

Anyway, each year Lizzie threw a big birthday party for herself in her father's house in Plainfield, and we all went, her friends, because of course we couldn't bear to disappoint her and add ourselves to her roster of worldwide enemies. It was invariably a miserable party—everyone drunk on bourbon, and Lizzie, eager to recreate the slumber parties of her childhood, dancing around in pink pajamas with feet. We were making s'mores over the gas stove—shoving the chocolate bars and the graham crackers onto fondue forks rather than old sticks—and *Beach Blanket Bingo* was playing on the VCR and no one was having a good time, particularly Nathan, who was overdressed in a beige Giorgio Armani linen suit he'd bought in Italy, and was standing in the corner idly pressing his neck, feeling for swollen lymph nodes. Lizzie's circle dwindled each year, as her friends moved on, or found ways to get out of it. This year eight of us had made it to the party, plus a newcomer from Lizzie's office, a very fat girl with very red nails named Dorrie Friedman, who, in spite of her heaviness, was what my mother would have called dainty. She ate a lot, but unless you were observant, you'd never have noticed it. The image of the fat person stuffing food into her face is mythic: I know from experience, when fat you eat slowly, chew methodically, in order not to draw attention to your mouth. Over the course of an hour I watched Dorrie Friedman put away six of those s'mores with a tidiness worthy of Emily Post, I watched her dab her cheek with her napkin after each bite, and I understood: This was shame, but also, in some peculiar way, this was innocence. A state to envy.

There is a point in Lizzie's parties when she invariably suggests we play Deprivation, a game that had been terribly popular among our crowd in college. The way you play it is you sit in a big circle, and everyone is given ten pennies. (In this case the pennies were unceremoniously taken from a huge bowl that sat on top of Lizzie's mother's refrigerator, and that she had upended on the linoleum floor—no doubt a long-contemplated act of desecration.) You go around the circle, and each person announces something he or she has never done, or a place they've never been—"I've never been to Borneo" is a good example—and then everyone who has been to Borneo is obliged to throw you a penny. Needless to say, especially in college, the game degenerates rather quickly to matters of sex and drugs.

I remembered the first time I ever played Deprivation, my sophomore year, I had been reading Blake's *Songs of Innocence* and *Songs of Experience.* Everything in our lives seemed a question of innocence and experience back then, so this seemed appropriate. There was a tacit assumption among my friends that "experience"—by that term we meant, I think, almost exclusively sex and drugs—was something you strove to get as much of as you could, that innocence, for all the praise it received in literature, was a state so essentially tedious that those of us still stuck in it deserved the childish recompense of shiny new pennies. (None of us, of course, imagining that five years from now the "experiences" we urged on one another might spread a murderous germ, that five years from now some of our friends, still in their youth, would be lost. Youth! You were supposed to sow your wild oats, weren't you? Those of us who didn't—we were the ones who failed, weren't we?)

One problem with Deprivation is that the older you get, the less interesting it becomes; every year, it seemed, my friends had fewer gaps in their lives to confess, and as our embarrassments began to stack up on the positive side, it was what we *had* done that was titillating. Indeed, Nick Walsh, who was to Lizzie what Nathan was to me, complained as the game began, "I can't play this. There's nothing I haven't done." But Lizzie, who has a naive faith in ritual, merely smiled and said, "Oh come on, Nick. No one's done *everything.* For instance, you could say, 'I've never been to Togo,' or 'I've never been made love to simultaneously by twelve Arab boys in a back alley on Mott Street.'"

"Well, Lizzie," Nick said, "it *is* true that I've never been to Togo." His leering smile surveyed the circle, and of course, there *was* someone there—Gracie Wong, I think—who had, in fact, been to Togo.

The next person in the circle was Nathan. He's never liked this game, but he also plays it more cleverly than anyone. "Hmm," he said, stroking his chin as if there were a beard there, "let's see . . . Ah, I've got it. I've never had sex with anyone in this group." He smiled boldly, and everyone laughed—everyone, that is, except for me and Bill Darlington, and Lizzie herself—all three of us now, for the wretched experiments of our early youth, obliged to throw Nathan a penny.

Next was Dorrie Friedman's turn, which I had been dreading. She sat on the floor, her legs crossed under her, her very fat fingers intertwined, and said, "Hmm . . . Something I've never done. Well—I've never ridden a bicycle."

An awful silence greeted this confession, and then a tinkling sound, like wind chimes, as the pennies flew. "Gee," Dorrie Friedman said, "I won big that time." I couldn't tell if she was genuinely pleased.

And as the game went on, we settled, all of us, into more or less parallel states of innocence and experience, except for Lizzie and Nick, whose piles had rapidly dwindled, and Dorrie Friedman, who, it seemed, by virtue of life-long fatness, had done nearly nothing. She had never been to Europe; she had never swum; she had never played tennis; she had never skied; she had never been on a boat. Even someone else's turn could be an awful moment for Dorrie, as when Nick said, "I've never had a vaginal orgasm." But fortunately, there, she did throw in her penny. I was relieved; I don't think I could have stood it if she hadn't.

After a while, in an effort not to look at Dorrie and her immense pile of pennies, we all started trying to trip up Lizzie and Nick, whose respective caches of sexual experience seemed limitless. "I've never had sex in my parents' bed," I offered. The pennies flew. "I've never had sex under a dry-docked boat." "I've never had sex with more than one other person." "Two other people." "Three other people." By then Lizzie was out of pennies, and declared the game over.

"I guess I won," Dorrie said rather softly. She had her pennies neatly piled in identically sized stacks.

I wondered if Lizzie was worried. I wondered if she was thinking about the disease, if she was frightened, the way Nathan was, or if she just assumed death was coming anyway, the final blow in her life of unendurable misfortunes. She started to gather the pennies back into their bowl, and I glanced across the room at Nathan, to see if he was ready to go. All through the game, of course, he had been looking pretty miserable—he always looks miserable at parties. Worse, he has a way of turning his misery around, making me responsible for it. Across the circle of our nearest and dearest friends he glared at me angrily, and I knew that by the time we were back in his car and on our way home to Manhattan he would have contrived a way for the evening to be my fault. And yet tonight, his occasional knowing sneers, inviting my complicity in looking down on the party, only enraged me. I was angry at him, in advance, for what I was sure he was going to do in the car, and I was also angry at him for being such a snob, for having no sympathy toward this evening, which, in spite of all its displeasures, was nevertheless an event of some interest, perhaps the very last hurrah of our youth, our own little big chill. And that was something: Up until now I had always assumed Nathan's version of things to be the correct one, and cast my own into the background. Now his perception seemed meager, insufficient: Here was an historic night, after all, and all he seemed to want to think about was his own boredom, his own unhappiness.

Finally, reluctantly, Lizzie let us go, and relinquished from her grip, we got into Nathan's car and headed onto the Garden State Parkway. "Never again," Nathan was saying, "will I allow you to convince me to attend one of Lizzie Fischman's awful parties. This is the last." I didn't even bother answering, it all seemed so predictable. Instead I just settled back into the comfortable velour of the car seat and switched on the radio. Dionne Warwick and Elton John were singing "That's What Friends Are For," and Nathan said, "You know, of course, that that's the song they wrote to raise money for AIDS."

"I'd heard," I said.

"Have you seen the video? It makes me furious. All these famous singers up there, grinning these huge grins, rocking back and forth. Why the hell are they smiling, I'd like to ask?"

For a second, I considered answering that question, then decided I'd better not. We were slipping into the Holland Tunnel, and by the time we got through to Manhattan I was ready to call it a night. I wanted to get back to my apartment and see if Roy had left a message on my answering machine. But Nathan said, "It's Saturday night, Celia, it's still early. Won't you have a drink with me or something?"

"I don't want to go to any more gay bars, Nathan, I told you that."

"So we'll go to a straight bar. I don't care. I just can't bear to go back to my apartment at eleven o'clock." We stopped for a red light, and he leaned closer to me. "The truth is, I don't think I can bear to be alone. Please."

"All right," I said. What else could I say?

"Goody," Nathan said.

We parked the car in a garage and walked to a darkish café on Greenwich Avenue, just a few doors down from the huge gay bar Nathan used to frequent, and which he jokingly referred to as "the airport." No mention was made of that bar in the café, however, where he ordered latte machiato for both of us. "Aren't you going to have some dessert?" he said. "I know I am. Baba au rhum, perhaps. Or tiramisu. You know *'tirami su'* means 'pick me up,' but if you want to offend an Italian waiter, you say 'I'll have the *tiramilo su,'* which means 'pick up my dick.'"

"I'm trying to lose weight, Nathan," I said. "Please don't encourage me to eat desserts."

"Sorry." He coughed. Our latte machiatos came, and Nathan raised his cup and said, "Here's to us. Here's to Lizzie Fischman. Here's to never playing that dumb game again as long as we live." These days, I noticed, Nathan used the phrase "as long as we live" a bit too frequently for comfort.

Reluctantly I touched my glass to his. "You know," he said, "I think I've always hated that game. Even in college, when I won, it made me jealous. Everyone else had done so much more than me. Back then I figured I'd have time to explore the sexual world. Guess the joke's on me, huh?"

I shrugged. I wasn't sure.

"What's with you tonight, anyway?" he said. "You're so distant."

"I just have things on my mind, Nathan, that's all."

"You've been acting weird ever since I got back from Europe, Celia. Sometimes I think you don't even want to see me."

Clearly he was expecting reassurances to the contrary. I didn't say anything.

"Well," he said, "is that it? You don't want to see me?"

I twisted my shoulders in confusion. "Nathan—"

"Great," he said, and laughed so that I couldn't tell if he was kidding. "Your best friend for nearly ten years. Jesus."

"Look, Nathan, don't melodramatize," I said. "It's not that simple. It's just that I have to think a little about myself. My own life, my own needs. I mean, I'm going to be thirty soon. You know how long it's been since I've had a boyfriend?"

"I'm not against your having a boyfriend," Nathan said. "Have I ever tried to stop you from having a boyfriend?"

"But, Nathan," I said, "I never get to meet anyone when I'm with you all the time. I love you and I want to be your friend, but you can't expect me to just keep giving and giving and giving my time to you without anything in return. It's not fair."

I was looking away from him as I said this. From the corner of my vision I could see him glancing to the side, his mouth a small, tight line.

"You're all I have," he said quietly.

"That's not true, Nathan," I said.

"Yes it is true, Celia."

"Nathan, you have lots of other friends."

"But none of them count. No one but you counts."

The waitress arrived with his goblet of tiramisu, put it down in front of him. "Go on with your life, you say," he was muttering. "Find a boyfriend. Don't you think I'd do the same thing if I could? But all those options are closed to me, Celia. There's nowhere for me to go, no route that isn't dangerous. I mean, getting on with my life—I just can't talk about that simply anymore, the way you can." He leaned closer, over the table. "Do you want to know something?" he said. "Every time I see someone I'm attracted to I go into a cold sweat. And I imagine that they're dead, that if I touch them, the part of them I touch will die. Don't you see? It's bad enough to be afraid you might get it. But to be afraid you might give it—and to someone you loved—" He shook his head, put his hand to his forehead.

What could I say to that? What possibly was there to say? I took his hand, suddenly, I squeezed his hand until the edges of his fingers were white. I was remembering how Nathan looked the first time I saw him, in line at a college dining hall, his hands on his hips, his head erect, staring worriedly at the old lady dishing out food, as if he feared she might run out, or not give him enough. I have always loved the boyish hungers—for food, for sex—because they are so perpetual, so faithful in their daily revival, and even though I hadn't met Nathan yet, I think, in my mind, I already understood: I wanted to feed him, to fill him up; I wanted to give him everything.

Across from us, now, two girls were smoking cigarettes and talking about what art was. A man and a woman, in love, intertwined their fingers. Nathan's hand was getting warm and damp in mine, so I let it go, and eventually he blew his nose and lit a cigarette.

"You know," he said after a while, "it's not the sex, really. That's not what I regret missing. It's just that— Do you realize, Celia, I've never been in love? Never once in my life have I actually been in love?" And he looked at me very earnestly, not knowing, not having the slightest idea, that once again he was counting me for nothing.

"Nathan," I said. "Oh, my Nathan." Still, he didn't seem satisfied, and I knew he had been hoping for something better than my limp consolation. He looked away from me, across the café, listening, I suppose, for that wind-chime peal as all the world's pennies flew his way.

QUESTIONS AND CONSIDERATIONS

1. How does the relationship between Nathan and Celia develop and change as the story unfolds? What factors cause their relationship to change?

2. How does knowing that the story is told from Celia's point of view influence your interpretation of the major events and characters? How do you imagine Nathan would have narrated the same events?

3. Explain how the game "A Place I've Never Been" is played. What relationship between innocence and experience does the game establish? Would this game be of primary interest to people in their teens and early twenties?

4. Interpret the meaning of the last sentence of the story in the context of the rules of the game and the themes of innocence and experience: "He looked away from me, across the café, listening, I suppose, for that wind-chime peal as all the world's pennies flew his way."

5. The story brings up a range of perplexing social and psychological issues about relationships between men and women today; discuss several of the issues explored in the story that you think would be of most relevance and concern to your generation.

6. Of what is Nathan most afraid? Of what is Celia most afraid? Do you think that the fear of AIDS is the major issue in either of their lives, or is the fear of AIDS for them more of a more physical manifestation of other, less tangible fears?

IDEAS FOR WRITING

1. Write a short story using the game that you discussed in your prereading journal as the thematic focus or symbol as does Leavitt in "A Place I've Never Been."

2. Write an essay that discusses one or two of the most perplexing social issues that people of your generation face as they enter into intimate relationships. You might refer to some of the issues raised in "A Place I've Never Been," such as trust, commitment, or the fear of AIDS.

Sonny's Blues

James Baldwin

Journal

Write about a time when one of your relatives got into trouble with school or legal authorities. What was your response? Did you try to help out? Did you find it difficult to believe your relative had done something wrong, or did you blame him or her for the problem?

I read about it in the paper, in the subway, on my way to work. I read it, and I couldn't believe it, and I read it again. Then perhaps I just stared at it, at the newsprint spelling out his name, spelling out the story. I stared at it in the swinging lights of the subway car, and in the faces and bodies of the people, and in my own face, trapped in the darkness which roared outside.

It was not to be believed and I kept telling myself that, as I walked from the subway station to the high school. And at the same time I couldn't doubt it. I was scared, scared for Sonny. He became real to me again. A great block of ice got settled in my belly and kept melting there slowly all day long, while I taught my classes algebra. It was a special kind of ice. It kept melting, sending trickles of ice water all up and down my veins, but it never got less. Sometimes it hardened and seemed to expand until I felt my guts were going to come spilling out or that I was going to choke or scream. This would always be at a moment when I was remembering some specific thing Sonny had once said or done.

When he was about as old as the boys in my classes his face had been bright and open, there was a lot of copper in it; and he'd had wonderfully direct brown eyes, and great gentleness and privacy. I wondered what he looked like now. He had been picked up, the evening before, in a raid on an apartment downtown, for peddling and using heroin.

I couldn't believe it: but what I mean by that is that I couldn't find any room for it anywhere inside me. I had kept it outside me for a long time. I hadn't wanted to know. I had had suspicions, but I didn't name them, I kept putting them away. I told myself that Sonny was wild, but he wasn't crazy. And he'd always been a good boy, he hadn't ever turned hard or evil or disrespectful, the way kids can, so quick, so quick, especially in Harlem. I didn't want to believe that I'd ever see my brother going down, coming to nothing, all that light in his face gone out, in the condition I'd already seen so many others. Yet it had happened and here I was, talking about algebra to a lot of boys who might, every one of them for all I knew, be popping off needles every time they went to the head. Maybe it did more for them than algebra could.

I was sure that the first time Sonny had ever had horse, he couldn't have been much older than these boys were now. These boys, now, were living as we'd been living then, they were growing up with a rush and their heads bumped abruptly against the low ceiling of their actual possibilities. They were filled with rage. All they really knew were two darknesses, the darkness of their lives, which was now closing in on them, and the darkness of the movies, which had blinded them to that other darkness, and in which they now, vindictively, dreamed, at once more together than they were at any other time, and more alone.

When the last bell rang, the last class ended, I let out my breath. It seemed I'd been holding it for all that time. My clothes were wet—I may have looked as though I'd been sitting in a steam bath, all dressed up, all afternoon. I sat alone in the classroom a long time. I listened to the boys outside, downstairs, shouting and cursing and laughing. Their laughter struck me for perhaps the first time. It was not the joyous laughter which—God knows why—one associates with children. It was mocking and insular, its intent to denigrate. It was disenchanted, and in this, also, lay the authority of their curses. Perhaps I was listening to them because I was thinking about my brother and in them I heard my brother. And myself.

One boy was whistling a tune, at once very complicated and very simple, it seemed to be pouring out of him as though he were a bird, and it sounded very cool and moving through all that harsh, bright air, only just holding its own through all those other sounds.

I stood up and walked over to the window and looked down into the courtyard. It was the beginning of the spring and the sap was rising in the boys. A teacher passed through them every now and again, quickly, as though he or she couldn't wait to get out of that courtyard, to get those boys out of their sight and off their minds. I started collecting my stuff. I thought I'd better get home and talk to Isabel.

The courtyard was almost deserted by the time I got downstairs. I saw this boy standing in the shadow of a doorway, looking just like Sonny. I almost called his name. Then I saw that it wasn't Sonny, but somebody we used to know, a boy from around our block. He'd been Sonny's friend. He'd never been mine, having been too young for me, and, anyway, I'd never liked him. And now, even though he was a grown-up man, he still hung around that block, still spent hours on the street corners, was always high and raggy. I used to run into him from time to time and he'd often work around to asking me for a quarter or fifty cents. He always had some real good excuse, too, and I always gave it to him, I don't know why.

But now, abruptly, I hated him. I couldn't stand the way he looked at me, partly like a dog, partly like a cunning child. I wanted to ask him what the hell he was doing in the school courtyard.

He sort of shuffled over to me, and he said, "I see you got the papers. So you already know about it."

"You mean about Sonny? Yes, I already know about it. How come they didn't get you?"

He grinned. It made him repulsive and it also brought to mind what he'd looked like as a kid. "I wasn't there. I stay away from them people."

"Good for you." I offered him a cigarette and I watched him through the smoke. "You come all the way down here just to tell me about Sonny?"

"That's right." He was sort of shaking his head and his eyes looked strange, as though they were about to cross. The bright sun deadened his damp dark brown skin and it made his eyes look yellow and showed up the dirt in his kinked hair. He smelled funky. I moved a little away from him and I said, "Well, thanks. But I already know about it and I got to get home."

"I'll walk you a little ways," he said. We started walking. There were a couple of kids still loitering in the courtyard and one of them said goodnight to me and looked strangely at the boy beside me.

"What're you going to do?" he asked me. "I mean, about Sonny?"

"Look. I haven't seen Sonny for over a year. I'm not sure I'm going to do anything. Anyway, what the hell *can* I do?"

"That's right," he said quickly, "ain't nothing you can do. Can't much help old Sonny no more, I guess."

It was what I was thinking and so it seemed to me he had no right to say it.

"I'm surprised at Sonny, though," he went on—he had a funny way of talking, he looked straight ahead as though he were talking to himself—"I thought Sonny was a smart boy, I thought he was too smart to get hung."

"I guess he thought so too," I said sharply, "and that's how he got hung. And now about you? You're pretty goddamn smart, I bet."

Then he looked directly at me, just for a minute. "I ain't smart," he said. "If I was smart, I'd have reached for a pistol a long time ago."

"Look. Don't tell *me* your sad story, if it was up to me, I'd give you one." Then I felt guilty—guilty, probably, for never having supposed that the poor bastard *had* a story of his own, much less a sad one, and I asked, quickly, "What's going to happen to him now?"

He didn't answer this. He was off by himself some place. "Funny thing," he said, and from his tone we might have been discussing the quickest way to get to Brooklyn, "when I saw the papers this morning, the first thing I asked myself was if I had anything to do with it. I felt sort of responsible."

I began to listen more carefully. The subway station was on the corner, just before us, and I stopped. He stopped, too. We were in front of a bar and he ducked slightly, peering in, but whoever he was looking for didn't seem to be there. The juke box was blasting away with something black and bouncy and I half watched the barmaid as she danced her way from the juke box to her place behind the bar. And I watched her face as she laughingly responded to something someone said to her, still keeping time to the music. When she smiled one saw the little girl, one sensed the doomed, still-struggling woman beneath the battered face of the semi-whore.

"I never *give* Sonny nothing," the boy said finally, "but a long time ago I come to school high and Sonny asked me how it felt." He paused, I couldn't bear to watch him, I watched the barmaid, and I listened to the music which seemed to be causing the pavement to shake. "I told him it felt great." The music stopped, the barmaid paused and watched the juke box until the music began again. "It did."

All this was carrying me some place I didn't want to go. I certainly didn't want to know how it felt. It filled everything, the people, the houses, the music, the dark, quicksilver barmaid, with menace; and this menace was their reality.

"What's going to happen to him now?" I asked again.

"They'll send him away some place and they'll try to cure him." He shook his head. "Maybe he'll even think he's kicked the habit. Then they'll let him loose"—he gestured, throwing his cigarette into the gutter. "That's all."

"What do you mean, that's *all*?"

But I knew what he meant.

"I *mean,* that's *all*." He turned his head and looked at me, pulling down the corners of his mouth. "Don't you know what I mean?" he asked, softly.

"How the hell *would* I know what you mean?" I almost whispered it, I don't know why.

"That's right," he said to the air, "how would *he* know what I mean?" He turned toward me again, patient and calm, and yet I somehow felt him shaking, shaking as though he were going to fall apart. I felt that ice in my guts again, the dread I'd felt all afternoon; and again I watched the barmaid, moving about the bar, washing glasses, and singing. "Listen. They'll let him out and then it'll just start all over again. That's what I mean."

"You mean—they'll let him out. And then he'll just start working his way back in again. You mean he'll never kick the habit. Is that what you mean?"

"That's right," he said, cheerfully. "*You* see what I mean."

"Tell me," I said at last, "why does he want to die? He must want to die, he's killing himself, why does he want to die?"

He looked at me in surprise. He licked his lips. "He don't want to die. He wants to live. Don't nobody want to die, ever."

Then I wanted to ask him—too many things. He could not have answered, or if he had, I could not have borne the answers. I started walking. "Well, I guess it's none of my business."

"It's going to be rough on old Sonny," he said. We reached the subway station. "This is your station?" he asked. I nodded. I took one step down. "Damn!" he said, suddenly. I looked up at him. He grinned again. "Damn it if I didn't leave all my money home. You ain't got a dollar on you, have you? Just for a couple of days, is all."

All at once something inside gave and threatened to come pouring out of me. I didn't hate him any more. I felt that in another moment I'd start crying like a child.

"Sure," I said. "Don't sweat." I looked in my wallet and didn't have a dollar, I only had a five. "Here," I said. "That hold you?"

He didn't look at it—he didn't want to look at it. A terrible closed look came over his face, as though he were keeping the number on the bill a secret from him and me. "Thanks," he said, and now he was dying to see me go. "Don't worry about Sonny. Maybe I'll write him or something."

"Sure," I said. "You do that. So long."

"Be seeing you," he said. I went on down the steps.

And I didn't write Sonny or send him anything for a long time. When I finally did, it was just after my little girl died, he wrote me back a letter which made me feel like a bastard.

Here's what he said:

Dear brother,

You don't know how much I needed to hear from you. I wanted to write you many a time but I dug how much I must have hurt you and so I didn't write. But now I feel like a man who's been trying to climb up out of some deep, real deep and funky hole and just saw the sun up there, outside. I got to get outside.

I can't tell you much about how I got here. I mean I don't know how to tell you. I guess I was afraid of something or I was trying to escape from something and you know I have never been very strong in the head (smile). I'm glad Mama and Daddy are dead and can't see what's happened to their son and I swear if I'd known what I was doing I would never have hurt you so, you and a lot of other fine people who were nice to me and who believed in me.

I don't want you to think it had anything to do with me being a musician. It's more than that. Or maybe less than that. I can't get anything straight in my head down here and I try not to think about what's going to happen to me when I get outside again. Sometime I think I'm going to flip and *never* get outside and sometime I think I'll come straight back. I tell you one thing, though, I'd rather blow my brains out than go through this again. But that's what they all say, so they tell me. If I tell you when I'm coming to New York and if you could meet me, I sure would appreciate it. Give my love to Isabel and the kids and I was sure sorry to hear about little Gracie. I wish I could be like Mama and say the Lord's will be done, but I don't know it seems to me that trouble is the one thing that never does get stopped and I don't know what good it does to blame it on the Lord. But maybe it does some good if you believe it.

Your brother,
Sonny

Then I kept in constant touch with him and I sent him whatever I could and I went to meet him when he came back to New York. When I saw him many things I thought I had forgotten came flooding back to me. This was because I had begun, finally, to wonder about Sonny, about the life that Sonny lived inside. This life, whatever it was, had made him older and thinner and it had deepened the distant stillness in which he had always moved. He looked very unlike my baby brother. Yet, when he smiled, when we shook hands, the baby brother I'd never known looked out from the depths of his private life, like an animal waiting to be coaxed into the light.

"How you been keeping?" he asked me.

"All right. And you?"

"Just fine." He was smiling all over his face. "It's good to see you again."

"It's good to see you."

The seven years' difference in our ages lay between us like a chasm: I wondered if these years would ever operate between us as a bridge. I was remembering, and it made it hard to catch my breath, that I had been there when he was born; and I had heard the first words he had ever spoken. When he started to walk, he walked from our mother straight to me. I caught him just before he fell when he took the first steps he ever took in this world.

"How's Isabel?"

"Just fine. She's dying to see you."

"And the boys?"

"They're fine, too. They're anxious to see their uncle."

"Oh, come on. You know they don't remember me."

"Are you kidding? Of course they remember you."

He grinned again. We got into a taxi. We had a lot to say to each other, far too much to know how to begin.

As the taxi began to move, I asked, "You still want to go to India?"

He laughed. "You still remember that. Hell, no. This place is Indian enough for me."

"It used to belong to them," I said.

And he laughed again. "They damn sure knew what they were doing when they got rid of it."

Years ago, when he was around fourteen, he'd been all hipped on the idea of going to India. He read books about people sitting on rocks, naked, in all kinds of weather, but mostly bad, naturally, and walking barefoot through hot coals and arriving at wisdom. I used to say that it sounded to me as though they were getting away from wisdom as fast as they could. I think he sort of looked down on me for that.

"Do you mind," he asked, "if we have the driver drive alongside the park? On the west side—I haven't seen the city in so long."

"Of course not," I said. I was afraid that I might sound as though I were humoring him, but I hoped he wouldn't take it that way.

So we drove along, between the green of the park and the stony, lifeless elegance of hotels and apartment buildings, toward the vivid, killing streets of our childhood. These streets hadn't changed, though housing projects jutted up out of them now like rocks in the middle of a boiling sea. Most of the houses in which we had grown up had vanished, as had the stores from which we had stolen, the basements in which we had first tried sex, the rooftops from which we had hurled tin cans and bricks. But houses exactly like the houses of our past yet dominated the landscape, boys exactly like the boys we once had been found themselves smothering in these houses, came down into the streets for light and air and found themselves encircled by disaster. Some escaped the trap, most didn't. Those who got out always left something of themselves behind, as some animals amputate a leg and leave it in the trap. It might be said, perhaps, that I had escaped, after all, I was a school teacher; or that Sonny had, he hadn't lived in Harlem for years. Yet, as the cab moved up-town through streets which seemed, with a rush, to darken with dark people, and as I covertly studied Sonny's face, it came to me that what we both were seeking through our separate cab windows was that part of ourselves which had been left behind. It's always at the hour of trouble and confrontation that the missing member aches.

We hit 110th Street and started rolling up Lenox Avenue. And I'd known this avenue all my life, but it seemed to me again, as it had seemed on the day I'd first heard about Sonny's trouble, filled with a hidden menace which was its very breath of life.

"We almost there," said Sonny.

"Almost." We were both too nervous to say anything more.

We live in a housing project. It hasn't been up long. A few days after it was up it seemed uninhabitably new, now, of course, it's already rundown. It looks like a parody of the good, clean, faceless life—God knows the people who live in it do their best to make it a parody. The beat-looking grass lying around isn't enough to make their lives green, the hedges will never hold out the streets, and they know it. The big windows fool no one, they aren't big enough to make space out of no space. They don't bother with the windows, they watch the TV screen instead. The playground is most popular with the children who don't play at jacks, or skip rope, or roller skate, or swing, and they can be found in it after dark. We moved in partly because it's not too far from where I teach, and partly for the kids; but it's really just like the houses in which Sonny and I grew up. The same things happen, they'll have the same things to remember. The moment Sonny and I started into the house I had the feeling that I was simply bringing him back into the danger he had almost died trying to escape.

Sonny has never been talkative. So I don't know why I was sure he'd be dying to talk to me when supper was over the first night. Everything went fine, the oldest boy remembered him, and the youngest boy liked him, and Sonny had remembered to bring something for each of them; and Isabel, who is really much nicer than I am, more open and giving, had gone to a lot of trouble about dinner and was genuinely glad to see him. And she's always been able to tease Sonny in a way that I haven't. It was nice to see her face so vivid again and to hear her laugh and watch her make Sonny laugh. She wasn't, or, anyway, she didn't seem to be, at all uneasy or embarrassed. She chatted as though there were no subject which had to be avoided and she got Sonny past his first, faint stiffness. And thank God she was there, for I was filled with that icy dread again. Everything I did seemed awkward to me, and everything I said sounded freighted with hidden meaning. I was trying to remember everything I'd heard about dope addiction and I couldn't help watching Sonny for signs. I wasn't doing it out of malice. I was trying to find out something about my brother. I was dying to hear him tell me he was safe.

"Safe!" my father grunted, whenever Mama suggested trying to move to a neighborhood which might be safer for children. "Safe, hell! Ain't no place safe for kids, nor nobody."

He always went on like this, but he wasn't, ever, really as bad as he sounded, not even on weekends, when he got drunk. As a matter of fact, he was always on the lookout for "something a little better," but he died before he found it. He died suddenly, during a drunken weekend in the middle of the war, when Sonny was fifteen. He and Sonny hadn't ever got on too well. And this was partly because Sonny was the apple of his father's eye. It was because he loved Sonny so much and was frightened for him, that he was always fighting with him. It doesn't do any good to fight with Sonny. Sonny just moves back, inside himself, where he can't be reached. But the principal reason that they never hit it off is that they were so much alike. Daddy was big and rough and loud-talking, just the opposite of Sonny, but they both had— that same privacy.

Mama tried to tell me something about this, just after Daddy died. I was home on leave from the army.

This was the last time I ever saw my mother alive. Just the same, this picture gets all mixed up in my mind with pictures I had of her when she was younger. The way I always see her is the way she used to be on a Sunday afternoon, say, when the old folks were talking after the big Sunday dinner. I always see her wearing pale blue. She'd be sitting on the sofa. And my father would be sitting in the easy chair, not far from her. And the living room would be full of church folks and relatives. There they sit, in chairs all around the living room, and the night is creeping up outside, but nobody knows it yet. You can see the darkness growing against the windowpanes and you hear the street noises every now and again, or maybe the jangling beat of a tambourine from one of the churches close by, but it's real quiet in the room. For a moment nobody's talking, but every face looks darkening, like the sky outside. And my mother rocks a little from the waist, and my father's eyes are closed. Everyone is looking at something a child can't see. For a minute they've forgotten the children. Maybe a kid is lying on the rug, half asleep. Maybe somebody's got a kid in his lap and is absent-mindedly stroking the kid's head. Maybe there's a kid, quiet and big-eyed, curled up in a big chair in the corner. The silence, the darkness coming, and the darkness in the faces frightens the child obscurely. He hopes that the hand which strokes his forehead will never stop—will never die. He hopes that there will never come a time when the old folks won't be sitting around the living room, talking about where they've come from, and what they've seen, and what's happened to them and their kinfolk.

But something deep and watchful in the child knows that this is bound to end, is already ending. In a moment someone will get up and turn on the light. Then the old folks will remember the children and they won't talk any more that day. And when light fills the room, the child is filled with darkness. He knows that everytime this happens he's moved just a little closer to that darkness outside. The darkness outside is what the old folks have been talking about. It's what they've come from. It's what they endure. The child knows that they won't talk any more because if he knows too much about what's happened to *them*, he'll know too much too soon, about what's going to happen to *him*.

The last time I talked to my mother, I remember I was restless. I wanted to get out and see Isabel. We weren't married then and we had a lot to straighten out between us.

There Mama sat, in black, by the window. She was humming an old church song, *Lord, you brought me from a long ways off*. Sonny was out somewhere. Mama kept watching the streets.

"I don't know," she said, "if I'll ever see you again, after you go off from here. But I hope you'll remember the things I tried to teach you."

"Don't talk like that," I said, and smiled. "You'll be here a long time yet."

She smiled, too, but she said nothing. She was quiet for a long time. And I said, "Mama, don't you worry about nothing. I'll be writing all the time, and you be getting the checks. . . ."

"I want to talk to you about your brother," she said, suddenly. "If anything happens to me he ain't going to have nobody to look out for him."

"Mama," I said, "ain't nothing going to happen to you *or* Sonny. Sonny's all right. He's a good boy and he's got good sense."

"It ain't a question of his being a good boy," Mama said, "nor of his having good sense. It ain't only the bad ones, nor yet the dumb ones that gets sucked under." She stopped, looking at me. "Your Daddy once had a brother," she said, and she smiled in a way that made me feel she was in pain. "You didn't never know that, did you?"

"No," I said, "I never knew that," and I watched her face.

"Oh, yes," she said, "your Daddy had a brother." She looked out of the window again. "I know you never saw your Daddy cry. But *I* did—many a time, through all these years."

I asked her, "What happened to his brother? How come nobody's ever talked about him?"

This was the first time I ever saw my mother look old.

"His brother got killed," she said, "when he was just a little younger than you are now. I knew him. He was a fine boy. He was maybe a little full of the devil, but he didn't mean nobody no harm."

Then she stopped and the room was silent, exactly as it had sometimes been on those Sunday afternoons. Mama kept looking out into the streets.

"He used to have a job in the mill," she said, "and, like all young folks, he just liked to perform on Saturday nights. Saturday nights, him and your father would drift around to different places, go to dances and things like that, or just sit around with people they knew, and your father's brother would sing, he had a fine voice, and play along with himself on his guitar. Well, this particular Saturday night, him and your father was coming home from some place, and they were both a little drunk and there was a moon that night, it was bright like day. Your father's brother was feeling kind of good, and he was whistling to himself, and he had his guitar slung over his shoulder. They was coming down a hill and beneath them was a road that turned off from the highway. Well, your father's brother, being always kind of frisky, decided to run down this hill, and he did, with that guitar banging and clanging behind him, and he ran across the road, and he was making water behind a tree. And your father was sort of amused at him and he was still coming down the hill, kind of slow. Then he heard a car motor and that same minute his brother stepped from behind the tree, into the road, in the moonlight. And he started to cross the road. And your father started to run down the hill, he says he don't know why. This car was full of white men. They was all drunk, and when they seen your father's brother they let out a great whoop and holler and they aimed the car straight at him. They was having fun, they just wanted to scare him, the way they do sometimes, you know. But they was drunk. And I guess the boy, being drunk, too, and scared, kind of lost his head. By the time he jumped it was too late. Your father says he heard his brother scream when the car rolled over him, and he heard the wood of that guitar when it give, and he heard them strings go flying, and he heard them white men shouting, and the car kept on a-going and it ain't stopped till this day. And, time your father got down the hill, his brother weren't nothing but blood and pulp."

Tears were gleaming on my mother's face. There wasn't anything I could say.

"He never mentioned it," she said, "because I never let him mention it before you children. Your Daddy was like a crazy man that night and for many a night thereafter. He says he never in his life seen anything as dark as that road after the lights of that car had gone away. Weren't nothing, weren't nobody on that road, just your Daddy and his brother and that busted guitar. Oh, yes. Your Daddy never did really get right again. Till the day he died he weren't sure but that every white man he saw was the man that killed his brother."

She stopped and took out her handkerchief and dried her eyes and looked at me.

"I ain't telling you all this," she said, "to make you scared or bitter or to make you hate nobody. I'm telling you this because you got a brother. And the world ain't changed."

I guess I didn't want to believe this. I guess she saw this in my face. She turned away from me, toward the window again, searching those streets.

"But I praise my Redeemer," she said at last, "that He called your Daddy home before me. I ain't saying it to throw no flowers at myself, but, I declare, it keeps me from feeling too cast down to know I helped your father get safely through this world. Your father always acted like he was the roughest, strongest man on earth. And everybody took him to be like that. But if he hadn't had *me* there—to see his tears!"

She was crying again. Still, I couldn't move. I said, "Lord, Lord, Mama, I didn't know it was like that."

"Oh, honey," she said, "there's a lot that you don't know. But you are going to find it out." She stood up from the window and came over to me. "You got to hold on to your brother," she said, "and don't let him fall, no matter what it looks like is happening to him and no matter how evil you gets with him. You going to be evil with him many a time. But don't you forget what I told you, you hear?"

"I won't forget," I said. "Don't you worry, I won't forget. I won't let nothing happen to Sonny."

My mother smiled as though she were amused at something she saw in my face. Then, "You may not be able to stop nothing from happening. But you got to let him know you's *there.*"

Two days later I was married, and then I was gone. And I had a lot of things on my mind and I pretty well forgot my promise to Mama until I got shipped home on a special furlough for her funeral.

And, after the funeral, with just Sonny and me alone in the empty kitchen, I tried to find out something about him.

"What do you want to do?" I asked him.

"I'm going to be a musician," he said.

For he had graduated, in the time I had been away, from dancing to the juke box to finding out who was playing what, and what they were doing with it, and he had bought himself a set of drums.

"You mean, you want to be a drummer?" I somehow had the feeling that being a drummer might be all right for other people but not for my brother Sonny.

"I don't think," he said, looking at me very gravely, "that I'll ever be a good drummer. But I think I can play a piano."

I frowned. I'd never played the role of the older brother quite so seriously before, had scarcely ever, in fact, *asked* Sonny a damn thing. I sensed myself in the presence of something I didn't really know how to handle, didn't understand. So I made my frown a little deeper as I asked: "What kind of musician do you want to be?"

He grinned. "How many kinds do you think there are?"

"Be *serious,*" I said.

He laughed, throwing his head back, and then looked at me. "I *am* serious."

"Well, then, for Christ's sake, stop kidding around and answer a serious question. I mean, do you want to be a concert pianist, you want to play classical music and all that, or—or what?" Long before I finished he was laughing again. "For Christ's *sake,* Sonny!"

He sobered, but with difficulty. "I'm sorry. But you sound so—*scared!*" and he was off again.

"Well, you may think it's funny now, baby, but it's not going to be so funny when you have to make your living at it, let me tell you *that.*" I was furious because I knew he was laughing at me and I didn't know why.

"No," he said, very sober now, and afraid, perhaps, that he'd hurt me, "I don't want to be a classical pianist. That isn't what interests me. I mean"—he paused, looking hard at me, as though his eyes would help me to understand, and then gestured helplessly, as though perhaps his hand would help—"I mean, I'll have a lot of studying to do, and I'll have to study *everything,* but, I mean, I want to play *with*—jazz musicians." He stopped. "I want to play jazz," he said.

Well, the word had never before sounded as heavy, as real, as it sounded that afternoon in Sonny's mouth. I just looked at him and I was probably frowning a real frown by this time. I simply couldn't see why on earth he'd want to spend his time hanging around nightclubs, clowning around on bandstands, while people pushed each other around a dance floor. It seemed—beneath him, somehow. I had never thought about it before, had never been forced to, but I suppose I had always put jazz musicians in a class with what Daddy called "good-time people."

"Are you *serious*?"

"Hell, *yes,* I'm serious."

He looked more helpless than ever, and annoyed, and deeply hurt.

I suggested, helpfully: "You mean—like Louis Armstrong?"

His face closed as though I'd struck him. "No. I'm not talking about none of that old-time, down home crap."

"Well, look, Sonny, I'm sorry, don't get mad. I just don't altogether get it, that's all. Name somebody—you know, a jazz musician you admire."

"Bird."

"Who?"

"Bird! Charlie Parker! Don't they teach you nothing in the goddamn army?"

I lit a cigarette. I was surprised and then a little amused to discover that I was trembling. "I've been out of touch," I said. "You'll have to be patient with me. Now. Who's this Parker character?"

"He's just one of the greatest jazz musicians alive," said Sonny, sullenly, his hands in his pockets, his back to me. "Maybe *the* greatest," he added, bitterly, "that's probably why *you* never heard of him."

"All right," I said, "I'm ignorant. I'm sorry. I'll go out and buy all the cat's records right away, all right?"

"It don't," said Sonny, with dignity, "make any difference to me. I don't care what you listen to. Don't do me no favors."

I was beginning to realize that I'd never seen him so upset before. With another part of my mind I was thinking that this would probably turn out to be one of those things kids go through and that I shouldn't make it seem important by pushing it too hard. Still, I didn't think it would do any harm to ask: "Doesn't all this take a lot of time? Can you make a living at it?"

He turned back to me and half leaned, half sat, on the kitchen table. "Everything takes time," he said, "and—well, yes, sure, I can make a living at it. But what I don't seem to be able to make you understand is that it's the only thing I want to do."

"Well, Sonny," I said, gently, "you know people can't always do exactly what they *want* to do—"

"*No,* I don't know that," said Sonny, surprising me. "I think people *ought* to do what they want to do, what else are they alive for?"

"You getting to be a big boy," I said desperately, "it's time you started thinking about your future."

"I'm thinking about my future," said Sonny, grimly. "I think about it all the time."

I gave up. I decided, if he didn't change his mind, that we could always talk about it later. "In the meantime," I said, "you got to finish school." We had already decided that he'd have to move in with Isabel and her folks. I knew this wasn't the ideal arrangement because Isabel's folks are inclined to be dicty and they hadn't especially wanted Isabel to marry me. But I didn't know what else to do. "And we have to get you fixed up at Isabel's."

There was a long silence. He moved from the kitchen table to the window. "That's a terrible idea. You know it yourself."

"Do you have a *better* idea?"

He just walked up and down the kitchen for a minute. He was as tall as I was. He had started to shave. I suddenly had the feeling that I didn't know him at all.

He stopped at the kitchen table and picked up my cigarettes. Looking at me with a kind of mocking, amused defiance, he put one between his lips. "You mind?"

"You smoking already?"

He lit the cigarette and nodded, watching me through the smoke. "I just wanted to see if I'd have the courage to smoke in front of you." He grinned and blew a great cloud of smoke to the ceiling. "It was easy." He looked at my face. "Come on, now. I bet you was smoking at my age, tell the truth."

I didn't say anything but the truth was on my face, and he laughed. But now there was something very strained in his laugh. "Sure. And I bet that ain't all you was doing."

He was frightening me a little. "Cut the crap," I said. "We already decided that you was going to go and live at Isabel's. Now what's got into you all of a sudden?"

"*You* decided it," he pointed out. "*I* didn't decide nothing." He stopped in front of me, leaning against the stove, arms loosely folded. "Look, brother. I don't want to stay in Harlem no more, I really don't." He was very earnest. He looked at me, then over toward the kitchen window. There was something in his eyes I'd never seen before, some thoughtfulness, some worry all his own. He rubbed the muscle of one arm. "It's time I was getting out of here."

"Where do you want to *go*, Sonny?"

"I want to join the army. Or the navy, I don't care. If I say I'm old enough, they'll believe me."

Then I got mad. It was because I was so scared. "You must be crazy. You goddamn fool, what the hell do you want to go and join the *army* for?"

"I just told you. To get out of Harlem."

"Sonny, you haven't even finished *school*. And if you really want to be a musician, how do you expect to study if you're in the *army*?"

He looked at me, trapped, and in anguish. "There's ways. I might be able to work out some kind of deal. Anyway, I'll have the G.I. Bill when I come out."

"*If* you come out." We stared at each other. "Sonny, please. Be reasonable. I know the setup is far from perfect. But we got to do the best we can."

"I ain't learning nothing in school," he said. "Even when I go." He turned away from me and opened the window and threw his cigarette out into the narrow alley. I watched his back. "At least, I ain't learning nothing you'd want me to learn." He slammed the window so hard I thought the glass would fly out, and turned back to me. "And I'm sick of the stink of these garbage cans!"

"Sonny," I said, "I know how you feel. But if you don't finish school now, you're going to be sorry later that you didn't." I grabbed him by the shoulders. "And you only got another year. It ain't so bad. And I'll come back and I swear I'll help you do *whatever* you want to do. Just try to put up with it till I come back. Will you please do that? For me?"

He didn't answer and he wouldn't look at me.

"Sonny. You hear me?"

He pulled away. "I hear you. But you never hear anything *I* say."

I didn't know what to say to that. He looked out of the window and then back to me. "OK," he said, and sighed. "I'll try."

Then I said, trying to cheer him up a little, "They got a piano at Isabel's. You can practice on it."

And as a matter of fact, it did cheer him up for a minute. "That's right," he said to himself. "I forgot that." His face relaxed a little. But the worry, the thoughtfulness, played on it still, the way shadows play on a face which is staring into the fire.

But I thought I'd never hear the end of that piano. At first, Isabel would write me, saying how nice it was that Sonny was so serious about his music and how, as soon as he came in from school, or wherever he had been when he was supposed to be at school, he went straight to that piano and stayed there until suppertime. And, after supper, he went back to that piano and stayed there until everybody went to bed. He was at the piano all day Saturday and all day Sunday. Then he bought a record player and started playing records. He'd play one record over and over again, all day long sometimes, and he'd improvise along with it on the piano. Or he'd play one section of the record, one chord, one change, one progression, then he'd do it on the piano. Then back to the record. Then back to the piano.

Well, I really don't know how they stood it. Isabel finally confessed that it wasn't like living with a person at all, it was like living with sound. And the sound didn't make any sense to her, didn't make any sense to any of them— naturally. They began, in a way, to be afflicted by this presence that was living in their home. It was as though Sonny were some sort of god, or monster. He moved in an atmosphere which wasn't like theirs at all. They fed him and he ate, he washed himself, he walked in and out of their door; he certainly wasn't nasty or unpleasant or rude, Sonny isn't any of those things; but it was as though he were all wrapped up in some cloud, some fire, some vision all his own; and there wasn't any way to reach him.

At the same time, he wasn't really a man yet, he was still a child, and they had to watch out for him in all kinds of ways. They certainly couldn't throw him out. Neither did they dare to make a great scene about that piano because even they dimly sensed, as I sensed, from so many thousands of miles away, that Sonny was at that piano playing for his life.

But he hadn't been going to school. One day a letter came from the school board and Isabel's mother got it—there had, apparently, been other letters but Sonny had torn them up. This day, when Sonny came in, Isabel's mother showed him the letter and asked where he'd been spending his time. And she finally got it out of him that he'd been down in Greenwich Village, with musicians and other characters, in a white girl's apartment. And this scared her and she started to scream at him and what came up, once she began—though she denies it to this day—was what sacrifices they were making to give Sonny a decent home and how little he appreciated it.

Sonny didn't play the piano that day. By evening, Isabel's mother had calmed down but then there was the old man to deal with, and Isabel herself. Isabel says she did her best to be calm but she broke down and started crying. She says she just watched Sonny's face. She could tell, by watching him, what was happening with him. And what was happening was that they penetrated his cloud, they had reached him. Even if their fingers had been a thousand times more gentle than human fingers ever are, he could hardly help feeling that they had stripped him naked and were spitting on that nakedness. For he also had to see that his presence, that music, which was life or death to him, had been torture for them and that they had endured it, not at all for his sake, but only for mine. And Sonny couldn't take that. He can take it a little better today than he could then but he's still not very good at it and, frankly, I don't know anybody who is.

The silence of the next few days must have been louder than the sound of all the music ever played since time began. One morning, before she went to work, Isabel was in his room for something and she suddenly realized that all of his records were gone. And she knew for certain that he was gone. And he was. He went as far as the navy would carry him. He finally sent me a postcard from some place in Greece and that was the first I knew that Sonny was still alive. I didn't see him any more until we were both back in New York and the war had long been over.

He was a man by then, of course, but I wasn't willing to see it. He came by the house from time to time, but we fought almost every time we met. I didn't like the way he carried himself, loose and dreamlike all the time, and I didn't like his friends, and his music seemed to be merely an excuse for the life he led. It sounded just that weird and disordered.

Then we had a fight, a pretty awful fight, and I didn't see him for months. By and by I looked him up, where he was living, in a furnished room in the Village, and I tried to make it up. But there were lots of people in the room and Sonny just lay on his bed, and he wouldn't come downstairs with me, and he treated these other people as though they were his family and I weren't. So I got mad and then he got mad, and then I told him that he might just as well be dead as live the way he was living. Then he stood up and he told me not to worry about him any more in life, that he *was* dead as far as I was concerned. Then he pushed me to the door and the other people looked on as though nothing were happening, and he slammed the door behind me. I stood in the hallway, staring at the door. I heard somebody laugh in the room and then the tears came to my eyes. I started down the steps, whistling to keep from crying, I kept whistling to myself, *You going to need me, baby, one of these cold, rainy days.*

I read about Sonny's trouble in the spring. Little Grace died in the fall. She was a beautiful little girl. But she only lived a little over two years. She died of polio and she suffered. She had a slight fever for a couple of days, but it didn't seem like anything and we just kept her in bed. And we would certainly have called the doctor, but the fever dropped, she seemed to be all right. So we thought it had just been a cold. Then, one day, she was up, playing, Isabel was in the kitchen fixing lunch for the two boys when they'd come in from school, and she heard Grace fall down in the living room. When you have a lot of children you don't always start running when one of them falls, unless they start screaming or something. And, this time, Grace was quiet. Yet, Isabel says that when she heard that *thump* and then that silence, something happened in her to make her afraid. And she ran to the living room and there was little Grace on the floor, all twisted up, and the reason she hadn't screamed was that she couldn't get her breath. And when she did scream, it was the worst sound, Isabel says, that she'd ever heard in all her life, and she still hears it sometimes in her dreams. Isabel will sometimes wake me up with a low, moaning, strangled sound and I have to be quick to awaken her and hold her to me and where Isabel is weeping against me seems a mortal wound.

I think I may have written Sonny the very day that little Grace was buried. I was sitting in the living room in the dark, by myself, and I suddenly thought of Sonny. My trouble made his real.

One Saturday afternoon, when Sonny had been living with us, or, anyway, been in our house, for nearly two weeks, I found myself wandering aimlessly about the living room, drinking from a can of beer, and trying to work up the courage to search Sonny's room. He was out, he was usually out whenever I was home, and Isabel had taken the children to see their grandparents. Suddenly I was standing still in front of the living room window, watching Seventh Avenue. The idea of searching Sonny's room made me still. I scarcely dared to admit to myself what I'd be searching for. I didn't know what I'd do if I found it. Or if I didn't.

On the sidewalk across from me, near the entrance to a barbecue joint, some people were holding an old-fashioned revival meeting. The barbecue cook, wearing a dirty white apron, his conked hair reddish and metallic in the pale sun, and a cigarette between his lips, stood in the doorway, watching them. Kids and older people paused in their errands and stood there, along with some older men and a couple of very tough-looking women who watched everything that happened on the avenue, as though they owned it, or were maybe owned by it. Well, they were watching this, too. The revival was being carried on by three sisters in black, and a brother. All they had were their voices and their Bibles and a tambourine. The brother was testifying and while he testified two of the sisters stood together, seeming to say, amen, and the third sister walked around with the tambourine outstretched and a couple of people dropped coins into it. Then the brother's testimony ended and the sister who had been taking up the collection dumped the coins into her palm and transferred them to the pocket of her long black robe. Then she raised both hands, striking the tambourine against the air, and then against one hand, and she started to sing. And the two other sisters and the brother joined in.

It was strange, suddenly, to watch, though I had been seeing these street meetings all my life. So, of course, had everybody else down there. Yet, they paused and watched and listened and I stood still at the window. *"Tis the old ship of Zion,"* they sang, and the sister with the tambourine kept a steady, jangling beat, *"it has rescued many a thousand!"* Not a soul under the sound of their voices was hearing this song for the first time, not one of them had been rescued. Nor had they seen much in the way of rescue work being done around them. Neither did they especially believe in the holiness of the three sisters and the brother, they knew too much about them, knew where they lived, and how. The woman with the tambourine, whose voice dominated the air, whose face was bright with joy, was divided by very little from the woman who stood watching her, a cigarette between her heavy, chapped lips, her hair a cuckoo's nest, her face scarred and swollen from many beatings, and her black eyes glittering like coal. Perhaps they both knew this, which was why, when, as rarely, they addressed each other, they addressed each other as Sister. As the singing filled the air the watching, listening faces underwent a change, the eyes focusing on something within; the music seemed to soothe a poison out of them; and time seemed, nearly, to fall away from the sullen, belligerent, battered faces, as though they were fleeing back to their first condition, while dreaming of their last. The barbecue cook half shook his head and smiled, and dropped his cigarette and disappeared into his joint. A man fumbled in his pockets for change and stood holding it in his hand impatiently, as though he had just remembered a pressing appointment further up the avenue. He looked furious. Then I saw Sonny, standing on the edge of the crowd. He was carrying a wide, flat notebook with a green cover, and it made him look, from where I was standing, almost like a schoolboy. The coppery sun brought out the copper in his skin, he was very faintly smiling, standing very still. Then the singing stopped, the tambourine turned into a collection plate again. The furious man dropped in his coins and vanished, so did a couple of the women, and Sonny dropped some change in the plate, looking directly at the woman with a little smile. He started across the avenue, toward the house. He has a slow, loping walk, something like the way Harlem hipsters walk, only he's imposed on this his own half-beat. I had never really noticed it before.

I stayed at the window, both relieved and apprehensive. As Sonny disappeared from my sight, they began singing again. And they were still singing when his key turned in the lock.

"Hey," he said.

"Hey, yourself. You want some beer?"

"No. Well, maybe." But he came up to the window and stood beside me, looking out. "What a warm voice," he said.

They were singing *If I could only hear my mother pray again!*

"Yes," I said, "and she can sure beat that tambourine."

"But what a terrible song," he said, and laughed. He dropped his notebook on the sofa and disappeared into the kitchen. "Where's Isabel and the kids?"

"I think they went to see their grandparents. You hungry?"

"No." He came back into the living room with his can of beer. "You want to come some place with me tonight?"

I sensed, I don't know how, that I couldn't possibly say no. "Sure. Where?"

He sat down on the sofa and picked up his notebook and started leafing through it. "I'm going to sit in with some fellows in a joint in the Village."

"You mean, you're going to play, tonight?"

"That's right." He took a swallow of his beer and moved back to the window. He gave me a sidelong look. "If you can stand it."

"I'll try," I said.

He smiled to himself and we both watched as the meeting across the way broke up. The three sisters and the brother, heads bowed, were singing *God be with you till we meet again.* The faces around them were very quiet. Then the song ended. The small crowd dispersed. We watched the three women and the lone man walk slowly up the avenue.

"When she was singing before," said Sonny, abruptly, "her voice reminded me for a minute of what heroin feels like sometimes—when it's in your veins. It makes you feel sort of warm and cool at the same time. And distant. And—and sure." He sipped his beer, very deliberately not looking at me. I watched his face. "It makes you feel—in control. Sometimes you've got to have that feeling."

"Do you?" I sat down slowly in the easy chair.

"Sometimes." He went to the sofa and picked up his notebook again. "Some people do."

"In order," I asked, "to play?" And my voice was very ugly, full of contempt and anger.

"Well"—he looked at me with great, troubled eyes, as though, in fact, he hoped his eyes would tell me things he could never otherwise say—"they *think* so. And *if* they think so—!"

"And what do *you* think?" I asked.

He sat on the sofa and put his can of beer on the floor. "I don't know," he said, and I couldn't be sure if he were answering my question or pursuing his thoughts. His face didn't tell me. "It's not so much to *play.* It's to *stand* it, to be able to make it at all. On any level." He frowned and smiled: "In order to keep from shaking to pieces."

"But these friends of yours," I said, "they seem to shake themselves to pieces pretty goddamn fast."

"Maybe." He played with the notebook. And something told me that I should curb my tongue, that Sonny was doing his best to talk, that I should listen. "But of course you only know the ones that've gone to pieces. Some don't—or at least they haven't *yet* and that's just about all *any* of us can say." He paused. "And then there are some who just live, really, in hell, and they know it and they see what's happening and they go right on. I don't know." He sighed, dropped the notebook, folded his arms. "Some guys, you can tell from the way they play, they on something *all* the time. And you can see that, well, it makes something real for them. But of course," he picked up his beer from the floor and sipped it and put the can down again, "they *want* to, too, you've got to see that. Even some of them that say they don't—*some, not all.*"

"And what about you?" I asked—I couldn't help it. "What about you? Do *you* want to?"

He stood up and walked to the window and remained silent for a long time. Then he sighed. "Me," he said. Then: "While I was downstairs before, on my way here, listening to that woman sing, it struck me all of a sudden how much suffering she must have had to go through—to sing like that. It's *repulsive* to think you have to suffer that much."

I said: "But there's no way not to suffer—is there, Sonny?"

"I believe not," he said and smiled, "but that's never stopped anyone from trying." He looked at me. "Has it?" I realized, with this mocking look, that there stood between us, forever, beyond the power of time or forgiveness, the fact that I had held silence—so long!—when he had needed human speech to help him. He turned back to the window. "No, there's no way not to suffer. But you try all kinds of ways to keep from drowning in it, to keep on top of it, and to make it seem—well, like *you.* Like you did something, all right, and now you're suffering for it. You know?" I said nothing. "Well you know," he said, impatiently, "why *do* people suffer? Maybe it's better to do something to give it a reason, *any* reason."

"But we just agreed," I said "that there's no way not to suffer. Isn't it better, then, just to—take it?"

"But nobody just takes it," Sonny cried, "that's what I'm telling you! *Everybody* tries not to. You're just hung up on the *way* some people try—it's not *your* way!"

The hair on my face began to itch, my face felt wet. "That's not true," I said, "that's not true. I don't give a damn what other people do, I don't even care how they suffer. I just care how *you* suffer." And he looked at me. "Please believe me," I said, "I don't want to see you—die—trying not to suffer."

"I won't," he said, flatly, "die trying not to suffer. At least, not any faster than anybody else."

"But there's no need," I said, trying to laugh, "is there? in killing yourself."

I wanted to say more, but I couldn't. I wanted to talk about will power and how life could be—well, beautiful. I wanted to say that it was all within; but was it? or, rather, wasn't that exactly the trouble? And I wanted to promise that I would never fail him again. But it would all have sounded—empty words and lies.

So I made the promise to myself and prayed that I would keep it.

"It's terrible sometimes, inside," he said, "that's what's the trouble. You walk these streets, black and funky and cold, and there's not really a living ass to talk to, and there's nothing shaking, and there's no way of getting it out—that storm inside. You can't talk it and you can't make love with it, and when you finally try to get with it and play it, you realize *nobody's* listening. So *you've* got to listen. You got to find a way to listen."

And then he walked away from the window and sat on the sofa again, as though all the wind had suddenly been knocked out of him. "Sometimes you'll do *anything* to play, even cut your mother's throat." He laughed and looked at me. "Or your brother's." Then he sobered. "Or your own." Then: "Don't worry. I'm all right now and I think I'll *be* all right. But I can't forget—where I've been. I don't mean just the physical place I've been, I mean where I've *been*. And *what* I've been."

"What have you been, Sonny?" I asked.

He smiled—but sat sideways on the sofa, his elbow resting on the back, his fingers playing with his mouth and chin, not looking at me. "I've been something I didn't recognize, didn't know I could be. Didn't know anybody could be." He stopped, looking inward, looking helplessly young, looking old. "I'm not talking about it now because I feel *guilty* or anything like that—maybe it would be better if I did, I don't know. Anyway, I can't really talk about it. Not to you, not to anybody," and now he turned and faced me. "Sometimes, you know, and it was actually when I was most *out* of the world, I felt that I was in it, that I was *with* it, really, and I could play or I didn't really have to *play,* it just came out of me, it was there. And I don't know how I played, thinking about it now, but I know I did awful things, those times, sometimes, to people. Or it wasn't that I *did* anything to them—it was that they weren't real." He picked up the beer can; it was empty; he rolled it between his palms: "And other times—well, I needed a fix, I needed to find a place to lean, I needed to clear a space to *listen*—and I couldn't find it, and I—went crazy, I did terrible things to *me,* I was terrible *for* me." He began pressing the beer can between his hands, I watched the metal begin to give. It glittered, as he played with it, like a knife, and I was afraid he would cut himself, but I said nothing. "Oh well. I can never tell you. I was all by myself at the bottom of something, stinking and sweating and crying and shaking, and I smelled it, you know? *my* stink, and I thought I'd die if I couldn't get away from it and yet, all the same, I knew that everything I was doing was just locking me in with it. And I didn't know," he paused, still flattening the beer can, "I didn't know, I still *don't* know, something kept telling me that maybe it was good to smell your own stink, but I didn't think that *that* was what I'd been trying to do—and—who can stand it?" and he abruptly dropped the ruined beer can, looking at me with a small, still smile, and then rose, walking to the window as though it were the lodestone rock. I watched his face, he watched the avenue. "I couldn't tell you when Mama died—but the reason I wanted to leave Harlem so bad was to get away from drugs. And then, when I ran away, that's what I was running from—really. When I came back, nothing had changed, *I* hadn't changed, I was just—older." And he stopped, drumming with his fingers on the windowpane. The sun had vanished, soon darkness would fall. I watched his face. "It can come again," he said, almost as though speaking to himself. Then he turned to me. "It can come again," he repeated. "I just want you to know that."

"All right," I said, at last. "So it can come again, All right."

He smiled, but the smile was sorrowful. "I had to try to tell you," he said.

"Yes," I said. "I understand that."

"You're my brother," he said, looking straight at me, and not smiling at all.

"Yes," I repeated, "yes. I understand that."

He turned back to the window, looking out. "All that hatred down there," he said, "all that hatred and misery and love. It's a wonder it doesn't blow the avenue apart."

We went to the only nightclub on a short, dark street, downtown. We squeezed through the narrow, chattering, jam-packed bar to the entrance of the big room, where the bandstand was. And we stood there for a moment, for the lights were very dim in this room and we couldn't see. Then, "Hello, boy," said a voice and an enormous black man, much older than Sonny or myself, erupted out of all that atmospheric lighting and put an arm around Sonny's shoulder. "I been sitting right here," he said, "waiting for you."

He had a big voice, too, and heads in the darkness turned toward us.

Sonny grinned and pulled a little away, and said, "Creole, this is my brother. I told you about him."

Creole shook my hand. "I'm glad to meet you, son," he said, and it was clear that he was glad to meet me *there,* for Sonny's sake. And he smiled, "You got a real musician in *your* family," and he took his arm from Sonny's shoulder and slapped him, lightly, affectionately, with the back of his hand.

"Well. Now I've heard it all," said a voice behind us. This was another musician, and a friend of Sonny's, a coal-black, cheerful-looking man, built close to the ground. He immediately began confiding to me, at the top of his lungs, the most terrible things about Sonny, his teeth gleaming like a lighthouse and his laugh coming up out of him like the beginning of an earthquake. And it turned out that everyone at the bar knew Sonny, or almost everyone; some were musicians, working there, or nearby, or not working, some were simply hangers-on, and some were there to hear Sonny play. I was introduced to all of them and they were all very polite to me. Yet, it was clear that, for them, I was only Sonny's brother. Here, I was in Sonny's world. Or, rather: his kingdom. Here, it was not even a question that his veins bore royal blood.

They were going to play soon and Creole installed me, by myself, at a table in a dark corner. Then I watched them, Creole, and the little black man, and Sonny, and the others, while they horsed around, standing just below the bandstand. The light from the bandstand spilled just a little short of them and, watching them laughing and gesturing and moving about, I had the feeling that they, nevertheless, were being most careful not to step into that circle of light too suddenly: that if they moved into the light too suddenly, without thinking, they would perish in flame. Then, while I watched, one of them, the small, black man, moved into the light and crossed the bandstand and started fooling around with his drums. Then—being funny and being, also, extremely ceremonious—Creole took Sonny by the arm and led him to the piano. A woman's voice called Sonny's name and a few hands started clapping. And Sonny, also being funny and being ceremonious, and so touched, I think, that he could have cried, but neither hiding it nor showing it, riding it like a man, grinned, and put both hands to his heart and bowed from the waist.

Creole then went to the bass fiddle and a lean, very bright-skinned brown man jumped up on the bandstand and picked up his horn. So there they were, and the atmosphere on the bandstand and in the room began to change and tighten. Someone stepped up to the microphone and announced them. Then there were all kinds of murmurs. Some people at the bar shushed others. The waitress ran around, frantically getting in the last orders, guys and chicks got closer to each other, and the lights on the bandstand, on the quartet, turned to a kind of indigo. Then they all looked different there. Creole looked about him for the last time, as though he were making certain that all his chickens were in the coop, and then he—jumped and struck the fiddle. And there they were.

All I know about music is that not many people ever really hear it. And even then, on the rare occasions when something opens within, and the music enters, what we mainly hear, or hear corroborated, are personal, private, vanishing evocations. But the man who creates the music is hearing something else, is dealing with the roar rising from the void and imposing order on it as it hits the air. What is evoked in him, then, is of another order, more terrible because it has no words, and triumphant, too, for that same reason. And his triumph, when he triumphs, is ours. I just watched Sonny's face. His face was troubled, he was working hard, but he wasn't with it. And I had the feeling that, in a way, everyone on the bandstand was waiting for him, both waiting for him and pushing him along. But as I began to watch Creole, I realized that it was Creole who held them all back. He had them on a short rein. Up there, keeping the beat with his whole body, wailing on the fiddle, with his eyes half closed, he was listening to everything, but he was listening to Sonny. He was having a dialogue with Sonny. He wanted Sonny to leave the shoreline and strike out for the deep water. He was Sonny's witness that deep water and drowning were not the same thing—he had been there, and he knew. And he wanted Sonny to know. He was waiting for Sonny to do the things on the keys which would let Creole know that Sonny was in the water.

And, while Creole listened, Sonny moved, deep within, exactly like some-one in torment. I had never before thought of how awful the relationship must be between the musician and his instrument. He has to fill it, this instrument, with the breath of life, his own. He has to make it do what he wants it to do. And a piano is just a piano. It's made out of so much wood and wires and little hammers and big ones, and ivory. While there's only so much you can do with it, the only way to find this out is to try; to try and make it do everything.

And Sonny hadn't been near a piano for over a year. And he wasn't on much better terms with his life, not the life that stretched before him now. He and the piano stammered, started one way, got scared, stopped; started an-other way, panicked, marked time, started again; then seemed to have found a direction, panicked again, got stuck. And the face I saw on Sonny I'd never seen before. Everything had been burned out of it, and, at the same time, things usually hidden were being burned in, by the fire and fury of the battle which was occurring in him up there.

Yet, watching Creole's face as they neared the end of the first set, I had the feeling that something had happened, something I hadn't heard. Then they finished, there was scattered applause, and then, without an instant's warning, Creole started into something else, it was almost sardonic, it was *Am I Blue.* And, as though he commanded, Sonny began to play. Something began to happen. And Creole let out the reins. The dry, low, black man said something awful on the drums, Creole answered, and the drums talked back. Then the horn insisted, sweet and high, slightly detached perhaps, and Creole listened, commenting now and then, dry, and driving, beautiful and calm and old. Then they all came together again, and Sonny was part of the family again. I could tell this from his face. He seemed to have found, right there beneath his fin-gers, a damn brand-new piano. It seemed that he couldn't get over it. Then, for awhile, just being happy with Sonny, they seemed to be agreeing with him that brand-new pianos certainly were a gas.

Then Creole stepped forward to remind them that what they were playing was the blues. He hit something in all of them, he hit something in me, myself, and the music tightened and deepened, apprehension began to beat the air. Creole began to tell us what the blues were all about. They were not about anything very new. He and his boys up there were keeping it new, at the risk of ruin, destruction, madness, and death, in order to find new ways to make us listen. For, while the tale of how we suffer, and how we are delighted, and how we may triumph is never new, it always must be heard. There isn't any other tale to tell, it's the only light we've got in all this darkness.

And this tale, according to that face, that body, those strong hands on those strings, has another aspect in every country, and a new depth in every generation. Listen, Creole seemed to be saying, listen. Now these are Sonny's blues. He made the little black man on the drums know it, and the bright, brown man on the horn. Creole wasn't trying any longer to get Sonny in the water. He was wishing him Godspeed. Then he stepped back, very slowly, fill-ing the air with the immense suggestion that Sonny speak for himself.

Then they all gathered around Sonny and Sonny played. Every now and again one of them seemed to say, amen. Sonny's fingers filled the air with life, his life. But that life contained so many others. And Sonny went all the way back, he really began with the spare, flat statement of the opening phrase of the song. Then he began to make it his. It was very beautiful because it wasn't hurried and it was no longer a lament. I seemed to hear with what burning he had made it his, with what burning we had yet to make it ours, how we could cease lamenting. Freedom lurked around us and I understood, at last, that he could help us to be free if we would listen, that he would never be free until we did. Yet, there was no battle in his face now. I heard what he had gone through, and would continue to go through until he came to rest in earth. He had made it his: that long line, of which we knew only Mama and Daddy. And he was giving it back, as everything must be given back, so that, passing through death, it can live forever. I saw my mother's face again, and felt, for the first time, how the stones of the road she had walked on must have bruised her feet. I saw the moonlit road where my father's brother died. And it brought something else back to me, and carried me past it. I saw my little girl again and felt Isabel's tears again, and I felt my own tears begin to rise. And I was yet aware that this was only a moment, that the world waited outside, as hungry as a tiger, and that trouble stretched above us, longer than the sky.

Then it was over. Creole and Sonny let out their breath, both soaking wet, and grinning. There was a lot of applause and some of it was real. In the dark, the girl came by and I asked her to take drinks to the bandstand. There was a long pause, while they talked up there in the indigo light and after awhile I saw the girl put a Scotch and milk on top of the piano for Sonny. He didn't seem to notice it, but just before they started playing again, he sipped from it and looked toward me, and nodded. Then he put it back on top of the piano. For me, then, as they began to play again, it glowed and shook above my brother's head like the very cup of trembling.

QUESTIONS AND CONSIDERATIONS

1. The narrator uses several images to describe his shock at the realization of Sonny's drug problem. What images does the narrator use to describe his feelings about Sonny, and what do these images reveal about the narrator's personality and his relationship with his brother?

2. How does the death of the narrator's child Gracie have an impact on his attitude toward and relationship with Sonny? What does Sonny's letter about Gracie's death reveal about Sonny and his relationship with his family?

3. What does the story the mother tells about the father's brother reveal about the legacy of close relationships in the narrator's family? What special burden of responsibility does the narrator feel as a consequence of knowing this story? Does he assume the responsibility asked of him by his mother?

4. Why is the narrator critical of Sonny's musical interests and his attitude toward formal schooling? Do his criticisms and fears seem justified? How does Sonny respond to the narrator's expressions of concern?

5. What does the narrator understand about Sonny and about his own community as he observes Sonny on the street among the revival singers? What is Sonny doing there? What does the conversation between the two brothers immediately following the street scene reveal about their relationship and particular attitudes toward music, drugs, and suffering?

6. What does the narrator realize about family relationships and cultural traditions in the scene in which Sonny plays with Creole and his jazz group at the nightclub? What is the significance of the final image in the story, the "cup of trembling" above Sonny's piano?

IDEAS FOR WRITING

1. Write an essay about a discussion with a friend or relative with whom you differed on a significant issue—politics, life style, or drug use. What was the nature of your difference, and how, if at all, were your differences reconciled?

2. Write an analysis of the relationship between the two brothers in "Sonny's Blues." Contrast the major differences that you perceive in their personalities and life styles. How do these differences make it difficult for them to communicate with and accept one another? By the end of the story, have they made any progress toward fuller communication with and acceptance of one another? Why?

A Wife's Story
Bharati Mukherjee

Journal

Write about a relationship that you had with a person from a different culture. Focus on one or two incidents that point up the differences in your values.

Imre says forget it, but I'm going to write David Mamet. So Patels are hard to sell real estate to. You buy them a beer, whisper Glengarry Glen Ross, and they smell swamp instead of sun and surf. They work hard, eat cheap, live ten to a room, stash their savings under futons in Queens, and before you know it they own half of Hoboken. You say, where's the sweet gullibility that made this nation great?

Polish jokes, Patel jokes: that's not why I want to write Mamet.

Seen their women?

Everybody laughs. Imre laughs. The dozing fat man with the Barnes & Noble sack between his legs, the woman next to him, the usher, everybody. The theater isn't so dark that they can't see me. In my red silk sari I'm conspicuous. Plump, gold paisleys sparkle on my chest.

The actor is just warming up. *Seen their women?* He plays a salesman, he's had a bad day and now he's in a Chinese restaurant trying to loosen up. His face is pink. His wool-blend slacks are creased at the crotch. We bought our tickets at half-price, we're sitting in the front row, but at the edge, and we see things we shouldn't be seeing. At least I do, or think I do. Spittle, actors goosing each other, little winks, streaks of makeup.

Maybe they're improvising dialogue too. Maybe Mamet's provided them with insult kits, Thursdays for Chinese, Wednesdays for Hispanics, today for Indians. Maybe they get together before curtain time, see an Indian woman settling in the front row off to the side, and say to each other: "Hey, forget Friday. Let's get *her* today. See if she cries. See if she walks out." Maybe, like the salesmen they play, they have a little bet on.

Maybe I shouldn't feel betrayed.

Their women, he goes again. *They look like they've just been fucked by a dead cat.*

The fat man hoots so hard he nudges my elbow off our shared armrest.

"Imre. I'm going home." But Imre's hunched so far forward he doesn't hear. English isn't his best language. A refugee from Budapest, he has to listen hard. "I didn't pay eighteen dollars to be insulted."

I don't hate Mamet. It's the tyranny of the American dream that scares me. First, you don't exist. Then you're invisible. Then you're funny. Then you're disgusting. Insult, my American friends will tell me, is a kind of acceptance. No instant dignity here. A play like this, back home, would cause riots. Communal, racist, and antisocial. The actors wouldn't make it off stage. This play, and all these awful feelings, would be safely locked up.

I long, at times, for clear-cut answers. Offer me instant dignity, today, and I'll take it.

"What?" Imre moves toward me without taking his eyes off the actor. "Come again?"

Tears come. I want to stand, scream, make an awful scene. I long for ugly, nasty rage.

The actor is ranting, flinging spittle. *Give me a chance. I'm not finished, I can get back on the board. I tell that asshole, give me a real lead. And what does that asshole give me? Patels. Nothing but Patels.*

This time Imre works an arm around my shoulders. "Panna, what is Patel? Why are you taking it all so personally?"

I shrink from his touch, but I don't walk out. Expensive girls' schools in Lausanne and Bombay have trained me to behave well. My manners are exquisite, my feelings are delicate, my gestures refined, my moods undetectable. They have seen me through riots, uprootings, separation, my son's death.

"I'm not taking it personally."

The fat man looks at us. The woman looks too, and shushes.

I stare back at the two of them. Then I stare, mean and cool, at the man's elbow. Under the bright blue polyester Hawaiian shirt sleeve, the elbow looks soft and runny. "Excuse me," I say. My voice has the effortless meanness of well-bred displaced Third World women, though my rhetoric has been learned elsewhere. "You're exploiting my space."

Startled, the man snatches his arm away from me. He cradles it against his breast. By the time he's ready with comebacks, I've turned my back on him. I've probably ruined the first act for him. I know I've ruined it for Imre.

It's not my fault; it's the *situation*. Old colonies wear down. Patels—the new pioneers—have to be suspicious. Idi Amin's lesson is permanent. AT&T wires move good advice from continent to continent. Keep all assets liquid. Get into 7-11s, get out of condos and motels. I know how both sides feel, that's the trouble. The Patel sniffing out scams, the sad salesmen on the stage: postcolonialism has made me their referee. It's hate I long for; simple, brutish, partisan hate.

After the show Imre and I make our way toward Broadway. Sometimes he holds my hand; it doesn't mean anything more than that crazies and drunks are crouched in doorways. Imre's been here over two years, but he's stayed very old-world, very courtly, openly protective of women. I met him in a seminar on special ed. last semester. His wife is a nurse somewhere in the Hungarian countryside. There are two sons, and miles of petitions for their emigration. My husband manages a mill two hundred miles north of Bombay. There are no children.

"You make things tough on yourself," Imre says. He assumed Patel was a Jewish name or maybe Hispanic; everything makes equal sense to him. He found the play tasteless, he worried about the effect of vulgar language on my sensitive ears. "You have to let go a bit." And as though to show me how to let go, he breaks away from me, bounds ahead with his head ducked tight, then dances on amazingly jerky legs. He's a Magyar, he often tells me, and deep down, he's an Asian too. I catch glimpses of it, knife-blade Attila cheekbones, despite the blondish hair. In his faded jeans and leather jacket, he's a rock video star. I watch MTV for hours in the apartment when Charity's working the evening shift at Macy's. I listen to WPLJ on Charity's earphones. Why should I be ashamed? Television in India is so uplifting.

Imre stops as suddenly as he'd started. People walk around us. The summer sidewalk is full of theatergoers in seersucker suits; Imre's year-round jacket is out of place. European. Cops in twos and threes huddle, lightly tap their thighs with night sticks and smile at me with benevolence. I want to wink at them, get us all in trouble, tell them the crazy dancing man is from the Warsaw Pact. I'm too shy to break into dance on Broadway. So I hug Imre instead.

The hug takes him by surprise. He wants me to let go, but he doesn't really expect me to let go. He staggers, though I weigh no more than 104 pounds, and with him, I pitch forward slightly. Then he catches me, and we walk arm in arm to the bus stop. My husband would never dance or hug a woman on Broadway. Nor would my brothers. They aren't stuffy people, but they went to Anglican boarding schools and they have a well-developed sense of what's silly.

"Imre." I squeeze his big, rough hand. "I'm sorry I ruined the evening for you."

"You did nothing of the kind." He sounds tired. "Let's not wait for the bus. Let's splurge and take a cab instead."

Imre always has unexpected funds. The Network, he calls it, Class of '56.

In the back of the cab, without even trying, I feel light, almost free. Memories of Indian destitutes mix with the hordes of New York street people, and they float free, like astronauts, inside my head. I've made it. I'm making something of my life. I've left home, my husband, to get a Ph.D. in special ed. I have a multiple-entry visa and a small scholarship for two years. After that, we'll see. My mother was beaten by her mother-in-law, my grandmother, when she'd registered for French lessons at the Alliance Française. My grandmother, the eldest daughter of a rich zamindar, was illiterate.

Imre and the cabdriver talk away in Russian. I keep my eyes closed. That way I can feel the floaters better. I'll write Mamet tonight. I feel strong, reckless. Maybe I'll write Steven Spielberg too; tell him that Indians don't eat monkey brains.

We've made it. Patels must have made it. Mamet, Spielberg: they're not condescending to us. Maybe they're a little bit afraid.

Charity Chin, my roommate, is sitting on the floor drinking Chablis out of a plastic wineglass. She is five foot six, three inches taller than me, but weighs a kilo and a half less than I do. She is a "hands" model. Orientals are supposed to have a monopoly in the hands-modelling business, she says. She had her eyes fixed eight or nine months ago and out of gratitude sleeps with her plastic surgeon every third Wednesday.

"Oh, good," Charity says. "I'm glad you're back early. I need to talk."

She's been writing checks, MCI, Con Ed, Bonwit Teller. Envelopes, already stamped and sealed, form a pyramid between her shapely, knee-socked legs. The checkbook's cover is brown plastic, grained to look like cowhide. Each time Charity flips back the cover, white geese fly over sky-colored checks. She makes good money, but she's extravagant. The difference adds up to this shared, rent-controlled Chelsea one-bedroom.

"All right. Talk."

When I first moved in, she was seeing an analyst. Now she sees a nutritionist.

"Eric called. From Oregon."

"What did he want?"

"He wants me to pay half the rent on his loft for last spring. He asked me to move back, remember? He *begged* me."

Eric is Charity's estranged husband.

"What does your nutritionist say?" Eric now wears a red jumpsuit and tills the soil in Rajneeshpuram.

"You think Phil's a creep too, don't you? What else can he be when creeps are all I attract?"

Phil is a flutist with thinning hair. He's very touchy on the subject of *flautists* versus *flutists*. He's touchy on every subject, from music to books to foods to clothes. He teaches at a small college upstate, and Charity bought a used blue Datsun ("Nissan," Phil insists) last month so she could spend weekends with him. She returns every Sunday night, exhausted and exasperated.

Phil and I don't have much to say to each other—he's the only musician I know; the men in my family are lawyers, engineers, or in business—but I like him. Around me, he loosens up. When he visits, he bakes us loaves of pumpernickel bread. He waxes our kitchen floor. Like many men in this country, he seems to me a displaced child, or even a woman, looking for something that passed him by, or for something that he can never have. If he thinks I'm not looking, he sneaks his hands under Charity's sweater, but there isn't too much there. Here, she's a model with high ambitions. In India, she'd be a flat-chested old maid.

I'm shy in front of the lovers. A darkness comes over me when I see them horsing around.

"It isn't the money," Charity says. Oh? I think. "He says he still loves me. Then he turns around and asks me for five hundred."

What's so strange about that, I want to ask. She still loves Eric, and Eric, red jumpsuit and all, is smart enough to know it. Love is a commodity, hoarded like any other. Mamet knows. But I say, "I'm not the person to ask about love." Charity knows that mine was a traditional Hindu marriage. My parents, with the help of a marriage broker, who was my mother's cousin, picked out a groom. All I had to do was get to know his taste in food.

It'll be a long evening, I'm afraid. Charity likes to confess. I unpleat my silk sari—it no longer looks too showy—wrap it in muslin cloth and put it away in a dresser drawer. Saris are hard to have laundered in Manhattan, though there's a good man in Jackson Heights. My next step will be to brew us a pot of chrysanthemum tea. It's a very special tea from the mainland. Charity's uncle gave it to us. I like him. He's a humpbacked, awkward, terrified man. He runs a gift store on Mott Street, and though he doesn't speak much English, he seems to have done well. Once upon a time he worked for the railways in Chengdu, Szechwan Province, and during the Wuchang Uprising, he was shot at. When I'm down, when I'm lonely for my husband, when I think of our son, or when I need to be held, I think of Charity's uncle. If I hadn't left home, I'd never have heard of the Wuchang Uprising. I've broadened my horizons.

Very late that night my husband calls me from Ahmadabad, a town of textile mills north of Bombay. My husband is a vice president at Lakshmi Cotton Mills. Lakshmi is the goddess of wealth, but LCM (Priv.), Ltd., is doing poorly. Lockouts, strikes, rock-throwings. My husband lives on digitalis, which he calls the food for our *yuga* of discontent.

"We had a bad mishap at the mill today." Then he says nothing for seconds.

The operator comes on. "Do you have the right party, sir? We're trying to reach Mrs. Butt."

"Bhatt," I insist. "*B* for Bombay, *H* for Haryana, *A* for Ahmadabad, double *T* for Tamil Nadu." It's a litany. "This is she."

"One of our lorries was firebombed today. Resulting in three deaths. The driver, old Karamchand, and his two children."

I know how my husband's eyes look this minute, how the eye rims sag and the yellow corneas shine and bulge with pain. He is not an emotional man—the Ahmadabad Institute of Management has trained him to cut losses, to look on the bright side of economic catastrophes—but tonight he's feeling low. I try to remember a driver named Karamchand, but can't. That part of my life is over, the way *trucks* have replaced *lorries* in my vocabulary, the way Charity Chin and her lurid love life have replaced inherited notions of marital duty. Tomorrow he'll come out of it. Soon he'll be eating again. He'll sleep like a baby. He's been trained to believe in turnovers. Every morning he rubs his scalp with cantharidine oil so his hair will grow back again.

"It could be your car next." Affection, love. Who can tell the difference in a traditional marriage in which a wife still doesn't call her husband by his first name?

"No. They know I'm a flunky, just like them. Well paid, maybe. No need for undue anxiety, please."

Then his voice breaks. He says he needs me, he misses me, he wants me to come to him damp from my evening shower, smelling of sandalwood soap, my braid decorated with jasmines.

"I need you too."

"Not to worry, please," he says. "I am coming in a fortnight's time. I have already made arrangements."

Outside my window, fire trucks whine, up Eighth Avenue. I wonder if he can hear them, what he thinks of a life like mine, led amid disorder.

"I am thinking it'll be like a honeymoon. More or less."

When I was in college, waiting to be married, I imagined honeymoons were only for the more fashionable girls, the girls who came from slightly racy families, smoked Sobranies in the dorm lavatories and put up posters of Kabir Bedi, who was supposed to have made it as a big star in the West. My husband wants us to go to Niagara. I'm not to worry about foreign exchange. He's arranged for extra dollars through the Gujarati Network, with a cousin in San Jose. And he's bought four hundred more on the black market. "Tell me you need me. Panna, please tell me again."

I change out of the cotton pants and shirt I've been wearing all day and put on a sari to meet my husband at JFK. I don't forget the jewelry; the marriage necklace of *mangalsutra,* gold drop earrings, heavy gold bangles. I don't wear them every day. In this borough of vice and greed, who knows when, or whom, desire will overwhelm.

My husband spots me in the crowd and waves. He has lost weight, and changed his glasses. The arm, uplifted in a cheery wave, is bony, frail, almost opalescent.

In the Carey Coach, we hold hands. He strokes my fingers one by one. "How come you aren't wearing my mother's ring?"

"Because muggers know about Indian women," I say. They know with us it's 24-karat. His mother's ring is showy, in ghastly taste anywhere but India: a blood-red Burma rube set in a gold frame of floral sprays. My mother-in-law got her guru to bless the ring before I left for the States.

He looks disconcerted. He's used to a different role. He's the knowing, suspicious one in the family. He seems to be sulking, and finally he comes out with it. "You've said nothing about my new glasses." I compliment him on the glasses, how chic and Western-executive they make him look. But I can't help the other things, necessities until he learns the ropes. I handle the money, buy the tickets. I don't know if this makes me unhappy.

Charity drives her Nissan upstate, so for two weeks we are to have the apartment to ourselves. This is more privacy than we ever had in India. No parents, no servants, to keep us modest. We play at housekeeping. Imre has lent us a hibachi, and I grill saffron chicken breasts. My husband marvels at the size of the Perdue hens. "They're big like peacocks, no? These Americans, they're really something!" He tries out pizzas, burgers, McNuggets. He chews. He explores. He judges. He loves it all, fears nothing, feels at home in the summer odors, the clutter of Manhattan streets. Since he thinks that the American palate is bland, he carries a bottle of red peppers in his pocket. I wheel a shopping cart down the aisles of the neighborhood Grand Union, and he follows, swiftly, greedily. He picks up hair rinses and high-protein diet powders. There's so much I already take for granted.

One night, Imre stops by. He wants us to go with him to a movie. In his work shirt and red leather tie, he looks arty or strung out. It's only been a week, but I feel as though I am really seeing him for the first time. The yellow hair worn very short at the sides, the wide, narrow lips. He's a good-looking man, but self-conscious, almost arrogant. He's picked the movie we should see. He always tells me what to see, what to read. He buys the *Voice.* He's a natural avant-gardist. For tonight he's chosen *Numéro Deux.*

"Is it a musical?" my husband asks. The Radio City Music Hall is on his list of sights to see. He's read up on the history of the Rockettes. He doesn't catch Imre's sympathetic wink.

Guilt, shame, loyalty. I long to be ungracious, not ingratiate myself with both men.

That night my husband calculates in rupees the money we've wasted on Godard. "That refugee fellow, Nagy, must have a screw loose in his head. I paid very steep prices for dollars on the black market."

Some afternoons we go shopping. Back home we hated shopping, but now it is a lovers' project. My husband's shopping list startles me. I feel I am just getting to know him. Maybe, like Imre, freed from the dignities of old-world culture, he too could get drunk and squirt Cheez Whiz on a guest. I watch him dart into stores in his gleaming leather shoes. Jockey shorts on sale in outdoor bins on Broadway entrance him. White tube socks with different bands of color delight him. He looks for microcassettes, for anything small and electronic and smuggleable. He needs a garment bag. He calls it a "wardrobe," and I have to translate.

"All of New York is having sales, no?"

My heart speeds watching him this happy. It's the third week in August, almost the end of summer, and the city smells ripe, it cannot bear more heat, more money, more energy.

"This is so smashing! The prices are so excellent!" Recklessly, my prudent husband signs away traveler's checks. How he intends to smuggle it all back I don't dare ask. With a microwave, he calculates, we could get rid of our cook.

This has to be love, I think. Charity, Eric, Phil: they may be experts on sex. My husband doesn't chase me around the sofa, but he pushes me down on Charity's battered cushions, and the man who has never entered the kitchen of our Ahmadabad house now comes toward me with a dish tub of steamy water to massage away the pavement heat.

Ten days into his vacation my husband checks out brochures for sightseeing tours. Shortline, Grayline, Crossroads: his new vinyl briefcase is full of schedules and pamphlets. While I make pancakes out of a mix, he comparison-shops. Tour number one costs $10.95 and will give us the World Trade Center, Chinatown, and the United Nations. Tour number three would take us both uptown *and* downtown for $14.95, but my husband is absolutely sure he doesn't want to see Harlem. We settle for tour number four: Downtown and the Dame. It's offered by a new tour company with a small, dirty office at Eighth and Forty-eighth.

The sidewalk outside the office is colorful with tourists. My husband sends me in to buy the tickets because he has come to feel Americans don't understand his accent.

The dark man, Lebanese probably, behind the counter comes on too friendly. "Come on, doll, make my day!" He won't say which tour is his. "Number four? Honey, no! Look, you've wrecked me! Say you'll change your mind." He takes two twenties and gives back change. He holds the tickets, forcing me to pull. He leans closer. "I'm off after lunch."

My husband must have been watching me from the sidewalk. "What was the chap saying?" he demands. "I told you not to wear pants. He thinks you are Puerto Rican. He thinks he can treat you with disrespect."

The bus is crowded and we have to sit across the aisle from each other. The tour guide begins his patter on Forty-sixth. He looks like an actor, his hair bleached and blow-dried. Up close he must look middle-aged, but from where I sit his skin is smooth and his cheeks faintly red.

"Welcome to the Big Apple, folks." The guide uses a microphone. "Big Apple. That's what we native Manhattan degenerates call our city. Today we have guests from fifteen foreign countries and six states from this U. S. of A. That makes the Tourist Bureau real happy. And let me assure you that while we may be the richest city in the richest country in the world, it's okay to tip your charming and talented attendant." He laughs. Then he swings his hip out into the aisle and sings a song.

"And it's mighty fancy on old Delancey Street, you know. . . ."

My husband looks irritable. The guide is, as expected, a good singer. "The bloody man should be giving us histories of buildings we are passing, no?" I pat his hand, the mood passes. He cranes his neck. Our window seats have both gone to Japanese. It's the tour of his life. Next to this, the quick business trips to Manchester and Glasgow pale.

"And tell me what street compares to Mott Street, in July. . . ."

The guide wants applause. He manages a derisive laugh from the Americans up front. He's working the aisles now. "I coulda been somebody, right? I coulda been a star!" Two or three of us smile, those of us who recognize the parody. He catches my smile. The sun is on his harsh, bleached hair. "Right, your highness? Look, we gotta maharani with us! Couldn't I have been a star?"

"Right!" I say, my voice coming out a squeal. I've been trained to adapt; what else can I say?

We drive through traffic past landmark office buildings and churches. The guide flips his hands. "Art Deco," he keeps saying. I hear him confide to one of the Americans: "Beats me. I went to a cheap guide's school." My husband wants to know more about this Art Deco, but the guide sings another song.

"We made a foolish choice," my husband grumbles. "We are sitting in the bus only. We're not going into famous buildings." He scrutinizes the pamphlets in his jacket pocket. I think, at least it's air-conditioned in here. I could sit here in the cool shadows of the city forever.

Only five of us appear to have opted for the "Downtown and the Dame" tour. The others will ride back uptown past the United Nations after we've been dropped off at the pier for the ferry to the Statue of Liberty.

An elderly European pulls a camera out of his wife's designer tote bag. He takes pictures of the boats in the harbor, the Japanese in kimonos eating popcorn, scavenging pigeons, me. Then, pushing his wife ahead of him, he climbs back on the bus and waves to us. For a second I feel terribly lost. I wish we were on the bus going back to the apartment. I know I'll not be able to describe any of this to Charity, or to Imre. I'm too proud to admit I went on a guided tour.

The view of the city from the Circle Line ferry is seductive, unreal. The skyline wavers out of reach, but never quite vanishes. The summer sun pushes through fluffy clouds and dapples the glass of office towers. My husband looks thrilled, even more than he had on the shopping trips down Broadway. Tourists and dreamers, we have spent our life's savings to see this skyline, this statue.

"Quick, take a picture of me!" my husband yells as he moves toward a gap of railings. A Japanese matron has given up her position in order to change film. "Before the Twin Towers disappear!"

I focus, I wait for a large Oriental family to walk out of my range. My husband holds his pose tight against the railing. He wants to look relaxed, an international businessman at home in all the financial markets.

A bearded man slides across the bench toward me. "Like this," he says and helps me get my husband in focus. "You want me to take the photo for you?" His name, he says, is Goran. He is Goran from Yugoslavia, as though that were enough for tracking him down. Imre from Hungary. Panna from India. He pulls the old Leica out of my hand, signaling the Orientals to beat it, and clicks away. "I'm a photographer," he says. He could have been a camera thief. That's what my husband would have assumed. Somehow, I trusted. "Get you a beer?" he asks.

"I don't. Drink, I mean. Thank you very much." I say those last words very loud, for everyone's benefit. The odd bottles of Soave with Imre don't count.

"Too bad." Goran gives back the camera.

"Take one more!" my husband shouts from the railing. "Just to be sure!" The island itself disappoints. The Lady has brutal scaffolding holding her in. The museum is closed. The snack bar is dirty and expensive. My husband reads out the prices to me. He orders two french fries and two Cokes. We sit at picnic tables and wait for the ferry to take us back.

"What was that hippie chap saying?"

As if I could say. A day-care center has brought its kids, at least forty of them, to the island for the day. The kids, all wearing name tags, run around us. I can't help noticing how many are Indian. Even a Patel, probably a Bhatt if I looked hard enough. They toss hamburger bits at pigeons. They kick styrofoam cups. The pigeons are slow, greedy, persistent. I have to shoo one off the table top. I don't think my husband thinks about our son.

"What hippie?"

"The one on the boat. With the beard and the hair."

My husband doesn't look at me. He shakes out his paper napkin and tries to protect his french fries from pigeon feathers.

"Oh, him. He said he was from Dubrovnik." It isn't true, but I don't want trouble.

"What did he say about Dubrovnik?"

I know enough about Dubrovnik to get by. Imre's told me about it. And about Mostar and Zagreb. In Mostar white Muslims sing the call to prayer. I would like to see that before I die: white Muslims. Whole peoples have moved before me; they've adapted. The night Imre told me about Mostar was also the night I saw my first snow in Manhattan. We'd walked down to Chelsea from Columbia. We'd walked and talked and I hadn't felt tired at all.

"You're too innocent," my husband says. He reaches for my hand. "Panna," he cries with pain in his voice, and I am brought back from perfect, floating memories of snow, "I've come to take you back. I have seen how men watch you."

"What?"

"Come back, now. I have tickets. We have all the things we will ever need. I can't live without you."

A little girl with wiry braids kicks a bottle cap at his shoes. The pigeons wheel and scuttle around us. My husband covers his fries with spread-out fingers. "No kicking," he tells the girl. Her name, Beulah, is printed in green ink on a heart-shaped name tag. He forces a smile, and Beulah smiles back. Then she starts to flap her arms. She flaps, she hops. The pigeons go crazy for fries and scraps.

"Special ed. course is two years," I remind him. "I can't go back."

My husband picks up our trays and throws them into the garbage before I can stop him. He's carried disposability a little too far. "We've been taken," he says, moving toward the dock, though the ferry will not arrive for another twenty minutes. "The ferry costs only two dollars round-trip per person. We should have chosen tour number one for $10.95 instead of tour number four for $14.95."

With my Lebanese friend, I think. "But this way we don't have to worry about cabs. The bus will pick us up at the pier and take us back to midtown. Then we can walk home."

"New York is full of cheats and whatnot. Just like Bombay." He is not accusing me of infidelity. I feel dread all the same.

That night, after we've gone to bed, the phone rings. My husband listens, then hands the phone to me. "What is this woman saying?" He turns on the pink Macy's lamp by the bed. "I am not understanding these Negro people's accents."

The operator repeats the message. It's a cable from one of the directors of Lakshmi Cotton Mills. "Massive violent labor confrontation anticipated. Stop. Return posthaste. Stop. Cable flight details. Signed Kantilal Shah."

"It's not your factory," I say. "You're supposed to be on vacation."

"So, you are worrying about me? Yes? You reject my heartfelt wishes but you worry about me?" He pulls me close, slips the straps of my nightdress off my shoulder. "Wait a minute."

I wait, unclothed, for my husband to come back to me. The water is running in the bathroom. In the ten days he has been here he has learned American rites: deodorants, fragrances. Tomorrow morning he'll call Air India; tomorrow evening he'll be on his way back to Bombay. Tonight I should make up to him for my years away, the gutted trucks, the degree I'll never use in India. I want to pretend with him that nothing has changed.

In the mirror that hangs on the bathroom door, I watch my naked body turn, the breasts, the thighs glow. The body's beauty amazes. I stand here shameless, in ways he has never seen me. I am free, afloat, watching somebody else.

QUESTIONS AND CONSIDERATIONS

1. Why does Panna want to write to the playwright David Mamet? What would she say to him about the "Patels"? What do they represent to her?

2. Where did Panna meet Imre? Why have they established a relationship with one another? How well do they understand one another? Contrast the opening and closing scenes of the story to show how Panna has learned to communicate with men in a different way while living in New York.

3. In what ways is Panna's life style both nontraditional and, at the same time, reflective of traditional Indian values instilled in her through her family and her boarding school experiences? How do you think Panna feels about herself?

4. Panna thinks, "Love is a commodity, hoarded like any other." Explain both Panna's feelings about love in the context of what you know about her marriage in India and her life in Manhattan.

5. Why does Panna's husband come to visit her in Manhattan? What does he like and dislike about New York City? What do you think Panna's husband is implying about his feelings for his wife and her life in Manhattan when he comments, "New York is full of cheats and what not. Just like Bombay"? How do you think Panna feels about her husband? Refer to the story to support each of your responses.

6. Why won't Panna return with her husband to India? What does she realize that she has learned about herself through her experiences in New York? Interpret the meaning of Panna's final statement, "I am free, afloat, watching somebody else." Is she really free?

IDEAS FOR WRITING

1. Write an essay in which you discuss what you think are some of the most interesting issues about modern relationships between men and women, and how these relationships are changing in response to the cultural changes that the story raises. Refer to the text and to your own life experiences to support your main ideas.

2. Write an essay in which you try to predict several of the effects of the breakdown of values in traditional cultures on modern marriages.

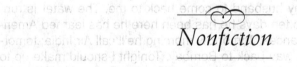

Nonfiction

Father Hunger
Michel Marriott

Journal

Write about a difference of opinion or a breakdown in communication between you and one of your parents. Has the difference been reconciled, or does it continue to affect your relationship?

Once, not too many years ago, I looked up from the scribble on my reporter's pad and stared into the hyperanimated face of Fidel Castro—and I saw my father. As part of a delegation of African-American journalists invited to Cuba in 1986, I counted myself lucky to be among the teeming Caribbeans crammed onto a dusty soccer field just outside a knot of empty shops, crowded flats and stands of sugarcane. Moreover, I felt a stab of surprise that I had somehow stepped, flesh and blood, into my father's dream.

Long disenchanted with what he called the "trick bag" of the United States, my father reveled in the sheer bravado of the Cuban revolution, its elevation of the Brown and Black to real power. He often talked, half jokingly, of course, of retiring someday to that island republic and having Uncle Sam send his Social Security checks to Havana.

In recognition of the special significance my journey might hold for him, I presented Dad with a gift on my return. To my disappointment, however, he barely accepted the carefully framed photograph I had taken of Castro and inscribed with words of tribute to my father's courage as a freethinker.

Why is it so difficult for us? I asked myself some weeks later when I discovered the picture pitched against a mound of disarray on my father's desk. After so many years of being buffeted by swirling currents of father–son tensions, intermittent hostilities and redeeming love, *why*, I mused, *does it remain so hard for us—two Black men—to, well, just get along?* There had been times when we had hurled hurtful words at each other like poison-tipped spears. We had even, in dizzying and terrifying fits of machismo, both reached for guns, prepared to shoot each other if need be.

Why wasn't it like television, where dads wore suits and ties to the dinner table and were ever ready to lend an ear or dispense fatherly advice with a knowing grin? Where was Fred MacMurray in blackface?

The truth is that for millions of Black men, our relationships with our fathers represent lifetimes of unfinished business. Much too often our most obvious models—from whom we begin to fashion our distinctive sense of a masculine identity—are marginal to our lives because of our fathers' physical or emotional absence from home. The issue is not new or exclusive to African-American men. James Herzog, a Harvard University Medical School assistant professor of psychiatry, coined the phrase "father hunger" to describe the psychological condition young children endure when long separated from their fathers. English professor Andrew Merton of the University of New Hampshire wrote in a 1986 article in *New Age* magazine of many men whose lives have been profoundly shaped and troubled by failures of intimacy with their fathers. Quoting author Samuel Osherson, Merton wrote: "The psychological or physical absence of fathers from their families is one of the great underestimated tragedies of our times."

What is so devastating for so many of us in search of our Black fathers is the realization that many of them were utter failures at nurturing us. And now, as many of us are fathers ourselves, we also find ourselves struggling with the identical phenomenon in relation to our own sons—as if this difficulty were inherent in our Black condition, as if it somehow passes from generation to generation in a recessive gene that we peculiarly carry. But, of course, it's sociological, not biological.

"The masculine role has clearly restricted our ability to relate to children," write Joseph H. Pleck and Jack Sawyer of American men in general, in their 1974 collection *Men and Masculinity.* "Our drive toward getting ahead means we often find little time or energy for being with children; moreover, we may project our own strivings for success upon them."

In the case of too many Black men, however, it is more likely that we project upon our sons our fear and profound sense of powerlessness and vulnerability in a society that daily crushes many of us. Countless Black boys, as a consequence, grow up in a tangle of fatherly love and loathing for what lies ahead for little Michael, little Jamil.

For example, my father would bristle with indignation whenever he discovered my brother and me, as young boys, watching Saturday-morning cartoons. "You don't have time for that bullshit," he'd say in a tone so sharp our child-joy would expire on the spot. "The white man wants you to look at Bugs Bunny while he's figuring out better ways to beat you. You better learn some math, read a book."

There'd be no hugs given or "good mornings" spoken. There was always so much harshness, a sternness very much like that I saw years later captured in Troy Maxson's rage and reason in August Wilson's play *Fences*. When Troy's teenage son, Cory, asks him why he doesn't like him, Troy responds with fury: "I done give you everything I had to give you. I gave you your life! Me and your mama worked that out between us. And liking your black ass wasn't part of the bargain. Don't you try and go through life worrying about if somebody like you or not. You best be making sure they doing right by you." Similarly, growing up with my father, at the time a factory worker at a synthetic-rubber manufacturing plant in Louisville, Kentucky, was like growing up in boot camp, training for the inevitable clashes with white racism and domination that waited just outside the nest of our segregated neighborhood.

Yet I identified with my father. I marveled at his strength—not merely muscular, since he was never a particularly large man. I was in awe of his accordionlike ability to expand on demand, to pump up his nerve and face down anyone who threatened him or his wife or three boys, whether a landlord, a police officer or a teacher who shirked responsibility. In that way, among many, I wanted to be like him: smart, tough, the relentless warrior.

James P. Comer, M.D., an African-American professor of child psychiatry at the Yale University Child Study Center says that while the concept of role modeling may sound like a cliché, it is nevertheless "very real" and necessary. "Kids are here without a road map, and you are like that map to them," he points out. According to Samuel Osherson in his popular 1986 book *Finding Our Fathers,* the need to "identify with father creates the crucial dilemma for boys. [Father is] often a shadowy figure at best, difficult to understand." The result can often be a troubling psychological limbo, explains Osherson, in which boys as young as 3 years old begin pulling away from their mothers but have no clear male model to identify with.

I've never forgotten the unshed tear in the voice of my best friend when I first asked him about his father, a man I'd never heard him talk about. Until that afternoon some years ago, my buddy had seemed to be a product of his mother's labors alone, a bloom from a self-pollinating black orchid.

But there was a man, from whom my friend's features had borrowed heavily. He had never married his mother. My buddy's only contact with the man was when, as a boy, he occasionally sat in the cluttered back room of the man's television-repair shop, a place cooled during the Philadelphia summers by an open door and the warm, breathy air of buzzing electric fans. After being told by his mother that the man in the shop was his father, one day my friend stoked up his nerve and asked the man if this was true.

"You're not any boy of mine," he replied, my friend told me. Wounded deeply, he never returned to the shop. Some years later his father died, a bridge between knowing and not knowing a part of himself forever swept away.

After having dozens of recent conversations with Black men about their relationships with their fathers, a common element emerges, regardless of age: Like a primal impulse, the men who have had injured relations with their fathers are busy trying to heal them. Those who enjoy mutually satis-fying, rich and rewarding relationships—if not the exaggerated bliss of *The Cosby Show*—find them invaluable. In an interview with astronaut Colonel Frederick Drew Gregory shortly before he became the first African-American to command a spacecraft in the late 1980's, he spoke with me at length about his father as mentor and role model. It was his father, he said, who inspired him to reach for heights that many, Black and white, would con-sider unattainable. James Comer writes lovingly of his late father in his 1988 book *Maggie's American Dream: The Life and Times of a Black Family.*

Comer, the father of a grown son and daughter, says it is not surprising that many Black men are trying to better understand and appreciate their fa-thers. "They realize what they have missed," he says. "In some cases there is a struggle for independence that can lead to a difficult relationship," though, he adds, "even bad times can be important once you have reestablished a good relationship." But at any time, Comer emphasizes, "it is important to reestab-lish the relationship."

Unfortunately that may be more problematic for boys born in the closing years of the twentieth century, since the numbers of African-American families headed by women continue to be substantial. And with alarming regularity, Black fathers are relegating themselves to being ghost dads of sorts. Many are lost to the streets, prisons, to successful careers or to legacies of poor rela-tionships with their own fathers, who had troubles with *their* fathers.

"Imagine what it must be like to have a part of you not there," says Terry M. Williams, author and sociologist at Yale, of boys who don't know or know well their fathers. "You think, *So where can I find it?*" Having the father pres-ent in the son's life is key, stresses Williams, even "if his role is not that strong."

Williams, author of the 1989 book *The Cocaine Kids: The Inside Story of a Teenage Drug Ring,* in which he chronicles some four years of observing a young crew of cocaine dealers in New York City, says many young men of color perceive themselves as being in a state of war. "They are acting out and trying to find a way to be men, through tough crews and homeboy networks. You can't deny that these are some of the negative sides of not having fathers around."

Williams, who has two sons, suggests that more Black men be more attentive to their roles as fathers and also reach out to be mentors and role models for other boys. Without positive role models, it is obvious that boys may turn to crime or antisocial behavior, says Williams.

As my own son nears his teenage years, I worry if our relationship will hold. His mother and I divorced when he was hardly a year old. But I have worked hard through the years to keep our father–son links strong and supportive, despite the hundreds of miles that separate us for most of the year. At the close of every telephone conversation, I tell him I love him. And he is careful to tell me he loves me, something my father has never been able to bring himself to say.

I love my father. Some of that love stems from my culture's obligation to honor him because he is my father. Yet another, much larger, part of that love flows from my understanding of him, my empathy with his life and wounds as a proud Black man dangling from a leafless tree of opportunities denied. At 63, my father is a man of enormous talents and, in his own estimation, of humble accomplishments. Many demons still stir in his soul.

For the past ten years we have moved, gently, to resolve our conflicts, to settle into roles reassigned to us by time and growth. In the last few years he has let me hug him when I see him now, which is all too infrequently. I, on the other hand, have reined in my juvenile urges to compete with him, to prove in battles of wit and wile that I am as much a man as he is.

For the last three years I've pulled out the same card of bright colors and upbeat prose I bought for Father's Day. But each year something prevents me from sending it. Procrastination abounds, moving me to return the card to my top drawer, more determined to actually send it to him the next year. Yet, as I wrote this article in the late summer, a process that forced me to refocus my feelings about Pop, I got out the card, signed it "I love you" and sent it homeward. I hope its arrival, though odd, will signal to him anew my homage to our connections, both involuntary and voluntary, both of the blood and of the heart.

I want my father to know that with each morning look into the bathroom mirror, I see a little more of his face peering through mine. Life's journey is circular, it appears. The years don't carry us away from our fathers—they return us to them.

If we are lucky, we will have our memories of them. If we are luckier still and work hard for it, we can enjoy with them laughter and tears of recognition, enjoy loving embraces of mutual appreciation and respect.

With each day, I feel luckier.

QUESTIONS AND CONSIDERATIONS

1. Why does Marriott give his father the carefully framed photo of Fidel Castro? Why does the father have trouble accepting his son's gift?

2. As a reflection on his relationship with his father, Marriott poses the question, "Why does it remain so hard for us—two black men—to, well, just get along?" What reasons does Marriott's essay propose?

3. How does Marriott define "father hunger"? Can you relate to his concept? If you are female, have you seen father hunger in yourself or in brothers, other relatives, or male friends with whom you are close? Consider the personal as well as societal implications of father hunger.

4. Why does Marriott argue that a black father's failure to nurture his son is "sociological and not biological"? Do you agree with him? According to the authorities cited in Marriott's essay, why do African-American youngsters and adult males particularly need their fathers?

5. Can you interpret this essay as a statement of Marriott's reconciliation with his father? What other motivations do you think he had for writing the essay?

IDEAS FOR WRITING

1. Write an essay that defines father hunger as you have understood it. Use examples from your own experiences, from popular culture, and from literature to illustrate your definition.

2. Write a short story that captures your definition of father hunger.

Asians
Richard Rodriguez

―――――

Journal

―――――

Write about a struggle you experienced between yourself and your parents or friends over a cultural misunderstanding.

For the child of immigrant parents the knowledge comes like a slap: America exists.

America exists everywhere in the city—on billboards; frankly in the smell of burgers and French fries. America exists in the slouch of the crowd, the pacing of traffic lights, the assertions of neon, the cry of freedom overriding the nineteenth-century melodic line.

Grasp the implications of American democracy in a handshake or in a stranger's Jeffersonian "hi." America is irresistible. Nothing to do with choosing.

Our parents came to America for the choices America offers. What the child of immigrant parents knows is that here is inevitability.

A Chinese boy says his high-school teacher is always after him to stand up, speak up, look up. Yeah, but then his father puts him down at home: "Since when have you started looking your father in the eye?"

I'd like you to meet Jimmy Lamm. Mr. Lamm was an architect in Saigon. Now he is a cabbie in San Francisco. Stalled in traffic in San Francisco, Jimmy tells me about the refugee camp in Guam where, for nearly two years, he and his family were quartered before their flight to America. A teenager surfs by on a skateboard, his hair cresting in purple spikes like an iron crown, his freedom as apparent, as deplorable, as Huck Finn's.

Damn kid. Honk. Honk.

The damn kid howls with pleasure. Flips us the bird.

Do you worry that your children will end up with purple hair?

Silence.

Then Jimmy says his children have too much respect for the struggle he and his wife endured. His children would never betray him so.

On the floor of Jimmy Lamm's apartment, next to the television, is a bowl of fruit and a burning wand of joss.

He means: his children would never *choose* to betray him.

Immigrant parents re-create a homeland in the parlor, tacking up post-cards or calendars of some impossible blue—lake or sea or sky.

The child of immigrant parents is supposed to perch on a hyphen, taking only the dose of America he needs to advance in America.

At the family picnic, the child wanders away from the spiced food and faceless stories to watch some boys playing baseball in the distance.

* * *

My Mexican father still regards America with skepticism from the high window of his morning paper. "Too much freedom," he says. Though he has spent most of his life in this country, my father yet doubts such a place as the United States of America exists. He cannot discern boundaries. How else to describe a country?

My father admires a flower bed on a busy pedestrian street in Zurich—he holds up the *National Geographic* to show me. "You couldn't have that in America," my father says.

When I was twelve years old, my father said he wished his children had Chinese friends—so polite, so serious are Chinese children in my father's estimation. The Spanish word he used was *formal*.

I didn't have any Chinese friends. My father did. Seventh and J Street was my father's Orient. My father made false teeth for several Chinese dentists downtown. When a Chinese family tried to move in a few blocks away from our house, I heard a friend's father boast that the neighbors had banded together to "keep out the Japs."

Many years pass.

In college, I was reading *The Merchant of Venice*—Shylock urging his daughter to avoid the temptation of the frivolous Christians on the lido. Come away from the window, Shylock commands. I heard my father's voice:

Hear you me, Jessica.
Lock up my doors, and when you hear the drum
And the vile squealing of the wry-necked fife,
Clamber not you up to the casements then,
Nor thrust your head into the public street
To gaze on Christian fools with varnished faces,
But stop my house's ears, I mean my casements.
Let not the sound of shallow foppery enter
My sober house.

*   *   *

I interview the mother on Evergreen Street for the *Los Angeles Times.* The mother says they came from Mexico ten years ago, and—look—already they have this nice house. Each year the kitchen takes on a new appliance.

Outside the door is Los Angeles; in the distance, the perpetual orbit of traffic. Here old women walk slowly under paper parasols, past the Vietnam vet who pushes his tinkling ice-cream cart past little green lawns, little green lawns, little green lawns. (Here teenagers have black scorpions tattooed into their biceps.)

Children here are fed and grow tall. They love Christmas. They laugh at cartoons. They go off to school with children from Vietnam, from Burbank, from Hong Kong. They get into fights. They come home and they say dirty words. Aw, Ma, they say. Gimme a break, they say.

The mother says she does not want American children. It is the thing about Los Angeles she fears, the season of adolescence, of Huck Finn and Daisy Miller.

Foolish mother. She should have thought of that before she came. She will live to see that America takes its meaning from adolescence. She will have American children.

*   *   *

The best metaphor of America remains the dreadful metaphor—the Melting Pot. Fall into the Melting Pot, ease into the Melting Pot, or jump into the Melting Pot—it makes no difference—you will find yourself a stranger to your parents, a stranger to your own memory of yourself.

A Chinese girl walks to the front of the classroom, unfolds several ruled pages, and begins to read her essay to a trio of judges (I am one of her judges).

The voice of the essay is the voice of an immigrant. Stammer and elision approximate naïveté (the judges squirm in their chairs). The narrator remembers her night-long journey to the United States aboard a Pan Am jet. The moon. Stars. Then a memory within a memory: in the darkened cabin of the plane, sitting next to her sleeping father, the little girl remembers bright China.

Many years pass.

The narrator's voice hardens into an American voice; her diction takes on rock and chrome. There is an ashtray on the table. The narrator is sitting at a sidewalk café in San Francisco. She is sixteen years old. She is with friends.

The narrator notices a Chinese girl passing on the sidewalk. The narrator remembers bright China. The passing girl's face turns toward hers. The narrator recognizes herself in the passing girl—herself less assimilated. Their connective glance lasts only seconds. The narrator is embarrassed by her double—she remembers the cabin of the plane, her sleeping father, the moon, stars. The stranger disappears.

   End of essay.

   The room is silent as the Chinese student raises her eyes from the text.

   One judge breaks the silence. Do you think your story is a sad story?

   No, she replies. It is a true story.

   What is the difference?

   (Slowly, then.)

   When you hear a sad story you cry, she says. When you hear a true story you cry even more.

* * *

   . . . With one breath people today speak of Hispanics and Asians—the new Americans. Between the two, Asians are the more admired—the model minority—more protestant than Protestants; so hardworking, self-driven; so bright. But the Asian remains more unsettling to American complacence, because the Asian is culturally more foreign.

   Hispanics may be reluctant or pushy or light or dark, but Hispanics are recognizably European. They speak a European tongue. They worship or reject a European God. The shape of the meat they eat is identifiable. But the Asian?

   Asians rounded the world for me. I was a Mexican teenager in America who had become an Irish Catholic. When I was growing up in the 1960s, I heard Americans describing their nation as simply bipartate: black and white. When black and white America argued, I felt I was overhearing some family quarrel that didn't include me. Korean and Chinese and Japanese faces in Sacramento rescued me from the simplicities of black and white America.

   I was in high school when my uncle from India died, my Uncle Raj, the dentist. After Raj died, we went to a succession of Chinese dentists, the first Asian names I connected with recognizable faces; the first Asian hands.

   In the 1960s, whole blocks of downtown Sacramento were to be demolished for a redevelopment. The *Sacramento Bee* reported several Chinese businessmen had declared their intention to build a ten-story office building downtown with a pagoda roof. About that same time, there was another article in the *Bee*. Mexican entrepreneurs would turn Sixth and K into a Mexican block with cobblestones, restaurants, colonial façades. My father was skeptical concerning the Mexican enterprise. "Guess which one will never get built?" my father intoned from the lamplight, snapping the spine of his newspaper.

   Dr. Chiang, one of our family dentists, had gone to the University of the Pacific. He encouraged the same school for me. Our entire conversational motif, repeated at every visit, was college—his path and my plans.

   Then there was Dr. Wang.

Not Dr. Wang! My sister refused. Dr. Wang didn't bother with Novocaine. Dr. Wang's office was a dark and shabby place.

My father said we owed it to Dr. Wang to be his patients. Dr. Wang referred business to my father.

Dr. Wang joked about my long nose. "Just like your father." And again: "Just like your father," as he pulled my nose up to open my mouth. Then China entered my mouth in a blast of garlic, a whorl of pain.

The Chinese businessmen built a ten-story office building downtown with a pagoda roof. Just as my father predicted they would.

* * *

. . . Americans are lonely now. Hispanics and Asians represent to us the alternatives of communal cultures at a time when Americans are demoralized. Americans are no longer sure that economic invincibility derives from individualism. Look at Japan! Americans learn chopsticks. Americans lustily devour what they say they fear to become. Sushi will make us lean, corporate warriors. Mexican Combination Plate #3, smothered in mestizo gravy, will burn a hole through our hearts.

No belief is more cherished by Americans, no belief is more typical of America, than the belief that one can choose to be free of American culture. One can pick and choose. Learn Spanish. Study Buddhism. . . . My Mexican father was never so American as when he wished his children might cultivate Chinese friends.

* * *

Many years pass.

Eventually I made my way through *Huckleberry Finn.* I was, by that time, a graduate student of English, able to trail Huck and Jim through thickets of American diction and into a clearing. Sitting in a university library, I saw, once more, the American river.

There is a discernible culture, a river, a thread, connecting Thomas Jefferson to Lucille Ball to Malcolm X to Sitting Bull. The panhandler at one corner is related to the pamphleteer at the next, who is related to the bank executive who is related to the Punk wearing a FUCK U T-shirt. The immigrant child sees this at once. But then he is encouraged to forget the vision.

When I was a boy who spoke Spanish, I saw America whole. I realized that there was a culture here because I lived apart from it. I didn't like America. Then I entered the culture. I entered the culture as you did, by going to school. I became Americanized. I ended up believing in choices as much as any of you do.

What my best teachers realized was their obligation to pass on to their students a culture in which the schoolmarm is portrayed as a minor villain.

* * *

When I taught Freshman English at Berkeley, I took the "F" bus from San Francisco. This was about the time when American educators were proclaiming Asians to be "whiz kids" and Asian academic triumphs fed the feature pages of American newspapers. There were lots of Asians on the "F" bus.

One day, sitting next to a Chinese student on the bus, I watched him study. The way he worried over the text was troubling to me. He knew something about the hardness of life, the seriousness of youth, that America had never taught me. I turned away; I looked out the bus window; I got off the bus at my usual stop. But consider the two of us on the "F" bus headed for Berkeley: the Chinese student poring over his text against some terrible test. Me sitting next to him, my briefcase full of English novels; lucky me. The Asian and the Hispanic. We represented, so many Americans then imagined, some new force in America, a revolutionary change, an undoing of the European line. But it was not so.

Immigrant parents send their children to school (simply, they think) to acquire the skills to "survive" in America. But the child returns home as America. Foolish immigrant parents.

By eight o'clock that morning—the morning of the bus ride—I stood, as usual, in a classroom in Wheeler Hall, lecturing on tragedy and comedy. Asian kids at the back of the room studied biochemistry, as usual, behind propped-up Shakespeares. I said nothing, made no attempt to recall them. At the end of the hour, I announced to the class that, henceforward, class participation would be a consideration in grading. Asian eyes peered over the blue rims of their Oxford Shakespeares.

Three Asian students came to my office that afternoon. They were polite. They had come to ask about the final exam—what did they need to know?

They took notes. Then one student (I would have said the most Americanized of the three) spoke up: "We think, Mr. Rodriguez, that you are prejudiced against Asian students. Because we do not speak up in class."

I made a face. Nonsense, I blustered. Freshman English is a course concerned with language. Is it so unreasonable that I should expect students to speak up in class? One Asian student is the best student in class . . . and so forth.

I don't remember how our meeting concluded. I recall my deliberation when I gave those three grades. And I think now the students were just. I did have a bias, an inevitable American bias, that favored the talkative student. Like most other American teachers, I equated intelligence with liveliness or defiance.

Another Asian student, a woman, an ethnic Chinese student from Vietnam or Cambodia, ended up with an F in one of my classes. It wasn't that she had no American voice, or even that she didn't know what to make of Thoreau. She had missed too many classes. She didn't even show up for the Final.

On a foggy morning during winter break, this woman came to my office with her father to remonstrate.

I was too embarrassed to look at her. I spoke to her father. She sat by the door.

I explained the five essay assignments. I showed him my grade book, the blank spaces next to her name. The father and I both paused a long time over my evidence. I suggested the university's remedial writing course. . . . *Really, you know, her counselor should never have* . . .

In the middle of my apology, he stood up; he turned and walked to where his daughter sat. I could see only his back as he hovered over her. I heard the slap. He moved away.

And then I saw her. She was not crying. She was looking down at her hands composed neatly on her lap.

Jessica!

QUESTIONS AND CONSIDERATIONS

1. Rodriguez claims, "The child of immigrant parents is supposed to perch on a hyphen, taking only the dose of America he needs to advance in America." Interpret the meaning of Rodriguez's image and then discuss several of the struggles in the clash of values between immigrant parents and their children that Rodriguez identifies in this selection.

2. Why is this selection entitled "Asians"? How do Rodriguez, his family, and their neighbors relate to Asians?

3. Why does Rodriguez include the quotation from Shylock in Shakespeare's *The Merchant of Venice*? What is Shylock's advice to his daughter Jessica, and why does the essay end with her name followed by an exclamation mark ("*Jessica!*")?

4. Why does Rodriguez argue that the "melting pot" remains the best metaphor for America? What is gained and lost in terms of intimate relationships through the melting-pot process? How does the image of the assimilated Asian youngster embarrassed by her "double" illustrate the loss involved in the melting-pot process?

5. Although Asians are more admired as a minority group than are Hispanics, why are they more "unsettling" to Americans? Explain Rodriguez's reasoning here.

6. As a teacher of English at Berkeley, Rodriguez experiences criticisms from his Asian students of his prejudices. What bias does Rodriguez admit to? How is his bias typical of "most other American teachers," and what does this bias suggest about the impact of American education on the values and cultural development of the children of immigrants?

IDEAS FOR WRITING

1. Write an essay in which you explain and illustrate how your early language experiences at grammar school shaped your self-concept, your identity as an American, and your ability to relate to your peers. Did Rodriguez's analysis of the problems that immigrants face help you to understand better your own struggle to learn the language of school and to become an American?

2. Write an essay in which you explain how the final example of the Chinese student reflects several of the basic paradoxes that Rodriguez presents in this selection. Conclude by explaining what you think are Rodriguez's most interesting insights and/or conclusions about relationships among Americans of different ethnic backgrounds and degrees of assimilation into mainstream American culture.

"Gossip"
From *You Just Don't Understand*
Deborah Tannen

Journal

Discuss the role that gossip plays in your relationships. Consider the ways that you think that gossip helps to create intimacy in relationships and the ways that you think it makes intimacy more difficult.

The impression that women talk too freely and too much in private situations is summed up in a word: *gossip.* Although gossip can be destructive, it isn't always; it can serve a crucial function in establishing intimacy—especially if it is not "talking against" but simply "talking about."

The label "gossip" casts a critical light on women's interest in talking about the details of people's lives. Evidence that the negativity of the term reflects men's interpretation of women's ways of talking can be seen in the following excerpt from Marge Piercy's novel *Fly Away Home.* Daria falls in love with Tom partly because he differs from her former husband, Ross, in this respect:

> It surprised her what he knew about the people around him. Ross would never have known that Gretta disliked her son's teacher, or that Fay had just given walking papers to her boyfriend because he drank too much in front of her boys. For a man, Tom had an uncommon interest in the details of people's lives. Gossip, Ross would call it, but she thought it was just being interested in people.

Not only men disparage an interest in the details of people's lives as "gossip." The great southern writer Eudora Welty, remembering her Mississippi childhood, writes that her mother tried to keep a talkative seamstress from telling stories about local people in front of her little girl: "'I don't want her exposed to gossip,'" Welty recalls her mother saying, "as if gossip were the measles and I could catch it." But far from having a bad influence on the child, the gossipy stories about people that Welty loved to hear inspired her to become a writer. When people talk about the details of daily lives, it is gossip; when they write about them, it is literature: short stories and novels.

Mary Catherine Bateson draws another parallel—between gossip and anthropology, the academic discipline that makes a career of documenting the details of people's lives. She recalls that her mother, Margaret Mead, told her she would never make an anthropologist because she wasn't interested enough in gossip.

In Gossip Begins Friendship

Telling details of others' lives is partly the result of women's telling their friends details of their own lives. These details become gossip when the friend to whom they are told repeats them to someone else—presumably another friend. Telling what's happening in your life and the lives of those you talk to is a grown-up version of telling secrets, the essence of girls' and women's friendships.

In Alice Mattison's story "New Haven," . . . Eleanor tells Patsy that she is falling in love with a married man. As soon as these words are out, Eleanor feels "a little ashamed to lack her secret suddenly," but "she also feels pleased; she doesn't have to guard it, for once. And it's exhilarating to talk about Peter." I was struck by Mattison's phrasing— "to lack her secret"—which captures the way that *having* a secret makes a person feel enhanced, and telling it is giving something away—in the sense of possession as well as the idiomatic sense of revelation. Mattison also captures the pleasure in not having to hide something, and being able to talk about what's really on your mind.

Not only is telling secrets evidence of friendship; it *creates* a friendship, when the listener responds in the expected way. Eleanor does not know Patsy well, but she would like to. There is an affinity and a budding friendship between them; they have taken to going together for coffee and ice cream following the rehearsals of the musical group in which they both play. By telling Patsy what was going on in her life, telling her secret, Eleanor promoted Patsy from acquaintance to friend.

Keeping friends up to date about the events in one's life is not only a privilege; for many women it is an obligation. One woman explained that she didn't enjoy telling the story of her breakup with her boyfriend over and over, but she had to, because if she had failed to inform any of her close friends about such an important development, they would have been deeply hurt when they found out. They would have taken her secrecy as a sign that she was curtailing their friendship, clipping its wings. The woman, furthermore, was incredulous when she learned that her boyfriend had not told anyone at all about their breakup. He had gone to work, gone to his gym, and played squash with his friends, all as if nothing had happened to change his life.

Because telling secrets is an essential part of friendship for most women, they may find themselves in trouble when they have no secrets to tell. For example, a woman I'll call Carol had several women friends she talked to every few days, exchanging stories about dates with men. They would share their excitement before a new date, and after the date took place, they would report in detail what had been said and done. So when Carol fell in love and formed a lasting relationship with a man, she ran out of material for talks with her friends. She also had less time to talk on the phone, since she now spent most of her free time with the man. This put a strain on her friendships; it was as if she had gathered up her marbles, reneging on her part in the partnership of talk that constituted the friendship.

Situations in which one person feels abandoned because the other forms a permanent relationship are not limited to women friends. In the story "Mendocino" by Ann Packer, the narrator, Bliss, finds it sad to visit her brother, who now lives with a woman, because his intimacy with the woman has diminished his intimacy with her. Bliss recalls their former closeness, when

> they would exchange work stories, and, into a second bottle of wine, confide in each other the news of their most recent failures at love. It amazes Bliss that until this moment she never once realized it was because they were failures that they talked about them. Now Gerald has his success, and it is as if the two of them had never been anything but what they are now: wary, cordial.

Because they are not exchanging secrets about relationships in one-on-one conversation, Bliss perceives her conversations with Gerald, now taking place in a group of three, to be wary and cordial—in a way, more like public speaking.

Many things conspire to separate people from their single friends if they find a stable relationship. I had a friend, a man, who had been single for many years and had developed a wide and strong network of women friends to whom he talked frequently. When he developed a stable relationship with a woman and they moved in together, his friends complained that he did not tell them anything anymore. "It's not that I'm keeping things from them," he told me. "It's just that Naomi and I get along fine and there's nothing to tell." By saying this, he did, however, tell me about a problem in his relationships—although it involved not his partner but his friends.

． ． ．

The Joy of Involvement

Despite the . . . appreciation of details in news stories, the usefulness of telling details in everyday conversation is not universally recognized. A woman told me that members of her family refer to her grandmother in a phrase that typifies the old woman's conversation: "I had a little ham, I had a little cheese." This affectionate yet disparaging mode of reference reveals that they find it boring when Grandmother tells them what she had for lunch. They wish she would give fewer details, or not report her lunch at all.

My great-aunt, for many years a widow, had a love affair when she was in her seventies. Obese, balding, her hands and legs misshapen by arthritis, she did not fit the stereotype of a woman romantically loved. But she was—by a man, also in his seventies, who lived in a nursing home but occasionally spent weekends with her in her apartment. In trying to tell me what this relationship meant to her, my great-aunt told of a conversation. One evening she had had dinner out, with friends. When she returned home, her male friend called and she told him about the dinner. He listened with interest and asked her, "What did you wear?" When she told me this, she began to cry: "Do you know how many years it's been since anyone asked me what I wore?"

When my great-aunt said this, she was saying that it had been years since anyone had cared deeply—intimately—about her. The exchange of relatively insignificant details about daily life sends a metamessage of rapport and caring.

Attention to details associated with a person is often a sign of romantic interest. In a novel titled *The Jealous One,* by Celia Fremlin, a woman sends her husband, Geoffrey, next door to deliver a dinner invitation to their new neighbor, who has moved in that day. Geoffrey returns full of excitement, bubbling with admiration for and details about the new neighbor. He announces, starry-eyed, that the neighbor has invited *them* to dinner in her not-yet-furnished home, and he asks his wife if she has a red ribbon for Shang Low, the neighbor's Pekingese, explaining that *Shang Low* is the opposite of *Shang High.* The wife responds with irony, but Geoffrey is slow to join in her ironic denigration of the neighbor's airs in ribboning her dog:

> She giggled in terrible solitude for a fraction of a second; and then Geoffrey joined in, a tiny bit too late and a tiny bit too loud. And the joke did not lead to another joke. Murmuring something about "having promised . . .", Geoffrey hurried away out of the kitchen and out of the house, without any red ribbon. And this piece of red ribbon, which they didn't look for, didn't find, and probably hadn't got, became the very first of the objects which couldn't ever again be mentioned between them.

Geoffrey's romantic interest in the new neighbor leaks out in his enthusiastic, uncritical recounting of details about her, such as the breed and name of her dog.

If recalling a detail or name is a sign of caring, failure to recall a name can be seen as a sign of lack of caring. Complaints are frequent from people whose parents disapprove of their partners or friends and seem to display their disapproval subtly by habitually referring to them by the wrong names or failing to recall their names. The same phenomenon can be manipulated for positive ends. This was the case with a woman who remained friends with the wife of an acquaintance of her former husband's. Her friend persisted in referring to the former husband's new wife as "what's her name." The divorced woman took the metamessage of this to be "Even though I see her occasionally, I don't really care about her. You are still the one who counts to me." Not remembering the new wife's name was offered as evidence of lack of caring about her—and, consequently, loyalty to the first wife.

Paying attention to details of a person's appearance can be a means of flirting. A woman had an appointment to meet a man she had met only once before, briefly. They were both married; the purpose of the meeting was business. But the man began their conversation by observing that she looked younger than he recalled, and her hair was different. "You were wearing a hat, then, weren't you?" he said. "And you were dressed in white then too." Simply saying that he had noticed her appearance the first time they had met was a kind of flirtation. It was not a displeasing one to her, though her husband found it displeasing when she recounted it to him.

The noticing of details shows caring and creates involvement. Men, however, often find women's involvement in details irritating. Because women are concerned first and foremost with establishing intimacy, they value the telling of details.

Conversely, many women complain that men don't tell enough details. A woman thus frustrated is Laura in Alice Mattison's story "Sleeping Giant." Laura and Dan are both troubled by their son-in-law's plan to buy an old, run-down house. In the past, when Laura tried to talk to her daughter about it, the daughter defended her husband. But Dan now assures Laura that their daughter sees her point of view, because she said as much to him. "Believe me," he says, "she's not happy about this." Laura wants more details about the conversation, but Dan won't supply them. Laura asks:

> "Well, why doesn't she tell him so?"
> He doesn't answer.
> "What did she say *exactly?*" Laura is searching in her canvas bag for her car keys. She's chilly after all, and there's a flannel shirt in the trunk of the car. She waits, holding the keys and the bag, but Dan still doesn't answer, and she drops the bag on the bench. "What did she *say?*"
> "Oh, I don't remember. General things."
> "What did *you* say?"
> "Oh, I don't know, Laura." Laura turns aside abruptly, opens the trunk, and stares into it for a moment, annoyed that Dan won't tell her more.

Laura sounds like innumerable flesh-and-blood women I've talked to. As one put it, "Men don't tell the whole story—who said what." Another complained of her husband: "It's like pulling teeth to get him to tell me, 'What did she *say? What did he *say?*'"

Yet another woman recalled a time that her best friend's husband tried unsuccessfully to take part in one of their conversations. Breaking with tradition, he tried to tell about an experience that he thought was similar to the ones they were discussing. The two women plied him with questions he couldn't answer about exactly what had been said and how and why. He backed off from the story, and didn't try to tell any more. Perhaps he was wondering to himself why the women were interested in all these unimportant details.

"Skip the Details"

Though many women value the recounting of subtle nuances in conversations with close friends, there are situations in which everyone feels oppressed by being told, or asked for, what seem like too many details. If interest in details is a sign of intimacy, a woman will resist such interest if it comes from someone she doesn't want to be intimate with. And everyone has had the experience of being told unwanted details—so many that they seem pointless, or demand longer or more intimate attention than one wants to give. Many of the examples I have collected of people piling on details in conversation involve old people. This may be because old people often want more involvement with young people than young people want with them, or because old people frequently cannot hear well, so they tell detailed stories to maintain interaction. Old people are also more inclined to reminisce about the past, consequently telling stories that are likely to include details.

It is a tenet of contemporary American psychology that mental health requires psychological separation from one's parents. One way of resisting overinvolvement, for some people at least, is resisting telling details. For example, one woman told me that her mother sought overinvolvement with her and had succeeded in achieving overinvolvement with her sister Jane. To support her claim, she said, "It's amazing, the details of Jane's life my mother knows." Later, she was explaining how she resists her mother's attempts to get overly involved in her life. As an example of her mother's prying, she said, "She's hungry for details. If I tell her I went somewhere, she asks, 'What did you wear?'"

The question that offended this woman was the same one that had brought my great-aunt such happiness. The difference is that my great-aunt was seeking involvement with the man who asked her what she wore. This woman was resisting what she perceived as the excessive involvement her mother sought with her. Presumably, however, when her sister Jane talks to their mother, she does not feel that the question "What did you wear?" is inappropriate. Perhaps, like my great-aunt, Jane values the show of caring and resulting involvement.

Mixing Business With Gossip

Many women mix talk about relatively important things, like business, with talk about relatively unimportant things, like clothes. On Monday morning, Marjorie walks into Beatrice's office to ask her opinion about a contract. After they have settled their business, or perhaps before, they bring each other up to date on their personal lives: Marjorie has her hands full with her ailing mother-in-law; Beatrice is feeling optimistic about a new relationship.

A woman who runs a counseling center noted that when she meets with women on her staff, it is not unusual for them to spend 75 percent of the time in personal talk and then efficiently take care of business in the remaining 25 percent. To men on the staff, this seems like wasting time. But the director places value on creating a warm, intimate working environment. She feels that such personal talk contributes to a sense of rapport that makes the women on her staff happy in their jobs and lays a foundation for the working relationship that enables them to conduct business so efficiently.

The mutual knowledge and trust that grows out of personal talk can precede a business relationship as well as grow out of it. A magazine article described a partnership between two women who own a construction company. The seed of their working relationship had been planted years before the business was founded, when the two women met regularly to exchange coffee and talk. When one of them decided to start a business, her working relationship with her partner was already in place.

For women who engage in frequent, regular social talk with friends, the machinery is up and running when a significant decision needs to be made. Elizabeth Loftus, a psychologist specializing in eyewitness testimony, was confronted with a moral dilemma when she was asked to testify on behalf of the man accused of being "Ivan the Terrible"—a notoriously sadistic Nazi war criminal. To be consistent, Loftus felt she should testify in this case as she had in many others. But her relatives and friends argued against it, and she recoiled at the prospect of undermining the testimony of the few witnesses who were alive to tell what Ivan had done—a mere fifty survivors of an estimated million of Ivan's victims. The dilemma was resolved when a friend dropped by for tea. Loftus recalls, "My friend, quoting Emerson, reminded me that 'A foolish consistency is the hobgoblin of little minds.'" With this comfort, Loftus decided not to testify. If women and men have different habits for social talk, they also make different use of it.

Differences in uses of social talk also begin early. One couple I talked to had different perspectives on their son's relationship with his best friend. The mother thought it odd that, despite the significant amount of time the boys spent together, for example playing football, their son found out what college his best friend was going to by reading it in their yearbook. One day a girl called him to ask whether his friend had a date for the prom. She was calling for *her* friend, who wanted to ask his friend, but not if he already had a date. Not only did their son not know whether his best friend had a date for the prom, but he was annoyed that the girl thought he should know. He gave her his friend's phone number and suggested she call to find out directly. He later commented that had he known his friend was going to the prom, he might have planned to go himself; not keeping up with such personal information deprived him of a chance to go.

All of this seemed very strange to the boy's mother, who could not imagine what it meant to be best friends if it didn't include knowing the basic developments in the other's life. To the boy's father, however, it seemed unremarkable.

Talking-About Versus Talking-Against

The relatively positive or negative value that is placed on talking about personal details—of one's own life or others'—is reflected in the positive and negative views of gossip. One man commented that he and I seemed to have different definitions of gossip. He said, "To you it seems to be discussion of personal details about people known to the conversationalists. To me, it's a discussion of the weaknesses, character flaws, and failures of third persons, so that the participants in the conversation can feel superior to them. This seems unworthy, hence gossip is bad."

This man's view parallels that of a woman who told me she was troubled by one of the women in her child care co-op who gossiped too much. But it turned out that this woman's gossip was all negative: putting down other members of the co-op and criticizing them. It was not the talking-*about* that was disturbing, but the talking-*against.* This distances the speakers from those they are talking about, rather than bringing them closer. Furthermore, it is natural to assume that someone who has only negative things to say about others will also say negative things about you when you aren't there.

Gossip as talking-against is related to a verbal game that Christine Cheepen calls "scapegoat." In conversations she analyzed, Cheepen found that speakers talked against someone who wasn't there to redress imbalances of power that had erupted. "Scapegoat" was a way for speakers to achieve parity with each other by teaming up against someone else.

In Cheepen's examples, however, the third party whom the conversationalists teamed up against wasn't just anyone—it was their boss. And this brings us back to the view of the man who told me why he considers gossip to be bad. To the extent that talking about someone who is not there brings an absent party into the room, the effect is to establish connection. But if that party is brought into the room to be *put down,* then the effect is negotiation of status. As always, connection and status are operating at once, so both views are valid. They are different takes on the same scene.

Women and Men on Their Own Terms

What is the solution, then, if women and men are talking at cross-purposes, about gossip as about other matters? How are we to open lines of communication? The answer is for both men and women to try to take each other on their own terms rather than applying the standards of one group to the behavior of the other. This is not a "natural" thing to do, because we tend to look for a single "right" way of doing things. Understandably, experts are as liable to do this as anyone else.

A national audience-participation talk show featured a psychologist answering questions about couples' relationships. A woman in the audience voiced a complaint: "My husband talks to his mother, but he won't talk to me. If I want to know how his day was, I listen to his conversation with his mother." The psychologist told this woman, "He probably trusts his mother more than he trusts you."

This comment reinforced the woman's own suspicions and worst fears. And what the psychologist said was perfectly legitimate and reasonable—within the framework of talk in women's friendships: The friend to whom you talk daily, telling all the little experiences you had, is your best friend. But how reasonable an interpretation is it from the man's point of view? I would wager that her husband did not think he needed to do anything special to create intimacy with his wife, because he was with her every day. But because his mother was alone, he humored her by telling her unimportant little things that she seemed to want to hear. His mother's need to hear such details would make sense to her son because she was alone and needed them as a substitute for the real thing, like watching life from her window. He wouldn't understand why his wife would want and need to hear such talk. Although it is possible that this man trusts his mother more than his wife, the evidence given does not warrant such a conclusion.

This therapist was judging the man's way of talking by women's standards. In a sense, the values of therapy are those more typically associated with women's ways of talking than with men's. This may be why a study showed that among inexperienced therapists, women do better than men. But over time, with experience, this gender difference disappears. Eventually, perhaps, men therapists—and men in therapy—learn to talk like women. This is all to the good. Assertiveness training, on the other hand, teaches women to talk more like men, and this too is to the good. Women and men would both do well to learn strategies more typically used by members of the other group—not to switch over entirely, but to have more strategies at their disposal.

Habitual ways of talking are hard to change. Learning to respect others' ways of talking may be a bit easier. Men should accept that many women regard exchanging details about personal lives as a basic ingredient of intimacy, and women should accept that many men do not share this view. Mutual acceptance will at least prevent the pain of being told you are doing something wrong when you are only doing things your way.

QUESTIONS AND CONSIDERATIONS

1. How does Tannen define gossip? Do you agree with her definition?

2. What are the main points that Tannen makes about the role that gossip plays in intimate relationships? How did this selection change your point of view about the role that gossip plays in establishing intimacy in relationships?

3. Tannen illustrates many of her ideas through references to literary works. Are her references convincing? Which of her examples seem most effective in clarifying her point?

4. What relationship do you see between the skills of a good gossip and the skills of an effective writer?

5. Apply one of Tannen's ideas about the role that gossip plays in establishing intimacy through reference to one or two of the selections in this chapter.

6. How do you think a man would have presented this topic? Compare and contrast the relationship issues and writing strategies that you think that a man might have developed to those that Tannen chose.

IDEAS FOR WRITING

1. Work on this writing assignment in a group of four, with two men and two women. Each group member should share a piece of gossip that he or she thinks would be interesting to group members. Then write a group definition of gossip that encompasses and synthesizes all of the examples presented by group members. Conclude your essay by discussing to what extent your group agrees with Tannen's perceptions about the ways that men and women value and use gossip as a strategy for creating intimacy.

2. Write an essay in which you respond to Tannen's conclusion: "Men should accept that many women regard exchanging details about personal lives as a basic ingredient of intimacy and women should accept that many men do not share this view." Do you agree or disagree with her point of view?

All Happy Clans Are Alike
In Search of the Good Family
Jane Howard

Journal

What is your definition of a family? Do you think that all members of a "family" need to be related biologically or through marriage?

Call it a clan, call it a network, call it a tribe, call it a family. Whatever you call it, whoever you are, you need one. You need one because you are human. You didn't come from nowhere. Before you, around you, and presumably after you, too, there are others. Some of these others must matter a lot—to you, and if you are very lucky, to one another. Their welfare must be nearly as important to you as your own. Even if you live alone, even if your solitude is elected and ebullient, you still cannot do without a clan or a tribe.

The trouble with the clans and tribes many of us were born into is not that they consist of meddlesome ogres but that they are too far away. In emergencies we rush across continents and if need be oceans to their sides, as they do to ours. Maybe we even make a habit of seeing them, once or twice a year, for the sheer pleasure of it. But blood ties seldom dictate our addresses. Our blood kin are often too remote to ease us from our Tuesdays to our Wednesdays. For this we must rely on our families of friends. If our relatives are not, do not wish to be, or for whatever reasons cannot be our friends, then by some complex alchemy we must try to transform our friends into our relatives. If blood and roots don't do the job, then we must look to water and branches, and sort ourselves into new constellations, new families.

These new families, to borrow the terminology of an African tribe (the Bangwa of the Cameroons), may consist either of friends of the road, ascribed by chance, or friends of the heart, achieved by choice. Ascribed friends are those we happen to go to school with, work with, or live near. They know where we went last weekend and whether we still have a cold. Just being around gives them a provisional importance in our lives, and us in theirs. Maybe they will still matter to us when we or they move away; quite likely they won't. Six months or two years will probably erase us from each other's thoughts, unless by some chance they and we have become friends of the heart.

Wishing to be friends, as Aristotle, wrote, is quick work, but friendship is a slowly ripening fruit. An ancient proverb he quotes in his *Ethics* had it that you cannot know a man until you and he together have eaten a peck of salt. Now a peck, a quarter of a bushel, is quite a lot of salt—more, perhaps, than most pairs of people ever have occasion to share. We must try though. We must sit together at as many tables as we can. We must steer each other through enough seasons and weathers so that sooner or later it crosses our minds that one of us, God knows which or with what sorrow, must one day mourn the other.

We must devise new ways, or revive old ones, to equip ourselves with kinfolk. Maybe such an impulse prompted whoever ordered the cake I saw in my neighborhood bakery to have it frosted to say "HAPPY BIRTHDAY SURROGATE." I like to think that this cake was decorated not for a judge but for someone's surrogate mother or surrogate brother: Loathsome jargon, but admirable sentiment. If you didn't conceive me or if we didn't grow up in the same house, we can still be related, if we decide we ought to be. It is never too late, I like to hope, to augment our families in ways nature neglected to do. It is never too late to choose new clans.

The best-chosen clans, like the best friendships and the best blood families, endure by accumulating a history solid enough to suggest a future. But clans that don't last have merit too. We can lament them but we shouldn't deride them. Better an ephemeral clan or tribe than none at all. A few of my life's most tribally joyous times, in fact, have been spent with people whom I have yet to see again. This saddens me, as it may them too, but dwelling overlong on such sadness does no good. A more fertile exercise is to think back on those times and try to figure out what made them, for all their brevity, so stirring. What can such times teach us about forming new and more lasting tribes in the future?

New tribes and clans can no more be willed into existence, of course, than any other good thing can. We keep trying, though. To try, with gritted teeth and girded loins, is after all American. That is what the two Helens and I were talking about the day we had lunch in a room up in a high-rise motel near the Kansas City airport. We had lunch there at the end of a two-day conference on families. The two Helens were social scientists, but I liked them even so, among other reasons because they both objected to that motel's coffee shop even more than I did. One of the Helens, from Virginia, disliked it so much that she had brought along homemade whole wheat bread, sesame butter, and honey from her parents' farm in South Dakota, where she had visited before the conference. Her picnic was the best thing that happened, to me at least, those whole two days.

"If you're voluntarily childless and alone," said the other Helen, who was from Pennsylvania by way of Puerto Rico, "it gets harder and harder with the passage of time. It's stressful. That's why you need support systems." I had been hearing quite a bit of talk about "support systems." The term is not among my favorites, but I can understand its currency. Whatever "support systems" may be, the need for them is clearly urgent, and not just in this country. Are there not thriving "megafamilies" of as many as three hundred people in Scandinavia? Have not the Japanese for years had an honored, enduring—if perhaps by our standards rather rigid—custom of adopting non-relatives to fill gaps in their families? Should we not applaud and maybe imitate such ingenuity?

And consider our own Unitarians. From Santa Barbara to Boston they have been earnestly dividing their congregations into arbitrary "extended families" whose members are bound to act like each other's relatives. Kurt Vonnegut, Jr., plays with a similar train of thought in his fictional *Slapstick*. In that book every newborn baby is assigned a randomly chosen middle name, like Uranium or Daffodil or Raspberry. These middle names are connected with hyphens to numbers between one and twenty, and any two people who have the same middle name are automatically related. This is all to the good, the author thinks, because "human beings need all the relatives they can get—as possible donors or receivers not of love but of common decency." He envisions these extended families as "one of the four greatest inventions by Americans," the others being *Robert's Rules of Order,* the Bill of Rights, and the principles of Alcoholics Anonymous.

This charming notion might even work, if it weren't so arbitrary. Already each of us is born into one family not of our choosing. If we're going to devise new ones, we might as well have the luxury of picking the members ourselves. Clever picking might result in new families whose benefits would surpass or at least equal those of the old. As a member in reasonable standing of six or seven tribes in addition to the one I was born to, I have been trying to figure which characteristics are common to both kinds of families.

1. Good families have a chief, or a heroine, or a founder—someone around whom others cluster, whose achievements, as the Yiddish word has it, let them *kvell,* and whose example spurs them on to like feats. Some blood dynasties produce such figures regularly; others languish for as many as five generations between demigods, wondering with each new pregnancy whether this, at last, might be the messianic baby who will redeem them. Look, is there not something gubernatorial about her footstep, or musical about the way he bangs with his spoon on his cup? All clans, of all kinds, need such a figure now and then. Sometimes clans based on water rather than blood harbor several such personages at one time. The Bloomsbury Group in London six decades ago was not much hampered by its lack of a temporal history.

2. Good families have a switchboard operator—someone who cannot help but keep track of what all the others are up to, who plays Houston Mission Control to everyone else's Apollo. This role is assumed rather than assigned. The person who volunteers for it often has the instincts of an archivist, and feels driven to keep scrapbooks and photograph albums up to date, so that the clan can see proof of its own continuity.

3. Good families are much to all their members, but everything to none. Good families are fortresses with many windows and doors to the outer world. The blood clans I feel most drawn to were founded by parents who are nearly as devoted to what they do outside as they are to each other and their children. Their curiosity and passion are contagious. Everybody, where they live, is busy. Paint is spattered on eyeglasses. Mud lurks under fingernails. Person-to-person calls come in the middle of the night from Tokyo and Brussels. Catcher's mitts, ballet slippers, overdue library books, and other signs of extrafamilial concerns are everywhere.

4. Good families are hospitable. Knowing that hosts need guests as much as guests need hosts, they are generous with honorary memberships for friends, whom they urge to come early and often and to stay late. Such clans exude a vivid sense of surrounding rings of relatives, neighbors, teachers, students, and godparents, any of whom at any time might break or slide into the inner circle. Inside that circle a wholesome, tacit emotional feudalism develops: you give me protection, I'll give you fealty. Such pacts begin with, but soon go far beyond, the jolly exchange of pie at Thanksgiving or cake on a birthday. They mean that you can ask me to supervise your children for the fortnight you will be in the hospital, and that however inconvenient this might be for me, I shall manage to do so. It means I can phone you on what for me is a dreary, wretched Sunday afternoon and for you is the eve of a deadline, knowing you will tell me to come right over, if only to watch you type. It means we need not dissemble. ("To yield to seeming," as Martin Buber wrote, "is man's essential cowardice, to resist it is his essential courage . . . one must at times pay dearly for life lived from the being, but it is never too dear.")

5. Good families deal squarely with direness. Pity the tribe that doesn't have, and cherish, at least one flamboyant eccentric. Pity too the one that supposes it can avoid for long the woes to which all flesh is heir. Lunacy, bankruptcy, suicide, and other unthinkable fates sooner or later afflict the noblest of clans with an undertow of gloom. Family life is a set of givens, someone once told me, and it takes courage to see certain givens as blessings rather than as curses. It surely does. Contradictions and inconsistencies are givens, too. So is the battle against what the Oregon patriarch Kenneth Babbs calls malarkey. "There's always malarkey lurking, bubbles in the cesspool, fetid bubbles that pop and smell. But I don't put up with malarkey, between my stepkids and my natural ones or anywhere else in the family."

6. Good families prize their rituals. Nothing welds a family more than these. Rituals are vital especially for clans without histories, because they evoke a past, imply a future, and hint at continuity. No line in the seder service at Passover reassures more than the last: "Next year in Jerusalem!" A clan becomes more of a clan each time it gathers to observe a fixed ritual (Christmas, birthdays, Thanksgiving, and so on), grieves at a funeral (anyone may come to most funerals; those who do declare their tribalness), and devises a new rite of its own. Equinox breakfasts can be at least as welding as Memorial Day pa-

rades. Several of my colleagues and I used to meet for lunch every Pearl Harbor Day, preferably to eat some politically neutral fare like smorgasbord, to "forgive" our only ancestrally Japanese friend, Irene Kubota Neves. For that and other things we became, and remain, a sort of family.

"Rituals," a California friend of mine said, "aren't just externals and holidays. They are the performances of our lives. They are a kind of shorthand. They can't be decreed. My mother used to try to decree them. She'd make such a goddamn fuss over what we talked about at dinner, aiming at Topics of Common Interest, topics that celebrated our cohesion as a family. These performances were always hollow, because the phenomenology of the moment got sacrificed for the *idea* of the moment. Real rituals are discovered in retrospect. They emerge around constitutive moments, moments that only happen once, around whose memory meanings cluster. You don't choose those moments. They choose themselves." A lucky clan includes a born mythologizer, like my blood sister, who has the gift for apprehending such a moment when she sees it, and who cannot help but invent new rituals everywhere she goes.

7. Good families are affectionate. This of course is a matter of style. I know clans whose members greet each other with gingerly handshakes or, in what pass for kisses, with hurried brushes of jawbones, as if the object were to touch not the lips but the ears. I don't see how such people manage. "The tribe that does not hug," as someone who has been part of many *ad hoc* families recently wrote to me, "is no tribe at all. More and more I realize that everybody, regardless of age, needs to be hugged and comforted in a brotherly or sisterly way now and then. Preferably now."

8. Good families have a sense of place, which these days is not achieved easily. As Susanne Langer wrote in 1957, "Most people have no home that is a symbol of their childhood, not even a definite memory of one place to serve that purpose . . . all the old symbols are gone." Once I asked a roomful of supper guests if anyone felt a strong pull to any certain spot on the face of the earth. Everyone was silent, except for a visitor from Bavaria. The rest of us seemed to know all too well what Walker Percy means in *The Moviegoer* when he tells of the "genie-soul of a place, which every place has or else is not a place [and which] wherever you go, you must meet and master or else be met and mastered." All that meeting and mastering saps plenty of strength. It also underscores our need for tribal bases of the sort which soaring real estate taxes and splintering families have made all but obsolete.

So what are we to do, those of us whose habit and pleasure and doom is our tendency, as a Georgia lady put it, to "fly off at every other whipstitch?" Think in terms of movable feasts, that's what. Live here, wherever here may be, as if we were going to belong here for the rest of our lives. Learn to hallow whatever ground we happen to stand on or land on. Like medieval knights who took their tapestries along on Crusades, like modern Afghanis with their yurts, we must pack such totems and icons as we can to make short-term quarters feel like home. Pillows, small rugs, watercolors can dispel much of the chilling anonymity of a motel room or sublet apartment. When we can, we should live in rooms with stoves or fireplaces or at least candlelight. The ancient saying is still true: Extinguished hearth, extinguished family.

Round tables help too, and as a friend of mine once put it, so do "too many comfortable chairs, with surfaces to put feet on, arranged so as to encourage a maximum of eye contact." Such rooms inspire good talk, of which good clans can never have enough.

9. Good families, not just the blood kind, find some way to connect with posterity. "To forge a link in the humble chain of being, encircling heirs to ancestors," as Michael Novak has written, "is to walk within a circle of magic as primitive as humans knew in caves." He is talking of course about babies, feeling them leap in wombs, giving them suck. Parenthood, however, is a state which some miss by chance and others by design, and a vocation to which not all are called. Some of us, like the novelist Richard P. Brickner, look on as others "name their children and their children in turn name their own lives, devising their own flags from their parents' cloth." What are we who lack children to do? Build houses? Plant trees? Write books or symphonies or laws? Perhaps, but even if we do these things, there should be children on the sidelines if not at the center of our lives.

It is a sadly impoverished tribe that does not allow access to, and make much of, some children. Not too much, of course; it has truly been said that never in history have so many educated people devoted so much attention to so few children. Attention, in excess, can turn to fawning, which isn't much better than neglect. Still, if we don't regularly see and talk to and laugh with people who can expect to outlive us by twenty years or so, we had better get busy and find some.

10. Good families also honor their elders. The wider the age range, the stronger the tribe. Jean-Paul Sartre and Margaret Mead, to name two spectacularly confident former children, have both remarked on the central importance of grandparents in their own early lives. Grandparents are now in much more abundant supply than they were a generation or two ago, when old age was more rare. If actual grandparents are not at hand, no family should have too hard a time finding substitute ones to whom to pay unfeigned homage. The Soviet Union's enchantment with day-care centers, I have heard, stems at least in part from the state's eagerness to keep children away from their presumably subversive grandparents. Let that be a lesson to clans based on interest as well as to those based on genes.

Of course there are elders and elders. Most people in America, as David T. Bazelon has written, haven't the slightest idea of what to do with the extra thirty years they have been given to live. Few are as briskly secure as Alice Roosevelt Longworth, who once, when I visited her for tea, showed a recent photograph and asked whether I didn't think it made her look like "a malevolent Eurasian concubine—an *aged* malevolent Eurasian concubine." I admitted that it did, which was just what she wanted to hear. But those of us whose fathers weren't Presidents may not grow old, if at all, with such style.

Sad stories abound. The mother of one friend of mine languished for years, never far from a coma, in a nursing home. Only when her husband and children sang one of her favorite old songs, such as "Lord Jeffrey Amherst," would a smile fleet across her face. But a man I know of in New Jersey, who couldn't stand the state of Iowa or babies, changed his mind on both counts when his daughter, who lived in Iowa, had a baby. Suddenly he took to inventing business trips to St. Louis, by way of Cedar Rapids, phoning to say he would be at the airport there at 11:31 P.M. and "Be sure to bring Jake!" That cheers me. So did part of a talk I had with a woman in Albuquerque, whom I hadn't seen since a trip some years before to the Soviet Union.

"Honey," she said when I phoned her during a short stopover and asked how she was, "if I were any better I'd blow up and *bust!* I can't *tell* you how *neat* it is to put some age on! A lot of it, of course, has to do with going to the shrink, getting uncorked, and of course it doesn't hurt to have money—no, we *don't* have a ranch; it's only 900 acres, so we call it a farm. But every year, as far as age is concerned, I seem to get better, doing more and more stuff I love to do. The only thing I've ever wanted and don't have is a good marriage. Nothing I do ever pleases the men I marry. The only reason I'm still married now is it's too much trouble not to be. But my girls are growing up to be just *neat* humans, and the men they're sharing their lives with are too. They pick nice guys, my girls. I wish I could say the same. But I'm a lot better off than many women my age. I go to parties where sixty-year-olds with blue bouffant hairdos are still telling the same jokes they told twenty-five or thirty years ago. Complacent? No, that's not it, exactly. What they are is sad—sad as the dickens. They don't seem to be *connected*."

Some days my handwriting resembles my mother's, slanting hopefully and a bit extravagantly eastward. Other days it looks more like my father's: resolute, vertical, guardedly free of loops. Both my parents will remain in my nerves and muscles and mind until the day I die, and so will my sister, but they aren't the only ones. If I were to die tomorrow, the obituary would note that my father and sister survived me. True, but not true enough. Like most official lists of survivors, this one would be incomplete.

Several of the most affecting relationships I have ever known of, or been part of, have sprung not from genes or contracts but from serendipitous, uncanny bonds of choice. I don't think enough can be said for the fierce tenderness such bonds can generate. Maybe the best thing to say is nothing at all, or very little. Midwestern preachers used to hold that "a heavy rain doesn't seep into the ground but rolls off—when you preach to farmers, your sermon should be a drizzle instead of a downpour." So too with any cause that matters: shouting and lapel-grabbing and institutionalizing can do more harm than good. A quiet approach works better.

"I wish it would hurry up and get colder," I said one warm afternoon several Octobers ago to a black man with whom I was walking in a park.

"Don't worry," he told me. "Like my grandmother used to say when I was a boy, 'Hawk'll be here soon enough.'"

"What did she mean by 'hawk'?"

"Hawk meant winter, cold, trouble. And she was right: the hawk always came."

With regard to families, many would say that the hawk has long been here, hovering. "I'd rather put up with being lonely now than have to put up with being still more lonely in the future," says a character in Natsume Soseki's novel *Kokoro*. "We live in an age of freedom, independence, and the self, and I imagine this loneliness is the price we have to pay for it." Seven decades earlier, in *Either/Or,* Sören Kierkegaard had written, "Our age has lost all the substantial categories of family, state, and race. It must leave the individual entirely to himself, so that in a stricter sense he becomes his own creator."

If it is true that we must create ourselves, maybe while we are about it we can also devise some new kinds of families, new connections to supplement the old ones. The second verse of a hymn by James Russell Lowell says,

> New occasions bring new duties;
> Time makes ancient good uncouth.

Surely one outworn "good" is the maxim that blood relatives are the only ones who can or should greatly matter. Or look at it another way: go back six generations, and each one of us has sixty-four direct ancestors. Go back twenty—only four or five centuries, not such a big chunk of human history—and we each have more than a million. Does it not stand to reason, since the world population was then so much smaller, that we all have a lot more cousins—though admittedly distant ones—than we were brought up to suspect? And don't these cousins deserve our attention?

One day after lunch at a friend's apartment I waited in his lobby while he collected his mail. Out of the elevator came two nurses supporting a wizened, staring woman who couldn't have weighed much more than seventy pounds. It was all the woman could do to make her way down the three steps to the sidewalk and the curb where a car was waiting. Those steps must have been to that woman what a steep mountain trail would be to me. The nurses guided her down them with infinite patience.

"Easy, darlin'," one nurse said to the woman.

"That's a good girl," said the other. The woman, my friend's doorman told us, was ninety. That morning she had fallen and hurt herself. On her forehead was something which, had it not been a bruise, we might have thought beautiful: a marvel of mauve and lavender and magenta. This woman, who was then being taken to a nursing home, had lived in my friend's apartment building for forty years. All her relatives were dead, and her few surviving friends no longer chose to see her.

"But how can that be?" I asked my friend. "*We* could never be that alone, could we?"

"Don't be so sure," said my friend, who knows more of such matters than I do. "Even if we were to end up in the same nursing home, if I was in markedly worse shape than you were, you might not want to see me, either."

"But I can't imagine not wanting to see you."

"It happens," my friend said.

Maybe we can keep it from happening. Maybe the hawk can be kept at bay, if we give more thought to our tribes and our clans and our several kinds of families. No aim seems to me more urgent, not any achievement more worthy of a psalm. So *hosanna in excelsis,* and blest be the tie that binds. And please pass the salt.

QUESTIONS AND DISCUSSIONS

1. Do you agree with Howard that people who are not married or blood relatives can form a kind of family? Discuss several types of families that are not bonded by blood relationships.

2. The title of this essay echoes the opening line of Tolstoy's *Anna Karenina:* "All happy families are alike, but unhappy families are unhappy after their own fashion." Do you agree or disagree with this point of view? Explain.

3. Howard's list of the characteristics of a happy family imply that there are many ways of defining an unhappy family. How would you define an unhappy family?

4. From her list of criteria for a happy family, what do you think Howard finds most important about relationships among family members? Do you agree with her? Can you think of additional characteristics of good family relationships?

5. How important do you think a happy family is to the well-being and success of an individual? Does Howard's essay address this issue thoroughly enough?

6. Do you agree with Howard's assertions about the importance of families and clans? Do you think a family should be more open to nurturing and accepting change or to establishing tradition and continuity of values and culture?

IDEAS FOR WRITING

1. Howard has created a list of the attributes of a good family. Drawing on her ideas when you want, create your own list of the ideal qualities of a good family in our modern world. Discuss the types of relationships among family members that you believe nurture the most positive types of communication. Develop examples to clarify and illustrate your criteria.

2. Consider a range and variety of groups in your community or on your campus that function like families. Discuss several of these by comparing and contrasting them to a family. How do these surrogate families and the relationships that are formed within them help individuals to function more happily within their own families?

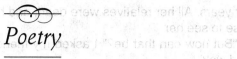

Poetry

When my love swears that she is made of truth

William Shakespeare

Journal

*Write about a time when you felt that not telling the whole truth to a lover would
be a better choice than complete honesty.*

When my love swears that she is made of truth,
I do believe her, though I know she lies,
That she might think me some untutor'd youth,
Unlearned in the world's false subtleties.
Thus vainly thinking that she thinks me young,   5
Although she knows my days are past the best,
Simply I credit her false-speaking tongue:
On both sides thus is simple truth supprest.
But wherefore says she not she is unjust?
And wherefore say not I that I am old?   10
O! love's best habit is in seeming trust,
And age in love loves not to have years told:
    Therefore I lie with her, and she with me,
    And in our faults by lies we flatter'd be.

QUESTIONS AND CONSIDERATIONS

1. What is the attitude of the speaker in the poem about his lover's "false speaking tongue"?

2. Shakespeare uses different meanings of the word "lie" to complicate the meaning of his poem and to point to the paradoxical nature of love. Analyze three different places in the poem where the narrator develops irony through the use of the word "lie."

3. What point does the sonnet make about the difference between youthful and mature love? Based on your own experiences, reading, and exposure to the popular media, do you agree or disagree with the poem's point of view on the nature of love?

4. Find an example of the narrator using clearly phrased opposite positions to emphasize the complexity of a love relationship.

5. After reading the poem several times, define several questions about the complex nature of adult love relationships that the poem poses.

6. This poem was written more than four hundred years ago. Do you think it still holds meaning and relevancy for the modern reader? Why?

IDEAS FOR WRITING

1. Write an essay in which you explore the relationship between honesty and truth, between being sensitive and being truthful in the context of a love relationship.

2. Write a poem that discusses and takes a position on several of the issues about the nature of love between adult lovers that Shakespeare explores in his sonnet. Try writing your poem using the sonnet form as Shakespeare does.

Starlight
Philip Levine

Journal

Write about an event during your childhood that helped you to understand some of the complex feelings one of your parents had about work, politics, family life, or spiritual issues.

My father stands in the warm evening
on the porch of my first house.
I am four years old and growing tired.
I see his head among the stars,
the glow of his cigarette, redder   5
than the summer moon riding
low over the old neighborhood. We
are alone, and he asks me if I am happy.
"Are you happy?" I cannot answer.
I do not really understand the word,   10
and the voice, my father's voice, is not
his voice, but somehow thick and choked,
a voice I have not heard before, but
heard often since. He bends and passes
a thumb beneath each of my eyes.   15
The cigarette is gone, but I can smell
the tiredness that hangs on his breath.
He has found nothing, and he smiles
and holds my head with both his hands.
Then he lifts me to his shoulder,   20
and now I too am there among the stars,
as tall as he. Are you happy? I say.

He nods in answer, Yes! oh yes! oh yes!
And in that new voice he says nothing,
holding my head tight against his head,   25
his eyes closed up against the starlight,
as though those tiny blinking eyes
of light might find a tall, gaunt child
holding his child against the promises
of autumn, until the boy slept   30
never to waken in that world again.

QUESTIONS AND CONSIDERATIONS

1. Why do you think the father in the poem asks his son if he is happy? Why can't the son answer his father's question?

2. What does the son sense about his father's emotional state?

3. Why does the father pass a "thumb beneath each of my [his son's] eyes"? What is he looking for?

4. Do you think that the father's positive answer to his son's question "Are you happy?" helps to lessen the son's apprehension? As you read the final lines of the poem, do you believe that the father is happy? Why or why not?

5. What does the last line of the poem, "never to waken in that world again," imply about how the narrator has been changed through his revelation about his father? What might it also imply about the father, who sees himself as a "tall, gaunt child"?

6. The poem's setting and imagery emphasize its mood. What do the following lines add to the feeling and implications of the poem: "the warm evening," "my first house," "the summer moon riding/low over the old neighborhood," "the starlight," "the promises/of autumn"?

IDEAS FOR WRITING

1. Write a poem or a short story about a time when you learned to understand something fundamental about your parents' values and emotional life. Use narrative strategies such as setting, dialogue, and detailed, descriptive images.

2. Write an essay in which you discuss the importance of moments of intense communication between children and parents. Provide examples from your own family life, the families of friends, or families as presented in literature and popular culture to support your insights.

The Hug
Tess Gallagher

Journal

Write about a time when you reached out to a stranger. What happened? Was the experience positive or disappointing?

A woman is reading a poem on the street
and another woman stops to listen. We stop too,
with our arms around each other. The poem
is being read and listened to out here
in the open. Behind us   5
no one is entering or leaving the houses.
Suddenly a hug comes over me and I'm
giving it to you, like a variable star shooting light
off to make itself comfortable, then
subsiding. I finish but keep on holding   10
you. A man walks up to us and we know he hasn't
come out of nowhere, but if he could, he
would have. He looks homeless because of how
he needs. "Can I have one of those?" he asks you,
and I feel you nod. I'm surprised,   15
surprised you don't tell him how
it is—that I'm yours, only
yours, etc., exclusive as a nose to
its face. Love—that's what we're talking about, love
that nabs you with "for me   20
only" and holds on.

So I walk over to him and put my
arms around him and try to
hug him like I mean it. He's got an overcoat on
so thick I can't feel   25
him past it. I'm starting the hug
and thinking, "How big a hug is this supposed to be?
How long shall I hold this hug?" Already
we could be eternal, his arms falling over my
shoulders, my hands not   30
meeting behind his back, he is so big!

I put my head into his chest and snuggle
in. I lean into him. I lean my blood and my wishes

into him. He stands for it. This is his
and he's starting to give it back so well I know he's   35
getting it. This hug. So truly, so tenderly
we stop having arms and I don't know if
my lover has walked away or what, or
if the woman is still reading the poem, or the houses—
what about them?—the houses.   40

Clearly, a little permission is a dangerous thing.
But when you hug someone you want it
to be a masterpiece of connection, the way the button
on his coat will leave the imprint of
a planet in my cheek   45
when I walk away. When I try to find some place
to go back to.

QUESTIONS AND CONSIDERATIONS

1. Why do you think the woman reading the poem on the street inspires the speaker of the poem to feel like hugging her lover?

2. Why is the narrator of the poem surprised when her lover agrees to allow the man who "looks homeless" to hug her? How does her partner's gesture begin to redefine the couple's traditional definition of romantic love?

3. Discuss the literal and metaphorical answers to the question the speaker asks: "How big a hug is this supposed to be?" What different meanings does the word "big" have in this sentence?

4. Why does the speaker lose herself in the hug?

5. Why does the speaker feel that "Clearly, a little permission is a dangerous thing"? Why has "the button on his coat left an imprint of a planet" in the speaker's cheek?

6. How is the concept of home developed as a symbol throughout the poem? Why does the speaker worry about where she will go back to once she has connected with the stranger? What connections does the poem seem to make between loving a special individual and loving people in your community?

IDEAS FOR WRITING

1. Write an essay in which you interpret the poem's perspective on the differences and similarities between an exclusive love for another person and about love for needy strangers in your community and elsewhere. Do you think it is possible to have an intense sense of love and caring for people you don't know personally?

2. Develop your journal entry into an essay or story that narrates your encounter with a stranger in your community. Discuss the impact that this experience had on your definition of love and caring, on your sense of responsibility for and connection to those who may be strangers but who nevertheless share your world.

Fever

Judith Ortiz Cofer

Journal

*Write about a ritual that you shared with one of your parents. How did it bring
you closer to them? What did the experience teach you about human
relationships?*

Father was to her, and to me,
like the wind—blowing through our house
on weekend leaves—and when we spoke to him,
he carried our voices away.

When he left,   5
and silence grew inside my mother like a child,
I would watch as she set the table for two,
then ate by herself in the kitchen, standing.

And she taught me this:
that silence is a thick and dark curtain,   10
the kind that pulls down over a shop window;

that love is the quick repercussion of a stone
bouncing off the same darkened window; that pain
is something you embrace, like a rag doll
no one will ask you to share.   15

Some nights, she allowed me in her bed.
Her skin was as cool as the surface
of the pillow the sick child clings to, awakening
from feverish dreams.

I would lay my head close to hers and listen   20
to the fine, knotted thread of her breath,
to her rosary of sighs,

her peace so deepened by sorrow, I know
it sustained me then, as the light
slipping past heavy, dark curtains might nourish   25
a small plant set, by accident, close
to the window.

QUESTIONS AND CONSIDERATIONS

1. Why is the father compared to the wind? What literal assumptions do you make from the metaphorical description of the father and his power in the opening stanza?

2. How does the speaker's mother define the silence, love, and pain that the father causes the mother? Why do you think the mother might experience her sense of abandonment, abuse, and rejection in this way?

3. Why does the speaker describe the pain of her mother in contrasting images? Analyze some of the images and comparisons used in the poem and explore their meanings and emotional impact.

4. How does the mother find peace in her pain? Why does the mother's sense of peace sustain the speaker?

5. The speaker compares the nourishment she receives from her mother's sorrowful sleep to "the light/slipping past heavy, dark curtains . . . a small plant set, by accident, close/to the window." What do these metaphors reveal about the speaker's relationship with her mother?

IDEAS FOR WRITING

1. Develop your journal writing into an essay, short story, or poem about a shared childhood ritual.

2. Write an essay in which you discuss what you feel are several important points that the poem "Fever" makes about the relationships between parents and children.

Let me not to the marriage of true minds admit impediments

William Shakespeare

Let me not to the marriage of true minds
Admit impediments: Love is not love
Which alters when it alteration finds,
Or bends with the remover to remove:
Oh, no! it is an ever-fixéd mark,   5
That looks on tempests and is never shaken;
It is the star to every wandering bark,
Whose worth's unknown, although his height be taken.
Love's not Time's fool, though rosy lips and cheeks
Within his bending sickle's compass come;   10
Love alters not with his brief hours and weeks,
But bears it out even to the edge of doom.
    If this be error and upon me proved,
    I never writ, nor no man ever loved.

QUESTIONS AND CONSIDERATIONS

1. According to the poem, what is love "not"? What positive definition of love does the poem create? How is the definition developed and supported? What comparison does the poem make between love and the stars? Between people and ships? How does the oath sworn by the speaker in the final couplet emphasize the poem's message?

2. Write an extended definition of love using examples and comparisons (metaphors and/or similes) from your own experience and imagination.

My Last Duchess
Robert Browning

Ferrara*

That's my last Duchess painted on the wall,
Looking as if she were alive. I call
That piece a wonder, now: Frà Pandolf's hands[†]
Worked busily a day, and there she stands.
Will't please you sit and look at her? I said   5
"Frá Pandolf' by design, for never read
Strangers like you that pictured countenance,
The depth and passion of its earnest glance,
But to myself they turned (since none puts by
The curtain I have drawn for you, but I)   10
And seemed as they would ask me, if they durst,
How such a glance came there; so, not the first
Are you to turn and ask thus. Sir, 'twas not
Her husband's presence only, called that spot
Of joy into the Duchess' cheek: perhaps   15
Frà Pandolf chanced to say "Her mantle laps
Over my lady's wrist too much," or "Paint
Must never hope to reproduce the faint
Half-flush that dies along her throat": such stuff
Was courtesy, she thought, and cause enough   20
For calling up that spot of joy. She had
A heart—how shall I say?—too soon made glad,
Too easily impressed; she liked whate'er
She looked on, and her looks went everywhere.

* Ferrara: Based loosely on the life of Alfonso II, Duke of Ferrara in Italy. Browning has the Duke speak in the poem. Alfonso's first wife, Lucrezia, a young girl, died in 1561 after three years of marriage.
[†] Frà Pandolf's hands: Brother Pandolf is an imaginary painter.

Sir, 'twas all one! My favor at her breast,   25
The dropping of the daylight in the West,
The bough of cherries some officious fool
Broke in the orchard for her, the white mule
She rode with round the terrace—all and each
Would draw from her alike the approving speech,   30
Or blush, at least. She thanked men—good! but thanked
Somehow—I know not how—as if she ranked
My gift of a nine-hundred-years-old name
With anybody's gift. Who'd stoop to blame
This sort of trifling? Even had you skill   35
In speech—(which I have not)—to make your will
Quite clear to such an one, and say, "Just this
Or that in you disgusts me; here you miss,
Or there exceed the mark"—and if she let
Herself be lessoned so, nor plainly set   40
Her wits to yours, forsooth, and made excuse
—E'en then would be some stooping; and I choose
Never to stoop. Oh sir, she smiled, no doubt,
Whene'er I passed her; but who passed without
Much the same smile? This grew; I gave commands;   45
Then all smiles stopped together. There she stands
As if alive. Will't please you rise? We'll meet
The company below, then. I repeat,
The Count your master's known munificence
Is ample warrant that no just pretense   50
Of mine for dowry will be disallowed;
Though his fair daughter's self, as I avowed
At starting, is my object. Nay, we'll go
Together down, sir. Notice Neptune, though,
Taming a sea horse, thought a rarity,   55
Which Claus of Innsbruck cast in bronze for me!

QUESTIONS

1. What does the Duke's creation of a work of art to replace his wife reveal about his personality and relationship with the Duchess? What did the Duchess do to offend the Duke? Do you consider her behavior appropriate? What is the significance of the Duke's final reference to a sculpture of "Neptune . . . /Taming a sea horse"? What impact do you think the Duke's speech will have on the Count, the father of the Duke's bride to be and "master" of the man to whom the Duke is speaking?

2. Using either prose or a poetic form similar to Browning's, write a letter to the Duke from the perspective of the Count or the Count's daughter. Explain why the Duke's proposal will or will not be accepted. Make references to the text of "My Last Duchess" to support your ideas.

February 13, 1980
Lucille Clifton

twenty-one years of my life you have been
the lost color in my eye. my secret blindness,
all my seeings turned grey with your going.
mother, i have worn your name like a shield.
it has torn but protected me all these years,   5
now even your absence comes of age.
i put on a dress called woman for this day
but i am not grown away from you
whatever i say.

QUESTIONS

1. To whom is the poem addressed? What anniversary does the date of the poem mark? In what sense is the poem about "secret blindness" or "lost color"? Why is the speaker's womanhood referred to as a "dress"?

2. Write a poem or essay addressed to a relative who has died with whom you continue to feel a sense of relationship or communion.

Digging
Seamus Heaney

Between my finger and my thumb
The squat pen rests; snug as a gun.

Under my window, a clean rasping sound
When the spade sinks into gravelly ground:
My father, digging. I look down   5

Till his straining rump among the flowerbeds
Bends low, comes up twenty years away
Stooping in rhythm through potato drills
Where he was digging.

The coarse boot nestled on the lug, the shaft   10
Against the inside knee was levered firmly.
He rooted out tall tops, buried the bright edge deep
To scatter new potatoes that we picked
Loving their cool hardness in our hands.

By God, the old man could handle a spade.   15
Just like his old man.

My grandfather cut more turf in a day
Than any other man on Toner's bog.
Once I carried him milk in a bottle
Corked sloppily with paper. He straightened up   20
To drink it, then fell to right away

Nicking and slicing neatly, heaving sods
Over his shoulder, going down and down
For the good turf. Digging.

The cold smell of potato mould, the squelch and slap   25
Of soggy peat, the curt cuts of an edge
Through living roots awaken in my head.
But I've no spade to follow men like them.

Between my finger and my thumb
The squat pen rests.   30
I'll dig with it.

QUESTIONS

1. How does the speaker in the poem contrast his connection to the tools of his profession with his father's and grandfather's relationship to the act of digging? What sharply observed and described images and details help to make the poem's contrasts more vivid? What resolution is suggested in the final three lines?

2. Write a poem or essay in which you compare and contrast your own professional needs and goals with those of your mother, father, or grandparents.

My Father
Dorotea Reyna

My father had the most
beautiful voice:
black keys on
white,
under the disdained   5
crown of a Mexican name

My father took to music—
violent his ways,
my father's days a pattern
of sunflowers & knives   10

Take a man gold
as the dust
on the sunflower's face,
a man darker even
than her dark face   15

Take a man more precise
than the sunflower's
sharp blade,
and place him in a cage—

More learned than the sum   20
on an abacus
of infinite terrain,

More primitive
than hate

My father more learned,   25
more primitive,
his heart a violent sonnet

QUESTIONS

1. What contrasts and contradictions does the speaker emphasize in her description of her father? Why was the father a man of contradictions? How and why is he compared to the sunflower? What caused him to be violent? Does the speaker blame or resent her father for being a violent man?

2. Write a poem or essay in which you try to capture a contradiction in the personality of a parent or relative, using contrasting metaphors and similes as Reyna does in "My Father."

Letter to My Sister

Maria Howe

We lived one life on the surface.
How could I have imagined your dark room?

I tell you I slept in the arms of the laddering beech
where even the numbing kitchen light
couldn't reach trembling in.   5

But this also is fiction.

I slept in fear. Then too
the beast crouched at my door
whimpering,

and it's true, I sometimes   10
offered you to him.

Forgive me the circumstances of my life.

This no one told us,
there is no such thing as family.

Nevertheless, today your voice reaches me,   15
deliberate on the wire,

and I, still older,
answer.

Perhaps this is the love we earn.

And if, with our words, the glass house cracks   20
and tumbles,

thus speaking, we stand clear,
the slivers sifting into our singular lives.

QUESTIONS

1. What did the narrator relate to her sister when they were growing up? Why has her life been different from that of her sister? Why does she ask her sister to forgive her? How do the sisters communicate now that they are adults?

2. In the form of prose or poetry, write a letter to a sister, brother, or other relative with whom you have some "unfinished business." In your letter, try to explain your feelings about the past and clear up any misunderstandings or feelings of guilt or resentment that you continue to have.

Standing in the Doorway, I Watch the Young Child Sleep

Sharon Hashimoto

Twenty months out of the womb,
your daughter lies still on the flat plane
of the twin bed, the sheet pulled taut
over her body like a second skin.

With her eyes closed to the dark,   5
does she remember the curve of your arms,
the slow pace and rhythm of your walk?
Or does she dream
of the swell and curl of the ocean,
drifting with the push of the moon,   10
the pull of the sun? That night,
you whimpered and clutched
at your pillow. Opening your eyes
to the dead quiet of the house,
you shrank away from the window   15
where a full moon hung pierced
on an apple tree's thin branches.
Your daughter rubs her cheek with her hand
and I can see our mother folding you
close into the creases of elbow and lap,   20
resting your head between the hills
of her breasts. Here, in this one shade
of night stretched over the room,
I can almost feel our mother's warm breath
as she leaned forward,   25
hiding your face
behind a fall of black hair.

QUESTIONS

1. The speaker in the poem addresses her younger sister, who has a child. How does the speaker feel as she watches her niece lying still on the twin bed? Why does the speaker feel her own mother's presence at this moment?

2. We sometimes see our parents' and even grandparents' influence in our own behavior and in that of our siblings. Write an essay in which you create a comparison between one of your siblings or yourself and either or both of your parents. How do you feel about your parents' influence on your behavior and character?

Married Love

Kuan Tao-Sheng
Translated by Kenneth Rexroth and Ling Chung

You and I
Have so much love
That it
Burns like a fire,
In which we bake a lump of clay   5
Molded into a figure of you
And a figure of me.

Then we take both of them,
And break them into pieces,
And mix the pieces with water,   10
And mold again a figure of you,
And a figure of me.
I am in your clay.
You are in my clay.
In life we share a single quilt.   15
In death we will share one bed.

QUESTIONS

1. The poem uses an extended metaphor or analogy to describe the love between a married couple. To what process does the metaphor compare love? Is the metaphor an effective one? Is the view of marriage it presents realistic?

2. Create your own analogy or extended metaphor to describe your view of the mixture or interchange of personalities that occurs in marriage or other long-term, committed relationship.

Grandfather and Grandmother in Love
David Mura

Now I will ask for one true word beyond
betrayal, that creaks and buoys like the bedsprings
used by the bodies that begot the bodies that begot me.
Now I will think of the moon bluing the white
sheets soaked in sweat, that heard him whisper   5
haiku of clover, azaleas, the cry of the cuckoo;
complaints of moles and beetles,
blight and bad debts, as the *biwa's* spirit
bubbled up between them, its song quavering.
Now I take this word and crack it, like a seed   10
between the teeth, spit it out into the world,
and let it seek the loam that nourished his greenhouse
roses, sputtering petals of chrysanthemum:
let it leave the sweet taste of *teriyaki,*
and a grain of rice lodges in my molars,   15
and the faint breath of *sake,* hot in the nostrils.
Now the drifting before writhing, now Buddha
stand back, now he bumps beside her,
otoo-san, okaa-san, calling each other.
Now there reverberates the *ran* of lovers,   20

and the bud of the past has burst through
into the other world,
where she, teasing, pushes him away, swats
his hand, like a pesky, tickling fly,
and then turns to his face that cries out   25
Laughing, and he is hauling her in, trawling
the caverns of her flesh, gathering gift
after gift from a sea that seems endless,
depths a boy dreams of, where dolphins
and fluorescent fins and fish with wings   30
suddenly spill their glittering scales
before him, and he, who was always baffled by beauty,
lets slip the net and dives under, and the night
washes over them, slipping from sight,
just the soft shushing of waves, drifting ground   35
swells, echoing the knocking tide of morning.

QUESTIONS

1. What is the "one true word beyond/betrayal" for which the speaker asks? What does he do with the word when he finds it? What memories and sexual fantasies about his grandparents does he have? How is fishing used as a metaphor for sexual relations? Why do you think the speaker needs to pursue these fantasies about his grandparents' relationship at this stage in his life?

2. Write a poem, story, or essay in which you imagine and explore the relationship between your parents or grandparents as it was before you were born. Interview family members to gather information.

The Meal

Suzanne E. Berger

They have washed their faces until they are pale,
their homework is beautifully complete.
They wait for the adults to lean towards each other.
The hands of the children are oval
and smooth as pine-nuts.   5

The girls have braided and rebraided their hair,
and tied ribbons without a single mistake.
The boy has put away his coin collection.
They are waiting for the mother to straighten her lipstick,
and for the father to speak.   10

They gather around the table, carefully
as constellations waiting to be named.
Their minds shift and ready, like dunes.
It is so quiet, all waiting stars and dunes.

Their forks move across their plates without scraping,   15
they wait for the milk and the gravy
at the table with its forgotten spices.
They are waiting for a happiness to lift their eyes,
like sudden light flaring in the trees outside.

The white miles of the meal continue,   20
the figures still travel across a screen:
the father carving the Sunday roast,
her mouth uneven as a torn hibiscus,
their braids still gleaming in the silence.

QUESTIONS

1. Characterize the values and life style of the family portrayed in this poem.
Do they seem happy? Do the children love and respect their parents? Do any of the
images and details reveal disturbing elements in the relationships among family
members?

2. Focus on a particular memory or select a photograph of a family meal or celebration. Write an essay or poem in which you describe the photograph or memory, using
vivid language, images, and details that suggest the complexities of the relationships
among family members.

Mending Wall
Robert Frost

Something there is that doesn't love a wall,
That sends the frozen-ground-swell under it,
And spills the upper boulders in the sun;
And makes gaps even two can pass abreast.
The work of hunters is another thing: 5
I have come after them and made repair
Where they have left not one stone on a stone,
But they would have the rabbit out of hiding,
To please the yelping dogs. The gaps I mean,
No one has seen them made or heard them made,   10
But at spring mending-time we find them there.

I let my neighbor know beyond the hill;
And on a day we meet to walk the line
And set the wall between us once again.
We keep the wall between us as we go. 15
To each the boulders that have fallen to each.
And some are loaves and some so nearly balls
We have to use a spell to make them balance:
'Stay whore you aro until our baoke aro turnod!'
We wear our fingers rough with handling them. 20
Oh, just another kind of outdoor game,
One on a side. It comes to little more:
There where it is we do not need the wall:
He is all pine and I am apple orchard.
My apple trees will never get across 25
And eat the cones under his pines, I tell him.
He only says, 'Good fences make good neighbors.'
Spring is the mischief in me, and I wonder
If I could put a notion in his head:
'*Why* do they make good neighbors? Isn't it 30
Where there are cows? But here there are no cows.
Before I built a wall I'd ask to know
What I was walling in or walling out,
And to whom I was like to give offense.
Something there is that doesn't love a wall, 35
That wants it down.' I could say 'Elves' to him,
But it's not elves exactly, and I'd rather
He said it for himself. I see him there
Bringing a stone grasped firmly by the top
In each hand, like an old-stone savage armed. 40
He moves in darkness as it seems to me,
Not of woods only and the shade of trees.
He will not go behind his father's saying,
And he likes having thought of it so well
He says again, 'Good fences make good neighbors.' 45

QUESTIONS

1. Why do the speaker and the neighbor work so hard to rebuild the wall between them, despite the fact that "Something there is that doesn't love a wall"? If rebuilding the wall is "just another kind of outdoor game," is it an important game, or a pointless and outmoded one? Why is the neighbor described as "like an old-stone savage"?

2. Write a response to the saying, "Good fences make good neighbors." What exactly does this saying mean? Do you agree or disagree with this view of relationships between neighbors?

We Real Cool
The Pool Players.
Seven at the Golden Shovel.

Gwendolyn Brooks

We real cool. We
Left school. We

Lurk late. We
Strike straight. We

Sing sin. We   5
Thin gin. We

Jazz June. We
Die soon.

QUESTIONS

　1. Why do you think the pool hall where the speakers congregate is called the
Golden Shovel? Why do the speakers in the poem only refer to themselves using the pronoun "we"? Why are the individual lines of the poem and its overall length so short? Is
the poem making a criticism of the speakers and their life style?

　2. Write a poem, story, or essay about a group of people who think and act alike,
using the pronoun "we" as Brooks does. Try to create appropriate images and details to
describe the life style of the "we."

A las Gatas

Lorna Dee Cervantes

**A Bird, Tiny, Mousie, Grumpy, Cat-Eyes, Flaca,
Sleepy, Princess y Betty la Boop**
We were nine lives, cat claws plunged in
the caterwauling of *la llorona* and the crying saints.
We believed in witches, wild cards, jokers
and the tricksters who lived without it.
Disciples of the pride, we preyed on fury's wing.   5
We lied. We stole the heart's desire. We never
got a cent, but feral, flew to another side
of glory. We came; this close to dying,
we gunned the engines of our grief, and gained.
Taught to live from hand to mouth, the moratorium   10
of our lives began at blood's first quickening.

Given to the beck and call so fast, we primed
our lives that instant when we slipped into the gap
between child and man—and slave. We chose
to stay, tough in the fist of our fathers'   15
mercy. No face cards in our deck, we dealt
the devil back his hand, we scorched the virgin
from our breasts, as the sweat of heat upon us
did not free us, but did not bind us either.
We had the power then, between three worlds,   20
to fuse our *bruja* pack, our pact to faith, not
in our futures but, in a present we could fix within
the diamond decks minted in our carboned eyes.
We were crystalline, runaway *rucas* on the prowl,
edge of night in our glassy throats, cut of class   25
in flyaway manes, the blood of oils on our slapped
cheeks, and with bit lips we smiled to
circling owls. No angels, no *novenas,* no past
spirits that we recognized, nobody's business
what we did, we know we earned our freedom,   30
and we did.

QUESTIONS

1. How is the central metaphor of cats *("gatas")* developed and how effective is it at creating an image of rebellion and independence? Between what "three worlds" do the speakers lie? Would you consider this poem critical of the "gatas" in the sense that Brooks' poem is critical of the "seven at the Golden Shovel"?

2. Write an essay about teenage rebellion. Do you think it is necessary for teenagers to rebel against the "program" laid out for them by their parents and their society in order to attain a real sense of identity and independence? Provide examples from your own experiences.

George
Dudley Randall

When I was a boy desiring the title of man
And toiling to earn it
In the inferno of the foundry knockout,
I watched and admired you working by my side,
As, goggled, with mask on your mouth and shoulders bright with sweat,   5
You mastered the monstrous, lumpish cylinder blocks,
And when they clotted the line and plunged to the floor
With force enough to tear your foot in two,
You calmly stepped aside.

One day when the line broke down and the blocks reared up   10
Groaning, grinding, and mounted like an ocean wave
And then rushed thundering down like an avalanche,
And we frantically dodged, then braced our heads together
To form an arch to life and stack them,
You gave me your highest accolade: 15
You said: "You not afraid of sweat. You strong as a mule."

Now, here, in the hospital,
In a ward where old men wait to die,
You sit, and watch time go by.
You cannot read the books I bring, not even   20
Those that are only picture books,
As you sit among the senile wrecks,
The psychopaths, the incontinent.

One day when you fell from your chair and stared at the air
With the look of fright which sight of death inspires,   25
I lifted you like a cylinder block, and said,
"Don't be afraid
Of a little fall, for you'll be here
A long time yet, because you're strong as a mule."

QUESTIONS

1. What memories does the speaker have of George? How do these memories contrast with George's present state? What impact has his contact with George had on the speaker's own life and values?

2. Write a poem or essay about an older person, a teacher or fellow worker, who had an important impact on you in your early years, who helped to form your values and beliefs.

To a Stranger
Walt Whitman

Passing stranger! you do not know how longingly I look upon you,
You must be he I was seeking, or she I was seeking (it comes to me
    as of a dream,)
I have somewhere surely lived a life of joy with you,
All is recall'd as we flit by each other, fluid, affectionate, chaste,   5
    matured,
You grew up with me, were a boy with me or a girl with me,
I ate with you and slept with you, your body has become not yours
    only nor left my body mine only,

You give me the pleasure of your eyes, face, flesh, as we pass, you   10
    take of my beard, breast, hands, in return,
I am not to speak to you, I am to think of you when I sit alone or
    wake at night alone,
I am to wait, I do not doubt I am to meet you again,
I am to see to it that I do not lose you.   15

QUESTIONS

1. What dream or fantasy relationship has the speaker had with the "passing stranger"? What does the speaker believe his or her relationship will be with the stranger in the future?

2. Write a poem or essay about an imagined relationship you have had with a stranger. If you met later and developed a relationship with the stranger, how did the "real" relationship differ from the initial fantasy?

Skydiving
Jim Wayne Miller

When I think of us seated in our separate days,
a hand under my breastbone tightens around a bar,
My seat tips back, rises, and my feet swing free,
as if I were riding a chair-lift in an amusement park.

We are strung out in five seats at fixed   5
distances from one another, dangling our feet
over treetops, over the heads of funny people
telescoped into themselves, whether thin or fat,

rising past several musics, past zebras and llamas
in their lots. Looking back at one another, we wave and clown.   10
One by one you turn ahead of me and, still climbing,
I touch my hand to yours as you pass, moving down.

When we are quiet in our separate rooms at night,
I think we are all skydivers falling through our
separate spaces. We float, lie prone in a circle.   15
Reaching out, we hold hands for a moment, then we're

off on our own currents, tumbling, backpedaling,
swimming or taking the sun in a playground
high over a brown yellow and green checkerboard
where roads run like lines in the palm of my hand.   20

It is pleasant and so still but we are falling
farther and farther apart through private corridors
of air. The earth grows under us, and begins
to be patches of ground the size of our shadows.

QUESTIONS

1. How does the extended description of riding a Ferris wheel with friends at the amusement park comment on the nature of friendship and camaraderie among young people? How does the second extended image of the poem, that of "skydivers falling through our/separate spaces" contrast to the first image of the Ferris wheel? What does the poem's final image, that of "patches of ground the size of our shadows" suggest?

2. Write a poem or essay in which you create an extended analogy or metaphor for the way friendship groups in high school or college grow apart while still remaining joined through shared memories and common values.

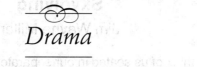

Drama

A Son, Come Home
Ed Bullins

Journal

Write about a vivid memory that you have of returning home after being away for an extended time. Focus on how you realized that your relationship with one of your parents had changed.

A Son, Come Home was first produced at the American Place Theatre on March 26th, 1968. It was directed by Robert MacBeth, with scenery by John Jay Moore and lighting by Roger Morgan. The cast was as follows:

MOTHER, *early 50's*	ESTELLE EVANS
SON, *30 years old*	WAYNE GRICE
THE GIRL	KELLY-MARIE BERRY
THE BOY	GARY BOLLING

Music for the production was composed by Gordon Watkins.

The BOY and the GIRL wear black tights and shirts. They move the action of the play and express the MOTHER'S and the SON'S moods and tensions. They become various embodiments recalled from memory and history: they enact a number of personalities and move from mood to mood.

The players are Black.

At rise: Scene: Bare stage but for two chairs positioned so as not to interfere with the actions of the BOY and the GIRL.

The MOTHER enters, sits in chair and begins to use imaginary iron and board. She hums a spiritual as she works.

MOTHER: You came three times . . . Michael? It took you three times to find me at home?

(The GIRL enters, turns and peers through the cracked, imaginary door)

SON'S VOICE *(offstage):* Is Mrs. Brown home?

GIRL *(an old woman):* What?

MOTHER: It shouldn't have taken you three times. I told you that I would be here by two and you should wait, Michael.

(The SON enters, passes the GIRL and takes his seat upon the other chair.

The BOY enters, stops on other side of the imaginary door and looks through at the GIRL)

BOY: Is Mrs. Brown in?

GIRL: Miss Brown ain't come in yet. Come back later . . . She'll be in before dark.

MOTHER: It shouldn't have taken you three times . . . You should listen to me, Michael. Standin' all that time in the cold.

SON: It wasn't cold, Mother.

MOTHER: I told you that I would be here by two and you should wait, Michael.

BOY: Please tell Mrs. Brown that her son's in town to visit her.

GIRL: You little Miss Brown's son? Well, bless the Lord.

(Calls over her shoulder)

Hey, Mandy, do you hear that? Little Miss Brown upstairs got a son . . . a great big boy . . . He's come to visit her.

BOY: You'll tell her, won't you?

GIRL: Sure, I'll tell her.

(Grins and shows gums)

I'll tell her soon as she gets in.

MOTHER: Did you get cold, Michael?

SON: No, Mother. I walked around some . . . sightseeing.

BOY: I walked up Twenty-third Street toward South. I had phoned that I was coming.

MOTHER: Sightseeing? But this is your home, Michael . . . always has been.

BOY: Just before I left New York I phoned that I was taking the bus. Two hours by bus, that's all. That's all it takes. Two hours.

SON: This town seems so strange. Different than how I remember it.

MOTHER: Yes, you have been away for a good while . . . How long has it been, Michael?

BOY: Two hours down the Jersey Turnpike, the trip beginning at the New York Port Authority Terminal . . .

SON: . . . and then straight down through New Jersey to Philadelphia . . .

GIRL: . . . and home . . . Just imagine . . . little Miss Brown's got a son who's come home.

SON: Yes, home . . . an anachronism.

MOTHER: What did you say, Michael?

BOY: He said . . .

GIRL *(late teens):* What's an anachronism, Mike?

SON: Anachronism: 1: an error in chronology; *esp:* a chronological misplacing of persons, events, objects, or customs in regard to each other 2: a person or a thing that is chronologically out of place—anachronistic/ *also* anachronic/ *or* anachronous—anachronistically/ *also* anachronously.

MOTHER: I was so glad to hear you were going to school in California.

BOY: College.

GIRL: Yes, I understand.

MOTHER: How long have you been gone, Michael?

SON: Nine years.

BOY: Nine years it's been. I wonder if she'll know me . . .

MOTHER: You've put on so much weight, son. You know that's not healthy.

GIRL *(20 years old):* And that silly beard . . . how . . .

SON: Oh . . . I'll take it off. I'm going on a diet tomorrow.

BOY: I wonder if I'll know her.

SON: You've put on some yourself, Mother.

MOTHER: Yes, the years pass. Thank the Lord.

BOY: I wonder if we've changed much.

GIRL: Yes, thank the Lord.

SON: The streets here seem so small.

MOTHER: Yes, it seems like that when you spend a little time in Los Angeles.

GIRL: I spent eighteen months there with your aunt when she was sick. She had nobody else to help her . . . she was so lonely. And you were in the service . . . away. You've always been away.

BOY: In Los Angeles the boulevards, the avenues, the streets . . .

SON: . . . are wide. Yes, they have some wide ones out West. Here, they're so small and narrow. I wonder how cars get through on both sides.

MOTHER: Why, you know how . . . we lived on Derby Street for over ten years, didn't we?

SON: Yeah, that was almost an alley.

MOTHER: Did you see much of your aunt before you left Los Angeles?

SON: What?

GIRL *(middle-aged woman) (to* BOY): Have you found a job yet, Michael?

MOTHER: Your aunt. My sister.

BOY: Nawh, not yet . . . Today I just walked downtown . . . quite a ways . . . this place is plenty big, ain't it?

SON: I don't see too much of Aunt Sophie.

MOTHER: But you're so much alike.

GIRL: Well, your bags are packed and are sitting outside the door.

BOY: My bags?

MOTHER: You shouldn't be that way, Michael. You shouldn't get too far away from your family.

SON: Yes, Mother.

BOY: But I don't have any money. I had to walk downtown today. That's how much money I have. I've only been here a week.

GIRL: I packed your bags, Michael.

MOTHER: You never can tell when you'll need or want your family, Michael.

SON: That's right, Mother.

MOTHER: You and she are so much alike.

BOY: Well, goodbye, Aunt Sophie.

GIRL:

(Silence)

MOTHER: All that time in California and you hardly saw your aunt. My baby sister.

BOY: Tsk tsk tsk.

SON: I'm sorry, Mother.

MOTHER: In the letters I'd get from both of you there'd be no mention of the other. All these years. Did you see her again?

SON: Yes.

GIRL *(on telephone):* Michael? Michael who? . . . Ohhh . . . Bernice's boy.

MOTHER: You didn't tell me about this, did you?

SON: No, I didn't.

BOY: Hello, Aunt Sophie. How are you?

GIRL: I'm fine, Michael. How arc you? You're looking well.

BOY: I'm getting on okay.

MOTHER: I prayed for you.

SON: Thank you.

MOTHER: Thank the Lord, Michael.

BOY: Got me a job working for the city.

GIRL: You did now.

BOY: Yes, I've brought you something.

GIRL: What's this, Michael . . . ohhh . . . it's money.

BOY: It's for the week I stayed with you.

GIRL: Fifty dollars. But, Michael, you didn't have to.

MOTHER: Are you still writing that radical stuff, Michael?

SON: Radical?

MOTHER: Yes . . . that stuff you write and send me all the time in those little books.

SON: My poetry, Mother?

MOTHER: Yes, that's what I'm talking about.

SON: No.

MOTHER: Praise the Lord, son. Praise the Lord. Didn't seem like anything I had read in school.

BOY (on telephone): Aunt Sophie? . . . Aunt Sophie? . . . It's me, Michael . . .

GIRL: Michael?

BOY: Yes . . . Michael . . .

GIRL: Oh . . . Michael . . . yes . . .

BOY: I'm in jail, Aunt Sophie . . . I got picked up for drunk driving.

GIRL: You did . . . how awful . . .

MOTHER: When you going to get your hair cut, Michael?

BOY: Aunt Sophie . . . will you please come down and sign my bail. I've got the money . . . I just got paid yesterday . . . They're holding more than enough for me . . . but the law says that someone has to sign for it.

MOTHER: You look almost like a hoodlum, Michael.

BOY: All you need to do is come down and sign . . . and I can get out.

MOTHER: What you tryin' to be . . . a savage or something? Are you keeping out of trouble, Michael?

GIRL: Ohhh . . . Michael . . . I'm sorry but I can't do nothin' like that . . .

BOY: But all you have to do is sign . . . I've got the money and everything.

GIRL: I'm sorry . . . I can't stick my neck out.

BOY: But, Aunt Sophie . . . if I don't get back to work I'll lose my job and everything . . . please . . .

GIRL: I'm sorry, Michael . . . I can't stick my neck out . . . I have to go now . . . Is there anyone I can call?

BOY: No.

GIRL: I could call your mother. She wouldn't mind if I reversed the charges on her, would she? I don't like to run my bills up.

BOY: No thanks.

MOTHER: You and your aunt are so much alike.

SON: Yes, Mother. Our birthdays are in the same month.

MOTHER: Yes, that year was so hot . . . so hot and I was carrying you . . .

(As the MOTHER speaks the BOY comes over and takes her by the hand and leads her from the chair, and they stroll around the stage, arm in arm.

The GIRL accompanies them and she and the BOY enact scenes from the MOTHER'S mind.)

. . . carrying you, Michael . . . and you were such a big baby . . . kicked all the time. But I was happy. Happy that I was having a baby of my own. . . . I worked as long as I could and bought you everything you might need . . . diapers . . . and bottles . . . and your own spoon . . . and even toys . . . and even books . . . And it was so hot in Philadelphia that year . . . Your Aunt Sophie used to come over and we'd go for walks . . . sometimes up on the avenue . . . I was living in West Philly then . . . in that old terrible section they called "The Bottom." That's where I met your father.

GIRL: You're such a fool, Bernice. No nigger . . . man or boy's . . . ever going to do a thing to me like that.

MOTHER: Everything's going to be all right, Sophia.

GIRL: But what is he going to do? How are you going to take care of a baby by yourself?

MOTHER: Everything's going to be all right, Sophia. I'll manage.

GIRL: You'll manage? How? Have you talked about marriage?

MOTHER: Oh, please, Sophia!

GIRL: What do you mean "please"? Have you?

MOTHER: I just can't. He might think . . .

GIRL: Think! That dirty nigger better think. He better think before he really messes up. And you better too. You got this baby comin' on. What are you going to do?

MOTHER: I don't know . . . I don't know what I can do.

GIRL: Is he still tellin' you those lies about . . .

MOTHER: They're not lies.

GIRL: Haaaa . . .

MOTHER: They're not.

GIRL: Some smooth-talkin' nigger comes up from Georgia and tells you he escaped from the chain gang and had to change his name so he can't get married 'cause they might find out . . . What kinda shit is that, Bernice?

MOTHER: Please, Sophia. Try and understand. He loves me. I can't hurt him.

GIRL: Loves you . . . and puts you through this?

MOTHER: Please . . . I'll talk to him . . . Give me a chance.

GIRL: It's just a good thing you got a family, Bernice. It's just a good thing. You know that, don't cha?

MOTHER: Yes, . . . yes, I do . . . but please don't say anything to him.

SON: I've only seen my father about a half dozen times that I remember, Mother. What was he like?

MOTHER: Down in The Bottom . . . that's where I met your father. I was young and hinkty then. Had big pretty brown legs and a small waist. Everybody used to to call me Bernie . . . and me and my sister would go to Atlantic City on the weekends and work as waitresses in the evenings and sit all afternoon on the black part of the beach at Boardwalk and Atlantic . . . getting blacker . . . and having the times of our lives. Your father probably still lives down in The Bottom . . . perched over some bar down there . . . drunk to the world . . . I can see him now . . . He had good white teeth then . . . not how they turned later when he started in drinkin' that wine and wouldn't stop . . . he was so nice then.

BOY: Awwww, listen, kid. I got my problems too.

GIRL: But Andy . . . I'm six months gone . . . and you ain't done nothin'.

BOY: Well, what can I do?

GIRL: Don't talk like that . . . What can you do? . . . You know what you can do.

BOY: You mean marry you? Now lissen, sweetheart . . .

GIRL: But what about our baby?

BOY: Your baby.

GIRL: Don't talk like that! It took more than me to get him.

BOY: Well . . . look . . . I'll talk to you later, kid. I got to go to work now.

GIRL: That's what I got to talk to you about too, Andy. I need some money.

BOY: Money! Is somethin' wrong with your head, woman? I ain't got no money.

GIRL: But I can't work much longer, Andy. You got to give me some money. Andy . . . you just gotta.

BOY: Woman . . . all I got to *ever* do is die and go to hell.

GIRL: Well, you gonna do that, Andy. You sho are . . . you know that, don't you? . . . You know that.

MOTHER: . . . Yes, you are, man. Praise the Lord. We all are . . . All of us . . . even though he ain't come for you yet to make you pay. Maybe he's waitin' for us to go together so I can be a witness to the retribution that's handed down. A witness to all that He'll bestow upon your sinner's head . . . A witness! . . . That's what I am, Andy! Do you hear me? . . . A witness!

SON: Mother . . . what's wrong? What's the matter?

MOTHER: Thank the Lord that I am not blinded and will see the fulfillment of divine . . .

SON: Mother!

MOTHER: Oh . . . is something wrong, Michael?

SON: You're shouting and walking around . . .

MOTHER: Oh . . . it's nothing, son. I'm just feeling the power of the Lord.

SON: Oh . . . is there anything I can get you, Mother?

MOTHER: No, nothing at all.

(She sits again and irons)

son: Where's your kitchen? . . . I'll get you some coffee . . . the way you like it. I bet I still remember how to fix it.

MOTHER: Michael . . . I don't drink anything like that no more.

SON: No?

MOTHER: Not since I joined the service of the Lord.

SON: Yeah? . . . Well, do you mind if I get myself a cup?

MOTHER: Why, I don't have a kitchen. All my meals are prepared for me.

SON: Oh . . . I thought I was having dinner with you.

MOTHER: No. There's nothing like that here.

SON: Well, could I take you out to a restaurant? . . . Remember how we used to go out all the time and eat? I've never lost my habit of liking to eat out. Remember . . . we used to come down to this part of town and go to restaurants. They used to call it home cooking then . . . now, at least where I been out West and up in Harlem . . . we call it soul food. I bet we could find a nice little restaurant not four blocks from here, Mother. Re-

member that old man's place we used to go to on Nineteenth and South? I
bet he's dead now . . . but . . .

MOTHER: I don't even eat out no more, Michael.

SON: No?

MOTHER: Sometimes I take a piece of holy bread to work . . . or some fruit . . .
if it's been blessed by my Spiritual Mother.

SON: I see.

MOTHER: Besides . . . we have a prayer meeting tonight.

SON: On Friday?

MOTHER: Every night. You'll have to be going soon.

SON: Oh.

MOTHER: You're looking well.

SON: Thank you.

MOTHER: But you look tired.

SON: Do I?

MOTHER: Yes, those rings around your eyes might never leave. Your father had
them.

SON: Did he?

MOTHER: Yes . . . and cowlicks . . . deep cowlicks on each side on his head.

SON: Yes . . . I remember.

MOTHER: Do you?

(The BOY *and the* GIRL *take crouching positions behind and in front of them. They are in a
streetcar. The* BOY *behind the* MOTHER *and* SON, *the* GIRL *across the aisle, a passenger)*

MOTHER *(young woman) (to the* BOY*):* Keep your damn hands off him, Andy!

BOY *(chuckles):* Awww, c'mon . . . Bernie. I ain't seen him since he was in the
crib.

MOTHER: And you wouldn't have seen neither of us . . . if I had anything to do
with it . . . Ohhh . . . why did I get on this trolley?

BOY: C'mon . . . Bernie . . . don't be so stuckup.

MOTHER: Don't even talk to us . . . and stop reaching after him.

BOY: Awww . . . c'mon . . . Bernie. Let me look at him.

MOTHER: Leave us alone. Look . . . people are looking at us.

(The GIRL *across the aisle has been peeking at the trio but looks toward front at the mention of herself)*

BOY: Hey, big boy . . . do you know who I am?

MOTHER: Stop it, Andy! Stop it, I say . . . Mikie . . . don't pay any attention to
him . . . you hear?

BOY: Hey, big boy . . . know who I am? . . . I'm your daddy. Hey, there . . .

MOTHER: Shut up . . . shut up, Andy . . . you nothin' to us.

BOY: Where you livin' at . . . Bernie? Let me come on by and see the little guy,
huh?

MOTHER: No! You're not comin' near us . . . ever . . . you hear?

BOY: But I'm his father . . . look . . . Bernie . . . I've been an ass the way I've
acted but . . .

MOTHER: He ain't got no father.

BOY: Oh, come off that nonsense, woman.

MOTHER: Mikie ain't got no father . . . his father's dead . . . you hear?

BOY: Dead?

MOTHER: Yes, dead. My son's father's dead.

BOY: What you talkin' about? . . . He's the spittin' image of me.

MOTHER: Go away . . . leave us alone, Andrew.

BOY: See there . . . he's got the same name as me. His first name is Michael after your father . . . and Andrew after me.

MOTHER: No, stop that, you hear?

BOY: Michael Andrew . . .

MOTHER: You never gave him no name . . . his name is Brown . . . Brown. The same as mine . . . and my sister's . . . and my daddy . . . You never gave him nothin' . . . and you're dead . . . go away and get buried.

BOY: You know that trouble I'm in . . . I got a wife down there, Bernie. I don't care about her . . . what could I do?

MOTHER (rises, pulling up the SON): We're leavin' . . . don't you try and follow us . . . you hear, Andy? C'mon . . . Mikie . . . watch your step now.

BOY: Well . . . bring him around my job . . . you know where I work. That's all . . . bring him around on payday.

MOTHER (leaving): We don't need anything from you . . . I'm working . . . just leave us alone.

(The BOY turns to the GIRL)

BOY (shrugs): That's the way it goes . . . I guess. Ships passing on the trolley car . . . Hey . . . don't I know you from up around 40th and Market?

(The GIRL turns away)

SON: Yeah . . . I remember him. He always had liquor on his breath.

MOTHER: Yes . . . he did. I'm glad that stuff ain't got me no more . . . Thank the Lord.

GIRL (35 years old): You want to pour me another drink, Michael?

BOY (15 years old): You drink too much, Mother.

GIRL: Not as much as some other people I know.

BOY: Well, me and the guys just get short snorts, Mother. But you really hide some port.

GIRL: Don't forget you talkin' to your mother. You gettin' more like your father every day.

BOY: Is that why you like me so much?

GIRL (grins drunkenly): Oh, hush up now, boy . . . and pour me a drink.

BOY: There's enough here for me too.

GIRL: That's okay . . . when Will comes in he'll bring something.

SON: How is Will, Mother?

MOTHER: I don't know . . . haven't seen Will in years.

SON: Mother.

MOTHER: Yes, Michael.

SON: Why you and Will never got married? . . . You stayed together for over ten years.

MOTHER: Oh, don't ask me questions like that, Michael.

SON: But why not?

MOTHER: It's just none of your business.

SON: But you could be married now . . . not alone in this room . . .

MOTHER: Will had a wife and child in Chester . . . you know that.

SON: He could have gotten a divorce, Mother . . . Why . . .

MOTHER: Because he just didn't . . . that's why.

SON: You never hear from him?

MOTHER: Last I heard . . . Will had cancer.

SON: Oh, he did.

MOTHER: Yes.

SON: Why didn't you tell me? . . . You could have written.

MOTHER: Why?

SON: So I could have known.

MOTHER: So you could have known? Why?

SON: Because Will was like a father to me . . . the only one I've really known.

MOTHER: A father? And you chased him away as soon as you got big enough.

SON: Don't say that, Mother.

MOTHER: You made me choose between you and Will.

SON: Mother.

MOTHER: The quarrels you had with him . . . the mean tricks you used to play . . . the lies you told to your friends about Will . . . He wasn't much . . . when I thought I had a sense of humor I us'ta call him just plain Will. But we was his family.

SON: Mother, listen.

MOTHER: And you drove him away . . . and he didn't lift a hand to stop you.

SON: Listen, Mother.

MOTHER: As soon as you were big enough you did all that you could to get me and Will separated.

SON: Listen.

MOTHER: All right, Michael . . . I'm listening.

(Pause)

SON: Nothing.

(Pause. Lifts an imaginary object)

Is this your tambourine?

MOTHER: Yes.

SON: Do you play it?

MOTHER: Yes.

SON: Well?

MOTHER: Everything I do in the service of the Lord I do as well as He allows.

SON: You play it at your meetings.

MOTHER: Yes, I do. We celebrate the life He has bestowed upon us.

SON: I guess that's where I get it from.
MOTHER: Did you say something, Michael?
SON: Yes. My musical ability.
MOTHER: Oh . . . you've begun taking your piano lessons again?
SON: No . . . I was never any good at that.
MOTHER: Yes, three different teachers and you never got past the tenth lesson.
SON: You have a good memory, Mother.
MOTHER: Sometimes, son. Sometimes.
SON: I play an electric guitar in a combo.
MOTHER: You do? That's nice.
SON: That's why I'm in New York. We got a good break and came East.
MOTHER: That's nice, Michael.
SON: I was thinking that Sunday I could rent a car and come down to get you and drive you up to see our show. You'll get back in plenty of time to rest for work Monday.
MOTHER: No, I'm sorry. I can't do that.
SON: But you would like it, Mother. We could have dinner up in Harlem, then go down and . . .
MOTHER: I don't do anything like that any more, Michael.
SON: You mean you wouldn't come to see me play even if I were appearing here in Philly?
MOTHER: That's right, Michael. I wouldn't come. I'm past all that.
SON: Oh, I see.
MOTHER: Yes, thank the Lord.
SON: But it's my life, Mother.
MOTHER: Good . . . then you have something to live for.
SON: Yes.
MOTHER: Well, you're a man now, Michael . . . I can no longer live it for you. Do the best with what you have.
SON: Yes . . . Yes, I will, Mother.
GIRL'S VOICE (offstage): Sister Brown . . . Sister Brown . . . hello.
MOTHER (uneasy; peers at watch): Oh . . . it's Mother Ellen . . . I didn't know it was so late.
GIRL (enters): Sister Brown . . . how are you this evening?
MOTHER: Oh, just fine, Mother.
GIRL: Good. It's nearly time for dinner.
MOTHER: Oh, yes, I know.
GIRL: We don't want to keep the others waiting at meeting . . . do we?
MOTHER: No, we don't.
GIRL (self-assured): Hello, son.
SON: Hello.
MOTHER: Oh, Mother . . . Mother . . .
GIRL: Yes, Sister Brown, what is it?
MOTHER: Mother . . . Mother . . . this is . . . this is . . .

(Pause)

. . . this is . . .

SON: Hello, I'm Michael. How are you?

MOTHER *(relieved):* Yes, Mother . . . This is Michael . . . my son.

GIRL: Why, hello, Michael. I've heard so much about you from your mother. She prays for you daily.

SON *(embarrassed):* Oh . . . good.

GIRL *(briskly):* Well . . . I have to be off to see about the others.

MOTHER: Yes, Mother Ellen.

GIRL *(as she exits; chuckles):* Have to tell everyone that you won't be keeping us waiting, Bernice.

(Silence)

SON: Well, I guess I better be going, Mother.

MOTHER: Yes.

SON: I'll write.

MOTHER: Please do.

SON: I will.

MOTHER: You're looking well . . . Thank the Lord.

SON: Thank you, so are you, Mother.

(He moves toward her and hesitates)

MOTHER: You're so much like your aunt. Give her my best . . . won't you?

SON: Yes, I will, Mother.

MOTHER: Take care of yourself, son.

SON: Yes, Mother. I will.

(The SON *exits. The* MOTHER *stands looking after him as the lights go slowly down to . . .)*
                                    Blackness

QUESTIONS AND CONSIDERATIONS

1. After reading the play aloud, discuss the impact that the changing roles of the Boy and the Girl had on your interpretation of the meaning of the dialogue between the mother and her son.

2. One of the central issues implied in the first scene of the play is that home is "an anachronism." Discuss how this point is developed in the play. Do you agree that home is an anachronism?

3. Explain the nature of the relationship between the Mother and Aunt Sophie as well as that between the Son and Aunt Sophie. Why does the Mother begin and end with the assertion that her son is like his Aunt Sophie?

4. What kind of relationship did Michael have with his real father? With Will? How have these relationships affected Michael's character?

5. Why does the Mother turn to the Lord to find retribution and salvation? What does the play imply about the Mother's decision? How do you feel about the Mother's decision to turn to religion?

6. Interpret the meaning of the relationship between the Girl and the Boy. What values do they represent?

IDEAS FOR WRITING

1. Relate your understanding of the mother-son relationship explored in the play to your own relationship or to the relationships that you have observed through personal experience, through popular culture, and in literature. In what ways is their relationship representative of qualities that are common to many mother-son relationships?

2. Write an essay in which you discuss whether or not you think that home is an anachronism. Refer to the play, other selections in this chapter, personal experiences, and popular culture to support your point of view.

And the Soul Shall Dance
Wakako Yamauchi

Journal

Write about the tensions within a first-generation immigrant family, either your own family, a family in your community, or one that you know of through popular culture. What was it that especially touched you about the conflict and struggle?

ACT ONE
Scene 1

Interior of the MURATA *house, afternoon. The set is spare. There is a kitchen table, four chairs, a bed, and on the wall, a calendar indicating the year and month: June, 1935. There is a doorway leading to the other room. Props are: a bottle of sake, two cups, a dish of chiles, a phonograph, and two towels hanging on pegs on the wall. A wide wooden bench sits outside.*

The bathhouse has just burned to the ground due to the carelessness of MASAKO, Nisei *daughter, eleven. Offstage there are sounds of* MURATA, *forty,* Issei *farmer, putting out the fire.*

Inside the house HANA MURATA, Issei *wife, in a drab house dress, confronts* MASAKO, *who is wearing a summer dress of the era.* MASAKO *is sullen and somewhat defiant.* HANA *breaks the silence.*

HANA: How could you be so careless, Masako? You know you should be extra careful with fire. How often have I told you? Now the whole bathhouse is gone. I told you time and again, when you stoke a fire, you should see that everything is swept into the fireplace.

MURATA *enters. He's dressed in old work clothes. He suffers from heat and exhaustion.*

MURATA *(coughing):* Shack went up like a matchbox. . . . This kind of weather dries everything . . . just takes a spark to make a bonfire out of dry timber.

HANA: Did you save any of it?

MURATA: No. Couldn't . . .

HANA *(to* MASAKO*):* How many times have I told you . . .

MASAKO *moves nervously.*

MURATA: No use crying about it now. *Shikata ga nai.* It's gone now. No more bathhouse. That's all there is to it.

HANA: But you've got to tell her. Otherwise she'll make the same mistake. You'll be building a bathhouse every year.

MURATA *removes his shirt and wipes off his face. He throws his shirt on a chair and sits at the table.*

MURATA: *Baka!* Ridiculous!

MASAKO: I didn't do it on purpose. *(She goes to the bed, opens a book)*

HANA *(follows* MASAKO*):* I know that but you know what this means? It means we bathe in a bucket . . . inside the house. Carry water in from the pond, heat it on the stove. . . . We'll use more kerosene.

MURATA: Tub's still there. And the fireplace. We can still build a fire under the tub.

HANA *(shocked):* But no walls! Everyone in the country can see us!

MURATA: Wait till dark then. Wait till dark.

HANA: We'll be using a lantern. They'll still see us.

MURATA: Angh! Who? Who'll see us? You think everyone in the country waits to watch us take a bath? Hunh! You know how stupid you sound? Ridiculous!

HANA *(defensively):* It'll be inconvenient.

HANA *is saved by a rap on the door.* OKA, Issei *neighbor, forty-five, enters. He is short and stout, dressed in faded work clothes.*

OKA: Hello! Hello! Oi! What's going on here? Hey! Was there some kind of fire?

HANA *rushes to the door to let* OKA *in. He stamps the dust from his shoes and enters.*

HANA: Oka-san! You just wouldn't believe. . . . We had a terrible thing happen.

OKA: Yeah. Saw the smoke from down the road. Thought it was your house. Came rushing over. Is the fire out?

MURATA *half rises and sits back again. He's exhausted.*

MURATA *(gesturing):* Oi, oi. Come in . . . sit down. No big problem. It was just our bathhouse.

OKA: Just the *furoba*, eh?

MURATA: Just the bath.

HANA: Our Masako was careless and the *furoba* caught fire. There's nothing left of it but the tub.

MASAKO *looks up from her book, pained. She makes a very small sound.*

OKA: Long as the tub's there, no problem. I'll help you with it. *(He starts to roll up his sleeves.* MURATA *looks at him)*

MURATA: What . . . now? Now?

OKA: Long as I'm here.

HANA: Oh, Papa. Aren't we lucky to have such friends?

MURATA *(to* HANA*):* Hell, we can't work on it now. The ashes are still hot. I just now put the damned fire out. Let me rest awhile. *(To* OKA*)* Oi, how about a little sake? *(Gesturing to* HANA*)* Make sake for Oka-san.

OKA *sits at the table.* HANA *goes to prepare the sake. She heats it, gets out the cups and pours it for the men.*

  I'm tired . . . I am *tired.*

HANA: Oka-san has so generously offered his help . . .

OKA *is uncomfortable. He looks around and sees* MASAKO *sitting on the bed.*

OKA: Hello, there, Masako-chan. You studying?

MASAKO: No, it's summer vacation.

MURATA *(sucking in his breath):* Kids nowadays . . . no manners . . .

HANA: She's sulking because I had to scold her.

MASAKO *makes a small moan.*

MURATA: Drink Oka-san.

OKA *(swallowing):* Ahhh, that's good.

MURATA: Eh, you not working today?

OKA: No . . . no . . . I took the afternoon off today. I was driving over to Nagatas' when I saw this big black cloud of smoke coming from your yard.

HANA: It went up so fast . . .

MURATA: What's up at Nagatas'? *(To* HANA*)* Get the chiles out. Oka-san loves chiles.

HANA *opens a jar of chiles and puts them on a plate. She serves the men and gets her mending basket and walks to* MASAKO. MASAKO *makes room for her on the bed.*

OKA *(helping himself):* Ah, chiles. (MURATA *looks at him, the question unanswered)* Well, I want to see him about my horse. I'm thinking of selling my horse.

MURATA: Sell your horse!

OKA *(scratches his head):* The fact is, I need some money. Nagata-san's the only one around made money this year, and I'm thinking he might want another horse.

MURATA: Yeah, he made a little this year. And he's talking big . . . big! Says he's leasing twenty more acres this fall.

OKA: Twenty acres?

MURATA: Yeah. He might want another horse.

OKA: Twenty acres, eh?

MURATA: That's what he says. But you know his old woman makes all the decisions.

OKA *scratches his head.*

HANA: They're doing all right.

MURATA: Henh. Nagata-kun's so hen-pecked, it's pathetic. *Peko-peko.* *(He makes motions of a hen pecking)*

OKA *(feeling the strain):* I better get over there.

MURATA: Why the hell you selling your horse?

OKA: I need cash.

MURATA: Oh, yeah. I could use some too. Seems like everyone's getting out of the depression but the poor farmers. Nothing changes for us. We go on and on planting our tomatoes and summer squash and eating them. . . . Well, at least it's healthy.

HANA: Papa, do you have lumber?

MURATA: Lumber? For what?

HANA: The bath.

MURATA (impatiently): Don't worry about that. We need more sake now.

HANA rises to serve him.

OKA: You sure Nagata-kun's working twenty more acres?

MURATA: Last I heard. What the hell; if you need a few bucks, I can loan you . .
.

OKA: A few hundred. I need a few hundred dollars.

MURATA: Oh, a few hundred. But what the hell you going to do without a horse? Out here a man's horse is as important as his wife.

OKA (seriously): I don't think Nagata will buy my wife.

The men laugh, but HANA doesn't find it so funny. MURATA glances at her. She fills the cups again. OKA makes a half-hearted gesture to stop her. MASAKO watches the pantomime carefully. OKA swallows his drink in one gulp.

I better get moving.

MURATA: What's the big hurry?

OKA: Like to get the horse business done.

MURATA: Ehhhh . . . relax. Do it tomorrow. He's not going to die, is he?

OKA (laughing): Hey, he's a good horse. I want to get it settled today. If Nagata-kun won't buy, I got to find someone else. You think maybe Kawaguchi . . . ?

MURATA: Not Kawaguchi. . . . Maybe Yamamoto.

HANA: What is all the money for, Oka-san? Does Emiko-san need an operation?

OKA: Nothing like that . . .

HANA: Sounds very mysterious.

OKA: No mystery, Mrs. No mystery. No sale, no money, no story.

MURATA (laughing): That's a good one. "No sale, no money, no. . . ." Eh, Mama.

He points to the empty cups. HANA fills the cups and goes back to MASAKO.

HANA (muttering): I see we won't be getting any work done today. (To MASAKO) Are you reading again? Maybe we'd still have a bath if you—

MASAKO: I didn't do it on purpose.

MURATA (loudly): I sure hope you know what you're doing, Oka-kun. What'd you do without a horse?

OKA: I was hoping you'd lend me yours now and then . . . (He looks at HANA) I'll pay for some of the feed.

MURATA (emphatically waving his hand): Sure! Sure!

OKA: The fact is, I need that money. I got a daughter in Japan and I just got to send for her this year.

Coming to life, HANA *puts down her mending and sits at the table.*

HANA: A daughter? You have a daughter in Japan? Why, I didn't know you had children. Emiko-san and you . . . I thought you were childless.

OKA *(scratching his head):* We are. I was married before.

MURATA: You son-of-a-gun!

HANA: Is that so? How old is your daughter?

OKA: Kiyoko must be . . . fifteen now. Yeah, fifteen.

HANA: Fifteen! Oh, that *would* be too old for Emiko-san's child. Is Kiyoko-san living with relatives in Japan?

OKA *(reluctantly):* Yeah, with grandparents. With Shizue's parents. Well, the fact is, Shizue, that's my first wife, and Emiko were sisters. They come from a family with no sons. I was a boy when I went to work for the family . . . as an apprentice . . . they're blacksmiths. Later I married Shizue and took on the family name—you know, *yoshi*—because they had no sons. My real name is Sakakihara.

MURATA: Sakakihara! That's a great name!

HANA: A magnificent name!

OKA: No one knows me by that here.

MURATA: Should have kept that . . . Sakakihara.

OKA *(muttering):* I don't even know myself by that name.

HANA: And Shizue-san passed away and you married Emiko-san?

OKA: Oh, yeah. Well, Shizue and I lived with the family for a while and we had the baby . . . that's, you know, Kiyoko. . . . *(The liquor has affected him and he's become less inhibited)* Well, while I was serving apprentice with the family, they always looked down their noses at me. After I married, it got worse. . . . That old man . . . angh! He was terrible! Always pushing me around, making me look bad in front of my wife and kid. That old man was mean . . . ugly!

MURATA: Yeah, I heard about that apprentice work—*detchi-boko* . . . . Heard it was damned humiliating.

OKA: That's the God's truth!

MURATA: Never had to do it myself. I came to America instead. They say *detchi-boko* is bloody hard work.

OKA: The work's all right. I'm not afraid of work. It's the humiliation! I hated them! Pushing me around like I was still a boy. . . . Me, a grown man! And married to their daughter! *(MURATA groans in sympathy)* Well, Shizue and I talked it over and we decided the best thing was to get away. We thought if I came to America and made some money . . . you know, send her money until we had enough, I'd go back and we'd leave the family . . . you know, move to another province . . . start a small business, maybe in the city, a noodle shop or something.

MURATA: That's everyone's dream. Make money, go home and live like a king.

OKA: I worked like a dog. Sent every penny to Shizue. And then she died. She died on me!

HANA *and* MURATA *observe a moment of silence in respect for* OKA'S *anguish.*

HANA: And you married Emiko-san.

OKA: I didn't marry her. They married her to me! Right after Shizue died.

HANA: But Oka-san, you were lucky . . .

OKA: Before the body was cold! No respect! By proxy. The old man wrote me they were arranging a marriage by proxy for me and Emiko. They said she'd grown to be a beautiful woman and would serve me well.

HANA: Emiko-san *is* a beautiful woman.

OKA: And they sent her to me. Took care of everything! Immigration, fare, everything.

HANA: But she's your sister-in-law—Kiyoko's aunt. It's good to keep the family together.

OKA: That's what I thought. But hear this: Emiko was the favored one. Shizue was not so pretty, not so smart. They were grooming Emiko for a rich man—his name was Yamoto—lived in a grand house in the village. They sent her to schools, you know, the culture thing: tea ceremony, you know, all that. They didn't even like me, and suddenly they married her to me.

MURATA: Yeah. You don't need all that formal training to make it over here. Just a strong back.

HANA: And a strong will.

OKA: It was all arranged. I couldn't do anything about it.

HANA: It'll be all right. With Kiyoko coming . . .

OKA *(dubiously):* I hope so . . . I never knew human beings could be so cruel. You know how they mistreated my daughter? You know after Emiko came over, things got from bad to worse and I *never* had enough money to send to Kiyoko.

MURATA: They don't know what it's like here. They think money's picked off the ground here.

OKA: And they treated Kiyoko so bad. They told her I forgot about her. They told her I didn't care—they said I abandoned her. Well, she knew better. She wrote to me all the time and I always told her I'd send for her . . . soon as I got the money. *(He shakes his head)* I just got to do something this year.

HANA: She'll be happier here. She'll know her father cares.

OKA: Kids tormented her for not having parents.

MURATA: Kids are cruel.

HANA: Masako will help her. She'll help her get started at school. She'll make friends . . . she'll be all right.

OKA: I hope so. She'll need friends. *(He considers he might be making a mistake after all)* What could I say to her? Stay there? It's not what you think over here? I can't help her? I just have to do this thing. I just have to do this one thing for her.

MURATA: Sure . . .

HANA: Don't worry. It'll work out fine.

MURATA *gestures to* HANA. *She fills the cups.*

MURATA: You talk about selling your horse, I thought you were pulling out.

OKA: I wish I could. But there's nothing else I can do.

MURATA: Without money, yeah . . .

OKA: You can go into some kind of business with money, but a man like me . . . no education . . . there's no kind of job I can do. I'd starve in the city.

MURATA: Dishwashing, maybe. Janitor . . .

OKA: At least here we can eat. Carrots, maybe, but we can eat.

MURATA: All the carrots we been eating 'bout to turn me into a rabbit.

They laugh. HANA *starts to pour more wine for* OKA *but he stops her.*

OKA: I better not drink any more. Got to drive to Nagata-san's yet. *(He rises and walks over to* MASAKO*)* You study hard, don't you? You'll teach Kiyoko English, eh? When she gets here . . .

HANA: Oh, yes. She will.

MURATA: Kiyoko-san could probably teach her a thing or two.

OKA: She won't know about American ways . . .

MASAKO: I'll help her.

HANA: Don't worry, Oka-san. She'll have a good friend in our Masako.

They move toward the door.

OKA: Well, thanks for the sake. I guess I talk too much when I drink. *(He scratches his head and laughs)* Oh. I'm sorry about the fire. By the way, come to my house for your bath . . . until you build yours again.

HANA *(hesitantly)*: Oh, uh . . . thank you. I don't know if . . .

MURATA: Good! Good! Thanks a lot. I need a good hot bath tonight.

OKA: Tonight, then.

MURATA: We'll be there.

HANA *(bowing)*: Thank you very much. Sayonara.

OKA *(nodding)*: See you tonight.

OKA *leaves.* HANA *faces her husband as soon as the door closes.*

HANA: Papa, I don't know about going over there.

MURATA *(surprised)*: Why?

HANA: Well, Emiko-san . . .

MURATA *(irritated)*: What's the matter with you? We need a bath and Oka's invited us over.

HANA *(to* MASAKO*)*: Help me clear the table.

MASAKO *reluctantly leaves her book and begins to clear the table.*

Papa, you know we've been neighbors already three, four years and Emiko-san's never been very hospitable.

MURATA: She's shy, that's all.

HANA: Not just shy . . . she's strange. I feel like she's pushing me off . . . she makes me feel like—I don't know—like I'm prying or something.

MURATA: Maybe you are.

HANA: And never puts out a cup of tea. . . . If she had all that training in the graces . . . why, a cup of tea . . .

MURATA: So if you want tea, ask for it.

HANA: I can't do that, Papa. She's strange . . . I don't know . . . *(To* MASAKO*)* When we go there, be very careful not to say anything wrong.

MASAKO: I never say anything anyway.

HANA *(thoughtfully):* Would you believe the story Oka-san just told? Why, I never knew . . .

MURATA: There're lot of things you don't know. Just because a man don't . . . talk about them, don't mean he don't feel . . . don't think about . . .

HANA *(looking around):* We'll have to take something . . . There's nothing to take . . . Papa, maybe you can dig up some carrots.

MURATA: God, Mama, be sensible. They got carrots. Everybody's got carrots.

HANA: Something . . . maybe I should make something.

MURATA: Hell, they're not expecting anything.

HANA: It's not good manners to go empty-handed.

MURATA: We'll take the sake.

HANA *grimaces.* MASAKO *sees the record player.*

MASAKO: I know, Mama. We can take the Victrola! We can play records for Mrs. Oka. Then nobody has to talk.

MURATA *laughs. Fade-out.*

Scene 2

That evening. We see the exterior wall of the OKAS' *weathered house. There is a workable screen door and a large screened window. Outside there is a wide wooden bench that can accommodate three or four people. There is one separate chair and a lantern stands against the house.*

The last rays of the sun light the area in a soft golden glow. This light grows gray as the scene progresses and it is quite dark at the end of the scene.

Through the screened window, EMIKO OKA, Issei *woman, thirty, can be seen walking erratically back and forth. She wears a drab cotton dress but her grace and femininity come through. Her hair is in a bun, in the style of Issei women of the era.*

OKA *sits cross-legged on the bench. He wears a yukata [summer robe] and fans himself with a round Japanese fan.*

The MURATAS *enter.* MURATA *carries towels and a bottle of sake.* HANA *carries the* Victrola, *and* MASAKO *a package containing their* yukatas.

OKA *(standing to receive the* MURATAS*):* Oh, you've come. Welcome!

MURATA: Yah. . . . Good of you to ask us.

HANA *(bowing):* Yes, thank you very much. *(To* MASAKO*)* Say "hello," Masako.

MASAKO: Hello.

HANA: And "thank you."

MASAKO: Thank you.

OKA *makes motion of protest.* EMIKO *stops her pacing and watches from the window.*

HANA *(glancing briefly at the window):* And how is Emiko-san this evening?

OKA *(turning toward the house):* Emi! Emiko!

HANA: That's all right. Don't call her out. She must be busy.

OKA *(half rising):* Emiko!

EMIKO *comes to the door.* HANA *starts a deep bow toward the door.*

MURATA: *Konbanwa* [Good evening]!

HANA: *Konbanwa,* Emiko-san. I feel so bad about this intrusion. Your husband has told you, our bathhouse was destroyed by fire and he graciously invited us to come use yours.

EMIKO *shakes her head.*

OKA: I didn't have a chance to . . .

HANA *(recovering and nudging* MASAKO*):* Say hello to Mrs. Oka.

MASAKO: Hello, Mrs. Oka.

HANA *lowers the Victrola onto the bench.*

OKA: What's this? You brought a phonograph?

MASAKO: It's a Victrola.

HANA *(laughing indulgently):* Yes. Masako wanted to bring this over and play some records.

MURATA *(extending the wine):* Brought a little sake too.

OKA *(taking the bottle):* Ah, now that I like. Emiko, bring out the cups.

He waves at his wife, but she doesn't move. He starts to ask again, but decides to get them himself. He enters the house and returns with two cups. EMIKO *seats herself on the single chair. The* MURATAS *unload their paraphernalia;* OKA *pours the wine, the men drink,* HANA *chatters and sorts the records.* MASAKO *stands by, helping her.*

HANA: Yes, our Masako loves to play records. I like records too . . . and Papa, he . . .

MURATA *(watching* EMIKO*):* They take me back home. The only way I can get there . . . in my mind.

HANA: Do you like music, Emiko-san? *(*EMIKO *looks vague but smiles faintly)* Okasan, you like them, don't you?

OKA: Yeah. But I don't have a player. No chance to hear them.

MURATA: I had to get this for them. They wouldn't leave me alone until I got it. Well . . . a phonograph . . . what the hell, they got to have some fun.

HANA: We don't have to play them, if you'd rather not . . .

OKA: Play. Play them.

HANA: I thought we could listen to them and relax. *(She extends some records to* EMIKO*)* Would you like to look through these, Emiko-san?

EMIKO *doesn't respond. She pulls out a sack of Bull Durham and starts to roll a cigarette.* HANA *pushes* MASAKO *to her.*

Take these to her.

MASAKO *moves toward* EMIKO *with the records.* MASAKO *stands watching her as she lights her cigarette.*

Some of these are very old. You might know them, Emiko-san. *(She sees* MASAKO *watching* EMIKO*)* Masako, bring those over here. *(She laughs uncom-*

fortably) **You might like this one, Emiko-san . . .** *(She starts the player)* **Do you know it?**

The record whines out "Kago No Tori." EMIKO *listens with her head cocked. She smokes her cigarette. She becomes wrapped in nostalgia and memories of the past.* MASAKO *watches her carefully.*

MASAKO *(whispering):* **Mama, she's crying.**

Startled, HANA *and* MURATA *look toward* EMIKO.

HANA *(pinching* MASAKO*):* **Shhh. The smoke is in her eyes.**

MURATA: **Did you bring the record I like, Mama?**

EMIKO *rises abruptly and enters the house.*

MASAKO: **They were tears, Mama.**

HANA: **From yawning, Masako.** *(Regretfully, to* OKA*)* **I'm afraid we've offended her.**

OKA *(unaware):* **Hunh? Aw . . . no . . . pay no attention . . . no offense . . .**

MASAKO *looks toward the window.* EMIKO *stands forlornly and slowly drifts into a dance.*

HANA: **I'm very sorry. Children, you know . . . they'll say anything, anything that's on their minds.**

MURATA *(notices* MASAKO *watching* EMIKO *through the window and tries to divert her attention):* **The needles. Masako, where're the needles?**

MASAKO *(still watching):* **I forgot them.**

HANA *sees what's going on.* OKA *is unaware.*

HANA: **Masako, go take your bath now. Masako . . .**

MASAKO *reluctantly picks up her towel and leaves.*

OKA: **Yeah, yeah . . . take your bath.**

MURATA *(sees* EMIKO *still dancing):* **Change the record, Mama.**

OKA *(still unaware):* **That's kind of sad.**

MURATA: **No use to get sick over a record. We're supposed to enjoy.**

HANA *stops the record.* EMIKO *disappears from the window.* HANA *selects a lively* ondo *[folk dance]—"Tokyo Ondo."*

HANA: **We'll find something more fun.**

The three begin to tap their feet to the music.

Can't you just see the festival? The dancers, the bright kimonos, the paper lanterns bobbing in the wind, the fireflies . . . how nostalgic. . . . Oh, how nostalgic . . .

From the side of the house, EMIKO *appears. Her hair is down, she wears an old straw hat. She dances in front of the* MURATAS. *They're startled. After the first shock, they watch with frozen smiles. They try to join* EMIKO'S *mood but something is missing.* OKA *is grieved. He finally stands as though he's had enough.* EMIKO, *now close to the door, ducks into the house.*

That was pretty . . . very nice . . .

OKA *settles down and grunts.* MURATA *clears his throat and* MASAKO *returns from her bath.*

MURATA: **You're done already?** *(He's glad to see her)*

MASAKO: I wasn't very dirty. The water was too hot.

MURATA: Good! Just the way I like it.

HANA: Not dirty?

MURATA (*picking up his towel*): Come on, Mama . . . scrub my back.

HANA (*laughing embarrassedly*): Oh, oh . . . well . . . *(She stops the player)* Masako, now don't forget . . . crank the machine and change the needle now and then.

MASAKO: I didn't bring them.

HANA: Oh. Oh . . . all right. I'll be back soon . . . don't forget . . . crank.

She leaves with her husband. OKA and MASAKO are alone. OKA is awkward and falsely hearty.

OKA: So! So you don't like hot baths, eh?

MASAKO: Not too hot.

OKA (*laughing*): I thought you like it real hot. Hot enough to burn the house down. That's a little joke.

MASAKO *busies herself with the records to conceal her annoyance.*

I hear you're real good in school. Always top of the class.

MASAKO: It's a small class. Only two of us.

OKA: When Kiyoko comes, you'll help her in school, yeah? You'll take care of her . . . a favor for me, eh?

MASAKO: Okay.

OKA: You'll be her friend, eh?

MASAKO: Okay.

OKA: That's good. That's good. You'll like her. She's a nice girl too. *(He stands, yawns, and stretches)* I'll go for a little walk now. *(He touches his crotch to indicate his purpose)*

MASAKO *turns her attention to the records and selects one—"The Soul Shall Dance"— and begins to sway to the music. The song draws EMIKO from the house. She looks out the window, sees MASAKO is alone and begins to slip into a dance.*

EMIKO: Do you like that song, Masa-chan?

MASAKO *is startled and draws back. She remembers her mother's warning. She doesn't know what to do. She nods.*

That's one of my favorite songs. I remember in Japan I used to sing it so often . . . my favorite song . . . *(She sings along with the record)*

Akai kuchibiru
Kappu ni yosete
Aoi sake nomya
Kokoro ga odoru . . .

Do you know what that means, Masa-chan?

MASAKO: I think so. . . . The soul will dance?

EMIKO: Yes, yes, that's right.

The soul shall dance.
Red lips against a glass
Drink the green . . .

MASAKO: Wine?

EMIKO *(nodding):* Drink the green wine.

MASAKO: Green? I thought wine is purple.

EMIKO *(nodding):* Wine is purple . . . but this is a green liqueur. *(She holds up one of the china cups as though it were crystal, and looks at it as though the light were shining through it and she sees the green liquid)* It's good . . . it warms your heart.

MASAKO: And the soul dances.

EMIKO: Yes.

MASAKO: What does it taste like? The green wine . . .

EMIKO: Oh, it's like . . . it's like . . .

The second verse starts. "Kurai yoru no yume/ Setsunasa yo/ Aoi sake nomya/ Yume mo odoru. . . ."

MASAKO: In the dark night . . .

EMIKO: Dreams are unbearable . . . insufferable . . . *(She turns sad)*

MASAKO: Drink the . . .

EMIKO *(nodding):* Drink the green wine . . .

MASAKO: And the dreams will dance.

EMIKO *(softly):* I'll be going back one day . . .

MASAKO: To where?

EMIKO: My home . . . Japan . . . my real home. I'm planning to go back.

MASAKO: By yourself?

EMIKO *(nodding):* Oh, yes. It's a secret. You can keep a secret?

MASAKO: Uh-huh. I have lots of secrets . . . all my own . . .

The music stops. EMIKO *sees* OKA *approaching and disappears into the house.* MASAKO *attends to the record and does not know* EMIKO *is gone.*

Secrets I never tell anyone.

OKA: Secrets? What kind of secrets? What did she say?

MASAKO: Oh. Nothing.

OKA: What did you talk about?

MASAKO: Nothing. . . . Mrs. Oka was talking about the song. She was telling me what it meant . . . about the soul.

OKA *(scoffing):* Heh! What does she know about soul? *(calming down)* Ehhh . . . some people don't have them . . . souls.

MASAKO *(timidly):* I thought . . . I think everyone has a soul. I read in a book . . .

OKA *(laughing):* Maybe . . . maybe you're right. I'm not an educated man, you know . . . I don't know too much about books. When Kiyoko comes you can talk to her about it. Kiyoko is very . . .

From inside the house, we hear EMIKO *begin to sing loudly at the name Kiyoko as though trying to drown it out.* OKA *stops talking. Then resumes.*

Kiyoko is very smart. You'll have a good time with her. She'll learn your language fast. How old did you say you are?

MASAKO: Almost twelve.

By this time OKA *and* MASAKO *are shouting, trying to be heard above* EMIKO'S *singing.*

OKA: Kiyoko is fifteen. . . . Kiyoko . . .

OKA *is exasperated. He rushes into the house seething.* MASAKO *hears* OKA'S *muffled rage: "Behave yourself," and "kitchigai" come through.* MASAKO *slinks to the window and looks in.* OKA *slaps* EMIKO *around.* MASAKO *reacts to the violence.* OKA *comes out.* MASAKO *returns to the bench in time. He pulls his fingers through his hair and sits next to* MASAKO. *She very slightly draws away.*

Want me to light a lantern?

MASAKO *(shaken):* No . . . ye— . . . okay . . .

OKA: We'll get a little light here . . .

He lights the lantern as the MURATAS *return from their bath. They are in good spirits.*

MURATA: Ahhhh . . . Nothing like a good hot bath.

HANA: So refreshing . . .

MURATA: A bath should be taken hot and slow. Don't know how Masako gets through so fast.

HANA: She probably doesn't get in the tub.

MASAKO: I do.

Everyone laughs.

Well I do.

EMIKO *comes out. She has a large purple welt on her face. She sits on the separate chair, hands folded, quietly watching the* MURATAS. *They look at her with alarm.* OKA *engages himself with his fan.*

HANA: Oh! Emiko-san . . . what . . . ah-ah . . . whaa . . . *(She draws a deep breath)* What a nice bath we had . . . such a lovely bath. We do appreciate your hos . . . pitality. Thank you so much.

EMIKO: Lovely evening, isn't it?

HANA: Very lovely. Very. Ah, a little warm, but nice. . . . Did you get a chance to hear the records? *(Turning to* MASAKO*)* Did you play the records for Mrs. Oka?

MASAKO: Ye— . . . no. . . . The needle was . . .

EMIKO: Yes, she did. We played the records together.

MURATA: Oh, you played the songs together?

EMIKO: Yes . . . yes . . .

MURATA: That's nice. . . . Masako can understand pretty good, eh?

EMIKO: She understands everything . . . everything I say.

MURATA *(withdrawing):* Oh, yeah? Eh, Mama, we ought to be going . . . *(He closes the player)* Hate to bathe and run but . . .

HANA: Yes, yes. Tomorrow is a busy day. Come, Masako.

EMIKO: Please . . . stay a little longer.

MURATA: Eh, well, we got to be going.

HANA: Why, thank you, but . . .

EMIKO: It's still quite early.

OKA (*indicating he's ready to say good-bye*): Enjoyed the music. And the sake.

EMIKO: The records are very nice. Makes me remember Japan. I sang those songs . . . those very songs. . . . Did you know I used to sing?

HANA (*politely*): Why, no . . . no. I didn't know that. You must have a very lovely voice.

EMIKO: Yes.

HANA: No, I didn't know that. That's very nice.

EMIKO: Yes, I sang. My parents were very strict . . . they didn't like it. They said it was frivolous. Imagine?

HANA: Yes, I can imagine. Things were like that . . . in those days singing was not considered proper for nice . . . I mean, only for women in the profess— . . .

MURATA: We better get home, Mama.

HANA: Yes, yes. What a shame you couldn't continue with it.

EMIKO: In the city I did do some classics: the dance, and the *koto,* and the flower, and of course, the tea . . . (*She makes the proper gesture for the different disciplines*) All those. Even some singing . . . classics, of course.

HANA (*politely*): Of course.

EMIKO: All of it is so disciplined . . . so disciplined. I was almost a *natori.*

HANA: Oh! How nice.

EMIKO: But everything changed.

HANA: Oh!

EMIKO: I was sent here to America. (*She glares at* OKA)

HANA: Oh, too bad . . . I mean, too bad about your *natori.*

MURATA (*loudly to* OKA): So did you see Nagata today?

OKA: Oh, yeah. Yeah.

MURATA: What did he say? Is he interested?

OKA: Yeah. Yeah. He's interested.

MURATA: He likes the horse, eh?

OKA: Ah . . . yeah.

MURATA: I knew he'd like him. I'd buy him myself if I had the money.

OKA: Well, I have to take him over tomorrow. He'll decide then.

MURATA: He'll buy . . . he'll buy. You'd better go straight over to the ticket office and get that ticket. Before you—ha-ha—spend the money.

OKA: Ha-ha. Yeah.

HANA: It'll be so nice when Kiyoko-san comes to join you. I know you're looking forward to it.

EMIKO (*confused*): Oh . . . oh . . .

HANA: Masako is so happy. It'll be good for her too.

EMIKO: I had more freedom in the city . . . I lived with an aunt and she let me . . . . She wasn't so strict.

MURATA *and* MASAKO *have their gear together and stand ready to leave.*

MURATA: Good luck on the horse tomorrow.

OKA: Yeah, thanks.

HANA *(bowing):* Many, many thanks.

OKA *(nodding toward the sake):* Thanks for the sake.

HANA *(bowing again):* Good night, Emiko-san. We'll see you again soon. We'll bring the records too.

EMIKO *(softly):* Those songs . . . those very songs . . .

MURATA: Let's go, Mama.

The MURATAS *pull away. Light follows them and grows dark on the* OKAS. *The* MURATAS *begin walking home.*

HANA: That was uncomfortable.

MASAKO: What's the matter with—

HANA: Shhhh!

MURATA: I guess Oka has his problems.

MASAKO: Is she really *kitchigai?*

HANA: Of course not. She's not crazy. Don't say that word, Masako.

MASAKO: I heard Mr. Oka call her that.

HANA: He called her that?

MASAKO: I . . . I think so.

HANA: You heard wrong, Masako. Emiko-san isn't crazy. She just likes her drinks. She had too much to drink tonight.

MASAKO: Oh.

HANA: She can't adjust to this life. She can't get over the good times she had in Japan. Well, it's not easy . . . but one has to know when to bend . . . like the bamboo. When the winds blow, bamboo bends. You bend or crack. Remember that, Masako.

MURATA *(laughing wryly):* Bend, eh? Remember that, Mama.

HANA *(softly):* You don't know . . . it isn't ever easy.

MASAKO: Do you want to go back to Japan, Mama?

HANA: Everyone does.

MASAKO: Do you, Papa?

MURATA: I'll have to make some money first.

MASAKO: I don't. Not me. Not Kiyoko . . .

HANA: After Kiyoko-san comes, Emiko will have company and things will straighten out. She has nothing to live on but memories. She doesn't have any friends. At least I have my friends at church . . . at least I have that. She must get awful lonely.

MASAKO: I know that. She tried to make friends with me.

HANA: She did? What did she say?

MASAKO: Well, sort of . . .

HANA: What did she say?

MASAKO: She didn't say anything. I just felt it. Maybe you should be her friend, Mama.

MURATA: Poor woman. We could have stayed longer.

HANA: But you wanted to leave. I tried to be friendly. You saw that. It's not easy to talk to Emiko. She either closes up, you can't pry a word from her, or else she goes on and on . . . all that . . . that . . . about the *koto* and tea and the flower . . . I mean, what am I supposed to say? She's so unpredictable. And the drinking . . .

MURATA: All right, all right, Mama.

MASAKO: Did you see her black eye?

HANA *(calming down):* She probably hurt herself. She wasn't very steady.

MASAKO: Oh, no. Mr. Oka hit her.

HANA: I don't think so.

MASAKO: He hit her. I saw him.

HANA: You saw that? Papa, do you hear that? She saw them. That does it. We're not going there again.

MURATA: Aww . . . Oka wouldn't do that. Not in front of a kid.

MASAKO: Well, they didn't do it in front of me. They were in the house.

MURATA: You see . . .

HANA: That's all right. You just have to fix the bathhouse. Either that or we're going to bathe at home . . . in a bucket. We're not going . . . we'll bathe at home. *(MURATA mutters to himself)* What?

MURATA: I said all right, it's the bucket then. I'll get to it when I can.

HANA *passes* MURATA *and walks ahead.*

Scene 3

Same evening. Lights cross-fade to the exterior of the OKA *house. The* MURATAS *have just left.* EMIKO *sits on the bench. Her back is to* OKA. OKA, *still standing, looks at her contemptuously as she takes the bottle and one of the cups to pour herself a drink.*

OKA: Nothing more disgusting than a drunk woman. *(EMIKO ignores him)* You made a fool of yourself. *Washi baka ni shite!* You made a fool of me!

EMIKO *doesn't move.*

EMIKO: One can only make a fool of oneself.

OKA: You learn that in the fancy schools, eh? *(EMIKO examines the pattern on her cup)* Eh? Eh? Answer me! *(EMIKO ignores him)* I'm talking to you. Answer me! *(Menacing)* You don't get away with that. You think you're so fine . . .

EMIKO *looks off into the horizon.* OKA *turns her roughly around.*

   When I talk, you listen!

EMIKO *turns away again.* OKA *pulls the cup from her hand.*

   Goddamnit! What'd you think my friends think of you? What kind of ass they think I am? *(He grabs her shoulders)*

EMIKO: Don't touch me . . . don't touch me.

OKA: Who the hell you think you are? "Don't touch me, don't touch me." Who the hell! High and mighty, eh? Too good for me, eh? Don't put on the act for me . . . I know who you are.

EMIKO: Tell me who I am, Mister Smart Peasant.

OKA: Shut your fool mouth, goddamnit! Sure! I'll tell you. I know all about you . . . Shizue told me. The whole village knows.

EMIKO: Shizue!

OKA: Yeah! Shizue. Embarrassed the hell out of her, your own sister.

EMIKO: Embarrassed? I have nothing to be ashamed of. I don't know what you're talking about.

OKA *(derisively)*: You don't know what I'm talking about. I know. The whole village knows. They're all laughing at you. At me! Stupid Oka got stuck with a second-hand woman. I didn't say anything because . . .

EMIKO: I'm not secondhand!

OKA: Who you trying to fool? I know. Knew long time ago. . . . Shizue wrote me all about your affairs in Tokyo. The men you were mess—

EMIKO: Affairs? Men?

OKA: That man you were messing with . . . I knew all along. I didn't say anything because you . . . I . . .

EMIKO: I'm not ashamed of it.

OKA: You're not ashamed! What the hell! Your father thought he was pulling a fast one on me . . . thought I didn't know nothing . . . thought I was some kind of dumb ass . . . I didn't say nothing because Shizue's dead . . . Shizue's dead. I was willing to give you a chance.

EMIKO *(laughing)*: A chance?

OKA: Yeah! A chance! Laugh! Give a *joro* another chance. Sure, I'm stupid . . . dumb.

EMIKO: I'm not a whore. I'm true . . . he knows I'm true.

OKA: True! Ha!

EMIKO: You think I'm untrue just because I let . . . let you. . . . There's only one man for me.

OKA: Let me *(obscene gesture)* you? I can do what I want with you. Your father palmed you off on me—like a dog or cat—an animal . . . couldn't do nothing with you. Even that rich dumb Yamato wouldn't have you. Your father—greedy father—so proud . . . making big plans for you . . . for himself. Ha! The whole village laughing at him . . . *(EMIKO hangs her head)* Shizue told me. And she was working like a dog . . . trying to keep your goddamn father happy . . . doing my work and yours.

EMIKO: My work?

OKA: Yeah, your work too! She killed herself working! She killed herself . . . *(He has tender memories of his dull, uncomplaining wife)* Up in the morning getting the fires started, working the bellows, cleaning the furnace, cooking, and late at night working with the sewing . . . tending the baby. . . . *(He mutters)* The goddamn family killed her. And you . . . you out there in Tokyo with the fancy clothes, doing the *(He sneers)* dance, the tea, the flower, the *koto,* and the . . . *(Obscene gesture)*

EMIKO *(hurting)*: Achhhh . . .

OKA: Did you have fun? Did you have fun on your sister's blood? *(EMIKO doesn't answer)* Did you? He must have been a son-of-a-bitch. . . . What would make that goddamn greedy old man send his prize mare to a plow horse like me? What kind of bum was he that your father—

EMIKO: He's not a bum . . . he's not a bum.

OKA: Was he Korean? Was he *Etta?* That's the only thing I could figure.

EMIKO: I'm true to him. Only him.

OKA: True? You think he's true to you? You think he waits for you? Remembers you? *Aho!* Think he cares?

EMIKO *(nodding quietly):* He does.

OKA: And waits ten years? *Baka!* Go back to Japan and see. You'll find out. Go back to Japan. *Kaire!*

EMIKO: In time.

OKA: In time? How about now?

EMIKO: I can't now.

OKA: Ha! Now! Go now! Who needs you? Who needs you? You think a man waits ten years for a woman? You think you're some kind of . . . of . . . diamond . . . treasure . . . he's going to wait his life for you? Go to him. He's probably married with ten kids. Go to him. Get out! Goddamn *joro* . . . Go! go!

He sweeps EMIKO *off the bench.*

EMIKO *(hurting):* Ahhhh! I . . . I don't have the money. Give me money to—

OKA: If I had money I would give it to you ten years ago. You think I been eating this *kuso* for ten years because I like it?

EMIKO: You're selling the horse. . . . Give me the—

OKA *(scoffing):* That's for Kiyoko. I owe you nothing.

EMIKO: Ten years, you owe me.

OKA: Ten years of what? Misery? You gave me nothing. I give you nothing. You want to go, pack your bag and start walking. Try cross the desert. When you get dry and hungry, think about me.

EMIKO: I'd die out there.

OKA: Die? You think I didn't die here?

EMIKO: I didn't do anything to you.

OKA: No, no you didn't. All I wanted was a little comfort and . . . you . . . no, you didn't. No. So you die. We all die. Shizue died. If she was here, she wouldn't treat me like this. . . . *(He thinks of his poor dead wife)* Ah, I should have brought her with me. She'd be alive now. We'd be poor but happy . . . like . . . like Murata and his wife . . . and the kid . . .

EMIKO: I wish she were alive too. I'm not to blame for her dying. I didn't know . . . I was away. I loved her. I didn't want her to die . . . I . . .

OKA *(softening):* I know that. I'm not blaming you for that. . . . And it's not my fault what happened to you either . . .

EMIKO *is silent and he mistakes that for a change in attitude. He is encouraged.*

You understand that, eh? I didn't ask for you. It's not my fault you're here in this desert . . . with . . . with me . . .

EMIKO *weeps.* OKA *reaches out.*

I know I'm too old for you. It's hard for me too . . . but this is the way it is. I just ask you be kinder . . . understand it wasn't my fault. Try make it easier for me . . . for yourself too.

OKA *touches her and she shrinks from his touch.*

EMIKO: Ach!

OKA (*humiliated again*): Goddamn it! I didn't ask for you! *Aho!* If you were smart you'd done as your father said . . . cut out that *saru shibai* with the *Etta* . . . married the rich Yamoto. Then you'd still be in Japan. Not here to make my life so miserable. (EMIKO *is silent*) And you can have your *Etta* . . . and anyone else you want. Take them all on . . . (*He is worn out. It's hopeless*) God, why do we do this all the time? Fighting, fighting all the time. There must be a better way to live . . . there must be another way.

OKA *waits for a response, gives up, and enters the house.* EMIKO *watches him leave and pours herself another drink. The storm has passed, the alcohol takes over. She turns to the door* OKA *disappeared into.*

EMIKO: Because I must keep the dream alive . . . the dream is all I live for. I am only in exile now. Because if I give in, all I've lived before . . . will mean nothing . . . will be for nothing. . . . Because if I let you make me believe this is all there is to my life, the dream would die . . . I would die . . . (*She pours another drink and feels warm and good*)

Fade-out.

End of Act One

ACT TWO

Scene 1

MURATAS' *kitchen, afternoon. The calendar reads September.* MASAKO *is at the kitchen table with several books. She thumbs through a Japanese magazine.* HANA *is with her, sewing.*

MASAKO: Do they always wear kimonos in Japan, Mama?

HANA: Most of the time.

MASAKO: I wonder if Kiyoko will be wearing a kimono like this?

HANA (*peering into* MASAKO's *magazine*): They don't dress like that . . . not for everyday.

MASAKO: I wonder what she's like.

HANA: Probably a lot like you. What do you think she's like?

MASAKO: She's probably taller.

HANA: Mr. Oka isn't tall.

MASAKO: And pretty . . .

HANA (*laughing*): Mr. Oka. . . . Well, I don't suppose she'll look like her father.

MASAKO: Mrs. Oka is pretty.

HANA: She isn't Kiyoko-san's real mother, remember.

MASAKO: Oh. That's right.

HANA: But they are related. Well, we'll soon see.

MASAKO: I thought she was coming in September. It's already September.

HANA: Papa said Oka-san went to San Pedro a few days ago. He should be back soon with Kiyoko-san.

MASAKO: Didn't Mrs. Oka go too?

HANA *(glancing toward the* OKA *house):* I don't think so. I see lights in their house at night.

MASAKO: Will they bring Kiyoko over to see us?

HANA: Of course. First thing, probably. You'll be very nice to her, won't you?

MASAKO *(leaves the table and finds another book):* Sure. I'm glad I'm going to have a friend. I hope she likes me.

HANA: She'll like you. Japanese girls are very polite, you know.

MASAKO: We have to be or our mamas get mad at us.

HANA: Then I should be getting mad at you more often.

MASAKO: It's often enough already, Mama. *(She opens a hardback book)* Look at this, Mama . . . I'm going to show her this book.

HANA: She won't be able to read at first.

MASAKO: I love this story. Mama, this is about people like us—settlers—it's about the prairie. We live in a prairie, don't we?

HANA: Prairie? Does that mean desert?

MASAKO: I think so.

HANA *(nodding and looking bleak):* We live in a prairie.

MASAKO: It's about the hardships and the floods and droughts and how they have nothing but each other.

HANA *(nodding):* We have nothing but each other. But these people—they're white people.

MASAKO *(nodding):* Sure, Mama. They come from the East. Just like you and Papa came from Japan.

HANA: We come from the Far Far East. That's different. White people are different from us.

MASAKO: I know that.

HANA: White people among white people . . . that's different from Japanese among white people. You know what I'm saying?

MASAKO: I know that. How come they don't write books about us . . . about Japanese people?

HANA: Because we're nobodies here.

MASAKO: If I didn't read these, there'd be nothing for me . . .

HANA: Some of the things you read, you're never going to know.

MASAKO: I can dream though.

HANA *(sighing):* Sometimes the dreaming makes the living harder. Better to keep your head out of the clouds.

MASAKO: That's not much fun.

HANA: You'll have fun when Kiyoko-san comes. You can study together, you can sew, and sometimes you can try some of those fancy American recipes.

MASAKO: Mama, you have to have chocolate and cream and things like that.

HANA: We'll get them.

We hear the putt-putt of OKA'S *old car.* MASAKO *and* HANA *pause and listen.* MASAKO *runs to the window.*

MASAKO: I think it's them!

HANA: The Okas?

MASAKO: It's them! It's them!

HANA stands and looks out. She removes her apron and puts away her sewing.

HANA: Two of them. Emiko-san isn't with them. Let's go outside.

OKA and KIYOKO, *fourteen, enter.* OKA *is wearing his going-out clothes: a sweater, white shirt, dark pants, but no tie.* KIYOKO *walks behind him. She is short, chunky, broad-chested and very self-conscious. Her hair is straight and banded into two shucks. She wears a conservative cotton dress, white socks and two-inch heels.* OKA *is proud. He struts in, his chest puffed out.*

OKA: Hello, hello. . . . We're here. We made it! *(He pushes* KIYOKO *forward)* This is my daughter, Kiyoko. *(To* KIYOKO*)* Murata-san . . . remember I was talking about? My friends . . .

KIYOKO *(barely audible as she speaks a standard formal greeting, bowing deeply):* Hajime mashite yoroshiku onegai shimasu . . .

HANA *(also bowing formally):* I hope your journey was pleasant.

OKA *(While the women are still bowing, he pushes* KIYOKO *toward* MASAKO.*)* This is Masako-chan; I told you about her . . .

MASAKO is shocked at KIYOKO'S *appearance. The girl she expected is already a woman. She stands with her mouth agape and withdraws noticeably.* HANA *rushes in to fill the awkwardness.*

HANA: Say hello, Masako. My goodness, where are your manners? *(She laughs apologetically)* In this country they don't make much to-do about manners. *(She stands back to examine* KIYOKO*)* My, my, I didn't picture you so grown up. My, my. . . . Tell me, how was your trip?

OKA *(proudly):* We just drove in from Los Angeles just this morning. We spent the night in San Pedro and the next two days we spent in Los Angeles . . . you know, Japanese town.

HANA: How nice!

OKA: Kiyoko was so excited. Twisting her head this way and that—couldn't see enough with her big eyes. *(He imitates her fondly)* She's from the country, you know . . . just a big country girl. Got all excited about the Chinese dinner—we had a Chinese dinner. She never ate it before.

KIYOKO *covers her mouth and giggles.*

HANA: Chinese dinner!

OKA: Oh, yeah. Duck, *pakkai,* chow mein, seaweed soup . . . the works!

HANA: A feast!

OKA: Oh, yeah. Like a holiday. Two holidays. Two holidays in one.

HANA *(pushes* MASAKO *forward):* Two holidays in one! Kiyoko-san, our Masako has been looking forward to meeting you.

KIYOKO *(bowing again):* Hajime mashite . . .

HANA: She's been thinking of all sorts of things she can do with you: sewing, cooking . . .

MASAKO: Oh, Mama.

KIYOKO *covers her mouth and giggles.*

HANA: It's true, Kiyoko-san. She's been looking forward to having a best friend.

KIYOKO *giggles again and* MASAKO *pulls away.*

OKA: Kiyoko, you shouldn't be so shy. The Muratas are my good friends and you should feel free with them. Ask anything, say anything . . . right?

HANA: Of course, of course. *(She is slightly annoyed with* MASAKO*)* Masako, go in and start the tea.

MASAKO *enters the house.*

I'll call Papa. He's in the yard. Papa! Oka-san is here! *(To* KIYOKO*)* Now tell me, how was your trip? Did you get seasick?

KIYOKO *(bowing and nodding):* Eh [Yes]. A little . . .

OKA: Tell her. Tell her how sick you got.

KIYOKO *covers her mouth and giggles.*

HANA: Oh, I know, I know. I was too. That was a long time ago. I'm sure things are improved now. Tell me about Japan . . . what is it like now? They say it's so changed . . . modern . . .

OKA: Kiyoko comes from the country . . . backwoods. Nothing changes much there from century to century.

HANA: Ah! That's true. That's why I love Japan. And you wanted to leave. It's unbelievable. To come here!

OKA: She always dreamed about it.

HANA: Well, it's not really that bad.

OKA: No, it's not that bad. Depends on what you make of it.

HANA: That's right. What you make of it. I was just telling Masako today . . .

MURATA *enters. He rubs his hands to take off the soil and comes in grinning. He shakes* OKA'S *hand.*

MURATA: *Oi, oi . . .*

OKA: Yah . . . I'm back. This is my daughter.

MURATA: No! She's beautiful!

OKA: Finally made it. Finally got her here.

MURATA *(to* KIYOKO*):* Your father hasn't stopped talking about you all summer.

HANA: And Masako too.

KIYOKO *(bowing):* Hajime mashite . . .

MURATA *(acknowledging with a short bow):* Yah. How'd you like the trip?

OKA: I was just telling your wife—had a good time in Los Angeles. Had a couple of great dinners, took in the cinema—Japanese pictures, bought her some American clothes.

HANA: Oh, you bought that in Los Angeles.

MURATA: Got a good price for your horse, eh? Lots of money, eh?

OKA: Nagata's a shrewd bargainer. Heh. It don't take much money to make her happy. She's a country girl.

MURATA: That's all right. Country's all right. Country girl's the best.

OKA: Had trouble on the way back.

MURATA: Yeah?

OKA: Fan belt broke.

MURATA: That'll happen.

OKA: Lucky I was near a gasoline station. We were in the mountains. Waited in a restaurant while it was getting fixed.

HANA: Oh, that was good.

OKA: Guess they don't see Japanese much. Stare? Terrible! Took them a long time to wait on us. Dumb waitress practically threw the food at us. Kiyoko felt bad.

HANA: Ah! That's too bad . . . too bad. That's why I always pack a lunch when we take trips.

MURATA: They'll spoil the day for you . . . those barbarians!

OKA: Terrible food too. Kiyoko couldn't swallow the dry bread and bologna.

HANA: That's the food they eat!

MURATA: Let's go in . . . have a little wine. Mama, we got wine? This is a celebration.

HANA: I think so . . . a little . . .

They enter the house talking. MASAKO *has made the tea, and* HANA *begins to serve the wine.*

How is your "mother"? Was she happy to see you?

KIYOKO: Oh, she . . . yes . . .

HANA: I just know she was surprised to see you so grown up. Of course, you remember her from Japan, don't you?

KIYOKO *(nodding): Eh.* I can barely remember. I was very young . . .

HANA: Of course. But you do, don't you?

KIYOKO: She was gone most of the time . . . at school in Tokyo. She was very pretty, I remember that.

HANA: She's still very pretty.

KIYOKO: *Eh.* She was She was always laughing. She was much younger then.

HANA: Oh now, it hasn't been that long ago.

MASAKO *leaves the room to go outside. The following dialogue continues muted as light goes dim in the house and focuses on* MASAKO. EMIKO *enters, is drawn to the* MURATA *window and listens.*

OKA: We stayed at an inn on East First Street. *Shizuokaya.* Whole inn filled with Shizuoka people . . . talking the old dialect. Thought I was in Japan again.

MURATA: That right?

OKA: Felt good. Like I was in Japan again.

HANA *(to* KIYOKO*):* Did you enjoy Los Angeles?

KIYOKO *(nodding): Eh.*

OKA: That's as close as I'll get to Japan.

MURATA: *Mattakuna!* That's for sure.

Outside MASAKO *becomes aware of* EMIKO.

MASAKO: Why don't you go in?

EMIKO: Oh. Oh. Why don't you?

MASAKO: They're all grownups in there. I'm not grown up.

EMIKO *(softly):* All grownups. . . . Maybe I'm not either. *(Her mood changes)* Masa-chan, do you have a boyfriend?

MASAKO: I don't like boys. They don't like me.

EMIKO: Oh, that will change. You will change. I was like that too.

MASAKO: Besides, there're none around here . . . Japanese boys. . . . There are some at school, but they don't like girls.

HANA *(calling from the kitchen).* Masako . . .

MASAKO *doesn't answer.*

EMIKO: Your mother is calling you.

MASAKO *(answering her mother): Nani* [What]?

HANA *(from the kitchen):* Come inside now.

EMIKO: You'll have a boyfriend one day.

MASAKO: Not me.

EMIKO: You'll fall in love one day. Someone will make the inside of you light up, and you'll know you're in love. *(She relives her own experience)* Your life will change . . . grow beautiful. It's good, Masa-chan. And this feeling you'll remember the rest of your life . . . will come back to you . . . haunt you . . . keep you alive . . . five, ten years . . . no matter what happens . . . keep you alive.

HANA *(from the kitchen):* Masako. . . . Come inside now.

MASAKO *turns aside to answer and* EMIKO *slips away.*

MASAKO: What, Mama?

HANA *(coming outside):* Come inside. Don't be so unsociable. Kiyoko wants to talk to you.

MASAKO *(watching* EMIKO *leave):* She doesn't want to talk to me. You're only saying that.

HANA: What's the matter with you? Don't you want to make friends with her?

MASAKO: She's not my friend. She's your friend.

HANA: Don't be so silly. She's only fourteen.

MASAKO: Fifteen. They said fifteen. She's your friend. She's an old lady.

HANA: Don't say that.

MASAKO: I don't like her.

HANA: Shhh! Don't say that.

MASAKO: She doesn't like me either.

HANA: Ma-chan. Remember your promise to Mr. Oka? You're going to take her to school, teach her the language, teach her the ways of Americans.

MASAKO: She can do it herself. You did.

HANA: That's not nice, Ma-chan.

MASAKO: I don't like the way she laughs. *(She imitates* KIYOKO *holding her hand to her mouth and giggling and bowing)*

HANA: Oh, how awful! Stop that. That's the way the girls do in Japan. Maybe she doesn't like your ways either. That's only a difference in manners. What you're doing now is considered very bad manners. *(She changes tone)*

Ma-chan . . . just wait—when she learns to read and speak, you'll have
so much to say to each other. Come on, be a good girl and come inside.

MASAKO: It's just old people in there, Mama. I don't want to go in.

HANA calls KIYOKO away from the table and speaks confidentially to her.

HANA: Kiyoko-san, please come here a minute. Maybe it's better for you to talk
to Masako alone.

KIYOKO leaves the table and walks to HANA outside.

Masako has a lot of things to tell you about . . . what to expect in school
and things . . .

MURATA *(calling from the table):* Mama, put out something . . . chiles . . . for Oka-
san.

*HANA leaves the two girls and enters the house. KIYOKO and MASAKO stand awkwardly,
KIYOKO glancing shyly at MASAKO.*

MASAKO: Do you like it here?

KIYOKO *(nodding): Eh.*

There's an uncomfortable pause.

MASAKO: School will be starting next week . . .

KIYOKO *(nodding): Eh.*

MASAKO: Do you want to walk to school with me?

KIYOKO *(nodding): Ah.*

MASAKO *(rolls her eyes and tries again):* I leave at 7:30.

KIYOKO: Ah.

There's a long pause. MASAKO finally gives up and moves offstage.

MASAKO: I have to do something.

*KIYOKO watches her leave and uncertainly moves back to the house. HANA looks up at
KIYOKO coming in alone, sighs, and quietly pulls out a chair for her. Fade-out.*

Scene 2

*November, night. Interior of the MURATA house. Lamps are lit. The family is at the
kitchen table. HANA sews, MASAKO does her homework, MURATA reads the paper.
They're dressed in warm robes and having tea. Outside, thunder rolls in the distance
and lightning flashes.*

HANA: It'll be *ohigan* [an autumn festival] soon.

MURATA: Something to look forward to.

HANA: We will need sweet rice for *omochi* [rice cakes].

MURATA: I'll order it next time I go to town.

HANA *(to MASAKO):* How is school? Getting a little harder?

MASAKO: Not that much. Sometimes the arithmetic is hard.

HANA: How is Kiyoko-san doing? Is she getting along all right?

MASAKO: She's good in arithmetic. She skipped a grade already.

HANA: Already? That's good news. Only November and she skipped a grade!
At this rate she'll be through before you.

MASAKO: Well, she's older.

MURATA: Sure, she's older, Mama.

HANA: Has she made any friends?

MASAKO: No. She follows me around all day. She understands okay, but she doesn't talk. She talks like, you know . . . she says "ranchi" for lunch and "ranchi" for ranch too, and like that. Kids laugh and copy behind her back. It's hard to understand her.

HANA: You understand her, don't you?

MASAKO: I'm used to it.

MURATA *smiles secretly.*

HANA: You should tell the kids not to laugh; after all, she's trying. Maybe you should help her practice those words . . . show her what she's doing wrong.

MASAKO: I already do. Our teacher told me to do that.

MURATA (*Looking up from his paper*): You ought to help her all you can.

HANA: And remember when you started school you couldn't speak English either.

MASAKO: I help her.

MURATA *rises and goes to the window. The night is cold. Lightning flashes and the wind whistles.*

MURATA: Looks like a storm coming up. Hope we don't have a freeze.

HANA: If it freezes, we'll have another bad year. Maybe we ought to start the smudge pots.

MURATA (*listening*): It's starting to rain. Nothing to do now but pray.

HANA: If praying is the answer, we'd be in Japan now . . . rich.

MURATA (*wryly*): We're not dead yet. We still have a chance. (HANA *glares at this small joke*) Guess I'll turn in.

HANA: Go to bed . . . go to bed. I'll sit up and worry.

MURATA: If worrying was the answer, we'd be around the world twice and in Japan. Come on, Mama. Let's go to bed. It's too cold tonight to be mad.

There's an urgent knock on the door. The family react to it.

(*Dareh da! Goes to the door and pauses*) Who is it!

KIYOKO (*weakly*): It's me . . . help me . . .

MURATA *opens the door and* KIYOKO *enters. She's dressed in a kimono with a shawl thrown over. Her legs are bare except for a pair of straw* zori. *Her hair is stringy from the rain and she trembles from the cold.*

MURATA: My God! Kiyoko-san! What's the matter?

HANA: Kiyoko-san! What is it?

MURATA: What happened?

KIYOKO (*gasping*): They're fighting . . . they're fighting.

MURATA: Ah . . . don't worry . . . those things happen. No cause to worry. Mama, make tea for her. Sit down and catch your breath. I'll take you home when you're ready.

HANA: Papa, I'll take care of it.

MURATA: Let me know when you're ready to go home.

HANA: It must be freezing out there. Try to get warm. Try to calm yourself.

MURATA: Kiyoko-san . . . don't worry.

HANA *waves* MASAKO *and* MURATA *off.* MURATA *leaves.* MASAKO *goes to her bed in the kitchen.*

HANA: Papa, I'll take care of it.

KIYOKO *(looking at* MURATA'S *retreating form):* I came to ask your help.

HANA: You ran down here without a lantern? You could have fallen and hurt yourself.

KIYOKO: I don't care . . . I don't care.

HANA: You don't know, Kiyoko-san. It's treacherous out there . . . snakes, spiders . . .

KIYOKO: I must go back . . . I . . . I . . . you . . . please come with me.

HANA: First, first, we must get you warm. . . . Drink your tea.

KIYOKO: But they might kill each other. They're fighting like animals. Help me stop them!

HANA *(goes to the stove to warm a pot of soup):* I cannot interfere in a family quarrel.

KIYOKO: It's not a quarrel . . . it's a . . .

HANA: That's all it is. A family squabble. You'll see. Tomorrow . . .

KIYOKO *(rises and puts her hand on* HANA'S *arm):* Not just a squabble . . . please!

She starts toward the door but HANA *restrains her.*

HANA: Now listen. Listen to me, Kiyoko-san. I've known your father and mother a little while now. I suspect it's been like this for years. Every family has some kind of trouble.

KIYOKO: Not like this . . . not like this.

HANA: Some have it better—some worse. When you get married, you'll under-stand. Don't worry. Nothing will happen. *(She takes a towel from the wall and dries* KIYOKO'S *hair)* You're chilled to the bone. You'll catch your death . . .

KIYOKO: I don't care . . . I want to die.

HANA: Don't be silly. It's not that bad.

KIYOKO: They started drinking early in the afternoon. They make some kind of brew and hide it somewhere in the desert.

HANA: It's illegal to make it. That's why they hide it. That home brew is poison to the body . . . and the mind too.

KIYOKO: It makes them crazy. They drink it all the time and quarrel constantly. I was in the other room studying. I try so hard to keep up with school.

HANA: We were talking about you just this evening. Masako says you're doing so well . . . you skipped a grade?

KIYOKO: It's hard . . . hard . . . I'm too old for the class and the children . . .
    (She remembers all her problems and starts to cry again)

HANA: It's always hard in a new country.

KIYOKO: They were bickering and quarreling all afternoon. Then something happened. All of a sudden I saw them on the floor . . . hitting and . . .

and . . . He was hitting her in the stomach, the face. . . . I tried to stop them, but they were so . . . drunk.

HANA: There, there. . . . It's probably all over now.

KIYOKO: Why does it happen like this? Nothing is right. Everywhere I go . . . Masa-chan is so lucky. I wish my life was like hers. I can hardly remember my real mother.

HANA: Emiko-san is almost a real mother to you. She's blood kin.

KIYOKO: She hates me. She never speaks to me. She's so cold. I want to love her but she won't let me. She hates me.

HANA: I don't think that's true, Kiyoko-san.

KIYOKO: I know it's true.

HANA: No. I don't think you have anything to do with it. It's this place. She hates it. This place is so lonely and alien.

KIYOKO: Then why didn't she go back? Why did they stay here?

HANA: You don't know. It's not so simple. Sometimes I think—

KIYOKO: Then why don't they make the best of it here? Like you?

HANA: That isn't easy either. Believe me. *(She goes to the stove to stir the soup)* Sometimes . . . sometimes the longing for homeland fills me with despair. Will I never return again? Will I never see my mother, my father, my sisters again? But what can one do? There are responsibilities here . . . children . . . *(She draws a sharp breath)* And another day passes . . . another month . . . another year. Eventually everything passes. *(She takes the soup to* KIYOKO*)* Did you have supper tonight?

KIYOKO *(bowing gratefully)*: Ah. When my . . . my aunt gets like this, she doesn't cook. No one eats. I don't get hungry anymore.

HANA: Cook for yourself. It's important to keep your health.

KIYOKO: I left Japan for a better life here . . .

HANA: It isn't easy for you, is it? But you must remember your filial duty.

KIYOKO: It's so hard.

HANA: But you can make the best of it here, Kiyoko-san. And take care of yourself. You owe that to yourself. Eat. Keep well. It'll be better, you'll see. And sometimes it'll seem worse. But you'll survive. We do, you know . . . we do . . . *(She looks around)* It's getting late.

KIYOKO *(apprehensively)*: I don't want to go back.

HANA: You can sleep with Masako tonight. Tomorrow you'll go back. And you'll remember what I told you.

She puts her arms around KIYOKO, *who is overcome with self-pity and begins to weep quietly.*

Life is never easy, Kiyoko-san. Endure. Endure. Soon you'll be marrying and going away. Things will not always be this way. And you'll look back on this . . . this night and you'll—

There is a rap on the door. HANA *exchanges glances with* KIYOKO *and goes to answer it. She opens it a crack.* OKA *has come looking for* KIYOKO. *He's dressed in an overcoat and holds a wet newspaper over his head.*

OKA: Ah! I'm sorry to bother you so late at night . . . the fact is . . .

HANA: Oka-san . . .

OKA *(jovially):* Good evening, good evening . . . *(He sees* KIYOKO*)* Ah . . . there you are. . . . Did you have a nice visit?

HANA *(irritated):* Yes, she's here.

OKA *(still cheerful):* Thought she might be. Ready to come home now?

HANA: She came in the rain.

OKA *(ignoring* HANA'S *tone):* That's foolish of you, Kiyoko. You might catch cold.

HANA: She was frightened by your quarreling. She came for help.

OKA *(laughing with embarrassment):* Oh! Kiyoko, that's nothing to worry about. It's just we had some disagreement . . .

HANA: That's what I told her, but she was frightened all the same.

OKA: Children are—

HANA: Not children, Oka-san. Kiyoko. Kiyoko was terrified. I think that was a terrible thing to do to her.

OKA *(rubbing his head):* Oh, I . . . I . . .

HANA: If you had seen her a few minutes ago . . . hysterical . . . shaking . . . crying . . . wet and cold to the bone . . . out of her mind with worry.

OKA *(rubbing his head):* Oh, I . . . I . . . don't know what she was so worried about.

HANA: You. You and Emiko fighting like you were going to kill each other.

OKA: *(There's nothing more to hide. He lowers his head in penitence)* Aaaaaachhhhhh . . .

HANA: I know I shouldn't tell you this, but there're one or two things I have to say: You sent for Kiyoko-san and now she's here. You said yourself she had a bad time in Japan, and now she's having a worse time. It isn't easy for her in a strange new country; the least you can do is try to keep her from worrying . . . especially about yourselves. I think it's terrible what you're doing to her . . . terrible!

OKA *(bowing in deep humility):* I am ashamed . . .

HANA: I think she deserves better. I think you should think about that.

OKA *(still in his bow):* I thank you for this reminder. It will never happen again. I promise.

HANA: I don't need that promise. Make it to Kiyoko-san.

OKA *(to* KIYOKO*):* Come with Papa now. He did a bad thing. He'll be a good papa from now. He won't worry his little girl again. All right? All right?

They move to the door.

KIYOKO: Thank you so much.

HANA *puts* MURATA'S *robe around* KIYOKO, *who tries to return it.*

OKA: Madam, I thank you again.

HANA *(to* KIYOKO*):* That's all right. You can bring it back tomorrow. *(Aside to* KIYOKO*)* Remember . . . remember what we talked about. *(Loudly)* Good night, Oka-san.

They leave. HANA *goes to* MASAKO, *who lies on the bed, and covers her.* MURATA *appears from the bedroom. He's heard it all. He and* HANA *exchange a glance and together they retire to their room. Fade-out.*

Scene 3

The next morning. The MURATA *house and yard.* HANA *and* MURATA *have already left the house to examine the rain damage in the fields.* MASAKO *prepares to go to school. She puts on a coat and picks up her books and lunch bag. Meanwhile,* KIYOKO *slips quietly into the yard. She wears a coat and carries* MURATA'S *robe. She sets it on the outside bench.* MASAKO *walks out and is surprised to see* KIYOKO.

MASAKO: Hi. I thought you'd be . . . sick today.

KIYOKO: Oh. I woke up late.

MASAKO *(scrutinizing* KIYOKO'S *face):* Your eyes are red.

KIYOKO *(averting her eyes):* Oh. I . . . got . . . sand in it. Yes.

MASAKO: Do you want to use eye drops? We have eye drops in the house.

KIYOKO: Oh . . . no. That's all right.

MASAKO: That's what you call bloodshot.

KIYOKO: Oh.

MASAKO: My father gets it a lot. When he drinks too much.

KIYOKO: Oh . . .

MASAKO *(notices* KIYOKO *doesn't have her lunch):* Where's your lunch bag?

KIYOKO: I . . . forgot it.

MASAKO: Did you make your lunch today?

KIYOKO: Yes. Yes, I did. But I forgot it.

MASAKO: Do you want to go back and get it?

KIYOKO: No, that's all right.

They are silent for a while.

   We'll be late.

MASAKO: Do you want to practice your words?

KIYOKO *(thoughtfully):* Oh . . .

MASAKO: Say, "My."

KIYOKO: My?

MASAKO: Eyes . . .

KIYOKO: Eyes.

MASAKO: Are . . .

KIYOKO: Are.

MASAKO: Red.

KIYOKO: Red.

MASAKO: Your eyes are red. *(*KIYOKO *doesn't repeat it)* I . . . *(*KIYOKO *doesn't cooperate)* Say, "I."

KIYOKO: I.

MASAKO: Got . . .

KIYOKO: Got.

MASAKO: Sand . . . *(KIYOKO balks)* Say, "I."

KIYOKO *(sighing):* I.

MASAKO: Reft . . .

KIYOKO: Reft.

MASAKO: My . . .

KIYOKO: My.

MASAKO: Runch . . .

KIYOKO: Run . . . lunch. *(She stops)* Masako-san, you are mean. You are hurting me.

MASAKO: It's a joke! I was just trying to make you laugh!

KIYOKO: I cannot laugh today.

MASAKO: Sure you can. You can laugh. Laugh! Like this! *(She makes a hearty laugh)*

KIYOKO: I cannot laugh when you make fun of me.

MASAKO: Okay, I'm sorry. We'll practice some other words then, okay? *(KIYOKO doesn't answer)* Say, "Okay."

KIYOKO *(reluctantly):* Okay . . .

MASAKO: Okay, then . . . um . . . um . . . *(She still teases and talks rapidly)* Say . . . um . . . "She sells sea shells on the sea shore."

KIYOKO *turns away indignantly.*

Aw, come on, Kiyoko! It's just a joke. Laugh!

KIYOKO *(imitating sarcastically):* Ha-ha-ha! Now you say, *"Kono kyaku wa yoku kaki ku kyaku da* [This guest eats a lot of persimmons]!"

MASAKO: Sure! I can say it! *Kono kyaku waki ku kyoku kaku . . .*

KIYOKO: That's not right.

MASAKO: *Koki kuki kya . . .*

KIYOKO: No.

MASAKO: Okay, then. You say, "Sea sells she shells . . . shu . . . sss . . ."

They both laugh, KIYOKO *with her hands over her mouth.* MASAKO *takes* KIYOKO'S *hands from her mouth.*

Not like that! Like this! *(She gives a big belly laugh)*

KIYOKO: Like this? *(She imitates* MASAKO*)*

MASAKO: Yeah, that's right! You're not mad anymore?

KIYOKO: I'm not mad anymore.

MASAKO: Okay. You can share my lunch today because we're . . .

KIYOKO: "Flends?"

MASAKO *looks at* KIYOKO, *they giggle and move on.* HANA *and* MURATA *come in from assessing the storm's damage. They are dressed warmly.* HANA *is depressed.* MURATA *tries hard to be cheerful.*

MURATA: It's not so bad, Mama.

HANA: Half the ranch is flooded . . . at least half.

MURATA: No-no. A quarter, maybe. It's sunny today . . . it'll dry.

HANA: The seedlings will rot.

MURATA: No, no. It'll dry. It's all right—better than I expected.

HANA: If we have another bad year, no one will lend us money for the next crop.

MURATA: Don't worry. If it doesn't drain by tomorrow, I'll replant the worst places. We still have some seed left. Yeah, I'll replant . . .

HANA: More work.

MURATA: Don't worry, Mama. It'll be all right.

HANA *(quietly)*: Papa, where will it end? Will we always be like this—always at the mercy of the weather—prices—always at the mercy of the gods?

MURATA *(patting HANA's back)*: Things will change. Wait and see. We'll be back in Japan by . . . in two years . . . guarantee. . . . Maybe sooner.

HANA *(dubiously)*: Two years . . .

MURATA *(Finds the robe on the bench)*: Ah, look, Mama. Kiyoko-san brought back my robe.

HANA *(sighing)*: Kiyoko-san . . . poor Kiyoko-san . . . and Emiko-san.

MURATA: Ah, Mama. We're lucky. We're lucky, Mama.

HANA *smiles sadly at* MURATA. *Fade-out.*

Scene 4

The following spring, afternoon. Exterior of the OKA *house.* OKA *is dressed to go out. He wears a sweater, long-sleeved white shirt, dark pants, no tie. He puts his foot on the bench to wipe off his shoe with the palm of his hand. He straightens his sleeve, removes a bit of lint, and runs his fingers through his hair. He hums under his breath.* KIYOKO *comes from the house. Her hair is frizzled with a permanent wave, she wears a gaudy new dress and a pair of new shoes. She carries a movie magazine—*Photoplay *or* Modern Screen.

OKA *(appreciatively)*: Pretty. Pretty.

KIYOKO *(turning for him)*: It's not too *hadeh?* I feel strange in colors.

OKA: Oh no. Young girls should wear bright colors. There's time enough to wear gray when you get old. Old-lady colors. *(KIYOKO giggles)* Sure you want to go to the picture show? It's such a nice day . . . shame to waste in a dark hall.

KIYOKO: Where else can we go?

OKA: We can go to the Muratas.

KIYOKO: All dressed up?

OKA: Or Nagatas. I'll show him what I got for my horse.

KIYOKO *(laughing)*: Oh, I love the pictures.

OKA: We don't have many nice spring days like this. Here the season is short. Summer comes in like a dragon . . . right behind . . . breathing fire . . . like a dragon. You don't know the summers here. They'll scare you. *(He tousles* KIYOKO'S *hair and pulls a lock of it. It springs back. He shakes his head in wonder)* Goddamn. Curly hair. Never thought curly hair could make you so happy.

KIYOKO *(giggling)*: All the American girls have curly hair.

OKA: Your friend Masako like it?

KIYOKO *(nodding)*: She says her mother will never let her get a permanent wave.

OKA: She said that, eh? Bet she's wanting one.

KIYOKO: I don't know about that.

OKA: Bet she's wanting some of your pretty dresses too.

KIYOKO: Her mother makes all her clothes.

OKA: Buying is just as good. Buying is better. No trouble that way.

KIYOKO: Masako's not so interested in clothes. She loves the pictures, but her mother won't let her go. Someday, can we take Masako with us?

OKA: If her mother lets her come. Her mother's got a mind of her own . . . a stiff back.

KIYOKO: But she's nice.

OKA (dubiously): Oh, yeah. Can't be perfect, I guess. Kiyoko, after the harvest I'll have money and I'll buy you the prettiest dress in town. I'm going to be lucky this year. I feel it.

KIYOKO: You're already too good to me . . . dresses, shoes, permanent wave . . . movies . . .

OKA: That's nothing. After the harvest, just wait . . .

KIYOKO: Magazines. . . . You do enough. I'm happy already.

OKA: You make me happy too, Kiyoko. You make me feel good . . . like a man again. . . . (That statement bothers him) One day you're going to make a young man happy. (KIYOKO giggles) Someday we going to move from here.

KIYOKO: But we have good friends here, Papa.

OKA: Next year our lease will be up and we got to move.

KIYOKO: The ranch is not ours?

OKA: No. In America, Japanese cannot own land. We lease and move every two, three years. Next year we going to go someplace where there's young fellows. There's none good enough for you here. (He watches KIYOKO giggle) Yeah. You going to make a good wife. Already a good cook. I like your cooking.

KIYOKO (a little embarrassed): Shall we go now?

OKA: Yeah. Put the magazine away.

KIYOKO: I want to take it with me.

OKA: Take it with you?

KIYOKO: Last time, after we came back, I found all my magazines torn in half.

OKA (looking toward the house): Torn?

KIYOKO: This is the only one I have left.

OKA (not wanting to deal with it): All right. All right.

The two prepare to leave when the door opens. EMIKO stands there, her hair is unkempt and she looks wild. She holds an empty can in one hand, the lid in the other.

EMIKO: Where is it?

OKA *tries to make a hasty departure.*

KIYOKO: Where is what?

OKA *pushes* KIYOKO *ahead of him, still trying to make a getaway.*

EMIKO: Where is it? Where is it? What did you do with it?

EMIKO *moves toward* OKA. *He can't ignore her and he stops.*

OKA (*with false unconcern to* KIYOKO): Why don't you walk on ahead to the Muratas?

KIYOKO: We're not going to the pictures?

OKA: We'll go. First you walk to the Muratas. Show them your new dress. I'll meet you there.

KIYOKO *picks up a small package and exits.* OKA *sighs and shakes his head.*

EMIKO (*shaking the can*): Where is it? What did you do with it?

OKA (*feigning surprise*): With what?

EMIKO: You know what. You stole it. You stole my money.

OKA: *Your* money?

EMIKO: I've been saving that money.

OKA: Yeah? Well, where'd you get it? Where'd you get it, eh? You stole it from me! Dollar by dollar. . . . You stole it from me! Out of my pocket!

EMIKO: I saved it!

OKA: From my pocket!

EMIKO: It's mine! I saved for a long time. . . . Some of it I brought from Japan.

OKA: *Bakayuna!* What'd you bring from Japan? Nothing but some useless kimonos.

OKA *starts to leave but* EMIKO *hangs on to him.*

EMIKO: Give back my money! Thief!

OKA (*swings around and balls his fists but doesn't strike*): Goddamn! Get off me!

EMIKO (*now pleading*): Please give it back . . . please . . . please . . .

She starts to stroke him. OKA *pulls her hands away and pushes her from him.*

Oni!

OKA (*seething*): *Oni?* What does that make you? *Oni baba?* Yeah, that's what you are . . . a devil!

EMIKO: It's mine! Give it back . . .

OKA: The hell! You think you can live off me and steal my money too? How stupid you think I am?

EMIKO (*tearfully*): But I've paid . . . I've paid . . .

OKA: With what?

EMIKO: You know I've paid.

OKA (*scoffing*): You call that paying?

EMIKO: What did you do with it?

OKA: I don't have it.

EMIKO: It's gone? It's gone?

OKA: Yeah! It's gone. I spent it. The hell! Every last cent.

EMIKO: The new clothes . . . the curls . . . restaurants . . . pictures . . . shoes. . . . My money . . . my going-home money . . .

OKA: You through?

EMIKO: What will I do? What will—

OKA: I don't care what you do. Walk. Use your feet. Swim to Japan. I don't care. I give you no more than you gave me. Now I don't want anything. I don't care what you do. (*He walks away*)

EMIKO *still holds the empty can. Offstage we hear* OKA'S *car door slam and the sound of his old car starting off. Accustomed to crying alone, she doesn't utter a sound. Her shoulders begin to shake, her dry soundless sobs turn to a silent laugh. She wipes the dust gently from the can as though comforting a friend. Her movements become sensuous, her hands move on to her own body, around her throat, over her breasts, to her hips, caressing, soothing, reminding her of her lover's hands. Fade-out.*

Scene 5

Same day, late afternoon. Exterior of the MURATA *house. The light is soft.* HANA *is sweeping the yard;* MASAKO *hangs a glass wind chime on the exposed wall.*

HANA *(directing* MASAKO*):* There . . . there. That's a good place.

MASAKO: Here?

HANA *(nodding):* It must catch the slightest breeze. *(sighing and listening)* It brings back so much. . . . That's the reason I never hung one before. I guess it doesn't matter much anymore . . .

MASAKO: I thought you liked to think about Japan.

HANA *(laughing sadly):* I didn't want to hear that sound so often . . . get too used to it. Sometimes you hear something too often, after a while you don't hear it anymore. . . . I didn't want that to happen. The same thing happens to feelings too, I guess. After a while you don't feel anymore. You're too young to understand that yet.

MASAKO: I understand, Mama.

HANA: Wasn't it nice of Kiyoko-san to give us the *furin?*

MASAKO: I love it. I don't know anything about Japan, but it makes me feel something too.

HANA: Maybe someday when you're grown up, gone away, you'll hear it and remember yourself as this little girl . . . remember this old house, the ranch, and . . . your old mama . . .

MASAKO: That's kind of scary.

EMIKO *enters unsteadily. She carries a bundle wrapped in a* furoshiki *[colorful scarf]. In the package are two beautiful kimonos.*

HANA: Emiko-san! What a pleasant surprise! Please sit down. We were just hanging the *furin.* It was so sweet of Kiyoko-san to give it to Masako. She loves it.

EMIKO *looks mildly interested. She acts as normal as she can throughout the scene, but at times drops her facade, revealing her desperation.*

EMIKO: Thank you. *(She sets her bundle on the bench but keeps her hand on it)*

HANA: Your family was here earlier. *(*EMIKO *smiles vaguely):* On their way to the pictures, I think. *(To* MASAKO*):* Make tea for us, Ma-chan.

EMIKO: Please don't . . .

HANA: Kiyoko-san was looking so nice—her hair all curly. . . . Of course, in our day, straight black hair was desirable. Of course, times change.

EMIKO: Yes.

HANA: But she did look fine. My, my, a colorful new dress, new shoes, a permanent wave—looked like a regular American girl. Did you choose her dress?

EMIKO: No . . . I didn't go.

HANA: You know, I didn't think so. Very pretty though. I liked it very much. Of course, I sew all Masako's clothes. It saves money. It'll be nice for you to make things for Kiyoko-san too. She'd be so pleased. I know she'd be pleased . . .

While HANA *talks,* EMIKO *plucks nervously at her package. She waits for* HANA *to stop talking.*

Emiko-san, is everything all right?

EMIKO *(smiling nervously):* Yes.

HANA: Masako, please go make tea for us. See if there aren't any more of those crackers left. Or did you finish them? *(To* EMIKO*)* We can't keep anything in this house. She eats everything as soon as Papa brings it home. You'd never know it, she's so skinny. We never have anything left for company.

MASAKO: We hardly ever have company anyway.

HANA *gives her daughter a strong look, and* MASAKO *goes into the house.* EMIKO *is lost in her own thoughts. She strokes her package.*

HANA: Is there something you . . . I can help you with? *(Very gently)* Emiko-san?

EMIKO *(suddenly frightened):* Oh no. I was thinking. . . . Now that . . . now that . . . Masa-chan is growing up . . . older . . .

HANA*(relieved):* Oh, yes. She's growing fast.

EMIKO: I was thinking . . . *(She stops, puts the package on her lap and is lost again)*

HANA: Yes, she is growing. Time goes so fast. I think she'll be taller than me soon. *(She laughs weakly, stops and looks puzzled)*

EMIKO: Yes.

EMIKO'S *depression pervades the atmosphere.* HANA *is affected by it. The two women sit in silence. A small breeze moves the wind chimes. For a moment light grows dim on the two lonely figures.* MASAKO *comes from the house with a tray of tea. The light returns to normal again.*

HANA *(gently):* You're a good girl.

MASAKO *looks first to* EMIKO *then to her mother. She sets the tray on the bench and stands near* EMIKO, *who seems to notice her for the first time.*

EMIKO: How are you?

HANA *(pours the tea and serves her):* Emiko-san, is there something I can do for you?

EMIKO: There's . . . I was . . . I . . . Masa-chan will be a young lady soon . . .

HANA: Oh, well, now I don't know about "lady."

EMIKO: Maybe she would like a nice . . . nice . . . *(She unwraps her package)* I have kimonos . . . I wore in Japan for dancing . . . maybe she can . . . if you like, I mean. They'll be nice on her . . . she's so slim . . .

EMIKO *shakes out a robe.* HANA *and* MASAKO *are impressed.*

HANA: Ohhhh! Beautiful!

MASAKO: Oh, Mama! Pretty!

HANA *and* MASAKO *finger the material.*

Gold threads, Mama.

HANA: Brocade!

EMIKO: Maybe Masa-chan would like them. I mean for her school programs . . . Japanese school . . .

HANA: Oh, no! Too good for country. People will be envious of us . . . wonder where we got them.

EMIKO: I mean for festivals . . . *Obon, Hana Matsuri* . . .

HANA: Oh, but you have Kiyoko-san now. You should give them to her. Has she seen them?

EMIKO: Oh . . . no . . .

HANA: She'll love them. You should give them to her . . . not our Masako.

EMIKO: I thought . . . I mean I was thinking of . . . if you could give me a little . . . if you could pay . . . manage to give me something for . . .

HANA: But these gowns, Emiko-san—they're worth hundreds.

EMIKO: I know, but I'm not asking for that. Whatever you can give . . . only as much as you can give.

MASAKO: Mama?

HANA: Masako, Papa doesn't have that kind of money.

EMIKO: Anything you can give . . . anything . . .

MASAKO: Ask Papa.

HANA: There's no use asking. I know he can't afford it.

EMIKO *(looking at* MASAKO*):* A little at a time.

MASAKO: Mama?

HANA *(firmly):* No, Masako. This is a luxury.

HANA *folds the gowns and puts them away.* MASAKO *is disappointed.* EMIKO *is devastated.* HANA *sees this and tries to find some way to help.*

Emiko-san, I hope you understand . . . *(*EMIKO *is silent, trying to gather her resources):* I know you can sell them and get the full price somewhere. Let's see . . . a family with a lot of growing daughters . . . someone who did well last year. . . . Nagatas have no girls. . . . Umedas have girls but no money. . . . Well, let's see. . . . Maybe not here in this country town. Ah. . . . You can take them to the city, Los Angeles, and sell them to a store . . . or Terminal Island . . . lots of wealthy fishermen there. Yes, that would be the place. Why, it's no problem, Emiko-san. Have your husband take them there. I know you'll get your money. He'll find a buyer. I know he will.

EMIKO: Yes. *(She finishes folding and ties the scarf. She sits quietly)*

HANA: Please have your tea. I'm sorry . . . I really would like to take them for Masako but it just isn't possible. You understand, don't you? *(*EMIKO *nods)* Please don't feel so . . . so bad. It's not really a matter of life or death, is it? Emiko-san?

EMIKO *nods again.* HANA *sips her tea.*

MASAKO: Mama? If you could ask Papa . . .

HANA: Oh, the tea is cold. Masako, could you heat the kettle?

EMIKO: No more. I must be going. *(She picks up her package and rises slowly)*

HANA *(looking helpless):* So soon? Emiko-san, please stay.

EMIKO *starts to go.*

    Masako will walk with you. *(She pushes* MASAKO *forward)*

EMIKO: It's not far.

HANA: Emiko-san? You'll be all right?

EMIKO: Yes . . . yes . . . yes *(She goes)*

HANA *(calling after her):* I'm sorry, Emiko-san.

EMIKO: Yes . . .

MASAKO *and* HANA *watch as* EMIKO *leaves. The light grows dim as though a cloud passes over.* EMIKO *is gone.* HANA *strokes* MASAKO'S *hair.*

HANA: Your hair is so black and straight . . . nice . . .

They stand close. The wind chimes tinkle; light grows dim. Light returns to normal. MURATA *enters. He sees this tableau of mother and child and is puzzled.*

MURATA: What's going on here?

The two women part.

HANA: Oh . . . nothing . . . nothing . . .

MASAKO: Mrs. Oka was here. She had two kimo—

HANA *(putting her hand on* MASAKO'S *shoulder):* It was nothing . . .

MURATA: *Eh?* What'd she want?

HANA: Later, Papa. Right now, I'd better fix supper.

MURATA *(looking at the sky):* Strange how that sun comes and goes. Maybe I didn't need to irrigate—looks like rain. *(He remembers and is exasperated)* Ach! I forgot to shut the water.

MASAKO: I'll do it, Papa.

HANA: Masako, that gate's too heavy for you.

MURATA: She can handle it. Take out the pin and let the gate fall all the way down. All the way. And put the pin back. Don't forget to put the pin back.

HANA: And be careful. Don't fall in the canal.

MASAKO *leaves.*

MURATA: What's the matter with that girl?

HANA: Nothing. Why?

MURATA: Usually have to beg her to do . . .

HANA: She's growing up.

MURATA: Must be that time of the month.

HANA: Oh, Papa, she's too young for that yet.

MURATA *(genially as they enter the house):* Got to start sometime. Looks like I'll be outnumbered soon. I'm outnumbered already.

HANA *glances at him and quietly sets about preparations for supper.* MURATA *removes his shirt and sits at the table with a paper. Light fades slowly.*

Scene 6

Same evening. Exterior, desert. There is at least one shrub. MASAKO appears, walking slowly. From a distance we hear EMIKO singing the song "And the Soul Shall Dance." MASAKO looks around, sees the shrub and crouches under it. EMIKO appears. She's dressed in one of her beautiful kimonos tied loosely at her waist. She carries a branch of sage. Her hair is loose.

EMIKO: *Akai kuchibiru*
     Kappu ni yosete
     Aoi sake nomya
     Kokoro ga odoru . . .
     Kurai yoru no yume
     Setsu nasa yo . . .

She breaks into a dance, laughs mysteriously, turns round and round, acting out a fantasy. MASAKO stirs uncomfortably. EMIKO senses a presence. She stops, drops her branch and walks offstage, singing as she goes.

     Aoi sake nomya
     Yume mo odoru . . .

MASAKO watches as EMIKO leaves. She rises slowly and picks up the branch EMIKO has left. She looks at the branch, moves forward a step and looks off to the point where EMIKO disappeared. Light slowly fades until only the image of MASAKO'S face remains etched in the mind.

End of Play

QUESTIONS AND CONSIDERATIONS

1. What are the sources of tension between Oka and Emiko? How does Kiyoko's return complicate their relationship and deepen their estrangement from one another?

2. Compare and contrast the marriage of Hana and Murata and of Emiko and Oka. What is the dramatic impact of the contrast in the couples' relationships? Does the play imply that marital relationships are seriously affected when it is necessary to redefine traditional cultural values?

3. Why is Emiko's favorite song "And the Soul Shall Dance"? Why is this also the play's title?

4. Emiko dreams of returning to Japan and Masako dreams of having a more exciting life, one that provides for the pleasures that she reads about in books about successful American whites. Hana's mother tells her, "Sometimes dreaming makes the living harder." What point of view does the play present about the potential for realizing one's dreams, for making a better life in America as an immigrant?

5. Why do Kiyoko and Masako finally become friends? What does each learn from the other?

6. How is Kiyoko changed by and used by her father? What effect do you think his treatment of her will have on her self-esteem as a young woman?

7. Why does the play end with Masako watching Emiko with her hair wild and her beautiful kimono loosely tied, dancing to "And the Soul Shall Dance"? How do you think Masako will be affected by Emiko's loneliness and longing?

IDEAS FOR WRITING

1. One of the major issues explored in the play is the way that changing cultural values break the bonds that exist within an immigrant family dedicated to the struggle to survive. Write an essay in which you discuss how immigrant families can maintain the close relationships and traditional cultural values that gave them the courage to come to a new land as they successfully assimilate and adjust to the demands of the mainstream culture.

2. Write a third act for the play that explores the lives of Masako and Kiyoko in their early twenties. What has happened to the marriages of Hana and Murata and Emiko and Oka? Explain your reasons for making conclusions about the way that the lives of these characters would unfold.

3. The play was written in 1935. Contrast the struggles of today's Asian-Americans with those in the play.

Student Writing

"Gossip and Intimacy in 'A Wife's Story' and Deborah Tannen's 'Gossip'"

Ryan Wesley Bounds

Ryan Bounds is from the small town of Hemiston, Oregon. He is a psychology major and thus is particularly interested in communication styles that promote caring and understanding relationships. Ryan Bounds wrote his essay to apply the advice given in Deborah Tannen's "Gossip" on the need for sharing intimate details of daily life to a particular work of fiction, Bharati Mukherjee's "A Wife's Story." As you read Bounds' essay, notice how he uses clear transitions, point-by-point analytical presentation of ideas, and strategies of comparison-contrast to emphasize the similarities and distinctions between Tannen's view of the function of gossip in male-female relationships and the communication styles of the characters in Mukherjee's story. Do you agree with the conclusions he draws about the two works? Does he provide an adequate number of relevant references to and quotations from each work to support his interpretations and evaluations? What additional points might he have made about the role of gossip in "A Wife's Story"?

Communication is the stuff of which interpersonal relationships are made, the foundation upon which they are built. A strong, intimate friendship or marriage requires a regular exchange of personally relevant information between partners so that closeness can be a psychological reality rather than a mere label. Both Deborah Tannen, in her analysis of gossip, and Bharati Murkherjee, in her fictional work, "A Wife's Story," explore the causes and effects of constrained communication between men and women. Tannen, in "Gossip," explores the role that revealing details about one's life plays in building and maintaining relationships; correspondingly, Mukherjee's "Wife's Story" depicts a marital relationship bereft of intimacy and seemingly devoid of idle conversation. However, whereas Tannen contends that it is women who gossip and men who avoid doing so, it is the narrator of "A Wife's Story"—a woman— who is depicted as least likely among her friends and husband to fall easily into a dialogue of self-revelation. The two works nevertheless share the idea that reticence or overly constrained conversation between men and women leads to a lack of intimacy in their relationships.

In her discussion of the subject, Tannen establishes two essential points about relaxed, detailed conversation, or gossip. The first is that, contrary to the popular conception, gossip is valuable and necessary for nurturing intimate relationships. Revealing part of one's self by discussing the details of one's life with another who is interested creates a rapport, a de facto relationship, between the speaker and the listener. Tannen writes: "Not only is telling secrets evidence of friendship; it creates friendship. . . ." Easy revelation also maintains relationships and the intimacy that characterizes them. Tannen observes that many women share painful experiences repeatedly, knowing that their friends would be deeply hurt if they discovered that the details of their friend's life—painful though they might be to report— had not been volunteered. More important is Tannen's comment on Ann Packer's "Mendocino," in which a woman laments her brother's emotional distance from her since his marriage (because they no longer privately share details of failed romantic endeavors). The lack of gossip has left their relationship more formal or "cordial—in a way like public speaking." In Tannen's estimation, intimacy in interpersonal relationships requires in several ways the mutually interesting exchange of personal details.

The second point that Tannen establishes in her analysis of

gossip is that women are likely to communicate through sharing
personal details whereas men tend to disparage doing so. This
disparity in communication styles leads to an inevitable decline
in intimacy as well as to strains in the relationship. Tannen
borrows from Marge Percy's "Fly Away Home," in which a woman,
Daria, falls in love with a man because he differs from her
former husband, Ross, in his interest in the lives of others:
"For a man, Tom had an uncommon interest in the details of
people's lives. Gossip, Ross would call it, but she [Daria]
thought it was just being interested in people." Women are thus
portrayed as being more likely than men to share in the details
of others' lives and more interested in breeding intimacy by
doing so.

The relationship between the narrator and her husband in
Mukherjee's "Wife's Story" depicts a relationship that seems to
suffer from a deficit of the very type of communication that
Tannen deems so vital for intimacy. It should not surprise
Tannen's readers, then, that the marriage in Mukherjee's
"Wife's Story" seems without intimacy and rapport. But, despite
Tannen's observation that women are generally more interested
in intimacy and detail-oriented conversation than men, it is
the narrator, the wife, who is the more constrained and formal
in her communication with friends and spouse. The narrator
comments of herself: "Expensive girls' schools in Lausanne and
Bombay have trained me to behave well. My manners are
exquisite, my feelings are delicate, my gestures refined, my
moods undetectable." The most obvious characteristic of the
narrator's personality is her reticence. When dealing with her
roommate, Charity, the narrator's impatience with having to
endure yet another lengthy conversation is conveyed in her curt
responses: "'Oh, good' Charity says. 'I'm glad you're back
early. I need to talk.' . . . 'All right. Talk.'" Later, the
narrator comments, "[i]t'll be a long evening, I'm afraid.
Charity likes to confess." The reader can, with a little
imagination, see the narrator's eyes roll emphatically at this
point. It becomes quite clear that the narrator does not like
to talk, even when dealing with her husband. At times, the
narrator shares feelings with the reader that she does not feel
the need to share with her doting husband; she speaks of
feeling lost, but does not volunteer her feelings to him.
Further, the narrator notices that her husband has lost weight
and changed the style of his spectacles, but fails to
acknowledge or compliment these changes until prodded to do so
by him. A clear pattern emerges in the story in which the
husband, who has come to the United States to ask his wife to
return home with him because he cannot live without her, asks
his wife what has happened or what she feels, and the wife
evades the question.

Appropriately, in light of Tannen's assertions in her

discussion of gossip, the marriage in "A Wife's Story" is
singularly detached and formal, at least by western standards.
When the narrator's husband reveals that he cannot live without
her and would like her to return with him to India, she responds
flatly, "Special ed. course is two years. I can't go back." Her
reaction to her husband's request seems inappropriately
dispassionate. This unemotional communication seems to be
standard between the couple. The narrator, being the only one to
have lived in the west, is responsible for taking care of money
and procuring tickets for sightseeing. She knows her husband
well enough to know that he likes to be in charge and might not
like the situation, but she must admit to knowing not exactly
how he does feel—nor does she ask. Throughout the story, there
is no hint of the intimacy or excitement that might stem from a
prolonged separation of a loving wife and her husband.
Correspondingly, the narrator makes no mention of much idle
conversation or leisurely sharing of personal happenings or
feelings between herself and her husband, who has traveled
thousands of miles to see her.

     In both Deborah Tannen's "Gossip" and Bharati Mukherjee's
"Wife's Story," the reader can observe the interaction of
communication styles and the intimacy of the corresponding
relationship. Each work suggests, in its own way, that intimacy
does not develop without a relaxed style of communication in
which both partners volunteer information about themselves and
their lives while the other attends to them. Tannen suggests
that men need to make more effort to gossip, to be willing to
value the details of other people's lives. In her estimation,
this is vital to the creation and maintenance of intimacy in
relationships. Mukherjee's story depicts a marriage starkly
devoid of intimacy or passion and, not coincidentally, without
much informal conversation between partners. Tannen's work is of
particular value because it delves deeper and more definitively
into the role of gossip in relationships, both among women and
between men and women. The contribution of the details of one's
life to a conversation plays a much larger part than merely
starting a discussion. Volunteering a part of one's self can
start new friendships, maintain lasting relationships, and
reinforce intimacy.

Connections: Ideas for Discussion and Writing

   1. Cultural differences can create obstacles to understanding and barriers to successful relationships. Write an essay in which you discuss and compare several readings in
this chapter that reflect on the way that cultural differences can lead to miscommunication within a relationship.

   2. The chapter begins with a folk tale about how men and women got together and

contains several selections about couple relationships at various stages of life. What did you learn about couples and relationships between the sexes through reading these selections? What different views of relationships and the problems that exist within male-female relationships did you notice? Write an essay comparing several of the selections in the chapter in terms of these issues.

3. A primary bond in most people's lives is that between child and parent. Compare several selections that comment on parent-child relationships. How do these selections explore issues such as a young child's admiration of a parental figure or teenage rebellion and separation from parents?

4. Compare several of the selections in this chapter that reflect on sibling relationships. How is the sibling relationship portrayed as both a valuable support and, at times, a struggle or a burden?

5. Compare selections from the chapter that make observations about friendship relations. Do such relationships seem as intense and meaningful as the family and romantic relationships presented in other chapter readings? In what ways are friendship relationships particularly important in modern life?

6. Write an essay of definition in which you explore the new ways that you have come to understand the meaning of the word "relationship" from reading this chapter.

7. Write about a relationship that you would like to change. Discuss the selections that have encouraged you to rethink your relationship and then discuss how you plan to change the relationship.

8. Write an essay that makes suggestions for the inclusion of several types of relationships that have not been explored in this chapter. Find poems, stories, essays, or plays to illustrate the type of relationship and the particular issues that you feel should be covered in this chapter.

Chapter 10

STRUGGLES

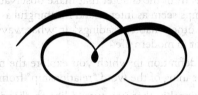

In every cry of every man,
In every infant's cry of fear,
In every voice, in every ban,
The mind-forged manacles I hear.
William Blake, "London"

No one knows
that I quit tonight,
maybe the mop
will push on without me . . .
They will call it Jorge
Martin Espada, "Jorge the Church Janitor Finally Quits"

. . . I choose
your only way, my small inheritor
and hand you off, trembling the selves we lose.
Go child, who is my sin and nothing more.
Anne Sexton, "Unknown Girl in the Maternity Ward"

We are caught in an inescapable network of mutuality, tied in a single garment of destiny.
Martin Luther King, Jr., "Letter from a Birmingham Jail"

Walking through the streets of London, the speaker in William Blake's poem "London" sees pain, poverty, prohibitions, and fear. The poet imagines that the pain has been internalized; he hears the grating and crushing of the mind's struggle against suffering: "The mind-forged manacles I hear." As Blake suggests

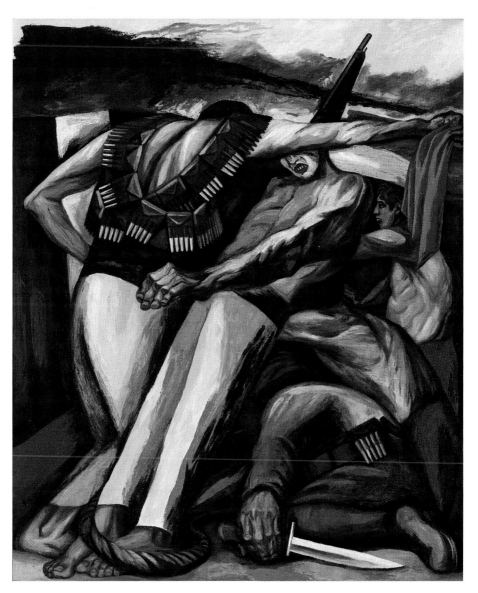

José Clemente Orozco. *Barricade.* 1931. Oil on canvas, 55 × 45″. The Museum of Modern Art, New York. Given Anonymously.

in his poem, while individuals struggle against the political and social institutions that can limit their external freedom, they also struggle within themselves
for inner freedom and peace.

Knowledge of human nature can bring disillusionment as people struggle to
feel joy and pain, to bear the humiliation of one's imperfect nature, and to make
the compromises that living within a family, workplace, or community sometimes necessitates. The essays, storys, poems, and plays in this chapter all focus
on this fundamental struggle of the human spirit to endure and triumph over the
losses and inequities that are inextricably woven into the fabric of our lives.

The speaker in Claribel Alegría's poem "I, Mirror" defines the struggle to be
alive in its most existential and personal form:

> I hurt
> therefore I exist

Yet the disillusioned speaker transforms herself into a mirror, blank, cold, and
"fleshless/scarcely keeping/a vague memory/of the pain." The struggle to exist in
a world of chaos and contradiction can numb us, just as the speaker in Alegría's
poem is dehumanized through suffering.

Children are often better barometers of feeling; frank and ingenuous, a child
often speaks the truth that adults avoid seeing or rationalize away. In the folk
tale "The Emperor's New Clothes," which opens this chapter's readings, Hans
Christian Andersen captures the folly of the adult world. In the tale's closing
lines the Emperor's vulnerability and foolishness are exposed by a young child
who acknowledges the nakedness he sees and speaks the truth: "He is not wearing anything." Hypocrisy and indifference to the truth are expressed through the
Emperor's final act in Andersen's story: Knowing that the child is right, the Emperor says, "I must go through with the procession." The charade continues.

The poem by Alegría and the folk tale by Andersen capture the opposite extremes of the struggles that are presented in the literature in this chapter. At one
end of the spectrum the poem shows the personal struggle not to feel, never to
remember the pain of suffering, whereas the folk tale reveals how political leaders can choose to be totally indifferent to the truth, committed only to meaningless rituals. As you read the selections, think about the ways that the writers
have expressed the tensions and conflicts in the personal struggle to feel, to care,
to cope with disappointment as well as the struggle against institutional indifference to pain, illness, poverty, and injustice. The selections explore political, economic, cultural, and gender-related issues of struggle and dissent.

Whereas "The Emperor's New Clothes" exposes the folly that oils the
wheels of political machines, in "Letter from a Birmingham Jail," Martin Luther
King, Jr., argues for civil rights claiming that "segregation distorts the soul and
damages the personality." Like Hans Christian Andersen, King expresses humankind's political struggles through the image of a garment: "We are caught in
an inescapable network of mutuality, tied in a single garment of destiny." In his

poem "The Man He Killed," Thomas Hardy reflects on the commonality of men's lives, the natural affection that members of a community feel, as he also reflects on their wanton killing of one another in what he sees as a senseless war. Reminiscent of "The Emperor's New Clothes," the short story "The Censors" by Luisa Valenzuela shows the reader how easily an individual can become trapped in a political machine. Sophocles' classic tragedy *Antigone* contrasts the political power of the state to the spiritual mandates of the gods. Like Martin Luther King, Sophocles argues for a belief in the spirit, in ethical action, as opposed to allegiance to a political regime.

Economic struggles are emphasized in many of the selections in this chapter. In the short story "A Loaf of Bread" James Alan McPherson explores the ways that economic policies can be changed through educating individuals in the community about the different cultural assumptions held by various ethnic groups. Whereas McPherson's story suggests that economic struggle within a community can lead to more equal treatment of citizens, in "Moments of Glory," Ngugi Wa Thiong'o presents a bleaker view of the economic struggles between men and women and Africans and white Christians, in East Africa. The brief triumph of the story's main character, an African prostitute, is accompanied by severe economic sanctions and imprisonment. In Lorna Dee Cervantes' poem, "Cannery Town in August," the economic mandates of the cannery dehumanize the lives of the citizens.

The effects of dislocation and loss of culture are explored in Louise Erdrich's "American Horse." In Erdrich's story a Native American mother struggles to keep her son, when government social workers come to take the boy away from what society has defined as an unfit home. In his poem "Jorge, the Church Janitor Finally Quits," Martin Espada reveals the white leaders' lack of interest in the Hispanic janitor's culture and their objectivification of his humanity; he is treated as if he were no more than a mop. Unlike the mother in "American Horse," Jorge can gain a limited satisfaction in his struggle against social institutions, but only by quitting his job. In her memoir "The Silent Girl" Maxine Hong Kingston reveals the confusion of a first-generation Chinese American child as she tries to adjust to elementary school; the angry child's fears lead to her nervous breakdown, from which she finally recovers after a year in bed.

Gender can also lead to struggles. The story "The Yellow Wallpaper," by Charlotte Perkins Gilman, questions the traditional gender struggle between a patronizing doctor/husband and his fragile and repressed patient/wife. In "Women, Home, and Community," Cynthia Hamilton argues that women have a stronger commitment to preserving a wholesome environment than male politicians because women's primary responsibility in life is to their children's well-being. In her poem, "Unknown Girl in the Maternity Ward," Anne Sexton implies that a young woman's decision to give up her newborn is related to lack of concern by the doctors in the maternity ward. She feels that no one can understand her feelings or help her.

Certainly you will be able to find more issues of struggle in the selections that follow. As you think about, define, and trace issues of struggle, also consider how reading about struggles affects your inner life. Question your relationship to the struggles addressed in these readings and reflect on the injustice, the pain, and the poverty in your own community. Perhaps reading and thinking about these selections will move you to feel pain and joy, to develop strategies that will help you to implement changes that will bring justice to your neighborhood and community and to the world.

Folk Tales

The Emperor's New Clothes
Hans Christian Andersen

Journal

Write about a time in your childhood when you realized that adults were not acknowledging a problem that was evident to you. How did having this insight make you feel?

Many years ago there lived an Emperor, who was so excessively fond of grand new clothes that he spent all his money upon them, that he might be very fine. He did not care about his soldiers, nor about the theatre, and only liked to drive out and show his new clothes. He had a coat for every hour of the day; and just as they say of a king, "He is in council," so they always said of him, "The Emperor is in the wardrobe."

In the great city in which he lived it was always very merry; every day came many strangers; one day two rogues came: they gave themselves out as weavers, and declared they could weave the finest stuff any one could imagine. Not only were their colors and patterns, they said, uncommonly beautiful, but the clothes made of the stuff possessed the wonderful quality that they became invisible to any one who was unfit for the office he held, or was incorrigibly stupid.

"Those would be capital clothes!" thought the Emperor. "If I wore those, I should be able to find out what men in my empire are not fit for the places they have; I could tell the clever from the dunces. Yes, the stuff must be woven for me directly!"

And he gave the two rogues a great deal of cash in hand, that they might begin their work at once.

As for them, they put up two looms, and pretended to be working; but they had nothing at all on their looms. They at once demanded the finest silk and the costliest gold; this they put into their own pockets, and worked at the empty looms till late into the night.

"I should like to know how far they have got on with the stuff," thought the Emperor. But he felt quite uncomfortable when he thought that those who were not fit for their offices could not see it. He believed, indeed, that he had nothing to fear for himself, but yet he preferred first to send some one else to see how matters stood. All the people in the city knew what peculiar power the stuff possessed, and all were anxious to see how bad or how stupid their neighbors were.

"I will send my honest old Minister to the weavers," thought the Emperor. "He can judge best how the stuff looks, for he has sense, and no one understands his office better than he."

Now the good old Minister went out into the hall where the two rogues sat working at the empty looms.

"Mercy on us!" thought the old Minister, and he opened his eyes wide. "I cannot see anything at all!" But he did not say this.

Both the rogues begged him to be so good as to come nearer, and asked if he did not approve of the colors and the pattern. Then they pointed to the empty loom, and the poor old Minister went on opening his eyes; but he could see nothing, for there was nothing to see.

"Mercy!" thought he, "can I indeed be so stupid: I never thought that, and not a soul must know it. Am I not fit for my office? No, it will never do for me to tell that I could not see the stuff."

"Don't you say anything to it?" asked one, as he went on weaving.

"O, it is charming—quite enchanting!" answered the old Minister, as he peered through his spectacles. "What a fine pattern, and what colors! Yes, I shall tell the Emperor that I am very much pleased with it."

"Well, we are glad of that," said both the weavers; and then they named the colors, and explained the strange pattern. The old Minister listened attentively, that he might be able to repeat it when the Emperor came. And he did so.

Now the rogues asked for more money, and silk and gold, which they declared they wanted for weaving. They put all into their own pockets, and not a thread was put upon the loom; they continued to work at the empty frames as before.

The Emperor soon sent again, dispatching another honest officer of the court, to see how the weaving was going on, and if the stuff would soon be ready. He fared just like the first: he looked and looked, but, as there was nothing to be seen but the empty looms, he could see nothing.

"Is not that a pretty piece of stuff?" asked the two rogues; and they displayed and explained the handsome pattern which was not there at all.

"I am not stupid!" thought the man: "it must be my good office, for which I am not fit. It is funny enough, but I must not let it be noticed." And so he praised the stuff which he did not see, and expressed his pleasure at the beautiful colors and charming pattern. "Yes, it is enchanting," he told the Emperor.

All the people in the town were talking of the gorgeous stuff. The Emperor wished to see it himself while it was still upon the loom. With a whole crowd of chosen men, among whom were also the two honest statesmen who had already been there, he went to the two cunning rogues, who were now weaving with might and main without fibre or thread.

"Is not that splendid?" said the two statesmen, who had already been there once. "Does not your Majesty remark the pattern and the colors?" And they pointed to the empty loom, for they thought that the others could see the stuff.

"What's this?" thought the Emperor. "I can see nothing at all! That is terrible. Am I stupid? Am I not fit to be Emperor? That would be the most dreadful thing that could happen to me. O, it is *very* pretty!" he said aloud. "It has our highest approbation." And he nodded in a contented way, and gazed at the empty loom, for he would not say that he saw nothing. The whole suite whom he had with him looked and looked, and saw nothing, any more than the rest; but, like the Emperor, they said, "That *is* pretty!" and counseled him to wear the splendid new clothes for the first time at the great procession that was presently to take place. "It is splendid, excellent!" went from mouth to mouth. On all sides there seemed to be general rejoicing, and the Emperor gave the rogues the title of Imperial Court Weavers.

The whole night before the morning on which the procession was to take place, the rogues were up, and kept more than sixteen candles burning. The people could see that they were hard at work, completing the Emperor's new clothes. They pretended to take the stuff down from the loom: they made cuts in the air with great scissors; they sewed with needles without thread; and at last they said, "Now the clothes are ready!"

The Emperor came himself with his noblest cavaliers; and the two rogues lifted up one arm as if they were holding something, and said, "See, here are the trousers! here is the coat! here is the cloak!" and so on. "It is as light as a spider's web: one would think one had nothing on; but that is just the beauty of it."

"Yes," said all the cavaliers; but they could not see anything, for nothing was there.

"Will your Imperial Majesty please to condescend to take off your clothes?" said the rogues; "then we will put on you the new clothes here in front of the great mirror."

The Emperor took off his clothes, and the rogues pretended to put on him each new garment as it was ready; and the Emperor turned round and round before the mirror.

"O, how well they look! how capitally they fit!" said all. "What a pattern! what colors! That *is* a splendid dress!"

"They are standing outside with the canopy which is to be borne above your Majesty in the procession!" announced the head Master of the Ceremonies.

"Well, I am ready," replied the Emperor. "Does it not suit me well?" And then he turned again to the mirror, for he wanted it to appear as if he contemplated his adornment with great interest.

The two chamberlains, who were to carry the train, stooped down with their hands toward the floor, just as if they were picking up the mantle; then they pretended to be holding something in the air. They did not dare to let it be noticed that they saw nothing.

So the Emperor went in procession under the rich canopy, and every one in the streets, said, "How incomparable are the Emperor's new clothes! what a train he has to his mantle! how it fits him!" No one would let it be perceived that he could see nothing, for that would have shown that he was not fit for his office, or was very stupid. No clothes of the Emperor's had ever had such a success as these.

"But he has nothing on!" a little child cried out at last.

"Just hear what that innocent says!" said the father: and one whispered to another what the child had said.

"But he has nothing on!" said the whole people at length. That touched the Emperor, for it seemed to him that they were right; but he thought within himself, "I must go through with the procession." And so he held himself a little higher, and the chamberlains held on tighter than ever, and carried the train which did not exist at all.

QUESTIONS AND CONSIDERATIONS

1. What is the weavers' con game? What strategies do they use to fool the emperor, courtiers, and the public? Why does the trick work so well?

2. What does the tale suggest about the power of language, particularly gossip?

3. Why does no one in the kingdom acknowledge the truth until the innocent child states the obvious: "But he has nothing on"?

4. Why does the ceremony continue despite the child's revelation?

5. Does this tale remind you of a recent political event? Which one?

Journals

From *The Diary of Che Guevara*

Che Guevara

Agosto, 1967

[1]

A quiet day, Miguel and Camba started the trail but only advanced a little over one kilometer due to the difficulties of the terrain and the vegetation. We killed a sly colt which should give us meat for five to six days. The small trenches to set an ambush were built in case the army should come around. If they should come tomorrow or the day after, the idea is to let them go by; if they don't discover the camp, to shoot them later on.

h = 650 ms.

[2]

The trail seems to have advanced well thanks to Benigno and Pablo who have followed it. It took them almost two hours to come back and reach the camp from the end of the road. They haven't given any news about us on the radio, since they announced the transfer of the corpse of an "anti-social one." My asthma struck me very hard and I have already used up the last anti-asthmatic injection; there is nothing left but tablets for about ten days.

[3]

The road turned out to be a fiasco; Miguel and Urbano took 57 minutes to return today; they advanced very slowly. There is no news. Pacho is recovering very well, but I, on the contrary, am ill. The day and the night were hard on me and a quick recovery is nowhere in sight. I tried the intravenous injection of novocaine to no avail.

[4]

The men came to a canyon which takes a course due southwest and may flow into the creeks which go into the Rio Grande. Tomorrow two pairs will cut the underbrush and Miguel will climb our canyon to explore what seems to be old *chacos*. My asthma has improved some.

[5]

Benigno, Camba, Urbano and Leon divided themselves into pairs to make better progress, but they came to a creek that flows into the Rosita and so today continued cross-country. Miguel went to explore the *chaco* but did not find it. We finished the horsemeat; tomorrow we shall try fishing, and the day after tomorrow we shall slaughter another animal. Tomorrow we will go as far as the new watering place. My asthma was implacable. Despite my reluctance for separation, I will have to send a group in advance. Benigno and Julio offered to be volunteers. Ñato's position needs to be examined.

[6]

The transfer of the camp was made; unfortunately there were not three hours on the road but one; which shows that we still have far to go. Benigno, Urbano, Camba and Leon continued breaking through, while Miguel and Aniceto went out to explore the new creek as far as its junction with the Rosita. By night they had not returned, and therefore precautions were taken, more so because I had heard something like a faraway mortar shot. Inti, Chapaco and I said a few words referring to today. Bolivian Independence Day.
h = 720 ms.

[7]

At 11 in the morning I had given up Miguel and Aniceto for lost, having ordered Benigno to advance cautiously as far as the outlet into the Rosita and study the direction they took, if they had gone that far. However at 13 the missing ones appeared. They had simply met with difficulties on the way, and night overtook them before reaching the Rosita. It was a bitter pill that Miguel made me swallow. We remained in the same place, but the trailbreakers found another creek, and tomorrow we shall move to it. Today our old horse Anselmo died. Now the only one we have left is our horse of burden. My asthma continues the same, and I am running out of medicine. Tomorrow I shall make a decision to send a group to the Ñacahuasu. Today marks exactly nine months since our arrival and the constitution of the guerrilla. Out of the first six, two are dead, one has disappeared and two are wounded; I have asthma which I do not know how to stop.

[8]

We walked effectively something like an hour, which seemed more like two to me due to the weariness of the little mare. In a moment of temper, I struck her in the neck with a whip, wounding her badly. The new camp must be the last one with water until the arrival at the Rosita or the Rio Grande; the *macheteros* are 40 minutes from here (two to three kilometers). A group of eight men were assigned to fulfill the following mission: they are to leave here tomorrow to walk all day long; the next day Camba should return with the news about whatever has happened; on the day after. Pablito and Dario should return with the news of that day. The remaining five will keep on until they reach Vargas' house and from there Coco and Aniceto should return with the news about how things are. Benigno, Julio and Ñato will go as far as the Ñacahuasu to look for my medicine. They should move with great care to avoid ambushes; we shall follow them and the points of meeting will be: the house of Vargas or further up, according to our speed, and the creek that is facing the cave in the Rio Grande, the Masicuri (Honorato) or the Ñacahuasu. The army announced that they have discovered a deposit of arms in one of our camps.

At night I brought everybody together and gave them the following lecture: we are in a difficult situation; Pacho has gotten better today but I am just a human carcass, and the episode of the little mare proves that at some moments I have lost control; that will be modified, but the situation must weigh squarely on everybody and whoever does not feel capable of sustaining it should say so.

It is one of those moments when great decisions must be taken; this type of struggle gives us the opportunity not only to turn ourselves into revolutionaries, the highest level of the human species, but it also allows us to graduate as men; those who cannot reach either one of these two stages should say so and leave the struggle.

All of the Cubans and some of the Bolivians expressed their desire to continue to the end; Eustaquio did the same but also criticized Muganga because he carried his knapsack on the mule instead of wood for fuel which provoked an angry reply from the latter; Julio chastized Moro and Pacho because of similar things, and there was a new angry answer, this time from Pacho. I finished the discussion by saying that there were two things being debated here of very different categories: one was whether the will to continue exists or not; the other deals with little grudges or internal problems of the guerrilla which wrests greatness from such a major decision. I did not like the questions raised by Eustaquio and Julio, but neither did I like the answers of Moro and Pacho. The essence is to be more revolutionary and set the example.

From *Digressions*
Gerald Early

. . . and the blues has got my heart.
—Louis Armstrong

November 24, 1987

Few activities can be as boring as attending academic conferences, listening to papers that you cannot understand, that are not worth the effort of trying to understand, that seem dutiful and unimaginative and filled with the current "hip" lingo of the business, terms like "megafiction" and "postmodern" and such. (As an uneducated friend once said to me, "Folks never know when they talking shit until somebody honest get an urge to wanna open some windows.") For in this too as in everything else in our culture one must be "current," even in the expressions of one's nostalgia. It is too much to listen to papers from people like yourself, unknowns who wish to be known, who are writing for job promotions, or to listen to the pomposity of the bigwigs, the stars, who have nothing to say that you did not already know and who do nothing but repeat the ideas of their latest book, which would not be so bad except the book has nothing much to offer. I know one thing: hardly any of these people would be here if they did not have to be; few would be writing if they could find another job which would pay them as poorly, give them as much fake prestige and free time, and that did not require "publications." It is unfortunate that people in this business are forced to talk endlessly when they have nothing to say and no way to say it, to borrow an old black saying.

I skipped most of the afternoon sessions to go to Harlem, just as I had skipped most of the morning sessions to walk in Central Park. I had been at the conference two days and had only heard one-half of one paper. I went to Harlem to do a spot of reading at the Schomburg, a place I had never set foot in before, despite being an Easterner, despite having gone to New York several times before, despite having been to Harlem.

Harlem looked worse than ever. I thought I was on a street somewhere in Bombay. So many unemployed people milling around, so many junkies milling around. A black woman, Jackie, who I believe is from Oregon, also attending the conference, accompanied me or rather I accompanied her as she approached me about the idea of going there. We were both well-dressed and this made us the target of panhandlers and beggars. One man was particularly insistent: "Aren't you a Christian?" he asked, but it was too late in the day to make an appeal based on religious guilt or the pious fake duty of doing good for people who, if truth were told, you really would not care were dead or alive. "You are black people too, you know," he shouted at us finally. And so he was right. But race guilt was not enough anymore either. At that moment my race was not enough, not nearly enough to make me one of these. I was torn between feeling: who are these black people? They are none of mine, not my black people, not my poor. Begone from me! But I felt as well the utter squalor, despair, dirt, lonesomeness, loathesomeness of the place was what I could bear because I had grown up black and I had grown up poor. But I could not bear it, not this much, not to this extreme. I only wished to turn my head in shame: To stop feeling a pounding dishonor that hammered in my head like a migraine because I had money, because I was well-dressed, because I was staying downtown at an expensive hotel that was really so close to this as to seem just outside my room window. I wanted to shout: "But I cannot afford to stay in such a hotel; someone else supports me here." I knew it would have made no difference for I had patrons who were willing to support me and they had none; I had access to money and they had none. Finally, I did not have to be there, in bright sunlight, watching in a kind of dreadful fascination, the voyeurism of the removed bourgeoisie, as a line of the dirtiest, most bedraggled people I have ever seen snaked its way through the street and into a store front building on Lennox Avenue. What was it? Why were they lined up there? At last, I discovered that someone, some agency, was giving away food. So this is autumn in New York; it *is* good to *live* it again.

I thought of Warner Sombart's *Why There Is No Socialism in the United States* and Oscar Wilde's "The Soul of Man Under Socialism" and thought that in a crude way the poor here do live under a kind of socialism. They deal with the state and only the state through its numerous agencies which are designed solely to keep the poor alive and to keep them miserable and contained. And they are, the poor, certainly all equal in the measurement of dispossession that has been allotted them. To look about the streets of Harlem is to see the soul of man under America's socialism, is to know that there is too much of a type of socialism in the United States. It is the socialism of the bourgeoisie who refuse to leave the poor alone and whose meddling does the poor little good. And it is all self-serving in the end. Give them food, give them drugs so they won't organize and turn the country upside down. Here we have people with so much leisure that they could cultivate themselves by using museums, libraries, and the parks; but we have so corrupted them with nonsense, made the parks, the libraries, and the museums the provinces of the bourgeoisie to use to cultivate their "precious" children, the playgrounds of the educated, that we scarcely permit the poor to enter these hallowed grounds of culture. That is the double tragedy: that we waste the poor by not putting them to useful work or useful leisure.

I stayed at the Schomberg for a few hours and then left to find a cab back to the hotel which soon became a matter of desperation as few cabs rumble up this way, I discovered, either by day or by night. I was not desperate to leave Harlem from fear. I felt no fear during the entire time I was there and indeed I have never felt fear strolling in any poor black neighborhood and I have walked in more than my share. I had to return to the hotel on time to deliver my paper. I was on. It was showtime in academe.

From *The Diary of Carolina Maria de Jesus*

Carolina Maria de Jesus

July 15, 1955

The birthday of my daughter Vera Eunice. I wanted to buy a pair of shoes for her, but the price of food keeps us from realizing our desires. Actually we are slaves to the cost of living. I found a pair of shoes in the garbage, washed them, and patched them for her to wear. . . .

I was ill all day. I thought I had a cold. At night my chest pained me. I started to cough. I decided not to go out at night to look for paper. I searched for my son João. He was . . . near the market. A bus had knocked a boy into the sidewalk and a crowd gathered. João was in the middle of it all. I poked him a couple of times and within five minutes he was home.

I washed the children, put them to bed, then washed myself and went to bed. I waited until 11:00 for a certain someone. He didn't come. I took an aspirin and laid down again. When I awoke the sun was sliding in space. My daughter Vera Eunice said: "Go get some water, Mother!"

July 16

I got up and obeyed Vera Eunice. I went to get the water. I made coffee. I told the children that I didn't have any bread, that they would have to drink their coffee plain . . . I was feeling ill and decided to cure myself. I stuck my finger down my throat twice, vomited, and knew I was under the evil eye . . . I thought of the worrisome life that I led. Carrying paper, washing clothes for the children, staying in the streets all day long. Yet I'm always lacking things, Vera doesn't have shoes and she doesn't like to go barefoot. For at least two years I've wanted to buy a meat grinder. And a sewing machine.

I came home and made lunch for the two boys. Rice, beans, and meat, and I'm going out to look for paper. I left the children, told them to play in the yard and not go into the street, because the terrible neighbors I have won't leave my children alone. I was feeling ill and wished I could lie down. But the poor don't rest nor are they permitted the pleasure of relaxation. I was nervous inside, cursing my luck. I collected two full sacks of paper. Afterward I went back and gathered up some scrap metal, some cans, and some kindling wood . . .

When I came home there was a crowd at my door. Children and women claiming José Carlos had thrown stones at their houses. They wanted me to punish him.

July 18

I got up at 7. Happy and content. Weariness would be here soon enough. . . .

Dona Silvia came to complain about my children. That they were badly educated. I don't look for defects in children. Neither in mine nor in others. I know that a child is not born with sense. When I speak with a child I use pleasant words. What infuriates me is that the parents come to my door to disrupt my rare moments of inner tranquillity. But when they upset me, I write. I know how to dominate my impulses. I only had two years of schooling, but I got enough to form my character. The only thing that does not exist in the favela is friendship. . . .

My kids are not kept alive by the church's bread. I take on all kinds of work to keep them. And those women have to beg or even steal. At night when they are begging I peacefully sit in my shack listening to Viennese waltzes. While their husbands break the boards of the shack, I and my children sleep peacefully.

I don't envy the married women of the favelas who lead lives like Indian slaves.

I never got married and I'm not unhappy. Those who wanted to marry me were mean and the conditions they imposed on me horrible.

July 19

. . . When those female witches invade my shack, my children throw stones at them. The women scream:

"What uneducated brats!"

I reply:

"My children are defending me. You are ignorant and can't understand that. I'm going to write a book about the favela, and I'm going to tell everything that happened here. And everything that you do to me. I want to write a book, and you with these disgusting scenes are furnishing me with the material."

Silvia asked me to take her name out of my book. . . .

July 21

I woke with the voice of Dona Maria asking me if I wanted to buy bananas or lettuce . . . Then I went to wash clothes. While the clothes were bleaching I sat on the sidewalk and wrote. A man passed by and asked me:

"What are you writing?"

"All the cheating that the favela dwellers practice. Those human wrecks."

He said:

"Write it and give it to an editor so he can make revisions."

. . . I spent the rest of the afternoon writing. At 4:30 . . . I gave the children a bath and got ready to go out. I went out to pick up paper but I felt ill. I hurried because it was cold. When I got home it was 10:30. I turned on the radio, took a bath, and heated some food. I read a little. I don't know how to sleep without reading. I like to leaf through a book. The book is man's best invention so far.

July 27

. . . Senhor Gino came to ask me to go to his shack. That I am neglecting him. I answered: no!

I am writing a book to sell. I am hoping that with this money I can buy a place and leave the favela. I don't have time to go to anybody's house. Senhor Gino insisted. He told me:

"Just knock and I'll open the door."

But my heart didn't ask me to go to his room.

May 15, 1958

. . . I classify São Paulo this way: The Governor's Palace is the living room. The mayor's office is the dining room and the city is the garden. And the favela is the back yard where they throw the garbage.

May 19

. . . What our President Senhor Juscelino has in his favor is his voice. He sings like a bird and his voice is pleasant to the ears. And now the bird is living in a golden cage called Catete Palace. Be careful, little bird, that you don't lose this cage, because cats when they are hungry think of birds in cages. The *favelados* are the cats, and they are hungry. . . .

I washed the floor because I'm expecting a visit from a future deputy and he wants me to make some speeches for him. He says he wants to know the favelas and if he is elected he's going to abolish them.

The sky was the color of indigo, and I understood that I adore my Brazil. My glance went over to the trees . . . the leaves moved by themselves. I thought: they are applauding my gesture of love to my country. I went on looking for paper. . . .

May 20

. . . my children ran to tell me that they had found some macaroni in the garbage. As the food supply was low I cooked some of the macaroni with beans. And my son João said to me:

"Uh, huh. You told me you weren't going to eat any more things from the garbage."

It was the first time I had failed to keep my word. I said:

"I had faith in President Kubitschek."

"You had faith, and now you don't have it any more?"

"No, my son, democracy is losing its followers. In our country everything is weakening. The money is weak. Democracy is weak and the politicians are very weak. Everything that is weak dies one day."

The politicians know that I am a poetess. And that a poet will even face death when he sees his people oppressed.

June 1

. . . I haven't said anything about my dear mother. She was very good. She wanted me to study to be a teacher. It was the uncertainties of life that made it impossible for her to realize her dream. But she formed my character, taught me to like the humble and the weak. That's why I have pity on the *favelados.* I know very well that there are contemptible people here, persons with perverted souls. Last night Amelia and her companion fought. She told him that he was with her only for the money she gave him. You only had to listen to Amelia's voice to know she enjoyed the argument. She had many children. Gave them all away. She has two boys at home that she doesn't want. She neglects children and collects men.

A man enters by the door. A child is the root of the heart. . . .

June 7

. . . When I was a girl my dream was to be a man to defend Brazil, because I read the history of Brazil and became aware that war existed. I read the masculine names of the defenders of the country, then I said to my mother:

"Why don't you make me become a man?"

She replied:

"If you walk under a rainbow, you'll become a man."

When a rainbow appeared I went running in its direction. But the rainbow was always a long way off. Just as the politicians are far from the people. I got tired and sat down. Afterward I started to cry. But the people must not get tired. They must not cry. They must fight to improve Brazil so that our children don't suffer as we are suffering. I returned and told my mother:

"The rainbow ran away from me."

QUESTIONS AND CONSIDERATIONS

1. What inner conflict do Che Guevara, Gerald Early, and Carolina Maria de Jesus feel in response to the struggles that they write about?

2. Why does each of the journal writers feel the need to turn to writing in order to express his or her feelings about injustice, instead of simply acting in response to injustice? In what sense is writing a "salvation" for each of these writers?

3. Gerald Early and Carolina Maria de Jesus make observations and use descriptions of the worlds of struggle and injustice. Contrast the way each author describes injustice and draws conclusions from his or her observations.

4. Each author tells one or more stories in his or her journal. What is the intention of each narrative? What point does each story make about the social struggles? Which author seems to be the most effective narrator?

5. Write in your journal about a social struggle that you have witnessed or been involved in. Describe the incident and explore your feelings about the struggle.

Fiction

The Yellow Wallpaper
Charlotte Perkins Gilman

Journal

Write about a nightmare in which you felt trapped or imprisoned. What did you learn about yourself after thinking about this dream?

It is very seldom that mere ordinary people like John and myself secure ancestral halls for the summer.

A colonial mansion, a hereditary estate, I would say a haunted house and reach the height of romantic felicity—but that would be asking too much of fate!

Still I will proudly declare that there is something queer about it.

Else, why should it be let so cheaply? And why have stood so long un-tenanted?

John laughs at me, of course, but one expects that.

John is practical in the extreme. He has no patience with faith, an intense horror of superstition, and he scoffs openly at any talk of things not to be felt and seen and put down in figures.

John is a physician, and *perhaps*—(I would not say it to a living soul, of course, but this is dead paper and a great relief to my mind)—*perhaps* that is one reason I do not get well faster.

You see, he does not believe I am sick! And what can one do?

If a physician of high standing, and one's own husband, assures friends and relatives that there is really nothing the matter with one but temporary nervous depression—a slight hysterical tendency—what is one to do?

My brother is also a physician, and also of high standing, and he says the same thing.

So I take phosphates or phosphites—whichever it is—and tonics, and air and exercise, and journeys, and am absolutely forbidden to "work" until I am well again.

Personally, I disagree with their ideas.

Personally, I believe that congenial work, with excitement and change, would do me good.

But what is one to do?

I did write for a while in spite of them; but it *does* exhaust me a good deal—having to be so sly about it, or else meet with heavy opposition.

I sometimes fancy that in my condition, if I had less opposition and more society and stimulus—but John says the very worst thing I can do is to think about my condition, and I confess it always makes me feel bad.

So I will let it alone and talk about the house.

The most beautiful place! It is quite alone, standing well back from the road, quite three miles from the village. It makes me think of English places that you read about, for there are hedges and walls and gates that lock, and lots of separate little houses for the gardeners and people.

There is a *delicious* garden! I never saw such a garden—large and shady, full of box-bordered paths, and lined with long grape-covered arbors with seats under them.

There were greenhouses, but they are all broken now.

There was some legal trouble, I believe, something about the heirs and co-heirs; anyhow, the place has been empty for years.

That spoils my ghostliness, I am afraid, but I don't care—there is something strange about the house—I can feel it.

I even said so to John one moonlight evening, but he said what I felt was a draught, and shut the window.

I get unreasonably angry with John sometimes. I'm sure I never used to be so sensitive. I think it is due to this nervous condition.

But John says if I feel so I shall neglect proper self-control; so I take pains to control myself—before him, at least, and that makes me very tired.

I don't like our room a bit. I wanted one downstairs that opened onto the piazza and had roses all over the window, and such pretty old-fashioned chintz hangings! But John would not hear of it.

He said there was only one window and not room for two beds, and no near room for him if he took another.

He is very careful and loving, and hardly lets me stir without special direction.

I have a schedule prescription of each hour in the day; he takes all care from me, and so I feel basely ungrateful not to value it more.

He said he came here solely on my account, that I was to have perfect rest and all the air I could get. "Your exercise depends on your strength, my dear," said he, "and your food somewhat on your appetite; but air you can absorb all the time." So we took the nursery at the top of the house.

It is a big, airy room, the whole floor nearly, with windows that look all ways, and air and sunshine galore. It was nursery first, and then playroom and gymnasium, I should judge, for the windows are barred for little children, and there are rings and things in the walls.

The paint and paper look as if a boys' school had used it. It is stripped off—the paper—in great patches all around the head of my bed, about as far as I can reach, and in a great place on the other side of the room low down. I never saw a worse paper in my life. One of those sprawling, flamboyant patterns committing every artistic sin.

It is dull enough to confuse the eye in following, pronouned enough constantly to irritate and provoke study, and when you follow the lame uncertain curves for a little distance they suddenly commit suicide—plunge off at outrageous angles, destroy themselves in unheard-of contradictions.

The color is repellent, almost revolting: a smouldering unclean yellow, strangely faded by the slow-turning sunlight. It is a dull yet lurid orange in some places, a stickly sulphur tint in others.

No wonder the children hated it! I should hate it myself if I had to live in this room long.

There comes John, and I must put this away—he hates to have me write a word.

We have been here two weeks, and I haven't felt like writing before, since that first day.

I am sitting by the window now, up in this atrocious nursery, and there is nothing to hinder my writings as much as I please, save lack of strength.

John is away all day, and even some nights when his cases are serious.

I am glad my case is not serious!

But these nervous troubles are dreadfully depressing.

John does not know how much I really suffer. He knows there is no reason to suffer, and that satisfies him.

Of course it is only nervousness. It does weigh on me so not to do my duty in any way!

I meant to be such a help to John, such a real rest and comfort, and here I am a comparative burden already!

Nobody would believe what an effort it is to do what little I am able—to dress and entertain, and order things.

It is fortunate Mary is so good with the baby. Such a dear baby!

And yet I *cannot* be with him, it makes me so nervous.

I suppose John never was nervous in his life. He laughs at me so about this wallpaper!

At first he meant to repaper the room, but afterward he said that I was letting it get the better of me, and that nothing was worse for a nervous patient than to give way to such fancies.

He said that after the wallpaper was changed it would be the heavy bedstead, and then the barred windows, and then that gate at the head of the stairs, and so on.

"You know the place is doing you good," he said, "and really, dear, I don't care to renovate the house just for a three months' rental."

"Then do let us go downstairs," I said. "There are such pretty rooms there."

Then he took me in his arms and called me a blessed little goose, and said he would go down cellar, if I wished, and have it whitewashed into the bargain.

But he is right enough about the beds and windows and things.

It is as airy and comfortable a room as anyone need wish, and, of course, I would not be so silly as to make him uncomfortable just for a whim.

I'm really getting quite fond of the big room, all but that horrid paper.

Out of one window I can see the garden—those mysterious deep-shaded arbors, the riotous old-fashioned flowers, and bushes and gnarly trees.

Out of another I get a lovely view of the bay and a little private wharf belonging to the estate. There is a beautiful shaded lane that runs down there from the house. I always fancy I see people walking in these numerous paths and arbors, but John has cautioned me not to give way to fancy in the least. He says that with my imaginative power and habit of story-making, a nervous weakness like mine is sure to lead to all manner of excited fancies, and that I ought to use my will and good sense to check the tendency. So I try.

I think sometimes that if I were only well enough to write a little it would relieve the press of ideas and rest me.

But I find I get pretty tired when I try.

It is so discouraging not to have any advice and companionship about my work. When I get really well, John says we will ask Cousin Henry and Julia down for a long visit; but he says he would as soon put fireworks in my pillowcase as to let me have those stimulating people about now.

I wish I could get well faster.

But I must not think about that. This paper looks to me as if it *knew* what a vicious influence it had!

There is a recurrent spot where the pattern lolls like a broken neck and two bulbous eyes stare at you upside down.

I get positively angry with the impertinence of it and the everlastingness. Up and down and sideways they crawl, and those absurd unblinking eyes are everywhere. There is one place where two breadths didn't match, and the eyes go all up and down the line, one a little higher than the other.

I never saw so much expression in an inanimate thing before, and we all know how much expression they have! I used to lie awake as a child and get more entertainment and terror out of blank walls and plain furniture than most children could find in a toy-store.

I remember what a kindly wink the knobs of our big old bureau used to have, and there was one chair that always seemed like a strong friend.

I used to feel that if any of the other things looked too fierce I could always hop into that chair and be safe.

The furniture in this room is no worse than inharmonious, however, for we had to bring it all from downstairs. I suppose when this was used as a play-room they had to take the nursery things out, and no wonder! I never saw such ravages as the children have made here.

The wallpaper, as I said before, is torn off in spots, and it sticketh closer than a brother—they must have had perseverance as well as hatred.

Then the floor is scratched and gouged and splintered, the plaster itself is dug out here and there, and this great heavy bed, which is all we found in the room, looks as if it had been through the wars.

But I don't mind it a bit—only the paper.

There comes John's sister. Such a dear girl as she is, and so careful of me! I must not let her find me writing.

She is a perfect and enthusiastic housekeeper, and hopes for no better profession. I verily believe she thinks it is the writing which made me sick!

But I can write when she is out, and see her a long way off from these windows.

There is one that commands the road, a lovely shaded winding road, and one that just looks off over the country. A lovely country, too, full of great elms and velvet meadows.

This wallpaper has a kind of subpattern in a different shade, a particularly irritating one, for you can only see it in certain lights, and not clearly then.

But in the places where it isn't faded and where the sun is just so—I can see a strange, provoking, formless sort of figure that seems to skulk about behind that silly and conspicuous front design.

There's sister on the stairs!

Well, the Fourth of July is over! The people are all gone, and I am tired out. John thought it might do me good to see a little company, so we just had Mother and Nellie and the children down for a week.

Of course I didn't do a thing. Jennie sees to everything now.

But it tired me all the same.

John says if I don't pick up faster he shall send me to Weir Mitchell in the fall.

But I don't want to go there at all. I had a friend who was in his hands once, and she says he is just like John and my brother, only more so!

Besides, it is such an undertaking to go so far.

I don't feel as if it was worthwhile to turn my hand over for anything, and I'm getting dreadfully fretful and querulous.

I cry at nothing, and cry most of the time.

Of course I don't when John is here, or anybody else, but when I am alone.

And I am alone a good deal just now. John is kept in town very often by serious cases, and Jennie is good and lets me alone when I want her to.

So I walk a little in the garden or down that lovely lane, sit on the porch under the roses, and lie down up here a good deal.

I'm getting really fond of the room in spite of the wallpaper. Perhaps *because* of the wallpaper.

It dwells in my mind so!

I lie here on this great immovable bed—it is nailed down, I believe—and follow that pattern about by the hour. It is as good as gymnastics, I assure you. I start, we'll say, at the bottom, down in the corner over there where it has not been touched, and I determine for the thousandth time that I *will* follow that pointless pattern to some sort of a conclusion.

I know a little of the principle of design, and I know this thing was not arranged on any laws of radiation, or alternation, or repetition, or symmetry, or anything else that I ever heard of.

It is repeated, of course, by the breadths, but not otherwise.

Looked at in one way, each breadth stands alone; the bloated curves and flourishes—a kind of "debased Romanesque" with dilirium tremens go waddling up and down in isolated columns of fatuity.

But, on the other hand, they connect diagonally, and the sprawling outlines run off in great slanting waves of optic horror, like a lot of wallowing sea-weeds in full chase.

The whole thing goes horizontally, too, at least it seems so, and I exhaust myself trying to distinguish the order of its going in that direction.

They have used a horizontal breadth for a frieze, and that adds wonderfully to the confusion.

There is one end of the room where it is almost intact, and there, when the crosslights fade and the low sun shines directly upon it, I can almost fancy radiation after all—the interminable grotesque seems to form around a common center and rush off in headlong plunges of equal distraction.

It makes me tired to follow it. I will take a nap, I guess.

I don't know why I should write this.

I don't want to.

I don't feel able.

And I know John would think it absurd. But I *must* say what I feel and think in some way—it is such a relief!

But the effort is getting to be greater than the relief.

Half the time now I am awfully lazy, and lie down ever so much. John says I mustn't lose my strength, and has me take cod liver oil and lots of tonics and things, to say nothing of ale and wines and rare meat.

Dear John! He loves me very dearly, and hates to have me sick. I tried to have a real earnest reasonable talk with him the other day, and tell him how I wish he would let me go and make a visit to Cousin Henry and Julia.

But he said I wasn't able to go, nor able to stand it after I got there; and I did not make out a very good case for myself, for I was crying before I had finished.

It is getting to be a great effort for me to think straight. Just this nervous weakness, I suppose.

And dear John gathered me up in his arms, and just carried me upstairs and laid me on the bed, and sat by me and read to me till it tired my head.

He said I was his darling and his comfort and all he had, and that I must take care of myself for his sake, and keep well.

He says no one but myself can help me out of it, that I must use my will and self-control and not let any silly fancies run away with me.

There's one comfort—the baby is well and happy, and does not have to occupy this nursery with the horrid wallpaper.

If we had not used it, that blessed child would have! What a fortunate escape! Why, I wouldn't have a child of mine, an impressionable little thing, live in such a room for worlds.

I never thought of it before, but it is lucky that John kept me here after all; I can stand it so much easier than a baby, you see.

Of course I never mention it to them any more—I am too wise—but I keep watch for it all the same.

There are things in the wallpaper that nobody knows about but me, or ever will.

Behind that outside pattern the dim shapes get clearer every day.

It is always the same shape, only very numerous.

And it is like a woman stooping down and creeping about behind that pattern. I don't like it a bit. I wonder—I begin to think—I wish John would take me away from here!

It is so hard to talk with John about my case, because he is so wise, and because he loves me so.

But I tried it last night.

It was moonlight. The moon shines in all around just as the sun does.

I hate to see it sometimes, it creeps so slowly, and always comes in by one window or another.

John was asleep and I hated to waken him, so I kept still and watched the moonlight on that undulating wallpaper till I felt creepy.

The faint figure behind seemed to shake the pattern, just as if she wanted to get out.

I got up softly and went to feel and see if the paper *did* move, and when I came back John was awake.

"What is it, little girl?" he said. "Don't go walking about like that—you'll get cold."

I thought it was a good time to talk, so I told him that I really was not gaining here, and that I wished he would take me away.

"Why, darling!" said he. "Our lease will be up in three weeks, and I can't see how to leave before.

"The repairs are not done at home, and I cannot possibly leave town just now. Of course, if you were in any danger, I could and would, but you really are better, dear, whether you can see it or not. I am a doctor, dear, and I know. You are gaining flesh and color, your appetite is better, I feel really much easier about you."

"I don't weigh a bit more," said I, "nor as much; and my appetite may be better in the evening when you are here but it is worse in the morning when you are away!"

"Bless her little heart!" said he with a big hug. "She shall be as sick as she pleases! But now let's improve the shining hours by going to sleep, and talk about it in the morning!"

"And you won't go away?" I asked gloomily.

"Why, how can I, dear? It is only three weeks more and then we will take a nice little trip for a few days while Jennie is getting the house ready. Really, dear, you are better!"

"Better in body perhaps--" I began, and stopped short, for he sat up straight and looked at me with such a stern, reproachful look that I could not say another word.

"My darling," said he, "I beg you, for my sake and for our child's sake, as well as for your own, that you will never for one instant let that idea enter your mind! There is nothing so dangerous, so fascinating, to a temperament like yours. It is a false and foolish fancy. Can you trust me as a physician when I tell you so?"

So of course, I said no more on that score, and we went to sleep before long. He thought I was asleep first, but I wasn't, and lay there for hours trying to decide whether that front pattern and the back pattern really did move together or separately.

On a pattern like this, by daylight, there is a lack of sequence, a defiance of law, that is a constant irritant to a normal mind.

The color is hideous enough, and unreliable enough, and infuriating enough, but the pattern is torturing.

You think you have mastered it, but just as you get well under way in following, it turns a back-somersault and there you are. It slaps you in the face, knocks you down, and tramples upon you. It is like a bad dream.

The outside pattern is a florid arabesque, reminding one of a fungus. If you can imagine a toadstool in joints, an interminable string of toadstools, budding and sprouting in endless convolutions—why, that is something like it.

That is, sometimes!

There is one marked peculiarity about this paper, a thing nobody seems to notice but myself, and that is that it changes as the light changes.

When the sun shoots in through the east window—I always watch for that first long, straight ray—it changes so quickly that I never can quite believe it.

That is why I watch it always.

By moonlight—the moon shines in all night when there is a moon—I wouldn't know it was the same paper.

At night in any kind of light, in twilight, candlelight, lamplight, and worst of all by moonlight, it becomes bars! The outside pattern, I mean, and the woman behind it is as plain as can be.

I didn't realize for a long time what the thing was that showed behind, that dim subpattern, but now I am quite sure it is a woman.

By daylight she is subdued, quiet. I fancy it is the pattern that keeps her so still. It is so puzzling. It keeps me quiet by the hour.

I lie down ever so much now. John says it is good for me, and to sleep all I can.

Indeed he started the habit by making me lie down for an hour after each meal.

It is a very bad habit, I am convinced, for you see, I don't sleep.

And that cultivates deceit, for I don't tell them I'm awake—oh, no!

The fact is I am getting a little afraid of John.

He seems very queer sometimes, and even Jennie has an inexplicable look.

It strikes me occasionally, just as a scientific hypothesis, that perhaps it is the paper!

I have watched John when he did not know I was looking, and come into the room suddenly on the most innocent excuses, and I've caught him several times *looking at the paper!* And Jennie too. I caught Jennie with her hand on it once.

She didn't know I was in the room, and when I asked her in a quiet, a very quiet voice, and the most restrained manner possible, what she was doing with the paper, she turned around as if she had been caught stealing, and looked quite angry—asked me why I should frighten her so!

Then she said that the paper stained everything it touched, that she had found yellow smooches on all my clothes and John's and she wishes we would be more careful!

Did not that sound innocent? But I know she was studying that pattern, and I am determined that nobody shall find it out but myself!

Life is very much more exciting now than it used to be. You see, I have something more to expect, to look forward to, to watch. I really do eat better, and am more quiet than I was.

John is so pleased to see me improve! He laughed a little the other day, and said I seemed to be flourishing in spite of my wallpaper.

I turned it off with a laugh. I had no intention of telling him it was *because* of the wallpaper—he would make fun of me. He might even want to take me away.

I don't want to leave now until I have found it out. There is a week more, and I think that will be enough.

I'm feeling so much better!

I don't sleep much at night, for it is so interesting to watch developments; but I sleep a good deal during the daytime.

In the daytime it is tiresome and perplexing.

There are always new shoots on the fungus, and new shades of yellow all over it. I cannot keep count of them, though I have tried conscientiously.

It is the strangest yellow, that wallpaper! It makes me think of all the yellow things I ever saw—not beautiful ones like buttercups, but old, foul, bad yellow things.

But there is something else about that paper—the smell! I noticed it the moment we came into the room, but with so much air and sun it was not bad. Now we have had a week of fog and rain, and whether the windows are open or not, the smell is here.

It creeps all over the house.

I find it hovering in the dining-room, skulking in the parlor, hiding in the hall, lying in wait for me on the stairs.

It gets into my hair.

Even when I go to ride, if I turn my head suddenly and surprise it—there is that smell!

Such a peculiar odor, too! I have spent hours in trying to analyze it, to find what it smelled like.

It is not bad—at first—and very gentle, but quite the subtlest, most enduring odor I ever met.

It used to disturb me at first. I thought seriously of burning the house—to reach the smell.

But now I am used to it. The only thing I can think of that it is like is the *color* of the paper! A yellow smell.

There is a very funny mark on this wall, low down, near the mopboard. A streak that runs round the room. It goes behind every piece of furniture, except the bed, a long straight, even *smooch,* as if it had been rubbed over and over.

I wonder how it was done and who did it, and what they did it for. Round and round and round—round and round and round—it makes me dizzy!

I really have discovered something at last.

Through watching so much at night, when it changes so, I have finally found out.

The front pattern *does* move—and no wonder! The woman behind shakes it!

Sometimes I think there are a great many women behind, and sometimes only one, and she crawls around fast, and her crawling shakes it all over.

Then in the very bright spots she keeps still, and in the very shady spots she just takes hold of the bars and shakes them hard.

And she is all the time trying to climb through. But nobody could climb through that pattern—it strangles so; I think that is why it has so many heads.

They get through and then the pattern strangles them off and turns them upside down, and makes their eyes white!

If those heads were covered or taken off it would not be half so bad.

I think that woman gets out in the daytime!

And I'll tell you why—privately—I've seen her!

I can see her out of every one of my windows!

It is the same woman, I know, for she is always creeping, and most women do not creep by daylight.

I see her in that long shaded lane, creeping up and down. I see her in those dark grape arbors, creeping all round the garden.

I see her on that long road under the trees, creeping along, and when a carriage comes she hides under the blackberry vines.

I don't blame her a bit. It must be very humiliating to be caught creeping by daylight!

I always lock the door when I creep by daylight. I can't do it at night, for I know John would suspect something at once.

And John is so queer now that I don't want to irritate him. I wish he would take another room! Besides, I don't want anybody to get that woman out at night but myself.

I often wonder if I could see her out of all the windows at once.

But, turn as fast as I can, I can only see out of one at one time.

And though I always see her, she *may* be able to creep faster than I can turn! I have watched her sometimes away off in the open country, creeping as fast as a cloud shadow in a wind.

If only that top pattern could be gotten off from the under one! I mean to try it, little by little.

I have found out another funny thing, but I shan't tell it this time! It does not do to trust people too much.

There are only two more days to get this paper off, and I believe John is beginning to notice. I don't like the look in his eyes.

And I heard him ask Jennie a lot of professional questions about me. She had a very good report to give.

She said I slept a good deal in the daytime.

John knows I don't sleep very well at night, for all I'm so quiet!

He asked me all sorts of questions too, and pretended to be very loving and kind.

As if I couldn't see through him!

Still, I don't wonder he acts so, sleeping under this paper for three months.

It only interests me, but I feel sure John and Jennie are affected by it.

Hurrah! This is the last day, but it is enough. John is to stay in town over night, and won't be out until this evening.

Jennie wanted to sleep with me—the sly thing; but I told her I should undoubtedly rest better for a night all alone.

That was clever, for really I wasn't alone a bit! As soon as it was moonlight and that poor thing began to crawl and shake the pattern, I got up and ran to help her.

I pulled and she shook. I shook and she pulled, and before morning we had peeled off yards of that paper.

A strip about as high as my head and half around the room.

And then when the sun came and that awful pattern began to laugh at me, I declared I would finish it today!

We go away tomorrow, and they are moving all my furniture down again to leave things as they were before.

Jennie looked at the wall in amazement, but I told her merrily that I did it out of pure spite at the vicious thing.

She laughed and said she wouldn't mind doing it herself, but I must not get tired.

How she betrayed herself that time!

But I am here, and no person touches this paper but Me—not *alive!*

She tried to get me out of the room—it was too patent! But I said it was so quiet and empty and clean now that I believed I would lie down again and sleep all I could, and not to wake me even for dinner—I would call when I woke.

So now she is gone, and the servants are gone, and the things are gone, and there is nothing left but that great bedstead nailed down, with the canvas mattress we found on it.

We shall sleep downstairs tonight, and take the boat home tomorrow.

I quite enjoy the room, now it is bare again.

How those children did tear about here!

This bedstead is fairly gnawed!

But I must get to work.

I have locked the door and thrown the key down into the front path.

I don't want to go out, and I don't want to have anybody come in, till John comes.

I want to astonish him.

I've got a rope up here that even Jennie did not find. If that woman does get out, and tries to get away, I can tie her!

But I forgot I could not reach far without anything to stand on!

This bed will *not* move!

I tried to lift and push it until I was lame, and then I got so angry I bit off a little piece at one corner—but it hurt my teeth.

Then I peeled off all the paper I could reach standing on the floor. It sticks horribly and the pattern just enjoys it! All those strangled heads and bulbous eyes and waddling fungus growths just shriek with derision!

I am getting angry enough to do something desperate. To jump out of the window would be admirable exercise, but the bars are too strong even to try.

Besides I wouldn't do it. Of course not. I know well enough that a step like that is improper and might be misconstrued.

I don't like to *look* out of the windows even—there are so many of those creeping women, and they creep so fast.

I wonder if they all come out of that wallpaper as I did!

But I am securely fastened now by my well-hidden rope—you don't get *me* out in the road there!

I suppose I shall have to get back behind the pattern when it comes night, and that is hard!

It is so pleasant to be out in this great room and creep around as I please!

I don't want to go outside. I won't, even if Jennie asks me to.

For outside you have to creep on the ground, and everything is green instead of yellow.

But here I can creep smoothly on the floor, and my shoulder just fits in that long smooch around the wall, so I cannot lose my way.

Why, there's John at the door!

It is no use, young man, you can't open it!

How he does call and pound!

Now he's crying to Jennie for an axe.

It would be a shame to break down that beautiful door!

"John, dear!" said I in the gentlest voice. "The key is down by the front steps, under a plantain leaf!"

That silenced him for a few moments.

Then he said, very quietly indeed, "Open the door, my darling!"

"I can't," said I. "The key is down by the front door under a plantain leaf!" And then I said it again, several times, very gently and slowly, and said it so often that he had to go and see, and he got it of course, and came in. He stopped short by the door.

"What is the matter?" he cried. "For God's sake, what are you doing!"

I kept on creeping just the same, but I looked at him over my shoulder.

"I've got out at last," said I, "in spite of you and Jane. And I've pulled off most of the paper, so you can't put me back!"

Now why should that man have fainted? But he did, and right across my path by the wall, so that I had to creep over him every time!

QUESTIONS AND CONSIDERATIONS

1. Why is the narrator spending her summer in the children's nursery of a colonial mansion? What is wrong with her? Why is she not allowed to see her child? Why is she not allowed to write?

2. Evaluate the relationship between John and the narrator. Can you think of any defense for the husband's behavior, considering the time when the story was written (late nineteenth century)? Do you think that similar types of struggles and conflicts between spouses occur in marriages today?

3. Why does the narrator see the wallpaper differently at night? Why does she become obsessed with the wallpaper?

4. Examine the images in the story that describe the wallpaper in the nursery. How do these images help us to understand the nature and significance of the narrator's entrapment as well as the state of women at the time the story was written?

5. Interpret the wallpaper as a symbol. Why does the narrator feel trapped in it? Is her husband, society, or herself imprisoning her? What does the narrator learn from reflecting on the women trapped in the wallpaper? What does the wallpaper symbolize to you?

6. What do you imagine happens to the narrator after the story's ending? How do you think her husband will respond to her rebellion? Will the narrator continue to liberate herself? Is the narrator healthier at the end of the story than she was earlier, or has she had a complete mental breakdown?

IDEAS FOR WRITING

1. Write a modern-day short story about a haunted house in which a woman is held prisoner. Who holds her prisoner, and what comment does your story make about the social and psychological forces that limit the freedom of women today?

2. Do some research into the treatment in the late nineteenth century of women with mental illness. Write an essay in which you point out how the story reveals typical social attitudes of the nineteenth century toward women who have a mental illness.

A Loaf of Bread
James Alan McPherson

Journal

*Write about a struggle you have observed between different ethnic groups
or social classes in your neighborhood. Begin by describing where
the conflict took place.*

It was one of those obscene situations, pedestrian to most people, but invested with meaning for a few poor folk whose lives are usually spent outside the imaginations of their fellow citizens. A grocer named Harold Green was caught red-handed selling to one group of people the very same goods he sold at lower prices at similar outlets in better neighborhoods. He had been doing this for many years, and at first he could not understand the outrage heaped upon him. He acted only from habit, he insisted, and had nothing personal against the people whom he served. They were his neighbors. Many of them he had carried on the cuff during hard times. Yet, through some mysterious access to a television station, the poor folk were now empowered to make grand denunciations of the grocer. Green's children now saw their father's business being picketed on the Monday evening news.

No one could question the fact that the grocer had been overcharging the people. On the news even the reporter grimaced distastefully while reading the statistics. His expression said, "It is my job to report the news, but sometimes even I must disassociate myself from it to protect my honor." This, at least, was the impression the grocer's children seemed to bring away from the television. Their father's name had not been mentioned, but there was a close-up of his store with angry black people and a few outraged whites marching in groups of three in front of it. There was also a close-up of his name. After seeing this, they were in no mood to watch cartoons. At the dinner table, disturbed by his children's silence, Harold Green felt compelled to say, "I am not a dishonest man." Then he felt ashamed. The children, a boy and his older sister, immediately left the table, leaving Green alone with his wife. "Ruth, I am not dishonest," he repeated to her.

Ruth Green did not say anything. She knew, and her husband did not, that the outraged people had also picketed the school attended by their children. They had threatened to return each day until Green lowered his prices. When they called her at home to report this, she had promised she would talk with him. Since she could not tell him this, she waited for an opening. She looked at her husband across the table.

"I did not make the world," Green began, recognizing at once the seriousness in her stare. "My father came to this country with nothing but his shirt. He was exploited for as long as he couldn't help himself. He did not protest or picket. He put himself in a position to play by the rules he had learned." He waited for his wife to answer, and when she did not, he tried again. "I did not make this world," he repeated. "I only make my way in it. Such people as these, they do not know enough to not be exploited. If not me, there would be a Greek, a Chinaman, maybe an Arab or a smart one of their own kind. Believe me, I deal with them. There is something in their style that lacks the patience to run a concern such as mine. If I closed down, take my word on it, someone else would do what has to be done."

But Ruth Green was not thinking of his leaving. Her mind was on other matters. Her children had cried when they came home early from school. She had no special feeling for the people who picketed, but she did not like to see her children cry. She had kissed them generously, then sworn them to silence. "One day this week," she told her husband, "you will give free, for eight hours, anything your customers come in to buy. There will be no publicity, except what they spread by word of mouth. No matter what they say to you, no matter what they take, you will remain silent." She stared deeply into him for what she knew was there. "If you refuse, you have seen the last of your children and myself."

Her husband grunted. Then he leaned toward her. "I will not knuckle under," he said. "I will *not* give!"

"We shall see," his wife told him.

The black pickets, for the most part, had at first been frightened by the audacity of their undertaking. They were peasants whose minds had long before become resigned to their fate as victims. None of them, before now, had thought to challenge this. But now, when they watched themselves on television, they hardly recognized the faces they saw beneath the hoisted banners and placards. Instead of reflecting the meekness they all felt, the faces looked angry. The close-ups looked especially intimidating. Several of the first pickets, maids who worked in the suburbs, reported that their employers, seeing the activity on the afternoon news, had begun treating them with new respect. One woman, midway through the weather report, called around the neighborhood to disclose that her employer had that very day given her a new china plate for her meals. The paper plates, on which all previous meals had been served, had been thrown into the wastebasket. One recipient of this call, a middle-aged woman known for her bashfulness and humility, rejoined that her husband, a sheet-metal worker, had only a few hours before been called "Mister" by his supervisor, a white man with a passionate hatred of color. She added the tale of a neighbor down the street, a widow woman named Murphy, who had at first been reluctant to join the picket; this woman now was insisting it should be made a daily event. Such talk as this circulated among the people who had been instrumental in raising the issue. As news of their victory leaked into the ears of others who had not participated, they received all through the night calls from strangers requesting verification, offering advice, and vowing support. Such strangers listened and then volunteered stories about indignities inflicted on them by city officials, policemen, other grocers. In this way, over a period of hours, the community became even more incensed and restless than it had been at the time of the initial picket.

Soon the man who had set events in motion found himself a hero. His name was Nelson Reed, and all his adult life he had been employed as an assembly-line worker. He was a steady husband, the father of three children, and a deacon in the Baptist church. All his life he had trusted in God and gotten along. But now something in him capitulated to the reality that came suddenly into focus. "I was wrong," he told people who called him. "The onliest thing that matters in this world is *money*. And when was the last time you seen a picture of Jesus on a dollar bill?" This line, which he repeated over and over, caused a few callers to laugh nervously, but not without some affirmation that this was indeed the way things were. Many said they had known it all along. Others argued that although it was certainly true, it was one thing to live without money and quite another to live without faith. But still most callers laughed and said, "You right. You *know* I know you right. Ain't it the truth, though?" Only a few people, among them Nelson Reed's wife, said nothing and looked very sad.

Why they looked sad, however, they would not communicate. And anyone observing their troubled faces would have to trust his own intuition. It is known that Reed's wife, Betty, measured all events against the fullness of her own experience. She was skeptical of everything. Brought to the church after a number of years of living openly with a jazz musician, she had embraced religion when she married Nelson Reed. But though she no longer believed completely in the world, she nonetheless had not fully embraced God. There was something in the nature of Christ's swift rise that had always bothered her, and something in the blood and vengeance of the Old Testament that was mellowing and refreshing. But she had never communicated these thoughts to anyone, especially her husband. Instead, she smiled vacantly while others professed leaps of faith, remained silent when friends spoke fiercely of their convictions. The presence of this vacuum in her contributed to her personal mystery; people said she was beautiful, although she was not outwardly so. Perhaps it was because she wished to protect this inner beauty that she did not smile now, and looked extremely sad, listening to her husband on the telephone.

Nelson Reed had no reason to be sad. He seemed to grow more energized and talkative as the days passed. He was invited by an alderman, on the Tuesday after the initial picket, to tell his story on a local television talk show. He sweated heavily under the hot white lights and attempted to be philosophical. "I notice," the host said to him, "that you are not angry at this exploitative treatment. What, Mr. Reed, is the source of your calm?" The assembly-line worker looked unabashedly into the camera and said, "I have always believed in *Justice* with a capital *J.* I was raised up from a baby believin' that God ain't gonna let nobody go *too* far. See, in *my* mind God is in charge of *all* the capital letters in the alphabet of this world. It say in the Scripture He is Alpha and Omega, the first and the last. He is just about the *onliest* capitalizer they is." Both Reed and the alderman laughed. "Now, when *men* start to capitalize, they gets *greedy.* They put a little *j* in *joy* and a littler one in *justice.* They raise up a big *G* in *Greed* and a big *E* in *Evil.* Well, soon as they commence to put a little *g* in *god,* you can expect some kind of reaction. The Savior will just raise up the *H* in *Hell* and go on from there. And that's just what I'm doin', giving these sharpies *HELL* with a big *H.*" The talk show host laughed along with Nelson Reed and the alderman. After the taping they drank coffee in the back room of the studio and talked about the sad shape of the world.

Three days before he was to comply with his wife's request, Green, the grocer, saw this talk show on television while at home. The words of Nelson Reed sent a chill through him. Though Reed had attempted to be philosophical, Green did not perceive the statement in this light. Instead, he saw a vindictive-looking black man seated between an ambitious alderman and a smug talk-show host. He saw them chatting comfortably about the nature of evil. The cameraman had shot mostly close-ups, and Green could see the set in Nelson Reed's jaw. The color of Reed's face was maddening. When his children came into the den, the grocer was in a sweat. Before he could think, he had shouted at them and struck the button turning off the set. The two children rushed from the room screaming. Ruth Green ran in from the kitchen. She knew why he was upset because she had received a call about the show, but she said nothing and pretended ignorance. Her children's school had been picketed that day, as it had the day before. But both children were still forbidden to speak of this to their father.

"Where do they get so much power?" Green said to his wife. "Two days ago nobody would have cared. Now everywhere, even in my home, I am condemned as a rascal. And what do I own? An airline? A multinational? Half of South America? *No!* I own three stores, one of which happens to be in a certain neighborhood inhabited by people who cost me money to run it." He sighed and sat upright on the sofa, his chubby legs spread wide. "A cabdriver has a meter that clicks as he goes along. I pay extra for insurance, iron bars, pilfering by customers and employees. Nothing clicks. But when I add a little overhead to my prices, suddenly everything clicks. But for someone else. When was there last such a world?" He pressed the palms of both hands to his temples, suggesting a bombardment of brain-stinging sounds.

This gesture evoked no response from Ruth Green. She remained standing by the door, looking steadily at him. She said, "To protect yourself, I would not stock any more fresh cuts of meat in the store until after the giveaway on Saturday. Also, I would not tell it to the employees until after the first customer of the day has begun to check out. But I would urge you to hire several security guards to close the door promptly at seven-thirty, as is usual." She wanted to say much more than this, but did not. Instead she watched him. He was looking at the blank gray television screen, his palms still pressed against his ears. "In case you need to hear again," she continued in a weighty tone of voice, "I said two days ago, and I say again now, that if you fail to do this you will not see your children again for many years."

He twisted his head and looked up at her. "What is the color of these people?" he asked.

"Black," his wife said.

"And what is the name of my children?"

"Green."

The grocer smiled. "There is your answer," he told his wife. "Green is the only color I am interested in."

His wife did not smile. "Insufficient," she said.

"The world is mad!" he moaned. "But it is a point of sanity with me to not bend. I will not bend." He crossed his legs and pressed one hand firmly atop his knee. *"I will not bend,"* he said.

"We will see," his wife said.

Nelson Reed, after the television interview, became the acknowledged leader of the disgruntled neighbors. At first a number of them met in the kitchen at his house; then, as space was lacking for curious newcomers, a mass meeting was held on Thursday in an abandoned theater. His wife and three children sat in the front row. Behind them sat the widow Murphy, Lloyd Dukes, Tyrone Brown, Les Jones—those who had joined him on the first picket line. Behind these sat people who bought occasionally at the store, people who lived on the fringes of the neighborhood, people from other neighborhoods come to investigate the problem, and the merely curious. The middle rows were occupied by a few people from the suburbs, those who had seen the talk show and whose outrage at the grocer proved much more powerful than their fear of black people. In the rear of the theater crowded aging, old-style leftists, somber students, cynical young black men with angry grudges to explain with inarticulate gestures. Leaning against the walls, huddled near the doors at the rear, tape-recorder-bearing social scientists looked as detached and serene as bookies at the track. Here and there, in this diverse crowd, a politician stationed himself, pumping hands vigorously and pressing his palms gently against the shoulders of elderly people. Other visitors passed out leaflets, buttons, glossy color prints of men who promoted causes, the familiar and obscure. There was a hubbub of voices, a blend of the strident and the playful, the outraged and the reverent, lending an undercurrent of ominous energy to the assembly.

Nelson Reed spoke from a platform on the stage, standing before a yellowed, shredded screen that had once reflected the images of matinee idols. "I don't mind sayin' that I have always been a sucker," he told the crowd. "All my life I have been a sucker for the words of Jesus. Being a natural-born fool, I just ain't never had the *sense* to learn no better. Even right today, while the whole world is sayin' wrong is right and up is down, I'm so dumb I'm *still* steady believin' what is wrote in the Good Book. . . ."

From the audience, especially the front rows, came a chorus singing, "Preach!"

"I have no doubt," he continued in a low baritone, "that it's true what is writ in the Good Book: 'The last shall be first and the first shall be last.' I don't know about y'all, but I have *always* been the last. I never wanted to be the first, but sometimes it look like the world get so bad that them that's holdin' onto the tree of life is the onliest ones left when God commence to blowin' dead leafs off the branches."

"Now you preaching," someone called.

In the rear of the theater a white student shouted an awkward "Amen."

Nelson Reed began walking across the stage to occupy the major part of his nervous energy. But to those in the audience, who now hung on his every word, it looked as though he strutted. "All my life," he said, "I have claimed to be a man without earnin' the right to call myself that. You know, the *average* man ain't really a man. The average man is a *bootlicker.* In fact, the *average* man would *run away* if he found hisself standing alone facin' down a adversary. I have done that *too many a time* in my life! But *not no more.* Better to be *once* was than *never* was a man. I will tell you tonight, there is somethin' *wrong* in being average. *I intend to stand up!* Now, if your average man that ain't really a man stand up, two things gonna happen: *one,* he gon bust through all the weights that been place on his head, and, *two,* he gon feel a lot of pain. But that same hurt is what make things fall in place. That, and gettin' your hands on one of these slick four-flushers tight enough so's you can squeeze him and say, *'No more!'* You do that, you g'on hurt some, but *you won't be average no more.* . . ."

"No *more!*" a few people in the front rows repeated.

"I say *no more!*" Nelson Reed shouted.

"No more! No more! No more!" The chant rustled through the crowd like the rhythm of an autumn wind against a shedding tree.

Then people laughed and chattered in celebration.

As for the grocer, from the evening of the television interview he had begun to make plans. Unknown to his wife, he cloistered himself several times with his brother-in-law, an insurance salesman, and plotted a course. He had no intention of tossing steaks to the crowd. "And why should I, Tommy?" he asked his wife's brother, a lean, bald-headed man named Thomas. "I don't cheat anyone. I have never cheated anyone. The businesses I run are always on the up-and-up. So why should I pay?"

"Quite so," the brother-in-law said, chewing an unlit cigarillo. "The world has gone crazy. Next they will say that people in my business are responsible for prolonging life. I have found that people who refuse to believe in death refuse also to believe in the harshness of life. I sell well by saying that death is a long happiness. I show people the realities of life and compare this to a funeral with dignity, *and* the promise of a bundle for every loved one salted away. When they look around hard at life, they usually buy."

"So?" asked Green. Thomas was a college graduate with a penchant for philosophy.

"So," Thomas answered. "You must fight to show these people the reality of both your situation and theirs. How would it be if you visited one of their meetings and chalked out, on a blackboard, the dollars and cents of your operation? Explain your overhead, your security fees, all the additional expenses. If you treat them with respect, they might understand."

Green frowned. "That I would never do," he said. "It would be admission of a certain guilt."

The brother-in-law smiled, but only with one corner of his mouth. "Then you have something to feel guilty about?" he asked.

The grocer frowned at him. *"Nothing!"* he said with great emphasis.

"So?" Thomas said.

This first meeting between the grocer and his brother-in-law took place on Thursday, in a crowded barroom.

At the second meeting, in a luncheonette, it was agreed that the grocer should speak privately with the leader of the group, Nelson Reed. The meeting at which this was agreed took place on Friday afternoon. After accepting this advice from Thomas, the grocer resigned himself to explain to Reed, in as finite detail as possible, the economic structure of his operation. He vowed to suppress no information. He would explain everything: inventories, markups, sale items, inflation, balance sheets, specialty items, overhead, and that mysterious item called profit. This last item, promising to be the most difficult to explain, Green and his brother-in-law debated over for several hours. They agreed first of all that a man should not work for free, then they agreed that it was unethical to ruthlessly exploit. From these parameters, they staked out an area between fifteen and forty percent, and agreed that someplace between these two borders lay an amount of return that could be called fair. This was easy, but then Thomas introduced the factor of circumstance. He questioned whether the fact that one serviced a risky area justified the earning of profits, closer to the forty-percent edge of the scale. Green was unsure. Thomas smiled. "Here is a case that will point out an analogy," he said, licking a cigarillo. "I read in the papers that a family wants to sell an electric stove. I call the home and the man says fifty dollars. I ask to come out and inspect the merchandise. When I arrive I see they are poor, have already bought a new stove that is connected, and are selling the old one for fifty dollars because they want it out of the place. The electric stove is in good condition, worth much more than fifty. But because I see what I see I offer forty-five."

Green, for some reason, wrote down this figure on the back of the sales slip for the coffee they were drinking.

The brother-in-law smiled. He chewed his cigarillo. "The man agrees to take forty-five dollars, saying he has had no other calls. I look at the stove again and see a spot of rust. I say I will give him forty dollars. He agrees to this, on condition that I myself haul it away. I say I will haul it away if he comes down to thirty. You, of course, see where I am going."

The grocer nodded. "The circumstances of his situation, his need to get rid of the stove quickly, placed him in a position where he has little room to bargain?"

"Yes," Thomas answered. "So? Is it ethical, Harry?"

Harold Green frowned. He had never liked his brother-in-law, and now he thought the insurance agent was being crafty. "But," he answered, "this man does not *have* to sell! It is his choice whether to wait for other calls. It is not the fault of the buyer that the seller is in a hurry. It is the right of the buyer to get what he wants at the lowest price possible. That is the rule. That has *always* been the rule. And the reverse of it applies to the seller as well."

"Yes," Thomas said, sipping coffee from the Styrofoam cup. "But suppose that in addition to his hurry to sell, the owner was also of a weak soul. There are, after all, many such people." He smiled. "Suppose he placed no value on the money?"

"Then," Green answered, "your example is academic. Here we are not talking about real life. One man lives by the code, one man does not. Who is there free enough to make a judgment?" He laughed. "Now you see," he told his brother-in-law. "Much more than a few dollars are at stake. If this one buyer is to be condemned, then so are most people in the history of the world. An examination of history provides the only answer to your question. This code will be here tomorrow, long after the ones who do not honor it are not."

They argued fiercely late into the afternoon, the brother-in-law leaning heavily on his readings. When they parted, a little before five o'clock, nothing had been resolved.

Neither was much resolved during the meeting between Green and Nelson Reed. Reached at home by the grocer in the early evening, the leader of the group spoke coldly at first, but consented finally to meet his adversary at a nearby drugstore for coffee and a talk. They met at the lunch counter, shook hands awkwardly, and sat for a few minutes discussing the weather. Then the grocer pulled two gray ledgers from his briefcase. "You have for years come into my place," he told the man. "In my memory I have always treated you well. Now our relationship has come to this." He slid the books along the counter until they touched Nelson Reed's arm.

Reed opened the top book and flipped the thick green pages with his thumb. He did not examine the figures. "All I know," he said, "is over at your place a can of soup cost me fifty-five cents, and two miles away at your other store for white folks you chargin' thirty-nine cents." He said this with the calm authority of an outraged soul. A quality of condescension tinged with pity crept into his gaze.

The grocer drummed his fingers on the counter top. He twisted his head and looked away, toward shelves containing cosmetics, laxatives, toothpaste. His eyes lingered on a poster of a woman's apple-red lips and milk-white teeth. The rest of the face was missing.

"Ain't no use to hide," Nelson Reed said, as to a child. "I know you wrong, *you* know you wrong, and before I finish, *everybody in this city* g'on know you wrong. God don't *like* ugly." He closed his eyes and gripped the cup of coffee. Then he swung his head suddenly and faced the grocer again. "Man, why you want to *do* people that way?" he asked. "We human, same as you."

"Before *God!*" Green exclaimed, looking squarely into the face of Nelson Reed. "Before God!" he said again. *"I am not an evil man!"* These last words sounded more like a moan as he tightened the muscles in his throat to lower the sound of his voice. He tossed his left shoulder as if adjusting the sleeve of his coat, or as if throwing off some unwanted weight. Then he peered along the counter top. No one was watching. At the end of the counter the waitress was scrubbing the coffee urn. "Look at these figures, please," he said to Reed.

The man did not drop his gaze. His eyes remained fixed on the grocer's face.

"All right," Green said. "Don't look. I'll tell you what is in these books, believe me if you want. I work twelve hours a day, one day off per week, running my business in three stores. I am not a wealthy person. In one place, in the area you call white, I get by barely by smiling lustily at old ladies, stocking gourmet stuff on the chance I will build a reputation as a quality store. The two clerks there cheat me; there is nothing I can do. In this business you must be friendly with everybody. The second place is on the other side of town, in a neighborhood as poor as this one. I get out there seldom. The profits are not worth the gas. I use the loss there as a write-off against some other properties," he paused. "Do you understand write-off?" he asked Nelson Reed.

"Naw," the man said.

Harold Green laughed. "What does it matter?" he said in a tone of voice intended for himself alone. "In this area I will admit I make a profit, but it is not so much as you think. But I do not make a profit here because the people are black. I make a profit because a profit is here to be made. I invest more here in window bars, theft losses, insurance, spoilage; I deserve to make more here than at the other places." He looked, almost imploringly, at the man seated next to him. "You don't accept this as the right of a man in business?"

Reed grunted. "Did the bear shit in the woods?" he said.

Again Green laughed. He gulped his coffee awkwardly, as if eager to go. Yet his motions slowed once he had set his coffee cup down on the blue plastic saucer. "Place yourself in *my* situation," he said, his voice high and tentative. "If *you* were running my store in this neighborhood, what would be *your* position? Say on a profit scale of fifteen to forty percent, at what point in between would you draw the line?"

Nelson Reed thought. He sipped his coffee and seemed to chew the liquid. "Fifteen to forty?" he repeated.

"Yes."

"I'm a churchgoin' man," he said. "Closer to fifteen than to forty."

"How close?"

Nelson Reed thought. "In church you tithe ten percent."

"In restaurants you tip fifteen," the grocer said quickly.

"All right," Reed said. "Over fifteen."

"How much over?"

Nelson Reed thought.

"Twenty, thirty, thirty-five?" Green chanted, leaning closer to Reed.

Still the man thought.

"Forty? Maybe even forty-five or fifty?" the grocer breathed in Reed's ear. "In the supermarkets, you know, they have more subtle ways of accomplishing such feats."

Reed slapped his coffee cup with the back of his right hand. The brown liquid swirled across the counter top, wetting the books. *"Damn this!"* he shouted.

Startled, Green rose from his stool.

Nelson Reed was trembling. "I ain't *you*," he said in a deep baritone. "I ain't the *supermarket* neither. All I is is a poor man that works *too* hard to see his pay slip through his fingers like rainwater. All I know is you done *cheat* me, you done *cheat* everybody in the neighborhood, and we organized now to get some of it *back!*" Then he stood and faced the grocer. "My daddy sharecropped down in Mississippi and bought in the company store. He owed them twenty-three years when he died. I paid off five of them years and then run away to up here. Now, I'm a deacon in the Baptist church. I raised my kids the way my daddy raise me and don't bother nobody. Now come to find out, after all my runnin', they done lift that *same company store* up out of Mississippi and slip it down on us here! Well, my daddy was a *fighter,* and if he hadn't owed all them years he would of raise him some hell. Me, I'm steady my daddy's child, plus I got seniority in my union. I'm a free man. Buddy, don't you know *I'm gonna raise me some hell!"*

Harold Green reached for a paper napkin to sop the coffee soaking into his books.

Nelson Reed threw a dollar on top of the books and walked away.

"I *will not* do it!" Harold Green said to his wife that same evening. They were in the bathroom of their home. Bending over the face bowl, she was washing her hair with a towel draped around her neck. The grocer stood by the door, looking in at her. "I will not bankrupt myself tomorrow," he said.

"I've been thinking about it, too," Ruth Green said, shaking her wet hair. "You'll do it, Harry."

"Why should I?" he asked. "You won't leave. You know it was a bluff. I've waited this long for you to calm down. Tomorrow is Saturday. This week has been a hard one. Tonight let's be realistic."

"Of course you'll do it," Ruth Green said. She said it the way she would say "Have some toast." She said, "You'll do it because you want to see your children grow up."

"And for what other reason?" he asked.

She pulled the towel tighter around her neck. "Because you are at heart a moral man."

He grinned painfully. "If I am, why should I have to prove it to *them?*"

"Not them," Ruth Green said, freezing her movements and looking in the mirror. "Certainly not them. By no means them. They have absolutely nothing to do with this."

"Who, then?" he asked, moving from the door into the room. "Who else should I prove something to?"

His wife was crying. But her entire face was wet. The tears moved secretly down her face.

"Who else?" Harold Green asked.

It was almost eleven P.M. and the children were in bed. They had also cried when they came home from school. Ruth Green said, "For yourself, Harry. For the love that lives inside your heart."

All night the grocer thought about this.

Nelson Reed also slept little that Friday night. When he returned home from the drugstore, he reported to his wife as much of the conversation as he could remember. At first he had joked about the exchange between himself and the grocer, but as more details returned to his conscious mind he grew solemn and then bitter. "He ask me to put myself in *his* place," Reed told his wife. "Can you imagine that kind of gumption? I never cheated nobody in my life. All my life I have lived on Bible principles. I am a deacon in the church. I have work all my life for other folks and I don't even own the house I live in." He paced up and down the kitchen, his big arms flapping loosely at his sides. Betty Reed sat at the table, watching. "This here's a low-down, ass-kicking world," he said. "I swear to God it is! All my life I have lived on principle and I ain't got a dime in the bank. Betty," he turned suddenly toward her, "don't you think I'm a fool?"

"Mr. Reed," she said. "Let's go on to bed."

But he would not go to bed. Instead, he took the fifth of bourbon from the cabinet under the sink and poured himself a shot. His wife refused to join him. Reed drained the glass of whiskey, and then another, while he resumed pacing the kitchen floor. He slapped his hands against his sides. "I think I'm a fool," he said. "Ain't got a dime in the bank, ain't got a pot to *pee* in or a wall to pitch it over, and that there *cheat* ask me to put myself inside *his* shoes. Hell, I can't even *afford* the kind of shoes he wears." He stopped pacing and looked at his wife.

"Mr. Reed," she whispered, "tomorrow ain't a work day. Let's go to bed."

Nelson Reed laughed, the bitterness in his voice rattling his wife. "The *hell* I will!" he said.

He strode to the yellow telephone on the wall beside the sink and began to dial. The first call was to Lloyd Dukes, a neighbor two blocks away and a lieu-tenant in the organization. Dukes was not at home. The second call was to McElroy's Bar on the corner of Sixty-fifth and Carroll, where Stanley Harper, another of the lieutenants, worked as a bartender. It was Harper who spread the word, among those men at the bar, that the organization would picket the grocer's store the following morning. And all through the night, in the bedroom of their house, Betty Reed was awakened by telephone calls coming from Lester Jones, Nat Lucas, Mrs. Tyrone Brown, the widow-woman named Mur-phy, all coordinating the time when they would march in a group against the store owned by Harold Green. Betty Reed's heart beat loudly beneath the cov-ers as she listened to the bitterness and rage in her husband's voice. On sev-eral occasions, hearing him declare himself a fool, she pressed the pillow against her eyes and cried.

The grocer opened later than usual this Saturday morning, but still it was early enough to make him one of the first walkers in the neighborhood. He parked his car one block from the store and strolled to work. There were no birds singing. The sky in this area was not blue. It was smog-smutted and gray, seeming on the verge of a light rain. The street, as always, was littered with cans, papers, bits of broken glass. As always the garbage cans overflowed. The morning breeze plastered a sheet of newspaper playfully around the sides of a rusted garbage can. For some reason, using his right foot, he loosened the paper and stood watching it slide into the street and down the block. The movement made him feel good. He whistled while unlocking the bars shielding the windows and door of his store. When he had unlocked the main door he stepped in quickly and threw a switch to the right of the jamb, before the shrill sound of the alarm could shatter his mood. Then he switched on the lights. Everything was as it had been the night before. He had already telephoned his two employees and given them the day off. He busied himself doing the usual things—hauling milk and vegetables from the cooler, putting cash in the till—not thinking about the silence of his wife, or the look in her eyes, only an hour before when he left home. He had determined, at some point while driving through the city, that today it would be business as usual. But he expected very few customers.

The first customer of the day was Mrs. Nelson Reed. She came in around nine-thirty A.M. and wandered about the store. He watched her from the check-out counter. She seemed uncertain of what she wanted to buy. She kept glancing at him down the center aisle. His suspicions aroused, he said finally, "Yes, may I help you, Mrs. Reed?" His words caused her to jerk, as if some devious thought had been perceived going through her mind. She reached over quickly and lifted a loaf of whole wheat bread from the rack and walked with it to the counter. She looked at him and smiled. The smile was a broad, shy one, that rare kind of smile one sees on virgin girls when they first confess love to themselves. Betty Reed was a woman of about forty-five. For some reason he could not comprehend, this gesture touched him. When she pulled a dollar from her purse and laid it on the counter, an impulse, from no place he could locate with his mind, seized control of his tongue. "Free," he told Betty Reed. She paused, then pushed the dollar toward him with a firm and determined thrust of her arm. "Free," he heard himself saying strongly, his right palm spread and meeting her thrust with absolute force. She clutched the loaf of bread and walked out of his store.

The next customer, a little girl, arriving well after ten-thirty A.M., selected a candy bar from the rack beside the counter. "Free," Green said cheerfully. The little girl left the candy on the counter and ran out of the store.

At eleven-fifteen A.M. a wino came in looking desperate enough to sell his soul. The grocer watched him only for an instant. Then he went to the wine counter and selected a half-gallon of medium-grade red wine. He shoved the jug into the belly of the wino, the man's sour breath bathing his face. "Free," the grocer said. "But you must not drink it in here."

He felt good about the entire world, watching the wino through the window gulping the wine and looking guiltily around.

At eleven twenty-five A.M. the pickets arrived.

Two dozen people, men and women, young and old, crowded the pavement in front of his store. Their signs, placards, and voices denounced him as a parasite. The grocer laughed inside himself. He felt lighthearted and wild, like a man drugged. He rushed to the meat counter and pulled a long roll of brown wrapping paper from the rack, tearing it neatly with a quick shift of his body resembling a dance step practiced fervently in his youth. He laid the paper on the chopping block and with the black-inked, felt-tipped marker scrawled, in giant letters, the word FREE. This he took to the window and pasted in place with many strands of Scotch tape. He was laughing wildly. "Free!" he shouted from behind the brown paper. "Free! Free! Free! Free! Free! Free!" He rushed to the door, pushed his head out, and screamed to the confused crowd, *"Free!"* Then he ran back to the counter and stood behind it, like a soldier at attention.

They came in slowly.

Nelson Reed entered first, working his right foot across the dirty tile as if tracking a squiggling worm. The others followed: Lloyd Dukes dragging a placard, Mr. and Mrs. Tyrone Brown, Stanley Harper walking with his fists clenched, Lester Jones with three of his children, Nat Lucas looking sheepish and detached, a clutch of winos, several bashful nuns, ironic-smiling teenagers and a few students. Bringing up the rear was a bearded social scientist holding a tape recorder to his chest. "Free!" the grocer screamed. He threw up his arms in a gesture that embraced, or dismissed, the entire store. *"All free!"* he shouted. He was grinning with the grace of a madman.

The winos began grabbing first. They stripped the shelf of wine in a matter of seconds. Then they fled, dropping bottles on the tile in their wake. The others, stepping quickly through this liquid, soon congealed it into a sticky, blood-like consistency. The young men went for the cigarettes and luncheon meats and beer. One of them had the prescience to grab a sack from the counter, while the others loaded their arms swiftly, hugging cartons and packages of cold cuts like long-lost friends. The students joined them, less for greed than for the thrill of the experience. The two nuns backed toward the door. As for the older people, men and women, they stood at first as if stuck to the wine-smeared floor. Then Stanley Harper, the bartender, shouted, "The man said *free,* y'all heard him." He paused. "Didn't you say *free* now?" he called to the grocer.

"I said free," Harold Green answered, his temples pounding.

A cheer went up. The older people began grabbing, as if the secret lusts of a lifetime had suddenly seized command of their arms and eyes. They grabbed toilet tissue, cold cuts, pickles, sardines, boxes of raisins, boxes of starch, cans of soup, tins of tuna fish and salmon, bottles of spices, cans of boned chicken, slippery cans of olive oil. Here a man, Lester Jones, burdened himself with several heads of lettuce, while his wife, in another aisle, shouted for him to drop those small items and concentrate on the gourmet section. She herself took imported sardines, wheat crackers, bottles of candied pickles, herring, anchovies, imported olives. French wafers, an ancient, half-rusted can of paté, stocked, by mistake, from the inventory of another store. Others packed their arms with detergents, hams, chocolate-coated cereal, whole chickens with hanging asses, wedges of bologna and salami like squashed footballs, chunks of cheeses, yellow and white, shriveled onions, and green peppers. Mrs. Tyrone Brown hung a curve of pepperoni around her neck and seemed to take on instant dignity, much like a person of noble birth in possession now of a long sought-after gem. Another woman, the widow Murphy, stuffed tomatoes into her bosom, holding a half-chewed lemon in her mouth. The more enterprising fought desperately over the three rusted shopping carts, and the victors wheeled these along the narrow aisles, sweeping into them bulk items—beer in six-packs, sacks of sugar, flour, glass bottles of syrup, toilet cleanser, sugar cookies, prune, apple and tomato juices—while others endeavored to snatch the carts from them. There were several fistfights and much cursing. The grocer, standing behind the counter, hummed and rang his cash register like a madman.

Nelson Reed, the first into the store, followed the nuns out, empty-handed.

In less than half an hour the others had stripped the store and vanished in many directions up and down the block. But still more people came, those late in hearing the news. And when they saw the shelves were bare, they cursed soberly and chased those few stragglers still bearing away goods. Soon only the grocer and the social scientist remained, the latter stationed at the door with his tape recorder sucking in leftover sounds. Then he, too, slipped away up the block.

By twelve-ten P.M. the grocer was leaning against the counter, trying to make his mind slow down. Not a man given to drink during work hours, he nonetheless took a swallow from a bottle of wine, a dusty bottle from beneath the wine shelf, somehow overlooked by the winos. Somewhat recovered, he was preparing to remember what he should do next when he glanced toward a figure at the door. Nelson Reed was standing there, watching him.

"All gone," Harold Green said. "My friend, Mr. Reed, there is no more." Still the man stood in the doorway, peering into the store.

The grocer waved his arms about the empty room. Not a display case had a single item standing. "All gone," he said again, as if addressing a stupid child. "There is nothing left to get. You, my friend, have come back too late for a second load. I am cleaned out."

Nelson Reed stepped into the store and strode toward the counter. He moved through wine-stained flour, lettuce leaves, red, green, and blue labels, bits and pieces of broken glass. He walked toward the counter.

"All day," the grocer laughed, not quite hysterically now, "all day long I have not made a single cent of profit. The entire day was a loss. This store, like the others, is *bleeding* me." He waved his arms about the room in a magnificent gesture of uncaring loss. "Now do you understand?" he said. "Now will you put yourself in my shoes? I have nothing here. Come, now, Mr. Reed, would it not be so bad a thing to walk in my shoes?"

"Mr. Green," Nelson Reed said coldly. "My wife bought a loaf of bread in here this mornin'. She forgot to pay you. I, myself, have come here to pay you your money."

"Oh," the grocer said.

"I think it was brown bread. Don't that cost more than white?"

The two men looked away from each other, but not at anything in the store.

"In my store, yes," Harold Green said. He rang the register with the most casual movement of his finger. The register read fifty-five cents.

Nelson Reed held out a dollar.

"And two cents tax," the grocer said.

The man held out the dollar.

"After all," Harold Green said. "We are all, after all, Mr. Reed, in debt to the government."

He rang the register again. It read fifty-seven cents.

Nelson Reed held out a dollar.

QUESTIONS AND CONSIDERATIONS

1. Why is it hard for Green to understand that he is cheating the people whom he thinks he serves? What rationalizations does he make for himself? Why do his wife and children see the situation differently?

2. Why does Ruth Green tell her husband to give his customers anything they want free for eight hours? Is her attitude altogether altruistic?

3. What impact does the picketing of Green's store have on the black community?

4. Nelson Reed, a Baptist minister, becomes a hero for saying, "The onliest thing that matters in this world is money. And when was the last time you seen a picture of Jesus on a dollar bill?" Although Nelson's statement helps to fuel the struggle and helps the black community to get a fair deal from Green, what critique does the story seem to make of Reed's values?

5. Do you think that Ruth Green's solution to the problem is an appropriate and effective one? How good is Green's brother-in-law's advice?

6. Why do Nelson Reed and Harold Green gain respect for one another? How is their conflict finally resolved?

IDEAS FOR WRITING

1. Write an analysis of the social and economic struggles explored in the story. What conclusions is the author making about these struggles, their causes, and the human consequences?

2. Write an essay that describes and then analyzes a situation in your own community that is similar to the one described in the story. Did reading the story help you to understand better the struggle within your own community?

Minutes of Glory
Ngugi Wa Thiong'o

Journal

Write about a time when you did something in order to have a "minute of glory" for which you later suffered. Was the struggle for glory worth the consequences?

Her name was Wanjiru. But she liked better her Christian one, Beatrice. It sounded more pure and more beautiful. Not that she was ugly; but she could not be called beautiful either. Her body, dark and full fleshed, had the form, yes, but it was as if it waited to be filled by the spirit. She worked in beer-halls where sons of women came to drown their inner lives in beer cans and froth. Nobody seemed to notice her. Except, perhaps, when a proprietor or an impatient customer called out her name, Beatrice; then other customers would raise their heads briefly, a few seconds, as if to behold the bearer of such a beautiful name, but not finding anybody there, they would resume their drinking, their ribald jokes, their laughter and play with the other serving girls. She was like a wounded bird in flight: a forced landing now and then but nevertheless wobbling from place to place so that she would variously be found in Alaska, Paradise, The Modern, Thome and other beer-halls all over Limuru. Sometimes it was because an irate proprietor found she was not attracting enough customers; he would sack her without notice and without salary. She would wobble to the next bar. But sometimes she was simply tired of nesting in one place, a daily witness of familiar scenes; girls even more decidedly ugly than she were fought over by numerous claimants at closing hours. What do they have that I don't have? she would ask herself, depressed. She longed for a bar-kingdom where she would be at least one of the rulers, where petitioners would bring their gifts of beer, frustrated smiles and often curses that hid more lust and love than hate.

She left Limuru town proper and tried the mushrooming townlets around. She worked at Ngarariga, Kamiritho, Rironi and even Tiekunu and everywhere the story was the same. Oh, yes, occasionally she would get a client; but none cared for her as she would have liked, none really wanted her enough to fight over her. She was always a hard-up customer's last resort. No make-believe even, not for her that sweet pretense that men indulged in after their fifth bottle of Tusker. The following night or during a pay-day, the same client would pretend not to know her; he would be trying his money-power over girls who already had more than a fair share of admirers.

She resented this. She saw in every girl a rival and adopted a sullen attitude. Nyagũthiĩ especially was the thorn that always pricked her wounded flesh. Nyagũthiĩ arrogant and aloof, but men always in her courtyard; Nyagũthiĩ fighting with men, and to her they would bring propitiating gifts which she accepted as of right. Nyagũthiĩ could look bored, impatient, or downright contemptuous and still men would cling to her as if they enjoyed being whipped with biting words, curled lips and the indifferent eyes of a free woman. Nyagũthiĩ was also a bird in flight, never really able to settle in one place, but in her case it was because she hungered for change and excitement: new faces and new territories for her conquest. Beatrice resented her very shadow. She saw in her the girl she would have liked to be, a girl who was both totally immersed in and yet completely above the underworld of bar violence and sex. Wherever Beatrice went the long shadow of Nyagũthiĩ would sooner or later follow her.

She fled Limuru for Ilmorog in Chiri District. Ilmorog had once been a ghost village, but had been resurrected to life by that legendary woman, Nyang'endo, to whom every pop group had paid their tribute. It was of her that the young dancing Muthuu and Muchun g'wa sang:

When I left Nairobi for Ilmorog
Never did I know
I would bear this wonder-child mine
Nyang'endo

As a result, Ilmorog was always seen as a town of hope where the weary and the down-trodden would find their rest and fresh water. But again Nyagũthiĩ followed her.

She found that Ilmorog, despite the legend, despite the songs and dances, was not different from Limuru. She tried various tricks. Clothes? But even here she never earned enough to buy herself glittering robes. What was seventy-five shillings a month without house allowance, posho, without salaried boy-friends? By that time, Ambi had reached Ilmorog, and Beatrice thought that this would be the answer. Had she not, in Limuru, seen girls blacker than herself transformed overnight from ugly sins into white stars by a touch of skin-lightening creams? And men would ogle them, would even talk with exaggerated pride of their newborn girl friends. Men were strange creatures, Beatrice thought in moments of searching analysis. They talked heatedly against Ambi, Butone, Firesnow, Moonsnow, wigs, straightened hair; but they always went for a girl with an Ambi-lightened skin and head covered with a wig made in imitation of European or Indian hair. Beatrice never tried to find the root cause of this black self-hatred, she simply accepted the contradiction and applied herself to Ambi with a vengeance. She had to rub out her black shame. But even Ambi she could not afford in abundance; she could only apply it to her face and her arms so that her legs and neck retained their blackness. Besides there were parts of her face she could not readily reach—behind the ears and above the eyelashes, for instance—and these were a constant source of shame and irritation for her Ambi-self.

She would always remember this Ambi period as one of her deepest humiliations before her later minutes of glory. She worked in Ilmorog Starlight Bar and Lodging. Nyagũthiĩ with her bangled hands, her huge earrings, served behind the counter. The owner was a good Christian soul who regularly went to church and paid all his dues to Harambee projects. Pot-belly. Grey hairs. Soft-spoken. A respectable family man, well known to Ilmorog. Hardworking even, for he would not leave the bar until the closing hours, or more precisely, until Nyagũthiĩ left. He had no eyes for any other girl; he hung around her, and surreptitiously brought her gifts of clothes without receiving gratitude in kind. Only the promise. Only the hope for tomorrow. Other girls he gave eighty shillings a month. Nyagũthiĩ had a room to herself. Nyagũthiĩ woke up whenever she like to take the stock. But Beatrice and the other girls had to wake up at five or so, make tea for the lodgers, clean up the bar and wash dishes and glasses. Then they would hang around the bar and in shifts until two o'clock when they would go for a small break. At five o'clock, they had to be in again, ready for customers whom they would now serve with frothy beers and smiles until twelve o'clock or for as long as there were customers thirsty for more Tuskers and Pilsners. What often galled Beatrice, although in her case it did not matter one way or another, was the owner's insistence that the girls should sleep in Starlight. They would otherwise be late for work, he said. But what he really wanted was for the girls to use their bodies to attract more lodgers in Starlight. Most of the girls, led by Nyagũthiĩ, defied the rule and bribed the watchman to let them out and in. They wanted to meet their regular or one-night boy-friends in places where they would be free and where they would be treated as not just barmaids. Beatrice always slept in. Her occasional one-night patrons wanted to spend the minimum. Came a night when the owner, refused by Nyagūthiī, approached her. He started by finding fault with her work; he called her names, then as suddenly he started praising her, although in a grudging almost contemptuous manner. He grabbed her, struggled with her, pot-belly, grey hairs, and everything. Beatrice felt an unusual revulsion for the man. She could not, she would not bring herself to accept that which had so recently been cast aside by Nyagūthiī. My God, she wept inside, what does Nyagūthiī have that I don't have? The man now humillated himself before her. He implored. He promised her gifts. But she would not yield. That night she too defied the rule. She jumped through a window; she sought a bed in another bar and only came back at six. The proprietor called her in front of all the others and dismissed her. But Beatrice was rather surprised at herself.

She stayed a month without a job. She lived from room to room at the capricious mercy of the other girls. She did not have the heart to leave Ilmorog and start all over again in a new town. The wound hurt. She was tired of wandering. She stopped using Ambi. No money. She looked at herself in the mirror. She had so aged, hardly a year after she had fallen from grace. Why then was she scrupulous, she would ask herself. But somehow she had a horror of soliciting lovers or directly bartering her body for hard cash. What she wanted was decent work and a man or several men who cared for her. Perhaps she took that need for a man, for a home and for a child with her to bed. Perhaps it was this genuine need that scared off men who wanted other things from barmaids. She wept late at nights and remembered home. At such moments, her mother's village in Nyeri seemed the sweetest place on God's earth. She would invest the life of her peasant mother and father with romantic illusions of immeasurable peace and harmony. She longed to go back home to see them. But how could she go back with empty hands? In any case the place was now a distant landscape in the memory. Her life was here in the bar among this crowd of lost strangers. Fallen from grace, fallen from grace. She was part of a generation which would never again be one with the soil, the crops, the wind and the moon. Not for them that whispering in dark hedges, not for her that dance and love-making under the glare of the moon, with the hill of Tumu Tumu rising to touch the sky. She remembered that girl from her home village who, despite a life of apparent glamour being the kept mistress of one rich man after another in Limuru, had gassed herself to death. This generation was now awed by the mystery of death, just as it was callous to the mystery of life; for how many unmarried mothers had thrown their babies into latrines rather than lose that glamour? The girl's death became the subject of jokes. She had gone metric—without pains, they said. Thereafter, for a week, Beatrice thought of going metric. But she could not bring herself to do it.

She wanted love; she wanted life.

A new bar was opened in Ilmorog. Treetop Bar, Lodging and Restaurant. Why Treetop, Beatrice could not understand unless because it was a storied building: tea-shop on the ground floor and beer-shop in a room at the top. The rest were rooms for five-minute or one-night lodgers. The owner was a retired civil servant but one who still played at politics. He was enormously wealthy with business sites and enterprises in every major town in Kenya. Big shots from all over the country came to his bar. Big men in Mercedes. Big men in their Bentleys. Big men in their Jaguars and Daimlers. Big men with uniformed chauffeurs drowsing with boredom in cars waiting outside. There were others not so big who came to pay respects to the great. They talked politics mostly. And about their work. Gossip was rife. Didn't you know? Indeed so and so has been promoted. Really? And so and so has been sacked. Embezzlement of public funds. So foolish you know. Not clever about it at all. They argued, they quarrelled, sometimes they fought it out with fists, especially during the elections campaign. The only point on which they were all agreed was that the Luo community was the root cause of all the trouble in Kenya; that intellectuals and University students were living in an ivory tower of privilege and arrogance; that Kiambu had more than a lion's share of developments; that men from Nyeri and Muranga had acquired all the big business in Nairobi and were even encroaching on Chiri District; that African workers, especially those on the farms, were lazy and jealous of 'us' who had sweated ourselves to sudden prosperity. Otherwise each would hymn his own praises or return compliments. Occasionally in moments of drunken ebullience and self-praise, one would order two rounds of beer for each man present in the bar. Even the poor from Ilmorog would come to Treetop to dine at the gates of the nouveaux riches.

Here Beatrice got a job as a sweeper and bedmaker. Here for a few weeks she felt closer to greatness. Now she made beds for men she had previously known as names. She watched how even the poor tried to drink and act big in front of the big. But soon fate caught up with her. Girls flocked to Treetop from other bars. Girls she had known at Limuru, girls she had known at Ilmorog. And most had attached themselves to one or several big men, often playing a hide-and-not-to-be found game with their numerous lovers. And Nyagũthĩĩ was there behind the counter, with the eyes of the rich and the poor fixed on her. And she, with her big eyes, bangled hands and earrings, maintained the same air of bored indifference. Beatrice as a sweeper and bedmaker became even more invisible. Girls who had fallen into good fortune looked down upon her.

She fought life with dreams. In between putting clean sheets on beds that had just witnessed a five-minute struggle that ended in a half-strangled cry and a pool, she would stand by the window and watch the cars and the chauffeurs, so that soon she knew all the owners by the number plates of their cars and the uniforms of their chauffeurs. She dreamt of lovers who would come for her in sleek Mercedes sports cars made for two. She saw herself linking hands with such a lover, walking in the streets of Nairobi and Mombasa, tapping the ground with high heels, quick, quick short steps. And suddenly she would stop in front of a display glass window, exclaiming at the same time, Oh darling, won't you buy me those. . . ? Those what? he would ask, affecting anger.

Those stockings, darling. It was as an owner of several stockings, ladderless and holeless, that she thought of her well-being. Never again would she mend torn things. Never, never, never. Do you understand? Never. She was next the proud owner of different coloured wigs, blonde wigs, brunette wigs, redhead wigs, Afro wigs, wigs, wigs, all the wigs in the world. Only then would the whole earth sing hallelujah to the one Beatrice. At such moments, she would feel exalted, lifted out of her murky self, no longer a floor sweeper and bed-maker for a five-minute instant love, but Beatrice, descendant of Wangu Mak-eri who made men tremble with desire at her naked body bathed in moonlight, daughter of Nyang'ondo, the founder of modern Ilmorog, of whom they often sang that she had worked several lovers into impotence.

Then she noticed him and he was the opposite of the lover of her dreams. He came one Saturday afternoon driving a big five-ton lorry. He carefully parked it beside the Benzes, the Jaguars and the Daimlers, not as a lorry, but as one of those sleek cream-bodied frames, so proud of it he seemed to be. He dressed in a baggy grey suit over which he wore a heavy khaki military overcoat. He removed the overcoat, folded it with care, and put it in the front seat. He locked all the doors, dusted himself a little, then walked round the lorry as if inspecting it for damage. A few steps before he entered Treetop, he turned round for a final glance at his lorry dwarfing the other things. At Treetop he sat in a corner and, with a rather loud defiant voice, ordered a Kenya one. He drank it with relish, looking around at the same time for a face he might recognize. He indeed did recognize one of the big ones and he immediately ordered for him a quarter bottle of Vat 69. This was accepted with a bare nod of the head and a patronising smile; but when he tried to follow his generosity with a conversation, he was firmly ignored. He froze, sank into his Muratina. But only for a time. He tried again: he was met with frowning faces. More pa-thetic were his attempts to join in jokes; he would laugh rather too loudly, which would make the big ones stop, leaving him in the air alone. Later in the evening he stood up, counted several crisp hundred shilling notes and handed them to Nyagũthiĩ behind the counter ostensibly for safekeeping. People whispered; murmured; a few laughed, rather derisively, though they were rather impressed. But this act did not win him immediate recognition. He stag-gered towards room no. 7 which he had hired. Beatrice brought him the keys. He glanced at her, briefly, then lost all interest.

Thereafter he came every Saturday. At five when most of the big shots were already seated. He repeated the same ritual, except the money act, and always met with defeat. He nearly always sat in the same corner and always rented room 7. Beatrice grew to anticipate his visits and, without being con-scious of it, kept the room ready for him. Often after he had been badly humili-ated by the big company, he would detain Beatrice and talk to her, or rather he talked to himself in her presence. For him, it had been a life of struggles. He had never been to school although getting an education had been his ambi-tion. He never had a chance. His father was a squatter in the European settled area in the Rift Valley. That meant a lot in those colonial days. It meant among other things a man and his children were doomed to a future of sweat and toil for the white devils and their children. He had joined the freedom struggle and like the others had been sent to detention. He came from detention the same as his mother had brought him to this world. Nothing. With independence he found he did not possess the kind of education which would have placed him in one of the vacancies at the top. He started as a charcoal burner, then a butcher, gradually working his own way to become a big transporter of vegetables and potatoes from the Rift Valley and Chiri districts to Nairobi. He was proud of his achievement. But he resented that others, who had climbed to their present wealth through loans and a subsidized education, would not recognize his like. He would rumble on like this, dwelling on education he would never have, and talking of better chances for his children. Then he would carefully count the money, put it under the pillow, and then dismiss Beatrice. Occasionally he would buy her a beer but he was clearly suspicious of women whom he saw as money-eaters of men. He had not yet married.

One night he slept with her. In the morning he scratched for a twenty shilling note and gave it to her. She accepted the money with an odd feeling of guilt. He did this for several weeks. She did not mind the money. It was useful. But he paid for her body as he would pay for a bag of potatoes or a sack of cabbages. With the one pound, he had paid for her services as a listener, a vessel of his complaints against those above, and as a one night receptacle of his man's burden. She was becoming bored with his ego, with his stories that never varied in content, but somehow, in him, deep inside, she felt that something had been there, a fire, a seed, a flower which was being smothered. In him she saw a fellow victim and looked forward to his visits. She too longed to talk to someone. She too longed to confide in a human being who would understand.

And she did it one Saturday night, suddenly interrupting the story of his difficult climb to the top. She did not know why she did it. Maybe it was the rain outside. It was softly drumming the corrugated iron sheets, bringing with the drumming a warm and drowsy indifference. He would listen. He had to listen. She came from Karatina in Nyeri. Her two brothers had been gunned down by the British soldiers. Another one had died in detention. She was, so to speak, an only child. Her parents were poor. But they worked hard on their bare strip of land and managed to pay her fees in primary school. For the first six years she had worked hard. In the seventh year, she must have relaxed a little. She did not pass with a good grade. Of course she knew many with similar grades who had been called to good government secondary schools. She knew a few others with lesser grades who had gone to very top schools on the strength of their connections. But she was not called to any high school with reasonable fees. Her parents could not afford fees in a Harambee school. And she would not hear of repeating standard seven. She stayed at home with her parents. Occasionally she would help them in the shamba and with house chores. But imagine: for the past six years she had led a life with a different rhythm from that of her parents. Life in the village was dull. She would often go to Karatina and to Nyeri in search of work. In every office, they would ask her the same questions: what work do you want? What do you know? Can you type? Can you take shorthand? She was desperate. It was in Nyeri, drinking Fanta in a shop, tears in her eyes, that she met a young man in a dark suit and sunglasses. He saw her plight and talked to her. He came from Nairobi. Looking for work? That's easy; in a big city there would be no difficulty with jobs. He would certainly help. Transport? He had a car—a cream-white Peugeot. Heaven. It was a beautiful ride, with the promise of dawn. Nairobi. He drove her to Terrace Bar. They drank beer and talked about Nairobi. Through the window she would see the neon-lit city and knew that here was hope. That night she gave herself to him, with the promise of dawn making her feel light and gay. She had a very deep sleep. When she woke in the morning, the man in the cream-white Peugeot was not there. She never saw him again. That's how she had started the life of a barmaid. And for one and a half years now she had not been once to see her parents. Beatrice started weeping. Huge sobs of self-pity. Her humiliation and constant flight were fresh in her mind. She had never been able to take to bar culture, she always thought that something better would come her way. But she was trapped, it was the only life she now knew, although she had never really learnt all its laws and norms. Again she heaved out and in, tears tossing out with every sob. Then suddenly she froze. Her sobbing was arrested in the air. The man had long covered himself. His snores were huge and unmistakable.

She felt a strange hollowness. Then a bile of bitterness spilt inside her. She wanted to cry at her new failure. She had met several men who had treated her cruelly, who had laughed at her scruples, at what they thought was an ill-disguised attempt at innocence. She had accepted. But not this, Lord, not this. Was this man not a fellow victim? Had he not, Saturday after Saturday, unburdened himself to her? He had paid for her human services; he had paid away his responsibility with his bottle of Tuskers and hard cash in the morning. Her innermost turmoil had been his lullaby. And suddenly something in her snapped. All the anger of a year and a half, all the bitterness against her humiliation were now directed at this man.

What she did later had the mechanical precision of an experienced hand.

She touched his eyes. He was sound asleep. She raised his head. She let it fall. Her tearless eyes were now cold and set. She removed the pillow from under him. She rummaged through it. She took out his money. She counted five crisp pink notes. She put the money inside her brassiere.

She went out of room no. 7. Outside it was still raining. She did not want to go to her usual place. She could not now stand the tiny cupboard room or the superior chatter of her roommate. She walked through mud and rain. She found herself walking towards Nyaguthii's room. She knocked at the door. At first she had no response. Then she heard Nyaguthii's sleepy voice above the drumming rain.

'Who is that?'

'It is me. Please open.'

'Who?'

'Beatrice,'

'At this hour of the night?'

'Please.'

Lights were put on. Bolts unfastened. The door opened. Beatrice stepped inside. She and Nyagũthiĩ stood there face to face. Nyagũthiĩ was in a see-through nightdress: on her shoulders she had a green pullover.

'Beatrice, is there anything wrong?' She at last asked, a note of concern in her voice.

'Can I rest here for a while? I am tired. And I want to talk to you.' Beatrice's voice carried assurance and power.

'But what has happened?'

'I only want to ask you a question, Nyagũthiĩ.'

They were still standing. Then, without a word, they both sat on the bed.

'Why did you leave home, Nyagũthiĩ?' Beatrice asked. Another silent moment. Nyagũthiĩ seemed to be thinking about the question. Beatrice waited. Nyagũthiĩ's voice when at last it came was slightly tremulous, unsteady.

'It is a long story, Beatrice. My father and mother were fairly wealthy. They were also good Christians. We lived under regulations. You must never walk with the heathen. You must not attend their pagan customs—dances and circumcision rites, for instance. There were rules about what, how and when to eat. You must even walk like a Christian lady. You must never be seen with boys. Rules, rules all the way. One day instead of returning home from school, I and another girl from a similar home ran away to Eastleigh. I have never been home once this last four years. That's all.'

Another silence. Then they looked at one another in mutual recognition.

'One more question, Nyagũthiĩ. You need not answer it. But I have always thought that you hated me, you despised me.'

'No, no, Beatrice, I have never hated you. I have never hated anybody. It is just that nothing interests me. Even men do not move me now. Yet I want, I need instant excitement. I need the attention of those false flattering eyes to make me feel myself, myself. But you, you seemed above all this—somehow you had something inside you that I did not have.'

Beatrice tried to hold her tears with difficulty.

Early the next day, she boarded a bus bound for Nairobi. She walked down Bazaar Street looking at the shops. Then down Government Road, right into Kenyatta Avenue, and Kimathi Street. She went into a shop near Hussein Suleiman's Street and bought several stockings. She put on a pair. She next bought herself a new dress. Again she changed into it. In a Bata Shoeshop, she bought high heeled shoes, put them on and discarded her old flat ones. On to an Akamba kiosk, and she fitted herself with earrings. She went to a mirror and looked at her new self. Suddenly she felt enormous hunger as if she had been hungry all her life. She hesitated in front of Moti Mahal. Then she walked on, eventually entering Fransae. There was a glint in her eyes that made men's eyes turn to her. This thrilled her. She chose a table in a corner and ordered Indian curry. A man left his table and joined her. She looked at him. Her eyes were merry. He was dressed in a dark suit and his eyes spoke of lust. He bought her a drink. He tried to engage her in conversation. But she ate in silence. He put his hand under the table and felt her knees. She let him do it. The hand went up and up her thigh. Then suddenly she left her unfinished food and her untouched drink and walked out. She felt good. He followed her. She knew this without once turning her eyes. He walked beside her for a few yards. She smiled at herself but did not look at him. He lost his confidence. She left him standing sheepishly looking at a glass window outside Gino's. In the bus back to Ilmorog, men gave her seats. She accepted this as of right. At Treetop bar she went straight to the counter. The usual crowd of big men were there. Their conversations stopped for a few seconds at her entry. Their lascivious eyes were turned to her. The girls stared at her. Even Nyagũthiĩ could not maintain her bored indifference. Beatrice bought them drinks. The manager came to her, rather unsure. He tried a conversation. Why had she left work? Where had she been? Would she like to work in the bar, helping Nyagũthiĩ behind the counter? Now and then? A barmaid brought her a note. A certain big shot wanted to know if she would join their table. More notes came from different big quarters with the one question; would she be free tonight? A trip to Nairobi even. She did not leave her place at the counter. But she accepted their drinks as of right. She felt a new power, confidence even.

She took out a shilling, put it in the slot and the juke box boomed with the voice of Robinson Mwangi singing *Hũnyũ wa Mashambani*. He sang of those despised girls who worked on farms and contrasted them with urban girls. Then she played a Kamaru and a D.K. Men wanted to dance with her. She ignored them, but enjoyed their flutter around her. She twisted her hips to the sound of yet another D.K. Her body was free. She was free. She sucked in the excitement and tension in the air.

Then suddenly at around six, the man with the five-ton lorry stormed into the bar. This time he had on his military overcoat. Behind him was a policeman. He looked around. Everybody's eyes were raised to him. But Beatrice went on swaying her hips. At first he could not recognize Beatrice in the girl celebrating her few minutes of glory by the juke box. Then he shouted In triumph. 'That is the girl! Thief! Thief!'

People melted back to their seats. The policeman went and handcuffed her. She did not resist. Only at the door she turned her head and spat. Then she went out followed by the policeman.

In the bar the stunned silence broke into hilarious laughter when someone made a joke about sweetened robbery without violence. They discussed her. Some said she should have been beaten. Others talked contemptuously about 'these bar girls.' Yet others talked with a concern noticeable in unbelieving shakes of their heads about the rising rate of crime. Shouldn't the Hanging Bill be extended to all thefts of property? And without anybody being aware of it the man with the five-ton lorry had become a hero. They now surrounded him with questions and demanded the whole story. Some even bought him drinks. More remarkable, they listened, their attentive silence punctuated by appreciative laughter. The averted threat to property had temporarily knit them into one family. And the man, accepted for the first time, told the story with relish.

But behind the counter Nyagūthiĩ wept.

QUESTIONS AND CONSIDERATIONS

1. Why does the narrator describe Wanjiru as a wounded bird? In what ways is this image appropriate?

2. Why is Wanjiru threatened by Nyagūthiĩ? How does she see Nyagūthiĩ as her shadow? What revelation does she have about Nyagūthiĩ later in the story?

3. Why does Wanjiru have two names? How does her second name reflect her confusion about living in a community that tolerates two religions, two races, and two cultures?

4. Why does Wanjiru lose her job in Ilmorog? Why is she unable to return to her home or to commit suicide ("go metric")?

5. What type of relationship does Wanjiru develop with the trucker she meets at Treetop? What does she learn from him? Why does she rebel against him?

6. What fantasy of herself does Wanjiru develop after she robs the trucker? How does the realization of her fantasy help her to develop self-confidence and at the same time hurt her? What will happen to her after her arrest and imprisonment? Do you see any positive consequences to her struggle?

IDEAS FOR WRITING

1. This story is set in Kenya. Write an essay in which you discuss how the story would turn out if it were set in the United States. Do you think poor women in this country are more optimistic about their futures than the women portrayed in "Minutes of Glory"?

2. Develop your journal into a short story or personal narrative in which you reflect further on the values, gains, and losses involved in the effort to achieve a "minute of glory."

American Horse
Louise Erdrich

Journal

Write about your feelings toward social workers. Do you think that they have empathy for the poor and minority families in your community?

The woman sleeping on the cot in the woodshed was Albertine American Horse. The name was left over from her mother's short marriage. The boy was the son of the man she had loved and let go. Buddy was on the cot too, sitting on the edge because he'd been awake three hours watching out for his mother and besides, she took up the whole cot. Her feet hung over the edge, limp and brown as two trout. Her long arms reached out and slapped at things she saw in her dreams.

Buddy had been knocked awake out of hiding in a washing machine while herds of policemen with dogs searched through a large building with many tiny rooms. When the arm came down, Buddy screamed because it had a blue cuff and sharp silver buttons. "Tss," his mother mumbled, half awake, "wasn't nothing." But Buddy sat up after her breathing went deep again, and he watched.

There was something coming and he knew it.

It was coming from very far off but he had a picture of it in his mind. It was a large thing made of metal with many barbed hooks, points, and drag chains on it, something like a giant potato peeler that rolled out of the sky, scraping clouds down with it and jabbing or crushing everything that lay in its path on the ground.

Buddy watched his mother. If he woke her up, she would know what to do about the thing, but he thought he'd wait until he saw it for sure before he shook her. She was pretty, sleeping, and he liked knowing he could look at her as long and close up as he wanted. He took a strand of her hair and held it in his hands as if it was the rein to a delicate beast. She was strong enough and could pull him along like the horse their name was.

Buddy had his mother's and his grandmother's name because his father had been a big mistake.

"They're all mistakes, even your father. But *you* are the best thing that ever happened to me."

That was what she said when he asked.

Even Kadie, the boyfriend crippled from being in a car wreck, was not as good a thing that had happened to his mother as Buddy was. "He was a medium-sized mistake," she said. "He's hurt and I shouldn't even say that, but it's the truth." At the moment, Buddy knew that being the best thing in his mother's life, he was also the reason they were hiding from the cops.

He wanted to touch the satin roses sewed on her pink T-shirt, but he knew he shouldn't do that even in her sleep. If she woke up and found him touching the roses, she would say, "Quit that, Buddy." Sometimes she told him to stop hugging her like a gorilla. She never said that in the mean voice she used when he oppressed her, but when she said that he loosened up anyway.

There were times he felt like hugging her so hard and in such a special way that she would say to him, "Let's get married." There were also times he closed his eyes and wished that she would die, only a few times, but still it haunted him that his wish might come true. He and Uncle Lawrence would be left alone. Buddy wasn't worried, though, about his mother getting married to somebody else. She had said to her friend, Madonna, "All men suck," when she thought Buddy wasn't listening. He had made an uncertain sound, and when they heard him they took him in their arms.

"Except for you, Buddy," his mother said. "All except for you and maybe Uncle Lawrence, although he's pushing it."

"The cops suck the worst, though," Buddy whispered to his mother's sleeping face, "because they're after us." He felt tired again, slumped down, and put his legs beneath the blanket. He closed his eyes and got the feeling that the cot was lifting up beneath him, that it was arching its canvas back and then traveling, traveling very fast and in the wrong direction for when he looked up he saw the three of them were advancing to meet the great metal thing with hooks and barbs and all sorts of sharp equipment to catch their bodies and draw their blood. He heard its insides as it rushed toward them, purring softly like a powerful motor and then they were right in its shadow. He pulled the reins as hard as he could and the beast reared, lifting him. His mother clapped her hand across his mouth.

"Okay," she said. "Lay low. They're outside and they're gonna hunt."

She touched his shoulder and Buddy leaned over with her to look through a crack in the boards.

They were out there all right, Albertine saw them. Two officers and that social worker woman. Vicki Koob. There had been no whistle, no dream, no voice to warn her that they were coming. There was only the crunching sound of cinders in the yard, the engine purring, the dust sifting off their car in a fine light brownish cloud and settling around them.

The three people came to a halt in their husk of metal—the car emblazoned with the North Dakota State Highway Patrol emblem which is the glowing profile of the Sioux policeman, Red Tomahawk, the one who killed Sitting Bull. Albertine gave Buddy the blanket and told him that he might have to wrap it around him and hide underneath the cot.

"We're gonna wait and see what they do." She took him in her lap and hunched her arms around him. "Don't you worry," she whispered against his ear. "Lawrence knows how to fool them."

Buddy didn't want to look at the car and the people. He felt his mother's heart beating beneath his ear so fast it seemed to push the satin roses in and out. He put his face to them carefully and breathed the deep, soft powdery woman smell of her. That smell was also in her little face cream bottles, in her brushes, and around the washbowl after she used it. The satin felt so unbearably smooth against his cheek that he had to press closer. She didn't push him away, like he expected, but hugged him still tighter until he felt as close as he had ever been to back inside her again where she said he came from. Within the smells of her things, her soft skin, and the satin of her roses, he closed his eyes then, and took his breaths softly and quickly with her heart.

They were out there, but they didn't dare get out of the car yet because of Lawrence's big, ragged dogs. Three of these dogs had loped up the dirt driveway with the car. They were rangy, alert, and bounced up and down on their cushioned paws like wolves. They didn't waste their energy barking, but positioned themselves quietly, one at either car door and the third in front of the bellied-out screen door to Uncle Lawrence's house. It was six in the morning but the wind was up already, blowing dust, ruffling their short moth-eaten coats. The big brown one on Vicki Koob's side had unusual black and white markings, stripes almost, like a hyena and he grinned at her, tongue out and teeth showing.

"Shoo!" Miss Koob opened her door with a quick jerk.

The brown dog sidestepped the door and jumped before her, tiptoeing. Its dirty white muzzle curled and its eyes crossed suddenly as if it was zeroing its cross-hair sights in on the exact place it would bite her. She ducked back and slammed the door.

"It's mean," she told Officer Brackett. He was printing out some type of form. The other officer, Harmony, a slow man, had not yet reacted to the car's halt. He had been sitting quietly in the back seat, but now he rolled down his window and with no change in expression unsnapped his holster and drew his pistol out and pointed it at the dog on his side. The dog smacked down on its belly, wiggled under the car and was out and around the back of the house before Harmony drew his gun back. The other dogs vanished with him. From wherever they had disappeared to they began to yap and howl, and the door to the low shoebox-style house fell open.

"Heya, what's going on?"

Uncle Lawrence put his head out the door and opened wide the one eye he had in working order. The eye bulged impossibly wider in outrage when he saw the police car. But the eyes of the two officers and Miss Vicki Koob were wide open too because they had never seen Uncle Lawrence in his sleeping get-up or, indeed, witnessed anything like it. For his ribs, which were cracked from a bad fall and still mending, Uncle Lawrence wore a thick white corset laced up the front with a striped sneakers' lace. His glass eye and his set of dentures were still out for the night so his face puckered here and there, around its absences and scars, like a damaged but fierce little cake. Although he had a few gray streaks now, Uncle Lawrence's hair was still thick, and because he wore a special contraption of elastic straps around his head every night, two oiled waves always crested on either side of his middle part. All of this would have been sufficient to astonish, even without the most striking part of his outfit—the smoking jacket. It was made of black satin and hung open around his corset, dragging a tasseled belt. Gold thread dragons struggled up the lapels and blasted their furry red breath around his neck. As Lawrence walked down the steps, he put his arms up in surrender and the gold tassels in the inner seams of his sleeves dropped into view.

"My heavens, what a sight." Vicki Koob was impressed.

"A character," apologized Officer Harmony.

As a tribal police officer who could be counted on to help out the State Patrol, Harmony thought he always had to explain about Indians or get twice as tough to show he did not favor them. He was slow-moving and shy but two jumps ahead of other people all the same, and now, as he watched Uncle

Lawrence's splendid approach, he gazed speculatively at the torn and bulging pocket of the smoking jacket. Harmony had been inside Uncle Lawrence's house before and knew that above his draped orange-crate shelf of war medals a blue-black German luger was hung carefully in a net of flat-headed nails and fishing line. Thinking of this deadly exhibition, he got out of the car and shambled toward Lawrence with a dreamy little smile of welcome on his face. But when he searched Lawrence, he found that the bulging pocket held only the lonesome-looking dentures from Lawrence's empty jaw. They were still dripping denture polish.

"I had been cleaning them when you arrived," Uncle Lawrence explained with acid dignity.

He took the toothbrush from his other pocket and aimed it like a rifle.

"Quit that, you old idiot." Harmony tossed the toothbrush away. "For once you ain't done nothing. We came for your nephew."

Lawrence looked at Harmony with a faint air of puzzlement.

"Ma Frere, listen," threatened Harmony amiably, "those two white people in the car came to get him for the welfare. They got papers on your nephew that give them the right to take him."

"Papers?" Uncle Lawrence puffed out his deeply pitted cheeks. "Let me see them papers."

The two of them walked over to Vicki's side of the car and she pulled a copy of the court order from her purse. Lawrence put his teeth back in and adjusted them with busy workings of his jaw.

"Just a minute," he reached into his breast pocket as he bent close to Miss Vicki Koob. "I can't read these without I have in my eye."

He took the eye from his breast pocket delicately, and as he popped it into his face the social worker's mouth fell open in a consternated O.

"What is this," she cried in a little voice.

Uncle Lawrence looked at her mildly. The white glass of the eye was cold as lard. The black iris was strangely charged and menacing.

"He's nuts," Bracket huffed along the side of Vicki's neck. "Never mind him."

Vicki's hair had sweated down her nape in tiny corkscrews and some of the hairs were so long and dangly now that they disappeared into the zippered back of her dress. Brackett noticed this as he spoke into her ear. His face grew red and the backs of his hands prickled. He slid under the steering wheel and got out of the car. He walked around the hood to stand with Leo Harmony.

"We could take you in too," said Brackett roughly. Lawrence eyed the officers in what was taken as defiance. "If you don't cooperate, we'll get out the handcuffs," they warned.

One of Lawrence's arms was stiff and would not move until he'd rubbed it with witch hazel in the morning. His other arm worked fine though, and he stuck it out in front of Brackett.

"Get them handcuffs," he urged them. "Put me in a welfare home."

Brackett snapped one side of the handcuffs on Lawrence's good arm and the other to the handle of the police car.

"That's to hold you," he said. "We're wasting our time. Harmony, you search that little shed over by the tall grass and Miss Koob and myself will search the house."

"My rights is violated!" Lawrence shrieked suddenly. They ignored him. He tugged at the handcuff and thought of the good heavy file he kept in his tool box and the German luger oiled and ready but never loaded, because of Buddy, over his shelf. He should have used it on these bad ones, even Harmony in his big-time white man job. He wouldn't last long in that job anyway before somebody gave him what for.

"It's a damn scheme," said Uncle Lawrence, rattling his chains against the car. He looked over at the shed and thought maybe Albertine and Buddy had sneaked away before the car pulled into the yard. But he sagged, seeing Albertine move like a shadow within the boards. "Oh, it's all a damn scheme," he muttered again.

"I want to find that boy and salvage him," Vicki Koob explained to Officer Brackett as they walked into the house. "Look at his family life—the old man crazy as a bedbug, the mother intoxicated somewhere."

Brackett nodded, energetic, eager. He was a short hopeful redhead who failed consistently to win the hearts of women. Vicki Koob intrigued him. Now, as he watched, she pulled a tiny pen out of an ornamental clip on her blouse. It was attached to a retractable line that would suck the pen back, like a child eating one strand of spaghetti. Something about the pen on its line excited Brackett to the point of discomfort. His hand shook as he opened the screendoor and stepped in, beckoning Miss Koob to follow.

They could see the house was empty at first glance. It was only one rectangular room with whitewashed walls and a little gas stove in the middle. They had already come through the cooking lean-to with the other stove and washstand and rusty old refrigerator. That refrigerator had nothing in it but some wrinkled potatoes and a package of turkey necks. Vicki Koob noted that in her perfect-bound notebook. The beds along the walls of the big room were covered with quilts that Albertine's mother, Sophie, had made from bits of old wool coats and pants that the Sisters sold in bundles at the mission. There was no one hiding beneath the beds. No one was under the little aluminum dinette table covered with a green oilcloth, or the soft brown wood chairs tucked up to it. One wall of the big room was filled with neatly stacked crates of things—old tools and springs and small half-dismantled appliances. Five or six television sets were stacked against the wall. Their control panels spewed colored wires and at least one was cracked all the way across. Only the topmost set, with coathanger antenna angled sensitively to catch the bounding signals around Little Shell, looked like it could possibly work.

Not one thing escaped Vicki Koob's trained and cataloguing gaze. She made note of the cupboard that held only commodity flour and coffee. The unsanitary tin oil drum beneath the kitchen window, full of empty surplus pork cans and beer bottles, caught her eye as did Uncle Lawrence's physical and mental deteriorations. She quickly described these "benchmarks of alcoholic dependency within the extended family of Woodrow (Buddy) American Horse" as she walked around the room with the little notebook open, pushed against her belly to steady it. Although Vicki had been there before, Albertine's presence had always made it difficult for her to take notes.

"Twice the maximum allowable space between door and threshold," she wrote now. "Probably no insulation. Two three-inch cracks in walls inadequately sealed with whitewashed mud." She made a mental note but could see no point in describing Lawrence's stuffed reclining chair that only reclined, the shadeless lamp with its plastic orchid in the bubble glass base, or the three-dimensional picture of Jesus that Lawrence had once demonstrated to her. When plugged in, lights rolled behind the water the Lord stood on so that he seemed to be strolling although he never actually went forward, of course, but only pushed the glowing waves behind him forever like a poor tame rat in a treadmill.

Brackett cleared his throat with a nervous rasp and touched Vicki's shoulder.

"What are you writing?"

She moved away and continued to scribble as if thoroughly absorbed in her work. "Officer Brackett displays an undue amount of interest in my person," she wrote. "Perhaps?"

He snatched playfully at the book, but she hugged it to her chest and moved off smiling. More curls had fallen, wetted to the base of her neck. Looking out the window, she sighed long and loud.

"All night on brush rollers for this. What a joke."

Brackett shoved his hands in his pockets. His mouth opened slightly, then shut with a small throttled cluck.

When Albertine saw Harmony ambling across the yard with his big brown thumbs in his belt, his placid smile, and his tiny black eyes moving back and forth, she put Buddy under the cot. Harmony stopped at the shed and stood quietly. He spread his arms to show her he hadn't drawn his big police gun.

"Ma Cousin," he said in the Michif dialect that people used if they were relatives or sometimes if they needed gas or a couple of dollars, "why don't you come out here and stop this foolishness?"

"I ain't your cousin," Albertine said. Anger boiled up in her suddenly. "I ain't related to no pigs."

She bit her lip and watched him through the cracks, circling, a big tan punching dummy with his boots full of sand so he never stayed down once he fell. He was empty inside, all stale air. But he knew how to get to her so much better than a white cop could. And now he was circling because he wasn't sure she didn't have a weapon, maybe a knife or the German luger that was the only thing that her father, Albert American Horse, had left his wife and daughter besides his name. Harmony knew that Albertine was a tall strong woman who took two big men to subdue when she didn't want to go in the drunk tank. She had hard hips, broad shoulders, and stood tall like her Sioux father, the American Horse who was killed threshing in Belle Prairie.

"I feel bad to have to do this," Harmony said to Albertine. "But for god-sakes, let's nobody get hurt. Come on out with the boy, why don't you? I know you got him in there."

Albertine did not give herself away this time. She let him wonder. Slowly and quietly she pulled her belt through its loops and wrapped it around and around her hand until only the big oval buckle with turquoise chunks shaped into a butterfly stuck out over her knuckles. Harmony was talking but she wasn't listening to what he said. She was listening to the pitch of his voice, the tone of it that would tighten or tremble at a certain moment when he decided to rush the shed. He kept talking slowly and reasonably, flexing the dialect from time to time, even mentioning her father.

"He was a damn good man. I don't care what they say, Albertine, I knew him."

Albertine looked at the stone butterfly that spread its wings across her fist. The wings looked light and cool, not heavy. It almost looked like it was ready to fly. Harmony wanted to get to Albertine through her father but she would not think about American Horse. She concentrated on the sky blue stone.

Yet the shape of the stone, the color, betrayed her.

She saw her father suddenly, bending at the grille of their old gray car. She was small then. The memory came from so long ago it seemed like a dream—narrowly focused, snapshot-clear. He was bending by the grille in the sun. It was hot summer. Wings of sweat, dark blue, spread across the back of his work shirt. He always wore soft blue shirts, the color of shade cloudier than this stone. His stiff hair had grown out of its short haircut and flopped over his forehead. When he stood up and turned away from the car, Albertine saw that he had a butterfly.

"It's dead," he told her. "Broke its wings and died on the grille."

She must have been five, maybe six, wearing one of the boy's T-shirts Mama bleached in Hilex-water. American Horse took the butterfly, a black and yellow one, and rubbed it on Albertine's collarbone and chest and arms until the color and the powder of it were blended into her skin.

"For grace," he said.

And Albertine had felt a strange lightening in her arms, in her chest, when he did this and said, "For grace." The way he said it, grace meant everything the butterfly was. The sharp delicate wings. The way it floated over grass. The way its wings seemed to breathe fanning in the sun. The wisdom of the way it blended into flowers or changed into a leaf. In herself she felt the same kind of possibilities and closed her eyes almost in shock or pain, she felt so light and powerful at that moment.

Then her father had caught her and thrown her high into the air. She could not remember landing in his arms or landing at all. She only remembered the sun filling her eyes and the world tipping crazily behind her, out of sight.

"He was a damn good man," Harmony said again.

Albertine heard his starched uniform gathering before his boots hit the ground. Once, twice, three times. It took him four solid jumps to get right where she wanted him. She kicked the plank door open when he reached for the handle and the corner.caught him on the jaw. He faltered, and Albertine hit him flat on the chin with the butterfly. She hit him so hard the shock of it went up her arm like a string pulled taut. Her fist opened, numb, and she let the belt unloop before she closed her hand on the tip end of it and sent the stone butterfly swooping out in a wide circle around her as if it was on the end of a leash. Harmony reeled backward as she walked toward him swinging the belt. She expected him to fall but he just stumbled. And then he took the gun from his hip.

Albertine let the belt go limp. She and Harmony stood within feet of each other, breathing. Each heard the human sound of air going in and out of the other person's lungs. Each read the face of the other as if deciphering letters carved into softly eroding veins of stone. Albertine saw the pattern of tiny arteries that age, drink, and hard living had blown to the surface of the man's face. She saw the spoked wheels of his iris and the arteries like tangled threads that sewed him up. She saw the living net of springs and tissue that held him together, and trapped him. She saw the random, intimate plan of his person.

She took a quick shallow breath and her face went strange and tight. She saw the black veins in the wings of the butterfly, roads burnt into a map, and then she was located somewhere in the net of veins and sinew that was the tragic complexity of the world so she did not see Officer Brackett and Vicki Koob rushing toward her, but felt them instead like flies caught in the same web, rocking it.

"Albertine!" Vicki Koob had stopped in the grass. Her voice was shrill and tight. "It's better this way, Albertine. We're going to help you."

Albertine straightened, threw her shoulders back. Her father's hand was on her chest and shoulders lightening her wonderfully. Then on wings of her father's hands, on dead butterfly wings, Albertine lifted into the air and flew toward the others. The light powerful feeling swept her up the way she had floated higher, seeing the grass below. It was her father throwing her up into the air and out of danger. Her arms opened for bullets but no bullets came. Harmony did not shoot. Instead, he raised his fist and brought it down hard on her head.

Albertine did not fall immediately, but stood in his arms a moment. Perhaps she gazed still farther back behind the covering of his face. Perhaps she was completely stunned and did not think as she sagged and fell. Her face rolled forward and hair covered her features, so it was impossible for Harmony to see with just what particular expression she gazed into the head-splitting wheel of light, or blackness, that overcame her.

Harmony turned the vehicle onto the gravel road that led back to town. He had convinced the other two that Albertine was more trouble than she was worth, and so they left her behind, and Lawrence too. He stood swearing in his cinder driveway as the car rolled out of sight. Buddy sat between the social worker and Officer Brackett. Vicki tried to hold Buddy fast and keep her arm down at the same time, for the words she'd screamed at Albertine had broken the seal of antiperspirant beneath her arms. She was sweating now as though she'd stored up an ocean inside of her. Sweat rolled down her back in a shallow river and pooled at her waist and between her breasts. A thin sheen of water came out on her forearms, her face. Vicki gave an irritated moan but Brackett seemed not to take notice, or take offense at least. Air-conditioned breezes were sweeping over the seat anyway, and very soon they would be comfortable. She smiled at Brackett over Buddy's head. The man grinned back. Buddy stirred. Vicki remembered the emergency chocolate bar she kept in her purse, fished it out, and offered it to Buddy. He did not react, so she closed his fingers over the package and peeled the paper off one end.

The car accelerated. Buddy felt the road and wheels pummeling each other and the rush of the heavy motor purring in high gear. Buddy knew that what he'd seen in his mind that morning, the thing coming out of the sky with barbs and chains, had hooked him. Somehow he was caught and held in the sour tin smell of the pale woman's armpit. Somehow he was pinned between their pounds of breathless flesh. He looked at the chocolate in his hand. He was squeezing the bar so hard that a thin brown trickle had melted down his arm. Automatically he put the bar in his mouth.

As he bit down he saw his mother very clearly, just as she had been when she carried him from the shed. She was stretched flat on the ground, on her stomach, and her arms were curled around her head as if in sleep. One leg was drawn up and it looked for all the world like she was running full tilt into the ground, as though she had been trying to pass into the earth, to bury herself, but at the last moment something had stopped her.

There was no blood on Albertine, but Buddy tasted blood now at the sight of her, for he bit down hard and cut his own lip. He ate the chocolate, every bit of it, tasting his mother's blood. And when he had the chocolate down inside him and all licked off his hands, he opened his mouth to say thank you to the woman, as his mother had taught him. But instead of a thank you coming out he was astonished to hear a great rattling scream, and then another, rip out of him like pieces of his own body and whirl onto the sharp things all around him.

QUESTIONS AND CONSIDERATIONS

1. What is the central conflict in the story? What point of view does each of the major characters in the story—Albertine, Buddy, Uncle Lawrence, Officer Harmony, Officer Brackett, and Vicki Koob—take in relation to this conflict?

2. What is the setting of the story? What key details make it vivid and real? How does the setting influence your feelings about the characters and their conflicts?

3. How do elements of Native American culture and heritage, such as the name American Horse and the symbol of the butterfly, add to the meaning and values of the story?

4. To some degree this is a story about a substitution of "mother figures"—Albertine and Vicki Koob. How are these two women contrasted in the story? What are the strengths and weaknesses of each?

5. In what ways are Albertine and Buddy's problems related to the fact that they are Native Americans? How might their problems be typical of those of any poor family?

6. Predict the future for Buddy and Albertine. Will the struggle portrayed in the story bring about any positive changes for them?

IDEAS FOR WRITING

1. Develop an essay in which you argue for or against the wisdom of removing a child such as Buddy from his home.

2. Native American families have many problems in adjusting to popular American culture, problems such as maintaining a sense of heritage, struggling with poverty, coping with alcohol, and dealing with bureaucracy. Write an essay in which you explore one of these problems. Present the historical causes of the problem as well as some possible ways of alleviating some of the suffering involved.

Action Will Be Taken

An Action-Packed Story

Heinrich Böll
Translated from the German by Leila Vennewitz

Journal

Write about a time when you realized that overwork or frantic activity could be a waste of your time and even self-destructive. What did you learn about yourself from this experience?

Probably one of the strangest interludes in my life was the time I spent as an employee in Alfred Wunsiedel's factory. By nature I am inclined more to pensiveness and inactivity than to work, but now and again prolonged financial difficulties compel me—for pensiveness is no more profitable than inactivity—to take on a so-called job. Finding myself once again at a low ebb of this kind, I put myself in the hands of the employment office and was sent with seven other fellow-sufferers to Wunsiedel's factory, where we were to undergo an aptitude test.

The exterior of the factory was enough to arouse my suspicions: the factory was built entirely of glass brick, and my aversion to well-lit buildings and well-lit rooms is as strong as my aversion to work. I became even more suspicious when we were immediately served breakfast in the well-lit, cheerful coffee shop: pretty waitresses brought us eggs, coffee and toast, orange juice was served in tastefully designed jugs, goldfish pressed their bored faces against the sides of pale-green aquariums. The waitresses were so cheerful that they appeared to be bursting with good cheer. Only a strong effort of will—so it seemed to me—restrained them from singing away all day long. They were as crammed with unsung songs as chickens with unlaid eggs.

Right away I realized something that my fellow-sufferers evidently failed to realize: that this breakfast was already part of the test; so I chewed away reverently, with the full appreciation of a person who knows he is supplying his body with valuable elements. I did something which normally no power on earth can make me do: I drank orange juice on an empty stomach, left the coffee and egg untouched, as well as most of the toast, got up, and paced up and down in the coffee shop, pregnant with action.

As a result I was the first to be ushered into the room where the questionnaires were spread out on attractive tables. The walls were done in a shade of green that would have summoned the word "delightful" to the lips of interior decoration enthusiasts. The room appeared to be empty, and yet I was so sure of being observed that I behaved as someone pregnant with action behaves when he believes himself unobserved: I ripped my pen impatiently from my pocket, unscrewed the top, sat down at the nearest table and pulled the questionnaire toward me, the way irritable customers snatch at the bill in a restaurant.

Question No. 1: Do you consider it right for a human being to possess only two arms, two legs, eyes, and ears?

Here for the first time I reaped the harvest of my pensive nature and wrote without hesitation: "Even four arms, legs and ears would not be adequate for my driving energy. Human beings are very poorly equipped."

Question No. 2: How many telephones can you handle at one time?

Here again the answer was as easy as simple arithmetic: "When there are only seven telephones," I wrote, "I get impatient; there have to be nine before I feel I am working to capacity."

Question No. 3: How do you spend your free time?

My answer: "I no longer acknowledge the term free time—on my fifteenth birthday I eliminated it from my vocabulary, for in the beginning was the act."

I got the job. Even with nine telephones I really didn't feel I was working to capacity. I shouted into the mouthpieces: "Take immediate action!" or: "Do something!—We must have some action—Action will be taken—Action has been taken—Action should be taken." But as a rule—for I felt this was in keeping with the tone of the place—I used the imperative.

Of considerable interest were the noon-hour breaks, when we consumed nutritious foods in an atmosphere of silent good cheer. Wunsiedel's factory was swarming with people who were obsessed with telling you the story of their lives, as indeed vigorous personalities are fond of doing. The story of their lives is more important to them than their lives, you have only to press a button, and immediately it is covered with spewed-out exploits.

Wunsiedel had a right-hand man called Broschek, who had in turn made a name for himself by supporting seven children and a paralyzed wife by working night-shifts in his student days, and successfully carrying on four business agencies, besides which he had passed two examinations with honors in two years. When asked by reporters: "When do you sleep, Mr. Broschek?" he had replied: "It's a crime to sleep!"

Wunsiedel's secretary had supported a paralyzed husband and four children by knitting, at the same time graduating in psychology and German history as well as breeding shepherd dogs, and she had become famous as a night-club singer where she was known as *Vamp Number Seven.*

Wunsiedel himself was one of those people who every morning, as they open their eyes, make up their minds to act. "I must act," they think as they briskly tie their bathrobe belts around them. "I must act," they think as they shave, triumphantly watching their beard hairs being washed away with the lather: these hirsute vestiges are the first daily sacrifices to their driving energy. The more intimate functions also give these people a sense of satisfaction: water swishes, paper is used. Action has been taken. Bread gets eaten, eggs are decapitated.

With Wunsiedel, the most trivial activity looked like action: the way he put on his hat, the way—quivering with energy—he buttoned up his overcoat, the kiss he gave his wife, everything was action.

When he arrived at his office he greeted his secretary with a cry of "Let's have some action!" And in ringing tones she would call back: "Action will be taken!" Wunsiedel then went from department to department, calling out his cheerful: "Let's have some action!" Everyone would answer: "Action will be taken!" And I would call back to him too, with a radiant smile, when he looked into my office: "Action will be taken!"

Within a week I had increased the number of telephones on my desk to eleven, within two weeks to thirteen, and every morning on the streetcar I enjoyed thinking up new imperatives, or chasing the words *take action* through various tenses and modulations: for two whole days I kept saying the same sentence over and over again because I thought it sounded so marvelous: "Action ought to have been taken;" for another two days it was: "Such action ought not to have been taken."

So I was really beginning to feel I was working to capacity when there actually was some action. One Tuesday morning—I had hardly settled down at my desk—Wunsiedel rushed into my office crying his "Let's have some action!" But an inexplicable something in his face made me hesitate to reply, in a cheerful gay voice as the rules dictated: "Action will be taken!" I must have paused too long, for Wunsiedel, who seldom raised his voice, shouted at me: "Answer! Answer, you know the rules!" And I answered, under my breath, reluctantly, like a child who is forced to say: I am a naughty child. It was only by a great effort that I managed to bring out the sentence: "Action will be taken," and hardly had I uttered it when there really was some action: Wunsiedel dropped to the floor. As he fell he rolled over onto his side and lay right across the open doorway. I knew at once, and I confirmed it when I went slowly around my desk and approached the body on the floor: he was dead.

Shaking my head I stepped over Wunsiedel, walked slowly along the corridor to Broschek's office, and entered without knocking. Broschek was sitting at his desk, a telephone receiver in each hand, between his teeth a ballpoint pen with which he was making notes on a writing pad, while with his bare feet he was operating a knitting machine under the desk. In this way he helps to clothe his family. "We've had some action," I said in a low voice.

Broschek spat out the ballpoint pen, put down the two receivers, reluctantly detached his toes from the knitting machine.

"What action?" he asked.

"Wunsiedel is dead," I said.

"No," said Broschek.

"Yes," I said, "come and have a look!"

"No," said Broschek, "that's impossible," but he put on his slippers and followed me along the corridor.

"No," he said, when we stood beside Wunsiedel's corpse, "no, no!" I did not contradict him. I carefully turned Wunsiedel over onto his back, closed his eyes, and looked at him pensively.

I felt something like tenderness for him, and realized for the first time that I had never hated him. On his face was that expression which one sees on children who obstinately refuse to give up their faith in Santa Claus, even though the arguments of their playmates sound so convincing.

"No," said Broschek, "no."

"We must take action," I said quietly to Broschek.

"Yes," said Broschek, "we must take action."

Action was taken: Wunsiedel was buried, and I was delegated to carry a wreath of artificial roses behind his coffin, for I am equipped with not only a penchant for pensiveness and inactivity but also a face and figure that go extremely well with dark suits. Apparently as I walked along behind Wunsiedel's coffin carrying the wreath of artificial roses I looked superb. I received an offer from a fashionable firm of funeral directors to join their staff as a professional mourner. "You are a born mourner," said the manager, "your outfit would be provided by the firm. Your face—simply superb!"

I handed in my notice to Broschek, explaining that I had never really felt I was working to capacity there; that, in spite of the thirteen telephones, some of my talents were going to waste. As soon as my first professional appearance as a mourner was over I knew: This is where I belong, this is what I am cut out for.

Pensively I stand behind the coffin in the funeral chapel, holding a simple bouquet, while the organ plays Handel's *Largo*, a piece that does not receive nearly the respect it deserves. The cemetery café is my regular haunt; there I spend the intervals between my professional engagements, although sometimes I walk behind coffins which I have not been engaged to follow, I pay for flowers out of my own pocket and join the welfare worker who walks behind the coffin of some homeless person. From time to time I also visit Wunsiedel's grave, for after all I owe it to him that I discovered my true vocation, a vocation in which pensiveness is essential and inactivity my duty.

It was not till much later that I realized I had never bothered to find out what was being produced in Wunsiedel's factory. I expect it was soap.

QUESTIONS AND CONSIDERATIONS

1. Why does the narrator apply for a job at Wunsiedel's factory? How does he reconcile his basically passive, lethargic personality with the frantic pace at the factory?

2. Why is the narrator such a successful employee? What is ironic about his success?

3. How does the narrator get a job at a funeral parlor? Is he being serious or ironic when he claims that the position is perfectly suited to his personality?

4. Why does the author wait until the end of the story to have the narrator admit that he had forgotten to ask what type of product was produced at the factory? Why does the narrator assume that soap was produced? What does soap suggest to you?

5. Are pensiveness and inactivity synonymous in this story? Why or why not?

6. What point does this story make about work and struggle in the workplace? How does the author's use of humor help to make the story's points more incisive and memorable?

IDEAS FOR WRITING

1. Wunsiedel's factory is a place where people are encouraged literally to work themselves to death for maximum production. Write about your own experiences working at a fast-paced, demanding job.

2. Do you think such "speed-up" strategies are effective in the long run? In contrast, have you had employers who motivated you to work in a less oppressive way? Write an essay about your vision of the ideal workplace, where high productivity could be achieved with a minimum of stress and unhappiness. How could such an ideal be attained?

The Censors
Luisa Valenzuela

Journal

Write about a time when you joined a group to study or to change it, yet found that once you had joined, your own attitudes changed significantly. Why do you think this happened? How did you change?

Poor Juan! One day they caught him with his guard down before he could even realize that what he had taken as a stroke of luck was really one of fate's dirty tricks. These things happen the minute you're careless and you let down your guard, as one often does. Juancito let happiness—a feeling you can't trust—get the better of him when he received from a confidential source Mariana's new address in Paris and he knew that she hadn't forgotten him. Without thinking twice, he sat down at his table and wrote her a letter. *The* letter that keeps his mind off his job during the day and won't let him sleep at night (what had he scrawled, what had he put on that sheet of paper he sent to Mariana?)

Juan knows there won't be a problem with the letter's contents, that it's irreproachablo, harmless. But wl at about the rest? He knows that they examine, sniff, feel, and read between the lines of each and every letter, and check its tiniest comma and most accidental stain. He knows that all letters pass from hand to hand and go through all sorts of tests in the huge censorship offices and that, in the end, very few continue on their way. Usually it takes months, even years, if there aren't any snags; all this time the freedom, maybe even the life, of both sender and receiver is in jeopardy. And that's why Juan's so down in the dumps: thinking that something might happen to Mariana because of his letters. Of all people, Mariana, who must finally feel safe there where she always dreamed she'd live. But he knows that the *Censor's Secret Command* operates all over the world and cashes in on the discount in air rates; there's nothing to stop them from going as far as that hidden Paris neighborhood, kidnapping Mariana, and returning to their cozy homes, certain of having fulfilled their noble mission.

Well, you've got to beat them to the punch, do what everyone tries to do: sabotage the machinery, throw sand in its gears, get to the bottom of the problem so as to stop it.

This was Juan's sound plan when he, like many others, applied for a censor's job—not because he had a calling or needed a job: no, he applied simply to intercept his own letter, a consoling but unoriginal idea. He was hired immediately, for each day more and more censors are needed and no one would bother to check on his references.

Ulterior motives couldn't be overlooked by the *Censorship Division,* but they needn't be too strict with those who applied. They knew how hard it would be for those poor guys to find the letter they wanted and even if they did, what's a letter or two when the new censor would snap up so many others? That's how Juan managed to join the *Post Office's Censorship Division,* with a certain goal in mind.

The building had a festive air on the outside which contrasted with its inner staidness. Little by little, Juan was absorbed by his job and he felt at peace since he was doing everything he could to get his letter for Mariana. He didn't even worry when, in his first month, he was sent to *Section K* where envelopes are very carefully screened for explosives.

It's true that on the third day, a fellow worker had his right hand blown off by a letter, but the division chief claimed it was sheer negligence on the victim's part. Juan and the other employees were allowed to go back to their work, albeit feeling less secure. After work, one of them tried to organize a strike to demand higher wages for unhealthy work, but Juan didn't join in; after thinking it over, he reported him to his superiors and thus got promoted.

You don't form a habit by doing something once, he told himself as he left his boss's office. And when he was transferred to *Section J,* where letters are carefully checked for poison dust, he felt he had climbed a rung in the ladder.

By working hard, he quickly reached *Section E* where the work was more interesting, for he could now read and analyze the letters' contents. Here he could even hope to get hold of his letter which, judging by the time that had elapsed, had gone through the other sections and was probably floating around in this one.

Soon his work became so absorbing that his noble mission blurred in his mind. Day after day he crossed out whole paragraphs in red ink, pitilessly chucking many letters into the censored basket. These were horrible days when he was shocked by the subtle and conniving ways employed by people to pass on subversive messages; his instincts were so sharp that he found behind a simple "the weather's unsettled" or "prices continue to soar" the wavering hand of someone secretly scheming to overthrow the Government.

His zeal brought him swift promotion. We don't know if this made him happy. Very few letters reached him in *Section B*—only a handful passed the other hurdles—so he read them over and over again, passed them under a magnifying glass, searched for microprint with an electronic microscope, and tuned his sense of smell so that he was beat by the time he made it home. He'd barely manage to warm up his soup, eat some fruit, and fall into bed, satisfied with having done his duty. Only his darling mother worried, but she couldn't get him back on the right road. She'd say, though it wasn't always true: Lola called, she's at the bar with the girls, they miss you, they're waiting for you. Or else she'd leave a bottle of red wine on the table. But Juan wouldn't overdo it: any distraction could make him lose his edge and the perfect censor had to be alert, keen, attentive, and sharp to nab cheats. He had a truly patriotic task, both self-denying and uplifting.

His basket for censored letters became the best fed as well as the most cunning basket in the whole *Censorship Division.* He was about to congratulate himself for having finally discovered his true mission, when his letter to Mariana reached his hands. Naturally, he censored it without regret. And just as naturally, he couldn't stop them from executing him the following morning, another victim of his devotion to his work.

QUESTIONS AND CONSIDERATIONS

1. Why does Juan take the job working for the censors? Why does he continue to get promoted regularly?

2. How and why does Juan get so involved with his job as a censor that he loses sight of his original purpose?

3. Clarify the struggle that the story explores, as you understand it. What other approaches might Juan have taken so that his struggle could have been less self-destructive?

4. Why does Juan eventually censor his own letter to Mariana "without regret"? Is there really anything worth censoring in the letter? What are the implications of his actions here and their relationship to the struggle that the story explores?

5. Consider Juan's attitude toward his job: Have you known people who were similar to Juan in their relationship to work? In what ways?

6. Valenzuela shows how the political system in Argentina controls its citizens. In what ways does our own government control the lives of its citizens?

IDEAS FOR WRITING

1. Write an essay that clarifies what you think are the most serious ways that the government and media censor information or curtail our freedom as citizens. Propose several ways that American citizens can fight this censorship.

2. Write a short story or fable about censorship, set either in your own community or in an imaginary society.

Shooting an Elephant
George Orwell

Journal

Write about a time when you were in a position of power. How did you feel about your responsibilities and your role?

In Moulmein, in Lower Burma, I was hated by large numbers of people—the only time in my life that I have been important enough for this to happen to me. I was sub-divisional police officer of the town, and in an aimless, petty kind of way anti-European feeling was very bitter. No one had the guts to raise a riot, but if a European woman went through the bazaars alone somebody would probably spit betel juice over her dress. As a police officer I was an obvious target and was baited whenever it seemed safe to do so. When a nimble Burman tripped me up on the football field and the referee (another Burman) looked the other way, the crowd yelled with hideous laughter. This happened more than once. In the end the sneering yellow faces of young men that met me everywhere, the insults hooted after me when I was at a safe distance, got badly on my nerves. The young Buddhist priests were the worst of all. There were several thousands of them in the town and none of them seemed to have anything to do except stand on street corners and jeer at Europeans.

All this was perplexing and upsetting. For at that time I had already made up my mind that imperialism was an evil thing and the sooner I chucked up my job and got out of it the better. Theoretically—and secretly, of course—I was all for the Burmese and all against their oppressors, the British. As for the job I was doing, I hated it more bitterly than I can perhaps make clear. In a job like that you see the dirty work of Empire at close quarters. The wretched prisoners huddling in the stinking cages of the lock-ups, the grey, cowed faces of the long-term convicts, the scarred buttocks of the men who had been flogged with bamboos—all these oppressed me with an intolerable sense of guilt. But I could get nothing into perspective. I was young and ill-educated and I had had to think out my problems in the utter silence that is imposed on every Englishman in the East. I did not even know that the British Empire is dying, still less did I know that it is a great deal better than the younger empires that are going to supplant it. All I knew was that I was stuck between my hatred of the empire I served and my rage against the evil-spirited little beasts who tried to make my job impossible. With one part of my mind I thought of the British Raj as an unbreakable tyranny, as something clamped down, in *saecula saeculorum,* upon the will of the prostrate peoples; with another part I thought that the greatest joy in the world would be to drive a bayonet into a Buddhist priest's guts. Feelings like these are normal by-products of imperialism; ask any Anglo-Indian official, if you can catch him off duty.

One day something happened which in a roundabout way was enlightening. It was a tiny incident in itself, but it gave me a better glimpse than I had had before of the real nature of imperialism—the real motives for which despotic governments act. Early one morning the sub-inspector at a police station the other end of town rang me up on the 'phone and said that an elephant was ravaging the bazaar. Would I please come and do something about it? I did not know what I could do, but I wanted to see what was happening and I got on to a pony and started out. I took my rifle, an old .44 Winchester and much too small to kill an elephant, but I thought the noise might be useful *in terrorem.* Various Burmans stopped me on the way and told me about the elephant's doings. It was not, of course, a wild elephant, but a tame one which had gone "must." It had been chained up, as tame elephants always are when their attack of "must" is due, but on the previous night it had broken its chain and escaped. Its mahout, the only person who could manage it when it was in that state, had set out in pursuit, but had taken the wrong direction and was now twelve hours' journey away, and in the morning the elephant had suddenly reappeared in the town. The Burmese population had no weapons and were quite helpless against it. It had already destroyed somebody's bamboo hut, killed a cow and raided some fruit-stalls and devoured the stock; also it had met the municipal rubbish van and, when the driver jumped out and took to his heels, had turned the van over and inflicted violences upon it.

The Burmese sub-inspector and some Indian constables were waiting for me in the quarter where the elephant had been seen. It was a very poor quarter, a labyrinth of squalid bamboo huts, thatched with palmleaf, winding all over a steep hillside. I remember that it was a cloudy, stuffy morning at the beginning of the rains. We began questioning the people as to where the elephant had gone and, as usual, failed to get any definite information. That is invariably the case in the East; a story always sounds clear enough at a distance, but the nearer you get to the scene of events the vaguer it becomes.

Some of the people said that the elephant had gone in one direction, some said that he had gone in another, some professed not even to have heard of any elephant. I had almost made up my mind that the whole story was a pack of lies, when we heard yells a little distance away. There was a loud, scandalized cry of "Go away, child! Go away this instant!" and an old woman with a switch in her hand came round the corner of a hut, violently shooing away a crowd of naked children. Some more women followed, clicking their tongues and exclaiming; evidently there was something that the children ought not to have seen. I rounded the hut and saw a man's dead body sprawling in the mud. He was an Indian, a black Dravidian coolie, almost naked, and he could not have been dead many minutes. The people said that the elephant had come suddenly upon him round the corner of the hut, caught him with its trunk, put its foot on his back and ground him into the earth. This was the rainy season and the ground was soft, and his face had scored a trench a foot deep and a couple of yards long. He was lying on his belly with arms crucified and head sharply twisted to one side. His face was coated with mud, the eyes wide open, the teeth bared and grinning with an expression of unendurable agony. (Never tell me, by the way, that the dead look peaceful. Most of the corpses I have seen looked devilish.) The friction of the great beast's foot had stripped the skin from his back as neatly as one skins a rabbit. As soon as I saw the dead man I sent an orderly to a friend's house nearby to borrow an elephant rifle. I had already sent back the pony, not wanting it to go mad with fright and throw me if it smelt the elephant.

The orderly came back in a few minutes with a rifle and five cartridges, and meanwhile some Burmans had arrived and told us that the elephant was in the paddy fields below, only a few hundred yards away. As I started forward practically the whole population of the quarter flocked out of the houses and followed me. They had seen the rifle and were all shouting excitedly that I was going to shoot the elephant. They had not shown much interest in the elephant when he was merely ravaging their homes, but it was different now that he was going to be shot. It was a bit of fun to them, as it would be to an English crowd; besides they wanted the meat. It made me vaguely uneasy. I had no intention of shooting the elephant—I had merely sent for the rifle to defend myself if necessary—and it is always unnerving to have a crowd following you. I marched down the hill, looking and feeling a fool, with the rifle over my shoulder and an ever-growing army of people jostling at my heels. At the bottom, when you got away from the huts, there was a metalled road and beyond that a miry waste of paddy fields a thousand yards across, not yet ploughed but soggy from the first rains and dotted with coarse grass. The elephant was standing eight yards from the road, his left side towards us. He took not the slightest notice of the crowd's approach. He was tearing up bunches of grass, beating them against his knees to clean them and stuffing them into his mouth.

I had halted on the road. As soon as I saw the elephant I knew with perfect certainty that I ought not to shoot him. It is a serious matter to shoot a working elephant—it is comparable to destroying a huge and costly piece of machinery—and obviously one ought not to do it if it can possibly be avoided. And at that distance, peacefully eating, the elephant looked no more danger- ous than a cow. I thought then and I think now that his attack of "must" was al- ready passing off; in which case he would merely wander harmlessly about until the mahout came back and caught him. Moreover, I did not in the least want to shoot him. I decided that I would watch him for a little while to make sure that he did not turn savage again, and then go home.

But at that moment, I glanced round at the crowd that had followed me. It was an immense crowd, two thousand at the least and growing every minute. It blocked the road for a long distance on either side. I looked at the sea of yellow faces above the garish clothes—faces all happy and excited over this bit of fun, all certain that the elephant was going to be shot. They were watching me as they would watch a conjuror about to perform a trick. They did not like me, but with the magical rifle in my hands I was momentarily worth watching. And suddenly I realized that I should have to shoot the ele- phant after all. The people expected it of me and I had got to do it; I could feel their two thousand wills pressing me forward, irresistibly. And it was at this moment, as I stood there with the rifle in my hands, that I first grasped the hollowness, the futility of the white man's dominion in the East. Here was I, the white man with his gun, standing in front of the unarmed native crowd—seemingly the leading actor of the piece; but in reality I was only an absurd puppet pushed to and fro by the will of those yellow faces behind. I perceived in this moment that when the white man turns tyrant it is his own freedom that he destroys. He becomes a sort of hollow, posing dummy, the conventionalized figure of a sahib. For it is the condition of his rule that he shall spend his life in trying to impress the "natives," and so in every crisis he has got to do what the "natives" expect of him. He wears a mask, and his face grows to fit it. I had got to shoot the elephant. I had committed myself to doing it when I sent for the rifle. A sahib has got to act like a sahib; he has got to appear resolute, to know his own mind and do definite things. To come all that way, rifle in hand, with two thousand people marching at my heels, and then to trail feebly away, having done nothing—no, that was impossible. The crowd would laugh at me. And my whole life, every white man's life in the East, was one long struggle not to be laughed at.

But I did not want to shoot the elephant. I watched him beating his bunch of grass against his knees, with that preoccupied grandmotherly air that ele- phants have. It seemed to me that it would be murder to shoot him. At that age I was not squeamish about killing animals, but I had never shot an elephant and never wanted to. (Somehow it always seems worse to kill a *large* animal.) Besides, there was the beast's owner to be considered. Alive, the elephant was worth at least a hundred pounds; dead, he would only be worth the value of his tusks, five pounds, possibly. But I had got to act quickly. I turned to some experienced-looking Burmans who had been there when we arrived, and asked them how the elephant had been behaving. They all said the same thing: he took no notice of you if you left him alone, but he might charge if you went too close to him.

It was perfectly clear to me what I ought to do. I ought to walk up to within, say, twenty-five yards of the elephant and test his behavior. If he charged, I could shoot; if he took no notice of me, it would be safe to leave him until the mahout came back. But also I knew that I was going to do no such thing. I was a poor shot with a rifle and the ground was soft mud into which one would sink at every step. If the elephant charged and I missed him, I should have about as much chance as a toad under a steam-roller. But even then I was not thinking particularly of my own skin, only of the watchful yellow faces behind. For at that moment, with the crowd watching me, I was not afraid in the ordinary sense, as I would have been if I had been alone. A white man mustn't be frightened in front of "natives"; and so, in general, he isn't frightened. The sole thought in my mind was that if anything went wrong those two thousand Burmans would see me pursued, caught, trampled on and reduced to a grinning corpse like that Indian up the hill. And if that happened it was quite probable that some of them would laugh. That would never do. There was only one alternative. I shoved the cartridges into the magazine and lay down on the road to get a better aim.

The crowd grew very still, and a deep, low, happy sigh, as of people who see the theatre curtain go up at last, breathed from innumerable throats. They were going to have their bit of fun after all. The rifle was a beautiful German thing with cross-hair sights. I did not then know that in shooting an elephant one would shoot to cut an imaginary bar running from ear-hole to ear-hole. I ought, therefore, as the elephant was sideways on, to have aimed straight at his ear-hole; actually I aimed several inches in front of this, thinking the brain would be further forward.

When I pulled the trigger I did not hear the bang or feel the kick—one never does when a shot goes home—but I heard the devilish roar of glee that went up from the crowd. In that instant, in too short a time, one would have thought, even for the bullet to get there, a mysterious, terrible change had come over the elephant. He neither stirred nor fell, but every line of his body had altered. He looked suddenly stricken, shrunken, immensely old, as though the frightful impact of the bullet had paralysed him without knocking him down. At last, after what seemed a long time—it might have been five seconds, I dare say—he sagged flabbily to his knees. His mouth slobbered. An enormous senility seemed to have settled upon him. One could have imagined him thousands of years old. I fired again into the same spot. At the second shot he did not collapse but climbed with desperate slowness to his feet and stood weakly upright, with legs sagging and head drooping. I fired a third time. That was the shot that did for him. You could see the agony of it jolt his whole body and knock the last remnant of strength from his legs. But in falling he seemed for a moment to rise, for as his hind legs collapsed beneath him he seemed to tower upward like a huge rock toppling, his trunk reaching skywards like a tree. He trumpeted, for the first and only time. And then down he came, his belly towards me, with a crash that seemed to shake the ground even where I lay.

I got up. The Burmans were already racing past me across the mud. It was obvious that the elephant would never rise again, but he was not dead. He was breathing very rhythmically with long rattling gasps, his great mound of a side painfully rising and falling. His mouth was wide open. I could see far down into caverns of pale pink throat. I waited a long time for him to die, but his breathing did not weaken. Finally I fired my two remaining shots into the spot where I thought his heart must be. The thick blood welled out of him like red velvet, but still he did not die. His body did not even jerk when the shots hit him, the tortured breathing continued without a pause. He was dying, very slowly and in great agony, but in some world remote from me where not even a bullet could damage him further. I felt I had to put an end to that dreadful noise. It seemed dreadful to see the great beast lying there, powerless to move and yet powerless to die, and not even to be able to finish him. I sent back for my small rifle and poured shot after shot into his heart and down his throat. They seemed to make no impression. The tortured gasps continued as steadily as the ticking of a clock.

In the end I could not stand it any longer and went away. I heard later that it took him half an hour to die. Burmans were bringing dahs and baskets even before I left, and I was told they had stripped his body almost to the bones by the afternoon.

Afterwards, of course, there were endless discussions about the shooting of the elephant. The owner was furious, but he was only an Indian and could do nothing. Besides, legally I had done the right thing, for a mad elephant has to be killed, like a mad dog, if its owner fails to control it. Among the Europeans opinion was divided. The older men said I was right, the younger men said it was a damn shame to shoot an elephant for killing a coolie, because the elephant was worth more than any damn Coringhee coolie. And afterwards I was very glad that the coolie had been killed; it put me legally in the right and it gave me sufficient pretext for shooting the elephant. I often wondered whether any of the others grasped that I had done it solely to avoid looking a fool.

QUESTIONS AND CONSIDERATIONS

1. Why does the narrator initially go to the bazaar to find out more about the elephant in "must"? He brings an old gun that he knows could not kill an elephant; what happens that makes him request an elephant gun?

2. Select several passages in the text that reflect Orwell's expertise at capturing details effectively. Explain why the details you selected are effective and deepen the meaning of the passage.

3. Why doesn't the narrator want to shoot the elephant? Why does he? Why is he most afraid of ridicule by the crowd of Burmese?

4. What is the effect of the detailed description of the elephant's death? Why does the narrator leave before the elephant dies?

5. Does the narrator think that the death of the elephant is more important than the death of the coolie? What are the various reactions from natives and government officials to the elephant's death? What does the death of the elephant come to symbolize?

6. What does the narrator learn from his experience of killing the elephant?

IDEAS FOR WRITING

1. Orwell states that "I perceived in this moment that when the white man turns tyrant it is his own freedom that he destroys." In what sense does a tyrant destroy his own freedom? Write an essay in which you argue either in support of or against this assertion from Orwell's essay.

2. Analyze in detail a conflict you experienced when you were in a position of power. What did you learn from this experience about the use and misuse of power and responsibility? What did you learn about the resentment felt by the powerless toward the powerful?

Letter from Birmingham Jail*
Martin Luther King, Jr.

Journal

Would you ever be willing to go to jail for something you believe in strongly? Why or why not?

My Dear Fellow Clergymen:

While confined here in the Birmingham city jail, I came across your recent statement calling my present activities "unwise and untimely." Seldom do I pause to answer criticism of my work and ideas. If I sought to answer all the criticisms that cross my desk, my secretaries would have little time for anything other than such correspondence in the course of the day, and I would have no time for constructive work. But since I feel that you are men of genuine good will and that your criticisms are sincerely set forth, I want to try to answer your statement in what I hope will be patient and reasonable terms.

*This response to a published statement by eight fellow clergymen from Alabama (Bishop C. C. J. Carpenter, Bishop Joseph A. Durick, Rabbi Milton L. Grafman, Bishop Paul Hardin, Bishop Holan B. Harmon, the Reverend George M. Murray, the Reverend Edward V. Ramage and the Reverend Earl Stallings) was composed under somewhat constricting circumstances. Begun on the margins of the newspaper in which the statement appeared while I was in jail, the letter was continued on scraps of writing paper supplied by a friendly Negro trusty, and concluded on a pad my attorneys were eventually permitted to leave me. Although the text remains in substance unaltered, I have indulged in the author's prerogative of polishing it for publication [King's note].

I think I should indicate why I am here in Birmingham, since you have been influenced by the view which argues against "outsiders coming in." I have the honor of serving as president of the Southern Christian Leadership Conference, an organization operating in every southern state, with headquarters in Atlanta, Georgia. We have some eighty-five affiliated organizations across the South, and one of them is the Alabama Christian Movement for Human Rights. Frequently we share staff, educational, and financial resources with our affiliates. Several months ago the affiliate here in Birmingham asked us to be on call to engage in a nonviolent direct-action program if such were deemed necessary. We readily consented, and when the hour came we lived up to our promise. So I, along with several members of my staff, am here because I was invited here. I am here because I have organizational ties here.

But more basically, I am in Birmingham because injustice is here. Just as the prophets of the eighth century B.C. left their villages and carried their "thus saith the Lord" far beyond the boundaries of their home towns, and just as the Apostle Paul left his village of Tarsus and carried the gospel of Jesus Christ to the far corners of the Greco-Roman world, so am I compelled to carry the gospel of freedom beyond my own home town. Like Paul, I must constantly respond to the Macedonian call for aid.

Moreover, I am cognizant of the interrelatedness of all communities and states. I cannot sit idly by in Atlanta and not be concerned about what happens in Birmingham. Injustice anywhere is a threat to justice everywhere. We are caught in an inescapable network of mutuality, tied in a single garment of destiny. Whatever affects one directly, affects all indirectly. Never again can we afford to live with the narrow, provincial "outside agitator" idea. Anyone who lives inside the United States can never be considered an outsider anywhere within its bounds.

You deplore the demonstrations taking place in Birmingham. But your statement, I am sorry to say, fails to express a similar concern for the conditions that brought about the demonstrations. I am sure that none of you would want to rest content with the superficial kind of social analysis that deals merely with effects and does not grapple with underlying causes. It is unfortunate that demonstrations are taking place in Birmingham, but it is even more unfortunate that the city's white power structure left the Negro community with no alternative.

In any nonviolent campaign there are four basic steps: collection of the facts to determine whether injustices exist; negotiation; self-purification; and direct action. We have gone through all these steps in Birmingham. There can be no gainsaying the fact that racial injustice engulfs this community. Birmingham is probably the most thoroughly segregated city in the United States. Its ugly record of brutality is widely known. Negroes have experienced grossly unjust treatment in the courts. There have been more unsolved bombings of Negro homes and churches in Birmingham than in any other city in the nation. These are the hard, brutal facts of the case. On the basis of these conditions,

Negro leaders sought to negotiate with the city fathers. But the latter consistently refused to engage in good-faith negotiation.

Then, last September, came the opportunity to talk with leaders of Birmingham's economic community. In the course of the negotiations, certain promises were made by the merchants—for example, to remove the stores' humiliating racial signs. On the basis of these promises, the Reverend Fred Shuttlesworth and the leaders of the Alabama Christian Movement for Human Rights agreed to a moratorium on all demonstrations. As the weeks and months went by, we realized that we were the victims of a broken promise. A few signs, briefly removed, returned; the others remained.

As in so many past experiences, our hopes had been blasted, and the shadow of deep disappointment settled upon us. We had no alternative except to prepare for direct action, whereby we would present our very bodies as a means of laying our case before the conscience of the local and the national community. Mindful of the difficulties involved, we decided to undertake a process of self-purification. We began a series of workshops on nonviolence, and we repeatedly asked ourselves: "Are you able to accept blows without retaliating?" "Are you able to endure the ordeal of jail?" We decided to schedule our direct-action program for the Easter season, realizing that except for Christmas, this is the main shopping period of the year. Knowing that a strong economic-withdrawal program would be the by-product of direct action, we felt that this would be the best time to bring pressure to bear on the merchants for the needed change.

Then it occurred to us that Birmingham's mayoral election was coming up in March, and we speedily decided to postpone action until after election day. When we discovered that the Commissioner of Public Safety, Eugene "Bull" Connor, had piled up enough votes to be in the run-off, we decided again to postpone action until the day after the run-off so that the demonstrations could not be used to cloud the issues. Like many others, we wanted to see Mr. Connor defeated, and to this end we endured postponement after postponement. Having aided in this community need, we felt that our direct-action program could be delayed no longer.

You may well ask, "Why direct action? Why sit-ins, marches, and so forth? Isn't negotiation a better path?" You are quite right in calling for negotiation. Indeed, this is the very purpose of direct action. Nonviolent direct action seeks to create such a crisis and foster such a tension that a community which has constantly refused to negotiate is forced to confront the issue. It seeks so to dramatize the issue that it can no longer be ignored. My citing the creation of tension as part of the work of the nonviolent-resister may sound rather shocking. But I must confess that I am not afraid of the word "tension." I have earnestly opposed violent tension, but there is a type of constructive, nonviolent tension which is necessary for growth. Just as Socrates felt that it was necessary to create a tension in the mind so that individuals could rise from the bondage of myths and half-truths to the unfettered realm of creative analysis and objective appraisal, so must we see the need for nonviolent gadflies to create the kind of tension in society that will help men rise from the dark depths of prejudice and racism to the majestic heights of understanding and brotherhood.

The purpose of our direct-action program is to create a situation so crisis-packed that it will inevitably open the door to negotiation. I therefore concur with you in your call for negotiation. Too long has our beloved Southland been bogged down in a tragic effort to live in monologue rather than dialogue.

One of the basic points in your statement is that the action that I and my associates have taken in Birmingham is untimely. Some have asked: "Why didn't you give the new city administration time to act?" The only answer that I can give to this query is that the new Birmingham administration must be prodded about as much as the outgoing one, before it will act. We are sadly mistaken if we feel that the election of Albert Boutwell as mayor will bring the millennium to Birmingham. While Mr. Boutwell is a much more gentle person than Mr. Connor, they are both segregationists, dedicated to maintenance of the status quo. I have hoped that Mr. Boutwell will be reasonable enough to see the futility of massive resistance to desegregation. But he will not see this without pressure from devotees of civil rights. My friends, I must say to you that we have not made a single gain in civil rights without determined legal and nonviolent pressure. Lamentably, it is an historical fact that privileged groups seldom give up their privileges voluntarily. Individuals may see the moral light and voluntarily give up their unjust posture; but, as Reinhold Niebuhr has reminded us, groups tend to be more immoral than individuals.

We know through painful experience that freedom is never voluntarily given by the oppressor; it must be demanded by the oppressed. Frankly, I have yet to engage in a direct-action campaign that was "well timed" in the view of those who have not suffered unduly from the disease of segregation. For years now I have heard the word "Wait!" It rings in the ear of every Negro with piercing familiarity. This "Wait" has almost always meant "Never." We must come to see, with one of our distinguished jurists, that "justice too long delayed is justice denied."

We have waited for more than 340 years for our constitutional and God-given rights. The nations of Asia and Africa are moving with jetlike speed toward gaining political independence, but we still creep at horse-and-buggy pace toward gaining a cup of coffee at a lunch counter. Perhaps it is easy for those who have never felt the stinging darts of segregation to say, "Wait." But when you have seen vicious mobs lynch your mothers and fathers at will and drown your sisters and brothers at whim; when you have seen hate-filled policemen curse, kick, and even kill your black brothers and sisters; when you see the vast majority of your twenty million Negro brothers smothering in an airtight cage of poverty in the midst of an affluent society; when you suddenly find your tongue twisted and your speech stammering as you seek to explain to your six-year-old daughter why she can't go to the public amusement park that has just been advertised on television, and see tears welling up in her eyes when she is told that Funtown is closed to colored children, and see ominous clouds of inferiority beginning to form in her little mental sky, and see her beginning to distort her personality by developing an unconscious bitterness toward white people; when you have to concoct an answer for a five-year-old son who is asking, "Daddy, why do white people treat colored people so mean?"; when you take a cross-country drive and find it necessary to sleep night after night in the uncomfortable corners of your automobile because no motel will accept you; when you are humiliated day in and day out by nagging signs reading "white" and "colored"; when your first name becomes "nigger," your middle name becomes "boy" (however old you are) and your last name becomes "John," and your wife and mother are never given the respected title "Mrs."; when you are harried by day and haunted by night by the fact that you are a Negro, living constantly at tiptoe stance, never quite knowing what to expect next, and are plagued with inner fears and outer resentments; when you are forever fighting a degenerating sense of "nobodiness"—then you will understand why we find it difficult to wait. There comes a time when the cup of endurance runs over, and men are no longer willing to be plunged into the abyss of despair. I hope, sirs, you can understand our legitimate and unavoidable impatience.

You express a great deal of anxiety over our willingness to break laws. This is certainly a legitimate concern. Since we so diligently urge people to obey the Supreme Court's decision of 1954 outlawing segregation in the public schools, at first glance it may seem rather paradoxical for us consciously to break laws. One may well ask: "How can you advocate breaking some laws and obeying others?" The answer lies in the fact that there are two types of laws: just and unjust. I would be the first to advocate obeying just laws. One has not only a legal but a moral responsibility to obey just laws. Conversely, one has a moral responsibility to disobey unjust laws. I would agree with St. Augustine that "an unjust law is no law at all."

Now, what is the difference between the two? How does one determine whether a law is just or unjust? A just law is a man-made code that squares with the moral law or the law of God. An unjust law is a code that is out of harmony with the moral law. To put it in the terms of St. Thomas Aquinas: An unjust law is a human law that is not rooted in eternal law and natural law. Any law that uplifts human personality is just. Any law that degrades human personality is unjust. All segregation statutes are unjust because segregation distorts the soul and damages the personality. It gives the segregator a false sense of superiority and the segregated a false sense of inferiority. Segregation, to use the terminology of the Jewish philosopher Martin Buber, substitutes an "I-it" relationship for an "I-thou" relationship and ends up relegating persons to the status of things. Hence segregation is not only politically, economically, and sociologically unsound, it is morally wrong and sinful. Paul Tillich has said that sin is separation. Is not segregation an existential expression of man's tragic separation, his awful estrangement, his terrible sinfulness? Thus it is that I can urge men to obey the 1954 decision of the Supreme

Court, for it is morally right; and I can urge them to disobey segregation ordinances, for they are morally wrong.

Let us consider a more concrete example of just and unjust laws. An unjust law is a code that a numerical or power majority group compels a minority group to obey but does not make binding on itself. This is *difference* made legal. By the same token, a just law is a code that a majority compels a minority to follow and that it is willing to follow itself. This is *sameness* made legal.

Let me give another explanation. A law is unjust if it is inflicted on a minority that, as a result of being denied the right to vote, had no part in enacting or devising the law. Who can say that the legislature of Alabama which set up that state's segregation laws was democratically elected? Throughout Alabama all sorts of devious methods are used to prevent Negroes from becoming registered voters, and there are some counties in which, even though Negroes constitute a majority of the population, not a single Negro is registered. Can any law enacted under such circumstances be considered democratically structured?

Sometimes a law is just on its face and unjust in its application. For instance, I have been arrested on a charge of parading without a permit. Now, there is nothing wrong in having an ordinance which requires a permit for a parade. But such an ordinance becomes unjust when it is used to maintain segregation and to deny citizens the First-Amendment privilege of peaceful assembly and protest.

I hope you are able to see the distinction I am trying to point out. In no sense do I advocate evading or defying the law, as would the rabid segregationist. That would lead to anarchy. One who breaks an unjust law must do so openly, lovingly, and with a willingness to accept the penalty. I submit that an individual who breaks a law that conscience tells him is unjust, and who willingly accepts the penalty of imprisonment in order to arouse the conscience of the community over its injustice, is in reality expressing the highest respect for law.

Of course, there is nothing new about this kind of civil disobedience. It was evidenced sublimely in the refusal of Shadrach, Meshach, and Abednego to obey the laws of Nebuchadnezzar, on the ground that a higher moral law was at stake. It was practiced superbly by the early Christians, who were willing to face hungry lions and the excruciating pain of chopping blocks rather than submit to certain unjust laws of the Roman Empire. To a degree, academic freedom is a reality today because Socrates practiced civil disobedience. In our own nation, the Boston Tea Party represented a massive act of civil disobedience.

We should never forget that everything Adolf Hitler did in Germany was "legal" and everything the Hungarian freedom fighters did in Hungary was "illegal." It was "illegal" to aid and comfort a Jew in Hitler's Germany. Even so, I am sure that, had I lived in Germany at the time, I would have aided and comforted my Jewish brothers. If today I lived in a Communist country where certain principles dear to the Christian faith are suppressed, I would openly advocate disobeying that country's anti-religious laws.

I must make two honest confessions to you, my Christian and Jewish brothers. First, I must confess that over the past few years I have been gravely disappointed with the white moderate. I have almost reached the regrettable conclusion that the Negro's great stumbling block in his stride toward freedom is not the White Citizen's Counciler or the Ku Klux Klanner, but the white moderate, who is more devoted to "order" than to justice; who prefers a negative peace which is the absence of tension to a positive peace which is the presence of justice; who constantly says, "I agree with you in the goal you seek, but I cannot agree with your methods of direct action"; who paternalistically believes he can set the timetable for another man's freedom; who lives by a mythical concept of time and who constantly advises the Negro to wait for a "more convenient season." Shallow understanding from people of good will is more frustrating than absolute misunderstanding from people of ill will. Lukewarm acceptance is much more bewildering than outright rejection.

I had hoped that the white moderate would understand that law and order exist for the purpose of establishing justice and that when they fail in this purpose they become the dangerously structured dams that block the flow of social progress. I had hoped that the white moderate would understand that the present tension in the South is a necessary phase of the transition from an obnoxious negative peace, in which the Negro passively accepted his unjust plight, to a substantive and positive peace, in which all men will respect the dignity and worth of human personality. Actually, we who engage in nonviolent direct action are not the creators of tension. We merely bring to the surface the hidden tension that is already alive. We bring it out in the open, where it can be seen and dealt with. Like a boil that can never be cured so long as it is covered up but must be opened with all its ugliness to the natural medicines of air and light, injustice must be exposed, with all the tension its exposure creates, to the light of human conscience and the air of national opinion, before it can be cured.

In your statement you assert that our actions, even though peaceful, must be condemned because they precipitate violence. But is this a logical assertion? Isn't this like condemning a robbed man because his possession of money precipitated the evil act of robbery? Isn't this like condemning Socrates because his unswerving commitment to truth and his philosophical inquiries precipitated the act by the misguided populace in which they made him drink hemlock? Isn't this like condemning Jesus because his unique God-consciousness and never-ceasing devotion to God's will precipitated the evil act of crucifixion? We must come to see that, as the federal courts have consistently affirmed, it is wrong to urge an individual to cease his efforts to gain his basic constitutional rights because the quest may precipitate violence. Society must protect the robbed and punish the robber.

I had also hoped that the white moderate would reject the myth concerning time in relation to the struggle for freedom. I have just received a letter from a white brother in Texas. He writes: "All Christians know that the colored people will receive equal rights eventually, but it is possible that you are in too great a religious hurry. It has taken Christianity almost two thousand years to

accomplish what it has. The teachings of Christ take time to come to earth."
Such an attitude stems from a tragic misconception of time, from the strangely
irrational notion that there is something in the very flow of time that will inevitably cure all ills. Actually, time itself is neutral; it can be used either de-
structively or constructively. More and more I feel that the people of ill will have
used time much more effectively than have the people of good will. We will
have to repent in this generation not merely for the hateful words and actions
of the bad people, but for the appalling silence of the good people. Human
progress never rolls in on wheels of inevitability; it comes through the tireless
efforts of men willing to be co-workers with God, and without this hard work,
time itself becomes an ally of the forces of social stagnation. We must use
time creatively, in the knowledge that the time is always ripe to do right. Now is
the time to make real the promise of democracy and transform our pending
national elegy into a creative psalm of brotherhood. Now is the time to lift our
national policy from the quicksand of racial injustice to the solid rock of human
dignity.

You speak of our activity in Birmingham as extreme. At first I was rather
disappointed that fellow clergymen would see my nonviolent efforts as those of
an extremist. I began thinking about the fact that I stand in the middle of two
opposing forces in the Negro community. One is a force of complacency,
made up in part of Negroes who, as a result of long years of oppression, are
so drained of self-respect and a sense of "somebodiness" that they have adjusted to segregation; and in part of a few middle-class Negroes who, because
of a degree of academic and economic security and because in some ways
they profit by segregation, have become insensitive to the problems of the
masses. The other force is one of bitterness and hatred, and it comes per-
ilously close to advocating violence. It is expressed in the various black nationalist groups that are springing up across the nation, the largest and best-
known being Elijah Muhammad's Muslim movement. Nourished by the
Negro's frustration over the continued existence of racial discrimination, this
movement is made up of people who have lost faith in America, who have absolutely repudiated Christianity, and who have concluded that the white man is
an incorrigible "devil."

I have tried to stand between these two forces, saying that we need emulate neither the "do-nothingism" of the complacent nor the hatred and despair
of the black nationalist. For there is the more excellent way of love and nonviolent protest. I am grateful to God that, through the influence of the Negro
church, the way of nonviolence became an integral part of our struggle.

If this philosophy had not emerged, by now many streets of the South
would, I am convinced, be flowing with blood. And I am further convinced that
if our white brothers dismiss as "rabblerousers" and "outside agitators" those
of us who employ nonviolent direct action, and if they refuse to support our
nonviolent efforts, millions of Negroes will, out of frustration and despair, seek
solace and security in black-nationalist ideologies—a development that would
inevitably lead to a frightening racial nightmare.

Oppressed people cannot remain oppressed forever. The yearning for freedom eventually manifests itself, and that is what has happened to the American Negro. Something within has reminded him of his birthright of freedom, and something without has reminded him that it can be gained. Consciously or unconsciously, he has been caught up by the *Zeitgeist,* and with his black brothers of Africa and his brown and yellow brothers of Asia, South America, and the Caribbean, the United States Negro is moving with a sense of great urgency toward the promised land of racial justice. If one recognizes this vital urge that has engulfed the Negro community, one should readily understand why public demonstrations are taking place. The Negro has many pent-up resentments and latent frustrations, and he must release them. So let him march; let him make prayer pilgrimages to the city hall; let him go on freedom rides—and try to understand why he must do so. If his repressed emotions are not released in nonviolent ways, they will seek expression through violence; this is not a threat but a fact of history. So I have not said to my people, "Get rid of your discontent." Rather, I have tried to say that this normal and healthy discontent can be channeled into the creative outlet of nonviolent direct action. And now this approach is being termed extremist.

But though I was initially disappointed at being categorized as an extremist, as I continued to think about the matter I gradually gained a measure of satisfaction from the label. Was not Jesus an extremist for love: "Love your enemies, bless them that curse you, do good to them that hate you, and pray for them which despitefully use you, and persecute you." Was not Amos an extremist for justice: "Let justice roll down like waters and righteousness like an ever-flowing stream." Was not Paul an extremist for the Christian gospel: "I bear in my body the marks of the Lord Jesus." Was not Martin Luther an extremist: "Here I stand; I cannot do otherwise, so help me God." And John Bunyan: "I will stay in jail to the end of my days before I make a butchery of my conscience." And Abraham Lincoln: "This nation cannot survive half slave and half free." And Thomas Jefferson: "We hold these truths to be self-evident, that all men are created equal. . . ." So the question is not whether we will be extremists, but what kind of extremists we will be. Will we be extremists for hate or for love? Will we be extremists for the preservation of injustice or for the extension of justice? In that dramatic scene on Calvary's hill three men were crucified. We must never forget that all three were crucified for the same crime—the crime of extremism. Two were extremists for immorality, and thus fell below their environment. The other, Jesus Christ, was an extremist for love, truth, and goodness, and thereby rose above his environment. Perhaps the South, the nation, and the world are in dire need of creative extremists.

I had hoped that the white moderate would see this need. Perhaps I was too optimistic; perhaps I expected too much. I suppose I should have realized that few members of the oppressor race can understand the deep groans and passionate yearnings of the oppressed race, and still fewer have the vision to see that injustice must be rooted out by strong, persistent, and determined action. I am thankful, however, that some of our white brothers in the South have grasped the meaning of this social revolution and committed themselves to it. They are still all too few in quantity, but they are big in quality. Some—such as Ralph McGill, Lillian Smith, Harry Golden, James McBridge Dabbs, Ann Braden, and Sarah Patton Boyle—have written about our struggle in eloquent and prophetic terms. Others have marched with us down nameless streets of the South. They have languished in filthy, roach-infested jails, suffering the abuse and brutality of policemen who view them as "dirty nigger-lovers." Unlike so many of their moderate brothers and sisters, they have recognized the urgency of the moment and sensed the need for powerful "action" antidotes to combat the disease of segregation.

Let me take note of my other major disappointment. I have been so greatly disappointed with the white church and its leadership. Of course, there are some notable exceptions. I am not unmindful of the fact that each of you has taken some significant stands on this issue. I commend you, Reverend Stallings, for your Christian stand on this past Sunday, in welcoming Negroes to your worship service on a nonsegregated basis. I commend the Catholic leaders of this state for integrating Spring Hill College several years ago.

But despite these notable exceptions, I must honestly reiterate that I have been disappointed with the church. I do not say this as one of those negative critics who can always find something wrong with the church. I say this as a minister of the gospel, who loves the church; who was nurtured in its bosom; who has been sustained by its spiritual blessings and who will remain true to it as long as the cord of life shall lengthen.

When I was suddenly catapulted into the leadership of the bus protest in Montgomery, Alabama, a few years ago, I felt we would be supported by the white church. I felt that the white ministers, priests, and rabbis of the South would be among our strongest allies. Instead, some have been outright opponents, refusing to understand the freedom movement and misrepresenting its leaders; all too many others have been more cautious than courageous and have remained silent behind the anesthetizing security of stainedglass windows.

In spite of my shattered dreams, I came to Birmingham with the hope that the white religious leadership of this community would see the justice of our cause and, with deep moral concern, would serve as the channel through which our just grievances could reach the power structure. I had hoped that each of you would understand. But again I have been disappointed.

I have heard numerous southern religious leaders admonish their worshipers to comply with a desegregation decision because it is the law, but I have longed to hear white ministers declare: "Follow this decree because integration is morally right and because the Negro is your brother." In the midst of blatant injustices inflicted upon the Negro, I have watched white churchmen stand on the sideline and mouth pious irrelevancies and sanctimonious trivialities. In the midst of a mighty struggle to rid our nation of racial and economic injustice, I have heard many ministers say: "Those are social issues, with which the gospel has no real concern." And I have watched many churches commit themselves to a completely otherworldly religion which makes a strange, un-Biblical distinction between body and soul, between the sacred and the secular.

I have traveled the length and breadth of Alabama, Mississippi, and all the other southern states. On sweltering summer days and crisp autumn mornings I have looked at the South's beautiful churches with their lofty spires pointing heavenward. I have beheld the impressive outlines of her massive religious-education buildings. Over and over I have found myself asking: "What kind of people worship here? Who is their God? Where were their voices when the lips of Governor Barnett dripped with words of interposition and nullification? Where were they when Governor Wallace gave a clarion call for defiance and hatred? Where were their voices of support when bruised and weary Negro men and women decided to rise from the dark dungeons of complacency to the bright hills of creative protest?"

Yes, these questions are still in my mind. In deep disappointment I have wept over the laxity of the church. But be assured that my tears have been tears of love. There can be no deep disappointment where there is not deep love. Yes, I love the church. How could I do otherwise? I am in the rather unique position of being the son, the grandson, and the great-grandson of preachers. Yes, I see the church as the body of Christ. But, oh! How we have blemished and scarred that body through social neglect and through fear of being nonconformists.

There was a time when the church was very powerful—in the time when the early Christians rejoiced at being deemed worthy to suffer for what they believed. In those days the church was not merely a thermometer that recorded the ideas and principles of popular opinion; it was a thermostat that trans-formed the mores of society. Whenever the early Christians entered a town, the people in power became disturbed and immediately sought to convict the Christians for being "disturbers of the peace" and "outside agitators." But the Christians pressed on, in the conviction that they were "a colony of heaven," called to obey God rather than man. Small in number, they were big in commit-ment. They were too God-intoxicated to be "astronomically intimidated." By their effort and example they brought an end to such ancient evils as infanti-cide and gladiatorial contests.

Things are different now. So often the contemporary church is a weak, in-effectual voice with an uncertain sound. So often it is an arch-defender of the status quo. Far from being disturbed by the presence of the church, the power structure of the average community is consoled by the church's silent—and often even vocal—sanction of things as they are.

But the judgment of God is upon the church as never before. If today's church does not recapture the sacrificial spirit of the early church, it will lose its authenticity, forfeit the loyalty of millions, and be dismissed as an irrelevant social club with no meaning for the twentieth century. Every day I meet young people whose disappointment with the church has turned into outright disgust.

Perhaps I have once again been too optimistic. Is organized religion too inextricably bound to the status quo to save our nation and the world? Perhaps I must turn my faith to the inner spiritual church, the church within the church, as the true *ekklesia* and the hope of the world. But again I am thankful to God that some noble souls from the ranks of organized religion have broken loose from the paralyzing chains of conformity and joined us as active partners in the struggle for freedom. They have left their secure congregations and walked the streets of Albany, Georgia, with us. They have gone down the highways of the South on tortuous rides for freedom. Yes, they have gone to jail with us. Some have been dismissed from their churches, have lost the support of their bishops and fellow ministers. But they have acted in the faith that right defeated is stronger than evil triumphant. Their witness has been the spiritual salt that has preserved the true meaning of the gospel in these troubled times. They have carved a tunnel of hope through the dark mountain of disappointment.

I hope the church as a whole will meet the challenge of this decisive hour. But even if the church does not come to the aid of justice, I have no despair about the future. I have no fear about the outcome of our struggle in Birmingham, even if our motives are at present misunderstood. We will reach the goal of freedom in Birmingham and all over the nation, because the goal of America is freedom. Abused and scorned though we may be, our destiny is tied up with America's destiny. Before the pilgrims landed at Plymouth, we were here. Before the pen of Jefferson etched the majestic words of the Declaration of Independence across the pages of history, we were here. For more than two centuries our forebears labored in this country without wages; they made cotton king; they built the homes of their masters while suffering gross injustice and shameful humiliation—and yet out of a bottomless vitality they continued to thrive and develop. If the inexpressible cruelties of slavery could not stop us, the opposition we now face will surely fail. We will win our freedom because the sacred heritage of our nation and the eternal will of God are embodied in our echoing demands.

Before closing I feel impelled to mention one other point in your statement that has troubled me profoundly. You warmly commended the Birmingham police force for keeping "order" and "preventing violence." I doubt that you would have so warmly commended the police force if you had seen its dogs sinking their teeth into unarmed, nonviolent Negroes. I doubt that you would so quickly commend the policemen if you were to observe their ugly and inhumane treatment of Negroes here in the city jail; if you were to watch them push and curse old Negro women and young Negro girls; if you were to see them slap and kick old Negro men and young boys; if you were to observe them, as they did on two occasions, refuse to give us food because we wanted to sing our grace together. I cannot join you in your praise of the Birmingham police department.

It is true that the police have exercised a degree of discipline in handling the demonstrators. In this sense they have conducted themselves rather "nonviolently" in public. But for what purpose? To preserve the evil system of segregation. Over the past few years I have consistently preached that nonviolence demands that the means we use must be as pure as the ends we seek. I have tried to make clear that it is wrong to use immoral means to attain moral ends. But now I must affirm that it is just as wrong, or perhaps even more so, to use moral means to preserve immoral ends. Perhaps Mr. Connor and his policemen have been rather nonviolent in public, as was Chief Pritchett in Albany, Georgia, but they have used the moral means of nonviolence to maintain the immoral end of racial injustice. As T. S. Eliot has said, "The last temptation is the greatest treason: To do the right deed for the wrong reason."

I wish you had commended the Negro sit-inners and demonstrators of Birmingham for their sublime courage, their willingness to suffer, and their amazing discipline in the midst of great provocation. One day the South will recognize its real heroes. They will be the James Merediths, with the noble sense of purpose that enables them to face jeering and hostile mobs, and with the agonizing loneliness that characterizes the life of the pioneer. They will be old, oppressed, battered Negro women, symbolized in a seventy-two-year-old woman in Montgomery, Alabama, who rose up with a sense of dignity and with her people decided not to ride segregated buses, and who responded with ungrammatical profundity to one who inquired about her weariness: "My feets is tired, but my soul is at rest." They will be the young high school and college students, the young ministers of the gospel and a host of their elders, courageously and nonviolently sitting in at lunch counters and willingly going to jail for conscience' sake. One day the South will know that when these disinherited children of God sat down at lunch counters, they were in reality standing up for what is best in the American dream and for the most sacred values in our Judaeo-Christian heritage, thereby bringing our nation back to those great wells of democracy which were dug deep by the founding fathers in their formulation of the Constitution and the Declaration of Independence.

Never before have I written so long a letter. I'm afraid it is much too long to take your precious time. I can assure you that it would have been much shorter if I had been writing from a comfortable desk, but what else can one do when he is alone in a narrow jail cell, other than write long letters, think long thoughts, and pray long prayers?

If I have said anything in this letter that overstates the truth and indicates an unreasonable impatience, I beg you to forgive me. If I have said anything that understates the truth and indicates my having a patience that allows me to settle for anything less than brotherhood, I beg God to forgive me.

I hope this letter finds you strong in the faith. I also hope that circumstances will soon make it possible for me to meet each of you, not as an integrationist or a civil-rights leader but as a fellow clergyman and a Christian brother. Let us all hope that the dark clouds of racial prejudice will soon pass away and the deep fog of misunderstanding will be lifted from our fear-drenched communities, and in some not too distant tomorrow the radiant stars of love and brotherhood will shine over our great nation with all their scintillating beauty.

Yours for the cause of Peace and Brotherhood,
Martin Luther King, Jr.

QUESTIONS AND CONSIDERATIONS

1. Why does King compare himself to the Apostle Paul? How does this comparison help to establish his authority, his wisdom, and his purpose in the letter?

2. What action is King protesting by being arrested? What practical political wisdom is behind his decision about when to stage the protest? What are the moral and philosophical principles that support his tactic of nonviolent protest?

3. In laying the foundation of his argument against the racist policies in Birmingham why does King establish the point that "groups tend to be more immoral than individuals?" Do you agree with King's point?

4. "Segregation distorts the soul and damages the personality." How does King apply this insight to discredit the unjust laws in Birmingham and throughout the United States? Can you apply King's principle to what you consider an unjust law in your community or at your college?

5. What examples of civil disobedience does King present? What conclusions can you draw from his examples? Are his examples persuasive?

6. In one of his initial metaphors in this letter, King says, "We are caught in an inescapable network of mutuality, tied in a single garment of destiny." Interpret King's metaphor and discuss why it has a different effect than a more literal statement of the idea would have had. Interpret the meanings of several other metaphors that King develops in his letter.

7. How does King refute the white moderates' assertion that "our actions, even though peaceful, must be condemned because they precipitate violence"? Do you agree or disagree? Do you think King's essay convinced his audience?

8. Why is King disappointed in the Christian leadership? Whom does King identify as the real heroes and heroines of the struggle for racial equality in our country?

IDEAS FOR WRITING

1. Write an essay in which you agree or disagree with King's feeling about the need for immediate action on the issues of civil rights. Do you agree that social change needs to be accelerated through protest movements, or do you favor a calmer, more gradual approach?

2. If King were alive, what do you think he would have said about the Rodney King verdicts and the Los Angeles riots? Do you feel that King's nonviolent approach is still effective in the struggle to improve the status of African Americans? Write an essay in which you present an argument in response to this issue.

The Silent Girl

Maxine Hong Kingston

Journal

---

*Write about an argument or disagreement that you had with someone
close to you that awakened an inner struggle. How were you changed through
your conflicts?*

She was a year older than I and was in my class for twelve years. During all
those years she read aloud but would not talk. Her older sister was usually beside her; their parents kept the older daughter back to protect the younger
one. They were six and seven years old when they began school. Although I
had flunked kindergarten, I was the same age as most other students in our
class; my parents had probably lied about my age, so I had had a head start
and came out even. My younger sister was in the class below me; we were
normal ages and normally separated. The parents of the quiet girl, on the
other hand, protected both daughters. When it sprinkled, they kept them home
from school. The girls did not work for a living the way we did. But in other
ways we were the same.

  We were similar in sports. We held the bat on our shoulders until we
walked to first base. (You got a strike only when you actually struck at the
ball.) Sometimes the pitcher wouldn't bother to throw to us. "Automatic walk,"
the other children would call, sending us on our way. By fourth or fifth grade,
though, some of us would try to hit the ball. "Easy out," the other kids would
say. I hit the ball a couple of times. Baseball was nice in that there was a definite spot to run to after hitting the ball. Basketball confused me because when
I caught the ball I didn't know whom to throw it to. "Me. Me," the kids would be
yelling. "Over here." Suddenly it would occur to me I hadn't memorized which
ghosts were on my team and which were on the other. When the kids said,
"Automatic walk," the girl who was quieter than I kneeled with one end of the
bat in each hand and placed it carefully on the plate. Then she dusted her
hands as she walked to first base, where she rubbed her hands softly, fingers
spread. She always got tagged out before second base. She would whisper-
read but not talk. Her whisper was as soft as if she had no muscles. She
seemed to be breathing from a distance. I heard no anger or tension.

  I joined in at lunchtime when the other students, the Chinese too, talked
about whether or not she was mute, although obviously she was not if she
could read aloud. People told how *they* had tried *their* best to be friendly. *They*
said hello, but if she refused to answer, well, they didn't see why they had to
say hello anymore. She had no friends of her own but followed her sister
everywhere, although people and she herself probably thought I was her
friend. I also followed her sister about, who was fairly normal. She was almost
two years older and read more than anyone else.

I hated the younger sister, the quiet one. I hated her when she was the last chosen for her team and I, the last chosen for my team. I hated her for her China doll hair cut. I hated her at music time for the wheezes that came out of her plastic flute.

One afternoon in the sixth grade (that year I was arrogant with talk, not knowing there were going to be high school dances and college seminars to set me back), I and my little sister and the quiet girl and her big sister stayed late after school for some reason. The cement was cooling, and the tetherball poles made shadows across the gravel. The hooks at the rope ends were clinking against the poles. We shouldn't have been so late; there was laundry work to do and Chinese school to get to by 5:00. The last time we had stayed late, my mother had phoned the police and told them we had been kidnapped by bandits. The radio stations broadcast our descriptions. I had to get home before she did that again. But sometimes if you loitered long enough in the schoolyard, the other children would have gone home and you could play with the equipment before the office took it away. We were chasing one another through the playground and in and out of the basement, where the playroom and lavatory were. During air raid drills (it was during the Korean War, which you knew about because every day the front page of the newspaper printed a map of Korea with the top part red and going up and down like a window shade), we curled up in this basement. Now everyone was gone. The playroom was army green and had nothing in it but a long trough with drinking spigots in rows. Pipes across the ceiling led to the drinking fountains and to the toilets in the next room. When someone flushed you could hear the water and other matter, which the children named, running inside the big pipe above the drinking spigots. There was one playroom for girls next to the girls' lavatory and one playroom for boys next to the boys' lavatory. The stalls were open and the toilets had no lids, by which we knew that ghosts have no sense of shame or privacy.

Inside the playroom the lightbulbs in cages had already been turned off. Daylight came in x-patterns through the caging at the windows. I looked out and, seeing no one in the schoolyard, ran outside to climb the fire escape upside down, hanging on to the metal stairs with fingers and toes.

I did a flip off the fire escape and ran across the schoolyard. The day was a great eye, and it was not paying much attention to me now. I could disappear with the sun; I could turn quickly sideways and slip into a different world. It seemed I could run faster at this time, and by evening I would be able to fly. As the afternoon wore on we could run into the forbidden places—the boys' big yard, the boys' playroom. We could go into the boys' lavatory and look at the urinals. The only time during school hours I had crossed the boys' yard was when a flatbed truck with a giant thing covered with canvas and tied down with ropes had parked across the street. The children had told one another that it was a gorilla in captivity; we couldn't decide whether the sign said "Trail of the Gorilla" or "Trial of the Gorilla." The thing was as big as a house. The teachers couldn't stop us from hysterically rushing to the fence and clinging to the wire mesh. Now I ran across the boys' yard clear to the Cyclone fence and thought about the hair that I had seen sticking out of the canvas. It was going to be summer soon, so you could feel that freedom coming on too.

I ran back into the girls' yard, and there was the quiet sister all by herself. I ran past her, and she followed me into the girls' lavatory. My footsteps rang hard against cement and tile because of the taps I had nailed into my shoes. Her footsteps were soft, padding after me. There was no one in the lavatory but the two of us. I ran all around the rows of twenty-five open stalls to make sure of that. No sisters. I think we must have been playing hide-and-go-seek. She was not good at hiding by herself and usually followed her sister; they'd hide in the same place. They must have gotten separated. In this growing twilight, a child could hide and never be found.

I stopped abruptly in front of the sinks, and she came running toward me before she could stop herself, so that she almost collided with me. I walked closer. She backed away, puzzlement, then alarm in her eyes.

"You're going to talk," I said, my voice steady and normal, as it is when talking to the familiar, the weak, and the small. "I am going to make you talk, you sissy-girl." She stopped backing away and stood fixed.

I looked into her face so I could hate it close up. She wore black bangs, and her cheeks were pink and white. She was baby-soft. I thought that I could put my thumb on her nose and push it bonelessly in, indent her face. I could poke dimples into her cheeks. I could work her face around like dough. She stood still, and I did not want to look at her face anymore; I hated fragility. I walked around her, looked her up and down the way the Mexican and Negro girls did when they fought, so tough. I hated her weak neck, the way it did not support her head but let it droop; her head would fall backward. I stared at the curve of her nape. I wished I was able to see what my own neck looked like from the back and sides. I hoped it did not look like hers; I wanted a stout neck. I grew my hair long to hide it in case it was a flower-stem neck. I walked around to the front of her to hate her face some more.

I reached up and took the fatty part of her cheek, not dough, but meat, between my thumb and finger. This close, and I saw no pores. "Talk," I said. "Are you going to talk?" Her skin was fleshy, like squid out of which the glassy blades of bones had been pulled. I wanted tough skin, hard brown skin. I had callused my hands; I had scratched dirt to blacken the nails, which I cut straight across to make stubby fingers. I gave her face a squeeze. "Talk." When I let go, the pink rushed back into my white thumbprint on her skin. I walked around to her side. "Talk!" I shouted into the side of her head. Her straight hair hung, the same all these years, no ringlets or braids or permanents. I squeezed her other cheek. "Are you? Huh? Are you going to talk?" She tried to shake her head, but I had hold of her face. She had no muscles to jerk away. Her skin seemed to stretch. I let go in horror. What if it came away in my hand? "No, huh?" I said, rubbing the touch of her off my fingers. "Say 'No,' then," I said. I gave her another pinch and a twist. "Say 'No.'" She shook her head, her straight hair turning with her head, not swinging side to side like the pretty girls'. She was so neat. Her neatness bothered me. I hated the way she folded the wax paper from her lunch; she did not wad her brown paper bag and her school papers. I hated her clothes—the blue pastel cardigan, the white blouse with the collar that lay flat over the cardigan, the homemade flat, cotton skirt she wore when everybody else was wearing flared skirts. I hated pastels; I would wear black always. I squeezed again, harder, even though her cheek had a weak rubbery feeling I did not like. I squeezed one cheek, then the other, back and forth until the tears ran out of her eyes as if I had pulled them out. "Stop crying," I said, but although she habitually followed me around, she did not obey. Her eyes dripped; her nose dripped. She wiped her eyes with her papery fingers. The skin on her hands and arms seemed powdery-dry, like tracing paper, onion paper. I hated her fingers. I could snap them like breadsticks. I pushed her hands down. "Say 'Hi,'" I said. "'Hi'. Like that. Say your name. Go ahead. Say it. Or are you stupid? You're so stupid, you don't know you own name, is that it? When I say, 'What's your name?' you just blurt it out, O.K.? What's your name?" Last year the whole class had laughed at a boy who couldn't fill out a form because he didn't know his father's name. The teacher sighed, exasperated and was very sarcastic, "Don't you notice things? What does your mother call him?" she said. The class laughed at how dumb he was not to notice things. "She calls him father of me," he said. Even we laughed although we knew that his mother did not call his father by name, and a son does not know his father's name. We laughed and were relieved that our parents had had the foresight to tell us some names we could give the teachers. "If you're not stupid," I said to the quiet girl, "what's you name?" She shook her head, and some hair caught in the tears; wet black hair stuck to the side of the pink and white face. I reached up (she was taller than I) and took a strand of hair. I pulled it. "Well, then, let's honk your hair," I said. "Honk. Honk." Then I pulled the other side—"ho-o-n-nk"—a long pull; "ho-o-n-n-nk"—a longer pull. I could see her little white ears, like white cutworms curled underneath the hair. "Talk!" I yelled into each cutworm.

I looked right at her. "I know you talk," I said. "I've heard you." Her eyebrows flew up. Something in those black eyes was startled, and I pursued it. "I was walking past your house when you didn't know I was there. I heard you yell in English and in Chinese. You weren't just talking. You were shouting. I heard you shout. You were saying, 'Where are you?' Say that again. Go ahead, just the way you did at home." I yanked harder on the hair, but steadily, not jerking. I did not want to pull it out. "Go ahead. Say, 'Where are you?' Say it loud enough for your sister to come. Call her. Make her come help you. Call her name. I'll stop if she comes. So call. Go ahead."

She shook her head, her mouth curved down, crying. I could see her tiny white teeth, baby teeth. I wanted to grow big strong yellow teeth. "You do have a tongue," I said. "So use it." I pulled the hair at her temples, pulled the tears out of her eyes. "Say, 'Ow'" I said. "Just 'Ow.' Say, 'Let go.' Go ahead. Say it. I'll honk you again if you don't say, 'Let me alone.' Say, 'Leave me alone,' and I'll let you go. I will. I'll let go if you say it. You can stop this anytime you want to, you know. All you have to do is tell me to stop. Just say, 'Stop.' You're just asking for it, aren't you? You're just asking for another honk. Well then, I'll have to give you another honk. Say, 'Stop.'" But she didn't. I had to pull again and again.

Sounds did come out of her mouth, sobs, chokes, noises that were almost words. Snot ran out of her nose. She tried to wipe it on her hands, but there was too much of it. She used her sleeve. "You're disgusting," I told her. "Look at you, snot streaming down your nose, and you won't say a word to stop it. You're such a nothing." I moved behind her and pulled the hair growing out of her weak neck. I let go. I stood silent for a long time. Then I screamed, "Talk!" I would scare the words out of her. If she had had little bound feet, the toes twisted under the balls, I would have jumped up and landed on them— crunch!—stomped on them with my iron shoes. She cried hard, sobbing aloud. "Cry, 'Mama,'" I said. "Come on. Cry, 'Mama.' Say, 'Stop it.'"

I put my finger on her pointed chin. "I don't like you. I don't like the weak little toots you make on your flute. Wheeze. Wheeze. I don't like the way you don't swing at the ball. I don't like the way you're the last one chosen. I don't like the way you can't make a fist for tetherball. Why don't you make a fist? Come on. Get tough. Come on. Throw fists." I pushed at her long hands; they swung limply at her sides. Her fingers were so long, I thought maybe they had an extra joint. They couldn't possibly make fists like other people's. "Make a fist," I said. "Come on. Just fold those fingers up; fingers on the inside, thumbs on the out- side. Say something. Honk me back. You're so tall, and you let me pick on you.

"Would you like a hanky? I can't get you one with embroidery on it or cro- cheting along the edges, but I'll get you some toilet paper if you tell me to. Go ahead. Ask me. I'll get it for you if you ask." She did not stop crying. "Why don't you scream, 'Help'?" I suggested. "Say, 'Help.' Go ahead." She cried on. "O.K. O.K. Don't talk. Just scream, and I'll let you go. Won't that feel good? Go ahead. Like this." I screamed not too loudly. My voice hit the tile and rang it as if I had thrown a rock at it. The stalls opened wider and the toilets wider and darker. Shadows leaned at angles I had not seen before. I was very late. Maybe a janitor had locked me in with this girl for the night. Her black eyes blinked and stared, blinked and stared. I felt dizzy from hunger. We had been in this lavatory together forever. My mother would call the police again if I didn't bring my sister home soon. "I'll let you go if you say just one word," I said. "You can even say 'a' or 'the,' and I'll let you go. Come on. Please." She didn't shake her head anymore, only cried steadily, so much water coming out of her. I could see the two duct holes where the tears welled out. Quarts of tears but no words. I grabbed her by the shoulder. I could feel bones. The light was coming in queerly through the frosted glass with the chicken wire embedded in it. Her crying was like an animal's—a seal's—and it echoed around the base- ment. "Do you want to stay here all night?" I asked. "Your mother is wondering what happened to her baby. You wouldn't want to have her mad at you. You'd better say something." I shook her shoulder. I pulled her hair again. I squeezed her face. "Come on! Talk! Talk! Talk!" She didn't seem to feel it anymore when I pulled her hair. "There's nobody here but you and me. This isn't a classroom or a playground or a crowd. I'm just one person. You can talk in front of one person. Don't make me pull harder and harder until you talk." But her hair seemed to stretch; she did not say a word. "I'm going to pull harder. Don't made me pull anymore, or your hair will come out and you're going to be bald. Do you want to be bald? You don't want to be bald, do you?"

Far away, coming from the edge of town, I heard whistles blow. The cannery was changing shifts, letting out the afternoon people, and still we were here at school. It was a sad sound—work done. The air was lonelier after the sound died.

"Why won't you talk?" I started to cry. What if I couldn't stop, and everyone would want to know what happened? "Now look what you've done," I scolded. "You're going to pay for this. I want to know why. And you're going to tell me why. You don't see I'm trying to help you out, do you? Do you want to be like this, dumb (do you know what dumb means?), your whole life? Don't you ever want to be a cheerleader? Or a pompon girl? What are you going to do for a living? Yeah, you're going to have to work because you can't be a housewife. Somebody has to marry you before you can be a housewife. And you, you are a plant. Do you know that? That's all you are if you don't talk. If you don't talk, you can't have a personality. You'll have no personality and no hair. You've got to let people know you have a personality and a brain. You think somebody is going to take care of you all your stupid life? You think you'll always have your big sister? You think somebody's going to marry you, is that it? Well, you're not the type that gets dates, let alone gets married. Nobody's going to notice you. And you have to talk for interviews, speak right up in front of the boss. Don't you know that? You're so dumb. Why do I waste my time on you?" Sniffling and snorting, I couldn't stop crying and talking at the same time. I kept wiping my nose on my arm, my sweater lost somewhere (probably not worn because my mother said to wear a sweater). It seemed as if I had spent my life in that basement, doing the worst thing I had yet done to another person. "I'm doing this for your own good," I said. "Don't you dare tell anyone I've been bad to you. Talk. Please talk."

I was getting dizzy from the air I was gulping. Her sobs and my sobs were bouncing wildly off the tile, sometimes together, sometimes alternating. "I don't understand why you won't say just one word," I cried, clenching my teeth. My knees were shaking, and I hung on to her hair to stand up. Another time I'd stayed too late, I had had to walk around two Negro kids who were bonking each other's head on the concrete. I went back later to see if the concrete had cracks in it. "Look. I'll give you something if you talk. I'll give you my pencil box. I'll buy you some candy. O.K.? What do you want? Tell me. Just say it, and I'll give it to you. Just say, 'yes,' or, 'O.K.,' or, 'Baby Ruth.'" But she didn't want anything.

I had stopped pinching her cheek because I did not like the feel of her skin. I would go crazy if it came away in my hands. "I skinned her," I would have to confess.

Suddenly I heard footsteps hurrying through the basement, and her sister ran into the lavatory calling her name. "Oh, there you are," I said. "We've been waiting for you. I was only trying to teach her to talk. She wouldn't cooperate, though." Her sister went into one of the stalls and got handfuls of toilet paper and wiped her off. Then we found my sister, and we walked home together. "Your family really ought to force her to speak," I advised all the way home. "You mustn't pamper her."

The world is sometimes just, and I spent the next eighteen months sick in bed with a mysterious illness. There was no pain and no symptoms, though the middle line in my left palm broke in two. Instead of starting junior high school, I lived like the Victorian recluses I read about. I had a rented hospital bed in the living room, where I watched soap operas on TV, and my family cranked me up and down. I saw no one but my family, who took good care of me. I could have no visitors, no other relatives, no villagers. My bed was against the west window, and I watched the seasons change the peach tree. I had a bell to ring for help. I used a bedpan. It was the best year and a half of my life. Nothing happened.

But one day my mother, the doctor, said, "You're ready to get up today. It's time to get up and go to school." I walked about outside to get my legs working, leaning on a staff I cut from the peach tree. The sky and trees, the sun were immense—no longer framed by a window, no longer grayed with a fly screen. I sat down on the sidewalk in amazement—the night, the stars. But at school I had to figure out again how to talk. I met again the poor girl I had tormented. She had not changed. She wore the same clothes, hair cut, and manner as when we were in elementary school, no make-up on the pink and white face, while the other Asian girls were starting to tape their eyelids. She continued to be able to read aloud. But there was hardly any reading aloud anymore, less and less as we got into high school. . . .

QUESTIONS AND CONSIDERATIONS

1. Why does the narrator hate the silent girl? How does she try to change her?

2. What freedoms does the narrator experience before meeting the silent girl in the lavatory? How might her previous sense of power have affected her attitude toward the silent sister?

3. Why does the narrator want the quiet girl to talk? Why does the silent girl refuse to say anything in spite of the narrator's bullying, persecution, and physical attacks? In what sense are both girls struggling against cultural stereotypes of Asian women?

4. Have you ever hated someone for being like a part of yourself that you did not like or accept? Do you think this rejection of a part of oneself as seen reflected in another person is a common cause for interpersonal struggle?

5. Why does the narrator finally start to cry herself? Why is she crying?

6. How do you interpret the narrator's mysterious illness? Why does she eventually get better?

IDEAS FOR WRITING

1. Write about a relationship that was so intense that you lost perspective on the differences or ego boundaries between yourself and the other person. What did you learn from this struggle?

2. Write an essay about the cultural stereotypes that you have had to struggle against in school. How have these struggles helped you to develop more self-awareness and self-confidence?

Women, Home, and Community: The Struggle in an Urban Environment

Cynthia Hamilton

Journal

Describe a political change implemented by women in your community.

In 1956, women in South Africa began an organized protest against the pass laws. As they stood in front of the office of the prime minister, they began a new freedom song with the refrain "now you have touched the women, you have struck a rock." This refrain provides a description of the personal commitment and intensity women bring to social change. Women's actions have been characterized as "spontaneous and dramatic," women in action portrayed as "intractable and uncompromising."[1] Society has summarily dismissed these as negative attributes. When in 1986 the City Council of Los Angeles decided that a 13-acre incinerator called LANCER (for Los Angeles City Energy Recovery Project), burning 2,000 tons a day of municipal waste, should be built in a poor residential, black, and Hispanic community, the women there said "No." Officials had indeed dislodged a boulder of opposition. According to Charlotte Bullock, one of the protestors, "I noticed when we first started fighting the issue how the men would laugh at the women . . . they would say, 'Don't pay no attention to them, that's only one or two women . . . they won't make a difference.' But now since we've been fighting for about a year the smiles have gone."[2]

Minority communities shoulder a disproportionately high share of the by-products of industrial development: waste, abandoned factories and ware-

[1] See Cynthia Cockburn, "When Women Get Involved in Community Action," in Marjorie Mayo (ed.), *Women in the Community* (London: Routledge & Kegan Paul, 1977).
[2] All of the quotes from Charlotte Bullock and Robin Cannon are personal communications, 1986.

houses, leftover chemicals and debris. These communities are also asked to house the waste and pollution no longer acceptable in white communities, such as hazardous landfills or dump sites. In 1987, the Commission for Racial Justice of the United Church of Christ published *Toxic Wastes and Race.* The commission concluded that race is a major factor related to the presence of hazardous wastes in residential communities throughout the United States. Three out of every five black and Hispanic Americans live in communities with uncontrolled toxic sites; 75 percent of the residents in rural areas in the Southwest, mainly Hispanics, are drinking pesticide-contaminated water; more than 2 million tons of uranium tailings are dumped on Native-American reservations each year, resulting in Navajo teenagers having seventeen times the national average of organ cancers; more than 700,000 inner city children, 50 percent of them black, are said to be suffering from lead poisoning, resulting in learning disorders. Working-class minority women are therefore motivated to organize around very pragmatic environmental issues, rather than those associated with more middle-class organizations. According to Charlotte Bullock, "I did not come to the fight against environmental problems as an intellectual but rather as a concerned mother. . . . People say, 'But you're not a scientist, how do you know it's not safe?' I have common sense. I know if dioxin and mercury are going to come out of an incinerator stack, somebody's going to be affected."

When Concerned Citizens of South Central Los Angeles came together in 1986 to oppose the solid waste incinerator planned for the community, no one thought much about environmentalism or feminism. These were just words in a community with a 78 percent unemployment rate, an average income ($8,158) less than half that of the general Los Angeles population, and a residential density more than twice that of the whole city. In the first stages of organization, what motivated and directed individual actions was the need to protect home and children; for the group this individual orientation emerged as a community centered battle. What was left in this deteriorating district on the periphery of the central business and commercial district had to be defended—a "garbage dump" was the final insult after years of neglect, watching downtown flourish while residents were prevented from borrowing enough to even build a new roof.

The organization was never gender restricted but it became apparent after a while that women were the majority. The particular kind of organization the group assumed, the actions engaged in, even the content of what was said, were all a product not only of the issue itself, the waste incinerator, but also a function of the particular nature of women's oppression and what happens as the process of consciousness begins.

Women often play a primary part in community action because it is about things they know best. Minority women in several urban areas have found themselves part of a new radical core as the new wave of environmental action, precipitated by the irrationalities of capital-intensive growth, has catapulted them forward. These individuals are responding not to "nature" in the abstract but to the threat to their homes and to the health of their children. Robin Cannon, another activist in the fight against the Los Angeles incinerator, says, "I have asthma, my children have asthma, my brothers and sisters have asthma, there are a lot of health problems that people living around an incinerator might be subjected to and I said, "They can't do this to me and my family.'"

Women are more likely than men to take on these issues precisely because the home has been defined and prescribed as a woman's domain. According to British sociologist Cynthia Cockburn, "In a housing situation that is a health hazard, the woman is more likely to act than the man because she lives there all day and because she is impelled by fear for her children. Community action of this kind is a significant phase of class struggle, but it is also an element of women's liberation."[3]

This phenomenon was most apparent in the battle over the Los Angeles incinerator. Women who had had no history of organizing responded as protectors of their children. Many were single parents, others were older women who had raised families. While the experts were convinced that their smug dismissal of the validity of the health concerns these women raised would send them away, their smugness only reinforced the women's determination. According to Charlotte Bullock:

> People's jobs were threatened, ministers were threatened . . . but I said, "I'm not going to be intimidated." My child's health comes first. . . . that's more important than my job.
>
>   In the 1950s the city banned small incinerators in the yard and yet they want to build a big incinerator . . . the Council is going to build something in my community which might kill my child. . . . I don't need a scientist to tell me that's wrong.

None of the officials were prepared for the intensity of concern or the consistency of agitation. In fact, the consultants they hired had concluded that these women did not fit the prototype of opposition. The consultants had concluded:

> Certain types of people are likely to participate in politics, either by virtue of their issue awareness or their financial resources, or both. Members of middle or higher socioeconomic strata (a composite index of level of education, occupational prestige, and income) are more likely to organize into effective groups to express their political interests and views. All socioeconomic groupings tend to resent the nearby siting of major facilities, but the middle and upper socioeconomic strata possess better resources to effectuate their opposition. Middle and higher socioeconomic strata neighborhoods should not fall at least within the one mile and five mile radii of the proposed site.

---

[3] Cockburn, "When Women," p. 62.

. . . although environmental concerns cut across all subgroups, people with a college education, young or middle aged, and liberal in philosophy are most likely to organize opposition to the siting of a major facility. Older people, with a high school education or less, and those who adhere to a free market orientation are least likely to oppose a facility.[4]

The organizers against the incinerator in South Central Los Angeles are the antithesis of the prototype: they are high school educated or less, above middle age and young, nonprofessionals and unemployed and low-income, without previous political experience. The consultants and politicians thus found it easy to believe that opposition from this group could not be serious.

The intransigence of the City Council intensified the agitation, and the women became less willing to compromise as time passed. Each passing month gave them greater strength, knowledge, and perseverance. The council and its consultants had a more formidable enemy than they had expected, and in the end they have had to compromise. The politicians have backed away from their previous embrace of incineration as a solution to the trash crisis, and they have backed away from this particular site in a poor, black and Hispanic, residential area. While the issues are far from resolved, it is important that the willingness to compromise has become the official position of the city as a result of the determination of "a few women."

The women in South Central Los Angeles were not alone in their battle. They were joined by women from across the city. White, middle-class, and professional women. As Robin Cannon puts it, "I didn't know we all had so many things in common . . . millions of people in the city had something in common with us—the environment." These two groups of women, together, have created something previously unknown in Los Angeles—unity of purpose across neighborhood and racial lines. According to Charlotte Bullock, "We are making a difference . . . when we come together as a whole and stick with it, we can win because we are right."

This unity has been accomplished by informality, respect, tolerance of spontaneity, and decentralization. All of the activities that we have been told destroy organizations have instead worked to sustain this movement. For example, for a year and a half the group functioned without a formal leadership structure. The unconscious acceptance of equality and democratic process resulted practically in rotating the chair's position at meetings. Newspeople were disoriented when they asked for the spokesperson and the group responded that everyone could speak for the neighborhood.

It may be the case that women, unlike men, are less conditioned to see the value of small advances.[5] These women were all guided by their vision of

[4] Cerrell Associates, *Political Difficulties Facing Waste to Energy Conversion Plant Siting* (Los Angeles: Califonia Waste Management Board, 1984), pp. 42–43.

[5] See Cockburn, "When Women," p. 63.

the possible: that it *was* possible to completely stop the construction of the incinerator, that it is possible in a city like Los Angeles to have reasonable growth, that it is possible to humanize community structures and services. As Robin Cannon says, "My neighbors said, 'You can't fight City Hall . . . and besides, you work there.' I told them I would fight anyway."

None of these women was convinced by the consultants and their traditional justifications for capital-intensive growth: that it increases property values by intensifying land use, that it draws new businesses and investment to the area, that it removes blight and deterioration—and the key argument used to persuade the working class—that growth creates jobs. Again, to quote Robin Cannon, "They're not bringing real development to our community. . . . They're going to bring this incinerator to us, and then say 'We're going to *give* you fifty jobs when you get this plant.' Meanwhile they're going to shut down another factory [in Riverside] and eliminate two hundred jobs to buy more pollution rights. . . . They may close more shops."

Ironically, the consultants' advice backfired. They had suggested that emphasizing employment and a gift to the community (of $2 million for a community development fund for park improvement) would persuade the opponents. But promises of heated swimming pools, air-conditioned basketball courts and fifty jobs at the facility were more insulting than encouraging. Similarly, at a public hearing, an expert witness's assurance that health risks associated with dioxin exposure were less than those associated with "eating peanut butter" unleashed a flurry of derision.

The experts' insistence on referring to congenital deformities and cancers as "acceptable risks" cut to the hearts of women who rose to speak of a child's asthma, or a parent's influenza, or the high rate of cancer, heart disease, and pneumonia in this poverty-stricken community. The callous disregard of human concerns brought the women closer together. They came to rely on each other as they were subjected to the sarcastic rebuffs of men who referred to their concerns as "irrational, uninformed, and disruptive." The contempt of the male experts was directed at professionals and the unemployed, at Whites and Blacks—all the women were castigated as irrational and uncompromising. As a result, new levels of consciousness were sparked in these women.

The reactions of the men backing the incinerator provided a very serious learning experience for the women, both professionals and nonprofessionals, who came to the movement without a critique of patriarchy. They developed their critique in practice. In confronting the need for equality, these women forced the men to a new level of recognition—that working-class women's concerns cannot be simply dismissed.

Individual transformations accompanied the group process. As the struggle against the incinerator proceeded to take on some elements of class struggle, individual consciousness matured and developed. Women began to recognize something of their own oppression as women. This led to new forms of action not only against institutions but to the transformation of social relations in the home as well. As Robin Cannon explains:

> My husband didn't take me seriously at first either. . . . He just saw a whole lot of women meeting and assumed we wouldn't get anything done. . . . I had to split my time . . . I'm the one who usually comes home from work, cooks, helps the kids with their homework, then I watch a little TV and go to bed to get ready for the next morning. Now I would rush home, cook, read my materials on LANCER. . . . now the kids were on their own . . . I had my own homework . . . My husband still wasn't taking me seriously. . . . After about 6 months everyone finally took me seriously. My husband had to learn to allocate more time for baby sitting. Now on Saturdays, if they went to the show or to the park, I couldn't attend . . . in the evening there were hearings . . . I was using my vacation time to go to hearings during the workday.

As parents, particularly single parents, time in the home was strained for these women. Children and husbands complained that meetings and public hearings had taken priority over the family and relations in the home. According to Charlotte Bullock, "My children understand, but then they don't want to understand. . . . They say, 'You're not spending time with me.'" Ironically, it was the concern for family, their love of their families, that had catapulted these women into action to begin with. But, in a pragmatic sense, the home did have to come second in order for health and safety to be preserved. These were hard learning experiences. But meetings in individual homes ultimately involved children and spouses alike—everyone worked and everyone listened. The transformation of relations continued as women spoke up at hearings and demonstrations and husbands transported children, made signs, and looked on with pride and support at public forums.

The critical perspective of women in the battle against LANCER went far beyond what the women themselves had intended. For these women, the political issues were personal and in that sense they became feminist issues. These women, in the end, were fighting for what they felt was "right" rather than what men argued might be reasonable. The coincidence of the principles of feminism and ecology that Carolyn Merchant explains in *The Death of Nature* (San Francisco: Harper & Row, 1981) found expression and developed in the consciousness of these women: the concern for Earth as a home, the recognition that all parts of a system have equal value, the acknowledgment of process, and, finally, that capitalist growth has social costs. As Robin Cannon says, "This fight has really turned me around, things are intertwined in ways I hadn't realized. . . . All these social issues as well as political and economic issues are really intertwined. Before, I was concerned only about health and then I began to get into the politics, decision making, and so many things."

In two years, what started as the outrage of a small group of mothers has transformed the political climate of a major metropolitan area. What these women have aimed for is a greater level of democracy, a greater level of involvement, not only in their organization but in the development process of the city generally. They have demanded accountability regarding land use and ownership, very subversive concerns in a capitalist society. In their organizing, the group process, collectivism, was of primary importance. It allowed the women to see their own power and potential and therefore allowed them to consolidate effective opposition. The movement underscored the role of principles. In fact, we citizens have lived so long with an unquestioning acceptance of profit and expediency that sometimes we forget that our objective is to do "what's right." Women are beginning to raise moral left us no other choice but to follow our own moral convictions rather than accept neutrality and capitulate in the face of crisis.

The environmental crisis will escalate in this decade and women are sure to play pivotal roles in the struggle to save our planet. If women are able to sustain for longer periods some of the qualities and behavioral forms they have displayed in crisis situations (such as direct participatory democracy and the critique of patriarchal bureaucracy), they may be able to reintroduce equality and democracy into progressive action. They may also reintroduce the value of being moved by principle and morality. Pragmatism has come to dominate all forms of political behavior and the results have often been disastrous. If women resist the "normal" organizational thrust to barter, bargain, and fragment ideas and issues, they may help set new standards for action in the new environment movement.

QUESTIONS AND CONSIDERATIONS

1. How does Hamilton define the women's response to the LANCER project? How do the men in the community react to the women's political goals?

2. The environmental struggle over the solid waste incinerator is staged by minority women. Why do they have more to lose than middle-class or professional women? Why are they successful? How do they reach out to women from all classes throughout the country?

3. Why is the example of the struggle against the incinerator especially appropriate support for the larger generalizations that Hamilton makes about women's commitment to saving the environment for their children? How does the metaphor of the incinerator as garbage dump for the rebuilt and elegant downtown area heighten the impact of her argument?

4. What does Hamilton see as the connection between feminism and environmental issues? Do you agree or disagree with her position?

5. How does the National Organization of Women's fighting the environmental pollution in Los Angeles show that the oppressed have power over their oppressors?

6. Did Hamilton's essay convince you of her position that women have the potential to act more ethically toward the environment because of their traditional roles as caretakers of the home and of children?

IDEAS FOR WRITING

1. Do research into the topic of feminism and environmentalism to find additional information that either supports or refutes Hamilton's position.

2. Discuss an environmental project that was implemented in your community. What was the project? Who initiated it? Who implemented it? Was the project successful?

Poetry

London
William Blake

Journal

Write about a walk down a city street when you confronted a social or racial conflict. What was happening? What was your response?

I wander through each chartered street,
Near where the chartered Thames does flow,
And mark in every face I meet
Marks of weakness, marks of woe.

In every cry of every man,   5
In every infant's cry of fear,
In every voice, in every ban,
The mind-forged manacles I hear.

How the chimney-sweeper's cry
Every black'ning church appalls;   10
And the hapless soldier's sigh
Runs in blood down palace walls.

But most through midnight streets I hear
How the youthful harlot's curse
Blasts the new born infant's tear,   15
And blights with plagues the marriage hearse.

QUESTIONS AND CONSIDERATIONS

1. What signs of despair and struggle does the speaker observe on his walk through the streets of London?

2. How would you characterize the speaker in the poem? Based on what you know about London in the late eighteenth century, do you think that the speaker's observations are accurate? What biases might the speaker have? What might he or she fail to notice?

3. The first stanza of the poem presents two crucial examples of repetition; the word *marks* is repeated three times, each time with a slightly different connotation, and the word *chartered* is also repeated. What do these repetitions add to the poem's tone and meaning?

4. The poem's diction includes words such as "chartered," "bans," "manacles." How do these key words help to reinforce the poem's meaning?

5. Two social institutions are mentioned in the third stanza: the church ("black'ning church") and the royalty ("palace walls"). What comment does the poem make about the relationship between these institutions and social struggle?

6. The final stanza brings up the issue of syphilis, which was transmitted by infected prostitutes to their customers and their families. How does this knowledge of the ravages of syphilis add to your understanding of the paradoxical expression in the last line of the poem, "marriage hearse"? How does the awareness of the threat of syphilis influence your interpretation of the phrase "youthful harlot's curse"? How else might the last stanza be interpreted?

IDEAS FOR WRITING

1. Write an updated version of "London," using either the form of a poem or narrative essay, based on a walk down a typical modern city street. What different struggles and what new versions of the issues raised in the Blake poem would be encountered?

2. Write an essay in which you discuss whether the comments in the last stanza of Blake's poem could also apply to today's AIDS epidemic. Do you think that modern society feels as helpless before the specter of AIDS as eighteenth-century England did in response to syphilis? Do you think that the social struggles in American cities are as serious and devastating as those described in Blake's poem?

I, Mirror

Claribel Alegría
Translated by Electa Arenal and Keitha Sapsin

Journal
———
Write about an experience in which the pain and the struggles of the people around you made you feel numb inside.

Water sparkles
on my skin
I don't feel it
water streams
down my back   5
I don't feel it
I rub myself with a towel
I pinch myself in the arm
I feel nothing
I begin to get dressed   10
stumbling
from the corners

like lightning bolts
shouts burst forth
tortured eyes   15
rats run
teeth
still I feel nothing
I wander through the streets:
children with dirty faces   20
ask me for money
child prostitutes
not yet fifteen
wound-filled streets
tanks approach   25
bayonets raised
bodies fall
weeping
at last I feel my arm
I am no longer a phantom   30
I hurt
therefore I exist
again I watch the scene:
children run
streaming blood   35
women with panic
on their faces
this time it hurts me less
I pinch myself again
and can feel nothing   40
I simply reflect
what is happening next to me
the tanks
are not tanks
nor the shouts   45
shouts
I am a blank mirror
that nothing penetrates
my surface
is hard   50
is brilliant
is polished
I became the mirror
I am fleshless
barely keeping   55
a vague memory
of the pain.

QUESTIONS AND CONSIDERATIONS

1. In the opening lines the speaker establishes that she does not feel pain—not from her senses, from her emotions, for herself, or for others. Why doesn't she feel pain?

2. A turning point in the speaker's consciousness and in the poem occurs at line 29: "weeping/at last I feel my arm . . . I hurt/therefore I exist." Interpret the speaker's meaning here in the context of what she has already told her audience. Why does hurting imply existence?

3. Does the chaos in the streets hurt the speaker less when she returns to them after her realization that her hurt confirms her existence?

4. As the poem closes, the speaker sees herself as a "blank mirror." Why would she perceive herself as a mirror?

5. Interpret the speaker's symbolic transformation. Why does she become "hard," "brilliant," "polished," and "fleshless"? Can you identify with the struggle that the speaker is experiencing? Is her transformation a positive one?

6. What alternatives are there to "mirroring" an unjust and violent social reality?

IDEAS FOR WRITING

1. Write an essay in which you explore several reasons why people may force themselves to remain seemingly unfeeling or distant in the face of human suffering. Is this a negative human trait, or an emotional survival technique? Develop several examples to illustrate your views.

2. Write a short story that expresses a character's struggle to identify and help those who are in pain and whose lives seem hopeless.

Unknown Girl in the Maternity Ward
Anne Sexton

Journal

How do you think you would feel if you had to give your child away for adoption or if your partner decided to give up your child for adoption?

Child, the current of your breath is six days long.
You lie, a small knuckle on my white bed;
lie, fisted like a snail, so small and strong
at my breast. Your lips are animals; you are fed
with love. At first hunger is not wrong.   5
The nurses nod their caps; you are shepherded
down starch halls with the other unnested throng
in wheeling baskets. You tip like a cup; your head

moving to my touch. You sense the way we belong.
But this is an institution bed.   10
You will not know me very long.

The doctors are enamel. They want to know
the facts. They guess about the man who left me,
some pendulum soul, going the way men go
and leave you full of child. But our case history   15
stays blank. All I did was let you grow.
Now we are here for all the ward to see.
They thought I was strange, although
I never spoke a word. I burst empty
of you, letting you learn how the air is so.   20
The doctors chart the riddle they ask of me
and I turn my head away. I do not know.

Yours is the only face I recognize.
Bone at my bone, you drink my answers in.
Six times a day I prize   25
your need, the animals of your lips, your skin
growing warm and plump. I see your eyes
lifting their tents. They are blue stones, they begin
to outgrow their moss. You blink in surprise
and I wonder what you can see, my funny kin,   30
as you trouble my silence. I am a shelter of lies
Should I learn to speak again, or hopeless in
such sanity will I touch some face I recognize?

Down the hall the baskets start back. My arms
fit you like a sleeve, they hold   35
catkins of your willows, the wild bee farms
of your nerves, each muscle and fold
of your first days. Your old man's face disarms
the nurses. But the doctors return to scold
me. I speak. It is you my silence harms.   40
I should have known; I should have told
them something to write down. My voice alarms
my throat. 'Name of father—none.' I hold
you and name you bastard in my arms.

And now that's that. There is nothing more   45
that I can say or lose.
Others have traded life before
and could not speak. I tighten to refuse
your owling eyes, my fragile visitor.

I touch your cheeks, like flowers. You bruise   50
against me. We unlearn. I am a shore
rocking you off. You break from me. I choose
your only way, my small inheritor
and hand you off, trembling the selves we lose.
Go child, who is my sin and nothing more.   55

QUESTIONS AND CONSIDERATIONS

1. What is the impact of the first stanza? How is the tone of this stanza different from the tone in the rest of the poem?

2. How does the speaker feel about the doctors who deliver the unknown child? How and why does the speaker connect the doctors with the man who left her pregnant?

3. There are many images in the poem that suggest a connection and tenderness between the speaker and her newborn; discuss several that you find especially expressive and reflective of the mother's pain in giving up her child.

4. Why is the anonymity of the title especially fitting for this poem? Why won't the speaker reveal the name of her child's father?

5. The young mother in the poem concludes: "Go child, who is my sin and nothing more." Does the poem support her statement or contradict it?

6. Why does the speaker fear sanity? What does she fear recognizing?

IDEAS FOR WRITING

1. Supporting your ideas through specific reference to the text, discuss how the ideas and images in this poem help you to understand the struggles of women who have given up their children for adoption.

2. Sexton's poem was written some years ago. Does it seem dated? Do you think that the position taken by the speaker in the poem would be a common one for a young unwed mother today? Write an essay in which you discuss why you think an unwed mother today would choose either to keep or to abandon her child.

Jorge the Church Janitor Finally Quits
Martin Espada

Journal

Write about the way that you think people cope with jobs in which they are treated more like machines than humans. Give an example from your experience, if possible.

No one asks
where I am from,
I must be
from the country of janitors,
I have always mopped this floor.   5
Honduras, you are a squatter's camp
outside the city
of their understanding.

No one can speak
my name,   10
I host the *fiesta*
of the bathroom,
stirring the toilet
like a punchbowl.
The Spanish music of my name   15
is lost
when the guests complain
about toilet paper.

What they say
must be true: 20
I am smart,
but I have a bad attitude.

No one knows
that I quit tonight,
maybe the mop   25
will push on without me,
sniffing along the floor
like a crazy squid
with stringy gray tentacles.
They will call it Jorge.   30

QUESTIONS AND CONSIDERATIONS

1. Why does the speaker claim that those whom he serves believe that he is "from the country of janitors"? Where was he actually born? Why is "the country of janitors" a "squatter's camp"? Why is it "outside of the city/of their understanding"?

2. In the second stanza, what is the effect of integrating the opposing ideas of cleaning a toilet bowl and stirring punch?

3. The speaker imagines that the mop is "like a crazy squid/with stringy gray tentacles." How does this image add to your sense of the speaker's self-concept? Considering the images developed in this poem, how would you characterize the tone?

4. Why does the speaker imagine that the mop will clean the bathrooms without him, that it will become Jorge? What does this imply about Jorge's self-concept? Have you ever imagined that if you left a job, an object or machine might take over your responsibilities?

5. Develop an image you had of yourself that expresses how you felt when you were being exploited by the people who employed you.

6. Have you known people who have had to struggle through the degradation that Jorge faces? How did you relate to their struggle?

IDEAS FOR WRITING

1. Write an essay directed to an audience of people who "serve" (janitors, waiters, drivers, etc.) whom you feel are exploited. Explain some of the feelings you have about their status, and what they could do to help themselves.

2. Write a story about Jorge after he quits. What will become of him? In the future, what will be his approach to work?

The Man He Killed

Thomas Hardy

"Had he and I but met
By some old ancient inn,
We should have sat us down to wet
Right many a nipperkin!

"But ranged as infantry,   5
And staring face to face,
I shot at him as he at me,
And killed him in his place.

"I shot him dead because—
   Because he was my foe,   10
Just so: my foe of course he was;
   That's clear enough; although

"He thought he'd 'list, perhaps,
   Off-hand-like—just as I—
Was out of work—had sold his traps—   15
   No other reason why.

"Yes; quaint and curious war is!
   You shoot a fellow down
You'd treat if met where any bar is,
   Or help to half-a crown."   20

QUESTIONS

1. What feelings does the speaker in the poem express about his "foe"? How does the speaker's language reveal his status in life and his uncertainty about the obligations of war?

2. Write an essay in which you argue for or against the attitude toward war expressed in the poem. For example, do you agree that most soldiers in a war come from the lower classes in society and that they often have no idea what they are fighting for?

Patterns

Amy Lowell

I walk down the garden paths,
And all the daffodils
Are blowing, and the bright blue squills
I walk down the patterned garden-paths
In my stiff, brocaded gown.   5
With my powdered hair and jewelled fan,
I too am a rare
Pattern. As I wander down
The garden paths.

My dress is richly figured,   10
And the train
Makes a pink and silver stain
On the gravel, and the thrift
Of the borders.

Just a plate of current fashion,   15
Tripping by in high-heeled, ribboned shoes.
Not a softness anywhere about me,
Only whalebone and brocade.
And I sink on a seat in the shade
Of a lime tree. For my passion   20
Wars against the stiff brocade.
The daffodils and squills
Flutter in the breeze
As they please.
And I weep;   25
For the lime-tree is in blossom
And one small flower has dropped upon my bosom.
And the plashing of waterdrops
In the marble fountain
Comes down the garden-paths   30
The dripping never stops.
Underneath my stiffened gown
Is the softness of a woman bathing in a marble basin,
A basin in the midst of hedges grown
So thick, she cannot see her lover hiding,   35
But she guesses he is near,
And the sliding of the water
Seems the stroking of a dear
Hand upon her.
What is Summer in a fine brocaded gown!   40
I should like to see it lying in a heap upon the ground.
All the pink and silver crumpled up on the ground.

I would be the pink and silver as I ran along the paths,
And he would stumble after,
Bewildered by my laughter.   45
I should see the sun flashing from his sword-hilt and the
buckles on his shoes.
I would choose
To lead him in a maze along the patterned paths,
A bright and laughing maze for my heavy-booted lover.   50
Till he caught me in the shade,
And the buttons of his waistcoat bruised my body as he
clasped me,
Aching, melting, unafraid.
With the shadows of the leaves and the sundrops   55
And the plopping of the waterdrops,
All about us in the open afternoon—

I am very like to swoon
With the weight of this brocade,
For the sun sifts through the shade.   60

Underneath the fallen blossom
In my bosom,
Is a letter I have hid.
It was brought to me this morning by a rider from the Duke.   65
"Madam, we regret to inform you that Lord Hartwell
Died in action Thursday se'nnight."
As I read it in the white, morning sunlight,
The letters squirmed like snakes.
"Any answer, Madam?" said my footman.   70
"No," I told him.
"See that the messenger takes some refreshment.
No, no answer."
And I walked into the garden,
Up and down the patterned paths,   75
In my stiff, correct brocade.
The blue and yellow flowers stood up proudly in the sun,
Each one.
I stood upright too,   80
Held rigid to the pattern
By the stiffness of my gown.
Up and down I walked.
Up and down.

In a month he would have been my husband.   85
In a month, here, underneath this lime,
We would have broke the pattern;
He for me, and I for him,
He as Colonel, I as Lady,
On this shady seat.   90
He had a whim
That sunlight carried blessing.
And I answered, "It shall be as you have said."
Now he is dead.

In Summer and in Winter I shall walk   95
Up and down
The patterned garden-paths
In my stiff, brocaded gown.
The squills and daffodils
Will give place to pillared roses, and to asters, and to snow   100

I shall go
Up and down,
In my gown.
Gorgeously arrayed,
Boned and stayed.   105
And the softness of my body will be guarded from embrace
By each button, hook, and lace.
For the man who should loose me is dead,
Fighting with the Duke in Flanders,
In a pattern called a war.   110
Christ! What are patterns for?

QUESTIONS

1. What "patterns" are explored by the speaker in the poem? How do these patterns
restrict and finally destroy the speaker's chances for happiness? How does the poet contrast human patterns to more natural rhythms?

2. Write an essay that discusses the ways social patterns, rituals, and obligations restrict our freedom and deprive us of happiness. Provide examples and illustrations drawn
from a particular social pattern: war, marriage, legal restrictions. Why are such social rituals felt to be necessary, and what perpetuates them?

Nighttime Fires
Regina Barreca

When I was five in Louisville
we drove to see nighttime fires. Piled seven of us,
all pajamas and running noses, into the Olds,
drove fast toward smoke. It was after my father
lost his job, so not getting up in the morning   5
gave him time: awake past midnight, he read old newspapers
with no news, tried crosswords until he split the pencil
between his teeth, mad. When he heard
the wolf whine of the siren, he woke my mother,
and she pushed and shoved   10
us all into waking. Once roused we longed for burnt wood
and a smell of flames high into the pines. My old man liked
driving to rich neighborhoods best, swearing in a good mood
as he followed fire engines that snaked like dragons
and split the silent streets. It was festival, carnival.   15

If there were a Cadillac or any car

in a curved driveway, my father smiled a smile
from a secret, brittle heart.
His face lit up in the heat given off by destruction
like something was being made, or was being set right.   20
I bent my head back to see where sparks
ate up the sky. My father who never held us
would take my hand and point to falling cinders that
covered the ground like snow, or, excited, show us
the swollen collapse of a staircase. My mother   25
watched my father, not the house. She was happy
only when we were ready to go, when it was finally over
and nothing else could burn.
Driving home, she would sleep in the front seat
as we huddled behind. I could see his quiet face in the   30
rearview mirror, eyes like hallways filled with smoke.

QUESTIONS

1. Why does the speaker's father like to drive to nighttime fires in rich neighborhoods? How is he treated by his family? What does the poem reveal about unemployment and its impact on workers and their families?

2. Using as examples of experiences of your own or those of your friends, write an essay about the immediate and long-term effects of unemployment on workers and their families.

The Mother

Gwendolyn Brooks

Abortions will not let you forget.
You remember the children you got that you did not get,
The damp small pulps with a little or with no hair,
The singers and workers that never handled the air.
You will never neglect or beat   5
Them, or silence or buy with a sweet.
You will never wind up the sucking-thumb
Or scuttle off ghosts that come.
You will never leave them, controlling your luscious sigh,
Return for a snack of them, with gobbling mother-eye.   10

I have heard in the voices of the wind the voices of my dim
    killed children.
I have contracted. I have eased
My dim dears at the breasts they could never suck.

I have said, Sweets, if I sinned, if I seized
Your luck   15
And your lives from your unfinished reach,
If I stole your births and your names,
Your straight baby tears and your games,
Your stilted or lovely loves, your tumults, your marriages, aches,
    and your deaths,
If I poisoned the beginnings of your breaths,   20
Believe that even in my deliberateness I was not deliberate.
Though why should I whine,
Whine that the crime was other than mine?—
Since anyhow you are dead.
Or rather, or instead,   25
You were never made.
But that too, I am afraid,
Is faulty: oh, what shall I say, how is the truth to be said?
You were born, you had body, you died.
It is just that you never giggled or planned or cried.   30

Believe me, I loved you all.
Believe me, I knew you, though faintly, and I loved, I loved you
All.

QUESTIONS

    1. What haunts the speaker? What apologies does she make to her aborted child?
What defense does she make for her actions? What does she mean by the statement
"even in my deliberateness I was not deliberate."

    2. Write an essay or a short story that explores your feelings and thoughts about
abortion.

Cannery Town in August
Lorna Dee Cervantes

All night it humps the air.
Speechless, the steam rises
from the cannery columns. I hear
the night bird rave about work
or lunch, or sing the swing shift
home. I listen, while bodyless
uniforms and spinach specked shoes
drift in monochrome down the dark
moon-possessed streets. Women

who smell of whiskey and tomatoes,   10
peach fuzz reddening their lips and eyes—
I imagine them not speaking, dumbed
by the can's clamor and drop
to the trucks that wait, grunting
in their headlights below.   15
They spotlight those who walk
like a dream, with no one
waiting in the shadows
to palm them back to living.

QUESTIONS

1. What distinctive sound, sights, and smells does the speaker use to re-create the environment of the cannery town? How does the poem appeal to the imagination as well as the senses of the reader? What impact does work in the cannery have on the minds of the workers?

2. Write a descriptive poem or essay about a workplace where you have spent some time. In your description show the impact that the environment of the workplace had on the workers.

My Mother, Who Came from China, Where She Never Saw Snow

Laureen Mar

In the huge, rectangular room, the ceiling
a machinery of pipes and fluorescent lights,
ten rows of women hunch over machines,
their knees pressing against pedals
and hands pushing the shiny fabric thick as tongues   5
through metal and thread.
My mother bends her head to one of these machines.
Her hair is coarse and wiry, black as burnt scrub.
She wears glasses to shield her intense eyes.
A cone of orange thread spins. Around her,   10
talk flutters harshly in Toisan wah.[1]
Chemical stings. She pushes cloth
through a pounding needle, under, around, and out,
breaks thread with a snap against fingerbone, tooth.

[1] A Chinese dialect.

Sleeve after sleeve, sleeve.   15
It is easy. The same piece.
For eight or nine hours, sixteen bundles maybe,
250 sleeves to ski coats, all the same.
It is easy, only once she's run the needle
through her hand. She earns money   20
by each piece, on a good day,
thirty dollars. Twenty-four years.
It is frightening how fast she works.
She and the women who were taught sewing
terms in English as Second Language.   25
Dull thunder passes through their fingers.

QUESTIONS

1. What repeated words and details does the speaker in the poem use to capture the
repetitious quality of work in the sewing factory? What comment does the poem make
about the expectations and training of immigrants in America? What does the poem's
final line suggest?

2. Write a poem or essay that captures the repetitious, speeded-up quality of modern work, using examples, details, and repeated words and phrases.

Des Moines Iowa Rap

June Jordan

So his wife and his daughters could qualify
Lester Williams told the people he was gonna try suicide:
suicide.
He promised the papers he would definitely try
so his wife and his babies could qualify for welfare   5
in the new year.
Welfare.
In the new year.

I wanna job so bad I can taste it I won't waste it
Wanna job so bad   10

36 years old and home from the Navy
Take my blood, he said, and my bones, he said,
for the meat and the gravy / I'm a vet from the Navy!
Take my meat. Take my bones.
I'm a blood, he said.   15

Tried suicide. Tried suicide.

Lester Williams made the offer and the offer made news
Wasn't all that much to dispute and confuse
Wouldn't hide in no closet and under no bed
Said he'd straightaway shoot himself dead instead 20
Like a man
Like a natural man
Like a natural man wanna job so bad he
can taste it
he can taste it 25

Took the wife in his arms. Held the children in his heart.
Took the gun from his belt. Held the gun to his head.
Like a man.
Like a natural man.
Like a natural man wanna job so bad gotta waste it. 30
Gotta waste it.

Tried Suicide.
Tried Suicide.

QUESTIONS

1. What comment does the poem make on the connections between unemployment, pride, bureaucracy, and suicide? How does the poem resemble actual rap songs, both in its language pattern and its content?

2. Create a rap poem or song of your own that expresses your strong feelings on a subject such as work, welfare, or some social struggle.

Words, Words, Words

Sipho Sepamla

We don't speak of tribal wars anymore
we say simple faction fights
there are no tribes around here
only nations
it makes sense you see 5
'cause' from there
one moves to multinational
it makes sense you get me
'cause from there
one gets one's homeland 10

which is a reasonable idea
'cause from there
one can dabble with independence
which deserves warm applause
—the bloodless revolution   15

we are talking of words
words tossed around as if
denied location by the wind
we mean those words some spit
others grab   20
dress them up for the occasion
fling them on the lap of an audience
we are talking of those words
that stalk our lives like policemen
words no dictionary can embrace   25
words that change sooner than seasons
we mean words
that spell out our lives
words, words, words
for there's a kind of poetic license   30
doing the rounds in these parts

QUESTIONS

1. What particular political words and phrases does the speaker use as examples of "words tossed around as if/denied location by the wind"? How do the misused words "stalk our lives like policemen"? In what sense do they "spell out our lives"?

2. Write an essay that discusses words that reflect on struggles in your community or on your campus, words that are frequently "tossed around" in modern politics in such a way that they arouse strong feelings, yet have no clear meaning.

Cloudy Day

Jimmy Santiago Baca

It is windy today. A wall of wind crashes against,
windows clunk against, iron frames
as wind swings past broken glass
and seethes, like a frightened cat
in empty spaces of the cellblock.   5

In the exercise yard
we sat huddled in our prison jackets,
on our haunches against the fence,
and the wind carried our words
over the fence,   10
while the vigilant guard on the tower
held his cap at the sudden gust.

I could see the main tower from where I sat,
and the wind in my face
gave me the feeling I could grasp   15
the tower like a cornstalk,
and snap it from its roots of rock.
The wind plays it like a flute,
this hollow shoot of rock.
The brim girded with barbwire   20
with a guard sitting there also,
listening intently to the sounds
as clouds cover the sun.

I thought of the day I was coming to prison,
in the back seat of a police car,   25
hands and ankles chained, the policeman pointed,
    "See that big water tank? The big
    silver one out there, sticking up?
    That's the prison."

And here I am, I cannot believe it.   30
Sometimes it is such a dream, a dream,
where I stand up in the face of the wind,
like now, it blows at my jacket,
and my eyelids flick a little bit.
while I stare disbelieving. . . .   35

The third day of spring,
and four years later, I can tell you,
how a man can endure, how a man
can become so cruel, how he can die
or become so cold. I can tell you this,   40
I have seen it every day, every day,
and still I am strong enough to love you,
love myself and feel good;
even as the earth shakes and trembles,
and I have not a thing to my name,   45
I feel as if I have everything, everything.

QUESTIONS

1. What images does Baca use to capture the degrading quality of life in prison? How does the poem's setting on a windy, cloudy day emphasize the speaker's emotional response to prison life? In the final stanza, what realization does the speaker come to about his own strengths and survival abilities?

2. Write a poem or essay about a situation in which you felt trapped and humiliated, yet found the inner strength to survive.

For the Student Strikers
Richard Wilbur

Go talk with those who are rumored to be unlike you,
And whom, it is said, you are so unlike.
Stand on the stoops of their houses and tell them why
You are out on strike.

It is not yet time for the rock, the bullet, the blunt   5
Slogan that fuddles the mind toward force.
Let the new sound in our streets be the patient sound
Of your discourse.

Doors will be shut in your faces, I do not doubt.
Yet here or there, it may be, there will start,   10
Much as the lights blink on in a block at evening,
Changes of heart.

They are your houses; the people are not unlike you;
Talk with them, then, and let it be done
Even for the grey wife of your nightmare sheriff   15
And the guardsman's son.

QUESTIONS

1. What advice does the speaker in the poem have for the student strikers? Are they likely to listen to his advice? What reasons does he give to support his views? What does the speaker mean in the phrase "They are your houses" (line 13)?

2. Write a poem or essay that offers a response to the advice given by the speaker in the poem. Do you agree or disagree with the speaker?

Picketing Supermarkets
Tom Wayman

Because all this food is grown in the store
do not take the leaflet.
Cabbages, broccoli and tomatoes
are raised at night in the aisles.
Milk is brewed in the rear storage areas.   5
Beef produced in vats in the basement.
Do not take the leaflet.
Peanut butter and soft drinks
are made fresh each morning by store employees.
Our oranges and grapes   10
are so fine and round
that when held up to the lights they cast no shadow.
Do not take the leaflet.

And should you take one
do not believe it.   15
This chain of stores has no connection
with anyone growing food someplace else.
How could we have an effect on local farmers?
Do not believe it.

The sound here is Muzak, for your enjoyment.   20
It is not the sound of children crying.
There *is* a lady offering samples
to mark Canada Cheese Month.
There is no dark-skinned man with black hair beside her
wanting to show you the inside of a coffin.   25
You would not have to look if there was.
And there are no Nicaraguan heroes
in any way connected with the bananas.

Pay no attention to these people.
The manager is a citizen.   30
All this food is grown in the store.

QUESTIONS

1. Who is the speaker in the poem? What is the speaker's response to the leafletting of the supermarket? What details and observations made by the speaker encourage you to accept or reject his view? For example, does the speaker have difficulty acknowledging any connections between ideas or aspects of reality that seem clear and obvious to you?

2. Go to a supermarket or other commercial enterprise in your community where picketing or leafletting is taking place. Read the leaflets; talk to the picketers and managers; then write up your own conclusions in an evaluative essay about the appropriateness of the cause or action that is being taken against the targeted business.

Roses and Revolutions
Dudley Randall

Musing on roses and revolutions,
I saw night close down on the earth like a great dark wing,
and the lighted cities were like tapers in the night,
and I heard the lamentations of a million hearts
regretting life and crying for the grave,   5
and I saw the Negro lying in the swamp with his face blown
    off,
and in northern cities with his manhood maligned and felt
    the writhing
of his viscera like that of the hare hunted down or the bear   10
    at bay,
and I saw men working and taking no joy in their work
and embracing the hard-eyed whore with joyless excitement
and lying with wives and virgins in impotence.

And as I groped in darkness   15
and felt the pain of millions,
gradually, like day driving night across the continent,
I saw dawn upon them like the sun a vision
of a time when all men walk proudly through the earth
and the bombs and missiles lie at the bottom of the ocean   20
like the bones of dinosaurs buried under the shale of eras,
and men strive with each other not for power or the accu-
    mulation of paper
but in joy create for others the house, the poem, the game of
    athletic beauty.   25

Then washed in the brightness of this vision,
I saw how in its radiance would grow and be nourished and
    suddenly
burst into terrible and splendid bloom
the blood-red flower of revolution.   30

QUESTIONS

1. What visions of the present and the future does the speaker have while "musing on roses and revolutions"? What major changes in values occur in the world of the future? How might the "blood-red flower of revolution" help bring the speaker's vision of the future into reality?

2. In the form of a poem or essay, write a response to the speaker in this poem. Do you agree with or object to the speaker's values and goals? Do you think that some form of revolution will be needed to bring such a "new world" into being?

Susumu, My Name

Russell Endo

You are entitled to overhear
Susumu, my name, means
    "progress" in Japanese,
The progress of prosperity
    and of good fortune.   5
The dust that seeped through
    makeshift barracks in Arizona
Whet my parents' taste for the
    American Dream.
But my luck shall have to be   10
    different
I want my wheels to skim like
    the blades of the wind
    Across all ruts.
I want my wheels to spin so fast   15
    That we stand still.
Are you with me?
Then may we whisper in the
    summer breeze
Susumu.   20

QUESTIONS

1. What does the speaker's name mean in Japanese? Why might his parents' incarceration in the World War II relocation camps for Japanese Americans have led them to give him this name? Contrast the speaker's point of view about the "American dream" and progress to that of his parents. What central image does the speaker use to clarify his vision of the future?

2. Write an essay about your personal goal or vision for the future. What struggles in your life have helped to create your goal or vision? How will your future be different from your parents' lives?

Drama

Antigonê

Sophocles

An English Version by Dudley Fitts and Robert Fitzgerald

Journal

*Write about an issue that involves a conflict between religious belief or custom
and secular beliefs or laws. What is your position on the issue?*

LIST OF CHARACTERS

ANTIGONÊ	TEIRESIAS
ISMENÊ	A SENTRY
EURYDICÊ	A MESSENGER
CREON	CHORUS
HAIMON	

Scene. Before the palace of CREON, *king of Thebes. A central double door, and
two lateral doors. A platform extends the length of the façade, and from this
platform three steps lead down into the "orchestra," or chorus-ground.*

*Time. Dawn of the day after the repulse of the Argive army from the assault on
Thebes.*

PROLOGUE

ANTIGONÊ *and* ISMENÊ *enter from the central door of the palace.*

ANTIGONÊ: Ismenê, dear sister,
  You would think that we had already suffered enough
  For the curse on Oedipus°
  I cannot imagine any grief

---

³ According to Greek legend, Oedipus was told by the Delphic oracle that he would kill his father
and marry his mother. Although he tried his utmost to avoid his fate, both parts of this prophecy
came true. Unwittingly he killed his father Laius, King of Thebes, and married Laius's widow, Jocasta, thereby becoming King of Thebes. Oedipus and Jocasta had four children: Polyneicês, Eteoclês,
Antigonê and Ismenê. When Oedipus learned what he had done, he blinded himself and left
Thebes. Eteoclês and Polyneicês quarreled and killed each other in battle. Creon who became King
of Thebes decreed Polyneicês a traitor and ordered that he should not be buried.

That you and I have not gone through. And now— 5
    Have they told you of the new decree of our King Creon?
ISMENÊ: I have heard nothing: I know
    That two sisters lost two brothers, a double death
    In a single hour; and I know that the Argive army
    Fled in the night; but beyond this, nothing. 10
ANTIGONÊ: I thought so. And that is why I wanted you
    To come out here with me. There is something we must do.
ISMENÊ: Why do you speak so strangely?
ANTIGONÊ: Listen, Ismenê:
    Creon buried our brother Eteoclês 15
    With military honors, gave him a soldier's funeral,
    And it was right that he should; but Polyneicês,
    Who fought as bravely and died as miserably,—
    They say that Creon has sworn
    No one shall bury him, no one mourn for him, 20
    But his body must lie in the fields, a sweet treasure
    For carrion birds to find as they search for food.
    That is what they say, and our good Creon is coming here
    To announce it publicly; and the penalty—
    Stoning to death in the public square! 25
                       There it is,
    And now you can prove what you are:
    A true sister, or a traitor to your family.
ISMENÊ: Antigonê, you are mad! What could I possibly do?
ANTIGONÊ: You must decide whether you will help me or not. 30
ISMENÊ: I do not understand you. Help you in what?
ANTIGONÊ: Ismenê, I am going to bury him. Will you come?
ISMENÊ: Bury him! You have just said the new law forbids it.
ANTIGONÊ: He is my brother. And he is your brother, too.
ISMENÊ: But think of the danger! Think what Creon will do!
ANTIGONÊ: Creon is not strong enough to stand in my way. 35
ISMENÊ: Ah sister!
    Ocdipus died, everyone hating him
    For what his own search brought to light, his eyes
    Ripped out by his own hand; and Iocastê died,
    His mother and wife at once: she twisted the cords 40
    That strangled her life; and our two brothers died,
    Each killed by the other's sword. And we are left:
    But oh, Antigonê,
    Think how much more terrible than these
    Our own death would be if we should go against Creon 45
    And do what he has forbidden! We are only women,
    We cannot fight with men, Antigonê!
    The law is strong, we must give in to the law

In this thing, and in worse. I beg the Dead
To forgive me, but I am helpless: I must yield   50
To those in authority. And I think it is dangerous business
To be always meddling.
ANTIGONÊ: If that is what you think,
I should not want you, even if you asked to come.
You have made your choice, you can be what you want to be.   55
But I will bury him; and if I must die,
I say that this crime is holy: I shall lie down
With him in death, and I shall be as dear
To him as he to me.
                             It is the dead,
Not the living, who make the longest demands:
We die for ever . . .   You may do as you like,   60
Since apparently the laws of the gods mean nothing to you.
ISMENÊ: They mean a great deal to me; but I have no strength
To break laws that were made for the public good.
ANTIGONÊ: That must be your excuse, I suppose. But as for me,
I will bury the brother I love.
ISMENÊ: Antigonê,   65
I am so afraid for you!
ANTIGONÊ: You need not be:
You have yourself to consider, after all.
ISMENÊ: But no one must hear of this, you must tell no one!
I will keep it a secret, I promise!
ANTIGONÊ: O tell it! Tell everyone!
Think of how they'll hate you when it all comes out   70
If they learn that you knew about it all the time!
ISMENÊ: So fiery! You should be cold with fear.
ANTIGONÊ: Perhaps. But I am doing only what I must.
ISMENÊ: But can you do it? I say that you cannot.
ANTIGONÊ: Very well: when my strength gives out,
I shall do no more.   75
ISMENÊ: Impossible things should not be tried at all.
ANTIGONÊ: Go away, Ismenê:
I shall be hating you soon, and the dead will too,
For your words are hateful. Leave me my foolish plan:
I am not afraid of the danger; if it means death,   80
It will not be the worst of deaths—death without honor.
ISMENÊ: Go then, if you feel that you must.
You are unwise,
But a loyal friend indeed to those who love you.

Exit into the palace. ANTIGONÊ *goes off, left. Enter the* CHORUS.

PÁRODOS

CHROUS: Now the long blade of the sun, lying   *Strophe 1*
    Level east to west, touches with glory
    Thebes of the Seven Gates. Open, unlidded
    Eye of golden day! O marching light
    Across the eddy and rush of Dircê's stream,°   5
    Striking the white shields of the enemy
    Thrown headlong backward from the blaze of morning!
CHORAGOS:° Polyneicês their commander
    Roused them with windy phrases,
    He the wild eagle screaming   10
    Insults above our land,
    His wings their shields of snow,
    His crest their marshalled helms.
CHORUS: Against our seven gates in a yawning ring   *Antistrophe 1*
    The famished spears came onward in the night;   15
    But before his jaws were sated with our blood,
    Or pine fire took the garland of our towers,
    He was thrown back; and as he turned, great Thebes—
    No tender victim for his noisy power—
    Rose like a dragon behind him, shouting war.   20
CHORAGOS: For God hates utterly
    The bray of bragging tongues;
    And when he beheld their smiling,
    Their swagger of golden helms,
    The frown of his thunder blasted   25
    Their first man from our walls.
CHORUS: We heard his shout of triumph high in the air   *Strophe 2*
    Turn to a scream; far out in a flaming arc
    He fell with his windy torch, and the earth struck him.
    And others storming in fury no less than his   30
    Found shock of death in the dusty joy of battle.
CHORAGOS: Seven captains at seven gates
    Yielded their clanging arms to the god
    That bends the battle-line and breaks it.
    These two only, brothers in blood,   35
    Face to face in matchless rage,
    Mirroring each the other's death,
    Clashed in long combat.

---

[5] *Dircê's stream*   a stream west of Thebes
[8] *Choragos*   leader of the Chorus

CHORUS: But now in the beautiful morning of victory   Antistrophe 2
    Let Thebes of the many chariots sing for joy!   40
    With hearts for dancing we'll take leave of war:
    Our temples shall be sweet with hymns of praise,
    And the long nights shall echo with our chorus.

                            Scene I

CHORAGOS: But now at last our new King is coming:
    Creon of Thebes, Menoikeus' son.
    In this auspicious dawn of his reign
    What are the new complexities
    That shifting Fate has woven for him?   5
    What is his counsel? Why has he summoned
    The old men to hear him?

Enter CREON *from the palace, center. He addresses the* CHORUS *from the top step.*

CREON: Gentlemen: I have the honor to inform you that our Ship of
    State, which recent storms have threatened to destroy, has
    come safely to harbor at last, guided by the merciful wisdom of   10
    Heaven. I have summoned you here this morning because I
    know that I can depend upon you: your devotion to King Laios
    was absolute; you never hesitated in your duty to our late ruler
    Oedipus; and when Oedipus died, your loyalty was transferred
    to his children. Unfortunately, as you know, his two sons, the   15
    princes Eteoclês and Polyneicês, have killed each other in bat-
    tle; and I, as the next in blood, have succeeded to the full
    power of the throne.

        I am aware, of course, that no Ruler can expect complete
    loyalty from his subjects until he has been tested in office.   20
    Nevertheless, I say to you at the very outset that I have nothing
    but contempt for the kind of Governor who is afraid, for what-
    ever reason, to follow the course that he knows is best for the
    State; and as for the man who sets private friendship above the
    public welfare,—I have no use for him, either. I call God to wit-   25
    ness that if I saw my country headed for ruin, I should not be
    afraid to speak out plainly; and I need hardly remind you that I
    would never have any dealings with an enemy of the people.
    No one values friendship more highly than I; but we must
    remember that friends made at the risk of wrecking our Ship   30
    are not real friends at all.

        These are my principles, at any rate, and that is why I have
    made the following decision concerning the sons of Oedipus:
    Eteoclês, who died as a man should die, fighting for his coun-
    try, is to be buried with full military honors, with all the cere-   35

mony that is usual when the greatest heroes die; but his brother Polyneicês, who broke his exile to come back with fire and sword against his native city and the shrines of his fathers' gods, whose one idea was to spill the blood of his blood and sell his own people into slavery—Polyneicês, I say, is to have no burial: no man is to touch him or say the least prayer for him; he shall lie on the plain, unburied; and the birds and the scavenging dogs can do with him whatever they like. 40

    This is my command, and you can see the wisdom behind it. As long as I am King, no traitor is going to be honored with the loyal man. But whoever shows by word and deed that he is on the side of the State,—he shall have my respect while he is living and my reverence when he is dead. 45

CHORAGOS: If that is your will, Creon son of Menoikeus,
    You have the right to enforce it: we are yours. 50

CREON: That is my will. Take care that you do your part.

CHORAGOS: We are old men: let the younger ones carry it out.

CREON: I do not mean that: the sentries have been appointed.

CHORAGOS: Then what is it that you would have us do?

CREON: You will give no support to whoever breaks this law. 55

CHORAGOS: Only a crazy man is in love with death!

CREON: And death it is; yet money talks, and the wisest
    Have sometimes been known to count a few coins too many.

Enter SENTRY *from left.*

SENTRY: I'll not say that I'm out of breath from running, King, because every time I stopped to think about what I have to tell you, I felt like going back. And all the time a voice kept saying, "You fool, don't you know you're walking straight into trouble?"; and then another voice: "Yes, but if you let somebody else get the news to Creon first, it will be even worse than that for you!" But good sense won out, at least I hope it was good sense, and here I am with a story that makes no sense at all; but I'll tell it anyhow, because, as they say, what's going to happen's going to happen and 60 65

CREON: Come to the point. What have you to say?

SENTRY: I did not do it. I did not see who did it. You must not punish me for what someone else has done. 70

CREON: A comprehensive defense! More effective, perhaps,
    If I knew its purpose. Come: what is it?

SENTRY: A dreadful thing . . . I don't know how to put it—

CREON: Out with it! 75

SENTRY: Well, then;
    The dead man—
        Polyneicês—

Pause. The SENTRY *is overcome, fumbles for words.* CREON *waits impassively.*

out there—

someone,—

New dust on the slimy flesh!

Pause. No sign from CREON.

Someone has given it burial that way, and   80
Gone . . .

Long pause. CREON *finally speaks with deadly control.*

CREON: And the man who dared do this?

SENTRY: I swear I
Do not know! You must believe me!

Listen:

The ground was dry, not a sign of digging, no,   85
Not a wheeltrack in the dust, no trace of anyone.
It was when they relieved us this morning: and one of them,
The corporal, pointed to it.

There it was,

The strangest—

Look: 90
The body, just mounded over with light dust: you see?
Not buried really, but as if they'd covered it
Just enough for the ghost's peace. And no sign
Of dogs or any wild animal that had been there.
And then what a scene there was! Every man of us   95
Accusing the other: we all proved the other man did it,
We all had proof that we could not have done it.
We were ready to take hot iron in our hands,
Walk through fire, swear by all the gods,
It was not I!   100
I do not know who it was, but it was not I!

CREON's *rage has been mounting steadily, but the* SENTRY *is too intent upon his story to notice it.*

And then, when this came to nothing, someone said
A thing that silenced us and made us stare
Down at the ground: you had to be told the news,
And one of us had to do it! We threw the dice,
And the bad luck fell to me. So here I am   105
No happier to be here than you are to have me:
Nobody likes the man who brings bad news.

CHORAGOS: I have been wondering, King: can it be that the gods have
done this?

CREON *(furiously):* Stop!

Must you doddering wrecks   110
Go out of your heads entirely? "The gods"!

Intolerable!
The gods favor this corpse? Why? How had he served them?
Tried to loot their temples, burn their images,
Yes, and the whole State, and its laws with it! 115
Is it your senile opinion that the gods love to honor bad men?
A pious thought!—
                    No, from the very beginning
There have been those who have whispered together,
Stiff-necked anarchists, putting their heads together,
Scheming against me in alleys. These are the men, 120
And they have bribed my own guard to do this thing.
(Sententiously.) Money!
There's nothing in the world so demoralizing as money.
Down go your cities,
Homes gone, men gone, honest hearts corrupted, 125
Crookedness of all kinds, and all for money!
(To SENTRY.*)*   But you—!
I swear by God and by the throne of God,
The man who has done this thing shall pay for it!
Find that man, bring him here to me, or your death 130
Will be the least of your problems: I'll string you up
Alive, and there will be certain ways to make you
Discover your employer before you die;
And the process may teach you a lesson you seem to have
     missed:
The dearest profit is sometimes all too dear: 135
That depends on the source. Do you understand me?
A fortune won is often misfortune.
SENTRY: King, may I speak?
CREON: Your very voice distresses me.
SENTRY: Are you sure that it is my voice, and not your conscience? 140
CREON: By God, he wants to analyze me now!
SENTRY: It is not what I say, but what has been done, that hurts you.
CREON: You talk too much.
SENTRY: Maybe; but I've done nothing.
CREON: Sold your soul for some silver: that's all you've done.
SENTRY: How dreadful it is when the right judge judges wrong! [145]
CREON: Your figures of speech
     May entertain you now; but unless you bring me the man,
     You will get little profit from them in the end.
Exit CREON *into the palace.*
SENTRY: "Bring me the man"—!
     I'd like nothing better than bringing him the man! [150]
     But bring him or not, you have seen the last of me here.
     At any rate, I am safe!   *(Exit* SENTRY.*)*

Ode I

CHORUS: Numberless are the world's wonders, but none   *Strophe 1*
    More wonderful than man; the stormgray sea
    Yields to his prows, the huge crests bear him high;
    Earth, holy and inexhaustible, is graven
    With shining furrows where his plows have gone   5
    Year after year, the timeless labor of stallions.

    The lightboned birds and beasts that cling to cover,   *Antistrophe 1*
    The lithe fish lighting their reaches of dim water,
    All are taken, tamed in the net of his mind;
    The lion on the hill, the wild horse windy-maned,   10
    Resign to him; and his blunt yoke has broken
    The sultry shoulders of the mountain bull.

    Words also, and thought as rapid as air,   *Strophe 2*
    He fashions to his good use; statecraft is his,
    And his the skill that deflects the arrows of snow,   15
    The spears of winter rain: from every wind
    He has made himself secure—from all but one:
    In the late wind of death he cannot stand.

    O clear intelligence, force beyond all measure!   *Antistrophe 2*
    O fate of man, working both good and evil!   20
    When the laws are kept, how proudly his city stands!
    When the laws are broken, what of his city then?
    Never may the anarchic man find rest at my hearth,
    Never be it said that my thoughts are his thoughts.

Scene II

Reenter SENTRY *leading* ANTIGONÊ

CHORAGOS: What does this mean? Surely this captive woman
    Is the Princess, Antigonê. Why should she be taken?
SENTRY: Here is the one who did it! We caught her
    In the very act of burying him.—Where is Creon?
CHORAGOS: Just coming from the house.

Enter CREON, *center.*

CREON: What has happened?   5
    Why have you come back so soon? O King,
SENTRY *(expansively)*:
    A man should never be too sure of anything:
    I would have sworn
    That you'd not see me here again: your anger

Frightened me so, and the things you threatened me with;   10
But how could I tell then
That I'd be able to solve the case so soon?
No dice-throwing this time: I was only too glad to come!
Here is this woman. She is the guilty one:
We found her trying to bury him.   15
Take her, then; question her; judge her as you will.
I am through with the whole thing now, and glad of it.
CREON: But this is Antigonê! Why have you brought her here?
SENTRY: She was burying him, I tell you!
CREON *(severely):*   Is this the truth?
SENTRY: I saw her with my own eyes. Can I say more?   20
CREON: The details: come, tell me quickly!
SENTRY: It was like this:
After those terrible threats of yours, King,
We went back and brushed the dust away from the body.
The flesh was soft by now, and stinking,
So we sat on a hill to windward and kept guard.   25
No napping this time! We kept each other awake.
But nothing happened until the white round sun
Whirled in the center of the round sky over us:
Then, suddenly,
A storm of dust roared up from the earth, and the sky   30
Went out, the plain vanished with all its trees
In the stinging dark. We closed our eyes and endured it.
The whirlwind lasted a long time, but it passed;
And then we looked, and there was Antigonê!
I have seen   35
A mother bird come back to a stripped nest, heard
Her crying bitterly a broken note or two
For the young ones stolen. Just so, when this girl
Found the bare corpse, and all her love's work wasted,
She wept, and cried on heaven to damn the hands   40
That had done this thing.
                                    And then she brought more dust
And sprinkled wine three times for her brother's ghost.
We ran and took her at once. She was not afraid,
Not even when we charged her with what she had done.
She denied nothing.
                                    And this was a comfort to me,   45
And some uneasiness: for it is a good thing
To escape from death, but it is no great pleasure
To bring death to a friend.
                                    Yet I always say
There is nothing so comfortable as your own safe skin!

CREON (*slowly, dangerously*): And you, Antigonê,   50
    You with your head hanging,—do you confess this thing?
ANTIGONÊ : I do. I deny nothing.
CREON (*to* SENTRY):   You may go.   (*Exit* SENTRY.)
    (*To* ANTIGONÊ.) Tell me, tell me briefly:
    Had you heard my proclamation touching this matter?
ANTIGONÊ: It was public. Could I help hearing it?   55
CREON: And yet you dared defy the law.
ANTIGONÊ:
    It was not God's proclamation. That final Justice
    That rules the world below makes no such laws.
    Your edict, King, was strong,
    But all your strength is weakness itself against   60
    The immortal unrecorded laws of God.
    They are not merely now: they were, and shall be,
    Operative for ever, beyond man utterly.
    I knew I must die, even without your decree:
    I am only mortal. And if I must die   65
    Now, before it is my time to die,
    Surely this is no hardship: can anyone
    Living, as I live, with evil all about me,
    Think Death less than a friend? This death of mine
    Is of no importance; but if I had left my brother   70
    Lying in death unburied, I should have suffered.
    Now I do not.
                You smile at me. Ah Creon,
    Think me a fool, if you like; but it may well be
    That a fool convicts me of folly.
CHORAGOS: Like father, like daughter: both headstrong, deaf to
    reason!   75
    She has never learned to yield:
CREON: She has much to learn.
    The inflexible heart breaks first, the toughest iron
    Cracks first, and the wildest horses bend their necks
    At the pull of the smallest curb.
                Pride? In a slave?
    This girl is guilty of a double insolence,   80
    Breaking the given laws and boasting of it.
    Who is the man here,
    She or I, if this crime goes unpunished?
    Sister's child, or more than sister's child,
    Or closer yet in blood—she and her sister   85
    Win bitter death for this!
    (*To* SERVANTS.)   Go, some of you,
    Arrest Ismenê. I accuse her equally.

Bring her: you will find her sniffling in the house there.
Her mind's a traitor: crimes kept in the dark
Cry for light, and the guardian brain shudders;   90
But how much worse than this
Is brazen boasting of barefaced anarchy!
ANTIGONÊ: Creon, what more do you want than my death?
CREON: Nothing.
    That gives me everything.
ANTIGONÊ: Then I beg you: kill me.
    This talking is a great weariness: your words   95
    Are distasteful to me, and I am sure that mine
    Seem so to you. And yet they should not seem so:
    I should have praise and honor for what I have done.
    All these men here would praise me
    Were their lips not frozen shut with fear of you.   100
    (Bitterly.) Ah the good fortune of kings,
    Licensed to say and do whatever they please!
CREON: You are alone here in that opinion.
ANTIGONÊ: No, they are with me. But they keep their tongues in leash.
CREON: Maybe. But you are guilty, and they are not.   105
ANTIGONÊ: There is no guilt in reverence for the dead.
CREON: But Eteoclês—was he not your brother too?
ANTIGONÊ: My brother too.
CREON: And you insult his memory?
ANTIGONÊ (softly): The dead man would not say that I insult it.
CREON: He would: for you honor a traitor as much as him.   110
ANTIGONÊ: His own brother, traitor or not, and equal in blood.
CREON: He made war on his country. Eteoclês defended it.
ANTIGONÊ: Nevertheless, there are honors due all the dead.
CREON: But not the same for the wicked as for the just.
ANTIGONÊ: Ah Creon, Creon,   115
    Which of us can say what the gods hold wicked?
CREON: An enemy is an enemy, even dead.
ANTIGONÊ: It is my nature to join in love, not hate.
CREON (finally losing patience): Go join them then; if you must have
        your love,
    Find it in hell!   120
CHORAGOS: But see, Ismenê comes:

Enter ISMENÊ, guarded.

    Those tears are sisterly, the cloud
    That shadows her eyes rains down gentle sorrow.
CREON: You too, Ismenê,
    Snake in my ordered house, sucking my blood   125
    Stealthily—and all the time I never knew

That these two sisters were aiming at my throne!

                                              Ismenê,

Do you confess your share in this crime, or deny it?

Answer me.

ISMENÊ: Yes, if she will let me say so. I am guilty.   130

ANTIGONÊ *(coldly):* No, Ismenê. You have no right to say so.

    You would not help me, and I will not have you help me.

ISMENÊ : But now I know what you meant; and I am here

    To join you, to take my share of punishment.

ANTIGONÊ: The dead man and the gods who rule the dead   135

    Know whose act this was. Words are not friends.

ISMENÊ: Do you refuse me, Antigonê? I want to die with you:

    I too have a duty that I must discharge to the dead.

ANTIGONÊ: You shall not lessen my death by sharing it.

ISMENÊ: What do I care for life when you are dead?   140

ANTIGONÊ: Ask Creon. You're always hanging on his opinions.

ISMENÊ: You are laughing at me. Why, Antigonê?

ANTIGONÊ: It's a joyless laughter, Ismenê.

ISMENÊ: But can I do nothing?

ANTIGONÊ: Yes. Save yourself. I shall not envy you.

    There are those who will praise you; I shall have honor, too.   145

ISMENÊ: But we are equally guilty!

ANTIGONÊ: No more, Ismenê.

    You are alive, but I belong to Death.

CREON *(to the* CHORUS*):* Gentlemen, I beg you to observe these girls:

    One has just now lost her mind; the other,

    It seems, has never had a mind at all.   150

ISMENÊ: Grief teaches the steadiest minds to waver, King.

CREON: Yours certainly did, when you assumed guilt with the guilty!

ISMENÊ: But how could I go on living without her?

CREON: You are.

    She is already dead.

ISMENÊ: But your own son's bride!

CREON: There are places enough for him to push his plow.   155

    I want no wicked women for my sons!

ISMENÊ: O dearest Haimon, how your father wrongs you!

CREON: I've had enough of your childish talk of marriage!

CHORAGOS: Do you really intend to steal this girl from your son?

CREON: No; Death will do that for me.

CHORAGOS: Then she must die?   160

CREON *(ironically):* You dazzle me.

                       —But enough of this talk!

(To GUARDS.*)* You, there, take them away and guard them well:

For they are but women, and even brave men run

When they see Death coming.

                          Exeunt ISMENÊ, ANTIGONÊ, *and* GUARDS.

Ode II

CHORUS: Fortunate is the man who has never tasted God's *Strophe 1*
    vengeance!
  Where once the anger of heaven has struck, that house is
    shaken
  For ever: damnation rises behind each child
  Like a wave cresting out of the black northeast,
  When the long darkness under sea roars up   5
  And bursts drumming death upon the windwhipped sand.

  I have seen this gathering sorrow from time long past *Antistrophe 1*
  Loom upon Oedipus' children: generation from generation
  Takes the compulsive rage of the enemy god.
  So lately this last flower of Oedipus' line   10
  Drank the sunlight! but now a passionate word
  And a handful of dust have closed up all its beauty.

    What mortal arrogance *Strophe 2*
    Transcends the wrath of Zeus?
  Sleep cannot lull him nor the effortless long months   15
  Of the timeless gods: but he is young for ever,
  And his house is the shining day of high Olympos.
    All that is and shall be,
    And all the past, is his.
  No pride on earth is free of the curse of heaven.   20

  The straying dreams of men *Antistrophe 2*
    May bring them ghosts of joy:
  But as they drowse, the waking embers burn them;
  Or they walk with fixed eyes, as blind men walk.
  But the ancient wisdom speaks for our own time: 25
    Fate works most for woe
    With Folly's fairest show.
  Man's little pleasure is the spring of sorrow.

Scene III

CHORAGOS: But here is Haimon, King, the last of all your sons.
  Is it grief for Antigonê that brings him here,
  And bitterness at being robbed of his bride?

Enter HAIMON.

CREON: We shall soon see, and no need of diviners.
                        —Son
  You have heard my final judgment on that girl: 5
  Have you come here hating me, or have you come
  With deference and with love, whatever I do?

HAIMON: I am your son, father. You are my guide.
   You make things clear for me, and I obey you.
   No marriage means more to me than your continuing wisdom.   10
CREON: Good. That is the way to behave: subordinate
   Everything else, my son, to your father's will.
   This is what a man prays for, that he may get
   Sons attentive and dutiful in his house,
   Each one hating his father's enemies,   15
   Honoring his father's friends. But if his sons
   Fail him, if they turn out unprofitably,
   What has he fathered but trouble for himself
   And amusement for the malicious?
                             So you are right
   Not to lose your head over this woman.   20
   Your pleasure with her would soon grow cold, Haimon,
   And then you'd have a hellcat in bed and elsewhere.
   Let her find her husband in Hell!
   Of all the people in this city, only she
   Has had contempt for my law and broken it.   25

   Do you want me to show myself weak before the people?
   Or to break my sworn word? No, and I will not.
   The woman dies.
   I suppose she'll plead "family ties." Well, let her.
   If I permit my own family to rebel,   30
   How shall I earn the world's obedience?
   Show me the man who keeps his house in hand,
   He's fit for public authority.
                     I'll have no dealings
   With lawbreakers, critics of the government:
   Whoever is chosen to govern should be obeyed—   35
   Must be obeyed, in all things, great and small,
   Just and unjust! O Haimon,
   The man who knows how to obey, and that man only,
   Knows how to give commands when the time comes.
   You can depend on him, no matter how fast   40

   The spears come: he's a good soldier, he'll stick it out.
   Anarchy, anarchy! Show me a greater evil!
   This is why cities tumble and the great houses rain down,
   This is what scatters armies!
   No, no: good lives are made so by discipline.   45
   We keep the laws then, and the lawmakers,
   And no woman shall seduce us. If we must lose,
   Let's lose to a man, at least! Is a woman stronger than we?

CHORAGOS: Unless time has rusted my wits,
    What you say, King, is said with point and dignity.   50
HAIMON *(boyishly earnest):* Father:
    Reason is God's crowning gift to man, and you are right
    To warn me against losing mine. I cannot say—
    I hope that I shall never want to say!—that you
    Have reasoned badly. Yet there are other men   55
    Who can reason, too; and their opinions might be helpful
    You are not in a position to know everything
    That people say or do, or what they feel:
    Your temper terrifies—everyone
    Will tell you only what you like to hear.   60
    But I, at any rate, can listen; and I have heard them
    Muttering and whispering in the dark about this girl.
    They say no woman has ever, so unreasonably,
    Died so shameful a death for a generous act:
    "She covered her brother's body. Is this indecent?   65
    She kept him from dogs and vultures. Is this a crime?
    Death?—She should have all the honor that we can give her!"

    This is the way they talk out there in the city.

    You must believe me:
    Nothing is closer to me than your happiness.   70
    What could be closer? Must not any son
    Value his father's fortune as his father does his?
    I beg you, do not be unchangeable:
    Do not believe that you alone can be right.
    The man who thinks that,   75
    The man who maintains that only he has the power
    To reason correctly, the gift to speak, the soul—
    A man like that, when you know him, turns out empty

    It is not reason never to yield to reason!

    In flood time you can see how some trees bend,   80
    And because they bend, even their twigs are safe,
    While stubborn trees are torn up, roots and all.
    And the same thing happens in sailing:
    Make your sheet fast, never slacken,—and over you go,
    Head over heels and under: and there's your voyage.   85
    Forget you are angry! Let yourself be moved!
    I know I am young; but please let me say this:
    The ideal condition
    Would be, I admit, that men should be right by instinct;

But since we are all too likely to go astray,   90
The reasonable thing is to learn from those who can teach.
CHORAGOS: You will do well to listen to him, King,
    If what he says is sensible. And you, Haimon,
    Must listen to your father.—Both speak well.
CREON: You consider it right for a man of my years and experience   95
    To go to school to a boy?
HAIMON: It is not right
    If I am wrong. But if I am young, and right,
    What does my age matter?
CREON: You think it right to stand up for an anarchist?
HAIMON: Not at all. I pay no respect to criminals.   100
CREON: Then she is not a criminal?
HAIMON: The City would deny it, to a man.
CREON: And the City proposes to teach me how to rule?
HAIMON: Ah. Who is it that's talking like a boy now?
CREON: My voice is the one voice giving orders in this City!   105
HAIMON: It is no City if it takes orders from one voice.
CREON: The State is the King!
HAIMON: Yes, if the State is a desert.

Pause.

CREON: This boy, it seems, has sold out to a woman.
HAIMON: If you are a woman: my concern is only for you.
CREON: So? Your "concern"! In a public brawl with your father!   110
HAIMON: How about you, in a public brawl with justice?
CREON: With justice, when all that I do is within my rights?
HAIMON: You have no right to trample on God's right.
CREON *(completely out of control)*: Fool, adolescent fool! Taken in by
    a woman!
HAIMON: You'll never see me taken in by anything vile.   115
CREON: Every word you say is for her!
HAIMON *(quietly, darkly)*:   And for you.
    And for me. And for the gods under the earth.
CREON: You'll never marry her while she lives.
HAIMON: Then she must die.—But her death will cause another.
CREON: Another?   120
    Have you lost your senses? Is this an open threat?
HAIMON: There is no threat in speaking to emptiness.
CREON: I swear you'll regret this superior tone of yours!
    You are the empty one!
HAIMON: If you were not my father,
    I'd say you were perverse.   125
CREON: You girlstruck fool, don't play at words with me!
HAIMON: I am sorry. You prefer silence.

CREON: Now, by God—!
    I swear, by all the gods in heaven above us,
    You'll watch it, I swear you shall!
    (To the SERVANTS*)*   Bring her out!
    Bring the woman out! Let her die before his eyes!   130
    Here, this instant, with her bridegroom beside her!
HAIMON: Not here, no; she will not die here, King.
    And you will never see my face again.
    Go on raving as long as you've a friend to endure you.

                                          (Exit HAIMON.*)*

CHORAGOS: Gone, gone.   135
    Creon, a young man in a rage is dangerous!
CREON: Let him do, or dream to do, more than a man can.
    He shall not save these girls from death.
CHORAGOS: These girls?
    You have sentenced them both?
CREON: No, you are right.
    I will not kill the one whose hands are clean.   140
CHORAGOS: But Antigonê?
CREON *(somberly):*   I will carry her far away
    Out there in the wilderness, and lock her
    Living in a vault of stone. She shall have food,
    As the custom is, to absolve the State of her death.
    And there let her pray to the gods of hell: 145
    They are her only gods:
    Perhaps they will show her an escape from death,
    Or she may learn,
                 through late,
    That piety shown the dead is pity in vain.   *(Exit* CREON.*)*

Ode III

CHORUS: Love, unconquerable   *Strophe*
    Waster of rich men, keeper
    Of warm lights and all-night vigil
    In the soft face of a girl:
    Sea-wanderer, forest-visitor!   5
    Even the pure Immortals cannot escape you,
    And mortal man, in his one day's dusk,
    Trembles before your glory.

    Surely you swerve upon ruin   *Antistrophe*
    The just man's consenting heart,   10
    As here you have made bright anger
    Strike between father and son—

And none has conquered but Love!
A girl's glance working the will of heaven:
Pleasure to her alone who mocks us,   15
Merciless Aphroditê.°

Scene IV

CHORAGOS (as ANTIGONÊ enters guarded): But I can no longer stand in
    awe of this,
Nor, seeing what I see, keep back my tears.
Here is Antigonê, passing to that chamber
Where all find sleep at last.

ANTIGONÊ: Look upon me, friends, and pity me   *Strophe 1*
Turning back at the night's edge to say
Good-by to the sun that shines for me no longer;
Now sleepy Death
Summons me down to Acheron,° that cold shore:
There is no bridesong there, nor any music.   10

CHORUS: Yet not unpraised, not without a kind of honor,
You walk at last into the underworld;
Untouched by sickness, broken by no sword.
What woman has ever found your way to death?

ANTIGONÊ: How often I have heard the story of Niobê,°   *Antistrophe 1*
Tantalos' wretched daughter, how the stone
Clung fast about her, ivy-close: and they say
The rain falls endlessly
And sifting soft snow; her tears are never done.
I feel the loneliness of her death in mine.   20

CHORUS: But she was born of heaven, and you
Are woman, woman-born. If her death is yours,
A mortal woman's, is this not for you
Glory in our world and in the world beyond?

ANTIGONÊ: You laugh at me. Ah, friends, friends,   *Strophe 2*
Can you not wait until I am dead? O Thebes,
O men many-charioted, in love with Fortune,
Dear springs of Dircê, sacred Theban grove,
Be witnesses for me, denied all pity,
Unjustly judged! and think a word of love   30
For her whose path turns
Under dark earth, where there are no more tears.

Ode III. ^{16} *Aphroditê*   goddess of love
Scene IV. ^{9} *Acheron*a   river of the underworld, which was ruled by Hades
^{15} *Niobê,* the daughter of Tantalos, boasted about her dozen children thereby provoking Artemis and
Apollo to kill them all. Crying inconsolably, Niobê fled to Mount Sipylus where Zeus turned her into
a stone image that wept perpetually.

CHORUS: You have passed beyond human daring and come at last
    Into a place of stone where Justice sits.
    I cannot tell   35
    What shape of your father's guilt appears in this.
ANTIGONÊ: You have touched it at last: that bridal bed   *Antistrophe 2*
    Unspeakable, horror of son and mother mingling:
    Their crime, infection of all our family!
    O Oedipus, father and brother!   40
    Your marriage strikes from the grave to murder mine.
    I have been a stranger here in my own land:
    All my life
    The blasphemy of my birth has followed me.
CHORUS: Reverence is a virtue, but strength   45
    Lives in established law: that must prevail.
    You have made your choice,
    Your death is the doing of your conscious hand.
ANTIGONÊ: Then let me go, since all your words are bitter,   *Epode*
    And the very light of the sun is cold to me.   50
    Lead me to my vigil, where I must have
    Neither love nor lamentation; no song, but silence.

CREON *interrupts impatiently.*

CREON: If dirges and planned lamentations could put off death,
    Men would be singing for ever.
    (To the SERVANTS.*)*   Take her, go!
    You know your orders: take her to the vault   55
    And leave her alone there. And if she lives or dies,
    That's her affair, not ours: our hands are clean.
ANTIGONÊ: O tomb, vaulted bride-bed in eternal rock,
    Soon I shall be with my own again
    Where Persephonê° welcomes the thin ghosts underground: 60
    And I shall see my father again, and you, mother,
    And dearest Polyneicês
                  —dearest indeed
    To me, since it was my hand
    That washed him clean and poured the ritual wine:
    And my reward is death before my time!   65
    And yet, as men's hearts know, I have done no wrong,
    I have not sinned before God. Or if I have,
    I shall know the truth in death. But if the guilt
    Lies upon Creon who judged me, then, I pray,
    May his punishment equal my own.   70

---

[60] *Persephonê*   queen of the underworld

CHORAGOS: O passionate heart,
    Unyielding, tormented still by the same winds!
CREON: Her guards shall have good cause to regret their delaying.
ANTIGONÊ: Ah! That voice is like the voice of death!
CREON: I can give you no reason to think you are mistaken.   75
ANTIGONÊ: Thebes, and you my fathers' gods,
    And rulers of Thebes, you see me now, the last
    Unhappy daughter of a line of kings,
    Your kings, led away to death. You will remember
    What things I suffer, and at what men's hands,   80
    Because I would not transgress the laws of heaven.
    (To the GUARDS, *simply.)* Come: let us wait no longer.

                              (Exit ANTIGONÊ, *left, guarded.)*

Ode IV

CHORUS: All Danaê's beauty was locked away   *Strophe 1*
    In a brazen cell where the sunlight could not come:
    A small room still as any grave, enclosed her.
    Yet she was a princess too.
    And Zeus in a rain of gold poured love upon her.   5
    O child, child.
    No power in wealth or war
    Or tough sea-blackened ships
    Can prevail against untiring Destiny!

    And Dryas' son° also, that furious king,   *Antistrophe 1*
    Bore the god's prisoning anger for his pride:
    Sealed up by Dionysos in deaf stone,
    His madness died among echoes.
    So at the last he learned what dreadful power
    His tongue had mocked: 15
    For he had profaned the revels,
    And fired the wrath of the nine
    Implacable Sisters° that love the sound of the flute.
    And old men tell a half-remembered tale   *Strophe 2*
    Of horror where a dark ledge splits the sea   20
    And a double surf beats on the gray shores:
    How a king's new woman,° sick
    With hatred for the queen he had imprisoned,
    Ripped out his two sons' eyes with her bloody hands

---

[10] *Dryas' son*   Lycurgus, King of Thrace
[18] *Sisters*   the Muses

While grinning Ares° watched the shuttle plunge   25
Four times: four blind wounds crying for revenge,

Crying, tears and blood mingled.—Piteously born,   *Antistrophe 2*
Those sons whose mother was of heavenly birth!
Her father was the god of the North Wind
And she was cradled by gales,   30
She raced with young colts on the glittering hills
And walked untrammeled in the open light:
But in her marriage deathless Fate found means
To build a tomb like yours for all her joy.

Scene V

Enter blind TEIRESIAS, *led by a boy. The opening speeches of* TEIRESIAS *should be in singsong contrast to the realistic lines of* CREON.

TEIRESIAS: This is the way the blind man comes, Princes, Princes,
    Lock-step, two heads lit by the eyes of one.
CREON: What new thing have you to tell us, old Teiresias?
TEIRESIAS: I have much to tell you: listen to the prophet, Creon.
CREON: I am not aware that I have ever failed to listen.   5
TEIRESIAS: Then you have done wisely, King, and ruled well.
CREON: I admit my debt to you. But what have you to say?
TEIRESIAS: This, Creon: you stand once more on the edge of fate.
CREON: What do you mean? Your words are a kind of dread.
TEIRESIAS: Listen, Creon: 10
    I was sitting in my chair of augury, at the place
    Where the birds gather about me. They were all a-chatter,
    As is their habit, when suddenly I heard
    A strange note in their jangling, a scream, a
    Whirring fury; I knew that they were fighting,   15
    Tearing each other, dying
    In a whirlwind of wings clashing. And I was afraid.
    I began the rites of burnt-offering at the altar,
    But Hephaistos° failed me: instead of bright flame,
    There was only the sputtering slime of the fat thigh-flesh   20
    Melting: the entrails dissolved in gray smoke,
    The bare bone burst from the welter. And no blaze!

---

[22] *king's new woman*   Eidothea, second wife of King Phineus, blinded her stepsons. Their mother, Cleopatra, had been imprisoned in a cave. Phineus was the son of a king, and Cleopatra, his first wife, was the daughter of Boreas, the North wind, but this illustrious ancestry could not protect his sons from violence and darkness.
[25] *Ares*   god of war
[19] *Hephaistos*   god of fire

This was a sign from heaven. My boy described it,
Seeing for me as I see for others.

I tell you, Creon, you yourself have brought   25
This new calamity upon us. Our hearths and altars
Are stained with the corruption of dogs and carrion birds
That glut themselves on the corpse of Oedipus' son.
The gods are deaf when we pray to them, their fire
Recoils from our offering, their birds of omen   30
Have no cry of comfort, for they are gorged
With the thick blood of the dead.
                                        O my son,
These are no trifles! Think: all men make mistakes,
But a good man yields when he knows his course is wrong,
And repairs the evil. The only crime is pride.   35
Give in to the dead man, then: do not fight with a corpse—
What glory is it to kill a man who is dead?
Think, I beg you:
It is for your own good that I speak as I do.
You should be able to yield for your own good.   40
CREON: It seems that prophets have made me their especial
      province.
All my life long
I have been a kind of butt for the dull arrows
Of doddering fortune-tellers
                                  No, Teiresias:
If your birds—if the great eagles of God himself   45
Should carry him stinking bit by bit to heaven,
I would not yield. I am not afraid of pollution:
No man can defile the gods.
                                  Do what you will,
Go into business, make money, speculate
In India gold or that synthetic gold from Sardis,   50
Get rich otherwise than by my consent to bury him.
Teiresias, it is a sorry thing when a wise man
Sells his wisdom, lets out his words for hire!
TEIRESIAS: Ah Creon! Is there no man left in the world—
CREON: To do what?—Come, let's have the aphorism!   55
TEIRESIAS: No man who knows that wisdom outweighs any wealth?
CREON: As surely as bribes are baser than any baseness.
TEIRESIAS: You are sick, Creon! You are deathly sick!
CREON: As you say: it is not my place to challenge a prophet.
TEIRESIAS: Yet you have said my prophecy is for sale.   60
CREON: The generation of prophets has always loved gold.
TEIRESIAS: The generation of kings has always loved brass.

CREON: You forget yourself! You are speaking to your King.

TEIRESIAS: I know it. You are a king because of me.

CREON: You have a certain skill; but you have sold out. 65

TEIRESIAS: King, you will drive me to words that—

CREON: Say them, say them!
Only remember: I will not pay you for them.

TEIRESIAS: No, you will find them too costly.

CREON: No doubt. Speak.
Whatever you say, you will not change my will.

TEIRESIAS: Then take this, and take it to heart! 70
The time is not far off when you shall pay back
Corpse for corpse, flesh of your own flesh.
You have thrust the child of this world into living night,
You have kept from the gods below the child that is theirs:
The one in a grave before her death, the other, 75
Dead, denied the grave. This is your crime:
And the Furies and the dark gods of Hell
Are swift with terrible punishment for you.
Do you want to buy me now, Creon?
Not many days,
And your house will be full of men and women weeping, 80
And curses will be hurled at you from far
Cities grieving for sons unburied, left to rot
Before the walls of Thebes.

These are my arrows, Creon: they are all for you.

(To BOY.*)* But come, child: lead me home. 85
Let him waste his fine anger upon younger men.
Maybe he will learn at last
To control a wiser tongue in a better head. *(Exit* TEIRESIAS.*)*

CHORAGOS: The old man has gone, King, but his words
Remain to plague us. I am old, too, 90
But I cannot remember that he was ever false.

CREON: That is true. . . . It troubles me.
Oh it is hard to give in! but it is worse
To risk everything for stubborn pride.

CHORAGOS: Creon: take my advice.

CREON: What shall I do? 95

CHORAGOS: Go quickly: free Antigonê from her vault
And build a tomb for the body of Polyneicês.

CREON: You would have me do this!

CHORAGOS: Creon, yes!
And it must be done at once: God moves
Swiftly to cancel the folly of stubborn men. 100

CREON: It is hard to deny the heart! But I
    Will do it: I will not fight with destiny.
CHORAGOS: You must go yourself, you cannot leave it to others.
CREON: I will go.—Bring axes, servants: Come with me to the tomb.
               I buried her, I   105
    Will set her free.
                  Oh quickly! My mind misgives—
    The laws of the gods are mighty, and a man must serve them
    To the last day of his life!   *(Exit* CREON.*)*

PAEAN°

CHORAGOS: God of many names   *Strophe 1*
CHORUS: O Iacchos
                         son
    of Kadmeian Sémelê
               O born of the thunder!
    Guardian of the West
              Regent
    of Eleusis' plain
            O Prince of maenad Thebes
    and the Dragon Field by rippling Ismenós:°   5
CHORAGOS: God of many names   *Antistrophe 1*
CHORUS: the flame of torches
    flares on our hills
            the nymphas of Iacchos
    dance at the spring of Castalia:
    from the vine-close mountain
              come ah come in ivy:
    Evohé evohé! sings through the streets of Thebes   10
CHORAGOS: God of many names   *Strophe 2*
CHORUS: Iacchos of Thebes
    heavenly child
           of Sémelê bride of the Thunderer!
    The shadow of plague is upon us:
            come
    with clement feet
           oh come from Parnasos
    down the long slopes
           across the lamenting water   15

Paean a hymn of praise. This paean is dedicated to Iacchos, also known as Dionysos, the son of Zeus and Sémelê, daughter of Kadmos. Iacchos's worshipers were the Maenads, whose cry was *"Evohê evohê."*
5 *Ismenosa* river near Thebes. Kadmos sowed a crop of dragon's teeth near the Ismenos. From these teeth sprang men who were ancestors of Theban nobility.

CHORAGOS: Iô Fire! Chorister of the throbbing stars!   *Antistrophe 2*
    O purest among the voices of the night!
    Thou son of God, blaze for us!
CHORUS: Come with choric rapture of circling Maenads
    Who cry *Iô Iacche!*
                     God of many names!   20

EXODOS

Enter MESSENGER *from left.*

MESSENGER: Men of the line of Kadmos,° you who live
    Near Amphion's citadel,°
                 I cannot say
  Of any condition of human life "This is fixed,
  This is clearly good, or bad." Fate raises up,
  And Fate casts down the happy and unhappy alike: 5
  No man can fortell his Fate.
                Take the case of Creon:
  Creon was happy once, as I count happiness:
  Victorious in battle, sole governor of the land,
  Fortunate father of children nobly born.
  And now it has all gone from him! Who can say   10
  That a man is still alive when his life's joy fails?
  He is a walking dead man. Grant him rich,
  Let him live like a king in his great house:
  If his pleasure is gone, I would not give
  So much as the shadow of smoke for all he owns.   15
CHORAGOS: Your words hint at sorrow: what is your news for us?
MESSENGER: They are dead. The living are guilty of their death.
CHORAGOS: Who is guilty? Who is dead? Speak!
MESSENGER: Haimon.
  Haimon is dead; and the hand that killed him
  Is his own hand.
CHORAGOS: His father's? or his own?   20
MESSENGER: His own, driven mad by the murder his father had done.
CHORAGOS: Teiresias, Teiresias, how clearly you saw it all!
MESSENGER: This is my news: you must draw what conclusions you
    can from it.
CHORAGOS: But look: Eurydicê, our Queen:
  Has she overheard us?   25

Enter EURYDICÊ *from the palace, center.*

---

[1] *Kadmos,*   see notes on page 736. Kadmos founded Thebes.
[3] *Amphion's citadel*   Amphion, a son of Zeus, played such sweet music that stones moved of their own will to form a wall around Thebes.

EURYDICÊ : I have heard something, friends:
          As I was unlocking the gate of Pallas'° shrine,
          For I needed her help today, I heard a voice
          Telling of some new sorrow. And I fainted
          There at the temple with all my maidens about me.   30
          But speak again: whatever it is, I can bear it:
          Grief and I are no strangers.
MESSENGER: Dearest Lady,
          I will tell you plainly all that I have seen.
          I shall not try to comfort you: what is the use,
          Since comfort could lie only in what is not true?   35
          The truth is always best.
                              I went with Creon
          To the outer plain where Polyneicês was lying,
          No friend to pity him, his body shredded by dogs.
          We made our prayers in that place to Hecatê
          And Pluto,° that they would be merciful. And we bathed   40
          The corpse with holy water, and we brought
          Fresh-broken branches to burn what was left of it,
          And upon the urn we heaped up a towering barrow
          Of the earth of his own land.
                              When we were done, we ran
          To the vault where Antigonê lay on her couch of stone.   45
          One of the servants had gone ahead,
          And while he was yet far off he heard a voice
          Grieving within the chamber, and he came back
          And told Creon. And as the King went closer,
          The air was full of wailing, the words lost,   50
          And he begged us to make all haste. "Am I a prophet?"
          He said, weeping, "And must I walk this road,
          The saddest of all that I have gone before?
          My son's voice calls me on. Oh quickly, quickly!
          Look through the crevice there, and tell me   55
          If it is Haimon, or some deception of the gods!"

          We obeyed: and in the cavern's farthest corner
          We saw her lying:
          She had made a noose of her fine linen veil
          And hanged herself. Haimon lay beside her,   60
          His arms about her waist, lamenting her,
          His love lost under ground, crying out
          That his father had stolen her away from him.

---

[27] *Pallas, Pallas Athene* goddess of wisdom
[39-40] *Hecatê/And Pluto* Hecatê and Pluto (also known as Hades) were deities of the underworld.

When Creon saw him the tears rushed to his eyes
And he called to him: "What have you done, child? Speak to me.   65
What are you thinking that makes your eyes so strange?
O my son, my son, I come to you on my knees!"
But Haimon spat in his face. He said not a word,
Staring—
        And suddenly drew his sword
And lunged. Creon shrank back, the blade missed; and the boy,   70
Desperate against himself, drove it half its length
Into his own side, and fell. And as he died
He gathered Antigonê close in his arms again,
Choking, his blood bright red on her white cheek.
And now he lies dead with the dead, and she is his   75
At last, his bride in the house of the dead.

                        Exit EURYDICÊ *into the palace.*

CHORAGOS: She has left us without a word. What can this mean?
MESSENGER: It troubles me, too: yet she knows what is best,
    Her grief is too great for public lamentation,
    And doubtless she has gone to her chamber to weep   80
    For her dead son, leading her maidens in his dirge.

Pause.

CHORAGOS: It may be so: but I fear this deep silence.
MESSENGER: I will see what she is doing. I will go in.

                       Exit MESSENGER *into the palace.*

Enter CREON *with attendants, bearing* HAIMON's *body.*

CHORAGOS: But here is the king himself: oh look at him,
    Bearing his own damnation in his arms.   85
CREON: Nothing you say can touch me any more.
    My own blind heart has brought me
    From darkness to final darkness. Here you see
    The father murdering, the murdered son—
    And all my civic wisdom!   90
    Haimon my son, so young, so young to die,
    I was the fool, not you; and you died for me.
CHORAGOS: That is the truth; but you were late in learning it.
CREON: This truth is hard to bear. Surely a god
    Has crushed me beneath the hugest weight of heaven,   95
    And driven me headlong a barbaric way
    To trample out the thing I held most dear.
    The pains that men will take to come to pain!

Enter MESSENGER *from the palace.*

MESSENGER: The burden you carry in your hands is heavy,
    But it is not all: you will find more in your house.   100

CREON: What burden worse than this shall I find there?

MESSENGER: The Queen is dead.

CREON: O port of death, deaf world,
    Is there no pity for me? And you, Angel of evil,
    I was dead, and your words are death again. 105
    Is it true, boy? Can it be true?
    Is my wife dead? Has death bred death?

MESSENGER: You can see for yourself.

The doors are opened and the body of EURYDICÊ *is disclosed within.*

CREON: Oh pity!
    All true, all true, and more than I can bear! 110
    O my wife, my son!

MESSENGER: She stood before the altar, and her heart
    Welcomed the knife her own hand guided,
    And a great cry burst from her lips for Megareus° dead,
    And for Haimon dead, her sons; and her last breath 115
    Was a curse for their father, the murderer of her sons.
    And she fell, and the dark flowed in through her closing eyes.

CREON: O God, I am sick with fear.
    Are there no swords here? Has no one a blow for me?

MESSENGER: Her curse is upon you for the deaths of both. 120

CREON: It is right that it should be. I alone am guilty.
    I know it, and I say it. Lead me in,
    Quickly, friends.
    I have neither life nor substance. Lead me in.

CHORAGOS: You are right, if there can be right in so much wrong. 125
    The briefest way is best in a world of sorrow.

CREON: Let it come,
    Let death come quickly, and be kind to me.
    I would not ever see the sun again.

CHORAGOS: All that will come when it will; but we, meanwhile, 130
    Have much to do. Leave the future to itself.

CREON: All my heart was in that prayer!

CHORAGOS: Then do not pray any more: the sky is deaf.

CREON: Lead me away. I have been rash and foolish.
    I have killed my son and my wife. 135
    I look for comfort; my comfort lies here dead.
    Whatever my hands have touched has come to nothing.
    Fate has brought all my pride to a thought of dust.

As CREON *is being led into the house, the* CHORAGOS *advances and speaks directly to the audience.*

---

[114] *Megareus* brother of Haimon, had died in the assault on Thebes.

CHORAGOS: There is no happiness where there is no wisdom;
    No wisdom but in submission to the gods.   140
    Big words are always punished,
    And proud men in old age learn to be wise.

QUESTIONS AND CONSIDERATIONS

1. What is the decree of King Creon that is discussed by Antigonê and Ismenê in the Prologue? What position is taken by each sister in response to the decree? How does each defend her position, and what does the position and argumentative style of each sister reveal about her character and values?

2. The role of the chorus in a Greek tragedy provides an important dramatic element of poetry, song, and dance to the play, while clarifying the mythical and theological, historical, and political background against which the central characters play out their conflicts. Discuss how the chorus in *Antigonê* accomplishes such complex aims, pointing out particular speeches and dramatic moments.

3. Discuss Creon's values. Point out particular speeches, such as his initial address and his speeches to Antigonê and Haimon, which embody his values. Does Creon have any of the qualities of a good leader? What makes it difficult for him to be an effective king?

4. Several characters in the play find themselves in conflict with Creon; each of these characters holds a different vision of "law and order" from Creon's. How do characters such as Antigonê, Haimon, the Sentry, and Teiresias take issue with Creon's concept of kingship, power, and law?

5. *Antigonê* is the final play in Sophocles' Theban Trilogy, which begins with *Oedipus Rex*. How does the history of Oedipus' incest, his fall, and his family line form a background that helps to deepen the meaning and the tragedy of the events in *Antigonê*? Does Sophocles suggest that the conflicts and reversals in this play flow inevitably from the events of the earlier plays, or do the characters in *Antigonê* take their positions and make their mistakes as free choices?

6. The ending of the play provides an example of a scene of "recognition," the awareness that Greek dramatists believed was necessary for a full realization of the movement of the tragedy and the evolution of the tragic character's consciousness. What is Creon's recognition in the play? What does he learn from his mistakes? How would you predict his future as a ruler and as a man?

IDEAS FOR WRITING

1. Choose a character from the play whose ideas on law and order you closely identify with. Write an essay in which you present the ideas of this character, using key lines and events from the play to support your analysis. Discuss the reasons why you find yourself in agreement with this character's perspective as well as what you consider to be the limits and flaws in the character's outlook.

2. Develop your journal entry for *Antigonê* into an essay in which you explore a conflict between religious and secular law involved in a contemporary social issue. What is your position on this issue, and why?

The Cuban Swimmer
Milcha Sanchez-Scott

Journal

Write about a time when you felt that your parents, school, or peers were pushing you to excel. Did you resist or go along willingly? Were the effects positive or negative?

CHARACTERS

MARGARITA SUÁREZ *The swimmer.*
EDUARDO SUÁREZ *Her father, the coach.*
SIMÓN SUÁREZ *Her brother.*
AÍDA SUÁREZ *The mother.*
ABUELA *Her grandmother.*
VOICE OF MEL MUNSON
VOICE OF MARY BETH WHITE
VOICE OF RADIO OPERATOR

SETTING

The Pacific Ocean between San Pedro and Catalina Island.

TIME

Summer.

Live conga drums can be used to punctuate the action of the play.

Scene 1

Pacific Ocean. Midday. On the horizon, in perspective, a small boat enters upstage left, crosses to upstage right, and exits. Pause. Lower on the horizon, the same boat, in larger perspective, enters upstage right, crosses and exits upstage left. Blackout.

Scene 2

Pacific Ocean. Midday. The swimmer, MARGARITA SUÁREZ, *is swimming. On the boat following behind her are her father,* EDUARDO SUÁREZ, *holding a megaphone, and* SIMÓN, *her brother, sitting on top of the cabin with his shirt off, punk sunglasses on, binoculars hanging on his chest.*

EDUARDO *(learning forward, shouting in time to* MARGARITA's *swimming):* **Uno, dos, uno, dos. Y uno, dos** . . . keep your shoulders parallel to the water.

SIMÓN: I'm gonna take these glasses off and look straight into the sun.

EDUARDO *(through megaphone):* *Muy bien, muy bien* . . . but punch those arms in, baby.

SIMÓN *(looking directly at the sun through binoculars):* Come on, come on, zap me. Show me something. *(He looks behind at the shoreline and ahead at the sea.)* Stop! Stop, *Papi!* Stop!

*(*AÍDA SUÁREZ *and* ABUELA, *the swimmer's mother and grandmother, enter running from the back of the boat.)*

AÍDA and ABUELA: *Qué? Qué es?*

AÍDA: *Es un* shark?

EDUARDO: Eh?

ABUELA: *Que es un* shark *dicen?*

*(*EDUARDO *blows whistle.* MARGARITA *looks up at the boat.)*

SIMÓN: No, *Papi*, no shark, no shark. We've reached the halfway mark.

ABUELA *(looking into the water):* *A dónde está?*

AÍDA: It's not in the water.

ABUELA: Oh, no? Oh, no?

AÍDA: No! *A poco* do you think they're gonna have signs in the water to say you are halfway to Santa Catalina? No. It's done very scientific. *A ver, hijo,* explain it to your grandma.

SIMÓN: Well, you see, Abuela— *(He points behind.)* There's San Pedro. *(He points ahead.)* And there's Santa Catalina. Looks halfway to me.

*(*ABUELA *shakes her head and is looking back and forth, trying to make the decision, when suddenly the sound of a helicopter is heard.)*

ABUELA *(looking up):* Virgencita de la Caridad del Cobre. *Qué es eso?*

(Sound of helicopter gets closer. MARGARITA *looks up.)*

MARGARITA: Papi, Papi!

(A small commotion on the boat, with everybody pointing at the helicopter above. Shadows of the helicopter fall on the boat. SIMÓN *looks up at it through binoculars.)*

Papi—qué es? What is it?

EDUARDO *(through megaphone):* Uh . . . uh . . . uh, *un momentico* . . . *mi hija.* . . . Your *papi's* got everything under control, understand? Uh . . . you just keep stroking. And stay . . . uh . . . close to the boat.

SIMÓN: Wow, *Papi!* We're on TV, man! Holy Christ, we're all over the fucking U.S.A.! It's Mel Munson and Mary Beth White!

AÍDA: *Por Dios!* Simón, don't swear. And put on your shirt.

*(*AÍDA *fluffs her hair, puts on her sunglasses and waves to the helicopter.* SIMÓN *leans over the side of the boat and yells to* MARGARITA.*)*

SIMÓN: Yo, Margo! You're on TV, man.

EDUARDO: Leave your sister alone. Turn on the radio.

MARGARITA: *Papi! Qué está pasando?*

ABUELA: *Que es la televisión dicen? (She shakes her head.) Porque como yo no puedo ver nada sin mis espejuelos.*

(ABUELA rummages through the boat, looking for her glasses. Voices of MEL MUNSON *and* MARY BETH WHITE *are heard over the boat's radio.)*

MEL'S VOICE: As we take a closer look at the gallant crew of *La Havana* . . . and there . . . yes, there she is . . . the little Cuban swimmer from Long Beach, California, nineteen-year-old Margarita Suárez. The unknown swimmer is our Cinderella entry . . . a bundle of tenacity, battling her way through the choppy, murky waters of the cold Pacific to reach the Island of Romance . . . Santa Catalina . . . where should she be the first to arrive, two thousand dollars and a gold cup will be waiting for her.

AÍDA: Doesn't even cover our expenses.

ABUELA: *Qué dice?*

EDUARDO: Shhhh!

MARY BETH'S VOICE: This is really a family effort, Mel, and—

MEL'S VOICE: Indeed it is. Her trainer, her coach, her mentor, is her father, Eduardo Suárez. Not a swimmer himself, it says here, Mr. Suárez is head usher of the Holy Name Society and the owner-operator of Suárez Treasures of the Sea and Salvage Yard. I guess it's one of those places—

MARY BETH'S VOICE: If I might interject a fact here, Mel, assisting in this swim is Mrs. Suárez, who is a former Miss Cuba.

MEL'S VOICE: And a beautiful woman in her own right. Let's try and get a closer look.

(Helicopter sound gets louder. MARGARITA, *frightened, looks up again.)*

MARGARITA: *Papi!*

EDUARDO *(through megaphone): Mi hija,* don't get nervous . . . it's the press. I'm handling it.

AÍDA: I see how you're handling it.

EDUARDO *(through megaphone):* Do you hear? Everything is under control. Get back into your rhythm. Keep your elbows high and kick and kick and kick and kick . . .

ABUELA *(finds her glasses and puts them on): Ay sí, es la televisión* . . . *(She points to helicopter.) Qué lindo mira* . . . *(She fluffs her hair, gives a big wave.) Aló América! Viva mi Margarita, viva todo los Cubanos en los Estados Unidos!*

AÍDA: *Ay por Dios,* Cecilia, the man didn't come all this way in his helicopter to look at you jumping up and down, making a fool of yourself.

ABUELA: I don't care. I'm proud.

AÍDA: He can't understand you anyway.

ABUELA: *Viva* . . . *(She stops.) Simón, comó se dice viva?*

SIMÓN: Hurray.

ABUELA: Hurray for *mi Margarita y* for all the Cubans living *en* the United States, *y un abrazo* . . . *Simón, abrazo* . . .

SIMÓN: A big hug.

ABUELA: *Sí,* a big hug to all my friends in Miami, Long Beach, Union City, except for my son Carlos, who lives in New York in sin! He lives . . . *(She crosses herself.)* in Brooklyn with a Puerto Rican woman in sin! *No decente* . . .

SIMÓN: Decent.

ABUELA: Carlos, *no decente.* This family, *decente.*

AÍDA: Cecilia, *por Dios.*

MEL'S VOICE: Look at that enthusiasm. The whole family has turned out to cheer little Margarita on to victory! I hope they won't be too disappointed.

MARY BETH'S VOICE: She seems to be making good time, Mel.

MEL'S VOICE: Yes, it takes all kinds to make a race. And it's a testimonial to the all-encompassing fairness . . , the greatness of this, the Wrigley Invitational Women's Swim to Catalina, where among all the professionals there is still room for the amateurs . . . like these, the simple people we see below us on the ragtag *La Havana,* taking their long-shot chance to victory. *Vaya con Dios!*

(Helicopter sound fading as family, including MARGARITA, *watch silently. Static as* SIMÓN *turns radio off.* EDUARDO *walks to bow of boat, looks out on the horizon.)*

EDUARDO *(to himself):* Amateurs.

AÍDA: Eduardo, that person insulted us. Did you hear, Eduardo? That he called us a simple people in a ragtag boat? Did you hear . . . ?

ABUELA *(clenching her fist at departing helicopter):* *Mal-Rayo los parta!*

SIMÓN *(same gesture):* Asshole!

*(*AÍDA *follows* EDUARDO *as he goes to side of boat and stares at* MARGARITA.*)*

AÍDA: This person comes in his helicopter to insult your wife, your family, your daughter . . .

MARGARITA *(pops her head out of the water):* *Papi?*

AÍDA: Do you hear me, Eduardo? I am not simple.

ABUELA: *Sí.*

AÍDA: I am complicated.

ABUELA: *Sí, demasiada complicada.*

AÍDA: Me and my family are not so simple.

SIMÓN: Mom, the guy's an asshole.

ABUELA *(shaking her fist at helicopter):* Asshole!

AÍDA: If my daughter was simple, she would not be in that water swimming.

MARGARITA: Simple? *Papi . . . ?*

AÍDA: *Ahora,* Eduardo, this is what I want you to do. When we get to Santa Catalina, I want you to call the TV station and demand an apology.

EDUARDO: *Cállete mujer! Aquí mando yo.* I will decide what is to be done.

MARGARITA: *Papi,* tell me what's going on.

EDUARDO: Do you understand what I am saying to you, Aída?

SIMÓN *(leaning over side of boat, to* MARGARITA*):* Yo Margo! You know that Mel Munson guy on TV? He called you a simple amateur and said you didn't have a chance.

ABUELA *(leaning directly behind* SIMÓN*):* *Mi hija, insultó a la familia. Desgraciado!*

AÍDA *(leaning in behind* ABUELA*):* He called us peasants! And your father is not doing anything about it. He just knows how to yell at me.

EDUARDO *(through megaphone):* Shut up! All of you! Do you want to break her concentration? Is that what you are after? Eh?

(ABUELA, AÍDA and SIMÓN *shrink back.* EDUARDO *paces before them.)*

>Swimming is rhythm and concentration. You win a race *aquí. (Pointing to his head.)* Now . . . *(To* SIMÓN.*)* you, take care of the boat, Aída y *Mama* . . . do something. Anything. Something practical.

(ABUELA and AÍDA *get on knees and pray in Spanish.)*

>Hija, give it everything, eh? . . . *por la familia. Uno . . . dos.* . . . You must win.

*(*SIMÓN *goes into cabin. The prayers continue as lights change to indicate bright sunlight, later in the afternoon.)*

Scene 3

Tableau for a couple of beats. EDUARDO *on bow with timer in one hand as he counts strokes per minute.* SIMÓN *is in the cabin steering, wearing his sunglasses, baseball cap on backward.* ABUELA *and* AÍDA *are at the side of the boat, heads down, hands folded, still muttering prayers in Spanish.*

AÍDA and ABUELA *(crossing themselves): En el nombre del Padre, del Hijo y del Espíritu Santo amén.*

EDUARDO *(through megaphone):* You're stroking seventy-two!

SIMÓN *(singing):* Mama's stroking, Mama's stroking seventy-two. . . .

EDUARDO *(through megaphone):* You comfortable with it?

SIMÓN *(singing):* Seventy-two, seventy-two, seventy-two for you.

AÍDA *(looking at the heavens): Ay,* Eduardo, *ven acá,* we should be grateful that *Nuestro Señor* gave us such a beautiful day.

ABUELA *(crosses herself): Sí, gracias a Dios.*

EDUARDO: She's stroking seventy-two, with no problem *(He throws a kiss to the sky.)* It's a beautiful day to win.

AÍDA: *Qué hermoso!* So clear and bright. Not a cloud in the sky. *Mira! Mira!* Even rainbows on the water . . . a sign from God.

SIMÓN *(singing):* Rainbows on the water . . . you in my arms . . .

ABUELA and EDUARDO *(looking the wrong way): Dónde?*

AÍDA *(pointing toward* MARGARITA*):* There, dancing in front of Margarita, leading her on . . .

EDUARDO: Rainbows on . . . *Ay coño!* It's an oil slick! You . . . you . . . *(To* SIMÓN.*)* Stop the boat. *(Runs to bow, yelling.)* Margarita! Margarita!

(On the next stroke, MARGARITA *comes up all covered in black oil.)*

MARGARITA: *Papi! Papi . . . !*

(Everybody goes to the side and stares at MARGARITA, *who stares back.* EDUARDO *freezes.)*

AÍDA: *Apúrate,* Eduardo, move . . . what's wrong with you . . . *no me oíste,* get my daughter out of the water.

EDUARDO *(softly):* We can't touch her. If we touch her, she's disqualified.

AÍDA: But I'm her mother.

EDUARDO: Not even by her own mother. Especially by her own mother. . . .

You always want the rules to be different for you, you always want to be the exception. *(To* SIMÓN.*)* And you . . . you didn't see it, eh? You were playing again?

SIMÓN: *Papi,* I was watching . . .

AÍDA *(interrupting):* *Pues,* do something Eduardo. You are the big coach, the monitor.

SIMÓN: Mentor! Mentor!

EDUARDO: How can a person think around you? *(He walks off to bow, puts head in hands.)*

ABUELA *(looking over side):* *Mira como todos los* little birds are dead. *(She crosses herself.)*

AÍDA: Their little wings are glued to their sides.

SIMÓN: Christ, this is like the La Brea tar pits.

AÍDA: They can't move their little wings.

ABUELA: *Esa niña tiene que moverse.*

SIMÓN: Yeah, Margo, you gotta move, man.

*(*ABUELA *and* SIMÓN *gesture for* MARGARITA *to move.* AÍDA *gestures for her to swim.)*

ABUELA: *Anda niña, muévete.*

AÍDA: Swim, *hija,* swim or the *aceite* will stick to your wings.

MARGARITA: *Papi?*

ABUELA *(taking megaphone):* Your *papi* say "move it!"

*(*MARGARITA *with difficulty starts moving.)*

ABUELA, AÍDA and SIMÓN *(laboriously counting):* *Uno, dos . . . uno, dos . . . anda . . . uno, dos.*

EDUARDO *(running to take megaphone from* ABUELA*):* *Uno, dos . . .*

*(*SIMÓN *races into cabin and starts the engine.* ABUELA, AÍDA *and* EDUARDO *count together.)*

SIMÓN *(looking ahead):* *Papi,* it's over there!

EDUARDO: Eh?

SIMÓN *(pointing ahead and to the right):* It's getting clearer over there.

EDUARDO *(through megaphone):* Now pay attention to me. Go to the right.

*(*SIMÓN, ABUELA, AÍDA *and* EDUARDO *all lean over side. They point ahead and to the right, except* ABUELA, *who points to the left.)*

FAMILY *(Shouting together):* *Para yá! Para yá!*

(Lights go down on boat. A special light on MARGARITA, *swimming through the oil, and on* ABUELA, *watching her.)*

ABUELA: *Sangre de mi sangre,* you will be another to save us. En Bolondron, where your great-grandmother Luz Suárez was born, they say one day it rained blood. All the people, they run into their houses. They cry, they pray, *pero* your great-grandmother Luz she had cojones like a man. She run outside. She look straight at the sky. She shake her fist. And she say to the evil one, "Mira . . . *(Beating her chest.) coño, Diablo, aquí estoy si me quieres."* And she open her mouth, and she drunk the blood.

Blackout.

Scene 4

Lights up on boat. AÍDA *and* EDUARDO *are on deck watching* MARGARITA *swim. We hear the gentle, rhythmic lap, lap, lap of the water, then the sound of inhaling and exhaling as* MARGARITA's *breathing becomes louder. Then* MARGARITA's *heartbeat is heard, with the lapping of the water and the breathing under it. These sounds continue beneath the dialogue to the end of the scene.*

AÍDA: *Dios mío.* Look how she moves through the water. . . .

EDUARDO: You see, it's very simple. It is a matter of concentration.

AÍDA: The first time I put her in water she came to life, she grew before my eyes. She moved, she smiled, she loved it more than me. She didn't want my breast any longer. She wanted the water.

EDUARDO: And of course, the rhythm. The rhythm takes away the pain and helps the concentration.

(Pause. AÍDA *and* EDUARDO *watch* MARGARITA.*)*

AÍDA: Is that my child or a seal. . . .

EDUARDO: Ah, a seal, the reason for that is that she's keeping her arms very close to her body. She cups her hands, and then she reaches and digs, reaches and digs.

AÍDA: To think that a daughter of mine . . .

EDUARDO: It's the training, the hours in the water. I used to tie weights around her little wrists and ankles.

AÍDA: A spirit, an ocean spirit, must have entered my body when I was carrying her.

EDUARDO *(to* MARGARITA*):* Your stroke is slowing down.

(Pause. We hear MARGARITA's *heartbeat with the breathing under, faster now.)*

AÍDA: Eduardo, that night, the night on the boat . . .

EDUARDO: Ah, the night on the boat again . . . the moon was . . .

AÍDA: The moon was full. We were coming to America. . . . *Qué romantico.*

(Heartbeat and breathing continue.)

EDUARDO: We were cold, afraid, with no money, and on top of everything, you were hysterical, yelling at me, tearing at me with your nails. *(Opens his shirt, points to the base of his neck.)* Look, I still bear the scars . . . telling me that I didn't know what I was doing . . . saying that we were going to die. . . .

AÍDA: You took me, you stole me from my home . . . you didn't give me a chance to prepare. You just said we have to go now, now! Now, you said. You didn't let me take anything. I left everything behind. . . . I left everything behind.

EDUARDO: Saying that I wasn't good enough, that your father didn't raise you so that I could drown you in the sea.

AÍDA: You didn't let me say even a good-bye. You took me, you stole me, you tore me from my home.

EDUARDO: I took you so we could be married.

AÍDA: That was in Miami. But that night on the boat, Eduardo. . . . We were not married, that night on the boat.

EDUARDO: *No pasó nada!* Once and for all get it out of your head, it was cold, you hated me, and we were afraid. . . .

AÍDA: *Mentiroso!*

EDUARDO: A man can't do it when he is afraid.

AÍDA: Liar! You did it very well.

EDUARDO: I did?

AÍDA: *Sí.* Gentle. You were so gentle and then strong . . . my passion for you so deep. Standing next to you . . . I would ache . . . looking at your hands I would forget to breathe, you were irresistible.

EDUARDO: I was?

AÍDA: You took me into your arms, you touched my face with your fingertips . . . you kissed my eyes . . . *la esquina de la boca y . . .*

EDUARDO: *Sí, sí,* and then . . .

AÍDA: I look at your face on top of mine, and I see the lights of Havana in your eyes. That's when you seduced me.

EDUARDO: Shhh, they're gonna hear you.

(Lights go down. Special on AÍDA.*)*

AÍDA: That was the night. A woman doesn't forget those things . . . and later that night was the dream . . . the dream of a big country with fields of fertile land and big, giant things growing. And there by a green, slimy pond I found a giant pea pod and when I opened it, it was full of little, tiny baby frogs.

*(*AÍDA *crosses herself as she watches* MARGARITA. *We hear louder breathing and heartbeat.)*

MARGARITA: Santa Teresa. Little Flower of God, pray for me. San Martín de Porres, pray for me. Santa Rosa de Lima, *Virgencita de la Caridad del Cobre,* pray for me. . . . Mother pray for me.

Scene 5

Loud howling of wind is heard, as lights change to indicate unstable weather, fog and mist. FAMILY *on deck, braced and huddled against the wind.* SIMÓN *is at the helm.*

AÍDA: *Ay Dios mío, qué viento.*

EDUARDO *(through megaphone):* Don't drift out . . . that wind is pushing you out. *(To* SIMÓN.*)* You! Slow down. Can't you see your sister is drifting out?

SIMÓN: It's the wind, *Papi.*

AÍDA: Baby, don't go so far. . . .

ABUELA *(to heaven):* *Ay Gran Poder de Dios, quita este maldito viento.*

SIMÓN: Margo! Margo! Stay close to the boat.

EDUARDO: Dig in. Dig in hard. . . . Reach down from your guts and dig in.

ABUELA *(to heaven):* *Ay Virgen de la Caridad del Cobre, por lo más tú quieres a pararla.*

AÍDA *(Putting her hand out, reaching for* MARGARITA*)*: **Baby, don't go far.**

*(*ABUELA *crosses herself. Action freezes. Lights get dimmer, special on* MARGARITA. *She keeps swimming, stops, starts again, stops, then, finally exhausted, stops altogether. The boat stops moving.)*

EDUARDO: **What's going on here? Why are we stopping?**

SIMÓN: *Papi,* **she's not moving! Yo Margo!**

(The FAMILY *all run to the side.)*

EDUARDO: *Hija!* . . . *Hijita!* **You're tired, eh?**

AÍDA: *Por supuesto* **she's tired. I like to see you get in the water, waving your arms and legs from San Pedro to Santa Catalina. A person isn't a machine, a person has to rest.**

SIMÓN: **Yo, Mama! Cool out, it ain't fucking brain surgery.**

EDUARDO *(to* SIMÓN*)*: **Shut up, you.** *(Louder to* MARGARITA.*)* **I guess your mother's right for once, huh? . . . I guess you had to stop, eh? . . . Give your brother, the idiot . . . a chance to catch up with you.**

SIMÓN *(clowning like Mortimer Snerd)*: **Dum dee dum dee dum ooops, ah shucks . . .**

EDUARDO: **I don't think he's Cuban.**

SIMÓN *(like Ricky Ricardo)*: *Oye,* **Lucy! I'm home! Ba ba lu!**

EDUARDO *(joins in clowning, grabbing* SIMÓN *in a headlock)*: **What am I gonna do with this idiot, eh? I don't understand this idiot. He's not like us, Margarita.** *(Laughing.)* **You think if we put him into your bathing suit with a cap on his head . . .** *(He laughs hysterically.)* **You think anyone would know . . . huh? Do you think anyone would know?** *(Laughs.)*

SIMÓN *(vamping)*: **Ay,** *mi amor.* **Anybody looking for tits would know.**

*(*EDUARDO *slaps* SIMÓN *across the face, knocking him down.* AÍDA *runs to* SIMÓN's *aid.* ABUELA *holds* EDUARDO *back.)*

MARGARITA: *Mía culpa! Mía culpa!*

ABUELA: *Qué dices hija?*

MARGARITA: *Papi,* **it's my fault, it's all my fault. . . . I'm so cold, I can't move. . . . I put my face in the water . . . and I hear them whispering . . . laughing at me. . . .**

AÍDA: **Who is laughing at you?**

MARGARITA: **The fish are all biting me . . . they hate me . . . they whisper about me. She can't swim, they say. She can't glide. She has no grace. . . . Yellowtails, bonita, tuna, man-o'-war, snub-nose sharks,** *los baracudas* **. . . they all hate me . . . only the dolphins care . . . and sometimes I hear the whales crying . . . she is lost, she is dead. I'm so numb, I can't feel.** *Papi! Papi!* **Am I dead?**

EDUARDO: *Vamos,* **baby, punch those arms in. Come on . . . do you hear me?**

MARGARITA: *Papi* . . . *Papi* . . . **forgive me. . . .**

(All is silent on the boat. EDUARDO *drops his megaphone, his head bent down in dejection.* ABUELA, AÍDA, SIMÓN, *all leaning over the side of the boat.* SIMÓN *slowly walks away.)*

AÍDA: *Mi hija, qué tienes?*

SIMÓN: Oh, Christ, don't make her say it. Please don't make her say it.

ABUELA: Say what? *Qué cosa?*

SIMÓN: She wants to quit, can't you see she's had enough?

ABUELA: *Mira, para eso. Esta niña* is turning blue.

AÍDA: *Oyeme, mi hija.* Do you want to come out of the water?

MARGARITA: *Papi?*

SIMÓN *(to* EDUARDO*):* She won't come out until *you* tell her.

AÍDA: Eduardo . . . answer your daughter.

EDUARDO: *Le dije* to concentrate . . . concentrate on your rhythm. Then the rhythm would carry her . . . ay, it's a beautiful thing, Aída. It's like yoga, like meditation, the mind over matter . . . the mind controlling the body . . . that's how the great things in the world have been done. I wish you . . . I wish my wife could understand.

MARGARITA: *Papi?*

SIMÓN *(to* MARGARITA*):* Forget him.

AÍDA *(imploring):* Eduardo, *por favor.*

EDUARDO *(walking in circles):* Why didn't you let her concentrate? Don't you understand, the concentration, the rhythm is everything. But no, you wouldn't listen. *(Screaming to the ocean.)* Goddamn Cubans, why, God, why do you make us go everywhere with our families? *(He goes to back of boat.)*

AÍDA *(opening her arms):* *Mi hija, ven,* come to *Mami. (Rocking.)* Your *mami* knows.

*(*ABUELA *has taken the training bottle, puts it in a net. She and* SIMÓN *lower it to* MARGARITA*.)*

SIMÓN: Take this. Drink it. *(As* MARGARITA *drinks,* ABUELA *crosses herself.)*

ABUELA: *Sangre de mi sangre.*

(Music comes up softly. MARGARITA *drinks, gives the bottle back, stretches out her arms, as if on a cross. Floats on her back. She begins a graceful backstroke. Lights fade on boat as special lights come up on* MARGARITA. *She stops. Slowly turns over and starts to swim, gradually picking up speed. Suddenly as if in pain she stops, tries again, then stops in pain again. She becomes disoriented and falls to the bottom of the sea. Special on* MARGARITA *at the bottom of the sea.)*

MARGARITA: *Ya no puedo* . . . I can't . . . A person isn't a machine . . . *es mi culpa* . . . Father forgive me . . . *Papi! Papi!* One, two. *Uno, dos. (Pause.) Papi! A dónde estás? (Pause.)* One, two, one, two. *Papi! Ay, Papi!* Where are you . . . ? Don't leave me. . . . Why don't you answer me? *(Pause. She starts to swim, slowly.) Uno, dos, uno, dos.* Dig in, dig in. *(Stops swimming.) Por favor, Papi! (Starts to swim again.)* One, two, one, two. Kick from your hip, kick from your hip. *(Stops swimming. Starts to cry.)* Oh God, please. . . . *(Pause.)* Hail Mary, full of grace . . . dig in, dig in . . . the Lord is with thee. . . . *(She swims to the rhythm of her Hail Mary.)* Hail Mary, full of grace . . . dig in, dig in . . . the Lord is with thee . . . dig in, dig in. . . . Blessed art thou among women. . . . *Mami,* it hurts. You let go of my hand. I'm lost. . . . And blessed is the fruit of thy womb, now and at the hour of our death. Amen. I don't want to die, I don't want to die.

*(*MARGARITA *is still swimming. Blackout. She is gone.)*

Scene 6

Lights up on boat, we hear radio static. There is a heavy mist. On deck we see only black outline of ABUELA *with shawl over her head. We hear the voices of* EDUARDO, AÍDA, *and* RADIO OPERATOR.

EDUARDO'S VOICE: La Havana! Coming from San Pedro. Over.

RADIO OPERATOR'S VOICE: Right, DT6-6, you say you've lost a swimmer.

AÍDA'S VOICE: Our child, our only daughter . . . listen to me. Her name is Margarita Inez Suárez, she is wearing a black one-piece bathing suit cut high in the legs with a white racing stripe down the sides, a white bathing cap with goggles and her whole body covered with a . . . with a . . .

EDUARDO'S VOICE: With lanolin and paraffin.

AÍDA'S VOICE: *Sí . . . con lanolin and paraffin.*

(More radio static. Special on SIMÓN, *on the edge of the boat.)*

SIMÓN: Margo! Yo Margo! *(Pause.)* Man don't do this. *(Pause.)* Come on. . . . Come on. . . . *(Pause.)* God, why does everything have to be so hard? *(Pause.)* Stupid. You know you're not supposed to die for this. Stupid. It's his dream and he can't even swim. *(Pause.)* Punch those arms in. Come home. Come home. I'm your little brother. Don't forget what Mama said. You're not supposed to leave me behind. *Vamos,* Margarita, take your little brother, hold his hand tight when you cross the street. He's so little. *(Pause.)* Oh, Christ, give us a sign. . . . I know! I know! Margo, I'll send you a message . . . like mental telepathy. I'll hold my breath, close my eyes, and I'll bring you home. *(He takes a deep breath; a few beats.)* This time I'll beep . . . I'll send out sonar signals like a dolphin. *(He imitates dolphin sounds.)*

(The sound of real dolphins takes over from SIMÓN, *then fades into sound of* ABUELA *saying the Hail Mary in Spanish, as full lights come up slowly.)*

Scene 7

EDUARDO *coming out of cabin, sobbing,* AÍDA *holding him.* SIMÓN *anxiously scanning the horizon.* ABUELA *looking calmly ahead.*

EDUARDO: *Es mi culpa, sí, es mi culpa. (He hits his chest.)*

AÍDA: *Ya, ya viejo . . .* it was my sin . . . I left my home.

EDUARDO: Forgive me, forgive me. I've lost our daughter, our sister, our granddaughter, *mi carne, mi sangre, mis ilusiones. (To heaven.) Dios mío,* take me . . . take me, I say . . . Goddammit, take me!

SIMÓN: I'm going in.

AÍDA and EDUARDO: No!

EDUARDO *(grabbing and holding* SIMÓN, *speaking to heaven):* God, take me, not my children. They are my dreams, my illusions . . . and not this one, this one is my mystery . . . he has my secret dreams. In him are the parts of me I cannot see.

(EDUARDO embraces SIMÓN. *Radio static becomes louder.)*

AÍDA: I . . . I think I see her.

SIMÓN: No, it's just a seal.

ABUELA (*looking out with binoculars*): ***Mi nietacita, dónde estás?*** (*She feels her heart.*) I don't feel the knife in my heart . . . my little fish is not lost.

(*Radio crackles with static. As lights dim on boat,* VOICES OF MEL *and* MARY BETH *are heard over the radio.*)

MEL'S VOICE: Tragedy has marred the face of the Wrigley Invitational Women's Race to Catalina. The Cuban swimmer, little Margarita Suárez, has reportedly been lost at sea. Coast Guard and divers are looking for her as we speak. Yet in spite of this tragedy the race must go on because . . .

MARY BETH'S VOICE (*interrupting loudly*): Mel!

MEL'S VOICE (*startled*): What!

MARY BETH'S VOICE: Ah . . . excuse me, Mel . . . we have a winner. We've just received word from Catalina that one of the swimmers is just fifty yards from the breakers . . . it's, oh, it's . . . Margarita Suárez!

(*Special on* FAMILY *in cabin listening to radio.*)

MEL'S VOICE: What? I thought she died!

(*Special on* MARGARITA, *taking off bathing cap, trophy in hand, walking on the water.*)

MARY BETH'S VOICE: Ahh . . . unless . . . unless this is a tragic . . . No . . . there she is, Mel. Margarita Suárez! The only one in the race wearing a black bathing suit cut high in the legs with a racing stripe down the side.

(FAMILY *cheering, embracing.*)

SIMÓN (*screaming*): Way to go, Margo!

MEL'S VOICE: This is indeed a miracle! It's a resurrection! Margarita Suárez, with a flotilla of boats to meet her, is now walking on the waters, through the breakers . . . onto the beach, with crowds of people cheering her on. What a jubilation! This is a miracle!

(*Sound of crowds cheering. Lights and cheering sounds fade.*)

Blackout.

QUESTIONS AND CONSIDERATIONS

1. What are the attitudes of the various members of the Suárez family toward the swimmer, Margarita? Which members of the family seem most sympathetic with her struggle? Which seem most inclined to want to push her beyond her limits or to treat her in a dehumanized way?

2. Margarita, the "heroine" of the play, has very few lines and generally asks questions of her family rather than making statements. Do you think that Margarita is capable of taking charge of her life? Does she seem to enjoy her struggle or to be personally involved with it?

3. How do the act of swimming, the ocean, and the image of the boat correspond symbolically to the struggles of immigrants in America and to Cubans in particular? What symbols might be used to represent the struggle to succeed of a different immigrant group, such as Asians or the Irish?

4. What social values are represented by the announcers, Mel and Mary Beth, and the contest which they promote, the Wrigley Invitational Women's Swim to Catalina? How do the concerns of the announcers differ from those of Margarita's family?

5. Comment on the ending of the play—the seeming death, resurrection, and victory of Margarita, who leaves the ocean "walking on the water." What will her future be in relation to her family and to herself as an individual? How does the play evaluate her accomplishment?

6. *The Cuban Swimmer* is an experimental, multimedia play that would be difficult to stage. What problems would be encountered in attempting to produce and stage this drama? How would elements of lighting, film, and audiotape need to be integrated into the production in order for it to be dramatically effective?

IDEAS FOR WRITING

1. Write a review of *The Cuban Swimmer* for a community newspaper, commenting on your response to the script. Would you recommend this play to your readers? Why or why not?

2. Write an essay in which you argue for or against the tendency of families to push their children to excel in sports or academics in order to bring honor to the family. Do you feel this kind of behavior will help or harm the child?

Student Writing

King's "Letter from Birmingham Jail" Today
Jeremy Taylor

Jeremy Taylor grew up in Willows, a rural community in northern California. His first year at college in the San Francisco Bay area introduced him to many new people, thoughts, and ideas. After reading Martin Luther King, Jr.'s, "Letter from a Birmingham Jail," Jeremy Taylor wrote the following essay to explore the path that race relations and ways of protest have taken since the days of King and the civil rights movement of the 1960s. Specifically, Taylor tries to predict King's reaction to the Rodney King verdict and its violent aftermath. As you read Taylor's essay, notice how he integrates the voice of the original King essay with the voices and rhetoric of today's African Americans. Is Taylor's evidence sufficient to support the general statements he makes about the changes of attitude evident in today's African-American community?

Over the past few years I have consistently preached
that nonviolence demands that the means we use must be
as pure as the ends we seek. I have tried to make
clear that it is wrong to use immoral means to attain
moral ends.

This quotation from Martin Luther King's "Letter from
Birmingham Jail" shows his belief that change must come by
lawful means. Martin Luther King, Jr., would have been appalled
at the outcome of the Rodney King trial, but he would have been
equally appalled at the violent aftermath that engulfed Los
Angeles.

The parallel between Birmingham of King's time and Los
Although King preached about bringing change through nonviolent means and civil disobedience, he was a strong follower
of the law. King stated in his letter that "I would be the first
to advocate obeying just laws." He saw nonviolent protest as a
way to bring about the changing of unjust laws, but he also felt
that just laws were to be obeyed. This is a key factor in trying
to determine what his reaction would have been to the riots
which followed the Rodney King verdict. During the L.A. riots,
laws were non-existent. Crimes of looting, arson, and physical
assault affected the lives of many. Although Martin Luther King,
Jr., would not have approved of this rampant destruction,
brutality, and disregard for law, he would not have been
surprised by the violence that occurred, for as he argues in his
"Letter from Birmingham Jail," "If [the African-American
people's] . . . emotions are not released in nonviolent ways,
they will seek expression through violence; this is not a threat
but a fact of history." King would not have condoned the
violence which followed the L.A riots, but he realized that most
human beings can only be kicked so many times before they will
kick back. This trait of human nature was observed in both the
Birmingham and Los Angeles revolts.

The parallel between Birmingham of King's time and Los
Angeles today is easily drawn. The "white power structure" of
Birmingham, which King attacks in his letter, can be compared
to the white jury which acquitted Rodney King's attackers,
while the demonstrations in Birmingham, although nonviolent,
can be compared to the Los Angeles uprising. This shows that
King would not be blind to the Black community's feeling that
the white power structure had left the people few viable
options.

Although Martin Luther King's advocacy of nonviolent protest
is still seen by many as the best way to bring about change,
aggressive rhetoric and means are becoming more prevalent in our
generation. As rapper Ice-T stated in a recent appearance at
Stanford University,

April 29 was the happiest day of my life. What you saw
in Los Angeles on April 29 was the consequences of the
system's fuck up. I am so proud that people got out
there and made some . . . noise.
                                    (qtd. in Marcus 1)

Ice-T speaks for many African Americans who feel that the
Los Angeles riots were needed to send a message to the general
uninformed public. Los Angeles gang member Randy Strictland
shares this view: "They just kicked us right in the face with
the Rodney King verdict. And we wanted to voice our opinion in
the only way we knew how. And that was to make some noise. It
was the only way people would listen to us" (qtd. in Monroe 38).
     What we are seeing is a transition from a more moderate
generation of African Americans to a generation that will not be
satisfied with the status quo, who are unwilling to wait for
justice. As Angela, a student at Clark Atlanta University stated
in a *Newsweek* interview following the riots, "If we can't have
justice, there's not going to be any peace. . . . It doesn't work.
It does not work" (qtd. in "Race: Our Dilemma Still" 51).
Professionals are seeing the problems and solutions in new ways
too. Norman Amaker, a Loyola University law professor, says that
"African Americans will draw from this[the verdict] the lesson
they've always known. Our lives aren't worth shit" (qtd. in "Race:
Our Dilemma Still" 44).
     Young people everywhere are looking for real change and
more equality. The generational gap was clearly seen at a
gathering for peace and nonviolence at South Central Los
Angeles' First African Methodist Episcopal Church. During the
uprising, while parents sang and prayed that there would be no
more bloodshed, "one young woman stood up and said, 'We can no
longer afford to listen to pretty speeches'" (qtd. in Matthews
34). Although this more aggressive attitude may come as a
surprise to some, listeners to rap music were not caught off
guard; now, due to L.A.'s uprising, people are beginning to take
notice of the violent lyrics of groups such as NWA, Public
Enemy, and Ice-T. After the Rodney King verdict, anger,
frustration, and disbelief were finally vented, not only at the
King verdict, but at the slow progress of overall race
relations.
     Although Martin Luther King, Jr., never would have condoned
this violence, the impact was enormous. The riots brought a new,
intense awareness to the general public. Newspaper headlines and
television reports blared details concerning this monumental
case and its unprecedented aftermath. Suddenly, schools were
sponsoring forums on racial relations, and people started to
scrutinize their own beliefs and examine the underlying issues
that brought about this violence. In another positive
development, leaders representing over 12,000 gang members came

to Los Angeles community gang worker Charles Norman to help in
keeping the peace. "We know it's going to be difficult to sustain
the peace," Norman says. "But it's the answer to a lot of prayers
from mothers, grandmothers, and other folks in the community"
(qtd. in Monroe 37).

What if the riots had not taken place? Would Rodney King's
trial have been forgotten like any other? Would there have been
a second trial, and would any of the police officers involved in
the King beating have been convicted? The destruction and harm
the riots caused were devastating, but perhaps because of them,
important issues that have been repeatedly denied and overlooked
are now being taken seriously.

I hope a social crisis such as the Los Angeles riots never
happens again, but since the the riots did occur, I hope they
will be remembered as a learning experience. Although methods of
expression have changed, the desire is still the same: equality
for all. Hopefully, history will prove the Rodney King trial and
its aftermath a turning point in the road to equal rights for
all. In late February of 1993, just as the civil rights trial of
the accused police officers was beginning in Los Angeles, Ice-T
warned: "Don't believe that America is so intellectual that we
are beyond revolution . . . it can happen anywhere" (qtd. in
Marcus 1).

Let's hope that violence will never again be implemented in
order to achieve change. Although a more aggressive attitude is
beginning to prevail, all of society pays when violence is the
law of the land. In Martin Luther King, Jr.'s, words, "Injustice
anywhere is a threat to justice everywhere."

Works Cited

King, Jr., Martin Luther. "Letter from Birmingham Jail."
    Imagining Worlds. Ed. Marjorie Ford and Jon Ford. New York:
    McGraw-Hill, 1994: 661–674.
Marcus, Lindsey. "Ice-T Warns of Revolution Against System."
    Stanford Daily 22 Feb. 1993: 1.
Matthews, Tom, et al. "The Siege of L.A." *Newsweek* 11 May 1992:
    30–38.
Monroe, Sylvester. "Life in the 'Hood." *Time* 15 June 1992:
    37–38.
"Race: Our Dilemma Still." *Newsweek* 11 May 1992: 44–51.

Connections: Ideas for Discussion and Writing

1. Lorna Dee Cervantes, James Alan McPherson, Martin Espada, and other writers
in this chapter expose struggles in the workplace and the dehumanizing quality of modern work. Write an essay in which you discuss and compare the ideas of several of these
writers about the exploitation of workers.

2. War in the modern world is often seen in literature, as in life, as a destructive and fundamentally pointless enterprise. Compare several of the visions of war and its consequences presented by writers in this chapter. Which of these views is most similar to your own view and experiences of war?

3. Racial differences and misunderstandings can be the source of much inner and public struggle and conflict. Write an essay on the ways in which authors such as Martin Luther King, Jr., James Alan McPherson, and Louise Erdrich reveal the varied dimensions of struggles related to race.

4. Poverty and class division create many conflicts and result in seemingly unending struggles. Compare the way such authors as McPherson, Jordon, Espada, Thiong'o, and Barreca reflect on issues of poverty and class.

5. Many personal and social struggles are related to gender roles and the inequalities between the sexes. Compare several of the selections in this chapter, or elsewhere in the text, that reflect on or exemplify struggles related to gender. What conclusions and advice do you have to offer?

6. The struggle for social change can be intense and exhilarating, as well as dangerous and at times destructive. Compare several of the writings that comment on this aspect of struggle.

NATURAL WORLDS

NATURAL WORLDS

It is the marriage of the soul with Nature that makes the intellect fruitful, and gives
birth to the imagination.
Henry David Thoreau, *Journal*

Nature cares nothing for logic, our human logic: she has her own, which we do not recognize
and do not acknowledge until we are crushed under its wheel.
Ivan Turgenev, *Smoke*

Nature is what we know—
Yet have no art to say—
So impotent Our Wisdom is
To her simplicity.
Emily Dickinson

Much of the most powerful literature—in expository form, in writings based on personal experience, in fictional narratives, and in lyric poetry—grapples with the complexities of the essential connection that people have always felt with nature. Although sometimes people try to dominate or to insulate themselves from nature, every human being is linked to the natural world. Trying to define the human response to nature and to express in language these feelings and attitudes can bring up many issues of controversy and paradox: What is "natural" about nature? What is human-made or cultivated in this world that is so marked by human endeavors?

As we follow our daily routine, we may sometimes think about whether or not it is possible to perceive of the elements of earth, air, water, and fire without

Georgia O'Keeffe, 1887–1986. *Red Canna.* © 1923. Oil on canvas mounted on masonite, 36 × 29⅞". Collection of The University of Arizona Museum of Art, Gift of Oliver James. (50.1.4)

human influences and controls. Our air is polluted by many toxic substances invented by humans in their efforts to improve their lives. Water, an abundant resource, essential to the nourishment of life, is subject to an infinite variety of techniques of channeling, transportation, and marketing. As in the myth of the phoenix rising from its ashes, fire, a wanton, destructive, and creative element in nature, destroys old life so that new vegetation can spring forth from the ashes. Yet fire is seen by human beings as an eternal adversary, to be suffocated or controlled at all costs. The earth itself, the birthplace and tomb of humanity, is often treated as a dangerous enemy, to be monitored carefully. We fear earthquakes, blizzards, hurricanes. We use the earth as our factory for producing crops with powerful chemical fertilizers, elaborate irrigation systems, while we take the fruits of the earth to be sold and distributed to people who have no connection to the land that gave birth to the fruits and vegetables that nourish their bodies.

For centuries scientists, psychologists, and anthropologists have puzzled over our literal and metaphorical relationship to the animal world. Do we have an obligation and a necessity to preserve animal species, or do animals exist to serve us and to be processed as food for our tables? Should we try to "rise above" natural urges, controlling and sublimating our "animal side," our instinctual behavior? In what ways are our unconscious minds dominated by our instinctual drives? Will understanding the animal world help us to understand ourselves better?

As modern town- and city-dwelling human beings, residing in housing complexes and driving automobiles to work each day, how can we relate to nature at all? Can we, like primitive peoples who live in harmony with the land, ever come to find in nature a source of spiritual nourishment, a path to self-understanding and self-acceptance?

Coming from different cultures and reflecting a diversity of values, each of the authors in this chapter defines nature and perceives humankind's relationship with it in a unique way; at the same time, these writers share many common concerns for the planet. Many of the selections in the chapter are critical of modern science's treatment of nature that encourages people to stand apart from nature, to perceive it as existing for humans to experiment upon, use, and "improve." In Nathaniel Hawthorne's story, "Rappaccini's Daughter," the scientist Rappaccini creates a garden full of hybrid plants that poison the air, whereas the speaker in Walt Whitman's poem, "When I Heard the Learn'd Astronomer," wanders away from a classroom lecture to look up in awe at the night sky. In the modern Native American story by Elizabeth Woody, "HomeCooking," science is seen as an attempt to understand nature through a kind of materialist mythology that often fails to grasp nature's mysteries.

Other writers in the chapter voice a respect for the power of nature, emphasizing that people need to develop strategies to survive in a harsh natural environment. Gretel Ehrlich explores this theme in her essay "On Water," as she chronicles the periodic floods and droughts that menace the life of sheep and cattle ranchers in the West. John Synge's powerful play, *Riders to the Sea,* Stephen Crane's classic story of survival, "The Open Boat," and Ray Young Bear's lyric poem, "The Reason Why I Am Afraid . . ." all ask readers to be aware of the unpredictable power of the natural world, to acknowledge the vulnerabilities of human beings to its changes.

Despite the human need to establish some controls over nature in order to survive, many writers feel that people today are re-creating and taming nature in a way that privileges the artificial at the expense of the truly natural. Thoreau's essay "Walking," Wordsworth's poem "The World Is Too Much with Us," Rilke's tragic poem "The Panther," and a number of the other stories and poems included explore the ways in which human culture has succeeded so well at taming and grooming nature that it has lost its power to move people profoundly, to inspire us as the wilderness can.

Whereas some writers see nature as too distant and tame, others continue to draw spiritual insight and revelation from their connections with the natural world. Native American essayist Leslie Marmon Silko, in "Landscape, History, and the Pueblo Imagination," describes a close, reciprocal relationship with nature, as does essayist Loren Eiseley, who experiences a number of powerful natural revelations in "The Judgment of the Birds." Poets Gladys Cardiff in "Pretty Bird," Jorie Graham in "Wanting a Child," and Gerard Manley Hopkins in his devotional poem "The Windhover" each presents a unique view of how nature provides inspiration and spiritual strength.

The selections in this chapter raise crucial issues and significant objections to the current attitudes about the relationship between humans and their natural world. Instead of providing solutions, the writers see nature in memorable ways, relying especially on vivid descriptions, fascinating creatures, and intense moments of revelation to engage readers. As you reflect on the selections that follow, we hope that you will be encouraged to raise further questions and begin to formulate possible solutions to the problems that make it difficult for people to live in harmony with nature. More importantly, we hope that the inspirational qualities of many of the writings will help you to become more closely in touch with the natural world, more appreciative of its wonders.

Folk Tales

The Tiger of Chao-Ch'êng
P'U Sung Ling

Journal

Write about an experience of "taming" or disciplining an animal. How did you feel about this experience, and what did you learn from it?

The following folk tale from seventeenth-century China is included in the popular collection *Strange Tales from a Chinese Studio* by the prolific story teller P'U Sung Ling.

At Chao-ch'êng there lived an old woman more than seventy years of age, who had an only son. One day he went up to the hills and was eaten by a tiger, at which his mother was so overwhelmed with grief that she hardly wished to live. With tears and lamentations she ran and told her story to the magistrate of the place, who laughed and asked her how she thought the law could be brought to bear on a tiger. But the old woman would not be comforted, and at length the magistrate lost his temper and bade her begone. Of this, however, she took no notice; and then the magistrate, in compassion for her great age and unwilling to resort to extremities, promised her that he would have the tiger arrested. Even then she would not go until the warrant had been actually issued; so the magistrate, at a loss what to do, asked his attendants which of them would undertake the job. Upon this one of them, Li Nêng, who happened to be gloriously drunk, stepped forward and said that he would; whereupon the warrant was immediately issued and the old woman went away. When our friend, Li Nêng, got sober, he was sorry for what he had done; but reflecting that the whole thing was a mere trick of his master's to get rid of the old woman's importunities, did not trouble himself much about it, handing in the warrant as if the arrest had been made. 'Not so,' cried the magistrate, 'you said you could do this, and now I shall not let you off.' Li Nêng was at his wits' end, and begged that he might be allowed to impress the hunters of the district. This was conceded; so collecting together these men, he proceeded to spend day and night among the hills in the hope of catching a tiger, and thus making a show of having fulfilled his duty.

A month passed away, during which he received several hundred blows with the bamboo, and at length, in despair, he betook himself to the Ch'êng-huang temple in the eastern suburb, where, falling on his knees, he prayed and wept by turns. By-and-by a tiger walked in, and Li Nêng, in a great fright, thought he was going to be eaten alive. But the tiger took no notice of anything, remaining seated in the doorway. Li Nêng then addressed the animal as follows:—'O tiger, if thou didst slay that old woman's son, suffer me to bind thee with this cord;' and, drawing a rope from his pocket, threw it over the animal's neck. The tiger drooped its ears, and allowing itself to be bound, followed Li Nêng to the magistrate's office. The latter then asked it, saying, 'Did you eat the old woman's son?' to which the tiger replied by nodding its head; whereupon the magistrate rejoined, 'That murderers should suffer death has ever been the law. Besides, this old woman had but one son, and by killing him you took from her the sole support of her declining years. But if now you will be as a son to her, your crime shall be pardoned.' The tiger again nodded assent, and accordingly the magistrate gave orders that he should be released, at which the old woman was highly incensed, thinking that the tiger ought to have paid with its life for the destruction of her son.

Next morning, however, when she opened the door of her cottage, there lay a dead deer before it; and the old woman, by selling the flesh and skin, was able to purchase food. From that day this became a common event, and sometimes the tiger would even bring her money and valuables, so that she became quite rich, and was much better cared for than she had been even by her own son. Consequently, she became very well-disposed to the tiger, which often came and slept in the verandah, remaining for a whole day at a time, and giving no cause of fear either to man or beast. In a few years the old woman died, upon which the tiger walked in and roared its lamentations in the hall. However, with all the money she had saved, she was able to have a splendid funeral; and while her relatives were standing round the grave, out rushed a tiger and sent them all running away in fear. But the tiger merely went up to the mound, and after roaring like a thunder-peal, disappeared again. Then the people of that place built a shrine in honour of the Faithful Tiger, and it remains there to this day.

QUESTIONS AND CONSIDERATIONS

1. Why does Li Nêng pursue and arrest the tiger? Does the tiger's sentence seem just?

2. Describe the relationship that evolves between the old woman and the tiger. Is it equal, harmonious, and reciprocal? Does each seem to have equally strong feelings about the other? Do the two help one another?

3. Why do the townspeople build a shrine to honor the tiger? What has the tiger done to deserve such an honor?

4. What issues do the tiger's crime, his punishment, and his "rehabilitation" raise about the appropriateness of taming animals or holding them to human standards of behavior? What does an animal gain and give up through adjusting itself to human ways?

Journals

From *The Journals*

Ralph Waldo Emerson

July 13. [1833]

I carried my ticket from Mr. Warden to the Cabinet of Natural History in the Garden of Plants. How much finer things are in composition than alone. 'Tis wise in man to make cabinets. When I was come into the Ornithological Chambers I wished I had come only there. The fancy-coloured vests of these elegant beings make me as pensive as the hues and forms of a cabinet of shells, formerly. It is a beautiful collection and makes the visitor as calm and genial as a bridegroom. The limits of the possible are enlarged, and the real is stranger than the imaginary. Some of the birds have a fabulous beauty. One parrot of a fellow called *Psittacus erythropterus* from New Holland deserves as special mention as a picture of Raphael in a gallery. He is the beau of all birds. Then the humming birds, little and gay. Least of all is the *Trochilus Niger.* I have seen beetles larger. The *Trochilus pella* hath such a neck of gold and silver and fire! *Trochilus Delalandi* from Brazil is a glorious little tot, *la mouche magnifique.* Among the birds of Paradise I remarked the *Manucode* or *Paradisea regia* from New Guinea, the *Paradisea Apoda,* and *Paradisea rubra.* Forget not the *Veuve à epaulettes,* or *Emberiza longicauda,* black with fine shoulder-knots; nor the *Ampelis cotinga;* nor the *Phasianus Argus,* a peacock-looking pheasant; nor the *Trogon pavoninus,* called also *Couroncou pavonin.*

I saw black swans and white peacocks; the ibis, the sacred and the rosy; the flamingo, with a neck like a snake; the toucan rightly called *rhinoceros;* and a vulture whom to meet in the wilderness would make your flesh quiver, so like an executioner he looked.

In the other rooms I saw amber containing perfect musquitoes, grand blocks of quartz, native gold in all its forms of crystallization,—threads, plates, crystals, dust; and silver, black as from fire. Ah! said I, this is philanthropy, wisdom, taste,—to form a cabinet of natural history. Many students were there with grammar and note-book, and a class of boys with their tutor from some school.

Here we are impressed with the inexhaustible riches of nature. The universe is a more amazing puzzle than ever, as you glance along this bewildering series of animated forms,—the hazy butterflies, the carved shells, the birds, beasts, fishes, insects, snakes, and the upheaving principle of life everywhere incipient, in the very rock aping organized forms. Not a form so grotesque, so savage, nor so beautiful but is an expression of some property inherent in man the observer,—an occult relation between the very scorpions and man. I feel the centipede in me,—cayman, carp, eagle, and fox. I am moved by strange sympathies; I say continually "I will be a naturalist."

November 2. [1833]

Nature is a language, and every new fact that we learn is a new word; but rightly seen, taken all together, it is not merely a language, but the language put together into a most significant and universal book. I wish to learn the language, not that I may learn a new set of nouns and verbs, but that I may read the great book which is written in that tongue.

From *Notebooks and Papers*

Gerard Manley Hopkins

March 12—A fine sunset: the higher sky dead clear blue bridged by a broad slant causeway rising from right to left of wisped or grass cloud, the wisps lying across; the sundown yellow, moist with light but ending at the top in a foam of delicate white pearling and spotted with big tufts of cloud in colour russet between brown and purple but edged with brassy light. But what I note it all for is this: before I had always taken the sunset and the sun as quite out of gauge with each other, as indeed physically they are for the eye after looking at the sun is blunted to everything else and if you look at the rest of the sunset you must cover the sun, but today I inscaped them together and made the sun the true eye and ace of the whole, as it is. It was all active and tossing out light and started as strongly forward from the field as a long stone or a boss in the knop of the chalice-stem: it is indeed by stalling it so that it falls into scape with the sky.

May 12 Wych-elms not out till today.—The chestnuts down by St. Joseph's were a beautiful sight: each spike had its own pitch, yet each followed in its place in the sweep with a deeper and deeper stoop. When the wind tossed them they plunged and crossed one another without losing their inscape. (Observe that motion multiplies inscape only when inscape is discovered, otherwise it disfigures.)

One day when the bluebells were in bloom I wrote the following. I do not think I have ever seen anything more beautiful than the bluebell I have been looking at. I know the beauty of our Lord by it. It[s inscape] is [mixed of] strength and grace, like an ash [tree]. The head is strongly drawn over [backwards] and arched down like a cutwater [drawing itself back from the line of the keel]. The lines of the bells strike and overlie this, rayed but not symmetrically, some lie parallel. They look steely against [the] paper, the shades lying between the bells and behind the cockled petal-ends and nursing up the precision of their distinctness, the petal-ends themselves being delicately lit. Then there is the straightness of the trumpets in the bells softened by the slight entasis and [by] the square splay of the mouth. One bell, the lowest, some way detached and carried on a longer footstalk, touched out with the tips of the petals an oval / not like the rest in a plane perpendicular to the axis of the bell but a little atilt, and so with [the] square-in-rounding turns of the petals. . . . There is a little drawing of this detached bell.—It looks square-cut in the original

Sept. 24—First saw the Northern Lights. My eye was caught by beams of light and dark very like the crown of horny rays the sun makes behind a cloud. At first I thought of silvery cloud until I saw that these were more luminous and did not dim the clearness of the stars in the Bear. They rose slightly radiating thrown out from the earthline. Then I saw soft pulses of light one after another rise and pass upwards arched in shape but waveringly and with the arch broken. They seemed to float, not following the warp of the sphere as falling stars look to do but free though concentrical with it. This busy working of nature wholly independent of the earth and seeming to go on in a strain of time not reckoned by our reckoning of days and years but simpler and as if correcting the preoccupation of the world by being preoccupied with and appealing to and dated to the day of judgment was like a new witness to God and filled me with delightful fear

From *The Journals*

Gretel Ehrlich

June 19

Watched Ray Hunt work with young colts today. He says: "You have to find the life in the body of the horse. It's a force that either tries to escape or gets redirected in circular shapes. Everything goes in a circle, the world ain't flat, and a wheel moves smoothly. When the horse is smooth you can feel the life going through from the hind end, through the feet, into the mind. When the horse's mind gets congested, when his thoughts get wadded up, when he's acting out of control with no thought for the person—there can be a lot of anguish in this. Watch him. When he begins letting his energy go all the way through, when he begins doing the right thing, the easy thing, then he's at peace with the world and with himself."

June 26

Irrigating the lower place, I smell something sweet and look up to see irises blooming. Planted fifty years ago by the homesteader, they still bloom, untended, with no house or gardener nearby. Amazing, in this harsh place where almost nothing grows, where flowers are stunted by deer, elk, cattle, horses, or by miserable heat or cold. Dream that the lights in a tall Manhattan building going on and off all night are really flowers.

July 1

A wild wind comes up. Rain begins and stops. Now it's just blowing and no rain comes out of it; it's blowing the dryness around, mocking our desert needs, blowing the water out of the creeks, blowing the cows down. My colt bucks in place as if the wind had lifted his hind quarters. The sudden lightness we feel is gravity bucking in a wild wind.

July 2

Flaubert: "What a heavy oar the pen is and what a strong current ideas are to row in."

July 4

Cowcamp. Go to bed in the back of my pickup because the bunkhouses were full. The stars above a lone pine tree look like a Ukiyoe print. A string of clouds passes, shaped like carpenter's tools shaken out across the sky. I feel happy and forlorn.

July 15

Then the days stretch out like single rods
the color of rust, nicked and scored by the various
sexual heats, limbic vines twist and travel, bunching
out in grapes, their green antennae vining my arms,
and all that we know, which, twisted against who
we are, climbs the trellis of the day.

July 17

98° in the shade. A whirling leaf catching the light falls like a cinder.

August 2

"Phillip looked away, as he sometimes looked away from the great pictures where visible forms suddenly become inadequate for the things they have shown to us."—E. M. Forster.

August 5

Rain finally. And then, still unbound, the clatter of cicadas clacking high up in every tree, over the wide square of the lake. The mind dappled by sound. Everything resembles the mind, big and small, or, the mind resembles everything in nature, the diffident, resounding chaos. Feel sick, then hungry, then a fast trip to the outhouse. Lie naked in the sun, then sit up with shirt on. Shoes on, then off, all the while, the green that came as suddenly as a blaze because of the rains, loses its tint as if drought blanched and bleached everything it touched, blades of grass are brown fingers of death pointing. A conference of sedimentologists crawls up and down the dry hills on this once-upon-a-time ocean: David Love, Mary Kraus, David Uhlir all say: each rock, each stratum of soil tells such a deep, unfolding story of how the continent was made. Sitting on the lawn outside the banker's house, Tom Brown says, "Knowledge is an upside-down pyramid, starting at a narrow point and forever expanding . . ."

Go home and watch the moon rise through binoculars. It is more spectacular for its not being quite full, for its imperfection, and Jupiter's tiny moons are like earrings. From this night on, there will be geologists in my life.

Morning. I walk. I don't cry *about* my life, but cry because of its fullness. The road is dry, kiln-dried with the glaze cracked or is it porcelain without a sheen? The birds' flight grows effortless as the drought continues, pulls the drawstring of moisture. In the colorless sky—what is there?—the geologists visit again and I turn groundward from shifting shadows and heats, changing breezes, wafting sounds of another drainage; choke-cherries ripening and the grass dying and the squash growing obscenely large in soil that cradled shallow seas and submitted to ash that fell continuously for ten thousand years. . . .

August 14

Why is my heart racing? I open the window. Have I been holding my breath all my life? Rocks dance. Their jetés are violent upthrusts, unlimbed blunt percussions. I skitter on subduction faults, detachment faults—like Heart Mountain, which moved twice; and down its rock face, red streaks—like the Buddhist's red threads of passion. Night. The back legs of running horses emit sparks; the moonless sky gathers them.

I lie in bed. The day is motionless, or so I think. But the tectonic plates are at odds. In my California home, they crash against each other, the continent moving west and the Pacific plates moving east. Here, granite pushes against sedimentary rock, producing undulations—synclines and anticlines result and rock, big as a mountain, is thrust up, upended.

From *A Country Year*

Winter

Sue Hubbell

A group of people concerned about a proposal to dam the river came over to my place last evening to talk. The first to arrive was my nearest neighbor. He burst excitedly into the cabin, asking me to bring a flashlight and come back to his pickup; he had something to show me. I followed him to his truck, where he took the flashlight and switched it on to reveal a newly killed bobcat stretched out in the bed of his truck. The bobcat was a small one, probably a female. Her broad face was set off by longer hair behind her jaws, and her pointed ears ended in short tufts of fur. Her tawny winter coat, heavy and full, was spotted with black, and her short stubby tail had black bars. Her body was beginning to stiffen in death, and I noticed a small trickle of blood from her nostrils.

"They pay thirty-five dollars a pelt now over at the country seat," my neighbor explained. "That's groceries for next week," he said proudly. None of us back here on the river has much money, and an opportunity to make next week's grocery money was fortunate for him, I knew. "And I guess you'll thank me because that's surely the varmint that's been getting your chickens," he added, for I had said nothing yet.

But I wasn't grateful. I was shocked and sad in a way that my neighbor would not have understood.

I had not heard a shot and didn't see the gun that he usually carries in the rack in his pickup, so I asked him how he had killed her.

"It was just standing there in the headlights when I turned the corner before your place," he said, "so I rammed it with the pickup bumper and knocked it out, and then I got out and finished it off with the tire iron."

His method of killing sounds more savage than it probably was. Animals in slaughterhouses are stunned before they are killed. Once stunned, the important thing was to kill the bobcat quickly, and I am sure my neighbor did so, for he is a practiced hunter.

Others began to arrive at the meeting and took note of the kill. One of them, a trapper, said that the going price of $35 a pelt was a good one. Not many years ago, the pelt price was under $2. Demand for the fur, formerly scorned for its poor quality, was created by a ban on imported cat fur and a continuing market for fur coats and trim.

My neighbor and the trapper are both third-generation Ozarkers. They could have gone away from here after high school, as did many of their classmates, and made easy money in the cities, but they stayed because they love the land. This brings us together in our opposition to damming the river to create a recreational lake, but our sensibilities are different, the product of different personalities and backgrounds. They come from families who have lived off the land from necessity; they have a deep practical knowledge of it and better skills than I have for living here with very little money. The land, the woods and the rivers, and all that are in and on them are resources to be used for those who have the knowledge and skills. They can cut and sell timber, clear the land for pasture, sell the gravel from the river. Ozarkers pick up wild black walnuts and sell them to the food-processing companies that bring hulling machines to town in October. There are fur buyers, too, so they trap animals and sell the pelts. These Ozarkers do not question the happy fact that they are at the top of the food chain, but kill to eat what swims in the river and walks in the woods, and accept as a matter of course that it takes life to maintain life. In this they are more responsible than I am; I buy my meat in neat sanitized packages from the grocery store.

Troubled by this a few years back, I raised a dozen chickens as meat birds, then killed and dressed the lot, but found that killing chicken Number Twelve was no easier than killing chicken Number One. I didn't like taking responsibility for killing my own meat, and went back to buying it at the grocery store. I concluded sourly that righteousness and consistency are not my strong points, since it bothered me not at all to pull a carrot from the garden, an act quite as life-ending as shooting a deer.

I love this land, too, and I was grateful that we could all come together to stop it from being destroyed by an artificial lake. But my aesthetic is a different one, and comes from having lived in places where beauty, plants and animals are gone, so I place a different value on what remains than do my Ozark friends and neighbors. Others at the meeting last night had lived at one time in cities, and shared my prejudices. In our arrogance, we sometimes tell one another that we are taking a longer view. But in the very long run I'm not so sure, and as in most lofty matters, like my failed meat project, I suspect that all our opinions are simply an expression of a personal sense of what is fitting and proper.

Certainly my reaction to seeing the dead bobcat was personal. I knew that bobcat, and she probably knew me somewhat better, for she would have been a more careful observer than I.

Four or five years ago, a man from town told me he had seen a mountain lion on Pigeon Hawk Bluff, the cliffs above the river just to the west of my place. There is a rocky outcropping there, and he had left his car on the road and walked out to it to look at the river two hundred and fifty feet below. He could see a dead turkey lying on a rock shelf, and climbed down to take a closer look. As he reached out to pick up the bird, he was attacked by a mountain lion who came out of a small cave he had not been able to see from above. He showed me the marks along his forearm—scars, he claimed, where the mountain lion had raked him before he could scramble away. There were marks on his arm, to be sure, but I don't know that a mountain lion or any other animal put them there. I suspect that the story was an Ozark stretcher, for the teller, who logs in many hours with the good old boys at the café in town, is a heavy and slow-moving man; it is hard to imagine him climbing nimbly up or down a steep rock face. Nor would I trust his identification of a mountain lion, an animal more talked of at the café than ever seen in this country.

Mountain lions are large, slender, brownish cats with long tails and small rounded ears. This area used to be part of their range, but as men moved in to cut timber and hunt deer, the cats' chief prey, their habitat was destroyed and they retreated to the west and south. Today they are seen regularly in Arkansas, but now and again there are reports of mountain lions in this part of the Ozarks. With the deer population growing, as it has in recent years under the Department of Conservation's supervision, wildlife biologists say that mountain lions will return to rocky and remote places to feed on them.

After the man told me his story, I watched around Pigeon Hawk Bluff on the outside chance that he might really have seen a mountain lion but in the years since I have never spotted one. I did, however, see a bobcat one evening, near the rock outcropping. This part of the Ozarks is still considered a normal part of bobcat range, but they are threatened by the same destruction of habitat that pushed the mountain lion back to wilder places, and they are uncommon.

Bobcats also kill and feed on deer, but for the most part they eat smaller animals: mice, squirrels, opossums, turkey, quail and perhaps some of my chickens. They are night hunters, and seek out caves or other suitable shelters during the day. In breeding season, the females often chose a rocky cliff cave as a den. I never saw the bobcat's den, but it may have been the cave below the lookout point on the road, although that seems a trifle public for a bobcat's taste. The cliff is studded with other caves of many sizes, and most are inaccessible to all but the most sure-footed. I saw the bobcat several times after that, walking silently along the cliff's edge at dusk. Sometimes in the evening I heard the piercing scream of a bobcat from that direction, and once, coming home late at night, I caught her in the road in the pickup's headlight beam. She stood there, blinded, until I switched off the headlights. Then she padded away into the shadows.

That stretch of land along the river, with its thickets, rocky cliffs and no human houses, would make as good a home ground as any for a bobcat. Females are more particular about their five miles or so of territory than are males, who sometimes intrude upon one another's bigger personal ranges, but bobcats all mark their territories and have little contact with other adults during their ten years or so of life.

I don't know for sure that the bobcat I have seen and heard over the past several years was always the same one, but it probably was, and last night probably I saw her dead in the back of my neighbor's pickup truck.

QUESTIONS AND CONSIDERATIONS

1. Nature journals are usually distinguished for their quality of observation. How do Ehrlich, Emerson, and Hopkins observe nature? What physical qualities stand out in nature for each writer? How does each use description to capture the essence of what has been experienced in the natural world? Point out especially moving images and details from each journal.

2. In addition to powers of observation, nature-oriented journals allow writers to reflect philosophically, to place nature within the context of their own beliefs and values. What unique philosophical view of nature is seen in each journal? With which perspective did you find yourself most sympathetic, and why?

3. Each author has a slightly different response to and definition of the beautiful in nature. What unique sense of the beauty of nature is revealed in each journal entry?

4. Both Gretel Ehrlich and Sue Hubbell are concerned about the uses of nature, particularly in terms of the relationship between humans and animals. Compare the different attitudes toward animals and their uses by humans that can be seen in the journals of these two authors.

5. Write an entry for your journal based on a day or a part of a day that you choose to spend in natural surroundings—at a park, a national forest, a garden, or even in your own backyard. Describe your observations and insights about nature and your responses to it. How are your responses to nature different from or similar to those of the journal writers in this chapter?

Fiction

Rappaccini's Daughter
Nathaniel Hawthorne

Journal

Freewrite on the subject of gardens or describe your favorite garden. What associations, personal and cultural, does the word garden have for you? In what ways do you consider a garden a natural place? In what ways do gardens seem artificial?

A young man, named Giovanni Guasconti, came, very long ago, from the more southern region of Italy, to pursue his studies at the University of Padua. Giovanni, who had but a scanty supply of gold ducats in his pocket, took lodgings in a high and gloomy chamber of an old edifice which looked not unworthy to have been the palace of a Paduan noble, and which, in fact, exhibited over its entrance the armorial bearings of a family long since extinct. The young stranger, who was not unstudied in the great poem of his country, recollected that one of the ancestors of this family, and perhaps an occupant of this very mansion, had been pictured by Dante as a partaker of the immortal agonies of his Inferno. These reminiscences and associations, together with the tendency to heartbreak natural to a young man for the first time out of his native sphere, caused Giovanni to sigh heavily as he looked around the desolate and ill-furnished apartment.

"Holy Virgin, signor!" cried old Dame Lisabetta, who, won by the youth's remarkable beauty of person, was kindly endeavoring to give the chamber a habitable air, "what a sigh was that to come out of a young man's heart! Do you find this old mansion gloomy? For the love of Heaven, then, put your head out of the window, and you will see as bright sunshine as you have left in Naples."

Guasconti mechanically did as the old woman advised, but could not quite agree with her that the Paduan sunshine was as cheerful as that of southern Italy. Such as it was, however, it fell upon a garden beneath the window and expended its fostering influences on a variety of plants, which seemed to have been cultivated with exceeding care.

"Does this garden belong to the house?" asked Giovanni.

"Heaven forbid, signor, unless it were fruitful of better pot herbs than any that grow there now," answered old Lisabetta. "No; that garden is cultivated by the own hands of Signor Giacomo Rappaccini, the famous doctor, who, I warrant him, has been heard of as far as Naples. It is said that he distils these plants into medicines that are as potent as a charm. Oftentimes you may see the signor doctor at work, and perchance the signora, his daughter, too, gathering the strange flowers that grow in the garden."

The old woman had now done what she could for the aspect of the chamber; and, commending the young man to the protection of the saints, took her departure.

Giovanni still found no better occupation than to look down into the garden beneath his window. From its appearance, he judged it to be one of those botanic gardens which were of earlier date in Padua than elsewhere in Italy or in the world. Or, not improbably, it might once have been the pleasure-place of an opulent family; for there was the ruin of a marble fountain in the centre, sculptured with rare art, but so woefully shattered that it was impossible to trace the original design from the chaos of remaining fragments. The water, however, continued to gush and sparkle into the sunbeams as cheerfully as ever. A little gurgling sound ascended to the young man's window and made him feel as if the fountain were an immortal spirit, that sung its song unceasingly and without heeding the vicissitudes around it, while one century imbodied it in marble and another scattered the perishable garniture on the soil. All about the pool into which the water subsided grew various plants, that seemed to require a plentiful supply of moisture for the nourishment of gigantic leaves, and, in some instances, flowers gorgeously magnificent. There was one shrub in particular, set in a marble vase in the midst of the pool, that bore a profusion of purple blossoms, each of which had the lustre and richness of a gem; and the whole together made a show so resplendent that it seemed enough to illuminate the garden, even had there been no sunshine. Every portion of the soil was peopled with plants and herbs, which, if less beautiful, still bore tokens of assiduous care, as if all had their individual virtues, known to the scientific mind that fostered them. Some were placed in urns, rich with old carving, and others in common garden pots; some crept serpent-like along the ground or climbed high, using whatever means of ascent was offered them. One plant had wreathed itself round a statue of Vertumnus, which was thus quite veiled and shrouded in a drapery of hanging foliage, so happily arranged that it might have served a sculptor for a study.

While Giovanni stood at the window he heard a rustling behind a screen of leaves, and became aware that a person was at work in the garden. His figure soon emerged into view, and showed itself to be that of no common laborer, but a tall, emaciated, sallow, and sickly-looking man, dressed in a scholar's garb of black. He was beyond the middle term of life, with gray hair, a thin, gray beard, and a face singularly marked with intellect and cultivation, but which could never, even in his more youthful days, have expressed much warmth of heart.

Nothing could exceed the intentness with which this scientific gardener examined every shrub which grew in his path: it seemed as if he was looking into their inmost nature, making observations in regard to their creative essence, and discovering why one leaf grew in this shape and another in that, and wherefore such and such flowers differed among themselves in hue and perfume. Nevertheless, in spite of this deep intelligence on his part, there was no approach to intimacy between himself and these vegetable existences. On the contrary, he avoided their actual touch or the direct inhaling of their odors with a caution that impressed Giovanni most disagreeably; for the man's demeanor was that of one walking among malignant influences, such as savage beasts, or deadly snakes, or evil spirits, which, should he allow them one moment of license, would wreak upon him some terrible fatality. It was strangely frightful to the young man's imagination to see this air of insecurity in a person cultivating a garden, that most simple and innocent of human toils, and which had been alike the joy and labor of the unfallen parents of the race. Was this garden, then, the Eden of the present world? And this man, with such a perception of harm in what his own hands caused to grow,—was he the Adam?

The distrustful gardener, while plucking away the dead leaves or pruning the too luxuriant growth of the shrubs, defended his hands with a pair of thick gloves. Nor were these his only armor. When, in his walk through the garden, he came to the magnificent plant that hung its purple gems beside the marble fountain, he placed a kind of mask over his mouth and nostrils, as if all this beauty did but conceal a deadlier malice; but, finding his task still too dangerous, he drew back, removed the mask, and called loudly, but in the infirm voice of a person affected with inward disease,—

"Beatrice! Beatrice!"

"Here am I, my father. What would you?" cried a rich and youthful voice from the window of the opposite house—a voice as rich as a tropical sunset, and which made Giovanni, though he knew not why, think of deep hues of purple or crimson and of perfumes heavily delectable. "Are you in the garden?"

"Yes, Beatrice," answered the gardener; "and I need your help."

Soon there emerged from under a sculptured portal the figure of a young girl, arrayed with as much richness of taste as the most splendid of the flowers, beautiful as the day, and with a bloom so deep and vivid that one shade more would have been too much. She looked redundant with life, health, and energy; all of which attributes were bound down and compressed, as it were, and girdled tensely, in their luxuriance, by her virgin zone. Yet Giovanni's fancy must have grown morbid while he looked down into the garden; for the impression which the fair stranger made upon him was as if there were another flower, the human sister of those vegetable ones, as beautiful as they, more beautiful than the richest of them, but still to be touched only with a glove, nor to be approached without a mask. As Beatrice came down the garden path, it was observable that she handled and inhaled the odor of several of the plants which her father had most sedulously avoided.

"Here, Beatrice," said the latter, "see how many needful offices require to be done to our chief treasure. Yet, shattered as I am, my life might pay the penalty of approaching it so closely as circumstances demand. Henceforth, I fear, this plant must be consigned to your sole charge."

"And gladly will I undertake it," cried again the rich tones of the young lady, as she bent towards the magnificent plant and opened her arms as if to embrace it. "Yes, my sister, my splendor, it shall be Beatrice's task to nurse and serve thee; and thou shalt reward her with thy kisses and perfumed breath, which to her is as the breath of life."

Then, with all the tenderness in her manner that was so strikingly expressed in her words, she busied herself with such attentions as the plant seemed to require; and Giovanni, at his lofty window, rubbed his eyes, and almost doubted whether it were a girl tending her favorite flower, or one sister performing the duties of affection to another. The scene soon terminated. Whether Dr. Rappaccini had finished his labors in the garden, or that his watchful eye had caught the stranger's face, he now took his daughter's arm and retired. Night was already closing in; oppressive exhalations seemed to proceed from the plants and steal upward past the open window; and Giovanni, closing the lattice, went to his couch and dreamed of a rich flower and beautiful girl. Flower and maiden were different, and yet the same, and fraught with some strange peril in either shape.

But there is an influence in the light of morning that tends to rectify whatever errors of fancy, or even of judgment, we may have incurred during the sun's decline, or among the shadows of the night, or in the less wholesome glow of moonshine. Giovanni's first movement, on starting from sleep, was to throw open the window and gaze down into the garden which his dreams had made so fertile of mysteries. He was surprised, and a little ashamed, to find how real and matter-of-fact an affair it proved to be, in the first rays of the sun which gilded the dewdrops that hung upon leaf and blossom, and, while giving a brighter beauty to each rare flower, brought every thing within the limits of ordinary experience. The young man rejoiced that, in the heart of the barren city, he had the privilege of overlooking this spot of lovely and luxuriant vegetation. It would serve, he said to himself, as a symbolic language to keep him in communication with Nature. neither the sickly and thoughtworn Dr. Giacomo Rappaccini, it is true, nor his brilliant daughter, were now visible; so that Giovanni could not determine how much of the singularity which he attributed to both was due to their own qualities and how much to his wonderworking fancy; but he was inclined to take a most rational view of the whole matter.

In the course of the day he paid his respects to Signor Pietro Baglioni, professor of medicine in the university, a physician of eminent repute, to whom Giovanni had brought a letter of introduction. The professor was an elderly personage, apparently of genial nature and habits that might almost be called jovial. He kept the young man to dinner, and made himself very agreeable by the freedom and liveliness of his conversation, especially when warmed by a flask or two of Tuscan wine. Giovanni, conceiving that men of science, inhabitants of the same city, must needs be on familiar terms with one another, took an opportunity to mention the name of Dr. Rappaccini. But the professor did not respond with so much cordiality as he had anticipated.

"Ill would it become a teacher of the divine art of medicine," said Professor Pietro Baglioni, in answer to a question of Giovanni, "to withhold due and well-considered praise of a physician so eminently skilled as Rappaccini; but, on the other hand, I should answer it but scantily to my conscience were I to permit a worthy youth like yourself, Signor Giovanni, the son of an ancient friend, to imbibe erroneous ideas respecting a man who might hereafter chance to hold your life and death in his hands. The truth is, our worshipful Dr. Rappaccini has as much science as any member of the faculty—with perhaps one single exception—in Padua, or all Italy; but there are certain grave objections to his professional character."

"And what are they?" asked the young man.

"Has my friend Giovanni any disease of body or heart, that he is so inquisitive about physicians?" said the professor, with a smile. "But as for Rappaccini, it is said of him—and I, who know the man well, can answer for its truth—that he cares infinitely more for science than for mankind. His patients are interesting to him only as subjects for some new experiment. He would sacrifice human life, his own among the rest, or whatever else was dearest to him, for the sake of adding so much as a grain of mustard seed to the great heap of his accumulated knowledge."

"Methinks he is an awful man indeed," remarked Guasconti, mentally recalling the cold and purely intellectual aspect of Rappaccini. "And yet, worshipful professor, is it not a noble spirit? Are there many men capable of so spiritual a love of science?"

"God forbid," answered the professor, somewhat testily; "at least, unless they take sounder views of the healing art than those adopted by Rappaccini. It is his theory that all medicinal virtues are comprised within those substances which we term vegetable poisons. These he cultivates with his own hands, and is said even to have produced new varieties of poison more horribly deleterious than Nature, without the assistance of this learned person, would ever have plagued the world withal. That the signor doctor does less mischief than might be expected with such dangerous substances, is undeniable. Now and then, it must be owned, he has effected, or seemed to effect, a marvellous cure; but, to tell you my private mind, Signor Giovanni, he should receive little credit for such instances of success,—they being probably the work of chance,—but should be held strictly accountable for his failures, which may justly be considered his own work."

The youth might have taken Baglioni's opinions with many grains of allowance had he known that there was a professional warfare of long continuance between him and Dr. Rappaccini, in which the latter was generally thought to have gained the advantage. If the reader be inclined to judge for himself, we refer him to certain black-letter tracts on both sides, preserved in the medical department of the University of Padua.

"I know not, most learned professor," returned Giovanni, after musing on what had been said of Rappaccini's exclusive zeal for science,—"I know not how dearly this physician may love his art; but surely there is one object more dear to him. He has a daughter."

"Aha!" cried the professor, with a laugh. "So now our friend Giovanni's secret is out. You have heard of this daughter, whom all the young men in Padua are wild about, though not half a dozen have ever had the good hap to see her face. I know little of the Signora Beatrice save that Rappaccini is said to have instructed her deeply in his science, and that, young and beautiful as fame reports her, she is already qualified to fill a professor's chair. Perchance her father destines her for mine! Other absurd rumors there be, not worth talking about or listening to. So now, Signor Giovanni, drink off your glass of lachryma."

Guasconti returned to his lodgings somewhat heated with the wine he had quaffed, and which caused his brain to swim with strange fantasies in reference to Dr. Rappaccini and the beautiful Beatrice. On his way, happening to pass by a florist's, he bought a fresh bouquet of flowers.

Ascending to his chamber, he seated himself near the window, but within the shadow thrown by the depth of the wall, so that he could look down into the garden with little risk of being discovered. All beneath his eye was a solitude. The strange plants were basking in the sunshine, and now and then nodding gently to one another, as if in acknowledgment of sympathy and kindred. In the midst, by the shattered fountain, grew the magnificent shrub, with its purple gems clustering all over it; they glowed in the air, and gleamed back again out of the depths of the pool, which thus seemed to overflow with colored radiance from the rich reflection that was steeped in it. At first, as we have said, the garden was a solitude. Soon, however,—as Giovanni had half hoped, half feared, would be the case,—a figure appeared beneath the antique sculptured portal, and came down between the rows of plants, inhaling their various perfumes as if she were one of those beings of old classic fable that lived upon sweet odors. On again beholding Beatrice, the young man was even startled to perceive how much her beauty exceeded his recollection of it; so brilliant, so vivid, was its character, that she glowed amid the sunlight, and, as Giovanni whispered to himself, positively illuminated the more shadowy intervals of the garden path. Her face being now more revealed than on the former occasion, he was struck by its expression of simplicity and sweetness—qualities that had not entered into his idea of her character, and which made him ask anew what manner of mortal she might be. Nor did he fail again to observe, or imagine, an analogy between the beautiful girl and the gorgeous shrub that hung its gemlike flowers over the fountain—a resemblance which Beatrice seemed to have indulged a fantastic humor in heightening, both by the arrangement of her dress and the selection of its hues.

Approaching the shrub, she threw open her arms, as with a passionate ardor, and drew its branches into an intimate embrace-so intimate that her features were hidden in its leafy bosom and her glistening ringlets all intermingled with the flowers.

"Give me thy breath, my sister," exclaimed Beatrice; "for I am faint with common air. And give me this flower of thine, which I separate with gentlest fingers from the stem and place it close beside my heart."

With these words the beautiful daughter of Rappaccini plucked one of the richest blossoms of the shrub, and was about to fasten it in her bosom. But now, unless Giovanni's draughts of wine had bewildered his senses, a singular incident occurred. A small orange-colored reptile, of the lizard or chameleon species, chanced to be creeping along the path, just at the feet of Beatrice. It appeared to Giovanni,—but, at the distance from which he gazed, he could scarcely have seen anything so minute,—it appeared to him, however, that a drop or two of moisture from the broken stem of the flower descended upon the lizard's head. For an instant the reptile contorted itself violently, and then lay motionless in the sunshine. Beatrice observed this remarkable phenomenon, and crossed herself, sadly, but without surprise; nor did she therefore hesitate to arrange the fatal flower in her bosom. There it blushed, and almost glimmered with the dazzling effect of a precious stone, adding to her dress and aspect the one appropriate charm which nothing else in the world could have supplied. But Giovanni, out of the shadow of his window, bent forward and shrank back, and murmured and trembled.

"Am I awake? Have I my senses?" said he to himself. "What is this being? Beautiful shall I call her, or inexpressibly terrible?"

Beatrice now strayed carelessly through the garden, approaching closer beneath Giovanni's window, so that he was compelled to thrust his head quite out of its concealment in order to gratify the intense and painful curiosity which she excited. At this moment there came a beautiful insect over the garden wall: it had, perhaps, wandered through the city, and found no flowers or verdure among those antique haunts of men until the heavy perfumes of Dr. Rappaccini's shrubs had lured it from afar. Without alighting on the flowers this winged brightness seemed to be attracted by Beatrice, and lingered in the air and fluttered about her head. Now, here it could not be but that Giovanni Guasconti's eyes deceived him. Be that as it might be, he fancied that, while Beatrice was gazing at the insect with childish delight, it grew faint and fell at her feet; its bright wings shivered; it was dead—from no cause that he could discern, unless it were the atmosphere of her breath. Again Beatrice crossed herself and sighed heavily as she bent over the dead insect.

An impulsive movement of Giovanni drew her eyes to the window. There she beheld the beautiful head of the young man—rather a Grecian than an Italian head, with fair, regular features, and a glistening of gold among his ringlets—gazing down upon her like a being that hovered in mid air. Scarcely knowing what he did, Giovanni threw down the bouquet which he had hitherto held in his hand.

"Signora," said he, "there are pure and healthful flowers. Wear them for the sake of Giovanni Guasconti."

"Thanks, signor," replied Beatrice, with her rich voice, that came forth as it were like a gush of music, and with a mirthful expression half childish and half womanlike. "I accept your gift, and would fain recompense it with this precious purple flower; but, if I toss it into the air, it will not reach you. So Signor Guasconti must even content himself with my thanks."

She lifted the bouquet from the ground, and then, as if inwardly ashamed at having stepped aside from her maidenly reserve to respond to a stranger's greeting, passed swiftly homeward through the garden. But, few as the moments were, it seemed to Giovanni, when she was on the point of vanishing beneath the sculptured portal, that his beautiful bouquet was already beginning to wither in her grasp. It was an idle thought; there could be no possibility of distinguishing a faded flower from a fresh one at so great a distance.

For many days after this incident the young man avoided the window that looked into Dr. Rappaccini's garden, as if something ugly and monstrous would have blasted his eyesight had he been betrayed into a glance. He felt conscious of having put himself, to a certain extent, within the influence of an unintelligible power by the communication which he had opened with Beatrice. The wisest course would have been, if his heart were in any real danger, to quit his lodgings and Padua itself at once; the next wiser, to have accustomed himself, as far as possible, to the familiar and daylight view of Beatrice—thus bringing her rigidly and systematically within the limits of ordinary experience. Least of all, while avoiding her sight, ought Giovanni to have remained so near this extraordinary being that the proximity and possibility even of intercourse should give a kind of substance and reality to the wild vagaries which his imagination ran riot continually in producing. Guasconti had not a deep heart—or, at all events, its depths were not sounded now; but he had a quick fancy, and an ardent southern temperament, which rose every instant to a higher fever pitch. Whether or no Beatrice possessed those terrible attributes, that fatal breath, the affinity with those so beautiful and deadly flowers which were indicated by what Giovanni had witnessed, she had at least instilled a fierce and subtle poison into his system. It was not love, although her rich beauty was a madness to him; nor horror, even while he fancied her spirit to be imbued with the same baneful essence that seemed to pervade her physical frame; but a wild offspring of both love and horror that had each parent in it, and burned like one and shivered like the other. Giovanni knew not what to dread; still less did he know what to hope; yet hope and dread kept a continual warfare in his breast; alternately vanquishing one another and starting up afresh to renew the contest. Blessed are all simple emotions, be they dark or bright! It is the lurid intermixture of the two that produces the illuminating blaze of the infernal regions.

Sometimes he endeavored to assuage the fever of his spirit by a rapid walk through the streets of Padua or beyond its gates: his footsteps kept time with the throbbing of his brain, so that the walk was apt to accelerate itself to a race. One day he found himself arrested; his arm was seized by a portly personage, who had turned back on recognizing the young man and expended much breath in overtaking him.

"Signor Giovanni! Stay, my young friend!" cried he. "Have you forgotten me? That might well be the case if I were as much altered as yourself."

It was Baglioni, whom Giovanni had avoided ever since their first meeting, from a doubt that the professor's sagacity would look too deeply into his secrets. Endeavoring to recover himself, he stared forth wildly from his inner world into the outer one and spoke like a man in a dream.

"Yes; I am Giovanni Guasconti. You are Professor Pietro Baglioni. Now let me pass!"

"Not yet, not yet, Signor Giovanni Guasconti," said the professor, smiling, but at the same time scrutinizing the youth with an earnest glance. "What! did I grow up side by side with your father? and shall his son pass me like a stranger in these old streets of Padua? Stand still, Signor Giovanni; for we must have a word or two before we part."

"Speedily, then, most worshipful professor, speedily," said Giovanni, with feverish impatience. "Does not your worship see that I am in haste?"

Now, while he was speaking there came a man in black along the street, stooping and moving feebly like a person in inferior health. His face was all overspread with a most sickly and sallow hue, but yet so pervaded with an expression of piercing and active intellect that an observer might easily have overlooked the merely physical attributes and have seen only this wonderful energy. As he passed, this person exchanged a cold and distant salutation with Baglioni, but fixed his eyes upon Giovanni with an intentness that seemed to bring out whatever was within him worthy of notice. Nevertheless, there was a peculiar quietness in the look, as if taking merely a speculative, not a human, interest in the young man.

"It is Dr. Rappaccini!" whispered the professor when the stranger had passed. "Has he ever seen your face before?"

"Not that I know," answered Giovanni, starting at the name.

"He *has* seen you! he must have seen you!" said Baglioni, hastily. "For some purpose or other, this man of science is making a study of you. I know that look of his! It is the same that coldly illuminates his face as he bends over a bird, a mouse, or a butterfly; which, in pursuance of some experiment, he has killed by the perfume of a flower; a look as deep as Nature itself, but without Nature's warmth of love. Signor Giovanni, I will stake my life upon it, you are the subject of one of Rappaccini's experiments!"

"Will you make a fool of me?" cried Giovanni, passionately. "*That,* signor professor, were an untoward experiment."

"Patience! patience!" replied the imperturbable professor. "I tell thee, my poor Giovanni, that Rappaccini has a scientific interest in thee. Thou hast fallen into fearful hands! And the Signora Beatrice,—what part does she act in this mystery?"

But Guasconti, finding Baglioni's pertinacity intolerable, here broke away, and was gone before the professor could again seize his arm. He looked after the young man intently and shook his head.

"This must not be," said Baglioni to himself. "The youth is the son of my old friend, and shall not come to any harm from which the arcana of medical science can preserve him. Besides, it is too insufferable an impertinence in Rappaccini thus to snatch the lad out of my own hands, as I may say, and make use of him for his infernal experiments. This daughter of his! It shall be looked to. Perchance, most learned Rappaccini, I may foil you where you little dream of it!"

Meanwhile Giovanni had pursued a circuitous route, and at length found himself at the door of his lodgings. As he crossed the threshold he was met by old Lisabetta, who smirked and smiled, and was evidently desirous to attract his attention; vainly, however, as the ebullition of his feelings had momentarily subsided into a cold and dull vacuity. He turned his eyes full upon the withered face that was puckering itself into a smile, but seemed to behold it not. The old dame, therefore, laid her grasp upon his cloak.

"Signor! signor!" whispered she, still with a smile over the whole breadth of her visage, so that it looked not unlike a grotesque carving in wood, darkened by centuries. "Listen, signor! There is a private entrance into the garden!"

"What do you say?" exclaimed Giovanni, turning quickly about, as if an inanimate thing should start into feverish life. "A private entrance into Dr. Rappaccini's garden?"

"Hush! hush! not so loud!" whispered Lisabetta, putting her hand over his mouth. "Yes; into the worshipful doctor's garden, where you may see all his fine shrubbery. Many a young man in Padua would give gold to be admitted among those flowers."

Giovanni put a piece of gold into her hand.

"Show me the way," said he.

A surmise, probably excited by his conversation with Baglioni, crossed his mind, that this interposition of old Lisabetta might perchance be connected with the intrigue, whatever were its nature, in which the professor seemed to suppose that Dr. Rappaccini was involving him. But such a suspicion, though it disturbed Giovanni, was inadequate to restrain him. The instant that he was aware of the possibility of approaching Beatrice, it seemed an absolute necessity of his existence to do so. It mattered not whether she were angel or demon; he was irrevocably within her sphere, and must obey the law that whirled him onward, in ever-lessening circles, towards a result which he did not attempt to foreshadow; and yet, strange to say, there came across him a sudden doubt whether this intense interest on his part were not delusory; whether it were really of so deep and positive a nature as to justify him in now thrusting himself into an incalculable position; whether it were not merely the fantasy of a young man's brain, only slightly or not at all connected with his heart.

He paused, hesitated, turned half about, but again went on. His withered guide led him along several obscure passages, and finally undid a door, through which, as it was opened, there came the sight and sound of rustling leaves, with the broken sunshine glimmering among them. Giovanni stepped forth, and, forcing himself through the entanglement of a shrub that wreathed its tendrils over the hidden entrance, stood beneath his own window in the open area of Dr. Rappaccini's garden.

How often is it the case that, when impossibilities have come to pass and dreams have condensed their misty substance into tangible realities, we find ourselves calm, and even coldly self-possessed, amid circumstances which it would have been a delirium of joy or agony to anticipate! Fate delights to thwart us thus. Passion will choose his own time to rush upon the scene, and lingers sluggishly behind when an appropriate adjustment of events would seem to summon his appearance. So was it now with Giovanni. Day after day his pulses had throbbed with feverish blood at the improbable idea of an interview with Beatrice, and of standing with her, face to face, in this very garden, basking in the Oriental sunshine of her beauty, and snatching from her full gaze the mystery which he deemed the riddle of his own existence. But now there was a singular and untimely equanimity within his breast. He threw a glance around the garden to discover if Beatrice or her father were present, and, perceiving that he was alone, began a critical observation of the plants.

The aspect of one and all of them dissatisfied him; their gorgeousness seemed fierce, passionate, and even unnatural. There was hardly an individual shrub which a wanderer, straying by himself through a forest, would not have been startled to find growing wild, as if an unearthly face had glared at him out of the thicket. Several also would have shocked a delicate instinct by an appearance of artificialness indicating that there had been such commixture, and, as it were, adultery of various vegetable species, that the production was no longer of God's making, but the monstrous offspring of man's depraved fancy, glowing with only an evil mockery of beauty. They were probably the result of experiment, which in one or two cases had succeeded in mingling plants individually lovely into a compound possessing the questionable and ominous character that distinguished the whole growth of the garden. In fine, Giovanni recognized but two or three plants in the collection, and those of a kind that he well knew to be poisonous. While busy with these contemplations he heard the rustling of a silken garment, and, turning, beheld Beatrice emerging from beneath the sculptured portal.

Giovanni had not considered with himself what should be his deportment; whether he should apologize for his intrusion into the garden, or assume that he was there with the privity at least, if not by the desire, of Dr. Rappaccini or his daughter; but Beatrice's manner placed him at his ease, though leaving him still in doubt by what agency he had gained admittance. She came lightly along the path and met him near the broken fountain. There was surprise in her face, but brightened by a simple and kind expression of pleasure.

"You are a connoisseur in flowers, signor," said Beatrice, with a smile, alluding to the bouquet which he had flung her from the window. "It is no marvel, therefore, if the sight of my father's rare collection has tempted you to take a nearer view. If he were here, he could tell you many strange and interesting facts as to the nature and habits of these shrubs; for he has spent a lifetime in such studies, and this garden is his world."

"And yourself, lady," observed Giovanni, "if fame says true,—you likewise are deeply skilled in the virtues indicated by these rich blossoms and these spicy perfumes. Would you deign to be my instructress, I should prove an apter scholar than if taught by Signor Rappaccini himself."

"Are there such idle rumors?" asked Beatrice, with the music of a pleasant laugh. "Do people say that I am skilled in my father's science of plants? What a jest is there! No; though I have grown up among these flowers, I know no more of them than their hues and perfume; and sometimes methinks I would fain rid myself of even that small knowledge. There are many flowers here, and those not the least brilliant, that shock and offend me when they meet my eye. But pray, signor, do not believe these stories about my science. Believe nothing of me save what you see with your own eyes."

"And must I believe all that I have seen with my own eyes?" asked Giovanni, pointedly, while the recollection of former scenes made him shrink. "No, signora; you demand too little of me. Bid me believe nothing save what comes from your own lips."

It would appear that Beatrice understood him. There came a deep flush to her cheek; but she looked full into Giovanni's eyes, and responded to his gaze of uneasy suspicion with a queenlike haughtiness.

"I do so bid you, signor," she replied. "Forget whatever you may have fancied in regard to me. If true to the outward senses, still it may be false in its essence; but the words of Beatrice Rappaccini's lips are true from the depths of the heart outward. Those you may believe."

A fervor glowed in her whole aspect and beamed upon Giovanni's consciousness like the light of truth itself; but while she spoke there was a fragrance in the atmosphere around her, rich and delightful, though evanescent, yet which the young man, from an indefinable reluctance, scarcely dared to draw into his lungs. It might be the odor of the flowers. Could it be Beatrice's breath which thus embalmed her words with a strange richness, as if by steeping them in her heart? A faintness passed like a shadow over Giovanni and flitted away; he seemed to gaze through the beautiful girl's eyes into her transparent soul, and felt no more doubt or fear.

The tinge of passion that had colored Beatrice's manner vanished; she became gay, and appeared to derive a pure delight from her communion with the youth not unlike what the maiden of a lonely island might have felt conversing with a voyager from the civilized world. Evidently her experience of life had been confined within the limits of that garden. She talked now about matters as simple as the daylight or summer clouds, and now asked questions in reference to the city, or Giovanni's distant home, his friends, his mother, and his sisters—questions indicating such seclusion, and such lack of familiarity with modes and forms, that Giovanni responded as if to an infant. Her spirit gushed out before him like a fresh rill that was just catching its first glimpse of the sunlight and wondering at the reflections of earth and sky which were flung into its bosom. There came thoughts, too, from a deep source, and fantasies of a gemlike brilliancy, as if diamonds and rubies sparkled upward among the bubbles of the fountain. Ever and anon there gleamed across the young man's mind a sense of wonder that he should be walking side by side with the being who had so wrought upon his imagination, whom he had idealized in such hues of terror, in whom he had positively witnessed such manifestations of dreadful attributes—that he should be conversing with Beatrice like a brother, and should find her so human and so maidenlike. But such reflections were only momentary; the effect of her character was too real not to make itself familiar at once.

In this free intercourse they had strayed through the garden, and now, after many turns among its avenues, were come to the shattered fountain, beside which grew the magnificent shrub, with its treasury of glowing blossoms. A fragrance was diffused from it which Giovanni recognized as identical with that which he had attributed to Beatrice's breath, but incomparably more powerful. As her eyes fell upon it, Giovanni beheld her press her hand to her bosom as if her heart were throbbing suddenly and painfully.

"For the first time in my life," murmured she, addressing the shrub, "I had forgotten thee."

"I remember, signora," said Giovanni, "that you once promised to reward me with one of these living gems for the bouquet which I had the happy boldness to fling to your feet. Permit me now to pluck it as a memorial of this interview."

He made a step towards the shrub with extended hand; but Beatrice darted forward, uttering a shriek that went through his heart like a dagger. She caught his hand and drew it back with the whole force of her slender figure. Giovanni felt her touch thrilling through his fibres.

"Touch it not!" exclaimed she, in a voice of agony. "Not for thy life! It is fatal!"

Then, hiding her face, she fled from him and vanished beneath the sculptured portal. As Giovanni followed her with his eyes, he beheld the emaciated figure and pale intelligence of Dr. Rappaccini, who had been watching the scene, he knew not how long, within the shadow of the entrance.

No sooner was Guasconti alone in his chamber than the image of Beatrice came back to his passionate musings, invested with all the witchery that had been gathering around it ever since his first glimpse of her, and now likewise imbued with a tender warmth of girlish womanhood. She was human; her nature was endowed with all gentle and feminine qualities; she was worthiest to be worshipped; she was capable, surely, on her part, of the height and heroism of love. Those tokens which he had hitherto considered as proofs of a frightful peculiarity in her physical and moral system were now either forgotten or by the subtle sophistry of passion transmitted into a golden crown of enchantment, rendering Beatrice the more admirable by so much as she was the more unique. Whatever had looked ugly was now beautiful; or, if incapable of such a change, it stole away and hid itself among those shapeless half ideas which throng the dim region beyond the daylight of our perfect consciousness. Thus did he spend the night, nor fell asleep until the dawn had begun to awake the slumbering flowers in Dr. Rappaccini's garden, whither Giovanni's dreams doubtless led him. Up rose the sun in his due season, and, flinging his beams upon the young man's eyelids, awoke him to a sense of pain. When thoroughly aroused, he became sensible of a burning and tingling agony in his hand—in his right hand—the very hand which Beatrice had grasped in her own when he was on the point of plucking one of the gemlike flowers. On the back of that hand there was now a purple print like that of four small fingers, and the likeness of a slender thumb upon his wrist.

O, how stubbornly does love,—or even that cunning semblance of love which flourishes in the imagination, but strikes no depth of root into the heart,—how stubbornly does it hold its faith until the moment comes when it is doomed to vanish into thin mist! Giovanni wrapped a handkerchief about his hand and wondered what evil thing had stung him, and soon forgot his pain in a revery of Beatrice.

After the first interview, a second was in the inevitable course of what we call fate. A third; a fourth; and a meeting with Beatrice in the garden was no longer an incident in Giovanni's daily life, but the whole space in which he might be said to live; for the anticipation and memory of that ecstatic hour made up the remainder. Nor was it otherwise with the daughter of Rappaccini. She watched for the youth's appearance and flew to his side with confidence as unreserved as if they had been playmates from early infancy—as if they were such playmates still. If, by any unwonted chance, he failed to come at the appointed moment, she stood beneath the window and sent up the rich sweetness of her tones to float around him in his chamber and echo and reverberate throughout his heart: "Giovanni! Giovanni! Why tarriest thou? Come down!" And down he hastened into that Eden of poisonous flowers.

But, with all this intimate familiarity, there was still a reserve in Beatrice's demeanor, so rigidly and invariably sustained that the idea of infringing it scarcely occurred to his imagination. By all appreciable signs, they loved; they had looked love with eyes that conveyed the holy secret from the depths of one soul into the depths of the other, as if it were too sacred to be whispered by the way; they had even spoken love in those gushes of passion when their spirits darted forth in articulated breath like tongues of long hidden flame; and yet there had been no seal of lips, no clasp of hands, nor any slightest caress such as love claims and hallows. He had never touched one of the gleaming ringlets of her hair; her garment—so marked was the physical barrier between them—had never been waved against him by a breeze. On the few occasions when Giovanni had seemed tempted to overstep the limit, Beatrice grew so sad, so stern, and withal wore such a look of desolate separation, shuddering at itself, that not a spoken word was requisite to repel him. At such times he was startled at the horrible suspicions that rose, monster-like, out of the caverns of his heart and stared him in the face; his love grew thin and faint as the morning mist; his doubts alone had substance. But, when Beatrice's face brightened again after the momentary shadow, she was transformed at once from the mysterious, questionable being whom he had watched with so much awe and horror; she was now the beautiful and unsophisticated girl whom he felt that his spirit knew with a certainty beyond all other knowledge.

A considerable time had now passed since Giovanni's last meeting with Baglioni. One morning, however, he was disagreeably surprised by a visit from the professor, whom he had scarcely thought of for whole weeks, and would willingly have forgotten still longer. Given up as he had long been to a pervading excitement, he could tolerate no companions except upon condition of their perfect sympathy with his present state of feeling. Such sympathy was not to be expected from Professor Baglioni.

The visitor chatted carelessly for a few moments about the gossip of the city and the university, and then took up another topic.

"I have been reading an old classic author lately," said he, "and met with a story that strangely interested me. Possibly you may remember it. It is of an Indian prince, who sent a beautiful woman as a present to Alexander the Great. She was as lovely as the dawn and gorgeous as the sunset; but what especially distinguished her was a certain rich perfume in her breath—richer than a garden of Persian roses. Alexander, as was natural to a youthful conqueror, fell in love at first sight with this magnificent stranger; but a certain sage physician, happening to be present, discovered a terrible secret in regard to her."

"And what was that?" asked Giovanni, turning his eyes downward to avoid those of the professor.

"That this lovely woman," continued Baglioni, with emphasis, "had been nourished with poisons from her birth upward, until her whole nature was so imbued with them that she herself had become the deadliest poison in existence. Poison was her element of life. With that rich perfume of her breath she blasted the very air. Her love would have been poison—her embrace death. Is not this a marvellous tale?"

"A childish fable," answered Giovanni, nervously starting from his chair. "I marvel how your worship finds time to read such nonsense among your graver studies."

"By the by," said the professor, looking uneasily about him, "what singular fragrance is this in your apartment? Is it the perfume of your gloves? It is faint, but delicious; and yet, after all, by no means agreeable. Were I to breathe it long, methinks it would make me ill. It is like the breath of a flower; but I see no flowers in the chamber."

"Nor are there any," replied Giovanni, who had turned pale as the professor spoke; "nor, I think, is there any fragrance except in your worship's imagination. Odors, being a sort of element combined of the sensual and the spiritual, are apt to deceive us in this manner. The recollection of a perfume, the bare idea of it, may easily be mistaken for a present reality."

"Ay; but my sober imagination does not often play such tricks," said Baglioni; "and, were I to fancy any kind of odor, it would be that of some vile apothecary drug, wherewith my fingers are likely enough to be imbued. Our worshipful friend Rappaccini, as I have heard, tinctures his medicaments with odors richer than those of Araby. Doubtless, likewise, the fair and learned Signora Beatrice would minister to her patients with draughts as sweet as a maiden's breath; but woe to him that sips them!"

Giovanni's face evinced many contending emotions. The tone in which the professor alluded to the pure and lovely daughter of Rappaccini was a torture to his soul; and yet the intimation of a view of her character, opposite to his own, gave instantaneous distinctness to a thousand dim suspicions, which now grinned at him like so many demons. But he strove hard to quell them and to respond to Baglioni with a true lover's perfect faith.

"Signor professor," said he, "you were my father's friend; perchance, too, it is your purpose to act a friendly part towards his son. I would fain feel nothing towards you save respect and deference; but I pray you to observe, signor, that there is one subject on which we must not speak. You know not the Signora Beatrice. You cannot, therefore, estimate the wrong—the blasphemy, I may even say—that is offered to her character by a light or injurious word."

"Giovanni! my poor Giovanni!" answered the professor, with a calm expression of pity, "I know this wretched girl far better than yourself. You shall hear the truth in respect to the poisoner Rappaccini and his poisonous daughter; yes, poisonous as she is beautiful. Listen; for, even should you do violence to my gray hairs, it shall not silence me. That old fable of the Indian woman has become a truth by the deep and deadly science of Rappaccini and in the person of the lovely Beatrice."

Giovanni groaned and hid his face.

"Her father," continued Baglioni, "was not restrained by natural affection from offering up his child in this horrible manner as the victim of his insane zeal for science; for, let us do him justice, he is as true a man of science as ever distilled his own heart in an alembic. What, then, will be your fate? Beyond a doubt you are selected as the material of some new experiment. Perhaps the result is to be death; perhaps a fate more awful still. Rappaccini, with what he calls the interest of science before his eyes, will hesitate at nothing."

"It is a dream," muttered Giovanni to himself; "surely it is a dream."

"But," resumed the professor, "be of good cheer, son of my friend. It is not yet too late for the rescue. Possibly we may even succeed in bringing back this miserable child within the limits of ordinary nature, from which her father's madness has estranged her. Behold this little silver vase! It was wrought by the hands of the renowned Benvenuto Cellini, and is well worthy to be a love gift to the fairest dame in Italy. But its contents are invaluable. One little sip of this antidote would have rendered the most virulent poisons of the Borgias innocuous. Doubt not that it will be as efficacious against those of Rappaccini. Bestow the vase, and the precious liquid within it, on your Beatrice, and hopefully await the result."

Baglioni laid a small, exquisitely wrought silver vial on the table and withdrew, leaving what he had said to produce its effect upon the young man's mind.

"We will thwart Rappaccini yet," thought he, chuckling to himself, as he descended the stairs; "but, let us confess the truth of him, he is a wonderful man—a wonderful man indeed; a vile empiric, however, in his practice, and therefore not to be tolerated by those who respect the good old rules of the medical profession."

Throughout Giovanni's whole acquaintance with Beatrice, he had occasionally, as we have said, been haunted by dark surmises as to her character; yet so thoroughly had she made herself felt by him as a simple, natural, most affectionate, and guileless creature, that the image now held up by Professor Baglioni looked as strange and incredible as if it were not in accordance with his own original conception. True, there were ugly recollections connected with his first glimpses of the beautiful girl; he could not quite forget the bouquet that withered in her grasp, and the insect that perished amid the sunny air, by no ostensible agency save the fragrance of her breath. These incidents, however, dissolving in the pure light of her character, had no longer the efficacy of facts, but were acknowledged as mistaken fantasies, by whatever testimony of the senses they might appear to be substantiated. There is something truer and more real than what we can see with the eyes and touch with the finger. On such better evidence had Giovanni founded his confidence in Beatrice, though rather by the necessary force of her high attributes than by any deep and generous faith on his part. But now his spirit was incapable of sustaining itself at the height to which the early enthusiasm of passion had exalted it; he fell down, grovelling among earthly doubts, and defiled therewith the pure whiteness of Beatrice's image. Not that he gave her up; he did but distrust. He resolved to institute some decisive test that should satisfy him, once for all, whether there were those dreadful peculiarities in her physical nature which could not be supposed to exist without some corresponding monstrosity of soul. His eyes, gazing down afar, might have deceived him as to the lizard, the insect, and the flowers; but if he could witness, at the distance of a few paces, the sudden blight of one fresh and beautiful flower in Beatrice's hand, there would be room for no further question. With this idea he hastened to the florist's and purchased a bouquet that was still gemmed with the morning dewdrops.

It was now the customary hour of his daily interview with Beatrice. Before descending into the garden, Giovanni failed not to look at his figure in the mirror—a vanity to be expected in a beautiful young man, yet, as displaying itself at that troubled and feverish moment, the token of a certain shallowness of feeling and insincerity of character. He did gaze, however, and said to himself that his features had never before possessed so rich a grace, nor his eyes such vivacity, nor his cheeks so warm a hue of superabundant life.

"At least," thought he, "her poison has not yet insinuated itself into my system. I am no flower to perish in her grasp."

With that thought he turned his eyes on the bouquet, which he had never once laid aside from his hand. A thrill of indefinable horror shot through his frame on perceiving that those dewy flowers were already beginning to droop; they wore the aspect of things that had been fresh and lovely yesterday. Giovanni grew white as marble, and stood motionless before the mirror, staring at his own reflection there as at the likeness of something frightful. He remembered Baglioni's remark about the fragrance that seemed to pervade the chamber. It must have been the poison in his breath! Then he shuddered—shuddered at himself. Recovering from his stupor, he began to watch with curious eye a spider that was busily at work hanging its web from the antique cornice of the apartment, crossing and recrossing the artful system of interwoven lines—as vigorous and active a spider as ever dangled from an old ceiling. Giovanni bent towards the insect, and emitted a deep, long breath. The spider suddenly ceased its toil; the web vibrated with a tremor originating in the body of the small artisan. Again Giovanni sent forth a breath, deeper, longer, and imbued with a venomous feeling out of his heart: he knew not whether he were wicked, or only desperate. The spider made a convulsive gripe with his limbs and hung dead across the window.

"Accursed! accursed!" muttered Giovanni, addressing himself. "Hast thou grown so poisonous that this deadly insect perishes by thy breath?"

At that moment a rich, sweet voice came floating up from the garden.

"Giovanni! Giovanni! It is past the hour! Why tarriest thou? Come down!"

"Yes," muttered Giovanni again. "She is the only being whom my breath may not slay! Would that it might!"

He rushed down, and in an instant was standing before the bright and loving eyes of Beatrice. A moment ago his wrath and despair had been so fierce that he could have desired nothing so much as to wither her by a glance; but with her actual presence there came influences which had too real an existence to be at once shaken off; recollections of the delicate and benign power of her feminine nature, which had so often enveloped him in a religious calm; recollections of many a holy and passionate outgush of her heart, when the pure fountain had been unsealed from its depths and made visible in its transparency to his mental eye; recollections which, had Giovanni known how to estimate them, would have assured him that all this ugly mystery was but an earthly illusion, and that, whatever mist of evil might seem to have gathered over her, the real Beatrice was a heavenly angel. Incapable as he was of such high faith, still her presence had not utterly lost its magic. Giovanni's rage was quelled into an aspect of sullen insensibility. Beatrice, with a quick spiritual sense, immediately felt that there was a gulf of blackness between them which neither he nor she could pass. They walked on together, sad and silent, and came thus to the marble fountain and to its pool of water on the ground, in the midst of which grew the shrub that bore gemlike blossoms. Giovanni was affrighted at the eager enjoyment—the appetite, as it were—with which he found himself inhaling the fragrance of the flowers.

"Beatrice," asked he, abruptly, "whence came this shrub?"

"My father created it," answered she, with simplicity.

"Created it! created it!" repeated Giovanni. "What mean you, Beatrice?"

"He is a man fearfully acquainted with the secrets of Nature," replied Beatrice; "and, at the hour when I first drew breath, this plant sprang from the soil, the offspring of his science, of his intellect, while I was but his earthly child. Approach it not!" continued she, observing with terror that Giovanni was drawing nearer to the shrub. "It has qualities that you little dream of. But I, dearest Giovanni,—I grew up and blossomed with the plant and was nourished with its breath. It was my sister, and I loved it with a human affection; for, alas!—hast thou not suspected it?—there was an awful doom."

Here Giovanni frowned so darkly upon her that Beatrice paused and trembled. But her faith in his tenderness reassured her, and made her blush that she had doubted for an instant.

"There was an awful doom," she continued, "the effect of my father's fatal love of science, which estranged me from all society of my kind. Until Heaven sent thee, dearest Giovanni, O, how lonely was thy poor Beatrice!"

"Was it a hard doom?" asked Giovanni, fixing his eyes upon her.

"Only of late have I known how hard it was," answered she, tenderly. "O, yes; but my heart was torpid, and therefore quiet."

Giovanni's rage broke forth from his sullen gloom like a lightning flash out of a dark cloud.

"Accursed one!" cried he, with venomous scorn and anger. "And, finding thy solitude wearisome, thou hast severed me likewise from all the warmth of life and enticed me into thy region of unspeakable horror!"

"Giovanni!" exclaimed Beatrice, turning her large bright eyes upon his face. The force of his words had not found its way into her mind; she was merely thunderstruck.

"Yes, poisonous thing!" repeated Giovanni, beside himself with passion. "Thou hast done it! Thou hast blasted me! Thou hast filled my veins with poison! Thou hast made me as hateful, as ugly, as loathsome and deadly a creature as thyself—a world's wonder of hideous monstrosity! Now, if our breath be happily as fatal to ourselves as to all others, let us join our lips in one kiss of unutterable hatred, and so die!"

"What hast befallen me?" murmured Beatrice, with a low moan out of her heart. "Holy Virgin, pity me, a poor heart-broken child!"

"Thou,—dost thou pray?" cried Giovanni, still with the same fiendish scorn. "Thy very prayers, as they come from thy lips, taint the atmosphere with death. Yes, yes; let us pray! Let us to church and dip our fingers in the holy water at the portal! They that come after us will perish as by a pestilence! Let us sign crosses in the air! It will be scattering curses abroad in the likeness of holy symbols!"

"Giovanni," said Beatrice calmly, for her grief was beyond passion, "why dost thou join thyself with me thus in those terrible words? I, it is true, am the horrible thing thou namest me. But thou,—what hast thou to do, save with one other shudder at my hideous misery to go forth out of the garden and mingle with thy race, and forget that there ever crawled on earth such a monster as poor Beatrice?"

"Dost thou pretend ignorance?" asked Giovanni, scowling upon her. "Behold! this power have I gained from the pure daughter of Rappaccini."

There was a swarm of summer insects flitting through the air in search of the food promised by the flower odors of the fatal garden. They circled round Giovanni's head, and were evidently attracted towards him by the same influence which had drawn them for an instant within the sphere of the shrubs. He sent forth a breath among them, and smiled bitterly at Beatrice as at least a score of the insects fell dead upon the ground.

"I see it! I see it!" shrieked Beatrice. "It is my father's fatal science! No, no, Giovanni; it was not I! Never! never! I dreamed only to love thee and be with thee a little time, and so to let thee pass away, leaving but thine image in mine heart; for, Giovanni, believe it, though my body be nourished with poison, my spirit is God's creature, and craves love as its daily food. But my father,—he has united us in this fearful sympathy. Yes; spurn me, tread upon me, kill me! O, what is death after such words as thine? But it was not I. Not for a world of bliss would I have done it."

Giovanni's passion had exhausted itself in its outburst from his lips. There now came across him a sense, mournful, and not without tenderness, of the intimate and peculiar relationship between Beatrice and himself. They stood, as it were, in an utter solitude, which would be made none the less solitary by the densest throng of human life. Ought not, then, the desert of humanity around them to press this insulated pair closer together? If they should be cruel to one another, who was there to be kind to them? Besides, thought Giovanni, might there not still be a hope of his returning within the limits of ordinary nature, and leading Beatrice, the redeemed Beatrice, by the hand? O, weak, and selfish, and unworthy spirit, that could dream of an earthly union and earthly happiness as possible, after such deep love had been so bitterly wronged as was Beatrice's love by Giovanni's blighting words! No, no; there could be no such hope. She must pass heavily, with that broken heart, across the borders of Time—she must bathe her hurts in some fount of paradise, and forget her grief in the light of immortality, and *there* be well.

But Giovanni did not know it.

"Dear Beatrice," said he, approaching her, while she shrank away as always at his approach, but now with a different impulse, "dearest Beatrice, our fate is not yet so desperate. Behold! there is a medicine, potent, as a wise physician has assured me, and almost divine in its efficacy. It is composed of ingredients the most opposite to those by which thy awful father has brought this calamity upon thee and me. It is distilled of blessed herbs. Shall we not quaff it together, and thus be purified from evil?"

"Give it to me!" said Beatrice, extending her hand to receive the little silver vial which Giovanni took from his bosom. She added, with a peculiar emphasis, "I will drink; but do thou await the result."

She put Baglioni's antidote to her lips; and, at the same moment, the figure of Rappaccini emerged from the portal and came slowly towards the marble fountain. As he drew near, the pale man of science seemed to gaze with a triumphant expression at the beautiful youth and maiden, as might an artist who should spend his life in achieving a picture or a group of statuary and finally be satisfied with his success. He paused; his bent form grew erect with conscious power; he spread out his hands over them in the attitude of a father imploring a blessing upon his children; but those were the same hands that had thrown poison into the stream of their lives. Giovanni trembled. Beatrice shuddered nervously, and pressed her hand upon her heart.

"My daughter," said Rappaccini, "thou art no longer lonely in the world. Pluck one of those precious gems from thy sister shrub and bid thy bridegroom wear it in his bosom. It will not harm him now. My science and the sympathy between thee and him have so wrought within his system that he now stands apart from common men, as thou dost, daughter of my pride and triumph, from ordinary women. Pass on, then, through the world, most dear to one another and dreadful to all besides!"

"My father," said Beatrice, feebly,—and still as she spoke she kept her hand upon her heart,—"wherefore didst thou inflict this miserable doom upon thy child?"

"Miserable!" exclaimed Rappaccini. "What mean you, foolish girl? Dost thou deem it misery to be endowed with marvellous gifts against which no power nor strength could avail an enemy—misery, to be able to quell the mightiest with a breath—misery, to be as terrible as thou art beautiful? Wouldst thou, then, have preferred the condition of a weak woman, exposed to all evil and capable of none?"

"I would fain have been loved, not feared," murmured Beatrice, sinking down upon the ground. "But now it matters not. I am going, father, where the evil which thou hast striven to mingle with my being will pass away like a dream—like the fragrance of these poisonous flowers, which will no longer taint my breath among the flowers of Eden. Farewell, Giovanni! Thy words of hatred are like lead within my heart; but they, too, will fall away as I ascend. O, was there not, from the first, more poison in thy nature than in mine?"

To Beatrice,—so radically had her earthly part been wrought upon by Rappaccini's skill,—as poison had been life, so the powerful antidote was death; and thus the poor victim of man's ingenuity and of thwarted nature, and of the fatality that attends all such efforts of perverted wisdom, perished there, at the feet of her father and Giovanni. Just at that moment Professor Pietro Baglioni looked forth from the window, and called loudly, in a tone of triumph mixed with horror, to the thunderstricken man of science,—

"Rappaccini! Rappaccini! and is *this* the upshot of your experiment?"

QUESTIONS AND CONSIDERATIONS

1. Characterize Giovanni, comparing his personality and values to those of Baglioni. Why does Giovanni avoid Baglioni?

2. What is Baglioni's view of Rappaccini? What was your first response to Baglioni's opinion of his fellow professor? How did your opinion of Rappaccini change as the story progressed?

3. What does Giovanni see in Rappaccini's garden that disturbs him? Why does he ignore his initial misgivings about Beatrice and the garden?

4. When Giovanni enters the garden and observes the plants, how are they described? What vision of nature does the story present through the plants, particularly the "magnificent shrub," which Giovanni wants to touch?

5. What are the implications of Baglioni's parable of the poisonous woman sent to visit Alexander the Great? What does the parable suggest about the relationship between Giovanni and Beatrice and, in a broader sense, about the relationship among women, sexuality, and nature?

6. When Rappaccini enters the garden, what is revealed about his philosophy of science and the reasoning behind his experiment with his daughter and Giovanni? In what sense can Rappaccini and his ideas be seen as a criticism of science and the human will to maintain power over nature? Does Rappaccini have any redeeming or appealing qualities?

IDEAS FOR WRITING

1. "Rappaccini's Daughter" reflects the attitudes of the Romantic movement toward science, love, and nature. Do some research into the ideas of the Romantics; then explain how you see this story as supportive of their attitudes about nature.

2. Write a modern version of this story in the form of a tale or parable in which science "poisons" nature or breaks our natural connection with the world.

The Open Boat
A Tale Intended to be after the Fact:
Being the Experience of Four Men from
the Sunk Steamer *Commodore*
Stephen Crane

Journal

Write about an experience when you saw nature as a dangerous adversary.
What did you learn from your struggle?

I

None of them knew the color of the sky. Their eyes glanced level, and were fastened upon the waves that swept toward them. These waves were of the hue of slate, save for the tops, which were of foaming white, and all of the men knew the colors of the sea. The horizon narrowed and widened, and dipped and rose, and at all times its edge was jagged with waves that seemed thrust up in points like rocks.

Many a man ought to have a bathtub larger than the boat which here rode upon the sea. These waves were most wrongfully and barbarously abrupt and tall, and each frothtop was a problem in small-boat navigation.

The cook squatted in the bottom, and looked with both eyes at the six inches of gunwale which separated him from the ocean. His sleeves were rolled over his fat forearms, and the two flaps of his unbuttoned vest dangled as he bent to bail out the boat. Often he said, "Gawd! that was a narrow clip." As he remarked it he invariably gazed eastward over the broken sea.

The oiler, steering with one of the two oars in the boat, sometimes raised himself suddenly to keep clear of water that swirled in over the stern. It was a thin little oar, and it seemed often ready to snap.

The correspondent, pulling at the other oar, watched the waves and wondered why he was there.

The injured captain, lying in the bow, was at this time buried in that profound dejection and indifference which comes, temporarily at least, to even the bravest and most enduring when, willy-nilly, the firm fails, the army loses, the ship goes down. The mind of the master of a vessel is rooted deep in the timbers of her, though he command for a day or a decade, and this captain had on him the stern impression of a scene in the grays of dawn of seven turned faces, and later a stump of a topmast with a white ball on it, that slashed to and fro at the waves, went low and lower, and down. Thereafter there was something strange in his voice. Although steady, it was deep with mourning, and of a quality beyond oration or tears.

"Keep 'er a little more south, Billie," said he.

"A little more south, sir," said the oiler in the stern.

A seat in this boat was not unlike a seat upon a bucking broncho, and by the same token a broncho is not much smaller. The craft pranced and reared and plunged like an animal. As each wave came, and she rose for it, she seemed like a horse making at a fence outrageously high. The manner of her scramble over these walls of water is a mystic thing, and, moreover, at the top of them were ordinarily these problems in white water, the foam racing down from the summit of each wave requiring a new leap, and a leap from the air. Then, after scornfully bumping a crest, she would slide and race and splash down a long incline, and arrive bobbing and nodding in front of the next menace.

A singular disadvantage of the sea lies in the fact that after successfully surmounting one wave you discover that there is another behind it just as important and just as nervously anxious to do something effective in the way of swamping boats. In a ten-foot dinghy one can get an idea of the resources of the sea in the line of waves that is not probable to the average experience which is never at sea in a dinghy. As each slaty wall of water approached, it shut all else from the view of the men in the boat, and it was not difficult to imagine that this particular wave was the final outburst of the ocean, the last effort of the grim water. There was a terrible grace in the move of the waves, and they came in silence, save for the snarling of the crests.

In the wan light the faces of the men must have been gray. Their eyes must have glinted in strange ways as they gazed steadily astern. Viewed from a balcony, the whole thing would doubtless have been weirdly picturesque. But the men in the boat had no time to see it, and if they had had leisure, there were other things to occupy their minds. The sun swung steadily up the sky, and they knew it was broad day because the color of the sea changed from slate to emerald green streaked with amber lights, and the foam was like tumbling snow. The process of the breaking day was unknown to them. They were aware only of this effect upon the color of the waves that rolled toward them.

In disjointed sentences the cook and the correspondent argued as to the difference between a life-saving station and a house of refuge. The cook had said: "There's a house of refuge just north of the Mosquito Inlet Light, and as soon as they see us they'll come off in their boat and pick us up."

"As soon as who see us?" said the correspondent.

"The crew," said the cook.

"Houses of refuge don't have crews," said the correspondent. "As I understand them, they are only places where clothes and grub are stored for the benefit of shipwrecked people. They don't carry crews."

"Oh, yes, they do," said the cook.

"No, they don't," said the correspondent.

"Well, we're not there yet, anyhow," said the oiler, in the stern.

"Well," said the cook, "perhaps it's not a house of refuge that I'm thinking of as being near Mosquito Inlet Light; perhaps it's a life-saving station."

"We're not there yet," said the oiler in the stern.

II

As the boat bounced from the top of each wave the wind tore through the hair of the hatless men, and as the craft plopped her stern down again the spray slashed past them. The crest of each of these waves was a hill, from the top of which the men surveyed for a moment a broad tumultuous expanse, shining and wind-riven. It was probably splendid, it was probably glorious, this play of the free sea, wild with lights of emerald and white and amber.

"Bully good thing it's an on-shore wind," said the cook. "If not, where would we be? Wouldn't have a show."

"That's right," said the correspondent.

The busy oiler nodded his assent.

Then the captain, in the bow, chuckled in a way that expressed humor, contempt, tragedy, all in one. "Do you think we've got much of a show now, boys?" said he.

Whereupon the three were silent, save for a trifle of hemming and hawing. To express any particular optimism at this time they felt to be childish and stupid, but they all doubtless possessed this sense of the situation in their minds. A young man thinks doggedly at such times. On the other hand, the ethics of their condition was decidedly against any open suggestion of hopelessness. So they were silent.

"Oh, well," said the captain, soothing his children, "we'll get ashore all right."

But there was that in his tone which made them think; so the oiler quoth, "Yes! if this wind holds."

The cook was bailing. "Yes! if we don't catch hell in the surf."

Canton-flannel gulls flew near and far. Sometimes they sat down on the sea, near patches of brown seaweed that rolled over the waves with a movement like carpets on a line in a gale. The birds sat comfortably in groups, and they were envied by some in the dinghy, for the wrath of the sea was no more to them than it was to a covey of prairie chickens a thousand miles inland. Often they came very close and stared at the men with black bead-like eyes. At these times they were uncanny and sinister in their unblinking scrutiny, and the men hooted angrily at them, telling them to be gone. One came, and evidently decided to alight on the top of the captain's head. The bird flew parallel to the boat and did not circle, but made short sidelong jumps in the air in chicken-fashion. His black eyes were wistfully fixed upon the captain's head. "Ugly brute," said the oiler to the bird. "You look as if you were made with a jacknife." The cook and the correspondent swore darkly at the creature. The captain naturally wished to knock it away with the end of the heavy painter, but he did not dare do it, because anything resembling an emphatic gesture would have capsized this freighted boat; and so, with his open hand, the captain gently and carefully waved the gull away. After it had been discouraged from the pursuit the captain breathed easier on account of his hair, and others breathed easier because the bird struck their minds at this time as being somehow gruesome and ominous.

In the meantime the oiler and the correspondent rowed. And also they rowed. They sat together in the same seat, and each rowed an oar. Then the oiler took both oars; then the correspondent took both oars; then the oiler; then the correspondent. They rowed and they rowed. The very ticklish part of the business was when the time came for the reclining one in the stern to take his turn at the oars. By the very last star of truth, it is easier to steal eggs from under a hen than it was to change seats in the dinghy. First the man in the stern slid his hand along the thwart and moved with care, as if he were of Sèvres. Then the man in the rowing-seat slid his hand along the other thwart. It was all done with the most extraordinary care. As the two sidled past each other, the whole party kept watchful eyes on the coming wave, and the captain cried: "Look out, now! Steady, there!"

The brown mats of seaweed that appeared from time to time were like islands, bits of earth. They were travelling, apparently, neither one way nor the other. They were, to all intents, stationary. They informed the men in the boat that it was making progress slowly toward the land.

The captain, rearing cautiously in the bow after the dinghy soared on a great swell, said that he had seen the lighthouse at Mosquito Inlet. Presently the cook remarked that he had seen it. The correspondent was at the oars then, and for some reason he too wished to look at the lighthouse; but his back was toward the far shore, and the waves were important, and for some time he could not seize an opportunity to turn his head. But at last there came a wave more gentle than the others, and when at the crest of it he swiftly scoured the western horizon.

"See it?" said the captain.

"No," said the correspondent, slowly; "I didn't see anything."

"Look again," said the captain. He pointed. "It's exactly in that direction."

At the top of another wave the correspondent did as he was bid, and this time his eyes chanced on a small, still thing on the edge of the swaying horizon. It was precisely like the point of a pin. It took an anxious eye to find a lighthouse so tiny.

"Think we'll make it, Captain?"

"If this wind holds and the boat don't swamp, we can't do much else," said the captain.

The little boat, lifted by each towering sea and splashed viciously by the crests, made progress that in the absence of seaweed was not apparent to those in her. She seemed just a wee thing wallowing, miraculously top up, at the mercy of five oceans. Occasionally a great spread of water, like white flames, swarmed into her.

"Bail her, cook," said the captain, serenely.

"All right, Captain," said the cheerful cook.

III

It would be difficult to describe the subtle brotherhood of men that was here established on the seas. No one said that it was so. No one mentioned it. But it dwelt in the boat, and each man felt it warm him. They were a captain, an oiler, a cook, and a correspondent, and they were friends—friends in a more curiously iron-bound degree than may be common. The hurt captain, lying against the water-jar in the bow, spoke always in a low voice and calmly; but he could never command a more ready and swiftly obedient crew than the motley three of the dinghy. It was more than a mere recognition of what was best for the common safety. There was surely in it a quality that was personal and heart-felt. And after this devotion to the commander of the boat, there was this comradeship, that the correspondent, for instance, who had been taught to be cynical of men, knew even at the time was the best experience of his life. But no one said that it was so. No one mentioned it.

"I wish we had a sail," remarked the captain. "We might try my overcoat on the end of an oar, and give you two boys a chance to rest." So the cook and the correspondent held the mast and spread wide the overcoat; the oiler steered; and the little boat made good way with her new rig. Sometimes the oiler had to scull sharply to keep a sea from breaking into the boat, but otherwise sailing was a success.

Meanwhile the lighthouse had been growing slowly larger. It had now almost assumed color, and appeared like a little gray shadow on the sky. The man at the oars could not be prevented from turning his head rather often to try for a glimpse of this little gray shadow.

At last, from the top of each wave, the men in the tossing boat could see land. Even as the lighthouse was an upright shadow on the sky, this land seemed but a long black shadow on the sea. It certainly was thinner than paper. "We must be about opposite New Smyrna," said the cook, who had coasted this shore often in schooners. "Captain, by the way, I believe they abandoned that life-saving station there about a year ago."

"Did they?" said the captain.

The wind slowly died away. The cook and the correspondent were not now obliged to slave in order to hold high the oar. But the waves continued their old impetuous swooping at the dinghy, and the little craft, no longer under way, struggled woundily over them. The oiler or the correspondent took the oars again.

Shipwrecks are apropos of nothing. If men could only train for them and have them occur when the men had reached pink condition, there would be less drowning at sea. Of the four in the dinghy none had slept any time worth mentioning for two days and two nights previous to embarking in the dinghy, and in the excitement of clambering about the deck of a foundering ship they had also forgotten to eat heartily.

For these reasons, and for others, neither the oiler nor the correspondent was fond of rowing at this time. The correspondent wondered ingenuously how in the name of all that was sane could there be people who thought it amusing to row a boat. It was not an amusement; it was a diabolical punishment, and even a genius of mental aberrations could never conclude that it was anything but a horror to the muscles and crime against the back. He mentioned to the boat in general how the amusement of rowing struck him, and the weary-faced oiler smiled in full sympathy. Previously to the foundering, by the way, the oiler had worked double watch in the engine-room of the ship.

"Take her easy now, boys," said the captain. "Don't spend yourselves. If we have to run a surf you'll need all your strength, because we'll sure have to swim for it. Take your time."

Slowly the land arose from the sea. From a black line it became a line of black and a line of white—trees and sand. Finally the captain said that he could make out a house on the shore. "That's the house of refuge, sure," said the cook. "They'll see us before long, and come out after us."

The distant lighthouse reared high. "The keeper ought to be able to make us out now, if he's looking through a glass," said the captain. "He'll notify the life-saving people."

"None of those other boats could have got ashore to give word of the wreck," said the oiler, in a low voice, "else the life-boat would be out hunting us."

Slowly and beautifully the land loomed out of the sea. The wind came again. It had veered from the north-east to the south-east. Finally a new sound struck the ears of the men in the boat. It was the low thunder of the surf on the shore. "We'll never be able to make the lighthouse now," said the captain. "Swing her head a little more north, Billie."

"A little more north, sir," said the oiler.

Whereupon the little boat turned her nose once more down the wind, and all but the oarsman watched the shore grow. Under the influence of this expansion doubt and direful apprehension were leaving the minds of the men. The management of the boat was still most absorbing, but it could not prevent a quiet cheerfulness. In an hour, perhaps, they would be ashore.

Their backbones had become thoroughly used to balancing in the boat, and they now rode this wild colt of a dinghy like circus men. The correspondent thought that he had been drenched to the skin, but happening to feel in the top pocket of his coat, he found therein eight cigars. Four of them were soaked with seawater; four were perfectly scatheless. After a search, somebody produced three dry matches; and thereupon the four waifs rode impudently in their little boat and, with an assurance of an impending rescue shining in their eyes, puffed at the big cigars, and judged well and ill of all men. Everybody took a drink of water.

IV

"Cook," remarked the captain, "there don't seem to be any signs of life about your house of refuge."

"No," replied the cook. "Funny they don't see us!"

A broad stretch of lowly coast lay before the eyes of the men. It was of low dunes topped with dark vegetation. The roar of the surf was plain, and sometimes they could see the white lip of a wave as it spun up the beach. A tiny house was blocked out black upon the sky. Southward, the slim lighthouse lifted its little gray length.

Tide, wind, and waves were swinging the dinghy northward. "Funny they don't see us," said the men.

The surf's roar was here dulled, but its tone was nevertheless thunderous and mighty. As the boat swam over the great rollers the men sat listening to this roar. "We'll swamp sure," said everybody.

It is fair to say here that there was not a life-saving station within twenty miles in either direction; but the men did not know this fact, and in consequence they made dark and opprobrious remarks concerning the eyesight of the nation's life-savers. Four scowling men sat in the dinghy and surpassed records in the invention of epithets.

"Funny they don't see us."

The light-heartedness of a former time had completely faded. To their sharpened minds it was easy to conjure pictures of all kinds of incompetency and blindness and, indeed, cowardice. There was the shore of the populous land, and it was bitter and bitter to them that from it came no sign.

"Well," said the captain, ultimately, "I suppose we'll have to make a try for ourselves. If we stay out here too long, we'll none of us have strength left to swim after the boat swamps."

And so the oiler, who was at the oars, turned the boat straight for the shore. There was a sudden tightening of muscles. There was some thinking. "If we don't all get ashore," said the captain—"if we don't all get ashore, I suppose you fellows know where to send news of my finish?"

They then briefly exchanged some addresses and admonitions. As for the reflections of the men, there was a great deal of rage in them. Perchance they might be formulated thus: "If I am going to be drowned—if I am going to be drowned—if I am going to be drowned, why, in the name of the seven made gods who rule the sea, was I allowed to come thus far and contemplate sand and trees? Was I brought here merely to have my nose dragged away as I was about to nibble the sacred cheese of life? It is preposterous. If this old ninny-woman, Fate, cannot do better than this, she should be deprived of the management of men's fortunes. She is an old hen who knows not her intention. If she has decided to drown me, why did she not do it in the beginning and save me all this trouble? The whole affair is absurd.—But no; she cannot mean to drown me. She dare not drown me. She cannot drown me. Not after all this work." Afterward the man might have had an impulse to shake his fist at the clouds. "Just you drown me, now, and then hear what I call you!"

The billows that came at this time were more formidable. They seemed always just about to break and roll over the little boat in a turmoil of foam. There was a preparatory and long growl in the speech of them. No mind unused to the sea would have concluded that the dinghy could ascend these sheer heights in time. The shore was still afar. The oiler was a wily surfman. "Boys," he said swiftly, "she won't live three minutes more, and we're too far out to swim. Shall I take her to sea again, Captain?"

"Yes; go ahead!" said the captain.

This oiler, by a series of quick miracles and fast and steady oarsmanship, turned the boat in the middle of the surf and took her safely to sea again.

There was a considerable silence as the boat bumped over the furrowed sea to deeper water. Then somebody in gloom spoke: "Well, anyhow, they must have seen us from the shore by now."

The gulls went in slanting flight up the wind toward the gray, desolate east. A squall, marked by dinghy clouds and clouds brick-red like smoke from a burning building, appeared from the south-east.

"What do you think of those life-saving people? Ain't they peaches?"

"Funny they haven't seen us."

"Maybe they think we're out here for sport! Maybe they think we're fishin'. Maybe they think we're damned fools."

It was a long afternoon. A changed tide tried to force them southward, but wind and wave said northward. Far ahead, where coast-line, sea, and sky formed their mighty angle, there were little dots which seemed to indicate a city on the shore.

"St. Augustine?"

The captain shook his head. "Too near Mosquito Inlet."

And the oiler rowed, and then the correspondent rowed; then the oiler rowed. It was a weary business. The human back can become the seat of more aches and pains than are registered in books for the composite anatomy of a regiment. It is a limited area, but it can become the theatre of innumerable muscular conflicts, tangles, wrenches, knots, and other comforts.

"Did you ever like to row, Billie?" asked the correspondent.

"No," said the oiler; "hang it!"

When one exchanged the rowing-seat for a place in the bottom of the boat, he suffered a bodily depression that caused him to be careless of everything save an obligation to wiggle one finger. There was cold sea-water swashing to and fro in the boat, and he lay in it. His head, pillowed on a thwart, was within an inch of the swirl of a wave-crest, and sometimes a particularly obstreperous sea came inboard and drenched him once more. But these matters did not annoy him. It is almost certain that if the boat had capsized he would have tumbled comfortably upon the ocean as if he felt sure that it was a great soft mattress.

"Look! There's a man on the shore!"

"Where?"

"There! See 'im?"

"Yes, sure! He's walking along."

"Now he's stopped. Look! He's facing us!"

"He's waving at us!"

"So he is! By thunder!"

"Ah, now we're all right! Now we're all right! There'll be a boat out here for us in half an hour."

"He's going on. He's running. He's going up to that house there."

The remote beach seemed lower than the sea, and it required a searching glance to discern the little black figure. The captain saw a floating stick, and they rowed to it. A bath towel was by some weird chance in the boat, and, trying this on the stick, the captain waved it. The oarsman did not dare turn his head, so he was obliged to ask questions.

"What's he doing now?"

"He's standing still again. He's looking, I think.—There he goes again—toward the house.—Now he's stopped again."

"Is he waving at us?"

"No, not now; he was, though."

"Look! There comes another man!"

"He's running."

"Look at him go, would you!"

"Why, he's on a bicycle. Now he's met the other man. They're both waving at us. Look!"

"There comes something up the beach."

"What the devil is that thing?"

"Why, it looks like a boat."

"Why, certainly, it's a boat."

"No; it's on wheels."

"Yes, so it is. Well, that must be the life-boat. They drag them along shore on a wagon."

"That's the life-boat, sure."

"No, by God, it's—it's an omnibus."

"I tell you it's a life-boat."

"It is not! It's an omnibus. I can see it plain. See? One of the these big hotel omnibuses."

"By thunder, you're right. It's an omnibus, sure as fate. What do you suppose they are doing with an omnibus? Maybe they are going around collecting the life-crew, hey?"

"That's it, likely. Look! There's a fellow waving a little black flag. He's standing on the steps of the omnibus. There come those other two fellows. Now they're all talking together. Look at the fellow with the flag. Maybe he ain't waving it!"

"That ain't a flag, is it? That's his coat. Why, certainly, that's his coat."

"So it is; it's his coat. He's taken it off and is waving it around his head. But would you look at him swing it!"

"Oh, say, there isn't any life-saving station there. That's just a winter-resort hotel omnibus that has brought over some of the boarders to see us drown."

"What's that idiot with the coat mean? What's he signalling, anyhow?"

"It looks as if he were trying to tell us to go north. There must be a life-saving station up there."

"No; he thinks we're fishing. Just giving us a merry hand. See? Ah, there, Willie!"

"Well, I wish I could make something out of those signals. What do you suppose he means?"

"He don't mean anything; he's just playing."

"Well, if he'd just signal us to try the surf again, or to go to sea and wait, or go north, or go south, or go to hell, there would be some reason in it. But look at him! He just stands there and keeps his coat revolving like a wheel. The ass!"

"There come more people."

"Now there's quite a mob. Look! Isn't that a boat?"

"Where? Oh, I see where you mean. No, that's no boat."

"That fellow is still waving his coat."

"He must think we like to see him do that. Why don't he quit it? It don't mean anything."

"I don't know. I think he is trying to make us go north. It must be that there's a life-saving station there somewhere."

"Say, he ain't tired yet. Look at 'im wave!"

"Wonder how long he can keep that up. He's been revolving his coat ever since he caught sight of us. He's an idiot. Why aren't they getting men to bring a boat out? A fishingboat—one of those big yawls—could come out here all right. Why don't he do something?"

"Oh, it's all right now."

"They'll have a boat out here for us in less than no time, now that they've seen us."

A faint yellow tone came into the sky over the low land. The shadows on the sea slowly deepened. The wind bore coldness with it, and the men began to shiver.

"Holy smoke!" said one, allowing his voice to express his impious mood, "If we keep on monkeying out here! If we've got to flounder out here all night!"

"Oh, we'll never have to stay here all night! Don't you worry. They've seen us now, and it won't be long before they'll come chasing out after us."

The shore grew dusky. The man waving a coat blended gradually into this gloom, and it swallowed in the same manner the omnibus and the group of people. The spray, when it dashed uproariously over the side, made the voyagers shrink and swear like men who were being branded.

"I'd like to catch the chump who waved the coat. I feel like socking him one, just for luck."

"Why? What did he do?"

"Oh, nothing, but then he seemed so damned cheerful."

In the meantime the oiler rowed, and then the correspondent rowed, and then the oiler rowed. Gray-faced and bowed forward, they mechanically, turn by turn, plied the leaden oars. The form of the lighthouse had vanished from the southern horizon, but finally a pale star appeared, just lifting from the sea. The streaked saffron in the west passed before the all-merging darkness, and the sea to the east was black. The land had vanished, and was expressed only by the low and dreary thunder of the surf.

"If I am going to be drowned—if I am going to be drowned—if I am going to be drowned, why, in the name of the seven gods who rule the sea, was I allowed to come thus far and contemplate sand and trees? Was I brought here merely to have my nose dragged away as I was about to nibble the sacred cheese of life?"

The patient captain, drooped over the water-jar, was sometimes obliged to speak to the oarsman.

"Keep her head up! Keep her head up!"

"Keep her head, up, sir." The voices were weary and low.

This was surely a quiet evening. All save the oarsman lay heavily and listlessly in the boat's bottom. As for him, his eyes were just capable of noting the tall black waves that swept forward in a most sinister silence, save for an occasional subdued growl of a crest.

The cook's head was on a thwart, and he looked without interest at the water under this nose. He was deep in other scenes. Finally he spoke. "Billie," he murmured, dreamfully, "what kind of pie do you like best?"

V

"Pie!" said the oiler and the correspondent, agitatedly. "Don't talk about those things, blast you!"

"Well," said the cook, "I was just thinking about ham sandwiches, and—"

A night on the sea in an open boat is a long night. As darkness settled finally, the shine of the light, lifting from the sea in the south, changed to full gold. On the northern horizon a new light appeared, a small bluish gleam on the edge of the waters. These two lights were the furniture of the world. Otherwise there was nothing but waves.

Two men huddled in the stern, and distances were so magnificent in the dinghy that the rower was enabled to keep his feet partly warm by thrusting them under his companions. Their legs indeed extended far under the rowingseat until they touched the feet of the captain forward. Sometimes, despite the efforts of the tired oarsman, a wave came piling into the boat, an icy wave of the night, and the chilling water soaked them anew. They would twist their bodies for a moment and groan, and sleep the dead sleep once more, while the water in the boat gurgled about them as the craft rocked.

The plan of the oiler and the correspondent was for one to row until he lost the ability, and then arouse the other from his sea-water couch in the bottom of the boat.

The oiler plied the oars until his head drooped forward and the overpowering sleep blinded him; and he rowed yet afterward. Then he touched a man in the bottom of the boat, and called his name. "Will you spell me for a little while?" he said meekly.

"Sure, Billie," said the correspondent, awaking and dragging himself to a sitting position. They exchanged places carefully, and the oiler, cuddling down in the sea-water at the cook's side, seemed to go to sleep instantly.

The particular violence of the sea had ceased. The waves came without snarling. The obligation of the man at the oars was to keep the boat headed so that the tilt of the roller would not capsize her, and to preserve her from filling when the crests rushed past. The black waves were silent and hard to be seen in the darkness. Often one was almost upon the boat before the oarsman was aware.

In a low voice the correspondent addressed the captain. He was not sure that the captain was awake, although this iron man seemed to be always awake. "Captain, shall I keep her making for that light north, sir?"

The same steady voice answered him. "Yes. Keep it about two points off the port bow."

The cook had tied a life-belt around himself in order to get even the warmth which this clumsy cork contrivance could donate, and he seemed almost stove-like when a rower, whose teeth invariably chattered wildly as soon as he ceased his labor, dropped down to sleep.

The correspondent, as he rowed, looked down at the two men sleeping underfoot. The cook's arm was around the oiler's shoulders, and, with their fragmentary clothing and haggard faces, they were the babes of the sea—a grotesque rendering of the old babes in the wood.

Later he must have grown stupid at his work, for suddenly there was a growling of water, and a crest came with a roar and a swash into the boat, and it was a wonder that it did not set the cook afloat in his life-belt. The cook continued to sleep, but the oiler sat up, blinking his eyes and shaking with the new cold.

"Oh, I'm awful sorry, Billie," said the correspondent, contritely.

"That's all right, old boy," said the oiler, and lay down again and was asleep.

Presently it seemed that even the captain dozed, and the correspondent thought that he was the one man afloat on all the oceans. The wind had a voice as it came over the waves, and it was sadder than the end.

There was a long, loud swishing astern of the boat, and a gleaming trail of phosphorescence, like blue flame, was furrowed on the black waters. It might have been made by a monstrous knife.

Then there came a stillness, while the correspondent breathed with open mouth and looked at the sea.

Suddenly there was another swish and another long flash of bluish light, and this time it was alongside the boat, and might almost have been reached with an oar. The correspondent saw an enormous fin speed like a shadow through the water, hurling the crystalline spray and leaving the long glowing trail.

The correspondent looked over his shoulder at the captain. His face was hidden, and he seemed to be asleep. He looked at the babes of the sea. They certainly were asleep. So, being bereft of sympathy, he leaned a little way to one side and swore softly into the sea.

But the thing did not then leave the vicinity of the boat. Ahead or astern, on one side or the other, at intervals long or short, fled the long sparkling streak, and there was to be heard the *whirroo* of the dark fin. The speed and power of the thing was greatly to be admired. It cut the water like a gigantic and keen projectile.

The presence of this biding thing did not affect the man with the same horror that it would if he had been a picnicker. He simply looked at the sea dully and swore in an undertone.

Nevertheless, it is true that he did not wish to be alone with the thing. He wished one of his companions to awake by chance and keep him company with it. But the company hung motionless over the water-jar, and the oiler and the cook in the bottom of the boat were plunged in slumber.

VI

"If I am going to be drowned—if I am going to be drowned—if I am going to be drowned, why, in the name of the seven mad gods who rule the sea, was I allowed to come thus far and contemplate sand and trees?"

During this dismal night, it may be remarked that a man would conclude that it was really the intention of the seven mad gods to drown him, despite the abominable injustice of it. For it was certainly an abominable injustice to drown a man who had worked so hard, so hard. The man felt it would be a crime most unnatural. Other people had drowned at sea since galleys swarmed with painted sails, but still—

When it occurs to a man that nature does not regard him as important, and that she feels she would not maim the universe by disposing of him, he at first wishes to throw bricks at the temple, and he hates deeply the fact that there are no bricks and no temples. Any visible expression of nature would surely be pelleted with his jeers.

Then, if there be no tangible thing to hoot, he feels, perhaps, the desire to confront a personification and indulge in pleas, bowed to one knee, and with hands supplicant, saying, "Yes, but I love myself."

A high cold star on a winter's night is the word he feels that she says to him. Thereafter he knows the pathos of his situation.

The men in the dinghy had not discussed these matters, but each had, no doubt, reflected upon them in silence and according to his mind. There was seldom any expression upon their faces save the general one of complete weariness. Speech was devoted to the business of the boat.

To chime the notes of his emotion, a verse mysteriously entered the correspondent's head. He had even forgotten that he had forgotten this verse, but it suddenly was in his mind.

> A soldier of the Legion lay dying in Algiers;
> There was lack of woman's nursing, there was dearth of woman's tears;
> But a comrade stood beside him, and he took that comrade's hand,
> And he said, "I never more shall see my own, my native land."

In his childhood the correspondent had been made acquainted with the fact that a soldier of the Legion lay dying in Algiers, but he had never regarded the fact as important. Myriads of his school-fellows had informed him of the soldier's plight, but the dinning had naturally ended by making him perfectly indifferent. He had never considered it his affair that a soldier of the Legion lay dying in Algiers, nor had it appeared to him as a matter for sorrow. It was less to him than the breaking of a pencil's point.

Now, however, it quaintly came to him as a human, living thing. It was no longer merely a picture of a few throes in the breast of a poet, meanwhile drinking tea and warming his feet at the grate; it was an actuality—stern, mournful, and fine.

The correspondent plainly saw the soldier. He lay on the sand with his feet out straight and still. While his pale left hand was upon his chest in an attempt to thwart the going of his life, the blood came between his fingers. In the far Algerian distance, a city of low square forms was set against a sky that was faint with the last sunset hues. The correspondent, plying the oars and dreaming of the slow and slower movements of the lips of the soldier, was moved by a profound and perfectly impersonal comprehension. He was sorry for the soldier of the Legion who lay dying in Algiers.

The thing which had followed the boat and waited had evidently grown bored at the delay. There was no longer to be heard the slash of the cutwater, and there was no longer the flame of the long trail. The light in the north still glimmered, but it was apparently no nearer to the boat. Sometimes the boom of the surf rang in the correspondent's ears, and he turned the craft seaward then and rowed harder. Southward, some one had evidently built a watch-fire on the beach. It was too low and too far to be seen, but it made a shimmering, roseate reflection upon the bluff in back of it, and this could be discerned from the boat. The wind came stronger, and sometimes a wave suddenly raged out like a mountain cat, and there was to be seen the sheen and sparkle of a broken crest.

The captain, in the bow, moved on his water-jar and sat erect. "Pretty long night," he observed to the correspondent. He looked at the shore. "Those life-saving people take their time."

"Did you see that shark playing around?"

"Yes, I saw him. He was a big fellow, all right."

"Wish I had known you were awake."

Later the correspondent spoke into the bottom of the boat.

"Billie!" There was a slow and gradual disentanglement.

"Billie, will you spell me?"

"Sure," said the oiler.

As soon as the correspondent touched the cold, comfortable sea-water in the bottom of the boat and had huddled close to the cook's life-belt he was deep in sleep, despite the fact that his teeth played all the popular airs. This sleep was so good to him that it was but a moment before he heard a voice call his name in a tone that demonstrated the last stages of exhaustion. "Will you spell me?"

"Sure, Billie."

The light in the north had mysteriously vanished, but the correspondent took his course from the wide-awake captain.

Later in the night they took the boat farther out to sea, and the captain directed the cook to take one oar at the stern and keep the boat facing the seas. He was to call out if he should hear the thunder of the surf. This plan enabled the oiler and the correspondent to get respite together. "We'll give those boys a chance to get into shape again," said the captain. They curled down and, after a few preliminary chatterings and trembles, slept once more the dead sleep. Neither knew they had bequeathed to the cook the company of another shark, or perhaps the same shark.

As the boat caroused on the waves, spray occasionally bumped over the side and gave them a fresh soaking, but this had no power to break their repose. The ominous slash of the wind and the water affected them as it would have affected mummies.

"Boys," said the cook, with the notes of every reluctance in his voice, "she's drifted in pretty close. I guess one of you had better take her to sea again." The correspondent, aroused, heard the crash of the toppled crests.

As he was rowing, the captain gave him some whisky-and-water, and this steadied the chills out of him. "If I ever get ashore and anybody shows me even a photograph of an oar—"

At last there was a short conversation.

"Billie!—Billie, will you spell me?"

"Sure," said the oiler.

VII

When the correspondent again opened his eyes, the sea and sky were each of the gray hue of the dawning. Later, carmine and gold was painted upon the waters. The morning appeared finally, in its splendor, with a sky of pure blue, and the sunlight flamed on the tips of the waves.

On the distant dunes were set many little black cottages, and a tall white windmill reared above them. No man, nor dog, nor bicycle appeared on the beach. The cottages might have formed a deserted village.

The voyagers scanned the shore. A conference was held in the boat. "Well," said the captain, "if no help is coming, we might better try a run through the surf right away. If we stay out here much longer we will be too weak to do anything for ourselves at all." The others silently acquiesced in this reasoning. The boat was headed for the beach. The correspondent wondered if none ever ascended the tall wind-tower, and if they never looked seaward. This tower was a giant, standing with its back to the plight of the ants. It represented in a degree, to the correspondent, the serenity of nature amid the struggles of the individual—nature in the wind, and nature in the vision of men. She did not seem cruel to him then, nor beneficent, nor treacherous, nor wise. But she was indifferent, flatly indifferent. It is, perhaps, plausible that a man in this situation, impressed with the unconcern of the universe, should see the innumerable flaws of life, and have them taste wickedly in his mind, and wish for another chance. A distinction between right and wrong seems absurdly clear to him, then, in this new ignorance of the grave-edge, and he understands that if he were given another opportunity he would mend his conduct and his words, and be better and brighter during an introduction or at a tea.

"Now, boys," said the captain, "she is going to swamp sure. All we can do is to work her in as far as possible, and then when she swamps, pile out and scramble for the beach. Keep cool now, and don't jump until she swamps sure."

The oiler took the oars. Over his shoulders he scanned the surf. "Captain," he said, "I think I'd better bring her about and keep her head-on to the seas and back her in."

"All right, Billie," said the captain. "Back her in." The oiler swung the boat then, and, seated in the stern, the cook and the correspondent were obliged to look over their shoulders to contemplate the lonely and indifferent shore.

The monstrous inshore rollers heaved the boat high until the men were again enabled to see the white sheets of water scudding up the slanted beach. "We won't get in very close," said the captain. Each time a man could wrest his attention from the rollers, he turned his glance toward the shore, and in the expression of the eyes during this contemplation there was a singular quality. The correspondent, observing the others, knew that they were not afraid, but the full meaning of their glances was shrouded.

As for himself, he was too tired to grapple fundamentally with the fact. He tried to coerce his mind into thinking of it, but the mind was dominated at this time by the muscles, and the muscles said they did not care. It merely occurred to him that if he should drown it would be a shame.

There were no hurried words, no pallor, no plain agitation. The men simply looked at the shore. "Now, remember to get well clear of the boat when you jump," said the captain.

Seaward the crest of a roller suddenly fell with a thunderous crash, and the long white comber came roaring down upon the boat.

"Steady now," said the captain. The men were silent. They turned their eyes from the shore to the comber and waited. The boat slid up the incline, leaped at the furious top, bounced over it, and swung down the long back of the wave. Some water had been shipped, and the cook bailed it out.

But the next crest crashed also. The tumbling, boiling flood of white water caught the boat and whirled it almost perpendicular. Water swarmed in from all sides. The correspondent had his hands on the gunwale at this time, and when the water entered at that place he swiftly withdrew his fingers, as if he objected to wetting them.

The little boat, drunken with this weight of water, reeled and snuggled deeper into the sea.

"Bail her out, cook! Bail her out!" said the captain.

"All right, Captain," said the cook.

"Now, boys, the next one will do for us sure," said the oiler. "Mind to jump clear of the boat."

The third wave moved forward, huge, furious, implacable. It fairly swallowed the dinghy, and almost simultaneously the men tumbled into the sea. A piece of life-belt had lain in the bottom of the boat, and as the correspondent went overboard he held this to his chest with his left hand.

The January water was icy, and he reflected immediately that it was colder than he had expected to find it off the coast of Florida. This appeared to his dazed mind as a fact important enough to be noted at the time. The coldness of the water was sad; it was tragic. This fact was somehow mixed and confused with his opinion of his own situation, so that it seemed almost a proper reason for tears. The water was cold.

When he came to the surface he was conscious of little but the noisy water. Afterward he saw his companions in the sea. The oiler was ahead in the race. He was swimming strongly and rapidly. Off to the correspondent's left, the cook's great white and corked back bulged out of the water; and in the rear the captain was hanging with his one good hand to the keel of the overturned dinghy.

There is a certain immovable quality to a shore, and the correspondent wondered at it amid the confusion of the sea.

It seemed also very attractive; but the correspondent knew that it was a long journey, and he paddled leisurely. The piece of life-preserver lay under him, and sometimes he whirled down the incline of a wave as if he were on a handsled.

But finally he arrived at a place in the sea where travel was beset with difficulty. He did not pause swimming to inquire what manner of current had caught him, but there his progress ceased. The shore was set before him like a bit of scenery on a stage, and he looked at it and understood with his eyes each detail of it.

As the cook passed, much farther to the left, the captain was calling to him, "Turn over on your back, cook! Turn over on your back and use the oar."

"All right, sir." The cook turned on his back, and, paddling with an oar, went ahead as if he were a canoe.

Presently the boat also passed to the left of the correspondent, with the captain clinging with one hand to the kneel. He would have appeared like a man raising himself to look over a board fence if it were not for the extraordinary gymnastics of the boat. The correspondent marvelled that the captain could still hold to it.

They passed on nearer to shore—the oiler, the cook, the captain—and following them went the water-jar, bouncing gaily over the seas.

The correspondent remained in the grip of this strange new enemy—a current. The shore, with its white slope of sand and its green bluff topped with little silent cottages, was spread like a picture before him. It was very near to him then, but he was impressed as one who, in a gallery, looks at a scene from Brittany or Algiers.

He thought: "I am going to drown? Can it be possible? Can it be possible? Can it be possible?" Perhaps an individual must consider his own death to be the final phenomenon of nature.

But later a wave perhaps whirled him out of this small deadly current, for he found suddenly that he could again make progress toward the shore. Later still he was aware that the captain, clinging with one hand to the keel of the dinghy, had his face turned away from the shore and toward him, and was calling his name. "Come to the boat! Come to the boat!"

In his struggle to reach the captain and the boat, he reflected that when one gets properly wearied drowning must really be a comfortable arrangement—a cessation of hostilities accompanied by a large degree of relief; and he was glad of it, for the main thing in his mind for some moments had been horror of the temporary agony. He did not wish to be hurt.

Presently he saw a man running along the shore. He was undressing with most remarkable speed. Coat, trousers, shirt, everything flew magically off him.

"Come to the boat!" called the captain.

"All right, Captain." As the correspondent paddled, he saw the captain let himself down to bottom and leave the boat. Then the correspondent performed his one little marvel of the voyage. A large wave caught him and flung him with ease and supreme speed completely over the boat and far beyond it. It struck him even then as an event in gymnastics and a true miracle of the sea. An overturned boat in the surf is not a plaything to a swimming man.

The correspondent arrived in water that reached only to his waist, but his condition did not enable him to stand for more than a moment. Each wave knocked him into a heap, and the undertow pulled at him.

Then he saw the man who had been running and undressing, and undressing and running, come bounding into the water. He dragged ashore the cook, and then waded toward the captain; but the captain waved him away and sent him to the correspondent. He was naked—naked as a tree in winter; but a halo was about his head, and he shone like a saint. He gave a strong pull, and a long drag, and a bully heave at the correspondent's hand. The correspondent, schooled in the minor formulae, said, "Thanks, old man." But suddenly the man cried, "What's that?" He pointed a swift finger. The correspondent said, "Go."

In the shallows, face downward, lay the oiler. His forehead touched sand that was periodically, between each wave, clear of the sea.

The correspondent did not know all that transpired afterward. When he achieved safe ground he fell, striking the sand with each particular part of his body. It was as if he had dropped from a roof, but the thud was grateful to him.

It seems that instantly the beach was populated with men with blankets, clothes, and flasks, and women with coffee-pots and all the remedies sacred to their minds. The welcome of the land to the men from the sea was warm and generous; but a still and dripping shape was carried slowly up the beach, and the land's welcome for it could only be the different and sinister hospitality of the grave.

When it came night, the white waves paced to and fro in the moonlight, and the wind brought the sound of the great sea's voice to the men on the shore, and they felt that they could then be interpreters.

QUESTIONS AND CONSIDERATIONS

1. Characterize the relationship between the men in the boat and nature. What is indicated by the first line of the story, "No one knew the color of the sky"? What does this description of the sea suggest: "waves . . . most wrongfully and barbarously abrupt and tall"?

2. How does each passenger react to being in an open boat in a high sea? What do their responses have in common?

3. What is revealed about the relationship of people to nature through the comparison "the craft pranced and reared and plunged like an animal"? Do the passengers in the open boat seem to have any control over their destiny?

4. What is suggested about the quality of beauty in a natural scene through the line "It was probably glorious, this play of the free sea, wild with lights of emerald."? How do these lines alter the first descriptions of nature included in the story? How are birds and sharks portrayed in the story? Are they "glorious" in any way?

5. Crane describes a "subtle brotherhood" that develops among the men in the boat. What comment does the story make about the relationship between brotherhood and the human struggle against nature? Do you agree with the view of brotherhood expressed in "The Open Boat"?

6. What is the correspondent's "one little marvel of the voyage"? What ironic comment does this "miracle" make about the struggle with nature for survival?

IDEAS FOR WRITING

1. Crane attempts to capture the frustration the men feel after seeing the "beautiful land" only to have salvation elude them: "If I am going to be drowned . . . why, in the name of the seven mad gods who rule the sea, was I allowed to come thus far? . . . The whole affair is absurd." Write an essay on your response to the view of nature and fate expressed in these lines. Do you believe that nature has a meaningful or just pattern?

2. At the end of the story the men believe that they "could then be interpreters" of the "great sea's voice." Write an essay in response to this belief. Do you feel that an encounter with a natural disaster such as a storm or shipwreck can help people to understand the "voice" or meaning of nature, or is nature silent, impenetrable, and elusive?

A White Heron
Sarah Orne Jewett

Journal

Contrast an experience of living in the city with time spent in a rural or "wild" environment. Which did you prefer? Why?

I

The woods were already filled with shadows one June evening, just before eight o'clock, though a bright sunset still glimmered faintly among the trunks of the trees. A little girl was driving home her cow, a plodding, dilatory, provoking creature in her behavior, but a valued companion for all that. They were going away from the western light, and striking deep into the dark woods, but their feet were familiar with the path, and it was no matter whether their eyes could see it or not.

There was hardly a night the summer through when the old cow could be found waiting at the pasture bars; on the contrary, it was her greatest pleasure to hide herself away among the high huckleberry bushes, and though she wore a loud bell she had made the discovery that if one stood perfectly still it would not ring. So Sylvia had to hunt for her until she found her and call Co'! Co'! with never an answering Moo, until her childish patience was quite spent. If the creature had not given good milk and plenty of it, the case would have seemed very different to her owners. Besides, Sylvia had all the time there was, and very little use to make of it. Sometimes in pleasant weather it was a consolation to look upon the cow's pranks as an intelligent attempt to play hide and seek, and as the child had no playmates she lent herself to this amusement with a good deal of zest. Though this chase had been so long that the wary animal herself had given an unusual signal of her whereabouts, Sylvia had only laughed when she came upon Mistress Moolly at the swamp-side, and urged her affectionately homeward with a twig of birch leaves. The old cow was not inclined to wander farther, she even turned in the right direction for once as they left the pasture, and stepped along the road at a good pace. She was quite ready to be milked now, and seldom stopped to browse. Sylvia wondered what her grandmother would say because they were so late. It was a great while since she had left home at half past five o'clock, but everybody knew the difficulty of making this errand a short one. Mrs. Tilley had chased the horned torment too many summer evenings herself to blame any one else for lingering, and was only thankful as she waited that she had Sylvia, nowadays, to give such valuable assistance. The good woman suspected that Sylvia loitered occasionally on her own account, there never was such a child for straying about out-of-doors since the world was made! Everybody said that it was a good change for a little maid who had tried to grow for eight years in a crowded manufacturing town, but, as for Sylvia herself, it seemed as if she never had been alive at all before she came to live at the farm. She thought often with wistful compassion of a wretched dry geranium that belonged to a town neighbor.

"'Afraid of folks,'" old Mrs. Tilley said to herself, with a smile, after she had made the unlikely choice of Sylvia from her daughter's houseful of children, and was returning to the farm. "'Afraid of folks,' they said! I guess she won't be troubled no great with 'em up to the old place!" When they reached the door of the lonely house and stopped to unlock it, and the cat came to purr loudly, and rub against them, a deserted pussy, indeed, but fat with young robins, Sylvia whispered that this was a beautiful place to live in, and she never should wish to go home.

The companions followed the shady wood-road, the cow taking slow steps, and the child very fast ones. The cow stopped long at the brook to drink, as if the pasture were not half a swamp, and Sylvia stood still and waited, letting her bare feet cool themselves in the shoal water, while the great twilight moths struck softly against her. She waded on through the brook as the cow moved away, and listened to the thrushes with a heart that beat fast with pleasure. There was a stirring in the great boughs overhead. They were full of little birds and beasts that seemed to be wide-awake, and going about their world, or else saying good-night to each other in sleepy twitters. Sylvia herself felt sleepy as she walked along. However, it was not much farther to the house, and the air was soft and sweet. She was not often in the woods so late as this, and it made her feel as if she were a part of the gray shadows and the moving leaves. She was just thinking how long it seemed since she first came to the farm a year ago, and wondering if everything went on in the noisy town just the same as when she was there; the thought of the great red-faced boy who used to chase and frighten her made her hurry along the path to escape from the shadow of the trees.

Suddenly this little woods-girl is horror-stricken to hear a clear whistle not very far away. Not a bird's whistle, which would have a sort of friendliness, but a boy's whistle, determined, and somewhat aggressive. Sylvia left the cow to whatever sad fate might await her, and stepped discreetly aside into the bushes, but she was just too late. The enemy had discovered her, and called out in a very cheerful and persuasive tone, "Halloa, little girl, how far is it to the road?" and trembling Sylvia answered almost inaudibly, "A good ways."

She did not dare to look boldly at the tall young man, who carried a gun over his shoulder, but she came out of her bush and again followed the cow, while he walked alongside.

"I have been hunting for some birds," the stranger said kindly, "and I have lost my way, and need a friend very much. Don't be afraid," he added gallantly. "Speak up and tell me what your name is, and whether you think I can spend the night at your house, and go out gunning early in the morning."

Sylvia was more alarmed than before. Would not her grandmother consider her much to blame? But who could have foreseen such an accident as this? It did not appear to be her fault, and she hung her head as if the stem of it were broken, but managed to answer, "Sylvy," with much effort when her companion again asked her name.

Mrs. Tilley was standing in the doorway when the trio came into view. The cow gave a loud moo by way of explanation.

"Yes, you'd better speak up for yourself, you old trial! Where'd she tucked herself away this time, Sylvy?" Sylvia kept an awed silence; she knew by instinct that her grandmother did not comprehend the gravity of the situation. She must be mistaking the stranger for one of the farmer-lads of the region.

The young man stood his gun beside the door, and dropped a heavy game-bag beside it; then he bade Mrs. Tilley good-evening, and repeated his wayfarer's story, and asked if he could have a night's lodging.

"Put me anywhere you like," he said. "I must be off early in the morning, before day; but I am very hungry, indeed. You can give me some milk at any rate, that's plain."

"Dear sakes, yes," responded the hostess, whose long slumbering hospitality seemed to be easily awakened. "You might fare better if you went out on the main road a mile or so, but you're welcome to what we've got. I'll milk right off, and you make yourself at home. You can sleep on husks or feathers," she proffered graciously. "I raised them all myself. There's good pasturing for geese just below here towards the ma'sh. Now step round and set a plate for the gentleman, Sylvy!" And Sylvia promptly stepped. She was glad to have something to do, and she was hungry herself.

It was a surprise to find so clean and comfortable a little dwelling in this New England wilderness. The young man had known the horrors of its most primitive housekeeping, and the dreary squalor of that level of society which does not rebel at the companionship of hens. This was the best thrift of an old-fashioned farmstead, though on such a small scale that it seemed like a hermitage. He listened eagerly to the old woman's quaint talk, he watched Sylvia's pale face and shining gray eyes with ever growing enthusiasm, and insisted that this was the best supper he had eaten for a month; then, afterward, the new-made friends sat down in the doorway together while the moon came up.

Soon it would be berry-time, and Sylvia was a great help at picking. The cow was a good milker, though a plaguy thing to keep track of, the hostess gossiped frankly, adding presently that she had buried four children, so that Sylvia's mother, and a son (who might be dead) in California were all the children she had left. "Dan, my boy, was a great hand to go gunning," she explained sadly. "I never wanted for pa'tridges or gray squer'ls while he was to home. He's been a great wand'rer, I expect, and he's no hand to write letters. There, I don't blame him, I'd ha' seen the world myself if it had been so I could.

"Sylvia takes after him," the grandmother continued affectionately, after a minute's pause. "There ain't a foot o' ground she don't know her way over, and the wild creatur's counts her one o' themselves. Squer'ls she'll tame to come an' feed right out o' her hands, and all sorts o' birds. Last winter she got the jay-birds to bangeing here, and I believe she'd 'a' scanted herself of her own meals to have plenty to throw out amongst 'em, if I hadn't kep' watch. Anything but crows, I tell her, I'm willin' to help support,—though Dan he went an' tamed one o' them that did seem to have reason same as folks. It was round here a good spell after he went away. Dan an' his father they didn't hitch,—but he never held up his head ag'in after Dan had dared him an' gone off."

The guest did not notice this hint of family sorrows in his eager interest in something else.

"So Sylvy knows all about birds, does she?" he exclaimed, as he looked round at the little girl who sat, very demure but increasingly sleepy, in the moonlight. "I am making a collection of birds myself. I have been at it ever since I was a boy." (Mrs. Tilley smiled.) "There are two or three very rare ones I have been hunting for these five years. I mean to get them on my own ground if they can be found."

"Do you cage 'em up?" asked Mrs. Tilley doubtfully, in response to this enthusiastic announcement.

"Oh, no, they're stuffed and preserved, dozens and dozens of them," said the ornithologist, "and I have shot or snared every one myself. I caught a glimpse of a white heron three miles from here on Saturday, and I have followed it in this direction. They have never been found in this district at all. The little white heron, it is," and he turned again to look at Sylvia with the hope of discovering that the rare bird was one of her acquaintances.

But Sylvia was watching a hop-toad in the narrow footpath.

"You would know the heron if you saw it," the stranger continued eagerly. "A queer tall white bird with soft feathers and long thin legs. And it would have a nest perhaps in the top of a high tree, made of sticks, something like a hawk's nest."

Sylvia's heart gave a wild beat; she knew that strange white bird, and had once stolen softly near where it stood in some bright green swamp grass, away over at the other side of the woods. There was an open place where the sunshine always seemed strangely yellow and hot, where tall, nodding rushes grew, and her grandmother had warned her that she might sink in the soft black mud underneath and never be heard of more. Not far beyond were the salt marshes and beyond those was the sea, the sea which

Sylvia wondered and dreamed about, but never had looked upon, though its great voice could often be heard above the noise of the woods on stormy nights.

"I can't think of anything I should like so much as to find that heron's nest," the handsome stranger was saying. "I would give ten dollars to anybody who could show it to me," he added desperately, "and I mean to spend my whole vacation hunting for it if need be. Perhaps it was only migrating, or had been chased out of its own region by some bird of prey."

Mrs. Tilley gave amazed attention to all this, but Sylvia still watched the toad, not divining, as she might have done at some calmer time, that the creature wished to get to its hole under the doorstep, and was much hindered by the unusual spectators at that hour of the evening. No amount of thought, that night, could decide how many wished-for treasures the ten dollars, so lightly spoken of, would buy.

The next day the young sportsman hovered about the woods, and Sylvia kept him company, having lost her first fear of the friendly lad, who proved to be most kind and sympathetic. He told her many things about the birds and what they knew and where they lived and what they did with themselves. And he gave her a jack-knife, which she thought as great a treasure as if she were a desert-islander. All day long he did not once make her troubled or afraid except when he brought down some unsuspecting singing creature from its bough. Sylvia would have liked him vastly better without his gun; she could not understand why he killed the very birds he seemed to like so much. But as the day waned, Sylvia still watched the young man with loving admiration. She had never seen anybody so charming and delightful; the woman's heart, asleep in the child, was vaguely thrilled by a dream of love. Some premonition of that great power stirred and swayed these young foresters who traversed the solemn woodlands with soft-footed silent care. They stopped to listen to a bird's song; they pressed forward again eagerly, parting the branches—speaking to each other rarely and in whispers; the young man going first and Sylvia following, fascinated, a few steps behind, with her gray eyes dark with excitement.

She grieved because the longed-for white heron was elusive, but she did not lead the guest, she only followed, and there was no such thing as speaking first. The sound of her own unquestioned voice would have terrified her—it was hard enough to answer yes or no when there was need of that. At last evening began to fall, and they drove the cow home together, and Sylvia smiled with pleasure when they came to the place where she heard the whistle and was afraid only the night before.

II

Half a mile from home, at the farther edge of the woods, where the land was highest, a great pine-tree stood, the last of its generation. Whether it was left for a boundary mark, or for what reason, no one could say; the woodchoppers who had felled its mates were dead and gone long ago, and a whole forest of sturdy trees, pines and oaks and maples, had grown again. But the stately head of this old pine towered above them all and made a landmark for sea and shore miles and miles away. Sylvia knew it well. She had always believed that whoever climbed to the top of it could see the ocean; and the little girl had often laid her hand on the great rough trunk and looked up wistfully at those dark boughs that the wind always stirred, no matter how hot and still the air might be below. Now she thought of the tree with a new excitement, for why, if one climbed it at break of day, could not one see all the world, and easily discover whence the white heron flew, and mark the place, and find the hidden nest?

What a spirit of adventure, what wild ambition! What fancied triumph and delight and glory for the later morning when she could make known the secret! It was almost too real and too great for the childish heart to bear.

All night the door of the little house stood open, and the whippoorwills came and sang upon the very step. The young sportsman and his old hostess were sound asleep, but Sylvia's great design kept her broad awake and watching. She forgot to think of sleep. The short summer night seemed as long as the winter darkness, and at last when the whippoorwills ceased, and she was afraid the morning would after all come too soon, she stole out of the house and followed the pasture path through the woods, hastening toward the open ground beyond, listening with a sense of comfort and companionship to the drowsy twitter of a half-awakened bird, whose perch she had jarred in passing. Alas, if the great wave of human interest which flooded for the first time this dull little life should sweep away the satisfactions of an existence heart to heart with nature and the dumb life of the forest!

There was the huge tree asleep yet in the paling moonlight, and small and hopeful Sylvia began with utmost bravery to mount to the top of it, with tingling, eager blood coursing the channels of her whole frame, with her bare feet and fingers, that pinched and held like bird's claws to the monstrous ladder reaching up, up, almost to the sky itself. First she must mount the white oak tree that grew alongside, where she was almost lost among the dark branches and the green leaves heavy and wet with dew; a bird fluttered off its nest, and a red squirrel ran to and fro and scolded pettishly at the harmless housebreaker. Sylvia felt her way easily. She had often climbed there, and knew that higher still one of the oak's upper branches chafed against the pine trunk, just where its lower boughs were set close together. There, when she made the dangerous pass from one tree to the other, the great enterprise would really begin.

She crept out along the swaying oak limb at last, and took the daring step across into the old pine-tree. The way was harder than she thought; she must reach far and hold fast, the sharp dry twigs caught and held her and scratched her like angry talons, the pitch made her thin little fingers clumsy and stiff as she went round and round the tree's great stem, higher and higher upward. The sparrows and robins in the woods below were beginning to wake and twitter to the dawn, yet it seemed much lighter there aloft in the pine-tree, and the child knew that she must hurry if her project were to be of any use.

The tree seemed to lengthen itself out as she went up, and to reach farther and farther upward. It was like a great main-mast to the voyaging earth; it must truly have been amazed that morning through all its ponderous frame as it felt this determined spark of human spirit creeping and climbing from higher branch to branch. Who knows how steadily the least twigs held themselves to advantage this light, weak creature on her way! The old pine must have loved his new dependent. More than all the hawks, and bats, and moths, and even the sweet-voiced thrushes, was the brave, beating heart of the solitary gray-eyed child. And the tree stood still and held away the winds that June morning while the dawn grew bright in the east.

Sylvia's face was like a pale star, if one had seen it from the ground, when the last thorny bough was past, and she stood trembling and tired but wholly triumphant, high in the tree-top. Yes, there was the sea with the dawning sun making a golden dazzle over it, and toward that glorious east flew two hawks with slow-moving pinions. How low they looked in the air from that height when before one had only seen them far up, and dark against the blue sky. Their gray feathers were as soft as moths; they seemed only a little way from the tree, and Sylvia felt as if she too could go flying away among the clouds. Westward, the woodlands and farms reached miles and miles into the distance; here and there were church steeples, and white villages; truly it was a vast and awesome world.

The birds sang louder and louder. At last the sun came up bewilderingly bright. Sylvia could see the white sails of ships out at sea, and the clouds that were purple and rose-colored and yellow at first began to fade away. Where was the white heron's nest in the sea of green branches, and was this wonderful sight and pageant of the world the only reward for having climbed to such a giddy height? Now look down again, Sylvia, where the green marsh is set among the shining birches and dark hemlocks; there where you saw the white heron once you will see him again; look, look! a white spot of him like a single floating feather comes up from the dead hemlock and grows larger, and rises, and comes close at last, and goes by the landmark pine with steady sweep of wing and outstretched slender neck and crested head. And wait! wait! do not move a foot or a finger, little girl, do not send an arrow of light and consciousness from your two eager eyes, for the heron has perched on a pine bough not far beyond yours, and cries back to his mate on the nest, and plumes his feathers for the new day!

The child gives a long sigh a minute later when a company of shouting cat-birds comes also to the tree, and vexed by their fluttering and lawlessness the solemn heron goes away. She knows his secret now, the wild, light, slender bird that floats and wavers, and goes back like an arrow presently to his home in the green world beneath. Then Sylvia, well satisfied, makes her perilous way down again, not daring to look far below the branch she stands on, ready to cry sometimes because her fingers ache and her lamed feet slip.

Wondering over and over again what the stranger would say to her, and what he would think when she told him how to find his way straight to the heron's nest.

"Sylvy, Sylvy!" called the busy old grandmother again and again, but nobody answered, and the small husk bed was empty, and Sylvia had disappeared.

The guest waked from a dream, and remembering his day's pleasure hurried to dress himself that It might sooner begin. He was sure from the way the shy little girl looked once or twice yesterday that she had at least seen the white heron, and now she must really be persuaded to tell. Here she comes now, paler than ever, and her worn old frock is torn and tattered, and smeared with pine pitch. The grandmother and the sportsman stand in the door together and question her, and the splendid moment had come to speak of the dead hemlock-tree by the green marsh.

But Sylvia does not speak after all, though the old grandmother fretfully rebukes her, and the young man's kind appealing eyes are looking straight in her own. He can make them rich with money; he has promised it, and they are poor now. He is so well worth making happy, and he waits to hear the story she can tell.

No, she must keep silence! What is it that suddenly forbids her and makes her dumb? Has she been nine years growing, and now, when the great world for the first time puts out a hand to her, must she thrust it aside for a bird's sake? The murmur of the pine's green branches is in her ears, she remembers how the white heron came flying through the golden air and how they watched the sea and the morning together, and Sylvia cannot speak; she cannot tell the heron's secret and give its life away.

Dear loyalty, that suffered a sharp pang as the guest went away disappointed later in the day, that could have served and followed him and loved him as a dog loves! Many a night Sylvia heard the echo of his whistle haunting the pasture path as she came home with the loitering cow. She forgot even her sorrow at the sharp report of his gun and the piteous sight of thrushes and sparrows dropping silent to the ground, their songs hushed and their pretty feathers stained and wet with blood. Were the birds better friends than their hunter might have been,—who can tell? Whatever treasures were lost to her, woodlands and summer-time, remember! Bring your gifts and graces and tell your secrets to this lonely country child!

QUESTIONS AND CONSIDERATIONS

1. How does Sylvia treat the old cow, Mistress Moolly? What does Sylvia's attitude toward the cow suggest about her way of relating to natural creatures?

2. How does the story contrast town and country life in terms of the impact that each has had on Sylvia? Which way of life seems to be preferable?

3. How would you characterize the "tall young man" that Sylvia meets in the woods? What different attitudes toward nature are held by the young man and Sylvia?

4. What does the young man mean when he refers to "collecting" birds? How do you feel about his hobby?

5. How does Sylvia respond to the prospect of hunting the heron and the possibility of a ten-dollar reward for finding it? How does her attitude toward the stranger change during their day in the woods?

6. What is the significance of Sylvia's climbing the lone pine tree to find the nest? Why does she keep the success of her quest a secret? Do you think she made the best decision?

IDEAS FOR WRITING

1. Write an essay in which you argue either for or against the scientific study of nature, if this study means killing natural creatures and using them as specimens or in experiments.

2. Write a narrative about a day or more that you spent in nature or in a wilderness area. What impact did this experience have on your relationship with and perspective on the natural world?

She Unnames Them
Ursula K. Le Guin

Journal

Write about an experience of naming an animal. How did you select a name? Was the animal changed for you by renaming it?

Most of them accepted namelessness with the perfect indifference with which they had so long accepted and ignored their names. Whales and dolphins, seals and sea otters consented with particular grace and alacrity, sliding into anonymity as into their element. A faction of yaks, however, protested. They said that "yak" sounded right, and that almost everyone who knew they existed called them that. Unlike the ubiquitous creatures such as rats and fleas, who had been called by hundreds or thousands of different names since Babel, the yaks could truly say, they said, that they had a *name*. They discussed the matter all summer. The councils of the elderly females finally agreed that though the name might be useful to others it was so redundant from the yak point of view that they never spoke it themselves and hence might as well dispense with it. After they presented the argument in this light to their bulls, a full consensus was delayed only by the onset of severe early blizzards. Soon after the beginning of the thaw, their agreement was reached and the designation "yak" was returned to the donor.

Among the domestic animals, few horses had cared what anybody called them since the failure of Dean Swift's attempt to name them from their own vocabulary. Cattle, sheep, swine, asses, mules, and goats, along with chickens, geese, and turkeys, all agreed enthusiastically to give their names back to the people to whom—as they put it—they belonged.

A couple of problems did come up with pets. The cats, of course, steadfastly denied ever having had any name other than those self-given, unspoken, ineffably personal names which, as the poet named Eliot said, they spend long hours daily contemplating—though none of the contemplators has ever admitted that what they contemplate is their names and some onlookers have wondered if the object of that meditative gaze might not in fact be the Perfect, or Platonic, Mouse. In any case, it is a moot point now. It was with the dogs, and with some parrots, lovebirds, ravens, and mynahs, that the trouble arose. These verbally talented individuals insisted that their names were important to them, and flatly refused to part with them. But as soon as they understood that the issue was precisely one of individual choice, and that anybody who wanted to be called Rover, or Froufrou, or Polly, or even Birdie in the personal sense, was perfectly free to do so, not one of them had the least objection to parting with the lowercase (or, as regards German creatures, uppercase) generic appellations "poodle," "parrot," "dog," or "bird," and all the Linnaean qualifiers that had trailed along behind them for two hundred years like tin cans tied to a tail.

The insects parted with their names in vast clouds and swarms of ephemeral syllables buzzing and stinging and humming and flitting and crawling and tunnelling away.

As for the fish of the sea, their names dispersed from them in silence throughout the oceans like faint, dark blurs of cuttlefish ink, and drifted off on the currents without a trace.

None were left now to unname, and yet how close I felt to them when I saw one of them swim or fly or trot or crawl across my way or over my skin, or stalk me in the night, or go along beside me for a while in the day. They seemed far closer than when their names had stood between myself and them like a clear barrier: so close that my fear of them and their fear of me became one same fear. And the attraction that many of us felt, the desire to smell one another's smells, feel or rub or caress one another's scales or skin or feathers or fur, taste one another's blood or flesh, keep one another warm—that attraction was now all one with the fear, and the hunter could not be told from the hunted, nor the eater from the food.

This was more or less the effect I had been after. It was somewhat more powerful than I had anticipated, but I could not now, in all conscience, make an exception for myself. I resolutely put anxiety away, went to Adam, and said, "You and your father lent me this—gave it to me, actually. It's been really useful, but it doesn't exactly seem to fit very well lately. But thanks very much! It's really been very useful."

It is hard to give back a gift without sounding peevish or ungrateful, and I did not want to leave him with that impression of me. He was not paying much attention, as it happened, and said only, "Put it down over there, O.K.?" and went on with what he was doing.

One of my reasons for doing what I did was that talk was getting us nowhere, but all the same I felt a little let down. I had been prepared to defend my decision. And I thought that perhaps when he did notice he might be upset and want to talk. I put some things away and fiddled around a little, but he continued to do what he was doing and to take no notice of anything else. At last I said, "Well, goodbye, dear. I hope the garden key turns up."

He was fitting parts together, and said, without looking around, "O.K., fine, dear. When's dinner?"

"I'm not sure," I said. "I'm going now. With the—" I hesitated, and finally said, "With them, you know," and went on out. In fact, I had only just then realized how hard it would have been to explain myself. I could not chatter away as I used to do, taking it all for granted. My words now must be as slow, as new, as single, as tentative as the steps I took going down the path away from the house, between the dark-branched, tall dancers motionless against the winter shining.

QUESTIONS AND CONSIDERATIONS

1. According to the narrator, why do most animals accept namelessness with "perfect indifference"? What does this suggest about the custom of naming animals and other living things?

2. What animals resisted giving up their names, and why?

3. How does Le Guin use the sounds of language, including onomatopoeia, or words that sound like what they are describing, to emphasize her "revisioning" of the relations of humans to the animal kingdom? Can you think of any animals that actually resemble the names people have given them?

4. How do the relationships between the narrator and the creatures of the earth, air, and water change after the unnaming? What does this imply about the barriers that names create between people and animals?

5. What is the significance of the narrator's conversation with Adam and her parting remarks to him? Why does Adam fail to respond to her decision to "give back" her name?

6. If the narrator is Eve, and if she has decided to leave Adam, where will she go? How does the last phrase of the story show her new sense of language and awareness of nature?

IDEAS FOR WRITING

1. Write an essay in which you explain why you agree or disagree with the argument "She Unnames Them" develops about the custom of naming natural creatures and the ill-effects of such naming.

2. Do some research in the library, looking up the names of a several familiar animals, fish, insects, reptiles, and birds. What does the dictionary reveal about the origins

and emotional implications of the names of these creatures? What new insights about creature naming did you develop through your research? Write an essay in which you argue for the appropriateness or inappropriateness of some of the names you have researched.

HomeCooking
Elizabeth Woody

Journal

Write about a particular food or special meal that you remember your parents or grandparents preparing for you when you were a child. What did you like best about the meal? What personal and cultural associations do you continue to have with this food or meal?

The flat teeth of the morning sun chew at the blisters of the old, tar-papered house. In the garden that thrives under a cloak of sagging cheesecloth, the grasshoppers pose on the promise of a meal. Granma is framed in the kitchen window as the tongues of curtains remain out from the morning breeze. Even with the hollyhocks' colorful bonnets, up tight against the wall, the house can appear as barren as a piano without ivory. There is a swarm of colors about the screen door, of calicos, tabbys, sylvesters and blackies. They mew for their meal, in a chorus. As I turn back the covers from my floor bed, I hear humming and a spoon scratching the sides of a pan.

Watching the swill of leftovers sop up the milk, Granma turns to take the pan to the cats, twenty-some wild ones. She is pleased to see me up so early and smiles a toothless greeting. "Hi, honey, got to feed my livestock." She sings her good-morning, almost, in the sweet, high-voiced, rhythmic, dialect of Warm Springs English, that sounds Indian. She is no bigger than five feet and no more than ninety-eight pounds. I see her hook the cats in her path expertly with her toes to flip them aside, with a dancer's grace, a certain harmless precision. I once had balked at Granpa's joke about putting up little goalposts in the yard, for Granma to improve her "cat-punting." That was some years ago. Now, I am oblivious to her harmless way of walking through the fur mass of cats that stay for the one meal, and all the mice and grasshoppers they can eat in the garden.

As I settle at the table, I think of the music my grandmother makes, that evokes some aspect of the world I had forgotten since the last visit. Like toads slurping up great moths at night, or the ripple and tumble of water over the rocks in the river, that is how her songs sound to me. I breathe in the sweet smell of old age that lingers after my mother's mother. The Nivea, the cleanliness of air-dried cotton, the oiled hair. I notice two rainbow trout on the counter and move to clean them.

She returns quietly, upon seeing me work to clean the plump trout, tells me, "You can fry up those fish. Someone brought them over real early. One relative, I don't know at all. All these kids look like strangers to me. I guess it's just old age that makes me forget how many of all you kids there are." She laughs a little as she looks to my response out of her eye-corners, sitting behind her coffee at the table.

"Oh, Granma," I say, catching her mood, tease back, "I know you have to remember me. If not for my family resemblance, but just for the trouble you took to wind me, catch me, to make me come inside from playing." I eye her, likewise with cornered eyes. I see her catch her coffee in her lips, in her effort to keep from spitting the liquid and by laughing encourage me. She responds quickly by saying that my mother could outrun her. Usually, she ends this comment on my mother's great speed in childhood, by saying that "she was just too tired to whip her for her naughtiness." Listening to the house groan in the ceiling, Granma changes the subject, to the building of our ranch house up Tenino Valley.

"Your Grandfather's people made that old ranch house over there. All from one tree. All the people came to do what they could. Pound the nails. Split the wood. The women butchered and barbecued the steers. Everyone helped then. They drug the tree there by horse team. Those days our people knew how to do everything for themselves. Not like nowadays, where we have to hire big shots to come in and boss us around."

The pan snaps from the wet skin of the fish as I begin to fry them up. I know that she did not witness the building of this ranch house. She has only merged her stories with my grandfather's, a merging they wanted, symbolized by the two cedar trees that they both planted, side by side, when they married. Saying to one another, that these trees would grow together, like they would, intermingle their roots and branches as one, while still letting the winds of life blow between them. I say, to bring her back to the moment, "These are pretty trout, Granma. About as good as the ones we used to catch, that made Granpa so mad, when I was a kid."

Granma reaches up to arrange the folds of her navy blue western bandanna on her head. It is folded, tri-cornered and knotted on top. She tilts her chin upward. "Oh, how he would get mad. He always said I had more luck than sense. I had a good dream about him last night. That he and I and Baby were fishing. Baby and I caught a fish and we were screaming, and then we were jumping up and down around it, squealing. Granpa said we were scaring away his fish. He always wanted the fish to just jump on his hook."

I laugh, "Granma, I must have been that baby. Sometimes, I wish that we had some poles, so we could fish. But then, we never did learn how to tie a good knot for the hooks. Oh, how we chased the grasshoppers for bait. You laughed so hard at me, jumping as hard as the bugs. We just had to sit down in the cheat grass and hold our sides and our dresses close to our legs, so the grasshoppers wouldn't jump on them. But what really got Granpa, was the fish we caught and you would just flip them up in the air behind us. He said that was no way to treat a fish."

Granma, nodding her head, retorts, "We only used a pin and bait. He had to spend our money on the fancy lures, the steelhead poles. He had his science and some notion that he treated the fish better when he made some big game out of it. We just needed fish for our table, not the fireplace. Your Granpa was a good man, even though he had a soft heart about killing things, like the deer."

The heat intensifies outside and the "hotbugs" sing their legs into a zzzing without pause. Granma sips her coffee, intermittently stirs the spoon in her cup. She eyes the spiral and begins to dream, like she dreams during the day, between words.

These stories of old days are magical. I'm gullible and young enough to still believe in magic. The magic is this soft rumble of blood-life, laughter, our great heart under the land. I hear that great tree and the cedars breathe through this house, too, on occasion. Up the valley, I can see the mountain hold a cap of a cloud. That mountain is as storied as our lives. He walked, lived, and lusted after a young woman mountain, fought with Wy-East, for her, in a time way before the Changer came to have all this chaos beaded up into some monstrously big Dreamer design. The design I only sense from the perspective of a bead. Sometimes I dream of this. I see segments of this power hanging from the hands of old ladies as they dance at gatherings. When I told my boyfriend this, he just said I was too way-out for him. That's how he seems to be anymore. Despite all his singing, sweating, he's too heavy with war and struggle to see the story. Yet, love always seems to knock men down to drag them back to these houses of magic. Just like love knocks us down and pulls us out to the sticks, to follow that guy anywhere he wants to go. Keep an eye on him, just in case something might take him away by terrible magic. Yes, the age of the Changer has passed, but the bloodline is still with us, and the inspiring thread of women's labor, the beads, the Great Transformer and the talk of love. The Beautiful Woman in Earth still whispers into the ears of her children.

"Owwww-witch!" I holler, as the grease sizzles on the skin of my hand. The fish get one last bite on me.

"Watch your cooking. You might just get as bad as me. I never got the hang of cooking on electric stoves. I always cooked on wood stoves or campfires, especially the first days I was married to your grandfather. We lived in a tent to put his brother through college, you know."

"Yeah, Gram, but I think it isn't your cooking abilities, I inherited, but the old Dreamer brain. I wasn't thinking about the fish in the pan."

At this point she chuckles deeply, bobbing her head, which turns her bandanna a nudge-worth out of place. A meadowlark tinkles a song from the yard. She tilts her head, so her bandanna looks correct, and says, "He sings about the rain that will come soon. Of course, in Indian, he makes his song. That's why it is so beautiful." She taps her finger on the neck handle of her eternal coffee cup. She waits, as she always waits, in a meditation. She waits through her chores. She waits as she waters the lawn with her green hoses, thumb holding the spray over the grass and shadows of juniper. She waits for her children to come and visit as I visit, answering her call for company.

As I pull out the enamel, shallow-bowled dishes, I remain quiet so as not to interrupt the thoughts I see about her, probably a prayer. She responds to me out of courtesy, since her thoughts linger over her long life, and the memories that are so rare and necessary.

I again think about the music I hear. I hear songs in my dreams. Which is unusual, since I do not know any songs, or even know Indian. I think of it as this, the music comes from the tapping of her finger, beating out the occasional soft song. The way a river sounds while we fish, and the sound of the life—dragonflies whirring, singing to me—the music mingles and makes these songs that sound through my dreams. Maybe I catch the hum of the mountain over there too. He's waiting, you see, to get involved with that fiery young woman he sees at the corner of his eyes. Mountain love is a real shaky, fired-up affair. They push up great hilly ranges, bed over the lakes, rub up against one another so wildly, that it takes years to cover up all that passionate rumbling and love talk. Once my grandmother said that her great-grandmother and aunt had to run their horses into a lake to cover themselves with wet hides to keep from getting burned. The water was so hot, it took all their courage to stay put. I believe that was the last rumble before the mountains curled up for a good sleep.

When I told one of my science teachers about this, he said that these stories are just myth, not fact, and that mountains don't love or even erupt anymore. I believed him until Mount St. Helens erupted. It erased all innocent belief in the fable of absolute science for me. Thank goodness, I had heard some "fact" about those mountains way before I entered school.

I give my grandmother her share of the fish, and she says as she always says, "Oh, honey, that is too much. Put some back. I'm not company."

"Eat, Granma, we have plenty for many lifetimes over." I settle my "husky" body down to savor the fish. "You know I sure miss Granpa. I miss his whistling in the mornings. When you and him would cook together. You remember that?"

Granma retorts, "I have spent half of my life cooking for all of you. But it was your grandfather who could cook the best. He knew all the dishes of this and that. Just like he knew all that wild music. High-wy-ahn, I think it was called. He was a great singer as well as a great jokester. You tell a story as tall as he could, but I always thought you hung around him too much."

I smile, then say, "You both were pretty wild examples for me to follow. I think a lot about how you two would play in the kitchen, while you cooked, what you called a farmer's breakfast, the potatoes, ham steaks, eggs. Between flipping over the food, you would dance to western music on the transistor radio, the jitterbug, the Charleston. Yeah, I remember how you two carried on while you thought I was still asleep." I smile thinking of how agile Granma was, dancing, diaper pins on her dress, blue tennis shoes toeing in and out. Granpa, twirling her around, in his sleeveless white undershirt, pants always neatly belted with a smile wide in pleasure, watching Granma's face spin like a light in the morning dawn. Granpa had a grin so wide, it was as if it could go halfway around his head, especially when he had Granma going, or getting her aggravated from his teasing. Then he'd grin all the more while he sweet-talked his way back into her good humor.

"It seemed that you always ended up your dancing with a good fight, box-ing, with your dukes curled over. You always won with your 'Appalachian apple cut' half a wind up, a quick strike to Granpa's 'glass jaw.' Then you'd grab his pants seat and have him in your mercy. He'd holler, 'I give up, honey! I give up, I'll marry you!'"

We both laughed a great laugh at the memory. Granma tucked the trout meat into a pooch in her soft cheek, tilted her chin toward me, and said in a quiet, matter-of-fact tone, "Your grandfather didn't marry me for my homecook-ing. I thought you always knew that."

QUESTIONS AND CONSIDERATIONS

1. How does the grandmother relate to the wild cats? How are her songs a way of interpreting nature?

2. Contrast the grandmother's relationship to nature and its creatures with that of her granddaughter, the narrator of the story.

3. What is the symbolism of the two cedar trees in the grandmother's front yard? How are the trees related to the grandmother's stories and to the view of nature reflected in the story as a whole?

4. What is the myth of the mountain that the narrator recalls as she cooks? How does the mountain myth help her to remember other Native American tales and stories about nature? What do these myths reveal about the narrator's heritage and values?

5. How did the narrator's science teacher react to her stories about the lovemaking and eruption of the mountains? What caused the narrator to doubt "the fable of absolute science"?

6. Describe the relationship between the grandmother and grandfather in the story. What kept their relationship lively and vital?

IDEAS FOR WRITING

1. "HomeCooking" raises some interesting questions about the scientific view of na-ture as opposed to the mythical vision. Write an essay in which you define the scientific interpretation of nature and its origins, contrasting it with the mythological or religious perspective presented in "HomeCooking." What are the advantages and disadvantages of each way of "explaining" and relating to nature? Which do you most prefer, and why?

2. Much of the prepared food we eat is not truly "natural." How important do you think it is that food be grown without pesticides and prepared simply without elaborate sauces, heavy spices, and additives or preservatives?

Essays

Walking
Henry David Thoreau

Journal

*Write about a walking or hiking experience in a wilderness area. What thoughts
went through your mind while you were walking?*

The West of which I speak is but another name for the Wild; and what I have
been preparing to say is, that in Wildness is the preservation of the World.
Every tree sends its fibres forth in search of the Wild. The cities import it at any
price. Men plough and sail for it. From the forest and wilderness come the tonics and barks which brace mankind. Our ancestors were savages. The story of
Romulus and Remus being suckled by a wolf is not a meaningless fable. The
founders of every state which has risen to eminence have drawn their nourishment and vigor from a similar wild source. It was because the children of the
Empire were not suckled by the wolf that they were conquered and displaced
by the children of the northern forests who were.

I believe in the forest, and in the meadow, and in the night in which the
corn grows. We require an infusion of hemlock-spruce or arbor-vitae in our
tea. There is a difference between eating and drinking for strength and from
mere gluttony. The Hottentots eagerly devour the marrow of the koodoo and
other antelopes raw, as a matter of course. Some of our Northern Indians eat
raw the marrow of the Arctic reindeer, as well as the various other parts, including the summits of the antlers, as long as they are soft. And herein, perchance, they have stolen a march on the cooks of Paris. They get what usually
goes to feed the fire. This is probably better than stall-fed beef and slaughter-
house pork to make a man of. Give me a wildness whose glance no civilization
can endure,—as if we lived on the marrow of koodoos devoured raw.

There are some intervals which border the strain of the wood-thrush, to
which I would migrate,—wild lands where no settler has squatted; to which,
methinks, I am already acclimated.

The African hunter Cummings tells us that the skin of the eland, as well as
that of most other antelopes just killed, emits the most delicious perfume of
trees and grass. I would have every man so much like a wild antelope, so
much a part and parcel of Nature, that his very person should thus sweetly ad-
vertise our senses of his presence, and remind us of those parts of Nature
which he most haunts. I feel no disposition to be satirical, when the trapper's

coat emits the odor of musquash even; it is a sweeter scent to me than that which commonly exhales from the merchant's or the scholar's garments. When I go into their wardrobes and handle their vestments, I am reminded of no grassy plains and flowery meads which they have frequented, but of dusty merchants' exchanges and libraries rather.

A tanned skin is something more than respectable, and perhaps olive is a fitter color than white for a man,—a denizen of the woods. "The pale white man!" I do not wonder that the African pitied him. Darwin the naturalist says, "A white man bathing by the side of a Tahitian was like a plant bleached by the gardener's art, compared with a fine, dark green one, growing vigorously in the open fields."

Ben Jonson exclaims,—

"How near to good is what is fair!"

So I would say,—

How near to good is what is *wild!*

Life consists with wildness. The most alive is the wildest. Not yet subdued to man, its presence refreshes him. One who pressed forward incessantly and never rested from his labors, who grew fast and made infinite demands on life, would always find himself in a new country or wilderness, and surrounded by the raw material of life. He would be climbing over the prostrate stems of primitive forest-trees.

Hope and the future for me are not in lawns and cultivated fields, not in towns and cities, but in the impervious and quaking swamps. When, formerly, I have analyzed my partiality for some farm which I had contemplated purchasing, I have frequently found that I was attracted solely by a few square rods of impermeable and unfathomable bog,—a natural sink in one corner of it. That was the jewel which dazzled me. I derive more of my subsistence from the swamps which surround my native town than from the cultivated gardens in the village. There are no richer parterres to my eyes than the dense beds of dwarf andromeda *(Cassandra calyculata)* which cover these tender places on the earth's surface. Botany cannot go farther than tell me the names of the shrubs which grow there,—the high-blueberry, panicled andromeda, lamb-kill, azalea, and rhodora,—all standing in the quaking sphagnum. I often think that I should like to have my house front on this mass of dull red bushes, omitting other flower plots and borders, transplanted spruce and trim box, even graveled walks,—to have this fertile spot under my windows, not a few imported barrow-fulls of soil only to cover the sand which was thrown out in digging the cellar. Why not put my house, my parlor, behind this plot, instead of behind that meagre assemblage of curiosities, that poor apology for a Nature and Art, which I call my front yard? It is an effort to clear up and make a decent appearance when the carpenter and mason have departed, though done as much for the passer-by as the dweller within. The most tasteful front-yard fence was never an agreeable object of study to me; the most elaborate ornaments, acorn-tops, or what not, soon wearied and disgusted me. Bring your sills up to the very edge of the swamp, then (though it may not be the best place for a dry cellar), so that there be no access on that side to citizens. Front yards are not made to walk in, but, at most, through, and you could go in the back way.

Yes, though you may think me perverse, if it were proposed to me to dwell in the neighborhood of the most beautiful garden that ever human art contrived, or else of a Dismal Swamp, I should certainly decide for the swamp. How vain, then, have been all your labors, citizens, for me!

My spirits infallibly rise in proportion to the outward dreariness. Give me the ocean, the desert, or the wilderness! In the desert, pure air and solitude compensate for want of moisture and fertility. The traveler Burton says of it: "Your *morale* improves; you become frank and cordial, hospitable and single-minded. . . . In the desert, spirituous liquors excite only disgust. There is a keen enjoyment in a mere animal existence." They who have been traveling long on the steppes of Tartary say: "On reëntering cultivated lands, the agitation, perplexity, and turmoil of civilization oppressed and suffocated us; the air seemed to fail us, and we felt every moment as if about to die of asphyxia." When I would recreate myself, I seek the darkest wood, the thickest and most interminable and, to the citizen, most dismal swamp. I enter a swamp as a sacred place,—a *sanctum sanctorum*. There is the strength, the marrow of Nature. The wild-wood covers the virgin-mould,—and the same soil is good for men and for trees. A man's health requires as many acres of meadow to his prospect as his farm does loads of muck. There are the strong meats on which he feeds. A town is saved, not more by the righteous men in it than by the woods and swamps that surround it. A township where one primitive forest waves above while another primitive forest rots below,—such a town is fitted to raise not only corn and potatoes, but poets and philosophers for the coming ages. In such a soil grew Homer and Confucius and the rest, and out of such a wilderness comes the Reformer eating locusts and wild honey.

To preserve wild animals implies generally the creation of a forest for them to dwell in or resort to. So it is with man. A hundred years ago they sold bark in our streets peeled from our own woods. In the very aspect of those primitive and rugged trees there was, methinks, a tanning principle which hardened and consolidated the fibres of men's thoughts. Ah! already I shudder for these comparatively degenerate days of my native village, when you cannot collect a load of bark of good thickness,—and we no longer produce tar and turpentine.

The civilized nations—Greece, Rome, England—have been sustained by the primitive forests which anciently rotted where they stand. They survive as long as the soil is not exhausted. Alas for human culture! little is to be expected of a nation, when the vegetable mould is exhausted, and it is compelled to make manure of the bones of its fathers. There the poet sustains himself merely by his own superfluous fat, and the philosopher comes down on his marrow-bones.

It is said to be the task of the American "to work the virgin soil," and that "agriculture here already assumes proportions unknown everywhere else." I think that the farmer displaces the Indian even because he redeems the meadow, and so makes himself stronger and in some respects more natural. I was surveying for a man the other day a single straight line one hundred and thirty-two rods long, through a swamp, at whose entrance might have been written the words which Dante read over the entrance to the infernal regions,—"Leave all hope, ye that enter,"—that is, of ever getting out again; where at one time I saw my employer actually up to his neck and swimming for his life in his property, though it was still winter. He had another similar swamp which I could not survey at all, because it was completely under water, and nevertheless, with regard to a third swamp, which I did *survey* from a distance, he remarked to me, true to his instincts, that he would not part with it for any consideration, on account of the mud which it contained. And that man intends to put a girdling ditch round the whole in the course of forty months, and so redeem it by the magic of his spade. I refer to him only as the type of a class.

The weapons with which we have gained our most important victories, which should be handed down as heirlooms from father to son, are not the sword and the lance, but the bushwhack, the turf-cutter, the spade, and the boghoe, rusted with the blood of many a meadow, and begrimed with the dust of many a hard-fought field. The very winds blew the Indian's corn-field into the meadow, and pointed out the way which he had not the skill to follow. He had no better implement with which to intrench himself in the land than a clam-shell. But the farmer is armed with plough and spade.

In literature it is only the wild that attracts us. Dullness is but another name for tameness. It is the uncivilized free and wild thinking in "Hamlet" and the "Iliad," in all the Scriptures and Mythologies, not learned in the schools, that delights us. As the wild duck is more swift and beautiful than the tame, so is the wild—the mallard—thought, which 'mid falling dews wings its way above the fens. A truly good book is something as natural, and as unexpectedly and unaccountably fair and perfect, as a wild flower discovered on the prairies of the West or in the jungles of the East. Genius is a light which makes the darkness visible, like the lightning's flash, which perchance shatters the temple of knowledge itself,—and not a taper lighted at the hearthstone of the race, which pales before the light of common day.

English literature, from the days of the minstrels to the Lake Poets,—Chaucer and Spenser and Milton, and even Shakespeare, included,—breathes no quite fresh and, in this sense, wild strain. It is an essentially tame and civilized literature, reflecting Greece and Rome. Her wilderness is a greenwood, her wild man a Robin Hood. There is plenty of genial love of Nature, but not so much of Nature herself. Her chronicles inform us when her wild animals, but not when the wild man in her, became extinct.

The science of Humboldt is one thing, poetry is another thing. The poet to-day, notwithstanding all the discoveries of science, and the accumulated learning of mankind, enjoys no advantage over Homer.

Where is the literature which gives expression to Nature? He would be a poet who could impress the winds and streams into his service, to speak for him; who nailed words to their primitive senses, as farmers drive down stakes in the spring, which the frost has heaved; who derived his words as often as he used them,—transplanted them to his page with earth adhering to their roots; whose words were so true and fresh and natural that they would appear to expand like the buds at the approach of spring, though they lay half-smoth-ered between two musty leaves in a library,—ay, to bloom and bear fruit there, after their kind, annually, for the faithful reader, in sympathy with surrounding Nature.

I do not know of any poetry to quote which adequately expresses this yearning for the Wild. Approached from this side, the best poetry is tame. I do not know where to find in any literature, ancient or modern, any account which contents me of that Nature with which even I am acquainted. You will perceive that I demand something which no Augustan nor Elizabethan age, which no *culture,* in short, can give. Mythology comes nearer to it than anything. How much more fertile a Nature, at least, has Grecian mythology its root in than English literature! Mythology is the crop which the Old World bore before its soil was exhausted, before the fancy and imagination were affected with blight; and which it still bears, wherever its pristine vigor is unabated. All other litera-tures endure only as the elms which overshadow our houses; but this is like the great dragon-tree of the Western Isles, as old as mankind, and, whether that does or not, will endure as long; for the decay of other literatures makes the soil in which it thrives.

The West is preparing to add its fables to those of the East. The valleys of the Ganges, the Nile, and the Rhine having yielded their crop, it remains to be seen what the valleys of the Amazon, the Plate, the Orinoco, the St. Lawrence, and the Mississippi will produce. Perchance, when, in the course of ages, American liberty has become a fiction of the past,—as it is to some ex-tent a fiction of the present,—the poets of the world will be inspired by Ameri-can mythology.

The wildest dreams of wild men, even, are not the less true, though they may not recommend themselves to the sense which is most common among Englishmen and Americans to-day. It is not every truth that recommends itself to the common sense. Nature has a place for the wild clematis as well as for the cabbage. Some expressions of truth are reminiscent,—others merely *sen-sible,* as the phrase is,—others prophetic. Some forms of disease, even, may prophesy forms of health. The geologist has discovered that the figures of ser-pents, griffins, flying dragons, and other fanciful embellishments of heraldry, have their prototypes in the forms of fossil species which were extinct before man was created, and hence "indicate a faint and shadowy knowledge of a previous state of organic existence." The Hindoos dreamed that the earth rest-ed on an elephant, and the elephant on a tortoise, and the tortoise on a ser-pent; and though it may be an unimportant coincidence, it will not be out of place here to state, that a fossile tortoise has lately been discovered in Asia large enough to support an elephant. I confess that I am partial to these wild fancies, which transcend the order of time and development. They are the sublimest recreation of the intellect. The partridge loves peas, but not those that go with her into the pot.

In short, all good things are wild and free. There is something in a strain of music, whether produced by an instrument or by the human voice,—take the sound of a bugle in a summer night, for instance,—which by its wildness, to speak without satire, reminds me of the cries emitted by wild beasts in their native forests. It is so much of their wildness as I can understand. Give me for my friends and neighbors wild men, not tame ones. The wildness of the savage is but a faint symbol of the awful ferity with which good men and lovers meet.

I love even to see the domestic animals reassert their native rights,—any evidence that they have not wholly lost their original wild habits and vigor; as when my neighbor's cow breaks out of her pasture early in the spring and boldly swims the river, a cold, gray tide, twenty-five or thirty rods wide, swollen by the melted snow. It is the buffalo crossing the Mississippi. This exploit confers some dignity on the herd in my eyes,—already dignified. The seeds of instinct are preserved under the thick hides of cattle and horses, like seeds in the bowels of the earth, an indefinite period.

Any sportiveness in cattle is unexpected. I saw one day a herd of a dozen bullocks and cows running about and frisking in unwieldy sport, like huge rats, even like kittens. They shook their heads, raised their tails, and rushed up and down a hill, and I perceived by their horns, as well as by their activity, their relation to the deer tribe. But, alas! a sudden loud *Whoa!* would have damped their ardor at once, reduced them from venison to beef, and stiffened their sides and sinews like the locomotive. Who but the Evil One has cried, "Whoa!" to mankind? Indeed, the life of cattle, like that of many men, is but a sort of locomotiveness; they move a side at a time, and man, by his machinery, is meeting the horse and the ox half-way. Whatever part the whip has touched is thenceforth palsied. Who would ever think of a *side* of any of the supple cat tribe, as we speak of a *side* of beef?

I rejoice that horses and steers have to be broken before they can be made the slaves of men, and that men themselves have some wild oats still left to sow before they become submissive members of society. Undoubtedly, all men are not equally fit subjects for civilization; and because the majority, like dogs and sheep, are tame by inherited disposition, this is no reason why the others should have their natures broken that they may be reduced to the same level. Men are in the main alike, but they were made several in order that they might be various. If a low use is to be served, one man will do nearly or quite as well as another; if a high one, individual excellence is to be regarded. Any man can stop a hole to keep the wind away, but no other man could serve so rare a use as the author of this illustration did. Confucius says, "The skins of the tiger and the leopard, when they are tanned, are as the skins of the dog and the sheep tanned." But it is not the part of a true culture to tame tigers, any more than it is to make sheep ferocious; and tanning their skins for shoes is not the best use to which they can be put.

QUESTIONS AND CONSIDERATIONS

1. Why does Thoreau believe that in "wilderness is the preservation of the world"? What historical evidence does he present? Is his evidence convincing?

2. Why does Thoreau believe that it is better to smell like nature than to smell of "merchant's exchanges and libraries"? Do you agree?

3. Why is Thoreau attracted to bogs and "quaking swamps"? Why does he consider a swamp a "sacred place"? How can a swamp "save" a town?

4. What parallel does Thoreau create between preserving wild animals and preserving humans? Is his analogy valid?

5. Thoreau makes several comparisons between the wildness in nature and the quality of the "wild" or the "natural" that attracts us in culture. He states that "mythology was the crop the old world bore before its soil was exhausted," and comments on intellectual activity: "Genius . . . makes darkness visible, like the lightning's flash." What reasoning does Thoreau use to clarify and support these and other comparisons that he makes? Are his comparisons effective?

6. Thoreau ends his essay with a statement of his feelings about domesticated and wild animals, which he in turn compares with domesticated versus wild or untamed humans. Is it possible for humans to be truly "wild" and "natural"? Does our human culture inevitably tame us?

IDEAS FOR WRITING

1. Write an essay in which you make an extended comparison between human culture and animal patterns of behavior. In what ways are humans both like and unlike animals? What, if anything, can humans learn from animals?

2. Develop a reflective essay or story about a solitary trip into the wilderness; discuss what either you or your main character learned from the experience.

The Judgment of the Birds
Loren Eiseley

Journal

Write about a time when you had a revelation or a moment of heightened, intense awareness after a period of close observation of a natural creature or event.

It is a commonplace of all religious thought, even the most primitive, that the man seeking visions and insight must go apart from his fellows and live for a time in the wilderness. If he is of the proper sort, he will return with a message. It may not be a message from the god he set out to seek, but even if he has failed in that particular, he will have had a vision or seen a marvel, and these are always worth listening to and thinking about.

The world, I have come to believe, is a very queer place, but we have been part of this queerness for so long that we tend to take it for granted. We rush to and fro like Mad Hatters upon our peculiar errands, all the time imagining our surroundings to be dull and ourselves quite ordinary creatures. Actually, there is nothing in the world to encourage this idea, but such is the mind of man, and this is why he finds it necessary from time to time to send emissaries into the wilderness in the hope of learning of great events, or plans in store for him, that will resuscitate his waning taste for life. His great news services, his worldwide radio network, he knows with a last remnant of healthy distrust will be of no use to him in this matter. No miracle can withstand a radio broadcast, and it is certain that it would be no miracle if it could. One must seek, then, what only the solitary approach can give—a natural revelation.

Let it be understood that I am not the sort of man to whom is entrusted direct knowledge of great events or prophecies. A naturalist, however, spends much of his life alone, and my life is no exception. Even in New York City there are patches of wilderness, and a man by himself is bound to undergo certain experiences falling into the class of which I speak. I set mine down, therefore: a matter of pigeons, a flight of chemicals, and a judgment of birds, in the hope that they will come to the eye of those who have retained a true taste for the marvelous, and who are capable of discerning in the flow of ordinary events the point at which the mundane world gives way to quite another dimension.

New York is not, on the whole, the best place to enjoy the downright miraculous nature of the planet. There are, I do not doubt, many remarkable stories to be heard there and many strange sights to be seen, but to grasp a marvel fully it must be savored from all aspects. This cannot be done while one is being jostled and hustled along a crowded street. Nevertheless, in any city there are true wildernesses where a man can be alone. It can happen in a hotel room, or on the high roofs at dawn.

One night on the twentieth floor of a midtown hotel I awoke in the dark and grew restless. On an impulse I climbed upon the broad old-fashioned window sill, opened the curtains, and peered out. It was the hour just before dawn, the hour when men sigh in their sleep or, if awake, strive to focus their wavering eyesight upon a world emerging from the shadows. I leaned out sleepily through the open window. I had expected depths, but not the sight I saw.

I found I was looking down from that great height into a series of curious cupolas or lofts that I could just barely make out in the darkness. As I looked, the outlines of these lofts became more distinct because the light was being reflected from the wings of pigeons who, in utter silence, were beginning to float outward upon the city. In and out through the open slits in the cupolas passed the white-winged birds on their mysterious errands. At this hour the city was theirs, and quietly, without the brush of a single wing tip against stone in that high, eerie place, they were taking over the spires of Manhattan. They were pouring upward in a light that was not yet perceptible to human eyes, while far down in the black darkness of the alleys it was still midnight.

As I crouched half-asleep across the sill, I had a moment's illusion that the world had changed in the night, as in some immense snowfall, and that, if I were to leave, it would have to be as these other inhabitants were doing, by the window. I should have to launch out into that great bottomless void with the simple confidence of young birds reared high up there among the familiar chimney pots and interposed horrors of the abyss.

I leaned farther out. To and fro went the white wings, to and fro. There were no sounds from any of them. They knew man was asleep and this light for a little while was theirs. Or perhaps I had only dreamed about man in this city of wings—which he could surely never have built. Perhaps I, myself, was one of these birds dreaming unpleasantly a moment of old dangers far below as I teetered on a window ledge.

Around and around went the wings. It needed only a little courage, only a little shove from the window ledge, to enter that city of light. The muscles of my hands were already making little premonitory lunges. I wanted to enter that city and go away over the roofs in the first dawn. I wanted to enter it so badly that I drew back carefully into the room and opened the hall door. I found my coat on the chair, and it slowly became clear to me that there was a way down through the floors, that I was, after all, only a man.

I dressed then and went back to my own kind, and I have been rather more than usually careful ever since not to look into the city of light. I had seen, just once, man's greatest creation from a strange inverted angle, and it was not really his at all. I will never forget how those wings went round and round, and how, by the merest pressure of the fingers and a feeling for air, one might go away over the roofs. It is a knowledge, however, that is better kept to oneself. I think of it sometimes in such a way that the wings, beginning far down in the black depths of the mind, begin to rise and whirl till all the mind is lit by their spinning, and there is a sense of things passing away, but lightly, as a wing might veer over an obstacle.

To see from an inverted angle, however, is not a gift allotted merely to the human imagination. I have come to suspect that within their degree it is sensed by animals, though perhaps as rarely as among men. The time has to be right; one has to be, by chance or intention, upon the border of two worlds. And sometimes these two borders may shift or interpenetrate and one sees the miraculous.

I once saw this happen to a crow.

This crow lives near my house, and though I have never injured him, he takes good care to stay up in the very highest trees and, in general, to avoid humanity. His world begins at about the limit of my eyesight.

On the particular morning when this episode occurred, the whole countryside was buried in one of the thickest fogs in years. The ceiling was absolutely zero. All planes were grounded, and even a pedestrian could hardly see his outstretched hand before him.

I was groping across a field in the general direction of the railroad station, following a dimly outlined path. Suddenly out of the fog, at about the level of my eyes, and so closely that I flinched, there flashed a pair of immense black wings and a huge beak. The whole bird rushed over my head with a frantic cawing outcry of such hideous terror as I have never heard in a crow's voice before and never expect to hear again.

He was lost and startled, I thought, as I recovered my poise. He ought not to have flown out in this fog. He'd knock his silly brains out.

All afternoon that great awkward cry rang in my head. Merely being lost in a fog seemed scarcely to account for it—especially in a tough, intelligent old bandit such as I knew that particular crow to be. I even looked once in the mirror to see what it might be about me that had so revolted him that he had cried out in protest to the very stones.

Finally, as I worked my way homeward along the path, the solution came to me. It should have been clear before. The borders of our worlds had shifted. It was the fog that had done it. That crow, and I knew him well, never under normal circumstances flew low near men. He had been lost all right, but it was more than that. He had thought he was high up, and when he encountered me looming gigantically through the fog, he had perceived a ghastly and, to the crow mind, unnatural sight. He had seen a man walking on air, desecrating the very heart of the crow kingdom, a harbinger of the most profound evil a crow mind could conceive of—air-walking men. The encounter, he must have thought, had taken place a hundred feet over the roofs.

He caws now when he sees me leaving for the station in the morning, and I fancy that in that note I catch the uncertainty of a mind that has come to know things are not always what they seem. He has seen a marvel in his heights of air and is no longer as other crows. He has experienced the human world from an unlikely perspective. He and I share a viewpoint in common: our worlds have interpenetrated, and we both have faith in the miraculous.

It is a faith that in my own case has been augmented by two remarkable sights. I once saw some very odd chemicals fly across a waste so dead it might have been upon the moon, and once, by an even more fantastic piece of luck, I was present when a group of birds passed a judgment upon life.

On the maps of the old voyageurs it is called *Mauvaises Terres,* the evil lands, and, slurred a little with the passage through many minds, it has come down to us anglicized as the badlands. The soft shuffle of moccasins has passed through its canyons on the grim business of war and flight, but the last of those slight disturbances of immemorial silences died out almost a century ago. The land, if one can call it a land, is a waste as lifeless as that valley in which lie the kings of Egypt. Like the Valley of the Kings, it is a mausoleum, a place of dry bones in what once was a place of life. Now it has silences as deep as those in the moon's airless chasms.

Nothing grows among its pinnacles; there is no shade except under great toadstools of sandstone whose bases have been eaten to the shape of wine glasses by the wind. Everything is flaking, cracking, disintegrating, wearing away in the long, imperceptible weather of time. The ash of ancient volcanic outbursts still sterilizes its soil, and its colors in that waste are the colors that flame in the lonely sunsets on dead planets. Men come there but rarely, and for one purpose only, the collection of bones.

It was a late hour on a cold, wind-bitten autumn day when I climbed a great hill spined like a dinosaur's back and tried to take my bearings. The tumbled waste fell away in waves in all directions. Blue air was darkening into purple along the bases of the hills. I shifted my knapsack, heavy with the petrified bones of long-vanished creatures, and studied my compass. I wanted to be out of there by nightfall, and already the sun was going sullenly down in the west.

It was then that I saw the flight coming on. It was moving like a little close-knit body of black specks that danced and darted and closed again. It was pouring from the north and heading toward me with the undeviating relentlessness of a compass needle. It streamed through the shadows rising out of monstrous gorges. It rushed over towering pinnacles in the red light of the sun or momentarily sank from sight within their shade. Across that desert of eroding clay and wind-worn stone they came with a faint wild twittering that filled all the air about me as those tiny living bullets hurtled past into the night.

It may not strike you as a marvel. It would not, perhaps, unless you stood in the middle of a dead world at sunset, but that was where I stood. Fifty million years lay under my feet, fifty million years of bellowing monsters moving in a green world now gone so utterly that its very light was traveling on the farther edge of space. The chemicals of all that vanished age lay about me in the ground. Around me still lay the shearing molars of dead titanotheres, the delicate sabers of soft-stepping cats, the hollow sockets that had held the eyes of many a strange, outmoded beast. Those eyes had looked out upon a world as real as ours; dark, savage brains had roamed and roared their challenges into the steaming night.

Now they were still here, or, put it as you will, the chemicals that made them were here about me in the ground. The carbon that had driven them ran blackly in the eroding stone. The stain of iron was in the clays. The iron did not remember the blood it had once moved within, the phosphorus had forgot the savage brain. The little individual moment had ebbed from all those strange combinations of chemicals as it would ebb from our living bodies into the sinks and runnels of oncoming time.

I had lifted up a fistful of that ground. I held it while that wild flight of southbound warblers hurtled over me into the oncoming dark. There went phosphorus, there went iron, there went carbon, there beat the calcium in those hurrying wings. Alone on a dead planet I watched that incredible miracle speeding past. It ran by some true compass over field and waste land. It cried its individual ecstasies into the air until the gullies rang. It swerved like a single body, it knew itself, and, lonely, it bunched close in the racing darkness, its individual entities feeling about them the rising night. And so, crying to each other their identity, they passed away out of my view.

I dropped my fistful of earth. I heard it roll inanimate back into the gully at the base of the hill: iron, carbon, the chemicals of life. Like men from those wild tribes who had haunted these hills before me seeking visions, I made my sign to the great darkness. It was not a mocking sign, and I was not mocked. As I walked into my camp late that night, one man, rousing from his blankets beside the fire, asked sleepily, "What did you see?"

"I think, a miracle," I said softly, but I said it to myself. Behind me that vast waste began to glow under the rising moon.

I have said that I saw a judgment upon life, and that it was not passed by men. Those who stare at birds in cages or who test minds by their closeness to our own may not care for it. It comes from far away out of my past, in a place of pouring waters and green leaves. I shall never see an episode like it again if I live to be a hundred, nor do I think that one man in a million has ever seen it, because man is an intruder into such silences. The light must be right, and the observer must remain unseen. No man sets up such an experiment. What he sees, he sees by chance.

You may put it that I had come over a mountain, that I had slogged through fern and pine needles for half a long day, and that on the edge of a little glade with one long, crooked branch extending across it, I had sat down to rest with my back against a stump. Through accident I was concealed from the glade, although I could see into it perfectly.

The sun was warm there, and the murmurs of forest life blurred softly away into my sleep. When I awoke, dimly aware of some commotion and outcry in the clearing, the light was slanting down through the pines in such a way that the glade was lit like some vast cathedral. I could see the dust motes of wood pollen in the long shaft of light, and there on the extended branch sat an enormous raven with a red and squirming nestling in his beak.

The sound that awoke me was the outraged cries of the nestling's parents, who flew helplessly in circles about the clearing. The sleek black monster was indifferent to them. He gulped, whetted his beak on the dead branch a moment, and sat still. Up to that point the little tragedy had followed the usual pattern. But suddenly, out of all that area of woodland, a soft sound of complaint began to rise. Into the glade fluttered small birds of half a dozen varieties drawn by the anguished outcries of the tiny parents.

No one dared to attack the raven. But they cried there in some instinctive common misery, the bereaved and the unbereaved. The glade filled with their soft rustling and their cries. They fluttered as though to point their wings at the murderer. There was a dim intangible ethic he had violated, that they knew. He was a bird of death.

And he, the murderer, the black bird at the heart of life, sat on there, glistening in the common light, formidable, unmoving, unperturbed, untouchable.

The sighing died. It was then I saw the judgment. It was the judgment of life against death. I will never see it again so forcefully presented. I will never hear it again in notes so tragically prolonged. For in the midst of protest, they forgot the violence. There, in that clearing, the crystal note of a song sparrow lifted hesitantly in the hush. And finally, after painful fluttering, another took the song, and then another, the song passing from one bird to another, doubtfully at first, as though some evil thing were being slowly forgotten. Till suddenly they took heart and sang from many throats joyously together as birds are known to sing. They sang because life is sweet and sunlight beautiful. They sang under the brooding shadow of the raven. In simple truth they had forgotten the raven, for they were the singers of life, and not of death.

I was not of that airy company. My limbs were the heavy limbs of an earthbound creature who could climb mountains, even the mountains of the mind, only by a great effort of will. I knew I had seen a marvel and observed a judgment, but the mind which was my human endowment was sure to question it and to be at me day by day with its heresies until I grew to doubt the meaning of what I had seen. Eventually darkness and subtleties would ring me round once more.

And so it proved until, on the top of a stepladder, I made one more observation upon life. It was cold that autumn evening, and, standing under a suburban street light in a spate of leaves and beginning snow, I was suddenly conscious of some huge and hairy shadows dancing over the pavement. They seemed attached to an odd, globular shape that was magnified above me. There was no mistaking it. I was standing under the shadow of an orb-weaving spider. Gigantically projected against the street, she was about her spinning when everything was going underground. Even her cables were magnified upon the sidewalk and already I was half-entangled in their shadows.

"Good Lord," I thought, "she has found herself a kind of minor sun and is going to upset the course of nature."

I procured a ladder from my yard and climbed up to inspect the situation. There she was, the universe running down around her, warmly arranged among her guy ropes attached to the lamp supports—a great black and yellow embodiment of the life force, not giving up to either frost or stepladders. She ignored me and went on tightening and improving her web.

I stood over her on the ladder, a faint snow touching my cheeks, and surveyed her universe. There were a couple of iridescent green beetle cases turning slowly on a loose strand of web, a fragment of luminescent eye from a moth's wing and a large indeterminable object, perhaps a cicada, that had struggled and been wrapped in silk. There were also little bits and slivers, little red and blue flashes from the scales of anonymous wings that had crashed there.

Some days, I thought, they will be dull and gray and the shine will be out of them; then the dew will polish them again and drops hang on the silk until everything is gleaming and turning in the light. It is like a mind, really, where everything changes but remains, and in the end you have these eaten-out bits of experience like beetle wings.

I stood over her a moment longer, comprehending somewhat reluctantly that her adventure against the great blind forces of winter, her seizure of this warming globe of light, would come to nothing and was hopeless. Nevertheless it brought the birds back into my mind, and that faraway song which had traveled with growing strength around a forest clearing years ago—a kind of heroism, a world where even a spider refuses to lie down and die if a rope can still be spun on to a star. Maybe man himself will fight like this in the end, I thought, slowly realizing that the web and its threatening yellow occupant had been added to some luminous store of experience, shining for a moment in the fogbound reaches of my brain.

The mind, it came to me as I slowly descended the ladder, is a very remarkable thing; it has gotten itself a kind of courage by looking at a spider in a street lamp. Here was something that ought to be passed on to those who will fight our final freezing battle with the void. I thought of setting it down carefully as a message to the future: *In the days of the frost seek a minor sun.*

But as I hesitated, it became plain that something was wrong. The marvel was escaping—a sense of bigness beyond man's power to grasp, the essence of life in its great dealings with the universe. It was better, I decided, for the emissaries returning from the wilderness, even if they were merely descending from a stepladder, to record their marvel, not to define its meaning. In that way it would go echoing on through the minds of men, each grasping at that beyond out of which the miracles emerge, and which, once defined, ceases to satisfy the human need for symbols.

In the end I merely made a mental note: One specimen of Epeira observed building a web in a street light. Late autumn and cold for spiders. Cold for men, too. I shivered and left the lamp glowing there in my mind. The last I saw of Epeira she was hauling steadily on a cable. I stepped carefully over her shadow as I walked away.

QUESTIONS AND CONSIDERATIONS

1. Why does Eiseley believe it is important to enter the wilderness, to remain apart from other humans, in order to experience profound insights and revelations? Do you agree with Eiseley? Explain your answer.

2. What was the "patch of wilderness" that Eiseley encountered in New York City? What revelation about nature did he have there? What did Eiseley learn about nature from his encounter with the crow? In what ways was this encounter both different from and similar to his previous one with the pigeons?

3. What new, deeper insight into the natural world and its elements does Eiseley gain from his encounter with the flock of warblers in the desert?

4. The essay takes its title from a fourth natural revelation, in which the author feels that a flock of birds is judging an intruder, a bird of prey. Why does Eiseley believe the smaller birds are judging the raven? What evidence does he present for his inference

about the birds? Does his inference seem accurate, or do you think it is a projection onto the birds of Eiseley's humanistic values?

5. Eiseley's final revelation is much less dramatic than the others in his essay. Why does Eiseley conclude with the anecdote of the spider? What meaning does he perceive in the spider's activity?

6. At the end of his essay, Eiseley seems to retreat from some of the "meaning" he has seen in the spider's act and, presumably, those of the creatures he observed earlier. Why does he come to feel that it is inappropriate to create meanings to explain natural phenomena? Do you accept his reasoning here?

IDEAS FOR WRITING

1. Write an essay in response to Eiseley's conclusion. Do you feel that people should refrain from projecting human meaning and values onto nature?

2. Develop a narrative about an observation of nature and a revelation you have had about a living creature. From this experience what did you learn about yourself, your values, and the way you observe, think, and feel?

On Water

Gretel Ehrlich

Journal

Write about an experience that helped you to understand the consequences to people and the economy of either too much or too little water or some other natural resource.

Frank Hinckley, a neighboring rancher in his seventies, would rather irrigate than ride a horse. He started spreading water on his father's hay- and grain-fields when he was nine, and his long-term enthusiasm for what's thought of disdainfully by cowboys as "farmers' work" is an example of how a discipline— a daily chore—can grow into a fidelity. When I saw Frank in May he was standing in a dry irrigation ditch looking toward the mountains. The orange tarp dams, hung like curtains from ten-foot-long poles, fluttered in the wind like prayer flags. In Wyoming we are supplicants, waiting all spring for the water to come down, for the snow pack to melt and fill the creeks from which we irrigate. Fall and spring rains amount to less than eight inches a year, while above our ranches, the mountains hold their snows like a secret: no one knows when they will melt or how fast. When the water does come, it floods through the state as if the peaks were silver pitchers tipped forward by mistake. When I looked in, the ditch water had begun dripping over Frank's feet. Then we heard a sound that might have been wind in a steep patch of pines. "Jumpin' Jesus, here it comes," he said, as a head of water, brown and foamy as beer, snaked toward us. He set five dams, digging the bright edges of plastic into silt. Water filled them the way wind fattens a sail, and from three notches cut in the ditch above each dam, water coursed out over a hundred acres of hayfield. When he finished, and the beadwork wetness had spread through the grass, he lowered himself to the ditch and rubbed his face with water.

A season of irrigating here lasts four months. Twenty, thirty, or as many as two hundred dams are changed every twelve hours, ditches are repaired and head gates adjusted to match the inconsistencies of water flow. By September it's over: all but the major Wyoming rivers dry up. Running water is so seasonal it's thought of as a mark on the calendar—a vague wet spot—rather than a geographical site. In May, June, July, and August, water is the sacristy at which we kneel; it equates time going by too fast.

Waiting for water is just one of the ways Wyoming ranchers find themselves at the mercy of weather. The hay they irrigate, for example, has to be cut when it's dry but baled with a little dew on it to preserve the leaf. Three days after Frank's water came down, a storm dumped three feet of snow on his alfalfa and the creeks froze up again. His wife, "Mike," who grew up in the arid Powder River country, and I rode to the headwaters of our creeks. The elk we startled had been licking ice in a draw. A snow squall rose up from behind a bare ridge and engulfed us. We built a twig fire behind a rock to warm ourselves, then rode home. The creeks didn't thaw completely until June.

Despite the freak snow, April was the second driest in a century; in the lower elevations there had been no precipitation at all. Brisk winds forwarded thunderclouds into local skies—commuters from other states—but the streamers of rain they let down evaporated before touching us. All month farmers and ranchers burned their irrigation ditches to clear them of obstacles and weeds—optimistic that water would soon come. Shell Valley resembled a battlefield: lines of blue smoke banded every horizon and the cottonwoods that had caught fire by mistake, their outstretched branches blazing, looked human. April, the cruelest month, the month of dry storms.

Six years ago, when I lived on a large sheep ranch, a drought threatened. Every water hole on 100,000 acres of grazing land went dry. We hauled water in clumsy beet-harvest trucks forty miles to spring range, and when we emptied them into a circle of stock tanks, the sheep ran toward us. They pushed to get at the water, trampling lambs in the process, then drank it all in one collective gulp. Other Aprils have brought too much moisture in the form of deadly storms. When a ground blizzard hit one friend's herd in the flatter, eastern part of the state, he knew he had to keep his cattle drifting. If they hit a fence line and had to face the storm, snow would blow into their noses and they'd drown. "We cut wire all the way to Nebraska," he told me. During the same storm another cowboy found his cattle too late: they were buried in a draw under a fifteen-foot drift.

High water comes in June when the runoff peaks, and it's another bugaboo for the ranchers. The otherwise amiable thirty-foot-wide creeks swell and change courses so that when we cross them with livestock, the water is belly-deep or more. Cowboys in the 1800s who rode with the trail herds from Texas often worked in the big rivers on horseback for a week just to cross a thousand head of longhorn steers, losing half of them in the process. On a less-grand scale we have drownings and near drownings here each spring. When we crossed a creek this year the swift current toppled a horse and carried the rider under a log. A cowboy who happened to look back saw her head go under, dove in from horseback, and saved her. At Trapper Creek, where Owen Wister spent several summers in the 1920s and entertained Mr. Hemingway, a cloudburst slapped down on us like a black eye. Scraps of rainbow moved in vertical sweeps of rain that broke apart and disappeared behind a ridge. The creek flooded, taking out a house and a field of corn. We saw one resident walking in a flattened alfalfa field where the river had flowed briefly. "Want to go fishing?" he yelled to us as we rode by. The fish he was throwing into a white bucket were trout that had been "beached" by the flood.

Westerners are ambivalent about water because they've never seen what it can create except havoc and mud. They've never walked through a forest of wild orchids or witnessed the unfurling of five-foot-high ferns. "The only way I like my water is if there's whiskey in it," one rancher told me as we weaned calves in a driving rainstorm. That day we spent twelve hours on horseback in the rain. Despite protective layers of clothing: wool union suits, chaps, ankle-length yellow slickers, neck scarves and hats, we were drenched. Water drips off hat brims into your crotch; boots and gloves soak through. But to stay home out of the storm is deemed by some as a worse fate: "Hell, my wife had me cannin' beans for a week," one cowboy complained. "I'd rather drown like a muskrat out there."

Dryness is the common denominator in Wyoming. We're drenched more often in dust than in water; it is the scalpel and the suit of armor that make westerners what they are. Dry air presses a stockman's insides outward. The secret, inner self is worn not on the sleeve but in the skin. It's an unlubricated condition: there's not enough moisture in the air to keep the whole emotional machinery oiled and working. "What you see is what you get, but you have to learn to look to see all that's there," one young rancher told me. He was physically reckless when coming to see me or leaving. That was his way of saying he had and would miss me, and in the clean, broad sweeps of passion between us, there was no heaviness, no muddy residue. Cowboys have learned not to waste words from not having wasted water, as if verbosity would create a thirst too extreme to bear. If voices are raspy, it's because vocal cords are coated with dust. When I helped ship seven thousand head of steers one fall, the dust in the big, roomy sorting corrals churned as deeply and sensually as water. We wore scarves over our noses and mouths; the rest of our faces blackened with dirt so we looked like raccoons or coal miners. The westerner's face is stiff and dark red as jerky. It gives no clues beyond the discerning look that says, "You've been observed." Perhaps the too-early lines of aging that pull across these ranchers' necks are really cracks in a wall through which we might see the contradictory signs of their character: a complacency, a restlessness, a shy, boyish pride.

I knew a sheepherder who had the words "hard luck" tattooed across his knuckles. "That's for all the times I've been dry," he explained. "And when you've been as thirsty as I've been, you don't forget how something tastes."

That's how he mapped out the big ranch he worked for: from thirst to thirst, whiskey to whiskey. To follow the water courses in Wyoming—seven rivers and a network of good-sized creeks—is to trace the history of settlement here. After a few bad winters the early ranchers quickly discovered the necessity of raising feed for livestock. Long strips of land on both sides of the creeks and rivers were grabbed up in the 1870s and '80s before Wyoming was a state. Land was cheap and relatively easy to accumulate, but control of water was crucial. The early ranches such as the Swan Land & Cattle Company, the Budd Ranch, the M-L, the Bug Ranch, and the Pitchfork took up land along the Chugwater, Green, Greybull, Big Horn, and Shoshone rivers. It was not long before feuds over water began. The old law of "full and undiminished flow" to those who owned land along a creek was changed to one that adjudicated and allocated water by the acre foot to specified pieces of land. By 1890 residents had to file claims for the right to use the water that flowed through their ranches. These rights were, and still are, awarded according to the date a ranch was established regardless of ownership changes. This solved the increasing problem of upstream-downstream disputes, enabling the first ranch established on a creek to maintain the first water right, regardless of how many newer settlements occurred upstream.

Land through which no water flowed posed another problem. Frank's father was one of the Mormon colonists sent by Brigham Young to settle and put under cultivation the arid Big Horn Basin. The twenty thousand acres they claimed were barren and waterless. To remedy this problem they dug a canal thirty-seven miles long, twenty-seven feet across, and sixteen feet deep by hand. The project took four years to complete. Along the way a huge boulder gave the canal diggers trouble: it couldn't be moved. As a last resort the Mormon men held hands around the rock and prayed. The next morning the boulder rolled out of the way.

Piousness was not always the rule. Feuds over water became venomous as the population of the state grew. Ditch riders—so called because they monitored on horseback the flow and use of water—often found themselves on the wrong end of an irrigating shovel. Frank remembers when the ditch rider in his district was hit over the head so hard by the rancher whose water he was turning off that he fell unconscious into the canal, floating on his back until he bumped into the next head gate.

With the completion of the canal, the Mormons built churches, schools, and houses communally, working in unison as if taking their cue from the water that snaked by them. "It was a socialistic sonofabitch from the beginning," Frank recalls, "a beautiful damned thing. These 'western individualists' forget how things got done around here and not so damned many years ago at that."

Frank is the opposite of the strapping, conservative western man. Sturdy, but small-boned, he has an awkward, knock-kneed gait that adds to his chronic amiability. Though he's made his life close to home, he has a natural, panoramic vision as if he had upped-periscope through the Basin's dust clouds and had a good look around. Frank's generosity runs like water: it follows the path of least resistance and, tumbling downhill, takes on a fullness so replete and indiscriminate as to sometimes appear absurd. "You can't cheat an honest man," he'll tell you and laugh at the paradox implied. His wide face and forehead indicate the breadth of his unruly fair-mindedness—one that includes not just local affections but the whole human community.

When Frank started irrigating there were no tarp dams. "We plugged up those ditches with any old thing we had—rags, bones, car parts, sod." Though he could afford to hire an irrigator now he prefers to do the work himself, and when I'm away he turns my water as well, then mows my lawn. "Irrigating is a contemptible damned job. I've been fighting water all my life. Mother Nature is a bitter old bitch, isn't she? But we have to have that challenge. We crave it and I'll be goddamned if I know why. I feel sorry for these damned rich ranchers with their pumps and sprinkler systems and gated pipe because they're missing out on something. When I go to change my water at dawn and just before dark, it's peaceful out there, away from everybody. I love the fragrances— grass growing, wild rose on the ditch bank—and hearing the damned old birds twittering away. How can we live without that?"

Two thousand years before the Sidon Canal was built in Wyoming, the Hohokam, a people who lived in what became Arizona, used digging sticks to channel water from the Salt and Gila rivers to dry land. Theirs was the most extensive irrigation system in aboriginal North America. Water was brought thirty miles to spread over fields of corn, beans, and pumpkins—crops inherited from tribes in South and Central America. "It's a primitive damned thing," Frank said about the business of using water. "The change from a digging stick to a shovel isn't much of an evolution. Playing with water is something all kids have done, whether it's in creeks or in front of fire hydrants. Maybe that's how agriculture got started in the first place."

Romans applied their insoluble cement to waterways as if it could arrest the flux and impermanence they knew water to signify. Of the fourteen aqueducts that brought water from mountains and lakes to Rome, several are still in use today. On a Roman latifundium—their equivalent of a ranch—they grew alfalfa, a hot-weather crop introduced by way of Persia and Greece around the fifth century B.C., and fed it to their horses as we do here. Feuds over water were common: Nero was reprimanded for bathing in the canal that carried the city's drinking water, the brothels tapped aqueducts on the sly until once the whole city went dry. The Empire's staying power began to collapse when the waterways fell into disrepair. Crops dried up and the water that had carried life to the great cities stagnated and became breeding grounds for mosquitoes until malaria, not water, flowed into the heart of Rome.

There is nothing in nature that can't be taken as a sign of both mortality and invigoration. Cascading water equates loss followed by loss, a momentum of things falling in the direction of death, then life. In Conrad's *Heart of Darkness,* the river is a redundancy flowing through rain forest, a channel of solitude, a solid thing, a trap. Hemingway's Big Two-Hearted River is the opposite: it's an accepting, restorative place. Water can stand for what is unconscious, instinctive, and sexual in us, for the creative swill in which we fish for ideas. It carries, weightlessly, the imponderable things in our lives: death and creation. We can drown in it or else stay buoyant, quench our thirst, stay alive.

In Navajo mythology, rain is the sun's sperm coming down. A Crow woman I met on a plane told me that. She wore a flowered dress, a man's wool jacket with a package of Vantages stuck in one pocket, and calf-high moccasins held together with two paper clips. "Traditional Crow think water is medicinal," she said as we flew over the Yellowstone River which runs through the tribal land where she lives. "The old tribal crier used to call out every morning for our people to drink all they could, to make water touch their bodies. 'Water is your body,' they used to say." Looking down on the seared landscape below, it wasn't difficult to understand the real and imagined potency of water. "All that would be a big death yard," she said with a sweep of her arm. That's how the drought would come: one sweep and all moisture would be banished. Bluebunch and June grass would wither. Elk and deer would trample sidehills into sand. Draws would fill up with dead horses and cows. Tucked under ledges of shale, dens of rattlesnakes would grow into city-states of snakes. The roots of trees would rise to the surface and flail through dust in search of water.

Everything in nature invites us constantly to be what we are. We are often like rivers: careless and forceful, timid and dangerous, lucid and muddied, eddying, gleaming, still. Lovers, farmers, and artists have one thing in common, at least—a fear of "dry spells," dormant periods in which we do no blooming, internal droughts only the waters of imagination and psychic release can civilize. All such matters are delicate of course. But a good irrigator knows this: too little water brings on the weeds while too much degrades the soil the way too much easy money can trivialize a person's initiative. In his journal Thoreau wrote, "A man's life should be as fresh as a river. It should be the same channel but a new water every instant."

This morning I walked the length of a narrow, dry wash. Slabs of stone, broken off in great squares, lay propped against the banks like blank mirrors. A sagebrush had drilled a hole through one of these rocks. The roots fanned out and down like hooked noses. Farther up, a quarry of red rock bore the fossilized marks of rippling water. Just yesterday, a cloudburst sent a skinny stream beneath these frozen undulations. Its passage carved the same kind of watery ridges into the sand at my feet. Even in this dry country, where internal and external droughts always threaten, water is self-registering no matter how ancient, recent, or brief.

QUESTIONS AND CONSIDERATIONS

1. Ehrlich uses many images and comparisons in the first paragraph of her essay. How do these figures of speech, such as "mountains hold their snows like a secret" and "tarp dams . . . fluttered in the wind like prayer flags" help to establish a tone and mood

for the essay while emphasizing the need for irrigation in the arid ranch country of Wyoming?

2. What examples does Ehrlich use to support her assertion that "Wyoming ranchers find themselves at the mercy of the weather"? Are her examples effective?

3. What conditions and problems related to weather do the Wyoming ranchers have to confront during the different seasons of the year? Why are these ranchers "ambivalent about water"?

4. How does Ehrlich create a causal relationship between the ranchers' personality and physical appearance and the weather that is often their adversary? Do her images and examples, such as her extended portrait of the rancher Frank Hinckley, help her to create clear causal relationships?

5. How does Ehrlich's brief historic account of water use in Roman times, among the Hohokam, and in the frontier days of the American West give depth and clarity to her portrait of modern ranch life?

6. Ehrlich's last four paragraphs create an extended conclusion for her essay. What point does she make about water and its meaning through the diverse literary and cultural comparisons and striking images included in these paragraphs? With what final impression of the power and meaning of water in relationship to human life and imagination does the essay leave you?

IDEAS FOR WRITING

1. Pick a vital natural resource—forests, land, water, or air—that you feel is not being respected in our culture. Write an essay in which you provide suggestions for more effective management and preservation of this crucial resource.

2. Write an essay similar to Ehrlich's in which you explore the connections between human personality, culture, imagination, and survival and one of the four key elements of earth, air, fire, or water. Focus on your own region or local community for examples, as Ehrlich does with the Wyoming ranch country.

Landscape, History, and the Pueblo Imagination
From a High Arid Plateau in New Mexico
Leslie Marmon Silko

Journal

Freewrite or cluster for about five minutes on the words landscape *and* imagination. *Describe a landscape that you love.*

You see that after a thing is dead, it dries up. It might take weeks or years, but eventually if you touch the thing, it crumbles under your fingers. It goes back to dust. The soul of the thing has long since departed. With the plants and wild game the soul may have already been borne back into bones and blood or thick green stalk and leaves. Nothing is wasted. What cannot be eaten by people or in some way used must then be left where other living creatures may benefit. What domestic animals or wild scavengers can't eat will be fed to the plants. The plants feed on the dust of these few remains.

The ancient Pueblo people buried the dead in vacant rooms or partially collapsed rooms adjacent to the main living quarters. Sand and clay used to construct the roof make layers many inches deep once the roof has collapsed. The layers of sand and clay make for easy gravedigging. The vacant room fills with cast-off objects and debris. When a vacant room has filled deep enough, a shallow but adequate grave can be scooped in a far corner. Archaeologists have remarked over formal burials complete with elaborate funerary objects excavated in trash middens of abandoned rooms. But the rocks and adobe mortar of collapsed walls were valued by the ancient people. Because each rock had been carefully selected for size and shape, then chiseled to an even face. Even the pink clay adobe melting with each rainstorm had to be prayed over, then dug and carried some distance. Corn cobs and husks, the rinds and stalks and animal bones were not regarded by the ancient people as filth or garbage. The remains were merely resting at a mid-point in their journey back to dust. Human remains are not so different. They should rest with the bones and rinds where they all may benefit living creatures—small rodents and insects—until their return is completed. The remains of things—animals and plants, the clay and the stones—were treated with respect. Because for the ancient people all these things had spirit and being. The antelope merely consents to return home with the hunter. All phases of the hunt are conducted with love. The love the hunter and the people have for the Antelope People. And the love of the antelope who agree to give up their meat and blood so that human beings will not starve. Waste of meat or even the thoughtless handling of bones cooked bare will offend the antelope spirits. Next year the hunters will vainly search the dry plains for antelope. Thus it is necessary to return carefully the bones and hair, and the stalks and leaves to the earth who first created them. The spirits remain close by. They do not leave us.

The dead become dust, and in this becoming they are once more joined with the Mother. The ancient Pueblo people called the earth the Mother Creator of all things in this world. Her sister, the Corn Mother, occasionally merges with her because all succulent green life rises out of the depths of the earth.

Rocks and clay are part of the Mother. They emerge in various forms, but at some time before, they were smaller particles or great boulders. At a later time they may again become what they once were. Dust.

A rock shares this fate with us and with animals and plants as well. A rock has being or spirit, although we may not understand it. The spirit may differ from the spirit we know in animals or plants or in ourselves. In the end we all originate from the depths of the earth. Perhaps this is how all beings share in the spirit of the Creator. We do not know.

From the Emergence Place

Pueblo potters, the creators of petroglyphs and oral narratives, never conceived of removing themselves from the earth and sky. So long as the human consciousness remains *within* the hills, canyons, cliffs, and the plants, clouds, and sky, the term *landscape,* as it has entered the English language, is misleading. "A portion of territory the eye can comprehend in a single view" does not correctly describe the relationship between the human being and his or her surroundings. This assumes the viewer is somehow *outside* or *separate* from the territory he or she surveys. Viewers are as much a part of the landscape as the boulders they stand on. There is no high mesa edge or mountain peak where one can stand and not immediately be part of all that surrounds. Human identity is linked with all the elements of Creation through the clan: you might belong to the Sun Clan or the Lizard Clan or the Corn Clan or the Clay Clan.[1] Standing deep within the natural world, the ancient Pueblo understood the thing as it was—the squash blossom, grasshopper, or rabbit itself could never be created by the human hand. Ancient Pueblos took the modest view that the thing itself (the landscape) could not be improved upon. The ancients did not presume to tamper with what had already been created. Thus *realism,* as we now recognize it in painting and sculpture, did not catch the imaginations of Pueblo people until recently.

The squash blossom itself is *one thing:* itself. So the ancient Pueblo potter abstracted what she saw to be the key elements of the squash blossom—the four symmetrical petals, with four symmetrical stamens in the center. These key elements, while suggesting the squash flower, also link it with the four cardinal directions. By representing only its intrinsic form, the squash flower is released from a limited meaning or restricted identity. Even in the most sophisticated abstract form, a squash flower or a cloud or a lightning bolt became intricately connected with a complex system of relationships which the ancient Pueblo people maintained with each other, and with the populous natural world they lived within. A bolt of lightning is itself, but at the same time it may mean much more. It may be a messenger of good fortune when summer rains are needed. It may deliver death, perhaps the result of manipulations by the Gunnadeyahs, destructive necromancers. Lightning may strike down an evildoer. Or lightning may strike a person of good will. If the person survives, lightning endows him or her with heightened power.

Pictographs and petroglyphs of constellations or elk or antelope draw their magic in part from the process wherein the focus of all prayer and concentration is upon the thing itself, which, in its turn, guides the hunter's hand. Connection with the spirit dimensions requires a figure or form which is all-inclusive. A "lifelike" rendering of an elk is too restrictive. Only the elk *is* itself. A

---

1 *Clan*—A social unit composed of families sharing common ancestors who trace their lineage back to the Emergence where their ancestors allied themselves with certain plants or animals or elements. [Silko's note]

realistic rendering of an elk would be only one particular elk anyway. The purpose of the hunt rituals and magic is to make contact with *all* the spirits of the Elk.

The land, the sky, and all that is within them—the landscape—includes human beings. Interrelationships in the Pueblo landscape are complex and fragile. The unpredictability of the weather, the aridity and harshness of much of the terrain in the high plateau country explain in large part the relentless attention the ancient Pueblo people gave the sky and the earth around them. Survival depended upon harmony and cooperation not only among human beings, but among all things—the animate and the less animate, since rocks and mountains were known to move, to travel occasionally.

The ancient Pueblos believed the Earth and the Sky were sisters (or sister and brother in the post-Christian version). As long as good family relations are maintained, then the Sky will continue to bless her sister, the Earth, with rain, and the Earth's children will continue to survive. But the old stories recall incidents in which troublesome spirits or beings threaten the earth. In one story, a malicious ka'tsina, called the Gambler, seizes the Shiwana, or Rainclouds, the Sun's beloved children.[2] The Shiwana are snared in magical power late one afternoon on a high mountain top. The Gambler takes the Rainclouds to his mountain stronghold where he locks them in the north room of his house. What was his idea? The Shiwana were beyond value. They brought life to all things on earth. The Gambler wanted a big stake to wager in his games of chance. But such greed, even on the part of only one being, had the effect of threatening the survival of all life on earth. Sun Youth, aided by old Grandmother Spider, outsmarts the Gambler and the rigged game, and the Rainclouds are set free. The drought ends, and once more life thrives on earth.

Through the Stories We Hear Who We Are

All summer the people watch the west horizon, scanning the sky from south to north for rain clouds. Corn must have moisture at the time the tassels form. Otherwise pollination will be incomplete, and the ears will be stunted and shriveled. An inadequate harvest may bring disaster. Stories told at Hopi, Zuni, and at Acoma and Laguna describe drought and starvation as recently as 1900. Precipitation in west-central New Mexico averages fourteen inches annually. The western pueblos are located at altitudes over 5,600 feet above sea level, where winter temperatures at night fall below freezing. Yet evidence of their presence in the high desert plateau country goes back ten thousand years. The ancient Pueblo people not only survived in this environment, but many years they thrived. In A.D. 1100 the people at Chaco Canyon had built cities with apartment buildings of stone five stories high. Their sophistication as sky-watchers was surpassed only by Mayan and Inca astronomers. Yet this

---

2 *Ka'tsina*—Ka'tsinas are spirit beings who roam the earth and who inhabit kachina masks worn in Pueblo ceremonial dances. [Silko's note]

vast complex of knowledge and belief, amassed for thousands of years, was never recorded in writing.

Instead, the ancient Pueblo people depended upon collective memory through successive generations to maintain and transmit an entire culture, a world view complete with proven strategies for survival. The oral narrative, or "story," became the medium in which the complex of Pueblo knowledge and belief was maintained. Whatever the event or the subject, the ancient people perceived the world and themselves within that world as part of an ancient continuous story composed of innumerable bundles of other stories.

The ancient Pueblo vision of the world was inclusive. The impulse was to leave nothing out. Pueblo oral tradition necessarily embraced all levels of human experience. Otherwise, the collective knowledge and beliefs comprising ancient Pueblo culture would have been incomplete. Thus stories about the Creation and Emergence of human beings and animals into this World continue to be retold each year for four days and four nights during the winter solstice. The "humma-hah" stories related events from the time long ago when human beings were still able to communicate with animals and other living things. But, beyond these two preceding categories, the Pueblo oral tradition knew no boundaries. Accounts of the appearance of the first Europeans in Pueblo country or of the tragic encounters between Pueblo people and Apache raiders were no more and no less important than stories about the biggest mule deer ever taken or adulterous couples surprised in cornfields and chicken coops. Whatever happened, the ancient people instinctively sorted events and details into a loose narrative structure. Everything became a story.

Traditionally everyone, from the youngest child to the oldest person, was expected to listen and to be able to recall or tell a portion, if only a small detail, from a narrative account or story. Thus the remembering and retelling were a communal process. Even if a key figure, an elder who knew much more than others, were to die unexpectedly, the system would remain intact. Through the efforts of a great many people, the community was able to piece together valuable accounts and crucial information that might otherwise have died with an individual.

Communal storytelling was a self-correcting process in which listeners were encouraged to speak up if they noted an important fact or detail omitted. The people were happy to listen to two or three different versions of the same event or the same humma-hah story. Even conflicting versions of an incident were welcomed for the entertainment they provided. Defenders of each version might joke and tease one another, but seldom were there any direct confrontations. Implicit in the Pueblo oral tradition was the awareness that loyalties, grudges, and kinship must always influence the narrator's choices as she emphasizes to listeners this is the way *she* has always heard the story told. The ancient Pueblo people sought a communal truth, not an absolute. For them this truth lived somewhere within the web of differing versions, disputes over minor points, outright contradictions tangling with old feuds and village rivalries.

A dinner-table conversation, recalling a deer hunt forty years ago when the largest mule deer ever was taken, inevitably stimulates similar memories in listeners. But hunting stories were not merely after-dinner entertainment. These accounts contained information of critical importance about behavior and migration patterns of mule deer. Hunting stories carefully described key landmarks and locations of fresh water. Thus a deer-hunt story might also serve as a "map." Lost travelers, and lost piñon-nut gathers, have been saved by sighting a rock formation they recognize only because they once heard a hunting story describing this rock formation.

The importance of cliff formations and water holes does not end with hunting stories. As offspring of the Mother Earth, the ancient Pueblo people could not conceive of themselves within a specific landscape. Location, or "place," nearly always plays a central role in the Pueblo oral narratives. Indeed, stories are most frequently recalled as people are passing by a specific geographical feature or the exact place where a story takes place. The precise date of the incident often is less important than the place or location of the happening. "Long, long ago," "a long time ago," "not too long ago," and "recently" are usually how stories are classified in terms of time. But the places where the stories occur are precisely located, and prominent geographical details recalled, even if the landscape is well-known to listeners. Often because the turning point in the narrative involved a peculiarity or special quality of a rock or tree or plant found only at that place. Thus, in the case of many of the Pueblo narratives, it is impossible to determine which came first: the incident or the geographical feature which begs to be brought alive in a story that features some unusual aspect of this location.

There is a giant sandstone boulder about a mile north of Old Laguna, on the road to Paguate. It is ten feet tall and twenty feet in circumference. When I was a child, and we would pass this boulder driving to Paguate village, someone usually made reference to the story about Kochininako, Yellow Woman, and the Estrucuyo, a monstrous giant who nearly ate her. The Twin Hero Brothers saved Kochininako, who had been out hunting rabbits to take home to feed her mother and sisters. The Hero Brothers had heard her cries just in time. The Estrucuyo had cornered her in a cave too small to fit its monstrous head. Kochininako had already thrown to the Estrucuyo all her rabbits, as well as her moccasins and most of her clothing. Still the creature had not been satisfied. After killing the Estrucuyo with their bows and arrows, the Twin Hero Brothers slit open the Estrucuyo and cut out its heart. They threw the heart as far as they could. The monster's heart landed there, beside the old trail to Paguate village, where the sandstone boulder rests now.

It may be argued that the existence of the boulder precipitated the creation of a story to explain it. But sandstone boulders and sandstone formations of strange shapes abound in the Laguna Pueblo area. Yet most of them do not have stories. Often the crucial element in a narrative is the terrain—some specific detail of the setting.

A high dark mesa rises dramatically from a grassy plain fifteen miles southeast of Laguna, in an area known as Swanee. On the grassy plain one hundred and forty years ago, my great-grandmother's uncle and his brother-in-law were grazing their herd of sheep. Because visibility on the plain extends for over twenty miles, it wasn't until the two sheepherders came near the high dark mesa that the Apaches were able to stalk them. Using the mesa to obscure their approach, the raiders swept around from both ends of the mesa. My great-grandmother's relatives were killed, and the herd lost. The high dark mesa played a critical role: the mesa had compromised the safety which the openness of the plains had seemed to assure. Pueblo and Apache alike relied upon the terrain, the very earth herself, to give them protection and aid. Human activities or needs were maneuvered to fit the existing surroundings and conditions. I imagine the last afternoon of my distant ancestors as warm and sunny for late September. They might have been traveling slowly, bringing the sheep closer to Laguna in preparation for the approach of colder weather. The grass was tall and only beginning to change from green to a yellow which matched the late-afternoon sun shining off it. There might have been comfort in the warmth and the sight of the sheep fattening on good pasture which lulled my ancestors into their fatal inattention. They might have had a rifle whereas the Apaches had only bows and arrows. But there would have been four or five Apache raiders, and the surprise attack would have canceled any advantage the rifles gave them.

Survival in any landscape comes down to making the best use of all available resources. On that particular September afternoon, the raiders made better use of the Swanee terrain than my poor ancestors did. Thus the high dark mesa and the story of the two lost Laguna herders became inextricably linked. The memory of them and their story resides in part with the high black mesa. For as long as the mesa stands, people within the family and clan will be reminded of the story of that afternoon long ago. Thus the continuity and accuracy of the oral narratives are reinforced by the landscape—and the Pueblo interpretation of that landscape is *maintained*.

The Migration Story: An Interior Journey

The Laguna Pueblo migration stories refer to specific places—mesas, springs, or cottonwood trees—not only locations which can be visited still, but also locations which lie directly on the state highway route linking Paguate village with Laguna village. In traveling this road as a child with older Laguna people I first heard a few of the stories from that much larger body of stories linked with the Emergence and Migration.[3] It may be coincidental that Laguna people continue to follow the same route which, according to the Migration story, the an-

---

3 *The Emergence*—All the human beings, animals, and life which had been created emerged from the four worlds below when the earth became habitable.

The Migration—The Pueblo people emerged into the Fifth World, but they had already been warned they would have to travel and search before they found the place they were meant to live. [Silko's note]

cestors followed south from the Emergence Place. It may be that the route is merely the shortest and best route for car, horse, or foot traffic between Laguna and Paguate villages. But if the stories about boulders, springs, and hills are actually remnants from a ritual that retraces the creation and emergence of the Laguna Pueblo people as a culture, as the people they became, then continued use of that route creates a unique relationship between the ritual-mythic world and the actual, everyday world. A journey from Paguate to Laguna down the long incline of Paguate Hill retraces the original journey from the Emergence Place, which is located slightly north of the Paguate village. Thus the landscape between Paguate and Laguna takes on a deeper significance: the landscape resonates the spiritual or mythic dimension of the Pueblo world even today.

Although each Pueblo culture designates a specific Emergence Place—usually a small natural spring edged with mossy sandstone and full of cattails and wild watercress—it is clear that they do not agree on any single location or natural spring as the one and only true Emergence Place. Each Pueblo group recounts its own stories about Creation, Emergence, and Migration, although they all believe that all human beings, with all the animals and plants, emerged at the same place and at the same time.[4]

Natural springs are crucial sources of water for all life in the high desert plateau country. So the small spring near Paguate village is literally the source and continuance of life for the people in the area. The spring also functions on a spiritual level, recalling the original Emergence Place and linking the people and the spring water to all other people and to that moment when the Pueblo people became aware of themselves as they are even now. The Emergence was an emergence into a precise cultural identity. Thus the Pueblo stories about the Emergence and Migration are not to be taken as literally as the anthropologists might wish. Prominent geographical features and landmarks which are mentioned in the narratives exist for ritual purposes, not because the Laguna people actually journeyed south for hundreds of years from Chaco Canyon or Mesa Verde, as the archaeologists say, or eight miles from the site of the natural springs at Paguate to the sandstone hilltop at Laguna.

The eight miles, marked with boulders, mesas, springs, and river crossings, are actually a ritual circuit or path which marks the interior journey the Laguna people made: a journey of awareness and imagination in which they emerged from being within the earth and from everything included in earth to the culture and people they became, differentiating themselves for the first time from all that had surrounded them, always aware that interior distances cannot be reckoned in physical miles or in calendar years.

---

4 *Creation*—Tse'itsi'nako, Thought Woman, the Spider, thought about it, and everything she thought came into being. First she thought of three sisters for herself, and they helped her think of the rest of the Universe, including the Fifth World and the four worlds below. *The Fifth World* is the world we are living in today. There are four previous worlds below this world. [Silko's note]

The narratives linked with prominent features of the landscape between Paguate and Laguna delineate the complexities of the relationship which human beings must maintain with the surrounding natural world if they hope to survive in this place. Thus the journey was an interior process of the imagination, a growing awareness that being human is somehow different from all other life—animal, plant, and inanimate. Yet we are all from the same source: the awareness never deteriorated into Cartesian duality, cutting off the human from the natural world.

The people found the opening into the Fifth World too small to allow them or any of the animals to escape. They had sent a fly out through the small hole to tell them if it was the world which the Mother Creator had promised. It was, but there was the problem of getting out. The antelope tried to butt the opening to enlarge it, but the antelope enlarged it only a little. It was necessary for the badger with her long claws to assist the antelope, and at last the opening was enlarged enough so that all the people and animals were able to emerge up into the Fifth World. The human beings could not have emerged without the aid of antelope and badger. The human beings depended upon the aid and charity of the animals. Only through interdependence could the human beings survive. Families belonged to clans, and it was by clan that the human being joined with the animal and plant world. Life on the high arid plateau became viable when the human beings were able to imagine themselves as sisters and brothers to the badger, antelope, clay, yucca, and sun. Not until they could find a viable relationship to the terrain, the landscape they found themselves in, could they *emerge.* Only at the moment the requisite balance between human and *other* was realized could the Pueblo people become a culture, a distinct group whose population and survival remained stable despite the vicissitudes of climate and terrain.

Landscape thus has similarities with dreams. Both have the power to seize terrifying feelings and deep instincts and translate them into images—visual, aural, tactile—into the concrete where human beings may more readily confront and channel the terrifying instincts or powerful emotions into rituals and narratives which reassure the individual while reaffirming cherished values of the group. The identity of the individual as a part of the group and the greater Whole is strengthened, and the terror of facing the world alone is extinguished.

Even now, the people at Laguna Pueblo spend the greater portion of social occasions recounting recent incidents or events which have occurred in the Laguna area. Nearly always, the discussion will precipitate the retelling of older stories about similar incidents or other stories connected with a specific place. The stories often contain disturbing or provocative material, but are nonetheless told in the presence of children and women. The effect of these inter-family or inter-clan exchanges is the reassurance for each person that she or he will never be separated or apart from the clan, no matter what might happen. Neither the worst blunders or disasters nor the greatest financial prosperity and joy will ever be permitted to isolate anyone from the rest of the group. In the ancient times, cohesiveness was all that stood between extinction and survival, and, while the individual certainly was recognized, it was always as an individual simultaneously bonded to family and clan by a complex bundle of custom and ritual. You are never the first to suffer a grave loss or profound humiliation. You are never the first, and you understand that you will probably not be the last to commit or be victimized by a repugnant act. Your family and clan are able to go on at length about others now passed on, others older or more experienced than you who suffered similar losses.

The wide deep arroyo near the Kings Bar (located across the reservation borderline) has over the years claimed many vehicles. A few years ago, when a Viet Nam veteran's new red Volkswagen rolled backwards into the arroyo while he was inside buying a six-pack of beer, the story of his loss joined the lively and large collection of stories already connected with that big arroyo. I do not know whether the Viet Nam veteran was consoled when he was told the stories about the other cars claimed by the ravenous arroyo. All his savings of combat pay had gone for the red Volkswagen. But this man could not have felt any worse than the man who, some years before, had left his children and mother-in-law in his station wagon with the engine running. When he came out of the liquor store his station wagon was gone. He found it and its passengers upside down in the big arroyo. Broken bones, cuts and bruises, and a total wreck of the car. The big arroyo has a wide mouth. Its existence needs no explanation. People in the area regard the arroyo much as they might regard a living being, which has a certain character and personality. I seldom drive past that wide deep arroyo without feeling a familiarity with and even a strange affection for this arroyo. Because as treacherous as it may be, the arroyo maintains a strong connection between human beings and the earth. The arroyo demands from us the caution and attention that constitute respect. It is this sort of respect the old believers have in mind when they tell us we must respect and love the earth.

Hopi Pueblo elders have said that the austere and, to some eyes, barren plains and hills surrounding their mesa-top villages actually help to nurture the spirituality of the Hopi *way*. The Hopi elders say the Hopi people might have settled in locations far more lush where daily life would not have been so grueling. But there on the high silent sandstone mesas that overlook the sandy arid expanses stretching to all horizons, the Hopi elders say the Hopi people must "live by their prayers" if they are to survive. The Hopi way cherishes the intangible: the riches realized from interaction and interrelationships with all beings above all else. Great abundances of material things, even food, the Hopi elders believe, tend to lure human attention away from what is most valuable and important. The views of the Hopi elders are not much different from those elders in all the Pueblos.

The bare vastness of the Hopi landscape emphasizes the visual impact of every plant, every rock, every arroyo. Nothing is overlooked or taken for granted. Each ant, each lizard, each lark is imbued with great value simply because the creature is there, simply because the creature is alive in a place where any life at all is precious. Stand on the mesa edge at Walpai and look west over the bare distances toward the pale blue outlines of the San Francisco peaks where the ka'tsina spirits reside. So little lies between you and the sky. So little lies between you and the earth. One look and you know that simply to survive is a great triumph, that every possible resource is needed, every possible ally—even the most humble insect or reptile. You realize you will be speaking with all of them if you intend to last out the year. Thus it is that the Hopi elders are grateful to the landscape for aiding them in their quest as spiritual people.

QUESTIONS AND CONSIDERATIONS

1. What comparisons does Silko make between the Pueblo attitude toward human remains and other organic remains, such as corncobs and animal bones? Why are the spirits concerned with each?

2. How does Silko contrast the meaning and connotations of the English word *landscape* with the way a Native American regards the relationship among people, earth, and sky? What examples does Silko provide? Are they clear and convincing?

3. Why did it take a long time for the Pueblos to develop realism in their art? What view of nature is reflected in the style of traditional Pueblo art? How is this art related to magic and ritual? What examples does Silko use to clarify these ideas?

4. According to Silko, why do the Pueblos rely on stories to explain their world-view? How are these stories perpetuated and related to permanent features of the landscape? How are the stories like a "map" that helps the Pueblos to survive?

5. What is the Pueblo emergence myth? How is it related both to the inner world of the Pueblo and their relationship with nature? According to Silko, how is the Pueblo vision of landscape related to the world of dreams?

6. What was the relationship between people and animals in the time of the Emergence? How is this human-animal interdependence reflected in the clan structure of Pueblo society?

IDEAS FOR WRITING

1. Write an essay in which you contrast the burial rituals in your own culture with those of the Native Americans profiled in this essay. Which form of burial would you choose? Why?

2. Contrast the Pueblo creation myth of the Emergence with the biblical myth of creation in Genesis. What different views of the relationships among humans, gods, and the natural world are reflected in each version? Which version do you prefer, and why?

Poetry

The Windhover

Gerard Manley Hopkins

Journal

Write about a natural creature that you admire, think of as a religious symbol, or represents some of your highest ideals.

To Christ Our Lord

I caught this morning morning's minion, king-
    dom of daylight's dauphin, dapple-dawn-drawn Falcon, in his
riding
    Of the rolling level underneath him steady air, and striding
High there, how he rung upon the rein of a wimpling wing
In his ecstasy! then off, off forth on swing,   5
    As a skate's heel sweeps smooth on a bow-bend: the hurl and
gliding
    Rebuffed the big wind. My heart in hiding
Stirred for a bird,—the achieve of, the mastery of the thing!

Brute beauty and valour and act, oh, air, pride, plume, here
    Buckle! AND the fire that breaks from thee then, a billion   10
Times told lovelier, more dangerous, O my chevalier!

    No wonder of it: shéer plód makes plough down sillion
Shine, and blue-bleak embers, ah my dear,
    Fall, gall themselves, and gash gold-vermilion.

QUESTIONS AND CONSIDERATIONS

    1. What does the speaker in the poem mean when he says that he "caught" the windhover? In what sense is the poem itself an example of this "catching"?

    2. Why is the poem dedicated to "Christ Our Lord"? In what sense can the falcon be interpreted as an emblem of Christ? Do you think it is appropriate to use natural creatures as religious emblems or symbols?

3. Hopkins alludes to the "ecstasy" of the falcon's flight. What is ecstatic about the way the falcon is flying on this particular morning? Do you think this is an accurate interpretation of the bird's flight?

4. Hopkins develops an extended comparison in his poem between the falcon and a "chevalier," a type of noble, swashbuckling soldier with "valour," "pride," "plume," and "buckle"—presumably, the buckling on of a sword. Does this description seem appropriate? Does it create a contrast to the religious implications of the dedication of the poem to Christ?

5. Explain your interpretation of "the fire that breaks from thee then." What is the fire and what does it represent? Why is the "fire" compared, in the poem's final stanza, to the plowing of a field ("sheer plod makes plow down sillon/Shine")?

6. Hopkins is famous for the control of the line and rhythms of his poetry. Read the poem aloud and discuss the way that the dramatic rhythms of the language, his rhymes, and the abrupt, unusual endings of his lines create a dynamic portrait of the falcon in full flight.

IDEAS FOR WRITING

1. Develop your journal entry into a poem or a descriptive essay about a natural creature that you admire. Try to use comparisons as Hopkins does to clarify how the creature represents certain values and ideals for you.

2. Write an essay in which you either agree or disagree with Hopkins' view of the falcon. Do you think that the falcon is a noble, spiritual creature, as the poem implies, or is the bird simply an instinct-driven predator?

The Animals in that Country
Margaret Atwood

Journal

Provide an example to contrast the different ways that various peoples and cultures perceive or value animals.

In that country the animals
have the faces of people:

the ceremonial
cats possessing the streets

the fox run   5
politely to earth, the huntsmen
standing around him, fixed
in their tapestry of manners

the bull, embroidered
with blood and given   10
an elegant death, trumpets, his name
stamped on him, heraldic brand
because

(when he rolled
on the sand, sword in his heart, the teeth   15
in his blue mouth were human)

he is really a man

even the wolves, holding resonant
conversations in their
orests thickened with legend.   20

In this country the animals
have the faces of
animals.

Their eyes
flash once in car headlights   25
and are gone.

Their deaths are not elegant.

They have the faces of
no-one.

QUESTIONS AND CONSIDERATIONS

1. Atwood, a Canadian, entitles her poem "The Animals in that Country." Is she referring to a particular country or continent here? If so, which one(s)?

2. What does Atwood mean when she says that the animals in "that country" have "the faces of people"? Can you think of any such animals in your own country?

3. In what sense do the foxes run "politely"? Why are the huntsmen described as "fixed/in their tapestry of manners"?

4. Atwood follows her description of the fox hunt with a similar description of a bullfight. How does the language of this stanza, with its use of such words as "elegant," "embroidered," and "heraldic" echo the language used in the previous stanza? What similar language can be found in the next stanza?

5. How do the final stanzas of the poem, beginning with "In this country," contrast with the descriptions of cultural perceptions of animals in the previous stanza?

6. What evaluation does the poem present about the values of "this country" as opposed to "that country" in regard to animals? Do you feel that animals should have "the faces of/no-one"?

IDEAS FOR WRITING

1. Write an essay in which you reflect on the causes for the historical differences between cultures, such as those that Atwood describes in her poem. Why do you think that certain cultures have a more "personified," ritualized view and others have a less ritualized attitude toward the animal kingdom? Develop one or two examples to support your point of view.

2. Analyze a sport such as the fox hunt or the bullfight that presents a ritualized, symbolic relationship between humans and animals. In what ways does the sport embody the values and history of the culture that produced it?

The Reason Why I Am Afraid Even Though I Am a Fisherman
Ray A. Young Bear

Journal

Write about a time when you felt afraid of nature. Why were you afraid?

Who is there
to witness the ice
as it gradually forms itself
from the cold rock-hard banks
to the middle of the river?   5
Is the wind chill a factor?
Does the water at some point
negotiate and agree to stop
moving and become frozen?
When you do not know the answers   10
to these immediately you are afraid,
and to even think in this inquisitive
manner is contrary to the precept
that life is in everything.
Me, I am not a man;   15
I respect the river
for not knowing its secret,
for answers have nothing
to do with cause and occurrence.
It doesn't matter how early   20
I wake to see the sun shine
through the ice-hole;
only the ice along

with my foolishness
decides when   25
to break.

QUESTIONS AND CONSIDERATIONS

1. Why is the speaker in the poem afraid?

2. Why might the fact that the speaker is a fisherman make him less afraid?

3. What questions does the speaker begin the poem with? How does he attempt to answer them?

4. What is ironic about the speaker's personification of the water as possibly "negotiat[ing] and agree[ing] to stop moving"? What unrealistic perception of nature is suggested here?

5. Despite his initial rational question, the speaker has a view of the world as a place in which "life is in everything." What are the implications of such a view? How is this perspective related to the poem's final lines, "only the ice along/with my foolishness/decides when/to break"?

6. What does the speaker mean by his comment, "Me, I am not a man"? What definition of manhood or human consciousness does he seem to reject here?

IDEAS FOR WRITING

1. Write an essay in which you create a definition of a human being. Do you believe that a human is superior to nature and its creatures? Why or why not?

2. Do you believe that it is possible really to know nature, to feel altogether safe in relation to it? Develop your response in an essay in which you state your belief on this issue and provide examples from your experiences with or knowledge of natural events.

Wanting a Child
Jorie Graham

Journal

Write about a personal insight that came to you through observing nature.

How hard it is for the river here to re-enter
the sea, though it's most beautiful, of course, in the waste
of time where it's almost
turned back. Then
it's yoked,   5
trussed. . . . The river
has been everywhere, imagine, dividing, discerning,
cutting deep into the parent rock,

scouring and scouring
its own bed.   10
Nothing is whole
where it has been. Nothing
remains unsaid.
Sometimes I'll come this far from home
merely to dip my fingers in this glittering, archaic   15
sea that renders everything
identical, flesh
where mind and body
blur. The seagulls squeak, ill-fitting
hinges, the beach is thick   20
with shells. The tide
is always pulsing upward, inland, into the river's rapid
argument, pushing
with its insistent tragic waves—the living echo,
says my book, of some great storm far out at sea, too far   25
to be recalled by us
but transferred
whole onto this shore by waves, so that erosion
is its very face.

QUESTIONS AND CONSIDERATIONS

1. What does the title of the poem imply about the emotional state of the speaker? If the poem had no title, would you read it differently?

2. Where is the "here," the setting of the poem? Explain the conflict between the river and the ocean described in the poem.

3. In light of the title of the poem, discuss a possible double meaning of the phrase "waste/of time"?

4. What are the literal and symbolic meanings of the words "yoked/trussed" and the phrase "cutting deep into the parent rock"?

5. What is the symbolism of the "glittering, archaic/sea that renders everything/identical"? What anxiety of the speaker do these lines emphasize?

6. In describing the "great storm far out at sea," of which the pushing of the ocean's waves up river is "the living echo," why does the speaker refer to "my book" as the source of this information? What does the reference to a book reveal about the consciousness and concerns of the speaker?

IDEAS FOR WRITING

1. Based on the evidence provided in the poem, write a description of the speaker in the poem and her values. What is her relationship with nature and with other people? Do you think she will have a child? Why or why not?

2. If you have ever given birth to or wanted to have a child, write a poem or descriptive essay in which you describe your feelings about childbirth and pregnancy, comparing your feelings to some other natural event: the flow of a river, a storm, an earthquake.

The World Is Too Much with Us
William Wordsworth

The world is too much with us; late and soon,
Getting and spending, we lay waste our powers;
Little we see in Nature that is ours;
We have given our hearts away, a sordid boon!
This Sea that bares her bosom to the moon;   5
The winds that will be howling at all hours,
And are up-gathered now like sleeping flowers;
For this, for everything, we are out of tune;
It moves us not. Great God! I'd rather be
A Pagan suckled in a creed outworn;   10
So might I, standing on this pleasant lea,
Have glimpses that would make me less forlorn;
Have sight of Proteus rising from the sea;
Or hear old Triton blow his wreathèd horn.

QUESTIONS

1. What is the poem's view of the modern response to nature? What details and examples from nature are used to support these views? Why would a "Pagan suckled in a
creed outworn" be likely to enjoy a more intimate relationship with nature than a modern person?

2. Write an essay or poem in response to Wordsworth's view of the relationship between people and nature as presented in his poem. Do you agree that people today are
alienated from nature? Provide examples from personal experience, reading, and
observations.

When I Heard the Learn'd Astronomer
Walt Whitman

When I heard the learn'd astronomer,
When the proofs, the figures, were ranged in columns before me,
When I was shown the charts and diagrams, to add, divide, and
    measure them.
When I sitting heard the astronomer where he lectured with much
    applause in the lecture-room,
How soon unaccountable I became tired and sick,   5
Till rising and gliding out I wander'd off by myself,
In the mystical moist night-air, and from time to time,
Look'd up in perfect silence at the stars.

QUESTIONS

1. What view of scientific learning about nature is presented in this poem? What images of education does Whitman create to emphasize his views? How do the images in the last four lines of the poem contrast to those in the first section? Which part of the poem did you prefer, and why?

2. Write an essay that discusses your experiences with the scientific study of nature through such courses as biology and astronomy. Have these courses helped you to develop a more genuine and tangible relationship with the natural world?

After Apple-Picking

Robert Frost

My long two-pointed ladder's sticking through a tree
Toward heaven still,
And there's a barrel that I didn't fill
Beside it, and there may be two or three
Apples I didn't pick upon some bough.   5
But I am done with apple-picking now.
Essence of winter sleep is on the night,
The scent of apples: I am drowsing off.
I cannot rub the strangeness from my sight
I got from looking through a pane of glass   10
I skimmed this morning from the drinking trough
And held against the world of hoary grass.
It melted, and I let it fall and break.
But I was well
Upon my way to sleep before it fell,   15
And I could tell
What form my dreaming was about to take.
Magnified apples appear and disappear,
Stem end and blossom end,
And every fleck of russet showing clear.   20
My instep arch not only keeps the ache,
It keeps the pressure of a ladder-round.
I feel the ladder sway as the boughs bend.
And I keep hearing from the cellar bin
The rumbling sound   25
Of load on load of apples coming in.
For I have had too much
Of apple-picking: I am overtired
Of the great harvest I myself desired.
There were ten thousand thousand fruit to touch,   30
Cherish in hand, lift down, and not let fall.

For all
That struck the earth,
No matter if not bruised or spiked with stubble,
Went surely to the cider-apple heap   35
As of no worth.
One can see what will trouble
This sleep of mine, whatever sleep it is.
Were he not gone,
The woodchuck could say whether it's like his   40
Long sleep, as I describe its coming on,
Or just some human sleep.

QUESTIONS

1. Why are the setting and time of year in the poem significant? How does the speaker feel about apple picking? About sleep and dreaming? What is the speaker's relationship to nature and particularly to animals, such as the woodchuck?

2. Write an essay, poem, or story in which you explore your feelings about an experience working out-of-doors: cutting grass, laying bricks, sweeping leaves, picking fruit. Did the task help you to feel closer to nature and rejuvenate your spirit, or did it alienate you from the natural world?

The Tropics in New York
Claude McKay

Bananas ripe and green, and ginger root,
    Cocoa in pods and alligator pears,
And tangerines and mangoes and grape fruit,
    Fit for the highest prize at parish fairs.

Set in the window, bringing memories   5
    Of fruit-trees laden by low-singing rills,
And dewy dawns, and mystical blue skies
    In benediction over nun-like hills.

My eyes grew dim, and I could no more gaze;
    A wave of longing through my body swept,   10
And, hungry for the old familiar ways,
    I turned aside and bowed my head and wept.

QUESTIONS

1. What is the effect of the long list of fruits in the first stanza of the poem? How is the speaker affected by the sight of these tropical fruits? Why does the speaker turn aside and weep?

2. Write a descriptive and reflective poem or a personal essay about a kind of fruit or vegetable that reminds you of your home or of another significant place and time in your life.

[A Narrow Fellow In The Grass]
Emily Dickinson

A narrow Fellow in the Grass
Occasionally rides—
You may have met Him—did you not
His notice sudden is—

The Grass divides as with a Comb—   5
A spotted shaft is seen—
And then it closes at your feet
And opens further on—

He likes a Boggy Acre
A Floor too cool for Corn—   10
Yet when a Boy, and Barefoot—
I more than once at Noon
Have passed, I thought, a Whip lash
Unbraiding in the Sun
When stooping to secure it   15
It wrinkled, and was gone—

Several of Nature's People
I know, and they know me—
I feel for them a transport
Of cordiality   20

But never met this Fellow
Attended, or alone
Without a tighter breathing
And Zero at the Bone—

QUESTIONS

1. How does the speaker feel about the snake and other natural creatures? Do the rhythms and line breaks, as well as the movement of the poem as a whole, seem to re-create the snake's movement through the grass? Why?

2. Write a poem or an essay about an animal or reptile that both fascinates and repels you. Explain your feelings for this creature and what it is that evokes this response in you.

A Blessing

James Wright

Just off the highway to Rochester, Minnesota,
Twilight bounds softly forth on the grass,
And the eyes of those two Indian ponies
Darken with kindness.
They have come gladly out of the willows   5
To welcome my friend and me.
We step over the barbed wire into the pasture
Where they have been grazing all day, alone.
They ripple tensely, they can hardly contain their happiness
That we have come.   10
They bow shyly as wet swans. They love each other.
There is no loneliness like theirs.
At home once more,
They begin munching the young tufts of spring in the darkness.
I would like to hold the slenderer one in my arms,   15
For she has walked over to me
And nuzzled my left hand.
She is black and white,
Her mane falls wild on her forehead,
And the light breeze moves me to caress her long ear   20
That is delicate as the skin over a girl's wrist.
Suddenly I realize
That if I stepped out of my body I would break
Into blossom.

QUESTIONS

1. What is the speaker's initial response to the Indian ponies? How does his response change and develop? What descriptive details does the speaker use to describe both the ponies and his physical and emotional response to them? Explain the speaker's realization in the last three lines of the poem.

2. Write a poem or essay in which you describe a moment of intense communion with a natural creature. Discuss what you learned about yourself and about nature from this experience. Use descriptive details and metaphors to illustrate your responses.

The Panther
In the Jardin des Plantes, Paris
Rainer Maria Rilke
Translated from the German by Stephen Mitchell

His vision, from the constantly passing bars,
has grown so weary that it cannot hold
anything else. It seems to him there are
a thousand bars; and behind the bars, no world.

As he paces in cramped circles, over and over,   5
the movement of his powerful soft strides
is like a ritual dance around a center
in which a mighty will stands paralyzed.

Only at times, the curtain of the pupils
lifts, quietly—. An image enters in,   10
rushes down through the tensed, arrested muscles,
plunges into the heart and is gone.

QUESTIONS

1. How does the poet present the inner world of the caged panther? How does the panther perceive the world within and outside the cage? What happens to him when "An image enters in"? Is the panther a symbol of particular types of people? If so, what types?

2. Write an essay in which you discuss your attitude about zoos. How do you think animals adapt to being kept in a cage? Do you believe that zoos serve a useful function in our culture? Are zoos a form of cruelty to animals?

A Work of Artifice
Marge Piercy

The bonsai tree
in the attractive pot
could have grown eighty feet tall
on the side of a mountain
till split by lightning.   5
But a gardener
carefully pruned it.

It is nine inches high.
Every day as he
whittles back the branches 10
the gardener croons,
It is your nature
to be small and cozy,
domestic and weak;
how lucky, little tree, 15
to have a pot to grow in.
With living creatures
one must begin very early
to dwarf their growth:
the bound feet, 20
the crippled brain,
the hair in curlers,
the hands you
love to touch.

QUESTIONS

1. What comment does the poem make about nature and artifice? Why is the gardener's comment to the tree ironic: "It is your nature/to be small and cozy,/domestic and weak"? How is the criticism of the domestication of nature compared to the stunting of the growth of women? Which of the poem's images of stunting are most effective?

2. Write an essay about your views on nature and artifice. How much of nature as you know it is in some degree artificial, the product of selective breeding and human cultivation? Do you think that artificially designing and breeding creatures to please humans is necessary, or is it a violation of the world's natural order?

Pretty Bird

Gladys Cardiff

While morning lifts its green blanket,
he waits, radiant, a little god
in the emerald light of his cage.

He wants out. He wants the height
of his perch. His impatience is charged 5
and crackles in a plumage of blue volts.

Yellow eyes stare from the ornate
mask of his face with its black chin
and ebony beak. His cheeks are white

and warm, like a Japanese dancer's skin.   10
Little black feathers, singular and distinct
as the dark acts we choose, stripe each cheek.

As I unlock his cage, I wonder if we wear
our demerits in some ancestral grain
like the reptilian yellow of his stare.   15

He climbs the pole, his feathers shimmering
like green leaves moving in a constant wind,
or water rippling in a cape of blue harmonics.

He is made for the tallest trees.
His back is blue sky, and his breast   20
the gold gap of sun through branches.

But here, the ground below him is littered
like a boneyard with wood chips and husks.
Clearly, he is excavating the wood

from beneath himself. One day, the perch   25
will split and separate, and he will know
the delicious sway of mountain branches

and abandonment. Two sharp terminals
will charge the void. And he will fall
the way a crippled bird must, in a long   30

downward spiral, his one clipped wing
pivotal.

QUESTIONS

1. In what sense is the bird in the poem godlike? Can the poem itself be interpreted
as an act of worship to the bird? How does the bird's plumage reflect or comment on
human frailties? What sensory details are used to create a vivid, attractive picture of the
bird? Is the bird diminished by captivity in the same sense that the panther is diminished
in Rilke's poem?

2. Birds and animals are revered and even worshiped in many cultures. Write a
poem or essay about a particular animal or bird that you admire. What heroic or godlike
qualities does this creature embody?

The Dragonfly
Louise Bogan

You are made of almost nothing
But of enough
To be great eyes
And diaphanous double vans;
To be ceaseless movement,   5
Unending hunger
Grappling love.

Link between water and air,
Earth repels you.
Light touches you only to shift into iridescence   10
Upon your body and wings.
Twice-born, predator,
You split into the heat.
Swift beyond calculation or capture
You dart into the shadow   15
Which consumes you.

You rocket into the day.
But at last, when the wind flattens the grasses,
For you, the design and purpose stop.
And you fall   20
With the other husks of summer.

QUESTIONS

1. What human qualities does the speaker project onto the dragonfly, and why? How does the dragonfly move among and connect the four elements—water, air, earth, and fire (or light)? What comment does the poem make about mortality in the natural world?

2. When natural creatures die, they often awaken feelings of loss and fears of mortality in us. Write an essay or poem about the thoughts and feelings you have experienced after witnessing or learning about the death of an animal.

Traveling through the Dark
William Stafford

Traveling through the dark I found a deer
dead on the edge of the Wilson River road.
It is usually best to roll them into the canyon:
that road is narrow; to swerve might make more dead.

By glow of the tail-light I stumbled back of the car
and stood by the heap, a doe, a recent killing;
she had stiffened already, almost cold.
I dragged her off; she was large in the belly.

My fingers touching her side brought me the reason—
her side was warm; her fawn lay there waiting,   10
alive, still, never to be born.
Beside that mountain road I hesitated.

The car aimed ahead its lowered parking lights;
under the hood purred the steady engine.
I stood in the glare of the warm exhaust turning red;   15
around our group I could hear the wilderness listen.

I thought hard for us all—my only swerving—,
then pushed her over the edge into the river.

QUESTIONS

  1. What central conflict does the speaker have that leads him to hesitate before
pushing the dead deer over the edge of the canyon? What does the imagery of darkness
in the poem suggest to you? What relationship among death, life, and survival does the
poem establish?

  2. Even though we may love nature and its creatures, there are times when human
survival depends on the sacrifice of animal life. Write an essay about situations in which
you believe it is necessary to sacrifice animals for human survival; then contrast these occasions with times when it may be possible to avoid such sacrifices.

Woodchucks

Maxine Kumin

Gassing the woodchucks didn't turn out right.
The knockout bomb from the Feed and Grain Exchange
was featured as merciful, quick at the bone
and the case we had against them was airtight,
both exits shoehorned shut with puddingstone,   5
but they had a sub-sub-basement out of range.

Next morning they turned up again, no worse
for the cyanide than we for our cigarettes
and state-store Scotch, all of us up to scratch.
They brought down the marigolds as a matter of course   10
and then took over the vegetable patch
nipping the broccoli shoots, beheading the carrots.

The food from our mouths, I said, righteously thrilling
to the feel of the .22, the bullets' neat noses.
I, a lapsed pacifist fallen from grace   15
puffed with Darwinian pieties for killing,
now drew a bead on the littlest woodchuck's face.
He died down in the everbearing roses.

Ten minutes later I dropped the mother. She
flipflopped in the air and fell, her needle teeth   20
still hooked in a leaf of early Swiss chard.
Another baby next. O one-two-three
the murderer inside me rose up hard,
the hawkeye killer came on stage forthwith.

There's one chuck left. Old wily fellow, he keeps   25
me cocked and ready day after day after day.

QUESTIONS

1. What is the speaker's attitude toward killing the woodchucks? How is humor
used in the poem? In what ways are the woodchucks compared to humans, such as the
speaker and her family? What comment does the poem make on human violence?

2. Write an essay in which you express some of your views on hunting. Do you
think there is a justification for hunting animals for sport or to avoid animal overpopula-
tion or protect crops and livestock?

The Heaven of Animals

James Dickey

Here they are. The soft eyes open.
If they have lived in a wood
It is a wood.
If they have lived on plains
It is grass rolling   5
Under their feet forever.

Having no souls, they have come,
Anyway, beyond their knowing.
Their instincts wholly bloom
And they rise.   10
The soft eyes open.

To match them, the landscape flowers,
Outdoing, desperately
Outdoing what is required:
The richest wood,   15
The deepest field.

For some of these,
It could not be the place
It is, without blood.
These hunt, as they have done,   20
But with claws and teeth grown perfect,

More deadly than they can believe.
They stalk more silently,
And crouch on the limbs of trees,
And their descent   25
Upon the bright backs of their prey

May take years
In a sovereign floating of joy.
And those that are hunted
Know this as their life,   30
Their reward: to walk

Under such trees in full knowledge
Of what is in glory above them,
And to feel no fear,
But acceptance, compliance.   35
Fulfilling themselves without pain

At the cycle's center,
They tremble, they walk
Under the tree,
They fall, they are torn,   40
They rise, they walk again.

QUESTIONS

1. How does the speaker describe the heaven of the animals? How do animal heavens differ from those of humans? How do the animals' ideas of heaven vary according to how they lived their lives? Is the same true for humans?

2. Write an essay about your idea of heaven, comparing and contrasting your view of heaven to the "heaven of animals" as described by James Dickey.

Offering

Zuni

Adapted by Robert Bly from the translation by Ruth Bunzel

This is what I want to happen: that our earth mother
may be clothed in ground corn four times over;
that frost flowers cover her over entirely;
that the mountain pines far away over there
may stand close to each other in the cold;   5
that the weight of snow crack some branches!
In order that the country may be this way
I have made my prayer sticks into something alive.

QUESTIONS

1. What does the speaker in the poem hope will occur in the natural world? What is meant by the "offering" in the poem, "I have made my prayer sticks into something alive"?

2. Write a poem based on the Zuni offering that describes your ideal vision of nature.

Drama

Riders to the Sea

John Millington Synge

Journal

Write about an experience with nature in which you or someone you know
suffered great loss, a significant financial loss, a loss of life, a loss of loved ones.
What was the response to this loss?

CHARACTERS

MAURYA, *an old woman*
BARTLEY, *her son*
CATHLEEN, *her daughter*
NORA, *a younger daughter*
MEN AND WOMEN

SCENE

An Island off the West of Ireland.

Cottage kitchen, with nets, oil-skins, spinning-wheel, some new boards standing by the wall, etc. CATHLEEN, a girl of about twenty, finishes kneading cake, and puts it down in the pot-oven by the fire; then wipes her hands, and begins to spin at the wheel. NORA, a young girl, puts her head in at the door.

NORA (in a low voice): Where is she?

CATHLEEN: She's lying down, God help her, and may be sleeping, if she's able.

NORA comes in softly, and takes a bundle from under her shawl.

CATHLEEN (spinning the wheel rapidly): What is it you have?

NORA: The young priest is after bringing them. It's a shirt and a plain stocking were got off a drowned man in Donegal.

CATHLEEN stops her wheel with a sudden movement, and leans out to listen.

NORA: We're to find out if it's Michael's they are, some time herself will be down looking by the sea.

CATHLEEN: How would they be Michael's, Nora? How would he go the length of that way to the far north?

NORA: The young priest says he's known the like of it. "If it's Michael's they are," says he, "you can tell yourself he's got a clean burial by the grace of God, and if they're not his, let no one say a word about them, for she'll be getting her death," says he, "with crying and lamenting."

The door which NORA half-closed is blown open by a gust of wind.

CATHLEEN (looking out anxiously): Did you ask him would he stop Bartley going this day with the horses to the Galway fair?

NORA: "I won't stop him," says he, "but let you not be afraid. Herself does be saying prayers half through the night, and the Almighty God won't leave her destitute," says he, "with no son living."

CATHLEEN: Is the sea bad by the white rocks, Nora?

NORA: Middling bad, God help us. There's a great roaring in the west, and it's worse it'll be getting when the tide's turned to the wind.

She goes over to the table with the bundle.

Shall I open it now?

CATHLEEN: Maybe she'd wake up on us, and come in before we'd done. (Coming to the table.) It's a long time we'll be, and the two of us crying.

NORA (goes to the inner door and listens): She's moving about on the bed. She'll be coming in a minute.

CATHLEEN: Give me the ladder, and I'll put them up in the turf-loft, the way she won't know of them at all, and maybe when the tide turns she'll be going down to see would he be floating from the east.

They put the ladder against the gable of the chimney; CATHLEEN goes up a few steps and hides the bundle in the turf-loft. MAURYA comes from the inner room.

MAURYA *(looking up at* CATHLEEN *and speaking querulously):* Isn't it turf enough you have for this day and evening?

CATHLEEN: There's a cake baking at the fire for a short space *(throwing down the turf)* and Bartley will want it when the tide turns if he goes to Connemara.

NORA *picks up the turf and puts it round the pot-oven.*

MAURYA *(sitting down on a stool at the fire):* He won't go this day with the wind rising from the south and west. He won't go this day, for the young priest will stop him surely.

NORA: He'll not stop him, mother, and I heard Eamon Simon and Stephen Pheety and Colum Shawn saying he would go.

MAURYA: Where is he itself?

NORA: He went down to see would there be another boat sailing in the week, and I'm thinking it won't be long till he's here now, for the tide's turning at the green head, and the hooker's tacking from the east.

CATHLEEN: I hear some one passing the big stones.

NORA *(looking out):* He's coming now, and he in a hurry.

BARTLEY *(comes in and looks round the room. Speaking sadly and quietly):* Where is the bit of new rope, Cathleen, was bought in Connemara?

CATHLEEN *(coming down):* Give it to him, Nora; it's on a nail by the white boards. I hung it up this morning, for the pig with the black feet was eating it.

NORA *(giving him a rope):* Is that it, Bartley?

MAURYA: You'd do right to leave that rope, Bartley, hanging by the boards. *(BARTLEY *takes the rope.)* It will be wanting in this place. I'm telling you, if Michael is washed up to-morrow morning, or the next morning, or any morning in the week, for it's a deep grave we'll make him by the grace of God.

BARTLEY *(beginning to work with the rope):* I've no halter the way I can ride down on the mare, and I must go now quickly. This is the one boat going for two weeks or beyond it, and the fair will be a good fair for horses I heard them saying below.

MAURYA: It's a hard thing they'll be saying below if the body is washed up and there's no man in it to make the coffin, and I after giving a big price for the finest white boards you'd find in Connemara.

She looks round at the boards.

BARTLEY: How would it be washed up, and we after looking each day for nine days, and a strong wind blowing a while back from the west and south?

MAURYA: If it wasn't found itself, that wind is raising the sea, and there was a star up against the moon, and it rising in the night. If it was a hundred horses, or a thousand horses you had itself, what is the price of a thousand horses against a son where there is one son only?

BARTLEY *(working at the halter, to* CATHLEEN*):* Let you go down each day, and see the sheep aren't jumping in on the rye, and if the jobber comes you can sell the pig with the black feet if there is a good price going.

MAURYA: How would the like of her get a good price for a pig?

BARTLEY *(to* CATHLEEN*):* If the west wind holds with the last bit of the moon let you and Nora get up weed enough for another cock for the kelp. It's hard set we'll be from this day with no one in it but one man to work.

MAURYA: It's hard set we'll be surely the day you're drownd'd with the rest. What way will I live and the girls with me, and I an old woman looking for the grave?

BARTLEY *lays down the halter, takes off his old coat, and puts on a newer one of the same flannel.*

BARTLEY *(to* NORA*):* Is she coming to the pier?

NORA *(looking out):* She's passing the green head and letting fall her sails.

BARTLEY *(getting his purse and tobacco):* I'll have half an hour to go down, and you'll see me coming again in two days, or in three days, or maybe in four days if the wind is bad.

MAURYA *(turning round to the fire, and putting her shawl over her head):* Isn't it a hard and cruel man won't hear a word from an old woman, and she holding him from the sea?

CATHLEEN: It's the life of a young man to be going on the sea, and who would listen to an old woman with one thing and she saying it over?

BARTLEY *(taking the halter):* I must go now quickly. I'll ride down on the red mare, and the gray pony'll run behind me. . . . The blessing of God on you.

He goes out.

MAURYA *(crying out as he is in the door):* He's gone now, God spare us, and we'll not see him again. He's gone now, and when the black night is falling I'll have no son left me in the world.

CATHLEEN: Why wouldn't you give him your blessing and he looking round in the door? Isn't it sorrow enough is on every one in this house without your sending him out with an unlucky word behind him, and a hard word in his ear?

MAURYA *takes up the tongs and begins raking the fire aimlessly without looking round.*

NORA *(turning towards her):* You're taking away the turf from the cake.

CATHLEEN *(crying out):* The Son of God forgive us, Nora, we're after forgetting his bit of bread.

She comes over to the fire.

NORA: And it's destroyed he'll be going till dark night, and he after eating nothing since the sun went up.

CATHLEEN *(turning the cake out of the oven):* It's destroyed he'll be, surely. There's no sense left on any person in a house where an old woman will be talking for ever.

MAURYA *sways herself on her stool.*

CATHLEEN *(cutting off some of the bread and rolling it in a cloth; to* MAURYA*):* Let you go down now to the spring well and give him this and he passing. You'll see him then and the dark word will be broken, and you can say "God speed you," the way he'll be easy in his mind.

MAURYA *(taking the bread):* Will I be in it as soon as himself?

CATHLEEN: If you go now quickly.

MAURYA *(standing up unsteadily):* It's hard set I am to walk.

CATHLEEN *(looking at her anxiously):* Give her the stick, Nora, or maybe she'll slip on the big stones.

NORA: What stick?

CATHLEEN: The stick Michael brought from Connemara.

MAURYA *(taking a stick* NORA *gives her):* In the big world the old people do be leaving things after them for their sons and children, but in this place it is the young men do be leaving things behind for them that do be old.

She goes out slowly. NORA *goes over to the ladder.*

CATHLEEN: Wait, Nora, maybe she'd turn back quickly. She's that sorry, God help her, you wouldn't know the thing she'd do.

NORA: Is she gone around by the bush?

CATHLEEN *(looking out):* She's gone now. Throw it down quickly, for the Lord knows when she'll be out of it again.

NORA *(getting the bundle from the loft):* The young priest said he'd be passing tomorrow, and we might go down and speak to him below if it's Michael's they are surely.

CATHLEEN *(taking the bundle):* Did he say what way they were found?

NORA *(coming down):* "There were two men," says he, "and they rowing round with poteen before the cocks crowed, and the oar of one of them caught the body, and they passing the black cliffs of the north."

CATHLEEN *(trying to open the bundle):* Give me a knife, Nora, the strings perished with the salt water, and there's a black knot on it you wouldn't loosen in a week.

NORA *(giving her a knife):* I've heard tell it was a long way to Donegal.

CATHLEEN *(cutting the string):* It is surely. There was a man in here a while ago— the man sold us that knife—and he said if you set off walking from the rock beyond, it would be seven days you'd be in Donegal.

NORA: And what time would a man take, and he floating?

CATHLEEN *opens the bundle and takes out a bit of a stocking. They look at them eagerly.*

CATHLEEN *(in a low voice):* The Lord spare us, Nora! isn't it a queer hard thing to say if it's his they are surely?

NORA: I'll get his shirt off the hook the way we can put the one flannel on the other. *(She looks through some clothes hanging in the corner.):* It's not with them, Cathleen, and where will it be?

CATHLEEN: I'm thinking Bartley put it on him in the morning, for his own shirt was heavy with the salt in it. *(Pointing to the corner.):* There's a bit of a sleeve was of the same stuff. Give me that and it will do.

NORA *brings it to her and they compare the flannel.*

CATHLEEN: It's the same stuff, Nora; but if it is itself aren't there great rolls of it in the shops of Galway, and isn't it many another man may have a shirt of it as well as Michael himself?

NORA *(who has taken up the stocking and counted the stitches, crying out):* It's Michael, Cathleen, it's Michael; God spare his soul, and what will herself say when she hears this story, and Bartley on the sea?

CATHLEEN *(taking the stocking):* It's a plain stocking.

NORA: It's the second one of the third pair I knitted, and I put up three score stitches, and I dropped four of them.

CATHLEEN *(counts the stitches):* It's that number is in it. *(Crying out.)* Ah, Nora, isn't it a bitter thing to think of him floating that way to the far north, and no one to keen him but the black hags that do be flying on the sea?

NORA *(swinging herself round, and throwing out her arms on the clothes.):* And isn't it a pitiful thing when there is nothing left of a man who was a great rower and fisher, but a bit of an old shirt and a plain stocking?

CATHLEEN *(after an instant):* Tell me is herself coming, Nora? I hear a little sound on the path.

NORA *(looking out):* She is, Cathleen. She's coming up to the door.

CATHLEEN: Put these things away before she'll come in. Maybe it's easier she'll be after giving her blessing to Bartley, and we won't let on we've heard anything the time he's on the sea.

NORA *(helping* CATHLEEN *to close the bundle):* We'll put them here in the corner.

They put them into a hole in the chimney corner. CATHLEEN *goes back to the spinning-wheel.*

NORA: Will she see it was crying I was?

CATHLEEN: Keep your back to the door the way the light'll not be on you.

NORA *sits down at the chimney corner, with her back to the door.* MAURYA *comes in very slowly, without looking at the girls, and goes over to her stool at the other side of the fire. The cloth with the bread is still in her hand. The girls look at each other, and* NORA *points to the bundle of bread.*

CATHLEEN *(after spinning for a moment):* You didn't give him his bit of bread?

MAURYA *begins to keen softly, without turning round.*

CATHLEEN: Did you see him riding down?

MAURYA *goes on keening.*

CATHLEEN *(a little impatiently):* God forgive you; isn't it a better thing to raise your voice and tell what you seen, than to be making lamentation for a thing that's done? Did you see Bartley, I'm saying to you.

MAURYA *(with a weak voice):* My heart's broken from this day.

CATHLEEN *(as before):* Did you see Bartley?

MAURYA: I seen the fearfulest thing.

CATHLEEN *(leaves her wheel and looks out):* God forgive you; he's riding the mare now over the green head, and the gray pony behind him.

MAURYA *(starts, so that her shawl falls back from her head and shows her white tossed hair. With a frightened voice):* The gray pony behind him.

CATHLEEN *(coming to the fire):* What is it ails you, at all?

MAURYA *(speaking very slowly):* I've seen the fearfulest thing any person has seen, since the day Bride Dara seen the dead man with the child in his arms.

CATHLEEN AND NORA: Uah.

They crouch down in front of the old woman at the fire.

NORA: Tell us what it is you seen.

MAURYA: I went down to the spring well, and I stood there saying a prayer to myself. Then Bartley came along, and he riding on the red mare with the gray pony behind him. *(She puts up her hands, as if to hide something from her eyes.)* The Son of God spare us, Nora!

CATHLEEN: What is it you seen?

MAURYA: I seen Michael himself.

CATHLEEN*(speaking softly):* You did not mother; it wasn't Michael you seen, for his body is after being found in the far north, and he's got a clean burial by the grace of God.

MAURYA *(a little defiantly):* I'm after seeing him this day, and he riding and galloping. Bartley came first on the red mare; and I tried to say "God speed you," but something choked the words in my throat. He went by quickly; and "the blessing of God on you," says he, and I could say nothing. I looked up then, and I crying, at the gray pony, and there was Michael upon it—with fine clothes on him, and new shoes on his feet.

CATHLEEN *(begins to keen):* It's destroyed we are from this day. It's destroyed, surely.

NORA: Didn't the young priest say the Almighty God wouldn't leave her destitute with no son living?

MAURYA *(in a low voice, but clearly):* It's little the like of him knows of the sea. . . . Bartley will be lost now, and let you call in Eamon and make me a good coffin out of the white boards, for I won't live after them. I've had a husband, and a husband's father, and six sons in this house—six fine men, though it was a hard birth I had with every one of them and they coming to the world—and some of them were found and some of them were not found, but they're gone now the lot of them. . . . There were Stephen, and Shawn, were lost in the great wind, and found after in the Bay of Gregory of the Golden Mouth, and carried up the two of them on the one plank, and in by that door.

She pauses for a moment, the girls start as if they heard something through the door that is half open behind them.

NORA *(in a whisper):* Did you hear that, Cathleen? Did you hear a noise in the north-east?

CATHLEEN *(in a whisper):* There's some one after crying out by the seashore.

MAURYA *(continues without hearing anything):* There was Sheamus and his father, and his own father again, were lost in a dark night, and not a stick or sign was seen of them when the sun went up. There was Patch after was drowned out of a curagh that turned over. I was sitting here with Bartley, and he a baby, lying on my two knees, and I seen two women, and three women, and four women coming in, and they crossing themselves, and not saying a word. I looked out then, and there were men coming after them, and they holding a thing in the half of a red sail, and water dripping out of it—it was a dry day, Nora—and leaving a track to the door.

She pauses again with her hand stretched out towards the door. It opens softly and old women begin to come in, crossing themselves on the threshold, and kneeling down in front of the stage with red petticoats over their heads.

MAURYA (*half in a dream, to* CATHLEEN): Is it Patch, or Michael, or what is it at all?

CATHLEEN: Michael is after being found in the far north, and when he is found there how could he be here in this place?

MAURYA: There does be a power of young men floating round in the sea, and what way would they know if it was Michael they had, or another man like him, for when a man is nine days in the sea, and the wind blowing, it's hard set his own mother would be to say what man was it.

CATHLEEN: It's Michael, God spare him, for they're after sending us a bit of his clothes from the far north.

She reaches out and hands MAURYA *the clothes that belonged to Michael.* MAURYA *stands up slowly and takes them in her hand.* NORA *looks out.*

NORA: They're carrying a thing among them and there's water dripping out of it and leaving a track by the big stones.

CATHLEEN (*in a whisper to the women who have come in*): Is it Bartley it is?

ONE OF THE WOMEN: It is surely, God rest his soul.

Two younger women come in and pull out the table. Then men carry in the body of BARTLEY, *laid on a plank, with a bit of sail over it, and lay it on the table.*

CATHLEEN (*to the women, as they are doing so*): What way was he drowned?

ONE OF THE WOMEN: The gray pony knocked him into the sea, and he was washed out where there is a great surf on the white rocks.

MAURYA has gone over and knelt down at the head of the table. The women are keening softly and swaying themselves with a slow movement. CATHLEEN *and* NORA *kneel at the other end of the table. The men kneel near the door.*

MAURYA (*raising her head and speaking as if she did not see the people around her*): They're all gone now, and there isn't anything more the sea can do to me. . . . I'll have no call now to be up crying and praying when the wind breaks from the south and you can hear the surf is in the east, and the surf is in the west, making a great stir with the two noises, and they hitting one on the other. I'll have no call now to be going down and getting Holy Water in the dark nights after Samhain, and I won't care what way the sea is when the other women will be keening. (*To* NORA.) Give me the Holy Water, Nora, there's a small sup still on the dresser.

NORA *gives it to her.*

MAURYA (*drops Michael's clothes across* BARTLEY's *feet, and sprinkles the Holy Water over him.*): It isn't that I haven't prayed for you, Bartley, to the Almighty God. It isn't that I haven't said prayers in the dark night till you wouldn't know what I'd be saying; but it's a great rest I'll have now, and it's time surely. It's a great rest I'll have now, and great sleeping in the long nights after

Samhain, if it's only a bit of wet flour we do have to eat, and maybe a fish that would be stinking.

She kneels down again, crossing herself, and saying prayers under her breath.

CATHLEEN *(to an old man):* Maybe yourself and Eamon would make a coffin when the sun rises. We have fine white boards herself bought, God help her, thinking Michael would be found, and I have a new cake you can eat while you'll be working.

THE OLD MAN *(looking at the boards):* Are there nails with them?

CATHLEEN: There are not, Colum; we didn't think of the nails.

ANOTHER MAN: It's a great wonder she wouldn't think of the nails, and all the coffins she's been made already.

CATHLEEN: It's getting old she is, and broken.

MAURYA *stands up again very slowly and spreads out the pieces of Michael's clothes beside the body, sprinkling them with the last of the Holy Water.*

NORA *(in a whisper to* CATHLEEN*):* She's quiet now and easy; but the day Michael was drowned you could hear her crying out from this to the spring well. It's fonder she was of Michael, and would any one have thought that?

CATHLEEN *(slowly and clearly):* An old woman will be soon tired with anything she will do, and isn't it nine days herself is after crying and keening, and making great sorrow in the house?

MAURYA *(puts the empty cup mouth downwards on the table, and lays her hands together on* BARTLEY's *feet):* They're all together this time, and the end is come. May the Almighty God have mercy on Bartley's soul, and on Michael's soul, and on the souls of Sheamus and Patch, and Stephen and Shawn *(bending her head);* and may He have mercy on my soul, Nora, and on the soul of every one is left living in the world.

She pauses, and the keen rises a little more loudly from the women, then sinks away.

MAURYA *(continuing):* Michael has a clean burial in the far north, by the grace of the Almighty God. Bartley will have a fine coffin out of the white boards, and a deep grave surely. What more can we want than that? No man at all can be living for ever, and we must be satisfied.

She kneels down again and the curtain falls slowly.

QUESTIONS AND CONSIDERATIONS

1. What impression of Maurya's family is created in the opening setting? Can you imagine what it would be like to live in such an austere, impoverished community?

2. What is the significance of the clothing Nora displays at the beginning of the play? To whom do they seem to belong? Do the priest's words offer any consolation? At what point is the issue of ownership of the clothing resolved? How does this "resolution" add to the drama and pathos of the play?

3. Maurya is first presented through the dialogue of her children. What picture of her emerges through their discussion? Is their view of her an accurate one?

4. What is the conflict that Maurya and Bartley have over the use of the piece of rope? How does this conflict help to emphasize dramatically their different outlooks on life?

5. How does Maurya's "keening," along with repeated phrases and lines, help to emphasize the play's tone of lamentation? Refer to examples from the text.

6. Discuss the ritual elements in the last scene. How do the physical elements of the ritual—the kneeling of Maurya and the old women, the sprinkling of holy water, the laying out of clothing, the upending of the cup—help to emphasize the tone and values of the play?

IDEAS FOR WRITING

1. Discuss the attitude toward the power of nature reflected in *Riders to the Sea*. How does the play suggest that people can come to terms with the need to coexist with and survive losses sustained at the hands of nature?

2. Develop your journal entry into an essay in which you reflect on your feelings about and how you survived a loss due to a natural disaster.

The Swamp Dwellers
Wole Soyinka

Journal

Write about an experience in which you traveled to a new, sophisticated environment, and upon returning home, saw your family and their values from a different perspective.

CHARACTERS

ALU *an old woman*   IGWEZU *son to Alu*
MAKURI *her husband*   A DRUMMER
A BEGGAR   ATTENDANTS TO KADIYE
KADIYE PRIEST

A village in the swamps.
Frogs, rain and other swamp noises.

The scene is a hut on stilts, built on one of the scattered semi-firm islands in the swamps. Two doors on the left lead into other rooms, and the one on the right leads outside. The walls are marsh stakes plaited with hemp ropes.
The room is fairly large, and is used both as the family workshop and as the 'parlour' for guests. About the middle of the right half of the stage is a barber's swivel chair, a very ancient one. On a small table against the right wall is

a meagre row of hairdressing equipment—a pair of clippers, scissors, local combs, lather basin and brush, razor—not much else. A dirty white voluminous agbada serves for the usual customer's sheet.

MAKURI, an old man of about sixty, stands by the window, looking out. Near the left downstage are the baskets he makes from the rushes which are strewn in front of him. Upstage left, his equally aged wife, ALU, sits on a mat, busy at her work, unravelling the patterns in dyed 'adire' cloths. ALU appears to suffer more than the normal viciousness of the swamp flies. She has a flick by her side which she uses frequently, yelling whenever a bite has caught her unawares.

It is near dusk, and there is a gentle wash of rain outside.

ALU: Can you see him?

MAKURI: See who?

ALU: My son Igwezu. Who else?

MAKURI: I did not come to look for him. Came only to see if the rain looks like stopping.

ALU: Well, does it?

MAKURI *(grunts):*

ALU *(goes back to her work. Then—):* It is time he was back. He went hours and hours ago.

MAKURI: He knows the way. He's a grown-up man, with a wife.

ALU *(flaring up with aged lack of heat):* If you had any good at all in you, you'd go and look for him.

MAKURI: And catch my death of cramp? Not likely . . . And anyway, *(getting warmer)* what's preventing you from going?

ALU: I want to be here when he gives me the news. I don't want to fall down dead out in the open.

MAKURI: The older you get, the more of a fraud you become. Every day for the past ten years, you've done nothing but swear that your son was dead in the marshes. And now you sit there like a crow and tell me that you're waiting for news about him.

ALU *(stubbornly):* I know he's dead.

MAKURI: Then what do you want Igwezu to tell you?

ALU: I only want to know if . . . I only want to ask him . . . I . . . I . . . He shouldn't have rushed off like that . . . dashing off like a madman before anyone could ask him a thing.

MAKURI *(insistently):* Before anyone could ask him WHAT?

ALU *(flares up again):* You're always trying to make me a liar.

MAKURI: I don't have to make you one.

ALU: Bah! Frog-face! *(resumes her work)* . . . Dropped his bundle and rushed off before I could ask him a thing . . . And to think he could have found him after all. To think he could have found him in the city . . .

MAKURI: Dead men don't go to the city. They go to hell.

ALU: I know one dead man who is sitting right here instead of going quietly to hell.

MAKURI: Now see who is calling who . . . .

ALU: You're so useless now that it takes you nearly a whole week to make one basket . . . and to think you don't even cut your own rushes!

MAKURI: If you had to get up so often to shave the heads of the whole village . . . and most of them crusted with kraw-kraw so that a man has to scrape and scrape until . . .

ALU *(yells suddenly and slaps herself on the arm).*

MAKURI *(looks at her for a moment):* Ha! Don't tell me now that a fly has been trying to suck blood from your dried-up veins.

ALU: If you had enough blood to hold you up, you'd prove it by going to look for your own son, and bring him home to supper.

MAKURI: He'll come home when he's hungry.

ALU: Suppose he's lost his way? Suppose he went walking in the swamps and couldn't find his way back?

MAKURI *(in bewilderment):* Him? Get lost? Woman, isn't it your son we're speaking of? The one who was born here, and has lived here all his life?

ALU: But he has been away now for some time. You cannot expect him to find his way about so quickly.

MAKURI: No, no. Of course not. The poor child has been away for eight . . . . whole . . . months . . . ! Tch, tch. You'd drive a man to drown himself in the swamps—just to get away from your fussing.

ALU *(puts aside her work and rises):* I'm going after him. I don't want to lose him too. I don't want him missing his foothold and vanishing without a cry, without a chance for anyone to save him.

MAKURI: Stay where you are.

(ALU crosses to doorpost and looks out.)

ALU: I'm going out to shout his name until he hears me. I had another son before the mire drew him into the depths. I don't want Igwezu going the same way.

MAKURI *(follows her):* You haven't lost a son yet in the slough, but you will soon if you don't stop calling down calamities on their heads.

ALU: It's not what I say. The worst has happened already. Awuchike was drowned.

MAKURI: You're a blood-thirsty woman. Awuchike got sick of this place and went into the city. That's where you'll find him, fadding it out with the gentlemen. But you'll be satisfied with nothing less than a festering corpse beneath the mire . . .

ALU: It's the truth.

MAKURI: It's a lie. All the young men go into the big town to try their hand at making money . . . only some of them remember their folk and send word once in a while.

ALU: You'll see. When Igwezu returns, you'll find that he never saw a trace of him.

MAKURI: And if he didn't? The city is a large place. You could live there all your life and never meet half the people in it.

ALU: They are twins. Their close birth would have drawn them together even if they were living at the opposite ends of the town.

MAKURI: Bah!

ALU: Bah to yourself. Nobody has ever seen him. Nobody has ever heard of him, and yet you say to me . . .

MAKURI: Nobody? Did you say nobody?

ALU: No one that really knew him. No one that could swear it was he.

MAKURI *(despairingly):* No one. No one that could swear . . . Ah, what a woman you are for deceiving yourself.

ALU: No one knows. Only the Serpent can tell. Only the Serpent of the swamps, the Snake that lurks beneath the slough.

MAKURI: The serpent be . . . ! Bah! You'll make me voice a sacrilege before I can stop my tongue. The traders came. They came one year, and they came the next. They looked at Igwezu and asked, Has he a twin? Has he a twin brother who lives in the town?

ALU: There are many people who look alike.

MAKURI *(sits down and takes up his work):* Well, I'll not perform the death rites for a son I know to be living.

ALU: If you felt for him like a true father, you'd know he was dead. But you haven't any feelings at all. Anyone would think they weren't your own flesh and blood.

MAKURI: Well, I have only your own word for that.

ALU: Ugh! You always did have a dirty tongue.

MAKURI *(slyly):* The land is big and wide, Alu, and you were often out by yourself, digging for crabs. And there were all those shifty-eyed traders who came to hunt for crocodile skins . . . Are you sure they didn't take your own skin with them . . . you old crocodile!

ALU: And if they did?

MAKURI: Poor luck to them. They couldn't have minded much which crocodile they took.

ALU: You're asking . . . Ayi! *(Slaps off a fly and continues more furiously.)* You're asking to have your head split and the wind let out.

MAKURI: And to think . . .

ALU *(makes a move to rise):* And I'll do it for you if you carry on the same . . .

MAKURI: Now, now, Alu. You know I didn't mean a word of that.

(ALU tightens her lips and resumes her work.)

(In a hurriedly placating tone.) There wasn't a woman anywhere more faithful than you, Alu; I never had a moment of worry in the whole of my life . . . *(His tone grows more sincere)* Not every man can look his wife in the face and make that boast, Alu. Not every man can do it. *(ALU remains inflexible.)* And the chances you could have taken. Those traders—every one of them wanted you to go back with him; promised he'd make you live like a lady, clothe you in silks and have servants to wait on your smallest wants . . . You don't belong here, they used to tell you. Come back with us to the city where men know the value of women . . . No, there was no doubt about

it. You could have had your choice of them. You turned their heads like a
pot of cane brew.

(ALU *begins to smile in spite of herself.*)

MAKURI: And the way I would go walking with you, and I could hear their heads
turning round, and one tongue hanging out and saying to the other, Now I
wonder what she sees in him . . . Poor fools . . . if only they knew. If only
they could see me take you out into the mangrove, and I so strong that I
could make you gripe and sweat and sink your teeth into my cheeks.

ALU: You were always one for boasting.

MAKURI: And you with your eyes shut so tight that I thought the skin would tear
itself. Your eyes always shut, so that up till this day, you cannot tell what I
looked like when the spirit took me, and I waxed as hot as the devil himself.

ALU: Be quiet.

MAKURI: You never feared the swamp then. You could walk across it day and
night and go to sleep in the middle of it . . . Alu, do you remember our
wedding night?

ALU (*pleased just the same*): We're past that kind of talk now. Have you no shame?

MAKURI: Come on, my own Alu. Tell old Makuri what you did on the night of our
wedding.

ALU: No.

MAKURI: You're a stubborn old hen . . . Won't you even tell how you dragged
me from the house and we went across the swamps, though it was so
dark that I could not see the whites of your eyes?

ALU (*stubbornly*): I do not remember.

MAKURI: And you took me to the point where the streams meet, and there you
said . . . (*Pauses.*)

ALU (*shyly*): Well, it was my mother who used to say it.

MAKURI: Tell me just the same . . . just as you said it that night when I thought
they were your own words.

ALU: My memory is not so good . . . but . . .

MAKURI: It will come. Think slowly.

ALU (*with a shy smile*): She said I had to say it on my bridal bed.

MAKURI: Just where we stood. Go on, say it again.

ALU: 'Where the rivers meet, there the marriage must begin. And the river bed
itself is the perfect bridal bed.'

MAKURI (*thoughtfully*): Ay-ii . . . The bed of the river itself . . . the bed of the
river . . . (*Bursts suddenly into what appears to be illogical laughter.*)

ALU: Eh? Why? What are you laughing at now?

MAKURI (*futile effort to control himself*): Ay—ya-ya! The river bed . . . (*Bursts out
laughing again.*)

ALU: Are you well Makuri?

MAKURI: Ay—ii! You must be really old, Alu. If you don't remember this, you're
too old to lie on another river bed.

ALU: I don't . . . What are you . . . ?

MAKURI: Think hard woman. Do you not remember? We did not know that the swamp came up as far as that part of the stream . . . The ground . . . gave . . . way beneath us!

ALU *(beginning to laugh):* It is all beginning to come back . . . yes, yes, so it did. So it did!

MAKURI: And can you remember that you were left kicking in the mire . . . ha ha!

ALU *(no longer amused).* I was? I suppose you never even got your fingers muddy?

MAKURI: Well, I jumped up in time, didn't I? But you went down just as you were, flat on your back. And there I stood looking at you . . .

ALU: Ay. Gawking and yelling your head off with laughter. I can remember now.

MAKURI: You'd have laughed too if you had stood where I did and seen what could be seen of you.

ALU: Call yourself a man? And all my ribs bruised because you stood on me trying to get me out.

MAKURI: If you hadn't been thrashing about so much, I'd have got you out much quicker . . .

(ALU has tightened her lips again. Bends rigidly over her work. Pause.)

MAKURI: The whole village said that the twins were the very colour of the swamp. . . . eh . . . Alu?

(ALU remains deaf to him.)

MAKURI: Ah well . . . Those were the days . . . those days were really good. Even when times were harsh and the swamp overran the land, we were able to laugh with the Serpent . . . *(Continues to work)* . . . but these young people . . . They are no sooner born than they want to get out of the village as if it carried a plague . . . *(Looks up suddenly.)* I bet none of them has ever taken his woman into the swamps.

ALU: They have more sense than that. *(She says this with an effort and immediately resumes her frigidity.)*

MAKURI: It is not sense they have . . . not sense at all. Igwezu was hardly joined to his wife before he took her off into the city. What would a girl like Desala do in a place like that, I ask you. What would she find to do in the city?

ALU *(primly):* If you'd kept your eyes about you, you would have known that she made him promise to take her there before she would wed him.

MAKURI: It ruins them. The city ruins them. What do they seek there except money? They talk to the traders, and then they cannot sit still . . . There was Gonushi's son for one . . . left his wife and children . . . not a word to anyone.

ALU *(almost between her teeth):* It was the swamp . . . He went the same way as my son . . .

MAKURI *(throwing down his basket):* Woman . . . ! *(He is interrupted by the sound of footsteps on the planks outside.)*

MAKURI: That must be Igwezu now.

ALU: Thank heavens. It will soon be dark.

MAKURI: You'd better make the most of him. He might be going back tomorrow.

ALU: Why should he?

MAKURI: He came for his crops. Now that he knows they've been ruined by the floods, he'll be running back to the city.

ALU: He will stay a few days at least.

MAKURI *(licking his lips):* With a full-bosomed woman like Desala waiting for him in the city . . . ? You must be getting old.

ALU: It's a let-down for him—coming all the way back and finding no harvest.

MAKURI: Now don't you start. We've had worse years before this.

ALU *(flaring):* But you haven't journeyed three days only to be cheated of your crops . . .

(The footsteps are right at the door. There is a knock on the wall.)

ALU: That's a queer mood he's in. Why is he knocking?

MAKURI: It's not Igwezu . . . I didn't think they were his footsteps. *(Goes towards the door and pulls aside the door matting.)* A good evening to you, stranger.

VOICE OFFSTAGE: Allah protect you.

MAKURI: Were you sent to me? Come in. Come into the house.

(The caller enters, feeling his way with a staff.)

MAKURI *(picks up the bundle from the floor):* Alu, take this bundle out of here . . . And bring some light. It is too dark in here.

BEGGAR: No, no. Not on my account. It makes no difference whatever to me.

MAKURI *(in a bewildered manner):* Oh . . . oh . . . I understand. *(Takes hold of the other end of the staff and leads him to the swivel chair.)* Sit here . . . Ah. *(Touches the stranger's forehead, and then his, saying devoutly—)* Blessed be the afflicted of the gods.

BEGGAR: Allah grant everlasting peace to this house.

(The blind man is tall and straight. It is obvious from his dress that he is a stranger to these parts. He wears a long, tubular gown, white, which comes below his calf, and a little skull cap. Down one ear hangs a fairly large ear-ring, and he wears a thick ring on one of his fingers. He has a small beard, which, with the skull cap, accentuates the length of his face and emphasizes its ebony-carving nature. His feet are muddy above the ankles. The rest of him is lightly wet. His bearing is of quiet dignity.)

MAKURI: You have journeyed far?

BEGGAR: Very far. I came all the way down the river.

MAKURI: Walking?

BEGGAR: Most of the way. Wherever it was possible, I walked. But sometimes, I was forced to accept a lift from the ferries.

MAKURI *(looks rapidly down his legs):* Alu! Some water for the man to wash his feet.

ALU *(coming in with the taper):* Give me time. I can't do everything at once, can I? *(Lights the oil lamps which are hanging from the rafters. Goes back again.)*

MAKURI: Have you met anyone in the village? Were you directed here?

BEGGAR: No. This happened to be the first house on my way . . . Are you the head of this house?

MAKURI: Y-yes, yes I am.

BEGGAR: Then it is with you I must speak.

MAKURI: We haven't much, but you can have shelter for the night, and food for . . .

BEGGAR: I have not come to beg for alms.

MAKURI: Oh? Do you know anyone here?

BEGGAR: No. I come from far away in the North. Have you ever heard of Bukanji?

MAKURI: Bukanji? Bukan . . . ? Ah, is that not the village of beggars?

BEGGAR: So it is known by the rest of the world . . . the village of beggars . . . but I have not come to beg.

MAKURI: Bukanji! That is a march of several weeks!

BEGGAR: I have been journeying for longer than that. I resolved to follow the river as far as it went, and never turn back. If I leave here, it will be to continue in the same direction.

MAKURI: But this is the end—this is where the river ends!

BEGGAR: No, friend. There are many more miles left of this river.

MAKURI: Yes, yes . . . But the rest is all swamp. Between here and the sea, you'll not find a human soul.

BEGGAR: I must stay here or walk on. I have sworn to tread only where the soil is moist.

MAKURI: You'll not get far in that direction. This is the end. This is as far as human beings can go, even those who have the use of their sight.

BEGGAR: Then I must stay here.

MAKURI: What do you want?

BEGGAR: Work.

MAKURI: Work?

BEGGAR: Yes, work. I wish to work on the soil. I wish to knead it between my fingers.

MAKURI: But you're blind. Why don't you beg like others? There is no true worshipper who would deny you this charity.

BEGGAR: I want a home, and I wish to work with my hands.

MAKURI *(in utter bewilderment):* You . . . the afflicted of the gods! Do you really desire to work, when even the least devout lives under the strict injunction of hospitality towards you?

BEGGAR *(getting up):* No more, no more. All the way down the river the natives read me the code of the afflicted, according to their various faiths. Some fed and clothed me. Others put money in my hands, food and drink in my bag. With some, it was the children and their stones, and sometimes the dogs followed me and whetted their teeth on my ankles . . . Good-bye. I shall follow the river to the end.

MAKURI: Wait. You are very hasty. Did you never learn that the blind man does not hurry for fear he out-walks his guide? Sit down again . . . Alu! Alu! When is that supper coming?

ALU *(from inside):* What supper? The last time it was water for washing his feet.

MAKURI: Well, hurry . . . *(Helps the blind man back into the chair.)* There . . . Now tell me all about your journey . . . Did you come through any of the big cities?

BEGGAR: One or two, but I did not stop there. I walked right through them without a halt.

MAKURI: And you have been on the road for . . . how long did you say?

BEGGAR: I have lost all count of time. To me, one day is just like another . . . ever since my sight became useless.

MAKURI: It must be strange . . . living in perpetual dark.

BEGGAR: I did not have many years to enjoy the benefit of the eyes. Four or five years at the most, and then . . . You have heard of the fly sickness?

MAKURI *(shaking his head):* Who hasn't? Who hasn't?

BEGGAR: It is fatal to cattle. The human beings fall ill and suffer agonies. When the sickness is over, the darkness begins . . . At first, it is mystifying and then . . . *(smiles).* When it happened to me, I thought I was dead and that I had gone to a paradise where my earthly eyes were unsuffering.

MAKURI: You did? If it had been old Makuri, he would have thought that he was in the darkest corner of hell.

BEGGAR *(smiling still):* But I was only a child, and I knew that I had committed no sins. Moreover, my faith promises paradise for all true believers—paradise in the company of Muhammad and all the prophets . . . *(Becoming serious.)* Those few moments were the happiest in my life. Any moment, I thought, and my eyes would be opened to the wonders around me. I heard familiar voices, and I rejoiced, because I thought that they were dead also, and were in paradise with me . . . And then slowly, the truth came to me, and I knew that I was living—but blind.

MAKURI: The gods be merciful.

BEGGAR: Even before anyone told me, I knew exactly what I had to do to live. A staff, a bowl, and I was out on the roads begging for alms from travellers, singing my prayers, pouring out blessings upon them which were not mine to give . . .

MAKURI: No, my friend. The blessings were yours. My faith teaches me that every god shakes a beggar by the hand, and his gifts are passed into his heart so that every man he blesses . . .

BEGGAR: Ah, but did I bless them from the heart? Were they not so many that I blessed without thought, and took from whatever hand was willing, however vile it was? Did I know if the alms came from a pure heart or from a robber and taker of lives, from the devout or the profane . . . ? I thanked and blessed them equally, even before I had the time to discover the size of their bounty . . . *(Begins to nod his head in time to his chanting.)*

(His chanting is tonal. No clear words. Faint drumming can now be heard offstage. The BEGGAR *hears it and stops abruptly, listening hard for the sound.)*

BEGGAR: Have you a festivity in the village tonight?

MAKURI: No. Why?

BEGGAR: I can hear drumming.

MAKURI *(after listening for a moment):* It must be the frogs. There is a whole city of them in the marshes.

BEGGAR: No, this is drumming. And it is coming this way . . . yes, it is drawing nearer.

MAKURI: Y—yes . . . I think I can hear it now . . . Alu!

ALU *(from inside):* What now?

MAKURI: Can you hear the drumming?

ALU: What drumming?

MAKURI: That means you can't. *(Confidentially.)* She was deaf the day she was born. *(Goes to the door and looks out.)* They are not within sight yet, whoever it is . . . Ah, I know who it must be . . . My son.

BEGGAR: You have a son?

MAKURI: Yes. He only came back today. He has been in the city making money.

BEGGAR: So he is wealthy?

MAKURI: We don't know yet. He hardly said a word to anyone before he rushed off again to see what the floods had done to his farm . . . The man is a fool. I told him there wasn't a thing to see except the swamp water, but he rushed out like a madman, dropping his bundle on the floor. He said he had to see for himself before he would believe it.

BEGGAR: Was there much damage to the farm?

MAKURI: Much damage? Not a grain was saved, not one tuber in the soil . . . And what the flood left behind was poisoned by the oil in the swamp water. *(Shakes his head.)* . . . It is hard for him, coming back for a harvest that isn't there.

BEGGAR: But it is possible then. It is possible to plant on this land in spite of the swamp?

MAKURI *(straining his eyes into the dark outside):* Oh yes. There are little bits of land here and there where a man can sow enough to keep his family, and even take to the market . . . Not much, but . . . I can't see them . . . But I'm sure it is he. He must have run into one of the drummers and been merry-making all afternoon. You can trust Luyaka to drum him back to his own house in welcome.

BEGGAR: Is there land here which a man can till? Is there any land to spare for a man who is willing to give his soul to the soil?

MAKURI *(shakes his head):* No, friend. All the land that can take the weight of a hoe is owned by someone in the village. Even the few sheep and goats haven't any land on which to graze. They have to be fed on cassava and other roots.

BEGGAR: But if a man is willing to take a piece of the ground and redeem it from the swamp—will they let him? If a man is willing to drain the filth away and make the land yield coco-yams and lettuce—will they let him?

MAKURI *(stares wildly):* Mind what you are saying, son. Mind what profanities you utter in this house.

BEGGAR *(surprised):* I merely ask to be given a little of what land is useless to the people.

MAKURI: You wish to rob the Serpent of the Swamps? You wish to take the food out of his mouth?

BEGGAR: The Serpent? The Serpent of the Swamps?

MAKURI: The land that we till and live on has been ours from the beginning of time. The bounds are marked by ageless iroko trees that have lived since the birth of the Serpent, since the birth of the world, since the start of time itself. What is ours is ours. But what belongs to the Serpent may never be taken away from him.

BEGGAR: I beg your forgiveness. *(Rises.)* I have not come to question your faith. Allah reward you for your hospitality . . . I must continue my journey . . .

MAKURI: Wait. *(He listens for a moment to the drumming which is now just outside the door.)* That is the drummer of the priest . . . *(Enter* ALU *running.)* Alu, is that not the priest's salutations coming from the drums?

ALU: Yes. It must be the Kadiye.

MAKURI: It is. It is . . . Well, don't stand there. Get the place fit to receive him . . . Clear away all the litter . . .

ALU *begins to tidy the room hastily. She takes away* MAKURI'*s baskets and rushes, returns to fetch her own things and takes them out of the room. She trims the lamp wicks and takes away any oddments lying around.)*

MAKURI: And see if there is any brew in the attic. The Kadiye might like some.

ALU *(grumbling):* Take this away . . . Prepare supper . . . See if there is any brew in the . . . Why don't you try and do something to help . . . !

MAKURI: Do you want me to be so ill-mannered as to leave my guest by himself? . . . *(Takes the blind man by the arm and leads him towards his stool.)* . . . You mustn't pay any attention to that ill-tempered hen . . . She always gets in a flutter when the Kadiye honours our house. *(Picks up his stool and moves off towards* ALU'*s corner.)* . . . He's probably come to offer prayers of thanks for the safe return of our son . . . He's our holy man, the Servant and Priest of the Serpent of the Swamp . . . *(Puts down the stool.)* Here. Sit down here. We must continue our talk when he is gone.

(The DRUMMER *is now at the door, and footsteps come up the gangway.*

The DRUMMER *is the first to enter. He bows in backwards, drumming praises of the* KADIYE. *Next comes the* KADIYE *himself, a big, voluminous creature of about fifty, smooth-faced except for little tufts of beard around his chin. His head is shaved clean. He wears a kind of loin-cloth, white, which comes down to below his knees and a flap of which hangs over his left arm. He is bare above the waist. At least half of the* KADIYE'*s fingers are ringed. He is followed by a servant, who brushes the flies off him with a horse-tail flick.)*

MAKURI *(places his arm across his chest and bows):* My house is open to you, Kadiye. You are very welcome.

(The KADIYE *places a hand on his head.)*

*(*ALU *hurries into the room and kneels. The* KADIYE *blesses her also.)*

KADIYE *(looks at the* BEGGAR *who remains sitting. Signs to the* DRUMMER *to stop.):* Did Igwezu bring a friend with him?

MAKURI: No Kadiye. This is a stranger who called at my house for charity. He is blind.

KADIYE: The gods protect you, friend.

BEGGAR: Allah shield you from all evil.

KADIYE *(startled):* Allah? is he from the North?

MAKURI: He is. He journeyed all the way from Bukanji.

KADIYE: Ah, from Bukanji. *(To the* SERVANT*)* Kundigu, give the man something.

(The SERVANT *brings out a purse and approaches the* BEGGAR. *When he is about a foot away, the* BEGGAR, *without a change of expression turns his bowl upside down. The* SERVANT *stands puzzled and looks to his master for further instructions.* KADIYE *looks quickly away, and the* SERVANT *tries to turn the bowl inside up. But the* BEGGAR *keeps it firmly downwards. The* SERVANT *looks backwards at the* KADIYE—*who by now has hemmed and begun to talk to* MAKURI—*slips the money into his own pocket, pulls the strings shut and returns to his place.)*

KADIYE: Ahem . . . Where is your son? I hear he has returned.

MAKURI: Yes he has. He went out in the afternoon to see his . . . He must have been detained by old friends and their sympathizing.

KADIYE: Yes, it is a pity. But, then, he is not the only one. Others lost even more than he did . . . And anyway, he has probably made himself a fortune in the city . . . Hasn't he?

MAKURI: I don't know. He hasn't told us . . . Won't you sit here . . . ?

KADIYE *(sits in the swivel chair):* They all do. They all make money.

MAKURI: Well, I only hope he has. He'll need something on which he can fall back.

KADIYE *(patting the arm of the chair):* Didn't he send you this chair within a few weeks of his arriving in the city?

MAKURI: Yes, he did. He's a man for keeping his word. Before he left, he said to me, With the first money I make, I am going to buy you one of those chairs which spin like a top. And you can put your customers in it and spin them until they are giddy.

KADIYE *(pushing his toes into the ground to turn the chair):* Ay—It is comfortable.

MAKURI: It is. When I have no customers, I sit in it myself. It is much better than a rocking chair . . . Alu!

ALU: Coming.

MAKURI: When are we having something to drink? Are you going to keep us waiting all night . . . ? *(Back to the* KADIYE—*)* And when they were bringing it over the water, it knocked a hole in the bottom of the canoe and nearly sank it . . . But that wasn't all. The carrier got stuck in the swamps and they had to dig him out . . . Alu!

ALU *(comes out with a gourd and a number of calabash-cups):* Here it is . . . There is no need to split your guts with shouting.

MAKURI *(takes the gourd from her and serves the drinks.* ALU *takes it round. She curtseys to the* KADIYE *when she hands him his cup.* MAKURI *takes a smell at the liquor before he begins to pour it out.):* A-a-ah! You'll find this good, Kadiye . . .

KADIYE: Has it been long fermenting?

MAKURI: Months and months. I pulped the canes nearly . . .

ALU: *You* did?

MAKURI: If you'd only give me a chance, woman! . . . I was going to say that my son pulped the canes before he left for the city.

ALU *(looking out of the door in between serving the drinks):* I wish he'd come. I wish he'd hurry up and come home. It is so dark and the swamps are . . .

MAKURI *(impatiently):* Here, here, take this to the drummer and stop your cackling. It will be his own fault if he doesn't come and we finish the lot. Pah! He's probably used to drinking bottled beer by now, instead of thriving on good wholesome cane brew, fermented in the froth of the swamp itself.

(Everyone now has a drink, except the BEGGAR, *who, in spite of a dumb persuasive attempt by* ALU, *refuses a cup. The* KADIYE *waits for* MAKURI *to come and taste his drink.)*

MAKURI *(takes the cup from the* KADIYE*):* If my face belies my thoughts, may the venom grip at once. *(Drinks a mouthful and hands it back.)*

KADIYE: The protection of the heavens be on us all. *(Drinks and smacks his lips. Then he looks round the room and announces gravely—)* The rains have stopped.

MAKURI *(shakes his head in distrust):* They have stopped too often Kadiye. It is only a lull.

KADIYE: No. They have stopped finally. My soothsayers have confirmed it. The skies are beginning to open: what few clouds there are, are being blown along the river.

MAKURI *(shrugs, without much enthusiasm):* The gods be praised.

KADIYE: The floods are over . . . The river will recede and we can plant again . . . I am now released of my vow.

MAKURI: Your vow, Kadiye?

KADIYE: Yes, When the floods began and the swamps overran the land, I vowed to the Serpent that I would neither shave nor wash until the rains ceased altogether . . .

MAKURI *(drops his cup):* I had no idea . . . is that the reason for your visit?

KADIYE: Yes, of course. Did you not guess?

MAKURI *(getting out the lather):* I will only be a moment . . .

KADIYE: No, old man. I shall wait for your son.

MAKURI: For Igwezu? . . . As you please, Kadiye . . . I hope he still remembers his trade. It must be a long time since he last wielded a razor.

KADIYE: Be it as it may, his hand is steadier than yours.

MAKURI *(replacing the lather):* True. True . . . We must all get old some time.

KADIYE: Has he been out long?

MAKURI: All day . . . But he should be back any moment now. He must be drinking with his friends . . . they haven't seen him for a whole season, and they won't let him go in a hurry . . .

ALU: He ought to be back by now. Who of his friends could have kept him so long?

KADIYE: Did he bring his wife?

ALU: No. He wouldn't want to expose her to the flooded roads and other discomforts of the journey.

MAKURI *(disgustedly):* Ah! They're soft. This younger generation is as soft as . . .

ALU: Aw, shut up in a while. Igwezu himself was lucky to get here at all. He would have had to turn back at the river if it wasn't for old Wazuri who is still ferrying travellers across the swollen stream. All the other fishermen have hung up their boats with their nets. *(Goes into the house.)*

MAKURI: And isn't that what I am telling you? As soon as the floods came, the younger men ran home to their wives. But not Wazuri! He's as old as the tortoise himself, but he keeps the paddle in his hand.

(The SERVANT *comes up and whispers in* KADIYE's *ear.)*

KADIYE: Ah yes . . . I nearly forgot. *(Drains his cup and gives it to* MAKURI.*)* I must go first to Daruga. His son is going to be circumcised tonight and he wants me to say the usual prayers . . . I'll call again on my way back. *(Rises, the* SERVANT *helping him.)*

MAKURI: Just as you please, Kadiye. And if Igwezu returns I shall tell him to prepare for you.

KADIYE: I shall send a man to find him out . . . *(Rubs his chin.)* This nest is beginning to attract the swamp flies. I must get it off tonight.

(Goes out, preceded by his DRUMMER *who drums him out as before, bowing backwards.)*

MAKURI: *(who has held the matting aside for them. Looks after them as the drumming dies away. Sighs.)* What a day! What a day! The whole world seems to have picked the same day to drop into my house . . . *(Stops suddenly as he is smitten by a recollection . . .)* The pot-bellied pig! So I am too old to shave him now, am I? Too old! Why he's nearly as old as the Serpent himself . . . Bah! I hope Igwezu has been celebrating with his friends and comes home drunk. He-he! We'll see who has the steady hand then. We'll see who goes from here with his chin all slashed and bleeding . . . He-he . . . *(Stops again, thinking hard . . .)* Now where was I before . . . ? Alu!

ALU *(enters simultaneously with a bowl of warm water):* If you want to bellow, go out into the swamp and talk to the frogs.

MAKURI: Aha, is that the water? No, no, bring it over here . . . Come on, my friend . . . come over here. It will be easier to wash your feet sitting in this chair . . . *(Leading him to the swivel chair . . .)* Do you realize it? You've brought good luck with you.

BEGGAR: Have I?

MAKURI: Well, didn't you hear what the Kadiye said? The rains have stopped . . . the floods are over. You must carry luck with your staff.

BEGGAR: Yes, I could feel the air growing lighter, and the clouds clearing over my head. I think the worst of your season is over.

MAKURI: I hope so. Only once or twice in my whole lifetime have we had it so bad.

BEGGAR: How thankful we would have been for the excess that you had here. If we had had the hundredth part of the fall you had, I would not be sitting under your roof this moment.

MAKURI: Is it really dry up country?

BEGGAR *(smiles indulgently):* A little worse than that.

MAKURI: Drought? Did you have a drought?

(While the BEGGAR *is speaking,* ALU *squats down and washes his feet. When this is finished, she wipes them dry, takes a small jar from one of the shelves, and rubs his feet with some form of ointment.)*

BEGGAR: We are used to droughts. Our season is one long continuous drought . . . But we were used to it. Even when it rained, the soil let the water run right through it and join some stream in the womb of the earth. All that we knew, and were content to live on alms . . . Until one day, about a year or more ago . . .

(There is only the gentle lapping of the water in the bowl. MAKURI *has brought his stool and is sitting on the left side of the chair, looking up at the* BEGGAR.*)*

. . . then we had more rain than I had ever known in my life. and the soil not only held the water, but it began to show off a leaf here and there . . . even on kola trees which had been stunted from birth. Wild millet pushed its way through the soil, and little tufts of elephant grass appeared from seeds which had lain forgotten season upon season . . . Best of all, hope began to spring in the heart of everyone . . . It is true that the land had lain barren for generations, that the fields had yielded no grain for the lifetime of the eldest in the village. We had known nothing but the dryness of the earth. Dry soil. Dry crumbs of dust. Clouds of dust even when there was no wind, but only a vulture flying low and flapping its wings over the earth . . . But now . . . we could smell the sweetness of lemon leaves, and the feel of the fronds of desert palm was a happiness which we had never known . . . The thought was no sooner born than we set to work before the soil changed its mind and released its moisture. We deserted the highways and marched on this land, hoes and mattocks in hand—and how few of these there were! The village had been long unused to farming, and there was no more than a handful of hoes. But we took our staffs and drove them into the earth. We sharpened stakes and picked the sand and the pebble until they bled . . . And it seemed as if the heavens rejoiced in our labour, for their blessings were liberal, and their good will on our side. The rains came when we wanted it. And the sun shone and the seeds began to ripen.

*(*IGWEZU *enters quietly, and remains by the door, unobserved.)*

Nothing could keep us from the farms from the moment that the shoots came through the surface, and all through the months of waiting. We went round the plantains and rubbed our skins against them, lightly, so that the tenderest bud could not be hurt. This was the closest that we had ever felt to one another. This was the moment that the village became a clan, and the clan a household, and even that was taken by Allah in one of his large hands and kneaded together with the clay of the earth. We loved the sound of a man's passing footsteps as if the rustle of his breath it was that gave life to the sprouting wonder around us. We even forgot to beg, and lived on the marvel of this new birth of the land, and the rich smell of its goodness . . . But it turned out to have been an act of spite. The feast was not meant for us—but for the locusts.

MAKURI *(involuntarily):* Locusts!

BEGGAR: They came in hordes, and squatted on the land. It only took an hour or two, and the village returned to normal.

ALU *(moaning):* Ay-ii, Ay-ii . . .

(MAKURI *buries his head in his hands.)*

BEGGAR: I headed away from my home, and set my face towards the river. When I said to the passing stranger, Friend, set my face towards the river, he replied, which river? But I only said to him, Towards any river, towards any stream; set my face towards the seas itself. But let there be water, because I am sick of the dryness.

MAKURI: Ay-ii, the hands of the gods are unequal. Their gifts become the burden of . . .

(ALU, *who has now finished her task, takes the bowl and rises. She is startled by suddenly seeing* IGWEZU, *and she drops the bowl in her fright.)*

ALU: My son!

MAKURI: Hm? Oh, he's back at last . . . *(Wakes suddenly to the dropped bowl, shouts—)* But was that a reason for you to be drowning the whole house? Now go and wipe it up instead of gawking at the man . . . Come on here, Igwezu. Come and sit down.

BEGGAR *(rising):* Your son? Is that the son you spoke of?

MAKURI: Yes . . . Now hurry up. Hurry up and dry the place.

(The BEGGAR *feels for his staff and moves out of the chair.* IGWEZU *sits down. He appears indifferent to his surroundings.)*

MAKURI: What held you? Have you been carousing?

IGWEZU: No. I went for a walk by myself.

MAKURI: All afternoon?

(IGWEZU *nods.)*

Do you mean to tell me . . . ? *(anxiously)* Son, are you feeling well?

ALU *(coming into the room with a piece of rag, overhears the last question):* Is he unwell? What is the matter with him?

MAKURI: He is not unwell. I merely asked him how he felt.

ALU *(on her knees, begins to wipe the floor):* Well, how does he feel?

IGWEZU *(without any kind of feeling):* Glad to be home. Glad to be once again with my own people . . . Is that not what every home-coming son should feel?

MAKURI *(after watching him for a moment):* Have you seen the farm?

(IGWEZU *is silent.)*

Son, you mustn't take it so hard. There is nothing that . . . *(Shakes his head in energetic despair and sees* ALU *still wiping the floor.)* **Hurry up, woman! Is the man not to get any supper after walking around by himself all day?**

*(*ALU *gasps.)*

IGWEZU: No, don't give yourself the trouble. I want no supper.

MAKURI: But you've eaten nothing all day.

IGWEZU: I have had my feast of welcome. I found it on the farm where the beans and the corn had made an everlasting pottage with the mud.

BEGGAR *(coming forward):* Master, it will thrive again.

IGWEZU *(He looks up at the* BEGGAR, *as if seeing him for the first time.)* Who are you? And why do you call me master?

BEGGAR: I am a wanderer, a beggar by birth and fortunes. But you own a farm. I have stood where your soil is good and cleaves to the toes like the clay of bricks in the mixing; but it needs the fingers of drought whose skin is parchment. I shall be your bondsman. I shall give myself to you and work the land for your good. I feel I can make it yield in my hands like an obedient child.

IGWEZU *(looks from* ALU *to* MAKURI, *who only shrugs his shoulders):* Where do you come from?

BEGGAR: Bukanji.

IGWEZU *(relapsing into his former manner):* Bukanji. Yes, I have heard of it, I have heard of it . . .

(The KADIYE's *drum has begun again to sound offstage.)*

MAKURI: The Kadiye! I had forgotten. Son, the Kadiye has been here. I think I can hear him returning now. He wants you to shave him tonight.

IGWEZU: Does he?

MAKURI: Yes. Now that the rains have ceased, his vow is come to an end. He wanted me to do it, but I said, No, Kadiye; I am still strong and healthy, but my fingers shake a little now and then, and your skin is tender.

IGWEZU: Yes. Is it not strange that his skin is tender? Is it not strange that he is smooth and well-preserved?

BEGGAR *(eagerly):* Is he fat, master? When he spoke, I detected a certain bulk in his voice.

IGWEZU: Ay, he is fat. He rolls himself like a fat and greasy porpoise.

ALU: Son, you must speak better of the holy man.

MAKURI *(tut-tutting):* The city has done him no good. No good at all.

BEGGAR: Master, is it true what they say? Do you speak ill of the holy man because your heart is in the city?

IGWEZU: Why? What does it matter to you?

BEGGAR: The bondsman must know the heart of the master; then he may serve him well.

*(*IGWEZU *continues to stare at the* BEGGAR, *puzzled.)*

BEGGAR: Do you serve the Serpent, master? Do you believe with the old man— that the land may not be redeemed? That the rotting swamps may not be purified?

IGWEZU: You make a strange slave with your questioning? What is all this to you?

BEGGAR: Even a slave may know the bounds of his master's kingdom.

IGWEZU: You know that already.

BEGGAR: Perhaps. I know that the Serpent has his share, but not who sets the boundaries . . . Is is the priest, or is it the master?

IGWEZU: What does it matter?

BEGGAR: I am a free bondsman. I give myself willingly. I gave without the asking. But I must know whom I serve, for then I will not stint my labour.

IGWEZU: Serve whom you please. It does not matter to Igwezu.

BEGGAR: Does the priest live well? Is the Serpent well kept and nourished?

IGWEZU: You may see for yourself. His thighs are like skinfuls of palm oil . . .

(The BEGGAR *throws back his head and laughs. It is the first time he has done so, and the effect is immediate on* MAKURI *and* ALU, *who stare at him in wonder.* IGWEZU *looks up ordinarily.)*

IGWEZU: It is a careless bondsman who laughs before his master.

BEGGAR: How does the Serpent fare in times of death? Does he thrive on the poisonous crabs? Does he drink the ooze of the mire?

MAKURI *(trembling with anger):* Beware. That borders upon sacrilege. That trespasses on the hospitality of this house.

BEGGAR *(with dignity):* I beg your forgiveness. It is for the master to question not the slave. *(He feels his way to the far corner, and remains there, standing.)*

IGWEZU *(thoughtfully):* Ay. So it is . . . So it is . . . and yet, I saw him come into this house; but I turned and went away again, back to the Serpent with whom I'd talked all afternoon.

MAKURI: You did what? Who are you talking about?

IGWEZU: The Kadiye. I saw him when he entered this house, but I went away and continued my walk in the swamps.

MAKURI: You did?

IGWEZU: Yes, I did not trust myself.

MAKURI: You did not trust yourself. Why? What has the Kadiye ever done to you?

IGWEZU: I do not know. At this moment, I do not know. So perhaps it is as well that he comes. Perhaps he can explain. Perhaps he can give meaning to what seems dark and sour . . . When I met with harshness in the city, I did not complain. When I felt the nakedness of its hostility, I accepted it. When I saw its knife sever the ties and the love of kinship, and turn brother against brother . . .

ALU: *(quickly):* You met him then. You found your brother in the city.

IGWEZU: Did I?

ALU: Your silence has deceived no one, Igwezu. Do you think I did not know all the time?

IGWEZU: He is dead. You've said so yourself. You have said it often enough.

ALU: Which death did he die—that is all I want to know. Surely a mother may say that much, and be forgiven the sin of lying to herself—even at the moment of the asking. And he is still my son, Igwezu; he is still your own twin.

(IGWEZU *remains silent.*)

ALU: I am too old to be a pilgrim to his grave. I am too weak to seek to bring him back to life . . . I only seek to know . . . Igwezu, did you find my son?

(*After a moment,* IGWEZU *nods slowly.*)

ALU: Let me hear it through your lips, and then I will know it is no trick of my eyes. Does my son live?

IGWEZU (*wearily*): He lives.

ALU (*nodding*): He lives. What does it matter that he breathes a foreign air. Perhaps there is something in the place that makes men forget. (*Going.*) What if he lives sufficient only to himself. He lives. One cannot ask too much. (*Goes into the house.*)

MAKURI (*ordinarily*): Was he well?

(IGWEZU *nods.*)

MAKURI (*obviously uncertain how to proceed. He keeps his eyes on the ground, from where he spies on* IGWEZU. *Slowly, and with hesitation . . .*) Did you . . . did you often . . . meet?

IGWEZU: I lived under his roof—for a while.

MAKURI (*shouting at the departed* ALU): Did you hear that? Did you hear that you stubborn old crow? . . . Was he . . . Did . . . er . . . ? You did say he was in good health?

IGWEZU: Healthier than you or I. And a thousand times as wealthy.

MAKURI: There! (*shouting out again*) Did you hear? Did I not always say so? (*more confidently now*) How did he make his money?

IGWEZU: In timber. He felled it and floated it over the seas . . . He is wealthy, and he is big.

MAKURI: Did he ever talk of his father? Does he remember his own home?

IGWEZU: Awuchike is dead to you and to this house. Let us not raise his ghost.

MAKURI (*stands bewildered for a moment. Then, with a sudden explosiveness . . .*): What did he do son? What happened in the city?

IGWEZU: Nothing but what happens to a newcomer to the race. The city reared itself in the air, and with the strength of its legs of brass kicked the adventurer in the small of his back.

MAKURI: And Awuchike? Was he on the horse that kicked? (IGWEZU *is silent.*)

MAKURI: Did your own brother ride you down, Igwezu? . . . Son, talk to me. What took place between you two? (IGWEZU *is silent again, and then*)

IGWEZU: The wound heals quicker if it is left unopened. What took place is not worth the memory . . . Does it not suffice that in the end I said to myself . . . I have a place, a home, and though it lies in the middle of the slough, I will go back to it. And I have a little plot of land which has rebelled against the waste that surrounds it, and yields a little fruit for the asking. I sowed this land before I went away. Now is the time for harvesting, and the cocoa-pods must be bursting with fullness . . . I came back with hope, with consolation in my heart. I came back with the assurance of one who has lived with his land and tilled it faithfully . . .

MAKURI: It is the will of the heavens . . .

IGWEZU: It was never in my mind . . . the thought that the farm could betray me so totally, that it could drive the final wedge into this growing loss of touch . . .

(The KADIYE's *drum has become more audible.)*

BEGGAR: Master, I think the Serpent approaches.

IGWEZU: I can hear him, bondsman. I can hear him.

(The KADIYE's *party arrives at the door.* MAKURI *runs to hold the matting aside, and the party enters as before.* ALU *comes out again and curtseys.)*

KADIYE: Is he back? Ah Igwezu, it is good to see you again. *(*IGWEZU *rises unhurriedly. The* KADIYE *tries to bless him but* IGWEZU *avoids this, as if by accident.)* I am glad to see you safe and well . . . *(Seats himself in the chair.)* Ah, what an affair that was. The child was crying loud enough to drown all the frogs in the swamp . . .

MAKURI *(leaning down to him. With fiendishness on his face—):* Did it happen, Kadiye? Did the child take his revenge?

KADIYE: Oh yes, he did. He drenched the healer with a sudden gush!

*(*MAKURI *dances delightedly, laughing in his ghoulish manner.)*

KADIYE: And that wasn't all. The foolish mother! She heard the cries and tried to get to her son from where she has been locked.

MAKURI: And pollute her own son!

KADIYE: Amazing, is it not? The mothers can never be trusted . . . And to think that she did succeed in the end!

MAKURI *(snapping his fingers over his head):* The gods forbid it!

KADIYE: She did. I had to purify the boy and absolve him from the crime of contamination. That is the fourth circumcision where I have known it to happen.

MAKURI: The best thing is to send the mother out of the house.

KADIYE: Do you think that hasn't been tried? It is harder to shift them than to get the child to stay still.

MAKURI: Ay. That is true enough. All women are a blood-thirsty lot. They love to hear the child wailing and crying out in pain. Then they can hug themselves and say, Serve you right, you little brat. Now you'll know what pains I went through, giving birth to you.

KADIYE: Ah, that is the truth of it . . . Anyway, it is all over now . . . all over and done with . . . *(Hems with pomposity and turns to* IGWEZU.*)* And how is the city gentleman? Have you been making a lot of money, Igwezu?

IGWEZU: None . . . where must I shave, Kadiye?

KADIYE *(puzzled):* Where?

IGWEZU: Is it the head or the chin?

MAKURI *(gasps. Then tries to force a casualness in his tone):* Pay no attention, Kadiye. It is only the humour of the townsmen.

KADIYE: A-ah . . . The chin, Igwezu. Shave off the beard.

IGWEZU *(begins to prepare the instruments)*: Did you make other vows, Kadiye? Were there other pleasures from which you abstained until the rains abated?

KADIYE: Oh, yes. Oh, yes indeed. I vowed that my body would remain unwashed.

IGWEZU: Ah. Did you keep within doors?

KADIYE: No. I had my duties . . . People still die, you know. And mothers give birth to children.

IGWEZU: And it rained throughout? Almost without a stop?

KADIYE: Yes, it did.

IGWEZU: Then perhaps once or twice you were out in the rain . . .?

MAKURI *(quickly)*: Igwezu . . . you . . . you . . . you were going to tell Kadiye about the big town.

IGWEZU: Was I?

KADIYE: Ah, yes. Tell me about the place. Was business as good as they say?

IGWEZU: For some people.

KADIYE: And you? Did your business thrive?

IGWEZU: No more than my farming has done.

KADIYE: Come now, Igwezu. I am not trying to obtain the promise of an ox for sacrifice . . . You did make some money?

IGWEZU: No.

KADIYE: I see he must be coaxed . . . Admit you've made enough to buy this village—men, livestock and all.

IGWEZU *(slips the agbada over the KADIYE's head)*: No, Kadiye. I made none at all.

KADIYE: A-ah, they are all modest . . . Did you make a little then?

IGWEZU: No I made none at all.

KADIYE *(looks hard at him. He is obviously disturbed by IGWEZU's manner. Speaks nervously.)*: Well, never mind, never mind. To some it comes quickly; to others a little more slowly. But your own turn will come soon, Igwezu; it will come before long.

IGWEZU: I'm afraid I have had my turn already. I lost everything; my savings, even my standing as a man. I went into debt.

KADIYE: Impossible!

IGWEZU: Shall I tell you what I offered as security? Would you like to know, Kadiye?

KADIYE: Not your pretty wife, I hope. *(guffawing)* I notice you had to come without her.

IGWEZU: No, holy one. It was not my wife. But what I offered had a lot in common with her. I put down the harvest from my farm.

MAKURI: Ha?

ALU: Igwezu. My poor Igwezu.

KADIYE *(laughing)*: Now what do you take us for? As if anyone in the city would lend money on a farm which he had never even seen. Are they such fools—these business men of yours?

IGWEZU: No. They are not fools; my brother least of all. He is anything but a fool.

ALU: Awuchike!

MAKURI: My own son? Your own flesh and blood?

(ALU *remains staring at* IGWEZU *for several moments. Then, shaking her head in complete and utter bewilderment, she turns round slowly and goes into the house, more slouched than ever before.*)

IGWEZU (*in the same calm relentlessness*): Wait, mother . . . I have not told you all. (*He begins to lather the* KADIYE's *face.*)

ALU: I know enough. (*She has stopped but does not turn round.*) But I no longer understand. I feel tired, son. I think I'll go to sleep.

IGWEZU: Don't you want news of my wife? Have you no interest in the simple and unspoilt child whom you wooed on my behalf?

(ALU *goes slowly out of the room.*

IGWEZU *begins to shave the* KADIYE. *There is silence.*)

IGWEZU (*without stopping*): Father. Tell me, father, is my brother a better man than I?

MAKURI: No, son. His heart is only more suited to the city.

IGWEZU: And yet we are twins. And in spite of that, he looked at my wife, and she went to him of her own accord . . . Tell me father, are women so easily swayed by wealth? Are all women the same?

MAKURI: Alu was different. She turned their heads but she kept her own.

IGWEZU: Thank you, father. Now where is the stranger who would be my bondsman?

BEGGAR: Here, master.

IGWEZU: You sightless ones are known to be gifted with more than human wisdom. You detected from the Kadiye's voice that he was fat . . . Keep still, priest of the swamps; this razor is keen and my hand is unsettled . . . Have I still your attention, bondsman? You have listened to me. It there anything in my voice which tells you what is lacking? Does something in my voice tell you why the bride of less than a season deserts her husband's side?

BEGGAR: I must seek that answer in the voice of the bride.

IGWEZU: That was wisely spoken. You have all the makings of a true bondsman.

MAKURI: You talk strangely, Igwezu. What is running in your head?

IGWEZU: It is only a game of children, father. Only a game of riddles and you have answered yours. So has my bondsman. Now it is the turn of the Kadiye.

KADIYE: I am prepared.

IGWEZU: With you, holy one, my questions must be roundabout. But you will unravel them, because you speak with the voice of gods . . . ?

KADIYE: As I said before, I am ready.

IGWEZU: Who must appease the Serpent of the Swamps?

KADIYE: The Kadiye.

IGWEZU: Who takes the gifts of the people, in order that the beast may be gorged and made sleepy-eyed with the feast of sacrifice.

KADIYE: The Kadiye.

IGWEZU *(His speech is increasing in speed and intensity):* On whom does the land depend for the benevolence of the reptile? Tell me that, priest. Answer in one word.

KADIYE: Kadiye.

IGWEZU: Can you see my mask, priest? Is it of this village?

KADIYE: Yes.

IGWEZU: Was the wood grown in this village?

KADIYE: Yes.

IGWEZU: Does it sing with the rest? Cry with the rest? Does it till the swamps with the rest of the tribe?

KADIYE: Yes.

IGWEZU: And so that the Serpent might not vomit at the wrong season and drown the land, so that He might not swallow at the wrong moment and gulp down the unwary traveller, do I not offer my goats to the priest?

KADIYE: Yes.

MAKURI: Igwezu, sometimes the guardians of the air are hard to please . . .

IGWEZU: Be quiet, father! . . . and did he offer them in turn to the Serpent?

KADIYE: He did.

IGWEZU: Everything which he received, from the grain to the bull?

KADIYE: Everything.

IGWEZU: The goat and the white cockerel which I gave before I left?

KADIYE: Every hair and feather of them.

IGWEZU: And he made it clear—that the offering was from me? That I demanded the protection of the heavens on me and my house, on my father and my mother, on my wife, land and chattels?

KADIYE: All the prayers were repeated.

IGWEZU: And ever since I began to till the soil, did I not give the soil his due? Did I not bring the first of the lentils to the shrine, and pour the first oil upon the altar?

KADIYE: Regularly.

IGWEZU: And when the Kadiye blessed my marriage, and tied the heaven-made knot, did he not promise a long life? Did he not promise children? Did he not promise happiness?

(IGWEZU has shaved off all except a last smear of lather. He remains standing with one hand around the KADIYE's jowl, the other retaining an indifferent hold on the razor, on the other side of his face.)

KADIYE *(does not reply this time)*

IGWEZU *(slowly and disgustedly):* Why are you so fat, Kadiye? *(The DRUMMER stares, hesitates, and runs out. The SERVANT moves nearer the door.)*

MAKURI *(snapping his fingers round his head):* May heaven forgive what has been uttered here tonight. May earth reject the folly, spoken by my son.

IGWEZU: You lie upon the land, Kadiye, and choke it in the folds of a serpent.

MAKURI: Son, listen to me . . .

IGWEZU: If I slew the fatted calf, Kadiye, do you think the land might breathe again? If I slew all the cattle in the land and sacrificed every measure of goodness, would it make any difference to our lives, Kadiye? Would it make any difference to our fates?

(The SERVANT *runs out also.)*

KADIYE *(in a choking voice):* Makuri, speak to your son . . .

BEGGAR: Master . . . master . . .

*(*IGWEZU *suddenly shaves off the final smear of lather with a rapid stroke which makes the* KADIYE *flinch. Releases him and throws the razor on the table.*

KADIYE *scrambles up at once, tearing the cloth from his neck. Makes for the door.)*

KADIYE *(panting):* You shall pay for this . . . I swear I shall make you pay for this . . . Do you think that you can make an ass of the Kadiye? . . . Do you think that you can pour your sacrilege into my ears with impunity?

IGWEZU: Go quickly, Kadiye. *(Sinks into the chair.)* And the next time that you wish to celebrate the stopping of the rains, do not choose a barber whose harvest rots beneath the mire.

KADIYE: You will pay, I swear it . . . You will pay for this. *(Flings off the sheet and goes out.)*

MAKURI: Son, what have you done?

IGWEZU: I know that the floods can come again. That the swamp will continue to laugh at our endeavours. I know that we can feed the Serpent of the Swamp and kiss the Kadiye's feet—but the vapours will still rise and corrupt the tassels of the corn.

MAKURI: I must go after him or he'll stir up the village against us. *(Stops at the door.)* This is your home, Igwezu, and I would not drive you from it for all the world. But it might be best for you if you went back to the city until this is forgotten.

(Exit.)

(Pause.)

BEGGAR *(softly):* Master . . . master . . . slayer of serpents.

IGWEZU *(in a tired voice):* I wonder what drove me on.

BEGGAR: What, master?

IGWEZU: Do you think that my only strength was that of despair? Or was there something of a desire to prove myself?

(The BEGGAR *remains silent.)*

IGWEZU: Your fat friend is gone. But will he stay away?

BEGGAR: I think that the old man was right. You should go back to the city.

IGWEZU: Is it of any earthly use to change one slough for another?

BEGGAR: I will come and keep you company. If necessary, I will beg for you.

IGWEZU *(stares at him, slowly shaking his head):* What manner of man are you? How have I deserved so much of you that you would beg for me?

BEGGAR: I made myself your bondsman. This means that I must share your hardships.

IGWEZU: I am too tired to see it all. I think we all ought to go to bed. Have they given you a place to sleep?

BEGGAR: Will I return with you to the city?

IGWEZU: No, friend. You like this soil. You love to scoop it up in your hands. You dream of cleaving ridges under the flood and making little balls of mud in which wrap your seeds. Is that not so?

BEGGAR: Yes, master.

IGWEZU: And you have faith, have you not? Do you not still believe in what you sow? That it will sprout and see the harvest sun?

BEGGAR: It must. In my wanderings, I think that I have grown a healer's hand.

IGWEZU: Then stay. Stay here and take care of the farm. I must go away.

(He crosses the room as if to go into the house.

Hesitates at the door, then turns round and walks slowly away.)

Tell my people I could not stop to say good-bye.

BEGGAR: You are not going now, master?

IGWEZU: I must not be here when the people call for blood.

BEGGAR: But the water is high. You should wait until the floods subside.

IGWEZU: No I want to paddle as I go.

BEGGAR: Is it not night? Is it not dark outside?

IGWEZU: It is.

BEGGAR: Then I shall come with you. I know the dark. Let me come with you over the swamp, as far as the river's edge.

IGWEZU: Two blind men groping in the dark? No.

BEGGAR: And how would you cross the river? There is no ferryman to be found after dark.

IGWEZU *(still looking out of the window. Pauses. He walks away, picks up the old man's work in absent movements. He drops it and looks up.)*

Only the children and the old stay here, bondsman. Only the innocent and the dotards. *(Walks slowly off.)*

BEGGAR: But you will return, master?

(IGWEZU checks briefly, but does not stop.)

BEGGAR: The swallows find their nest again when the cold is over. Even the bats desert dark holes in the trees and flap wet leaves with wings of leather. There were wings everywhere as I wiped my feet against your threshold. I heard the cricket scratch himself beneath the armpit as the old man said to me . . .

(The door swings to. The BEGGAR sighs, gestures a blessing and says.)

I shall be here to give account.

(The oil lamps go out slowly and completely. The BEGGAR remains on the same spot, the moonlight falling on him through the window.)

The End

QUESTIONS AND CONSIDERATIONS

1. What life style, social class, and occupations are suggested by the opening setting of the play in the interior of the hut? What mood is established?

2. Contrast the characters of Alu and Makuri. Who is dominant? For whom do you feel more sympathy?

3. Although the play's tone is somber, it does have comic moments. Give examples of humor, indicating the purpose and effect of the humor in the play as a whole.

4. How is the physical setting of the swamp, with its darkness, rising river, incessant rain, and rotting crops used to emphasize the mood and decisions that the characters must make? How is the world of the swamp contrasted to other settings, such as the village of the beggars and the city where Igwezu has lost his wife and fortune? What portrait of Nigerian society and its shifting values during the early 1960s is presented through these varied environments?

5. What is the function of the fat priest of the Serpent, Kadiye? Does the religion he professes actually help or console the swamp dwellers? Are you sympathetic with the priest when he is menaced by Igwezu?

6. What contrasting values are represented by Awuchike, his twin brother Igwezu, and the blind beggar who offers to be a bondsman to Igwezu? What are their losses, and what hopes, if any, does each continue to hold? Which of the three, if any of them, seems the most heroic?

IDEAS FOR WRITING

1. Do some research into the socioeconomic, religious, and ecological problems in a developing country then write an essay in which you explore some of these issues further, making references both to the play and to outside sources and references.

2. Write a narrative or a brief play in which you present a family of rural or urban Americans who struggle with some of the same economic and spiritual problems as the characters in *The Swamp Dwellers*. Consider how your characters might attempt to resolve their dilemmas.

And on the Eighth Day She Unnamed Them
Matt D. Rostoker

Matt Rostoker wrote the following essay, a response to Ursula Le Guin's story "She Unnames Them," as an attempt to explore the reasoning behind the story and the effects of the unnaming of living creatures on the animals, on the human relationship with nature, as well as on the relationship between men and women. Rostoker is interested in ecological issues and approaches the story from a pro-ecology and feminist perspective. His greatest obstacle in understanding and responding to the story was Le Guin's wide range of literary references, which include T. S. Eliot's *Practical Cats,* the Book of Genesis, and

Swift's *Gulliver's Travels.* Thus, writing his response became a project in literary research as well as a journey in understanding the logic and ideology behind Le Guin's unusual fantasy. A stylistic problem that concerned Rostoker in later drafts of his essay was the use of pronouns: If the animals are unnamed and reinvented, if the relationship between Eve and Adam is to be changed utterly, how should a writer refer to the creatures and characters in the story? Should one use terms like "animals" or refer to the creatures simply as "them"? Should "humans" be termed "men," as in the old world of Genesis, or should some new terms be found? Finally, how does a reader evaluate the cause and effect relations in Le Guin's story? For instance, would "unnaming" the creatures of nature really modify our relationship with nature, or do the words we use to name and describe nature reflect deeper needs that are not so easily changed? As you read his essay, ask yourself if the solutions Matt Rostoker has found to the problems he encountered in writing his essay are workable and insightful.

The complex environmental problems of the modern world are the result of generations of human habitation and a life style based on domination over nature. The idea of control of nature relies on the belief that humans are the highest form of life on Earth. Ursula Le Guin's "She Unnames Them" attacks this way of thinking. Le Guin proposes an entirely different ideal, one in which animals are shed of their human-derived "names" and receive respect as beings equal to humans. She takes issue with labeling and categorizing other life forms, humans' lack of awareness of species-centered behavior, and the disregard for other forms of life. Le Guin's "She Unnames Them" proposes a divergent view of nature from that of the biblical Genesis. Le Guin believes that if on the eighth day Eve had "unnamed" the animal kingdom, our views and life styles would be harmonious with nature.

As a fictional, feminist, and naturalist work, Le Guin's story combines her repertoire of biblical and literary knowledge to illustrate the evolution by which animals and the environment have been subject to human domination. The daughter of a pair of anthropological and literary scholars at the University of California at Berkeley, Dorothy and Alfred Kroeber, Le Guin's academic heritage and upbringing are evident in her references to both biblical and literary sources, as well as to Native American belief systems. These references permit Le Guin to transcend contemporary issues by invoking a timeless theme of unity between human and nature.

As the origin myth of Western culture, the Book of Genesis provides the framework which Le Guin follows as she explores the evolution of man's feelings of superiority over nature. In Genesis, God provided the Heaven and the Earth, and created Adam and Eve, the first man and woman. The critical references here are from Genesis, Ch. 2, verses 19-20:

> And out of the ground the Lord God formed every <u>beast</u>
> of the field, and every fruit of the air; and brought
> them unto Adam to see what he would call them; and
> whatsoever Adam called every living creature, that was
> the name there of.

From this "divinely inspired," male-oriented belief system arose
Western European civilization. Adam and Eve begat Cain and Abel,
the fathers of domestic agriculture and animal husbandry, and
man's dominion over nature began.

In "She Unnames Them" the pronoun "them" replaces the
English noun "beast," a derogatory and hierarchical word; I
prefer to use the pronoun "them" as well. By challenging God and
Adam from the very beginning during Genesis, Le Guin proposes an
entirely new perception of the natural world, free of
categorization and domination, a world of equals.

Throughout her story, Le Guin parallels the progress of
humanity, including the scientific Linnaean qualifiers, as an
evolution of names for "them." She contrasts this by invoking
some past literary attempts to return to a more humanistic,
natural world order. Le Guin alludes to the names made up for
animals encountered on a journey to an imaginary world of
intelligent horses in Jonathan Swift's <u>Gulliver's Travels:</u> "Among
the domestic animals, few horses had cared what anybody called
them since the <u>failure</u> of Dean Swift's attempt to name them from
their own vocabulary."

It is the failure of humankind to regard all living things
as equals that now imperils the planet with global ecological
destruction. Swift, as Le Guin invites us to infer, made
conscious attempts to understand and respect the horse-people,
devoting many chapters to describing the life of a land
inhabited by a society of intelligent horses, whom he
onomatopoetically refers to in their native tongue as
"Houyhnhnms." With similar purpose, Le Guin mentions T. S.
Eliot's collection of poems, <u>The Book of Practical Cats</u>, which
concerns intelligent, complex cats with unique personalities.
She hints of other attempts to have animals name themselves, and
"give their names back to the people to whom—-as they put it—-
they belonged." Eliot, Swift, and Le Guin believe "the issue was
precisely one of individual choice." Here, the ultimate
revolutionary reversal of naming arises through the rejection of
all scientific, Latin, and manmade labels and names:

> Anybody who wanted to be called Rover, or Froufrou, or
> Polly, or even Birdie in the personal sense, was
> perfectly free to do so, not one of them had the least
> objection to parting with the lowercase (or, as
> regards German creatures, uppercase) generic
> appellations "poodle," "parrot," "dog," or "bird," and

all the Linnaean qualifiers that had trailed along
behind them for two hundred years like tin cans tied
to a tail.

Thus, Le Guin unravels the awkward pigeon-holing,
nonsensical, utilitarian names and categories imposed and
created by humans. She sets out to unname "them," to liberate our
oppressed and downtrodden cohabitors of the planet, our fellow
creatures. The results of unnaming are multifold: Labels and
stereotypes can be abolished, hierarchical relationships leveled
into equals, and a peaceful, sensual, unified world of natural
diversity can be embraced. Instead of "human versus nature," a
"human is one with nature," so that a unified idea can be
imparted, an intimate connection emphasized between all living
things. The following passage illustrates the new relationships
that evolve between humans and animals after the "unnaming"
ceremony:

> None were left now to unname, and yet how close I felt
> to them when I saw one of them swim or fly or crawl
> across my way or over my skin, or stalk me in the
> night, or go along beside me in the day. They seemed
> far closer than when their names had stood between
> myself and them like a clear barrier: so close that my
> fear of them and their fear of me became one same fear
> . . . and the hunter could not be told from the
> hunted, nor the eater from the food.

With the multisensual and intimate style in this passage,
Le Guin re-creates the relationship between humans and animals;
their natural world is described in terms of how they live,
behave, and relate to one another, not according to where they
fit in man's world or under a categorization. Le Guin abolishes
barriers between mankind and nature, reverting to a Native
American worldview where the natural world is revered and
respected. Humans are part of a larger world, not above it, as
in Western cultures. From such a naturalist perspective, Le Guin
employs imaginative methods to illustrate nature and establish
an ecological worldview. Vibrant, richly sensory imagery helps
Le Guin to succeed in her quest of unnaming: "The insects parted
with their names in vast clouds and swarms of ephemeral
syllables buzzing and stinging and humming and flitting and
crawling and tunnelling away."
    At the end of the story, Eve hands back her name to Adam
and God, providing a turning point for a new holistic,
ecological worldview. The final dialogue between Eve and Adam
invites a feminist reading. While giving back her name to Adam
and God, Eve (now simply "She") attempts to carefully explain her
decision-making process relative to the unnaming. Adam is

oblivious, preoccupied, and ignores her. Lacking awareness outside of himself, focusing only on his trivial activities, he is self-centered and self-motivated: "He continued to do what he was doing and to take no notice of anything else." It is this noncommunicative and closed-minded trait of men that Le Guin cites as another way people create barriers between men, women, and nature. By unnaming "them" and herself, and then walking out on Adam, Eve reverses her subordinate role to her husband and forges a new concept and approach to living. She empowers herself and simultaneously establishes a new worldview.

Through a process of detailing the origins of Western European Judeo-Christian values, Le Guin revises Genesis and proposes an entirely different concept regarding man's role in nature. One wonders whether Eve returns to Adam to bear Cain and Abel. If she did not, modern humans and their machines, global warming, and the atomic bomb would not exist. By freeing nature of labels and subordination to humans, Le Guin permits the evolution of a natural, holistic world order. It is such a view that offers us some hope, that if it is adopted, we may have a chance to ameliorate centuries of accumulating and logarithmically exploding human populations and ecological decline. When Ursula Le Guin asserts "She Unnames Them," she insists on a new religion, a new worldview, grounded on precepts of harmony, equality, understanding, and intimacy between all living things. In Le Guin's vision, had Eve succeeded in unnaming "them," perhaps we would not be living in such a violent maelstrom of global environmental death. We would be closer to the Earth Summit logo of a globe, dove, and a hand: symbols of peace, cooperation, harmony, and global environmental health.

Connections: Ideas for Discussion and Writing

1. Compare the presentation of conflict between traditional cultural values and the need for survival in the face of a hostile environment as seen in the plays *Riders to the Sea, The Swamp Dwellers,* and August Wilson's *The Piano Lesson* (see Chapter 7).

2. Compare the conflict between urban and rural life, particularly in terms of the natural environment and its consolations, as seen in works from this chapter such as the story "The White Heron," the play *The Swamp Dwellers,* the essay "Walking," and poems such as "The World Is Too Much with Us."

3. Many of the selections in this chapter reflect on the way that humans have caged and oppressed animals, making it difficult for them to be "natural." Compare several poems, stories, or essays that focus on this issue.

4. Several of the readings suggest that our personalities are shaped by our involvement with nature. Compare the way that works such as Silko's "Landscape, History, and the Pueblo Imagination," Ehrlich's "On Water," Soyinta's *The Swamp Dwellers,* and Crane's "The Open Boat" reflect on this theme.

5. A number of the selections make a comment on artifice, trying to create a view of the natural as opposed to the artificial. Compare the way that readings such as "She Unnames Them," "Rappaccini's Daughter," "The Animals in that Country," "When I Heard the Learn'd Astronomer," and "A Work of Artifice" explore the distinctions between artifice and nature.

6. The Native American view of nature, as represented by as Ray Young Bear, Elizabeth Woody, Gladys Cardiff, and Leslie Marmon Silko, relies on a complex set of myths and spiritual concepts as well as a sense of interdependence with the natural world that is quite distinct from the traditional Western European and American view. Discuss the way several of the Native American writers in this chapter perceive and present nature.

7. A number of the readings in this chapter criticize the scientific and rational view of nature that sets nature apart as something to be used, studied, and controlled. Explore the critique of scientific rationalism as seen in works by such authors as Hawthorne, Thoreau, Whitman, Woody, Young Bear, Le Guin, Jewett, and Eiseley. Do you agree or disagree with the criticism of science made by these writers?

HAUNTINGS AND REFLECTIONS

HAUNTINGS
AND REFLECTIONS

Touching this vision here,
It is an honest ghost, that let me tell you.
Shakespeare, *Hamlet*, 1.5, lines 143–144

They cannot scare me with their empty spaces
Between stars—on stars where no human race is.
I have it in me so much nearer home
To scare myself with my own desert places.
Robert Frost, "Desert Places"

One need not be a chamber—to be Haunted—
One need not be a House—
The Brain has Corridors—surpassing
Material Place—
Emily Dickinson

Earlier chapters in *Imagining Worlds* have focused on the effort to develop creativity, to understand the process of maturation, to build supportive relationships, to overcome social and political struggles, and to solve environmental problems. This final chapter of selections encourages you to reflect on losses and accomplishments, to think about the meaning of your life, and to develop a sense of appreciation for the lives of others. The death of a family member or a close friend, a serious illness, or a natural disaster can lead one to think about fundamental questions: Is there a meaningful pattern to life and to human history? Is there an afterlife, either literally or metaphorically? The works of litera-

Georges de La Tour, 1593–1652. *The Penitent Magdalen.* Oil on canvas, 52½ × 40¼′. The Metropolitan Museum of Art. Gift of Mr. and Mrs. Charles Wrightsman, 1978. (1978.517)

ture that we have included in this chapter explore such questions within the framework of a meditation over experiences from the past.

Spiritual leaders, philosophers, historians, social scientists, doctors, psychologists—all remind us of the importance of reflecting on the past and the futility of trying to escape from our personal past, from the legacy of our culture and our nation. As Emily Dickinson suggests in the lines that introduce this chapter, the mind houses our spiritual past with a permanence that surpasses any material home; thus experiences from the distant past can come to seize our imaginations and our unconscious minds, obsessing us and demanding explanations.

People are literally and metaphorically haunted by human history, by past decisions, by what the poet Robert Frost refers to as "the road not taken." People also are haunted by their failures and losses: financial losses, physical losses, and emotional losses involving those about whom one has cared deeply. Sometimes individuals rethink already familiar situations and translate their thoughts into written reflections that can take the form of a journal entry, a personal essay, a story, poem, or even a play. In some cases reflection can evolve into a unique personal philosophy or worldview.

Reflective writing focuses on turning-point experiences in life, experiences of revelation that may have been overlooked, neglected, or forgotten with the need to respond to the daily demands of getting ahead or just surviving. Built from the particulars, the realistic details of an event, the reflective journal, essay, story, poem, or play develops the initial experience into an exploration of a more general human issue through symbols and metaphors based on experience. For example, in his classic play *Hamlet,* Shakespeare develops images of rot and decay into powerful metaphors that reflect the insidious, evil, and pervasive political and human corruption in the state of Denmark. The writer of a reflective work begins by leading the reader along the path of the author's own experience; as the writer re-creates in clear detail and emotional authenticity a crucial event or turning point for readers to relive, he or she explores the human paradoxes and conflicts implied in the event.

Because reflective writing assumes that exploring the issues implied in a situation is more important than coming to a definitive conclusion or persuading the reader of the "correctness" of a point of view, reflective works are questioning and open-ended in their structure rather than directed toward an argumentative conclusion. The reader is invited to bring his or her own experiences and ideas into a final interpretation and evaluation of the issues explored in the work, to become a collaborative partner, a co-author, a full participant in the text.

The majority of the stories, poems, essays, and journal entries in this chapter reflect on similar issues: childhood memories, solitude, the aging process, loss of loved ones, questions about the legacy of heritage and culture, questions about the meaning of life itself and the afterlife. A number of the readings raise fundamental questions about memory and the past, particularly focusing on ways people can rethink their past so that it no longer haunts them but instead is put in a perspective that gives them direction for shaping their future.

Several of the works included here focus on the dangers that can occur if a promise or commitment made during youth, either to oneself or to another, is not kept or resolved. Elizabeth Bowen's "The Demon Lover" is a disturbing story of a middle-aged woman who is obsessed with a fiancé who disappeared in World War I. Yukio Mishima's "Swaddling Clothes" also explores the theme of broken promises from the past that continue to haunt the present. The guilty obsession of the main character leads her to risk her life. In contrast, hauntings from the past can serve as signposts or warnings that help an individual to understand the past. Hamlet's vision of his dead father, for example, leads him to perceive more clearly that "something is rotten in the state of Denmark" and to seek vengeance for his father's murder. Visions of a long-dead lover help the narrator in Becky Birtha's "In the Life" to find comfort in her lonely present-day existence. Similarly, in Alberto Ríos' poem "Mi Abuelo," a young man is able to use his imagination to reconnect with images and feelings about his grandfather that bring purpose and guidance to his life in the present.

The imagination, visions, hauntings—can they be trusted? Can our premonitions, our dreams, our nightmares help us to reflect on our problems and find solutions, or might they lead us into madness and self-destruction? Defining the boundaries between a belief in the power of a vision to reveal the truth and a descent into confusion and madness is a central issue in many of the selections in this chapter. In part because he cannot know for certain if he should trust and seek guidance from his vision of the ghost of his father, Hamlet postpones his revenge and falls into a state of obsessive reflection and despair. In her essay "A Field of Silence," Annie Dillard shows how she comes to see the meaning of eternity through a vision, and at the same time feels completely overwhelmed because the moment cannot be comprehended rationally. Although she must turn away from its intensity, her vision leads her to reflect deeply on the spiritual in nature and in daily life.

Exhausted from competitive struggle, E. M. Forster's young hero in "The Other Side of the Hedge" has great difficulty acknowledging his vision of a relaxed, cooperative life on the "other side." In contrast, the diplomat's wife in Isabel Allende's "Phantom Palace" finds herself so enchanted by the visions of the native past that pervade the dictator's summer palace in the jungle that she loses herself in the magic of the place, finally refusing to return to "civilization" at all.

Sometimes the visions and voices that speak to us in our dreams and in moments of serious reflection may represent parts of ourselves that we have long avoided facing. How do individuals integrate or silence these voices of "the other" within themselves? Alice Walker explores this issue in her essay "Beauty: When the Other Dancer Is the Self," as she comes to reconcile two conflicting images of herself, one as a beautiful child who is maimed for life by a tragic accident, the other as a mature woman who has lost the sight in one eye but has found the meaning of inner beauty and love. Judith Ortiz Cofer explores the disowned erotic side of the self in her poem "The Other"; in his poem "Fog-Horn" W. S. Merwin creates a powerful metaphor of a foghorn calling from the dangerous dark places inside us, calling to awaken us.

Tragic life situations often lead people to reflect on their own mortality and on that of friends and loved ones. The Native American myth that begins the chapter, "The End of the World," presents an image of an old woman and a dog who coexist as a self-sustaining unit, made up equally of creative and destructive elements that balance each other out, helping to maintain the existence of the world. The journal entries in this chapter, such as Carl Gustav Jung's "Retrospect" and Elizabeth Gray Vining's "Being Seventy," focus on the way that the successes and failures of life need to be acknowledged and put in perspective through reflection. Poets like John Donne in "Death Be Not Proud" and Dylan Thomas in "Do Not Go Gentle into That Good Night" wrestle with the reality of death as they devise rhetorical challenges that assert the ultimate survival of life over death. Maxine Kumin in her poem "The Envelope" perceives the individual life as one extended through a series of lives, through all of the family members who have gone before and are nestled together inside each individual, contained in memory and therefore surviving physical death.

Reflection on the way the past survives in the present is placed within specific historical contexts in chapter readings such as James Dickey's poem, "Hunting Civil War Relics at Nimblewill Creek." Through a reflection upon a ruined statue from a vanished civilization, Percy Bysshe Shelley's "Ozymandias" explores the vanity of human wishes for immortality in historical deeds. Roberta Hill Whiteman in her poem "Star Quilt" creates connections between a quilt whose pattern reflects her Native American heritage and the way that heritage guides her present family life. Scott Momaday in the essay "Grandmother's Country" explores the geography and historical events that gave his Kiowa grandmother's life a special meaning and that gives meaningful values and a sense of direction to his own life.

Reflective writing engages the imagination and extends personal experience and thought: *outward,* to one's distant past and to the past of vanished ancestors; *inward,* to buried and internalized memories; *forward,* to shape personal, social, and religious values. We hope that reading the selections in this chapter will help you to explore fundamental cultural and philosophical issues and the ways that such issues play a role in your own life.

Folk Tales

The End of the World

American Indian (White River Sioux)

Journal

Describe a physical or spiritual force or forces that have the potential to destroy the world or maintain and sustain it.

The following modern tale from the White River Sioux tribe encourages readers to reflect on the relationship between creation and destruction.

Somewhere at a place where the prairie and the Maka Sicha, the Badlands, meet, there is a hidden cave. Not for a long, long time has anyone been able to find it. Even now, with so many highways, cars, and tourists, no one has discovered this cave.

In it lives a woman so old that her face looks a shriveled-up walnut. She is dressed in rawhide, the way people used to be before the white man came. She has been sitting there for a thousand years or more, working on a blanket strip for her buffalo robe. She is making the strip out of dyed porcupine quills, the way our ancestors did before white traders brought glass beads to this turtle continent. Resting beside her, licking his paws, watching her all the time is Shunka Sapa, a huge black dog. His eyes never wander from the old woman, whose teeth are worn flat, worn down to little stumps, she has used them to flatten so many porcupine quills.

A few steps from where the old woman sits working on her blanket strip, a huge fire is kept going. She lit this fire a thousand or more years ago and has kept it alive ever since. Over the fire hangs a big earthen pot, the kind some Indian peoples used to make before the white man came with his kettles of iron. Inside the big pot, *wojapi* is boiling and bubbling. *Wojapi* is berry soup, good and sweet and red. That soup has been boiling in the pot for a long time, ever since the fire was lit.

Every now and then the old woman gets up to stir the *wojapi* in the huge earthen pot. She is so old and feeble that it takes her a while to get up and hobble over to the fire. The moment her back is turned, the huge black dog starts pulling the porcupine quills out of her blanket strip. This way she never makes any progress, and her quillwork remains forever unfinished. The Sioux people used to say that if the old woman ever finishes her blanket strip, then at the very moment that she threads the last porcupine quill to complete the design, the world will come to an end.

QUESTIONS AND CONSIDERATIONS

1. Why is it significant that this story is set in the modern world of "highways, cars, and tourists"? How are modern fears and concerns about our planet and culture reflected in the story?

2. Why is the age of the woman in the story significant? What is her role in the story?

3. What meaning is implied by the image of the old woman weaving a blanket strip from porcupine quills, "the way our ancestors did before the white traders brought glass beads"?

4. What is the role of the dog in the story? What larger forces might the dog represent?

5. Develop your own myth or fantasy about the end of the world or about saving the world from destruction.

Journals

Diaries

Linda Hogan

May 3, 1977

I went to the Vapor Caves and spent hours there, underground. I walked down the old stairs into stone beneath the ground. In the long tunnel I began to feel the steaming heat, to smell the sulfur and minerals of earth condensing on my body. The slow drips of water wearing holes into the stone. Walls coated in white crystal, salty to taste, and green algae. I lay down on a warm marble slab, feeling a small amount of fear at being alone underground with only the sounds of earth.

Even objects placed inside the cave by people seemed primitive and were becoming overgrown with natural elements. Some bricks were coated with a green deposit. The marble slabs placed inside as seats were slowly being shaped by the moving water. I liked the feeling of balance and naturalness, as if nothing could withstand the slow passing of time. Also the feeling of being inside the powerful subconscious of the physical world. I kept thinking that certain spirits or spirit thoughts were stored here. Old people, years ago, healed in these caves, left something of themselves. Alone, I felt these energies. There was the heat, the vapor and steam, the odor of being inside ground, buried in the center of a potent vibrance. Then the water steamed up, bubbled from some core inside the stones and made gurgling noises. Occasionally the rock itself would open, groaning. And myself a part of all that, detached in some way, not static, not long-lasting in the physical world but still somehow connected to that energy and it to me, as if we fed each other.

Two large white women entered. I heard them come down the narrow staircase into the ground. They merged with the marble slabs, all white until their bodies and the stone were one piece, a frieze, half body and no back. One had very pale blond hair and pale eyes and when she moved her heavy body I thought of the fish that live on cave floors, the white crickets. The water surrounded us and was constantly flowing out, seeping down into the ground. Although my own skin is not very dark, the women were strange-looking to me, soft and wanting to talk. They were unaware of the presence of the earth, of being inside it. Because of this I resented their intrusion.

But they soon left. I stayed all day. Above me the air and light, but here with all the slow movements, the life of earth creating itself, was something that welled strong emotions in me, something that brought back the voices of the people who lived before this time. Out of the stone, I heard whispers of people that live in my body, grandparents, ancestors, voices that were changing my life, and when I left, cleansed, I knew it would be to enter a new world.

May 10

I have neglected, for many years, the cultural influences that were part of my childhood. I have spent years in silence about this, partly out of my own confusion and partly because it seems like something I imagined, to have lived these two lives. I remember hearing Buckminster Fuller speak, saying that he had seen so many changes in the past century. And though I am young, I have seen many changes too, from Oklahoma, where we went to town in a wagon drawn by horses, to big cities with four-lane highways.

It seems suddenly very crucial that I pay attention to that breach in my life between the Indian culture and the Anglo, and I feel that these things need to be said, if only to order them. My father's background has created a dislocation for us. Even though he has worked at assimilating himself into a white working-class life, he has yet to lose his hold on the past. His memories and stories take me back to Oklahoma. But they are colored with a racism he has learned, a feeling of worthlessness. He spent so many years trying to forget his background, to deny it. He married a white woman, hoped for light-skinned children. And my mother, too, would like to forget Oklahoma, the place of no water, no plumbing, nothing but dust and heat.

My own memories are of my grandparents, the small shack that was in the center of a dried field, the dry pond where the snapping turtle lived, surviving the evaporation of water and even the deadly heat of the summers. It seems mystical now, the rains of fish, the turtle, armadillos and tarantulas. It is difficult to reconcile this past with the city where we now live.

May 14

Being in the vapor caves opened something inside of me and memories have been returning. Mostly family memories, my father during the Korean War, my

mother ironing all day and night to support us. It must have been a difficult life
for her, being separated and without much money. The letters we received
from my father's Japanese girl friend. I realize that marriage must have destroyed my mother in so many ways. There was never anything left over for
herself. Physically, from the labor.

I think it was hard for my mother to be married to an Indian. She still does
not want to talk about it. And she does not want to be a part of the community
here. The singing and drums give her headaches. It is difficult for me, since
this is a large part of my own identity, and I feel guilt, as if by not pretending to
be only white, which is what she wants, I am rejecting my mother.

May 15

A spirit being appears to me. I call her Lucy after my grandmother. This was a
person I created out of my imagination. But she has become real and has
taken her own shape, giving up the form I tried to impose upon her. Originally I
tried to create her in the image of my grandmother because I needed her
sweet words and laugh. I hoped the imaginary being would offer spiritual guidance. But this woman seems so old, so primal, that she could be an ancestor
of my grandmother. Her age, as her appearance, changes, but she is old.
Often she appears with black bangs and long hair, a round face with a slight
Oriental cast to it. Or she is wearing a part in the middle of her hair. At other
times, her face is angular and long, lips full but rather tight. Sometimes she is
old, with white coarse strands running through her hair, and it is pulled back
and fastened behind her head. She may wear a cotton old-woman's house-
dress, faded and loose around her full breasts. Or a traditional buckskin dress,
plain and unbeaded, like the one I remember from childhood. She is sometimes barefoot, sometimes wearing old-woman's thick stockings and black
laced shoes. But she appears in an egg of golden light and her dark eyes are
always alert, honest and warm, her voice is always the same. I believe the
changes are different ages and times summoned to me. She chooses which
one is necessary when I create her.

She gives me a form of power. She does not come to me unless I enter a
quiet place, her space and time. I go there and I am patient, and she comes. I
read that imagination is the only reality, that we create material worlds in our
dreams and fantasies. Perhaps this woman is the material of this world that
has been created from imagination and then materialized into a bright molecu-
lar substance. I think that I am the ethereal spirit and I am haunting her with
my powerlessness and my conflicts.

Today she appeared as a young woman with long dark hair, pushed back
over the left shoulder in a wave nearly solid, like black water. Then she
merged herself into the old woman I have grown mostly accustomed to. She
was sturdy and her face was calm. The wrinkles were many. While she was
changing, an old man came out of one side of her body, diminishing in form
because of his age. His hair was white and shining. His face was dark, heavy
lids angled over his black eyes, and he was nearly feeble, but a great deal of

power entered with his spirit. He came from her side, from her rib, a male counterpart to the biblical creation myth. He was bent and humble. He was never separate from her but hung suspended from her side in profile as she faced me and showed me her powers of transformation.

Often she is found in a forest, deep and green. Giant ferns arch down to the ground. Trees are large and thick with hanging moss. The floor is damp with black earth and old leaves crumbling back into themselves. Sometimes she is in a desert and appears very large in the barrenness of earth and horizon. Sometimes she is indoors, inside a small square room, very warm, with light opaque through the windows, which look like oiled parchment.

Today she reached for me and gently tugged at me. As I began to leave myself, I kept thinking: I live in my brain, where this pressure is. I live in my chest. I live in my genitals, my spine, my breasts, my stomach. I wondered all the while if it is possible for a person to be located in her own body. As if that person is a face submerged in flesh, bone, muscle. All the nerves branch over it like a maze that keeps us from seeing the buried face.

May 18

I feel I have never had a home. All my life moving from place to place. The only thing that remained the same, that was stable, was Oklahoma. Even the landscape never changed. The towns there never grew up into cities. The people were the same each year, wearing the same clothing, saying the same things.

The search for a homeland is part of the Chickasaw migration legend. It was ordained by the deities and began in the past when the people lived in the land of the "setting sun." During the days they would walk over the land, searching for their home. The priests carried a pole. They carried it in their hands by day and planted it each night. During the night it moved about and by morning it would be pointing the direction they were to travel. For a while it commanded the people to journey east, toward the morning sun. They crossed the Mississippi River eventually, and on the other side, the pole finally ceased to move during the night. The land was settled, crops were planted. It became known as the Old Fields. But one morning the pole leaned westward. The people gathered together and began the long journey back. They abandoned their village but did not feel sorrow because the pole had commanded it.

And I am still moving, looking for a home. I don't know if I will ever escape my tradition, my past. It goes with me everywhere, like a shadow.

June 3

I recognize these headaches. The splitting of my head is symbolic of the pulling apart of myself by these two lives. After the pain goes away I wonder at my ability to survive it, the breaking apart of brain cells, the electrically charged chemicals being pushed into themselves, all things compressed and pressed by the swelling of blood vessels.

Colors are painful, everything so intensified that the world is out of proportion. The environment becomes large and menacing. A shadow is black velvet. The smallest sound of a cricket is deafening. I am afraid that I do this to myself by my inability to reconcile the two people I have become.

It is like a disturbance in the earth, splitting itself, hot lava, stone melted from inside and unable to contain itself. And the heat flowing down over me, burning. Years later these places will be more fertile because of the ash. I hope that I am like the earth. That I will split out of myself, end this war, the two factions locked inside the same bones.

November 15

I asked my sister questions about Oklahoma and how it had affected her. I asked her about what being a Chickasaw meant to her. I really wanted to see if some of her feelings and perceptions would clarify my own. Lately I have been in such conflict. I have never been able to identify myself with the Anglo culture or feel comfortable with many white people, and yet I am not dark.

She seemed to have some strong feelings but couldn't verbalize them. She also feels fragmented. One memory that intensified as she spoke was that of bathing outside in the metal tub. Whatever water was left over from the day's cooking, washing or drinking went into the tub for our baths and we sat outside in the middle of the yard, two girls naked, our skin pale, our nipples flat and pink. The men, uncles and cousins, never seemed to notice how light-skinned we were, never seemed to notice! She was older and felt shame for having a woman's body. I remember feeling so naked that I would scrub at myself with the brush and the medicinal soap that would kill chiggers.

But Donna mentioned her Norwegian husband and blond sons. They are not interested in what my father says, in what our lives were. And why should they be? It is really not their life. And yet it is difficult to see it go. Much easier not to think about it at all.

November 24

It doesn't take much to put everything back in its place. Two days ago, out petting some horses and feeding them grass from places they couldn't reach. A dark one, a roan with a white forehead, a white ragged young male. I can still smell that fresh horse smell, a combination of earth, herbs, dry grass. They smell like autumn, old rotting apples. And their eyes are beautiful and sad, dark with a pale circle around the outside.

I am always running outside to watch the geese, walking to see snakes and horses and coyotes. To me the land and world is sacred and it is where my life comes from.

June 1978

Something that is a process I can barely name is taking effect. I have been going through so many changes and they are both difficult, alien and pleasant. I have been feeling great energy. I can pinpoint a turning in my life since I visited the Vapor Caves and it grows more intense daily and begins to dictate how I live and how I see the world.

This is fragmented because I am not certain I understand. Yesterday morning there was a herd of deer. Lucy is growing stronger inside me, giving me direction. This morning when I woke up, there was a dream voice saying: "The creation of islands of electricity and shift." And then a feather blew in through the window, about twelve inches long. That is my third accumulation of unusual events which have spoken to me. I don't want to go into the others.

There is this need I feel to make a break with ordinary reality, the way I've been struggling to live out my life. Against all my inner impulses, I have been forcing myself to do what is expected, but now that no longer holds or seems important. Something inside is opening and changing. I am learning new things and they aren't of the physical world. This began so many years ago, but the evolution has been a long road of detours. Now I am beginning another new path. Always beginning. It is always beginning.

Retrospect
Carl Gustav Jung

When people say I am wise, or a sage, I cannot accept it. A man once dipped a hatful of water from a stream. What did that amount to? I am not that stream. I am at the stream, but I do nothing. Other people are at the same stream, but most of them find they have to do something with it. I do nothing. I never think that I am the one who must see to it that cherries grow on stalks. I stand and behold, admiring what nature can do.

There is a fine old story about a student who came to a rabbi and said, "In the olden days there were men who saw the face of God. Why don't they any more?" The rabbi replied, "Because nowadays no one can stoop so low."

One must stoop a little in order to fetch water from the stream.

The difference between most people and myself is that for me the "dividing walls" are transparent. That is my peculiarity. Others find these walls so opaque that they see nothing behind them and therefore think nothing is there. To some extent I perceive the processes going on in the background, and that gives me an inner certainty. People who see nothing have no certainties and can draw no conclusions—or do not trust them even if they do. I do not know what started me off perceiving the stream of life. Probably the unconscious itself. Or perhaps my early dreams. They determined my course from the beginning.

Knowledge of processes in the background early shaped my relationship to the world. Basically, that relationship was the same in my childhood as it is to this day. As a child I felt myself to be alone, and I am still, because I know things and must hint at things which others apparently know nothing of, and for the most part do not want to know. Loneliness does not come from having no people about one, but from being unable to communicate the things that seem important to oneself, or from holding certain views which others find inadmissible. The loneliness began with the experiences of my early dreams, and reached its climax at the time I was working on the unconscious. If a man knows more than others, he becomes lonely. But loneliness is not necessarily inimical to companionship, for no one is more sensitive to companionship than the lonely man, and companionship thrives only when each individual remembers his individuality and does not identify himself with others.

It is important to have a secret, a premonition of things unknown. It fills life with something impersonal, a *numinosum*. A man who has never experienced that has missed something important. He must sense that he lives in a world which in some respects is mysterious; that things happen and can be experienced which remain inexplicable; that not everything which happens can be anticipated. The unexpected and the incredible belong in this world. Only then is life whole. For me the world has from the beginning been infinite and ungraspable.

I have had much trouble getting along with my ideas. There was a daimon in me, and in the end its presence proved decisive. It overpowered me, and if I was at times ruthless it was because I was in the grip of the daimon. I could never stop at anything once attained. I had to hasten on, to catch up with my vision. Since my contemporaries, understandably, could not perceive my vision, they saw only a fool rushing ahead.

I have offended many people, for as soon as I saw that they did not understand me, that was the end of the matter so far as I was concerned. I had to move on. I had no patience with people—aside from my patients. I had to obey an inner law which was imposed on me and left me no freedom of choice. Of course I did not always obey it. How can anyone live without inconsistency?

For some people I was continually present and close to them so long as they were related to my inner world; but then it might happen that I was no longer with them, because there was nothing left which would link me to them. I had to learn painfully that people continued to exist even when they had nothing more to say to me. Many excited in me a feeling of living humanity, but only when they appeared within the magic circle of psychology; next moment, when the spotlight cast its beam elsewhere, there was nothing to be seen. I was able to become intensely interested in many people; but as soon as I had seen through them, the magic was gone. In this way I made many enemies. A creative person has little power over his own life. He is not free. He is captive and driven by his daimon.

> *Shamefully*
> *A power wrests away the heart from us,*
>   *For the Heavenly Ones each demand sacrifice;*
>   *But if it should be withheld*
>   *Never has that led to good,*

says Hölderlin.

This lack of freedom has been a great sorrow to me. Often I felt as if I were on a battlefield, saying, "Now you have fallen, my good comrade, but I must go on." For "shamefully a power wrests away the heart from us." I am fond of you, indeed I love you, but I cannot stay. There is something heart-rending about that. And I myself am the victim; I *cannot* stay. But the daimon manages things so that one comes through, and blessed inconsistency sees to it that in flagrant contrast to my "disloyalty" I can keep faith in unsuspected measure.

Perhaps I might say: I need people to a higher degree than others, and at the same time much less. When the daimon is at work, one is always too close and too far. Only when it is silent can one achieve moderation.

The daimon of creativity has ruthlessly had its way with me. The ordinary undertakings I planned usually had the worst of it—though not always and not everywhere. By the way of compensation, I think, I am conservative to the bone. I fill my pipe from my grandfather's tobacco jar and still keep his alpen-stock, topped with a chamois horn, which he brought back from Pontresina after having been one of the first guests at that newly opened *Kurort.*

I am satisfied with the course my life has taken. It has been bountiful, and has given me a great deal. How could I ever have expected so much? Nothing but unexpected things kept happening to me. Much might have been different if I myself had been different. But it was as it had to be; for all came about be-cause I am as I am. Many things worked out as I planned them to, but that did not always prove of benefit to me. But almost everything developed naturally and by destiny. I regret many follies which sprang from my obstinacy; but with-out that trait I would not have reached my goal. And so I am disappointed and not disappointed. I am disappointed with people and disappointed with myself. I have learned amazing things from people, and have accomplished more than I expected of myself. I cannot form any final judgment because the phenome-non of life and the phenomenon of man are too vast. The older I have become, the less I have understood or had insight into or known about myself.

I am astonished, disappointed, pleased with myself. I am distressed, de-pressed, rapturous. I am all these things at once, and cannot add up the sum. I am incapable of determining ultimate worth or worthlessness; I have no judg-ment about myself and my life. There is nothing I am quite sure about. I have no definite convictions—not about anything, really. I know only that I was born and exist, and it seems to me that I have been carried along. I exist on the foundation of something I do not know. In spite of all uncertainties, I feel a so-lidity underlying all existence and a continuity in my mode of being.

The world into which we are born is brutal and cruel, and at the same time of divine beauty. Which element we think outweighs the other, whether mean-inglessness or meaning, is a matter of temperament. If meaninglessness were absolutely preponderant, the meaningfulness of life would vanish to an in-creasing degree with each step in our development. But that is—or seems to me—not the case. Probably, as in all metaphysical questions, both are true: Life is—or has—meaning and meaninglessness. I cherish the anxious hope that meaning will preponderate and win the battle.

When Lao-tzu says: "All are clear, I alone am clouded," he is expressing what I now feel in advanced old age. Lao-tzu is the example of a man with superior insight who has seen and experienced worth and worthlessness, and who at the end of his life desires to return into his own being, into the eternal unknowable meaning. The archetype of the old man who has seen enough is eternally true. At every level of intelligence this type appears, and its lineaments are always the same, whether it be an old peasant or a great philosopher like Lao-tzu. This is old age, and a limitation. Yet there is so much that fills me: plants, animals, clouds, day and night, and the eternal in man. The more uncertain I have felt about myself, the more there has grown up in me a feeling of kinship with all things. In fact it seems to me as if that alienation which so long separated me from the world has become transferred into my own inner world, and has revealed to me an unexpected unfamiliarity with myself.

From
Being Seventy:
The Measure of a Year
Elizabeth Gray Vining

Tuesday, March 20

Chapel Hill was lovely this morning with redbud and daffodils blooming everywhere. I drove along North Street past the little house that Morgan and I built forty-three years ago. It stands among its trees (oaks, elms, cedars) gray-shingled with white trim, with an air of elegance, tiny though it is. All the other small houses built at the same time look shabby and tacky. It was pain to see it—and joy. Those two golden young people who lived there for three years belonged in another age, and perhaps to a fairy tale.

> Fear no more the heat o' th' sun
> Nor the furious winter's rages;
> Thou thy worldly task hast done,
> Home art gone and ta'en thy wages.
> Golden lads and girls all must,
> Like chimney-sweepers, come to dust.

These, I think, are some of the most beautiful lines ever written—and all with the simple words that everyone may use, but so fitted to the thought and the sound and to one another that together they take on a beauty and mystery far beyond their separate qualities.

She was young, Imogen, and actually not dead, only preserved by a potion until it was safe for her to live. But Arviragus and Guiderius, her brothers, thought that she was dead and said those perfect words over her as they strewed flowers on her body.

> Thou thy worldly task hast done,
> Home art gone and ta'en thy wages

expresses my fundamental conviction about death—and life. We each have some earthly task to do, and when it is done, we go home. When someone dies swiftly, of a heart attack, perhaps, full of years and honors, it is obvious that his time has come, his task done. But what of those who die young, like Morgan in full stride, his Ph.D. within his grasp? Or those who like Violet suffer year after year of strokes, living on, yet not really alive, to eighty-five or more?

The task, I think, is not an obvious one, not visible to the outward eye even of love. It must be some inner act of growth, some hidden contract to be met, some ripening to be accomplished. "Men must endure/their going hence," says Edgar in *King Lear,* "even as their coming hither;/Ripeness is all." Some ripen young; some take a long time to it.

And how can I be so sure of this, without believing in an anthropomorphic god or a bookkeeper in heaven? Only because I know—I *know* —that there is meaning in the universe, not chaos, and that love is at the heart of it. . . .

Wednesday, April 11

The day before yesterday Howard Brinton died. He was eighty-nine, lame and blind, and he had for the last two or three years been a transparent shell through which the light shone. Up to the end he was dictating his articles on the early Friends, his mind clear and retentive, his spirit shining. More than anyone else, except possibly Rufus Jones, Howard Brinton has for me expressed the essence of Quakerism today. And as a person he was lovable, gentle, wise, humorous, clear-sighted. He had had a stroke a few days earlier and was in the hospital under oxygen; at the end his speech returned and his mind was clear. Yuki, his wife, was with him day and night. His death was a serene transition.

What makes one dying peaceful and another painful? I have been reading the last volume of Leon Edel's great biography of Henry James. "The Master" at seventy-three had a stroke. He had servants, nurses, a devoted secretary around him. His sister-in-law, his niece, and his nephew came from America to London to be with him and to take charge. It took him nearly three restless, uncomfortable, irritable months to die. During that time his mind was much occupied with that which had been the absorption of his life—writing. He dictated to his secretary letters to Napoleon and others, essays, many meaningless but beautifully worded paragraphs. On February 24, four days before the end, he spoke of having had a night of "horror and terror." Altogether it was a protracted and difficult dying.

Whittier died at eighty-four. He was staying with a friend and cousin, Sarah A. Gove, at her place, Elmfield, at Hampton Falls, New Hampshire. On September 3, 1892, he had a stroke. His much-loved niece, Elizabeth Pritchard, came from Portland to be with him. For the three days that he lived, he was full of acceptance—"It is all right. Everybody is so kind"—and of love. Over and over he said, "Love, love to all the world." On September 6, as the sun was rising, he died. It was a peaceful and beautiful dying, and brief.

Violet had two years of immobility and silence and apparently of unconsciousness after her last stroke, and then died alone in her room in the nursing home. I was not there. I could have been. I went to see her several times a week, but I did not know that the change was coming. This I can hardly bear, even now, after more than three years. Even if she knew nothing, I would have sat beside her. I would have been there.

Teilhard de Chardin prayed for a "good end" and died swiftly of a heart attack. Two years or so ago I wrote such a prayer for myself.

> O God our Father, spirit of the universe, I am old in years and in the sight of others, but I do not feel old within myself. I have hopes and purposes, things I wish to do before I die. A surging of life within me cries, "Not yet! Not yet!" more strongly than it did ten years ago, perhaps because the nearer approach of death arouses the defensive strength of the instinct to cling to life.
>
> Help me to loosen, fiber by fiber, the instinctive strings that bind me to the life I know. Infuse me with Thy spirit so that it is Thee I turn to, not the old ropes of habit and thought. Make me poised and free, ready when the intimation comes to go forward eagerly and joyfully into the new phase of life that we call death.
>
> Help me to bring my work each day to an orderly state so that it will not be a burden to those who must fold it up and put it away when I am gone. Keep me ever aware and ever prepared for the summons.
>
> If pain comes before the end help me not to fear it or struggle against it but to welcome it as a hastening of the process by which the strings that bind me to life are untied. Give me joy in awaiting the great change that comes after this life of many changes, let my self be merged in Thy Self as a candle's wavering light is caught up into the sun.

This prayer, like many others, is really addressed more to myself than to God. And I am not at all sure that by the time one has reached seventy one can do anything at all about the manner of one's dying. Whittier and Teilhard de Chardin and Howard Brinton had won their way of dying by their way of living over the years before.

Friday, August 5

Iris Murdoch is one of the few women novelists whom the critics take seriously. In *The Black Prince* she says, speaking in her own person as author, not as one of her characters: "Life is horrible, without metaphysical sense, wrecked by chance, pain and the close prospect of death."

She states this opinion with more pungency than most people, perhaps, but she is not alone in her view. Indeed it seems to me that it has become a modern cliché, with no more truth than most clichés. Unquestionably there is much pain, physical and mental, in the world. We can never forget the anguish of those who suffered in the German death camps, at Hiroshima and Nagasaki, in the villages of Vietnam: the three great crimes of the modern world. And pain goes on in prisons, ghettos, labor camps, in bombed villages and places where political prisoners are tortured. But pain is not cumulative. It is individual. When an individual has too much to bear, he is eased by death, which comes as a friend. And no one's life is wholly pain; each has some moments of beauty, of happiness.

To me it seems childish and churlish to say that life is horrible and without meaning. Life is a trust, given into our hands, to hold carefully, to use well, to enjoy, to give back when the time comes. Oh, I know I have been fortunate beyond most people and far beyond my deserts. Perhaps I lack that "tragic sense" which Europeans are said to have and in which Americans are reported to be deficient. I do not think that life lacks metaphysical sense, even if I cannot say explicitly what that sense is, and I am sure that life has meaning, that I have work to do, that when it is finished I shall abandon this body and enter the unknown.

Meanwhile there is the beauty of the sunrise, of a misty, salty sea coast with the bell buoy intoning, of a great pine tree against the sky. There is the deep joy of friendship, of human love, the challenge of writing, the excitement of watching the world careening on its way, the small steady comforts of cold water, of bed, of a shower bath, of a new-laid egg, and hot coffee; the stimulus of books and reading and ideas that stir one to agreement or rejection or question.

QUESTIONS AND CONSIDERATIONS

1. All three of the journals in this chapter reflect on the insight that comes with maturity and age. What changes in self-understanding or in their relationship with their inner world have Hogan, Jung, and Vining experienced? What events have led them to new insights?

2. In their quests for self-understanding and self-acceptance, Vining and Hogan take solace and inspiration from nature. Discuss how nature is an integral part of these writers' insights and inspirations.

3. Vining, Hogan, and Jung all reflect on regrets they have about people from their past who are no longer a part of their lives. What different kinds of regret do they discuss? To what extent are they able to forgive themselves for past events in their lives that have distanced them from old friends or family members?

4. Jung and Vining wrote their journal entries when they were quite elderly: Jung was 81 and Vining was 70. What attitudes toward mortality and the afterlife are expressed in their reflections? In what different ways have they come to accept the inevitability of dying?

5. Hogan and Jung are in touch with inner forces, spirit presences that motivate and inspire them: Jung has his "daimon"; Hogan has the spirit being she calls "Lucy." Discuss how these presences influence Hogan and Jung in their lives and in their writing.

6. Write a journal entry or brief essay in which you reflect on the pattern your life has taken so far. What regrets and hopes do you have, and what future directions do you see for yourself?

Fiction

The Other Side of the Hedge

E. M. Forster

Journal

Write a fantasy about a society without stress and competition.

My pedometer told me that I was twenty-five; and, though it is a shocking thing to stop walking, I was so tired that I sat down on a milestone to rest. People outstripped me, jeering as they did so, but I was too apathetic to feel resentful, and even when Miss Eliza Dimbleby, the great educationist, swept past, exhorting me to persevere, I only smiled and raised my hat.

At first I thought I was going to be like my brother, whom I had had to leave by the roadside a year or two round the corner. He had wasted his breath on singing, and his strength on helping others. But I had travelled more wisely, and now it was only the monotony of the highway that oppressed me—dust under foot and brown crackling hedges on either side, ever since I could remember.

And I had already dropped several things—indeed, the road behind was strewn with the things we all had dropped; and the white dust was settling down on them, so that already they looked no better than stones. My muscles were so weary that I could not even bear the weight of those things I still carried. I slid off the milestone into the road, and lay there prostrate, with my face to the great parched hedge, praying that I might give up.

A little puff of air revived me. It seemed to come from the hedge; and, when I opened my eyes, there was a glint of light through the tangle of boughs and dead leaves. The hedge could not be as thick as usual. In my weak, morbid state, I longed to force my way in, and see what was on the other side. No one was in sight, or I should not have dared to try. For we of the road do not admit in conversation that there is another side at all.

I yielded to the temptation, saying to myself that I would come back in a minute. The thorns scratched my face, and I had to use my arms as a shield, depending on my feet alone to push me forward. Halfway through I would have gone back, for in the passage all the things I was carrying were scraped off me, and my clothes were torn. But I was so wedged that return was impossible, and I had to wiggle blindly forward, expecting every moment that my strength would fail me, and that I should perish in the undergrowth.

Suddenly cold water closed round my head, and I seemed sinking down for ever. I had fallen out of the hedge into a deep pool. I rose to the surface at last, crying for help, and I heard someone on the opposite bank laugh and say: "Another!" And then I was twitched out and laid panting on the dry ground.

Even when the water was out of my eyes, I was still dazed, for I had never been in so large a space, nor seen such grass and sunshine. The blue sky was no longer a strip, and beneath it the earth had risen grandly into hills— clean, bare buttresses, with beech trees in their folds, and meadows and clear pools at their feet. But the hills were not high, and there was in the landscape a sense of human occupation—so that one might have called it a park, or garden, if the words did not imply a certain triviality and constraint.

As soon as I got my breath, I turned to my rescuer and said:

"Where does this place lead to?"

"Nowhere, thank the Lord!" said he, and laughed. He was a man of fifty or sixty—just the kind of age we mistrust on the road—but there was no anxiety in his manner, and his voice was that of a boy of eighteen.

"But it must lead somewhere!" I cried, too much surprised at his answer to thank him for saving my life.

"He wants to know where it leads!" he shouted to some men on the hill side, and they laughed back, and waved their caps.

I noticed then that the pool into which I had fallen was really a moat which bent round to the left and to the right, and that the hedge followed it continually. The hedge was green on this side—its roots showed through the clear water, and fish swam about in them—and it was wreathed over with dog-roses and Traveller's Joy. But it was a barrier, and in a moment I lost all pleasure in the grass, the sky, the trees, the happy men and women, and realized that the place was but a prison, for all its beauty and extent.

We moved away from the boundary, and then followed a path almost parallel to it, across the meadows. I found it difficult walking, for I was always trying to out-distance my companion, and there was no advantage in doing this if the place led nowhere. I had never kept step with anyone since I left my brother.

I amused him by stopping suddenly and saying disconsolately, "This is perfectly terrible. One cannot advance: one cannot progress. Now we of the road——"

"Yes. I know."

"I was going to say, we advance continually."

"I know."

"We are always learning, expanding, developing. Why, even in my short life I have seen a great deal of advance—the Transvaal War, the Fiscal Question, Christian Science, Radium. Here for example—"

I took out my pedometer, but it still marked twenty-five, not a degree more.

"Oh, it's stopped! I meant to show you. It should have registered all the time I was walking with you. But it makes me only twenty-five."

"Many things don't work in here," he said. "One day a man brought in a Lee-Metford, and that wouldn't work."

"The laws of science are universal in their application. It must be the water in the moat that has injured the machinery. In normal conditions everything works. Science and the spirit of emulation—those are the forces that have made us what we are."

I had to break off and acknowledge the pleasant greetings of people whom we passed. Some of them were singing, some talking, some engaged in gardening, hay-making, or other rudimentary industries. They all seemed happy; and I might have been happy too, if I could have forgotten that the place led nowhere.

I was startled by a young man who came sprinting across our path, took a little fence in fine style, and went tearing over a ploughed field till he plunged into a lake, across which he began to swim. Here was true energy, and I exclaimed: "A cross-country race! Where are the others?"

"There are no others," my companion replied; and, later on, when we passed some long grass from which came the voice of a girl singing exquisitely to herself, he said again: "There are no others." I was bewildered at the waste in production, and murmured to myself, "What does it all mean?"

He said: "It means nothing but itself"—and he repeated the words slowly, as if I were a child.

"I understand," I said quietly, "but I do not agree. Every achievement is worthless unless it is a link in the chain of development. And I must not trespass on your kindness any longer. I must get back somehow to the road and have my pedometer mended."

"First, you must see the gates," he replied, "for we have gates, though we never use them."

I yielded politely, and before long we reached the moat again, at a point where it was spanned by a bridge. Over the bridge was a big gate, as white as ivory, which was fitted into a gap in the boundary hedge. The gate opened outwards, and I exclaimed in amazement, for from it ran a road—just such a road as I had left—dusty under foot, with brown crackling hedges on either side as far as the eye could reach.

"That's my road!" I cried.

He shut the gate and said: "But not your part of the road. It is through this gate that humanity went out countless ages ago, when it was first seized with the desire to walk."

I denied this, observing that the part of the road I myself had left was not more than two miles off. But with the obstinacy of his years he repeated: "It is the same road. This is the beginning, and though it seems to run straight away from us, it doubles so often, that it is never far from our boundary and sometimes touches it." He stooped down by the moat, and traced on its moist margin an absurd figure like a maze. As we walked back through the meadows, I tried to convince him of his mistake.

"The road sometimes doubles to be sure, but that is part of our discipline. Who can doubt that its general tendency is onward? To what goal we know not—it may be to some mountain where we shall touch the sky, it may be over precipices into the sea. But that it goes forward—who can doubt that? It is the thought of that that makes us strive to excel, each in his own way, and gives us an impetus which is lacking with you. Now that man who passed us—it's true that he ran well, and jumped well, and swam well; but we have men who can run better, and men who can jump better, and who can swim better. Specialization has produced results which would surprise you. Similarly, that girl—"

Here I interrupted myself to exclaim: "Good gracious me! I could have sworn it was Miss Eliza Dimbleby over there, with her feet in the fountain!"

He believed that it was.

"Impossible! I left her on the road, and she is due to lecture this evening at Tunbridge Wells. Why, her train leaves Cannon Street in—of course my watch has stopped like everything else. She is the last person to be here."

"People always are astonished at meeting each other. All kinds come through the hedge, and come at all times—when they are drawing ahead in the race, when they are lagging behind, when they are left for dead. I often stand near the boundary listening to the sounds of the road—you know what they are—and wonder if anyone will turn aside. It is my great happiness to help someone out of the moat, as I helped you. For our country fills up slowly, though it was meant for all mankind."

"Mankind have other aims," I said gently, for I thought him well-meaning; "and I must join them." I bade him good evening, for the sun was declining, and I wished to be on the road by nightfall. To my alarm, he caught hold of me, crying: "You are not to go yet!" I tried to shake him off, for we had no interests in common, and his civility was becoming irksome to me. But for all my struggles the tiresome old man would not let go; and, as wrestling is not my specialty, I was obliged to follow him.

It was true that I could have never found alone the place where I came in, and I hoped that, when I had seen the other sights about which he was worrying, he would take me back to it. But I was determined not to sleep in the country, for I mistrusted it, and the people too, for all their friendliness. Hungry though I was, I would not join them in their evening meals of milk and fruit, and, when they gave me flowers, I flung them away as soon as I could do so unobserved. Already they were lying down for the night like cattle—some out on the bare hillside, others in groups under the beeches. In the light of an orange sunset I hurried on with my unwelcome guide, dead tired, faint from want of food, but murmuring indomitably: "Give me life, with its struggles and victories, with its failures and hatreds, with its deep moral meaning and its unknown goal!"

At last we came to a place where the encircling moat was spanned by another bridge, and where another gate interrupted the line of the boundary hedge. It was different from the first gate; for it was half transparent like horn, and opened inwards. But through it, in the waning light, I saw again just such a road as I had left—monotonous, dusty, with brown crackling hedges on either side, as far as the eye could reach.

I was strangely disquieted at the sight, which seemed to deprive me of all self-control. A man was passing us, returning for the night to the hills, with a scythe over his shoulder and a can of some liquid in his hand. I forgot the destiny of our race. I forgot the road that lay before my eyes, and I sprang at him, wrenched the can out of his hand, and began to drink.

It was nothing stronger than beer, but in my exhausted state it overcame me in a moment. As in a dream, I saw the old man shut the gate, and heard him say: "This is where your road ends, and through this gate humanity—all that is left of it—will come in to us."

Though my senses were sinking into oblivion, they seemed to expand ere they reached it. They perceived the magic song of nightingales, and the odour of invisible hay, and stars piercing the fading sky. The man whose beer I had stolen lowered me down gently to sleep off its effects, and, as he did so, I saw that he was my brother.

QUESTIONS AND CONSIDERATIONS

1. What are the narrator's concerns at the beginning of the story? How old is he? Why is he tired? How does he feel about his brother?

2. Discuss the symbols that the story develops: the dusty road strewn with "the things we had all dropped," the milestone on which the narrator sits to rest, and the hedge. What does each symbol represent and how are they related?

3. What is implied by the narrator's difficult passage through the hedge, the loss of his clothes, and his emergence in a "deep pool" on the other side?

4. How does the narrator feel about life on the other side of the hedge? What is his response to the older man who pulls him out of the pool and into the noncompetitive world of the other side?

5. What is significant about the gates that allow people in and out of the world on "the other side"? Do you agree with the narrator's interpretation of their meaning?

6. How do you interpret the ending of the story, the narrator's drinking of the beer, his vision, and his final realization about his brother?

IDEAS FOR WRITING

1. Central to the meaning of this story is a debate on the nature and purpose of competitive behavior. Write an essay in which you argue that competition and specialization lead to improvements in human life; or take another position, possibly one closer to that of the older man in the story and the citizens on the "other side."

2. Do some research into the way people lived in farming communities in the past. Does the evidence suggest that people were happier in such communities than in today's hi-tech, fast-paced world? After thinking about the story and the research that you have completed, present your point of view on the advantages or disadvantages of the competitive way of life in urban America.

Phantom Palace

Isabel Allende

Journal

Write about how you imagine previous residents of your neighborhood, going
back even to early settlers or native peoples, organized their lives. What values
and ethical assumptions might they have upheld? How do you think they would
feel about your life style?

When five centuries earlier the bold renegades from Spain with their bone-
weary horses and armor candescent beneath an American sun stepped upon
the shores of Quinaroa, Indians had been living and dying in that same place
for several thousand years. The conquistadors announced with heralds and
banners the "discovery" of a new land, declared it a possession of a remote
emperor, set in place the first cross, and named the place San Jerónimo, a
name unpronounceable to the natives. The Indians observed these arrogant
ceremonies with some amazement, but the news had already reached them of
the bearded warriors who advanced across the world with their thunder of iron
and powder; they had heard that wherever these men went they sowed sorrow
and that no known people had been capable of opposing them: all armies had
succumbed before that handful of centaurs. These Indians were an ancient
tribe, so poor that not even the most befeathered chieftain had bothered to
exact taxes from them, and so meek that they had never been recruited for
war. They had lived in peace since the dawn of time and were not eager to
change their habits because of some crude strangers. Soon, nevertheless,
they comprehended the magnitude of the enemy and they understood the futility of attempting to ignore them; their presence was overpowering, like a heavy
stone bound to every back. In the years that followed, the Indians who had not
died in slavery or as a result of the different tortures improvised to entrench
the new gods, or as victims of unknown illnesses, scattered deep into the jungle and gradually lost even the name of their people. Always in hiding, like
shadows among the foliage, they survived for centuries, speaking in whispers
and mobilizing by night. They came to be so skillful in the art of dissimulation
that history did not record them, and today there is no evidence of their passage through time. Books do not mention them, but the *campesinos* who live
in the region say they have heard them in the forest, and every time the belly
of a young unmarried woman begins to grow round and they cannot point to
the seducer, they attribute the baby to the spirit of a lustful Indian. People of
that place are proud of carrying a few drops of the blood of those invisible beings mingled with the torrential flow from English pirates, Spanish soldiers,
African slaves, adventurers in search of El Dorado, and, later, whatever immigrant stumbled onto these shores with his pack on his back and his head filled
with dreams.

Europe consumed more coffee, cocoa, and bananas than we as a nation could produce, but all that demand was no bonanza for us; we continued to be as poor as ever. Events took a sudden turn when a black man digging a well along the coast drove his pick deep into the ground and a stream of petroleum spurted over his face. Toward the end of the Great War there was a widely held notion that ours was a prosperous country, when in truth most of the inhabitants still squished mud between their toes. The fact was that gold flowed only into the coffers of El Benefactor and his retinue, but there was hope that someday a little would spill over for the people. Two decades passed under this democratic totalitarianism, as the President for Life called his government, during which any hint of subversion would have been crushed in the name of his greater glory. In the capital there were signs of progress; motorcars, movie houses, ice cream parlors, a hippodrome, and a theater that presented spectaculars from New York and Paris. Every day dozens of ships moored in the port, some carrying away petroleum and others bringing in new products, but the rest of the country drowsed in a centuries-long stupor.

One day the people of San Jerónimo awakened from their siesta to the deafening pounding that presaged the arrival of the steam engine. The railroad tracks would unite the capital with this small settlement chosen by El Benefactor as the site for his Summer Palace, which was to be constructed in the style of European royalty—no matter that no one knew how to distinguish summer from winter, since both were lived under nature's hot, humid breath. The sole reason for erecting such a monumental work on this precise spot was that a certain Belgian naturalist had affirmed that if there was any truth to the myth of the Earthly Paradise, this landscape of incomparable beauty would have been the location. According to his observations the forest harbored more than a thousand varieties of brightly colored birds and numerous species of wild orchids, from the *Brassia,* which is as large as a hat, to the tiny *Pleurothallis,* visible only under a magnifying glass.

The idea of the Palace had originated with some Italian builders who had called on His Excellency bearing plans for a hodgepodge of a villa, a labyrinth of countless columns, wide colonnades, curving staircases, arches, domes and capitals, salons, kitchens, bedchambers, and more than thirty baths decorated with gold and silver faucets. The railroad was the first stage in the enterprise, indispensable for transporting tons of materials and hundreds of workmen to this remote corner of the world, in addition to the supervisors and craftsmen brought from Italy. The task of putting together that jigsaw puzzle lasted four years: flora and fauna were transmuted in the process, and the cost was equivalent to that of all the warships of the nation's fleet, but it was paid for punctually with the dark mineral that flowed from the earth, and on the anniversary of the Glorious Ascent to Power the ribbon was cut to inaugurate the Summer Palace. For the occasion the locomotive of the train was draped in the colors of the flag, and the freight cars were replaced by parlor cars upholstered in plush and English leather; the formally attired guests include members of the oldest aristocracy who, although they detested the cold-blooded Andean who had usurped the government, did not dare refuse his invitation.

El Benefactor was a crude man with the comportment of a peon; he bathed in cold water and slept on a mat on the floor with his boots on and his pistol within arm's reach; he lived on roast meat and maize, and drank nothing but water and coffee. His black cigars were his one luxury; he considered anything else a vice befitting degenerates or homosexuals—including alcohol, which he disapproved of and rarely offered at his table. With time, nevertheless, he was forced to accept a few refinements, because he understood the need to impress diplomats and other eminent visitors if they were not to carry the report abroad that he was a barbarian. He did not have a wife to mend his Spartan ways. He believed that love was a dangerous weakness. He was convinced that all women, except his own mother, were potentially perverse and that the most prudent way to treat them was to keep them at arm's length. He had always said that a man asleep in an amorous embrace was as vulnerable as a premature baby; he demanded, therefore, that his generals sleep in the barracks and limit their family life to sporadic visits. No woman had ever spent the night in his bed or could boast of anything more than a hasty encounter. No woman, in fact, had ever made a lasting impression until Marcia Lieberman entered his life.

The celebration for the inauguration of the Summer Palace was a stellar event in the annals of El Benefactor's government. For two days and two nights alternating orchestras played the most current dance tunes and an army of chefs prepared an unending banquet. The most beautiful mulatto women in the Caribbean, dressed in sumptuous gowns created for the occasion, whirled through salons with officers who had never fought in a battle but whose chests were covered with medals. There was every sort of diversion: singers imported from Havana and New Orleans, flamenco dancers, magicians, jugglers and trapeze artists, card games and dominoes, and even a rabbit hunt. Servants released the rabbits from their cages, and the guests pursued the scampering pack with finely bred greyhounds; the chase came to an end when one wit blasted all the black-necked swans gliding across the lake. Some guests passed out in their chairs, drunk with dancing and liquor, while others jumped fully clothed into the swimming pool or drifted off in pairs to the bedchambers. El Benefactor did not want to know the details. After greeting his guests with a brief speech, and beginning the dancing with the most aristocratic lady present, he had returned to the capital without a farewell. Parties put him in a bad humor. On the third day the train made the return journey, carrying home the enervated *bons vivants*. The Summer Palace was left in a calamitous state: the baths were dunghills, the curtains were dripping with urine, the furniture was gutted, and the plants drooped in their flowerpots. It took the servants a week to clean up the ravages of that hurricane.

The Palace was never again the scene of a bacchanal. Occasionally El Benefactor went there to get away from the pressures of his duties, but his repose lasted no more than three or four days, for fear that a conspiracy might be hatched in his absence. The government required eternal vigilance if power was not to slip through his fingers. The only people left in all that enormous edifice were the personnel entrusted with its maintenance. When the clatter of the construction equipment and the train had stilled, and the echoes of the inaugural festivities died down, the region was once again calm, and the orchids flowered and birds rebuilt their nests. The inhabitants of San Jerónimo returned to their habitual occupations and almost succeeded in forgetting the presence of the Summer Palace. That was when the invisible Indians slowly returned to occupy their territory.

The first signs were so subtle that no one paid attention to them; footsteps and whispers, fleeting silhouettes among the columns, the print of a hand on the clean surface of a table. Gradually food began to disappear from the kitchens, and bottles from the wine cellars; in the morning, some beds seemed to have been slept in. The servants blamed one another but never raised their voices because no one wanted the officer of the guard to take the matter into his hands. It was impossible to watch the entire expanse of that house, and while they were searching one room they would hear sighs in the adjoining one; but when they opened that door they would find only a curtain fluttering, as if someone had just stepped through it. The rumor spread that the Palace was under a spell, and soon the fear spread even to the soldiers, who stopped walking their night rounds and limited themselves to standing motionless at their post, eyes on the surrounding landscape, weapons at the ready. The frightened servants stopped going down to the cellars and, as a precaution, locked many of the rooms. They confined their activities to the kitchen and slept in one wing of the building. The remainder of the mansion was left unguarded, in the possession of the incorporeal Indians who had divided the rooms with invisible lines and taken up residence there like mischievous spirits. They had survived the passage of history, adapting to changes when they were inevitable, and when necessary taking refuge in a dimension of their own. In the rooms of the Palace they at last found refuge; there they noiselessly made love, gave birth without celebration, and died without tears. They learned so thoroughly all the twists and turns of that marble maze that they were able to exist comfortably in the same space with the guards and servants, never so much as brushing against them, as if they existed in a different time.

Ambassador Lieberman debarked in the port with his wife and a full cargo of personal belongings. He had traveled with his dogs, all his furniture, his library, his collection of opera recordings, and every imaginable variety of sports equipment, including a sailboat. From the moment his new destination had been announced, he had detested that country. He had left his post as Vice Consul in Vienna motivated by the ambition to obtain an ambassadorship, even if it meant South America, a bizarre continent for which he had not an ounce of sympathy. Marcia, his wife, took the appointment with better humor. She was prepared to follow her husband throughout his diplomatic pilgrim-

age—even though each day she felt more remote from him and had little interest in his mundane affairs—because she was allowed a great deal of freedom.
She had only to fulfill certain minimal wifely requirements, and the remainder
of her time was her own. In fact, her husband was so immersed in his work
and his sports that he was scarcely aware of her existence; he noticed her
only when she was not there. Lieberman's wife was an indispensable complement to his career; she lent brilliance to his social life and efficiently managed
his complicated domestic staff. He thought of her as a loyal partner, but he had
never been even slightly curious about her feelings. Marcia consulted maps
and an encyclopedia to learn the particulars of that distant nation, and began
studying Spanish. During the two weeks of the Atlantic crossing she read
books by the famous Belgian naturalist and, even before arriving, was enam-
ored of that heat-bathed geography. As she was a rather withdrawn woman,
she was happier in her garden than in the salons where she had to accompany her husband, and she concluded that in the new post she would have fewer
social demands and could devote herself to reading, painting, and exploring
nature.

Lieberman's first act was to install fans in every room of his residence. Immediately thereafter he presented his credentials to the government authorities.
When El Benefactor received him in his office, the couple had been in the city
only a few days, but the gossip that the Ambassador's wife was a beautiful
woman had already reached the caudillo's ears. For reasons of protocol he invited them to dinner, although he found the diplomat's arrogance and garrulity
insufferable. On the appointed night Marcia Lieberman entered the Reception
Hall on her husband's arm and, for the first time in a long lifetime, a woman
caused El Benefactor to gasp for breath. He had seen more lithe figures, and
faces more beautiful, but never such grace. She awakened memories of past
conquests, fueling a heat in his blood that he had not felt in many years. He
kept his distance that evening, observing the Ambassador's wife surreptitiously,
seduced by the curve of her throat, the shadow in her eyes, the movement of
her hands, the solemnity of her bearing. Perhaps it crossed his mind that he
was more than forty years older than she and that any scandal would have
repercussions far beyond the national boundaries, but that did not discourage
him; on the contrary, it added an irresistible ingredient to his nascent passion.

Marcia Lieberman felt the man's eyes fastened on her like an indecent caress, and she was aware of the danger, but she did not have the strength to
escape. At one moment she thought of telling her husband they should leave,
but instead remained seated, hoping the old man would approach her and at
the same time ready to flee if he did. She could not imagine why she was
trembling. She had no illusions about her host; the signs of age were obvious
from where she was sitting: the wrinkled and blemished skin, the dried-up
body, the hesitant walk. She could imagine his stale odor and knew intuitively
that his hands were claws beneath the white kid gloves. But the dictator's
eyes, clouded by age and the exercise of so much cruelty, still held a gleam of
power that held her frozen in her chair.

El Benefactor did not know how to pay court to a woman; until that moment he had never had need to do so. That fact acted in his favor, for had he
harassed Marcia with a Lothario's gallantries she would have found him repulsive and would have retreated with scorn. Instead she could not refuse him
when a few days later he knocked at her door, dressed in civilian clothes and
without his guards, looking like a dreary great-grandfather, to tell her that he
had not touched a woman for ten years and that he was past temptations of
that sort but, with all respect, he was asking her to accompany him that afternoon to a private place where he could rest his head in her queenly lap and
tell her how the world had been when he was still a fine figure of a macho and
she had not yet been born.

"And my husband?" Marcia managed to ask in a whisper-thin voice.

"Your husband does not exist, my child. Now only you and I exist," the
President for Life replied as he led her to his black Packard.

Marcia did not return home, and before the month was out Ambassador
Lieberman returned to his country. He had left no stone unturned in searching
for his wife, refusing at first to accept what was no secret, but when the evidence of the abduction became impossible to ignore, Lieberman had asked for
an audience with the Chief of State and demanded the return of his wife. The
interpreter tried to soften his words in translation, but the President captured
the tone and seized the excuse to rid himself once and for all of that imprudent
husband. He declared that Lieberman had stained the honor of the nation with
his absurd and unfounded accusations and gave him three days to leave the
country. He offered him the option of withdrawing without a scandal, to protect
the dignity of the country he represented, since it was to no one's interest to
break diplomatic ties and obstruct the free movement of the oil tankers. At the
end of the interview, with the expression of an injured father, he added that he
could understand the Ambassador's dilemma and told him not to worry, because in his absence, he, El Benefactor, would continue the search for his
wife. As proof of his good intents he called the Chief of Police and issued instructions in the Ambassador's presence. If at any moment Lieberman had
thought of refusing to leave without Marcia, a second thought must have made
clear to him that he was risking a bullet in the brain, so he packed his belongings and left the country before the three days were up.

Love had taken El Benefactor by surprise at an age when he no longer remembered the heart's impatience. This cataclysm rocked his senses and
thrust him back into adolescence, but not sufficiently to dull his vulpine cunning. He realized that his was a passion of sensuality, and he could not imagine that Marcia returned his emotions. He did not know why she had followed
him that afternoon, but his reason indicated that it was not for love, and, as he
knew nothing about women, he supposed that she had allowed herself to be
seduced out of a taste for adventure, or greed for power. In fact, she had fallen
prey to compassion. When the old man embraced her, anxiously, his eyes watering with humiliation because his manhood did not respond as it once had,
she undertook, patiently and with good will, to restore his pride. And thus after

several attempts the poor man succeeded in passing through the gates and lingering a few brief instants in the proffered warm gardens, collapsing immediately thereafter with his heart filled with foam.

"Stay with me," El Benefactor begged, as soon as he had recovered from fear of succumbing upon her.

And Marcia had stayed, because she was moved by the aged caudillo's loneliness, and because the alternative of returning to her husband seemed less interesting than the challenge of slipping past the iron fence this man had lived behind for eighty years.

El Benefactor kept Marcia hidden on one of his estates, where he visited her daily. He never stayed the night with her. Their time together was spent in leisurely caresses and conversation. In her halting Spanish she told him about her travels and the books she had read; he listened, not understanding much, content simply with the cadence of her voice. In turn he told her stories of his childhood in the arid lands of the Andes, and of his life as a soldier; but if she formulated some question he immediately threw up his defenses, observing her from the corner of his eyes as if she were the enemy. Marcia could not fail to note this implacable stoniness and realized that his habit of distrust was much stronger than his need to yield to tenderness, and so, after a few weeks, she resigned herself to defeat. Once she had renounced any hope of winning him over with love, she lost interest in him and longed to escape the walls that sequestered her. But it was too late. El Benefactor needed her by his side because she was the closest thing to a companion he had known; her husband had returned to Europe and she had nowhere to turn in this land; and even her name was fading from memory. The dictator perceived the change in her and his mistrust intensified, but that did not cause him to stop loving her. To console her for the confinement to which she was now condemned—her appearance outside would have confirmed Lieberman's accusations and shot international relations to hell—he provided her with all the things she loved: music, books, animals. Marcia passed the hours in a world of her own, every day more detached from reality. When she stopped encouraging him, El Benefactor found it impossible to embrace her, and their meetings resolved into peaceful evenings of cookies and hot chocolate. In his desire to please her, El Benefactor invited her one day to go with him to the Summer Palace, so she could see the paradise of the Belgian naturalist she had read so much about.

The train had not been used since the inaugural celebration ten years before and was so rusted that they had to make the trip by automobile, escorted by a caravan of guards; a crew of servants had left a week before, taking everything needed to restore the Palace to its original luxury. The road was no more than a trail defended by chain gangs against encroaching vegetation. In some stretches they had to use machetes to clear the ferns, and oxen to haul the cars from the mud, but none of that diminished Marcia's enthusiasm. She was dazzled by the landscape. She endured the humid heat and the mosquitoes as if she did not feel them, absorbed by a nature that seemed to welcome her in its embrace. She had the impression that she had been there before, perhaps in dreams or in another life, that she belonged there, that until that moment she had been a stranger in the world, and that her instinct had dictated every step she had taken, including that of leaving her husband's house to follow a trembling old man, for the sole purpose of leading her here. Even before she saw the Summer Palace, she knew that it would be her last home. When the edifice finally rose out of the foliage, encircled by palm trees and shimmering in the sun, Marcia breathed a deep sigh of relief, like a shipwrecked sailor when he sees home port.

Despite the frantic preparations that had been made to receive them, the mansion still seemed to be under a spell. The Roman-style structure, conceived as the center of a geometric park and grand avenues, was sunk in the riot of a gluttonous jungle growth. The torrid climate had changed the color of the building materials, covering them with a premature patina; nothing was visible of the swimming pool and gardens. The greyhounds had long ago broken their leashes and were running loose, a ferocious, starving pack that greeted the newcomers with a chorus of barking. Birds had nested in the capitals of the columns and covered the reliefs with droppings. On every side were signs of disorder. The Summer Palace had been transformed into a living creature defenseless against the green invasion that had surrounded and overrun it. Marcia leapt from the automobile and ran to the enormous doors where the servants awaited, oppressed by the heat of the dog days. One by one she explored all the rooms, the great salons decorated with crystal chandeliers that hung from the ceilings like constellations and French furniture whose tapestry upholstery was now home to lizards, bedchambers where bed canopies were blanched by intense sunlight, baths where moss had grown in the seams of the marble. Marcia never stopped smiling; she had the face of a woman recovering what was rightfully hers.

When El Benefactor saw Marcia so happy, a touch of the old vigor returned to warm his creaking bones, and he could embrace her as he had in their first meetings. Distractedly, she acceded. The week they had planned to spend there lengthened into two, because El Benefactor had seldom enjoyed himself so much. The fatigue accumulated in his years as tyrant disappeared, and several of his old man's ailments abated. He strolled with Marcia around the grounds, pointing out the many species of orchids climbing the treetrunks or hanging like grapes from the highest branches, the clouds of white butterflies that covered the ground, and the birds with iridescent feathers that filled the air with their song. He frolicked with her like a young lover, he fed her bits of the delicious flesh of wild mangoes, with his own hands he bathed her in herbal infusions, and he made her laugh by serenading her beneath her window. It had been years since he had been away from the capital, except for brief flights to provinces where his presence was required to put down some insurrection and to renew the people's belief that his authority was not to be questioned. This unexpected vacation had put him in a fine frame of mind; life suddenly seemed more fun, and he had the fantasy that with this beautiful woman beside him he could govern forever. One night he unintentionally fell asleep in her arms. He awoke in the early morning, terrified, with the clear sensation of having betrayed himself. He sprang out of bed, sweating, his heart galloping, and observed Marcia lying there, a white odalisque in repose, her copper hair spilling across her face. He informed his guards that he was returning to the city. He was not surprised when Marcia gave no sign of going with him. Perhaps in his heart he preferred it that way, since he understood that she represented his most dangerous weakness, that she was the only person who could make him forget his power.

El Benefactor returned to the capital without Marcia. He left behind a half-dozen soldiers to guard the property and a few employees to serve her, and he promised he would maintain the road so that she could receive his gifts, provisions, mail, and newspapers and magazines. He assured her that he would visit her often, as often as his duties as Chief of State permitted, but when he said goodbye they both knew they would never meet again. El Benefactor's caravan disappeared into the ferns and for a moment silence fell over the Summer Palace. Marcia felt truly free for the first time in her life. She removed the hairpins holding her hair in a bun, and shook out her long hair. The guards unbuttoned their jackets and put aside their weapons, while the servants went off to hang their hammocks in the coolest corners they could find.

For two weeks the Indians had observed the visitors from the shadows. Undeceived by Marcia Lieberman's fair skin and marvelous curly hair, they recognized her as one of their own but they had not dared materialize in her presence because of the habit of centuries of clandestinity. After the departure of the old man and his retinue, they returned stealthily to occupy the space where they had lived for generations. Marcia knew intuitively that she was never alone, that wherever she went a thousand eyes followed her, that she moved in a ferment of constant murmuring, warm breathing, and rhythmic pulsing, but she was not afraid; just the opposite, she felt protected by friendly spirits. She became used to petty annoyances: one of her dresses disappeared for several days, then one morning was back in a basket at the foot of her bed; someone devoured her dinner before she entered the dining room; her watercolors and books were stolen, but also she found freshly cut orchids on her table, and some evenings her bath waited with mint leaves floating in the cool water; she heard ghostly notes from pianos in the empty salons, the panting of lovers in the armoires, the voices of children in the attics. The servants had no explanation for those disturbances and she stopped asking, because she imagined they themselves were part of the benevolent conspiracy. One night she crouched among the curtains with a flashlight, and when she felt the thudding of feet on the marble, switched on the beam. She thought she saw shadowy, naked forms that for an instant gazed at her mildly and then vanished. She called in Spanish, but no one answered. She realized she would need enormous patience to uncover those mysteries, but it did not matter because she had the rest of her life before her.

A few years later the nation was jolted by the news that the dictatorship had come to an end for a most surprising reason: El Benefactor had died. He was a man in his dotage, a sack of skin and bones that for months had been decaying in life, and yet very few people imagined that he was mortal. No one remembered a time before him; he had been in power so many decades that people had become accustomed to thinking of him as an inescapable evil, like the climate. The echoes of the funeral were slow to reach the Summer Palace. By then most of the guards and servants, bored with waiting for replacements that never came, had deserted their posts. Marcia listened to the news without emotion. In fact, she had to make an effort to remember her past, what had happened beyond the jungle, and the hawk-eyed old man who had changed the course of her destiny. She realized that with the death of the tyrant the reasons for her remaining hidden had evaporated; she could return to civilization, where now, surely, no one was concerned with the scandal of her kidnapping. She quickly discarded that idea, however, because there was nothing outside the snarl of the surrounding jungle that interested her. Her life passed peacefully among the Indians; she was absorbed in the greenness, clothed only in a tunic, her hair cut short, her body adorned with tattoos and feathers. She was utterly happy.

A generation later, when democracy had been established in the nation and nothing remained of the long history of dictators but a few pages in scholarly books, someone remembered the marble villa and proposed that they restore it and found an Academy of Art. The Congress of the Republic sent a commission to draft a report, but their automobiles were not up to the grueling trip, and when finally they reached San Jerónimo no one could tell them where the Summer Palace was. They tried to follow the railroad tracks, but the rails had been ripped from the ties and the jungle had erased all traces. Then the Congress sent a detachment of explorers and a pair of military engineers who flew over the area in a helicopter; the vegetation was so thick that not even they could find the site. Details about the Palace were misplaced in people's memories and the municipal archives; the notion of its existence became gossip for old women; reports were swallowed up in the bureaucracy and, since the nation had more urgent problems, the project of the Academy of Art was tabled.

Now a highway has been constructed that links San Jerónimo to the rest of the country. Travelers say that sometimes after a storm, when the air is damp and charged with electricity, a white marble palace suddenly rises up beside the road, hovers for a few brief moments in the air, like a mirage, and then noiselessly disappears.

QUESTIONS AND CONSIDERATIONS

1. Describe the Indians of San Jerónimo. How do they respond to the encroachment of "civilization"? What allows them to survive and to prevail?

2. Characterize El Benefactor. What are his values, and what qualities of political power in the New World does he represent? Why is his regime able to survive for so many years?

3. What is the nature of the relationship between Ambassador Lieberman and his wife, Marcia? Why is Lieberman willing to leave without his wife? What critique is Allende making about "civilized" relationships through her portrayal of the Lieberman marriage?

4. What is the nature of the relationship between Marcia and El Benefactor? What does she represent for him? What advantages does the relationship have for her?

5. What type of person is Marcia? How does she change as the story develops?

6. Describe the phantom palace. How does it change physically? What might the various transformations of the palace represent? What is the significance of its loss and rebirth as a ghost house or legend?

IDEAS FOR WRITING

1. Do research into and then write about a "lost civilization", for example, the Mayan or the ancient Minoan. Based on current knowledge and speculation, what values did this vanished civilization uphold? What can we learn from the accomplishments and mistakes of this civilization?

2. A major theme of "Phantom Palace" is the survival of Native American culture, despite relentless encroachment by Western values and artifacts. Do some research into and write about the ways that Native American culture has influenced the culture and values of the New World, either in North or South America.

Swaddling Clothes
Yukio Mishima

Journal

Write about feelings you have about violating a particular social custom or "taboo".

He was always busy, Toshiko's husband. Even tonight he had to dash off to an appointment, leaving her to go home alone by taxi. But what else could a woman expect when she married an actor—an attractive one? No doubt she had been foolish to hope that he would spend the evening with her. And yet he must have known how she dreaded going back to their house, unhomely with its Western-style furniture and with the bloodstains still showing on the floor.

Toshiko had been oversensitive since girlhood: that was her nature. As the result of constant worrying she never put on weight, and now, an adult woman, she looked more like a transparent picture than a creature of flesh and blood. Her delicacy of spirit was evident to her most casual acquaintance.

Earlier that evening, when she had joined her husband at a night club, she had been shocked to find him entertaining friends with an account of "the incident." Sitting there in his American-style suit, puffing at a cigarette, he had seemed to her almost a stranger.

"It's a fantastic story," he was saying, gesturing flamboyantly as if in an attempt to outweigh the attractions of the dance band. "Here this new nurse for our baby arrives from the employment agency, and the very first thing I notice about her is her stomach. It's enormous—as if she had a pillow stuck under her kimono! No wonder, I thought, for I soon saw that she could eat more than the rest of us put together. She polished off the contents of our rice bin like that. . . ." He snapped his fingers. "'Gastric dilation'—that's how she explained her girth and her appetite. Well, the day before yesterday we heard groans and moans coming from the nursery. We rushed in and found her squatting on the floor, holding her stomach in her two hands, and moaning like a cow. Next to her our baby lay in his cot, scared out of his wits and crying at the top of his lungs. A pretty scene, I can tell you!"

"So the cat was out of the bag?" suggested one of their friends, a film actor like Toshiko's husband.

"Indeed it was! And it gave me the shock of my life. You see, I'd completely swallowed that story about 'gastric dilation.' Well, I didn't waste any time. I rescued our good rug from the floor and spread a blanket for her to lie on. The whole time the girl was yelling like a stuck pig. By the time the doctor from the maternity clinic arrived, the baby had already been born. But our sitting room was a pretty shambles!"

"Oh, that I'm sure of!" said another of their friends, and the whole company burst into laughter.

Toshiko was dumbfounded to hear her husband discussing the horrifying happening as though it were no more than an amusing incident which they chanced to have witnessed. She shut her eyes for a moment and all at once she saw the newborn baby lying before her: on the parquet floor the infant lay, and his frail body was wrapped in bloodstained newspapers.

Toshiko was sure that the doctor had done the whole thing out of spite. As if to emphasize his scorn for this mother who had given birth to a bastard under such sordid conditions, he had told his assistant to wrap the baby in some loose newspapers, rather than proper swaddling. This callous treatment of the newborn child has offended Toshiko. Overcoming her disgust at the entire scene, she had fetched a brand-new piece of flannel from her cupboard and, having swaddled the baby in it, had lain him carefully in an armchair.

This all had taken place in the evening after her husband had left the house. Toshiko had told him nothing of it, fearing that he would think her oversoft, oversentimental; yet the scene had engraved itself deeply in her mind. Tonight she sat silently thinking back on it, while the jazz orchestra brayed and her husband chatted cheerfully with his friends. She knew that she would never forget the sight of the baby, wrapped in stained newspapers and lying on the floor—it was a scene fit for a butchershop. Toshiko, whose own life had been spent in solid comfort, poignantly felt the wretchedness of the illegitimate baby.

I am the only person to have witnessed its shame, the thought occurred to her. The mother never saw her child lying there in its newspaper wrappings, and the baby itself of course didn't know. I alone shall have to preserve that terrible scene in my memory. When the baby grows up and wants to find out about his birth, there will be no one to tell him, so long as I preserve silence. How strange that I should have this feeling of guilt! After all, it was I who took him up from the floor, swathed him properly in flannel, and laid him down to sleep in the armchair.

They left the night club and Toshiko stepped into the taxi that her husband had called for her. "Take this lady to Ushigome," he told the driver and shut the door from the outside. Toshiko gazed through the window at her husband's smiling face and noticed his strong, white teeth. Then she leaned back in the seat, oppressed by the knowledge that their life together was in some way too easy, too painless. It would have been difficult for her to put her thoughts into words. Through the rear window of the taxi she took a last look at her husband. He was striding along the street toward his Nash car, and soon the back of his rather garish tweed coat had blended with the figures of the passers-by.

The taxi drove off, passed down a street dotted with bars and then by a theatre, in front of which the throngs of people jostled each other on the pavement. Although the performance had only just ended, the lights had already been turned out and in the half dark outside it was depressingly obvious that the cherry blossoms decorating the front of the theatre were merely scraps of white paper.

Even if that baby should grow up in ignorance of the secret of his birth, he can never become a respectable citizen, reflected Toshiko, pursuing the same train of thoughts. Those soiled newspaper swaddling clothes will be the symbol of his entire life. But why should I keep worrying about him so much? Is it because I feel uneasy about the future of my own child? Say twenty years from now, when our boy will have grown up into a fine, carefully educated young man, one day by a quirk of fate he meets that other boy, who then will also have turned twenty. And say that the other boy, who has been sinned against, savagely stabs him with a knife. . . .

It was a warm, overcast April night, but thoughts of the future made Toshiko feel cold and miserable. She shivered on the back seat of the car.

No, when the time comes I shall take my son's place, she told herself suddenly. Twenty years from now I shall be forty-three. I shall go to that young man and tell him straight out about everything—about his newspaper swaddling clothes, and about how I went and wrapped him in flannel.

The taxi ran along the dark wide road that was bordered by the park and by the Imperial Palace moat. In the distance Toshiko noticed the pinpricks of light which came from the blocks of tall office buildings.

Twenty years from now that wretched child will be in utter misery. He will be living a desolate, hopeless, poverty-stricken existence—a lonely rat. What else could happen to a baby who has had such a birth? He'll be wandering through the streets by himself, cursing his father, loathing his mother.

No doubt Toshiko derived a certain satisfaction from her somber thoughts: she tortured herself with them without cease. The taxi approached Hanzomon and drove past the compound of the British Embassy. At that point the famous rows of cherry trees were spread out before Toshiko in all their purity. On the spur of the moment she decided to go and view the blossoms by herself in the dark night. It was a strange decision for a timid and unadventurous young woman, but then she was in a strange state of mind and she dreaded the return home. That evening all sorts of unsettling fancies had burst open in her mind.

She crossed the wide street—a slim, solitary figure in the darkness. As a rule when she walked in the traffic Toshiko used to cling fearfully to her companion, but tonight she darted alone between the cars and a moment later had reached the long narrow park that borders the Palace moat. Chidorigafuchi, it is called—the Abyss of the Thousand Birds.

Tonight the whole park had become a grove of blossoming cherry trees. Under the calm cloudy sky the blossoms formed a mass of solid whiteness. The paper lanterns that hung from wires between the trees had been put out; in their place electric light bulbs, red, yellow, and green, shone dully beneath the blossoms. It was well past ten o'clock and most of the flowerviewers had gone home. As the occasional passers-by strolled through the park, they would automatically kick aside the empty bottles or crush the waste paper beneath their feet.

Newspapers, thought Toshiko, her mind going back once again to those happenings. Bloodstained newspapers. If a man were ever to hear of that piteous birth and know that it was he who had lain there, it would ruin his entire life. To think that I, a perfect stranger, should from now on have to keep such a secret—the secret of a man's whole existence. . . .

Lost in these thoughts, Toshiko walked on through the park. Most of the people still remaining there were quiet couples; no one paid her any attention. She noticed two people sitting on a stone bench beside the moat, not looking at the blossoms, but gazing silently at the water. Pitch black it was, and swathed in heavy shadows. Beyond the moat the somber forest of the Imperial Palace blocked her view. The trees reached up, to form a solid dark mass against the night sky. Toshiko walked slowly along the path beneath the blossoms hanging heavily overhead.

On a stone bench, slightly apart from the others, she noticed a pale object—not, as she had at first imagined, a pile of cherry blossoms, nor a garment forgotten by one of the visitors to the park. Only when she came closer did she see that it was a human form lying on the bench. Was it, she wondered, one of those miserable drunks often to be seen sleeping in public places? Obviously not, for the body had been systematically covered with newspapers, and it was the whiteness of those papers that had attracted Toshiko's attention. Standing by the bench, she gazed down at the sleeping figure.

It was a man in a brown jersey who lay there, curled up on layers of newspapers, other newspapers covering him. No doubt this had become his normal night residence now that spring had arrived. Toshiko gazed down at the man's dirty, unkempt hair, which in places had become hopelessly matted. As she observed the sleeping figure wrapped in its newspapers, she was inevitably reminded of the baby who had lain on the floor in its wretched swaddling clothes. The shoulder of the man's jersey rose and fell in the darkness in time with his heavy breathing.

It seemed to Toshiko that all her fears and premonitions had suddenly taken concrete form. In the darkness the man's pale forehead stood out, and it was a young forehead, though carved with the wrinkles of long poverty and hardship. His khaki trousers had been slightly pulled up; on his sockless feet he wore a pair of a battered gym shoes. She could not see his face and suddenly had an overmastering desire to get one glimpse of it.

She walked to the head of the bench and looked down. The man's head was half buried in his arms, but Toshiko could see that he was surprisingly young. She noticed the thick eyebrows and the fine bridge of his nose. His slightly open mouth was alive with youth.

But Toshiko had approached too close. In the silent night the newspaper bedding rustled, and abruptly the man opened his eyes. Seeing the young woman standing directly beside him, he raised himself with a jerk, and his eyes lit up. A second later a powerful hand reached out and seized Toshiko by her slender wrist.

She did not feel in the least afraid and made no effort to free herself. In a flash the thought had struck her. Ah, so the twenty years have already gone by! The forest of the Imperial Palace was pitch dark and utterly silent.

QUESTIONS AND CONSIDERATIONS

1. This story takes place in modern, urban Japan, a society that is undergoing rapid transformation. What Japanese cultural issues does the story reflect upon? Does the story seem accepting or critical of modern Japanese values and customs?

2. What past events and imaginary future scenarios haunt the central character of the story?

3. Characterize Toshiko: What are her values? Her strengths and weaknesses? How does she relate to other people?

4. How do the values and personality of Toshiko's husband differ from Toshiko's? What are his primary interests? Does he understand his wife's feelings and point of view? Why do you think Mishima gave him a professional identity as an actor?

5. How do the symbols, such as the newspaper swaddling clothes, the cherry blossoms, the taxi cab, and the three main settings of the story—a nightclub, Toshiko's home, and an urban park—contribute to the meaning of the events in the story?

6. Interpret the meaning of the story's ending: Why did Toshiko, usually so timid, allow herself to take such risks by leaving the cab at night? Why does Toshiko acquiesce to the "powerful hand" of the homeless man on the park bench? How is the final scene related to her fantasy about the illegitimate son of the nurse and her feelings of protectiveness about her own child?

IDEAS FOR WRITING

1. It could be argued that Toshiko's self-destructive actions are caused in part by her guilty feelings about the violation of taboos and social obligations in her home. Discuss the potentially destructive power of a taboo or social obligation in your culture.

2. People sometimes feel haunted, as Toshiko does in the story, by individuals from their past whom they think they have insulted or with whom they have unfinished business. Write an essay about a person from your past who continues to haunt you. What impact might your relationship with this individual have had on his or her development? What would you like to say to him or her?

The Demon Lover
Elizabeth Bowen

Journal

Write about a time in your life when you were alone and began to reflect upon people and events from your past.

Towards the end of her day in London Mrs. Drover went round to her shut-up house to look for several things she wanted to take away. Some belonged to herself, some to her family, who were by now used to their country life. It was late August; it had been a steamy, showery day: at the moment the trees down the pavement glittered in an escape of humid yellow afternoon sun. Against the next batch of clouds, already piling up ink-dark, broken chimneys and parapets stood out. In her once familiar street, as in any unused channel, an unfamiliar queerness had silted up: a cat wove itself in and out of railings, but no human eye watched Mrs. Drover's return. Shifting some parcels under her arm, she slowly forced round her latchkey in an unwilling lock, then gave the door, which had warped, a push with her knee. Dead air came out to meet her as she went in.

The staircase window having been boarded up, no light came down into the hall. But one door, she could just see, stood ajar, so she went quickly through into the room and unshuttered the big window in there. Now the prosaic woman, looking about her, was more perplexed than she knew by everything that she saw, by traces of her long former habit of life—the yellow smoke-stain up the white marble mantelpiece, the ring left by a vase on the top of the escritoire; the bruise in the wallpaper where, on the door being thrown open widely, the china handle had always hit the wall. The piano, having gone away to be stored, had left what looked like claw-marks on its part of the parquet. Though not much dust and seeped in, each object wore a film of another kind; and, the only ventilation being the chimney, the whole drawing-room smelled of the cold hearth. Mrs. Drover put down her parcels on the escritoire and left the room to proceed upstairs; the things she wanted were in a bedroom closet.

She had been anxious to see how the house was—the part-time caretaker she shared with some neighbours was away this week on his holiday, known to be not yet back. At the best of times he did not look in often, and she was never sure that she trusted him. There were some cracks in the structure, left by the last bombing, on which she was anxious to keep an eye. Not that one could do anything—

A shaft of refracted daylight now lay across the hall. She stopped dead and stared at the hall table—on this lay a letter addressed to her.

She thought first—then the caretaker *must* be back. All the same, who, seeing the house shuttered, would have dropped a letter in at the box? It was not a circular, it was not a bill. And the post office redirected, to the address in the country, everything for her that came through the post. The caretaker (even if he *were* back) did not know she was due in London today—her call here had been planned to be a surprise—so his negligence in the manner of this letter, leaving it to wait in the dusk and the dust, annoyed her. Annoyed, she picked up the letter, which bore no stamp. But it cannot be important, or they would know. . . . She took the letter rapidly upstairs with her, without a stop to look at the writing till she reached what had been her bedroom, where she let in light. The room looked over the garden and other gardens: the sun had gone in; as the clouds sharpened and lowered, the trees and rank lawns seemed already to smoke with dark. Her reluctance to look again at the letter came from the fact that she felt intruded upon—and by someone contemptuous of her ways. However, in the tenseness preceding the fall of rain she read it: it was a few lines.

> Dear Kathleen: You will not have forgotten that today is our anniversary, and the day we said. The years have gone by at once slowly and fast. In view of the fact that nothing has changed, I shall rely upon you to keep your promise. I was sorry to see you leave London, but was satisfied that you would be back in time. You may expect me, therefore, at the hour arranged. Until then . . .
>
>   K.

Mrs. Drover looked for the date: it was today's. She dropped the letter on to the bed-springs, then picked it up to see the writing again—her lips, beneath the remains of lipstick, beginning to go white. She felt so much the change in her own face that she went to the mirror, polished a clear patch in it, and looked at once urgently and stealthily in. She was confronted by a woman of forty-four, with eyes starting out under a hat-brim that had been rather carelessly pulled down. She had not put on any more powder since she left the shop where she ate her solitary tea. The pearls her husband had given her on their marriage hung loose around her now rather thinner throat, slipping in the V of the pink wool jumper her sister knitted last autumn as they sat round the fire. Mrs. Drover's most normal expression was one of controlled worry, but of assent. Since the birth of the third of her little boys, attended by a quite serious illness, she had had an intermittent muscular flicker to the left of her mouth, but in spite of this she could always sustain a manner that was at once energetic and calm.

Turning from her own face as precipitately as she had gone to meet it, she went to the chest where the things were, unlocked it, threw up the lid, and knelt to search. But as rain began to come crashing down she could not keep from looking over her shoulder at the stripped bed on which the letter lay. Behind the blanket of rain the clock of the church that still stood struck six—with rapidly heightening apprehension she counted each of the slow strokes. "The hour arranged . . . My God," she said, "*what* hour? How should I . . . ? After twenty-five years . . ."

The young girl talking to the soldier in the garden had not ever completely seen his face. It was dark; they were saying goodbye under a tree. Now and then—for it felt, from not seeing him at this intense moment, as though she had never seen him at all—she verified his presence for these few moments longer by putting out a hand, which he each time pressed, without very much kindness, and painfully, on to one of the breast buttons of his uniform. That cut of the button on the palm of her hand was, principally, what she was to carry away. This was so near the end of a leave from France that she could only wish him already gone. It was August 1916. Being not kissed, being drawn away from and looked at intimidated Kathleen till she imagined spectral glitters in the place of his eyes. Turning away and looking back up the lawn she saw, through branches of trees, the drawing-room window light: she caught a breath for the moment when she could go running back there into the safe arms of her mother and sister, and cry: "What shall I do, what shall I do? He has gone?"

Hearing her catch her breath, her fiancé said, without feeling: "Cold?"

"You're going away such a long way."

"Not so far as you think."

"I don't understand."

"You don't have to," he said. "You will. You know what we said."

"But that was—suppose you—I mean, suppose."

"I shall be with you," he said, "sooner or later. You won't forget that. You need do nothing but wait."

Only a little more than a minute later she was free to run up the silent lawn. Looking in through the window at her mother and sister, who did not for the moment perceive her, she already felt that unnatural promise drive down between her and the rest of all human kind. No other way of having given herself could have made her feel so apart, lost and foresworn. She could not have plighted a more sinister troth.

Kathleen behaved well when, some months later, her fiancé was reported missing, presumed killed. Her family not only supported her but were able to praise her courage without stint because they could not regret, as a husband for her, the man they knew almost nothing about. They hoped she would, in a year or two, console herself—and had it been only a question of consolation things might have gone much straighter ahead. But her trouble, behind just a little grief, was a complete dislocation from everything. She did not reject other lovers, for these failed to appear: for years she failed to attract men—and with the approach of her thirties she became natural enough to share her family's anxiousness on this score. She began to put herself out, to wonder; and at thirty-two she was very greatly relieved to find herself being courted by William Drover. She married him, and the two of them settled down in this quiet, arboreal part of Kensington: in this house the years piled up, her children were born, and they all lived till they were driven out by the bombs of the next war. Her movements as Mrs. Drover were circumscribed, and she dismissed any idea that they were still watched.

As things were—dead or living the letter-writer sent her only a threat. Unable, for some minutes, to go on kneeling with her back exposed to the empty room, Mrs. Drover rose from the chest to sit on an upright chair whose back was firmly against the wall. The desuetude of her former bedroom, her married London home's whole air of being a cracked cup from which memory, with its reassuring power, had either evaporated or leaked away, made a crisis—and at just this crisis the letter-writer had, knowledgeably, struck. The hollowness of the house this evening cancelled years on years of voices, habits, and steps. Through the shut windows she only heard rain fall on the roofs around. To rally herself, she said she was in a mood—and for two or three seconds shutting her eyes, told herself that she had imagined the letter. But she opened them—there it lay on the bed.

On the supernatural side of the letter's entrance she was not permitting her mind to dwell. Who, in London, knew she meant to call at the house today? Evidently, however this had been known. The caretaker, *had* he come back, had had no cause to expect her: he would have taken the letter in his pocket, to forward it, at his own time, through the post. There was no other sign that the caretaker had been in—but, if not? Letters dropped in at doors of deserted houses do not fly or walk to tables in halls. They do not sit on the dust of empty tables with the air of certainty that they will be found. There is needed some human hand—but nobody but the caretaker had a key. Under circumstances she did not care to consider, a house can be entered without a key. It was possible that she was not alone now. She might be being waited for, downstairs. Waited for—until when? Until "the hour arranged." At least that was not six o'clock: six has struck.

She rose from the chair and went over and locked the door.

The thing was, to get out. To fly? No, not that: she had to catch her train. As a woman whose utter dependability was the keystone of her family life she was not willing to return to the country, to her husband, her little boys, and her sister, without the objects she had come up to fetch. Resuming work at the chest she set about making up a number of parcels in a rapid, fumbling-decisive way. These, with her shopping parcels, would be too much to carry; these meant a taxi—at the thought of the taxi her heart went up and her normal breathing resumed. I will ring up the taxi now; the taxi cannot come too soon: I shall hear the taxi out there running its engine, till I walk calmly down to it through the hall. I'll ring up—But no: the telephone is cut off . . . She tugged at a knot she had tied wrong.

The idea of flight. . . . He was never kind to me, not really. I don't remember him kind at all. Mother said he never considered me. He was set on me, that was what it was—not love. Not love, not meaning a person well. What did he do, to make me promise like that? I can't remember—But she found that she could.

She remembered with such dreadful acuteness that the twenty-five years since then dissolved like smoke and she instinctively looked for the weal left by the button on the palm of her hand. She remembered not only all that he said and did but the complete suspension of *her* existence during that August week. I was not myself—they all told me so at the time. She remembered—but with one white burning blank as where acid has dropped on a photograph: *under no conditions* could she remember his face.

So, wherever he may be waiting, I shall not know him. You have no time to run from a face you do not expect.

The thing was to get to the taxi before any clock struck what could be the hour. She would slip down the street and round the side of the square to where the square gave on the main road. She would return in the taxi, safe, to her own door, and bring the solid driver into the house with her to pick up the parcels from room to room. The idea of the taxi driver made her decisive, bold: she unlocked her door, went to the top of the staircase, and listened down.

She heard nothing—but while she was hearing nothing the *passé* air of the staircase was disturbed by a draught that travelled up to her face. It emanated from the basement: down there a door or window was being opened by someone who chose this moment to leave the house.

The rain had stopped; the pavements steamily shone as Mrs. Drover let herself out by inches from her own front door into the empty street. The unoccupied houses opposite continued to meet her look with their damaged stare. Making towards the thoroughfare and the taxi, she tried not to keep looking behind. Indeed, the silence was so intense—one of those creeks of London silence exaggerated this summer by the damage of war—that no tread could have gained on hers unheard. Where her street debouched on the square where people went on living, she grew conscious of, and checked, her unnatural pace. Across the open end of the square two buses impassively passed each other: women, a perambulator, cyclists, a man wheeling a barrow signalized, once again, the ordinary flow of life. At the square's most populous corner should be—and was—the short taxi rank. This evening, only one taxi—but this, although it presented its blank rump, appeared already to be alertly waiting for her. Indeed, without looking round the driver started his engine as she panted up from behind and put her hand on the door. As she did so, the clock struck seven. The taxi faced the main road: to make the trip back to her house it would have to turn—she had settled back on the seat and the taxi *had* turned before she, surprised by its knowing movement, recollected that she had not "said where." She leaned forward to scratch at the glass panel that divided the driver's head from her own.

The driver braked to what was almost a stop, turned round, and slid the glass panel back: the jolt of this flung Mrs. Drover forward till her face was almost into the glass. Through the aperture driver and passenger, not six inches between them, remained for an eternity eye to eye. Mrs. Drover's mouth hung open for some seconds before she could issue her first scream. After that she continued to scream freely and to beat with her gloved hands on the glass all round as the taxi, accelerating without mercy, made off with her into the hinterland of deserted streets.

QUESTIONS AND CONSIDERATIONS

1. What happened in Mrs. Drover's life just prior to the events described in the story? Why is she in her London home alone? Why is her home empty? Why are there "cracks in the structure"? What might these cracks signify?

2. Mrs. Drover notices marks or scars left by furnishings that have been removed from her home: a yellow smoke stain, a "ring left by a vase," a "bruise" on the wall, even "claw marks" where a piano has rested on the wooden floor. What symbolism is suggested by these marks?

3. Where did the letter that Mrs. Drover finds on the hall table come from? What is mysterious about the letter? How would you describe its contents and the author's attitude toward Mrs. Dover? Why do you think the letter is signed with the single initial "K"?

4. As Mrs. Drover considers the letter and its possible author, she thinks back on a promise she made twenty-five years ago, during World War I. What was the nature of her promise? To whom did she make this promise, and why?

5. What happens to Kathleen after her fiancé is reported missing? How would you describe her mental state during these years? How does her outlook change when she meets Mr. Drover?

6. At the end of the story Mrs. Drover gets into a waiting cab and is driven screaming through the "hinterland of deserted streets." Who do you think is driving the cab, and why is Mrs. Drover screaming? What will happen to her?

IDEAS FOR WRITING

1. The story's conclusion invites interpretation. There can be several possible explanations for the letter Mrs. Dover finds and for the story's ending. Do you think this to be a story about a ghost or demon, a story about a psychotic individual who loves Kathleen and returns to take her away, or is it a psychological portrait of a woman who is haunted by her past and can't live completely in the present? Perhaps you have yet another interpretation. Write an essay in which you interpret the key events of the story and its meaning.

2. This story explores the impact of war on relationships, family life, and memories of the past. Using the events described in the story, your own experiences with war or interviews with people who have lived through a war, write an essay about the impact of war on memory and human relationships.

In the Life

Becky Birtha

Journal

*Write about a dream or fantasy you had about a person you were once close to
who is no longer alive or with whom you are no longer in contact. How did you
feel about the dream? What message did the dream or fantasy have for you?*

Grace come to me in my sleep last night. I feel somebody presence, in the
room with me, then I catch the scent of Posner's Bergamot Pressing Oil, and
that cocoa butter grease she use on her skin. I know she standing at the bedside, right over me, and then she call my name.

"Pearl."

My Christian name Pearl Irene Jenkins, but don't nobody ever call me that
no more. I been Jinx to the world for longer than I care to specify. Since my
mother passed away, Grace the only one ever use my given name.

"Pearl," she say again. "I'm just gone down to the garden awhile. I be
back."

I'm so deep asleep I have to fight my way awake, and when I do be fully
woke, Grace is gone. I ease my tired bones up and drag em down the stairs,
cross the kitchen in the dark, and out the back screen door onto the porch. I
guess I'm half expecting Gracie to be there waiting for me, but there ain't another soul stirring tonight. Not a sound but singing crickets, and nothing staring
back at me but that old weather-beaten fence I ought to painted this summer,
and still ain't made time for. I lower myself down into the porch swing, where
Gracie and I have sat so many still summer nights and watched the moon rising up over Old Mister Thompson's field.

I never had time to paint that fence back then, neither. But it didn't matter
none, cause Gracie had it all covered up with her flowers. She used to sit right
here on this swing at night, when a little breeze be blowing, and say she could
tell all the different flowers apart, just by they smell. The wind pick up a scent,
and Gracie say, "Smell that jasmine, Pearl?" Then a breeze come up from another direction, and she turn her head like somebody calling her and say, "Now
that's my honeysuckle, now."

It used to tickle me, cause she knowed I couldn't tell all them flowers of
hers apart when I was looking square at em in broad daylight. So how I'm
gonna do it by smell in the middle of the night? I just laugh and rock the swing
a little, and watch her enjoying herself in the soft moonlight.

I could never get enough of watching her. I always did think that Grace
Simmons was the prettiest woman north of the Mason-Dixon line. Now I've
lived enough years to know it's true. There's been other women in my life besides Grace, and I guess I loved them all, one way or another, but she was
something special—Gracie was something else again.

She was a dark brownskin woman—the color of fresh gingerbread hot out the oven. In fact, I used to call her that—my gingerbread girl. She had plenty enough of that pretty brownskin flesh to fill your arms up with something substantial when you hugging her, and to make a nice background for them dimples in her cheeks and other places I won't go into detail about.

Gracie could be one elegant good looker when she set her mind to it. I'll never forget the picture she made, that time the New Year's Eve party was down at the Star Harbor Ballroom. That was the first year we was in the Club, and we was going to every event they had. Dressed to kill. Gracie had on that white silk dress that set off her complexion so perfect, with her hair done up in all them little curls. A single strand of pearls that could have fooled anybody. Long gloves. And a little fur stole. We was serious about our partying back then! I didn't look too bad myself, with that black velvet jacket I used to have, and the pleats in my slacks pressed so sharp you could cut yourself on em. I weighed quite a bit less than I do now, too. Right when you come in the door of the ballroom, they have a great big floor to ceiling gold frame mirror, and if I remember rightly, we didn't get past that for quite some time.

Everybody want to dance with Gracie that night. And that's fine with me. Along about the middle of the evening, the band is playing a real hot number, and here come Louie and Max over to me, all long-face serious, wanting to know how I can let my woman be out there shaking her behind with any stranger that wander in the door. Now they know good and well ain't no strangers here. The Cinnamon & Spice Club is a private club, and all events is by invitation only.

Of course, there's some thinks friends is more dangerous than strangers. But I never could be the jealous, overprotective type. And the fact is, I just love to watch the woman. I don't care if she out there shaking it with the Virgin Mary, long as she having a good time. And that's just what I told Max and Lou. I could lean up against that bar and watch her for hours.

You wouldn't know, to look at her, she done it all herself. Made all her own dresses and hats, and even took apart a old ratty fur coat that used to belong to my great aunt Malinda to make that cute little stole. She always did her own hair—every week or two. She used to do mine, too. Always be teasing me about let her make me some curls this time. I'd get right aggravated. Cause you can't have a proper argument with somebody when they standing over your head with a hot comb in they hand. You kinda at they mercy. I'm sitting fuming and cursing under them towels and stuff, with the sweat dripping all in my eyes in the steamy kitchen—and she just laughing. "Girl," I'm telling her, "you know won't no curls fit under my uniform cap. Less you want me to stay home this week and you gonna go work my job and your job too."

Both of us had to work, always, and we still ain't had much. Everybody always think Jinx and Grace doing all right, but we was scrimping and saving all along. Making stuff over and making do. Half of what we had to eat grew right here in this garden. Still and all, I guess we *was* doing all right. We had each other.

Now I finally got the damn house paid off, and she ain't even here to appreciate it with me. And Gracie's poor bedraggled garden is just struggling along on its last legs—kinda like me. I ain't the kind to complain about my lot, but truth to tell, I can't be down crawling around on my hands and knees no more—this body I got put up such a fuss and holler. Can't enjoy the garden at night proper nowadays, nohow. Since Mister Thompson's land was took over by the city and they built them housing projects where the field used to be, you can't even see the moon from here, till it get up past the fourteenth floor. Don't no moonlight come in my yard no more. And I guess I might as well pick my old self up and go on back to bed.

Sometimes I still ain't used to the fact that Grace is passed on. Not even after these thirteen years without her. She the only woman I ever lived with—and I lived with her more than half my life. This house her house, too, and she oughta be here in it with me.

I rise up by six o'clock most every day, same as I done all them years I worked driving for the C.T.C. If the weather ain't too bad, I take me a walk—and if I ain't careful, I'm liable to end up down at the Twelfth Street Depot, waiting to see what trolley they gonna give me this morning. There ain't a soul working in that office still remember me. And they don't even run a trolley on the Broadway line no more. They been running a bus for the past five years.

I forgets a lot of things these days. Last week, I had just took in the clean laundry off the line, and I'm up in the spare room fixing to iron my shirts, when I hear somebody pass through that squeaky side gate and go on around to the back yard. I ain't paid it no mind at all, cause that's the way Gracie most often do when she come home. Go see about her garden fore she even come in the house. I always be teasing her she care more about them collards and string beans than she do about me. I hear her moving around out there while I'm sprinkling the last shirt and plugging in the iron—hear leaves rustling, and a crate scraping along the walk.

While I'm waiting for the iron to heat up, I take a look out the window, and come to see it ain't Gracie at all, but two a them sassy little scoundrels from over the projects—one of em standing on a apple crate and holding up the other one, who is picking my ripe peaches off my tree, just as brazen as you please. Don't even blink a eyelash when I holler out the window. I have to go running down all them stairs and out on the back porch, waving the cord I done jerked out the iron—when Doctor Matthews has told me a hundred times I ain't supposed to be running or getting excited about nothing, with my pressure like it is. And I ain't even supposed to be *walking* up and down no stairs.

When they seen the ironing cord in my hand, them two little sneaks had a reaction all right. The one on the bottom drop the other one right on his padded quarters and lit out for the gate, hollering, "Look out, Timmy! Here come Old Lady Jenkins!"

When I think about it now, it was right funny, but at the time I was so mad it musta took me a whole half hour to cool off. I sat there on that apple crate just boiling.

Eventually, I begun to see how it wasn't even them two kids I was so mad at. I was mad at time. For playing tricks on me the way it done. So I don't even remember that Grace Simmons has been dead now for the past thirteen years. And mad at time just for passing—so fast. If I had my life to live over, I wouldn't trade in none of them years for nothing. I'd just slow em down.

The church sisters around here is always trying to get me to be thinking about dying, myself. They must figure, when you my age, that's the only excitement you got left to look forward to. Gladys Hawkins stopped out front this morning, while I was mending a patch in the top screen of the front door. She was grinning from ear to ear like she just spent the night with Jesus himself.

"Morning, Sister Jenkins. Right pretty day the good Lord seen fit to send us, ain't it?"

I ain't never known how to answer nobody who manages to bring the good Lord into every conversation. If I nod and say yes, she'll think I finally got religion. But if I disagree, she'll think I'm crazy, cause it truly is one pretty August morning. Fortunately, it don't matter to her whether I agree or not, cause she gone right on talking according to her own agenda anyway.

"You know, this Sunday is Women's Day over at Blessed Endurance. Reverend Solomon Moody is gonna be visiting, speaking on 'A Woman's Place in the Church.' Why don't you come and join us for worship? You'd be most welcome."

I'm tempted to tell her exactly what come to my mind—that I ain't never heard of no woman name Solomon. However, I'm polite enough to hold my tongue, which is more than I can say for Gladys.

She ain't waiting for no answer from me, just going right on. "I don't spose you need me to point it out to you, Sister Jenkins, but you know you ain't as young as you used to be." As if both of our ages wasn't common knowledge to each other, seeing as we been knowing one another since we was girls. "You reaching that time of life when you might wanna be giving a little more attention to the spiritual side of things than you been doing. . . ."

She referring, politely as she capable of, to the fact that I ain't been seen inside a church for thirty-five years.

". . . And you know what the good Lord say. 'Watch therefore, for ye know neither the day nor the hour . . .' But, 'He that believeth on the Son hath everlasting life . . .'"

It ain't no use to argue with her kind. The Lord is on they side in every little disagreement, and he don't never give up. So when she finally wind down and ask me again will she see me in church this Sunday, I just say I'll think about it.

Funny thing, I been thinking about it all day. But not the kinda thoughts she want me to think, I'm sure. Last time I went to church was on a Easter Sunday. We decided to go on accounta Gracie's old meddling cousin, who was always nagging us about how we unnatural and sinful and a disgrace to her family. Seem like she seen it as her one mission in life to get us two sinners inside a church. I guess she figure, once she get us in there, God gonna take over the job. So Grace and me finally conspires that the way to get her off our backs is to give her what she think she want.

Course, I ain't had on a skirt since before the war, and I ain't aiming to change my lifelong habits just to please Cousin Hattie. But I did take a lotta pains over my appearance that day. I'd had my best tailor-made suit pressed fresh, and slept in my stocking cap the night before so I'd have every hair in place. Even had one a Gracie's flowers stuck in my buttonhole. And a brand new narrow-brim dove gray Stetson hat. Gracie take one look at me when I'm ready and shake her head. "The good sisters is gonna have a hard time concentrating on the preacher today!"

We arrive at her cousin's church nice and early, but of course it's a big crowd inside already on accounta it being Easter Sunday. The organ music is wailing away, and the congregation is dazzling—decked out in nothing but the finest and doused with enough perfume to outsmell even the flowers up on the altar.

But as soon as we get in the door, this kinda sedate commotion break out—all them good Christian folks whispering and nudging each other and trying to turn around and get a good look. Well, Grace and me, we used to that. We just find us a nice seat in one of the empty pews near the back. But this busy buzzing keep up, even after we seated and more blended in with the crowd. And finally it come out that the point of contention ain't even the bottom half of my suit, but my new dove gray Stetson.

This old gentleman with a grizzled head, wearing glasses about a inch thick is turning around and leaning way over the back of the seat, whispering to Grace in a voice plenty loud enough for me to hear, "You better tell your beau to remove that hat, entering in Jesus' Holy Chapel."

Soon as I get my hat off, some old lady behind me is grumbling. "I declare, some of these children haven't got no respect at all. Oughta know you sposed to keep your head covered, setting in the house of the Lord."

Seem like the congregation just can't make up its mind whether I'm supposed to wear my hat or I ain't.

I couldn't hardly keep a straight face all through the service. Every time I catch Gracie eye, or one or the other of us catch a sight of my hat, we off again. I couldn't wait to get outa that place. But it was worth it. Gracie and me was entertaining the gang with that story for weeks to come. And we ain't had no more problems with Cousin Hattie.

Far as life everlasting is concerned, I imagine I'll cross that bridge when I reach it. I don't see no reason to rush into things. Sure, I know Old Man Death is gonna be coming after me one of these days, same as he come for my mother and dad, and Gracie and, just last year, my old buddy Louie. But I ain't about to start nothing that might make him feel welcome. It might be different for Gladys Hawkins and the rest of them church sisters, but I got a whole lot left to live for. Including a mind fulla good time memories. When you in the life, one thing your days don't never be, and that's dull. Your nights neither. All these years I been in the life, I loved it. And you know Jinx ain't about to go off with no Old *Man* without no struggle, nohow.

To tell the truth, though, sometime I do get a funny feeling bout Old Death.

Sometime I feel like he here already—been here. Waiting on me and watching me and biding his time. Paying attention when I have to stop on the landing of the stairs to catch my breath. Paying attention if I don't wake up till half past seven some morning, and my back is hurting me so bad it take me another half hour to pull myself together and get out the bed.

The same night after I been talking to Gladys in the morning, it take me a long time to fall asleep. I'm lying up in bed waiting for the aching in my back and my joints to ease off some, and I can swear I hear somebody else in the house. Seem like I hear em downstairs, maybe opening and shutting the ice-box door, or switching off a light. Just when I finally manage to doze off, I hear somebody footsteps right here in the bedroom with me. Somebody tippy-toeing real quiet, creaking the floor boards between the bed and the dresser . . . over to the closet . . . back to the dresser again.

I'm almost scared to open my eyes. But it's only Gracie—in her old raggedy bathrobe and a silk handkerchief wrapped up around all them little braids in her head—putting her finger up to her lips to try and shush me so I won't wake up.

I can't help chuckling. "Hey Gingerbread Girl. Where you think you going in your house coat and bandana and it ain't even light out yet. Come on get back in this bed."

"You go on to sleep," she say. "I'm just going out back a spell."

It ain't no use me trying to make my voice sound angry, cause she so con-trary when it come to that little piece of ground down there I can't help laugh-ing. "What you think you gonna complish down there in the middle of the night? It ain't even no moon to watch tonight. The sky been filling up with clouds all evening, and the weather forecast say rain tomorrow."

"Just don't pay me no mind and go on back to sleep. It ain't the middle of the night. It's almost daybreak." She grinning like she up to something, and sure enough, she say, "This the best time to pick off them black and yellow beetles been making mildew outa my cucumber vines. So I'm just fixing to turn the tables around a little bit. You gonna read in the papers tomorrow morning bout how the entire black and yellow beetle population of number Twenty-seven Bank Street been wiped off the face of the earth—while you was up here sleeping."

Both of us is laughing like we partners in a crime, and then she off down the hall, calling out, "I be back before you even know I'm gone."

But the full light of day is coming in the window, and she ain't back yet.

I'm over to the window with a mind to holler down to Grace to get her be-hind back in this house, when the sight of them housing projects hits me right in the face: stacks of dirt-colored bricks and little caged-in porches, heaped up into the sky blocking out what poor skimpy light this cloudy morning brung.

It's a awful funny feeling start to come over me. I mean to get my house-coat, and go down there anyway, just see what's what. But in the closet I can see it ain't but my own clothes hanging on the pole. All the shoes on the floor is mine. And I know I better go ahead and get washed, cause it's a whole lot I want to get done fore it rain, and that storm is coming in for sure. Better pick the rest of them ripe peaches and tomatoes. Maybe put in some peas for fall picking, if my knees'll allow me to get that close to the ground.

The rain finally catch up around noon time and slow me down a bit. I never could stand to be cooped up in no house in the rain. Always make me itchy. That's one reason I used to like driving a trolley for the C.T.C. Cause you get to be out every day, no matter what kinda weather coming down—get to see people and watch the world go by. And it ain't as if you exactly out in the weather, neither. You get to watch it all from behind that big picture window.

Not that I woulda minded being out in it. I used to want to get me a job with the post office, delivering mail. Black folks could make good money with the post office, even way back then. But they wouldn't out you on no mail route. Always stick em off in a back room someplace, where nobody can't see em and get upset cause some little colored girl making as much money as the white boy working next to her. So I stuck with the C.T.C. all them years, and got my pension to prove it.

The rain still coming down steady along about three o'clock, when Max call me up say do I want to come over to her and Yvonne's for dinner. Say they fried more chicken that they can eat, and anyway Yvonne all involved in some new project she want to talk to me about. And I'm glad for the chance to get out the house. Max and Yvonne got the place all picked up for company. I can smell that fried chicken soon as I get in the door.

Yvonne don't never miss a opportunity to dress up a bit. She got the front of her hair braided up, with beads hanging all in her eyes, and a kinda loose robe-like thing, in colors look like the fruit salad at a Independence Day picnic. Max her same old self in her slacks and loafers. She ain't changed in all the years I known her—cept we both got more wrinkles and gray hairs. Yvonne a whole lot younger than us two, but she hanging in there. Her and Max been to-gether going on three years now.

Right away, Yvonne start to explain about this project she doing with her women's club. When I first heard about this club she in, I was kinda interested. But I come to find out it ain't no social club, like the Cinnamon & Spice Club used to be. It's more like a organization. Yvonne call it a collective. They never has no outings or parties or picnics or nothing—just meetings. And projects.

The project they working on right now, they all got tape recorders. And they going around tape-recording people story. Talking to people who been in the life for years and years, and asking em what it was like, back in the old days. I been in the life since before Yvonne born. But the second she stick that microphone in my face, I can't think of a blessed thing to say.

"Come on, Jinx, you always telling us all them funny old time stories."

Them little wheels is rolling round and round, and all that smooth, shiny brown tape is slipping off one reel and sliding onto the other, and I can't think of not one thing I remember.

"Tell how the Cinnamon & Spice Club got started," she say.

"I already told you about that before."

"Well tell how it ended, then. You never told me that."

"Ain't nothing to tell. Skip and Peaches broke up." Yvonne waiting, and the reels is rolling, but for the life of me I can't think of another word to say about it. And Max is sitting there grinning, like I'm the only one over thirty in the room and she don't remember a thing.

Yvonne finally give up and turn the thing off, and we go on and stuff ourselves on the chicken they fried and the greens I brung over from the garden. By the time we start in on the sweet potato pie, I have finally got to remembering. Telling Yvonne about when Skip and Peaches had they last big falling out, and they was both determine they was gonna stay in the Club—and couldn't be in the same room with one another for fifteen minutes. Both of em keep waiting on the other one to drop out, and both of em keep showing up, every time the gang get together. And none of the rest of us couldn't be in the same room with the two a them for even as long as they could stand each other. We'd be sneaking around, trying to hold a meeting without them finding out. But Peaches was the president and Skip was the treasurer, so you might say our hands was tied. Wouldn't neither one of em resign. They was both convince the Club couldn't go on without em, and by the time they was finished carrying on, they had done made sure it wouldn't.

Max is chiming in correcting all the details, every other breath come outa my mouth. And then when we all get up to go sit in the parlor again, it come out that Yvonne has sneaked that tape recording machine in here under that African poncho she got on, and has got down every word I said.

When time come to say good night, I'm thankful, for once, that Yvonne insist on driving me home—though it ain't even a whole mile. The rain ain't let up all evening, and is coming down in bucketfuls while we in the car. I'm half soaked just running from the car to the front door.

Yvonne is drove off down the street, and I'm halfway through the front door, when it hit me all of a sudden that the door ain't been locked. Now my mind may be getting a little threadbare in spots, but it ain't wore out yet. I know it's easy for me to slip back into doing things the way I done em twenty or thirty years ago, but I could swear I distinctly remember locking this door and hooking the key ring back on my belt loop, just fore Yvonne drove up in front. And now here's the door been open all this time.

Not a sign a nobody been here. Everything in its place, just like I left it. The slipcovers on the couch is smooth and neat. The candy dishes and ash trays and photographs is sitting just where they belong, on the end tables. Not even so much as a throw rug been moved a inch. I can feel my heart start to thumping like a blowout tire.

Must be, whoever come in here ain't left yet.

The idea of somebody got a nerve like that make me more mad than scared, and I know I'm gonna find out who it is broke in my house, even if it don't turn out to be nobody but them little peach-thieving rascals from round the block. Which I wouldn't be surprised if it ain't. I'm scooting from room to room, snatching open closet doors and whipping back curtains—tiptoeing down the hall and then flicking on the lights real sudden.

When I been in every room, I go back through everywhere I been, real slow, looking in all the drawers, and under the old glass doorstop in the hall, and in the back of the recipe box in the kitchen—and other places where I keep things. But it ain't nothing missing. No money—nothing.

In the end, ain't nothing left for me to do but go to bed. But I'm still feeling real uneasy. I know somebody or something done got in here while I was gone. And ain't left yet. I lay wake in the bed a long time, cause I ain't too particular about falling asleep tonight. Anyway, all this rain just make my joints swell up worse, and the pains in my knees just don't let up.

The next thing I know Gracie waking me up. She lying next to me and kissing me all over my face. I wake up laughing, and she say, "I never could see no use in shaking somebody I rather be kissing." I can feel the laughing running all through her body and mine, holding her up against my chest in the dark—knowing there must be a reason why she woke me up in the middle of the night, and pretty sure I can guess what it is. She kissing under my chin now, and starting to undo my buttons.

It seem like so long since we done this. My whole body is all a shimmer with this sweet, sweet craving. My blood is racing, singing, and her fingers is sliding inside my nightshirt. "Take it easy," I say in her ear. Cause I want this to take us a long, long time.

Outside, the sky is still wide open—the storm is throbbing and beating down on the roof over our heads, and pressing its wet self up against the window. I catch ahold of her fingers and bring em to my lips. Then I roll us both over so I can see her face. She smiling up at me through the dark, and her eyes is wide and shiny. And I run my fingers down along her breast, underneath her own nightgown. . . .

I wake up in the bed alone. It's still night. Like a flash I'm across the room, knowing I'm going after her, this time. The carpet treads is nubby and rough, flying past underneath my bare feet, and the kitchen linoleum cold and smooth. The back door standing wide open, and I push through the screen.

The storm is moved on. That fresh air feel good on my skin through the cotton nightshirt. Smell good, too, rising up outa the wet earth, and I can see the water sparkling on the leaves of the collards and kale, twinkling in the vines on the bean poles. The moon is riding high up over Thompson's field, spilling moonlight all over the yard, and setting all them blossoms on the fence to shining pure white.

There ain't a leaf twitching and there ain't a sound. I ain't moving either. I'm just gonna stay right here on this back porch. And hold still. And listen close. Cause I know Gracie somewhere in this garden. And she waiting for me.

QUESTIONS AND CONSIDERATIONS

1. What was the nature of the relationship between Jinx, the narrator, and Grace, the woman who appears in Jinx's dream? Why is Grace "the only one ever use my given name [Pearl]"?

2. What message does Grace have for Jinx when she appears in Jinx's dreams? Why does she lead Jinx to the garden? What significance did the garden have in their lives?

3. How did Jinx and Pearl manage to survive in spite of their poverty?

4. Jinx and Pearl have been fortunate to have found sympathetic friends such as Max and Yvonne who accept their lesbian relationship. What misunderstandings have they faced because of their relationship? How did they respond to these misunderstandings? How have the community's religious values made it especially difficult for the couple's life style to be tolerated?

5. What images in the story reveal the changes that have occurred in Pearl's life as she has aged? How well has she adjusted to growing older? How does she feel about her own mortality?

6. Contrast Grace's dream at the end of the story with her first dream? What is Pearl's response to the final dream, and what does her response suggest about her physical and mental state at the end of the story?

IDEAS FOR WRITING

1. Max and Yvonne attempt to get Jinx to tape-record her thoughts about her early years in "the life." Do some taped interviews with older people you know who have led unusual lives. Discuss and interpret the interviews; present some conclusions about how people change as they grow older and about how the quality of life in your community has changed.

2. Write a personal essay about a departed friend or relative who helped to shape your life and values. Discuss times when you feel conscious of the person's presence as a guiding force in your life. How and why do you think the people who have shaped our lives continue to influence us even after their death?

A Chagall Story
Richard Cortez Day

Journal

Write about a time when you felt as if you were outside of your body, observing and reflecting on your life.

One afternoon in Via della Spada, Guido Iannotti's chest knocked him over. He had been knocked over by lots of things in his long life. He remembered particularly a certain brown horse with a mean eye and a mule's trick of kicking sideways. Mamma, he almost hadn't gotten up that time. But never before had his own chest knocked him down.

As he lay there on the street, he saw faces bending over him—Paolo the greengrocer from around the corner, Fulvia from the bakery—and farther back a circle of others, acquaintances from the quarter, passersby, a tourist or two.

How serious they all were! Fulvia, with both hands to her cheeks, said, *"È morto?"* and Paolo replied, *"Morto, sì."*

Dead? Guido Iannotti dead? If they would give him a few minutes, let him rest a little, he would scramble to his feet and do a dance. But as he saw himself there on the stones, mouth open, gulping like a fish, he had to admit that they might have a point. The sickly gray color of his face, the caved-in cheeks: even at eighty a man should look better than that. Perhaps if someone would straighten his hat . . .

An ambulance nosed into the narrow street, siren howling, and the crowd parted respectfully. But it kept right on going. Guido rose to follow it with his eyes. *Madonna Santa,* it was on another mission! He looked down and saw a second ambulance, this one silent, stopping beside the form on the sidewalk. Two men got out, in no rush at all. They lifted him as if he weighed no more than a picture of himself. "Hey, easy—watch my hat!" he said.

One of the men picked up his hat and tossed it in after him. Guido dove for a look. He saw his shoe soles, like the letter *V,* and, within the *V,* the yellow flower in his buttonhole and the bottom of the jaw he'd been shaving for more than sixty years. The men closed the doors. They got in and drove away. Guido watched. No, they weren't heading for the hospital.

Fulvia, with flour on her cheeks, crossed herself. The passersby moved on. Paolo went back into his shop, where a customer was testing the pears. "Hey, signora," he said, "buy first, then squeeze!" Within a few minutes, life was back to normal in Via della Spada. Guido was gone and forgotten.

"So, I'm a spirit," he said. "So this is what it's like." He knocked a ripe pear onto the floor right under Paolo's nose. Paolo squinted and scratched his head. *"Aou,* I'm invisible," Guido said. He rolled three tomatoes out of the box, knocked another pear to the floor, and flung a bunch of grapes at Paolo's feet. Paolo was the kind who hid inferior fruit under the good ones, who short-changed you unless you counted every lira, who weighed his hand with the vegetables. Guido had bought that hand a thousand times. He turned the cashbox upside down and let the bills flutter. Paolo rolled his eyes, crossed himself, howled like a dog.

This was sport. This was revenge. How he'd longed to get even with that tyrant Paolo. He felt better than he'd felt for a long while. Where was the old ache in his hip? They must have carted it off in the ambulance. He felt like getting out and doing things. But since he wasn't sure how much time he had before going to heaven, he thought he should get home and put his affairs in order. He had always made duty his first priority. He didn't want to leave a mess for his daughter—it wouldn't be right.

In Via del Moro, how often he'd cursed the darkness. It wasn't a street, it was a slit between rows of houses. It might have been fine for an astronomer—you could set your clock by the flash the sun made as it passed over—but for the people who had to live there, well, he was surprised they weren't as blind as moles. What did they need eyes for? They got where they were going by touching the walls.

The stairway to his apartment had been his cross to bear. Eight flights, eighty-eight steps, and with what reward at the top? A cramped dungeon of a place, a kind of subcellar, as if they'd built the house upside down. He and his wife had raised three children there, the whole family pale as mushrooms, and then their daughter, Lisa, and her husband had moved in and raised their two, and now one of those two had come back with *her* husband, to raise yet more children in the gloom. There had always been plenty of children. Laura, bless her, had died ten years ago because of her weight. To climb the stairs, she'd had to work twice as hard as Guido. Finally, her heart gave out.

This time, he skipped up the steps and wasn't even winded. In the apartment he saw that the family had already heard. News travels fast in the Santa Maria Novella quarter; Lisa was already wearing black. But what was this? Her husband, Marco, who was too lazy to work and get an apartment of his own, was going through the dresser, throwing Guido's things out, putting his own clothes in the drawers. And look, there on the bed, all his personal belongings—his letters, the pictures he'd saved, Laura's wedding ring, his documents, his keys, his pocketknife, his own wedding ring! Lisa and Marco were going through everything, moving into his room, and him not even decently buried yet. Look at them, stretching out on the bed, bouncing, testing it! His own family, the ungrateful wretches!

But then a thought crossed his mind. Could there have been a funeral already, and he'd missed it? Perhaps they'd put him in the ground with proper ceremonies and tears, with the jonquil in his buttonhole, with his hat resting on his chest. While he'd been kicking fruit around Paolo's shop, perhaps the funeral had come and gone. In this spirit life, he could see, he was still a puppy. He had a lot to learn. Where, for example, did one catch the bus for heaven? Shouldn't there be an angel picking him up about now, or at least a notice pinned up somewhere?

He left his family to their predictable concerns. Life was for the living, and he wanted no part of it. Let Lisa and her husband have the sagging bed, the old backbreaker; let them go on dragging their bodies up the stairs. That was life? All that labor? And for what? Free as a bird, he took a few turns around Piazza Santa Maria Novella, keeping an eye out for the angel. On a cornice of the church, he sat next to a pigeon. Down below, two priests strolled in the April sunshine. There were young lovers, hurrying businessmen, gawking tourists. He dove from the ledge, swooped low, and like a lark fired up and over the buildings to the train station. Perhaps it wouldn't be a bus, but one of those trains, a funicular, like he'd ridden on his honeymoon at Vesuvius.

But there was nothing at the station, either. If he could find some other spirits . . . Where in Florence would spirits hang out? He sailed over the Arno and tried Santa Maria del Carmine, then Santo Spirito. Nothing doing. He swung back across the river to the big cathedral, the Duomo, and alighted on the main altar. There was a mass in progress. To get some attention, he hovered right over the priest's head, then blew out one of the candles, but the priest went right on with his sermon. Guido fanned his notes onto the floor, but he kept talking, the old fool. All is vanity, remember that you too will die, and so forth. The idiot. Guido, with exquisite pleasure, spiraled up into the dome, then plunged and did hair-raising turns at floor level around the rows of columns. Then he shot from the church right through a ten-foot-thick stone wall. He didn't get a scratch.

At Santa Croce and San Miniato al Monte, he fared no better than at the other churches. Nothing but people, no angels, no other spirits. Had he missed the helicopter? Where was the elevator? He drifted into All Saints' for a look around, and there, in the right transept, in a glass case, he saw the *corpo incorrotto,* the uncorrupted remains, of Saint Giacomo Melanzane, who had been archbishop of Florence from A.D. 1389 until 1439.

The body wasn't exactly fresh, but it was still recognizable as a man's, though the face was shrunken, leathery, and brown, and the miter had tipped a bit forward on the brow. But there were the eyes, the nose, and the down-turned, sour-looking mouth. In fact, the saint, in Guido's estimation, looked pretty much like he himself would have looked with a few hundred more years on him.

But miracle of miracles! The eyes opened a little and looked sideways. With the smallest of gestures, but unmistakable in meaning, the head moved: come here.

"In there?" Guido said.

The saint nodded. With some distaste, Guido went through the glass.

It wasn't too bad. The see-through coffin, though not large, contained the two of them easily, and there was only a faint dusty smell, like very dry leaves. He said, "Thank you, Your Reverence. I was beginning to think I was alone in the universe."

"You are. And call me Giacco. It's good of you to call. I haven't had a decent conversation in God knows how long. It's too bad we can't have coffee. That's the one thing I miss most. I like it strong, black, sweet—almost syrup. It puts hair on your chest. Remember the taste? Remember how the first swallow goes straight to your brain?"

"Yes, I remember," Guido said. "But what I want to know is, how do I get to heaven? I seem to be stuck here, between two worlds. I must have missed something."

"Heaven? Ha, there isn't any."

"There isn't? Just hell, then? I thought . . ."

"No hell, either. I don't know where those notions come from—it was long before my time. Anyway, they're false."

"But there must be an afterlife. Look, we're talking, and we're both dead."

"We're that, all right. Look at me. Would you believe I used to be over six feet tall? You're lucky—they plopped you right in the ground. They tanned me like a horsehide and left me to be stared at. It's humiliating. The loathing, the disgust on people's faces—it's like being a leper. Everyone turns away."

"But you're Saint Melanzane. I thought saints were enthroned in splendor, close to God."

"You've been in the Baptistery, I see. Idiot artists! What thrones? What God? Anyway, where would you set up a throne? It's just air up there. It's less than air. What would you stand a throne on?"

"Then this is all there is?"

"It could be worse. Cheer up. Have you tried hovering and swooping? Sailing's a lot of fun. You can go through walls, you know, and play tricks on people."

"I've done all that. It's—forgive me—kind of boring, isn't it? Where are all the other spirits? There must be millions of us, somewhere."

"You're new at this. You've got to stop thinking of where and when, for there aren't any. Millions, you say? Billions—quadrillions. They're out in the universe, mostly. You almost never meet one. No, this is it—you're on your own. Do what you can with what you've got."

"But, Your Reverence—"

"Stop that. Do I look like a thing to be revered?"

"Well then, Giacco. The universe—you admit there is one. But you say there's no God. So where did the universe come from?"

"Oy, one of those. Just my luck. I never see anyone, and when someone comes along, he turns out to be a philosopher! Sludge, that's where it came from. A big gob of sludge."

"Then who created the sludge?"

"How do I know? It created itself, then diversified. It turned itself into sun and moons, trees, birds, bugs, and people, not to mention lions and lambs. It's all sludge, when you break it down."

"The soul?"

"Sludge."

"Christ? Mary? The Apostles?"

"Yep. Say, there's a nun in a box over at Santissima Annunziata. Saint Ambrosia, I think her name is. Why don't you coast over and have a chat with her? She might like some company. If I remember right, she was a real student of these questions. Augustine, Jerome, Aquinas—they were her boys. Pop over there, she's a laugh a minute, or used to be."

"All right, I'll go see her," Guido said. "But is this all you do, lie here and grump, until you get another body to inhabit?"

"Get another body? Does that happen?"

"I don't know, Giacco—you're the archbishop. I've heard of it, that's all I can say. It's called reincarnation."

"Wouldn't you know? As if once wasn't enough. Twice yet. But maybe it won't happen. I've never heard of it. Can we choose a body, do you think, or do we take potluck? What if it was a cow or pig? Or a toad? What if it was a woman? Imagine that!"

"Maybe it won't happen," Guido said. "Don't be upset. I'm sorry I brought it up."

"Another body, Jesus." He fell silent for a few moments. Then he brightened. "Say, would you like to go out for a while, hover some? We could shoot down to Rome. The Vatican's nice—very well kept up. Or we could swing down around Africa—"

"No thanks," Guido said. "I want to find my wife if I can. Her name is Laura—gray-haired, overweight? You haven't seen her, have you?"

"Ha. You've got lots to learn about the way things work. You're still too close to life—you think the way people think. What's a wife? Sludge—in a shape of sorts, soft, squishy, with a pocket to reach into and pull babies out of, eh? What say we whip out to Mars and back? Want to race?"

"Another time maybe. I think I'll hang around some. Maybe I'll come across her."

"Fat chance."

"Well, see you later."

"There isn't any. You're a case. There should be a school for infants like you. Later, before, after, once upon a time: you'll stop thinking like that. Take a swoop or two out in the universe. Come back smarter, kid."

Guido eased through the glass, through the side wall of the church, and shot up over the city. He did a parabola, falling to, through, the roof of Santissima Annunziata. Ah, there below the altar, in a glass coffin, was the nun that Giacco had mentioned. Now for some answers. "Psst," he said. "Psst, Ambrosia!" She lay, or her body did, in classic repose, hands folded on her breast. Where her spirit was, who could say? Maybe she'd gone for a spin. Maybe she was lost in theological speculation. He couldn't get a word out of her.

He noticed a very old but familiar-looking woman kneeling at the altar before the coffin. "Mamma?" he said. He hovered before the wrinkled face. Then he saw the rings—her own, Laura's, and one on her right thumb, his. Could it be? This ancient creature was his daughter Lisa, whom he'd just left that morning in Via del Moro.

Her husband had died? Her daughter, too? For her to be wearing the rings, the whole family must have died. Had there been an epidemic? Were all the Iannottis dead?

He fired from the church and zipped straight to Via del Moro. In the apartment he found a strange young woman nursing a baby. Lisa must have moved. He didn't recognize any of the furniture. Thoughtfully, he cruised Via delle Belle Donne, Via della Spada, and the other streets in the maze off Piazza Santa Maria Novella. Paolo was gone, his shop converted to a shoestore, and though Fulvia's bakery was still there, he knew neither the owner nor the customers. On the facade of the church, pigeons still perched, but who knew how many generations of pigeons had lived and died since he'd lived in the quarter?

Had lived? Did live! He was more alive now than ever! Like a hummingbird, he shot straight up into the haze above the city. That meandering path of blue light down there—it was his beloved river, the Arno—and the big patch of green: what else but Cascine Park, where he and Laura had walked on Sunday when they were young. The red tile roofs, the broad boulevards, the parks, the labyrinthine narrow streets: that was Florence down there, filling the valley, busy as an anthill, lovely. With a city that complex and fascinating, why would he want a universe!

He tipped forward and shot down into it. This was where she would be—she'd loved the city as much as he did. Yellow was her color. Laura and yellow. Why else had he worn a yellow flower in his buttonhole for all those years? There, just above that border of jonquils—Laura?

No, but this was where she would come to—this park. The universe might be endless, but so was eternity. That improved the odds considerably. He wove among the yellow flowers, wove a pattern in the air above the grass, constructing an attractive design. The jonquils moved in the April breeze. He hovered brightly, giving off all the light he had.

QUESTIONS AND CONSIDERATIONS

1. In the opening paragraphs of the story, what do we learn about Guido Iannotti? How old is he? Is he a "survivor" type? Is he a sophisticated person?

2. How does Guido gradually come to understand that he is, in fact, dead? What evidence is presented? What seems to have caused his death?

3. What is Guido's attitude toward his death? How does he use his new status for his own amusement and revenge?

4. What is Guido's attitude toward his family and his daughter, Lisa? How does his attitude change as the story develops?

5. How does Guido's attitude toward life and religion change as he comes to accept his new status as one of the dead? What does Saint Melanzane reveal to Guido about the universe, the existence of God, and creation? Do you agree with the ideas expressed by the saint?

6. At the end of the story, Guido finds himself in the future. How does he capture the soul of his long-deceased wife, Laura? What view of life and death is suggested by the story's final image: "He hovered brightly, giving off all the light he had"?

IDEAS FOR WRITING

1. Develop a fantasy, either in essay or story form, in which you imagine yourself free of your body as Guido is in this story. What would you do with your time? Where would you go? Who would you seek out? What questions would you want to have answered? What would you try to change?

2. Develop an essay that presents a response to the views of the saint with whom Guido converses in the church. Do you agree or disagree with the saint's perspective on God, creation, and the afterlife?

Essays

Grandmother's Country

N. Scott Momaday

Journal

Write about a place that has spiritual or ancestral significance for you: a family home, a public building, or a natural setting.

A single knoll rises out of the plain in Oklahoma, north and west of the Wichita Range. For my people, the Kiowas, it is an old landmark, and they gave it the name Rainy Mountain. The hardest weather in the world is there. Winter brings blizzards, hot tornadic winds arise in the spring, and in summer the prairie is an anvil's edge. The grass turns brittle and brown, and it cracks beneath your feet. There are green belts along the rivers and creeks, linear groves of hickory and pecan, willow and witch hazel. At a distance in July or August the steaming foliage seems almost to writhe in fire. Great green and yellow grasshoppers are everywhere in the tall grass, popping up like corn to sting the flesh, and tortoises crawl about on the red earth, going nowhere in the plenty of time. Loneliness is an aspect of the land. All things in the plain are isolate; there is no confusion of objects in the eye, but *one* hill or *one* tree or *one* man. To look upon that landscape in the early morning, with the sun at your back, is to lose the sense of proportion. Your imagination comes to life, and this, you think, is where Creation was begun.

I returned to Rainy Mountain in July. My grandmother had died in the spring, and I wanted to be at her grave. She had lived to be very old and at last infirm. Her only living daughter was with her when she died, and I was told that in death her face was that of a child.

I like to think of her as a child. When she was born, the Kiowas were living the last great moment of their history. For more than a hundred years they had controlled the open range from the Smoky Hill River to the Red, from the headwaters of the Canadian to the fork of the Arkansas and Cimarron. In alliance with the Comanches, they had ruled the whole of the southern Plains. War was their sacred business, and they were among the finest horsemen the world has ever known. But warfare for the Kiowas was preeminently a matter of disposition rather than of survival, and they never understood the grim, unrelenting advance of the U.S. Cavalry. When at last, divided and ill-provisioned, they were driven onto the Staked Plains in the cold rains of autumn, they fell into panic. In Palo Duro Canyon they abandoned their crucial stores to pillage and had nothing then but their lives. In order to save themselves, they surrendered to the soldiers at Fort Sill and were imprisoned in the old stone corral that now stands as a military museum. My grandmother was spared the humiliation of those high gray walls by eight or ten years, but she must have known from birth the affliction of defeat, the dark brooding of old warriors.

Her name was Aho, and she belonged to the last culture to evolve in North America. Her forebears came down from the high country in western Montana nearly three centuries ago. They were a mountain people, a mysterious tribe of hunters whose language has never been positively classified in any major group. In the late seventeenth century they began a long migration to the south and east. It was a journey toward the dawn, and it led to a golden age. Along the way the Kiowas were befriended by the Crows, who gave them the culture and religion of the Plains. They acquired horses, and their ancient nomadic spirit was suddenly free of the ground. They acquired Tai-me, the sacred Sun Dance doll, from that moment the object and symbol of their worship, and so shared in the divinity of the sun. Not least, they acquired the sense of destiny, therefore courage and pride. When they entered upon the southern Plains they had been transformed. No longer were they slaves to the simple necessity of survival; they were a lordly and dangerous society of fighters and thieves, hunters and priests of the sun. According to their origin myth, they entered the world through a hollow log. From one point of view, their migration was the fruit of an old prophecy, for indeed they emerged from a sunless world.

Although my grandmother lived out her long life in the shadow of Rainy Mountain, the immense landscape of the continental interior lay like memory in her blood. She could tell of the Crows, whom she had never seen, and of the Black Hills, where she had never been. I wanted to see in reality what she had seen more perfectly in the mind's eye, and traveled fifteen hundred miles to begin my pilgrimage.

Yellowstone, it seemed to me, was the top of the world, a region of deep lakes and dark timber, canyons and waterfalls. But, beautiful as it is, one might have the sense of confinement there. The skyline in all directions is close at hand, the high wall of the woods and deep cleavages of shade. There is a perfect freedom in the mountains, but it belongs to the eagle and the elk, the badger and the bear. The Kiowas reckoned their stature by the distance they could see, and they were bent and blind in the wilderness.

Descending eastward, the highland meadows are a stairway to the plain. In July the inland slope of the Rockies is luxuriant with flax and buckwheat, stonecrop and larkspur. The earth unfolds and the limit of the land recedes. Clusters of trees, and animals grazing far in the distance, cause the vision to reach away and wonder to build upon the mind. The sun follows a longer course in the day, and the sky is immense beyond all comparison. The great billowing clouds that sail upon it are shadows that move upon the grain like water, dividing light. Farther down, in the land of the Crows and Blackfeet, the plain is yellow. Sweet clover takes hold of the hills and bends upon itself to cover and seal the soil. There the Kiowas paused on their way; they had come to the place where they must change their lives. The sun is at home on the plains. Precisely there does it have the certain character of a god. When the Kiowas came to the land of the Crows, they could see the dark lees of the hills at dawn across the Bighorn River, the profusion of light on the grain shelves, the oldest deity ranging after the solstices. Not yet would they veer southward to the caldron of the land that lay below; they must wean their blood from the northern winter and hold the mountains a while longer in their view. They bore Tai-me in procession to the east.

A dark mist lay over the Black Hills, and the land was like iron. At the top of a ridge I caught sight of Devil's Tower upthrust against the gray sky as if in the birth of time the core of the earth had broken through its crust and the motion of the world was begun. There are things in nature that engender an awful quiet in the heart of man; Devil's Tower is one of them. Two centuries ago, because they could not do otherwise, the Kiowas made a legend at the base of the rock. My grandmother said:

> Eight children were there at play, seven sisters and their brother. Suddenly the boy was struck dumb; he trembled and began to run upon his hands and feet. His fingers became claws, and his body was covered with fur. Directly there was a bear where the boy had been. The sisters were terrified; they ran, and the bear after them. They came to the stump of a great tree, and the tree spoke to them. It bade them climb upon it, and as they did so it began to rise into the air. The bear came to kill them, but they were just beyond its reach. It reared against the tree and scored the bark all around with its claws. The seven sisters were borne into the sky, and they became the stars of the Big Dipper.

From that moment, and so long as the legend lives, the Kiowas have kinsmen in the night sky. Whatever they were in the mountains, they could be no more. However tenuous their well-being, however much they had suffered and would suffer again, they had found a way out of the wilderness.

My grandmother had a reverence for the sun, a holy regard that now is all but gone out of mankind. There was a wariness in her, and an ancient awe. She was a Christian in her later years, but she had come a long way about, and she never forgot her birthright. As a child she had been to the Sun Dances; she had taken part in those annual rites, and by them she had learned the restoration of her people in the presence of Tai-me. She was about seven when the last Kiowa Sun Dance was held in 1887 on the Washita River above Rainy Mountain Creek. The buffalo were gone. In order to consummate the ancient sacrifice—to impale the head of a buffalo bull upon the medicine tree—a delegation of old men journeyed into Texas, there to beg and barter for an animal from the Goodnight herd. She was ten when the Kiowas came together for the last time as a living Sun Dance culture. They could find no buffalo; they had to hang an old hide from the sacred tree. Before the dance could begin, a company of soldiers rode out from Fort Sill under orders to disperse the tribe. Forbidden without cause the essential act of their faith, having seen the wild herds slaughtered and left to rot upon the ground, the Kiowas backed away forever from the medicine tree. That was July 20, 1890, at the great bend of the Washita. My grandmother was there. Without bitterness, and for as long as she lived, she bore a vision of deicide.

Now that I can have her only in memory, I see my grandmother in the several postures that were peculiar to her: standing at the wood stove on a winter morning and turning meat in a great iron skillet; sitting at the south window, bent above her beadwork, and afterwards, when her vision failed, looking down for a long time into the fold of her hands; going out upon a cane, very slowly as she did when the weight of age came upon her; praying. I remember her most often at prayer. She made long, rambling prayers out of suffering and hope, having seen many things. I was never sure that I had the right to hear, so exclusive were they of all mere custom and company. The last time I saw her she prayed standing by the side of her bed at night, naked to the waist, the light of a kerosene lamp moving upon her dark skin. Her long, black hair, always drawn and braided in the day, lay upon her shoulders and against her breasts like a shawl. I do not speak Kiowa, and I never understood her prayers, but there was something inherently sad in the sound, some merest hesitation upon the syllables of sorrow. She began in a high and descending pitch, exhausting her breath to silence; then again and again—and always the same intensity of effort, of something that is, and is not, like urgency in the human voice. Transported so in the dancing light among the shadows of her room, she seemed beyond the reach of time. But that was illusion; I think I knew then that I should not see her again.

Houses are like sentinels in the plain, old keepers of the weather watch. There, in a very little while, wood takes on the appearance of great age. All colors wear soon away in the wind and rain, and then the wood is burned gray and the grain appears and the nails turn red with rust. The windowpanes are black and opaque; you imagine there is nothing within, and indeed there are many ghosts, bones given up to the land. They stand here and there against the sky, and you approach them for a longer time than you expect. They belong in the distance; it is their domain.

Once there was a lot of sound in my grandmother's house, a lot of coming and going, feasting and talk. The summers there were full of excitement and reunion. The Kiowas are a summer people; they abide the cold and keep to themselves, but when the season turns and the land becomes warm and vital they cannot hold still; an old love of going returns upon them. The aged visitors who came to my grandmother's house when I was a child were made of lean and leather, and they bore themselves upright. They wore great black hats and bright ample shirts that shook in the wind. They rubbed fat upon their hair and wound their braids with strips of colored cloth. Some of them painted their faces and carried the scars of old and cherished enmities. They were an old council of warlords, come to remind and be reminded of who they were. Their wives and daughters served them well. The women might indulge themselves; gossip was at once the mark and compensation of their servitude. They made loud and elaborate talk among themselves, full of jest and gesture, fright and false alarm. They went abroad in fringed and flowered shawls, bright beadwork and German silver. They were at home in the kitchen, and they prepared meals that were banquets.

There were frequent prayer meetings, and great nocturnal feasts. When I was a child I played with my cousins outside, where the lamplight fell upon the ground and the singing of the old people rose up around us and carried away into the darkness. There were a lot of good things to eat, a lot of laughter and surprise. And afterwards, when the quiet returned, I lay down with my grandmother and could hear the frogs away by the river and feel the motion of the air.

Now there is a funeral silence in the rooms, the endless wake of some final word. The walls have closed in upon my grandmother's house. When I returned to it in mourning, I saw for the first time in my life how small it was. It was late at night, and there was a white moon, nearly full. I sat for a long time on the stone steps by the kitchen door. From there I could see out across the land; I could see the long row of trees by the creek, the low light upon the rolling plains, and the stars of the Big Dipper. Once I looked at the moon and caught sight of a strange thing. A cricket had perched upon the handrail, only a few inches away from me. My line of vision was such that the creature filled the moon like a fossil. It had gone there, I thought, to live and die, for there, of all places, was its small definition made whole and eternal. A warm wind rose up and purled like the longing within me.

The next morning I awoke at dawn and went out on the dirt road to Rainy Mountain. It was already hot, and the grasshoppers began to fill the air. Still, it was early in the morning, and the birds sang out of the shadows. The long yellow grass on the mountain shone in the bright light, and a scissortail hied above the land. There, where it ought to be, at the end of a long and legendary way, was my grandmother's grave. Here and there on the dark stones were ancestral names. Looking back once, I saw the mountain and came away.

QUESTIONS AND CONSIDERATIONS

1. What is the significance of the knoll that the Kiowas call Rainy Mountain? Why does Momaday believe that Rainy Mountain seems to be "where Creation was begun"? How does the mountain make the imagination "come to life"?

2. Momaday describes Rainy Mountain as having "the hardest weather in the world." What details does he use to demonstrate the truth of this statement?

3. Why does Momaday travel fifteen hundred miles "to begin my pilgrimage"? What is the purpose and destination of his pilgrimage? What is Momaday trying to learn or discover?

4. What is the significance of the legend of Devil's Tower told to Momaday by his grandmother? What does this legend reveal about the values of the Kiowas? How is the legend evoked indirectly by the image of the cricket reflected against the moon? How do the legend and the image of the cricket finally help Momaday to reconcile himself to his grandmother's death?

5. What was the purpose of the Kiowa Sun Dance? What vision of defeat did Momaday's grandmother bear all her life, "without bitterness"? Why wasn't she bitter?

6. How do Momaday's vivid memories of his grandmother's home and the activities that took place there reinforce his sense of the value and significance of his grandmother's life and that of the Kiowa people?

IDEAS FOR WRITING

1. Choose a Native American culture or of another group and do research into the importance to this group of particular rituals such as the Sun Dance described in Momaday's essay. You might compare the function of the Native American rituals to the dominant rituals of devotion and continuity that are central in modern American culture. Write your conclusions in the form of a brief research paper.

2. Write an essay about revisiting a familiar place from your past that is haunted by "ghosts" of memory. What do these memories reveal to you about the differences between your present values and those that you were taught as a child?

Kubota
Garrett Hongo

Journal

Write a journal entry in which you reflect on the meaning of the life of one of your older relatives. Discuss how particular choices in this person's life have influenced your own decisions.

On December 8, 1941, the day after the Japanese attack on Pearl Harbor in Hawaii, my grandfather barricaded himself with his family—my grandmother, my teenage mother, her two sisters and two brothers—inside of his home in La'ie, a sugar plantation village on Oahu's North Shore. This was my maternal grandfather, a man most villagers called by his last name, Kubota. It could mean either "Wayside Field" or else "Broken Dreams," depending on which ideograms he used. Kubota ran La'ie's general store, and the previous night, after a long day of bad news on the radio, some locals had come by, pounded on the front door, and made threats. One was said to have brandished a machete. They were angry and shocked, as the whole nation was in the aftermath of the surprise attack. Kubota was one of the few Japanese Americans in the village and president of the local Japanese language school. He had become a target for their rage and suspicion. A wise man, he locked all his doors and windows and did not open his store the next day, but stayed closed and waited for news from some official.

He was a *kibei,* a Japanese American born in Hawaii (a U.S. territory then, so he was thus a citizen) but who was subsequently sent back by his father for formal education in Hiroshima, Japan, their home province. *Kibei* is written with two ideograms in Japanese: one is the word for "return" and the other is the word for "rice." Poetically, it means one who returns from America, known as the Land of Rice in Japanese (by contrast, Chinese immigrants called their new home Mountain of Gold).

Kubota was graduated from a Japanese high school and then came back to Hawaii as a teenager. He spoke English—and a Hawaiian creole version of it at that—with a Japanese accent. But he was well liked and good at numbers, scrupulous and hard working like so many immigrants and children of immigrants. Castle & Cook, a grower's company that ran the sugarcane business along the North Shore, hired him on first as a stock boy and then appointed him to run one of its company stores. He did well, had the trust of management and labor—not an easy accomplishment in any day—married, had children, and had begun to exert himself in community affairs and excel in his own recreations. He put together a Japanese community organization that backed a Japanese language school for children and sponsored teachers from Japan. Kubota boarded many of them, in succession, in his own home. This made dinners a silent affair for his talkative, Hawaiian-bred children, as their stern *sensei,* or teacher, was nearly always at table and their own abilities in the Japanese language were as delinquent as their attendance. While Kubota and the *sensei* rattled on about things Japanese, speaking Japanese, his children hurried through their suppers and tried to run off early to listen to the radio shows.

After dinner, while the *sensei* graded exams seated in a wicker chair in the spare room and his wife and children gathered around the radio in the front parlor, Kubota sat on the screened porch outside, reading the local Japanese newspapers. He finished reading about the same time as he finished the tea he drank for his digestion—a habit he'd learned in Japan—and then he'd get out his fishing gear and spread it out on the plank floors. The wraps on his rods needed to be redone, gears in his reels needed oil, and, once through with those tasks, he'd painstakingly wind on hundreds of yards of new line. Fishing was his hobby and his passion. He spent weekends camping along the North Shore beaches with his children, setting up umbrella tents, packing a rice pot and hibachi along for meals. And he caught fish. *Ulu'a* mostly, the huge surf-feeding fish known on the mainland as the jack crevalle, but he'd go after almost anything in its season. In Kawela, a plantation-owned bay nearby, he fished for mullet Hawaiian-style with a throw net, stalking the bottom-hugging, gray-backed schools as they gathered at the stream mouths and in the freshwater springs. In an outrigger out beyond the reef, he'd try for *aku*—the skipjack tuna prized for steaks and, sliced raw and mixed with fresh seaweed and cut onions, for *sashimi* salad. In Kahaluu and Ka'awa and on an offshore rock locals called Goat Island, he loved to go torching, stringing lanterns on bamboo poles stuck in the sand to attract *kumu'u,* the red goatfish, as they schooled at night just inside the reef. But in Lai'e on Laniloa Point near

Kahuku, the northernmost tip of Oahu, he cast twelve- and fourteen-foot surf rods for the huge, varicolored, and fast-running *ulu'a* as they ran for schools of squid and baitfish just beyond the biggest breakers and past the low sand flats wadable from the shore to nearly a half mile out. At sunset, against the western light, he looked as if he walked on water as he came back, fish and rods slung over his shoulders, stepping along the rock and coral path just inches under the surface of a running tide.

When it was torching season, in December or January, he'd drive out the afternoon before and stay with old friends, the Tanakas or Yoshikawas, shopkeepers like him who ran stores near the fishing grounds. They'd have been preparing for weeks, selecting and cutting their bamboo poles, cleaning the hurricane lanterns, tearing up burlap sacks for the cloths they'd soak with kerosene and tie onto sticks they'd poke into the soft sand of the shallows. Once lit, touched off with a Zippo lighter, these would be the torches they'd use as beacons to attract the schooling fish. In another time, they might have made up a dozen paper lanterns of the kind mostly used for decorating the summer folk dances outdoors on the grounds of the Buddhist church during O-Bon, the Festival for the Dead. But now, wealthy and modern and efficient killers of fish, Tanaka and Kubota used rag torches and Colemans and cast rods with tips made of Tonkin bamboo and butts of American-spun fiberglass. After just one good night, they might bring back a prize bounty of a dozen burlap bags filled with scores of bloody, rigid fish delicious to eat and even better to give away as gifts to friends, family, and special customers.

It was a Monday night, the day after Pearl Harbor, and there was a rattling knock at the front door. Two FBI agents presented themselves, showed identification, and took my grandfather in for questioning in Honolulu. He didn't return home for days. No one knew what had happened or what was wrong. But there was a roundup going on of all those in the Japanese-American community suspected of sympathizing with the enemy and worse. My grandfather was suspected of espionage, of communicating with offshore Japanese submarines launched from the attack fleet days before war began. Torpedo planes and escort fighters, decorated with the insignia of the Rising Sun, had taken an approach route from northwest of Oahu directly across Kahuku Point and on toward Pearl. They had strafed an auxiliary air station near the fishing grounds my grandfather loved and destroyed a small gun battery there, killing three men. Kubota was known to have sponsored and harbored Japanese nationals in his own home. He had a radio. He had wholesale access to firearms. Circumstances and an undertone of racial resentment had combined with wartime hysteria in the aftermath of the tragic naval battle to cast suspicion on the loyalties of my grandfather and all other Japanese Americans. The FBI reached out and pulled hundreds of them in for questioning in dragnets cast throughout the West Coast and Hawaii.

My grandfather was lucky; he'd somehow been let go after only a few days. Others were not as fortunate. Hundreds, from small communities in Washington, California, Oregon, and Hawaii, were rounded up and, after what appeared to be routine questioning, shipped off under Justice Department orders to holding centers in Leuppe on the Navaho reservation in Arizona, in Fort Missoula in Montana, and on Sand Island in Honolulu Harbor. There were other special camps on Maui in Ha'iku and on Hawaii—the Big Island—in my own home village of Volcano.

Many of these men—it was exclusively the Japanese-American men suspected of ties to Japan who were initially rounded up—did not see their families again for more than four years. Under a suspension of due process that was only after the fact ruled as warranted by military necessity, they were, if only temporarily, "disappeared" in Justice Department prison camps scattered in particularly desolate areas of the United States designated as militarily "safe." These were grim forerunners of the assembly centers and concentration camps for the 120,000 Japanese-American evacuees that were to come later.

I am Kubota's eldest grandchild, and I remember him as a lonely, habitually silent old man who lived with us in our home near Los Angeles for most of my childhood and adolescence. It was the fifties, and my parents had emigrated from Hawaii to the mainland in the hope of a better life away from the old sugar plantation. After some success, they had sent back for my grandparents and taken them in. And it was my grandparents who did the work of the household while my mother and father worked their salaried city jobs. My grandmother cooked and sewed, washed our clothes, and knitted in the front room under the light of a huge lamp with a bright three-way bulb. Kubota raised a flower garden, read up on soils and grasses in gardening books, and planted a zoysia lawn in front and a dichondra one in back. He planted a small patch near the rear block wall with green onions, eggplant, white Japanese radishes, and cucumber. While he hoed and spaded the loamless, clayey earth of Los Angeles, he sang particularly plangent songs in Japanese about plum blossoms and bamboo groves.

Once, in the mid-sixties, after a dinner during which, as always, he had been silent while he worked away at a meal of fish and rice spiced with dabs of Chinese mustard and catsup thinned with soy sauce, Kubota took his own dishes to the kitchen sink and washed them up. He took a clean jelly jar out of the cupboard—the glass was thick and its shape squatty like an old-fashioned. He reached around to the hutch below where he kept his bourbon. He made himself a drink and retired to the living room where I was expected to join him for "talk story," the Hawaiian idiom for chewing the fat.

I was a teenager and, though I was bored listening to stories I'd heard often enough before at holiday dinners, I was dutiful. I took my spot on the couch next to Kubota and heard him out. Usually, he'd tell me about his schooling in Japan where he learned judo along with mathematics and literature. He'd learned the *soroban* there—the abacus, which was the original pocket calculator of the Far East—and that, along with his strong, judo-trained back, got him his first job in Hawaii. This was the moral. "Study *ha-ahd*," he'd say with pidgin emphasis. "Learn read good. Learn speak da kine *good* English." The message is the familiar one taught to any children of immigrants: succeed through education. And imitation. But this time, Kubota reached down into his past and told me a different story. I was thirteen by then, and I suppose he thought me ready for it. He told me about Pearl Harbor, how the planes flew in wing after wing of formations over his old house in La'ie in Hawaii, and how, the next day, after Roosevelt had made his famous "Day of Infamy" speech about the treachery of the Japanese, the FBI agents had come to his door and taken him in, hauled him off to Honolulu for questioning, and held him without charge for several days. I thought he was lying. I thought he was making up a kind of horror story to shock me and give his moral that much more starch. But it was true. I asked around. I brought it up during history class in junior high school, and my teacher, after silencing me and stepping me off to the back of the room, told me that it was indeed so. I asked my mother and she said it was true. I asked my schoolmates, who laughed and ridiculed me for being so ignorant. We lived in a Japanese-American community, and the parents of most of my classmates were the *nisei* who had been interned as teenagers all through the war. But there was a strange silence around all of this. There was a hush, as if one were invoking the ill powers of the dead when one brought it up. No one cared to speak about the evacuation and relocation for very long. It wasn't in our history books, though we were studying World War II at the time. It wasn't in the family albums of the people I knew and whom I'd visit staying over weekends with friends. And it wasn't anything that the family talked about or allowed me to keep bringing up either. I was given the facts, told sternly and pointedly that "it was war" and that "nothing could be done." *"Shikatta ga nai"* is the phrase in Japanese, a kind of resolute and determinist pronouncement on how to deal with inexplicable tragedy. I was to know it but not to dwell on it. Japanese Americans were busy trying to forget it ever happened and were having a hard enough time building their new lives after "camp." It was as if we had no history for four years and the relocation was something unspeakable.

But Kubota would not let it go. In session after session, for months it seemed, he pounded away at his story. He wanted to tell me the names of the FBI agents. He went over their questions and his responses again and again. He'd tell me how one would try to act friendly toward him, offering him cigarettes while the other, who hounded him with accusations and threats, left the interrogation room. Good cop, bad cop, I thought to myself already superficially street wise from stories black classmates told of the Watts riots and from my having watched too many episodes of *Dragnet* and *The Mod Squad.* But Kubota was not interested in my experiences. I was not made yet, and he was determined that his stories be part of my making. He spoke quietly at first, mildly, but once into his narrative and after his drink was down, his voice would rise and quaver with resentment and he'd make his accusations. He gave his testimony to me and I held it at first cautiously in my conscience like it was an heirloom too delicate to expose to strangers and anyone outside of the world Kubota made with his words. "I give you story now," he once said, "and you learn speak good, eh?" It was my job, as the disciple of his preaching I had then become, Ananda to his Buddha, to reassure him with a promise. "You learn speak good like the Dillingham," he'd say another time, referring to the wealthy scion of the grower family who had once run, unsuccessfully, for one of Hawaii's first senatorial seats. Or he'd then invoke a magical name, the name of one of his heroes, a man he thought particularly exemplary and right- eous. "Learn speak dah good Ing-rish like *Mistah Inouye*," Kubota shouted. "He *lick* dah Dillingham even in debate. I saw on *terre-bision* myself." He was remembering the debates before the first senatorial election just before Hawaii was admitted to the Union as its fiftieth state. "You *tell* story," Kubota would end. And I had my injunction.

The town we settled in after the move from Hawaii is called Gardena, the independently incorporated city south of Los Angeles and north of San Pedro harbor. At its northern limit, it borders on Watts and Compton, black towns. To the southwest are Torrance and Redondo Beach, white towns. To the rest of L.A., Gardena is primarily famous for having legalized five-card draw poker after the war. On Vermont Boulevard, its eastern border, there is a dingy little Vegas-like strip of card clubs with huge parking lots and flickering neon signs that spell out "The Rainbow" and "The Horseshoe" in timed sequences of vari- colored lights. The town is only secondarily famous as the largest community of Japanese Americans in the United States outside of Honolulu, Hawaii. When I was in high school there, it seemed to me that every *sansei* kid I knew wanted to be a doctor, an engineer, or a pharmacist. Our fathers were garden- ers or electricians or nurserymen or ran small businesses catering to other Japanese Americans. Our mothers worked in civil service for the city or as cashiers for Thrifty Drug. What the kids wanted was a good job, good pay, a fine home, and no troubles. No one wanted to mess with the law—from either side—and no one wanted to mess with language or art. They all talked about getting into the right clubs so that they could go to the right schools. There was a certain kind of sameness, an intensely enforced system of conformity. Style was all. Boys wore moccasin-sewn shoes from Flagg Brothers, black A-1 slacks, and Kensington shirts with high collars. Girls wore their hair up in stiff bouffants solidified in hairspray and knew all the latest dances from the slau- son to the funky chicken. We did well in chemistry and in math, no one who was Japanese but me spoke in English class or in history unless called upon, and no one talked about World War II. The day after Robert Kennedy was assassinated, after winning the California Democratic primary, we worked on calculus and elected class coordinators for the prom, featuring the 5th Dimen- sion. We avoided grief. We avoided government. We avoided strong feelings and dangers of any kind. Once punished, we tried to maintain a concerted emotional and social discipline and would not willingly seek to fall out of the narrow margin of protective favor again.

But when I was thirteen, in junior high, I'd not understood why it was so difficult for my classmates, those who were themselves Japanese American, to talk about the relocation. They had cringed, too, when I tried to bring it up during our discussions of World War II. I was Hawaiian-born. They were main- land-born. Their parents had been in camp, had been the ones to suffer the complicated experience of having to distance themselves from their own history and all things Japanese in order to make their way back and into the American social and economic mainstream. It was out of this sense of shame and a fear of stigma I was only beginning to understand that the *nisei* had silenced themselves. And, for their children, among whom I grew up, they wanted no heritage, no culture, no contact with a defiled history. I recall the silence very well. The Japanese-American children around me were burdened in a way I was not. Their injunction was silence. Mine was to speak.

Away at college, in another protected world in its own way as magical to me as the Hawaii of my childhood, I dreamed about my grandfather. Tired from studying languages, practicing German conjugations or scripting an army's worth of Chinese ideograms on a single sheet of paper, Kubota would come to me as I drifted off into sleep. Or I would walk across the newly mown ball field in back of my dormitory, cutting through a street-side phalanx of ancient eucalyptus trees on my way to visit friends off campus, and I would think of him, his anger, and his sadness.

I don't know myself what makes someone feel that kind of need to have a story they've lived through be deposited somewhere, but I can guess. I think about *The Iliad, The Odyssey, The Peloponnesian Wars* of Thucydides, and a myriad of the works of literature I've studied. A character, almost a *topoi* he occurs so often, is frequently the witness who gives personal testimony about an event the rest of his community cannot even imagine. The sibyl is such a character. And Procne, the maid whose tongue is cut out so that she will not tell that she has been raped by her own brother-in-law, the king of Thebes. There are the dime novels, the epic blockbusters Hollywood makes into miniseries, and then there are the plain, relentless stories of witnesses who have suffered through horrors major and minor that have marked and changed their lives. I myself haven't talked to Holocaust victims. But I've read their survival stories and their stories of witness and been revolted and moved by them. My father-in-law, Al Thiessen, tells me his war stories again and again and I listen. A Mennonite who set aside the strictures of his own church in order to serve, he was a Marine codeman in the Pacific during World War II, in the Signal Corps on Guadalcanal, Morotai, and Bougainville. He was part of the island-hopping maneuver MacArthur had devised to win the war in the Pacific. He saw friends die from bombs which exploded not ten yards away. When he was with the 298th Signal Corps attached to the Thirteenth Air Force, he saw plane after plane come in and crash, just short of the runway, killing their crews, setting the jungle ablaze with oil and gas fires. Emergency wagons would scramble, bouncing over newly bulldozed land men used just the afternoon before for a football game. Every time we go fishing together, whether it's in a McKenzie boat drifting for salmon in Tillamook Bay or taking a lunch break from wading the riffles of a stream in the Cascades, he tells me about what happened to him and the young men in his unit. One was a Jewish boy from Brooklyn. One was a foul-mouthed kid from Kansas. They died. And he *has* to tell me. And I *have* to listen. It's a ritual payment the young owe their elders who have survived. The evacuation and relocation is something like that.

Kubota, my grandfather, had been ill with Alzheimer's disease for some time before he died. At the house he'd built on Kamehameha Highway in Hau'ula, a seacoast village just down the road from La'ie where he had his store, he'd wander out from the garage or greenhouse where he'd set up a workbench, and trudge down to the beach or up toward the line of pines he'd planted while employed by the Work Projects Administration during the thirties. Kubota thought he was going fishing. Or he thought he was back at work for Roosevelt, planting pines as a windbreak or soilbreak on the windward flank of the Ko'olau Mountains, emerald monoliths rising out of sea and cane fields from Waialua to Kaneohe. When I visited, my grandmother would send me down to the beach to fetch him. Or I'd run down Kam Highway a quarter mile or so and find him hiding in the cane field by the roadside, counting stalks, measuring circumferences in the claw of his thumb and forefinger. The look on his face was confused or concentrated, I didn't know which. But I guessed he was going fishing again. I'd grab him and walk him back to his house on the highway. My grandmother would shut him in a room.

Within a few years, Kubota had a stroke and survived it, then he had another one and was completely debilitated. The family decided to put him in a nursing home in Kahuku, just set back from the highway, within a mile or so of Kahuku Point and the Tanaka Store where he had his first job as a stock boy. He lived there three years, and I visited him once with my aunt. He was like a potato that had been worn down by cooking. Everything on him—his eyes, his teeth, his legs and torso—seemed like it had been sloughed away. What he had been was mostly gone now and I was looking at the nub of a man. In a wheelchair, he grasped my hands and tugged on them—violently. His hands were still thick and, I believed, strong enough to lift me out of my own seat into his lap. He murmured something in Japanese—he'd long ago ceased to speak any English. My aunt and I cried a little, and we left him.

I remember walking out on the black asphalt of the parking lot of the nursing home. It was heat-cracked and eroded already, and grass had veined itself into the interstices. There were coconut trees around, a cane field I could see across the street, and the ocean I knew was pitching a surf just beyond it. The green Ko'olaus came up behind us. Somewhere nearby, alongside the beach, there was an abandoned airfield in the middle of the canes. As a child, I'd come upon it playing one day, and my friends and I kept returning to it, day after day, playing war or sprinting games or coming to fly kites. I recognize it even now when I see it on TV—it's used as a site for action scenes in the detective shows Hollywood always sets in the islands: a helicopter chasing the hero racing away in a Ferrari, or gun dealers making a clandestine rendezvous on the abandoned runway. It was the old airfield strafed by Japanese planes the day the major flight attacked Pearl Harbor. It was the airfield the FBI thought my grandfather had targeted in his night fishing and signaling with the long surf poles he'd stuck in the sandy bays near Kahuku Point.

Kubota died a short while after I visited him, but not, I thought, without giving me a final message. I was on the mainland, in California studying for Ph.D. exams, when my grandmother called me with the news. It was a relief.

He'd suffered from his debilitation a long time and I was grateful he'd gone. I went home for the funeral and gave the eulogy. My grandmother and I took his ashes home in a small, heavy metal box wrapped in a black *furoshiki,* a large silk scarf. She showed me the name the priest had given to him on his death, scripted with a calligraphy brush on a long, narrow talent of plain wood. Buddhist commoners, at death, are given priestly names, received symbolically into the clergy. The idea is that, in their next life, one of scholarship and leisure, they might meditate and attain the enlightenment the religion is aimed at. *"Shaku Shūchi,"* the ideograms read. It was Kubota's Buddhist name, incorporating characters from his family and given names. It meant "Shining Wisdom of the Law." He died on Pearl Harbor Day, December 7, 1983.

After years, after I'd finally come back to live in Hawaii again, only once did I dream of Kubota, my grandfather. It was the same night I'd heard HR 442, the redress bill for Japanese Americans, had been signed into law. In my dream that night Kubota was "torching," and he sang a Japanese song, a querulous and wavery folk ballad, as he hung paper lanterns on bamboo poles stuck into the sand in the shallow water of the lagoon behind the reef near Kahuku Point. Then he was at a work table, smoking a hand-rolled cigarette, letting it dangle from his lips Bogart-style as he drew, daintily and skillfully, with a narrow trim brush, ideogram after ideogram on a score of paper lanterns he had hung in a dark shed to dry. He had painted a talismanic mantra onto each lantern, the ideogram for the word "red" in Japanese, a bit of art blended with some superstition, a piece of sympathetic magic appealing to the magenta coloring on the rough skins of the schooling, night-feeding fish he wanted to attract to his baited hooks. He strung them from pole to pole in the dream then, hiking up his khaki worker's pants to his white ankles showed and wading through the shimmering black waters of the sand flats and then the reef. "The moon is leaving, leaving," he sang in Japanese. "Take me deeper in the savage sea." He turned and crouched like an ice racer then, leaning forward so that his unshaven face almost touched the light film of water. I could see the light stubble of beard like a fine, gray ash covering the lower half of his face. I could see his gold-rimmed spectacles. He held a small wooden boat in his cupped hands and placed it lightly on the sea and pushed it away. One of his lanterns was on it and, written in small neat rows like a sutra scroll, it had been decorated with the silvery names of all our dead.

QUESTIONS AND CONSIDERATIONS

1. What was Kubota's life like before Pearl Harbor? How had he succeeded in Hawaii? How did he try to keep Japanese cultural traditions alive? How did the events of December 8, 1941, irreversibly change his life and the life of his family?

2. The first part of the essay presents a period in Kubota's life before the narrator was born. What memories does Hongo have of Kubota from his childhood? How does Kubota try to preserve his heritage and his connection with nature in Gardena, California?

3. Through the ritual of the talk story, Kubota attempts to pass on a vision of the past, both the ancestral past in Japan as well as the more recent years in Hawaii. What morals do Kubota's talk stories typically support? What is the "different story" that he tells his grandchildren one evening after drinking a glass of whiskey? Why doesn't his grandson believe the story?

4. What philosophical attitude is summed up by the Japanese expression *"Shikatta ga nai"*? How does this attitude help to explain the point of view in Hongo's community about the relocation camps and the war years?

5. What is meant by Hongo's remark about his conversation with Kubota: "I was not made yet"? In what ways did Kubota's stories and his injunctions help to "make" Hongo the adult he later became?

6. How do Kubota and his stories continue to influence Hongo throughout his college years and into his adult life? What similarities does Hongo perceive between the stories of Kubota and those of Al Thiessen, his father-in-law?

7. Although Kubota deteriorates physically and mentally as he ages, making direct communication impossible, Hongo believes that he gives his grandson a "final message" in the form of a dream. What is the dream and what message does it seem to hold for Hongo and for Japanese Americans in general? What external events might have triggered Hongo's dream about his grandfather?

IDEAS FOR WRITING

1. Write an essay about a story told to you by a relative or a dream you have had about a relative that provided you with a message or a direction in life. Explain how the story or dream influenced your thinking and your life.

2. Write an essay about a belief or cultural value you currently hold. Describe the belief or value and then reflect upon its origins in your family life and/or religious training. Discuss the ways that you have modified this belief to make it your own.

Beauty: When the Other Dancer Is the Self

Alice Walker

Journal

Write about a physical scar from your childhood that affected your sense of well-being and/or your self-concept. How did you change and grow as you came to accept the scar?

It is a bright summer day in 1947. My father, a fat, funny man with beautiful eyes and a subversive wit, is trying to decide which of his eight children he will take with him to the county fair. My mother, of course, will not go. She is knocked out from getting most of us ready: I hold my neck stiff against the pressure of her knuckles as she hastily completes the braiding and then beribboning of my hair.

My father is the driver for the rich old white lady up the road. Her name is Miss Mey. She owns all the land for miles around, as well as the house in which we live. All I remember about her is that she once offered to pay my mother thirty-five cents for cleaning her house, raking up piles of her magnolia leaves, and washing her family's clothes, and that my mother—she of no money, eight children, and a chronic earache—refused it. But I do not think of this in 1947. I am two and a half years old. I want to go everywhere my daddy goes. I am excited at the prospect of riding in a car. Someone has told me fairs are fun. That there is room in the car for only three of us doesn't faze me at all. Whirling happily in my starchy frock, showing off my biscuit-polished patent-leather shoes and lavender socks, tossing my head in a way that makes my ribbons bounce, I stand, hands on hips, before my father. "Take me, Daddy," I say with assurance; "I'm the prettiest!"

Later, it does not surprise me to find myself in Miss Mey's shiny black car, sharing the back seat with the other lucky ones. Does not surprise me that I thoroughly enjoy the fair. At home that night I tell the unlucky ones all I can remember about the merry-go-round, the man who eats live chickens, and the teddy bears, until they say: that's enough, baby Alice. Shut up now, and go to sleep.

It is Easter Sunday, 1950. I am dressed in a green, flocked, scalloped-hem dress (handmade by my adoring sister, Ruth) that has its own smooth satin petticoat and tiny hot-pink roses tucked into each scallop. My shoes, new T-strap patent leather, again highly biscuit-polished. I am six years old and have learned one of the longest Easter speeches to be heard that day, totally unlike the speech I said when I was two: "Easter lilies/pure and white/blossom in/the morning light." When I rise to give my speech I do so on a great wave of love and pride and expectation. People in the church stop rustling their new crinolines. They seem to hold their breath. I can tell they admire my dress, but it is my spirit, bordering on sassiness (womanishness), they secretly applaud.

"That girl's a little *mess*," they whisper to each other, pleased.

Naturally I say my speech without stammer or pause, unlike those who stutter, stammer, or, worst of all, forget. This is before the word "beautiful" exists in people's vocabulary, but "Oh, isn't she the *cutest* thing!" frequently floats my way. "And got so much sense!" they gratefully add . . . for which thoughtful addition I thank them to this day.

It was great fun being cute. But then, one day, it ended.

I am eight years old and a tomboy. I have a cowboy hat, cowboy boots, checkered shirt and pants, all red. My playmates are my brothers, two and four years older than I. Their colors are black and green, the only difference in the way we are dressed. On Saturday nights we all go to the picture show, even my mother; Westerns are her favorite kind of movie. Back home, "on the ranch," we pretend we are Tom Mix, Hopalong Cassidy, and Lash LaRue (we've even named one of our dogs Lash LaRue); we chase each other for hours rustling cattle, being outlaws, delivering damsels from distress. Then my parents decide to buy my brothers guns. These are not "real" guns. They shoot "BBs," copper pellets my brothers say will kill birds. Because I am a girl, I do not get a gun. Instantly I am relegated to the position of Indian. Now there appears a great distance between us. They shoot and shoot at everything with their new guns. I try to keep up with my bow and arrows.

One day while I am standing on top of our makeshift "garage"—pieces of tin nailed across some poles—holding my bow and arrow and looking out toward the fields, I feel an incredible blow in my right eye. I look down just in time to see my brother lower his gun.

Both brothers rush to my side. My eye stings, and I cover it with my hand. "If you tell," they say, "we will get a whipping. You don't want that to happen, do you?" I do not. "Here is a piece of wire," says the older brother, picking it up from the roof; "say you stepped on one end of it and the other flew up and hit you." The pain is beginning to start. "Yes," I say. "Yes, I will say that is what happened." If I do not say this is what happened, I know my brothers will find ways to make me wish I had. But now I will say anything that gets me to my mother.

Confronted by our parents we stick to the lie agreed upon. They place me on a bench on the porch and I close my left eye while they examine the right. There is a tree growing from underneath the porch that climbs past the railing to the roof. It is the last thing my right eye sees. I watch as its trunk, its branches, and then its leaves are blotted out by the rising blood.

I am in shock. First there is intense fever, which my father tries to break using lily leaves bound around my head. Then there are chills: my mother tries to get me to eat soup. Eventually, I do not know how, my parents learn what has happened. A week after the "accident" they take me to see a doctor. "Why did you wait so long to come?" he asks, looking into my eye and shaking his head. "Eyes are sympathetic," he says. "If one is blind, the other will likely become blind too."

This comment of the doctor's terrifies me. But it is really how I look that bothers me most. Where the BB pellet struck there is a glob of whitish scar tissue, a hideous cataract, on my eye. Now when I stare at people—a favorite pastime, up to now—they will stare back. Not at the "cute" little girl, but at her scar. For six years I do not stare at anyone, because I do not raise my head.

Years later, in the throes of a mid-life crisis, I ask my mother and sister whether I changed after the "accident." "No," they say, puzzled. "What do you mean?"

What do I mean?

I am eight, and, for the first time, doing poorly in school, where I have been something of a whiz since I was four. We have just moved to the place where the "accident" occurred. We do not know any of the people around us because this is a different county. The only time I see the friends I knew is when we go back to our old church. The new school is the former state penitentiary. It is a large stone building, cold and drafty, crammed to overflowing with boisterous, ill-disciplined children. On the third floor there is a huge circular imprint of some partition that has been torn out.

"What used to be here?" I ask a sullen girl next to me on our way past it to lunch.

"The electric chair," says she.

At night I have nightmares about the electric chair, and about all the people reputedly "fried" in it. I am afraid of the school, where all the students seem to be budding criminals.

"What's the matter with your eye?" they ask, critically.

When I don't answer (I cannot decide whether it was an "accident" or not), they shove me, insist on a fight.

My brother, the one who created the story about the wire, comes to my rescue. But then brags so much about "protecting" me, I become sick.

After months of torture at the school, my parents decide to send me back to our old community, to my old school. I live with my grandparents and the teacher they board. But there is no room for Phoebe, my cat. By the time my grandparents decide there is room, and I ask for my cat, she cannot be found. Miss Yarborough, the boarding teacher, takes me under her wing, and begins to teach me to play the piano. But soon she marries an African—a "prince" she says—and is whisked away to his continent.

At my old school there is at least one teacher who loves me. She is the teacher who "knew me before I was born" and bought my first baby clothes. It is she who makes life bearable. It is her presence that finally helps me turn on the one child at the school who continually calls me "one-eyed bitch." One day I simply grab him by his coat and beat him until I am satisfied. It is my teacher who tells me my mother is ill.

My mother is lying in bed in the middle of the day, something I have never seen. She is in too much pain to speak. She has an abscess in her ear. I stand looking down on her, knowing that if she dies, I cannot live. She is being treated with warm oils and hot bricks held against her cheek. Finally a doctor comes. But I must go back to my grandparents' house. The weeks pass but I am hardly aware of it. All I know is that my mother might die, my father is not so jolly, my brothers still have their guns, and I am the one sent away from home.

"You did not change," they say.

Did I imagine the anguish of never looking up?

I am twelve. When relatives come to visit I hide in my room. My cousin Brenda, just my age, whose father works in the post office and whose mother is a nurse, comes to find me. "Hello," she says. And then she asks, looking at my recent school picture, which I did not want taken, and on which the "glob," as I think of it, is clearly visible, "You still can't see out of that eye?"

"No," I say, and flop back on the bed over my book.

That night, as I do almost every night, I abuse my eye. I rant and rave at it, in front of the mirror. I plead with it to clear up before morning. I tell it I hate and despise it. I do not pray for sight. I pray for beauty.

"You did not change," they say.

I am fourteen and baby-sitting for my brother Bill, who lives in Boston. He is my favorite brother and there is a strong bond between us. Understanding my feelings of shame and ugliness he and his wife take me to a local hospital, where the "glob" is removed by a doctor named O. Henry. There is still a small bluish crater where the scar tissue was, but the ugly white stuff is gone. Almost immediately I become a different person from the girl who does not raise her head. Or so I think. Now that I've raised my head I win the boyfriend of my dreams. Now that I've raised my head I have plenty of friends. Now that I've raised my head classwork comes from my lips as faultlessly as Easter speeches did, and I leave high school as valedictorian, most popular student, and *queen,* hardly believing my luck. Ironically, the girl who was voted most beautiful in our class (and was) was later shot twice through the chest by a male companion, using a "real" gun, while she was pregnant. But that's another story in itself. Or is it?

"You did not change," they say.

It is now thirty years since the "accident." A beautiful journalist comes to visit and to interview me. She is going to write a cover story for her magazine that focuses on my latest book. "Decide how you want to look on the cover," she says. "Glamorous, or whatever."

Never mind "glamorous," it is the "whatever" that I hear. Suddenly all I can think of is whether I will get enough sleep the night before the photography session: if I don't, my eye will be tired and wander, as blind eyes will.

At night in bed with my lover I think up reasons why I should not appear on the cover of a magazine. "My meanest critics will say I've sold out," I say. "My family will now realize I write scandalous books."

"But what's the real reason you don't want to do this?" he asks.

"Because in all probability," I say in a rush, "my eye won't be straight."

"It will be straight enough," he says. Then, "Besides, I thought you'd made your peace with that."

And I suddenly remember that I have.

I remember:

I am talking to my brother Jimmy, asking if he remembers anything unusual about the day I was shot. He does not know I consider that day the last time my father, with his sweet home remedy of cool lily leaves, chose me, and that I suffered and raged inside because of this. "Well," he says, "all I remember is standing by the side of the highway with Daddy, trying to flag down a car. A white man stopped, but when Daddy said he needed somebody to take his little girl to the doctor, he drove off."

I remember:

I am in the desert for the first time. I fall totally in love with it. I am so overwhelmed by its beauty, I confront for the first time, consciously, the meaning of the doctor's words years ago: "Eyes are sympathetic. If one is blind, the other will likely become blind too." I realize I have dashed about the world madly, looking at this, looking at that, storing up images against the fading of the light. *But I might have missed seeing the desert!* The shock of that possibility—and gratitude for over twenty-five years of sight—sends me literally to my knees. Poem after poem comes—which is perhaps how poets pray.

> *On Sight*
>
> I am so thankful I have seen
> The Desert
> And the creatures in the desert
> And the desert Itself.
>
> The desert has its own moon
> Which I have seen
> With my own eye.
> There is no flag on it.
>
> Trees of the desert have arms
> All of which are always up
> That is because the moon is up
> The sun is up
> Also the sky
> The stars
> Clouds
> None with flags.
>
> If there *were* flags, I doubt
> the trees would point.
> Would you?

But mostly, I remember this:

I am twenty-seven, and my baby daughter is almost three. Since her birth I have worried about her discovery that her mother's eyes are different from other people's. Will she be embarrassed? I think. What will she say? Every day she watches a television program called "Big Blue Marble." It begins with a picture of the earth as it appears from the moon. It is bluish, a little battered-looking, but full of light, with whitish clouds swirling around it. Every time I see it I weep with love, as if it is a picture of Grandma's house. One day when I am putting Rebecca down for her nap, she suddenly focuses on my eye. Something inside me cringes, gets ready to try to protect myself. All children are cruel about physical differences, I know from experience, and that they don't always mean to be is another matter. I assume Rebecca will be the same.

But no-o-o-o. She studies my face intently as we stand, her inside and me outside her crib. She even holds my face maternally between her dimpled little hands. Then, looking every bit as serious and lawyerlike as her father, she says, as if it may just possibly have slipped my attention: "Mommy, there's a *world* in your eye." (As in, "Don't be alarmed, or do anything crazy.") And then, gently, but with great interest: "Mommy, where did you *get* that world in your eye?"

For the most part, the pain left then. (So what if my brothers grew up to buy even more powerful pellet guns for their sons and to carry real guns themselves. So what, if a young "Morehouse man" once nearly fell off the steps of Trevor Arnett Library because he thought my eyes were blue.) Crying and laughing I ran to the bathroom, while Rebecca mumbled and sang herself off to sleep. Yes indeed, I realized, looking into the mirror. There *was* a world in my eye. And I saw that it was possible to love it: that in fact, for all it had taught me of shame and anger and inner vision, I *did* love it. Even to see it drifting out of orbit in boredom, or rolling up out of fatigue, not to mention floating back at attention in excitement (bearing witness, a friend has called it), deeply suitable to my personality, and even characteristic of me.

That night I dream I am dancing to Stevie Wonder's song "Always" (the name of the song is really "As," but I hear it as "Always"). As I dance, whirling and joyous, happier than I've ever been in my life, another bright-faced dancer joins me. We dance and kiss each other and hold each other through the night. The other dancer has obviously come through all right, as I have done. She is beautiful, whole and free. And she is also me.

QUESTIONS AND CONSIDERATIONS

1. What are the most difficult aspects of Walker's adjustment to living with her damaged "glob eye"? Is the pain Walker endures portrayed as primarily negative, or is it an experience through which she grows?

2. Walker's family did not believe that Alice was changed by the accident. Are they correct? Why or why not?

3. Why does Walker fall in love with the desert? How is the poem "On Sight" thematically connected to the meaning of the essay as a whole?

4. How does Walker's daughter help her to make peace with her damaged eye? What does the daughter mean when she says, "Mommy, there's a *world* in your eye"? Why is Walker's final realization ironic?

5. Explain the meaning of the essay's title. Through reflecting on her experience, how has Walker's definition of beauty changed and grown? How has she come to accept the ghost of her lost eye and the reality of her partial blindness?

IDEAS FOR WRITING

1. Write about an experience in which you struggled to develop self-acceptance after an emotional or physical scar. Were you successful, as Walker seems to have been, or do you feel you are still involved in an ongoing effort?

2. Read other texts that try to define the nature of beauty; then write an essay in which you define beauty, drawing on your outside readings for ideas and examples. How is your definition similar to or different from the definition implied in Walker's essay? How has your definition evolved through your reading and life experiences?

A Field of Silence
Annie Dillard

Journal

Write about a time when you were alone in a natural setting and had an experience, insight, or revelation about an important personal, philosophical, or religious issue: the nature of solitude, eternity, the pattern or meaning of life.

There is a place called "the farm" where I lived once, in a time that was very lonely. Fortunately I was unconscious of my loneliness then, and felt it only deeply, bewildered, in the half-bright way that a puppy feels pain.

I loved the place, and still do. It was an ordinary farm, a calf-raising, hay-making farm, and very beautiful. Its flat, messy pastures ran along one side of the central portion of a quarter-mile road in the central part of an island, an island in Puget Sound, so that from the high end of the road you could look west toward the Pacific, to the Sound and its hundred islands, and from the other end—and from the farm—you could see east to the water between you and the mainland, and beyond it the mainland's mountains slicked smooth with snow.

I liked the clutter about the place, the way everything blossomed or seeded or rusted; I liked the hundred half-finished projects, the smells, and the way the animals always broke loose. It is calming to herd animals. Often a regular rodeo breaks out—two people and a clever cow can kill a morning—but still, it is calming. You laugh for a while, exhausted, and silence is restored; the beasts are back in their pastures, the fences not fixed but disguised as if they were fixed, ensuring the animals' temporary resignation; and a great calm descends, a lack of urgency, a sense of having to invent something to do until the next time you must run and chase cattle.

The farm seemed eternal in the crude way the earth does—extending, that is, a very long time. The farm was as old as earth, always there, as old as the island, the Platonic form of "farm," of human society itself and at large, a piece of land eaten and replenished a billion summers, a piece of land worked on, lived on, grown over, plowed under, and stitched again and again, with fingers or with leaves, in and out and into human life's thin weave. I lived there once.

I lived there once and I have seen, from behind the barn, the long roadside pastures heaped with silence. Behind the rooster, suddenly, I saw the silence heaped on the fields like trays. That day the green hayfields supported silence evenly sown; the fields bent just so under the even pressure of silence, bearing it, even, palming it aloft: cleared fields, part of a land, a planet, they did not buckle beneath the heel of silence, nor split up scattered to bits, but instead lay secret, disguised as time and matter a though that were nothing, ordinary—disguised as fields like those which bear the silence only because they are spread, and the silence spreads over them, great in size.

I do not want, I think, ever to see such a sight again. That there is loneliness here I had granted, in the abstract—but not, I thought, inside the light of God's presence, inside his sanction, and signed by his name.

I lived alone in the farmhouse and rented; the owners, Angus and Lynn in their twenties, lived in another building just over the yard. I had beer reading and restless for two or three days. It was morning. I had just read at breakfast an Updike story, "Packed Dirt, Churchgoing, A Dying Cat, A Traded Car," which moved me. I heard our own farmyard rooster and two or three roosters across the street screeching. I quit the house, hoping at heart to see Lynn or Angus, but immediately to watch our rooster as he crowed.

It was Saturday morning late in the summer, in early September, clear-aired and still. I climbed the barnyard fence between the poultry and the pastures; I watched the red rooster, and the rooster, reptilian, kept one alert and alien eye on me. He pulled his extravagant neck to its maximum length, hauled himself high on his legs, stretched his beak as if he were gagging, screamed, and blinked. It was a ruckus. The din came from everywhere, and only the most rigorous application of reason could persuade me that it proceeded in its entirety from this lone and maniac bird.

After a pause, the roosters across the street would start, answering the proclamation, or cranking out another round, arrhythmically, interrupting. In the same way there is no pattern nor sense to the massed stridulations of cicadas; their skipped beats, enjambments, and failed alterations jangle your spirits, as though each of those thousand insects, each with identical feelings, were stubbornly deaf to the others, and loudly alone.

I shifted along the fence to see if Lynn or Angus was coming or going. To the rooster I said nothing, but only stared. And he stared at me: we were both careful to keep the wooden fence slat from our line of sight, so that this profiled eye and my two eyes could meet. From time to time I looked beyond the pastures to learn if anyone might be seen on the road.

When I was turned away in this manner, the silence gathered and struck me. It bashed me broadside from nowhere, as if I'd been hit by a plank. It dropped from the heavens above me like yard goods; ten acres of fallen, invisible sky choked the fields. The pastures on either side of the road turned green in a surrealistic fashion, monstrous, impeccable, as if they were holding their breath. The roosters stopped. All the things of the world—the fields and the fencing, the road, a parked orange truck—were stricken and selfconscious. A world pressed down on their surfaces, a world battered just within their surfaces, and that real world, so near to emerging, had got struck.

There was only silence. It was the silence of matter caught in the act and embarrassed. There were no cells moving, and yet there were cells. I could see the shape of the land, how it lay holding silence. Its poise and its stillness were unendurable, like the ring of the silence you hear in your skull when you're little and notice you're living, the ring which resumes later in life when you're sick.

There were flies buzzing over the dirt by the henhouse, moving in circles and buzzing, black dreams in chips off the one long dream, the dream of the regular world. But the silent fields were the real world, eternity's outpost in time, whose look I remembered but never like this, this God-blasted, paralyzed day. I felt myself tall and vertical, in a blue shirt, selfconscious, and wishing to die. I heard the flies again; I looked at the rooster who was frozen looking at me.

Then at last I heard whistling, human whistling far on the air, and I was not able to bear it. I looked around, heartbroken; only at the big yellow Charolais farm far up the road was there motion—a woman, I think, dressed in pink, and pushing a wheelbarrow easily over the grass. It must have been she who was whistling and heaping on top of the silence those hollow notes of song. But the slow sound of the music—the beautiful sound of the music ringing the air like a stone bell—was isolate and detached. The notes spread into the general air and became the weightier part of silence, silence's last straw. The distant woman and her wheelbarrow were flat and detached, like mechanized and pink-painted properties for a stage. I stood in pieces, afraid I was unable to move. Something had unhinged the world. The houses and roadsides and pastures were buckling under the silence. Then a Labrador, black, loped up the distant driveway, fluid and cartoonlike, toward the pink woman. I had to try to turn away. Holiness is a force, and like the others can be resisted. It was given, but I didn't want to see it, God or no God. It was as if God had said, "I am here, but not as you have known me. This is the look of silence, and of loneliness unendurable: it too has always been mine, and now will be yours." I was not ready for a life of sorrow, sorrow deriving from knowledge I could just as well stop at the gate.

I turned away, willful, and the whole show vanished. The realness of things disassembled. The whistling became ordinary, familiar; the air above the fields released its pressure and the fields lay hooded as before. I myself could act. Looking to the rooster I whistled to him myself, softly, and some hens appeared at the chicken house window, greeted the day, and fluttered down.

Several months later, walking past the farm on the way to a volleyball game, I remarked to a friend, by way of information, "There are angels in those fields." Angels! That silence so grave and so stricken, that choked and unbearable green! I have rarely been so surprised at something I've said. Angels! What are angels? I had never thought of angels, in any way at all.

From that time I began to think of angels. I considered that sights such as I had seen of the silence must have been shared by the people who said they saw angels. I began to review the thing I had seen that morning. My impression now of those fields is of thousands of spirits—spirits trapped, perhaps, by my refusal to call them more fully, or by the paralysis of my own spirit at that time—thousands of spirits, angels in fact, almost discernible to the eye, and whirling. If pressed I would say they were three or four feet from the ground. Only their motion was clear (clockwise, if you insist); that, and their beauty unspeakable.

There are angels in those fields, and I presume, in all fields, and everywhere else. I would go to the lions for this conviction, to witness this fact. What all this means about perception, or language, or angels, or my own sanity, I have no idea.

QUESTIONS AND CONSIDERATIONS

1. Dillard describes the farm where she once spent time alone. What qualities made the farm special for Dillard? How did the quality of the life she led on the farm help to prepare her for the vision or realization that she describes in her essay?

2. Why does Dillard not wish "to see such a sight again"? Why does she feel her realization was unbearable?

3. Dillard describes her experience of the silence through metaphors and images. Which of her images did you find most effective? Is she successful in translating her vision into poetic language?

4. Dillard's vision could be considered theological, a vision of God. What religious insight does the vision hold for Dillard? Does her experience confirm the view of God with which you are familiar? Do you think Dillard's vision is a religious one?

5. Why does it take Dillard so long to come to the insight that "there are angels in those fields"? How does this insight and her subsequent description of the angels differ from her initial experience of silence and solitude?

6. How do you interpret Dillard's vision? Does it seem to be a purely subjective experience, or would you consider such a vision by a talented, intelligent writer and observer of the natural scene as "evidence of things unseen"?

IDEAS FOR WRITING

1. The news media frequently report on visions. Do some research into the subject of waking visions; then write an essay about your response to such paranormal experiences. Do you take such occurrences seriously, treat them with skepticism, or feel ambivalent about them? If such "visions" are actually mere hallucinations, what might cause them to occur? Provide examples.

2. Develop your journal entry about a moment of insight in natural solitude into a reflective essay about how your thinking about the initial incident has evolved.

Poetry

Desert Places

Robert Frost

Journal

Write about a physical place or inner feelings that sometimes frighten you.

Snow falling and night falling fast, oh, fast
In a field I looked into going past,
And the ground almost covered smooth in snow,
But a few weeds and stubble showing last.

The woods around it have it—it is theirs.   5
All animals are smothered in their lairs.
I am too absent-spirited to count;
The loneliness includes me unawares.

And lonely as it is that loneliness
Will be more lonely ere it will be less—   10
A blanker whiteness of benighted snow
With no expression, nothing to express.

They cannot scare me with their empty spaces
Between stars—on stars where no human race is.
I have it in me so much nearer home   15
To scare myself with my own desert places.

QUESTIONS AND CONSIDERATIONS

1. What is the significance of the snow that Frost mentions in the first three stanzas of the poem? What quality of the snow does Frost emphasize?

2. Night is another symbol developed in the poem: As the snow is falling heavily, so is the night "falling fast, oh, fast." What does night represent in the poem? How and why is the blackness of night compared and contrasted with the whiteness of the snow?

3. A major theme in the poem is loneliness: four times Frost repeats the word *lonely* or *loneliness.* How do the images in the poem help to represent and emphasize loneliness?

4. The fourth stanza of the poem shifts the focus of the imagery from the immediate (fields, weeds, animals, snow) to the distant: the "empty spaces" between stars. Why

don't these vast empty spaces frighten the speaker? What is the effect of the abrupt shift of focus in the last stanza?

5. Every line in this poem is iambic pentameter in rhythm; every stanza has four lines and is rhymed very tightly in an aaba pattern. What is the effect of writing this disturbing poem in such a simple, almost obsessively regular, pattern of meter and rhyme?

6. What do you think causes the kind of loneliness explored in the poem? Do you think the speaker chooses loneliness as a life style, or is the loneliness a circumstance the narrator wishes to break free from but cannot?

IDEAS FOR WRITING

1. Like the speaker in the poem, people are often frightened about what they see when they look within themselves: perhaps a tendency to act violently, to withdraw, or to become depressed. Write an essay about what you find most frightening: your inner world of thoughts and feelings, the social world, the reality of mortality, the separateness of human beings, or the potential insignificance of individual life.

2. Write an essay on loneliness: Is loneliness an important concern in your life? In what ways are loneliness and being alone different states of mind? What are the advantages and disadvantages of being alone?

The Other
Judith Ortiz Cofer

Journal

Write about the experience of being haunted by a hidden side of your personality.

A sloe-eyed dark woman shadows me.
In the morning she sings
Spanish love songs in a high
falsetto filling my shower stall
with echoes.   5
She is by my side
in front of the mirror as I slip
into my tailored skirt and she
into her red cotton dress.
She shakes out her black mane as I   10
run a comb through my close-cropped cap.
Her mouth is like a red bull's eye
daring me.
Everywhere I go I must
make room for her: she crowds me   15
in elevators where others wonder

at all the space I need.
At night her weight tips my bed, and
it is her wild dreams that run rampant
through my head exhausting me. Her heartbeats.   20
like dozens of spiders carrying the poison
of her restlessness over the small
distance that separates us,
drag their countless legs
over my bare flesh.   25

QUESTIONS AND CONSIDERATIONS

1. In what sense does the "dark woman" shadow the speaker? How is the word *shadow* developed here? In what ways is the woman "dark"?

2. What type of songs does the dark woman sing? Why is it significant that the dark woman sings in the speaker's shower and that her singing creates "echoes"?

3. What series of physical actions does the dark woman make that are opposed to the actions and choices made by the speaker? How does the dark woman dress? What do her hairdo and makeup suggest?

4. In crowded elevators, the speaker needs a lot of space around her. Why does she blame this on the dark woman within who is "crowding her"?

5. At night, the speaker has "wild dreams" that she attributes to the dark woman. Why does she have trouble accepting her dreams?

6. What is meant by the final comparison in the poem of the heartbeats of the dark woman to "dozens of spiders"? Is "restlessness" primarily a negative or a positive quality?

IDEAS FOR WRITING

1. Develop your journal into a poem or story about the conflict between different aspects of your personality.

2. Do some research into what causes disassociation between different parts of the self. What can be done to reintegrate the fragmented, or "split," personality?

Poem to My Grandmother
in Her Death
Michele Murray

Journal

Write a letter to a relative or friend whom you have not seen in many years. Try to explain how your life has changed since you last saw each other and why memories of the person continue to live on in your mind.

After a dozen years of death
even love wanders off, old faithful
dog tired of lying on stiff marble.

In any case you would not understand
this life, the plain white walls   5
& the books, a passion lost on you.

I do not know what forced your life
through iron years into a shape of giving—
an apple, squares of chocolate, a hand.

There should have been nothing left   10
after the mean streets, foaming washtubs,
the wild cries of births at home.

Never mind. It's crumbling in my hands,
too, what you gave. I've jumped from ledges
& landed oddly twisted, bleeding internally.   15

Thus I learn how to remember your injuries—
your sudden heaviness as fine rain fell,
or your silence over the scraped bread board.

Finding myself in the end is finding you
& if you are lost in the folds of your silence   20
then I find only to lose with you those years

I stupidly slung off me like ragged clothes
when I was ashamed to be the child
of your child. I scramble for them now

In dark closets because I am afraid.   25
I have forgotten so much. If I could meet you
again perhaps I could rejoin my own flesh.

And not lose whatever you called love.
I could understand your silences & speak them
& you would be as present to me as your worn ring.   30

In the shadows I reach for the bucket of fierce dahlias
you bought without pricing, the coat you shook
free of its snow, the blouse that you ironed.

> There's no love so pure it can thrive
> without its incarnations. I would like to know you   35
> once again over your chipped cups brimming with tea.

QUESTIONS AND CONSIDERATIONS

1. What does the first stanza of the poem say about the nature of love, memory, and absence?

2. How does the narrator of the poem contrast her current life style and attitude toward "giving" to the life and the outlook of her grandmother? How does the narrator come to understand the "injuries" of the grandmother?

3. What conflict did the narrator have with her mother? Does the conflict suggested in the poem seem to be a typical one?

4. In the last three stanzas the narrator refers to several items she has retained, either in reality or in memory, which evoke for her qualities of her grandmother. What do these symbols of memory suggest to you about the grandmother's values and outlook on life?

5. What is meant by the statement in the last stanza of the poem, "There's no love so pure it can thrive/without its incarnations"? Do you agree or disagree with this concept of love?

6. Do you think that the narrator has been successful in her efforts to revive the connection she once felt with her grandmother, or is this really a poem about the inevitability of loss and change?

IDEAS FOR WRITING

1. Write a reflective essay in which you select several objects that belonged to an absent or deceased friend or relative. Describe each briefly and discuss what memories and values are entwined with the object.

2. Develop the brief letter in your journal entry into a longer letter to a departed friend or relative in which you explore some unresolved feelings and haunting memories that continue to influence your life.

Visions and Interpretations
Li-Young Lee

Journal

Write about a vision or series of revelatory images that passed through your mind in a dream or while reading.

Because this graveyard is a hill,
I must climb up to see my dead,

stopping once midway to rest
beside this tree.

It was here, between the anticipation   5
of exhaustion, and exhaustion,
between vale and peak,
my father came down to me

and we climbed arm in arm to the top.
He cradled the bouquet I'd brought,   10
and I, a good son, never mentioned his grave,
erect like a door behind him.

And it was here, one summer day, I sat down
to read an old book. When I looked up
from the noon-lit page, I saw a vision   15
of a world about to come, and a world about to go.

Truth is, I've not seen my father
since he died, and, no, the dead
do not walk arm in arm with me.

If I carry flowers to them, I do so without their help,   20
the blossoms not always bright, torch-like,
but often heavy as sodden newspaper.

Truth is, I came here with my son one day,
and we rested against this tree,
and I fell asleep, and dreamed   25

a dream which, upon my boy waking me, I told.
Neither of us understood.
Then we went up.

Even this is not accurate.
Let me begin again: 30

Between two griefs, a tree.
Between my hands, white chrysanthemums, yellow chrysanthemums.

The old book I finished reading
I've since read again and again.

And what was far grows near,   35
and what is near grows more dear,

and all of my visions and interpretations
depend on what I see,

and between my eyes is always
the rain, the migrant rain.   40

QUESTIONS AND CONSIDERATIONS

1. What is the setting of the poem? How does the setting help to emphasize the issues and concerns of the speaker?

2. In what sense does the speaker's father come "down to" him? What is suggested by the image of the grave "erect like a door behind him"?

3. What kind of vision does the speaker have while reading "an old book"? How does his vision while reading relate to his earlier vision of his father?

4. In line 23 of the poem, beginning with the words "Truth is," the speaker seems to deny the truth of the vision he has just shared with the reader. What was the effect on you of this denial? Where in the poem did you consider that the speaker was being most truthful?

5. What do you think is the subject of the dream the speaker relates to his son after falling asleep against the tree? Why doesn't Lee share the dream directly with his readers?

6. In line 29, the speaker admits that he has still not been "accurate" and proceeds to restate his vision in the form of a final ten-line statement. Analyze the images and ideas of the final "vision and interpretation." How does Lee's final insight differ from the first two visions and interpretations explored in the poem? What is meant by the "two chrysanthemums"? The rereading of the old book? The image of "the migrant rain"?

IDEAS FOR WRITING

1. Write an interpretation of Lee's poem that discusses several of the different ideas that it explores. Explain the changed "visions and interpretations" that occur as the speaker reflects on his original experience and tries to express his experiences and ideas more fully and clearly.

2. Write an essay in which you compare several different interpretations that you have had over the years of the meaning of a book, a short text, or an experience. How has your understanding of the original incident or text changed as your thinking and view of the world have evolved or become more sophisticated?

Star Quilt

Roberta Hill Whiteman

There are notes to lightning in my bedroom.
A star forged from linen thread and patches.
Purple, yellow, red like diamond suckers, children

of the star gleam on sweaty nights. The quilt unfolds
against sheets, moving, warm clouds of Chinook.   5
It covers my cuts, my red birch clusters under pine.

Under it your mouth begins a legend,
and wide as the plain, I hope Wisconsin marshes
promise your caress. The candle locks

us in forest smells, your cheek tattered   10
by shadow. Sweetened by wings, my mothlike heart
flies nightly among geraniums.

We know of land that looks lonely,
but isn't, of beef with hides of velveteen,
of sorrow, an eddy in blood.   15

Star quilt, sewn from dawn light by fingers
of flint, take away those touches
meant for noisier skins,

anoint us with grass and twilight air,
so we may embrace, two bitter roots   20
pushing back into the dust.

QUESTIONS

  1. What images and comparisons does Whiteman use to describe the star quilt?
What traditional Native American values and cultural traits does it represent? How does
the quilt support the relationship of the couple in the poem, the "two bitter roots"?

  2. Write a poem, story, or essay about a family heirloom that helps you to maintain
your sense of heritage and brings you closer to those you love.

Ozymandias
Percy Bysshe Shelley

I met a traveller from an antique land
Who said: Two vast and trunkless legs of stone
Stand in the desert . . . Near them, on the sand,
Half sunk, a shattered visage lies, whose frown,
And wrinkled lip, and sneer of cold command,   5
Tell that its sculptor well those passions read
Which yet survive, stamped on these lifeless things,
The hand that mocked them, and the heart that fed:
And on the pedestal these words appear:
'My name is Ozymandias, king of kings: 10
Look on my works, ye Mighty, and despair!'
Nothing beside remains. Round the decay
Of that colossal wreck, boundless and bare
The lone and level sands stretch far away.

QUESTIONS

1. Describe the personality and character of King Ozymandias. What is ironic about the size of his statue, its present decay, and its inscription? How does Shelley use contrasting images of the statue and its present setting to heighten the irony of his portrait of the fallen king?

2. Write a poem or essay about a fallen leader. What physical images do you associate with the arrogance, pretensions, and downfall of the leader?

Fog-Horn
W. S. Merwin

Surely that moan is not the thing
That men thought they were making, when they
Put it there, for their own necessities.
That throat does not call to anything human
But to something men had forgotten,   5
That stirs under fog. Who wounded that beast
Incurably, or from whose pasture
Was it lost, full grown, and time closed round it
With no way back? Who tethered its tongue
So that its voice could never come   10
To speak out in the light of clear day,
But only when the shifting blindness

Descends and is acknowledged among us,
As though from under a floor it is heard,
Or as though from behind a wall, always   15
Nearer than we had remembered? If it
Was we that gave tongue to this cry
What does it bespeak in us, repeating
And repeating, insisting on something
That we never meant? We only put it there   20
To give warning of something we dare not
Ignore, lest we should come upon it
Too suddenly, recognize it too late,
As our cries were swallowed up and all hands lost.

QUESTIONS

1. How does Merwin manage to animate the foghorn, to give it a haunting, ghost-like presence? What is the foghorn's "warning"? How is this warning related to dreams and memory?

2. Write an essay about a warning you received from within yourself—a dream, or perhaps an illness, that seemed to be telling you to be careful about the way you were living your life and to pay attention to your inner life.

In a Dark Time
Theodore Roethke

In a dark time, the eye begins to see,
I meet my shadow in the deepening shade;
I hear my echo in the echoing wood—
A lord of nature weeping to a tree.
I live between the heron and the wren,   5
Beasts of the hill and serpents of the den.

What's madness but nobility of soul
At odds with circumstances? The day's on fire!
I know the purity of pure despair,
My shadow pinned against a sweating wall.   10
That place among the rocks—is it a cave,
Or winding path? The edge is what I have.

A steady storm of correspondences!
A night flowing with birds, a ragged moon,
And in broad day the midnight come again!   15
A man goes far to find out what he is—

Death of the self in a long, tearless night,
All natural shapes blazing unnatural light.

Dark, dark my light, and darker my desire.
My soul, like some heat-maddened summer fly,   20
Keeps buzzing at the sill. Which I is *I*?
A fallen man, I climb out of my fear.
The mind enters itself, and God the mind,
And one is One, free in the tearing wind.

QUESTIONS

1. What part of the self does the shadow that the speaker meets in the "deepening shade" represent? What is the speaker's mood at the beginning of the poem? How has he or she changed and grown by the time the poem reaches its final line: "And one is One, free in the tearing wind"? In what sense does the self of the speaker die in the course of the "night" of the poem? How is the speaker reborn?

2. Write a poem or essay about a time of crisis in your life, when you struggled with self-doubt and negative feelings. How did you change or grow through your struggle?

Mirror

Sylvia Plath

I am silver and exact. I have no preconceptions.
Whatever I see I swallow immediately
Just as it is, unmisted by love or dislike.
I am not cruel, only truthful—
The eye of a little god, four-cornered.   5
Most of the time I meditate on the opposite wall.
It is pink, with speckles. I have looked at it so long
I think it is a part of my heart. But it flickers.
Faces and darkness separate us over and over.

Now I am a lake. A woman bends over me,   10
Searching my reaches for what she really is.
Then she turns to those liars, the candles or the moon.
I see her back, and reflect it faithfully.
She rewards me with tears and an agitation of hands.
I am important to her. She comes and goes.   15
Each morning it is her face that replaces the darkness.
In me she has drowned a young girl, and in me an old woman
Rises toward her day after day, like a terrible fish.

QUESTIONS

1. How is the mirror like "the eye of a little god"? How is it like a lake? What does the mirror do for those who look into it? What do people look for in the mirror? In what sense do aspects of people's selves "drown" in the mirror?

2. Write an essay about vanity and appearance. Why are people in our society so concerned about their appearance? How does vanity make it difficult for people to accept the aging process?

Hunting Civil War Relics at Nimblewill Creek

James Dickey

As he moves the mine-detector
A few inches over the ground,
Making it vitally float
Among the ferns and weeds,
I come into this war   5
Slowly, with my one brother,
Watching his face grow deep
Between the earphones,
For I can tell
If we enter the buried battle   10
Of Nimblewill
Only by his expression.

Softly he wanders, parting
The grass with a dreaming hand.
No dead cry yet takes root   15
In his clapped ears
Or can be seen in his smile.
But underfoot I feel
The dead regroup,
The burst metals all in place,   20
The battle lines be drawn
Anew to include us
In Nimblewill,
And I carry the shovel and pick

More as if they were   25
Bright weapons that I bore.
A bird's cry breaks

In two, and into three parts.
We cross the creek; the cry
Shifts into another,   30
Nearer, bird, and is
Like the shout of a shadow—
Lived-with, appallingly close—
Or the soul, pronouncing
"Nimblewill":   35
Three tones; your being changes.

We climb the bank;
A faint light glows
On my brother's mouth.
I listen, as two birds fight   40
For a single voice, but he
Must be hearing the grave,
In pieces, all singing
To his clamped head,
For he smiles as if   45
He rose from the dead within
Green Nimblewill
And stood in his grandson's shape.

No shot from the buried war
Can kill me now,   50
For the dead have waited here
A hundred years to create
The look on a man's loved features,
While I stand, with
The same voice calling insanely   55
Like that of a sniper
Who throws down his rifle and yells
In the pure joy of missing me
At Nimblewill
And my brother beside me holds   60

A long-buried light on his lips.
I fall to my knees
To dig wherever he points,
To bring up mess-tin or bullet,
To go underground   65
Still singing, myself,
Like a hidden bird,
Or a man who renounces war,
Or one who shall lift up the past,

Not breathing 'Father,'   70
At Nimblewill,
But saying, 'Fathers! Fathers!'

QUESTIONS

1. What images does Dickey use to establish and draw us into the dreamlike mood
of the poem? What ghosts haunt the speaker in the poem? What comment does the
poem make on history, war, death, and family relationships? How do you interpret the
final quoted words of the poem, "Fathers! Fathers!"?

2. Write a poem or personal essay about an experience of digging through relics
from the past, looking at old family possessions stored in an attic, or visiting a museum.
How did this experience and your reflection about it change or deepen your sense of the
relationship between the past and the present?

Curandera
Pat Mora

They think she lives alone
on the edge of town in a two-room house
where she moved when her husband died
at thirty-five of a gunshot wound
in the bed of another woman. The *curandera*   5
and house have aged together to the rhythm
of the desert.

She wakes early, lights candles before
her sacred statues, brews tea of *yerbabuena*.
She moves down her porch steps, rubs   10
cool morning sand into her hands, into her arms.
Like a large black bird, she feeds on
the desert, gathering herbs for her basket.

Her days are slow, days of grinding
dried snake into powder, of crushing   15
wild bees to mix with white wine.
And the townspeople come, hoping
to be touched by her ointments,
her hands, her prayers, her eyes.
She listens to their stories, and she listens   20
to the desert, always, to the desert.

By sunset she is tired. The wind
strokes the strands of long, gray hair,

the smell of drying plants drifts
into her blood, the sun seeps   25
into her bones. She dozes
on her back porch. Rocking, rocking.

At night she cooks chopped cactus
and brews more tea. She brushes a layer
of sand from her bed, sand which covers   30
the table, stove, floor. She blows
the statues clean, the candles out.
Before sleeping, she listens to the message
of the owl and the coyote. She closes her eyes
and breathes with the mice and snakes   35
and wind.

QUESTIONS

1. How does the *curandera* pass her days? Why do the townspeople come to her? Does she have real magical or spiritual powers? If so, what seems to be the source of her power?

2. Write an essay about a mysterious older person whom people in your community believe has magical powers. What leads them to believe this?

Windigo
For Angela
Louise Erdrich

The Windigo is a flesh-eating, wintry demon with a man buried deep inside of it. In some Chippewa stories, a young girl vanquishes this monster by forcing boiling lard down its throat, thereby releasing the human at the core of ice.

You knew I was coming for you, little one,
when the kettle jumped into the fire.
Towels flapped on the hooks,
and the dog crept off, groaning,
to the deepest part of the woods.   5

In the hackles of dry brush a thin laughter started up.
Mother scolded the food warm and smooth in the pot
and called you to eat.
But I spoke in the cold trees:
New one, I have come for you, child hide and lie still.   10

The sumac pushed sour red cones through the air.
Copper burned in the raw wood.
You saw me drag toward you.
Oh touch me, I murmured, and licked the soles of your feet.

You dug your hands into my pale, melting fur.   15
I stole you off, a huge thing in my bristling armor.
Steam rolled from my wintry arms, each leaf shivered
from the bushes we passed
until they stood, naked, spread like the cleaned spines of fish.

Then your warm hands hummed over and shoveled themselves full   20
of the ice and the snow. I would darken and spill
all night running, until at last morning broke the cold earth
and I carried you home,
a river shaking in the sun.

QUESTIONS

1. How does the explanation of the Windigo legend that introduces the poem help readers to interpret the events and details in the poem? Is Erdrich suggesting that the Windigo literally spirits the child in the poem away, or should the poem be read as a nightmare? Is the ending of the poem a positive one? How has the child in the poem grown through her experience with the Windigo demon?

2. Write an essay, poem, or story about an imaginary modern demon that would frighten children. Describe the demon and its behavior and explain why it is particularly disturbing.

Mi Abuelo

Alberto Ríos

Where my grandfather is is in the ground
where you can hear the future like an
Indian with his ear at the tracks. A
pipe leads down to him so that sometimes
he whispers what will happen to a man   5
in town or how he will meet the best-
dressed woman tomorrow and how the best
man at her wedding will chew the ground
next to her. Mi abuelo is the man
who talks through all the mouths in my house. An   10
echo of me hitting the pipe sometimes
to stop him from saying "my hair is a
sieve" is the only other sound. It is a
phrase that among all others is the best,

he says, and "my hair is a sieve" is sometimes   15
repeated for hours out of the ground
when I let him, but mostly I don't. "An
abuelo should be much more than a man
like you!" He stops then, and speaks: "I am a man
who has served ants with the attitude of a   20
waiter, who has made each smile as only an
ant who is fat can, and they liked me best,
but there is nothing left." Yet, I know he ground
green coffee beans as a child, and sometimes
he will talk about his wife, and sometimes   25
about when he was deaf and a man
cured him by mail and he heard ground
hogs talking, or about how he walked with a
cane he chewed on when he got hungry. At best,
mi abuelo is a liar. I see an   30
old picture of him at nani's with an
off-white yellow center mustache and sometimes
that's all I know for sure. He talks best
about these hills, slowest waves, and where this man
is going, and I'm convinced his hair is a   35
sieve, that his fever is cool now in the ground.
Mi abuelo is an ordinary man.
I look down the pipe, sometimes, and see a
ripple-topped stream in its best suit, in the ground.

QUESTIONS

1. In what ways does the abuelo (grandfather) continue to communicate with the speaker? What is meant by the "message" of the grandfather, "my hair is a sieve"? What memories does the speaker maintain of his grandfather? What is the meaning of the speaker's final vision of his abuelo as a "ripple-topped stream in its best suit"?

2. Write an essay or poem in which you reflect on dreamlike memories and fantasies you have had about a friend or relative who has died.

Lost Sister

Cathy Song

1

In China,
even the peasants
named their first daughters
Jade—
the stone that in the far fields   5

could moisten the dry season,
could make men move mountains
for the healing green of the inner hills
glistening like slices of winter melon.

And the daughters were grateful: 10
they never left home.
To move freely was a luxury
stolen from them at birth.
Instead, they gathered patience,
learning to walk in shoes   15
the size of teacups,
without breaking—
the arc of their movements
as dormant as the rooted willow,
as redundant as the farmyard hens.   20
But they traveled far
in surviving,
learning to stretch the family rice,
to quiet the demons,
the noisy stomachs.   25

2

There is a sister
across the ocean,
who relinquished her name,
diluting jade green
with the blue of the Pacific.   30
Rising with a tide of locusts,
she swarmed with others
to inundate another shore.
In America,
there are many roads   35
and women can stride along with men.

But in another wilderness,
the possibilities,
the loneliness,
can strangulate like jungle vines.   40
The meager provisions and sentiments
of once belonging—
fermented roots, Mah-Jongg tiles and firecrackers—
set but a flimsy household
in a forest of nightless cities.   45
A giant snake rattles above,

spewing black clouds into your kitchen.
Dough-faced landlords
slip in and out of your keyholes,
making claims you don't understand,   50
tapping into your communication systems
of laundry lines and restaurant chains.

You find you need China:
your one fragile identification,
a jade link   55
handcuffed to your wrist.
You remember your mother
who walked for centuries,
footless—
and like her,   60
you have left no footprints,
but only because
there is an ocean in between,
the unremitting space of your rebellion.

QUESTIONS

1. What is the traditional role of the Chinese first daughter, as signified by the name "Jade"? Why and how does the "sister/across the ocean" rebel against her destiny and relinquish her name? Why does the rebellious immigrant daughter feel finally that she "need[s] China"?

2. Write an essay or poem directed to or reflecting on a sibling or friend who rebelled against his or her traditional culture and tried to develop a new identity. Try to clarify your feelings about how such a person needs both to rebel against and to reconcile himself or herself with the ghosts of the past.

Death Be Not Proud

John Donne

Death be not proud, though some have callèd thee
Mighty and dreadful, for thou art not so;
For those whom thou think'st thou dost overthrow
Die not, poor death, nor yet canst thou kill me.
From rest and sleep, which but thy pictures be,   5
Much pleasure, then from thee much more must flow,
And soonest our best men with thee do go,
Rest of their bones, and soul's delivery.
Thou art slave to fate, chance, kings, and desperate men,

And dost with poison, war, and sickness dwell,   10
And poppy, or charms can make us sleep as well,
And better than thy stroke; why swell'st thou then?
One short sleep past, we wake eternally,
And death shall be no more; death, thou shalt die.

QUESTIONS

1. Why does Donne think that Death should be "not proud"? In what sense do people take pleasure from the "pictures" of Death? To what is Death a slave? In what sense will Death itself "die"?

2. Write a poem or essay in which you personify death, making it into an adversary. Do you see death as a formidable adversary, or as an opponent who can be tricked or defeated, as Donne does?

Do Not Go Gentle into That Good Night
Dylan Thomas

Do not go gentle into that good night,
Old age should burn and rave at close of day;
Rage, rage against the dying of the light.

Though wise men at their end know dark is right,
Because their words had forked no lightning they   5
Do not go gentle into that good night.

Good men, the last wave by, crying how bright
Their frail deeds might have danced in a green bay,
Rage, rage against the dying of the light.

Wild men who caught and sang the sun in flight,   10
And learn, too late, they grieved it on its way,
Do not go gentle into that good night.

Grave men, near death, who see with blinding sight
Blind eyes could blaze like meteors and be gay,
Rage, rage against the dying of the light.   15

And you, my father, there on the sad height,
Curse, bless, me now with your fierce tears, I pray.
Do not go gentle into that good night.
Rage, rage against the dying of the light.

QUESTIONS

1. What arguments does the speaker in the poem use to persuade his father and his readers to resist death? How does the poem use repetition and examples of different types of people to support these arguments?

2. Write a poem or essay directed to a sick or troubled person, urging him or her to resist giving into despair. Use examples, images, and repetition to support your viewpoint.

A Supermarket in California
Allen Ginsberg

What thoughts I have of you tonight, Walt Whitman, for I walked
down the sidestreets under the trees with a headache self-conscious looking
at the full moon.
    In my hungry fatigue, and shopping for images, I went into the neon
fruit supermarket, dreaming of your enumerations!
    What peaches and what penumbras? Whole families shopping at night!
Aisles full of husbands! Wives in the avocados, babies in the
tomatoes!—and you, García Lorca, what were you doing down by the
watermelons?

    I saw you, Walt Whitman, childless, lonely old grubber, poking among
the meats in the refrigerator and eyeing the grocery boys.
    I heard you asking questions of each: Who killed the pork chops?
What price bananas? Are you my Angel?   5
    I wandered in and out of the brilliant stacks of cans following you, and
followed in my imagination by the store detective.
    We strode down the open corridors together in our solitary fancy
tasting artichokes, possessing every frozen delicacy, and never passing the
cashier.

    Where are we going, Walt Whitman? The doors close in a hour. Which way
does your beard point tonight?
    (I touch your book and dream of our odyssey in the supermarket and feel
absurd.)
    Will we walk all night through solitary streets? The trees add shade
to shade, lights out in the houses, we'll both be lonely.   10
    Will we stroll dreaming of the lost America of love past blue
automobiles in driveways, home to our silent cottage?
    Ah, dear father, graybeard, lonely old ccurage-teacher, what America
did you have when Charon quit poling his ferry and you got out on a
smoking bank and stood watching the boat disappear on the black waters
of Lethe?

QUESTIONS

1. Why does Ginsberg select poets Walt Whitman and Federico García Lorca as ghosts to appear in a modern supermarket? What comment does the poem make about America, homosexuality, commercialism, nature, and death?

2. Write a poem or essay about a supermarket at night. Observe the people there and the way you relate to the people and the physical environment. Of what literary figures do the people remind you? What do you think the shoppers will do or feel when they leave? Try to ask some questions or draw some conclusions about modern life as Ginsberg does in his poem.

The Envelope
Maxine Kumin

It is true, Martin Heidegger, as you have written,
I *fear to cease,* even knowing that at the hour
of my death my daughters will absorb me, even
knowing they will carry me about forever
inside them, an arrested fetus, even as I carry   5
the ghost of my mother under my navel, a nervy
little androgynous person, a miracle
folded in lotus position.

Like those old pear-shaped Russian dolls that open
at the middle to reveal another and another, down   10
to the pea-sized, irreducible minim,
may we carry our mothers forth in our bellies.
May we, borne onward by our daughters, ride
in the Envelope of Almost-Infinity,
that chain letter good for the next twenty-five   15
thousand days of their lives.

QUESTIONS

1. What helps the speaker to reconcile herself with the inevitability of death? How does the comparison with "those old pear-shaped Russian dolls" help to clarify the speaker's views on death and immortality? What is the "Envelope of Almost-Infinity," and how do women "ride" in it? In what sense is the envelope like a chain letter?

2. Do you agree with the speaker that people continue to live on through future generations of their family after physical death? Provide examples to support your point of view.

Drama

Hamlet
William Shakespeare

Journal

Write about a time when you acted wild or manic but really felt otherwise. What motivated you to act differently from the way you felt? Did acting "crazy" enable you to perceive others differently from the way you do ordinarily?

[DRAMATIS PERSONAE

GHOST *of Hamlet, the former King of Denmark*
CLAUDIUS, *King of Denmark, the former King's brother*
GERTRUDE, *Queen of Denmark, widow of the former King and now wife of Claudius*
HAMLET, *Prince of Denmark, son of the late King and of Gertrude*

POLONIUS, *councillor to the King*
LAERTES, *his son*
OPHELIA, *his daughter*
REYNALDO, *his servant*

HORATIO, *Hamlet's friend and fellow student*

VOLTIMAND,
CORNELIUS,
ROSENCRANTZ,
GUILDENSTERN, }*members of the Danish court*
OSRIC,
A GENTLEMAN,
A LORD,

BERNARDO,
FRANCISCO, }*officers and soldiers on watch*
MARCELLUS,

FORTINBRAS, *Prince of Norway*
CAPTAIN *in his army*

Three or Four PLAYERS, *taking the roles of* PROLOGUE, PLAYER
   KING, PLAYER QUEEN, *and* LUCIANUS
Two MESSENGERS
FIRST SAILOR
Two CLOWNS, *a gravedigger and his companion*
PRIEST
FIRST AMBASSADOR *from England*

Lords, Soldiers, Attendants, Guards, other Players, Followers of Laertes, other Sailors,
another Ambassador or Ambassadors from England

SCENE: Denmark]

ACT I

Scene 1

Enter BERNARDO *and* FRANCISCO, *two sentinels,* [*meeting*].
BERNARDO: Who's there?
FRANCISCO:
   Nay, answer me. Stand and unfold yourself.   2
BERNARDO: Long live the King!
FRANCISCO: Bernardo?
BERNARDO: He.
FRANCISCO:
   You come most carefully upon your hour.
BERNARDO:
   'Tis now struck twelve. Get thee to bed, Francisco.
FRANCISCO:
   For this relief much thanks. 'Tis bitter cold,
   And I am sick at heart.
BERNARDO: Have you had quiet guard?
FRANCISCO: Not a mouse stirring.
BERNARDO: Well, good night.
   If you do meet Horatio and Marcellus,
   The rivals of my watch, bid them make haste.   14

Enter HORATIO *and* MARCELLUS.

FRANCISCO:
   I think I hear them.—Stand, ho! Who is there?
HORATIO: Friends to this ground.   16

I.1. Location: Elsinore castle. A guard platform.
2 *me* (Francisco emphasizes that *he* is the sentry currently on watch.) *unfold yourself* reveal your
identity   14 *rivals* partners   16 *ground* country, land

MARCELLUS: And liegemen to the Dane.   17
FRANCISCO: Give you good night.   18
MARCELLUS:
O, farewell, honest soldier. Who hath relieved you?
FRANCISCO:
Bernardo hath my place. Give you good night.

Exit FRANCISCO.

MARCELLUS: Holla! Bernardo!
BERNARDO: Say, what, is Horatio there?
HORATIO: A piece of him.
BERNARDO:
Welcome, Horatio. Welcome, good Marcellus.
HORATIO:
What, has this thing appeared again tonight?
BERNARDO: I have seen nothing.
MARCELLUS:
Horatio says 'tis but our fantasy,   27
And will not let belief take hold of him
Touching this dreaded sight twice seen of us.
Therefore I have entreated him along   30
With us to watch the minutes of this night,   31
That if again this apparition come
He may approve our eyes and speak to it.   33
HORATIO:
Tush, tush, 'twill not appear.
BERNARDO: Sit down awhile,
And let us once again assail your ears,
That are so fortified against our story,
What we have two nights seen.   37
HORATIO: Well, sit we down,
And let us hear Bernardo speak of this.
BERNARDO: Last night of all,   39
When yond same star that's westward from the pole   40
Had made his course t' illume that part of heaven   41
Where now it burns, Marcellus and myself,
The bell then beating one—

Enter GHOST.

MARCELLUS:
Peace, break thee off! Look where it comes again!

---

17 *liegemen to the Dane* men sworn to serve the Danish king   18 *Give* i.e., may God give   27 *fantasy* imagination   30 *along* i.e., to come along   31 *watch* i.e., keep watch during   33 *approve* corroborate   37 *What* i.e., with what   39 *Last . . . all* i.e., this *very* last night. (Emphatic.)   40 *pole* polestar, north star   41 *his* its.   *illume* illuminate

BERNARDO:

    In the same figure like the King that's dead.

MARCELLUS:

    Thou art a scholar. Speak to it, Horatio.   46

BERNARDO:

    Looks 'a not like the King? Mark it, Horatio.   47

HORATIO:

    Most like. It harrows me with fear and wonder.

BERNARDO:

    It would be spoke to.

MARCELLUS: Speak to it, Horatio.   49

HORATIO:

    What art thou that usurp'st this time of night,   50

    Together with that fair and warlike form

    In which the majesty of buried Denmark   52

    Did sometime march? By heaven, I charge thee speak! 53

MARCELLUS:

    It is offended.

BERNARDO: See, it stalks away.

HORATIO:

    Stay! Speak, speak! I charge thee, speak!   *Exit* GHOST.

MARCELLUS: 'Tis gone and will not answer.

BERNARDO:

    How now, Horatio? You tremble and look pale.

    Is not this something more than fantasy?

    What think you on 't?   59

HORATIO:

    Before my God, I might not this believe

    Without the sensible and true avouch   61

    Of mine own eyes.

MARCELLUS: Is it not like the King?

HORATIO: As thou art to thyself.

    Such was the very armor he had on

    When he the ambitious Norway combated.   65

    So frowned he once when, in an angry parle,   66

    He smote the sledded Polacks on the ice.   67

    'Tis strange.

---

46 *scholar* one learned enough to know how to question a ghost properly 47 *'a* he 49 *It . . . to* (It was commonly believed that a ghost could not speak until spoken to.) 50 *usurp'st* wrongfully takes over 52 *buried Denmark* the buried King of Denmark 53 *sometime* formerly 59 *on 't* of it 61 *sensible* confirmed by the senses. *avouch* warrant, evidence 65 *Norway* King of Norway 66 *parle* parley 67 *sledded* traveling on sleds. *Polacks* Poles

MARCELLUS:
> Thus twice before, and jump at this dead hour,   69
> With martial stalk hath he gone by our watch.

HORATIO:
> In what particular thought to work I know not,   71
> But in the gross and scope of mine opinion   72
> This bodes some strange eruption to our state.

MARCELLUS:
> Good now, sit down, and tell me, he that knows,   74
> Why this same strict and most observant watch
> So nightly toils the subject of the land,   76
> And why such daily cast of brazen cannon   77
> And foreign mart for implements of war,   78
> Why such impress of shipwrights, whose sore task   79
> Does not divide the Sunday from the week.
> What might be toward, that this sweaty haste   81
> Doth make the night joint-laborer with the day?
> Who is 't that can inform me?

HORATIO: That can I;
> At least, the whisper goes so. Our last king,
> Whose image even but now appeared to us,
> Was, as you know, by Fortinbras of Norway,
> Thereto pricked on by a most emulate pride,   87
> Dared to the combat; in which our valiant Hamlet—
> For so this side of our known world esteemed him—   89
> Did slay this Fortinbras; who by a sealed compact   90
> Well ratified by law and heraldry
> Did forfeit, with his life, all those his lands
> Which he stood seized of to the conqueror;   93
> Against the which a moiety competent   94
> Was gagèd by our king, which had returned   95
> To the inheritance of Fortinbras
> Had he been vanquisher, as, by the same covenant   97
> And carriage of the article designed,   98
> His fell to Hamlet. Now, sir, young Fortinbras,

---

69 *jump* exactly   71 *to work* i.e., to collect my thoughts and try to understand this   72 *gross and scope* general drift   74 *Good now* (An expression denoting entreaty or expostulation.)   76 *toils* causes to toil. *subject* subjects   77 *cast* casting   78 *mart* buying and selling   79 *impress* impressment, conscription   81 *toward* in preparation   87 *Thereto . . . pride* (Refers to old Fortinbras, not the Danish King.) *pricked on* incited. *emulate* emulous, ambitious   89 *this . . . world* i.e., all Europe, the Western world   90 *sealed* certified, confirmed   93 *seized* possessed   94 *Against the* in return for. *moiety competent* sufficient portion   95 *gagèd* engaged, pledged   97 *covenant* i.e., the *sealed compact* of l. 90   98 *carriage* import, bearing. *article designed* article or clause drawn up or prearranged

Of unimprovèd mettle hot and full,   100
Hath in the skirts of Norway here and there   101
Sharked up a list of lawless resolutes   102
For food and diet to some enterprise   103
That hath a stomach in 't, which is no other—   104
As it doth well appear unto our state—
But to recover of us, by strong hand
And terms compulsatory, those foresaid lands
So by his father lost. And this, I take it,
Is the main motive of our preparations,
The source of this our watch, and the chief head   110
Of this posthaste and rummage in the land.   111

BERNARDO:
I think it be no other but e'en so.
Well may it sort that this portentous figure   113
Comes armèd through our watch so like the King
That was and is the question of these wars.   115

HORATIO:
A mote it is to trouble the mind's eye.   116
In the most high and palmy state of Rome,   117
A little ere the mightiest Julius fell,
The graves stood tenantless and the sheeted dead   119
Did squeak and gibber in the Roman streets;
As stars with trains of fire and dews of blood,   121
Disasters in the sun; and the moist star   122
Upon whose influence Neptune's empire stands   123
Was sick almost to doomsday with eclipse.   124
And even the like precurse of feared events,   125
As harbingers preceding still the fates   126
And prologue to the omen coming on,   127
Have heaven and earth together demonstrated
Unto our climatures and countrymen.   129

Enter GHOST.
But soft, behold! Lo, where it comes again!   130

100 *unimprovèd* unrestrained, undisciplined 101 *skirts* outlying regions, outskirts 102 *Sharked up* got together in irregular fashion. *list* i.e., troop. *resolutes* desperadoes 103 *For food and diet* i.e., they are to serve as *food,* or means, *to some enterprise* 104 *stomach* (1) a spirit of daring (2) an appetite that is fed by the *lawless resolutes* 110 *head* source 111 *rummage* bustle, commotion 113 *sort* suit 115 *question* focus of contention 116 *mote* speck of dust 117 *palmy* flourishing 119 *sheeted* shrouded 121 *As* (This abrupt transition suggests that matter is possibly omitted between ll. 120 and 121.) 122 *Disasters* unfavorable signs or aspects. *moist star* i.e., moon, governing tides 123 *Neptune* god of the sea. *stands* depends 124 *sick . . . doomsday* (See Matthew 24:29 and Revelation 6:12.) 125 *precurse* heralding, foreshadowing 126 *harbingers* forerunners. *still* continually 127 *omen* calamitous event 129 *climatures* regions 130 *soft* i.e., enough, break off

I'll cross it, though it blast me. *(It spreads his arms.)*
   Stay, illusion!   131
If thou hast any sound or use of voice,
  Speak to me!
If there be any good thing to be done
That may to thee do ease and grace to me,
Speak to me!
If thou art privy to thy country's fate,
Which, happily, foreknowing may avoid,   138
O, speak!
Or if thou hast uphoarded in thy life
Extorted treasure in the womb of earth,
For which, they say, you spirits oft walk in death,
Speak of it! *(The cock crows.)* Stay and speak!—
   Stop it, Marcellus.
MARCELLUS:
  Shall I strike at it with my partisan?   144
HORATIO: Do, if it will not stand.   *[They strike at it.]*
BERNARDO: 'Tis here!
HORATIO: 'Tis here!   *[Exit GHOST.]*
MARCELLUS: 'Tis gone.
  We do it wrong, being so majestical,
  To offer it the show of violence,
  For it is as the air invulnerable,
  And our vain blows malicious mockery.
BERNARDO:
  It was about to speak when the cock crew.
HORATIO:
  And then it started like a guilty thing
  Upon a fearful summons. I have heard
  The cock, that is the trumpet to the morn,   156
  Doth with his lofty and shrill-sounding throat
  Awake the god of day, and at his warning,
  Whether in sea or fire, in earth or air,
  Th' extravagant and erring spirit hies   160
  To his confine; and of the truth herein
  This present object made probation.   162
MARCELLUS:
  It faded on the crowing of the cock.
  Some say that ever 'gainst that season comes   164

---

131 *cross* stand in its path, confront. *blast* wither, strike with a curse *s.d. his* its 138 *happily* haply, perchance 144 *partisan* long-handled spear 156 *trumpet* trumpeter 160 *extravagant and erring* wandering beyond bounds. (The words have similar meaning.) 162 *probation* proof 164 *'gainst* just before

Wherein our Savior's birth is celebrated,
This bird of dawning singeth all night long,
And then, they say, no spirit dare stir abroad;
The nights are wholesome, then no planets strike,   168
No fairy takes, nor witch hath power to charm,   169
So hallowed and so gracious is that time.   170

HORATIO:
So have I heard and do in part believe it.
But, look, the morn in russet mantle clad
Walks o'er the dew of yon high eastward hill.
Break we our watch up, and by my advice
Let us impart what we have seen tonight
Unto young Hamlet; for upon my life,
This spirit, dumb to us, will speak to him.
Do you consent we shall acquaint him with it,
As needful in our loves, fitting our duty?

MARCELLUS:
Let's do 't, I pray, and I this morning know
Where we shall find him most conveniently.

Exeunt.

ACT I

Scene 2

Flourish. Enter CLAUDIUS, *King of Denmark,* GERTRUDE *the Queen,* [the] *Council, as* POLONIUS *and his son* LAERTES, HAMLET, *cum aliis* [*including* VOLTIMAND *and* CORNELIUS].

KING:
Though yet of Hamlet our dear brother's death
The memory be green, and that it us befitted
To bear our hearts in grief and our whole kingdom
To be contracted in one brow of woe,
Yet so far hath discretion fought with nature
That we with wisest sorrow think on him
Together with remembrance of ourselves.
Therefore our sometime sister, now our queen,   8
Th' imperial jointress to this warlike state,   9
Have we, as 'twere with a defeated joy—

---

168 *strike* destroy by evil influence   169 *takes* bewitches   170 *gracious* full of grace
I.2. Location: The castle.
s.d. as i.e., such as, including.   *cum aliis* with others   1 *our* my. (The royal "we"; also in the following lines.)   8 *sometime* former   9 *jointress* woman possessing property with her husband

With an auspicious and a dropping eye,   11
With mirth in funeral and with dirge in marriage,
In equal scale weighing delight and dole—   13
Taken to wife. Nor have we herein barred
Your better wisdoms, which have freely gone
With this affair along. For all, our thanks.
Now follows that you know young Fortinbras,   17
Holding a weak supposal of our worth,   18
Or thinking by our late dear brother's death
Our state to be disjoint and out of frame,
Colleaguèd with this dream of his advantage,   21
He hath not failed to pester us with message
Importing the surrender of those lands   23
Lost by his father, with all bonds of law,   24
To our most valiant brother. So much for him.
Now for ourself and for this time of meeting.
Thus much the business is: we have here writ
To Norway, uncle of young Fortinbras—
Who, impotent and bedrid, scarcely hears   29
Of this his nephew's purpose—to suppress
His further gait herein, in that the levies,   31
The lists, and full proportions are all made   32
Out of his subject; and we here dispatch   33
You, good Cornelius, and you, Voltimand,
For bearers of this greeting to old Norway,
Giving to you no further personal power
To business with the King more than the scope
Of these dilated articles allow.   [*He gives a paper.*]   38
Farewell, and let your haste commend your duty.   39
CORNELIUS, VOLTIMAND:
   In that, and all things, will we show our duty.
KING:
   We doubt it nothing. Heartily farewell.   41

                          [*Exeunt* VOLTIMAND *and* CORNELIUS.]

And now, Laertes, what's the news with you?
You told us of some suit; what is 't, Laertes?

11 *With . . . eye* with one eye smiling and the other weeping   13 *dole* grief   17 *know* be informed
(that)   18 *weak supposal* low estimate   21 *Colleaguèd with* joined to, allied with.   *dream . . . advantage* illusory hope of success. (His only ally is this hope.)   23 *Importing* pertaining to   24 *bonds* contracts   29 *impotent* helpless   31 *His* i.e., Fortinbras's.   *gait* proceeding   31–33 *in that . . . subject*
since the levying of troops and supplies is drawn entirely from the King of Norway's own subjects
38 *dilated* set out at length   39 *commend* recommend to friendly remembrance. (Their haste will impress the King with their attention to duty.)   41 *nothing* not at all

You cannot speak of reason to the Dane   44
And lose your voice. What wouldst thou beg, Laertes,   45
That shall not be my offer, not thy asking?
The head is not more native to the heart,   47
The hand more instrumental to the mouth,   48
Than is the throne of Denmark to thy father.
What wouldst thou have, Laertes?

LAERTES:
                               My dread lord,

Your leave and favor to return to France,   51
From whence though willingly I came to Denmark
To show my duty in your coronation,
Yet now I must confess, that duty done,
My thoughts and wishes bend again toward France
And bow them to your gracious leave and pardon.   56

KING:
Have you your father's leave? What says Polonius?

POLONIUS:
H'ath, my lord, wrung from me my slow leave   58
By laborsome petition, and at last
Upon his will I sealed my hard consent.   60
I do beseech you, give him leave to go.

KING:
Take thy fair hour, Laertes. Time be thine,   62
And thy best graces spend it at thy will!   63
But now, my cousin Hamlet, and my son—   64

HAMLET:
A little more than kin, and less than kind.   65

KING:
How is it that the clouds still hang on you?

HAMLET:
Not so, my lord. I am too much in the sun.   67

QUEEN:
Good Hamlet, cast thy nighted color off,   68
And let thine eye look like a friend on Denmark.   69

---

44 *the Dane* the Danish king   45 *lose your voice* waste your speech   47 *native* closely connected, related   48 *instrumental* serviceable   51 *leave and favor* kind permission   56 *leave and pardon* permission to depart   58 *H'ath* he has   60 *sealed* (as if sealing a legal document).   *hard* reluctant   62 *Take thy fair hour* enjoy your time of youth   63 *And . . . will* and may your finest qualities guide the way you choose to spend your time   64 *cousin* any kin not of the immediate family   65 *A little . . . . kind* i.e., closer than an ordinary nephew (since I am stepson), and yet more separated in natural feeling (with pun on *kind* meaning "affectionate" and "natural," "lawful." This line is often read as an aside, but it need not be. The King chooses perhaps not to respond to Hamlet's cryptic and bitter remark.)   67 *the sun* i.e., the sunshine of the King's royal favor (with pun on *son*)   68 *nighted color* (1) mourning garments of black (2) dark melancholy   69 *Denmark* the King of Denmark

Do not forever with thy vailèd lids   70
Seek for thy noble father in the dust.
Thou know'st 'tis common, all that lives must die,   72
Passing through nature to eternity.
HAMLET:
   Ay, madam, it is common.
QUEEN: If it be,
   Why seems it so particular with thee?   75
HAMLET:
   Seems, madam? Nay, it is. I know not "seems."
'Tis not alone my inky cloak, good Mother,
Nor customary suits of solemn black,   78
Nor windy suspiration of forced breath,   79
No, nor the fruitful river in the eye,   80
Nor the dejected havior of the visage,   81
Together with all forms, moods, shapes of grief,   82
That can denote me truly. These indeed seem,
For they are actions that a man might play.
But I have that within which passes show;
These but the trappings and the suits of woe.
KING:
   'Tis sweet and commendable in your nature, Hamlet,
To give these mourning duties to your father.
But you must know your father lost a father,
That father lost, lost his, and the survivor bound
In filial obligation for some term
To do obsequious sorrow. But to persever   92
In obstinate condolement is a course   93
Of impious stubbornness. 'Tis unmanly grief.
It shows a will most incorrect to heaven,
A heart unfortified, a mind impatient,   96
An understanding simple and unschooled.   97
For what we know must be and is as common
As any the most vulgar thing to sense,   99
Why should we in our peevish opposition
Take it to heart? Fie, 'tis a fault to heaven,
A fault against the dead, a fault to nature,
To reason most absurd, whose common theme

---

70 *vailèd lids* lowered eyes 72 *common* of universal occurrence. (But Hamlet plays on the sense of "vulgar" in l. 74.) 75 *particular* personal 78 *customary* (1) socially conventional (2) habitual with me 79 *suspiration* sighing 80 *fruitful* abundant 81 *havior* expression 82 *moods* outward expressions of feeling 92 *obsequious* suited to obsequies or funerals. *persever* persevere 93 *condolement* sorrowing 96 *unfortified* i.e., against adversity 97 *simple* ignorant 99 *As . . . sense* as the most ordinary experience

Is death of fathers, and who still hath cried,   104
From the first corpse till he that died today,   105
"This must be so." We pray you, throw to earth
This unprevailing woe and think of us   107
As of a father; for let the world take note,
You are the most immediate to our throne,   109
And with no less nobility of love
Than that which dearest father bears his son
Do I impart toward you. For your intent   112
In going back to school in Wittenberg,   113
It is most retrograde to our desire,   114
And we beseech you bend you to remain   115
Here in the cheer and comfort of our eye,
Our chiefest courtier, cousin, and our son.

QUEEN:
Let not thy mother lose her prayers, Hamlet.
I pray thee, stay with us, go not to Wittenberg.

HAMLET:
I shall in all my best obey you, madam.   120

KING:
Why, 'tis a loving and a fair reply.
Be as ourself in Denmark. Madam, come.
This gentle and unforced accord of Hamlet
Sits smiling to my heart, in grace whereof   124
No jocund health that Denmark drinks today   125
But the great cannon to the clouds shall tell,
And the King's rouse the heaven shall bruit again,   127
Respeaking earthly thunder. Come away.   128

                    Flourish. Exeunt all but HAMLET.

HAMLET:
O, that this too too sullied flesh would melt,   129
Thaw, and resolve itself into a dew!
Or that the Everlasting had not fixed
His canon 'gainst self-slaughter! O God, God,   132
How weary, stale, flat, and unprofitable
Seem to me all the uses of this world!   134

---

104 *still* always   105 *the first corpse* (Abel's)   107 *unprevailing* unavailing   109 *most immediate* next in succession   112 *impart toward* i.e., bestow my affection on.   *For* as for   113 *to school* i.e., to your studies.   *Wittenberg* famous German university founded in 1502   114 *retrograde* contrary   115 *bend you* incline yourself   120 *in all my best* to the best of my ability   124 *to* i.e., at.   *grace* thanksgiving 125 *jocund* merry   127 *rouse* drinking of a draft of liquor.   *bruit again* loudly echo   128 *thunder* i.e., of trumpet and kettledrum, sounded when the King drinks; see I.4.8–12   129 *sullied* defiled. (The early quartos read *sallied,* the Folio *solid.*)   132 *canon* law   134 *all the uses* the whole routine

Fie on 't, ah fie! 'Tis an unweeded garden
That grows to seed. Things rank and gross in nature
Possess it merely. That it should come to this!   137
But two months dead—nay, not so much, not two.
So excellent a king, that was to this   139
Hyperion to a satyr, so loving to my mother   140
That he might not beteem the winds of heaven   141
Visit her face too roughly. Heaven and earth,
Must I remember? Why, she would hang on him
As if increase of appetite had grown
By what it fed on, and yet within a month—
Let me not think on 't; frailty, thy name is woman!—
A little month, or ere those shoes were old   147
With which she followed my poor father's body,
Like Niobe, all tears, why she, even she—   149
O God, a beast, that wants discourse of reason,   150
Would have mourned longer—married with my uncle,
My father's brother, but no more like my father
Than I to Hercules. Within a month,
Ere yet the salt of most unrighteous tears
Had left the flushing in her gallèd eyes,   155
She married. O, most wicked speed, to post
With such dexterity to incestuous sheets!   157
It is not, nor it cannot come to good.
But break, my heart, for I must hold my tongue.

Enter HORATIO, MARCELLUS, *and* BERNARDO.

HORATIO:
   Hail to your lordship!
HAMLET: I am glad to see you well.
   Horatio!—or I do forget myself.
HORATIO:
   The same, my lord, and your poor servant ever.
HAMLET:
   Sir, my good friend; I'll change that name with you.   163

---

137 *merely* completely   139 *to* in comparison to   140 *Hyperion* Titan sun-god, father of Helios.
satyr a lecherous creature of classical mythology, half-human but with a goat's legs, tail, ears,
and horns   141 *beteem* allow   147 *or ere* even before   149 *Niobe* Tantalus' daughter, Queen of
Thebes, who boasted that she had more sons and daughters than Leto; for this, Apollo and
Artemis, children of Leto, slew her fourteen children. She was turned by Zeus into a stone that
continually dropped tears.   150 *wants . . . reason* lacks the faculty of reason   155 *gallèd* irritated, inflamed   157 *incestuous* (In Shakespeare's day, the marriage of a man like Claudius to his
deceased brother's wife was considered incestuous.)   163 *change* exchange (i.e., the name of
friend)

And what make you from Wittenberg, Horatio?—   164
Marcellus.

MARCELLUS: My good lord.

HAMLET:

I am very glad to see you. [*TO* BERNARDO.] Good even, sir.—
But what in faith make you from Wittenberg?

HORATIO:

A truant disposition, good my lord.

HAMLET:

I would not hear your enemy say so,
Nor shall you do my ear that violence
To make it truster of your own report
Against yourself. I know you are no truant.
But what is your affair in Elsinore?
We'll teach you to drink deep ere you depart.

HORATIO:

My lord, I came to see your father's funeral.

HAMLET:

I prithee, do not mock me, fellow student;
I think it was to see my mother's wedding.

HORATIO:

Indeed, my lord, it followed hard upon.   179

HAMLET:

Thrift, thrift, Horatio! The funeral baked meats   180
Did coldly furnish forth the marriage tables.   181
Would I had met my dearest foe in heaven   182
Or ever I had seen that day, Horatio!   183
My father!—Methinks I see my father.

HORATIO:

Where, my lord?

HAMLET: In my mind's eye, Horatio.

HORATIO:

I saw him once. 'A was a goodly king.   186

HAMLET:

'A was a man. Take him for all in all,
I shall not look upon his like again.

HORATIO:

My lord, I think I saw him yesternight.

HAMLET: Saw? Who?

HORATIO: My lord, the King your father.

HAMLET: The King my father?

---

164 *make* do   179 *hard* close   180 *baked meats* meat pies   181 *coldly* i.e., as cold leftovers   182
dearest closest (and therefore deadliest)   183 *Or ever* before   186 *'A* he

HORATIO:

    Season your admiration for a while   193

    With an attent ear till I may deliver,   194

    Upon the witness of these gentlemen,

    This marvel to you.

HAMLET: For God's love, let me hear!

HORATIO:

    Two nights together had these gentlemen,

    Marcellus and Bernardo, on their watch,

    In the dead waste and middle of the night,

    Been thus encountered. A figure like your father,

    Armèd at point exactly, cap-à-pie,   201

    Appears before them, and with solemn march

    Goes slow and stately by them. Thrice he walked

    By their oppressed and fear-surprisèd eyes

    Within his truncheon's length, whilst they, distilled   205

    Almost to jelly with the act of fear,   206

    Stand dumb and speak not to him. This to me

    In dreadful secrecy impart they did,

    And I with them the third night kept the watch,

    Where, as they had delivered, both in time,

    Form of the thing, each word made true and good,

    The apparition comes. I knew your father;

    These hands are not more like.

HAMLET: But where was this?

MARCELLUS:

    My lord, upon the platform where we watch.

HAMLET:

    Did you not speak to it?

HORATIO: My lord, I did,

    But answer made it none. Yet once methought

    It lifted up its head and did address   217

    Itself to motion, like as it would speak;   218

    But even then the morning cock crew loud,   219

    And at the sound it shrunk in haste away

    And vanished from our sight.

HAMLET: 'Tis very strange.

HORATIO:

    As I do live, my honored lord, 'tis true,

---

193 *Season your admiration* restrain your astonishment   194 *attent* attentive   201 *at point* correctly in every detail.   *cap-à-pie* from head to foot   205 *truncheon* officer's staff.   *distilled* dissolved 206 *act* action, operation   217–218 *did . . . speak* began to move as though it were about to speak 219 *even then* at that very instant

And we did think it writ down in our duty
To let you know of it.

HAMLET:

Indeed, indeed, sirs. But this troubles me.
Hold you the watch tonight?

ALL: We do, my lord.

HAMLET: Armed, say you?

ALL: Armed, my lord.

HAMLET: From top to toe?

ALL: My lord, from head to foot.

HAMLET: Then saw you not his face?

HORATIO:

O, yes, my lord, he wore his beaver up.   232

HAMLET: What looked he, frowningly?   233

HORATIO:

A countenance more in sorrow than in anger.

HAMLET: Pale or red?

HORATIO: Nay, very pale.

HAMLET: And fixed his eyes upon you?

HORATIO: Most constantly.

HAMLET: I would I had been there.

HORATIO: It would have much amazed you.

HAMLET: Very like, very like. Stayed it long?

HORATIO:

While one with moderate haste might tell a hundred.   242

MARCELLUS, BERNARDO: Longer, longer.

HORATIO: Not when I saw 't.

HAMLET: His beard was grizzled—no?   245

HORATIO:

It was, as I have seen it in his life,
A sable silvered.

HAMLET: I will watch tonight.   247
Perchance 'twill walk again.

HORATIO: I warrant it will.

HAMLET:

If it assume my noble father's person,
I'll speak to it though hell itself should gape
And bid me hold my peace. I pray you all,
If you have hitherto concealed this sight,
Let it be tenable in your silence still,   253
And whatsoever else shall hap tonight,

---

232 *beaver* visor on the helmet   233 *What* how   242 *tell* count   245 *grizzled* gray   247 *sable silvered* black mixed with white   253 *tenable* held tightly

Give it an understanding but no tongue.
I will requite your loves. So, fare you well.
Upon the platform twixt eleven and twelve
I'll visit you.

ALL: Our duty to your honor.

HAMLET:
Your loves, as mine to you. Farewell.

Exeunt [all but HAMLET*].*

My father's spirit in arms! All is not well.
I doubt some foul play. Would the night were come!   261
Till then sit still, my soul. Foul deeds will rise,
Though all the earth o'erwhelm them, to men's eyes.

Exit.

ACT I

Scene 3

Enter LAERTES *and* OPHELIA, *his sister.*

LAERTES:
My necessaries are embarked. Farewell.
And, sister, as the winds give benefit
And convoy is assistant, do not sleep   3
But let me hear from you.

OPHELIA: Do you doubt that?

LAERTES:
For Hamlet, and the trifling of his favor,
Hold it a fashion and a toy in blood,   6
A violet in the youth of primy nature,   7
Forward, not permanent, sweet, not lasting,   8
The perfume and suppliance of a minute—   9
No more.

OPHELIA: No more but so?

LAERTES: Think it no more.
For nature crescent does not grow alone   11
In thews and bulk, but as this temple waxes   12
The inward service of the mind and soul
Grows wide withal. Perhaps he loves you now,   14

---

261 *doubt* suspect
I.3. Location: Polonius's chambers.
3 *convoy is assistant* means of conveyance are available   6 *toy in blood* passing amorous fancy
7 *primy* in its prime, springtime   8 *Forward* precocious   9 *suppliance* supply, filler   11 *crescent*
growing, waxing   12 *thews* bodily strength. *temple* i.e., body   14 *Grows wide withal* grows along
with it

And now no soil nor cautel doth besmirch   15
The virtue of his will; but you must fear,   16
His greatness weighed, his will is not his own.   17
For he himself is subject to his birth.
He may not, as unvalued persons do,
Carve for himself, for on his choice depends   20
The safety and health of this whole state,
And therefore must his choice be circumscribed
Unto the voice and yielding of that body   23
Whereof he is the head. Then if he says he loves you,
It fits your wisdom so far to believe it
As he in his particular act and place   26
May give his saying deed, which is no further   27
Than the main voice of Denmark goes withal.   28
Then weigh what loss your honor may sustain
If with too credent ear you list his songs,   30
Or lose your heart, or your chaste treasure open
To his unmastered importunity.
Fear it, Ophelia, fear it, my dear sister,
And keep you in the rear of your affection,   34
Out of the shot and danger of desire.   35
The chariest maid is prodigal enough   36
If she unmask her beauty to the moon.   37
Virtue itself scapes not calumnious strokes.
The canker galls the infants of the spring   39
Too oft before their buttons be disclosed,   40
And in the morn and liquid dew of youth   41
Contagious blastments are most imminent.   42
Be wary then; best safety lies in fear.
Youth to itself rebels, though none else near.   44
OPHELIA:
I shall the effect of this good lesson keep
As watchman to my heart. But, good my brother,
Do not, as some ungracious pastors do,   47
Show me the steep and thorny way to heaven,

---

15 *soil* blemish. *cautel* deceit 16 *will* desire 17 *His greatness weighed* considering his high position 20 *Carve* i.e., choose 23 *voice and yielding* assent, approval 26 *in . . . place* in his particular restricted circumstances 27 *deed* effect 28 *main voice* general assent. *withal* along with 30 *credent* credulous. *list* listen to 34 *keep . . . affection* don't advance as far as your affection might lead you. (A military metaphor.) 35 *shot* range 36 *chariest* most scrupulously modest 37 *If she unmask* if she does no more than show her beauty. *moon* (Symbol of chastity.) 39 *canker galls* cankerworm destroys 40 *buttons* buds. *disclosed* opened 41 *liquid dew* i.e., time when dew is fresh and bright 42 *blastments* blights 44 *Youth . . . rebels* youth is inherently rebellious 47 *ungracious* ungodly

Whiles like a puffed and reckless libertine   49
Himself the primrose path of dalliance treads,
And recks not his own rede.

Enter POLONIUS.

LAERTES: O, fear me not.   51
I stay too long. But here my father comes.
A double blessing is a double grace;   53
Occasion smiles upon a second leave.   54

POLONIUS:
Yet here, Laertes? Aboard, aboard, for shame!
The wind sits in the shoulder of your sail,
And you are stayed for. There—my blessing with thee!
And these few precepts in thy memory
Look thou character. Give thy thoughts no tongue,   59
Nor any unproportioned thought his act.   60
Be thou familiar, but by no means vulgar.   61
Those friends thou hast, and their adoption tried,   62
Grapple them unto thy soul with hoops of steel,
But do not dull thy palm with entertainment   64
Of each new-hatched, unfledged courage. Beware   65
Of entrance to a quarrel, but being in,
Bear 't that th' opposèd may beware of thee.   67
Give every man thy ear, but few thy voice;
Take each man's censure, but reserve thy judgment.   69
Costly thy habit as thy purse can buy,   70
But not expressed in fancy; rich, not gaudy,   71
For the apparel oft proclaims the man,
And they in France of the best rank and station
Are of a most select and generous chief in that.   74
Neither a borrower nor a lender be,
For loan oft loses both itself and friend,
And borrowing dulls the edge of husbandry.   77
This above all: to thine own self be true,
And it must follow, as the night the day,
Thou canst not then be false to any man.

---

49 *puffed* bloated, or swollen with pride 51 *recks* heeds. *rede* counsel 53 *double* (Laertes has already bidden his father good-bye.) 54 *Occasion . . . leave* happy is the circumstance that provides a second leave-taking. (The goddess Occasion, or Opportunity, smiles.) 59 *Look* be sure that. *character* inscribe 60 *unproportioned* badly calculated, intemperate. *his* its 61 *familiar* sociable. *vulgar* common 62 *tried* tested 64 *dull thy palm* i.e., shake hands so often as to make the gesture meaningless 65 *courage* young man of spirit 67 *Bear 't that* manage it so that 69 *censure* opinion, judgment 70 *habit* clothing 71 *fancy* excessive ornament, decadent fashion 74 *Are . . . that* i.e., are of a most refined and well-bred preeminence in choosing what to wear 77 *husbandry* thrift

Farewell. My blessing season this in thee!   81
LAERTES:
Most humbly do I take my leave, my lord.
POLONIUS:
The time invests you. Go, your servants tend.   83
LAERTES:
Farewell, Ophelia, and remember well
What I have said to you.
OPHELIA: 'Tis in my memory locked,
And you yourself shall keep the key of it.
LAERTES: Farewell.   *Exit* LAERTES.
POLONIUS:
What is 't, Ophelia, he hath said to you?
OPHELIA:
So please you, something touching the Lord Hamlet.
POLONIUS: Marry, well bethought.   91
'Tis told me he hath very oft of late
Given private time to you, and you yourself
Have of your audience been most free and bounteous.
If it be so—as so 'tis put on me,   95
And that in way of caution—I must tell you
You do not understand yourself so clearly
As it behooves my daughter and your honor.   98
What is between you? Give me up the truth.
OPHELIA:
He hath, my lord, of late made many tenders   100
Of his affection to me.
POLONIUS:
Affection? Pooh! You speak like a green girl,
Unsifted in such perilous circumstance.   103
Do you believe his tenders, as you call them?
OPHELIA:
I do not know, my lord, what I should think.
POLONIUS:
Marry, I will teach you. Think yourself a baby
That you have ta'en these tenders for true pay   107
Which are not sterling. Tender yourself more dearly,   108
Or—not to crack the wind of the poor phrase,   109

81 *season* mature   83 *invests* besieges, presses upon.   *tend* attend, wait   91 *Marry* i.e., by the Virgin Mary. (A mild oath.)   95 *put on* impressed on, told to   98 *behooves* befits   100 *tenders* offers   103 *Unsifted* i.e., untried   107 *tenders* (with added meaning here of "promises to pay")   108 *sterling* legal currency.   *Tender* hold, look after, offer   109 *crack the wind* i.e., run it until it is broken-winded

Running it thus—you'll tender me a fool.   110
OPHELIA:
My lord, he hath importuned me with love
In honorable fashion.
POLONIUS:
Ay, fashion you may call it. Go to, go to.   113
OPHELIA:
And hath given countenance to his speech, my lord,   114
With almost all the holy vows of heaven.
POLONIUS:
Ay, springes to catch woodcocks. I do know,   116
When the blood burns, how prodigal the soul   117
Lends the tongue vows. These blazes, daughter,
Giving more light than heat, extinct in both
Even in their promise as it is a-making,   120
You must not take for fire. From this time
Be something scanter of your maiden presence.   122
Set your entreatments at a higher rate   123
Than a command to parle. For Lord Hamlet,   124
Believe so much in him that he is young,   125
And with a larger tether may he walk
Than may be given you. In few, Ophelia,   127
Do not believe his vows, for they are brokers,   128
Not of that dye which their investments show,   129
But mere implorators of unholy suits,   130
Breathing like sanctified and pious bawds   131
The better to beguile. This is for all: 132
I would not, in plain terms, from this time forth
Have you so slander any moment leisure   134
As to give words or talk with the Lord Hamlet.
Look to 't, I charge you. Come your ways.   136
OPHELIA: I shall obey, my lord.   *Exeunt.*

---

110 *tender me a fool* (1) show yourself to me as a fool (2) show me up as a fool (3) present me with a grandchild. (*Fool* was a term of endearment for a child.)   113 *fashion* mere form, pretense. *Go to* (An expression of impatience.)   114 *countenance* credit, confirmation   116 *springes* snares. *woodcocks* birds easily caught; here used to connote gullibility   117 *prodigal* i.e., prodigally   120 *it* i.e., the promise   122 *something* somewhat   123 *entreatments* negotiations for surrender. (A military term.)   124 *parle* discuss terms with the enemy. (Polonius urges his daughter, in the metaphor of military language, not to meet with Hamlet and consider giving in to him merely because he requests an interview.)   125 *so . . . him* this much concerning him   127 *In few* briefly   128 *brokers* go-betweens, procurers   129 *dye* color or sort. *investments* clothes. (The vows are not what they seem.)   130 *mere implorators* out and out solicitors   131 *Breathing* speaking   132 *for all* once for all, in sum   134 *slander* abuse, misuse. *moment* moment's   136 *Come your ways* come along

ACT I

Scene 4

Enter HAMLET, HORATIO, *and* MARCELLUS.

HAMLET:
    The air bites shrewdly; it is very cold.   1

HORATIO:
    It is a nipping and an eager air.   2

HAMLET:
    What hour now?

HORATIO: I think it lacks of twelve.   3

MARCELLUS:
    No, it is struck.

HORATIO: Indeed? I heard it not.
    It then draws near the season   5
    Wherein the spirit held his wont to walk.   6

                       A flourish of trumpets, and two pieces go off
                                      [within].

    What does this mean, my lord?

HAMLET:
    The King doth wake tonight and takes his rouse,   8
    Keeps wassail, and the swaggering upspring reels;   9
    And as he drains his drafts of Rhenish down,   10
    The kettledrum and trumpet thus bray out
    The triumph of his pledge.

HORATIO: Is it a custom?   12

HAMLET: Ay, marry, is 't,
    But to my mind, though I am native here
    And to the manner born, it is a custom   15
    More honored in the breach than the observance.   16
    This heavy-headed revel east and west   17
    Makes us traduced and taxed of other nations.   18
    They clepe us drunkards, and with swinish phrase   19
    Soil our addition; and indeed it takes   20
    From our achievements, though performed at height,   21

I.4. Location: The guard platform.

1 *shrewdly* keenly, sharply 2 *eager* biting 3 *lacks of* is just short of 5 *season* time 6 *held his wont* was accustomed *s.d. pieces* i.e., of ordnance, cannon 8 *wake* stay awake and hold revel. *rouse* carouse, drinking bout 9 *wassail* carousal. *upspring* wild German dance. *reels* dances 10 *Rhenish* Rhine wine 12 *the triumph . . . pledge* i.e., his feat in draining the wine in a single draft 15 *manner* custom (of drinking) 16 *More . . . observance* better neglected than followed 17 *east and west* i.e., everywhere 18 *taxed of* censured by 19 *clepe* call. *with swinish phrase* i.e., by calling us swine 20 *addition* reputation 21 *at height* outstandingly

The pith and marrow of our attribute.   22
So, oft it chances in particular men,
That for some vicious mole of nature in them,   24
As in their birth—wherein they are not guilty,
Since nature cannot choose his origin—   26
By their o'ergrowth of some complexion,   27
Oft breaking down the pales and forts of reason,   28
Or by some habit that too much o'erleavens   29
The form of plausive manners, that these men,   30
Carrying, I say, the stamp of one defect,
Being nature's livery or fortune's star,   32
His virtues else, be they as pure as grace,   33
As infinite as man may undergo,   34
Shall in the general censure take corruption   35
From that particular fault. The dram of evil   36
Doth all the noble substance often dout   37
To his own scandal.

Enter GHOST.

HORATIO: Look, my lord, it comes!   38
HAMLET:
Angels and ministers of grace defend us!
Be thou a spirit of health or goblin damned,   40
Bring with thee airs from heaven or blasts from hell,   41
Be thy intents wicked or charitable,   42
Thou com'st in such a questionable shape   43
That I will speak to thee. I'll call thee Hamlet,
King, Father, royal Dane. O, answer me!
Let me not burst in ignorance, but tell
Why thy canonized bones, hearsèd in death,   47
Have burst their cerements; why the sepulcher   48
Wherein we saw thee quietly inurned   49

---

22 *The pith . . . attribute* the essence of the reputation that others attribute to us   24 *for* on account of.   *mole of nature* natural blemish in one's constitution   26 *his* its.   27 *their o'ergrowth . . . complexion* the excessive growth in individuals of some natural trait   28 *pales* palings, fences (as of a fortification)   29 *o'erleavens* induces a change throughout (as yeast works in dough)   30 *plausive* pleasing   32 *nature's livery* sign of one's servitude to nature.   *fortune's star* the destiny that chance brings   33 *His virtues else* i.e., the other qualities of *these men* (l. 30)   34 *may undergo* can sustain   35 *general censure* general opinion that people have of him   36–38 *The dram . . . scandal* i.e., the small drop of evil blots out or works against the noble substance of the whole and brings it into disrepute. To *dout* is to blot out. (A famous crux.)   38 *To . . . scandal* i.e., with consequent ruin or disgrace to that man   40 *Be thou* i.e., whether you are.   *spirit of health* good angel   41 *Bring* i.e., whether you bring   42 *Be thy intents* i.e., whether your intents are   43 *questionable* inviting question   47 *canonize* buried according to the canons of the church.   *hearsèd* coffined   48 *cerements* grave-clothes   49 *inurned* entombed.

Hath oped his ponderous and marble jaws
To cast thee up again. What may this mean,
That thou, dead corpse, again in complete steel,   52
Revisits thus the glimpses of the moon,   53
Making night hideous, and we fools of nature   54
So horridly to shake our disposition   55
With thoughts beyond the reaches of our souls?
Say, why is this? Wherefore? What should we do?

                          [*The* GHOST] *beckons* [HAMLET].

HORATIO:
It beckons you to go away with it,
As if it some impartment did desire   59
To you alone.
MARCELLUS: Look with what courteous action
It wafts you to a more removèd ground.
But do not go with it.
HORATIO: No, by no means.
HAMLET:
It will not speak. Then I will follow it.
HORATIO:
Do not, my lord!
HAMLET: Why, what should be the fear?
I do not set my life at a pin's fee,   65
And for my soul, what can it do to that,
Being a thing immortal as itself?
It waves me forth again. I'll follow it.
HORATIO:
What if it tempt you toward the flood, my lord,   69
Or to the dreadful summit of the cliff
That beetles o'er his base into the sea,   71
And there assume some other horrible form
Which might deprive your sovereignty of reason   73
And draw you into madness? Think of it.
The very place puts toys of desperation,   75
Without more motive, into every brain
That looks so many fathoms to the sea
And hears it roar beneath.

---

52 *complete steel* full armor   53 *glimpses of the moon* pale and uncertain moonlight   54 *fools of nature*
mere men, limited to natural knowledge and subject to the caprices of nature   55 *So . . . disposition*
to distress our mental composure so violently   59 *impartment* communication   65 *fee* value   69
flood sea   71 *beetles o'er* overhangs threateningly (like bushy eyebrows). *his* its   73 *deprive . . .*
reason take away the rule of reason over your mind   75 *toys of desperation* fancies of desperate acts,
i.e., suicide

HAMLET:
It wafts me still.—Go on, I'll follow thee.
MARCELLUS:
You shall not go, my lord.   *[They try to stop him.]*
HAMLET: Hold off your hands!
HORATIO:
Be ruled. You shall not go.
HAMLET: My fate cries out,   81
And makes each petty artery in this body   82
As hardy as the Nemean lion's nerve.   83
Still am I called. Unhand me, gentlemen.
By heaven, I'll make a ghost of him that lets me!   85
I say, away!—Go on, I'll follow thee.

Exeunt GHOST *and* HAMLET.

HORATIO:
He waxes desperate with imagination.
MARCELLUS:
Let's follow. 'Tis not fit thus to obey him.
HORATIO:
Have after. To what issue will this come?   89
MARCELLUS:
Something is rotten in the state of Denmark.
HORATIO:
Heaven will direct it.
MARCELLUS: Nay, let's follow him.   *Exeunt.*   91

ACT I

Scene 5

Enter GHOST *and* HAMLET.

HAMLET:
Whither wilt thou lead me? Speak. I'll go no further.
GHOST:
Mark me.
HAMLET: I will.
GHOST: My hour is almost come,
When I to sulfurous and tormenting flames
Must render up myself.

---

81 *My fate cries out* my destiny summons me   82 *petty* weak.   *artery* (through which the vital spirits were thought to have been conveyed)   83 *Nemean lion* one of the monsters slain by Hercules in his twelve labors.   nerve sinew   85 *lets* hinder   89 *Have after* let's go after him.   *issue* outcome   91 *it* i.e., the outcome
I.5. Location: The battlements of the castle.

HAMLET: Alas, poor ghost!
GHOST:
    Pity me not, but lend thy serious hearing
    To what I shall unfold.
HAMLET :   Speak. I am bound to hear.   7
GHOST:
    So art thou to revenge, when thou shalt hear.
HAMLET: What?
GHOST: I am thy father's spirit,
    Doomed for a certain term to walk the night,
    And for the day confined to fast in fires,   12
    Till the foul crimes done in my days of nature   13
    Are burnt and purged away. But that I am forbid   14
    To tell the secrets of my prison house,
    I could a tale unfold whose lightest word
    Would harrow up thy soul, freeze thy young blood,   17
    Make thy two eyes like stars start from their spheres,   18
    Thy knotted and combinèd locks to part,   19
    And each particular hair to stand on end
    Like quills upon the fretful porpentine.   21
    But this eternal blazon must not be   22
    To ears of flesh and blood. List, list, O, list!
    If thou didst ever thy dear father love—
HAMLET: O God!
GHOST:
    Revenge his foul and most unnatural murder.
HAMLET: Murder?
GHOST:
    Murder most foul, as in the best it is,   28
    But this most foul, strange, and unnatural.
HAMLET:
    Haste me to know 't, that I, with wings as swift
    As meditation or the thoughts of love
    May sweep to my revenge.
GHOST: I find thee apt;
    And duller shouldst thou be than the fat weed   33
    That roots itself in ease on Lethe wharf,   34

---

7 *bound* (1) ready (2) obligated by duty and fate. (The Ghost, in l. 8, answers in the second sense.)
12 *fast* do penance   13 *crimes* sins   14 *But that* were it not   17 *harrow up* lacerate, tear   18 *spheres*
i.e., eye-sockets, here compared to the orbits or transparent revolving spheres in which, according to
Ptolemaic astronomy, the heavenly bodies were fixed   19 *knotted . . . locks* i.e., hair neatly arranged
and confined   21 *porpentine* porcupine   22 *eternal blazon* revelation of the secrets of eternity   28 *in
the best* even at best   33 *shouldst thou be* you would have to be.   *fat* torpid, lethargic   34 *Lethe* the
river of forgetfulness in Hades.   *wharf* bank

Wouldst thou not stir in this. Now, Hamlet, hear.
'Tis given out that, sleeping in my orchard,   36
A serpent stung me. So the whole ear of Denmark
Is by a forgèd process of my death   38
Rankly abused. But know, thou noble youth,   39
The serpent that did sting thy father's life
Now wears his crown.
HAMLET: O, my prophetic soul! My uncle!
GHOST:

Ay, that incestuous, that adulterate beast,   43
With witchcraft of his wit, with traitorous gifts—   44
O wicked wit and gifts, that have the power
So to seduce!—won to his shameful lust
The will of my most seeming-virtuous queen.
O Hamlet, what a falling off was there!
From me, whose love was of that dignity
That it went hand in hand even with the vow   50
I made to her in marriage, and to decline
Upon a wretch whose natural gifts were poor
To those of mine!   53
But virtue, as it never will be moved,   54
Though lewdness court it in a shape of heaven,   55
So lust, though to a radiant angel linked,
Will sate itself in a celestial bed   57
And prey on garbage.
But soft, methinks I scent the morning air.
Brief let me be. Sleeping within my orchard,
My custom always of the afternoon,
Upon my secure hour thy uncle stole,   62
With juice of cursèd hebona in a vial,   63
And in the porches of my ears did pour   64
The leprous distillment, whose effect   65
Holds such an enmity with blood of man
That swift as quicksilver it courses through
The natural gates and alleys of the body,
And with a sudden vigor it doth posset   69

---

36 *orchard* garden   38 *forgèd process* falsified account   39 *abused* deceived   43 *adulterate* adulterous
44 *gifts* (1) talents (2) presents   50 *even with the vow* with the very vow   53 *To* compared to
54 *virtue, as it* as virtue   55 *shape of heaven* heavenly form   57 *sate . . . bed* i.e., cease to find sexual
pleasure in a virtuously lawful marriage   62 *secure* confident, unsuspicious   63 *hebona* a poison.
(The word seems to be a form of *ebony,* though it is thought perhaps to be related to *henbane,* a poison, or to *ebenus,* yew.)   64 *porches of my ears* ears as a porch or entrance of the body   65 *leprous
distillment* distillation causing leprosy-like disfigurement   69 *posset* coagulate, curdle

And curd, like eager droppings into milk,   70
The thin and wholesome blood. So did it mine,
And a most instant tetter barked about,   72
Most lazar-like, with vile and loathsome crust,   73
All my smooth body.
Thus was I, sleeping, by a brother's hand
Of life, of crown, of queen at once dispatched,   76
Cut off even in the blossoms of my sin,
Unhouseled, disappointed, unaneled,   78
No reckoning made, but sent to my account   79
With all my imperfections on my head.
O, horrible! O, horrible, most horrible!
If thou hast nature in thee, bear it not.   82
Let not the royal bed of Denmark be
A couch for luxury and damnèd incest.   84
But, howsoever thou pursues this act,
Taint not thy mind nor let thy soul contrive
Against thy mother aught. Leave her to heaven
And to those thorns that in her bosom lodge,
To prick and sting her. Fare thee well at once.
The glowworm shows the matin to be near,   90
And 'gins to pale his uneffectual fire.   91
Adieu, adieu, adieu! Remember me.   [Exit.]
HAMLET:
O all you host of heaven! O earth! What else?
And shall I couple hell? O, fie! Hold, hold, my heart,   94
And you, my sinews, grow not instant old,   95
But bear me stiffly up. Remember thee?
Ay, thou poor ghost, whiles memory holds a seat
In this distracted globe. Remember thee?   98
Yea, from the table of my memory   99
I'll wipe away all trivial fond records,   100
All saws of books, all forms, all pressures past   101
That youth and observation copied there,
And thy commandment all alone shall live

---

70 *eager* sour, acid   72 *tetter* eruption of scabs.   *barked* covered with a rough covering, like bark on
a tree   73 *lazar-like* leper-like   76 *dispatched* suddenly deprived   78 *Unhouseled* without having received the Sacrament.   *disappointed* unready (spiritually) for the last journey.   *unaneled* without
having received extreme unction   79 *reckoning* settling of accounts   82 *nature* i.e., the promptings
of a son   84 *luxury* lechery   90 *matin* i.e., morning   91 *uneffectual fire* light rendered ineffectual
by the approach of bright day   94 *couple* add.   *Hold* hold together   95 *instant* instantly   98 *globe*
(1) head (2) world   99 *table* tablet, slate   100 *fond* foolish   101 *saws* wise sayings.   *forms* shapes
or images copied onto the slate; general ideas.   *pressures* impressions stamped

Within the book and volume of my brain,
Unmixed with baser matter. Yes, by heaven!
O most pernicious woman!
O villain, villain, smiling, damnèd villain!
My tables—meet it is I set it down   108
That one may smile, and smile, and be a villain.
At least I am sure it may be so in Denmark.   [*Writing.*]
So, unclo, there you are. Now to my word: 111
It is "Adieu, adieu! Remember me."
I have sworn 't.

Enter HORATIO *and* MARCELLUS.

HORATIO: My lord, my lord!
MARCELLUS: Lord Hamlet!
HORATIO: Heavens secure him!   116
HAMLET: So be it.
MARCELLUS: Hillo, ho, ho, my lord!
HAMLET: Hillo, ho, ho, boy! Come, bird, come.   119
MARCELLUS: How is 't, my noble lord?
HORATIO: What news, my lord?
HAMLET: O, wonderful!
HORATIO: Good my lord, tell it.
HAMLET: No, you will reveal it.
HORATIO: Not I, my lord, by heaven.
MARCELLUS: Nor I, my lord.
HAMLET:
    How say you, then, would heart of man once think it?   127
    But you'll be secret?
HORATIO, MARCELLUS: Ay, by heaven, my lord.
HAMLET:
    There's never a villain dwelling in all Denmark
    But he's an arrant knave.   130
HORATIO:
    There needs no ghost, my lord, come from the grave
    To tell us this.
HAMLET: Why, right, you are in the right.
    And so, without more circumstance at all,   133
    I hold it fit that we shake hands and part,
    You as your business and desire shall point you—

---

108 *tables* writing tablets.   *meet it is* it is fitting   111 *there you are* i.e., there, I've written that down
against you   116 *secure him* keep him safe   119 *Hillo . . . come* (A falconer's call to a hawk in air.
Hamlet mocks the hallooing as though it were a part of hawking.)   127 *once* ever   130 *arrant* thor-
oughgoing   133 *circumstance* ceremony, elaboration

For every man hath business and desire,
Such as it is—and for my own poor part,
Look you, I'll go pray.

HORATIO:
These are but wild and whirling words, my lord.

HAMLET:
I am sorry they offend you, heartily;
Yes, faith, heartily.

HORATIO: There's no offense, my lord.

HAMLET:
Yes, by Saint Patrick, but there is, Horatio,   142
And much offense too. Touching this vision here,   143
It is an honest ghost, that let me tell you.   144
For your desire to know what is between us,
O'ermaster 't as you may. And now, good friends,
As you are friends, scholars, and soldiers,
Give me one poor request.

HORATIO: What is 't, my lord? We will.

HAMLET:
Never make known what you have seen tonight.

HORATIO, MARCELLUS: My lord, we will not.

HAMLET: Nay, but swear 't.

HORATIO :   In faith, my lord, not I.   153

MARCELLUS: Nor I, my lord, in faith.

HAMLET: Upon my sword.   [He holds out his sword.]   155

MARCELLUS: We have sworn, my lord, already.   156

HAMLET: Indeed, upon my sword, indeed.

GHOST (cries under the stage):   Swear.

HAMLET:
Ha, ha, boy, sayst thou so? Art thou there, truepenny?   159
Come on, you hear this fellow in the cellarage.
Consent to swear.

HORATIO: Propose the oath, my lord.

HAMLET:
Never to speak of this that you have seen,
Swear by my sword.

GHOST [beneath]: Swear.   [They swear.]   164

---

142 *Saint Patrick* (The keeper of Purgatory and patron saint of all blunders and confusion.)
143 *offense* (Hamlet deliberately changes Horatio's "no offense taken" to "an offense against all decency.")   144 *an honest ghost* i.e., a real ghost and not an evil spirit   153 *In faith . . . I* i.e., I swear not to tell what I have seen. (Horatio is not refusing to swear.)   155 *sword* i.e., the hilt in the form of a cross   156 *We . . . already* i.e., we swore *in faith*   159 *truepenny* honest old fellow   164 s.d. *They swear* (Seemingly they swear here, and at ll. 170 and 190, as they lay their hands on Hamlet's sword. Triple oaths would have particular force; these three oaths deal with what they have seen, what they have heard, and what they promise about Hamlet's *antic disposition*.)

HAMLET:

   Hic et ubique? Then we'll shift our ground.   165

                             [He moves to another spot.]

   Come hither, gentlemen,

   And lay your hands again upon my sword.

   Swear by my sword

   Never to speak of this that you have heard.

GHOST *[beneath]:*   Swear by his sword.   *[They swear.]*

HAMLET:

   Well said, old mole. Canst work i' th' earth so fast?

   A worthy pioner! Once more remove, good friends.   172

                             [He moves again.]

HORATIO:

   O day and night, but this is wondrous strange!

HAMLET:

   And therefore as a stranger give it welcome.   174

   There are more things in heaven and earth, Horatio,

   Than are dreamt of in your philosophy.   176

   But come;

   Here, as before, never, so help you mercy,   178

   How strange or odd soe'er I bear myself—

   As I perchance hereafter shall think meet

   To put an antic disposition on—   181

   That you, at such times seeing me, never shall,

   With arms encumbered thus, or this headshake,   183

   Or by pronouncing of some doubtful phrase

   As "Well, we know," or "We could, an if we would,"   185

   Or "If we list to speak," or "There be, an if they might,"   186

   Or such ambiguous giving out, to note   187

   That you know aught of me—this do swear,   188

   So grace and mercy at your most need help you.

GHOST *[beneath]:*   Swear.   *[They swear.]*

HAMLET:

   Rest, rest, perturbèd spirit! So, gentlemen,

   With all my love I do commend me to you;   192

   And what so poor a man as Hamlet is

---

165 *Hic et ubique* here and everywhere. (Latin.)   172 *pioner* foot soldier assigned to dig tunnels and excavations   174 *as a stranger* i.e., since it is a stranger and hence needing your hospitality 176 *your philosophy* i.e., this subject called "natural philosophy" or "science" that people talk about 178 *so help you mercy* i.e., as you hope for God's mercy when you are judged   181 *antic* fantastic 183 *encumbered* folded or entwined   185 *an if* if   186 *list* wished. *There . . . might* i.e., there are people here (we, in fact) who could tell news if we were at liberty to do so   187 *giving out* intimidation, promulgating. *note* draw attention to the fact   188 *aught* i.e., something secret   192 *do . . . you* entrust myself to you

May do t' express his love and friending to you,   194
God willing, shall not lack. Let us go in together,   195
And still your fingers on your lips, I pray.   196
The time is out of joint. O cursèd spite   197
That ever I was born to set it right!

                              [They wait for him to leave first.]
Nay, come, let's go together.   *Exeunt.*   199

ACT II

Scene 1

Enter old POLONIUS *with his man* [REYNALDO].

POLONIUS:
Give him this money and these notes, Reynaldo.

                              [He gives money and papers.]
REYNALDO: I will, my lord.
POLONIUS:
You shall do marvelous wisely, good Reynaldo,   3
Before you visit him, to make inquire   4
Of his behavior.
REYNALDO: My lord, I did intend it.
POLONIUS:
Marry, well said, very well said. Look you, sir,
Inquire me first what Danskers are in Paris,   7
And how, and who, what means, and where they keep,   8
What company, at what expense; and finding
By this encompassment and drift of question   10
That they do know my son, come you more nearer   11
Than your particular demands will touch it.   12
Take you, as 'twere, some distant knowledge of him,   13
As thus, "I know his father and his friends,
And in part him." Do you mark this, Reynaldo?
REYNALDO: Ay, very well, my lord.
POLONIUS:
"And in part him, but," you may say, "not well.

---

194 *friending* friendliness   195 *lack* be lacking   196 *still* always   197 *The time* i.e., the state of affairs.   *spite* i.e., the spite of Fortune   199 *let's go together* (Probably they wait for him to leave first, but he refuses this ceremoniousness.)
II.1. Location: Polonius' chambers.
3 *marvelous* marvelously   4 *inquire* inquiry   7 *Danskers* Danes   8 *what means* what wealth (they have).   *keep* dwell   10 *encompassment* roundabout talking.   *drift* gradual approach or course
11–12 *come . . . it* i.e., you will find out more this way than by asking pointed questions (*particular demands*)   13 *Take you* assume, pretend

But if 't be he I mean, he's very wild,
Addicted so and so," and there put on him   19
What forgeries you please—marry, none so rank   20
As may dishonor him, take heed of that,
But, sir, such wanton, wild, and usual slips   22
As are companions noted and most known
To youth and liberty.
REYNALDO: As gaming, my lord.
POLONIUS: Ay, or drinking, fencing, swearing,
Quarreling, drabbing—you may go so far.   27
REYNALDO: My lord, that would dishonor him.
POLONIUS:
Faith, no, as you may season it in the charge.   29
You must not put another scandal on him
That he is open to incontinency;   31
That's not my meaning. But breathe his faults so
quaintly   32
That they may seem the taints of liberty,   33
The flash and outbreak of a fiery mind,
A savageness in unreclaimèd blood,   35
Of general assault.   36
REYNALDO: But, my good lord—
POLONIUS:
Wherefore should you do this?
REYNALDO: Ay, my lord, I would know that.
POLONIUS: Marry, sir, here's my drift,
And I believe it is a fetch of warrant.   41
You laying these slight sullies on my son,
As 'twere a thing a little soiled wi' the working   43
Mark you,
Your party in converse, him you would sound,   45
Having ever seen in the prenominate crimes   46
The youth you breathe of guilty, be assured   47
He closes with you in this consequence: 48
"Good sir," or so, or "friend," or "gentleman,"
According to the phrase or the addition   50

---

19 *put on* impute to   20 *forgeries* invented tales.   *rank* gross   22 *wanton* sportive, unrestrained
27 *drabbing* keeping company with loose women   29 *season* temper, soften   31 *incontinency* habitual sexual excess   32 *quaintly* artfully, subtly   33 *taints of liberty* faults resulting from free living
35–36 *A savageness . . . assault* a wildness in untamed youth that assails all indiscriminately
41 *fetch of warrant* legitimate trick   43 *soiled wi' the working* soiled by handling while it is being made
45 *converse* conversation.   *sound* i.e., sound out   46 *Having ever* if he has ever.   *prenominate crimes*
before-mentioned offenses   47 *breathe* speak   48 *closes . . . consequence* follows your lead in some
fashion as follows   50 *addition* title

Of man and country.

REYNALDO: Very good, my lord.

POLONIUS: And then, sir, does 'a this—'a does—what was I
about to say? By the Mass, I was about to say something.
Where did I leave?

REYNALDO: At "closes in the consequence."

POLONIUS:

At "closes in the consequence," ay, marry.
He closes thus: "I know the gentleman,
I saw him yesterday," or "th' other day,"
Or then, or then, with such or such, "and as you say,
There was 'a gaming," "there o'ertook in 's rouse,"   60
"There falling out at tennis," or perchance   61
"I saw him enter such a house of sale,"
Videlicet a brothel, or so forth. See you now,   63
Your bait of falsehood takes this carp of truth;   64
And thus do we of wisdom and of reach,   65
With windlasses and with assays of bias,   66
By indirections find directions out.   67
So by my former lecture and advice
Shall you my son. You have me, have you not?   69

REYNALDO:

My lord, I have.

POLONIUS: God b' wi' ye; fare ye well.   70

REYNALDO: Good my lord.

POLONIUS:

Observe his inclination in yourself.   72

REYNALDO: I shall, my lord.

POLONIUS: And let him ply his music.   74

REYNALDO: Well, my lord.

POLONIUS:

Farewell.   *Exit* REYNALDO.

Enter Ophelia.

                    How now, Ophelia, what's the matter?

OPHELIA:

O my lord, my lord, I have been so affrighted!

POLONIUS: With what, i' the name of God?

---

60 *o'ertook in 's rouse* overcome by drink   61 *falling out* quarreling   63 *Videlicet* namely   64 *carp* a
fish   65 *reach* capacity, ability   66 *windlasses* i.e., circuitous paths. (Literally, circuits made to head
off the game in hunting.)   *assays of bias* attempts through indirection (like the curving path of the
bowling ball which is biased or weighted to one side)   67 *directions* i.e., the way things really are
69 *have* understand   70 *b' wi'* be with   72 *in yourself* in your own person (as well as by asking
questions)   74 *let him ply* see that he continues to study

OPHELIA:

    My lord, as I was sewing in my closet,   79

    Lord Hamlet, with his doublet all unbraced,   80

    No hat upon his head, his stockings fouled,

    Ungartered, and down-gyvèd to his ankle,   82

    Pale as his shirt, his knees knocking each other,

    And with a look so piteous in purport   84

    As if he had been loosèd out of hell

    To speak of horrors—he comes before me.

POLONIUS:

    Mad for thy love?

OPHELIA: My lord, I do not know,

    But truly I do fear it.

POLONIUS: What said he?

OPHELIA:

    He took me by the wrist and held me hard.

    Then goes he to the length of all his arm,

    And with his other hand thus o'er his brow

    He falls to such perusal of my face

    As 'a would draw it. Long stayed he so.   93

    At last, a little shaking of mine arm

    And thrice his head thus waving up and down,

    He raised a sigh so piteous and profound

    As it did seem to shatter all his bulk   97

    And end his being. That done, he lets me go,

    And with his head over his shoulder turned

    He seemed to find his way without his eyes,

    For out o' doors he went without their helps,

    And to the last bended their light on me.

POLONIUS:

    Come, go with me. I will go seek the King.

    This is the very ecstasy of love,   104

    Whose violent property fordoes itself   105

    And leads the will to desperate undertakings

    As oft as any passion under heaven

    That does afflict our natures. I am sorry.

    What, have you given him any hard words of late?

OPHELIA:

    No, my good lord, but as you did command

    I did repel his letters and denied

---

79 *closet* private chamber 80 *doublet* close-fitting jacket. *unbraced* unfastened 82 *down-gyvèd* fallen to the ankles (like gyves or fetters) 84 *in purport* in what it expressed 93 *As* as if (also in l. 97) 97 *bulk* body 104 *ecstasy* madness 105 *property* nature. *fordoes* destroys

His access to me.

POLONIUS: That hath made him mad.
    I am sorry that with better heed and judgment
    I had not quoted him. I feared he did but trifle   114
    And meant to wrack thee. But beshrew my jealousy!   115
    By heaven, it is as proper to our age   116
    To cast beyond ourselves in our opinions   117
    As it is common for the younger sort
    To lack discretion. Come, go we to the King.
    This must be known, which, being kept close, might
      move   120
    More grief to hide than hate to utter love.   121
    Come.   *Exeunt.*

ACT II

Scene 2

Flourish. Enter KING *and* QUEEN, ROSENCRANTZ, *and* GUILDENSTERN [*with others*].

KING:
    Welcome, dear Rosencrantz and Guildenstern.
    Moreover that we much did long to see you,   2
    The need we have to use you did provoke
    Our hasty sending. Something have you heard
    Of Hamlet's transformation—so call it,
    Sith nor th' exterior nor the inward man   6
    Resembles that it was. What it should be,   7
    More than his father's death, that thus hath put him
    So much from th' understanding of himself,
    I cannot dream of. I entreat you both
    That, being of so young days brought up with him,   11
    And sith so neighbored to his youth and havior,   12
    That you vouchsafe your rest here in our court   13
    Some little time, so by your companies
    To draw him on to pleasures, and to gather

---

114 *quoted* observed 115 *wrack* i.e., ruin, seduce. *beshrew my jealousy* a plague upon my suspicious nature 116 *proper . . . age* characteristic of us (old) men 117 *cast beyond* overshoot, miscalculate 120 *close* secret 120–121 *might . . . love* i.e., might cause more grief (because of what Hamlet might do) by hiding the knowledge of Hamlet's strange behavior to Ophelia than unpleasantness by telling it

II.2. Location: The castle.

2 *Moreover that* besides the fact that 6 *Sith* since. *nor . . . nor* neither . . . nor 7 *that* what 11 *of . . . days* from such early youth 12 *And sith so neighbored to* i.e., and since you are (or, and since that time you are) intimately acquainted with. *havior* demeanor 13 *vouchsafe your rest* please to stay

So much as from occasion you may glean, 16
Whether aught to us unknown afflicts him thus
That, opened, lies within our remedy. 18
QUEEN:
Good gentlemen, he hath much talked of you,
And sure I am two men there is not living
To whom he more adheres. If it will please you
To show us so much gentry and good will 22
As to expend your time with us awhile
For the supply and profit of our hope, 24
Your visitation shall receive such thanks
As fits a king's remembrance.
ROSENCRANTZ: Both Your Majesties 26
Might, by the sovereign power you have of us, 27
Put your dread pleasures more into command 28
Than to entreaty.
GUILDENSTERN: But we both obey,
And here give up ourselves in the full bent 30
To lay our service freely at your feet,
To be commanded.
KING:
Thanks, Rosencrantz and gentle Guildenstern.
QUEEN:
Thanks, Guildenstern and gentle Rosencrantz.
And I beseech you instantly to visit
My too much changèd son. Go, some of you,
And bring these gentlemen where Hamlet is.
GUILDENSTERN:
Heavens make our presence and our practices 38
Pleasant and helpful to him!
QUEEN: Ay, amen!

Exeunt ROSENCRANTZ *and* GUILDENSTERN [*with
some attendants*].

Enter POLONIUS.

POLONIUS:
Th' ambassadors from Norway, my good lord,
Are joyfully returned.

---

16 *occasion* opportunity   18 *opened* being revealed   22 *gentry* courtesy   24 *supply . . . hope* aid and furtherance of what we hope for   26 *As fits . . . remembrance* i.e., as would be a fitting gift of a king who rewards true service   27 *of* over   28 *dread* inspiring awe   30 *in . . . bent* to the utmost degree of our capacity   38 *practices* doings

KING:
    Thou still hast been the father of good news.   42
POLONIUS:
    Have I, my lord? I assure my good liege
    I hold my duty, as I hold my soul,   44
    Both to my God and to my gracious king;
    And I do think, or else this brain of mine
    Hunts not the trail of policy so sure   47
    As it hath used to do, that I have found
    The very cause of Hamlet's lunacy.
KING:
    O, speak of that! That do I long to hear.
POLONIUS:
    Give first admittance to th' ambassadors.
    My news shall be the fruit to that great feast.   52
KING:
    Thyself do grace to them and bring them in.

                                  [*Exit* POLONIUS.]

    He tells me, my dear Gertrude, he hath found
    The head and source of all your son's distemper.
QUEEN:
    I doubt it is no other but the main   56
    His father's death and our o'erhasty marriage.

Enter AMBASSADORS [VOLTIMAND *and* CORNELIUS, *with* POLONIUS].

KING:
    Well, we shall sift him.—Welcome, my good friends!   58
    Say, Voltimand, what from our brother Norway?   59
VOLTIMAND:
    Most fair return of greetings and desires.   60
    Upon our first, he sent out to suppress   61
    His nephew's levies, which to him appeared
    To be a preparation 'gainst the Polack,
    But, better looked into, he truly found
    It was against Your Highness. Whereat grieved
    That so his sickness, age, and impotence   66
    Was falsely borne in hand, sends out arrests   67
    On Fortinbras, which he, in brief, obeys,
    Receives rebuke from Norway, and in fine   69

---

42 *still* always 44 *hold* maintain. *as* as firmly as 47 *policy* statecraft 52 *fruit* dessert 56 *doubt* fear, suspect. *main* chief point, principal concern 58 *sift him* i.e., question Polonius closely 59 *brother* i.e., fellow king 60 *desires* good wishes 61 *Upon our first* at our first words on the business 66 *impotence* helplessness 67 *borne in hand* deluded, taken advantage of. *arrests* orders to desist 69 *in fine* in conclusion

Makes vow before his uncle never more
To give th' assay of arms against Your Majesty.   71
Whereon old Norway, overcome with joy,
Gives him three thousand crowns in annual fee
And his commission to employ those soldiers,
So levied as before, against the Polack,
With an entreaty, herein further shown,

[Giving a paper]

That it might please you to give quiet pass
Through your dominions for this enterprise
On such regards of safety and allowance   79
As therein are set down.
KING: It likes us well,   80
And at our more considered time we'll read,   81
Answer, and think upon this business.
Meantime we thank you for your well-took labor.
Go to your rest; at night we'll feast together.
Most welcome home!   *Exeunt* AMBASSADORS.
POLONIUS: This business is well ended.
My liege, and madam, to expostulate   86
What majesty should be, what duty is,
Why day is day, night night, and time is time,
Were nothing but to waste night, day, and time.
Therefore, since brevity is the soul of wit,   90
And tediousness the limbs and outward flourishes,
I will be brief. Your noble son is mad.
Mad call I it, for, to define true madness,
What is 't but to be nothing else but mad?
But let that go.
QUEEN: More matter, with less art.
POLONIUS:
Madam, I swear I use no art at all.
That he's mad, 'tis true; 'tis true 'tis pity,
And pity 'tis 'tis true—a foolish figure,   98
But farewell it, for I will use no art.
Mad let us grant him, then, and now remains
That we find out the cause of this effect,
Or rather say, the cause of this defect,

                                                            103

---

71 *give th' assay* make trial of strength, challenge 79 *On . . . allowance* i.e., with such considerations or conditions for the safety of Denmark and terms of permission for Fortinbras 80 *likes* pleases 81 *considered* suitable for deliberation 86 *expostulate* expound, inquire into 90 *wit* sound sense or judgment, intellectual keenness 98 *figure* figure of speech

For this effect defective comes by cause.
Thus it remains, and the remainder thus.
Perpend.   105
I have a daughter—have while she is mine—
Who, in her duty and obedience, mark,
Hath given me this. Now gather and surmise.   108
[*He reads the letter.*] "To the celestial and my soul's idol,
the most beautified Ophelia"—
That's an ill phrase, a vile phrase; "beautified" is a vile
phrase. But you shall hear. Thus: [*He reads.*]
"In her excellent white bosom, these, etc."   113
QUEEN: Came this from Hamlet to her?
POLONIUS:
Good madam, stay awhile. I will be faithful.   115

                      [*He reads.*]

    "Doubt thou the stars are fire,
        Doubt that the sun doth move,
    Doubt truth to be a liar,   118
        But never doubt I love.
O dear Ophelia, I am ill at these numbers. I have not   120
art to reckon my groans. But that I love thee best, O   121
most best, believe it. Adieu.
        Thine evermore, most dear lady, whilst this
            machine is to him, Hamlet."   124
This in obedience hath my daughter shown me,
And, more above, hath his solicitings,   126
As they fell out by time, by means, and place,   127
All given to mine ear.
KING: But how hath she   128
Received his love?
POLONIUS: What do you think of me?
KING:
As of a man faithful and honorable.
POLONIUS:
I would fain prove so. But what might you think,   131
When I had seen this hot love on the wing—
As I perceived it, I must tell you that,

---

103 *For . . . cause* i.e., for this defective behavior, this madness, has a cause   105 *Perpend* consider
108 *gather and surmise* draw your own conclusions   113 *In . . . bosom* (The letter is poetically addressed to her heart.)   *these* i.e., the letter   115 *stay* wait.   *faithful* i.e., in reading the letter accurately   118 *Doubt* suspect   120 *ill . . . numbers* unskilled at writing verses   121 *reckon* (1) count
(2) number metrically, scan   124 *machine* i.e., body   126 *more above* moreover   127 *fell out* occurred.   *by* according to   128 *given . . . ear* i.e., told me about   131 *fain* gladly

Before my daughter told me—what might you,
Or my dear Majesty your queen here, think,
If I had played the desk or table book,   136
Or given my heart a winking, mute and dumb,   137
Or looked upon this love with idle sight?   138
What might you think? No, I went round to work,   139
And my young mistress thus I did bespeak: 140
"Lord Hamlet is a prince out of thy star;   141
This must not be." And then I prescripts gave her   142
That she should lock herself from his resort,   143
Admit no messengers, receive no tokens.
Which done, she took the fruits of my advice;
And he, repellèd—a short tale to make—
Fell into a sadness, then into a fast,
Thence to a watch, thence into a weakness,   148
Thence to a lightness, and by this declension   149
Into the madness wherein now he raves
And all we mourn for.
KING [*to* QUEEN]:   Do you think 'tis this?   151
QUEEN: It may be, very like.
POLONIUS:
Hath there been such a time—I would fain know that—
That I have positively said "'Tis so,"
When it proved otherwise?
KING: Not that I know.
POLONIUS:
Take this from this, if this be otherwise   156
If circumstances lead me, I will find
Where truth is hid, though it were hid indeed
Within the center.
KING: How may we try it further?   159
POLONIUS:
You know sometimes he walks four hours together
Here in the lobby.
QUEEN: So he does indeed.

136 *played . . . table book* i.e., remained shut up, concealing the information; or, acted as a go-between, provided communication 137 *given . . . winking* closed the eyes of my heart to this 138 *with idle sight* complacently or incomprehendingly 139 *round* roundly, plainly 140 *bespeak* address 141 *out of thy star* above your sphere, position 142 *prescripts* orders 143 *his resort* his visits 148 *watch* state of sleeplessness 149 *lightness* lightheadedness. *declension* decline, deterioration 151 *all* i.e., into everything that 156 *Take this from this* (The actor gestures, indicating that he means his head from his shoulders, or his staff of office or chain from his hands or neck, or something similar.) 159 *center* middle point of the earth (which is also the center of the Ptolemaic universe). *try* test, judge

POLONIUS:

    At such a time I'll loose my daughter to him.   162

    Be you and I behind an arras then.   163

    Mark the encounter. If he love her not

    And be not from his reason fallen thereon,   165

    Let me be no assistant for a state,

    But keep a farm and carters.

KING: We will try it.

Enter HAMLET [*reading on a book*].

QUEEN:

    But look where sadly the poor wretch comes reading.   168

POLONIUS:

    Away, I do beseech you both, away.

    I'll board him presently. O, give me leave.   170

                       Exeunt KING *and* QUEEN [*with attendants*].

    How does my good Lord Hamlet?

HAMLET: Well, God-a-mercy.   172

POLONIUS: Do you know me, my lord?

HAMLET: Excellent well. You are a fishmonger.   174

POLONIUS: Not I, my lord.

HAMLET: Then I would you were so honest a man.

POLONIUS: Honest, my lord?

HAMLET: Ay, sir. To be honest, as this world goes, is to be one man

picked out of ten thousand.

POLONIUS: That's very true, my lord.

HAMLET: For if the sun breed maggots in a dead dog, being a good

kissing carrion—Have you a daughter?   182

POLONIUS: I have, my lord.

HAMLET: Let her not walk i' the sun. Conception is a blessing, but as   184

your daughter may conceive, friend, look to 't.

POLONIUS [*aside*]:   How say you by that? Still harping on my daughter

Yet he knew me not at first; 'a said I was a fishmonger. 'A is far   187

gone. And truly in my youth I suffered much extremity for love,

very near this. I'll speak to him again.—What do you read, my

lord?

HAMLET: Words, words, words.

POLONIUS: What is the matter, my lord?   192

---

162 *loose* (as one might release an animal that is being mated) 163 *arras* hanging, tapestry
165 *thereon* on that account 168 *sadly* seriously 170 *board* accost. *presently* at once. *give me*
leave i.e., excuse me. (Said to those he hurries offstage, including the King and Queen.) 172 *God-a-*
mercy i.e., thank you 174 *fishmonger* fish merchant 182 *a good kissing carrion* i.e., a good piece of
flesh for kissing, or for the sun to kiss 184 *i' the sun* (with additional implication of the sunshine of
princely favors). *Conception* (1) understanding (2) pregnancy 187 *'a* he 192 *matter* substance.
(But Hamlet plays on the sense of "basis for a dispute.")

HAMLET: Between who?

POLONIUS: I mean, the matter that you read, my lord.

HAMLET: Slanders, sir; for the satirical rogue says here that old men have gray beards, that their faces are wrinkled, their eyes purging thick amber and plum-tree gum, and that they have aplentiful lack of wit, together with most weak hams. All which, sir, though I most powerfully and potently believe, yet I hold it not honesty to have it thus set down, for yourself, sir, shall grow old as I am, if like a crab you could go backward.

197
198

200
201

POLONIUS [*aside*]:   Though this be madness, yet there is method in 't.—Will you walk out of the air, my lord?

203

HAMLET: Into my grave.

POLONIUS: Indeed, that's out of the air. [*Aside.*] How pregnant sometimes his replies are! A happiness that often madness hits on, which reason and sanity could not so prosperously be delivered of. I will leave him and suddenly contrive the means of meeting between him and my daughter.—My honorable lord, I will most humbly take my leave of you.

205
206
207
208

HAMLET: You cannot, sir, take from me anything that I will more willingly part withal—except my life, except my life, except my life.

212

Enter GUILDENSTERN *and* ROSENCRANTZ.

POLONIUS: Fare you well, my lord.

HAMLET: These tedious old fools!

214

POLONIUS: You go to seek the Lord Hamlet. There he is.

ROSENCRANTZ [*to* POLONIUS]:   God save you, sir!

[*Exit* POLONIUS.]

GUILDENSTERN: My honored lord!

ROSENCRANTZ: My most dear lord!

HAMLET: My excellent good friends! How dost thou, Guildenstern? Ah, Rosencrantz! Good lads, how do you both?

ROSENCRANTZ:

As the indifferent children of the earth.

221

GUILDENSTERN:

Happy in that we are not overhappy.
On Fortune's cap we are not the very button.

HAMLET: Nor the soles of her shoe?

ROSENCRANTZ: Neither, my lord.

HAMLET: Then you live about her waist, or in the middle of her favors?

226

---

197 *purging* discharging.   *amber* i.e., resin, like the resinous *plum-tree gum*   198 *wit* understanding   200 *honesty* decency, decorum   201 *old* as old   203 *out of the air* (The open air was considered dangerous for sick people.)   205 *pregnant* quick-witted, full of meaning.   *happiness* felicity of expression   207 *prosperously* successfully   208 *suddenly* immediately   212 *withal* with   214 *old fools* i.e., old men like Polonius   221 *indifferent* ordinary, at neither extreme of fortune or misfortune   226 *favors* i.e., sexual favors

GUILDENSTERN: Faith, her privates we.   227

HAMLET: In the secret parts of Fortune? O, most true, she is a
strumpet. What news?   229

ROSENCRANTZ: None, my lord, but the world's grown honest.

HAMLET: Then is doomsday near. But your news is not true. Let me
question more in particular. What have you, my good friends, deserved at the hands of Fortune that she sends you to prison
hither?

GUILDENSTERN: Prison, my lord?

HAMLET: Denmark's a prison.

ROSENCRANTZ: Then is the world one.

HAMLET: A goodly one, in which there are many confines, wards,   238
and dungeons, Denmark being one o' the worst.

ROSENCRANTZ: We think not so, my lord.

HAMLET: Why then 'tis none to you, for there is nothing either good
or bad but thinking makes it so. To me it is a prison.

ROSENCRANTZ: Why then, your ambition makes it one. 'Tis too narrow for your mind.

HAMLET: O God, I could be bounded in a nutshell and count myself
a king of infinite space, were it not that I have bad dreams.

GUILDENSTERN: Which dreams indeed are ambition, for the very sub-   247
stance of the ambitious is merely the shadow of a dream.   248

HAMLET: A dream itself is but a shadow.

ROSENCRANTZ: Truly, and I hold ambition of so airy and light a quality
that it is but a shadow's shadow.

HAMLET: Then are our beggars bodies, and our monarchs and out-   252
stretched heroes the beggars' shadows. Shall we to the court?   253
For, by my fay, I cannot reason.   254

ROSENCRANTZ, GUILDENSTERN: We'll wait upon you.   255

HAMLET: No such matter. I will not sort you with the rest of my ser-   256
vants, for, to speak to you like an honest man, I am most dread-   257
fully attended. But, in the beaten way of friendship, what make   258
you at Elsinore?

ROSENCRANTZ: To visit you, my lord, no other occasion.

HAMLET: Beggar that I am, I am even poor in thanks; but I thank

---

227 *her privates we* i.e., (1) we are sexually intimate with Fortune, the fickle goddess who bestows
her favors indiscriminately (2) we are her ordinary citizens   229 *strumpet* prostitute. (A common ep-
ithet for indiscriminate Fortune; see l. 453 below.)   238 *confines* places of confinement.   *wards* cells
247–248 *the very . . . ambitious* that seemingly very substantial thing that the ambitious pursue   252
bodies i.e., solid substances rather than shadows (since beggars are not ambitious)   252–253 *outstretched* (1) far-reaching in their ambition (2) elongated as shadows   254 *fay* faith   255 *wait upon*
accompany, attend. (But Hamlet uses the phrase in the sense of providing menial service.)   256 *sort*
class, categorize   257–258 *dreadfully attended* waited upon in slovenly fashion   258 *beaten way* familiar path, tried-and-true course.   *make* do

you, and sure, dear friends, my thanks are too dear a halfpenny.   262
Were you not sent for? Is it your own inclining? Is it a free visita-   263
tion? Come, come, deal justly with me. Come, come; nay, speak.

GUILDENSTERN: What should we say, my lord?

HAMLET: Anything but to the purpose. You were sent for, and there is   266
a kind of confession in your looks which your modesties have   267
not craft enough to color. I know the good King and Queen have
sent for you.

ROSENCRANTZ: To what end, my lord?

HAMLET: That you must teach me. But let me conjure you, by the   271
rights of our fellowship, by the consonancy of our youth, by the   272
obligation of our ever-preserved love, and by what more dear a
better proposer could charge you withal, be even and direct with   274
me whether you were sent for or no.

ROSENCRANTZ [*aside to* GUILDENSTERN]:   What say you?

HAMLET [*aside*]:   Nay, then, I have an eye of you.—If you love me,   277
hold not off.   278

GUILDENSTERN: My lord, we were sent for.

HAMLET: I will tell you why; so shall my anticipation prevent your dis-   280
covery, and your secrecy to the King and Queen molt no feather.   281
I have of late—but wherefore I know not—lost all my mirth, for-
gone all custom of exercises; and indeed it goes so heavily with
my disposition that this goodly frame, the earth, seems to me a
sterile promontory; this most excellent canopy, the air, look you,
this brave o'erhanging firmament, this majestical roof fretted with   286
golden fire, why, it appeareth nothing to me but a foul and pesti-
lent congregation of vapors. What a piece of work is a man! How   288
noble in reason, how infinite in faculties, in form and moving how
express and admirable, in action how like an angel, in apprehen-   290
sion how like a god! The beauty of the world, the paragon of ani-   291
mals! And yet, to me, what is this quintessence of dust? Man de-   292
lights not me—no, nor woman neither, though by your smiling
you seem to say so.

ROSENCRANTZ: My lord, there was no such stuff in my thoughts.

262 *dear a halfpenny* expensive at the price of a halfpenny, i.e., of little worth   263 *free* voluntary
266 *Anything but to the purpose* anything except a straightforward answer. (Said ironically.)
267 *modesties* sense of shame. *color* disguise   271 *conjure* adjure, entreat   272 *the consonancy of our
youth* our closeness in our younger days   274 *better proposer* more skillful propounder. *charge* urge
even straight, honest   277 *of* on   278 *hold not off* don't hold back   280–281 *so . . . discovery* in that
way my saying it first will spare you from revealing the truth   281 *molt no feather* i.e., not diminish
in the least   286 *brave* splendid   286 *fretted* adorned (with fretwork, as in a vaulted ceiling)
288 *congregation* mass. *piece of work* masterpiece   290 *express* well-framed, exact, expressive (?)
290–291 *apprehension* power of comprehending   292 *quintessence* the fifth essence of ancient philosophy, beyond earth, water, air, and fire, supposed to be the substance of the heavenly bodies and to
be latent in all things

HAMLET: Why did you laugh then, when I said man delights not me?

ROSENCRANTZ: To think, my lord, if you delight not in man, what
Lenten entertainment the players shall receive from you. We   298
coted them on the way, and hither are they coming to offer you   299
service.

HAMLET: He that plays the king shall be welcome; His Majesty shall 301
have tribute of me. The adventurous knight shall use his foil and   302
target, the lover shall not sigh gratis, the humorous man shall   303
end his part in peace, the clown shall make those laugh whose   304
lungs are tickle o' the sear, and the lady shall say her mind   305
freely, or the blank verse shall halt for 't. What players are they? 306

ROSENCRANTZ: Even those you were wont to take such delight in,
the tragedians of the city.

HAMLET: How chances it they travel? Their residence, both in repu- 309
tation and profit, was better both ways.

ROSENCRANTZ: I think their inhibition comes by the means of the late 311
innovation.   312

HAMLET: Do they hold the same estimation they did when I was in
the city? Are they so followed?

ROSENCRANTZ: No, indeed are they not.

HAMLET: How comes it? Do they grow rusty?   316

ROSENCRANTZ: Nay, their endeavor keeps in the wonted pace. But   317
there is, sir, an aerie of children, little eyases, that cry out on the 318
top of question and are most tyrannically clapped for 't. These   319
are now the fashion, and so berattle the common stages—so   320
they call them—that many wearing rapiers are afraid of goose   321
quills and dare scarce come thither.

HAMLET: What, are they children? Who maintains 'em? How are
they escoted? Will they pursue the quality no longer than they   324
can sing? Will they not say afterwards, if they should grow them-   325

---

298 *Lenten entertainment* meager reception (appropriate to Lent)   299 *coted* overtook and passed by
301-302 *shall . . . of me* will receive my tribute of praise   302–303 *foil and target* sword and shield
303 *gratis* for nothing. *humorous man* eccentric character, dominated by one trait or "humor"
304 *in peace* i.e., with full license   305 *tickle o' the sear* easy on the trigger, ready to laugh easily. (A
sear is part of a gunlock.)   306 *halt* limp   309 *residence* remaining in one place, i.e., in the city
311 *inhibition* formal prohibition (from acting plays in the city)   311–312 *late* recent. *innovation*
i.e., the new fashion in satirical plays performed by boy actors in the "private" theaters; or possibly a
political uprising; or the strict limitations set on the theaters in London in 1600   316–336 *How . . .
load too* (The passage, omitted from the early quartos, alludes to the so-called War of the Theaters,
1599–1602, the rivalry between the children's companies and the adult actors.)   317 *keeps* continues. *wonted* usual   318 *aerie* nest. *eyases* young hawks   318–319 *cry . . . question* speak shrilly,
dominating the controversy (in decrying the public theaters)   319 *tyrannically* outrageously
320 *berattle* berate, clamor against. *common stages* public theaters   321 *many wearing rapiers* i.e.,
many men of fashion, afraid to patronize the common players for fear of being satirized by the
poets writing for the boy actors. *goose quills* i.e., pens of satirists   324 *escoted* maintained. *quality*
(acting) profession   324–325 *no longer . . . sing* i.e., only until their voices change

selves to common players—as it is most like, if their means are   326
no better—their writers do them wrong to make them exclaim   327
against their own succession?   328

ROSENCRANTZ: Faith, there has been much to-do on both sides, and   329
the nation holds it no sin to tar them to controversy. There was   330
for a while no money bid for argument unless the poet and the   331
player went to cuffs in the question.   332

HAMLET: Is 't possible?

GUILDENSTERN: O, there has been much throwing about of brains.

HAMLET: Do the boys carry it away?   335

ROSENCRANTZ: Ay, that they do, my lord—Hercules and his load too.   336

HAMLET: It is not very strange; for my uncle is King of Denmark, and
those that would make mouths at him while my father lived give   338
twenty, forty, fifty, a hundred ducats apiece for his picture in little. 339
'Sblood, there is something in this more than natural, if philoso-   340
phy could find it out.   341

A flourish [of trumpets within].

GUILDENSTERN: There are the players.

HAMLET: Gentlemen, you are welcome to Elsinore. Your hands,
come then. Th' appurtenance of welcome is fashion and cere-   344
mony. Let me comply with you in this garb, lest my extent to the   345
players, which, I tell you, must show fairly outwards, should   346
more appear like entertainment than yours. You are welcome.   347
But my uncle-father and aunt-mother are deceived.

GUILDENSTERN: In what, my dear lord?

HAMLET: I am but mad north-north-west. When the wind is southerly   350
I know a hawk from a handsaw.   351

Enter POLONIUS.

POLONIUS: Well be with you, gentlemen!

HAMLET: Hark you, Guildenstern, and you too; at each ear a hearer.
That great baby you see there is not yet out of his swaddling   354
clouts.   355

---

326 *common* regular, adult.   *like* likely   326–327 *if . . . better* if they find no better way to support
themselves   328 *succession* i.e., future careers   329 *to-do* ado   330 *tar* set on (as dogs)   331 *argument* plot for a play   332 *went . . . question* came to blows in the play itself   335 *carry it away*
i.e., win the day   336 *Hercules . . . load* (Thought to be an allusion to the sign of the Globe Theatre, which was Hercules bearing the world on his shoulder.)   338 *mouths* faces   339 *ducats* gold
coins.   *in little* in miniature   340 *'Sblood* by God's (Christ's) blood   340–341 *philosophy* i.e., scientific inquiry   344 *appurtenance* proper accompaniment   345 *comply* observe the formalities of
courtesy   345 *garb* i.e., manner.   *my extent* that which I extend, i.e., my polite behavior
346 *show fairly outwards* show every evidence of cordiality   347 *entertainment* a (warm) reception
350 *north-north-west* i.e., only partly, at times   351 *hawk, handsaw* i.e., two very different things,
though also perhaps meaning a mattock (or *hack*) and a carpenter's cutting tool respectively; also
birds, with a play on *hernshaw* or heron   354–355 *swaddling clouts* cloths in which to wrap a
newborn baby

ROSENCRANTZ: Haply he is the second time come to them, for they   356
   say an old man is twice a child.
HAMLET: I will prophesy he comes to tell me of the players; mark
   it.—You say right, sir, o' Monday morning, 'twas then indeed.
POLONIUS: My lord, I have news to tell you.
HAMLET: My lord, I have news to tell you. When Roscius was an   361
   actor in Rome—
POLONIUS: The actors are come hither, my lord.
HAMLET: Buzz, buzz!   364
POLONIUS: Upon my honor—
HAMLET: Then came each actor on his ass.
POLONIUS: The best actors in the world, either for tragedy, comedy,
   history, pastoral, pastoral-comical, historical-pastoral, tragical-
   historical, tragical-comical-historical-pastoral, scene individable,   369
   or poem unlimited. Seneca cannot be too heavy, nor Plautus too   370
   light. For the law of writ and the liberty, these are the only men.   371
HAMLET: O Jephthah, judge of Israel, what a treasure hadst thou!   372
POLONIUS: What a treasure had he, my lord?
HAMLET: Why,
     "One fair daughter, and no more,
     The which he lovèd passing well."   375
POLONIUS [aside]:   Still on my daughter.
HAMLET: Am I not i' the right, old Jephthah?
POLONIUS :   If you call me Jephthah, my lord, I have a daughter that I
   love passing well.
HAMLET: Nay, that follows not.
POLONIUS: What follows then, my lord?
HAMLET: Why,
     "As by lot, God wot,"   383
   and then, you know,
     "It came to pass, as most like it was"—   385
   the first row of the pious chanson will show you more,   386
   for look where my abridgment comes.   387

Enter the PLAYERS.

   You are welcome, masters; welcome, all. I am glad to see thee

---

356 *haply* perhaps   361 *Roscius* a famous Roman actor who died in 62 B.C.   364 *Buzz* (An interjec-
tion used to denote stale news.)   369 *scene individable* a play observing the unity of place; or
perhaps one that is unclassifiable   370 *poem unlimited* a play disregarding the unities of time and
place; one that is all-inclusive   370 *Seneca* writer of Latin tragedies.   *Plautus* writer of Latin comedy
371 *law . . . liberty* dramatic composition both according to rules and without rules, i.e., "classical"
and "romantic" dramas.   *these* i.e., the actors   372 *Jephthah . . . Israel* (Jephthah had to sacrifice his
daughter; see Judges 11. Hamlet goes on to quote from a ballad on the theme.)   375 *passing*
surpassingly   383 *lot* chance.   *wot* knows   385 *like* likely, probable   386 *row* stanza.   *chanson*
ballad, song   387 *my abridgment* something that cuts short my conversation; also, a diversion

well. Welcome, good friends. O, old friend! Why, thy face is
valanced since I saw thee last. Com'st thou to beard me in Den-   390
mark? What, my young lady and mistress! By 'r Lady, your lady-   391
ship is nearer to heaven than when I saw you last, by the altitude
of a chopine. Pray God your voice, like a piece of uncurrent gold,   393
be not cracked within the ring. Masters, you are all welcome.   394
We'll e'en to 't like French falconers, fly at anything we see. We'll 395
have a speech straight. Come, give us a taste of your quality.   396
Come, a passionate speech.

FIRST PLAYER: What speech, my good lord?

HAMLET: I heard thee speak me a speech once, but it was never
acted, or if it was, not above once, for the play, I remember,
pleased not the million; 'twas caviar to the general. But it was—   401
as I received it, and others, whose judgments in such matters
cried in the top of mine—an excellent play, well digested in the   403
scenes, set down with as much modesty as cunning. I remember   404
one said there were no sallets in the lines to make the matter sa-   405
vory, nor no matter in the phrase that might indict the author of   406
affection, but called it an honest method, as wholesome as
sweet, and by very much more handsome than fine. One speech   408
in 't I chiefly loved: 'twas Aeneas' tale to Dido, and thereabout of
it especially when he speaks of Priam's slaughter. If it live in your 410
memory, begin at this line: let me see, let me see—

    "The rugged Pyrrhus, like th' Hyrcanian beast"—   412
'Tis not so. It begins with Pyrrhus:

    "The rugged Pyrrhus, he whose sable arms,   414
    Black as his purpose, did the night resemble
    When he lay couchèd in the ominous horse,   416
    Hath now this dread and black complexion smeared

---

390 *valanced* fringed (with a beard). *beard* confront, challenge (with obvious pun). 391 *young lady* i.e., boy playing women's parts. *By 'r Lady* by Our Lady 393 *chopine* thick-soled shoe of Italian fashion. *uncurrent* not passable as lawful coinage 394 *cracked . . . ring* i.e., changed from adolescent to male voice, no longer suitable for women's roles. (Coins featured rings enclosing the sovereign's head; if the coin was cracked within this ring, it was unfit for currency.) 395 *e'en to 't* go at it 396 *straight* at once. *quality* professional skill 401 *caviar to the general* caviar to the multitude, i.e., a choice dish too elegant for coarse tastes 403 *cried in the top of* i.e., spoke with greater authority than 403 *digested* arranged, ordered 404 *modesty* moderation, restraint. *cunning* skill 405 *sallets* i.e., something savory, spicy improprieties 406 *indict* convict 408 *fine* elaborately ornamented, showy 410 *Priam's slaughter* the slaying of the ruler of Troy, when the Greeks finally took the city 412 *Pyrrhus* a Greek hero in the Trojan War, also known as Neoptolemus, son of Achilles—another avenging son. *Hyrcanian beast* i.e., tiger. (On the death of Priam, see Virgil, *Aeneid*, 2.506–558; compare the whole speech with Marlowe's *Dido Queen of Carthage*, 2.1.214 ff. On the *Hyrcanian* tiger, see *Aeneid*, 4.366–367. Hyrcania is on the Caspian Sea.) 414 *sable* black (for reasons of camouflage during the episode of the Trojan horse) 416 *couchèd* concealed. *ominous horse* Trojan horse, by which the Greeks gained access to Troy

With heraldry more dismal. Head to foot   418
Now is he total gules, horridly tricked   419
With blood of fathers, mothers, daughters, sons,
Baked and impasted with the parching streets,   421
That lend a tyrannous and a damnèd light
To their lord's murder. Roasted in wrath and fire,   423
And thus o'ersizèd with coagulate gore,   424
With eyes like carbuncles, the hellish Pyrrhus   425
Old grandsire Priam seeks."
So proceed you.

POLONIUS: 'Fore God, my lord, well spoken, with good accent and
good discretion.

FIRST PLAYER: "Anon he finds him
Striking too short at Greeks. His antique sword,
Rebellious to his arm, lies where it falls,
Repugnant to command. Unequal matched,   432
Pyrrhus at Priam drives, in rage strikes wide,
But with the whiff and wind of his fell sword   434
Th' unnervèd father falls. Then senseless Ilium,   435
Seeming to feel this blow, with flaming top
Stoops to his base, and with a hideous crash   437
Takes prisoner Pyrrhus' ear. For, lo! His sword,
Which was declining on the milky head   439
Of reverend Priam, seemed i' th' air to stick.
So as a painted tyrant Pyrrhus stood,   441
And, like a neutral to his will and matter,   442
Did nothing.
But as we often see against some storm   444
A silence in the heavens, the rack stand still,   445
The bold winds speechless, and the orb below   446
As hush as death, anon the dreadful thunder
Doth rend the region, so, after Pyrrhus' pause,   448
Arousèd vengeance sets him new a-work,
And never did the Cyclops' hammers fall   450
On Mars's armor forged for proof eterne   451

---

418 *dismal* ill-omened   419 *gules* red. (A heraldic term.)   *tricked* adorned, decorated   421 *impasted*
crusted, like a thick paste.   *with . . . streets* by the parching heat of the streets (because of the fires
everywhere)   423 *their lord's* i.e., Priam's   424 *o'ersizèd* covered as with size or glue   425 *carbuncles* large fiery-red precious stones thought to emit their own light   432 *Repugnant* disobedient, re-
sistant   434 *fell* cruel   435 *unnervèd* strengthless.   *senseless Ilium* inanimate citadel of Troy
437 *his* its   439 *declining* descending.   *milky* white-haired   441 *painted* i.e., painted in a picture
442 *like . . . matter* i.e., as though suspended between his intention and its fulfillment   444 *against*
just before   445 *rack* mass of clouds   446 *orb* globe, earth   448 *region* sky   450 *Cyclops* giant
armormakers in the smithy of Vulcan   451 *proof eterne* eternal resistance to assault

With less remorse than Pyrrhus' bleeding sword   452
Now falls on Priam.
Out, out, thou strumpet Fortune! All you gods
In general synod take away her power!   455
Break all the spokes and fellies from her wheel,   456
And bowl the round nave down the hill of heaven   457
As low as to the fiends!"

POLONIUS: This is too long.

HAMLET: It shall to the barber's with your beard.—Prithee, say on.
He's for a jig or a tale of bawdry, or he sleeps. Say on; come to   461
Hecuba.   462

FIRST PLAYER:
"But who, ah woe! had seen the moblèd queen"—   463

HAMLET: "The moblèd queen"?

POLONIUS: That's good. "Moblèd queen" is good.

FIRST PLAYER:
"Run barefoot up and down, threat'ning the flames
With bisson rheum, a clout upon that head   467
Where late the diadem stood, and, for a robe,   468
About her lank and all o'erteemèd loins   469
A blanket, in the alarm of fear caught up—
Who this had seen, with tongue in venom steeped,
'Gainst Fortune's state would treason have pronounced.   472
But if the gods themselves did see her then
When she saw Pyrrhus make malicious sport
In mincing with his sword her husband's limbs,
The instant burst of clamor that she made,
Unless things mortal move them not at all,
Would have made milch the burning eyes of heaven,   478
And passion in the gods."   479

POLONIUS: Look whe'er he has not turned his color and has tears in   480
's eyes. Prithee, no more.

HAMLET: 'Tis well. I'll have thee speak out the rest of this soon.—
Good my lord, will you see the players well bestowed? Do you   483
hear, let them be well used, for they are the abstract and brief   484
chronicles of the time. After your death you were better have a
bad epitaph than their ill report while you live.

---

454 *remorse* pity   455 *synod* assembly   456 *fellies* pieces of wood forming the rim of a wheel
457 *nave* hub   461 *jig* comic song and dance often given at the end of a play   462 *Hecuba* wife of
Priam   463 *who . . . had* anyone who had (also in l. 471).   *moblèd* muffled   467 *bisson rheum* blinding tears.   *clout* cloth   468 *late* lately   469 *o'erteemèd* worn out with bearing children   472 *state*
rule, managing.   *pronounced* proclaimed   478 *milch* milky, moist with tears   479 *passion* overpowering emotion   480 *whe'er* whether   483 *bestowed* lodged   484 *abstract* summary account

POLONIUS: My lord, I will use them according to their desert.

HAMLET: God's bodikin, man, much better. Use every man after his   488
   desert, and who shall scape whipping? Use them after your own
   honor and dignity. The less they deserve, the more merit is in
   your bounty. Take them in.

POLONIUS: Come, sirs.

HAMLET: Follow him, friends. We'll hear a play tomorrow. [*As they
   start to leave,* HAMLET *detains the* FIRST PLAYER.] Dost thou hear me,
   old friend? Can you play *The Murder of Gonzago?*

FIRST PLAYER: Ay, my lord.

HAMLET: We'll ha 't tomorrow night. You could, for a need, study a   497
   speech of some dozen or sixteen lines which I would set down
   and insert in 't, could you not?

FIRST PLAYER: Ay, my lord.

HAMLET: Very well. Follow that lord, and look you mock him not.   501
   (*Exeunt* POLONIUS *and* PLAYERS.) My good friends, I'll leave you till
   night. You are welcome to Elsinore.

ROSENCRANTZ: Good my lord!

Exeunt [ROSENCRANTZ *and* GUILDENSTERN].

HAMLET:

Ay, so, goodbye to you.—Now I am alone.
O, what a rogue and peasant slave am I!
Is it not monstrous that this player here,
But in a fiction, in a dream of passion,   508
Could force his soul so to his own conceit   509
That from her working all his visage wanned,   510
Tears in his eyes, distraction in his aspect,
A broken voice, and his whole function suiting   512
With forms to his conceit? And all for nothing!   513
For Hecuba!
What's Hecuba to him, or he to Hecuba,
That he should weep for her? What would he do
Had he the motive and the cue for passion
That I have? He would drown the stage with tears
And cleave the general ear with horrid speech,   519
Make mad the guilty and appall the free,   520
Confound the ignorant, and amaze indeed
The very faculties of eyes and ears. Yet I,

---

488 *God's bodikin* by God's (Christ's) little body, *bodykin.* (Not to be confused with *bodkin,* dagger.)
497 *ha 't* have it. *study* memorize   501 *mock* mimic derisively   508 *But* merely   509 *to* in accord
with. *conceit* conception   510 *from her working* as a result of, or in response to, his soul's activity.
wanned grew pale   512–513 *his whole . . . conceit* all his bodily powers responding with actions to
suit his thought   519 *the general ear* everyone's ear. *horrid* horrible   520 *appall* (Literally, make
pale.) *free* innocent

A dull and muddy-mettled rascal, peak   523
Like John-a-dreams, unpregnant of my cause,   524
And can say nothing—no, not for a king
Upon whose property and most dear life   526
A damned defeat was made. Am I a coward?   527
Who calls me villain? Breaks my pate across?
Plucks off my beard and blows it in my face?
Tweaks me by the nose? Gives me the lie i' the throat   530
As deep as to the lungs? Who does me this?
Ha, 'swounds, I should take it; for it cannot be   532
But I am pigeon-livered and lack gall   533
To make oppression bitter, or ere this   534
I should ha' fatted all the region kites   535
With this slave's offal. Bloody, bawdy villain!
Remorseless, treacherous, lecherous, kindless villain!   537
O, vengeance!
Why, what an ass am I! This is most brave,   539
That I, the son of a dear father murdered,
Prompted to my revenge by heaven and hell,
Must like a whore unpack my heart with words
And fall a-cursing, like a very drab,   543
A scullion! Fie upon 't, foh! About, my brain!   544
Hum, I have heard
That guilty creatures sitting at a play
Have by the very cunning of the scene   547
Been struck so to the soul that presently   548
They have proclaimed their malefactions;
For murder, though it have no tongue, will speak
With most miraculous organ. I'll have these players
Play something like the murder of my father
Before mine uncle. I'll observe his looks;
I'll tent him to the quick. If 'a do blench,   554
I know my course. The spirit that I have seen
May be the devil, and the devil hath power
T' assume a pleasing shape; yea, and perhaps,

523 *muddy-mettled* dull-spirited. *peak* mope, pine   524 *John-a-dreams* a sleepy, dreaming idler. *unpregnant of* not quickened by   526 *property* i.e., the crown; perhaps also character, quality   527 *defeat* destruction   530 *Gives me the lie* calls me a liar   532 *'swounds* by his (Christ's) wounds   533 *pigeon-livered* (The pigeon or dove was popularly supposed to be mild because it secreted no gall.)   534 *To . . . bitter* to make tyranny bitter to itself   535 *region kites* kites (birds of prey) of the air   537 *Remorseless* pitiless. *kindless* unnatural   539 *brave* fine, admirable. (Said ironically.)   543 *drab* prostitute   544 *scullion* menial kitchen servant (apt to be foulmouthed).   *About* about it, to work   547 *cunning* art, skill.   *scene* dramatic presentation   548 *presently* at once   554 *tent* probe. *blench* quail, flinch

Out of my weakness and my melancholy,
As he is very potent with such spirits,   559
Abuses me to damn me. I'll have grounds   559
More relative than this. The play's the thing   561
Wherein I'll catch the conscience of the King.   *Exit.*

ACT III

Scene 1

Enter KING, QUEEN, POLONIUS, OPHELIA, ROSENCRANTZ, GUILDENSTERN, *lords.*

KING:

And can you by no drift of conference   1
Get from him why he puts on this confusion,
Grating so harshly all his days of quiet
With turbulent and dangerous lunacy?

ROSENCRANTZ:

He does confess he feels himself distracted,
But from what cause 'a will by no means speak.

GUILDENSTERN:

Nor do we find him forward to be sounded,   7
But with a crafty madness keeps aloof
When we would bring him on to some confession
Of his true state.

QUEEN: Did he receive you well?

ROSENCRANTZ: Most like a gentleman.

GUILDENSTERN:

But with much forcing of his disposition.   12

ROSENCRANTZ:

Niggard of question, but of our demands   13
Most free in his reply.

QUEEN: Did you assay him   14
To any pastime?

ROSENCRANTZ:

Madam, it so fell out that certain players
We o'erraught on the way. Of these we told him,   17
And there did seem in him a kind of joy
To hear of it. They are here about the court,
And, as I think, they have already order
This night to play before him.

---

559 *spirits* humors (of melancholy)   560 *Abuses* deludes   561 *relative* cogent, pertinent
III.1. Location: The castle.
1 *drift of conference* directing of conversation   7 *forward* willing. *sounded* questioned   12 *disposition* inclination   13 *question* conversation   14 *assay* try to win   17 *o'erraught* overtook and passed

POLONIUS: 'Tis most true,
   And he beseeched me to entreat Your Majesties
   To hear and see the matter.
KING:
   With all my heart, and it doth much content me
   To hear him so inclined.
   Good gentlemen, give him a further edge   26
   And drive his purpose into these delights.
ROSENCRANTZ:
   We shall, my lord.   *Exeunt* ROSENCRANTZ *and* GUILDENSTERN.
KING: Sweet Gertrude, leave us too,
   For we have closely sent for Hamlet hither,   29
   That he, as 'twere by accident, may here
   Affront Ophelia.   31
   Her father and myself, lawful espials,   32
   Will so bestow ourselves that seeing, unseen,
   We may of their encounter frankly judge,
   And gather by him, as he is behaved,
   If 't be th' affliction of his love or no
   That thus he suffers for.
QUEEN: I shall obey you.
   And for your part, Ophelia, I do wish
   That your good beauties be the happy cause
   Of Hamlet's wildness. So shall I hope your virtues
   Will bring him to his wonted way again,
   To both your honors.
OPHELIA: Madam, I wish it may.
                              [*Exit* QUEEN.]

POLONIUS:
   Ophelia, walk you here.—Gracious, so please you,   43
   We will bestow ourselves. [*To* OPHELIA.] Read on this book,   44
                        [*Giving her a book*]
   That show of such an exercise may color   45
   Your loneliness. We are oft to blame in this—   46
   'Tis too much proved—that with devotion's visage   47
   And pious action we do sugar o'er
   The devil himself.
KING [*aside*]:   O, 'tis too true!
   How smart a lash that speech doth give my conscience!

---

26 *edge* incitement   29 *closely* privately   31 *Affront* confront, meet   32 *espials* spies   43 *Gracious* Your Grace (i.e., the King)   44 *bestow* conceal   45 *exercise* act of devotion. (The book she reads is one of devotion.)   *color* give a plausible appearance to   46 *loneliness* being alone   47 *too much proved* too often shown to be true, too often practiced

The harlot's cheek, beautied with plastering art,
Is not more ugly to the thing that helps it   53
Than is my deed to my most painted word.
O heavy burden!

POLONIUS:
I hear him coming. Let's withdraw, my lord.   56

[*The* KING *and* POLONIUS *withdraw.*]

Enter HAMLET. [OPHELIA *pretends to read a book.*]

HAMLET:
To be, or not to be, that is the question:
Whether 'tis nobler in the mind to suffer
The slings and arrows of outrageous fortune,   59
Or to take arms against a sea of troubles
And by opposing end them. To die, to sleep—
No more—and by a sleep to say we end
The heartache and the thousand natural shocks
That flesh is heir to. 'Tis a consummation
Devoutly to be wished. To die, to sleep;
To sleep, perchance to dream. Ay, there's the rub,   66
For in that sleep of death what dreams may come,
When we have shuffled off this mortal coil,   68
Must give us pause. There's the respect   69
That makes calamity of so long life.   70
For who would bear the whips and scorns of time,   71
Th' oppressor's wrong, the proud man's contumely,   72
The pangs of disprized love, the law's delay,   73
The insolence of office, and the spurns   74
That patient merit of th' unworthy takes,   75
When he himself might his quietus make   76
With a bare bodkin? Who would fardels bear,   77
To grunt and sweat under a weary life,
But that the dread of something after death,
The undiscovered country from whose bourn   80
No traveler returns, puzzles the will,
And makes us rather bear those ills we have
Than fly to others that we know not of?

---

53 *to* compared to. *the thing* i.e., the cosmetic 56 s.d. *withdraw* (The King and Polonius may retire behind an arras. The stage directions specify that they "enter" again near the end of the scene.) 59 *slings* missiles 66 *rub* (Literally, an obstacle in the game of bowls.) 68 *shuffled* sloughed, cast. *coil* turmoil 69 *respect* consideration 70 *of . . . life* so long-lived (also suggesting that long life is itself a calamity) 71 *time* the world we live in 72 *contumely* insolent abuse 73 *disprized* unvalued 74 *office* officialdom. *spurns* insults 75 *of . . . takes* receives from unworthy persons 76 *quietus* acquittance; here, death 77 *a bare* merely a. *bodkin* dagger. *fardels* burdens 80 *bourn* boundary

Thus conscience does make cowards of us all;
And thus the native hue of resolution   85
Is sicklied o'er with the pale cast of thought,   86
And enterprises of great pitch and moment   87
With this regard their currents turn awry   88
And lose the name of action.—Soft you now,   89
The fair Ophelia. Nymph, in thy orisons   90
Be all my sins remembered.
OPHELIA: Good my lord.
How does your honor for this many a day?
HAMLET:
I humbly thank you; well, well, well.
OPHELIA:
My lord, I have remembrances of yours,
That I have longèd long to redeliver.
I pray you, now receive them.   [*She offers tokens.*]
HAMLET:
No, not I. I never gave you aught.
OPHELIA:
My honored lord, you know right well you did,
And with them words of so sweet breath composed
As made the things more rich. Their perfume lost,
Take these again, for to the noble mind
Rich gifts wax poor when givers prove unkind.
There, my lord.   [*She gives tokens.*]
HAMLET: Ha, ha! Are you honest?   104
OPHELIA: My lord?
HAMLET: Are you fair?   106
OPHELIA: What means your lordship?
HAMLET: That if you be honest and fair, your honesty should admit   108
no discourse to your beauty.   109
OPHELIA: Could beauty, my lord, have better commerce than with   110
honesty?
HAMLET: Ay, truly, for the power of beauty will sooner transform hon-
esty from what it is to a bawd than the force of honesty can
translate beauty into his likeness. This was sometime a paradox,   114
but now the time gives it proof. I did love you once.   115
OPHELIA: Indeed, my lord, you made me believe so.

---

85 *native hue* natural color, complexion   86 *cast* tinge, shade of color   87 *pitch* height (as of a falcon's flight).   *moment* importance   88 *regard* respect, consideration.   *currents* courses   89 *Soft you*
i.e., wait a minute, gently   90 *orisons* prayers   104 *honest* (1) truthful (2) chaste   106 *fair* (1)
beautiful (2) just, honorable   108 *your honesty* your chastity   109 *discourse to* familiar dealings
with   110 *commerce* dealings, intercourse   114 *his* its   *sometime* formerly.   *a paradox* a view opposite to commonly held opinion.   115 *the time* the present age

HAMLET: You should not have believed me, for virtue cannot so   117
inoculate our old stock but we shall relish of it. I loved you not.   118

OPHELIA: I was the more deceived.

HAMLET: Get thee to a nunnery. Why wouldst thou be a breeder of   120
sinners? I am myself indifferent honest, but yet I could accuse   121
me of such things that it were better my mother had not borne
me: I am very proud, revengeful, ambitious, with more offenses
at my beck than I have thoughts to put them in, imagination to   124
give them shape, or time to act them in. What should such fellows as I do crawling between earth and heaven? We are arrant
knaves all; believe none of us. Go thy ways to a nunnery.
Where's your father?

OPHELIA: At home, my lord.

HAMLET: Let the doors be shut upon him, that he may play the fool
nowhere but in 's own house. Farewell.

OPHELIA: O, help him, you sweet heavens!

HAMLET: If thou dost marry, I'll give thee this plague for thy dowry:
be thou as chaste as ice, as pure as snow, thou shalt not escape
calumny. Get thee to a nunnery, farewell. Or, if thou wilt needs
marry, marry a fool, for wise men know well enough what mon-   136
sters you make of them. To a nunnery, go, and quickly too.   137
Farewell.

OPHELIA: Heavenly powers, restore him!

HAMLET: I have heard of your paintings too, well enough. God hath
given you one face, and you make yourselves another. You jig,   141
you amble, and you lisp, you nickname God's creatures, and   142
make your wantonness your ignorance. Go to, I'll no more on 't;   143
it hath made me mad. I say we will have no more marriage.
Those that are married already—all but one—shall live. The rest
shall keep as they are. To a nunnery, go.   *Exit.*

OPHELIA:

O, what a noble mind is here o'erthrown!
The courtier's, soldier's, scholar's, eye, tongue, sword,
Th' expectancy and rose of the fair state,   149
The glass of fashion and the mold of form,   150

117–118 *inoculate* graft, be engrafted to   118 *but . . . it* i.e., that we do not still have about us a
taste of the old stock, i.e., retain our sinfulness   120 *nunnery* convent (with possibly an awareness
that the word was also used derisively to denote a brothel)   121 *indifferent honest* reasonably virtuous   124 *beck* command   136–137 *monsters* (An allusion to the horns of a cuckold.)   *you* i.e., you
women   141 *jig* i.e., dance and sing affectedly and wantonly.   142 *amble* dance, move coquettishly
lisp (A wanton affectation.)   *nickname* find a new name for, transform (as in using cosmetics)
143 *make . . . ignorance* i.e., excuse your affectation on the grounds of your ignorance   *on 't* of it
149 *Th' expectancy . . . state* the hope and ornament of the kingdom made fair (by him)
150 *The glass . . . form* the mirror of true self-fashioning and the pattern of courtly behavior

Th' observed of all observers, quite, quite down!   151
And I, of ladies most deject and wretched,
That sucked the honey of his music vows,
Now see that noble and most sovereign reason
Like sweet bells jangled out of tune and harsh,
That unmatched form and feature of blown youth   156
Blasted with ocstasy. O, woe is me,   157
T' have seen what I have seen, see what I see!

Enter KING *and* POLONIUS.

KING:

Love? His affections do not that way tend;   159
Nor what he spake, though it lacked form a little,
Was not like madness. There's something in his soul
O'er which his melancholy sits on brood,   162
And I do doubt the hatch and the disclose   163
Will be some danger; which for to prevent,
I have in quick determination
Thus set it down: he shall with speed to England   166
For the demand of our neglected tribute.   167
Haply the seas and countries different
With variable objects shall expel   169
This something settled matter in his heart,   170
Whereon his brains still beating puts him thus   171
From fashion of himself. What think you on 't?   172

POLONIUS:

It shall do well. But yet do I believe
The origin and commencement of his grief
Sprung from neglected love.—How now, Ophelia?
You need not tell us what Lord Hamlet said;
We heard it all.—My lord, do as you please,
But, if you hold it fit, after the play
Let his queen-mother all alone entreat him   179
To show his grief. Let her be round with him;   180
And I'll be placed, so please you, in the ear
Of all their conference. If she find him not,   182

---

151 *Th' observed . . . observers* i.e., the center of attention and honor in the court   156 *blown* blooming   157 *Blasted* withered. *ecstasy* madness   159 *affections* emotions, feelings   162 *sits on brood* sits like a bird on a nest, about to *hatch* mischief (l. 163)   163 *doubt* fear. *disclose* disclosure, hatching   166 *set it down* resolved   167 *For . . . of* to demand   169 *variable objects* various sights and surroundings to divert him   170 *This something . . . heart* the strange unidentified matter settled in his heart   171 *still* continually   172 *From . . . himself* out of his natural manner   179 *queen-mother* queen and mother, not widowed dowager   180 *round* blunt   182 *find him not* fails to discover what is troubling him

    To England send him, or confine him where
    Your wisdom best shall think.
KING: It shall be so.
    Madness in great ones must not unwatched go.   *Exeunt.*

ACT III

Scene 2

Enter HAMLET *and three of the* PLAYERS.

HAMLET: Speak the speech, I pray you, as I pronounced it to you,
trippingly on the tongue. But if you mouth it, as many of our play-   2
ers do, I had as lief the town crier spoke my lines. Nor do not   3
saw the air too much with your hand, thus, but use all gently; for
in the very torrent, tempest, and, as I may say, whirlwind of your
passion, you must acquire and beget a temperance that may
give it smoothness. O, it offends me to the soul to hear a robus-   7
tious periwig-pated fellow tear a passion to tatters, to very rags,   8
to split the ears of the groundlings, who for the most part are ca-   9
pable of nothing but inexplicable dumb shows and noise. I would   10
have such a fellow whipped for o'erdoing Termagant. It out-   11
Herods Herod. Pray you, avoid it.   12

FIRST PLAYER: I warrant your honor.

HAMLET: Be not too tame neither, but let your own discretion be your
tutor. Suit the action to the word, the word to the action, with this
special observance, that you o'erstep not the modesty of nature.   16
For anything so o'erdone is from the purpose of playing, whose   17
end, both at the first and now, was and is to hold as 'twere the
mirror up to nature, to show virtue her feature, scorn her own   19
image, and the very age and body of the time his form and pres-   20
sure. Now this overdone or come tardy off, though it makes the   21
unskillful laugh, cannot but make the judicious grieve, the cen-   22
sure of the which one must in your allowance o'erweigh a whole   23
theater of others. O, there be players that I have seen play, and

---

III.2. Location: The castle.

2–3 *our players* (Indefinite use; i.e., players nowadays.)   3 *I had as lief* I would just as soon   7–8 *ro-bustious* violent, boisterous.   8 *periwig-pated* wearing a wig   9 *groundlings* spectators who paid least and stood in the yard of the theater.   9–10 *capable of* able to understand   11 *Termagant* a supposed deity of the Mohammedans, not found in any English medieval play but elsewhere portrayed as violent and blustering   12 *Herod* Herod of Jewry. (A character in *The Slaughter of the Innocents* and other cycle plays. The part was played with great noise and fury.)   16 *modesty* restraint, moderation   17 *from* contrary to   19 *scorn* i.e., something foolish and deserving of scorn   20 *the very . . . time* i.e., the present state of affairs.   *his* its   20–21 *pressure* stamp, impressed character   21 *come tardy off* inadequately done   21–22 *the unskillful* those lacking in judgment   22–23 *the censure . . . one* the judgment of even one of whom   23 *your allowance* your scale of values

heard others praise, and that highly, not to speak it profanely,   25
that, neither having th' accent of Christians nor the gait of Christ-   26
ian, pagan, nor man, have so strutted and bellowed that I have   27
thought some of nature's journeymen had made men and not   28
made them well, they imitated humanity so abominably.   29
FIRST PLAYER: I hope we have reformed that indifferently with us, sir.   30
HAMLET: O, reform it altogether. And let those that play your clowns
speak no more than is set down for them; for there be of them   32
that will themselves laugh, to set on some quantity of barren   33
spectators to laugh too, though in the meantime some necessary
question of the play be then to be considered. That's villainous,
and shows a most pitiful ambition in the fool that uses it. Go
make you ready.   [*Exeunt* PLAYERS.]

Enter POLONIUS, GUILDENSTERN, *and* ROSENCRANTZ.

How now, my lord, will the King hear this piece of work?
POLONIUS: And the Queen too, and that presently.   39
HAMLET: Bid the players make haste.   [*Exit* POLONIUS.]
Will you two help to hasten them?
ROSENCRANTZ:
Ay, my lord.   *Exeunt they two.*
HAMLET: What ho, Horatio!

Enter HORATIO.

HORATIO: Here, sweet lord, at your service.
HAMLET:
Horatio, thou art e'en as just a man
As e'er my conversation coped withal.   46
HORATIO:
O, my dear lord—
HAMLET: Nay, do not think I flatter,
For what advancement may I hope from thee
That no revenue hast but thy good spirits
To feed and clothe thee? Why should the poor be
    flattered?
No, let the candied tongue lick absurd pomp,   52
And crook the pregnant hinges of the knee   53
Where thrift may follow fawning. Dost thou hear?   54

---

25 *not . . . profanely* (Hamlet anticipates his idea in ll. 33–34 that some men were not made by God at all.)   26 *Christians* i.e., ordinary decent folk   27 *nor man* i.e., nor any human being at all   28 *journeymen* laborers not yet masters in their trade   29 *abominably* (Shakespeare's usual spelling, *abhominably,* suggests a literal though etymologically incorrect meaning, "removed from human nature.")   30 *indifferently* tolerably   32 *of them*   i.e., some among them   33 *barren* i.e., of wit   39 *presently* at once   46 *my . . . withal* my contact with people provided opportunity for encounter with   52 *candied* sugared, flattering   53 *pregnant* compliant   54 *thrift* profit

Since my dear soul was mistress of her choice
And could of men distinguish her election,   56
Sh' hath sealed thee for herself, for thou hast been   57
As one, in suffering all, that suffers nothing,
A man that Fortune's buffets and rewards
Hast ta'en with equal thanks; and blest are those
Whose blood and judgment are so well commeddled   61
That they are not a pipe for Fortune's finger
To sound what stop she please. Give me that man   63
That is not passion's slave, and I will wear him
In my heart's core, ay, in my heart of heart,
As I do thee.—Something too much of this.—
There is a play tonight before the King.
One scene of it comes near the circumstance
Which I have told thee of my father's death.
I prithee, when thou seest that act afoot,
Even with the very comment of thy soul   71
Observe my uncle. If his occulted guilt   72
Do not itself unkennel in one speech,   73
It is a damnèd ghost that we have seen,   74
And my imaginations are as foul
As Vulcan's stithy. Give him heedful note,   76
For I mine eyes will rivet to his face,
And after we will both our judgments join
In censure of his seeming.   79
HORATIO: Well, my lord.
    If 'a steal aught the whilst this play is playing   80
    And scape detecting, I will pay the theft.

[Fourish.] Enter trumpets and kettledrums, KING, QUEEN, POLONIUS, OPHELIA,
[ROSENCRANTZ, GUILDENSTERN, and other lords, with guards carrying torches].

HAMLET: They are coming to the play. I must be idle. Get you a place.   82

[The KING, QUEEN, and courtiers sit.]

KING: How fares our cousin Hamlet?   83

HAMLET: Excellent, i' faith, of the chameleon's dish: I eat the air,   84
    promise-crammed. You cannot feed capons so.   85

---

56 could . . . election could make distinguishing choices among men   57 sealed thee (Literally, as one
would seal a legal document to mark possession.)   61 blood passion.   commeddled commingled
63 stop hole in a wind instrument for controlling the sound   71 very . . . soul i.e., your most pene-
trating observation and consideration   72 occulted hidden   73 unkennel (As one would say of a fox
driven from its lair.)   74 damnèd in league with Satan   76 stithy smithy, place of stiths (anvils)
79 censure of his seeming judgment of his appearance or behavior   80 If 'a steal aught i.e., if he hides
anything   82 idle (1) unoccupied (2) mad   83 cousin i.e., close relative   84 chameleon's dish (Chame-
leons were supposed to feed on air. Hamlet deliberately misinterprets the King's fares as "feeds."
By his phrase eat the air he also plays on the idea of feeding himself with the promise of succession,
of being the heir.)   85 capons roosters castrated and crammed with feed to make them succulent

KING: I have nothing with this answer, Hamlet. These words are not   86
   mine.   87
HAMLET: No, nor mine now. [*To* POLONIUS.] My lord, you played once i'   88
   th' university, you say?
POLONIUS: That did I, my lord, and was accounted a good actor.
HAMLET: What did you enact?
POLONIUS: I did enact Julius Caesar. I was killed i' the Capitol; Bru-
   tus killed me.
HAMLET: It was a brute part of him to kill so capital a calf there.—Be   94
   the players ready?
ROSENCRANTZ: Ay, my lord. They stay upon your patience.
QUEEN: Come hither, my dear Hamlet, sit by me.
HAMLET: No, good Mother, here's metal more attractive.   98
POLONIUS [*to the* KING]:   Oho, do you mark that?
HAMLET: Lady, shall I lie in your lap?   [*Lying down at* OPHELIA*'s feet.*]
OPHELIA: No, my lord.
HAMLET: I mean, my head upon your lap?
OPHELIA: Ay, my lord.
HAMLET: Do you think I meant country matters?   104
OPHELIA: I think nothing, my lord.
HAMLET: That's a fair thought to lie between maids' legs.
OPHELIA: What is, my lord?
HAMLET: Nothing.   108
OPHELIA: You are merry, my lord.
HAMLET: Who, I?
OPHELIA: Ay, my lord.
HAMLET: O God, your only jig maker. What should a man do but be   112
   merry? For look you how cheerfully my mother looks, and my fa-
   ther died within 's two hours.   114
OPHELIA: Nay, 'tis twice two months, my lord.
HAMLET: So long? Nay then, let the devil wear black, for I'll have a
   suit of sables. O heavens! Die two months ago, and not forgot-   117
   ten yet? Then there's hope a great man's memory may outlive

---

86 *have . . . with* make nothing of, or gain nothing from   86–87 *are not mine* do not respond to what I asked   88 *nor mine now* (Once spoken, words are proverbially no longer the speaker's own— and hence should be uttered warily.)   94 *brute* (The Latin meaning of *brutus,* "stupid," was often used punningly with the name Brutus.)   *part* (1) deed (2) role   *calf* fool   98 *metal* substance that is *attractive,* i.e., magnetic, but with suggestion also of *mettle,* disposition   104 *country matters* the coarse and bawdy things that country folk do (with a pun on the first syllable of *country*)   108 *Nothing* the figure zero or naught, suggesting the female anatomy. (*Thing* not infrequently has a bawdy connota- tion of male or female anatomy, and the reference here could be male.)   112 *only jig maker* very best composer of jigs (song and dance). (Hamlet replies sardonically to Ophelia's observation that he is merry by saying, "If you're looking for someone who is really merry, you've come to the right per- son.")   114 *within 's* within this   117 *suit of sables* garments trimmed with the fur of the sable, and hence suited for a wealthy person, not a mourner (but with a pun on *sable,* black, ironically suggest- ing mourning once again)

his life half a year. But, by 'r Lady, 'a must build churches, then,
or else shall 'a suffer not thinking on, with the hobbyhorse,   120
whose epitaph is "For O, for O, the hobbyhorse is forgot."   121

The trumpets sound. Dumb show follows.

Enter a KING *and a* QUEEN [*very lovingly*]; *the* QUEEN *embracing him, and he her.* [*She kneels, and makes show of protestation unto him.*] *He takes her up, and declines his head upon her neck. He lies him down upon a bank of flowers. She, seeing him asleep, leaves him. Anon comes in another man, takes off his crown, kisses it, pours poison in the sleeper's ears, and leaves him. The* QUEEN *returns, finds the* KING *dead, makes passionate action. The* POISONER *with some three or four come in again, seem to condole with her. The dead body is carried away. The* POISONER *woos the* QUEEN *with gifts; she seems harsh awhile, but in the end accepts love.*

                                              [*Exeunt* PLAYERS.]

OPHELIA: What means this, my lord?
HAMLET: Marry, this' miching mallico; it means mischief.   123
OPHELIA: Belike this show imports the argument of the play.   124

Enter PROLOGUE.

HAMLET: We shall know by this fellow. The players cannot keep
           counsel; they'll tell all.   126
OPHELIA: Will 'a tell us what this show meant?
HAMLET: Ay, or any show that you will show him. Be not you   128
           ashamed to show, he'll not shame to tell you what it means.
OPHELIA: You are naught, you are naught. I'll mark the play.   130
PROLOGUE:
     For us, and for our tragedy,
     Here stooping to your clemency,   132
     We beg your hearing patiently.   [*Exit.*]
HAMLET: Is this a prologue, or the posy of a ring?   134
OPHELIA: 'Tis brief, my lord.
HAMLET: As woman's love.

Enter [*two* PLAYERS *as*] KING *and* QUEEN.

PLAYER KING:
     Full thirty times hath Phoebus' cart gone round   137

120 *suffer . . . on* undergo oblivion   121 *For . . . forgot* (Verse of a song occurring also in *Love's Labor's Lost,* 3.1.27–28. The hobbyhorse was a character made up to resemble a horse and rider, appearing in the morris dance and such May-game sports. This song laments the disappearance of such customs under pressure from the Puritans.)   123 *this' miching mallico* this is sneaking mischief   124 *Belike* probably.   *argument* plot   126 *counsel* secret   128 *Be not you* if you are not   130 *naught* indecent. (Ophelia is reacting to Hamlet's pointed remarks about not being ashamed to show all.)   132 *stooping* bowing   134 *posy . . . ring* brief motto in verse inscribed in a ring   137 *Phoebus' cart* the sun god's chariot, making its yearly cycle

Neptune's salt wash and Tellus' orbèd ground,   138
And thirty dozen moons with borrowed sheen   139
About the world have times twelve thirties been,
Since love our hearts and Hymen did our hands   141
  Unite commutual in most sacred bands.   142
PLAYER QUEEN:
So many journeys may the sun and moon
Make us again count o'er ere love be done!
But, woe is me, you are so sick of late,
So far from cheer and from your former state,
That I distrust you. Yet, though I distrust,   147
Discomfort you, my lord, it nothing must.   148
For women's fear and love hold quantity;   149
In neither aught, or in extremity.   150
Now, what my love is, proof hath made you know,   151
And as my love is sized, my fear is so.   152
Where love is great, the littlest doubts are fear;
Where little fears grow great, great love grows there.
PLAYER KING:
Faith, I must leave thee, love, and shortly too;
My operant powers their functions leave to do.   156
And thou shalt live in this fair world behind,   157
Honored, beloved; and haply one as kind
For husband shalt thou—
PLAYER QUEEN: O, confound the rest!
Such love must needs be treason in my breast.
In second husband let me be accurst!
None wed the second but who killed the first.   162
HAMLET: Wormwood, wormwood.
PLAYER QUEEN:
The instances that second marriage move   164
Are base respects of thrift, but none of love.   165
A second time I kill my husband dead
When second husband kisses me in bed.
PLAYER KING:
I do believe you think what now you speak,

---

138 *salt wash* the sea. *Tellus* goddess of the earth, of the *orbèd ground*   139 *borrowed* i.e., reflected 141 *Hymen* god of matrimony   142 *commutual* mutually. *bands* bonds   147 *distrust* am anxious about   148 *nothing* not at all   149 *hold quantity* keep proportion with one another   150 *In . . . extremity* i.e., women fear and love either too little or too much, but the two, fear and love, are equal in either case   151 *proof* experience   152 *sized* in size   156 *operant powers* vital functions. *leave to do* cease to perform   157 *behind* after I have gone   162 *None* i.e., let no woman. *but who* except her who   164 *instances* motives. *move* motivate   165 *base . . . thrift* ignoble considerations of material prosperity

But what we do determine oft we break.
Purpose is but the slave to memory,   169
Of violent birth, but poor validity,   170
Which now, like fruit unripe, sticks on the tree,   171
But fall unshaken when they mellow be.
Most necessary 'tis that we forget   173
To pay ourselves what to ourselves is debt.   174
What to ourselves in passion we propose,
The passion ending, doth the purpose lose.
The violence of either grief or joy
Their own enactures with themselves destroy.   178
Where joy most revels, grief doth most lament;   179
Grief joys, joy grieves, on slender accident.   180
This world is not for aye, nor 'tis not strange   181
That even our loves should with our fortunes change;
For 'tis a question left us yet to prove,
Whether love lead fortune, or else fortune love.
The great man down, you mark his favorite flies;   185
The poor advanced makes friends of enemies.   186
And hitherto doth love on fortune tend;   187
For who not needs shall never lack a friend,   188
And who in want a hollow friend doth try   189
Directly seasons him his enemy.   190
But, orderly to end where I begun,
Our wills and fates do so contrary run   192
That our devices still are overthrown;   193
Our thoughts are ours, their ends none of our own.   194
So think thou wilt no second husband wed,
But die thy thoughts when thy first lord is dead.

PLAYER QUEEN:
Nor earth to me give food, nor heaven light,   197
Sport and repose lock from me day and night,   198
To desperation turn my trust and hope,

---

169 *Purpose . . . memory* i.e., our good intentions are subject to forgetfulness   170 *validity* strength, durability   171 *Which* i.e., purpose   173–174 *Most . . . debt* i.e., it's inevitable that in time we forget the obligations we have imposed on ourselves   178 *enactures* fulfillments   179–180 *Where . . . accident* i.e., the capacity for extreme joy and grief go together, and often one extreme is instantly changed into its opposite on the slightest provocation   181 *aye* ever   185 *down* fallen in fortune   186 *The poor . . . enemies* i.e., when one of humble station is promoted, you see his enemies suddenly becoming his friends   187 *hitherto* up to this point in the argument, or, to this extent. *tend* attend   188 *who not needs* he who is not in need (of wealth)   189 *who in want* he who, being in need. *try* test (his generosity)   190 *seasons him* ripens him into   192 *Our . . . run* what we want and what we get go so contrarily   193 *devices still* intentions continually   194 *ends* results   197 *Nor* let neither   198 *Sport . . . night* may day deny me its pastimes and night its repose

An anchor's cheer in prison be my scope!   200
Each opposite that blanks the face of joy   201
Meet what I would have well and it destroy!   202
Both here and hence pursue me lasting strife   203
If, once a widow, ever I be a wife!

HAMLET: If she should break it now!

PLAYER KING:

'Tis deeply sworn. Sweet, leave me here awhile;
My spirits grow dull, and fain I would beguile   207
The tedious day with sleep.

PLAYER QUEEN: Sleep rock thy brain,
And never come mischance between us twain!

> *[He sleeps.] Exit* [PLAYER QUEEN].

HAMLET: Madam, how like you this play?

QUEEN: The lady doth protest too much, methinks.   212

HAMLET: O, but she'll keep her word.

KING: Have you heard the argument? Is there no offense in 't?   214

HAMLET: No, no, they do but jest, poison in jest. No offense i' the   215
world.

KING: What do you call the play?

HAMLET: *The Mousetrap.* Marry, how? Tropically. This play is the   218
image of a murder done in Vienna. Gonzago is the Duke's name,   219
his wife, Baptista. You shall see anon. 'Tis a knavish piece of
work, but what of that? Your Majesty, and we that have free   221
souls, it touches us not. Let the galled jade wince, our withers   222
are unwrung.   223

Enter LUCIANUS.

This is one Lucianus, nephew to the King.

OPHELIA: You are as good as a chorus, my lord.   225

HAMLET: I could interpret between you and your love, if I could see
the puppets dallying.   227

---

200 *anchor's cheer* anchorite's or hermit's fare.   *my scope* the extent of my happiness   201–202 *Each . . . destroy* may every adverse thing that causes the face of joy to turn pale meet and destroy everything that I desire to see prosper.   201 *blanks* causes to blanch or grow pale   203 *hence* in the life hereafter   207 *spirits* vital spirits   212 *doth . . . much* makes too many promises and protestations   214 *argument* plot   214–215 *offense . . . offense* cause for objection . . . crime   215 *jest* make believe   218 *Tropically* figuratively. (The first quarto reading, *trapically,* suggests a pun on *trap* in *Mousetrap.*)   219 *Duke's* i.e., King's. (A slip that may be due to Shakespeare's possible source, the actual murder of the Duke of Urbino by Luigi Gonzaga in 1538.)   221 *free* guiltless   222 *galled jade* horse whose hide is rubbed by saddle or harness.   *withers* the part between the horse's shoulder blades   223 *unwrung* not rubbed sore   225 *chorus* (In many Elizabethan plays the forthcoming action was explained by an actor known as the "chorus"; at a puppet show the actor who spoke the dialogue was known as an "interpreter," as indicated by the lines following.)   227 *puppets dallying* (With sexual suggestion, continued in *keen,* i.e., sexually aroused, *groaning,* i.e., moaning in pregnancy, and *edge,* i.e., sexual desire or impetuosity.)

OPHELIA: You are keen, my lord, you are keen.   228
HAMLET: It would cost you a groaning to take off mine edge.
OPHELIA: Still better, and worse.   230
HAMLET: So you mis-take your husbands.—Begin, murderer; leave   231
   thy damnable faces and begin. Come, the croaking raven doth
   bellow for revenge.
LUCIANUS:
   Thoughts black, hands apt, drugs fit, and time agreeing,
   Confederate season, else no creature seeing,   235
   Thou mixture rank, of midnight weeds collected,
   With Hecate's ban thrice blasted, thrice infected,   237
   Thy natural magic and dire property   238
   On wholesome life usurp immediately.

               [*He pours the poison into the sleeper's ear.*]

HAMLET: 'A poisons him i' the garden for his estate. His name's   240
   Gonzago. The story is extant, and written in very choice Italian.
   You shall see anon how the murderer gets the love of Gonzago's
   wife.   [CLAUDIUS *rises.*]
OPHELIA: The King rises.
HAMLET: What, frighted with false fire?   245
QUEEN: How fares my lord?
POLONIUS: Give o'er the play.
KING: Give me some light. Away!
POLONIUS: Lights, lights, lights!   *Exeunt all but* HAMLET *and* HORATIO.
HAMLET:
   "Why, let the strucken deer go weep,   250
      The hart ungallèd play.   251
   For some must watch, while some must sleep;   252
      Thus runs the world away."   253
   Would not this, sir, and a forest of feathers—if the rest of my   254
   fortunes turn Turk with me—with two Provincial roses on my   255
   razed shoes, get me a fellowship in a cry of players?   256

228 *keen* sharp, bitter   230 *Still . . . worse* more keen, always *bettering* what other people say with witty wordplay, but at the same time more offensive   231 *So* even thus (in marriage).   *mis-take* take erringly, falseheartedly. (The marriage vows say, "for better, for worse.")   235 *Confederate season* the time and occasion conspiring (to assist the murderer).   *else* otherwise   237 *Hecate's ban* the curse of Hecate, the goddess of witchcraft   238 *dire property* baleful quality   240 *estate* i.e., the kingship.   *His* i.e., the King's   245 *false fire* the blank discharge of a gun loaded with powder but no shot   250–253 *Why . . . away* (Probably from an old ballad, with allusion to the popular belief that a wounded deer retires to weep and die; cf. *As You Like It,* 2.1.66.)   251 *ungallèd* unafflicted   252 *watch* remain awake   253 *Thus . . . away* thus the world goes   254 *this* i.e., the play.   *feathers* (Allusion to the plumes that Elizabethan actors were fond of wearing.)   255 *turn Turk with* turn renegade against, go back on.   *Provincial roses* rosettes of ribbon like the roses of a part of France   256 *razed* with ornamental slashing.   *fellowship . . . players* partnership in a theatrical company.   *cry* pack (of hounds)

HORATIO: Half a share.

HAMLET: A whole one, I.

      "For thou dost know, O Damon dear,   259

        This realm dismantled was   260

      Of Jove himself, and now reigns here   261

        A very, very—pajock."   262

HORATIO: You might have rhymed.

HAMLET: O good Horatio, I'll take the ghost's word for a thousand pound. Didst perceive?

HORATIO: Very well, my lord.

HAMLET: Upon the talk of the poisoning?

HORATIO: I did very well note him.

Enter ROSENCRANTZ *and* GUILDENSTERN.

HAMLET: Aha! Come, some music! Come, the recorders.   269

      "For if the King like not the comedy,

      Why then, be like, he likes it not, perdy."   271

    Come, some music.

GUILDENSTERN: Good my lord, vouchsafe me a word with you.

HAMLET: Sir, a whole history.

GUILDENSTERN: The King, sir—

HAMLET: Ay, sir, what of him?

GUILDENSTERN: Is in his retirement marvelous distempered.   277

HAMLET: With drink, sir?

GUILDENSTERN: No, my lord, with choler.   279

HAMLET: Your wisdom should show itself more richer to signify this to the doctor, for for me to put him to his purgation would per-   281 haps plunge him into more choler.

GUILDENSTERN: Good my lord, put your discourse into some frame   283 and start not so wildly from my affair.

HAMLET: I am tame, sir. Pronounce.

GUILDENSTERN: The Queen, your mother, in most great affliction of spirit, hath sent me to you.

HAMLET: You are welcome.

---

259 *Damon* the friend of Pythias, as Horatio is friend of Hamlet; or, a traditional pastoral name 260 *dismantled* stripped, divested   261 *Of Jove* (Jove, like Hamlet's father, has been taken away, leaving only a peacock or an ass.)   262 *pajock* peacock, a bird with a bad reputation. (Here substituted for the obvious rhyme-word "ass.") Or possibly the word is *patchock*, savage, base person. 269 *recorders* wind instruments of the flute kind   271 *perdy* (A corruption of the French *par dieu,* "by God.")   277 *retirement* withdrawal to his chambers.   *distempered* out of humor. (But Hamlet deliberately plays on the wider application to any illness of mind or body, as in ll. 309–310, especially to drunkenness.)   279 *choler* i.e., anger. (But Hamlet takes the word in its more basic humors sense of "bilious disorder.")   281 *purgation* (Hamlet hints at something going beyond medical treatment to bloodletting and the extraction of confession.)   283 *frame* order.   *start* shy or jump away (like a horse; the opposite of *tame* in l. 309)

GUILDENSTERN: Nay, good my lord, this courtesy is not of the right
   breed. If it shall please you to make me a wholesome answer, I   290
   will do your mother's commandment; if not, your pardon and my   291
   return shall be the end of my business.

HAMLET: Sir, I cannot.

ROSENCRANTZ: What, my lord?

HAMLET: Make you a wholesome answer; my wit's diseased. But,
   sir, such answer as I can make, you shall command, or rather,
   as you say, my mother. Therefore no more, but to the matter. My
   mother, you say—

ROSENCRANTZ: Then thus she says: your behavior hath struck her
   into amazement and admiration.

HAMLET: O wonderful son, that can so stonish a mother! But is there
   no sequel at the heels of this mother's admiration? Impart.   302

ROSENCRANTZ: She desires to speak with you in her closet ere you   303
   go to bed.

HAMLET: We shall obey, were she ten times our mother. Have you
   any further trade with us?

ROSENCRANTZ: My lord, you once did love me.

HAMLET: And do still, by these pickers and stealers.   308

ROSENCRANTZ: Good my lord, what is your cause of distemper? You
   do surely bar the door upon your own liberty if you deny your   310
   griefs to your friend.

HAMLET: Sir, I lack advancement.

ROSENCRANTZ: How can that be, when you have the voice of the
   King himself for your succession in Denmark?

HAMLET: Ay, sir, but "While the grass grows"—the proverb is some-   315
   thing musty.   316

Enter the PLAYERS *with recorders.*

   O, the recorders. Let me see one. [*He takes a recorder.*] To with- 317
   draw with you: why do you go about to recover the wind of me,   318
   as if you would drive me into a toil?   319

GUILDENSTERN: O, my lord, if my duty be too bold, my love is too   320
   unmannerly.

HAMLET: I do not well understand that. Will you play upon this pipe? 322

GUILDENSTERN: My lord, I cannot.

---

290 *breed* (1) kind (2) breeding, manners   291 *pardon* permission to depart   302 *admiration* wonder
303 *closet* private chamber   308 *pickers and stealers* i.e., hands. (So called from the catechism, "to
keep my hands from picking and stealing.")   310 *deny* refuse to share   315 *While . . . grows* (The
rest of the proverb is "the silly horse starves"; Hamlet may not live long enough to succeed to the
kingdom.)   315–316 *something* somewhat   *s.d. Players* actors   317–318 *withdraw* speak privately
318 *recover the wind* get to the windward side (thus driving the game into the toil, or net)   319 *toil*
snare   320–321 *if . . . unmannerly* if I am using an unmannerly boldness, it is my love that occasions
it   322 *I . . . that* i.e., I don't understand how genuine love can be unmannerly

HAMLET: I pray you.

GUILDENSTERN: Believe me, I cannot.

HAMLET: I do beseech you.

GUILDENSTERN: I know no touch of it, my lord.

HAMLET: It is as easy as lying. Govern these ventages with your fin-   328
gers and thumb, give it breath with your mouth, and it will discourse most eloquent music. Look you, these are the stops.

GUILDENSTERN: But these cannot I command to any utterance of harmony. I have not the skill.

HAMLET: Why, look you now, how unworthy a thing you make of me!
You would play upon me, you would seem to know my stops,
you would pluck out the heart of my mystery, you would sound   335
me from my lowest note to the top of my compass, and there is   336
much music, excellent voice, in this little organ, yet cannot you 337
make it speak. 'Sblood, do you think I am easier to be played on
than a pipe? Call me what instrument you will, though you can
fret me, you cannot play upon me.   340

Enter POLONIUS.

God bless you, sir!

POLONIUS: My lord, the Queen would speak with you, and presently. 342

HAMLET: Do you see yonder cloud that's almost in shape of a
camel?

POLONIUS: By the Mass and 'tis, like a camel indeed.

HAMLET: Methinks it is like a weasel.

POLONIUS: It is backed like a weasel.

HAMLET: Or like a whale?

POLONIUS: Very like a whale.

HAMLET: Then I will come to my mother by and by. [*Aside.*] They fool 350
me to the top of my bent.—I will come by and by.   351

POLONIUS: I will say so.   [*Exit.*]

HAMLET: "By and by" is easily said. Leave me, friends.

[*Exeunt all but* HAMLET.]

'Tis now the very witching time of night,   354
When churchyards yawn and hell itself breathes out
Contagion to this world. Now could I drink hot blood   356
And do such bitter business as the day
Would quake to look on. Soft, now to my mother.

---

328 *ventages* stops of the recorder   335 *sound* (1) fathom (2) produce sound in   336 *compass* range
(of voice)   337 *organ* musical instrument   340 *fret* irritate (with a quibble on *fret* meaning the piece
of wood, gut, or metal that regulates the fingering on an instrument)   342 *presently* at once   350 *by
and by* quite soon   350–351 *fool me* make me play the fool. *top of my bent* limit of my ability or endurance. (Literally, the extent to which a bow may be bent.)   354 *witching time* time when spells are
cast and evil is abroad   356 *Now could I* i.e., now I might be tempted to

O heart, lose not thy nature! Let not ever
The soul of Nero enter this firm bosom.   360
Let me be cruel, not unnatural;
I will speak daggers to her, but use none.
My tongue and soul in this be hypocrites:
How in my words soever she be shent,   364
To give them seals never my soul consent!   *Exit.*   365

ACT III

Scene 3

Enter KING, ROSENCRANTZ, *and* GUILDENSTERN.

KING:
    I like him not, nor stands it safe with us   1
    To let his madness range. Therefore prepare you.
    I your commission will forthwith dispatch,   3
    And he to England shall along with you.
    The terms of our estate may not endure   5
    Hazard so near 's as doth hourly grow
    Out of his brows.   7
GUILDENSTERN: We will ourselves provide.
    Most holy and religious fear it is   8
    To keep those many many bodies safe
    That live and feed upon Your Majesty.
ROSENCRANTZ:
    The single and peculiar life is bound   11
    With all the strength and armor of the mind
    To keep itself from noyance, but much more   13
    That spirit upon whose weal depends and rests
    The lives of many. The cess of majesty   15
    Dies not alone, but like a gulf doth draw   16
    What's near it with it; or it is a massy wheel   17
    Fixed on the summit of the highest mount,
    To whose huge spokes ten thousand lesser things
    Are mortised and adjoined, which, when it falls,   20

---

360 *Nero* murderer of his mother, Agrippina   364 *How . . . soever* however much by my words.
shent rebuked   365 *give them seals* i.e., confirm them with deeds
III.3. Location: The castle.
1 *him* i.e., his behavior   3 *dispatch* prepare, cause to be drawn up   5 *terms* condition, circumstances. *our estate* my royal position   7 *brows* i.e., effronteries, threatening frowns, or contrivances
8 *religious fear* sacred duty   11 *single and peculiar* individual and private   13 *noyance* harm   15 *cess*
decease, cessation   16 *gulf* whirlpool   17 *massy* massive   20 *when it falls* i.e., when it descends,
like the wheel of Fortune, bringing a king down with it

Each small annexment, petty consequence, 21
Attends the boisterous ruin. Never alone 22
Did the King sigh, but with a general groan.

KING:

Arm you, I pray you, to this speedy voyage, 24
For we will fetters put about this fear,
Which now goes too free-footed.

ROSENCRANTZ: We will haste us.

Exeunt GENTLEMEN [ROSENCRANTZ *and* GUILDENSTERN].

Enter POLONIUS.

POLONIUS:

My lord, he's going to his mother's closet.
Behind the arras I'll convey myself 28
To hear the process. I'll warrant she'll tax him home, 29
And, as you said—and wisely was it said—
'Tis meet that some more audience than a mother, 31
Since nature makes them partial, should o'erhear
The speech, of vantage. Fare you well, my liege. 33
I'll call upon you ere you go to bed
And tell you what I know.

KING: Thanks, dear my lord.

Exit [POLONIUS].

O, my offense is rank, it smells to heaven;
It hath the primal eldest curse upon 't, 37
A brother's murder. Pray can I not,
Though inclination be as sharp as will; 39
My stronger guilt defeats my strong intent,
And like a man to double business bound 41
I stand in pause where I shall first begin,
And both neglect. What if this cursèd hand
Were thicker than itself with brother's blood,
Is there not rain enough in the sweet heavens
To wash it white as snow? Whereto serves mercy 46
But to confront the visage of offense? 47

---

21 *Each . . . consequence* i.e., every hanger-on and unimportant person or thing connected with the King 22 *Attends* participates in 24 *Arm* prepare 28 *arras* screen of tapestry placed around the walls of household apartments. (On the Elizabethan stage, the arras was presumably over a door or discovery space in the tiring-house facade.) 29 *process* proceedings. *tax him home* reprove him severely 31 *meet* fitting 33 *of vantage* from an advantageous place, or, in addition 37 *the primal eldest curse* the curse of Cain, the first murderer; he killed his brother Abel 39 *Though . . . will* though my desire is as strong as my determination 41 *bound* (1) destined (2) obliged. (The King wants to repent and still enjoy what he has gained.) 46–47 *Whereto . . . offense* i.e., for what function does mercy serve other than to undo the effects of sin

And what's in prayer but this twofold force,
To be forestallèd ere we come to fall,   49
Or pardoned being down? Then I'll look up.
My fault is past. But, O, what form of prayer
Can serve my turn? "Forgive me my foul murder"?
That cannot be, since I am still possessed
Of those effects for which I did the murder:
My crown, mine own ambition, and my queen.
May one be pardoned and retain th' offense?   56
In the corrupted currents of this world   57
Offense's gilded hand may shove by justice,   58
And oft 'tis seen the wicked prize itself   59
Buys out the law. But 'tis not so above.
There is no shuffling, there the action lies   61
In his true nature, and we ourselves compelled,   62
Even to the teeth and forehead of our faults,   63
To give in evidence. What then? What rests?   64
Try what repentance can. What can it not?
Yet what can it, when one cannot repent?
O wretched state! O bosom black as death!
O limèd soul, that, struggling to be free,   68
Art more engaged! Help, angels! Make assay.   69
Bow, stubborn knees, and heart with strings of steel,
Be soft as sinews of the newborn babe!
All may be well.   [*He kneels.*]

Enter HAMLET.

HAMLET:
      Now might I do it pat, now 'a is a-praying;   73
      And now I'll do 't. [*He draws his sword.*] And so 'a goes to heaven,
      And so am I revenged. That would be scanned: 75
      A villain kills my father, and for that,
      I, his sole son, do this same villain send
      To heaven.
      Why, this is hire and salary, not revenge.
      'A took my father grossly, full of bread,   80

---

49 *forestallèd* prevented (from sinning)   56 *th' offense* i.e., the thing for which one offended
57 *currents* courses   58 *gilded hand* hand offering gold as a bribe.   *shove by* thrust aside
59 *wicked prize* prize won by wickedness   61 *There* i.e., in heaven.   *shuffling* escape by trickery.
the action lies the accusation is made manifest, comes up for consideration. (A legal metaphor.)
62 *his* its   63 *to the teeth and forehead* face to face, concealing nothing   64 *give in* provide.   *rests*
remains   68 *limèd* caught as with birdlime, a sticky substance used to ensnare birds   69 *engaged*
embedded.   *assay* trial. (Said to himself.)   73 *pat* opportunely   75 *would be scanned* needs to be
looked into, or, would be interpreted as follows   80 *grossly* i.e., not spiritually prepared.   *full of
bread* i.e., enjoying his worldly pleasures. (See Ezekiel 16:49.)

With all his crimes broad blown, as flush as May;   81
And how his audit stands who knows save heaven?   82
But in our circumstance and course of thought   83
'Tis heavy with him. And am I then revenged,
To take him in the purging of his soul,
When he is fit and seasoned for his passage?   86
No!
Up, sword, and know thou a more horrid hent.   88

                                 [He puts up his sword.]

When he is drunk asleep, or in his rage,
Or in th' incestuous pleasure of his bed,
At game a-swearing, or about some act
That has no relish of salvation in 't—   92
Then trip him, that his heels may kick at heaven,
And that his soul may be as damned and black
As hell, whereto it goes. My mother stays.   95
This physic but prolongs thy sickly days.   *Exit.*   96
KING:
My words fly up, my thoughts remain below.
Words without thoughts never to heaven go.   *Exit.*

ACT III

Scene 4

Enter [QUEEN] GERTRUDE *and* POLONIUS.

POLONIUS:
'A will come straight. Look you lay home to him.   1
Tell him his pranks have been too broad to bear with,   2
And that Your Grace hath screened and stood between
Much heat and him. I'll shroud me even here.   4
Pray you, be round with him.   5
HAMLET (*within*):   Mother, Mother, Mother!
QUEEN: I'll warrant you, fear me not.
Withdraw, I hear him coming.

                            [POLONIUS hides behind the arras.]

---

81 *crimes broad blown* sins in full bloom. *flush* lusty 82 *audit* account 83 *in . . . thought* as we see it from our mortal perspective 86 *seasoned* matured, readied 88 *know . . . hent* await to be grasped by me on a more horrid occasion 92 *relish* trace, savor 95 *stays* awaits (me) 96 *physic* purging (by prayer) or, Hamlet's postponement of the killing

III.4. Location: The Queen's private chamber.

1 *lay* thrust (i.e., reprove him soundly) 2 *broad* unrestrained 4 *Much heat* i.e., the King's anger. *shroud* conceal (with ironic fitness to Polonius's imminent death. The word is only in the first quarto; the second quarto and the Folio read "silence.") 5 *round* blunt

Enter HAMLET.

HAMLET: Now, Mother, what's the matter?

QUEEN:

    Hamlet, thou hast thy father much offended.   10

HAMLET:

    Mother, you have my father much offended.

QUEEN:

    Come, come, you answer with an idle tongue.   12

HAMLET:

    Go, go, you question with a wicked tongue.

QUEEN:

    Why, how now, Hamlet?

HAMLET: What's the matter now?

QUEEN:

    Have you forgot me?   15

HAMLET: No, by the rood, not so:

    You are the Queen, your husband's brother's wife,

    And—would it were not so!—you are my mother.

QUEEN:

    Nay, then, I'll set those to you that can speak.

HAMLET:

    Come, come, and sit you down; you shall not budge.

    You go not till I set you up a glass

    Where you may see the inmost part of you.

QUEEN:

    What wilt thou do? Thou wilt not murder me?

    Help, ho!

POLONIUS [*behind the arras*]:   What ho! Help!

HAMLET [*drawing*]:

    How now? A rat? Dead for a ducat, dead!   25

                       [*He thrusts his rapier through the arras.*]

POLONIUS [*behind the arras*]:

    O, I am slain!   [*He falls and dies.*]

QUEEN: O me, what hast thou done?

HAMLET: Nay, I know not. Is it the King?

QUEEN:

    O, what a rash and bloody deed is this!

HAMLET:

    A bloody deed—almost as bad, good Mother,

    As kill a king and marry with his brother.

---

10 *thy father* i.e., your stepfather, Claudius   12 *idle* foolish   15 *forgot me* i.e., forgotten that I am your mother.   *rood* cross of Christ   25 *Dead for a ducat* i.e., I bet a ducat he's dead, whoever I killed; or, a ducat is his life's fee

QUEEN:
    As kill a king!
HAMLET: Ay, lady, it was my word.
                [He parts the arras and discovers POLONIUS.]
    Thou wretched, rash, intruding fool, farewell!
    I took thee for thy better. Take thy fortune.
    Thou find'st to be too busy is some danger.—   35
    Leave wringing of your hands. Peace, sit you down,
    And let me wring your heart, for so I shall,
    If it be made of penetrable stuff,
    If damnèd custom have not brazed it so   39
    That it be proof and bulwark against sense.   40
QUEEN:
    What have I done, that thou dar'st wag thy tongue
    In noise so rude against me?
HAMLET: Such an act
    That blurs the grace and blush of modesty,
    Calls virtue hypocrite, takes off the rose
    From the fair forehead of an innocent love
    And sets a blister there, makes marriage vows   47
    As false as dicers' oaths. O, such a deed
    As from the body of contraction plucks   49
    The very soul, and sweet religion makes   50
    A rhapsody of words. Heaven's face does glow   51
    O'er this solidity and compound mass   52
    With tristful visage, as against the doom,   53
    Is thought-sick at the act.   54
QUEEN: Ay me, what act,   55
    That roars so loud and thunders in the index?   56
HAMLET [*showing her two likenesses*]:
    Look here upon this picture, and on this,
    The counterfeit presentment of two brothers.   58
    See what a grace was seated on this brow:
    Hyperion's curls, the front of Jove himself,   60
    An eye like Mars to threaten and command,
    A station like the herald Mercury   62

---

35 *busy* playing the busybody 39 *damnèd custom* habitual wickedness. *brazed* brazened, hardened 40 *proof* armor. *sense* feeling 47 *sets a blister* i.e., brands as a harlot 49 *contraction* the marriage contract 50 *sweet religion makes* i.e., makes marriage vows 51 *rhapsody* senseless string 51–54 *Heaven's . . . act* heaven's face looks down upon this solid world, this compound mass, with sorrowful face as though the day of doom were near, and is thought-sick at the deed (i.e., Gertrude's marriage) 56 *index* table of contents, prelude or preface 58 *counterfeit presentment* portrayed representation 60 *Hyperion's* the sun god's. *front* brow 62 *station* manner of standing.

New-lighted on a heaven-kissing hill—   63
A combination and a form indeed
Where every god did seem to set his seal   65
To give the world assurance of a man.
This was your husband. Look you now what follows:
Here is your husband, like a mildewed ear,   68
Blasting his wholesome brother. Have you eyes?   69
Could you on this fair mountain leave to feed
And batten on this moor? Ha, have you eyes?   71
You cannot call it love, for at your age
They heyday in the blood is tame, it's humble,   73
And waits upon the judgment, and what judgment
Would step from this to this? Sense, sure, you have,   75
Else could you not have motion, but sure that sense
Is apoplexed, for madness would not err,   77
Nor sense to ecstasy was ne'er so thralled,
But it reserved some quantity of choice   79
To serve in such a difference. What devil was't   80
That thus hath cozened you at hoodman-blind?   81
Eyes without feeling, feeling without sight,
Ears without hands or eyes, smelling sans all,   83
Or but a sickly part of one true sense
Could not so mope. O shame, where is thy blush?   85
Rebellious hell,
If thou canst mutine in a matron's bones,   87
To flaming youth let virtue be as wax   88
And melt in her own fire. Proclaim no shame   89
When the compulsive ardor gives the charge,   90
Since frost itself as actively doth burn,   91
And reason panders will.   92
QUEEN: O Hamlet, speak no more!

63 *New-lighted* newly alighted   65 *set his seal* i.e., affix his approval   68 *ear* i.e., of grain   69 *Blast-ing* blighting   71 *batten* gorge.   *moor* barren upland (suggesting also "dark-skinned")   73 *heyday* state of excitement.   *blood* passion   75 *Sense* perception through the five senses (the functions of the middle or sensible soul)   77 *apoplexed* paralyzed. (Hamlet goes on to explain that without such a paralysis of will, mere madness would not so err, nor would the five senses so enthrall themselves to *ecstasy* or lunacy; even such deranged states of mind would be able to make the obvious choice between Hamlet Senior and Claudius.)   *err* so err   79 *But* but that   80 *To . . . difference* to help in making choice between two such men   81 *cozened* cheated.   *hoodman-blind* blindman's buff. (In this game, says Hamlet, the devil must have pushed Claudius toward Gertrude while she was blind-folded.)   83 *sans* without   85 *mope* be dazed, act aimlessly   87 *mutine* incite mutiny   88–89 *be as wax . . . fire* i.e., melt like a candle or stick of sealing wax held over its own flame   89–92 *Proclaim . . . will* call it no shameful business when the compelling ardor of youth delivers the attack, i.e., commits lechery, since the frost of advanced age burns with as active a fire of lust and reason per-verts itself by fomenting lust rather than restraining it

Thou turn'st my eyes into my very soul,
And there I see such black and grainèd spots   95
As will not leave their tinct.   96
HAMLET: Nay, but to live
In the rank sweat of an enseamèd bed,   97
Stewed in corruption, honeying and making love   98
Over the nasty sty!
QUEEN: O, speak to me no more!
These words like daggers enter in my ears.
No more, sweet Hamlet!
HAMLET: A murderer and a villain,
A slave that is not twentieth part the tithe   103
Of your precedent lord, a vice of kings,   104
A cutpurse of the empire and the rule,
That from a shelf the precious diadem stole
And put it in his pocket!
QUEEN: No more!

Enter GHOST [*in his nightgown*].

HAMLET: A king of shreds and patches—   109
Save me, and hover o'er me with your wings,
You heavenly guards! What would your gracious figure?
QUEEN: Alas, he's mad!
HAMLET:
Do you not come your tardy son to chide,
That, lapsed in time and passion, lets go by   114
Th' important acting of your dread command?   115
O, say!
GHOST:
Do not forget. This visitation
Is but to whet thy almost blunted purpose.
But look, amazement on thy mother sits.   119
O, step between her and her fighting soul!
Conceit in weakest bodies strongest works.   121
Speak to her, Hamlet.
HAMLET: How is it with you, lady?
QUEEN: Alas, how is 't with you,

---

95 *grainèd* dyed in grain, indelible   96 *leave their tinct* surrender their color   97 *enseamèd* saturated in the grease and filth of passionate lovemaking   98 *Stewed* soaked, bathed (with a suggestion of *stew,* brothel)   103 *tithe* tenth part   104 *precedent* former (i.e., the elder Hamlet).   *vice* buffoon. (A reference to the Vice of the morality plays.)   109 *shreds and patches* i.e., motley, the traditional costume of the clown or fool   114 *lapsed in time and passion* having allowed time to lapse and passion to cool, or, having lost momentum through excessive indulgence in passion   115 *important* importunate, urgent   119 *amazement* distraction   121 *Conceit* imagination

That you do bend your eye on vacancy,
And with th' incorporal air do hold discourse?   125
Forth at your eyes your spirits wildly peep,
And, as the sleeping soldiers in th' alarm,   127
Your bedded hair, like life in excrements,   128
Start up and stand on end. O gentle son,
Upon the heat and flame of thy distemper
Sprinkle cool patience. Whereon do you look?

HAMLET:

On him, on him! Look you how pale he glares!
His form and cause conjoined, preaching to stones,   133
Would make them capable.—Do not look upon me,   134
Lest with this piteous action you convert   135
My stern effects. Then what I have to do   136
Will want true color—tears perchance for blood.   137

QUEEN: To whom do you speak this?

HAMLET: Do you see nothing there?

QUEEN:

Nothing at all, yet all that is I see.

HAMLET: Nor did you nothing hear?

QUEEN: No, nothing but ourselves.

HAMLET:

Why, look you there, look how it steals away!
My father, in his habit as he lived!   144
Look where he goes even now out at the portal!

                                          Exit GHOST.

QUEEN:

This is the very coinage of your brain.   146
This bodiless creation ecstasy.   147
Is very cunning in.   148

HAMLET: Ecstasy?

My pulse as yours doth temperately keep time,
And makes as healthful music. It is not madness
That I have uttered. Bring me to the test,
And I the matter will reword, which madness   153

---

125 *incorporal* immaterial   127 *as . . . alarm* like soldiers called out of sleep by an alarum
128 *bedded* laid in smooth layers.   *like life in excrements* i.e., as though hair, an outgrowth of the
body, had a life of its own. (Hair was thought to be lifeless because it lacks sensation, and so its
standing on end would be unnatural and ominous.)   133 *His . . . conjoined* his appearance joined to
his cause for speaking   134 *capable* receptive   135–136 *convert . . . effects* divert me from my stern
duty   137 *want . . . blood* lack plausibility so that (with a play on the normal sense of *color*) I shall
shed colorless tears instead of blood   144 *habit* dress. *as* as when   146 *very* mere   147–148 *This
. . . in* madness is skillful in creating this kind of hallucination   153 *reword* repeat word for word

Would gambol from. Mother, for love of grace,   154
Lay not that flattering unction to your soul   155
That not your trespass but my madness speaks.
It will but skin and film the ulcerous place,   157
Whiles rank corruption, mining all within,   158
Infects unseen. Confess yourself to heaven,
Repent what's past, avoid what is to come,
And do not spread the compost on the weeds   161
To make them ranker. Forgive me this my virtue;   162
For in the fatness of these pursy times   163
Virture itself of vice must pardon beg,
Yea, curb and woo for leave to do him good.   165
QUEEN:
O Hamlet, thou hast cleft my heart in twain.
HAMLET:
O, throw away the worser part of it,
And live the purer with the other half.
Good night. But go not to my uncle's bed;
Assume a virtue, if you have it not.
That monster, custom, who all sense doth eat,   171
Of habits devil, is angel yet in this,   172
That to the use of actions fair and good
He likewise gives a frock or livery   174
That aptly is put on. Refrain tonight,   175
And that shall lend a kind of easiness
To the next abstinence; the next more easy;
For use almost can change the stamp of nature,   178
And either . . . the devil, or throw him out   179
With wondrous potency. Once more, good night;
And when you are desirous to be blest,   181
I'll blessing beg of you. For this same lord,   182

[*Pointing to* POLONIUS]

I do repent; but heaven hath pleased it so
To punish me with this, and this with me,

---

154 *gambol* skip away   155 *unction* ointment   157 *skin* grow a skin for   158 *mining* working under the surface   161 *compost* manure   162 *this is my virtue* my virtuous talk in reproving you   163 *fatness* grossness. *pursy* flabby, out of shape   165 *curb* bow, bend the knee. *leave* permission   171 *who . . . eat* which consumes all proper or natural feeling, all sensibility   172 *Of habits devil* devil-like in prompting evil habits   174 *livery* an outer appearance, a customary garb (and hence a predisposition easily assumed in time of stress)   175 *aptly* readily   178 *use* habit. *the stamp of nature* our inborn traits   *179 And either* (A defective line usually emended by inserting the word *master* after *either,* following the fourth quarto and early editors.)   181–182 *when . . . you* i.e., when you are ready to be penitent and seek God's blessing, I will ask your blessing as a dutiful son should (on the occasion of departure)

That I must be their scourge and minister.   185
I will bestow him, and will answer well   186
The death I gave him. So, again, good night.
I must be cruel only to be kind.
This bad begins, and worse remains behind.   189
One word more, good lady.

QUEEN: What shall I do?

HAMLET:

Not this by no means that I bid you do:
Let the bloat king tempt you again to bed,   192
Pinch wanton on your cheek, call you his mouse,   193
And let him, for a pair of reechy kisses,   194
Or paddling in your neck with his damned fingers,   195
Make you to ravel all this matter out   196
That I essentially am not in madness,
But mad in craft. 'Twere good you let him know,   198
For who that's but a queen, fair, sober, wise,
Would from a paddock, from a bat, a gib,   200
Such dear concernings hide? Who would do so?   201
No, in despite of sense and secrecy,
Unpeg the basket on the house's top,   203
Let the birds fly, and like the famous ape,   204
To try conclusions, in the basket creep   205
And break your own neck down.   206

QUEEN:

Be thou assured, if words be made of breath,
And breath of life, I have no life to breathe
What thou hast said to me.

HAMLET:

I must to England. You know that?

QUEEN: Alack,
I had forgot. 'Tis so concluded on.

HAMLET:

There's letters sealed, and my two schoolfellows,
Whom I will trust as I will adders fanged,

---

185 *their scourge and minister* i.e., agent of heavenly retribution. (By *scourge*, Hamlet also suggests that he himself will eventually suffer punishment in the process of fulfilling heaven's will.) 186 *bestow* stow, dispose of. *answer* account for 189 *This* i.e., the killing of Polonius. *behind* to come 192 *bloat* bloated 193 *Pinch wanton* i.e., leave his love pinches on your cheeks, branding you as wanton 194 *reechy* dirty, filthy 195 *paddling* fingering amorously 196 *ravel . . . out* unravel, disclose 198 *in craft* by cunning. *good* (Said sarcastically; also the following 8 lines.) 200 *paddock* toad. *gib* tomcat 201 *dear concernings* important affairs 203 *Unpeg the basket* open the cage, i.e., let out the secret 204 *famous ape* (in a story now lost) 205 *conclusions* experiments (in which the ape apparently enters a cage from which birds have been released and then tries to fly out of the cage as they have done, falling to his death) 206 *down* in the fall; utterly

They bear the mandate; they must sweep my way   214
And marshal me to knavery. Let it work.   215
For 'tis the sport to have the enginer   216
Hoist with his own petard, and 't shall go hard   217
But I will delve one yard below their mines   218
And blow them at the moon. O, 'tis most sweet
When in one line two crafts dirctly meet.   220
This man shall set me packing.   221
I'll lug the guts into the neighbor room.
Mother, good night indeed. This counselor
Is now most still, most secret, and most grave,
Who was in life a foolish prating knave.—
Come, sir, to draw toward an end with you.—   226
Good night, Mother.

Exeunt [separately, HAMLET
dragging in POLONIUS].

ACT IV

Scene 1

Enter KING *and* QUEEN, *with* ROSENCRANTZ *and* GUILDENSTERN.

KING:

There's matter in these sighs, these profound heaves.   1
You must translate; 'tis fit we understand them.
Where is your son?

QUEEN:

Bestow this place on us a little while.

[*Exeunt* ROSENCRANTZ *and* GUILDENSTERN.]

Ah, mine own lord, what have I seen tonight!

KING:

What, Gertrude? How does Hamlet?

214–215 *sweep . . . knavery* sweep a path before me and conduct me to some *knavery* or treachery prepared for me   215 *work* proceed   216 *enginer* maker of military contrivances   217 *Hoist with* blown up by.   *petard* an explosive used to blow in a door or make a breach   217–218 *'t shall . . . will* unless luck is against me, I will   218 *mines* tunnels used in warfare to undermine the enemy's emplacements; Hamlet will countermine by going under their mines   220 *in one line* i.e., mines and countermines on a collision course, or the countermines directly below the mines.   *crafts* acts of guile, plots   221 *set me packing* set me to making schemes, and set me to lugging (him), and, also, send me off in a hurry   226 *draw . . . end* finish up (with a pun on *draw*, pull)

IV.1. Location: The castle.

s.d. Enter . . . Queen (Some editors argue that Gertrude never exits in III.4 and that the scene is continuous here, but the second quarto marks an entrance for her and at 1. 35 Claudius speaks of Gertrude's *closet* as though it were elsewhere. A short time has elapsed during which the King has become aware of her highly wrought emotional state.)   1 *matter* significance

QUEEN:

    Mad as the sea and wind when both contend
    Which is the mightier. In his lawless fit,
    Behind the arras hearing something stir,
    Whips out his rapier, cries, "A rat, a rat!"
    And in this brainish apprehension kills   11
    The unseen good old man.

KING: O heavy deed!   12

    It had been so with us, had we been there.   13
    His liberty is full of threats to all—
    To you yourself, to us, to everyone.
    Alas, how shall this bloody deed be answered?   16
    It will be laid to us, whose providence   17
    Should have kept short, restrained, and out of haunt   18
    This mad young man. But so much was our love,
    We would not understand what was most fit,
    But, like the owner of a foul disease,
    To keep it from divulging, let it feed   22
    Even on the pith of life. Where is he gone?

QUEEN:

    To draw apart the body he hath killed,
    O'er whom his very madness, like some ore   25
    Among a mineral of metals base,   26
    Shows itself pure: 'a weeps for what is done.

KING: O Gertrude, come away!
    The sun no sooner shall the mountains touch
    But we will ship him hence, and this vile deed
    We must with all our majesty and skill
    Both countenance and excuse.—Ho, Guildenstern!

Enter ROSENCRANTZ *and* GUILDENSTERN.

    Friends both, go join you with some further aid.
    Hamlet in madness hath Polonius slain,
    And from his mother's closet hath he dragged him.
    Go seek him out, speak fair, and bring the body
    Into the chapel. I pray you, haste in this.

           [*Exeunt* ROSENCRANTZ *and* GUILDENSTERN.]

    Come, Gertrude, we'll call up our wisest friends
    And let them know both what we mean to do
    And what's untimely done.   40

---

11 *brainish apprehension* headstrong conception 12 *heavy* grievous 13 *us* i.e., me. (The royal "we"; also in l. 15.) 16 *answered* explained 17 *providence* foresight 18 *short* i.e., on a short tether. *out of haunt* secluded 22 *divulging* becoming evident 25 *ore* vein of gold 27 *mineral* mine 40 *And . . . done* (A defective line; conjectures as to the missing words include *So, haply, slander* [Capell and others]; *For, haply, slander* [Theobald and others]; and *So envious slander* [Jenkins].)

Whose whisper o'er the world's diameter,   41
As level as the cannon to his blank,   42
Transports his poisoned shot, may miss our name
And hit the woundless air. O, come away!   44
My soul is full of discord and dismay.   *Exeunt.*

ACT IV

Scene 2

Enter HAMLET.

HAMLET: Safely stowed.

ROSENCRANTZ , GUILDENSTERN (*within*): Hamlet! Lord Hamlet!

HAMLET: But soft, what noise? Who calls on Hamlet? O, here they
come.

Enter ROSENCRANTZ *and* GUILDENSTERN.

ROSENCRANTZ:
What have you done, my lord, with the dead body?

HAMLET:
Compounded it with dust, whereto 'tis kin.

ROSENCRANTZ:
Tell us where 'tis, that we may take it thence
And bear it to the chapel.

HAMLET: Do not believe it.

ROSENCRANTZ: Believe what?

HAMLET: That I can keep your counsel and not mine own. Besides,   11
to be demanded of a sponge, what replication should be made   12
by the son of a king?   13

ROSENCRANTZ: Take you me for a sponge, my lord?

HAMLET: Ay, sir, that soaks up the King's countenance, his rewards,   15
his authorities. But such officers do the King best service in the
end. He keeps them, like an ape, in the corner of his jaw, first
mouthed to be last swallowed. When he needs what you have
gleaned, it is but squeezing you, and, sponge, you shall be dry
again.

ROSENCRANTZ: I understand you not, my lord.

HAMLET: I am glad of it. A knavish speech sleeps in a foolish ear.   22

ROSENCRANTZ: My lord, you must tell us where the body is and go
with us to the King.

---

41 *diameter* extent from side to side 42 *As level* with as direct aim. *his blank* its target at point-
blank range 44 *woundless* invulnerable
IV.2. Location: The castle.
11 *That . . . own* (Perhaps Hamlet is suggesting that they have their secrets and he has his.)
12 *demanded of* questioned by *replication* reply 15 *countenance* favor 22 *sleeps in* has no meaning to

HAMLET: The body is with the King, but the King is not with the body.   25
    The King is a thing—
GUILDENSTERN: A thing, my lord?
HAMLET: Of nothing. Bring me to him. Hide fox, and all after   28

Exeunt.

ACT IV

Scene 3

Enter KING, *and two or three.*

KING:
    I have sent to seek him, and to find the body.
    How dangerous is it that this man goes loose!
    Yet must not we put the strong law on him.
    He's loved of the distracted multitude,   4
    Who like not in their judgment, but their eyes,   5
    And where 'tis so, th' offender's scourge is weighed,   6
    But never the offense. To bear all smooth and even,   7
    This sudden sending him away must seem
    Deliberate pause. Diseases desperate grown   9
    By desperate appliance are relieved,   10
    Or not at all.

Enter ROSENCRANTZ, [GUILDENSTERN,] *and all the rest.*
    How now, what hath befall'n?
ROSENCRANTZ:
    Where the dead body is bestowed, my lord,
    We cannot get from him.
KING: But where is he?
ROSENCRANTZ:
    Without, my lord; guarded, to know your pleasure.
KING:
    Bring him before us.
ROSENCRANTZ: Ho! Bring in the lord.

25 *The . . . body* (Perhaps alludes to the legal commonplace of "the king's two bodies," which drew a distinction between the sacred office of kingship and the particular mortal who possessed it at any given time. Hence, although Claudius's body is necessarily a part of him, true kingship is not contained in it. Similarly, Claudius will have Polonius's body when it is found, but there is no kingship in this business either.)   28 *Of nothing* (1) of no account (2) lacking the essence of kingship, as in ll. 25–26 and note   28 *Hide . . . after* (An old signal cry in the game of hide-and-seek, suggesting that Hamlet now runs away from them.)
IV.3. Location: The castle.
4 *distracted* fickle, unstable   5 *Who . . . eyes* who choose not by judgment but by appearance   6 *scourge* punishment.   *weighed* sympathetically considered   7 *To . . . even* to manage the business in an unprovocative way   9 *Deliberate pause* carefully considered action   10 *appliance* remedy, treatment

They enter [with HAMLET*].*

KING: Now, Hamlet, where's Polonius?

HAMLET: At supper.

KING: At supper? Where?

HAMLET: Not where he eats, but where 'a is eaten. A certain convocation of politic worms are e'en at him. Your worm is your only   21
emperor for diet. We fat all creatures else to fat us, and we fat
ourselves for maggots. Your fat king and your lean beggar is but
variable service—two dishes, but to one table. That's the end.   24

KING: Alas, alas!

HAMLET: A man may fish with the worm that hath eat of a king, and   26
eat of the fish that hath fed of that worm.

KING: What dost thou mean by this?

HAMLET: Nothing but to show you how a king may go a progress   29
through the guts of a beggar.

KING: Where is Polonius?

HAMLET: In heaven. Send thither to see. If your messenger find him
not there, seek him i' th' other place yourself. But if indeed you
find him not within this month, you shall nose him as you go up
the stairs into the lobby.

KING [*to some attendants*]:   Go seek him there.

HAMLET: 'A will stay till you come. [*Exeunt attendants.*]

KING:
Hamlet, this deed, for thine especial safety—
Which we do tender, as we dearly grieve   39
For that which thou hast done—must send thee hence
With fiery quickness. Therefore prepare thyself.
The bark is ready, and the wind at help,   42
Th' associates tend, and everything is bent   43
For England.

HAMLET: For England!

KING: Ay, Hamlet.

HAMLET: Good.

KING:
So is it, if thou knew'st our purposes.

HAMLET: I see a cherub that sees them. But come, for England!   49
Farewell, dear Mother.

---

21 *politic worms* crafty worms (suited to a master spy like Polonius).   *e'en* even now   21 *Your worm*
your average worm. (On *your,* compare *your fat king and your lean beggar* in l. 23.)   *diet* food, eating
(with a punning reference to the Diet of Worms, a famous *convocation* held in 1521)   24 *variable
service* different courses of a single meal   26 *eat* eaten. (Pronounced *et.*)   29 *progress* royal journey
of state   39 *tender* regard, hold dear.   *dearly* intensely   42 *bark* sailing vessel wait.   43 *tend* wait.
bent in readiness   49 *cherub* (Cherubim are angels of knowledge. Hamlet hints that both he and
heaven are onto Claudius's tricks.)

KING: Thy loving father, Hamlet.

HAMLET: My mother. Father and mother is man and wife, man and
wife is one flesh, and so, my mother. Come, for England!   *Exit.*

KING:

Follow him at foot; tempt him with speed aboard.   53
Delay it not. I'll have him hence tonight.
Away! For everything is sealed and done
That else leans on th' affair. Pray you, make haste.   56

[*Exeunt all but the* KING.]

And, England, if my love thou hold'st at aught—   57
As my great power thereof may give thee sense,   58
Since yet thy cicatrice looks raw and red   59
After the Danish sword, and thy free awe   60
Pays homage to us—thou mayst not coldly set   61
Our sovereign process, which imports at full,   62
By letters congruing to that effect,   63
The present death of Hamlet. Do it, England,   64
For like the hectic in my blood he rages,   65
And thou must cure me. Till I know 'tis done,
Howe'er my haps, my joys were ne'er begun.   *Exit.*   67

ACT IV

Scene 4

Enter FORTINBRAS *with his army over the stage.*

FORTINBRAS:

Go, Captain, from me greet the Danish king.
Tell him that by his license Fortinbras   2
Craves the conveyance of a promised march   3
Over his kingdom. You know the rendezvous.
If that His Majesty would aught with us,
We shall express our duty in his eye;   6
And let him know so.

CAPTAIN: I will do 't, my lord.

FORTINBRAS: Go softly on.   [*Exeunt all but the* CAPTAIN.]   9

---

53 *at foot* close behind, at heel 56 *leans on* bears upon, is related to 57 *England* i.e., King of
England. *at naught* at any value 58 *As . . . sense* for so my great power may give you a just
appreciation of the importance of valuing my love 59 *cicatrice* scar 60 *free awe* voluntary show
of respect 61 *coldly set* regard with indifference 62 *process* command. *imports at full* conveys
specific directions for 63 *congruing* agreeing 64 *present* immediate 65 *hectic* persistent fever
67 *haps* fortunes

IV.4. Location: The coast of Denmark.

2 *license* permission 3 *the conveyance of* escort during 6 *duty* respect. *eye* presence 9 *softly*
slowly, circumspectly

Enter HAMLET, ROSENCRANTZ, [GUILDENSTERN,] *etc.*

HAMLET: Good sir, whose powers are these?   10
CAPTAIN: They are of Norway, sir.
HAMLET: How purposed, sir, I pray you?
CAPTAIN: Against some part of Poland.
HAMLET: Who commands them, sir?
CAPTAIN:
   The nephew to old Norway, Fortinbras.
HAMLET:
   Goes it against the main of Poland, sir,   16
   Or for some frontier?
CAPTAIN:
   Truly to speak, and with no addition,   18
   We go to gain a little patch of ground
   That hath in it no profit but the name.
   To pay five ducats, five, I would not farm it;   21
   Nor will it yield to Norway or the Pole
   A ranker rate, should it be sold in fee.   23
HAMLET:
   Why, then the Polack never will defend it.
CAPTAIN:
   Yes, it is already garrisoned.
HAMLET:
   Two thousand souls and twenty thousand ducats
   Will not debate the question of this straw.   27
   This is th' impostume of much wealth and peace,   28
   That inward breaks, and shows no cause without
   Why the man dies. I humbly thank you, sir.
CAPTAIN:
   God b' wi' you, sir.   [*Exit.*]
ROSENCRANTZ: Will 't please you go, my lord?
HAMLET:
   I'll be with you straight. Go a little before.

             [*Exeunt all except* HAMLET.]

   How all occasions do inform against me   34
   And spur my dull revenge! What is a man,
   If his chief good and market of his time   36
   Be but to sleep and feed? A beast, no more.
   Sure he that made us with such large discourse,   38

---

10 *powers* forces   16 *main* main part   18 *addition* exaggeration   21 *To pay* i.e., for a yearly rental of.   *farm it* take a lease of it   23 *ranker* higher.   *in fee* fee simple, outright   27 *debate . . . straw* settle this trifling matter   28 *impostume* abscess   34 *inform against* denounce, betray; take shape against   36 *market of* profit of, compensation for   38 *discourse* power of reasoning

Looking before and after, gave us not
That capability and godlike reason
To fust in us unused. Now, whether it be   41
Bestial oblivion, or some craven scruple   42
Of thinking too precisely on th' event—   43
A thought which, quartered, hath but one part wisdom
And ever three parts coward—I do not know
Why yet I live to say "This thing's to do,"
Sith I have cause, and will, and strength, and means   47
To do 't. Examples gross as earth exhort me: 48
Witness this army of such mass and charge,   49
Led by a delicate and tender prince,   50
Whose spirit with divine ambition puffed
Makes mouths at the invisible event,   52
Exposing what is mortal and unsure
To all that fortune, death, and danger dare,
Even for an eggshell. Rightly to be great
Is not to stir without great argument,
But greatly to find quarrel in a straw
When honor's at the stake. How stand I then,   58
That have a father killed, a mother stained,
Excitements of my reason and my blood,   60
And let all sleep, while to my shame I see
The imminent death of twenty thousand men
That for a fantasy and trick of fame   63
Go to their graves like beds, fight for a plot   64
Whereon the numbers cannot try the cause,   65
Which is not tomb enough and continent   66
To hide the slain? O, from this time forth
My thoughts be bloody or be nothing worth!   *Exit.*

ACT IV

Scene 5

Enter HORATIO, [QUEEN] GERTRUDE, *and a* GENTLEMAN.

QUEEN:
   I will not speak with her.
GENTLEMAN: She is importunate,

---

41 *fust* grow moldy   42 *oblivion* forgetfulness   43 *precisely* scrupulously.   *event* outcome   47 *Sith*
since   48 *gross* obvious   49 *charge* expense   50 *delicate and tender* of fine and youthful qualities
52 *Makes mouths* makes scornful faces.   *invisible event* unforeseeable outcome   58 *at the stake* at risk
(in gambling)   60 *Excitements of* promptings by   63 *fantasy* fanciful caprice, illusion.   *trick* trifle,
deceit   64 *plot* i.e., of ground   65 *Whereon . . . cause* i.e., on which there is insufficient room for
the soldiers needed to engage in a military contest   66 *continent* receptacle, container
IV.5. Location: The castle.

Indeed distract. her mood will needs be pitied.   2
QUEEN: What would she have?
GENTLEMAN:
    She speaks much of her father, says she hears
    There's tricks i' the world, and hems, and beats her heart,   5
    Spurns enviously at straws, speaks things in doubt   6
    That carry but half sense. Her speech is nothing,
    Yet the unshapèd use of it doth move   8
    The hearers to collection; they yawn at it,   9
    And botch the words up fit to their own thoughts,   10
    Which, as her winks and nods and gestures yield them,   11
    Indeed would make one think there might be thought,   12
    Though nothing sure, yet much unhappily.   13
HORATIO:
    'Twere good she were spoken with, for she may strew
    Dangerous conjectures in ill-breeding minds.   15
QUEEN: Let her come in.   [*Exit* GENTLEMAN.]
    [*Aside.*] To my sick soul, as sin's true nature is,
    Each toy seems prologue to some great amiss.   18
    So full of artless jealousy is guilt,   19
    It spills itself in fearing to be spilt.   20

Enter OPHELIA [*distracted*].

OPHELIA:
    Where is the beauteous majesty of Denmark?
QUEEN: How now, Ophelia?
OPHELIA: (*She sings.*)
        "How should I your true love know
          From another one?
          By his cockle hat and staff,   25
          And his sandal shoon."   26
QUEEN:
    Alas, sweet lady, what imports this song?
OPHELIA : Say you? Nay, pray you, mark.
        "He is dead and gone, lady,   (*Song.*)
          He is dead and gone;

---

2 *distract* distracted   5 *tricks* deceptions.   *heart* i.e., breast   6 *Spurns . . . straws* kicks spitefully, takes offense at trifles.   *in doubt* obscurely   8 *unshapèd use* distracted manner   9 *collection* inference, a guess at some sort of meaning.   *yawn* gape, wonder; grasp. (The Folio reading, *aim,* is possible.)   10 *botch* patch   11 *Which* i.e., the words.   *yield* deliver, represent   12 *thought* conjectured   13 *much unhappily* very unskillfully, clumsily   15 *ill-breeding* prone to suspect the worst and to make mischief   18 *toy* trifle.   *amiss* calamity   19–20 *So . . . spilt* guilt is so full of suspicion that it unskillfully betrays itself in fearing betrayal   21 s.d. *Enter Ophelia* (In the first quarto, Ophelia enters "playing on a lute, and her hair down, singing.")   25 *cockle hat* hat with cockleshell stuck in it as a sign that the wearer had been a pilgrim to the shrine of Saint James of Compostella in Spain   26 *shoon* shoes

At his head a grass-green turf,
At his heels a stone."
OPHELIA: Oho!
QUEEN: Nay, but Ophelia—
OPHELIA: Pray you, mark.
    [Sings.] "White his shroud as the mountain snow"—
Enter KING.

QUEEN : Alas, look here, my lord.
OPHELIA:

       "Larded with sweet flowers;   *(Song.)*   38
        Which bewept to the ground did not go
           With true-love showers."   40

KING: How do you, pretty lady?
OPHELIA: Well, God 'ild you! They say the owl was a baker's daugh-   42
    ter. Lord, we know what we are, but know not what we may be.
    God be at your table!
KING: Conceit upon her father.   45
OPHELIA: Pray let's have no words of this; but when they ask you
    what it means, say you this:
       "Tomorrow is Saint Valentine's day,   *(Song.)*   48
        All in the morning betime,   49
        And I a maid at your window,
        To be your Valentine.
        Then up he rose, and donned his clothes,
        And dupped the chamber door,   53
        Let in the maid, that out a maid
        Never departed more."
KING: Pretty Ophelia—
OPHELIA: Indeed, la, without an oath, I'll make an end on 't:
    [Sings.] "By Gis and by Saint Charity,   58
        Alack, and fie for shame!
        Young men will do 't, if they come to 't;
        By Cock, they are to blame.   61
        Quoth she, 'Before you tumbled me,
        You promised me to wed.'"
    He answers:
       "'So would I ha' done, by yonder sun,
       An thou hadst not come to my bed.'"   66

---

38 *Larded* decorated 40 *showers* i.e., tears 42 *God 'ild* God yield or reward. *owl* (Refers to a
legend about a baker's daughter who was turned into an owl for refusing Jesus bread.) 45 *Conceit*
brooding 48 *Valentine's* (This song alludes to the belief that the first girl seen by a man on the
morning of this day was his valentine or truelove.) 49 *betime* early 53 *dupped* opened 58 *Gis*
Jesus 61 *Cock* (A perversion of "God" in oaths.) 66 *An* if

KING: How long hath she been thus?

OPHELIA: I hope all will be well. We must be patient, but I cannot
    choose but weep to think they would lay him i' the cold ground.
    My brother shall know of it. And so I thank you for your good
    counsel. Come, my coach! Good night, ladies, good night, sweet
    ladies, good night, good night.   *[Exit.]*

KING [*to* HORATIO]:
    Follow her close. Give her good watch, I pray you.

                                          [Exit HORATIO.]

    O, this is the poison of deep grief; it springs
    All from her father's death—and now behold!
    O Gertrude, Gertrude,
    When sorrows come, they come not single spies,   77
    But in battalions. First, her father slain;
    Next, your son gone, and he most violent author
    Of his own just remove; the people muddied,   80
    Thick and unwholesome in their thoughts and whispers
    For good Polonius' death—and we have done but greenly   82
    In hugger-mugger to inter him; poor Ophelia   83
    Divided from herself and her fair judgment,
    Without the which we are pictures or mere beasts;
    Last, and as much containing as all these,   86
    Her brother is in secret come from France,
    Feeds on his wonder, keeps himself in clouds,   88
    And wants not buzzers to infect his ear   89
    With pestilent speeches of his father's death,
    Wherein necessity, of matter beggared,   91
    Will nothing stick our person to arraign   92
    In ear and ear. O my dear Gertrude, this,   93
    Like to a murdering piece, in many places   94
    Gives me superfluous death.   *A noise within.*   95

QUEEN: Alack, what noise is this?

KING: Attend!   97
    Where are my Switzers? Let them guard the door.   98

Enter a MESSENGER.

    What is the matter?

---

77 *spies* scouts sent in advance of the main force   80 *muddied* stirred up, confused   82 *greenly* im-
prudently, foolishly   83 *hugger-mugger* secret haste   86 *as much containing* i.e., as full of serious
matter   88 *in clouds* i.e., of suspicion and rumor   89 *wants* lacks. *buzzers* gossipers, informers
91 *necessity* i.e., the need to invent some plausible explanation.   *of matter beggared* unprovided with
facts   92–93 *Will . . . ear* will not hesitate to accuse my (royal) person in everybody's
ears   94 *murdering piece* cannon loaded so as to scatter its shot   95 *Gives . . . death* kills me over
and over   97 *Attend* i.e., guard me   98 *Switzers* Swiss guards, mercenaries

MESSENGER: Save yourself, my lord!
   The ocean, overpeering of his list,   101
   Eats not the flats with more impetuous haste   102
   Than young Laertes, in a riotous head,   103
   O'erbears your officers. The rabble call him lord,
   And, as the world were now but to begin,   105
   Antiquity forgot, custom not known,
   The ratifiers and props of every word,   107
   They cry, "Choose we! Laertes shall be king!"
   Caps, hands, and tongues applaud it to the clouds,   109
   "Laertes shall be king, Laertes king!"   *A noise within.*

QUEEN:
   How cheerfully on the false trail they cry!
   O, this is counter, you false Danish dogs!   112

Enter LAERTES *with others.*

KING: The doors are broke.

LAERTES:
   Where is this King?—Sirs, stand you all without.

ALL: No, let's come in.

LAERTES: I pray you, give me leave.

ALL: We will, we will.

LAERTES:
   I thank you. Keep the door. [*Exeunt followers.*] O thou vile king,
   Give me my father!

QUEEN [*holding him*]:   Calmly, good Laertes.

LAERTES:
   That drop of blood that's calm proclaims me bastard,
   Cries cuckold to my father, brands the harlot
   Even here, between the chaste unsmirchèd brow   123
   Of my true mother.

KING: What is the cause, Laertes,
   That thy rebellion looks so giantlike?
   Let him go, Gertrude. Do not fear our person.   126
   There's such divinity doth hedge a king   127
   That treason can but peep to what it would,   128
   Acts little of his will. Tell me, Laertes,   129

---

101 *overpeering of his list* overflowing its shore, boundary   102 *flats* i.e., flatlands near shore. *impetuous* violent (also with the meaning of *impiteous* [*impitious*, Q2], pitiless)   103 *head* armed force   105 *as* as if   107 *The ratifiers . . . word* i.e., *antiquity* (or tradition) and *custom* ought to confirm (*ratify*) and underprop our every word or promise   109 *Caps* (The caps are thrown in the air.)   112 *counter* (A hunting term meaning to follow the trail in a direction opposite to that which the game has taken.)   123 *between* in the middle of   126 *fear our* fear for   127 *hedge* protect as with a surrounding barrier   128 *can . . . would* can only glance, as from afar off or through a barrier, at what it would intend   129 *Acts . . . will* (but) performs little of what it intends

Why thou art thus incensed. Let him go, Gertrude.
Speak, man.

LAERTES: Where is my father?

KING: Dead.

QUEEN:
   But not by him.

KING: Let him demand his fill.

LAERTES:
   How came he dead? I'll not be juggled with.   134
   To hell, allegiance! Vows, to the blackest devil!
   Conscience and grace, to the profoundest pit!
   I dare damnation. To this point I stand,
   That both the worlds I give to negligence,   138
   Let come what comes, only I'll be revenged
   Most throughly for my father.   140

KING: Who shall stay you?

LAERTES: My will, not all the world's.   142
   And for my means, I'll husband them so well
   They shall go far with little.

KING: Good Laertes,
   If you desire to know the certainty
   Of your dear father, is 't writ in your revenge
   That, swoopstake, you will draw both friend and foe,   147
   Winner and loser?

LAERTES: None but his enemies.

KING: Will you know them, then?

LAERTES:
   To his good friends thus wide I'll ope my arms,
   And like the kind life-rendering pelican   152
   Repast them with my blood.   153

KING: Why, now you speak
   Like a good child and a true gentleman.
   That I am guiltless of your father's death,
   And am most sensibly in grief for it,   156
   It shall as level to your judgment 'pear   157
   As day does to your eye.   *A noise within.*

LAERTES:
   How now, what noise is that?

---

134 *juggled with* cheated, deceived   138 *both . . . negligence* i.e., both this world and the next are of
no consequence to me   140 *throughly* thoroughly   142 *My will . . . world's* i.e., I'll stop *(stay)* when
my will is accomplished, not for anyone else's   147 *swoopstake* (Literally, taking all stakes on the
gambling table at once, i.e., indiscriminately; *draw* is also a gambling term.)   152 *pelican* (Refers to
the belief that the female pelican fed its young with its own blood.)   153 *Repast* feed   156 *sensibly*
feelingly   157 *level* plain

Enter OPHELIA.

KING: Let her come in.

LAERTES:

O heat, dry up my brains! Tears seven times salt
Burn out the sense and virtue of mine eye!   161
By heaven, thy madness shall be paid with weight   162
Till our scale turn the beam. O rose of May!   163
Dear maid, kind sister, sweet Ophelia!
O heavens, is 't possible a young maid's wits
Should be as mortal as an old man's life?
Nature is fine in love, and where 'tis fine   167
It sends some precious instance of itself   168
After the thing it loves.   169

OPHELIA:

"They bore him barefaced on the bier,   *(Song.)*
    Hey non nonny, nonny, hey nonny,
    And in his grave rained many a tear—"
Fare you well, my dove!

LAERTES:

Hadst thou thy wits and didst persuade revenge,   174
It could not move thus.

OPHELIA: You must sing "A-down a-down," and you "call him a-   176
down-a." O, how the wheel becomes it! It is the false steward   177
that stole his master's daughter.   178

LAERTES: This nothing's more than matter.   179

OPHELIA: There's rosemary, that's for remembrance; pray you, love, 180
remember. And there is pansies; that's for thoughts.   181

LAERTES: A document in madness, thoughts and remembrance fitted. 182

OPHELIA: There's fennel for you, and columbines. There's rue for 183
you, and here's some for me; we may call it herb of grace o' Sundays. You must wear your rue with a difference. There's a daisy.   185
I would give you some violets, but they withered all when my fa-   186
ther died. They say 'a made a good end—

---

161 *virtue* faculty, power   162 *paid with weight* repaid, avenged equally or more   163 *beam* crossbar
of a balance   167 *fine in* refined by   168 *instance* token   169 *After . . . loves* i.e., into the grave,
along with Polonius   174 *persuade* argue cogently for   176–177 *You . . . a-down-a* (Ophelia assigns
the singing of refrains, like her own "Hey non nonny," to various imaginary singers.)   177 *wheel*
spinning wheel as accompaniment to the song, or refrain   178 *false steward* (The story is unknown.)
179 *This . . . matter* this seeming nonsense is more eloquent than sane utterance   180 *rosemary*
(Used as a symbol of remembrance both at weddings and at funerals.)   181 *pansies* (Emblems of
love and courtship; perhaps from French *pensées,* thoughts.)   182 *document* instruction, lesson
183 *fennel* (Emblem of flattery.)   *columbines* (Emblems of unchastity or ingratitude.)   185 *rue* (Emblem of repentance; when mingled with holy water, it was known as *herb of grace.*)   185 *with a difference* (A device used in heraldry to distinguish one family from another on the coat of arms, here
suggesting that Ophelia and the Queen have different causes of sorrow and repentance; perhaps
with a play on *rue* in the sense of ruth, pity.)   *daisy* (Emblem of dissembling, faithlessness.)   186 *violets* (Emblems of faithfulness.)

[*Sings.*] "For bonny sweet Robin is all my joy."
LAERTES:
    Thought and affliction, passion, hell itself,   189
    She turns to favor and to prettiness.   190
OPHELIA:
       "And will 'a not come again?   (*Song.*)
       And will 'a not come again?
        No, no, he is dead.
        Go to thy deathbed,
       He never will come again.

       "His beard was as white as snow,
       All flaxen was his poll.   197
         He is gone, he is gone.
         And we cast away moan.
         God ha' mercy on his soul!"
    And of all Christian souls, I pray God. God b' wi' you. [*Exit.*]
LAERTES: Do you see this, O God?
KING:
    Laertes, I must commune with your grief,
    Or you deny me right. Go but apart,
    Make choice of whom your wisest friends you will,   205
    And they shall hear and judge twixt you and me.
    If by direct or by collateral hand   207
    They find us touched, we will our kingdom give,   208
    Our crown, our life, and all that we call ours
    To you in satisfaction; but if not,
    Be you content to lend your patience to us,
    And we shall jointly labor with your soul
    To give it due content.
LAERTES: Let this be so.
    His means of death, his obscure funeral—
    No trophy, sword, nor hatchment o'er his bones,   215
    No noble rite, nor formal ostentation—   216
    Cry to be heard, as 'twere from heaven to earth,
    That I must call 't in question.   218
KING: So you shall,
    And where th' offense is, let the great ax fall.
    I pray you, go with me.   *Exeunt.*

---

189 *Thought* melancholy   190 *favor* grace, beauty   197 *poll* head   205 *whom* whichever of
207 *collateral* indirect   208 *us touched* me implicated   215 *trophy* memorial. *hatchment* tablet displaying the armorial bearings of a deceased person   216 *ostentation* ceremony   218 *That* so that.
call 't in question demand an explanation

ACT IV

Scene 6

Enter HORATIO *and others.*

HORATIO:
   What are they that would speak with me?
GENTLEMAN: Seafaring men, sir. They say they have letters for you.
HORATIO: Let them come in.   [*Exit* GENTLEMAN.]
   I do not know from what part of the world
   I should be greeted, if not from Lord Hamlet.

Enter SAILORS.

FIRST SAILOR: God bless you, sir.
HORATIO: Let him bless thee too.
FIRST SAILOR: 'A shall, sir, an please him. There's a letter for you, sir   8
   —it came from th' ambassador that was bound for England—if   9
   your name be Horatio, as I am let to know it is.   [*He gives a letter.*]
HORATIO [*reads*]:   "Horatio, when thou shalt have overlooked this,   11
   give these fellows some means to the King; they have letters for   12
   him. Ere we were two days old at sea, a pirate of very warlike
   appointment gave us chase. Finding ourselves too slow of sail,   14
   we put on a compelled valor, and in the grapple I boarded them.
   On the instant they got clear of our ship, so I alone became their
   prisoner. They have dealt with me like thieves of mercy, but they   17
   knew what they did: I am to do a good turn for them. Let the
   King have the letters I have sent, and repair thou to me with as   19
   much speed as thou wouldest fly death. I have words to speak in
   thine ear will make thee dumb, yet are they much too light for the
   bore of the matter. These good fellows will bring thee where I   22
   am. Rosencrantz and Guildenstern hold their course for England. Of them I have much to tell thee. Farewell.
                              He that thou knowest thine, Hamlet."
   Come, I will give you way for these your letters,   26
   And do 't the speedier that you may direct me
   To him from whom you brought them.   *Exeunt.*

IV.6. Location: The castle.
8 *an* if it   9 *th' ambassador* (Evidently Hamlet. The sailor is being circumspect.)   11 *overlooked* looked over   12 *means* means of access   14 *appointment* equipage   17 *thieves of mercy* merciful thieves   19 *repair* come   22 *bore* caliber, i.e., importance   26 *way* means of access

ACT IV

Scene 7

Enter KING *and* LAERTES.

KING:

Now must your conscience my acquittance seal,   1
And you must put me in your heart for friend,
Sith you have heard, and with a knowing ear,   3
That he which hath your noble father slain
Pursued my life.

LAERTES: It well appears. But tell me
Why you proceeded not against these feats   6
So crimeful and so capital in nature,   7
As by your safety, greatness, wisdom, all things else,
You mainly were stirred up.   9

KING: O, for two special reasons,
Which may to you perhaps seem much unsinewed,   11
But yet to me they're strong. The Queen his mother
Lives almost by his looks, and for myself—
My virtue or my plague, be it either which—
She is so conjunctive to my life and soul   15
That, as the star moves not but in his sphere,   16
I could not but by her. The other motive
Why to a public count I might not go   18
Is the great love the general gender bear him,   19
Who, dipping all his faults in their affection,
Work like the spring that turneth wood to stone,   21
Convert his gyves to graces, so that my arrows,   22
Too slightly timbered for so loud a wind,   23
Would have reverted to my bow again   24
But not where I had aimed them.

LAERTES:

And so have I a noble father lost,
A sister driven into desperate terms   27
Whose worth, if praises may go back again,   28

IV.7. Location: The castle.

1 *my acquittance seal* confirm or acknowledge my innocence   3 *Sith* since   6 *feats* acts   7 *capital* punishable by death   9 *mainly* greatly   11 *unsinewed* weak   15 *conjunctive* closely united   16 *his* its.   *sphere* one of the hollow spheres in which, according to Ptolemaic astronomy, the planets were supposed to move   18 *count* account, reckoning, indictment   19 *general gender* common people   21 *Work* operate, act.   *spring* i.e., a spring with such a concentration of lime that it coats a piece of wood with limestone, in effect gilding it   22 *gyves* fetters (which, gilded by the people's praise, would look like badges of honor)   23 *slightly timbered* light.   *loud* strong   24 *reverted* returned   27 *terms* state, condition   28 *go back* i.e., recall what she was

Stood challenger on mount of all the age   29
For her perfections. But my revenge will come.
KING:
Break not your sleeps for that. You must not think
That we are made of stuff so flat and dull
That we can let our beard be shook with danger
And think it pastime. You shortly shall hear more.
I loved your father, and we love ourself;
And that, I hope, will teach you to imagine—

Enter a MESSENGER *with letters.*

How now? What news?
MESSENGER: Letters, my lord, from Hamlet:
This to Your Majesty, this to the Queen.

                                        [*He gives letters.*]

KING: From Hamlet? Who brought them?
MESSENGER:
Sailors, my lord, they say. I saw them not.
They were given me by Claudio. He received them
Of him that brought them.
KING: Laertes, you shall hear them.—
Leave us.   [*Exit* MESSENGER.]
[*Reads.*] "High and mighty, you shall know I am set naked on your   44
kingdom. Tomorrow shall I beg leave to see your kingly eyes,
when I shall, first asking your pardon, thereunto recount the oc-   46
casion of my sudden and more strange return.   Hamlet."
What should this mean? Are all the rest come back?
Or is it some abuse, and no such thing?   49
LAERTES:
Know you the hand?
KING: 'Tis Hamlet's character. "Naked!"   50
And in a postscript here he says "alone."
Can you devise me?   52
LAERTES:
I am lost in it, my lord. But let him come.
It warms the very sickness in my heart
That I shall live and tell him to his teeth,
"Thus didst thou."   56
KING: If it be so, Laertes—
As how should it be so? How otherwise?—   57

29 *on mount* set up on high 44 *naked* destitute, unarmed, without following 46 *pardon* permission 49 *abuse* deceit. *no such thing* no such thing has occurred 50 *character* handwriting
52 *devise* explain to 56 *Thus didst thou* i.e., here's for what you did to my father 57 *As . . . otherwise* how can this (Hamlet's return) be true? Yet how otherwise than true (since we have the evidence of his letter)

Will you be ruled by me?
LAERTES: Ay, my lord,
So you will not o'errule me to a peace.   59
KING:
To thine own peace. If he be now returned,
As checking at his voyage, and that he means   61
No more to undertake it, I will work him
To an exploit, now ripe in my device,   63
Under the which he shall not choose but fall;
And for his death no wind of blame shall breathe,
But even his mother shall uncharge the practice   66
And call it accident.
LAERTES: My lord, I will be ruled,
The rather if you could devise it so
That I might be the organ.   69
KING: It falls right.
You have been talked of since your travel much,
And that in Hamlet's hearing, for a quality
Wherein they say you shine. Your sum of parts   72
Did not together pluck such envy from him
As did that one, and that, in my regard,
Of the unworthiest siege.   75
LAERTES: What part is that, my lord?
KING:
A very ribbon in the cap of youth,
Yet needful too, for youth no less becomes   78
The light and careless livery that it wears
Than settled age his sables and his weeds   80
Importing health and graveness. Two months since   81
Here was a gentleman of Normandy.
I have seen myself, and served against, the French,
And they can well on horseback, but this gallant   84
Had witchcraft in 't; he grew unto his seat,
And to such wondrous doing brought his horse
As had he been incorpsed and demi-natured   87
With the brave beast. So far he topped my thought   88
That I in forgery of shapes and tricks   89

59 *So* provided that   61 *checking at* i.e., turning aside from (like a falcon leaving the quarry to fly at a chance bird).   *that if*   63 *device* devising, invention   66 *uncharge the practice* acquit the stratagem of being a plot   69 *organ* agent, instrument   72 *Your . . . parts* i.e., all your other virtues 75 *unworthiest siege* least important rank   78 *no less becomes* is no less suited by   80 *sables* rich robes furred with sable.   *weeds* garments   81 *Importing health* signifying a concern for health and dignified prosperity; also, giving an impression of comfortable prosperity   84 *can well* are skilled 87 *incorpsed and demi-natured* of one body and nearly of one nature (like the centaur)   88 *topped* surpassed   89 *forgery* imagining

    Come short of what he did.

LAERTES: A Norman was 't?

KING: A Norman.

LAERTES:

    Upon my life, Lamord.

KING: The very same.

LAERTES:

    I know him well. He is the brooch indeed   93
    And gem of all the nation.

KING: He made confession of you,   95
    And gave you such a masterly report
    For art and exercise in your defense,   97
    And for your rapier most especial,
    That he cried out 'twould be a sight indeed
    If one could match you. Th' escrimers of their nation,   100
    He swore, had neither motion, guard, nor eye
    If you opposed them. Sir, this report of his
    Did Hamlet so envenom with his envy
    That he could nothing do but wish and beg
    Your sudden coming o'er, to play with you.   105
    Now, out of this—

LAERTES: What out of this, my lord?

KING:

    Laertes, was your father dear to you?
    Or are you like the painting of a sorrow,
    A face without a heart?

LAERTES: Why ask you this?

KING:

    Not that I think you did not love your father,
    But that I know love is begun by time,   111
    And that I see, in passages of proof,   112
    Time qualifies the spark and fire of it.   113
    There lives within the very flame of love
    A kind of wick or snuff that will abate it,   115
    And nothing is at a like goodness still,   116
    For goodness, growing to a pleurisy,   117
    Dies in his own too much. That we would do,   118

93 *brooch* ornament   95 *confession* testimonial, admission of superiority   97 *For . . . defense* in respect to your skill and practice with your weapon   100 *escrimers* fencers   105 *play* fence   111 *begun by time* i.e., created by the right circumstance and hence subject to change   112 *passages of proof* actual instances   113 *qualifies* weakens, moderates   115 *snuff* the charred part of a candlewick   116 *nothing . . . still* nothing remains at a constant level of perfection   117 *pleurisy* excess, plethora. (Literally, a chest inflammation.)   118 *in . . . much* of its own excess.   *That* that which

We should do when we would; for this "would" changes
And hath abatements and delays as many   120
As there are tongues, are hands, are accidents,   121
And then this "should" is like a spendthrift sigh,   122
That hurts by easing. But, to the quick o' th' ulcer: 123
Hamlet comes back. What would you undertake
To show yourself in deed your father's son
More than in words?

LAERTES: To cut his throat i' the church.

KING:

No place, indeed, should murder sanctuarize;   127
Revenge should have no bounds. But good Laertes,
Will you do this, keep close within your chamber.   129
Hamlet returned shall know you are come home.
We'll put on those shall praise your excellence   131
And set a double varnish on the fame
The Frenchman gave you, bring you in fine together,   133
And wager on your heads. He, being remiss,   134
Most generous, and free from all contriving,   135
Will not peruse the foils, so that with ease,
Or with a little shuffling, you may choose
A sword unbated, and in a pass of practice   138
Requite him for your father.

LAERTES: I will do 't,
And for that purpose I'll anoint my sword.
I bought an unction of a mountebank   141
So mortal that, but dip a knife in it,
Where it draws blood no cataplasm so rare,   143
Collected from all simples that have virtue   144
Under the moon, can save the thing from death   145
That is but scratched withal. I'll touch my point
With this contagion, that if I gall him slightly,   147
It may be death.

KING: Let's further think of this,
Weigh what convenience both of time and means

---

120 *abatements* diminutions   121 *accidents* occurrences, incidents   122 *spendthrift sigh* (An allusion to the belief that sighs draw blood from the heart.)   123 *hurts by easing* i.e., costs the heart blood even while it affords emotional relief.   *quick o' th' ulcer* heart of the matter   127 *sanctuarize* protect from punishment. (Alludes to the right of sanctuary with which certain religious places were invested.)   129 *Will you do this* if you wish to do this   131 *put on those shall* arrange for some to   133 *in fine* finally   134 *remiss* negligently unsuspicious   135 *generous* noble-minded   138 *unbated* not blunted, having no button.   *pass of practice* treacherous thrust   141 *unction* ointment.   *mountebank* quack doctor   143 *cataplasm* plaster or poultice   144 *simples* herbs   145 *Under the moon* i.e., anywhere   147 *gall* graze, wound

May fit us to our shape. If this should fail,   150
And that our drift look through our bad performance,   151
'Twere better not assayed. Therefore this project
Should have a back or second, that might hold
If this did blast in proof. Soft, let me see.   154
We'll make a solemn wager on your cunnings—   155
I ha 't!
When in your motion you are hot and dry—
As make your bouts more violent to that end—   158
And that he calls for drink, I'll have prepared him
A chalice for the nonce, whereon but sipping,   160
If he by chance escape your venomed stuck,   161
Our purpose may hold there. [*A cry within.*] But stay, what noise?

Enter QUEEN.

QUEEN:
One woe doth tread upon another's heel,
So fast they follow. Your sister's drowned, Laertes.

LAERTES: Drowned! O, where?

QUEEN:
There is a willow grows askant the brook,   166
That shows his hoar leaves in the glassy stream;   167
Therewith fantastic garlands did she make
Of crowflowers, nettles, daisies, and long purples,   169
That liberal shepherds give a grosser name,   170
But our cold maids do dead men's fingers call them.   171
There on the pendent boughs her crownet weeds   172
Clamb'ring to hang, an envious sliver broke,   173
When down her weedy trophies and herself   174
Fell in the weeping brook. Her clothes spread wide,
And mermaidlike awhile they bore her up,
Which time she chanted snatches of old lauds,   177
As one incapable of her own distress,   178
Or like a creature native and endued   179
Unto that element. But long it could not be
Till that her garments, heavy with their drink,

---

150 *shape* part we propose to act   151 *drift . . . performance* i.e., intention should be made visible by our bungling   154 *blast in proof* burst in the test (like a cannon)   155 *cunnings* respective skills   158 *As* i.e., and you should   160 *nonce* occasion   161 *stuck* thrust. (From *stoccado,* a fencing term.)   166 *askant* aslant   167 *hoar* white or gray   169 *long purples* early purple orchids   170 *liberal* free-spoken.   *a grosser name* (The testicle-resembling tubers of the orchid, also in some cases resembling *dead men's fingers,* have earned various slang names like dogstones and cullions.)   171 *cold* chaste   172 *crownet* made into a chaplet or coronet   173 *envious sliver* malicious branch   174 *weedy* i.e., of plants   177 *lauds* hymns   178 *incapable* lacking capacity to apprehend   179 *endued* adapted by nature

Pulled the poor wretch from her melodious lay
To muddy death.
LAERTES: Alas, then she is drowned?
QUEEN: Drowned, drowned.
LAERTES:
Too much of water hast thou, poor Ophelia,
And therefore I forbid my tears. But yet
It is our trick; nature her custom holds,   187
Let shame say what it will. [*He weeps.*] When these are gone,   188
The woman will be out. Adieu, my lord.   189
I have a speech of fire that fain would blaze,
But that this folly douts it.   *Exit.*   191
KING: Let's follow, Gertrude.
How much I had to do to calm his rage!
Now fear I this will give it start again;
Therefore let's follow.   *Exeunt.*

ACT V

Scene 1

Enter two CLOWNS [*with spades and mattocks*].

FIRST CLOWN: Is she to be buried in Christian burial, when she will-
fully seeks her own salvation?   2
SECOND CLOWN: I tell thee she is; therefore make her grave straight.   3
The crowner hath sat on her, and finds it Christian burial.   4
FIRST CLOWN: How can that be, unless she drowned herself in her
own defense?
SECOND CLOWN: Why, 'tis found so.   7
FIRST CLOWN: It must be *se offendendo*, it cannot be else. For here   8
lies the point: if I drown myself wittingly, it argues an act, and an
act hath three branches—it is to act, to do, and to perform.
Argal, she drowned herself wittingly.   11
SECOND CLOWN: Nay, but hear you, goodman delver—   12

---

187 *It is our trick* i.e., weeping is our natural way (when sad)   188–189 *When . . . out* when my
tears are all shed, the woman in me will be expended, satisfied   191 *douts* extinguishes. (The second quarto reads "drowns.")
V.1. Location: A churchyard.
s.d. Clowns rustics   2 *salvation* (A blunder for "damnation," or perhaps a suggestion that Ophelia
was taking her own shortcut to heaven.)   3 *straight* straightway, immediately. (But with a pun on
strait, narrow.)   *crowner* coroner.   *sat on her* conducted a session on her case   4 *finds it* gives his official verdict that her means of death was consistent with   7 *found so* determined so in the coroner's
verdict   8 *se offendendo* (A comic mistake for *se defendendo,* term used in verdicts of justifiable homi-
cide.)   11 *Argal* (Corruption of *ergo,* therefore.)   12 *goodman* (An honorific title often used with the
name of a profession or craft.)

FIRST CLOWN: Give me leave. Here lies the water; good. Here
    stands the man; good. If the man go to this water and drown
    himself, it is, will he, nill he, he goes, mark you that. But if the   15
    water come to him and drown him, he drowns not himself. Argal,
    he that is not guilty of his own death shortens not his own life.

SECOND CLOWN: But is this law?

FIRST CLOWN: Ay, marry, is 't—crowner's quest law.   19

SECOND CLOWN: Will you ha' the truth on 't? If this had not been a
    gentlewoman, she should have been buried out o' Christian
    burial.

FIRST CLOWN: Why, there thou sayst. And the more pity that great   23
    folk should have countenance in this world to drown or hang   24
    themselves more than their even-Christian. Come, my spade.   25
    There is no ancient gentlemen but gardeners, ditchers, and
    grave makers. They hold up Adam's profession.   27

SECOND CLOWN: Was he a gentleman?

FIRST CLOWN: 'A was the first that ever bore arms.   29

SECOND CLOWN: Why, he had none.

FIRST CLOWN: What, art a heathen? How dost thou understand the
    Scripture? The Scripture says Adam digged. Could he dig with
    out arms? I'll put another question to thee. If thou answerest me   33
    not to the purpose, confess thyself—   34

SECOND CLOWN: Go to.

FIRST CLOWN: What is he that builds stronger than either the mason,
    the shipwright, or the carpenter?

SECOND CLOWN: The gallows maker, for that frame outlives a thou-   38
    sand tenants.

FIRST CLOWN: I like thy wit well, in good faith. The gallows does well.   40
    But how does it well? It does well to those that do ill. Now thou
    dost ill to say the gallows is built stronger than the church. Argal,
    the gallows may do well to thee. To 't again, come.

SECOND CLOWN: "Who builds stronger than a mason, a shipwright, or
    a carpenter?"

FIRST CLOWN: Ay, tell me that, and unyoke.   46

SECOND CLOWN: Marry, now I can tell.

FIRST CLOWN: To 't.

---

15 *will he, nill he* whether he will or no, willy-nilly 19 *quest* inquest 23 *there thou sayst* i.e., that's
right 24 *countenance* privilege 25 *even-Christian* fellow Christians. *ancient* going back to ancient
times 27 *hold up* maintain 29 *bore arms* (To be entitled to bear a coat of arms would make Adam
a gentleman, but as one who bore a spade our common ancestor was an ordinary delver in the
earth.) 33 *arms* i.e., the arms of the body 34 *confess thyself* (The saying continues, "and be
hanged.") 38 *frame* (1) gallows (2) structure 40 *does well* (1) is an apt answer (2) does a good turn
46 *unyoke* i.e., after this great effort you may unharness the team of your wits

SECOND CLOWN: Mass, I cannot tell.   49

Enter HAMLET *and* HORATIO [*at a distance*].

FIRST CLOWN: Cudgel thy brains no more about it, for your dull ass
    will not mend his pace with beating; and when you are asked
    this question next, say "a grave maker." The houses he makes
    lasts till doomsday. Go get thee in and fetch me a stoup of liquor.   53

                     [*Exit* SECOND CLOWN. FIRST CLOWN *digs.*]

                                       Song.

     "In youth, when I did love, did love,   54
      Methought it was very sweet,
     To contract—O—the time for—a—my behove,   56
      O, methought there—a—was nothing—a—meet."   57

HAMLET: Has this fellow no feeling of his business, 'a sings in grave-   58
    making?

HORATIO: Custom hath made it in him a property of easiness.   60

HAMLET: 'Tis e'en so. The hand of little employment hath the daintier   61
    sense.   62

FIRST CLOWN: *Song.*
     "But age with his stealing steps
      Hath clawed me in his clutch,
     And hath shipped me into the land,   65
      As if I had never been such."

                          [*He throws up a skull.*]

HAMLET: That skull had a tongue in it and could sing once. How the
    knave jowls it to the ground, as if 'twere Cain's jawbone, that did   68
    the first murder! This might be the pate of a politician, which   69
    this ass now o'erreaches, one that would circumvent God, might   70
    it not?

HORATIO: It might, my lord.

HAMLET: Or of a courtier, which could say, "Good morrow, sweet
    lord! How dost thou, sweet lord?" This might be my Lord Such-a-
    one, that praised my Lord Such-a-one's horse when 'a meant to
    beg it, might it not?

HORATIO: Ay, my lord.

---

49 *Mass* by the Mass   53 *stoup* two-quart measure   54 *In . . . love* (This and the two following stanzas, with nonsensical variations, are from a poem attributed to Lord Vaux and printed in *Tottel's Miscellany,* 1557. The O and *a* [for "ah"] seemingly are the grunts of the digger.)   56 *To contract . . . behove* i.e., to shorten the time for my own advantage. (Perhaps he means to *prolong* it.)   57 *meet* suitable, i.e., more suitable   58 *'a* that he   60 *property of easiness* i.e., something he can do easily and indifferently   61–62 *daintier sense* more delicate sense of feeling   65 *into the land* i.e., toward my grave (?) (But note the lack of rhyme in *steps, land.*)   68 *jowls* dashes   69 *politician* schemer, plotter   70 *o'erreaches* circumvents, gets the better of (with a quibble on the literal sense)

HAMLET: Why, e'en so, and now my Lady Worm's, chapless, and   78
    knocked about the mazard with a sexton's spade. Here's fine
    revolution, an we had the trick to see 't. Did these bones cost   80
    no more the breeding but to play at loggets with them? Mine   81
    ache to think on 't.   *Song.*

FIRST CLOWN:
        "A pickax and a spade, a spade,
            For and a shrouding sheet;   84
        O, a pit of clay for to be made
            For such a guest is meet."

                                    [He throws up another skull.]

HAMLET: There's another. Why may not that be the skull of a
    lawyer? Where be his quiddities now, his quillities, his cases, his   88
    tenures, and his tricks? Why does he suffer this mad knave now   89
    to knock him about the sconce with a dirty shovel, and will not   90
    tell him of his action of battery? Hum, this fellow might be in 's   91
    time a great buyer of land, with his statutes, his recognizances,   92
    his fines, his double vouchers, his recoveries. Is this the fine of   93
    his fines and the recovery of his recoveries, to have his fine pate   94
    full of fine dirt? Will his vouchers vouch him no more of his pur-   95
    chases, and double ones too, than the length and breadth of a
    pair of indentures? The very conveyances of his lands will   97
    scarcely lie in this box, and must th' inheritor himself have no   98
    more, ha?
HORATIO: Not a jot more, my lord.
HAMLET: Is not parchment made of sheepskins?
HORATIO: Ay, my lord, and of calves' skins too.
HAMLET: They are sheep and calves which seek out assurance in   103
    that. I will speak to this fellow.—Whose grave's this, sirrah?   104

---

78 *chapless* having no lower jaw.   *mazard* i.e., head. (Literally, a drinking vessel.)   80 *revolution* turn
of Fortune's wheel, change.   *an* if.   *trick to see* knack of seeing   80–81 *cost . . . but* involve so
little expense and care in upbringing that we may   81 *loggets* a game in which pieces of hard wood
shaped like Indian clubs or bowling pins are thrown to lie as near as possible to a stake   84 *For and*
and moreover   88 *quiddities* subtleties, quibbles. (From Latin *quid,* a thing.)   *quillities* verbal niceties,
subtle distinctions. (Variation of *quiddities.*)   89 *tenures* the holding of a piece of property or office,
or the conditions or period of such holding   90 *sconce* head   91 *action of battery* lawsuit about physical assault   92 *statutes, recognizances* legal documents guaranteeing a debt by attaching land and
property   93 *fines, recoveries* ways of converting entailed estates into "fee simple" or freehold.   *double* signed by two signatories.   *vouchers* guarantees of the legality of a title to real estate   93–95 *fine
of his fines . . . fine pate . . . fine dirt* end of his legal maneuvers . . . elegant head . . . minutely sifted
dirt   97 *pair of indentures* legal document drawn up in duplicate on a single sheet and then cut apart
on a zigzag line so that each pair was uniquely matched. (Hamlet may refer to two rows of teeth, or
dentures.)   *conveyances* deeds   98 *box* (1) deed box (2) coffin. ("Skull" has been suggested.)   *inheritor*
possessor, owner   103–104 *assurance in that* safety in legal parchments   104 *sirrah* (A term of address to inferiors.)

FIRST CLOWN: Mine, sir.
    [*Sings.*] "O, a pit of clay for to be made
        For such a guest is meet."
HAMLET: I think it be thine, indeed, for thou liest in 't.
FIRST CLOWN: You lie out on 't, sir, and therefore 'tis not yours. For
    my part, I do not lie in 't, yet it is mine.
HAMLET: Thou dost lie in 't, to be in 't and say it is thine. 'Tis for the
    dead, not for the quick; therefore thou liest.   112
FIRST CLOWN: 'Tis a quick lie, sir; 'twill away again from me to you.
HAMLET: What man dost thou dig it for?
FIRST CLOWN: For no man, sir.
HAMLET: What woman, then?
FIRST CLOWN: For none, neither.
HAMLET: Who is to be buried in 't?
FIRST CLOWN: One that was a woman, sir, but, rest her soul, she's
    dead.
HAMLET: How absolute the knave is! We must speak by the card, or   121
    equivocation will undo us. By the Lord, Horatio, this three years   122
    I have took note of it: the age is grown so picked that the toe of   123
    the peasant comes so near the heel of the courtier, he galls his   124
    kibe.—How long hast thou been grave maker?   125
FIRST CLOWN: Of all the days i' the year, I came to 't that day that our
    last king Hamlet overcame Fortinbras.
HAMLET: How long is that since?
FIRST CLOWN: Cannot you tell that? Every fool can tell that. It was
    that very day that young Hamlet was born—he that is mad and
    sent into England.
HAMLET: Ay, marry, why was he sent into England?
FIRST CLOWN: Why, because 'a was mad. 'A shall recover his wits
    there, or if 'a do not, 'tis no great matter there.
HAMLET: Why?
FIRST CLOWN: 'Twill not be seen in him there. There the men are as
    mad as he.
HAMLET: How came he mad?
FIRST CLOWN: Very strangely, they say.
HAMLET: How strangely?
FIRST CLOWN: Faith, e'en with losing his wits.
HAMLET: Upon what ground?   142

---

112 *quick* living   121 *absolute* strict, precise.   *by the card* by the mariner's card or chart on which
the points of the compass were marked, i.e., with precision   122 *equivocation* ambiguity in the use
of terms   123 *took* taken.   *picked* refined, fastidious   124–125 *galls his kibe* chafes the courtier's
chilblain   142 *ground* cause. (But in the next line the gravedigger takes the word in the sense of
"land," "country.")

FIRST CLOWN: Why, here in Denmark. I have been sexton here, man
   and boy, thirty years.

HAMLET: How long will a man lie i' th' earth ere he rot?

FIRST CLOWN: Faith, if 'a be not rotten before 'a die—as we have
   many pocky corpses nowadays that will scarce hold the laying   147
   in—'a will last you some eight year or nine year. A tanner will last 148
   you nine year.

HAMLET: Why he more than another?

FIRST CLOWN: Why, sir, his hide is so tanned with his trade that 'a will
   keep out water a great while, and your water is a sore decayer of   152
   your whoreson dead body. [He picks up a skull.] Here's a skull   153
   now hath lien you i' th' earth three-and-twenty years.   154

HAMLET: Whose was it?

FIRST CLOWN: A whoreson mad fellow's it was. Whose do you think it
   was?

HAMLET: Nay, I know not.

FIRST CLOWN: A pestilence on him for a mad rogue! 'A poured a
   flagon of Rhenish on my head once. This same skull, sir, was,   160
   sir, Yorick's skull, the King's jester.

HAMLET: This?

FIRST CLOWN: E'en that.

HAMLET: Let me see. [He takes the skull.] Alas, poor Yorick! I knew
   him, Horatio, a fellow of infinite jest, of most excellent fancy. He
   hath bore me on his back a thousand times, and now how   166
   abhorred in my imagination it is! My gorge rises at it. Here hung   167
   those lips that I have kissed I know not how oft. Where be your
   gibes now? Your gambols, your songs, your flashes of merriment
   that were wont to set the table on a roar? Not one now, to mock   170
   your own grinning? Quite chopfallen? Now get you to my lady's   171
   chamber and tell her, let her paint an inch thick, to this favor she   172
   must come. Make her laugh at that. Prithee, Horatio, tell me one
   thing.

HORATIO: What's that, my lord?

HAMLET: Dost thou think Alexander looked o' this fashion i' th'
   earth?

HORATIO: E'en so.

HAMLET: And smelt so? Pah!   [He puts down the skull.]

HORATIO: E'en so, my lord.

---

147 *pocky* rotten, diseased. (Literally, with the pox, or syphilis.)   147–148 *hold the laying in* hold together long enough to be interred   152 *sore* i.e., terrible, great   153 *whoreson* i.e., vile, scurvy
154 *lien you* lain. (*You* is used colloquially.)   160 *Rhenish* Rhine wine   166 *bore* borne   167 *My
gorge rises* i.e., I feel nauseated   170–171 *mock your own grinning* i.e., laugh at the faces you make
171 *chopfallen* (1) lacking the lower jaw (2) dejected   172 *favor* aspect, appearance

HAMLET: To what base uses we may return, Horatio! Why may not
imagination trace the noble dust of Alexander till 'a find it stopping a bunghole?   183
HORATIO: 'Twere to consider too curiously to consider so.   184
HAMLET: No, faith, not a jot, but to follow him thither with modesty   185
enough, and likelihood to lead it. As thus: Alexander died,
Alexander was buried, Alexander returneth to dust, the dust is
earth, of earth we make loam, and why of that loam whereto he   188
was converted might they not stop a beer barrel?
Imperious Caesar, dead and turned to clay,   190
Might stop a hole to keep the wind away.
O, that that earth which kept the world in awe
Should patch a wall t' expel the winter's flaw!   193

Enter KING, QUEEN, LAERTES, *and the corpse* [*of* OPHELIA,
   in procession, with PRIEST, *lords, etc.*].

But soft, but soft awhile! Here comes the King,   194
The Queen, the courtiers. Who is this they follow?
And with such maimèd rites? This doth betoken   196
The corpse they follow did with desperate hand
Fordo its own life. 'Twas of some estate.   198
Couch we awhile and mark.   199

> [*He and* HORATIO *conceal themselves.*
> OPHELIA'S *body is taken to the grave.*]

LAERTES: What ceremony else?
HAMLET [*to* HORATIO]:
That is Laertes, a very noble youth. Mark.
LAERTES: What ceremony else?
PRIEST:
Her obsequies have been as far enlarged
As we have warranty. Her death was doubtful,   204
And but that great command o'ersways the order   205
She should in ground unsanctified been lodged   206
Till the last trumpet. For charitable prayers,   207
Shards, flints, and pebbles should be thrown on her.   208
Yet here she is allowed her virgin crants,   209

---

183 *bunghole* hole for filling or emptying a cask   184 *curiously* minutely   185 *modesty* moderation
188 *loam* mortar consisting chiefly of moistened clay and straw   190 *Imperious* imperial   193 *flaw*
gust of wind   194 *soft* i.e., wait, be careful   196 *maimèd* mutilated, incomplete   198 *Fordo*
destroy.   *estate* rank   199 *Couch we* let's hide, lurk   204 *warranty* i.e., ecclesiastical authority
205 *great . . . order* orders from on high overrule the prescribed procedures   206 *She should . . .
lodged* i.e., she should have been buried in unsanctified ground   207 *For* in place of   208 *Shards*
broken bits of pottery   209 *crants* garlands betokening maidenhood

Her maiden strewments, and the bringing home   210
Of bell and burial.   211

LAERTES:
Must there no more be done?

PRIEST: No more be done.
We should profane the service of the dead
To sing a requiem and such rest to her   215
As to peace-parted souls.

LAERTES: Lay her i' th' earth,
And from her fair and unpolluted flesh
May violets spring! I tell thee, churlish priest,   218
A ministering angel shall my sister be
When thou liest howling.   220

HAMLET [*to* HORATIO]:   What, the fair Ophelia!

QUEEN [*scattering flowers*]:   Sweets to the sweet! Farewell.
I hoped thou shouldst have been my Hamlet's wife.
I thought thy bride-bed to have decked, sweet maid,
And not have strewed thy grave.

LAERTES: O, treble woe
Fall ten times treble on that cursèd head
Whose wicked deed thy most ingenious sense   226
Deprived thee of!—Hold off the earth awhile,
Till I have caught her once more in mine arms.   228

    [*He leaps into the grave and embraces* OPHELIA.]

Now pile your dust upon the quick and dead,
Till of this flat a mountain you have made
T' o'ertop old Pelion or the skyish head   231
Of blue Olympus.   232

HAMLET [*coming forward*]:   What is he whose grief
Bears such an emphasis, whose phrase of sorrow   234
Conjures the wandering stars and makes them stand   235
Like wonder-wounded hearers? This is I,   236
Hamlet the Dane.   237

LAERTES [*grappling with him*]:   The devil take thy soul!   238

---

210 *strewments* flowers strewn on a coffin   210–211 *bringing . . . burial* laying to rest of the body in
consecrated ground, to the sound of the bell   215 *such rest* i.e., to pray for such rest   216 *peace-
parted souls* those who have died at peace with God   218 *violets* (See IV.5.186 and note.)   220 *howling* i.e., in hell   226 *ingenious sense* a mind that is quick, alert, of fine qualities   228 *Till . . . arms*
(Implies an open coffin.)   231–232 *Pelion, Olympus* mountains in the north of Thessaly; see also
Ossa, below, at l. 265   234 *emphasis* i.e., rhetorical and florid emphasis. (*Phrase* has a similar rhetorical connotation.)   235 *wandering stars* planets   236 *wonder-wounded* struck with amazement   237
the Dane (This title normally signifies the King; see I.1.17 and note.)   238 *s.d. Grappling with him*
(Most editors think, despite the testimony of the first quarto that *"Hamlet leaps in after Laertes,"* that
Laertes jumps out of the grave to attack Hamlet.)

HAMLET: Thou pray'st not well.
    I prithee, take thy fingers from my throat,
    For though I am not splenitive and rash,   241
    Yet have I in me something dangerous,
    Which let thy wisdom fear. Hold off thy hand.
KING: Pluck them asunder.
QUEEN: Hamlet, Hamlet!
ALL: Gentlemen!
HORATIO: Good my lord, be quiet.

                          [HAMLET *and* LAERTES *are parted.*]

HAMLET:
    Why, I will fight with him upon this theme
    Until my eyelids will no longer wag.   249
QUEEN: O my son, what theme?
HAMLET:
    I loved Ophelia. Forty thousand brothers
    Could not with all their quantity of love
    Make up my sum. What wilt thou do for her?
KING: O, he is mad, Laertes.
QUEEN: For love of God, forbear him.   255
HAMLET:
    'Swounds, show me what thou'lt do.   256
    Woo't weep? Woo't fight? Woo't fast? Woo't tear thyself?   257
    Woo't drink up eisel? Eat a crocodile?   258
    I'll do 't. Dost come here to whine?
    To outface me with leaping in her grave?
    Be buried quick with her, and so will I.   261
    And if thou prate of mountains, let them throw
    Millions of acres on us, till our ground,
    Singeing his pate against the burning zone,   264
    Make Ossa like a wart! Nay, an thou'lt mouth,   265
    I'll rant as well as thou.
QUEEN: This is mere madness,   266
    And thus awhile the fit will work on him;
    Anon, as patient as the female dove

---

241 *splenitive* quick-tempered   249 *wag* move. (A fluttering eyelid is a conventional sign that life has not yet gone.)   255 *forbear him* leave him alone   255 *'Swounds* by His (Christ's) wounds 257 *Woo't* wilt thou   258 *drink up* drink deeply.   *eisel* vinegar.   *crocodile* (Crocodiles were supposed to shed hypocritical tears.)   261 *quick* alive   264 *his pate* its head, i.e., top.   *burning zone* zone in the celestial sphere containing the sun's orbit, between the tropics of Cancer and Capricorn 265 *Ossa* another mountain in Thessaly. (In their war against the Olympian gods, the giants attempted to heap Ossa, Pelion, and Olympus on one another to scale heaven.)   *an* if.   *mouth* i.e., rant   266 *mere* utter

When that her golden couplets are disclosed,   269
His silence will sit drooping.
HAMLET: Hear you, sir.
What is the reason that you use me thus?
I loved you ever. But it is no matter.
Let Hercules himself do what he may,   273
The cat will mew, and dog will have his day.   274
KING:
I pray thee, good Horatio, wait upon him.

Exit HAMLET *and* HORATIO.

[*To* LAERTES.] Strengthen your patience in our last night's speech;   276
We'll put the matter to the present push.—   277
Good Gertrude, set some watch over your son.—
This grave shall have a living monument.   279
An hour of quiet shortly shall we see;   280
Till then, in patience our proceeding be.   *Exeunt.*

ACT V

Scene 2

Enter HAMLET *and* HORATIO.

HAMLET:
So much for this, sir; now shall you see the other.   1
You do remember all the circumstance?
HORATIO: Remember it, my lord!
HAMLET:
Sir, in my heart there was a kind of fighting
That would not let me sleep. Methought I lay
Worse than the mutines in the bilboes. Rashly,   6
And praised be rashness for it—let us know   7
Our indiscretion sometimes serves us well   8
When our deep plots do pall, and that should learn us   9
There's a divinity that shapes our ends,
Rough-hew them how we will—
HORATIO: That is most certain.   11

---

269 *golden couplets* two baby pigeons, covered with yellow down. *disclosed* hatched 273–274 *Let
. . . day* i.e., (1) even Hercules couldn't stop Laertes's theatrical rant (2) I too will have my turn; i.e.,
despite any blustering attempts at interference, every person will sooner or later do what he must do
276 *in* i.e., by recalling 277 *present push* immediate test 279 *living* lasting; also refers (for
Laertes's benefit) to the plot against Hamlet 280 *hour of quiet* time free of conflict
V.2. Location: The castle.
1 *see the other* i.e., hear the other news 6 *mutines* mutineers. *bilboes* shackles. *Rashly* on impulse.
(This adverb goes with ll. 12ff.) 7 *know* acknowledge 8 *indiscretion* lack of foresight and judgment (not an indiscreet act) 9 *pall* fail, falter, go stale. *learn* teach 11 *Rough-hew* shape roughly,
botch

HAMLET: Up from my cabin,
    My sea-gown scarfed about me, in the dark   13
    Groped I to find out them, had my desire,
    Fingered their packet, and in fine withdrew   15
    To mine own room again, making so bold,
    My fears forgetting manners, to unseal
    Their grand commission; where I found, Horatio—
    Ah, royal knavery!—an exact command,
    Larded with many several sorts of reasons   20
    Importing Denmark's health and England's too,   21
    With, ho! such bugs and goblins in my life,   22
    That on the supervise, no leisure bated,   23
    No, not to stay the grinding of the ax,   24
    My head should be struck off.
HORATIO: Is 't possible?
HAMLET [*giving a document*]:
    Here's the commission. Read it at more leisure.
    But wilt thou hear now how I did proceed?
HORATIO: I beseech you.
HAMLET:
    Being thus benetted round with villainies—
    Ere I could make a prologue to my brains,   30
    They had begun the play—I sat me down,   31
    Devised a new commission, wrote it fair.   32
    I once did hold it, as our statists do,   33
    A baseness to write fair, and labored much   34
    How to forget that learning, but, sir, now
    It did me yeoman's service. Wilt thou know   36
    Th' effect of what I wrote?   37
HORATIO: Ay, good my lord.
HAMLET:
    An earnest conjuration from the King,   38
    As England was his faithful tributary,
    As love between them like the palm might flourish,
    As peace should still her wheaten garland wear   41
    And stand a comma 'tween their amities,   42

---

13 *sea-gown* seaman's coat.   *scarfed* loosely wrapped   15 *Fingered* pilfered, pinched.   *in fine* finally, in conclusion   20 *Larded* garnished, decorated   21 *Importing* relating to   22 *bugs* bugbears, hobgoblins.   *in my life* i.e., to be feared if I were allowed to live   23 *supervise* reading.   *leisure bated* delay allowed   24 *stay* await   30–31 *Ere . . . play* i.e., before I could consciously turn my brain to the matter, it had started working on a plan   32 *fair* in a clear hand   33 *statists* statesmen   34 *baseness* i.e., lower-class trait   36 *yeoman's* i.e., substantial, faithful, loyal. (In the British navy, the ship's yeoman is usually a scribe or clerk.)   37 *effect* purport   38 *conjuration* entreaty   41 *still* always.   *wheaten garland* (Symbolic of fruitful agriculture, of peace and plenty.)   42 *comma* (Indicating continuity, link.)

And many suchlike "as"es of great charge,   43
That on the view and knowing of these contents,
Without debatement further more or less,
He should those bearers put to sudden death,
Not shriving time allowed.   47

HORATIO: How was this sealed?
HAMLET:
Why, even in that was heaven ordinant.   48
I had my father's signet in my purse,   49
Which was the model of that Danish seal;   50
Folded the writ up in the form of th' other,   51
Subscribed it, gave 't th' impression, placed it safely,   52
The changeling never known. Now, the next day   53
Was our sea fight, and what to this was sequent
Thou knowest already.

HORATIO:
So Guildenstern and Rosencrantz go to 't.
HAMLET:
Why, man, they did make love to this employment.
They are not near my conscience. Their defeat   58
Does by their own insinuation grow.   59
'Tis dangerous when the baser nature comes   60
Between the pass and fell incensèd points   61
Of mighty opposites.   62

HORATIO: Why, what a king is this!
HAMLET:
Does it not, think thee, stand me now upon—   63
He that hath killed my king and whored my mother,
Popped in between th' election and my hopes,   65
Thrown out his angle for my proper life,   66
And with such cozenage—is 't not perfect conscience   67
To quit him with this arm? And is 't not to be damned   68
To let this canker of our nature come   69
In further evil?   70

43 *"as"es* (1) the "whereases" of a formal document (2) asses. *charge* (1) import (2) burden (appropriate to asses) 47 *shriving time* time for confession and absolution 48 *ordinant* directing 49 *signet* small seal 50 *model* replica 51 *writ* writing 52 *Subscribed* signed (with forged signature). *impression* i.e., with a wax seal 53 *changeling* i.e., the substituted letter. (Literally, a fairy child substituted for a human one.) 58 *defeat* destruction 59 *insinuation* intrusive intervention, sticking their noses in my business 60 *baser* of lower social station 61 *pass* thrust. *fell* fierce 62 *opposites* antagonists 63 *stand me now upon* become incumbent on me now 65 *election* (The Danish monarch was "elected" by a small number of high-ranking electors.) 66 *angle* fishing line. *proper* very 67 *cozenage* trickery 68 *quit* requite, pay back 69 *canker* ulcer 69–70 *come In* grow into

HORATIO:
> It must be shortly known to him from England
> What is the issue of the business there.

HAMLET:
> It will be short. The interim is mine,
> And a man's life's no more than to say "one."   74
> But I am very sorry, good Horatio,
> That to Laertes I forgot myself,
> For by the image of my cause I see
> The portraiture of his. I'll court his favors.
> But, sure, the bravery of his grief did put me   79
> Into a tow'ring passion.

HORATIO: Peace, who comes here?

Enter a COURTIER [OSRIC].

OSRIC: Your lordship is right welcome back to Denmark.

HAMLET: I humbly thank you, sir. [*To* HORATIO.] Dost know this water
fly?

HORATIO: No, my good lord.

HAMLET: Thy state is the more gracious, for 'tis a vice to know him.
He hath much land, and fertile. Let a beast be lord of beasts,   86
and his crib shall stand at the King's mess. 'Tis a chuff, but, as I   87
say, spacious in the possession of dirt.   88

OSRIC: Sweet lord, if your lordship were at leisure, I should impart a
thing to you from His Majesty.

HAMLET: I will receive it, sir, with all diligence of spirit.
Put your bonnet to his right use; 'tis for the head.   92

OSRIC: I thank your lordship, it is very hot.

HAMLET: No, believe me, 'tis very cold. The wind is northerly.

OSRIC: It is indifferent cold, my lord, indeed.   95

HAMLET: But yet methinks it is very sultry and hot for my complexion.   96

OSRIC: Exceedingly, my lord. It is very sultry, as 'twere—I cannot tell
how. My lord, His Majesty bade me signify to you that 'a has laid
a great wager on your head. Sir, this is the matter—

HAMLET: I beseech you, remember.

[HAMLET *moves him to put on his hat.*]

OSRIC: Nay, good my lord; for my ease, in good faith. Sir, here is   101
newly come to court Laertes—believe me, an absolute gentle-   102

---

74 *a man's . . . one* i.e., one's whole life occupies such a short time, only as long as it takes to count
to one   79 *bravery* bravado   86–87 *Let . . . mess* i.e., if a man, no matter how beastlike, is as rich in
possessions as Osric, he may eat at the King's table   87 *chuff* boor, churl. (The second quarto
spelling, *chough,* is a variant spelling that also suggests the meaning here of "chattering jackdaw.")
92 *bonnet* any kind of cap or hat.   *his* its   95 *indifferent* somewhat   96 *complexion* temperament
101 *for my ease* (A conventional reply declining the invitation to put his hat back on.)   102 *absolute*
perfect

man, full of most excellent differences, of very soft society and   103
great showing. Indeed, to speak feelingly of him, he is the card   104
or calendar of gentry, for you shall find in him the continent of   105
what part a gentleman would see.   106

HAMLET: Sir, his definement suffers no perdition in you, though I   107
know to divide him inventorially would dozy th' arithmetic of   108
memory, and yet but yaw neither in respect of his quick sail. But,   109
in the verity of extolment, I take him to be a soul of great article   110
and his infusion of such dearth and rareness as, to make true   111
diction of him, his semblable is his mirror and who else would   112
trace him his umbrage, nothing more.   113

OSRIC: Your lordship speaks most infallibly of him.

HAMLET: The concernancy, sir? Why do we wrap the gentleman in   115
our more rawer breath?   116

OSRIC: Sir?

HORATIO: Is 't not possible to understand in another tongue? You will   118
do 't, sir, really.   119

HAMLET: What imports the nomination of this gentleman?   120

OSRIC: Of Laertes?

HORATIO [to HAMLET]: His purse is empty already; all 's golden words
are spent.

HAMLET: Of him, sir.

OSRIC: I know you are not ignorant—

HAMLET: I would you did, sir. Yet in faith if you did, it would not much
approve me. Well, sir?   127

OSRIC: You are not ignorant of what excellence Laertes is—

HAMLET: I dare not confess that, lest I should compare with him in   129
excellence. But to know a man well were to know himself.   130

---

103 *differences* special qualities.   *soft society* agreeable manners.   104 *great showing* distinguished appearance.   *feelingly* with just perception.   *card* chart, map.   105 *calendar* guide.   *gentry* good breeding   105–106 *the continent . . . part* one who contains in him all the qualities. (A *continent* is that which contains.)   *what part* whatever part, any part which   107 *definement* definition. (Hamlet proceeds to mock Osric by using his lofty diction back at him.)   *perdition* loss, diminution   108 *divide him inventorially* i.e., enumerate his graces.   *dozy* dizzy   109 *yaw* swing unsteadily off course. (Said of a ship.)   *neither* for all that.   *in respect of* in comparison with   110 *in . . . extolment* in true praise (of him).   *of great article* one with many articles in his inventory   111 *infusion* essence, character infused into him by nature.   *dearth and rareness* rarity   111–112 *make true diction* speak truly   112 *semblable* only true likeness   112–113 *who . . . trace* any other person who would wish to follow   113 *umbrage* shadow   115 *concernancy* import, relevance   116 *rawer breath* i.e., speech which can only come short in praising him   118 *to understand . . . tongue* i.e., for you, Osric, to understand when someone else speaks your language. (Horatio twits Osric for not being able to understand the kind of flowery speech he himself uses, when Hamlet speaks in such a vein. Alternatively, all this could be said to Hamlet.)   118–119 *You will do 't* i.e., you can if you try   120 *nomination* naming   127 *approve* commend   129–130 *I dare . . . himself* i.e., I dare not boast of knowing Laertes's excellence lest I seem to compare his with my own, since to appreciate excellence in another one must possess it oneself; by the same token, it is presumptuous to claim the self-knowledge necessary to know another person well

OSRIC: I mean, sir, for his weapon; but in the imputation laid on him   131
    by them in his meed, he's unfellowed.   132
HAMLET: What's his weapon?
OSRIC: Rapier and dagger.
HAMLET: That's two of his weapons—but well.   135
OSRIC: The King, sir, hath wagered with him six Barbary horses,
    against the which he has impawned, as I take it, six French   137
    apiers and poniards, with their assigns, as girdle, hangers, and   138
    so. Three of the carriages, in faith, are very dear to fancy, very   139
    responsive to the hilts, most delicate carriages, and of very lib-   140
    eral conceit.   141
HAMLET: What call you the carriages?
HORATIO [*to* HAMLET]:   I knew you must be edified by the margent ere   143
    you had done.
OSRIC: The carriages, sir, are the hangers.
HAMLET: The phrase would be more germane to the matter if we
    could carry a cannon by our sides; I would it might be hangers till
    then. But, on: six Barbary horses against six French swords, their
    assigns, and three liberal-conceited carriages; that's the French
    bet against the Danish. Why is this impawned, as you call it?
OSRIC: The King, sir, hath laid, sir, that in a dozen passes between   151
    yourself and him, he shall not exceed you three hits. He hath laid
    on twelve for nine, and it would come to immediate trial, if your
    lordship would vouchsafe the answer.   154
HAMLET: How if I answer no?
OSRIC: I mean, my lord, the opposition of your person in trial.
HAMLET: Sir, I will walk here in the hall. If it please His Majesty, it is
    the breathing time of day with me. Let the foils be brought, the   158
    gentleman willing, and the King hold his purpose, I will win for him
    an I can; if not, I will gain nothing but my shame and the odd hits.
OSRIC: Shall I deliver you so?   161
HAMLET: To this effect, sir—after what flourish your nature will.

---

131 *for* i.e., with 131–132 *imputation . . . them* reputation given him by others 132 *meed* merit.
unfellowed unmatched 135 *but well* but never mind 137 *he* i.e., Laertes. *impawned* staked,
wagered 138 *poniards* daggers. *assigns* appurtenances. *hangers* straps on the sword belt
(*girdle*) from which the sword hung 138–139 *and so* and so on 139 *carriages* (An affected way of
saying *hangers;* literally, gun carriages.) *dear to fancy* fancifully designed, tasteful 140 *responsive* corresponding closely, matching or well adjusted. *delicate* (i.e., in workmanship) 140–141 *liberal conceit* elaborate design 143 *margent* margin of a book, place for explanatory notes 151 *laid* wagered
151 *passes* bouts. (The odds of the betting are hard to explain. Possibly the King bets that Hamlet
will win at least five out of twelve, at which point Laertes raises the odds against himself by betting
he will win nine.) 154 *vouchsafe the answer* be so good as to accept the challenge. (Hamlet deliberately takes the phrase in its literal sense.) 158 *breathing time* exercise period. *Let* i.e., if 161 *deliver*
report what you say

OSRIC: I commend my duty to your lordship.   163

HAMLET: Yours, yours. [*Exit* OSRIC.] 'A does well to commend it himself; there are no tongues else for 's turn.   165

HORATIO: This lapwing runs away with the shell on his head.   166

HAMLET: 'A did comply with his dug before 'a sucked it. Thus has   167
he—and many more of the same breed that I know the drossy   168
age dotes on—only got the tune of the time and, out of an habit   169
of encounter, a kind of yeasty collection, which carries them   170
through and through the most fanned and winnowed opinions;   171
and do but blow them to their trial, the bubbles are out.   172

Enter a LORD.

LORD: My lord, His Majesty commended him to you by young Osric,
who brings back to him that you attend him in the hall. He sends
to know if your pleasure hold to play with Laertes, or that you will   175
take longer time.

HAMLET: I am constant to my purposes; they follow the King's pleasure. If his fitness speaks, mine is ready; now or whensoever,   178
provided I be so able as now.

LORD: The King and Queen and all are coming down.

HAMLET: In happy time.   181

LORD: The Queen desires you to use some gentle entertainment to   182
Laertes before you fall to play.

HAMLET: She well instructs me.   [*Exit* LORD.]

HORATIO: You will lose, my lord.

HAMLET: I do not think so. Since he went into France, I have been in
continual practice; I shall win at the odds. But thou wouldst not
think how ill all's here about my heart; but it is no matter.

HORATIO: Nay, good my lord—

HAMLET: It is but foolery, but it is such a kind of gaingiving as would   190
perhaps trouble a woman.

HORATIO: If your mind dislike anything, obey it. I will forestall their
repair hither and say you are not fit.   193

163 *commend* commit to your favor. (A conventional salutation; but Hamlet wryly uses a more literal meaning, "recommend," in l. 164.)   165 *for 's turn* for his purposes, i.e., to do it for him   166 *lapwing* (A proverbial type of youthful forwardness. Also, a bird that draws intruders away from its
nest and was thought to run about when newly hatched with its head in the shell; a seeming reference to Osric's hat.)   167 *comply . . . dug* observe ceremonious formality toward his nurse's or
mother's teat   168 *drossy* laden with scum and impurities, frivolous   169 *tune* temper, mood, manner of speech   169–170 *habit of encounter* demeanor of social intercourse   170 *yeasty* frothy. *collection* i.e., of current phrases   171 *fanned and winnowed* select and refined. (Literally, like grain separated from its chaff. Osric is both the chaff and the bubbly froth on the surface of the liquor that is
soon blown away.)   172 *blow . . . out* i.e., put them to the test, and their ignorance is exposed
175 *that* if   178 *If . . . ready* if he declares his readiness, my convenience waits on his   181 *In
happy time* (A phrase of courtesy indicating acceptance.)   182 *entertainment* greeting   190 *gaingiving* misgiving   193 *repair* coming

HAMLET: Not a whit, we defy augury. There is special providence in
the fall of a sparrow. If it be now, 'tis not to come; if it be not to
come, it will be now; if it be not now, yet it will come. The readiness is all. Since no man of aught he leaves knows, what is 't to   197
leave betimes? Let be.   198

A table prepared. [Enter] trumpets, drums, and officers with cushions; KING,
QUEEN, *[*OSRIC,*] and all the state; foils, daggers, [and wine borne in;] and*
LAERTES.

KING:
Come, Hamlet, come and take this hand from me.

> *[The* KING *puts* LAERTES'S *hand into* HAMLET'S.]

HAMLET:
Give me your pardon, sir. I have done you wrong,
But pardon 't as you are a gentleman.
This presence knows,   202
And you must needs have heard, how I am punished
With a sore distraction. What I have done
That might your nature, honor, and exception   205
Roughly awake, I here proclaim was madness.
Was 't Hamlet wronged Laertes? Never Hamlet.
If Hamlet from himself be ta'en away,
And when he's not himself does wrong Laertes,
Then Hamlet does it not, Hamlet denies it.
Who does it, then? His madness. If 't be so,
hamlet is of the faction that is wronged;   212
His madness is poor Hamlet's enemy.
Sir, in this audience,
Let my disclaiming from a purposed evil
Free me so far in your most generous thoughts
That I have shot my arrow o'er the house   217
And hurt my brother.
LAERTES: I am satisfied in nature,   218
Whose motive in this case should stir me most   219
To my revenge. But in my terms of honor
I stand aloof, and will no reconcilement
Till by some elder masters of known honor
I have a voice and precedent of peace   223
To keep my name ungored. But till that time,   224

197–198 *Since . . . Let be* since no one has knowledge of what he is leaving behind, what does
an early death matter after all? Enough; don't struggle against it.   202 *presence* royal assembly
205 *exception* disapproval   212 *faction* party   217 *That I have* as if I had   218 *in nature* i.e., as to
my personal feelings   219 *motive* prompting   223 *voice* authoritative pronouncement.   *of peace*
for reconciliation   224 *name ungored* reputation unwounded

I do receive your offered love like love,
And will not wrong it.
HAMLET: I embrace it freely,
And will this brothers' wager frankly play.—   227
Give us the foils. Come on.
LAERTES: Come, one for me.
HAMLET:
I'll be your foil, Laertes. In mine ignorance   229
Your skill shall, like a star i' the darkest night,
Stick fiery off indeed.   231
LAERTES: You mock me, sir.
HAMLET: No, by this hand.
KING:
Give them the foils, young Osric. Cousin Hamlet,
You know the wager?
HAMLET: Very well, my lord.
Your Grace has laid the odds o' the weaker side.   235
KING:
I do not fear it; I have seen you both.
But since he is bettered, we have therefore odds.   237
LAERTES:
This is too heavy. Let me see another.

                          [He exchanges his foil for another.]

HAMLET:
This likes me well. These foils have all a length?   239

                                    [They prepare to play.]

OSRIC: Ay, my good lord.
KING:
Set me the stoups of wine upon that table.
If Hamlet give the first or second hit,
Or quit in answer of the third exchange,   243
Let all the battlements their ordnance fire.
The King shall drink to Hamlet's better breath,   245
And in the cup an union shall he throw   246
Richer than that which four successive kings
In Denmark's crown have worn. Give me the cups,

227 *frankly* without ill feeling or the burden of rancor   229 *foil* thin metal background which sets
a jewel off (with pun on the blunted rapier for fencing)   231 *Stick fiery off* stand out brilliantly
235 *laid the odds o'* bet on, backed   237 *is bettered* has improved; is the odds-on favorite. (Laertes's
handicap is the "three hits" specified in l. 152.)   239 *likes me* pleases me   243 *Or . . . exchange*
i.e., or requites Laertes in the third bout for having won the first two   245 *better breath* improved
vigor   246 *union* pearl. (So called, according to Pliny's *Natural History,* 9, because pearls are *unique,*
never identical.)

And let the kettle to the trumpet speak,   249
The trumpet to the cannoneer without,
The cannons to the heavens, the heaven to earth,
"Now the King drinks to Hamlet." Come, begin.

Trumpets the while.

And you, the judges, bear a wary eye.
HAMLET: Come on, sir.
LAERTES: Come, my lord. [*They play.* HAMLET *scores a hit.*]
HAMLET: One.
LAERTES: No.
HAMLET: Judgment.
OSRIC: A hit, a very palpable hit.

Drum, trumpets, and shot. Flourish.
A piece goes off.

LAERTES: Well, again.
KING:

Stay, give me drink. Hamlet, this pearl is thine.

[*He throws a pearl in* HAMLET'S *cup,*
and drinks.]

Here's to thy health. Give him the cup.
HAMLET:

I'll play this bout first. Set it by awhile.
Come. [*They play.*] Another hit; what say you?
LAERTES: A touch, a touch, I do confess 't.
KING:

Our son shall win.
QUEEN: He's fat and scant of breath.   265
Here, Hamlet, take my napkin, rub thy brows.   266
The Queen carouses to thy fortune, Hamlet.   267
HAMLET: Good madam!
KING: Gertrude, do not drink.
QUEEN:

I will, my lord, I pray you pardon me.   [*She drinks.*]
KING [*aside*]:

It is the poisoned cup. It is too late.
HAMLET:

I dare not drink yet, madam; by and by.
QUEEN: Come, let me wipe thy face.
LAERTES [*to the* KING]:

My lord, I'll hit him now.

---

249 *kettle* kettledrum   265 *fat* not physically fit, out of training   266 *napkin* handkerchief   267
carouses drinks a toast

KING: I do not think 't.

LAERTES [aside]:

And yet it is almost against my conscience.

HAMLET:

Come, for the third, Laertes. You do but dally.

I pray you, pass with your best violence;   277

I am afeard you make a wanton of me.   278

LAERTES: Say you so? Come on.   [They play.]

OSRIC: Nothing neither way.

LAERTES:

Have at you now!

[LAERTES *wounds* HAMLET; *then, in scuffling,*
they change rapiers, and HAMLET *wounds* LAERTES.]

KING: Part them! They are incensed.   282

HAMLET:

Nay, come, again.   [*The* QUEEN *falls.*]

OSRIC: Look to the Queen there, ho!

HORATIO:

They bleed on both sides. How is it, my lord?

OSRIC: How is 't, Laertes?

LAERTES:

Why, as a woodcock to mine own springe, Osric;   287

I am justly killed with mine own treachery.

HAMLET:

How does the Queen?

KING: She swoons to see them bleed.

QUEEN:

No, no, the drink, the drink—O my dear Hamlet—

The drink, the drink! I am poisoned.   [*She dies.*]

HAMLET:

O villainy! Ho, let the door be locked!

Treachery! Seek it out.   [LAERTES *falls. Exit* OSRIC.]

LAERTES:

It is here, Hamlet. Hamlet, thou art slain.

No med'cine in the world can do thee good;

In thee there is not half an hour's life.

The treacherous instrument is in thy hand,

Unbated and envenomed. The foul practice   298

---

277 *pass* thrust 278 *make . . . me* i.e., treat me like a spoiled child, holding back to give me an advantage 282 *s.d. in scuffling, they change rapiers* (This stage direction occurs in the Folio. According
to a widespread stage tradition, Hamlet receives a scratch, realizes that Laertes's sword is unbated,
and accordingly forces an exchange.) 287 *woodcock* a bird, a type of stupidity or as a decoy.
springe trap, snare 298 *Unbated* not blunted with a button. *practice* plot

Hath turned itself on me. Lo, here I lie,
Never to rise again. Thy mother's poisoned.
I can no more. The King, the King's to blame.
HAMLET:
The point envenomed too? Then, venom, to thy work.

[*He stabs the* KING .]

ALL: Treason! Treason!
KING:
O, yet defend me, friends! I am but hurt.
HAMLET [*forcing the* KING *to drink*]:
Here, thou incestuous, murderous, damnèd Dane,
Drink off this potion. Is thy union here?   306
Follow my mother.   [*The* KING *dies.*]
LAERTES: He is justly served.
It is a poison tempered by himself.   308
Exchange forgiveness with me, noble Hamlet.
Mine and my father's death come not upon thee,
Nor thine on me!   [*He dies.*]
HAMLET:
Heaven make thee free of it! I follow thee.
I am dead, Horatio. Wretched Queen, adieu!
You that look pale and tremble at this chance,   314
That are but mutes or audience to this act,   315
Had I but time—as this fell sergeant, Death,   316
Is strict in his arrest—O, I could tell you—   317
But let it be. Horatio, I am dead;
Thou livest. Report me and my cause aright
To the unsatisfied.
HORATIO: Never believe it.
I am more an antique Roman than a Dane.   321
Here's yet some liquor left.

[*He attempts to drink from the poisoned cup.*
HAMLET *prevents him.*]

HAMLET: As thou'rt a man,
Give me the cup! Let go! By heaven, I'll ha 't.
O God, Horatio, what a wounded name,
Things standing thus unknown, shall I leave behind me!
If thou didst ever hold me in thy heart,
Absent thee from felicity awhile,

---

306 *union* pearl. (See l. 246; with grim puns on the word's other meanings: marriage, shared death.)
308 *tempered* mixed   314 *chance* mischance   315 *mutes* silent observers   316 *fell* cruel.   *sergeant*
sheriff's officer   317 *strict* (1) severely just (2) unavoidable.   *arrest* (1) taking into custody (2) stopping my speech   321 *Roman* (It was the Roman custom to follow masters in death.)

And in this harsh world draw thy breath in pain
To tell my story. (*A march afar off* [*and a volley within*].)
   What warlike noise is this?

Enter OSRIC.

OSRIC:
   Young Fortinbras, with conquest come from Poland,
   To th' ambassadors of England gives
   This warlike volley.

HAMLET: O, I die, Horatio!
   The potent poison quite o'ercrows my spirit.   334
   I cannot live to hear the news from England,
   But I do prophesy th' election lights
   On Fortinbras. He has my dying voice.   337
   So tell him, with th' occurrents more and less   338
   Which have solicited—the rest is silence.   [*He dies.*]   339

HORATIO:
   Now cracks a noble heart. Good night, sweet prince,
   And flights of angels sing thee to thy rest!

                         [*March within.*]

   Why does the drum come hither?

Enter FORTINBRAS, *with the* [*English*] AMBASSADORS [*with drum,*
    colors, and attendants].

FORTINBRAS:
   Where is this sight?

HORATIO: What is it you would see?
   If aught of woe or wonder, cease your search.

FORTINBRAS:
   This quarry cries on havoc. O proud Death,   345
   What feast is toward in thine eternal cell,   346
   That thou so many princes at a shot
   So bloodily hast struck?

FIRST AMBASSADOR: The sight is dismal,
   And our affairs from England come too late.
   The ears are senseless that should give us hearing,
   To tell him his commandment is fulfilled,
   That Rosencrantz and Guildenstern are dead.
   Where should we have our thanks?

HORATIO: Not from his mouth,   353

---

334 *o'ercrows* triumphs over (like the winner in a cockfight)   337 *voice* vote   338 *occurrents* events,
incidents   339 *solicited* moved, urged. (Hamlet doesn't finish saying what the events have prompted; presumably his acts of vengeance, or his reporting those events to Fortinbras.)   345 *quarry* heap
of dead. *cries on havoc* proclaims a general slaughter   346 *feast* i.e., Death feasting on those who
have fallen. *toward* in preparation   353 *his* i.e., Claudius's

Had it th' ability of life to thank you.
He never gave commandment for their death.
But since, so jump upon this bloody question,   356
You from the Polack wars, and you from England,
Are here arrived, give order that these bodies
High on a stage be placèd to the view,   359
And let me speak to th' yet unknowing world
How these things came about. So shall you hear
Of carnal, bloody, and unnatural acts,
Of accidental judgments, casual slaughters,   363
Of deaths put on by cunning and forced cause,   364
And, in this upshot, purposes mistook
Fall'n on th' inventors' heads. All this can I
Truly deliver.
FORTINBRAS: Let us haste to hear it,
And call the noblest to the audience.
For me, with sorrow I embrace my fortune.
I have some rights of memory in this kingdom,   370
Which now to claim my vantage doth invite me.   371
HORATIO:
Of that I shall have also cause to speak,
And from his mouth whose voice will draw on more.   373
But let this same be presently performed,   374
Even while men's minds are wild, lest more mischance
On plots and errors happen.   376
FORTINBRAS: Let four captains
Bear Hamlet, like a soldier, to the stage,
For he was likely, had he been put on,   378
To have proved most royal; and for his passage,   379
The soldiers' music and the rite of war
Speak loudly for him.
Take up the bodies. Such a sight as this
Becomes the field, but here shows much amiss.   383
Go bid the soldiers shoot.

Exeunt [marching, bearing off the dead bodies;
a peal of ordnance is shot off].

---

356 *jump* precisely, immediately.   *question* dispute   359 *stage* platform   363 *judgments* retribu-
tions.   *casual* occurring by chance   364 *put on* instigated   370 *of memory* traditional, remembered,
unforgotten   371 *vantage* i.e., presence at this opportune moment   372 *voice . . . more* vote will influence still others   374 *presently* immediately   376 *On* on the basis of, on top of   378 *put on* i.e.,
invested in royal office, and so put to the test   379 *passage* death   383 *field* i.e., of battle

QUESTIONS AND CONSIDERATIONS

[Act I]

1. Discuss the first appearance of the Ghost in Act I.1. What speculation about its significance do Horatio and Marcellus make? What mood does this scene create for the action to follow?

2. In Act I.2, what is revealed about the tensions in the court and the nature of Claudius as a ruler? What frame of mind does Hamlet seem to be in, particularly as revealed by his interactions with Claudius and his soliloquy, lines 129–159? How does Hamlet's mood shift when Horatio informs him of the Ghost? Does Hamlet at this point strike you as decisive, as a potential "man of action"?

3. In Acts I.3 and II.1, what is revealed about Polonius' character? How does he relate to his children? Does he trust them? Is his advice to them sound?

4. In Act I.4–5, Hamlet encounters and responds to the Ghost's news. How does Hamlet await and respond to the news? Does he fully trust the Ghost? Is he enthusiastic or reluctant to undertake his revenge? Why or why not?

[Act II]

5. In Act II.1, what change of behavior has Ophelia noticed in Hamlet? Does Polonius' interpretation of Hamlet's behavior as "the very ecstasy of love" seem ironic to you? Why or why not?

6. How does Claudius' encouragement of Rosencrantz and Guildenstern to spy on Hamlet echo Polonius' advice to Reynaldo in the previous scene? What point do you think is being made by this juxtaposition? Do you think Rosencrantz and Guildenstern will be successful in their efforts to "gather/So much as . . . [they] may glean" from Hamlet? Are Claudius and Polonius likely to be any more successful in their spying on Hamlet's encounters with Ophelia?

7. Analyze the exchanges between Hamlet, Polonius, Rosencrantz and Guildenstern, and the player in Act II.2. How sane does Hamlet seem to be? Point out moments when he seems to loose control, other times when he seems to be ridiculing his interrogators.

[Act III]

8. What scheme does Hamlet develop with the Players? In what sense is he both author and director of the play within a play? Who is the true audience of the play? Is Hamlet successful in reaching his audience?

9. Analyze the famous "To Be or Not to Be" soliloquy (Act III.1, lines 57–89). Does Hamlet seem genuinely depressed and suicidal here? What are several possible meanings of the line "Thus conscience does make cowards of us all"? Does Hamlet seem to have a particularly strong conscience? For instance, does his conscience prevent him from killing the King in the chapel?

10. Analyze the interaction between Hamlet and Ophelia in Act III.1–2. Does he seem to have genuine feelings for her, or is he merely manipulative?

11. Analyze the exchange between Hamlet and his mother in Act III.4. Some critics have seen in this scene evidence for the Freudian interpretation of Hamlet, in which Hamlet's reluctance to kill the King is caused by Hamlet's own reawakened Oedipal fantasies, triggered by the King's "incestuous" marriage to Hamlet's mother and the slaying

of Hamlet's father. What evidence for the theory exists in this scene? For instance, does Hamlet seem unduly preoccupied with his mother's sex life?

[Act IV]

12. Act IV places special emphasis on imagery of decay and pestilence. Point out several of these images and comment on what they add to the tone and meaning of the play.

13. What is Claudius' scheme to rid himself of Hamlet? From Hamlet's behavior in this act, do you think the scheme will be successful? How has Hamlet's character changed since the killing of Polonius?

14. How do Ophelia's mad scene and Laertes' thirst for vengeance in Act IV.5 echo the tragedy within Hamlet's family? Does Laertes' eagerness to judge and to seek vengeance ("To cut his throat i' the church"—Act IV.7, line 125) reflect poorly on Hamlet, who seems to delay taking revenge against the killer of his father?

[Act V]

15. How does the dialogue between the Clown/Gravediggers and between Hamlet and Horatio help to establish a suitable mood for the final act of the play? In what sense are Hamlet and Horatio being compared to the Gravediggers? What reflection on death and the significance of life is made here? See particularly Act V.2, lines 183–216.

16. Compare Hamlet's meditation on fate as contained in Act V.2, lines 217–222 with his earlier speeches on fate, such as the "To Be or Not to Be" soliloquy. How has his thinking evolved?

17. In the swordplay between Laertes and Hamlet, the King's manipulative plan falls apart. Why does the King's plan fail? Is it a matter of chance, or a poor plan to begin with? Does fate play a hand, or does Hamlet control the outcome in some way?

18. How do Laertes' final words give Hamlet greater stature? How will Horatio complete Hamlet's redemption in the public eye?

19. Why does Hamlet give Fortinbras "th' election lights"? In what ways does Fortinbras resemble Hamlet? How is he different from the Prince? How do you imagine the future of Denmark under Fortinbras' rule? How would Hamlet have ruled?

IDEAS FOR WRITING

1. Critics have long disagreed about why Hamlet hesitates so long to kill King Claudius. Many theories have been advanced: that Hamlet is unsure of whether Claudius is in fact guilty and the Ghost reliable; that Hamlet is too gentle or has an overly conscientious temperament for such a violent deed; that he is too reflective, cynical, and philosophical to act decisively; or that he is neurotic, depressed, perhaps the victim of an Oedipus complex. Do some research into several of the theories that attempt to explain Hamlet's behavior. Discuss the issue of Hamlet's alleged failure to act in the play. Which theory seems to best explain his hesitation, if in fact, you believe that such hesitation exists?

2. *Hamlet* is one of Shakespeare's most frequently produced plays. Each generation has interpreted the play differently and produced it according to values and concerns of the age. If you were to produce a "modern" Hamlet that would use contemporary dress and emphasize the concerns of the 1990s, what decisions would you make about costuming, setting, and contemporary references?

3. *Hamlet* is a very reflective, thoughtful play. What are two enduring philosophical or political issues that the speeches, the characters, and the play seem to comment upon? Use particular lines and interactions as support for your interpretation.

Student Writing

"Hauntings"
David Wilkinson

Originally from Tacoma, Washington, David Wilkinson is a student of psychology and biology who is working toward a career in biomedical research. He enjoys playing the trombone, singing in an a cappella group, biking, and scuba diving. Wilkinson wrote the following essay in order to draw together a number of literary works that explore ways that loss, memories, and a better understanding of the distant past, although at times overwhelming, can have a positive impact, transforming a personality and provoking crucial decisions and actions. As you read the essay, ask yourself how successful the student has been at integrating his own story of his grandmother's death with the stories of the professional writers he compares. Consider how effectively he uses evidence from the play, novel, story, and essays about which he writes, and how clearly and insightfully he compares and contrasts the diverse works covered in his essay.

    This ridge, called Memorial Hill, was my place to be
absolutely alone when sorting out emotions. Cross-legged at the
crest of the hill, I was enveloped by a cold breeze. The bitter
chill of my numb body scarcely entered my mind, where a smiling,
kindly grandmother-figure was sitting on her porch-swing holding
the hand of a three-year-old boy. Just as she began to speak,
the jarring sound of a train whistle blaring from the snow-swept
valley below opened my eyes. Back across the commons, lights
from Frost Library beckoned through a veil of snowy trees. It
was still winter in Amherst, Massachusetts.
    Earlier that same evening, my great-grandmother, Iva, had
died. The spicy woman who brought laughter and a jar of pickled
beets to every gathering had just stopped breathing. As the wind
blew, my body shuddered with chills and unresolved memories from
my childhood. The odor of boiling ramen amidst the copper jello
molds and plastic magnets of Iva's kitchen served as the setting
for a more distant reality; in that world, Iva and two small
children, my sister and I, still talked and laughed.

Growing up with a great-grandmother so animated, vibrant, and alive is a blessing. Part of the luxury lies in the child's naive notion of "forever." Each year we would go back to Iva's house to find her waiting for us, the same dancing eyes and wrinkled smile as a greeting. Gradually, however, my great-grandmother's world faded into the background of the fast-paced world of my new independence. Iva's death proved to be a moment of reckoning for me as I realized that my memories of Iva's love, warmth and humor are reflected through my continued relationships with my family. Iva's passing helped me recognize her influence on many of the values and the close connection I feel with my family.

Just as Iva's death helped me see the links between her life and my values, other troubling experiences, such as the deaths of friends and loved ones, can haunt the memory and conscience of those left behind. These painful and emotionally challenging memories are often described as historical hauntings. They can precipitate understandings of self and of the patterns of individual and social history. In Shakespeare's Hamlet and Garrett Hongo's essay, "Kubota," haunting memories of loss challenge the main character's core values. Hauntings also affect the outlook and character of the narrators in Becky Birtha's story "In the Life" and in James Baldwin's essay on the death of his father, "Notes of a Native Son." Finally, Toni Morrison's novel Song of Solomon shows how a haunting vision of cultural and historical identity can awaken alienated individuals, leading them to a better understanding of their history as it relates to their culture and family values.

Shakespeare's Hamlet reveals how hauntings can promote profound changes in character. Prince Hamlet is haunted by the specter of his murdered father, as well as by his filial responsibility of revenge. Shakespeare held firm beliefs in the power of supernatural manifestations on the real world. Thus, the lurking spirit of Hamlet's father shadows Hamlet throughout the play, directing or at least influencing his actions. The ghost initially appears to Hamlet on the battlements, intimating his infernal punishment in "sulf'rous and tormenting flames." The shade exhorts Hamlet: "If thou didst ever thy dear father love-- . . . Revenge his most foul and unnatural murder" (Act 1.5, lines 24, 26).

Hamlet's father's ghost informs the prince of the wrongs perpetrated by Claudius, presenting itself at opportune moments throughout the play to harden Hamlet's resolve to act swiftly in revenge. In fact, the supernatural presence of Hamlet's father serves a catalytic role in Hamlet's internal turmoil, encouraging his halting transformation during the course of the play.

Hamlet is haunted not only by his late father, but also by his unavoidable responsibility to avenge the murder. With the

ghost's story of murder, Hamlet becomes accountable to kill
Claudius and regain the throne. Thus both the ghost of his
father and his nascent responsibility to right the historical
wrong of murder haunt Hamlet, who is forced to look into the
core of his being to rectify his duty of violent revenge with
his own contemplative nature. The hauntings of both ghost and
duty press the issue into Hamlet's mind. He is caught between
the bounds of his intellectual nature and the imperatives of his
situation. As the son of a murdered king, Hamlet must exact the
full price of revenge to restore honor to the throne of Denmark,
while as a philosopher and man of thought, he requires assurance
of the ghost's truth before he will act, and becomes overly
reflective when circumstances seem to call for direct action.
Hamlet thus is forced to confront the division that lies deep in
his own nature: "I,/A dull and muddy-mettled rascal, peak/ Like
John-a-dreams, unpregnant of my cause" (Act 2.2, lines 522-524).
Hamlet's mind, conscience, and soul are in turmoil throughout
the play, as he is haunted by the messages of his father's shade
and the imposed filial and societal duties of vengeance.

By the end of the play, Hamlet experiences a partial change
of character and comes to terms with his fated responsibility of
revenge. The players' performance convinces Hamlet that the king
was guilty of murder, while the attempt against his own life
discovered on the trip to England galvanizes Hamlet to act
against Claudius. In Act 5 of the play, Hamlet speaks resolutely
to Horatio about his imminent revenge; it is clear that he is no
longer haunted by doubt:

> [Claudius] hath killed my king and whored my mother,
> Popped in between th' election and my hopes,
> Thrown out his angle for my proper life,
> And with such cozenage—is 't not perfect conscience
> To quit him with this arm? (Act 5.2, lines 64-68)

Hamlet is finally convinced that he must act; however, only
after he has been poisoned in his fated duel with Laertes does
Hamlet actually kill Claudius. Hauntings of both supernatural
influences and fated duties enact an arduous transformation in
Hamlet's character, forcing him to look deeply into his own
nature. The evolution of his character comes too late to
preserve his own life. Thus, in Hamlet Shakespeare shows that
hauntings can initiate significant character changes yet can
also have dangerous or even fatal consequences.

A more positive resolution to the dilemmas of haunting
occurs in Garrett Hongo's essay "Kubota," which describes his
haunting by patterns of family history, cultural conflicts, and
discrimination that helped form his identity as a Japanese-
American. Growing up in Gardena, California, in the 1960s, Hongo
encountered many Japanese-Americans who distanced themselves

from their cultural past in favor of mainstream American culture. As Hongo recalls:

> It was out of this sense of shame and a fear of stigma
> I was only beginning to understand that the nisei had
> silenced themselves. And, for their children, among
> whom I grew up, they wanted no heritage, no culture,
> no contact with a defiled history (991).

In childhood, Hongo was surrounded by these silent children of the nisei. While his environment discouraged identification with a Japanese heritage, the author describes how his grandfather sparked an interest in his cultural past. Hongo's grandfather, Kubota, brought to life the history of his Japanese-American heritage. Kubota relived for his grandson fishing expeditions for kumu'u , the red goatfish, along the reefs in Hawaii, and related the pain of war-time prejudice and discrimination. Despite the post World War II societal imperative of silence, Kubota shared his past, countering the norms of denial that characterized his grandson's culture.

The haunting legacy of Kubota's Japanese heritage was a catalytic influence on Hongo's emerging identity. Hongo tells of a man driven to incorporate the experiences and knowledge of the past into the culture of his grandson. Kubota voiced the history of the Japanese experience in America, a set of haunting revelations, and profoundly affected Garrett Hongo: "I was not made yet, and he was determined that his stories be part of my making" (989). Hongo describes his experience with the rich culture of his family's past. Because of his closeness with his grandfather, Hongo was exposed to his Japanese heritage and chose to identify with that heritage in his academic studies and in his own poetry.

During his youth, Hongo was greatly influenced by Kubota's haunting witness to the past. Thus, the death of Kubota was a powerfully haunting experience for Hongo, causing him to realize the extent of his indebtedness to and mutual identity with Kubota. After his grandfather's death, Hongo became the living repository for Kubota's memories and vivid legacy. At the close of the essay, Hongo dreams of Kubota hanging fishing lanterns near Kahuku Point in Hawaii. Unlike the disabled, "nub of a man" that Hongo had seen in the nursing home, in the dream Kubota is seen "torching" amidst his painted lanterns:

> [Kubota] held a small wooden boat in his cupped hands
> and placed it lightly on the sea and pushed it away.
> One of his lanterns was on it and . . . it was
> decorated with the silvery names of all our dead. (993)

This dream, sparked by the redress bill compensating Japanese-

Americans for the injustices of war-time prejudice, revived
Hongo's memories of Kubota. Alive in the author's mind, Kubota
was able to liberate and commemorate the ghosts of those who had
died before the legal reaffirmation of Japanese-Americans' right
to their culture. In his vivid memories and dreams of Kubota,
and his keen interest in the plight of Japanese-Americans,
Garrett Hongo shows how the hauntings of Kubota and his culture
had a formative influence on his own identity and career.
Historical hauntings such as Kubota's stories can permanently
affect character.

Even if identity remains unchanged, reflection caused by a
haunting experience can cause a shift in perspective and
outlook, and can be reassuring and revitalizing in a time of
loneliness. Becky Birtha's story "In the Life," for example,
relates the story of Pearl Jenkins, called Jinx, a woman haunted
by the absence of her dead lover. Jinx is frequently visited by
the apparition of her lover, Grace: "Grace come to me in my
sleep last night. I feel somebody presence, in the room with me
then I catch the scent of Posner's Bergamot Pressing Oil . . .
she use on her skin" (964).

The two characters, one alive and one dead, exchange words,
glances and caresses in Jinx's vision. Her dreams are so
compelling that at one point Jinx runs down to the garden,
convinced she will find Grace. Becky Birtha presents a character
whose hauntings are so believable that she must struggle to
convince herself they are not reality; finally she gives in to
them and enjoys them as valid experiences. Jinx's hauntings echo
her past, while standing in distinct contrast with her current
life as an aged and lonely woman. Jinx's vivid fantasies are a
visionary call from her life as a young, vital person. These
waking recollections and nocturnal hauntings emphasize the
importance of her life with Grace, despite the changes that come
with age. In fact, only dissonant reminders of her age and the
change of her neighborhood jar Jinx into the present:

> I hear her moving around out there. . . . I take a
> look out the window, and come to see it ain't Gracie
> at all, but two a them sassy little scoundrels from
> over the projects. . . . Eventually I begun to see how
> it wasn't even them two kids I was so mad at. I was
> mad at time. For playing tricks on me the way it done.
> So I don't even remember that Grace Simmons has been
> dead now for the past thirteen years. (966–967)

Jinx's strong, emotionally compelling hauntings lead her to
believe that time has not passed. Birtha paints the picture of a
woman haunted by the loss of her life's partner, who through her
hauntings begins to formulate a new understanding and
perspective on her changes.

In "Notes of a Native Son," James Baldwin shows how a single, haunting occurrence can awaken and change the assumptions of an entire lifetime. Baldwin changes his negative perspective on his father following his father's death. Initially, he is troubled by the jaded life and solitary death of his father. He describes the aftermath of his father's death and his own attempts at understanding. Baldwin says that, "On the morning of the 3rd of August, we drove my father to the graveyard through a wilderness of smashed plate glass. . . . He had lived and died in an intolerable bitterness of spirit and it frightened me, as we drove through those unquiet, ruined streets, to see how powerful and overflowing this bitterness could be and to realize that this bitterness now was mine" (85, 88). The decline and solitary death of his once-powerful father confront Baldwin, causing him to reconsider his father. The haunting experiences associated with his father's death and funeral compel the author to reassess his father's ruin and his dubious share in the dilemmas that brought it about.

The death of his father triggers recollections of Baldwin's own experiences with racial hatred and violence. The author discovers many of the constraints imposed on his father's life, and also grows to understand the web of family problems, paranoia, and the immense weight of societal prejudice that destroyed his father. At his father's hospital bed, Baldwin saw the immense changes that had been brought to bear on his father: "The moment I saw him I knew why I had put off this visit so long. . . . I had hated him and I wanted to hold on to this hatred. I did not want to look on him as a ruin: it was not a ruin I had hated . . ." (101). The events marking his father's decline cause Baldwin to recognize the legacy of pain and destruction visited on his father. The death of his father forces him to account for the haunting specter of racial hatred and violence in both of their lives.

In an attempt to ease his mental disquiet, Baldwin begins to uncover the true father of his earliest memories. During a particular song during the funeral, he is haunted by memories of a smiling, care-free father he had all but forgotten. Baldwin eventually comes to an understanding of those influences that broke his father and his own susceptibility. He concludes that, "Now it had been laid to my charge to keep my own heart free of hatred and despair. . . . Now that my father was irrecoverable, I wished that he had been beside me so that I could have searched his face for the answers which only the future would give me now" (114).

The hollow silence of the city and of his dead, broken father impresses upon Baldwin the legacy of his black heritage. Sparked by the haunting death of his father, James Baldwin reevaluates his father's life, and his own share in his father's problems. Baldwin's experiences demonstrate how haunting

episodes can challenge long held feelings, stimulating self-
knowledge, and self-discovery.

    While some historical hauntings induce perspective or
personality changes, Toni Morrison's Song of Solomon describes a
character who initially lacks a sense history and belonging.
Early in the novel the character Milkman becomes troubled by his
lack of connection with any familial history or culture. Growing
up in the Lake Superior town of Mercy, Michigan, Milkman is
portrayed as a character alienated from his parents and sisters.
Ignorant of his past and family history, he holds very little
respect for his father, a wealthy, black real estate owner, not
understanding the events that formed his father's personality.
Milkman lives adrift amidst the neurosis of his immediate
family. While conversing with his friend Guitar, Milkman
realizes that, "Maybe Guitar was right-partly. His life was
pointless, aimless, and it was true that he didn't concern
himself an awful lot about other people. There was nothing he
wanted bad enough to risk anything for, inconvenience himself
for" (107). In the absence of any connection to his roots, or
understanding of the problems of his dysfunctional family,
Milkman disengages from his own life, motivated only by short-
sighted, hedonistic whims.

    As the novel progresses, however, Morrison describes
Milkman's growing yearning for direction. At first, his lack of
purpose or vision presents an apparently insurmountable problem,
but gradually, despite his disaffection, Milkman begins to
unravel the mysteries of his familial history. Milkman's only
initial knowledge of his family is that his legal name, Macon
Dead, was given to his grandfather by whites when freed slaves
were registered. With many of the details of his family heritage
locked within his father's silent, clouded mind, Milkman
eventually seeks his "name" and a familial connection with his
aunt Pilate. "I'll ask Pilate. Pilate knows. It's in that . . .
box hanging from her ear. Her own name and everybody else's. Bet
mine's in there too. I'm gonna ask her what my name is" (89).
While Morrison shows the emptiness in Milkman's life, with each
detail, his drive for meaning and association with his past
grows from mere curiosity to a near obsession. For example,
Milkman's incipient motive for searching out his familial roots
is a desire to recover gold that, according to Pilate, was lost
during his father's boyhood. However, when Milkman searches for
his father's childhood home, he begins to discover his "people,"
and a transformation begins.

    As Milkman explores his father's country and begins to
understand the character of his family, he comes to take pride
in them, and his quest for gold becomes transmuted by his
discoveries of family history. Song of Solomon is, largely, the
story of Milkman's character transformation. When he begins to

identify with the history of his family, Milkman becomes haunted
by a need to recover the previously lost names and places,
tracing his grandfather's past to Shalimar, Virginia:

> How many dead lives and fading memories were buried in
> and beneath the names of the places in this country.
> . . . When you know your name, you should hang on to
> it, for unless it is noted down and remembered, it
> will die when you do. (333)

Milkman eventually learns of his true name and heritage as
one of the children of Solomon, a legendary slave who returned
to his native Africa, escaping the bonds of slavery. More
importantly, however, as Milkman gains an understanding of his
previously haunting and absent familial past, he gains
confidence in himself and eventually discovers his spiritual and
ancestral home. At the close of the novel Guitar shoots Pilate,
killing her; Milkman stands over the bones of his grandfather
and the body of his aunt, imbued with direction and courage, and
at last begins to fight back. Toni Morrison shows how the
haunting call of the familial past can become overpowering,
eventually altering personality, and, in some cases, provoking
decisive action. In Song of Solomon , cultural and familial
history come to haunt Milkman, eventually forging in him a
powerful new sense of identity and purpose.
     Historical hauntings powerfully influence our lives and
conceptions of the world, inducing contemplation of the relation
between past and present. Such powerful experiences can
establish connection with and understanding of the past, cause
personality or perspective changes, or bring about wholesale
character transformations. The development of a unique personal
identity necessarily involves taking part in and adopting a
history, whether cultural, communal, or familial. The resulting
human bonds of identification and association tether the past
and present together; thus the haunting influences of the past
are both invaluable and unescapable.
     The identities formed during life wrap both past and
present into one single consciousness that is carried through
life. Never truly free of who we were, we are served though
hauntings of the past with vivid reminders of our deeper
identity and purpose. Forever in need of a "people," a culture,
and a history, hauntings from the past do not allow us to forget
who we are. I will not forget Iva Cooper. Having played a part
in my making and that of my family, she will always be part of
my being. . . .
     The door opens and a few snow flakes wander in, and then
that icy breeze begins to blow. Once again I am returning to
Memorial Hill. The familiar chill grips my body, while familiar

faces fill my mind. As I walk, I close my eyes and begin the
mental journey home. Concentrating carefully, the uneven, foot-
worn boards of Iva's deck come into view, melting away just as
quickly as I approach the porch-swing. Once again my smiling,
wrinkled great-grandmother sits on that swing with the same
three-year-old boy, and begins to speak. This time I will hear
what she has to say.

Works Cited

Baldwin, James. Notes of a Native Son. Boston: Beacon Press,
     1984.
Birtha, Becky. "In the Life." Imagining Worlds. Ed. Marjorie
     Ford and Jon Ford. New York: McGraw-Hill, 1994 964-972.
Hongo, Garrett. "Kubota." Imagining Worlds. Ed. Marjorie Ford
     and Jon Ford. New York: McGraw-Hill, 1994 985-993.
Morrison, Toni. Song of Solomon. New York: Signet, 1977.
Shakespeare, William. "Hamlet." Imagining Worlds. Ed. Marjorie
     Ford and Jon Ford. New York: McGraw-Hill, 1994 1027-1153.

Connections: Ideas for Discussion and Writing

1. People are often haunted by their past; the dead return in dreams and visions to
raise issues that we have not yet put to rest. How do people best resolve the past and put
the past behind them? When is it important to pay attention to "hauntings," replayings of
past traumas and events to learn from the past? Write a documented essay in which you
discuss how several works from this chapter as well as other readings reflect on this
issue. You might consider such works as Yukio Mishima's "Swaddling Clothes," Elizabeth Bowen's "The Demon Lover," Becky Birtha's "In the Life," Alberto Rios' "Mi
Abuelo," and Shakespeare's Hamlet.

2. What happens when a person has a vision of an alternative reality? When are
such visions to be trusted? Do they offer answers to our problems. Can they lead us into
madness and self-destruction? Write a documented essay in which you examine how
these issues are presented in outside readings as well as in such works as Charlotte
Perkins Gilman's "The Yellow Wallpaper," Isabel Allende's "Phantom Palace," E. M.
Forster's "The Other Side of the Hedge," Annie Dillard's "A Field of Silence," Theodore
Roethke's "In a Dark Time," and Shakespeare's Hamlet.

3. People's inner selves may at times haunt them in the form of "doubled" or alternative selves that may represent hidden potentials, ways people could have followed but
chose not to. How do people confront the "dark side of the soul," the "other"? Should
these voices be listened to, integrated into behavior, or dismissed as irrational distrac-
tions? Where do such images of the "double" or the "other" originate? Why do some
people seem to have multiple selves, whereas others feel comfortable just being who
they are, with one primary identity? Write an essay in which you discuss several such
issues in relation to works you have read in this text and elsewhere. You might consider
such readings as W. S. Merwin's "Fog-Horn," Robert Frost's "Desert Places," Judith Ortiz
Cofer's "The Other," Charlotte Perkins Gilman's "The Yellow Wallpaper," Theodore
Roethke's "In a Dark Time", Sylvia Plath's "Mirror," and Shakespeare's Hamlet.

4. History can include the history of one's own family or the history of a vanished civilization. How do we make sense of our lives in the present through studying the historic and familial past? How do patterns from the distant past continue to influence the present? Write an essay in which you discuss such issues related to history, making references to outside readings as well as such chapter selections as Isabel Allende's "Phantom Palace," James Dickey's "Hunting Civil War Relics at Nimblewill Creek," Percy Bysshe Shelley's "Ozymandias," Michele Murray's "Poem to My Grandmother in Her Death," Li-Young Lee's "Visions and Interpretations," Alberto Ríos' "Mi Abuelo," and Shakespeare's *Hamlet*

5. Beliefs in magic and the supernatural are an important part of many peoples' heritage, even though modern values tend to be more "reality based." What role can religion, magic, and superstition play in modern life? Is it important to maintain aspects of a heritage because of the way such beliefs keep the past alive, despite the fact that a person may logically reject the "superstitious" aspects of a culture or religion? Write an essay in which you explore such issues relative to magic and the supernatural, using outside readings as well as such chapter readings as N. Scott Momaday's "Grandmother's Country," Garrett Hongo's "Kubota," Richard Cortez Day's "A Chagall Story," Linda Hogan's "Diaries," Pat Mora's "Curandera," Louise Erdrich's "Windigo," and Roberta Hill Whiteman's "Star Quilt."

6. Death brings out many responses in people. How do we cope with death, struggling against it while learning to accept its ultimate reality? In what ways does life prevail over death? Write an essay in which you examine the ways outside readings as well as chapter readings confront and establish a dialogue with the reality of death and the survival of life. You might examine such chapter selections as the Native American folk tale "The End of the World," Elizabeth Gray Vining's "Being Seventy," Maxine Kumin's "The Envelope," John Donne's "Death Be Not Proud," Dylan Thomas' "Do Not Go Gentle into That Good Night," Richard Cortez Day's "A Chagall Story," and Shakespeare's *Hamlet.*

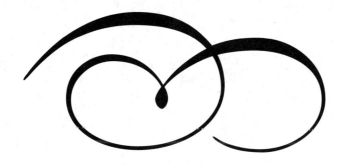

APPENDIX

RESEARCH WRITING

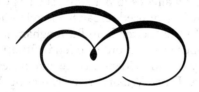

One of the reasons I decided to become a writer is that I love all aspects of the research process.
Roger Rapaport

As this quote from author and publisher Roger Rapaport suggests, doing class-room research can be exciting and creative, a complement to the imaginative journeys you have taken throughout the term as you have studied the readings in *Imagining Worlds*. Research is not necessarily a highly formal kind of writing that only takes place in a library; you can do research in many ways: while you are reading the newspaper or polling your friends about their opinions on a so-cial or political issue, when you are watching a film version of a story or inter-viewing an expert about his or her opinions on a subject. Writers do research throughout their careers. Each time an author of fiction or nonfiction begins a new book, research occupies a substantial part of his or her time; this might in-clude reviewing a number of texts and visual materials relative to the period in which a work is to be set. Research is often necessary once again during major revisions. When you read a text, the research may seem hidden because it has been synthesized and transformed through the writer's imagination.

All types of research require engagement with a broad range of materials. For example, if you are writing about a writer, examine photographs of the au-thor and his or her family; get to know something about the geographic region, the culture, and the literary schools that may have influenced him or her. Read widely in his or her fiction and nonfiction works, and try to see what others think: teachers, critics, contemporaries. Student writers of research papers, like fiction writers, can also draw on their own individual voices or visions of the world.

Formal research papers differ from the kind of writing a creative writer does in that such papers use formal documentation to indicate the author and page of quotations, facts, and ideas that come from a source. Formal research papers also use bibliographies or works cited pages to give a full reference for all sources cited in the body of the text or referred to in footnotes or endnotes.

Several student essays in *Imagining Worlds* illustrate the way that the strategic use of research can increase the effectiveness of a point of view. In the casebook on stories, for instance, Laurie Fiedler's interest and wide reading about the culture and dilemmas of the Vietnam war era helped to stimulate and focus her imagination in her sequel to Tim O'Brien's "Field Trip" while yielding insights into the character and his problems. Matt Rostoker used primary source research in his essay on Ursula Le Guin's "And She Unnamed Them," turning to the texts to which Le Guin alludes in her story, such as *Gulliver's Travels* and the Book of Genesis. Jeremy Taylor used research and references to several texts, including Martin Luther King's "Letter from Birmingham Jail" and a speech delivered on campus by rapper Ice-T, in order to lend authority to his comments on the continuing relevancy of King's ideas on race and protest.

Two student writers, David Wilkinson in "Hauntings" and Jeannie Chang in "The Dream Journal," have written extended research papers for *Imagining Worlds* of the kind sometimes referred to as "term projects." David Wilkinson's essay compares a universal theme he encountered in reading a series of different literary texts, whereas Jeannie Chang's essay is more like the kind of research project typically done in a humanities, economics, sociology, or psychology course; it is focused on the exploration of issues and ideas.

Because an extended research paper such as those undertaken by Wilkinson or Chang requires a great deal of planning and effort, it is helpful to divide the project into stages. We recommend that you keep a research journal as you work through the planning stages of your paper; your journal can include notes and ideas for your paper, an annotated bibliography of works you intend to use, and a day-to-day account of your research process and progress. Make an entry in your journal for each day you do work on the paper. Sum up each trip to the library, each study session or peer review activity, with a focus on what you learned on that particular occasion. The following journal entries were completed by a student who planned to write on how Aldous Huxley's family and upbringing influenced his writing of *Brave New World*.

RESEARCH JOURNAL ENTRIES

<u>Friday, April 2:</u> Today I decided what to write on! I had long been interested in thought provoking, futuristic works like Orwell's <u>1984</u> and Huxley's <u>Brave New World</u>. When I noticed that a chapter from <u>Brave New World</u> was included in my textbook, I decided to make Huxley the focus of my research. I felt that

reading additional works by and about Huxley would give me
additional insights into Huxley the man and Huxley the author
and enable me to understand what sparked his ideas and my
ability to identify with them.

Saturday, April 3: I am at home today baby-sitting, and I would
like to begin work on my paper; unfortunately I have no
reference materials available except for my Webster's New World
Dictionary, which seemed like a good place to start my research.
I read the entries on Aldous Huxley as well as the names of his
famous siblings, André Fielding and Sir Julian Huxley, as well
as his grandfather, the scientist Thomas Henry Huxley. Armed
with this information I plan to go to the San Francisco Library.

Monday, April 5: The San Francisco Main Library is a large
graystone building filled with books on just about every
imaginable subject. I hit the mother lode with regard to Aldous
Huxley. In addition to Brave New World, I found collections of
stories and essays, and a biography by Sybille Bedford. I took
extensive notes from the biography. I had no idea of the range
of Huxley's interests or his foray into the world of drug use.

Once you have started your research notebook, try to work through the following steps.

CHOOSING A TOPIC

Imagining Worlds provides writing assignments many of which would be good
ideas for researched writing. Each of the "Connections" questions can be developed into research projects. Students also can do research into a writer's life
and the ideas and experiences that may have led him or her to write a particular story, essay, play, or poem. You might also want to do further reading in the
works of a writer you have enjoyed reading in the text, as the student journal
writer does in her research on Aldous Huxley. If your instructor has designed
your course to emphasize issues and ideas rather than particular writers and literary works, you might choose to do further research into a subject raised in
one of the six thematic chapters in the book. Do some brainstorming, listing all
the topics that interest you; also try some freewriting on authors, topics, and issues raised in the course. Whatever author, work, or topic you choose to write
about, you will have to think about them for a number of weeks; if you choose
prematurely or pick a subject you don't really care deeply about, your research
experience may be tedious and unproductive. Consult with your classmates
and instructor before choosing a subject, and spend a few days browsing in the
library to see if there is enough material or if there seems to be too much to
handle in a short research essay. Sometimes librarians can give you ideas for

topics or help you to define vaguely worded topics in language that is closer to that of the subject headings in the card catalogs and computer databases at your library.

SEEKING INFORMATION

Begin your research in the reference room. For research into contemporary issues, check the subject catalog, computer databases such as Infotrac and Pro-Quest, as well as periodical indexes such as *Reader's Guide to Periodical Literature* and indexes such as the *Social Sciences and Humanities Index* and the *New York Times Index*. For literary research, *Contemporary Authors* is a good starting place to find information on writers, as is *A Dictionary of Literary Biography*. A multi-volume encyclopedia such as *Encyclopaedia Britannica* can be helpful for information on writers and literary movements. For more specialized information on critical articles, see *MLA International Bibliography of Books and Articles on the Modern Languages and Literature;* for information on particular literary genres, you might try a specialized index or a collection of recent criticism. For criticism on the novel, use *The Contemporary Novel: A Checklist of Critical Literature on the British and American Novel since 1945*. For critical opinion on plays, examine *Dramatic Criticism Index: A Bibliography of Commentaries on Playwrights from Ibsen to the Avant-Garde*. For poetry analysis, look into *Poetry Explication: A Checklist of Interpretation since 1925 of British and American Poems Past and Present*. For story criticism, try *Twentieth-Century Short Story Explication: Interpretations 1900–1975*. For essays, both critical and philosophical, check out *The Essay and General Literature Index*.

NARROWING AND FOCUSING YOUR TOPIC

You may be overwhelmed to find entire scholarly journals and dozens of books devoted to a subject you have an interest in. How can you begin to cover so much in so few pages? This was the dilemma that confronted student writer Jeannie Chang when she began to do research into dreams and sleep studies. Jeannie discovered that many psychologists and researchers have devoted their careers to deciding why we dream and what dreams reveal about the personality of the dreamer.

After spending several days reading broadly about the psychological theories of dreams, Chang decided to narrow her topic to the dream journal, for several reasons. It was something she was curious about and she had decided to keep a dream journal for her English class; and it wasn't too technical a subject, so that she felt competent to make sense of what others had written about it and to respond insightfully to the ideas of her sources. Plenty of information was available on the subject in the library at her college, and there were even several faculty members with whom she could confer for advice on directions for more recent research. Once you have a specific topic in mind, try to focus it first by stating it as a question: What influenced Aldous Huxley in the writing of *Brave New World*? Is the poem "My Papa's Waltz" really about child abuse? Can keeping a dream journal really lead to valuable personal insights? After a little more preliminary research, you can try to answer your initial question, creating a tentative thesis for your paper. But keep try to your thesis flexible, open to new points and ideas that come to you in your research.

SELECTING AND STUDYING YOUR SOURCES

Once you have acquainted yourself with the resources available at the library, choose a subject you have an interest in, and narrow it down somewhat. Now you need to begin your research in earnest. You may have already checked out several promising general texts or photocopied a few intriguing articles found in indexes or databanks, but this material will only get you so far. One simple approach to systematic research is to divide your topic into categories, even writing a preliminary scratch outline of your subject; then spend some time doing research into each major aspect of your subject. The student doing research on Aldous Huxley might spend time on each of the following subtopics: Huxley's grandparents, parents, and siblings; his childhood; his university years at Cambridge and the failure of his eyesight; his life living abroad, focusing particularly on his time spent with D. H. Lawrence in New Mexico. Gradually assemble information on your subject, using either traditional bibliography cards or a computerized notebook.

The following entry is from the research log of the student who was writing on Aldous Huxley and *Brave New World;* notice how her annotation helps her keep track of the major sources she has collected and provides notes on how they can be used in further research:

Bedford, Sybille. <u>Biography of Aldous Leonard Huxley</u>. New York: Random House, 1974.

    A thoughtfully written biography of the writer, from his early years through adulthood. Although primarily about Aldous, it gives us background and insights into the Huxley family, their life, loves, and the demons which drove them. Useful as a starting point leading one to understand Huxley's need to write about the human condition.

Huxley, Aldous Leonard. <u>The Doors of Perception and Heaven and Hell</u>. New York: Harper, 1954.

    Deals with the effects of peyote and visions on the mind;

indicates the extent that drugs, mind control and visionary
experience were a preoccupation in Huxley's life and thought.

Huxley, Aldous Leonard. Island. London: Chatto and Windus, 1962.
    This is a more positive utopia, an answer to the problems
of Brave New World. This novel shows Huxley's growth following
his experiences with drugs and the pacifist movement.

FINDING A BALANCE OF SOURCES

As you continue to investigate sources for your paper, remember to try for a balance of ideas and perspectives. Many students look too hard for sources with which they agree, in order to back up or justify a preliminary thesis statement. If you can't find research that supports your thesis, you may need to change your focus on the issue. Even if you do find plenty of support for your views, try to find some critics with whom you don't agree, who may even make you angry, in order to test your assumptions. Such sources can be used to give your paper balance, to show the range of positions typically taken on the issue, or to indicate perspectives with which you disagree and which you might want to refute or criticize.

EVALUATING SOURCES

Except for the biography by Sybille Bradford, the sources in this student's annotated bibliography are primary sources, that is, texts written by the author being studied in the paper. Such sources need to be evaluated only for relevancy: How does the source relate to the main thesis or focus of your paper? If the source is relevant, it needs to be analyzed and cited several times; if it is only of passing interest, a two- or three-sentence summary of the work will suffice, perhaps even treating it in a paragraph in which several other related works are mentioned briefly.

    More complex problems arise when evaluating secondary sources for research: critical articles, commentaries on works of fiction, arguments, and controversial research findings. In evaluating secondary sources, you may feel at a disadvantage because you don't know enough about the issue under consideration to be a discerning judge. The following questions will help; when in doubt, consult your instructor or an experienced research librarian.

1. Is this a recent source, and does the source cite other, up-to-date references?
2. Does the source simply state opinion, or is the opinion backed up by

specific textual references and references to other relevant primary and secondary sources?

3. Does the source come from a reputable journal in the field, or from a newspaper or general interest publication in which authors often have no specialized training in the area under discussion?

4. What are the credentials of the author of the article or book? Is the person affiliated with academic institutions and/or have previous publication credits in the area under discussion?

5. Does the source use language objectively and clearly, or is the meaning obscured by jargon or what seems to be argument that is imbalanced, overly emotional in thought and language?

In order to evaluate your sources more effectively, you might try making a dialogic journal entry for each major source in your research log. In your dialogic entry, copy several short, yet crucial passages from the source on one side of a page; on the other side, copy your own responses and answers to the sorts of questions just suggested. Sometimes it can be helpful to make your questioning irreverent ("So what?" "Really?" "Says who?") in order to break down the tendency most beginning writers have to see their sources as "gospel," as lofty fonts of wisdom.

NOTE TAKING

In your preliminary research, as in dialogic journal entries, you have already been involved in doing note taking; now is a good time to refine the process. If at all possible, use a computer to help you with this phase of your research; a laptop is the ideal research instrument, as it can be brought into the library to take notes on reference materials that are on reserve. The process of taking notes is similar, whether done on a computer or on the more familiar notecards. First of all, before you begin to take notes on a source, check to see that you have a complete bibliography card or a full entry on your annotated bibliography providing inclusive pages for an article, publisher, date, full author name, and title. Make sure that all quotations include the title of the article and a page number, so that this information will be readily available should you later choose to use the quotation in your paper. You can shorten a very long quotation by using the ellipsis marks (. . .) between quoted sentences or phrases. On a notecard or computer file you can include a mixture of paraphrasing (placing the idea of a passage in your own words) and summary (reducing a long passage, section or even an entire work to two or three sentences, as in an annotated bibliography entry). Make it clear by using quotation marks when the language used is exactly that of your source and when your own words are being used, as in a paraphrase or summary.

PARAPHRASING VERSUS PLAGIARIZING

One of the worst academic sins is plagiarizing, the unacknowledged appropriation of the words or ideas of another person. Often charges of plagiarism arise from sloppy or overly hasty research. Effective and careful note taking, along with appropriate documentation of your sources in the draft and final version of your paper, will protect you against any unintentional plagiarism. Remember, as you paraphrase sections of a source onto notecards, to do so systematically. One approach that works well is to read a passage over and then set it aside for a minute. Then without looking at it, convert the words on the page into your own language, using simple and direct expression and leaving out metaphorical language or lengthy "asides." After you have paraphrased a passage, read over the original again to make sure that you haven't unintentionally used a phrase or two or more words from the original; if you have, paraphrase that part again. If the phrase is so memorable that you want to preserve it, put quotation marks around any words from the original.

FROM RESEARCH TO WRITING

The time comes in your research process when you need to start assembling your library work into a paper. Don't worry if you feel your library work isn't quite finished; there are always a few loose ends of research to tie up, and you will probably need to return to the library after writing your first or even second draft of the essay.

Moving from research to writing a research paper can be daunting, but if you have been systematic in your research, it can be rewarding and exciting. Try to find a large area to spread out your materials; even if you are working on a computer, it is is a good idea to print out all the notes you have been keeping in files just to get an overview of what you actually have. Try to group notes in different areas that correspond roughly to the different sections of your topic.

DEVELOPING A THESIS AND OUTLINE

Once you have organized your notes and responses to your sources, try to refine your initial view of the essay and its form: Has your tentative early thesis changed in the course of your research? Are there new sections that have emerged because of the amount of material you discovered? Do certain sections need to be combined? What is the best overall order for your paper at this point? Answering these questions will lead you in the direction of a formal outline, which is important for writing a research paper because of the length and complexity involved. Following is an outline and thesis for Jeannie Chang's essay

"The Dream Journal: An Exploration of Your Inner Self."

```
  I. Thesis: Dreams are an important part of our lives that we
     can learn from; they should not be surrendered too easily;
     thus, it is important to keep a dream journal which will
     enhance our dream recall and understanding.

 II. Supporting Research and Arguments
     A. Everyone dreams each night; we spend at least 5 years of
        our lives dreaming, yet most people remember few of
        their dreams.
     B. Personal experience and research by Henry Reed have
        shown that keeping a dream journal enhances dream
        recall.
     C. Recalling dreams helps in self-understanding,
        understanding the inner world.
     D. Recalling dreams also helps us make sense of the meaning
        and pattern of our daily lives; patterns of dreams
        intimately related to patterns of waking life.
     E. Dreams can serve as "warnings," helping us to solve
        problems.
     F. Dreams are creative productions of the unconscious mind,
        and can give us insights into and help us resolve
        problems in our creative endeavors.
     G. To be effective, dream journal entries need to be
        developed and interpreted for what they reveal about
        ourselves, our problems, and our inner and outer worlds.

III. Conclusion: Although some people might not be able to deal
     with the emotion involved in trying to capture their
     dreams, for most people it can be a rewarding experience of
     self-knowledge.
```

WRITING THE DRAFT

From the outline, move on to writing drafts for sections of your paper and submitting the first draft of your paper. Writing the paper in sections is a good strategy, as the research paper is longer and each part of the paper can have special problems, ranging from clearly defining key terms and issues, to giving preliminary background, to indicating the different, conflicting ideas of your sources, to the final section in which you provide your own perspective on the issue as a whole. Try writing the sections rapidly rather than worrying about editing at this stage.

In drafting a research paper, there is a tendency to get bogged down in copying quotations. You might try numbering your quotations and longer paraphrases, spreading your cards or printed files out in order, and then simply putting a number in your text to correspond to a particular card or file. This makes it easier to for your drafting to approximate the speed of thought in normal composing; it will also make it easier to keep your own "voice" as a writer throughout the paper, rather than getting into an unintentional imitation of the powerful, assured voices of your sources. Write the main body of your paper first; then draft an attention-getting introduction and an effective, emphatic conclusion.

REVISING THE DRAFT

The revising process with a research paper is not that much different from the process discussed in the introduction to *Imagining Worlds*. The paper is simply longer, more complex in its reasoning and use of support, and requires more attention to effective use of source "voices" and documentation of sources. Before beginning your revision, set the draft aside for a few hours in order to relax and develop a distance from it. As you return to the draft, try to read through it as one of your peers might. Ask some general questions about the content and clarity of the ideas presented; think about whether the support is sound and if the paper has a sense of overall unity. You might compare the draft to the outline, to see whether the essay needs rearrangement. Consider combining topics, or exploring new issues that have arisen in the drafting process.

PEER SHARING THE DRAFT

Peer writing groups can be helpful in revising a research paper just as they are in revising shorter classroom essays. Because research papers are longer and more detailed than the essays you usually write, allow more time for reading and discussion. For the first stage of the peer-sharing process, print up enough copies of your draft for everyone in your group. Then critique each research paper following guidelines that are similar to those that you have used before in your writing group. While we encourage your group to develop a set of criteria in your own language or just to respond to the papers before beginning to analyze them, the following guidelines can be useful:

1. Did the paper hold your attention? Was it interesting and informative? What did you learn from it? Do you have any further questions that you would like the writer to answer?
2. Was the paper clearly focused and logically developed? Was it easy for you to grasp the writer's purpose as you read the paper? If the paper was difficult to follow in places, let the writer know what was unclear or where you lost the writer's sense of logic.

3. Was the evidence convincing? Were the statistics and examples relevant to the thesis being developed, and were they easy for you to understand and relate to your realm of experiences? Was any of the supporting evidence too technical, too detailed, or too particular to keep you interested?

4. Was the argument or point of view of the paper clear to you? Did the writer go off on tangents or stay focused on the issue at hand? If parts of the essay seemed irrelevant to the main point, let the writer know what you think should be rethought.

5. Did you feel that the writer of the paper was directing the point of view and always using the sources to support his or her ideas, or did the sources and their voices seem to dominate? Were there places in the paper when the writer's voice was replaced by the sources? Was information just restated and placed in the paper, or did you always feel that the writer had thought about the sources and put the information into his or her own language and point of view? A research paper should not rely excessively on the language or jargon of the discipline, but should be easy to grasp and of interest to everyone in the group.

6. Has the writer brought the authority of his or her sources into the body of the text clearly and effectively by introducing the writer of the source prior to quoting? Has the writer used a wide enough breadth of source opinion to be convincing and fair?

7. Are the quotations, summaries, or paraphrases clearly woven in with the writer's own style and point of view? Is the writer careful not to include very long quotations? Typically, a quotation should not be longer than two sentences; many will be even shorter.

8. Is the paper clear mechanically and grammatically? Check for subject-verb agreement, vague pronoun reference, run-on sentences or fragments, variety of sentence structure.

Allow enough time to go over each paper carefully. After this session, think about the suggestions your writing group has made for your paper; remember that there may be contradictory advice; it will be your responsibility to make the changes that you think will improve your paper. At this point you may have to go back to the library to do more research or gather more information through interviewing.

When you complete the first stage of peer sharing, turn the paper into your instructor for some further commentary; you might request a conference with him or her to get another perspective on the issues of form and content raised in the peer-sharing session.

REWRITING THE INITIAL DRAFT

At this point will be ready to do a rewrite of your initial draft, adding in fuller documentation and doing more library research if there was insufficient support for any of the points in the initial draft. Remember at this stage to make a fuller assessment of your use of parenthetical citation and sources on your works cited page. Do all the works cited on the final page appear in the body of the paper? Are all the works that are cited in the text included on the final works cited page? Have you been careful to use a parenthetical citation and page reference for all works either quoted, paraphrased, summarized, or from which a fact or idea is drawn that you make use of in your essay? Remember that if you haven't taken care with your use of citations, you may be accused of sloppy research or even of plagiarism.

PROOFREADING AND FINE-TUNING THE SECOND DRAFT

If time permits, try another peer-sharing session, this time focusing on issues of form. This process will involve a critique of the MLA parenthetical documentation style and the works cited page, as well as a closer look at your use of transition, smoothly blended and correctly punctuated quotations, spelling, and abbreviations. Bring a copy of the Modern Language Association style guidelines to this group meeting along with enough copies of your revised draft with the MLA parenthetical style in your paper as correct as you can get it. If your group simply cannot agree on how to cite a reference, or if there is disagreement about what form to use, ask your instructor for help.

FINAL REWRITE

Now you are ready to complete the final stage of the writing process, the corrected, "published" version of the paper. Consider all of the advice you have been given on your paper; then prepare the final version for your instructor and submit your paper. If you are really pleased with your efforts, you might consider submitting your paper to a community or campus publication or perhaps to a journal of student writing that is produced by your department.

MLA
DOCUMENTATION

Although you will probably be using the Modern Language Association format in this course, it is not the only research format you will encounter in your college research writing; in fact, it is always a good idea to ask instructors what format they prefer. Many disciplines in college use the American Psychological Association format, which uses a bibliography of works cited and consulted. The MLA format was designed to eliminate all footnotes or endnotes except for informational notes. Instead of a traditional lengthy bibliography, the MLA uses a "Works Cited" page that must include only works actually cited in the body of your text. The MLA format is appropriate for use in a paper in an English course, particularly one such as this one with a focus on reading literature. The MLA format is also useful in that its elimination of annoying footnotes speeds the composition and revising process, helping you to focus on your own writing rather than worrying excessively about documentation. However, despite its simplifications, the MLA format is as exacting in its rules as any other bibliographical format. We provide here only a few of the many types of entries available using the MLA format; for others, consult a complete English handbook or the *MLA Handbook for Writers of Research Papers* (3rd edition) by Joseph Gibaldi and Walter S. Achtert (New York: Modern Language Association, 1988).

PARENTHETICAL CITATIONS

Use parenthetical citations to give credit for lines of drama, poetry, sentences, or phrases taken directly from books, articles, or interviews; also use parenthetical citations when using ideas or facts taken from your sources, unless these ideas or facts are common knowledge. Most people agree, for instance, that Shakespeare is the greatest dramatist in the English language, and that modern poetry tends to reject regular rhyme and meter, so there is no need to indicate where these ideas came from. A parenthetical citation is just what it sounds like: a parenthesis, in which a work is "cited," or referred to in an abbreviated form. Parenthetical citations usually come at the end of a sentence or quotation.

Single Author Citation

The most common parenthetical citations include the author's last name and a page number. Notice that the period of the sentence comes after the close of the parentheses:

```
Many modern researchers believe that schizophrenia is
genetically transmitted (Morris 68).
```

Author Introduced Earlier

If the author of a quotation or idea is formally introduced earlier in the sentence or paragraph, only a page number is necessary within the parenthetical citation:

```
Waking associations are defined in Sloane's Psychoanalytic
Understanding of the Dream as "an actual part of one's previous
experience, including actions, spoken words, thoughts,
fantasies, and affects" (23).
```

No Author

If there is no author, use the title of the source, or a shortened version, within the parentheses:

```
Many African Americans today have little confidence in peaceful
solutions to their problems ("Race: Our Dilemma Still" 37-38).
```

Two or More Works by the Same Author

If there are two are more works on your Works Cited page by the same author, use the author's last name and a shortened version of the work's title in parentheses:

Elizabeth Bowen searched during the stories she wrote during
World War II for "indestructible landmarks in a destructible
world" (Bowen, "Preface" xi).

One Source Quoted within Another Source

Sometimes a source will cite another source, giving only a name and a quotation. In this case use the "qtd. in" format within parentheses:

In a letter to Virginia Woolf, after hearing that Woolf's house
had been destroyed by bombing, Elizabeth Bowen wrote, "All my
life I have said, 'Whatever happens there will always be tables
and chairs'—what a mistake" (qtd. in Glendinning 164).

Lines in a Poem or Verse Drama

In short quotations, indicate a line break with a slash mark (/); follow with
parentheses that give inclusive line numbers. Quotations of more than two lines
should be set off in a block. Give act, scene, and line number in plays. For example, "(IV.3.321)" would indicate Act IV, third scene, line 321.

David Mura ends his poem "Grandfather and Grandmother in Love"
with an image of the ocean that evokes associations of sleep,
sexuality, and renewal: "Just the soft shushing of waves,
drfting ground/swells, echoing the knocking tide of morning"
(lns. 35-36).

WORKS CITED ENTRIES

The MLA style Works Cited page is similar to a bibliography, except that it
must contain *only* the works cited in the body of your paper. The works should
be listed in alphabetical order, with the author's last name first. If there is no author, begin with the title of the work and alphabetize by the first word of the
title, excluding articles such as "a" or "the." Articles should not be numbered,
and the second line of entries should be indented, not the first line. Each Works
Cited entry should include basic information on the source, in the appropriate
sequence: author, title, title of a publication, place published, publisher, date,
and pages for articles. Following are some of the more common Works Cited
entries. Notice that names of presses are abbreviated, with names of longer
companies shortened ("Stanford UP" is short for Stanford University Press;
"Prentice" is short for Prentice Hall).

Book with One Author

Fiedler, Leslie. <u>Freaks: Myths and Images of the Secret Self.</u>
     New York: Simon and Schuster, 1977.

Book with Two Authors

Ullman, Montague, and Nan Zimmerman. <u>Working with Dreams.</u>
     London: Hutchinson, 1979.

Book with Several Authors

Maimon, Elaine P., et al. <u>Writing in the Arts and Sciences.</u>
     Cambridge, MA: Winthrop, 1981.

Two Books by the Same Author

Plath, Sylvia. <u>The Bell Jar.</u> New York: Harper, 1971.
---. <u>Collected Poems.</u> Ed. Ted Hughes. New York: Harper, 1981.

Book with Editor and/or Translator

Montaigne, Michel. <u>The Complete Works of Montaigne.</u> Ed. and
     trans. Donald M. Frame. Stanford: Stanford UP, 1958.

Preface or Introduction

Boothe, Wayne C. "Introduction." <u>Problems of Dostoevsky's
     Poetics.</u> By Mikhail Bakhtin. Ed. Caryl Emerson.
     Minneapolis: U of Minnesota P, 1986. xiii-xxviii.

An Edited Collection

Lauter, Paul, ed. <u>Reconstructing American Literature: Courses,
     Syllabi, Issues.</u> New York: Feminist P, 1983.

Article (or other text) in an Edited Collection

Armitage, Susan H. "Women's Literature and the American
     Frontier: A New Perspective on the Frontier Myth." <u>Women,
     Women Writers, and the West.</u> Ed. Lee and Merrill Lewis. New
     York: Whitson, 1979. 5-13.
Dickinson, Emily. "Poem 617." <u>The Complete Poems of Emily
     Dickinson.</u> Ed. Thomas H. Johnson. Boston: Little, Brown,
     1960. 304.

[Note: Pages of the article included; editors of collection should also be credited
as shown.]

Article in a Magazine (weekly)

Monroe, Sylvester, "Life in the 'Hood." <u>Time</u> 15 June 1992:
        37-38.

Article in a Magazine (monthly)

Rapping, Elayne. "Who Needs the Hollywood Left?" <u>The Progressive</u>
        Sept. 1993: 34 36.

Article in a Scholarly Journal

Reck, Rima Drell. "MLA Masterpieces: Canon, Ideology, and
        Audience." <u>College English</u> 48 (1986): 484-91.

Article in a Newspaper

Strum, Charles. "Malls Wrestle with the Blues." <u>New York Times</u>
        26 Sept. 1993: E5.

Article in an Encyclopaedia or Reference Book (unsigned)

"Steinbeck, John." <u>Encyclopedia Americana.</u> 1990 ed.

[Note that nothing is included about the publisher of this reference book, as it is
a well-known and readily available encyclopedia. The page and volume need
not be included, as the work is arranged alphabetically.]

SAMPLE STUDENT RESEARCH ESSAY

For an example of a literature-oriented student research paper using the MLA
format, see the essay by David Wilkinson at the end of Chapter 12. The student
research essay by Jeannie Chang that follows provides an example of an application of many aspects of the MLA format just discussed, in the context of a paper
that examines the dream journal. This is a typical research paper that might be
done for an English or humanities course. Notice how the student writer uses
parenthetical citations and a Works Cited page that contains all of the sources
referred to in the body of the paper. Notice also how Chang integrates paraphrase of studies and research findings, direct quotation from her sources, as
well as her own experiences with keeping a dream journal.

Jeannie Chang

Professor Ford

English 3

March 9, 1993

                    The Dream Journal: An Exploration

                              of Your Inner Self

        For the past few weeks I have been keeping a dream

journal. When I began the project, I wondered if

keeping the journal would actually enhance my memory

for details in dreams, especially details like color.

The journal project provided me with an opportunity to

discover firsthand the truth in this statement, as well

as an opportunity to reflect upon my dreams, a subject

which has fascinated me since a recurring childhood

nightmare in which a mad scientist would poison my

family, leaving me as the sole survivor of his malice.

Reflecting upon the reality revealed in that nightmare,

I began to wonder what purpose dreams serve, why we

dream, and why we don't pay more attention to our dream

worlds.

        Perhaps we are fooled into overlooking any

function of dreams because we misleadingly experience

them during the seemingly passive sleeping hours.

Ironically, however, the dreaming brain which functions

during sleep and is characterized by Rapid Eye

Movements (REM sleep) is more active than the waking

Chang 2

brain. Coupled with the consideration that a human being will spend approximately five years in the dream state, assuming a life span of 75 years (Dement, Sleep 12), we can only conclude that dreams are a significant part of life; they should not be surrendered to departure easily.

The ephemeral quality of dreams probably contributes to our social and cultural indifference to the dream world. How easy it is to awake and hastily discard a remembered dream after only a moment's notice! Not only do we often abandon any dreams we do recall, but we also often fail to recollect any at all. How can we allot significance to or analyze something which evades our conscious thought? Perhaps if we were more aware of our dreams, remembering a substantial number of them, we would assign them more waking importance. The fleeting nature of dreams presents our first obstacle: the problem of having no dreams to refer to, none to analyze.

The truth is that a non-dreamer does not exist. The average adult has four to six REM sleep periods-- the period during which dreams occur--per night (Dement, Sleep 58). A human is yet to be found who does not experience dreams, as confirmed in the laboratory. These laboratory tests involving control groups reveal that subjects awakened during each REM period of the night will report many more dreams than

do those who attempt to recall dreams simply in the
morning (Dement, Some 45). This reduction in recall is
attributed to the forgetting of dreams through the
course of the night. Several theories about the cause
of forgetfulness are described in Robbins's The
Psychology of Dreams. One hypothesis explains that the
discrepancy between recall of dreams among individuals
may be related to the discrepancy in "waking memory";
not everyone enjoys the same memory capacity for
visual data (52). Other evidenced theories include the
interference hypothesis which suggests that new,
distracting material upon waking decreases the
subsequent recall of dreams, and the salience
hypothesis which proposes that the more vivid the
dream, the likelier it will be remembered. Another
theory, however less persuasive and as yet unproved,
is the repression hypothesis: non-recallers
unconsciously block their dreams from conscious
awareness because of their painful nature (52-59).

Is there nothing then, that we can do if we cannot
remember a significant portion of our dreams? Before I
began my dream journal, I would often wake up without
the recollection of a dream, or with only fragments and
images which were soon lost in the bustle of morning
activity. I never would have characterized myself as a
frequent dreamer; I thought I dreamt at most three to
four times a week. However, I didn't consciously try to

Chang 4

remember my dreams, or elaborate on the portions I did
recollect. With the recent maintenance of a dream
journal, I seem to have had more dreams than usual, or
rather, I have remembered more of them. Writing in a
journal has challenged me to alter the magnitude of my
conscious effort to recollect dreams; I am motivated by
my curiosity for the content, details, and function of
my dreams. This new, conscious attitude I have assumed
about the potential disclosure of insights within the
dream world has motivated me to be diligent about
recording my dreams, persistent about eliciting more
recall, and intent about associating them with related
waking events. I have discovered that surprisingly
enough, upon meditation and reflection, I actually can
remember my dreams almost daily.

Confirming my observations, psychologist Henry
Reed, in his experiment with Princeton undergraduate
subjects, obtained similar results. He found his
subjects could control the quantity of dreams recalled
by the intensity of their motivation as evidenced by
their morning behavior. Reed also discovered that the
recollection of certain aspects of dreams such as
visual, auditory, and other sensory detail, color, and
emotions were enhanced over the course of the dream
record keeping experiment (40-41). His findings suggest
that "learning how to remember . . . dreams" is indeed
possible (44). Thus the illusory nature of dreams can

Chang 5

be overcome to an extent, and dreams can be captured
for analysis.

Now that we know dream recall can be improved upon
training, we have cleared the first obstacle hindering
our practical use of dreams. However, yet another
question surfaces: What do dreams tell us, if anything?
Why is it important to even recall and interpret dreams?

Sigmund Freud, the founder of psychoanalysis,
wrote that dream interpretation is "the royal road to a
knowledge of the unconscious activities of the mind"
(qtd. in Mattoon 5). Many of our unconscious fears,
wishes, and personality are revealed during sleep;
thus, dreams are an important reflection of the whole
of the individual. As dream analyst Carl Gustav Jung
stated, "only when the individual is willing to fulfill
the demands of rigorous self-examination and self-
knowledge" is one able to effectively relate with
intimates, the community, the world, and the universe
(qtd. in Mambert and Foster 3). Self-awareness and
understanding is a universal quest; it only makes sense
to include one's dreams in this search for the soul,
considering they are as much a part of ourselves as
waking thoughts.

The several similarities between waking and
dreaming thoughts form the basis for their comparable
importance. An obvious example is the similar content
of our daily and nocturnal worlds; dreams often embrace

Chang 6

the reality of our waking activity. Many of our
conscious problems, pleasures, and preoccupations flood
our dream world, occupying even our unconscious
thoughts. For example, I recorded a dream in which I
attended a party in a colorful full-length skirt. I
realized upon waking that this dream was reinforcing
the preoccupation I had about finding an appropriate
outfit to wear to a costume party that night; in
reality, I don't own a gypsy-like skirt, though I had
wished that I did. Other dreams held deeper meaning,
revealing issues and events I hadn't consciously
realized affected me to such an extent. One morning,
for example, I remembered the following dream:

> I was wearing my black flats that have <u>no</u>
> traction, especially on the carpeted stairs
> (that I later tried to climb), and the tight
> miniskirt (I was wearing) wouldn't let me move!
> So when we (my brother Allan and I) saw Kris (my
> older sister), we ran up a super long stairway.
> Al went first, then Kris, and she was telling me
> to hurry and I was saying I couldn't because of
> the outfit, and I remember thinking that I
> should take off my skirt and shoes rather than
> be caught by the pursuing, sleazy men.

After recording this dream, I realized upon association
that it captured several concerns I had during the
preceding days. The weekend before this dream, I had

worn my black flats which I noticed were very slippery
on carpeting; I went hiking in San Francisco and had
climbed a very long and steep set of stairs; I had
recently thought how much I missed my brother and
sister, whom I hadn't spoken with for awhile. I also
had been upset and concerned about my weight gain,
upset that all my clothes were snug; and I had been
disturbed the night before at a gathering at which I
had received womanizing stares and comments from the
Food Service workers. I didn't realize the impact any
of these events made on me until I had this single
dream which surprisingly incorporated all these
separate impressions. It was almost as if my
unconscious were pressing these issues to my attention,
in search of some sort of resolution.

These two personal examples of dreams illustrate
dream researcher Dr. Montague Ullman and writer Nan
Zimmerman's belief that "there is something to learn
about ourselves in each of our dreams although the
importance and significance to our lives will vary from
dream to dream" (24). The second of the two dreams,
like many others, demonstrates our tendency to dream
about our interactions with close friends and family
rather than about mere acquaintances and strangers, and
about issues and events that have changed our lives
rather than about those that have barely affected us on
a conscious level. Our unconscious mind often

integrates past events with present occurrences and old
friends with new companions, connecting our new
experiences with past ones.

Through this integrative nature of dreams, we are
reminded of recent occurrences and their relation to us
as individuals. Another personal example representing
this function of a dream is one I had in which I took
my Caucasian boyfriend out to dinner at a Korean
restaurant. The day before I experienced this dream, we
had seen a Korean flag in a store, and I had taught him
how to say "the Korean flag" in my language. The dream
called attention to my desire to educate him about my
cultural background; it was an issue I felt I was
neglecting. Dreams in this way may reveal even more
about ourselves than we can consciously perceive;
through their focus and content, dreams give us an
additional, fresh perspective about ourselves. Dreams
being an uninhibited expression of our innermost self,
bring to the surface unconscious struggles, wishes, and
concerns. As Ullman and Zimmerman suggest, "working
with [dreams] increases our store of knowledge about
ourselves" (24).

Not only do dreams hold similar content as in
waking activity, but they are also similar in several
other respects. Studies conducted by leading sleep
researchers Dr. Edward Wolpert and Dr. William Dement
have shown that the passage of time in dreams and

reality is equivalent (<u>Some</u> 47). Thus, our actions in
dreams take the same amount of time to perform as in
reality; "dreams are not instantaneous," as was
previously believed (46). Interestingly, our eye
movements in dreams also correlate to our eye movements
while awake. Dr. Dement and his colleague Howard
Roffwarg first conjectured this "scanning hypothesis"
when they noticed that eye movements seemed patterned
in accordance with the actions in subjects' dreams,
such as a dream reported about watching a Ping-Pong
match in which only horizontal movements were recorded.
Several subsequent experiments established the validity
of their theory, in particular, the study Dr. Edward
Wolpert and William Offenkranz conducted on blind
subjects (<u>Some</u> 50). As expected, the two researchers
found no eye movements in the congenitally blind during
dreaming, but observed eye movements in those who
became blind later in life. These results affirmed
Dement and Roffwarg's original belief that "the brain
is doing in the REM state essentially the same thing it
does in the waking state; a sensory input is being
elaborated" (51). Dement expands on this similarity
between waking and dreaming brain activity by
speculating that this similarity is part of the reason
why dreams seem so real (52).

Dreams also seem real because in them, "we are
fully conscious and aware of ourselves" (Dement, <u>Sleep</u>

231). This attribute of dreams--the incredible sense of
reality we feel while in the dream state--can help us
better connect with our feelings during consciousness.
Our emotions seem just as real in the realm of
dreaming; these emotions can be analyzed and applied to
our waking advantage. Fear of loss as I experienced in
my recurring nightmare attuned me to the importance of
my family; perhaps I could transform the negative
emotions of fear, death, and loneliness into positive
actions, like expressions of love, savoring of life,
and pleasure in companionship.

These negative emotions in dreams may serve a
preventive purpose: if I change my waking behavior to a
productive purpose, perhaps I can avoid future regrets
and unnecessary pain. An unpleasant outcome in a dream
may cause us to rethink or to change our conscious
activity, serving as a "warning dream" (Faraday 172).
Dr. Dement relates an example of a time when he was a
heavy smoker; he had a dream in which he was diagnosed
with lung cancer and endured the mental and physical
agony of the ordeal. His incredibly vivid dream
deterred him from smoking again; he quit (Some 102).

This dream allowed Dr. Dement to experience
something he hadn't as yet, and would rather not
experience in the future. Many dreams share this
capacity of allowing us to experience something
forbidden, new, and perhaps exciting: a handicapped

woman may perhaps find herself walking in her dreams, a
man may find himself able to fly, a sweet-toothed child
may find him/herself in a candy land. Dreams in this
way allow us to experience things we have never before
experienced; like literature, they let us enter another
world, offering us a different perspective.

The similarity apparent between literature and
dreams as an entrance into a new world provides an
opportunity for writers to incorporate their dreams
into their waking creativity. The uninhibited mind
working in dreams is a creative process in itself; this
effortless creativity can and should be applied to
creativity on paper. As Professors Marjorie and Jon
Ford, authors of <u>Dreams and Inward Journeys</u>, suggest,
"the process of understanding dreams leads to many
insights and images that you may find useful in your
more formal writing" (38). A well-known example of the
use of dreams in literature is Robert Louis Stevenson's
<u>The Strange Case of Dr. Jekyll and Mr. Hyde</u>; Stevenson
claims to have been inspired by his dreams in
developing the plot of the novel (Robbins 74).

Not only can we derive themes and ideas from
dreams, but we may also experience a dream which
presents a work of creativity in a more finished form.
Two famous examples of this occurrence include Samuel
Taylor Coleridge's "Kubla Khan" and A. C. Benson's "The
Phoenix" (Dement, <u>Sleep</u> 310). Although not everyone

will have an incredible piece of writing, song, or other creative image revealed in a dream, these experiences certainly suggest the value of being attentive to the content of our dreams. Just as several literary masterpieces have been revealed in the dream world, scientific discoveries and other problem solving have also surfaced nocturnally. Apparently the illusory structure of the benzene ring was discovered in German scientist Friedrich August Kékulé's dreams (Dement, Some 97). Again, not all of us will discover something of this nature; however, Professor Dement, in an experiment on college students, found that "the possibility . . . of problem solving during sleep" exists (Sleep 313). This phenomenon of solutions occurring during dreaming is most probably related to an extreme conscious preoccupation with the problem (312). As discussed above, we have the tendency to dream about daily concerns; dreaming of a solution may be a result of this constant search for a resolution.

Having thus described many of the advantages of tapping into the dream world, knowing how to keep an effective dream journal is important. I have personally experienced the transitory characteristic of dreams; they are quickly lost. Ann Faraday in her book Dream Power, describes the process: "The dream swirls away from memory, first fragmenting and then completely evaporating" (62). Ensuring that I would record the

Chang 13

maximum number of dreams before they faded away, I
found that if I kept my dream journal with a pen,
within easy reach of my bed, I would save the time and
trouble, and eliminate the potential problem of not
wanting to get out of my warm bed. It would then be at
my ready disposal at all hours of the night, in case I
awoke with a dream before morning; dreams, as dream
researcher Henry Reed's participants were instructed,
should be recorded "immediately upon awakening, whether
in the middle of the night or in the morning" (Reed
35).

Above all, a dream diary should "develop as
complete a profile as (possible of) . . . conscious and
unconscious activity" (Mambert and Foster 212). Thus
each entry should include the date, a complete record
of the dream, any waking associations with the dream,
reactions and feelings the dream evoked, and a personal
interpretation (121-213). Also, a detailed description
of the setting in which the dream takes place should
not be overlooked; it could represent an aspect of what
the is dreamer feeling: a storm may signal inner
turmoil, enclosed areas may signify restrictions
(Faraday 133). To increase the amount of dream material
recalled, subjects in Reed's study reported the
advantage of "remaining still and relaxed, letting the
mind float, and rehearsing previously recalled dream
images" (42).

In my dream journal, waking associations perform an especially important function. Waking associations are defined in Sloane's <u>Psychoanalytic Understanding of the Dream</u> as "an actual part of one's previous experience, including actions, spoken words, thoughts, fantasies, and affects" (23). By including such waking associations, the dream journal becomes much like a regular journal. I readily welcomed this duality in function since I had found that upon arrival at college, I had had less time and opportunity to reflect and record my thoughts and emotions in my daily journal. The dream journal provided a chance for me to continue some form of a reflective process while integrating a new, important aspect I previously ignored: the dream world.

However, the dream journal's most important function by far is the insight and understanding gained after the recording of the dream. To gain this self-awareness, dream entries need to be evaluated, interpreted, and investigated; as Ann Faraday recommends, it is important to commence as soon as possible with the "work on the dream" (320).

How do we know what our dreams are telling us? True, many books have been published on the interpretation and symbolism within dreams. However, although many published theories of eminent psychoanalysts, such as Freud's <u>Interpretation of </u>

<u>Dreams</u>, are available, I believe the dreamer to be the
best judge of the significance of his/her dream. I
found it satisfying to be able to figure out my own
dreams, interpreting them in the context of my life, my
personality, my experiences, and through my
perspective. I didn't believe I would be comfortable or
convinced by a psychoanalyst's interpretation; somehow,
I don't think I would accept a stranger informing me of
what my dream meant, or insisting that every elongated
object was a phallic symbol. However, I do realize the
importance of professional help for people who are
extremely disturbed or who may be extremely out of
touch with themselves and, thus, unable to read into
their dreams. For the most part, though, the majority
of individuals have the capacity to translate their own
dreams, gaining a more complete picture of themselves.
The satisfaction of knowing oneself, keen to inner
workings, should be ample motivation for anyone to keep
a dream journal.

Works Cited

Dement, William C. <u>Sleep and Dreams: A Course Reader</u>.

    Stanford, CA: Stanford Bookstore, 1992.

_____.<u>Some Must Watch While Some Must Sleep</u>. Stanford,

    CA: Stanford Alumni Association, 1972.

Faraday, Ann. <u>Dream Power</u>. London: Hodder and

    Stoughton, 1972.

Ford, Marjorie, and Jon Ford. <u>Dreams and Inward

    Journeys</u>. New York: HarperCollins, 1990.

Mambert, W. A., and B. Frank Foster. <u>A Trip into Your

    Unconscious</u>. Washington DC: Acropolis Books, 1973.

Mattoon, Mary Ann. <u>Understanding Dreams</u>. Dallas: Spring

    Publications, 1984.

Reed, Henry. "Learning to Remember Dreams." <u>Journal of

    Humanistic Psychology</u> 13.3 (1973): 33-48.

Robbins, Paul R. <u>The Psychology of Dreams</u>. London:

    McFarland, 1988.

Sloane, Paul. <u>Psychoanalytic Understanding of the

    Dream</u>. New York: Jason Aronson, 1979.

Ullman, Montague, and Nan Zimmerman. <u>Working with

    Dreams</u>. London: Hutchinson, 1979.

NOTES
ON AUTHORS

Achebe, Chinua (1930–) Considered to be the finest Nigerian novelist, Chinua Achebe has spent his life weaving together his Ibo culture and his English education. His novels, *Things Fall Apart* (1958), *Arrow of God* (1964), and *Anthills of the Savannah* (1988), cover Nigerian history from the first colonial encounters through the independence era of the 1960s. Achebe embraces the idea fundamental to the African oral tradition that "art is, and always was, at the service of man. Our ancestors created their myths and legends and told their stories for a human purpose. . . . [A]ny good story, any good novel, should have a message, should have a purpose."

Alegría, Claribel (1924–) Although a native of Nicaragua, Claribel Alegría spent her childhood in exile in El Salvador. Alegría returned to Nicaragua when the Somoza dictatorship was overthrown in 1979. A poet, novelist, and essayist whose first collection appeared in 1948, Alegría was introduced to North American readers in the bilingual collections *Flowers from the Volcano* (1982) and *Woman of he River* (1989). Carolyn Forché, who translated the earlier collection, writes of Alegría: "In her poems, we listen to the stark cry of the human spirit."

Allende, Isabel (1942–) Chilean writer Isabel Allende was born in Lima, Peru, and has lived for a number of years in California. As the niece of Chilean President Salvador Allende, her life changed radically when he was assassinated in 1973. Isabel Allende had been a noted journalist in Chile, but she was forced into exile. A letter from her grandfather inspired her to turn to fiction: "My grandfather thought people died only when you forgot them. I wanted to prove to him that I had forgotten nothing, that his spirit was going to live with us forever." Allende's memories formed the kernel of her first novel, *The House of the Spirits* (1985). Her recent books include *Of Love and Shadows* (1987), *Eva Luna* (1988), *The Stories of Eva Luna* (1991), and *Infinite Plan* (1993).

Andersen, Hans Christian (1805–1867) Danish author Hans Christian Andersen began his life in a small provincial town, with a shoemaker father and an almost illiterate mother. Andersen was fascinated with the theater, and soon moved to Copenhagen to act. His acting aspirations were unsuccessful, but Andersen impressed several people with his writing, and they supported further schooling for him. Andersen found fame in 1835 with the publication of his novel *The Improvisatore* and the first of his many fairy tales for children. The rest of his life was spent in writing, traveling, and associating with artists and the aristocracy.

Angelou, Maya (1928–) Maya Angelou grew up in the tiny town of Stamps, Arkansas, and spent time in St. Louis, San Francisco, and Los Angeles as a young woman. Angelou is best known for her autobiographical writing, especially *I Know Why the Caged Bird Sings* (1970); she also writes poetry and plays and has worked as a stage and screen performer and singer. In addition, Angelou has lectured all over the world and been active in the civil rights movement. Her autobiographical work, *All God's Children Need Traveling Shoes* (1986), describes her four-year stay in Ghana just as that African nation had won its independence. Her collection of essays *Wouldn't Take Nothing For My Journey* (1993) made the best sellers list upon its publication.

Atwood, Margaret (1939–) Born in Ottawa, Canada, Margaret Atwood received her B.A. at the University of Toronto and an M.A. from Radcliffe. She is the author of more than fifteen books of poetry, beginning with *Double Persephone* (1961) and including *Procedures for Underground* (1970) and *True Stories* (1981). Atwood has also written many novels, including *Surfacing* (1972), *The Handmaid's Tale* (1985), and *The Robber Bride* (1993). Her poetry has been described as focusing on "the contrast between the flux of life or nature and the fixity of man's artificial creations." Often noted for her feminist concerns, Atwood remarks, "I began as a profoundly apolitical writer, but then I began to do what all novelists and some poets do: I began to describe the world around me."

Baca, Jimmy Santiago (1952–) Jimmy Santiago Baca taught himself to read while in prison; he now lives and writes in Albuquerque, New Mexico. Of Chicano and Apache descent, Baca was abandoned by his parents, spent some time in a New Mexico orphanage, and ended up living on the streets at an early age. Prison life transformed his perspective: "I saw all these Chicanos going out to the fields and being treated like animals. I wanted to learn how to read and to write and to understand. . . . Had I not found the language, I would have been a guerrilla in the mountains." Baca's first collection, *Immigrants in Our Own Land* (1979), was praised for its sweep of emotions in describing the persistence of humanity amidst the desolation of prison. *Meditations on the South Valley* (1987) and *Black Mesa Poems* (1989) are more recent collections. His essays are collected in *Working in the Dark* (1991).

Baldwin, James (1924–1987) From a large, struggling family in Harlem, James Baldwin read voraciously on his own, in the libraries of Harlem and other parts of New York City.

His stepfather was a strict minister, and Baldwin himself preached from age 14 to 17, an experience that was the basis of his first novel, *Go Tell It on the Mountain* (1953). Baldwin went on to become an important novelist, essayist, and civil rights activist. Some of his best known works include *Notes of a Native Son* (1955), *The Fire Next Time* (1963), *In Another Country* (1967), and *Evidence of Things Not Seen* (1985). Baldwin always saw art as something active, vital: "You write in order to change the world. . . . The world changes according to the way people see it, and if you alter, even by a millimeter, the way a person looks or people look at reality, then you can change it."

Bambara, Toni Cade (1939–)   Born in New York City, Toni Cade Bambara received a B.A. at Queens College and an M.A. at City College; she also studied in Florence, Paris, and at the Katherine Dunham Dance Studio. In addition to writing fiction, Bambara has taught writing and literature, worked as a community organizer, and developed documentaries detailing the African-American experience. Her writing includes the short story collection *Gorilla, My Love* (1972) and the novels *The Salt Eaters* (1980) and *If Blessing Comes* (1987). In all of them her voice is distinctive for its movement from metaphorical heights to street corner poetry. As author John Wideman notes, Bambara "emphasizes the necessity for black people to maintain their best traditions, to remain healthy and whole as they struggle for political power."

Barreca, Regina   Regina Barreca received her Ph.D. from New York University. She is a professor of English at the University of Connecticut, with a specialty in feminist theory and modern British literature. Barreca is co-editor of the journal *Lit: Literature Interpretation Theory.* She has written poetry and cultural criticism and has edited several anthologies of fiction and nonfiction, including *Sex and Death in Victorian Literature.* Her essays have appeared in *Ms.* magazine and in a variety of academic periodicals. She has also written a feminist analysis of women's humor, *They Used to Call Me Snow White* (1991). Her poetry has appeared in the *Minnesota Review* and in other journals.

Basso, Keith H. (1940–)   Born in Asheville, North Carolina, Keith H. Basso went to Harvard as an undergraduate and to Stanford for a Ph.D. in anthropology. He is currently a professor at the University of New Mexico. His scholarship has centered on the Apache, including his latest book *Western Apache Language and Culture: Essays in Linguistic Anthropology* (1990). In addition to his teaching and writing, Basso serves as a consultant to the White Mountain and San Carlos Apache tribes.

Beattie, Ann (1947–)   A native of Washington, D.C., Ann Beattie received a B.A. at American University and an M.A. from the University of Connecticut. She has been a visiting writer and lecturer at a number of universities, and now resides in Charlottesville, Virginia. An author of short stories and novels, Beattie brought out her first collection, *Distortions,* in 1976. Her collection *Where You'll Find Me* (1986) found a national audience for her "almost hallucinatory particularity of detail." As Beattie puts it, "My stories are a lot about chaos." Some of her better known short story collections include *Secrets and Surprises* and *Falling in Place.* Her most recent novels are *Picturing Will* (1989) and *What Was Mine* (1991).

Benedict, Ruth (1887–1948)   Ruth Benedict completed her undergraduate work at Vassar, married a biochemist, and then returned to school for a Ph.D. in anthropology under the direction of Franz Boas. She remained at Columbia and Barnard as a professor until her death, teaching, among others, Margaret Mead. Benedict is best known for *Patterns of Culture* (1934), which elaborates on her theory that cultures could be seen as "personality writ large." Her other works include *Race: Science and Politics* (1940) and *The Chrysanthe-*

mum and the Sword: Patterns of Japanese Culture (1946). Throughout her life, Benedict also wrote poetry, an accomplishment she kept secret from most of her colleagues in anthropology.

Berger, Suzanne E. (1944–)   Born and raised in Texas Suzanne E. Berger traveled to Northwestern for her undergraduate education and then on to Johns Hopkins and Northeastern for graduate work, finishing with a master's in education. While writing poetry, Berger also teaches English in the Boston area. Her work can be found in *These Rooms* (1979) and *Legacies* (1984). When looking for a subject, Berger remarks, "I like to explore the human spirit in conflict with itself and the world, and also its brief moments of harmony."

Bidart, Frank (1939–)   The poet Frank Bidart lives in Cambridge, Massachusetts, and teaches literature at Wellesley College. Bidart grew up in Bakersfield and Bishop, California. He has always enjoyed movies, popular culture, and the arts. In college Bidart changed his major to literature and began to write poetry. His collection *In the Western Night* (1990) brings together all his work since 1965. Bidart sees poetry as a very human activity: "The drive to conceptualize, to understand our lives, is as fundamental and inevitable as any other need. So a poem must include it, make it part of its 'action.'"

Birtha, Becky (1948–)   Becky Birtha, who lives in Philadelphia, is a African-American, lesbian writer who works in both poetry and prose. Her stories have been published in *For Nights Like This One: Stories of Loving Women* (1983) and *Lovers' Choice* (1987). Birtha's poems can be found in *The Forbidden Poems* (1991). Birtha is a writer with a talent for representing the difficult course of women's lives and relationships with insight and a warm, distinctive voice.

Blake, William (1757–1827)   William Blake—poet, painter, engraver, and a spiritual visionary—was a life-long eccentric thought by many people to be insane. Blake lived his entire life in London supporting himself through his work as an engraver. As a child, Blake once saw a tree full of angels, and he maintained the power of eidetic vision, a condition in which human perception projects physical images so powerfully that the projector cannot easily tell the difference between them and images of the natural world. Blake's *The Marriage of Heaven and Hell* (1790) is a daring experimental work in prose. His most famous lyrics can be found in *Songs of Innocence and of Experience* (1794), where the reader is often presented with the same situation from varying points of view, a technique tied to Blake's motto: "Truth is always in the extremes—keep them."

Bogan, Louise (1897–1970)   Although born in Maine, poet, critic, and editor Louise Bogan spent most of her career in New York City working as poetry editor for the *New Yorker.* Her career as a published poet stretches from 1923 through 1968, and her poems are collected in *The Blue Estuaries* (1968). Bogan was also an accomplished critic and translator. Influenced by the English metaphysical poets, Bogan uses complex meters and imagery. Bogan's poetry maintains a personal quality through the economical use of an immediate and contemporary language.

Böll, Heinrich (1917–1985)   The 1972 Nobel Prize winner in literature, Heinrich Böll was born in Cologne, Germany, and has been praised for his part in the post–World War II rebirth of German literature. After reluctantly serving in the German army during the war, Böll began a career as a writer, publishing novels, stories, plays, poetry, and nonfiction while also working as a translator. Böll strives for simplicity, often taking on a satirical voice, as in his highly acclaimed novel *Group Portrait with Lady* (1971). For Böll, there is always a moral imperative, a conscience, in his writing, and his work clearly expresses his social ideal of a utopian Christian Marxism.

Bowen, Elizabeth (1899–1973)   The Irish writer Elizabeth Bowen was born in Dublin, worked in a hospital in Ireland during World War I, and saw action in the Second World War in the British Ministry of Information. Bowen's long career began with the novel *The Hotel* (1927) and ended with *Eva Trout; or, Changing Scenes* (1968). Her stories have been collected in several volumes; Bowen has also published a variety of nonfiction. Bowen's fiction is often labeled psychological realism, an aim that Bowen explains as follows: "Characters pre-exist. They are found. They reveal themselves slowly to the novelist's perception as might fellow-travellers seated opposite one in a very dimly-lit railway carriage."

Brooks, Gwendolyn (1917–)   Gwendolyn Brooks, a lifelong Chicagoan, began writing at age seven and was first published at thirteen. She went on to Wilson Junior College, jobs, marriage, and early publishing. She was the first African American to win the Pulitzer Prize for poetry, for *Annie Allen* (1949). Her collections include *The Bean Eaters* (1960), *In the Mecca* (1968), and recently, *Blacks* (1987). Reflecting on her career, Brooks remarked, "poets who happen also to be Negroes are twice tried," for they must both "write poetry and remember that they are Negroes."

Browning, Robert (1812–1889)   Brought up in London, Robert Browning received most of his education in his father's large and eclectic library. In the 1830s and early 1840s Browning published poems and wrote plays. After eloping with the well-known poet Elizabeth Barrett to Italy, where they lived until her death, he published his successful collection *Men and Women* (1855). This was followed by *Dramatis Personae* (1864) and *The Ring and the Book* (1868–69). His most popular poems were written as dramatic monologues by invented characters, confronting issues of history, art, philosophy, and religion.

Bullins, Ed (1935–)   Born in a Philadelphia ghetto, Ed Bullins was a gang member as a teenager. During the late 1960s Bullins cofounded a number of important West Coast black arts organizations and was involved with the influential New Lafayette Theater, a community-based playhouse in New York. Now living on the West Coast, Bullins works as an instructor in dramatic performance, play directing, and playwriting. He has published more than fifty dramatic works. In all his work, Bullins has helped shape a revolutionary "theater of black experience." But as one critic writes of pieces like *Clara's Ole Man* and *In the Wine Time,* "Individuals are locked together by need, trapped by their own material and biological necessities. Race is only one, and perhaps not even the dominant, reality."

Cardiff, Gladys (1942–)   Gladys Cardiff was born in Browning, Montana, and is part Cherokee. She studied at the University of Washington and has continued to reside in the state, writing and teaching poetry. Her poems have appeared in such publications as *Inscape, Northwest Review,* and *Puget Soundings,* as well as in anthologies such as *Carriers of the Dream Wheel* and *From the Belly of the Shark.* Her collection *To Frighten a Storm* came out in 1976. The close relationship with nature that is part of Native American culture is a dominant theme in much of Cardiff's poetry.

Cervantes, Lorna Dee (1954–)   A native of northern California with Chicano roots, Lorna Dee Cervantes received a B.A. at San Jose State and has also studied at the University of California, Santa Cruz. Her first book of poems, *Emplumada,* came out in 1981. Cervantes has also founded her own press and poetry magazine, *Mango.* Her poems often depict male-female and class struggles.

Clifton, Lucille (1936–)   Lucille Clifton grew up in Depew, New York, attended Howard University, and for a number of years, devoted herself to raising her six children. Most recently, she has been a professor of literature and creative writing at the University of California, Santa Cruz. In addition to several collections of poems, including *Good Times* (1969), *Two Headed Woman* (1980), and *Quilting* (1991), Clifton has written a memoir, *Generations* (1976) and many children's books. Speaking of her own work, Clifton says, "I am a woman and I write from that experience. I am a Black Woman and I write from that experience. I do not feel inhibited or bound by what I am."

Cofer, Judith Ortiz (1952–)   The daughter of a teenage mother and a career navy father, Judith Ortiz Cofer spent her childhood traveling between the United States and her native Puerto Rico reading books and listening to her grandmother's stories. She married in college, had a daughter, did graduate work in English at Oxford, and now resides in Florida where she teaches and writes poetry that traces the experience of those who live in more than one culture. Her collections include *Reaching for the Mainland* (1987) and *Terms of Survival* (1988). She has also written a novel, *The Line of the Sun* (1989), and a memoir, *Silent Dancing* (1990).

Crane, Stephen (1871–1900)   The son of a Methodist minister, Stephen Crane rejected religious and social traditions. Crane spent most of his childhood in Asbury Park, New Jersey, and attended Syracuse University for a time. He turned to journalism and lived for a while in New York City. Observing and living the grim life of the poor, urban immigrants, Crane wrote *Maggie, A Girl of the Streets* (1893). His most famous work, *The Red Badge of Courage* (1895), became widely successful. Whether in his fiction, poetry, or reportage, Crane's characteristic focus was the physical, emotional, and intellectual responses of humans under extreme pressure. He persistently explored the powerful role of nature and environment in shaping character and determining lives.

Cummings, E.E. (1894–1962)   From a distinguished New England intellectual family, E. E. Cummings spent much of his life trying to shock his readers. After studying both painting and poetry at Harvard, Cummings served as an ambulance driver in France during World War I, where he was put into a prison camp, an experience that he wrote about in *The Enormous Room* (1920). Upon returning to the United States, Cummings moved to Greenwich Village, in New York City, where he experimented with the visual appearance of the poems he was beginning to produce. His *Complete Poems (1910–1962)* appeared in 1982. Although his poetry often met with hostile criticism, Cummings's inventive language and technical skill have influenced and inspired many contemporary poets.

Day, Richard Cortez (1927–)   Richard Cortez Day is a college instructor of English at Humboldt State University in California and the author of one collection of short stories, *When in Florence* (1986). The stories in this collection are carefully wrought and dignified, mostly told from the point of view of an American who resides in Italy.

De Jesus, Carolina Maria (1913–?)   The Afro-Brazilian memoirist Carolina Maria de Jesus grew up poor in rural Minas Gerais. She migrated to Sao Paulo and ended up a desperate single mother living in a shantytown. De Jesus began to write in notebooks found in the trash, writing "anything and everything, for when I was writing I was in a golden palace, with crystal windows and silver chandeliers. . . . Then I put away my book and the smells came in through the rotting walls and rats ran over my feet." In 1958, a reporter discovered her writing, and de Jesus's edited diaries became the sensation of Brazil, telling an unacknowledged story of humanity amidst desperate poverty and hunger.

Dickey, James (1923–)   A native of Atlanta, James Dickey served in World War II and then attended Vanderbilt University. After beginning a teaching career in 1960, he became a full-time poet, although he has also taught at several universities. All of Dickey's work can be found in *The Whole Motion: Collected Poems, 1945–1992*. He is the author of the best-selling novel *Deliverance* (1970). In his poetry Dickey assumes an attitude of the beholder, "one who enters into objects and people and places with the sense of these things entering into him." Dickey believes that poetry is "the highest medium that mankind has ever come up with. It's language itself, which is a miraculous medium which makes everything else that man has ever done possible."

Dickinson, Emily (1830–1886)   Emily Dickinson lived her entire life in her parents' home in Amherst, Massachusetts. Although Dickinson attended nearby Amherst Academy, she was largely self-educated. Her lawyer father bought her many books and worried over their effect on his sensitive daughter. Dickinson focused her energies on a few intense friendships, her family, her household obligations, and her private poetry. She is the author of more than fifteen hundred poems, although only seven appeared in print during her lifetime and all anonymously. Yet her influence on writers and readers of the present century has been enormous.

Dillard, Annie (1945–)   Annie Dillard grew up in an affluent family in Pittsburgh, Pennsylvania, before going to Hollins College. Her parents encouraged her to be a free spirit and intellectually adventurous. Her writing reveals her knowledge of literature, art, philosophy, theology, natural science, history, and even quantum physics. Dillard is best known for her Pulitzer Prize–winning work of nonfiction, *Pilgrim at Tinker Creek* (1974), which suggests how an understanding of the divine can be sought through the study of the natural world. Dillard has also published poetry, literary criticism, a memoir, and a recent novel, *The Living* (1992).

Divakaruni, Chitra (1956–)   Originally from Calcutta, India, Chitra Divakaruni immigrated to the United States and earned a Ph.D. in English at the University of California at Berkeley. Divakaruni lives in the San Francisco Bay area and teaches creative writing at Foothill College. Her poetry has been collected in *Dark Like the River* (1987), *The Reason for Nasturtiums* (1990), and *Black Candle: Poems about Women from India, Pakistan, and Bangladesh* (1991). Quite often, Divakaruni's poems explore the inner worlds, the everyday acts, and historical exploitation of women of India.

Donne, John (1572–1631)   Born in the city of London into a devout Catholic family, John Donne renounced his Catholic faith as a young man. After becoming secretary to Sir Thomas Egerton, Lord Keeper of the Great Seal, and being elected a member of Parliament, Donne's civil career ceased when he secretly married Ann More, Lady Egerton's niece. In 1615, Donne became an Anglican priest, eventually gaining recognition as an excellent preacher and poet. In his poetry, usually labeled metaphysical, Donne is known for his unique blend of thought and passion, wit, seriousness, and a willful obscurity. The critic Mario Praz has said about Donne's style that it will always appeal to readers "whom the rhythm of thought itself attracts."

Dorris, Michael (1945–)   A member of the Modoc tribe from Washington State, Michael Dorris now makes his home in New Hampshire. He is a professor of anthropology and Native American studies at Dartmouth, and is married to the Native American writer Louise Erdrich. Dorris's works include a nonfiction memoir about his adopted son's struggle with fetal alcohol syndrome, *The Broken Cord* (1989), a novel *A Yellow Raft in Blue Water* (1987), and *The Crown of Columbus* (1991), a book he wrote with Erdrich.

Early, Gerald (1952–)   The son of a baker and a preschool teacher, the writer and scholar Gerald Early grew up in Philadelphia, attended the University of Pennsylvania, and then received his Ph.D. in English at Cornell. Since 1982, Early has been a professor of English and African and Afro-American studies at Washington University in St. Louis. His essays on American culture have appeared in a number of periodicals as well as the collections *Tuxedo Junction: Essays on American Culture* (1990) and *The Culture of Bruising: Essays on Literature, Prizefighting, and Modern American Culture* (1991). Early has also contributed his poetry to a number of reviews.

Ehrlich, Gretel (1946–)   Gretel Ehrlich was born and raised in California but moved to Wyoming in 1976. *The Solace of Open Spaces* (1985) recounts her experience of moving there permanently after the death of her fiancé. It describes in moving and careful detail human life in a place dominated by harsh nature. Her novel *Heart Mountain* (1988) focuses on the Japanese internment camp at Heart Mountain, Wyoming. Some of the same characters appear in the short story collection *Drinking Dry Clouds: Wyoming Stories* (1991). In all her writing, Ehrlich attempts to live up to a stark natural vision: "The truest art I would strive for in any work would be to give the page the same qualities as earth: weather would land on it harshly; light would elucidate the most difficult truths; wind would sweep away obtuse padding."

Eiseley, Loren (1907–1977)   A native of Nebraska, Loren Eiseley spent most of his life as a professor of anthropology and history of science at the University of Pennsylvania. He is known for his powerful prose writing on scientific topics for the general public. His works include *Firmament of Time* (1960), *The Night Country* (1971), and *The Star Thrower* (1978). He also published several volumes of poetry. A blend of anthropology, archaeology, natural history, and the history of science, Eiseley's work is written in a dramatic poetic prose. Eiseley often pondered the relationship between human awareness and nature: "No longer, as with the animal, can the world be accepted as given. It has to be perceived and consciously thought about, abstracted, and considered. The moment one does so, one is outside of the natural; objects are each one surrounded with an aura radiating meaning to man alone."

Eliot, George (1819–1880)   The youngest child of a farmer's daughter and an agent for the estate of a large landowner, Marian Evans, later to assume the pen name George Eliot, grew up in the Midlands of England in a provincial and deeply religious household. Although she moved to London at age 32, she always returned to the provinces in her novels, working over the material of her memory with her imagination. Her first novel, *Adam Bede,* appeared in 1859 with considerable success. Other important novels include *Silas Marner* (1861) and *Middlemarch* (1872), which is considered her finest work. Henry James speaks highly of her "extensive human sympathy . . . from which a novelist draws . . . inspiration." Moral concern for her characters is the essence of George Eliot's fiction.

Emerson, Ralph Waldo (1803–1882)   Preacher, poet, orator, and essayist, Ralph Waldo Emerson has often been called the father of American literature. Born in Boston, Emerson attended Harvard on scholarship and was an ordained Unitarian minister. After doubt about his role as spiritual leader led him to leave the church, Emerson moved to rural Concord and dedicated himself to writing. His thought-provoking essays "Nature" (1836) and "Self-Reliance" (1841) influenced the young writers of his day and continue to inspire new generations of readers. Emerson advocated "creative reading as well as creative writing. . . . No facts are to me sacred; none are profane; I simply experiment, an endless seeker, with no Past at my back."

Endo, Russell (1953–)   Russell Endo is a Japanese-American poet who currently resides in Philadelphia. His parents were interned in relocation camps during World War II, and his writing reflects on the cultural differences that exist between different generations in Japanese-American families. Endo is particularly concerned in his writing with the merging of the Asian cultural tradition with the American poetic tradition. His poetry has appeared in the *American Poetry Review,* the *Philadelphia Inquirer,* and in other literary magazines.

Erdrich, Louise (1954–)   Louise Erdrich grew up in Little Falls, Minnesota, where her parents worked for the Bureau of Indian Affairs. She is a member of the Turtle Mountain Chippewa tribe of North Dakota. After graduating from Dartmouth College and Johns Hopkins, Erdrich edited *The Circle,* a newspaper published by the Boston Indian Council. Erdrich works in both poetry and prose and gained considerable attention with her first novel, *Love Medicine* (1984), which details the relations among three Chippewa families on a North Dakota reservation in a series of separate narratives spanning a period of fifty years from 1934 to 1984. Her published works include the poetry collections *Jacklight* (1984) and *Baptism of Desire* (1989), as well as the novels *Beet Queen* (1986), *Tracks* (1989), and *The Bingo Palace* (1994).

Espada, Martin (1957–)   The Puerto Rican poet Martin Espada was born in Brooklyn and currently resides in Boston, where he works as a tenant lawyer. His writing reflects his diverse work and life experiences. *The Immigrant Iceboy's Bolero* (1986) and *Rebellion Is the Circle of a Lover's Hands* (1990) are two of Espada's collections. Commenting on Espada's selection for the PEN/Revson Fellowship, the jury wrote, "He brings to American poetry an imagination and a sense of history which it has not previously known. . . . The greatness of Espada's art . . . is that it gives dignity to the insulted and the injured of the earth."

Forster, E. M. (1879–1970)   The British novelist E. M. Forster grew up comfortably in a country household dominated by women. After attending Cambridge and a period of travel in Europe, Forster began to write novels that satirize the attitudes of English tourists abroad. More novels followed, including *A Room with a View* (1908) and *Howards End* (1910). Forster published his last novel, *A Passage to India,* in 1924 and devoted the remainder of his life to a wide range of literary activities, focusing especially on the fight against censorship. On the temper of the modern author, Forster once wrote: "Separation—that is the end that really satisfies him—not simply the separation that comes through death, but the more tragic separation of people who part before they need, or who part because they have seen each other too closely."

Frank, Anne (1929–1945)   Anne Frank was born in the German city of Frankfurt, but her family fled to Amsterdam in 1933 to avoid the Nazi persecution of the Jews. In 1942, with Holland under German occupation, the Franks went into hiding. It is during this period that Frank wrote her famous *The Diary of a Young Girl.* In 1944 the family was discovered in their secret annex and sent to Auschwitz. Soon separated, Anne Frank, her mother, and her sister died in concentration camps. Only her father and her own testimony through the diary survived the war.

Frost, Robert (1875–1963)   Best known as a New England farmer poet, Robert Frost was born in San Francisco and raised in the mill town of Lawrence, Massachusetts. Moving in and out of university, odd jobs, and teaching, Frost knew that he was to be a poet. He lived for a number of years with his family on a farm in New Hampshire, spent some time in England, and found success upon the publication of his second book of poems, *North of Boston* (1914). Frost became the best known of modern American poets, winning four Pulitzer Prizes and reading at John F. Kennedy's inauguration. For Frost, a poem "runs a course of lucky events, and ends in a clarification of life not necessarily a great clarification such as sects and culture are founded on, but in a momentary stay against confusion."

Fuentes, Carlos (1928–   )   A member of a Mexican diplomatic family, Fuentes also has served as a diplomat, but his primary occupation has been that of writer. Fuentes sees a thematic unity in his works: "In a sense my novels are one book with many chapters: *Where the Air Is Clear* (1960) is the biography of Mexico City; *The Death of Artemio Cruz* (1964) deals with an individual in that city; *A Change of Skin* (1968) is that city, that society, facing the world, coming to grips with the fact that it is part of civilization and that there is a world outside that intrudes into Mexico." Fuentes remarks that he writes "to create readers rather than to give something that readers are expecting."

Gallagher, Tess (1943–   )   The daughter of loggers, Tess Gallagher grew up in Port Angeles, Washington. She graduated from the University of Washington, went to the University of Iowa for an M.F.A, and has taught creative writing at a number of universities. Gallagher's first collection of poems was *Stepping Outside* (1974); her best known collection is *Under Stars* (1978), and she has recently written the volumes *Valentine Elegy* (1992) and *Moon Crossing Bridge* (1992). She also writes essays and short stories. In discussing her poetry, Gallagher notes, "My main obsession . . . has been with how memory works or doesn't work in the creating of what matters in our lives."

Geok-lin Lim, Shirley (1944–   )   Originally from Malaysia and currently residing in the United States, Shirley Geok-lin Lim is a widely published poet, critic, and teacher. Her first book of poetry, *Crossing the Peninsula,* won the Commonwealth Poetry Prize in 1980, and she also has published a book of poetry entitled *Modern Secrets, New and Selected Poems,* as well as other books of poetry and short stories. Her criticism has appeared in *Asia* and *Contact II.* She has edited anthologies of Asian-American poetry *(The Forbidden Stitch)* and world literature *(One World of Literature).* Her poetry and stories examine the experiences of Chinese Malaysians, both in Malaysia and as immigrants.

Gilman, Charlotte Perkins (1860–1935)   Born in Hartford, Connecticut, Gilman had a difficult childhood and a disastrous marriage. She was best known during her lifetime for her sociological studies, especially *Woman and Economics* (1898), a comprehensive analysis of women's past and present position in society and of the reasons for their subordination. Gilman concludes that women's economic dependency on men stunts not only the growth of women but of the human species as well. Gilman also wrote three utopian novels, the most famous being *Herland* (1915). Although considered the leading intellectual in the women's movement from the 1890s to 1920, Gilman's work was soon forgotten, only to be rediscovered in the 1970s by a new generation of feminist readers.

Ginsberg, Allen (1926–   )   After growing up in the New York area and graduating from Columbia University, Allen Ginsberg wrote poetry and worked a number of jobs, including merchant marine, night porter, and market research consultant. When "Howl" was published in 1956 and subsequently became the center of a trial for obscenity, Ginsberg became a spokesperson for the Beat generation, challenging social and poetic conformity all over the world. Well known for his political activities and his interest in the visionary, Ginsberg has consistently tied poetry to spiritual concerns: "Writing poetry is a form of discovering who I am, and getting beyond who I am to free awakeness of consciousness, to a self that isn't who I am."

Giovanni, Nikki (1943–)   Known for her poetry, essays, and autobiographical writings, Nikki Giovanni is a popular reader and lecturer who currently teaches at Virginia Polytechnic Institute. She has won a Ford Foundation grant and has received awards from the National Endowment for the Arts and the Harlem Cultural Council. Her first book, *Black Feeling, Black Talk,* appeared in 1968; she has since written a number of volumes of poetry, a memoir, *Gemini* (1971), and a collection of essays, *Sacred Cows* (1988). Giovanni's poetry is characterized by its conversational tone and her use of African-American dialect and jazz rhythms.

Graham, Jorie (1951–)   The poet Jorie Graham was born in New York City, but grew up in the south of France and in different parts of Italy. After being involved in the Paris student uprisings of 1968, Graham returned to the United States. Since 1983 she has been a professor and workshop instructor at the University of Iowa. The aesthetic and metaphysical concerns that Graham expresses in her poetry show the influence of her parents, a painter and a theological scholar. Her collections include *Hybrids of Plants and Ghosts* (1980), *The End of Beauty* (1987), and *Region of Unlikeness* (1991). Graham sees writing as a way to "clean the language of its current lies, to make it capable of connecting us to the world."

Guevara, Che (1928–1967)   Ernesto Guevara Serna, later to be known as "Che," was educated as a doctor of medicine and surgery in his native Buenos Aires. He became known as a courageous revolutionary military leader and eventually led the first rebel force against Batista into Havana. From 1959 through 1965, Guevara held a number of government posts in Cuba. He then became commander in chief of a guerrilla organization in Bolivia, where he was executed by the Bolivian army in 1967. This ill-fated expedition was part of his plan to ignite revolution throughout the Third World. Guevara published a number of nonfictional texts during his lifetime, including the widely known training manual *Guerrilla Warfare* (1961). *The Diary of Che Guevara* was published posthumously.

Hamilton, Cynthia   Cynthia Hamilton earned a B.A. at Stanford and a Ph.D. at Boston University. Currently she is a professor in the Pan American Studies Department at California State University, Los Angeles. A political activist as well as a scholar, Hamilton fought against the construction of a solid waste incinerator in Los Angeles. This struggle is the topic of her essay, "Women, Home and Community," that is anthologized in *Reweaving the World: The Emergence of Ecofeminism* (1990).

Hampl, Patricia (1946–)   A native of Minnesota, from a family that has its roots in Prague, Czechoslavakia, Patricia Hampl earned her B.A. in English from the University of Minnesota in 1968 and her M.F.A. from the University of Iowa in 1970. She has taught English at the University of Minnesota since 1984. Hampl writes both poetry and autobiography. Her first published memoir was *A Romantic Education* (1981); recently, she has published an account of her quest for religious understanding, *Virgin Time* (1992). In 1992 Patricia Hampl was awarded the prestigious MacArthur Award for creative achievement.

Hardy, Thomas (1840–1928)   Regarded as both a major late Victorian novelist and a major twentieth-century poet, Thomas Hardy was born in a modest cottage in the county of Dorset, far from modern civilization. His father was a builder, as was his grandfather, and this influenced Hardy's early career in architecture, a profession he worked at for sixteen years while submitting poems unsuccessfully to magazines. Hardy turned to fiction and saw his fame grow as he published such novels as *Return of the Native* (1878), *Tess of the D'Urbervilles* (1891), and *Jude the Obscure* (1895). For the last thirty years of his life,

Hardy wrote only poetry. Over the course of his life, Hardy wrote nearly one thousand lyric poems, as he put it, in order "to record impressions, not convictions."

Harjo, Joy (1951–) Born in Oklahoma, the daughter of a Creek father and a Chero-kee-French mother, Joy Harjo has always been proud of her Native American heritage. After finishing her education at the University of New Mexico and the University of Iowa, she taught at colleges throughout the Southwest. A talented artist-poet, screen writer, essayist, and saxophonist, Harjo has also served as a consultant for the Native American Public Broadcasting Consortium and the National Endowment for the Arts. *Secrets from the Center of the World* (1989) and *In Mad Love and War* (1990) are her most recent poetry collections. As a teacher and a writer, Harjo emphasizes the connections between oral and written culture, between art and the world: "Words are not just words but sounds, which are voices, which are connected, growing to others. The world is not static but shifts, changes."

Harper, Michael (1938–) Born in Brooklyn and educated in Los Angeles, the poet Michael S. Harper worked at the post office to put himself through school. Harper lives in Providence, Rhode Island, where he teaches at Brown University. His collections include *Dear John, Dear Coltrane* (1970), *Images of Kin* (1977), and *Healing Song for the Inner Ear* (1985). He has also co-edited an African-American anthology, *Chant of Saints* (1979). Harper notes particularly the effect travel has had on his work: "My travels made me look closely at the wealth of human materials in my own life, its ethnic richness, complexity of language and stylization."

Harrison, Jim (1937–) From a farming family in northern Michigan, Jim Harrison studied comparative literature at Michigan State and now lives on a farm in Michigan, writing novels, poetry, and screenplays. His first poetry collection was *Plain Song* (1965). His collection of novellas *Legends of the Fall* (1979) found a larger public. His latest novel is *The Woman Lit by Fireflies* (1990). Commenting on his own work, Harrison notes, "My sympathies run hotly to the impure, the inclusive, as the realm of poetry. A poet, at best, speaks in the out loud speech of his tribe, deals in essences whether political, social, or personal."

Hashimoto, Sharon (1953–) From a Japanese-American family with roots in Hawaii, Sharon Hashimoto resides in Seattle, where she was born, and educated at the University of Washington (M.A. in creative writing). She currently teaches literature and writing at Highline Community College. Hashimoto has published extensively in journals such as *Ironwood, The American Scholar,* and *Poetry; The Crane Wife* is a recent collection of her poems. Hashimoto's poetry stresses themes of family and heritage.

Hawthorne, Nathaniel (1804–1864) Since the publication of *The Scarlet Letter* in 1850, Nathaniel Hawthorne has been recognized as one of America's most important writers. Born in Salem, Massachusetts, he was the descendant of Puritan immigrants and the son of a ship's captain. After studying at Bowdoin College, Hawthorne dedicated himself to becoming a writer. He spent a number of years scraping by through the occasional position here or there and the sale of his tales to magazines. His *Twice-Told Tales* (1837) were widely praised, as were the stories in *Mosses from an Old Manse* (1846). Hawthorne's carefully wrought fiction centers on issues of the weight of the Puritan past, guilt, and morality. His characters are never simply good or bad but complex and engaged in intense inner struggles.

Heaney, Seamus (1939–) Born into a farming family in Northern Ireland, Heaney received his B.A. at Queen's University of Belfast. Since then, he has been a poet and an

English professor. His first collection, *Death of a Naturalist,* came out in 1966. His more recent books include *Station Island* (1984) and *The Haw Lantern* (1987). Heaney describes himself as one of a group of Catholics in Northern Ireland who "emerged from a hidden, a buried life and entered the realm of education." Speaking of his work, Heaney has said of the process, "The poem came, it came. I didn't go and fetch it. I prefer to think of myself as the host to the thing rather than a big game hunter."

Hemingway, Ernest (1899–1961)   Ernest Hemingway was born in Oak Park, Illinois, a suburb of Chicago. His mother was a music teacher and his father was a physician. Hemingway joined an ambulance corps during World War I, returned home, and then joined a group of expatriate artists in Paris, the so-called "lost generation." Writing for newspapers, Hemingway began to work on his fiction. His first novel, *The Sun Also Rises* (1926), brought him international recognition. When *For Whom the Bell Tolls* (1940) came out and Hemingway moved to Cuba, he was not just a well-known author but an international celebrity. *The Old Man and the Sea* (1952) won a Pulitzer Prize; Hemingway was awarded the Nobel Prize in 1954. On the value of creation, Hemingway remarked on literary invention as the making of "a whole new thing truer than any thing true and alive."

Henley, Beth (1952–   )   The daughter of an attorney and an actress, Beth Henley grew up in Mississippi and continues to represent that regional voice in her plays, even though she now resides in Los Angeles. Best known for her Pulitzer Prize–winning play, *Crimes of the Heart,* Henley first came to notice when her one-act play *Am I Blue* was produced while she was a student at Southern Methodist University. Typically, her work explores deep southern small-town life with a twist of black humor and a focus on women coping. Although she is interested in acting, Henley has continued writing, including her recent plays *Abundance* (1991) and *The Debutante Ball* (1991).

Hogan, Linda (1947–   )   A Chickasaw who grew up in Denver, Colorado, and attended the University of Colorado, Linda Hogan has worked as a dental assistant, waitress, homemaker, secretary, researcher, poet-in-schools, and since 1982, a professor, now at the University of Minnesota. Hogan's published writing includes the poetry collections *Calling Myself Home* (1979), *Seeing Through the Sun* (1985), and *Red Clay* (1991), which contains poems and stories, as well as the novel *Mean Spirit* (1990). Hogan has dedicated her writing to "gentle women" and their children, and her work looks to reconciliations for the survival of family, community, and the natural world with visions of Indian continuance and a strong sense of place.

Hongo, Garrett (1951–   )   Garrett Hongo is of Japanese descent but was born in Volcano, Hawaii, and spent most of his childhood in Los Angeles. After studying at Pomona College and the University of California, Irvine, Hongo founded the Asian Exclusion Act theater group in Seattle in 1975 and has since gone on to a career as an English professor at the University of Oregon. Hongo is the author of two collections of poetry, *Yellow Light* (1982) and *The River of Heaven* (1988), a prose memoir, *Volcano Journal,* (1995) and a collection of essays on Hawaii, *Letters from Paradise.* Hongo considers his art as "motivated by a search for origins of various kinds—quests for ethnic and familial roots, cultural identity, and poetic inspiration, all ultimately somehow connected with my need for an active imaginative and spiritual life."

hooks, bell (1952–   )   Gloria Watkins, who writes under the name bell hooks, teaches at Oberlin, writes poetry, and has produced a significant body of work about the history and theory of race and gender. These books include *Feminist Theory from Margin to Center* (1984), *Talking Back: Thinking Feminist, Thinking Black* (1989), and *Black Looks: Race and Representation* (1992). Her writing, whether in prose or poetry, uncovers lost parts of our history: hooks, for example, has not been afraid to discuss sexism in the black community and racism in the women's movement; she hopes to renew silenced voices. In dedicating *Ain't' I a Woman* to her mother, hooks wrote to Rosa Bell, "who told me when I was a child that she had once written poems—that I had inherited my love of reading and my longing to write from her."

Hopkins, Gerard Manley (1844–1889)   The English poet Gerard Manley Hopkins was raised in Stratford, Essex. Hopkins went to Oxford to become an Anglican minister. He became, instead, attracted to the Roman Catholic Church, so he converted and decided to become a Jesuit. His poetry was perceived to be too experimental and challenging for the general public, but it has significantly influenced poetry in the twentieth century. Ultimately, his poetic vision reconciles his life in the church with his solitary vision. As Hopkins believed, "All things are charged with God, and if we know how to touch them, give off sparks and take fire."

Howard, Jane (1935–   )   Jane Howard grew up in Springfield, Illinois, the daughter of a newspaperman and a housewife, and remained in the Midwest for her college studies at the University of Michigan. Most of Howard's adult life, however, has been spent working as a journalist for *Life* magazine, and she resides in New York City. Her books include *Please Touch: A Guided Tour of the Human Potential Movement* (1970), *Families* (1978), and *Margaret Mead: A Life* (1984). As one reviewer noted, Howard's talent is "a knack for bringing people out, [she] has a good reporter's eye for the details of their lives and an ear for what they say."

Howe, Marie (1950–   )   Marie Howe received her M.F.A. from Columbia University in 1983. In addition to writing, she has taught at Dartmouth, Tufts, and Warren Wilson College. Howe's poetry has been published in such magazines as *The Atlantic, The American Poetry Review,* and *The Partisan Review;* her first collection, *The Good Thief* (1988), appeared in the *National Poetry Series.* Novelist Margaret Atwood describes Howe's writing as "poems of obsession that transcend their own dark roots."

Hubbell, Sue (1935–   )   After a childhood in Michigan and working as a librarian on the East Coast, in 1973 Sue Hubbell moved to the Ozark Mountains in southern Missouri, where she earns a living as a beekeeper. Her widely acclaimed book of essays *A Country Year: Living the Questions* (1986) contains her reflections on that life. As Hubbell writes in describing her transition, "Wild things and wild places pull me more strongly than they did a few years ago, and domesticity, dusting and cookery interest me not at all."

Huggan, Isabel (1943–   )   A native of Kitchener, Ontario, Isabel Huggan has worked in publishing in Toronto, taught high school, and held positions as a reporter and photographer. Her first book, *The Elizabeth Stories,* came out in 1984. While maintaining that her main concern as a writer is to tell a good story, Huggan often examines the mother-daughter dynamic and the effect of middle-class values on the individual. As she describes it, "I am very interested in what repression has done to my generation of women, how we rebelled and grew."

Hughes, Ted (1930–   )   Born in England to a carpenter and a housewife, Ted Hughes went on to an education at Cambridge and gained a reputation as a poet of international stature from his first poetry collection. He has published more than 30 volumes of poetry, from *The Hawk in the Rain* (1957) to more recent collections like *Wolfwatching* (1989) and *Moortown Diary* (1989). Hughes was appointed Poet Laureate of England in 1984. His work also includes editing the writing of his wife, the poet Sylvia Plath, who committed suicide. Hughes's world is dominated by nature. As critic Thomas Nye comments, "He wanted to capture not just live animals, but the aliveness of animals in their natural state: their wildness, their quiddity, the fox-ness of the fox and the crow-ness of the crow."

Jewett, Sarah Orne (1849–1909) Descending from a prerevolutionary family involved in the shipping business, Sarah Orne Jewett grew up in the village of South Berwick, Maine. Her father was a physician, and she wished to follow that career, but her poor health made it impossible. Jewett began writing fiction upon graduating from Berwick Academy, dividing her time between Boston and the New England shore. Jewett's most important stories are included in *A White Heron and Other Stories* (1886) and *The Country of the Pointed Firs* (1896). She also published poetry and literature for children. Jewett is particularly skilled at rendering close friendships among women and an almost documentary record of landscape and dialect.

Jordan, June (1936–   ) A native of Harlem, June Jordan studied at Barnard and the University of Chicago and then returned to the New York area where she taught at several universities. She currently teaches at Berkeley. Jordan is a poet, novelist, essayist, dramatist, and writer of children's books. Her poetry collections include *Things That I Do in the Dark* (1977) and *Naming Our Destiny* (1989). *Technical Difficulties: African-American Notes on the State of the Union* (1992) is Jordan's most recent book of essays. In all of her writing, Jordan explores the black experience, combining the personal and the political.

Joyce, James (1882–1941) A native of Dublin who once considered entering the priesthood, James Joyce renounced both his religion and his native land when he moved to Trieste in 1904, later settling in Paris after World War I. *Dubliners* (1914), a collection of short stories, was greeted with enthusiasm. Joyce's autobiographical novel *Portrait of the Artist as a Young Man* (1914–1915) further enhanced his reputation, although he continued to struggle against poverty and increasing eye trouble. His monumental novel *Ulysses* was published in Paris in 1922. It took a landmark court decision against literary censorship before it could be published in America in 1933. Joyce's last novel, *Finnegans Wake* (1939), pushed his technique of stream of consciousness and his linguistic experiments to revolutionary extremes. Both novels have greatly influenced the development of twentieth-century fiction.

Jung, Carl Gustav (1875–1961) The Swiss psychiatrist Carl Gustav Jung is known as the most influential student of Sigmund Freud; Jung's theories of the human psyche have had an impact independent of his mentor. Jung began his studies at the University of Basel with the intention of entering medicine, but he was fascinated by mental phenomena, so he began to work with schizophrenic patients and to collaborate with Freud. Jung and Freud broke off their relationship in 1913 when Freud attacked Jung's *The Psychology of the Unconscious*. Among Jung's most important concepts is that of the collective unconscious which manifests itself through archetypes or common patterns of expression. As Jung explains, "The psyche is not of today; its ancestry goes back millions of years. Individual consciousness is only the flower and the fruit of the season, sprung from the perennial rhizome beneath the earth."

Keats, John (1795–1821) The British Romantic poet John Keats was born in London, the eldest son of a stable keeper. Apprenticed early to a surgeon, Keats abandoned medicine to write poetry. At age 24, in the midst of the critical failure of his first poems, his growing illness, and hopeless love for Fanny Brawne, Keats composed his famous odes. He died from tuberculosis in Rome at age 26. Commenting on the writing process, Keats once wrote, "I compare human life to a large Mansion of Many Apartments, two of which I can only describe, the doors of the rest being as yet shut upon me." Keats is remembered for his sonnets, the long narrative poems "The Eve of Saint Agnes" and "La

Belle Dame Sans Merci," and for his philosophical odes, including "Ode to a Grecian Urn" and "Ode to Melancholy."

King, Jr., Martin Luther (1929–1968) The son of a Baptist preacher and a teacher, Martin Luther King, Jr., grew up in Atlanta. After college, King assumed the pastorate of a church in Montgomery, Alabama. During demonstrations against segregation in Birmingham in 1962, King was jailed and wrote his famous protest letter. His "I Have a Dream" speech of 1963 influenced the passage of the Civil Rights Act of 1964, the year King received the Nobel Peace Prize. In the mid-1960s, he widened his attention from civil rights to economic rights. In 1968 King was assassinated while supporting striking garbage workers in Memphis. His collections of writings include *Stride Toward Freedom* and *Why We Can't Wait.* Believing in the possibility of collective action with nonviolence, King saw himself as "a drum major for justice, a drum major for peace, a drum major for righteousness."

Kingston, Maxine Hong (1940–) The child of Chinese immigrants, Maxine Hong Kingston grew up in Stockton, California, graduated from the University of California at Berkeley, and has taught both high school and college English. Her first book, *The Woman Warrior: Memoirs of a Girlhood Among Ghosts* (1976), won the National Book Critics Circle Award and was named one of the top ten nonfiction works of the 1970s. *China Men* (1980) and her most recent book, *Tripmaster Monkey* (1989), have also been much praised. In all of her work, Kingston forges a link between her present identity as an American and the China of her ancestral past, "[the] mythic China that influences some people's lives so strongly that they live for it or live by it."

Kollwitz, Käthe (1867–1945) The German artist Käthe Kollwitz was born in Konigsberg but spent most of her adult life living and working in Berlin. Kollwitz worked in a variety of media and is known especially for her very powerful prints and sculptures of the human figure. Although a very private person, Kollwitz was engaged with the public issues of the time, especially during the period between the wars. Having lost a son in World War I, she urged that the idealism and readiness for sacrifice of the young should be turned toward peaceful building and not war. Kollwitz was an early public critic of Nazism, although it meant losing her position and studio at the Academy of Arts in Berlin and her work being barred from public exhibitions.

Kumin, Maxine (1925–) Although born in Philadelphia, Maxine Kumin now resides on her farm in New Hampshire. Kumin's *Up Country: Poems of New England* won the 1973 Pulitzer Prize. Her most recent volume of poetry is *Looking for Luck* (1992). Kumin has also written many children's books, as well as a number of well-received novels. Kumin sees her roles in life as balanced between writing and motherhood, and her poetry sometimes serves as a kind of therapy for her. Her most discussed motifs refer back to the images and rhythms of New England rural life. She is also a very subtle observer of mother-daughter relations. Commenting on her craft, Kumin remarks, "I particularly observe things in nature because they interest me, but I don't think of it as observing. What I'm always after is to get the facts: to be true to the actuality."

Lauro, Shirley (1933–) From Des Moines, Iowa, and educated at Northwestern, the University of Wisconsin, and Columbia University, Shirley Lauro has spent her professional life in New York City. Lauro has worked as a film, television, and stage actress, as well as an instructor in speech and theater. She is best known for her plays. Her first published work was a novel, *The Edge* (1965), which she wrote because she had been discouraged from writing for the theater at that time. A number of award-winning plays have followed, including *The Contest* (1975); *The Coal Diamond* (1979), which explores the relationships of four women; and *Open Admissions* (1981), which takes a harsh look at discrimination and education.

Leavitt, David (1961–) The son of a professor, David Leavitt grew up in Pittsburgh and went on to study English at Yale University. After graduation, he went to New York to become a writer, and he spent some time working in publishing. *Family Dancing* (1984) is his first collection of short stories. This was followed by the novel *The Lost Language of Cranes* (1986), *A Place I've Never Been* (1990), and, most recently, *While England Sleeps* (1993). One reviewer noted that in many of his stories Leavitt "captures the deep rooted tensions between adult gays and their families and the efforts of childless gays to carve out families among their peers."

Lee, Li-Young (1957–) Li-Young Lee was born in Jakarta, Indonesia, of Chinese parents. In 1959, his father, after spending a year as a political prisoner, fled Indonesia with his family. They traveled in Hong Kong, Macau, and Japan, finally arriving in America in 1964. Currently residing in Chicago, Lee studied at several universities and has taught at Northwestern and the University of Iowa. Lee has been featured in Bill Moyers's *Voices of Memory* public television program and has published two collections of his work: *Rose* (1986) and *The City in Which I Love You* (1990). Gerald Stern feels that Lee's poetry is characterized by "a devotion to language, a belief in its holiness, a pursuit of certain Chinese ideas, or Chinese memories . . . and a moving personal search for redemption."

Le Guin, Ursula K. (1929–) The daughter of an anthropologist and a writer, Ursula Le Guin has combined these backgrounds in producing fictions about imaginary cultures. Known for her science fiction novels, Le Guin also writes juvenile books and poetry. *Always Coming Home* (1985) combines poetry and prose and includes stories, legends, autobiography, and a tape in depicting a people known as the Kesh who reside in northern California after a nuclear war. Le Guin's most recent novel is *Searoad: The Chronicles of Klatsand* (1991). Speaking of the process of creating or "discovering" the worlds of her fiction, Le Guin says, "It seems to me that most of an artist's job anyway not just a writer's is to be ready, to have the skills perfected. . . . You're just wandering around the wave lengths until something comes through."

Levertov, Denise (1923–) Raised in Essex, England, and privately educated, Denise Levertov worked as a nurse during World War II and then immigrated to the United States in 1948. She notes her father's Hasidic ancestry, her mother's Welsh intensity, and an interest in humanitarian politics as important inheritances. She has taught at a number of universities in the United States and was for many years a professor at Stanford. Levertov began publishing her poetry in the 1940s; this early work has been reprinted in *Collected Early Poems 1940–1960* (1979). Recent collections include *Candles in Babylon* (1982) and *A Door in the Hive* (1989). Levertov also writes essays on poetry, poetic form, and political issues. For her, a poet's work is "to summon the divine." Levertov writes, "To believe, as an artist, in inspiration or the intuitive . . . is to lie with a door of one's life open to the transcendent, the numinous."

Levine, Philip (1928–) Born in Detroit to a businessman and a bookseller, both Russian Jewish immigrants, Philip Levine went on to Wayne University and to the University of Iowa. Since that time, Levine has held a number of different teaching positions, and his poetry has won numerous awards. He has published some twenty collections, including *On the Edge* (1961), *7 Years from Somewhere* (1979), and the recent *What Work Is* (1991). Levine's poetic voice goes back to the 1950s when he worked in the automobile plants of Detroit. There, he decided, as he puts it, "to find a voice for the voiceless, the working men and women of America's industrial cities."

Lorde, Audre (1934–1992) Born of Caribbean immigrants who settled in New York City, Audre Lorde attended Hunter College High School and Hunter College and received an M.A. in library science from Columbia. In 1968, she left her job as head librarian of the City University of New York to be poet-in-residence at Tougaloo College in Mississippi, which led to her first book of poems, *The First Cities* (1970). She returned to New York, where she was Poet and Professor of English at Hunter College. Her later work celebrates the legends of strong black women, especially her mother. *Zami: A New Spelling of My Name* (1982), for example, combines autobiography, history, and myth to create a new literary form that Lorde called "biomythography." Lorde wrote, as she put it, "to speak the truth . . . and to attempt to speak it with as much precision and beauty as possible."

Lowell, Amy (1874–1925) Amy Lowell was born in Boston, a descendant of wealthy New England intellectuals. As a poet, biographer, and essayist, Lowell became the most outspoken proponent of imagism and a new American poetry. Lowell saw her variety of work as tied together in a larger project: "I find myself here as a prophet of you all and I feel that all of us working together will in twenty years reconstruct the taste of this country." Her poetry and prose were always experimental, and she was awarded the Pulitzer Prize posthumously for the "polymorphic prose" volume *What's O'Clock.* For Lowell, freedom of subject and the use of common speech were important, but above all, she maintained that "concentration is of the very essence of poetry."

Mar, Laureen A second-generation Chinese-American poet and story writer, from Seattle, Laureen Mar came from an immigrant working-class background. Her mother did piecework in the garment industry, and Mar's earliest memories are of her mother's ceaseless labors. Her poetry has appeared in the anthology *The Third Woman,* edited by Dexter Fisher (1980).

Marcus, Adrianne (1935–) Born in Massachusetts, Adrianne Marcus now resides in northern California, where she has made her home for more than two decades. Her poetry can be found in *Faced with Love* (1977), *Child of Earthquake Country* (1980), and *Divided Weather* (1985). An instructor of writing for a number of years, Marcus feels strongly about expressing herself in a variety of genres: "I write poetry because I have to, nonfiction because I like to write about what others do, and fiction because it permits me to combine poetry and nonfiction in different ways to discover something about the world that I did not understand when I began the story."

Marriott, Michel A reporter for the *New York Times,* Michel Marriott has written essays and stories for many periodicals, including *Essence* magazine, where his autobiographical essay "Father Hunger" first appeared.

McCluskey, John (1944–) Born in Middletown, Ohio, John McCluskey attended Harvard and went on to an M.A. at Stanford. He has been a professor of Afro-American literature and fiction writing at Indiana University since 1977. The author of two novels— *Look What They Done to My Song* (1974) and *Mr. America's Last Season Blues* (1983)—and much short fiction, McCluskey notes that he draws inspiration from African-American artists in a number of fields, from Ralph Ellison to Miles Davis. As one reviewer said, "For McCluskey, the Afro-American cultural experience has been a heroic one—one that has nurtured the individual and the group."

McKay, Claude (1889–1948) From the Clarendon Hills of Jamaica, Claude McKay came to the United States to study agriculture. He became an important figure in the Harlem Renaissance, although he spent much of his life in France, Great Britain, and North Africa. His literary output was varied: essays for radical journals, two hundred published poems, three novels, and other nonfictional books. Best known for his protest poems, McKay often put them in traditional verse forms like the sonnet. But his poetry also reaches back to his rural Jamaica and encompasses universal themes of nature, love, and beauty.

McPherson, James Alan (1943–) James Alan McPherson grew up in Savannah, Georgia, where he attended its segregated public schools. He went on to graduate from Harvard Law School and later earned an M.F.A. at the University of Iowa where he now teaches in the Writers Workshop. McPherson's reputation has been built on his well-crafted short stories, especially those in *Elbow-Room* (1977), for which he was awarded the Pulitzer Prize in fiction. Discussing his approach to characters in his stories, McPherson explains, "Certain of these people happen to be black, and certain of them happen to be white; but I have tried to keep the color part of most of them far in the background, where these things should rightly be kept."

Merwin, W. S. (1927–) W. S. Merwin was raised in Union City, New Jersey, and Scranton, Pennsylvania. After graduating from Princeton, Merwin lived for several years in London, translating French and Spanish classics for the British Broadcasting Corporation and writing plays. Merwin is best known as a poet, although he has published several volumes of essays. His collections span the decades, from *A Mask for Janus* (1952) and *The Lice* (1969) to *Opening the Hand* (1983) and *The Lost Upland* (1992). Merwin's poetry has been stylistically quite varied during his long career, but many of his works stress human alienation from nature. Since the 1980s, Merwin has been living in Hawaii and has become even more direct in voicing his ecological concerns.

Miller, Jim Wayne (1936–) Jim Wayne Miller grew up in North Carolina, went to school at Berea College, and completed a Ph.D. at Vanderbilt. He continues to live in the South, working as a professor of German at Western Kentucky University. In addition to poetry, Miller writes short stories, essays, and scholarly reviews. His volumes of poetry include *Copperhead Cane* (1964) and *Veins of Words* (1984). He says of his poetry that "I work like a bricoleur: He has materials lying around, odds and ends of all sorts, things that have just accumulated. He then conceives of something that can be made from them. Poets are people who put things together."

Milosz, Czeslaw (1911–) Born in Lithuania and raised in Poland, Czeslaw Milosz defected to the West in 1951, immigrating to the United States in 1960 and soon finding a home at the University of California, Berkeley. Milosz was involved in the Polish resistance during the Nazi occupation, and, after the war, he was posted as cultural attache in Paris. When called back to Poland, he defected to the United States. In 1980 Milosz was awarded the Nobel Prize for literature, primarily for his poetry. *Provinces* (1991) is his most recent collection in English. His essays in *Visions from San Francisco Bay* (1982) reflect on his life as a transplanted European and comment obliquely on the fascinating juxtapositions that make up the United States. Whether in poetry or prose, Milosz interweaves the personal and the historical, the East and the West.

Mishima, Yukio (1925–1970) Kimitake Hiraoka, who wrote under the name Yukio Mishima, spent his whole life in Tokyo, eventually taking his own life in a ritual suicide. Mishima was born into a family of samurai nobility, and he followed the tradition with its emphasis on the martial arts, control over mind and body, and great loyalty to the Emperor. In addition to writing in a variety of genres, Mishima was also a swordsman, singer, actor, and director of plays and films. His first novel, *Confessions of a Mask* (1949), created a furor in Japan and abroad with its elegant portrait of homosexuality. Mishima worked also on modernized versions of traditional Japanese No plays. His last text, completed just before his suicide, is the four-volume *Sea of Fertility*, a work tied to twentieth-century Japanese history yet universal in its focus on the dissolution of the individual.

Momaday, N. Scott (1934–) N. Scott Momaday comes from a varied background: Kiowa on his father's side and part Cherokee from his mother. His schooling was equally diverse, including reservation, public, and parochial schools and eventually Stanford where he earned a Ph.D. in English. Momaday has gone on to a number of professorships, extensive travel, and variety in literary output. *House Made of Dawn* (1968) was awarded the Pulitzer Prize for fiction. *The Way to Rainy Mountain* (1969) interweaves stories from Kiowa elders, short historical and personal commentaries, poems, and three lyric essays in retelling Kiowa history. Momaday's most recent novel is *The Ancient Child* (1989). What ties together Momaday's work is his dedication to preserving and presenting Native American concepts of being and culture.

Moore, Marianne (1887–1972) Marianne Moore was raised in Kirkwood, Missouri, and Carlisle, Pennsylvania, by a single mother under strict Presbyterianism. At Bryn Mawr she majored in biology, fostering a lifelong love of animal lore. Moore taught typing and bookkeeping at the Carlisle Indian School, worked at the New York Public Library, and then, from 1925 to 1929, edited *The Dial*, the leading literary review of the time. T. S. Eliot said that she was one of the few writers who had made a contribution to the language. Moore's *Collected Poems* (1951) won the National Book Award and the Pulitzer Prize. Her work has always been considered difficult yet rewarding, with its idiosyncratic line breaks and her keen wit. She never lost her passion for the well-made poem, brought about through endless revising, a fondness for exact detail, and the collecting of phrases from all over.

Mora, Pat (1942–) Pat Mora has spent her life in El Paso, Texas, where she now teaches at the University of Texas and directs the university museum. Mora writes poetry, essays, and children's books. Her poetry has been collected in *Chants* (1984), *Borders* (1986), and *Communion* (1991). Her most recent work is *Nepantla: Essays from the Land in the Middle* (1993). Mora describes a multiple impulse for writing: "I write, in part, because Hispanic perspectives need to be part of our literary heritage; I want to be part of that validation process. I also write because I am fascinated by the pleasure and power of words."

Mukherjee, Bharati (1940–) Born in Calcutta, India, the daughter of a chemist father and housewife, Bharati Mukherjee immigrated to the United States in 1961, went to Canada in 1968, and returned to the States in 1980. Her university education began in Calcutta and ended with a Ph.D. from the University of Iowa. She is now a professor of English at Skidmore College. Mukherjee is the author of short stories, nonfiction, and several novels, including *The Tiger's Daughter* (1972) and *Jasmine* (1989), and *Holder of the World* (1993). Speaking both of her own life and the tension that she explores in much of her writing, Mukherjee has said, "while changing citizenship is easy, swapping cultures is not."

Mura, David (1952–) A third-generation Japanese American, David Mura received his M.F.A. from Vermont College and currently resides in St. Paul, Minnesota. His writing reflects a weaving of different traditions. A poet and essayist, Mura has published the prize-winning prose work, *A Male Grief: Notes on Pornography and Addiction* (1987), as well as a collection of his poems, *After We Lost Our Way* (1989), which won the 1988 National Poetry Series contest. His most recent book, *Turning Japanese: Memoirs of a Sansei* (1991), combines travel writing and memoir as Mura reflects on his experience of living in Japan for a year.

Murray, Michele (1933–1974) Born in Brooklyn, a graduate of the New School for Social Research and the University of Connecticut, Michele Murray held teaching positions in English for a number of years, primarily in schools in the Washington, D.C., area. At the same time, Murray wrote children's books and poems, the latter collected posthumously in *The Great Mother* (1974). She also edited the ground-breaking anthology *A House of Good Proportion: Images of Women in Literature* (1973). After her early death by cancer, Clifford Redley of the *National Observer* commented: "What we most loved and admired about Michele was her absolutely breathtaking enthusiasm for her work."

Naipaul, V. S. (1932–) Born in Trinidad to descendants of Hindu immigrants from northern India, V. S. Naipaul attended Queen's Royal College in Trinidad and Oxford University in England. The author of more than twenty books, including histories and travel writing, Naipaul is best known for his novels. These include *A House for Mr. Biswas* (1961); *In a Free State* (1971), which won the Booker Prize for England's best novel of the year, and his most recent *The Enigma of Arrival* (1987). Describing himself as "content to be a colonial, without a past, without ancestors," Naipaul writes of the many psychic realities of exile.

O'Brien, Tim (1946–) A native of Austin, Minnesota, Tim O'Brien works now as a writer and a journalist, but served in Vietnam, an experience that led to his first book, *If I Die in a Combat Zone, Box Me Up and Ship Me Home* (1973). It persuasively conveys the feelings of those veterans who did their duty in a war that they privately despised. O'Brien has since published the novels *Northern Lights* (1974), *Going after Cacciato* (1978), and *The Nuclear Age* (1985).

Olds, Sharon (1942–) A native of San Francisco and a Stanford graduate with a Ph.D. from Columbia, the poet Sharon Olds now resides in New York City, where she writes and teaches poetry workshops. Olds has published several books of poems, including *Satan Says* (1980), *The Dead and the Living* (1984), and *The Father* (1992); her work has been included in numerous reviews and anthologies. Her poetry explores roles she has experienced as daughter, woman, and mother. Typically, Olds's very personal poems pull the reader into a violent, changing universe, a world of extreme emotions.

Olsen, Tillie (1912–) Born in Nebraska, Tillie Olsen left high school to work, raise four children, and continue the family tradition of labor organizing. Her work began to receive recognition when she won the O'Henry Prize in 1961 for her short story "Tell Me a Riddle." Her best known collection of four short stories is entitled *Tell Me a Riddle. Silences* (1978) is a collection of essays that explore the different circumstances that can make it possible for women to be creative. As Olsen describes it, she had little luxury to pursue her craft: Time to write came as "stolen moments . . . in the deep night hours for as long as I could stay awake, after the kids were in bed, after the household tasks were done, sometimes during. It is no accident that the first work I considered publishable began: 'I stand here ironing.'" Olsen has been writing and teaching ever since.

Orwell, George (1903–1950) Although a British citizen, George Orwell was born in Motihar, India. He soon returned to England with his mother while his father, a colonial civil servant, remained abroad. After graduating from Eton, Orwell worked as a police officer for the Indian Imperial Police before deciding to make a career in writing. Disturbed by the rise of Fascism, Orwell fought in the Spanish Civil War, a chilling experience he chronicled in *Homage to Catalonia* (1952). His most famous works are the novels *Animal Farm* (1945) and *Nineteen Eighty-Four* (1949), both of which warn of the growing power of modern governments. Orwell has always been known as a consummate writer of nonfictional prose. In all his mature work, Orwell expresses a combined concern for social welfare, individuality, and ethics with orthodoxies of any kind depicted as dangerous. As he puts it, "Liberty is telling people what they do not want to hear."

Paley, Grace (1922–) The daughter of Russian-Jewish immigrants, Grace Paley grew up in the Bronx and went on to study at Hunter College and New York University. Although she first wrote poetry, Paley is best known for her short stories in collections such as *The Little Disturbances of Man* (1959) and her most recent *Long Walks and Intimate Talks* (1991). Paley's stories tend to focus on conversation rather than plot. A longtime political activist as well as teacher and devoted mother, Paley admits that she often has been distracted from writing, but she sees no conflict in her varied roles: "It may come from my political feelings, but I think art, literature, fiction, poetry whatever it is, makes justice in the world."

Piercy, Marge (1936–) Born in Detroit to a Welsh English Protestant father and a Jewish mother of Russian and Lithuanian descent, Marge Piercy experienced poverty and prejudice early in life. Piercy focused on political and social activism during the 1960s. In 1970 she moved to Cape Cod and began a very productive period as a writer while continuing her activism. Her novel *Small Changes* (1973) received attention for its powerful portrayal of women's consciousness raising groups. Her latest work includes the book of poems *Mars and Her Children* (1992) and a novel, *He, She, and It* (1991). In combining her work as writer and activist, Piercy has stressed that she wants her writing to be "useful": "To find ourselves spoken for in art gives dignity to our pain, our anger, our lust, our losses."

Plath, Sylvia (1932–1963) The daughter of a professor and a teacher, Sylvia Plath was raised in rural New England. She attended Smith College and Cambridge University, where she met and married English poet Ted Hughes. Plath had a number of emotional breakdowns, including one in her junior year at Smith, which she chronicled in her novel *The Bell Jar (1963)*. Her books of poetry include *The Colossus* (1960) and *Ariel* (1965). Her journals appeared in 1982. Plath's writing has been called "confessional poetry," and its emotional intensity is unmistakable. Ted Hughes summarized her unique talent as follows: "She had free and controlled access to depths formerly reserved to the primitive ecstatic priests, shamans and Holy men. . . . She saw her world in the flame of the ultimate substance and the ultimate depth."

Randall, Dudley (1914–) Born in Washington, D.C., the son of a teacher and a Congregational minister, Dudley Randall grew up in Detroit. He attended Wayne University after having worked first as a foundry worker for the Ford Motor Company. He went on to earn a graduate degree in library science and studied in Ghana. As founder of Broadside Press and Detroit's first poet laureate, Randall's influence on the black poetry movement has been one of the strongest in recent times. As Suzanne Dolezal writes, "Broadside Press . . . provided a forum for just about every major black poet to come along" between 1965 and 1977. The collection *More to Remember* (1971) first brought Randall wide notice. *A Litany of Friends* (1981) has confirmed his reputation as a poet of the people of Detroit.

Reyna, Dorotea From the Rio Grande Valley of south Texas, Dorotea Reyna moved west to Stanford University for a degree in English. She returned to Texas for graduate study and now resides in the San Francisco Bay area. Reyna writes poetry, short stories, and plays.

Rilke, Rainer Maria (1875–1926) Born in Prague, Rainer Maria Rilke is considered the greatest lyrical poet of modern Germany. His childhood, however, was unhappy, for his mother treated him like a girl while his father sent him to military schools, which he despised. Rilke published his first volumes of poetry while still a student, but repudiated this work after two visits to Russia. There, Rilke acquired the mystical sense of the brotherhood of humans and things that underlies much of his poetry. After a visit to Paris, Rilke came under the influence of the sculptor Rodin; from this contact, Rilke learned to eliminate the personal element from his poems and to aim for universality of theme. *The Duino Elegies* and *Sonnets to Orpheus* are among his more important collections.

Ríos, Alberto (1952–) Born in Nogales, Arizona, to a nurse and a justice of the peace, Alberto Ríos considers himself a border person, both by location and by his split heritage; he had a Mexican father and an English mother. A writer of poetry, stories, and drama, Ríos' poetry can be found in *Whispering to Fool the Wind* (1982), *Five Indiscretions* (1985), and most recently, *Teodoro Luna's Two Kisses* (1990). *The Iguana Killer* (1984) contains twelve of his stories. On working in English as a bilingual writer, Ríos says, "I have been around other languages all my life, particularly Spanish. . . . Rather than filling out, a second name for something pushes it forward, forward and backward, and gives it another life."

Rodriguez, Richard (1944–) The son of Mexican-American immigrants, Richard Rodriguez grew up in Sacramento and could not speak English when he entered elementary school. Rodriguez went on to graduate from Stanford and Columbia and to continue his study of English Renaissance literature at the University of California, Berkeley. Turning down university positions, Rodriguez decided to become a full-time writer. His memoir *Hunger of Memory* (1982) brought him fame and notoriety with its negative view of bilingual education and critique of affirmative action. In his most recent work, *Days of Obligation* (1992), Rodriguez writes, "The youth of my life was defined by Protestant optimism. Now . . . I incline more toward the Mexican point of view, though some part of me continues to resist the cynical conclusions of Mexico."

Roethke, Theodore (1908–1963) The poet Theodore Roethke spent his childhood in and around his father's large commercial greenhouses in Saginaw, Michigan. Roethke sensed he was a poet in his youth and consciously devoted himself to the craft while a student at Michigan and then Harvard. He supported himself and his family through his lifelong teaching career, including a long period as a teacher of creative writing at the University of Washington. Commenting on his first volume, *Open House* (1941), Roethke boldly announced his "intention to use himself as the material for his art." Roethke continued to explore his inner world and to reflect on the natural mysteries of life in volumes such as *The Lost Son* (1948) and *Words for the Wind* (1957).

Rukeyser, Muriel (1913–1980) Poet and lifetime New Yorker, Muriel Rukeyser led a very active life, as social activist, teacher, biographer, screenwriter, dramatist, translator, and author of children's books. From her first award-winning work, *Theory of Flight* (1935), Rukeyser was known as a passionate talent. She published more than a dozen poetry collections and was often labeled a poet of social protest. She is noted for her social concerns and characteristic outpouring of energy. While not rejecting political poetry, her later collections display a wider range of interests, including the very personal.

Sanchez-Scott, Milcha (1955–) Milcha Sanchez-Scott was born in Bali to an Indonesian-Chinese-Dutch mother and a Colombian father. When she was a teenager, her family immigrated to La Jolla, California. Sanchez-Scott has written a number of plays that address her mixed heritage and variety of childhood experiences, including *Latina* (1980), *Dog Lady* (1984), *Evening Star* (1988), and *The Architect Piece* (1991).

Sarton, May (1912–1992) Originally from Belgium, May Sarton spent many years living in relative solitude at her home in northern New England. Sarton is best known for her poetry, novels, and journals. She received many awards for her writing including grants from the Guggenheim and the National Endowment for the Arts, and held honorary doctorates at colleges such as Colby and Bowdoin. *The Silence Now: New and Uncollected Earlier Poems* (1988) is the most recent of her fifteen books of poetry. *The Education of Harriet Hatfield* (1989) was her twenty-first work of fiction. *The Journal of a Solitude* (1973), a record of a period of her life spent living alone, is one of her best-known nonfiction works.

Sepamla, Sipho (1932–) Poet, playwright, and novelist, Sipho Sepamla was born in Krugersdorp, South Africa, and trained as a teacher, but has worked many years as the director of the Federated Union of Black Arts. Sepamla's poetry collections include *Hurry Up to It!* (1975), *The Soweto I Love* (1977), and *Children of the Earth* (1983). In his poetry, Sepamla typically skewers South African society and government with subtle irony. In his novel *A Ride on the Whirlwind* (1981), Sepamla sets out to explore the psychology of terrorism and the environment that fosters it through a novel set during the 1976 riots in Soweto.

Sexton, Anne (1928–1974) After attending a finishing school for women in Boston, Sexton eloped, gave birth to two daughters. She was hospitalized periodically for emotional disturbances that recurred throughout her life. In 1956, after a suicide attempt, a doctor advised her to write poetry. Sexton's first collection, *To Bedlam and Part Way Back* (1960), was controversial and celebrated, bringing with it notoriety and numerous awards. *Live or Die* (1966) received the Pulitzer Prize. In 1974, she committed suicide. Sexton is best known as a confessional poet, but through her personal, exploratory voice, she touches on many cultural concerns, particularly those that relate to women's conflicts in modern American society.

Shakespeare, William (1564–1616) The most famous dramatist in the world, William Shakespeare was born in the town of Stratford on Avon, not far from London, to a relatively well-off tradesman and his wife. He attended Stratford Grammar School but did not go on to university. Married at age 18 to Anne Hathaway, by 1589 Shakespeare was in London and involved in the theater. He soon became a shareholder in the Lord Chamberlain's Men, an acting company, then an actor, and their principal playwright, which he remained until retirement to Stratford in 1610. His sonnets were first published in 1609. As a sequence, they have a haunting quality, woven through with the complex theme of time and love. Shakespeare is known for his comedies such as *Much Ado about Nothing* and *Taming of the Shrew* and particularly for his tragedies that reflect on issues of politics, loyalty, rebellion, love, and fate: *Julius Caesar, Othello, Hamlet, Macbeth,* and *King Lear.*

Shelley, Percy Bysshe (1792–1822) Percy Bysshe Shelley's life and works exemplified the extremes of romanticism in both ecstasy and despair: rebellion against authority, close ties with nature, the power of visionary imagination and poetry, the pursuit of ideal love, and always, the untamed spirit in search of freedom. Shelley grew up in a traditional, wealthy British family and was destined for a parliamentary career. At Eton and Oxford his unconventional views brought him attention and problems, and he was expelled from the latter for publishing a pamphlet on atheism. His private life was equally stormy, attracting much notoriety. He eventually left England for Italy with his second wife, Mary, the author of the novel *Frankenstein*. In Italy Shelley wrote his best poems from 1818 through 1822. Percy Shelley died very young in a sailing accident. Many consider his long poem *Prometheus Unbound* to be his most important work.

Silko, Leslie Marmon (1948–) Leslie Marmon Silko grew up on the Laguna Pueblo Reservation in the house where her father was born, graduated from the University of New Mexico, and now resides in Tucson where she writes and teaches English at the University of Arizona. Silko first published a book of poems, *Laguna Woman* (1974), and then gained national attention with *Ceremony* (1977), which was the first full-length novel by a Native American woman to be published. She has followed this with more poems, stories, and essays, including her latest, *The Almanac of the Dead* (1992). Her writings center on Pueblo life and thought, and incorporate Native American story-telling techniques in their structure.

Smith, R. T. (1947–) Born in Washington, D.C., to parents of Scotch-Irish and Tuscarora heritage, R. T. Smith studied at the University of North Carolina and Appalachian State University. He has directed the creative writing program at Auburn University and has authored many poetry collections, including *Waking under Snow* (1975), *Rural Route* (1981), *Banish Misfortune* (1988), and his latest, *The Cardinal Heart* (1991).

Song, Cathy (1955–) The daughter of a Chinese mother and a Korean father, Cathy Song has spent most of her life in Honolulu, Hawaii. She went east to Wellesley and Boston University to study literature and creative writing, but has returned to her native Hawaii to teach and write poetry. Her poems in *Picture Bride* (1983), which won the Yale Series of Younger Poets Award, are often autobiographical and portrait-like, with a special focus on family relationships. *Frameless Windows, Squares of Light* (1988) is her most recent collection. Song has also edited the anthology of women's fiction and poetry, *Sister Stew* (1991).

Sophocles (496–405 B.C.) The Greek playwright Sophocles was born at Colonus, near Athens, where he also died. Sophocles was well educated in music and gymnastics and learned the art of writing tragedy from Aeschylus with whom he is often compared. He was also a public figure, being elected to the board of Hellenotamiai, the treasurers of the Athenian League. Only seven of the more than one hundred tragedies written by Sophocles survive. Those extant include the Theban Trilogy, (*Oedipus Rex, Oedipus at Colonus,* and *Antigone*) and *Electra.* His plays are marked by the idealized aspect of their heroes and the beauty of the choral odes.

Soto, Gary (1952–) A professor of English and Chicano studies at the University of California, Berkeley, Gary Soto has published works of poetry, memoirs, and fiction. His first poetry collection was *The Elements of San Joaquin* (1977), and he has more recently come out with poems in *Neighborhood Odes* (1992) and fiction in *Local News* (1993). A Mexican American from California's agricultural San Joaquin Valley, Soto is very conscious of his ethnic and class background, having worked as a migrant laborer during his childhood. However, he becomes angry when critics judge his work on whether it is "Chicano" enough: "Some critics want to keep Mexicans in the barrio and, once they get out of there, they point the finger and say, Shame, shame."

Soyinka, Wole (1934–) Africa's most famous playwright and a Nobel Prize winner, Wole Soyinka grew up in Abeokuta, Nigeria, attended university in Ibadan and Leeds, and then began a career in theater. Soyinka was imprisoned for his political views and left Nigeria in 1969, not to return until 1975. His writing, whether plays, poems, or essays, criticizes both European colonialism and the excesses of his own people. Similarly, his plays draw on traditional African, especially Yoruban, methods of presentation as well as on the techniques of European theater. *A Dance of the Forests* (1960) and *Death and the King's Horseman* (1976) are among his most celebrated works. Soyinka explains, "My writing grows more and more preoccupied with the theme of the oppressive boot, the irrelevance of the color of the foot that wears it, and the struggle for individuality."

Spender, Stephen (1909–) Born in London, England before the First World War, Stephen Spender is the last surviving poet of the British Generation of writers that came of age in the 1930s. Spender's poetry is most often associated with that of W. H. Auden and Christopher Isherwood. Spender is also known for his essays and plays as well as for his work as an editor and a translator. He has won numerous academic awards and honors. Spender was a Professor of English at the University of London from 1970–1977 and has taught in the United States at Northwestern University, Vanderbilt University, and Wesleyan College. Spender's published writings can be found in *Collected Poems 1939–1985* and in *Journals 1939–1983*.

Stafford, William (1914–1993) William Stafford was born and raised in Kansas, moved to Iowa where he earned a Ph.D. in English, and taught at Lewis and Clark College in Portland from 1948 until 1980. Stafford's poetry gained him the most renown, including a National Book Award for *Traveling through the Dark* (1963), but he was also the author of the nonfictional *Writing the Australian Crawl: Views on the Writer's Vocation* (1978). His last collection was *Passwords* (1991). With faith in the teaching power of nature and a belief in writing as experiment, Stafford was interested in the exploratory power of the pen: "I am headlong to discover."

Stevens, Wallace (1879–1955) An attorney's son from Reading, Pennsylvania, Wallace Stevens studied philosophy at Harvard and then went on to study law at New York University. Moving to Hartford, Connecticut, in 1916, Stevens became an insurance executive, a position he held until his death. In fact, many of his insurance associates did not even realize that he was a poet. Stevens published his poetry in reviews, and his first book of poems, *Harmonium,* came out in 1923. He did not receive national acclaim until his *Collected Poems* (1954) won the Pulitzer Prize and the National Book Award. Despite his focus in his poetry on the inner life, Stevens saw his work as representing an "accuracy with respect to the structure of reality."

Sung ling, P'U (1640–1715) P'U Sung ling is the author of folk tales that are as well known throughout China as the *Arabian Nights* is in the West. College educated, but unable to proceed to teaching in the university as he wished, Sung ling spent a private life at home in the society of books and friends. *Strange Stories from a Chinese Studio* (1679) is the volume with which he made his fame, although it circulated only in manuscript during his lifetime. In this collection, Sung ling mixed strange stories of Taoist magic, marvelous accounts of impossible countries beyond the sea, simple scenes of everyday Chinese life, and notices of extraordinary natural phenomena.

Synge, John Millington (1871–1909) John Millington Synge was born in a Dublin, Ireland, suburb to a formerly important Anglo-Irish Protestant family that had lost most of its wealth and land. From the hills south of Dublin, he proceeded to Trinity College and then to intellectual and physical wandering on the Continent. The Irish poet William Butler Yeats met him in Paris and suggested that he return to Ireland, live on the Aran islands, and tell the story of the isolated inhabitants there. Synge began to write plays, the first of which, *In the Shadow of the Glen,* was produced at the Irish National Theatre in 1903. Several more followed, including his most famous, *The Playboy of the Western World* (1907). Synge saw his art coming from the living poetry of those who work, the peasantry: "In Ireland, for a few years more, we have a popular imagination that is fiery, and magnificent, and tender."

Tan, Amy (1952–) The daughter of Chinese-American immigrants, Amy Tan grew up in Oakland, earned an M.A. at San Jose State, and continues to live in the San Francisco Bay area. Her mother was a vocational nurse, her father was both a minister and an electrical engineer. Tan began a career as a technical writer and then turned to fiction. Her novels *The Joy Luck Club* (1989) and *The Kitchen God's Wife* (1991) have been enthusiastically received by critics and the public. Both stories feature Chinese-American women who are ambivalent about their Chinese background. As Tan remarked, writing *The Joy Luck Club* helped her discover "how very Chinese I was. And how much had stayed with me that I had tried to deny."

Tannen, Deborah (1945–) Born in Brooklyn, New York, Deborah Tannen received her B.A. from SUNY, Binghamton, and then went on to complete a Ph.D. in linguistics from the University of California, Berkeley. Tannen has been a professor of linguistics at Georgetown University since 1979. Her last two books are *That's Not What I Meant!: How Conversational Style Makes or Breaks Your Relations with Others* (1986) and *You Just Don't Understand* (1990). She has also written a collection of short stories, *Greek Icons*. Discussing her professional goals, Tannen says, "I see one of my missions the presentation of linguistic research to a general audience as a means of understanding human communication and improving it."

Tao-sheng, Kuan (1262–1319) The wife of Chao Meng-fu, one of China's best known calligraphers and painters, Kuan Tao-sheng was also a famous artist and calligrapher. She is highly acclaimed as a poet whose images are emotionally charged, concete, and highly sensory.

Thiong'o, Ngugi Wa (1938–) Educated in his native Kenya and in England, Ngugi Wa Thiong'o spent years as a literature professor in Nairobi while becoming East Africa's most prominent writer. In 1982, he went into exile in London. His fiction has attracted the most critical attention, especially the novels *Weep Not, Child* (1964), *A Grain of Wheat* (1968), and *Petals of Blood* (1977). *Moving the Centre: The Struggle for Cultural Freedom* (1993) is his most recent collection of essays. In all his work, Thiong'o has been an outspoken critic of the many forms of oppression in Kenya and East Africa. In 1977, for example, he declared his intention to write only in Gikuyu or Swahili, not English: "Language is a carrier of a people's culture, culture is a carrier of a people's values. . . . And when you destroy a people's language, you are destroying that very important aspect of their heritage."

Thomas, Dylan (1914–1953) Dylan Thomas grew up in Swansea, Wales, attended the grammar school where his father was English master, but left at age 16 to pursue his career as a writer. Thomas had written poems from an early age—his first collection, *18 Poems* (1934), came out when he was just 19, but he soon became a writer-of-all-trades: journalism, broadcasting, filmmaking, and always, poetry. His humorous stories about his childhood are collected in *Portrait of the Artist as a Young Dog* (1940). Thomas's stage presence led to several enormously successful lecture–poetry reading trips to the United States. Although he gained a reputation for hard drinking and flamboyance, Thomas was a careful craftsman. His richly textured poems reveal a fascination with nature, death, and rejuvenation.

Thoreau, Henry David (1817–1862) Henry David Thoreau grew up in Concord, Massachusetts, home also to Emerson and Hawthorne, and attended nearby Harvard College. Thoreau spent the rest of his life in his home community. He is most famous for his retirement to a hut at the edge of Walden Pond, an experience he described in *Walden* (1854). This carefully constructed book adroitly combines a detailed, factual record of a particular experience with reflections on human experience at a more universal level. Thoreau published only one other book during his short lifetime, *A Week on the Concord and Merrimack Rivers* (1849), but he also kept a very detailed journal that is packed with acute observations of botanical phenomena. Thoreau was also a vocal opponent of slavery. Together, his work provides a critique of the materialistic values and the destruction of the natural environment tied to the rise of industrialism.

Tolkien, J. R. R. (1892–1973) Born in South Africa to English parents, J. R. R. Tolkien's life was centered in and around Oxford University—as a student, as a professor of Anglo-Saxon language and literature, and as a literary celebrity. He is most famous for his novels *The Hobbit* (1937) and the trilogy *The Lord of the Rings* (1954–1955), which chronicle the mysterious world Middle Earth. Although Tolkien considered his stories a language game, his imaginative world is not frivolous. Writing for Tolkien, "opens a door on Other Time, and if we pass through though only for a moment, we stand outside our own time, outside Time itself, maybe."

Valenzuela, Luisa (1938–) The Argentine writer Luisa Valenzuela grew up in Buenos Aires, although she has spent considerable time living in New York. Valenzuela has worked as a journalist, a free-lance writer, and a professor, but is best known for her experimental, dreamlike prose-fiction, which challenges political oppression as well as male-dominated ways of viewing the world. Her work has been translated into English in volumes such as *Strange Things Happen Here* (1979), *The Lizard's Tail* (1983), and most recently, *Black Novel with Argentines* (1992).

Vining, Elizabeth Gray (1902–) Elizabeth Gray Vining was raised in Philadelphia and attended Bryn Mawr College and Drexel University. Before World War II, Vining wrote many books for adults and children, including the Newbery Award winner *Adam of the Road*. After working for the American Friends Service Committee during World War II, Vining was appointed in 1946 tutor to Crown Prince Akihito of Japan, an experience that she related in the widely read *Windows for the Crown Prince*. Vining continued to write historical novels and biographies and in 1970 published her autobiography, *Quiet Pilgrimage*. Her latest book is the memoir of her seventieth year, *Being Seventy* (1978).

Walker, Alice (1944–) Alice Walker was born in Eatonton, Georgia, to a family of black sharecroppers. Her childhood was marked by the difficulties of segregation and poverty and by the nurturing of family and church. Walker began to write while attending Sarah Lawrence College. After moving back South in 1967, Walker published a book of poems and a novel, *The Third Life of Grange Copeland* (1970). Heading north again, Walker continued her work in poetry and prose while also completing her landmark essay collection *In Search of Our Mothers' Gardens*. Her novel *The Color Purple* (1982) won a Pulitzer Prize and was made into a successful film. Walker has recently published the novel *Possessing the Secret of Joy* (1992) and her collected poems, *Her Blue Body Everything We Know*. In all her work, Walker has emphasized the bravery and imagination of the black woman, "one of America's greatest heroes."

Wayman, Tom (1945–) Born in Hawkesbury, Ontario, Tom Wayman was educated at the University of British Columbia and the University of California, Irvine. Wayman has taught at various universities and has also worked as a construction worker and a factory assemblyman. Work of all kinds is at the heart of his writing and in the poems he has collected in the anthology *Abbot's Got the Contract, A Government Job at Last: An Anthology of Working Poems* (1976). His own poetry has been most recently collected in *Introducing Tom Wayman: Selected Poems, 1973–1980*. Wayman's poetic style uses satiric humor to make serious points about our society.

White, E. B. (1899–1985) The essayist E. B. White grew up in a rural suburb of New York and attended Cornell University. After an unsuccessful stint as a newspaper reporter, White took over the "Talk of the Town" section of the recently founded *New*

Yorker, providing the voice of the magazine for decades with his wry essays that typically began with a personal incident and moved on to larger questions. He was also the author of children's books, including *Charlotte's Web* (1952). For White, writing was always an act of faith and hope, as he described in a 1971 address: "Writing itself is an act of faith, nothing else. And it must be the writer, above all others, who keeps it alive choked with laughter, or with pain."

Whiteman, Roberta Hill (1947–) Roberta Hill Whiteman, a member of the Oneida tribe, was born in Baraboo, Wisconsin. After receiving a degree in psychology from the University of Wisconsin and an M.F.A. from the University of Montana, Whiteman was certain that writing was her vocation. Her poetry has been collected in *Star Quilt* (1984) as well as in a number of anthologies. Whiteman's poems frequently employ a confrontation with an object as a generative point for memory and imagination. Whiteman explains her poetry's relationship to her Native American heritage: "I think we [Indian people] sense . . . even as children, that we have an intuitive sense of our own exile."

Whitman, Walt (1819–1892) Born in a farmhouse on Long Island, Walt Whitman soon moved to Brooklyn with his family. Whitman was largely self-educated, and at age 12 began a series of jobs in the New York area: typesetter, schoolteacher, journalist, housebuilder. He self-published the first edition of his life work *Leaves of Grass* in 1855, which kept evolving to its final edition of 1891–1892. *Leaves of Grass* is a declaration of literary independence, a broad, bold and comprehensive book, as Whitman put it, "poems of freedom, and the . . . personality singing in high tones democracy and the New World."

Wilbur, Richard (1921–) Born in New York City, Richard Wilbur, poet laureate of the United States in 1987–1988, graduated from Amherst before fighting in World War II as an infantryman. Wilbur began his long teaching career in literature, primarily at Wesleyan and Smith. The author of many poetry collections, Wilbur is also known for his translations of plays by Molière, Voltaire, and Racine. His collection *Things of This World* (1956) won both the National Book Award and the Pulitzer Prize. Wilbur is a defender of order at several levels, for he views the care with words, rhythms, formal patterns, and rhyme that is evident in his poetry as essential for humans trying to comprehend the world. Wilbur feels that "the universe is full of glorious energy, that the energy tends to take pattern and shape, and that the ultimate character of things is comely and good."

Willard, Nancy (1936–) Born in Ann Arbor, Michigan, Nancy Willard stayed at the University of Michigan until she earned a Ph.D. Her career has been varied: poet, author of children's literature, literary critic, short story writer, and professor of English. Her first collection of poetry was *In His Country* (1966), and most recently she came out with *Water Walker* (1989). Willard emphasizes the affirmative role of poetry: "Art is not a mere selection from the world but a transformation of it into something that praises existence."

Williams, William Carlos (1883–1963) Williams's family spoke Spanish at home in Paterson, New Jersey. After medical school at the University of Pennsylvania and some time in Europe, Williams settled down to life as a physician in Rutherford, New Jersey. He was passionate about the arts and wrote constantly. His works include *The Collected Stories* (1961), the literary essays of *In the American Grain* (1925), and an autobiography. Williams is best known for his poetry, which can be found in *The Collected Poems, Volumes I and II.* Interested in developing an "American idiom," Williams was defiant of all conventions in his art. As he put it, "I think the artist, generally speaking, feels lonely. . . . He is usually in rebellion against the world."

Wilson, August (1945–) Growing up in poverty in Pittsburgh, Pennsylvania, August Wilson dropped out of school at age 16 and began to work at a series of menial jobs. Wilson founded the Black Horizons Theatre Company in 1968, "trying to raise conscious-ness through theater." His 1985 play *Ma Rainey's Black Bottom* brought him national recognition. *Fences* (1986) won many awards, including the Pulitzer Prize for drama. *Two Trains Running,* his most recent work, had a very successful run on Broadway. Wilson's writing process is arduous; he writes many revisions, but his plays begin as he sits in a café, listening to voices, writing down snatches of dialogue on napkins. When enough napkins have accumulated, he re-shapes the voices into drama.

Woo, Merle (1941–) Born in 1941, Merle Woo is the daughter of Chinese-Korean immigrants. Her essays, stories, and poems have been included in anthologies like *This Bridge Called My Back: Writings by Radical Women of Color* (1981) and in her own poetry collection, *Yellow Woman Speaks* (1986). Woo speaks of combining her work as teacher, activist, and poet: "We poets who are outspoken as Asian Americans, women, lesbians/gays, workers, cannot separate ourselves from the reality in which we live. We are freedom fighters with words as our weapons—on the page or on the picket sign."

Woody, Elizabeth (1959–) Elizabeth Woody is a Warm Springs, Wasco/Navajo Indi-an. She studied creative writing at the Institute of American Indian Arts, and her poetry and short fiction have appeared in many anthologies and periodicals. *Hand into Stone* (1988) is her first poetry collection. Typically, her work addresses the permanence of Na-tive American traditions amidst the constant change in the world around them.

Woolf, Virginia (1882–1941) Growing up in London, the daughter of eminent Victorian literary critic and agnostic Leslie Stephen, Virginia Woolf had little formal schooling, but educated herself in her father's vast library. Her life was punctuated by periods of depres-sion, the last leading to suicide. With her husband and friends, she formed the intellectual circle known as the Bloomsbury group. Woolf is most famous for her novels *Mrs. Dal-loway* (1925), *To the Lighthouse* (1927), and *The Waves* (1931), as well as the influential essay *A Room of One's Own* (1929). Her novels exhibit ceaseless experimentation, always striving to open up the inner life of individuals. A perfectionist when it came to her art, Woolf noted, "if one wishes to better the world one must, paradoxically enough, with-draw and spend more and more time fashioning one's sentences to perfection in soli-tude."

Wordsworth, William (1770–1850) Widely regarded as the central poet of the British Romantics, William Wordsworth was born in rural England to a comfortable middle-class family. After studying modern languages at Cambridge University, he spent considerable time in revolutionary France. From 1795 until 1808 he was at the height of his poetic powers, producing, among many poems, those contained in *Lyrical Ballads* (1798), while finishing most of his autobiographical masterpiece *The Prelude*. Nature, emotion, imagi-nation, and the self are his constant themes. Wordsworth believed above all that "All good poetry is the spontaneous overflow of powerful feeling."

Wright, James (1927–1980) Born in Martin's Ferry, Ohio, but a longtime resident of New York City, James Wright is best known as a poet, although he was a translator of poetry as well. After attending Kenyon College and the University of Washington, Wright began teaching literature while writing at the same time. Many consider the col-lection *The Branch Will Not Break* (1963) as his most important book; his *Collected Poems* won the 1972 Pulitzer Prize. Nature, loneliness, and alienation are Wright's major con-cerns.

Yamauchi, Wakako (1924–) A lifetime California resident, Wakako Yamauchi grew up in a community of Japanese immigrant farmers in the Imperial Valley. Her education was halted and her family lost everything when they were sent to an internment camp in Arizona during World War II. Yamauchi's writing career began when she took a short story course; this eventually led to the production of *And the Soul Shall Dance* in 1977. She has written some ten plays, including *The Music Lesson* (1980) and *The Chairman's Wife* (1990). Her perspective on relationships goes back to her mother: "Mother was a feminist in her time, and she always made me feel that I was somebody."

Yeats, William Butler (1865–1939) Although from a family of English ancestry, William Butler Yeats grew up in Dublin and spent much of his life fighting for Irish independence. His father was a painter, and Yeats, too, began studies at the School of Art in Dublin; at 21 he abandoned painting in favor of literature. Best known as a poet, Yeats was also a playwright and was instrumental in starting the Irish Literary Theatre. A student of Irish culture, mystic religion, and the supernatural, Yeats combined these elements into the highly individualized vision that comes through in his metaphysical autobiography, *A Vision,* and in his complex poetry that is collected in *The Collected Poems of William Butler Yeats* (1940). In 1923 he received the Nobel Prize for literature.

Young Bear, Ray A. (1950–) Ray A. Young Bear is a lifelong resident of the Mesquakie (Red Earth) Tribal Settlement in central Iowa. He was an art major at the University of Northern Iowa. His published work includes two collections of poetry, *Winter of the Salamander* (1980) and *The Invisible Musician* (1990), which combine dream, myth, and memory. Young Bear has taught at the Institute of American Indian Arts and the University of Iowa. He is also a singer and co-founder of the Woodland Song & Dance Troupe. Young Bear is very conscious of the tensions inherent in being a Native American writer for a wider audience: "I have attempted to maintain a delicate equilibrium with my tribal homeland's history and geographic surroundings and the world that changes its face along the borders."

GLOSSARY
OF TERMS

Absurdism, theater of the absurd a movement in theater and the arts that began after World War II and emphasized lack of meaning in social life and lack of communication among characters, to the point that normal logic and sequence of events often seems to break down.

Allegory a literary work that gives abstract moral qualities to characters, objects, plot, and setting, often for the purpose of moral or philosophical instruction.

Alliteration repeating consonant sounds for poetic effect.

Allusion enhancing meaning by references to other literary, religious, or philosophical works, ideas, or individuals.

Ambiguity a word, phrase, or situation in which more than one meaning or interpretation is possible.

Analogy a comparison of two items, ideas, or situations with similar attributes in order to clarify a point or support an argument. One item should be simpler or better known than the item that is intended to be explained or clarified through the analogy, as in the case of the analogy that seeks to explain an echo by comparing it with a ball bouncing off a wall.

Analysis breaking down a text into parts, sections, or points in order to understand it better. Literary interpretation begins with a close analytical reading and uses analysis to support and guide interpretation.

Antagonist the major character or force in a literary work whose efforts are opposed to those of the protagonist or central character.

Archetype image, symbol, type of character, story, or motif that occurs in literature in different cultures, universal or common to all humanity.

Argument a discussion or debate over a specific point, involving a presentation of evidence to support an assertion and refute contradictory evidence or claims. In expository writing, an argument is often a piece of writing in which the thesis has an "argumentative edge"; the body of the essay provides evidence supporting that thesis. Much expository writing and some expressive or literary writing involve some degree of argument.

Assonance device of poetic sound in which a series of vowel sounds are repeated in a line of poetry.

Assumptions prior ideas, values, and beliefs held by an arguer, reader, character, or author that condition further choices, statements, arguments, and beliefs.

Audience the readers of a written work or the viewers/listeners of a work in another medium such as drama or film. One's sense of audience helps to shape writing, determining many crucial choices of style and content: background information, selection of appeals, extent of narrative. The audience for a piece of writing or drama can be limited to a small circle, members of a particular class or group, or the work can attempt to reach out to a more general audience. A literary work is read by diverse audiences who tend to interpret texts differently.

Ballad a type of narrative poem that was set to music in the form of the folk ballad and originally shared in the form of folk music. A ballad usually uses a four-line stanza, rhymed a-b-a-b, with the lines in each stanza beginning with four beats, then going to three, then back to four, and ending in a three-beat line. The literary ballad (popular among the Romantic poets of the 19th century) is not designed to be sung but is a more sophisticated version of the folk ballad, written by a single author and designed to appear in print.

Blank verse unrhymed lines of poetry written in iambic pentameter which is close to the rhythms of ordinary English speech. Shakespeare's plays and many of the longer poems in the English language are written in blank verse.

Canon the selection of literary works that are widely accepted and commonly taught in schools or performed theatrically. Canonical works help to define—and to limit—a community's or nation's sense of "culture." Recently in academia the accepted canon of Western European cultural writings has been challenged by the introduction of modern and ancient works from previously excluded groups and cultures.

Catharsis the purgation of the emotions of pity and fear that Aristotle and the classical dramatists believed to be the true purpose of tragedy.

Cause and effect a type of thought, paragraph, or essay organization that considers an event or situation and looks back, analyzing origins and influences, or that looks to the future to discuss potential outcomes or results of an event. Writers must take special care in analyzing distant, coincidental, or immediate causes and in examining possible future effects.

Character fictional persons in a play, poem, or story. They may be realistically portrayed or display exaggerated traits for comical or satirical effect. Characters help writers to embody their ideas about human nature.

Chorus a group of citizens in a play who exhibit the characteristic attitudes of a culture or community. In classical drama the chorus often provides a religious, mythical, and social commentary on the main events of the play, which is appropriate because the chorus is a sort of collective voice of a religious community.

Classification refers to a means of developing a piece of writing through sorting or categorizing items, people, or ideals by class or type. In an essay, the classification should support a thesis and increase the reader's understanding; there also must be a clearly stated purpose supported by the process of categorization.

Cliché trite, overly used expression or figure of speech: "She was as pretty as a picture."

Climax the high point of the action in a literary work.

Clustering a graphic type of prorating activity involving grouping or connecting related ideas by drawing circles around items and connecting the circled items with lines.

Collaboration working together, especially in joint intellectual activity. In composition courses, students frequently collaborate in and out of class through peer workshops and study groups, responding to each other's drafts, working on exercises, studying readings, sometimes composing drafts together. Collaborative groups need to set guidelines for effective work, such as agreeing to come to class prepared, selecting a group leader and note taker, preparing time schedules, and carefully considering all members' observations.

Comedy a literary work in which the conflict leads to a happy ending, and the resolution is on a positive, integrative note, romantically and/or socially.

Comparison/contrast paragraph or essay organized so as to discuss similarities and/or differences between two things, places, peoples, or theories, in order to increase the reader's understanding of one or both and to support an assertion. Comparison/contrast can also be used to understand related literary works better, contrasting different characters, settings, or changes in mood.

Conclusion the closing part of an essay or other literary work. The conclusion of an essay drives home the point while often supplying a thought-provoking point to encourage the reader to reconsider the points made in the essay or to reflect on the long-term implications of the problem under discussion. Conclusions in stories or poems are usually less direct than conclusions in essays, leaving readers with more room for interpretation.

Conflict element of opposition, clash, or struggle in a story, poem, or play; often points to ideas that the author feels to be in contradiction or opposed. Conflict can be between people and society, between individuals, with nature, or internal. The ending of the literary work may provide a resolution of the main conflict.

Connotation/denotation connotation refers to the nonexplicit, unspoken associations a word has for various audiences. Denotation refers to the explicit, dictionary-style definitions of a word. "Home," for example, denotes "a place where one lives, a residence," while to many people it connotes belonging, comfort, and warmth.

Convention a traditional device or plot element used in a literary genre with which the audience has certain set expectations. For instance, a convention of comedy is the "happy ending," often with a reunion of characters who were previously at odds with one another.

Couplet a pair of end-rhymed lines of poetry. Often entire poems are written in couplets.

Criticism, literary refers to serious efforts to analyze literary works, usually for the purpose of interpretation and understanding. Literary criticism may be written from a number of different philosophical perspectives. Some critics focus on social issues as reflected in literary works, whereas others are more interested in psychological or linguistic aspects of literature.

Critique a critical review of a piece of writing or artistic production. Because a critique involves a judgment or evaluation, it needs to state clearly the underlying criteria or values upon which its evaluation rests as well as to provide specific references to the work under consideration.

Cultural diversity the presence of varied cultures within a society or a region.

Culture socially transmitted behaviors, beliefs, institutions, artistic artifacts, and other products of human work and thought characteristic of a community or a population.

Definition categorizes, amplifies, and explains what one means by a particular term. How and to what degree one defines largely depends on the overall purpose and audience for a particular piece of writing. A definition essay can be developed using a number of different writing techniques: comparison (with other similar, easily confused meanings), classification (different varieties or types), and argumentation (that your definition is the best one or the most appropriate).

Denouement literally the "unknotting" or unraveling of a plot; refers to the final scene where the last decisions and final recognitions (and, sometimes, deaths) take place.

Description the process of putting mental images or sense impressions into words. Description is often used to support claims or other strategies of writing. Although usually description adds realism to fictional writing, sometimes a crucial description in a work helps convey the mood of the narrator and makes points about the scene taking place and the story as a whole.

Dialogue a rendering of conversation in literary form, using a colon or quotation marks to set off each speaker's words. Much of the meaning of a play is presented in dialogue, unlike the short story, which relies more on the author's voice as well as presentation of the inner life of characters. Dialogue can be realistic speech, but it often involves stylized debate over social and philosophical issues, particularly in Greek drama, for in Greece formal debate and the Socratic dialogue were the primary tools for exploring conflicting ideas.

Diction a writer's characteristic choice of words. Diction can be characterized as abstract, concrete, high, medium, or low. Diction is an important component of an author's style and the overall impression made by a literary work.

Didactic a literary work designed to teach a moral or philosophical lesson. See allegory.

Drafting the process of writing a serious of preliminary, often rapidly composed, versions of a work, allowing the final version to emerge from the pattern established through successive drafts.

Drama a form of writing, including speeches and dialogue, settings, and stage directions, generally intended to be acted and performed live (usually in a theater) using actors to portray roles or "parts." Although modern drama employs mainly conversational language, some drama, such as that of the classical Greek theater, is written in poetic lines or in blank verse.

Dramatic irony a situation within a play in which the audience has more awareness about what the future holds in store for a character than does the character.

Dramatic monologue a poem in which a single character speaks from within a dramatic context, as in Robert Browning's "My Last Duchess."

Elegy a long, formal poem written to mourn the death of someone highly loved and respected.

Empathy one of the major ways that readers make an emotional connection with a literary work, through creating a strong sense of personal, emotional relatedness to one or more of the characters; a kind of bonding with fictional characters.

Essay a brief piece of writing, usually several pages in length, on a single subject, expressing the writer's point of view. An essay may be developed by any number of modes and organizational strategies.

Example an illustration to support or demonstrate a point, a specific representative of a group or whole. Examples are a common type of evidence used to support claims. Examples should be introduced clearly, with adequate transition and emphasis on the example's relevance to the main point of the paragraph in which it is found.

Explication an extremely close and detailed, line-by-line analysis of a work of literature, most frequently associated with close readings of poems. Explication could be considered a type of paraphrase that attempts to clarify the meaning of a text as it unfolds to the reader.

Exposition, expository in fiction, exposition refers to background explanation of events that took place before the events narrated in the story. In essay writing, exposition involves a careful explanation of events or ideas for purposes of enhancing the understanding of the reader. Strategies for expository writing include definition, process, classification, comparison, and, in some cases, cause-effect writing.

Expressionism a writing style or movement that tends to focus on inner reality and to distort the view of external reality; an extreme is the stream of consciousness narrative.

Fable a brief secular tale with a moral, similar to a parable or folk tale, designed to teach a practical or ethical lesson. Often, as in *Aesop's Fables,* the fable uses animals as its main characters.

Fairy tale a type of folk tale designed for the amusement and enlightenment of young people; often contains strong elements of the supernatural and features children as heroes. Fairy tales have been collected and written down by linguists and folklorists such as the Grimm Brothers. See also folk tale.

Fate the pattern of individual and social destiny. The Greeks believed there was a fate in store for us by, designed by the gods, which was not always apparent. Often the plot of a tragedy is a hero's quest to unravel and comprehend his or her personal fate. The hero often tries to avoid fate, always unsuccessfully—fate can't be tricked.

Feminist criticism a criticism that concentrates on the treatment of female characters and concerns in fiction by male and female authors, with a special emphasis on women writers and the need for greater acceptance and understanding of the particular mode of expression and themes explored by women writers.

Fiction anything not literally true, although the lines between fiction and nonfiction writing today are blurred, as biographers and journalists tend to invent imaginatively thoughts and emotions for the "real" people they write about. In contrast, some "fiction" may be so realistic as to be very "real," providing an intense experience.

Figurative language nonliteral, comparative language that makes use of metaphor (direct comparisons of two items that on the surface may seem to have little in common) and simile (comparisons using "like" or "as"). Poems often communicate their primary meaning through figurative language, whereas in essays figurative language is often used to create a mood or to add an extra, imaginative dimension to the discussion.

First person narrator a teller of a story who uses the first person pronoun. First person narrators can be characterized as reliable or unreliable, insightful or limited in their knowledge and understanding.

Flashback a movement back in time in the plot of a story, often triggered by an association with a similar moment in the present.

Flat character a simplified, stereotyped minor character, often associated closely with a certain social role: a sheriff, a waitress, and the like.

Foil in a drama, characters of similar backgrounds opposed by different value systems and personality traits; used for contrast: Hamlet and Laertes, for instance.

Folk tale a story transmitted orally over many generations; folk tales are a way that a preliterate culture expresses its values and communicates them to the next generation.

Foot a unit of metric division in a line of poetry involving two or three syllables, one or more of which is accented. See meter. Some of the more common poetic feet include the iambic (unaccented followed by accented syllable), the anapestic (two unaccented syllables followed by an accented one), the trochaic (one accented syllable followed by an unaccented one), and the spondaic (two accented syllables in a row).

Foreshadowing details that hint at the eventual outcome of a story and help create a certain mood or sustain tone.

Free verse a form of poetry in which the lines may be of varied length and rhythm.

Freewriting a form of prewriting in which a person writes rapidly without stopping for 10 to 15 minutes, allowing whatever comes to mind in response to a feeling or topic onto the paper. Freewriting also can be done as a first response to a reading. Such writing helps writers and readers to express underlying feelings and responses, and can help people find a direction for further, more directed writing.

Gaps, in texts jumps, blanks, or indeterminacies in a text that readers fill imaginatively through varied interpretations: What happened when a period of time was skipped over in a narrative? What takes place in a sketchily described scene? What happens before or after the story begins?

Genre one of the major forms or types of literature—story, poetry, literary essay, drama.

Hubris excessive pride. In classical tragedy, hubris was seen as one of the major causes for the fall of the hero.

Iambic pentameter the most common type of poetic line in English, a five-beat line of poetry involving five feet of poetry, each with an unaccented syllable followed by an accented syllable.

Ideology beliefs and values of a society, of a writer, and of a reader; includes both general ideology (politics, religion, life style) and literary ideology and theories. Ideology inevitably influences the way we read and relate to or evaluate an author's work.

Image, imagery a representation or a picture in the mind, often evoked through both literal and figurative language. An image and repeated images or "imagery" often make writing seem more vivid and concrete.

Interpretation an attempt to make sense of a work of literature by examining it in a systematic way, usually involves a very close reading of the work followed by an analysis of the techniques of written expression. Depending on one's view of the essence of literary expression, an interpretation may also take into account the period in which a work was written, information about the author's life. An interpretation may also include a reflection on the values and assumptions of the reader who is writing the interpretation.

Irony statement or situation that is the opposite of what we might expect. Authors use irony to emphasize that reality is different from our hopes and dreams. Irony underscores conflict, but may also be used for humorous effect.

Limited point of view a type of narrative viewpoint in which an author uses the third person pronoun (he, she), yet chooses to limit awareness of consciousness to the perspective of a single character: "He looked at the other people in the room and felt a sickness inside him: How could he ever be that clever?"

Line a brief unit of meaning in a poem. Lines may vary from only a few syllables in length to as many as twenty syllables. A line is set off from other adjacent lines by a break or return. A poem is composed of anywhere from two lines, as in a haiku, to hundreds, as in an epic poem.

Lyric a type of short poem that uses a first person speaker and that is highly emotional, imaginative, and songlike in its use of rhythm and other "musical" poetic effects. Lyric poems are often written on such themes as love, loss, and nature.

Magic realism a type of fiction, popular in Latin America and increasingly so in the United States, in which a realistic surface is punctuated by dreamlike events that may or may not be entirely real. Magic realism calls into question the relationship between the world of reality, fantasy, and dreams.

Memoir an account of the personal experiences of the author, such as an autobiography.

Metaphors nonliteral, implied comparisons, not using "like" or "as" between two things or levels of reality.

Meter a regular pattern of repeated accenting throughout a passage of poetry; often, one to three unaccented syllables are followed by an accented syllable (creating what is known as a "metric foot"); between two and six similarly accented metric feet then compose a typical poetic "line" in the poem. Meters are named by the numbers of poetic feet contained: a dimeter has two feet or "beats" to the line, a trimeter has three feet, a tetrameter has four feet, a pentameter has five, and so on.

Motif an element, expression, or device that is used often in a type of literary work. Frequently used in connection with folk literature: the motif of the glass slipper in "Cinderella," for instance.

Myth a symbolic and imaginative story, often repeated and retold, frequently dealing with a heroic or ancestral figure, and dealing with recurring themes such as creation, knowledge, ill, and redemption. Myths reflect the values of a culture.

Narration, narrative a story about a fictional or nonfictional event, involving a movement through time and space. Many essays contain strong narrative elements that serve as extended examples of more general points that the writer makes. Good narration involves strong, active verbs, and an abundance of descriptive detail, particular descriptions of movements as well as inner body sensations.

Naturalism a literary movement that emphasizes the overpowering forces of nature and natural law. The most famous naturalist story is Stephen Crane's "The Open Boat."

New criticism a type of criticism, popular in the 1950s and '60s, which paid extremely close attention to the form and techniques of literary texts. New critics emphasized humanistic values in literature, but believed that the most relevant evidence for an interpretation could be found in the text itself, rather than in the author's personal life, external philosophical theories, or in the reader's subjective responses.

Ode a formal and respectful, extended poem designed to celebrate a person, season, or object, as in John Keats's "Ode on a Grecian Urn."

Objective point of view a form of third person narration similar to that in a play, in which characters are seen "objectively," from without, with no effort made to capture directly their inner world.

Omniscient narrator a type of narrative point of view in fiction in which the narrator is not attached to a particular character but rather an all-seeing, all-knowing voice that is free to see into the minds and motivations of any character in the work.

Onomatopoeia the use in a poem of words that sound like what they describe: *buzz, bang, whiz, sizzle.*

Parable a brief narrative text designed to teach a moral or religious lesson, such as the parables of Jesus in the Bible. See allegory, didactic.

Paradox a poetic or logical figure of speech in which something that is presented as an apparent contradiction is shown to be, on a deeper level, true.

Paragraph a piece of writing set off from other parts by indentation and generally developing one topic or one aspect of a topic. Unlike journalists, who must write short paragraphs to fill narrow columns of print for quick reading, in expository essays the average paragraph is often seven or eight sentences in length, which allows for a clear topic sentence, one or two related examples, and other developing detail and supporting facts.

Paraphrase a type of writing done in order to understand or begin a commentary on a particular text, in which the original text (or a section of it) is rendered in the words of the author of the paraphrase, using fairly simple, direct diction. Any language from the original text must be set off in quotations.

Parody a kind of writing in which an author imitates (with exaggeration) a well-known work of writing or the style of another writer for purposes of humor and/or ridicule of the original.

Peer sharing and review the process of exchanging and reading papers in a classroom for the purpose of mutual, and supportive criticism; usually done at the draft stage of writing in order to enhance the rewriting process.

Persona the speaker in a poem when the speaker is not entirely equated with the author.

Personification a device that occurs usually in a poem but sometimes in a story or essay and gives inanimate objects or animals human qualities.

Plot the main events of a story or other narrative in their causal order. Plots may move forward in a temporal sequence, or they may travel back and forth in time, revealing important past events when necessary to make sense of an evolving action. A full plot involves the exposition, the initial unfolding of events, the introduction of conflict, the rising action as suspense mounts, the climax or high point of action, falling action, and the final resolution or ending of the story.

Poetry literary works in rhythmical language or verse. Modern poems often use open forms, without set meters or established lengths for lines. Poems are subtle and concentrated in their use of language. They usually involve a heightened sense of figurative language, such as extended metaphor, and may use a central speaking voice or persona to convey ideas. Sometimes the persona of the poem seems to espouse the poet's own views or to reflect on childhood experiences. Often, however, the poem and its imaginary world take on a life of their own and are subject to a wide range of interpretations.

Point of view perspective or vantage point from which a writer views reality or conveys action or information. Stories and poems are most often narrated in either first person point of view, third person limited (that is, limited to the awareness of a single character), or third person omniscient (the all-knowing narrative voice). Essays are sometimes told using the first person "I" point of view, as in the case of personal experience narratives. See also first person, objective point of view, limited, and omniscient narrator.

Prereading an early stage in the reading process in which the reader tries to determine what to expect from a particular work: Is it fiction? Written recently or long ago? From an unfamiliar culture or class perspective? Prereading helps the reader determine what orientation to take toward the work and what he or she needs to know to make sense of it. In prereading a long work a reader examines headnotes, names of major characters and settings, and titles of chapters and sections and skims through some of the section openers.

Process, in writing the act of writing can be seen as a process involving a number of phases: prewriting/planning, drafting, editing and revising, and proofreading. Good writing tends to evolve through spending adequate time on each of these phases, going over the piece frequently and sharing it with others to see it from different perspectives.

Protagonist the central character in a play or other fictional work. The protagonist often embodies positive virtues, as in the case of the hero.

Psychological criticism a kind of criticism that derives in part from Freud's ideas about literature. Freud believed that literature was like a dream and could be interpreted psychologically with an eye toward the unconscious motivation of the characters. Psychological critics consider many of the gestures and objects in literature as symbolic of inner states of mind and are particularly alert to sexual implications of behavior and objects in a work.

Reader response theory and criticism a type of criticism that believes the meaning of a work derives in large part from the assumptions and values of the reader rather than residing exclusively in the text. Reader responses to the same text will thus tend to vary widely among readers from different "interpretive communities" or backgrounds.

Reading process like writing, the reading process can be seen as a series of overlapping steps such as prereading, asking questions about main headings and topic sentences, making response entries in a reader's journal, then rereading and evaluating the selection as a whole.

Realism fiction that gives the impression of believable, everyday characters, settings, and situations. Usually realism contains large amounts of descriptive detail.

Recognition (anagnorisis) a moment of insight in the course of a story or play, often in a tragedy, in which a character realizes and accepts his or her errors and fate.

Reflective writing fictional or nonfictional literature in which authors examine aspects of personal experience to draw some larger conclusions about themselves, ideas, and the world they live in.

Refrain one or two lines of poetry that are repeated at the ends of stanzas or sections in order to emphasize the meaning and form of the poem.

Resolution the stage of the plot in which the conflicting elements are brought together. See also denouement, plot.

Response statement a record of the reader's immediate reaction to a text. Response statements may answer such questions as the following: How did you respond to the text? How did the text and you, as reader, affect that response? Did your response differ from what might be the intended reader response? What does your response tell you about yourself and your society? Response statements are often a point of departure for further reading and writing.

Reversal (perepetia) a moment in the course of a story or play, particularly in tragedy, when a character's plans and efforts clearly have failed or have turned out the opposite of what the character originally intended.

Rhyme use of words that sound alike: *fame/blame/game*. Rhyme is a device that links poetry to music. Most commonly seen in poetry is end rhyme, in which the final words of two or more lines in a stanza sound alike except for the first one or two letters. End rhyme can help to pattern an entire poem, creating the stanzaic form. Rhymes may be also be internal, that is, occurring within a single line of poetry.

Rhythm the sense of a "beat," a regular pattern of syllable emphasis in a poem. The rhythm of a poem adds to its meaning, unity, and intensity by holding the attention of a reader; subtle variations of a standard rhythm help to emphasize building emotions and new turns of thought. See also meter.

Romanticism a literary movement and style characterized by an emphasis on the pursuit of intense emotional relationships with art, with people, and with nature. Romantics tend to scorn intellectual restraint and conventional behavior, both in art and in life. Romanticism differs in this respect from sentimentalism, which is often expressed in traditional (even clichéd) literary forms and embraces traditional forms of behavior and relationships.

Round character a character with multiple dimensions, recognizable human traits, capable of growth and change. Usually only the major character in a literary work is "rounded."

Run-on line a line of poetry that continues without a pause in its sense, rhythm, or punctuation into the following line; also known as enjambment.

Satire a work of literature designed to ridicule through humor an element or trend in society of which the author is critical.

Scansion a stylized reading of a poem in which the reader attempts to determine the meter and to mark off the poetic feet and accented syllables.

Scene a short section of a story, or in a play, a portion of an act, unified by time and place.

Sentimental, sentimentalism a fictional work or artwork that appeals excessively and unrealistically to the emotions.

Sestina a type of poem in which a series of six words is repeated in a complex sequence, usually at the end of each line, throughout the poem. The first line of each stanza ends with the last word of the previous stanza. A sestina has seven stanzas. The first six stanzas have six lines each, and the poem concludes with a three-line stanza. Alberto Alvaro Ríos' "Nani" is a sestina.

Setting where a work of fiction or autobiography takes place. Setting also can include any details that indicate time of day, weather conditions, historical period, and the like.

Short story a brief fictional narrative, designed to create a strong emotional response in a reader or to make a point about a theme through skillful use of such fictional techniques as point of view, characters, plot, and setting.

Simile a nonliteral literary comparison using "like" or "as."

Soliloquy a speech by a character in a play delivered directly to the audience; a way for authors to allow a character to air inner thoughts without other characters overhearing.

Sonnet a type of lyric poetry written by Donne, Shakespeare, Milton, Wordsworth, and some modern poets. Typically a sonnet has 14 lines and a complex rhyme scheme. The Petrarchan sonnet form has an eight-line unit of rhymed lines (the octet) followed by a six-line unit or sestet. The overall rhyme scheme is a pattern such as *abbaabba/cdccdc*. Shakespearean sonnet changed this pattern slightly to a series of three quatrains followed by a couplet, rhymed in a pattern similar to *abab/cdcd/efef/gg*.

Stanza the poetic equivalent of a paragraph; a group of poetic lines, often of uniform length throughout the poem. Stanzaic types are named for their lengths: a tercet is a three-line stanza, a quatrain a five-line stanza, and so on.

Stereotype a character who lacks dimension, who is inseparable from his or her dominant motivation: the miser, the loose woman, the hypochondriac.

Stream of consciousness a type of writing in which the unconscious, unspoken perceptions of a character become the dominant narrative voice. Stream of consciousness writing avoids most punctuation and formally patterned sentences, following the logic of free association.

Structure the interaction and interrelationship between the parts and aspects of a work. In a story or play, structure includes an analysis of the various stages of the plot. In a poem, structure would involve the evolving pattern of an extended metaphor or other figurative language, as well as the pattern provided by the poem's movement in one of the traditional forms such as the sonnet. The structure of an essay might derive more from the pattern of its central argument and supports.

Style dominant language of a piece of writing—rhythm of sentences, diction, sound of the words, figurative language. Style helps to underscore the tone and meaning of the work. A style could be called plain, folksy, elaborate and formal, or dreamy and flowing.

Symbol, symbolism an object, place, or person that represents something else, often something invisible or intangible, by association, resemblance, or custom. Symbolism refers to the pattern or type of symbols present in a literary work; it also refers to a literary movement in which symbols played a significant stylistic role.

Theme an idea, point of view, or perception amplified or discussed in a work such as a literary work or composition.

Thesis the central point or core assertion in a piece of writing. The rest of the writing, typically an essay, develops and supports the thesis.

Tone the attitude of the author toward the world of the story, as transferred to the reader through literary techniques and strategies; tone may be mocking, sympathetic, tragic, comic, pathetic, or the like. However, because readers bring their own values to a literary text, they may disagree about the exact degree or shading of tone; thus discussions of tone are really acts of interpretation.

Tragedy a play of heightened values and emotional intensity in which a strong central figure, or hero, is brought down by a combination of forces: his or her own flaws and the power of fate.

Tragic hero the main character in a tragedy. The tragic hero is often a larger than life figure, more "noble" than the average person, a leader or spokesperson for a group or a people. Tragic heroes often suffer from flaws such as excessive pride, arrogance, or ignorance of their fate or true identity.

Villanelle a complexly rhymed poem of 19 lines with refrains (full line repetition). The villanelle is rhymed, has five three-line stanzas rhyming *aba,* and concludes with a quatrain rhymed *abaa.* The first and third lines of the poem are repeated in subsequent stanzas and create the couplet that concludes the poem. Dylan Thomas's "Do Not Go Gentle into That Good Night" is a modern example of the villanelle.

Voice refers to the sense of an author's personal presence as it is revealed in the language of a piece of writing—the style and tone of a writer that come through in the prose, giving the author's work a unique, lively quality.

PERMISSIONS
ACKNOWLEDGMENTS

Gerald Early, excerpt from "Digressions," in *Antæus*, No. 61 (Autumn, 1988), ed. Daniel Halpern. Reprinted by permission of Gerald Early.

Gretel Ehrlich, excerpt from "From the Journals," in *Antæus*, No. 61 (Autumn, 1988), ed. Daniel Halpern. Reprinted by permission of Darhansoff & Verrill, agent for Gretel Ehrlich.

Gretel Ehrlich, "On Water," from *The Solace of Open Spaces* by Gretel Ehrlich. Copyright © 1985 by Gretel Ehrlich. Used by permission of Viking Penguin, a division of Penguin Books USA Inc.

Loren Eiseley, "The Judgment of the Birds." From *The Immense Journey* by Loren Eiseley. Copyright © 1956 by Loren Eiseley. Reprinted by permission of Random House, Inc.

Russell Endo, "Susumu, My Name," from *The American Poetry Review*, 14, No. 3 (May/June 1985). Reprinted by permission of the author.

Louise Erdrich, "American Horse." Copyright © 1983 by Louise Erdrich. Reprinted by permission of the author. This story, in altered form, is part of Louise Erdrich's novel, *The Bingo Palace* (published by HarperCollins 1994).

Louise Erdrich, "Windigo" from *Jacklight* by Louise Erdrich. Copyright © 1984 by Louise Erdrich. Reprinted by permission of Henry Holt and Company, Inc.

Martín Espada, "Jorge the Church Janitor Finally Quits" from *Rebellion is the Circle of a Lover's Hands/Rebelión es el giro de manos del amante* by Martín Espada. Curbstone Press. Copyright 1991 by Martín Espada. Distributed by InBook. Used with permission of Curbstone Press.

E.M. Forster, "The Other Side of the Hedge." From *Collected Tales* by E.M. Forster. Published 1947 by Alfred A. Knopf, Inc. Reprinted by permission of Alfred A. Knopf, Inc., and Sidgwick & Jackson.

Anne Frank, "My Longing to Talk to Someone." From *The Diary of Anne Frank: The Critical Edition* by Anne Frank. Copyright © 1986 by Anne Frank-Fonds, Basle/Switzerland, for all texts of Anne Frank. Used by permission of Doubleday, a division of Bantam Doubleday Dell Publishing Group, Inc.

Robert Frost, "After Apple-Picking," "Birches," "Desert Places," and "Mending Wall" from *The Poetry of Robert Frost* edited by Edward Connery Lathem. Copyright 1936, 1944, © 1958 by Robert Frost. Copyright © 1964, 1967 by Lesley Frost Ballantine. Copyright 1916, 1930, 1939, © 1968, 1969 by Henry Holt and Company, Inc. Reprinted by permission of Henry Holt and Company, Inc.

Carlos Fuentes, "The Doll Queen" from *Burnt Water* by Carlos Fuentes, translated by Margaret Sayers Peden. Translation copyright © 1980 by Farrar, Straus & Giroux, Inc. Reprinted by permission of Farrar, Straus & Giroux, Inc.

Tess Gallagher, "The Hug" copyright 1984 by Tess Gallagher. Reprinted from *Willingly* with the permission of Graywolf Press, Saint Paul.

Allen Ginsberg, "A Supermarket in California" from *Collected Poems 1947-1980* by Allen Ginsberg. Copyright © 1955 by Allen Ginsberg. Copyright Renewed. Reprinted by permission of HarperCollins Publishers, Inc.

Nikki Giovanni, "Ego-tripping" from *The Women and the Men* by Nikki Giovanni. Copyright © 1970, 1974, 1975 by Nikki Giovanni. By permission of William Morrow & Company, Inc.

ing Back: Thinking Feminist, Thinking Black by bell hooks. Copyright © 1989 by Gloria Watkins. Reprinted by permission of South End Press. In " 'when i was a young soldier for the revolution': coming to voice," the lines from "A Litany for Survival" are reprinted from *The Black Unicorn, Poems* by Audre Lorde, by permission of W. W. Norton & Company, Inc. Copyright © 1978 by Audre Lorde.

"How Men and Women Got Together," from *American Indian Myths and Legends* by Richard Erdoes and Alfonso Ortiz. Copyright © 1984 by Richard Erdoes and Alfonso Ortiz. Reprinted by permission of Pantheon Books, a division of Random House, Inc.

"How Spider Obtained the Sky God's Stories," from *Akan-Ashanti Folk-Tales*, collected and translated by R.S. Rattray. Oxford University Press, 1930.

Jane Howard, "All Happy Clans Are Alike: In Search of the Good Family" from *Families* by Jane Howard. Copyright © 1978 by Jane Howard. Reprinted by permission of Simon & Schuster, Inc.

Marie Howe, "Letter to My Sister" from *The Good Thief* by Marie Howe. Copyright © 1988 by Marie Howe. Reprinted by permission of Persea Books, Inc.

Sue Hubbell, "Winter." From *A Country Year: Living the Questions* by Sue Hubbell. Copyright © 1983, 1984, 1985, 1986 by Sue Hubbell. Reprinted by permission of Random House, Inc.

Isabel Huggan, "Celia Behind Me," from *The Elizabeth Stories* by Isabel Huggan. Copyright © 1984 by Isabel Huggan. Used by permission of Viking Penguin, a division of Penguin Books USA Inc., and Oberon Press.

Ted Hughes, "The Thought-Fox." Copyright © 1956, 1957 by Ted Hughes. From *New Selected Poems* by Ted Hughes. Reprinted by permission of Faber and Faber Ltd.

June Jordan, "Des Moines Iowa Rap." From the book, *Living Room* by June Jordan. Copyright © 1985 by June Jordan. Used by permission of the publisher, Thunder's Mouth Press.

James Joyce, "Araby," from *Dubliners* by James Joyce. Copyright 1916 by B. W. Heubsch. Definitive text Copyright © 1967 by the Estate of James Joyce. Used by permission of Viking Penguin, a division of Penguin Books USA Inc.

Carl Gustav Jung, "Retrospect." From *Memories, Dreams and Reflections* by C.G. Jung. Copyright © 1962, 1963 and renewed 1989, 1990, 1991 by Random House, Inc. Reprinted by permission of Pantheon Books, a division of Random House, Inc.

Martin Luther King, Jr., "Letter from Birmingham Jail" from *Why We Can't Wait* by Martin Luther King, Jr. Reprinted by arrangement with The Heirs to the Estate of Martin Luther King, Jr., c/o Joan Daves Agency as agent for the proprietor. Copyright 1963 by the Estate of Martin Luther King, Jr. Copyright renewed 1991 by Coretta Scott King.

Maxine Hong Kingston, "The Silent Girl." From *The Woman Warrior* by Maxine Hong Kingston. Copyright © 1975, 1976 by Maxine Hong Kingston. Reprinted by permission of Alfred A. Knopf, Inc.

Käthe Kollwitz, excerpts from *The Diary and Letters of Käthe Kollwitz*, ed. Hans Kollwitz, trans. Richard and Clara Winston. © 1988 by Northwestern University Press. Reprinted by permission of Northwestern University Press. First published 1955 by The Henry Regnery Company.

Maxine Kumin, "The Envelope," copyright © 1982 by Maxine Kumin, from *Our Ground Time Here Will Be Brief* by Maxine Kumin. Used by permission of Viking Penguin, a division of Penguin Books USA Inc.

"The End of the World," from *American Indian Myths and Legends* by Richard Erdoes and Alphonso Ortiz. Copyright © 1984 by Richard Erdoes and Alfonso Ortiz. Reprinted by permission of Pantheon Books, a division of Random House, Inc.

Ngugi Wa Thiong'o, "Minutes of Glory." Reprinted by permission of Ngugi Wa Thiong'o: *Secret Lives* (Heinemann, A Division of Reed Publishing (USA) Inc., Portsmouth, NH, 1975).

Dylan Thomas, "Do Not Go Gentle into That Good Night" and "In My Craft or Sullen Art." From Dylan Thomas: *Poems of Dylan Thomas.* Copyright 1944, 1945 by The Trustees for the Copyrights of Dylan Thomas, 1952 by Dylan Thomas. Reprinted by permission of New Directions Publishing Corp., and J.M. Dent.

J.R.R. Tolkien, "Leaf by Niggle" from *Tree and Leaf* by J.R.R. Tolkien. Copyright © 1964 by George Allen and Unwin Ltd., © renewed 1992 by John F. R. Tolkien, Christopher R. Tolkien and Priscilla M.A.R. Tolkien. Reprinted by permission of Houghton Mifflin Co., and HarperCollins Publishers Ltd. All rights reserved.

Luisa Valenzuela, "The Censors," trans. David Unger. From *Open Door: Stories* by Luisa Valenzuela. North Point Press, 1988. Copyright © 1988, 1978, 1976 by Luisa Valenzuela. Reprinted by permission of Rosario Santos, agent for the author.

Elizabeth Gray Vining, from *Being Seventy* by Elizabeth Gray Vining. Copyright © 1978 by Elizabeth Gray Vining. Used by permission of Viking Penguin, a division of Penguin Books USA Inc.

Alice Walker, "Beauty: When the Other Dancer Is the Self" from *In Search of Our Mothers' Gardens: Womanist Prose,* copyright © 1983 by Alice Walker, reprinted by permission of Harcourt Brace & Company.

Tom Wayman, "Picketing Supermarkets." © 1973 by Tom Wayman. From *Did I Miss Anything? Selected Poems 1973-1993* by Tom Wayman. Harbour Publishing Co. Ltd., 1993. Reprinted by permission of Harbour Publishing Co. Ltd.

E.B. White, "Once More to the Lake" from *One Man's Meat* by E.B. White. Copyright 1941 by E.B. White. Reprinted by permission of HarperCollins Publishers, Inc.

Roberta Hill Whiteman, "Star Quilt" from *Star Quilt* (Holy Cow! Press, 1984). Copyright © by Roberta Hill Whiteman. Reprinted by permission of the publisher.

Richard Wilbur, "For the Student Strikers" from *The Mind-Reader,* copyright © 1971 by Richard Wilbur, reprinted by permission of Harcourt Brace & Company.

Nancy Willard, "Why I Never Answered Your Letter" is reprinted from *Carpenter of the Sun, Poems* by Nancy Willard, by permission of Liveright Publishing Corporation. Copyright © 1974 by Nancy Willard.

William Carlos Williams, "The Artist." From William Carlos Williams: *The Collected Poems of William Carlos Williams, 1939-1962,* vol. II. Copyright 1954 by William Carlos Williams. First printed in *The New Yorker.* Reprinted by permission of New Directions Publishing Corp.

August Wilson, *The Piano Lesson.* Copyright © 1988, 1990 by August Wilson. Used by permission of Dutton Signet, a division of Penguin Books USA Inc.

Merle Woo, "Poem for the Creative Writing Class, Spring 1982" from *Chinese American Poetry: An Anthology,* ed. L. Ling-chi Wang and Henry Yiheng Zhao. Asian American Studies, University of California, Santa Barbara, 1991. Reprinted by permission of Merle Woo.

SUBJECT INDEX

INDEX OF AUTHORS, TITLES, AND FIRST LINES

Italics indicate titles of works. Authors and first lines of poems are in roman type.